# INTRODUCTION TO
# LAW

## Fifth Edition

# INTRODUCTION TO
# LAW

## Fifth Edition

### Beth Walston-Dunham

DELMAR
CENGAGE Learning™

Australia • Brazil • Japan • Korea • Mexico • Singapore • Spain • United Kingdom • United States

**Introduction to Law, Fifth Edition**
Beth Walston-Dunham

Vice President, Career and Professional
Editorial: Dave Garza

Director of Learning Solutions:
Sandy Clark

Acquisitions Editor: Shelley Esposito

Managing Editor: Larry Main

Product Manager: Melissa Riveglia

Editorial Assistant: Lyss Zaza

Vice President, Career and Professional
Marketing: Jennifer McAvey

Marketing Director: Debbie Yarnell

Marketing Coordinator:
Jonathan Sheehan

Production Director: Wendy Troeger

Production Manager: Mark Bernard

Senior Content Project Manager:
Betty Dickson

Art Director: Joy Kocsis

Technology Project Manager:
Christopher Catalina

Production Technology Analyst:
Thomas Stover

For product information and technology assistance, contact us at
**Professional & Career Group Customer Support, 1-800-648-7450**

For permission to use material from this text or product,
submit all requests online at **cengage.com/permissions.**
Further permissions questions can be e-mailed to
**permissionrequest@cengage.com.**

Library of Congress Control Number: 2007941009

ISBN-13: 978-1-4283-1850-2

ISBN-10: 1-4283-1850-X

**Delmar**
5 Maxwell Drive
Clifton Park, NY 12065-2919
USA

Cengage Learning products are represented in Canada by Nelson Education, Ltd.

For your lifelong learning solutions, visit **delmar.cengage.com**

Visit our corporate website at **cengage.com.**

**Notice to the Reader**

Publisher does not warrant or guarantee any of the products described herein or perform any independent analysis in connection with any of the product information contained herein. Publisher does not assume, and expressly disclaims, any obligation to obtain and include information other than that provided to it by the manufacturer. The reader is expressly warned to consider and adopt all safety precautions that might be indicated by the activities described herein and to avoid all potential hazards. By following the instructions contained herein, the reader willingly assumes all risks in connection with such instructions. The reader is notified that this text is an educational tool, not a practice book. Since the law is in constant change, no rule or statement of law in this book should be relied upon for any service to any client. The reader should always refer to standard legal sources for the current rule or law. If legal advice or other expert assistance is required, the services of the appropriate professional should be sought. The publisher makes no representations or warranties of any kind, including but not limited to, the warranties of fitness for particular purpose or merchantability, nor are any such representations implied with respect to the material set forth herein, and the publisher takes no responsibility with respect to such material. The publisher shall not be liable for any special, consequential, or exemplary damages resulting, in whole or part, from the readers' use of, or reliance upon, this material.

Printed in the United States of America
1 2 3 4 5 X X 12 11 10 09 08

To Bobby, Sam, and Ben,
For continually introducing me to the
singular importance of each and every day.

Beth

# CONTENTS

## CHAPTER 1                                     1

### The Historical Basis and Current Structure of the American Legal System

## CHAPTER 2                                     26

### The Courts

## CHAPTER 3                                     55

### Legislation

**CHAPTER 4**         71

## The Executive Branch and Administrative Authority

**CHAPTER 5**         94

## The Legal Professional

**CHAPTER 6**         119

## The Law of Ethics

**CHAPTER 7**         149

## Substantive and Procedural Issues

## CHAPTER 8                                    187

### Jurisdiction

## CHAPTER 9                                    215

### Torts

CHAPTER 10                               273

Family Law

## CHAPTER 11                    341

### Estates and Probate

## CHAPTER 12                    369

### Property Law

## CHAPTER 13                    415

### The Law of Contracts

## CHAPTER 16                                   525

### Criminal Procedure

## APPENDIXES                                   567

# TABLE OF CASES

The purpose of this book is not to answer all of the student's questions about the law but to generate questions. As an introductory text, the goal of this book is to create an awareness and appreciation for the effect that law has on virtually every facet of life and society. The chapters guide the student from a basic introduction of the rationale behind the structure of the U.S. system of government to a discussion of each major area of law in the legal system. Regardless of the initial reason for picking up this book, the intended outcome of reading for the student remains the same: to gain a better understanding of not only how but also why law is such an integral part of our professional and personal lives and to gain some sense of the order and stability that law provides even as it remains adaptive to the ever-changing face of American society.

This text is aimed at the student who is studying law for the first time. Each chapter is designed to introduce the student to fundamental legal concepts and principles Chapters 1 to 6 provide an introduction to the U.S. legal system, the manner in which law is created and administered, and certain considerations that affect legal disputes. The balance, Chapters 7 to 16, concentrate on different areas of law by exploring basic principles and terminology. The areas covered include property, business, estates, tort, family, contract, and criminal law and procedure. Chapter 5 addresses the roles of legal professionals and their support staff. Throughout the text, and specifically in Chapter 6, discussion is given to the ethical considerations that affect legal professionals and subjects of law.

## CHANGES TO THE FIFTH EDITION

The fifth edition of *Introduction to Law* is designed to take an established and comprehensive text into the current realm of the U.S. legal system with cases, exhibits, examples, and assignments that reflect modern-day and developing legal standards. In an ever-changing society, the text addresses not only the long-held legal traditions but also more volatile and evolving areas of law such as the so-called right to die, medical malpractice, same-sex marriages, reproductive law, negotiable instruments, and major substantive law changes such as the recent overhaul of the bankruptcy code. These and many other current issues are addressed throughout the text.

Although the goal remains as always—to introduce the beginning student to the structure and function of the U.S. legal system, major areas of law, and relevant terminology—the new edition also touches on the areas familiar to so many in American culture. Each chapter begins with a "news" type article to introduce the student to the relevance of the chapter topic in contemporary society. This is followed by a brief outline and chapter objectives. With this prologue, the student should be prepared to consider the subsequent text with an idea of how it is relevant in real-world terms.

## CHAPTER FORMAT

Recent case law has been incorporated to provide a better view of the current position of courts across the nation. Chapter features include the following:

- **A Chapter Outline** provides an introduction to the major topics that will be addressed.

- **Chapter Objectives** at the beginning of each chapter focus students' attention on the main elements the student will learn.
- **New Hypothetical Applications** are interspersed through each chapter to illustrate chapter concepts. Points for Discussion follow the applications and provide a springboard for class discussion.
- **Longer Edited Cases,** most of them new to this edition, are followed by questions that encourage students to consider the major issues in each case.
- **Assignments Throughout Each Chapter,** the majority of which are new to this edition, test students' knowledge by asking them to apply the chapter material.
- **Ethical Considerations and Ethical Circumstances** in each chapter provide insight to the legal issues presented.
- **A chapter Summary** ends each chapter with a brief review of the main points covered.
- **Key Terms** are set in boldface type and defined in the margin where they first appear within the chapter. For easy review, each chapter also ends with a list of the key terms found in the chapter.
- **Review Questions** follow the chapter material, which allow students yet another opportunity to review the chapter content.
- **Helpful Web Sites** connect the text material to the most current resources.

Chapters conclude with Internet Assignments to introduce the student to the concept of Internet legal research.

## SUPPORT MATERIAL

This fifth edition is accompanied by a support package that will assist students in learning and aid instructors in teaching:

- An Instructor's Manual and Test Bank by Beth Walston-Dunham accompanies this edition and has been greatly expanded to incorporate all changes in the text and to provide comprehensive teaching support. It includes such items as sample syllabi, power point presentations, a lecture key consisting of a synopsis of all major concepts, information to guide classroom discussion in the Points for Discussion following applications, assignment and review questions, and answers. Also included are case briefs for all cases found in the text. A comprehensive test bank provides 480 objective test questions and answers. The test bank consists of questions that have already been successfully class tested.

### Student CD-ROM

The new accompanying CD-ROM provides additional material to help students master the important concepts in the course. This CD-ROM includes a study guide with Concept Summary Questions,

Matching Questions, and Applications of major concepts in the chapters.

### Instructor's eResource CD-ROM

The new e-Resource component provides instructors with all the tools they need in one convenient CD-ROM. Instructors will find that this resource provides them with a turnkey solution to help them teach by making available PowerPoint® slides for each chapter, a Computerized Test Bank and an electronic version of the Instructor's Manual. . . .

All of these Instructor materials are also posted on our web site, in the Online Resources section.

### WebTUTOR™ on WebCT and BlackBoard

The WebTutor™ supplement to accompany *Introduction to Law* allows you, as the instructor, to take learning beyond the classroom. This Online Courseware is designed to complement the text and benefit students and instructors alike by helping to better manage your time, prepare for exams, organize your notes, and more. WebTutor™ allows you to extend your reach beyond the classroom.

## Online Companion™

The Online Companion™ provides students with additional support materials in the form of Chapter Outlines and Review Quizzes. The Online Companion™ can be found at www.paralegal.delmar.cengage.com in the Online Companion™ section of the Web Site.

## Web Page

Come visit our web site at www.paralegal.delmar. cengage.com where you will find valuable information

such as hot links and sample materials to download, as well as other Delmar Cengage Learning products.

---

Please note that the internet resources are of a time-sensitive nature and URL addresses may often change or be deleted.

# ACKNOWLEDGMENTS

Thanks and appreciation are extended to the manuscript reviewers, instructors, and others who provided invaluable suggestions and support in the preparation of the fifth edition:

**Carol Halley**
National American University
Brooklyn Center, MN

**Christie Highlander**
SW Illinois Community College
Granite City, IL

**Robert Jacobs**
Central Washington University
Ellensburg, WA

**Janice Kazmier**
Tulane University
Jefferson, LA

**Nancy Simmons**
St. Louis Community College at Meramec
St. Louis, MO

**Debra Wicks**
Evans City, PA

# The Historical Basis and Current Structure of the American Legal System

The new government has finally been established. With the help of a committed military and citizenship, the Constitution was adopted and the first open elections were held. There is still unrest in many areas, and some conflicts continue. There are those who still maintain that a return to the former system of government is imminent and the best alternative for the public at large. However, the majority has spoken and established the new course for what promises to be a nation unlike any other that the people of this nation have ever known. Many look forward to the freedoms they have only dreamt of in the past. The new Congress has convened and is in the process of passing legislation to give structure to the government and protect the rights of individuals. A judiciary has been appointed, and now hears the cases coming before them from the citizens. High ranking officials hope that after so many years of struggle it is only a matter of time until foreign military forces leave the soil of the burgeoning nation, and peace will finally reign over this battle scarred country.

*The Boston Revolutionary Herald,* 1776

## CHAPTER OBJECTIVES

After reading this chapter, you should be able to:

- Distinguish the positivist, naturalist, and sociological theories.

- Explain the role of the political theories in the current system of American government.

- Discuss the weaknesses of the Articles of Confederation.

- Describe the function of each branch of government under the Constitution.

- Explain the differences between legislative, judicial, and administrative law.

- Distinguish the traditional and modern balance of application of laws.

- List the hierarchy of law and explain the exception to the rule of the hierarchy.

## THE HISTORICAL BASIS OF AMERICAN LAW

The historical path of democracy has been traveled many times since the creation of the American legal system. The newspaper article on the preceding page could have been written about many new governments, including the most recent attempt to establish a democratic system in Iraq. The concept is relatively straightforward. Citizens want a just and proper governmental authority that addresses inequality, reveres individual rights, and protects the population as a whole. In this chapter, the focus is on how these goals have been approached through the systematic development of the American legal system despite sociological and economic changes. Subsequent chapters examine both the mechanical aspects of the American legal system and fundamental concepts in the most common areas of legal practice within the system.

While the purpose of this text and this chapter is not to provide a course on American history, there are important facts to note. The longevity of the American legal system is derived from a complex equation that allows the laws to provide stability while also being responsive to the need for change. Understanding this basis, it is easier to see how and why the American government was established to withstand the tests of time.

### Before the Government

The American legal system was not developed hastily. The first settlers in the New World had no intention of creating an entirely new legal system. For more than a century, these people clung to the methods of law and order that they or their ancestors had known in Europe, predominately in England. These colonists not only adhered to many of the laws of England but also accepted and sanctioned the prevailing attitudes toward religion. Under these principles, people were charged and punished by the government for committing acts regarded as sinful and consequently illegal. As the American population grew, British and other European governments stepped up their efforts to establish a formal and permanent influence in America. These attempts included establishing the presence of foreign governments in the colonies by placing government officials there and attempting to enforce the laws of these foreign governments. Although the colonists were willing to adopt many legal principles, particularly from England, they were not interested in adopting a governmental structure that they felt was unresponsive to the will of the people. This was especially true because those foreign governments were the very structures the colonists had sought to avoid by coming to America.

During the revolutionary era that began in the mid-eighteenth century, the colonists realized that they had to establish some form of permanent governmental structure if they were to avoid rule by another country. Our modern structure derives from a combination of factors that influenced those who were responsible for establishing the American government. The founders' foresight is evidenced by many of the laws and procedures they created that remain in place more than two centuries later.

Initially, the colonists' primary legal concern was to deter and punish criminal acts as a means of maintaining order. As mentioned above, the founders sought to prosecute and punish those who committed what were seen as crimes against the morals of the predominantly religious population. Many of those in positions of authority in the new government were also members of the new American aristocracy. The focus of law in early American society thus was an attempt by this aristocracy to impress its perception of right and wrong on the working classes and to punish those whom the wealthy and powerful perceived to be improper or sinful.

The original system of justice in America was a simplistic theory of right and wrong. This theory, also known as the **naturalist theory**,[1] was based on the belief that all persons were born not only with the ability to distinguish the difference between right and wrong but also the knowledge that they were responsible for acting in the proper manner. However, the population increased, industry advanced and expanded, cultures mixed, and vast numbers of individuals with different opinions of right and wrong came together in communities. These developments rendered obsolete a justice system predicated on simple aristocratic beliefs of right and wrong. The people required a more detailed legal system that included written legal principles that could be applied to a myriad of circumstances and the entire population.

**naturalist theory**
Philosophy that all persons know inherently the difference between right and wrong.

As mentioned, with the increase in population and industry came nearly simultaneous attempts by other nations to control the colonies. Initially, colonies fought this control as individual governments without ties to the other colonies, but the colonists quickly realized that if any of them were to succeed against the attempts of others to take control, especially the British, the colonies must become unified.

## The Results of the Revolution

At the time of the Revolution, the colonies came together and issued their Declaration of Independence. To enforce such a document was not an easy task for a largely unsophisticated, poorly armed, and disorganized band of citizens who were matched against Great Britain's army and navy and any other country that might attempt to increase its power and position on the world stage. Nevertheless, the people formed a central government made up of individual states.

This new government was guided for eleven years by a document known as the Articles of Confederation. The Constitution as we know it was not passed until September 1787. The Articles bore little resemblance to the current Constitution. Under the Articles, each state sent delegates as members of Congress who then nominated and elected a president among themselves. The delegates passed laws, acted as judges in disputes among the states, negotiated treaties, and served as the government for the new nation. The duties assigned the president were to preside over sessions of Congress and act as an ambassador to, and receive representatives of, other governments. All legal disputes with respect to individuals continued to be dealt with by each state's own system of justice.

The founders quickly realized that the Articles of Confederation and Congress were largely ineffective. The national government had no "enforcement power": It had no judges, no jails, and no way to force collection of the monies each state was supposed to contribute. Moreover, there was no money or organization to support a national army. Nor was there a staff of government employees to operate the government when Congress was not in session. The president was only the head of a small group of delegates, not the leader of the nation. Clearly, if such a nation was to succeed, then a much more organized system would have to be created.

Interestingly, one of the very first real issues in creating a permanent government was whether to allow the states to continue in existence. Several delegates, including some from the South, believed that the individual states should be abolished and that all people and all legal issues should be governed by a central authority. In history, small states within a country had often ended up in conflict with one another over power struggles and other factors that produced civil war. However, in this instance the idea failed to gain popular support because the settlers were fiercely independent and sought to preserve as much personal freedom from government as possible. In the end, a government of separate state governments and a national government with specific functions was created. The states were left intact because they could respond effectively and quickly to the needs of their citizens and the individual state economies. Keep in mind that mass transit and communication were virtually nonexistent and a distant national government was seen as being uninformed and uninvolved on matters of local concern. The national government was formed to protect the fundamental rights of all citizens and ensure that the state governments would not interfere with individual rights. The national government would also handle national issues such as interstate commerce, Indian affairs, immigration, and international issues such as treaties for trade and nonaggression.

**Establishment of Branches of Government.** Once the issue of national statehood was decided, a Constitutional Convention set out to create a structure for the new federal government. The Constitutional Congress drafted the Constitution, which clearly defined the powers and limitations of the national and state governments with respect to each other and to individual citizens. The members of the Constitutional Congress agreed that there would be three distinct branches of government, each with separate duties and all with the obligation to cooperate with and monitor the other branches to ensure that no one branch obtained too much power. This separation of powers was a direct attempt to prevent the development of the monarchy type of government that so many colonists had rejected by coming to America.

The first branch of government created by the Constitutional Convention was the legislative branch. This Congress would be elected by the people (directly for the House of Representatives but indirectly for the Senate, whose members were elected by the state legislatures until the Seventeenth Amendment was ratified in 1913). Congress would retain the sole authority to make statutory law. In this way, the people as a whole would always have significant influence in making the laws that all persons were required to follow. As delegated by the Constitution, only Congress, and no other branch, has the power to create statutory law. In the past, when any other governmental source attempted to create statutory law, the law has been struck down as being in violation of what is known as the *delegation doctrine*. The delegation doctrine is based on the legal principle that Congress cannot delegate or give away its authority to make statutory law. Chapter 4 specifically discusses the development and application of the delegation doctrine more fully.

The executive was the second branch of government created in the Constitution. The president was given authority to head the executive branch at the national level. This is paralleled in the states, with each state executive branch headed by a governor. Under the Constitution, the president is elected indirectly by the people through the electoral college. Each state is entitled to appoint a number of electors equal to the state's total number of senators and representatives in Congress. A person cannot serve as both a member of Congress and an elector. Each state legislature determines the manner in which the electors are selected. The electors vote and elect the president by a majority. Generally, the electoral vote reflects the popular vote. In the event there is no one person with a majority, the House of Representatives is responsible for electing the president. The details of the electoral process can be found in Article II of the Constitution (Appendix A). Chapter 4 also discusses the executive branch.

The president has the power to approve or reject acts of Congress. The power is not absolute, however, and the president cannot deny Congress's authority to enact law if it is, in fact, the will of the majority that such law be enacted. Rejection by the president of a law enacted by Congress is known as an *exercise of the veto power* and can be overridden by a significant majority of Congress. The president also has several important functions with respect to foreign affairs and has the ultimate duty to enforce the laws of the United States. Consequently, federal law-enforcement agencies are considered part of the executive branch. A similar structure is in place at the state level between the governor and state law-enforcement personnel. The various powers and functions of the executive branch are discussed further in Chapter 4.

Finally, the Constitutional Convention determined that a third and separate branch of government was needed to serve as mediator of disputes, so it established the judicial branch. The judiciary has the task of judicial review. This branch of government has the authority and responsibility to interpret laws and protect the Constitution from violation by Congress, the president, or the states. Although the Constitution vests the ultimate authority to enforce laws in the president, in practice the judiciary also assists in enforcement when the courts apply law to specific cases.

**The Bill of Rights.** The three separate but related branches of government were designed to offer protection from a small number of persons gaining power over the entire population. By having the branches operate independently but with the power to influence one another, the people are better protected from one branch obtaining too much power or using its power unwisely. Through this system of *checks and balances,* each branch can use its specially designated powers to make sure the other branches act within their constitutionally prescribed limits.

In addition to framing the Constitution, the Congress, with the approval of the people, subsequently passed the Bill of Rights, which protects essential fundamental human freedoms. The Bill protects all citizens from government infringement on those matters that are presumed to be inherently personal and a matter of choice for all human beings. The following rights are specifically protected:

• Freedom of speech, religion, and press; peaceable assembly; petitions for governmental change (First Amendment).

- Right to bear arms (Second Amendment).
- Freedom from unreasonable invasion of home by the government for purposes of search and seizure of persons or property or for occupation by the military other than as prescribed (Third, Fourth Amendments).
- Right to have an independent judicial magistrate determine if probable cause exists before a search or arrest warrant can be issued (Fourth Amendment).
- Right not to be tried twice for the same crime (Fifth Amendment).
- Right not to have persons or property seized without due process (Fifth Amendment).
- Right to a speedy and public trial (Sixth Amendment).
- Right to an impartial jury in the jurisdiction where the alleged crime occurred or the dispute is governed by common law (Sixth, Seventh Amendments).
- Freedom from forced self-incrimination (Fifth Amendment).
- Right to counsel in criminal prosecutions (Sixth Amendment) .
- Right of the accused to know of the crime alleged (Sixth Amendment).
- Right of the accused to confront the witnesses for the prosecution (Sixth Amendment).
- Right not to be subjected to excessive bail (Eighth Amendment).
- Freedom from cruel or unusual punishment (Eighth Amendment).
- Freedom from use of the Constitution to limit individual rights not mentioned in it (Ninth Amendment).
- Right of the states to govern on matters not addressed in the Constitution or its amendments (Tenth Amendment).

The Bill of Rights establishes the standards of fundamental fairness by which the government must deal with its citizens. These standards have been and will continue to be protected by the U.S. Supreme Court.

**Additional Individual Rights.** In recent years, the Supreme Court has been increasingly asked to resolve issues that determine the rights of persons to be free from governmental intrusion into their private lives. Issues have ranged from abortion to the rights of law-enforcement officials to search and seize persons and evidence of criminal activity and even the death penalty. Frequently, news reports will discuss opinions of the Supreme Court that define the boundaries between the government obligations and individual freedoms with respect to the Bill of Rights. From time to time, additional language regarding these freedoms has been added through amendments to the Constitution as Congress and the people have deemed appropriate.

The Constitution and its amendments were not only created more than 200 years ago to establish a new government but also serve as the foundations of modern-day law. Every time Congress passes a statute, the executive branch enforces the law, or the judiciary interprets law applicable to a situation or an individual, such action must be taken in accordance with the requirements of the Constitution and its amendments. All law created in this country must be consistent with, and embody the spirit of, the rights guaranteed in the Constitution and its amendments. The Constitution and its amendments continue to be responsible for giving definition to the rights of citizens and government alike. More recently, the courts have used the Constitution and its amendments in high-profile opinions to prevent police from invading the privacy of individuals without a warrant, allow people the right to publicly express their religious and political beliefs, and encourage the public to take an active role in government through elections, petitions, and peaceful protests.

## ASSIGNMENT 1.1

Consider the following situations and identify which of the Bill of Rights would allegedly protect the behavior.

1. The right to have a parade to celebrate gay pride.
2. The right to create a religion that claims the U.S. government is an instrument of Satan.
3. The right to refuse entry to one's home by a police officer who does not have a warrant.
4. The right to have the government pay for some defendant's attorney's fees in a criminal prosecution.
5. The right to be released from jail before trial if the defendant deposits a sum with the court that is reasonably expected to deter the defendant from fleeing the jurisdiction or committing additional crimes.
6. The right to circulate a petition that supports the replacement of the democratic government with a dictatorship.
7. The right of media to be present during the trial in a criminal prosecution.
8. The right to carry a registered weapon in public.
9. The right to be informed of the charges against a defendant before the trial.
10. The right of a defendant to question the victim in an alleged case of sexual assault.

## ASSIGNMENT 1.2

Identify five modern-day situations in which the rights of an individual are at odds with the rights of the public as a whole.

*Example:* The right of a motorcyclist to choose whether to wear a helmet versus the right of the public to protect itself from the costs to the government in providing long-term care for individuals with severe brain injuries caused by motorcyclists who are injured when not wearing a helmet.

## The Influence of Political Theories

The functioning of the branches of government and the manner in which issues between government and citizens are decided are the product of distinct philosophies that have influenced the U.S. legal system since its inception. As Congress structured the new government, the naturalist theory became inadequate to deal with the complexity of legal issues that arose. As a result, other theories regarding the establishment of an orderly society were incorporated into the U.S. system of government and law. One influential theory was the **positivist theory**, which proposes that a government should have a single entity to determine what is right and wrong as a matter of law.[2] The law cannot be questioned or challenged. If a law is violated, punishment will automatically follow. This theory is evident in the court of last resort: the U.S. Supreme Court. Short of a constitutional amendment, the decisions of the Supreme Court are not subject to any other authority.

**positivist theory**
Political belief that there should be a superior governmental entity that is not subject to question or challenge.

Another political theory of law that has become an integral part of American law is rooted in social consciousness. This sociological view suggests that people as a group determine what is and is not acceptable, based on the needs of society at the time. **Sociological theory** holds that the law is in a constant state of change and adjusts accordingly to the needs of society. Society as a whole decides what is right and what is wrong.[3] In conjunction with the naturalist theory, the positivist and sociological theories provide the components for a successful and durable government. Today, the majority of law is created by representatives elected to Congress by the population. If citizens believe that a law is wrong, they can lobby to have it

**sociological theory**
Doctrine that follows the principle that government should adapt laws to reflect society's current needs and beliefs.

changed. If they believe their elected representatives are not enacting laws that embody the beliefs of the people, they can elect new legislators. If the legislature passes a law that appears to violate the Constitution, citizens can challenge the law in the courts, which have the power to resolve the issue by upholding the statute or invalidating it as unconstitutional.

## Balance as the Key to Success

In some respects, the U.S. government is a product of each of the three philosophies previously discussed. The naturalist theory is reflected in the language of the Constitution and especially the Bill of Rights, which state what was and continues to be considered fundamentally fair. The Constitution and the Bill of Rights also contain statements indicative of the positivist idea of an ultimate authority that interprets the laws and decides in what circumstances they apply and how they should be enforced. The ultimate rule has been embodied in the judiciary. Although laws can be challenged, in such cases the Supreme Court is generally the final authority on legal issues. A decision by this court can be affected only by a congressional constitutional enactment or in a decision wherein the Court revises a previous position (both are relatively rare occurrences). The Supreme Court helps ensure that the laws are applied consistently to all people. The duty of the Court is to guarantee that each individual's rights will be protected against government, persons, or entities that might violate those rights.

The sociological theory plays an important role in our governmental structure because society can influence the government and laws in many ways. The people have the right to periodically elect representatives to Congress and to select the president. They even have the right to approve or reject constitutional amendments and certain other laws. If society's needs change, the flexible system of government allows passage of laws, the election of representatives who will enact laws suited to the changing times, or both. Evidence of this can be seen in any governmental election. Theoretically, the members of Congress elected by the majority represent the beliefs of the people with regard to the law.

As a practical matter, citizens have more frequent personal contact with the judicial branch than with any other branch of government. Judges hear everything from traffic cases to domestic disputes to claims that Congress has exceeded the limits of its authority by passing laws that violate the Constitution. Since the beginning of the current system of government, courts have continually faced the task of balancing competing interests. These interests might be called the **traditional balance** and the **modern balance**, both of which are employed by judges when determining legal claims.

The traditional balance arose from the very heart of our governmental system. The people no longer wanted strictly positivist rule from a single source but wanted to have input into the laws by which they had to live. However, not everyone agrees as to what the law should be in a given situation. Under majority rule, laws are enacted based on what the majority thinks is necessary to protect the rights of the public as a whole. Some individuals, however, maintain that they have a valid right to disobey a particular law or that the law as written does not apply to their particular situation. In that case, the judiciary must examine the broadly written laws and apply them to individual circumstances. The challenge facing every judge is to enforce the laws to the extent necessary to protect the rights of the public while permitting the greatest amount of personal freedom possible for the individual. Simply stated, the traditional balance equals The Rights of the People versus The Rights of the Individual.

**traditional balance**
Goal of the judiciary to allow maximum personal freedom without detracting from the welfare of the general public.

**modern balance**
Goal of lawmaking authorities to balance the need for consistency and stability against the need for a flexible and adaptive government.

## APPLICATION 1.1

Barney owns an animal grooming, training, and boarding business known as Barks-a-lot Farms. The business was started by Barney's parents more than fifty years ago and has flourished. Recently, several homes in close proximity to the business have been purchased and leveled to make way for extremely upscale homes. As part of the overall development of the community, the city council wants to force the sale of Barks-a-lot Farms to make way for a private developer to put in a high-end shopping and restaurant complex. Barney does not want to sell. The city attempts to take the property through the eminent domain process on the grounds that it is for the greater public good. Barney wants to fight the forced sale of his family business and home.

This issue has arisen in recent years across the country as economic growth is balanced against individual rights. So far, the position of the courts has generally been that benefits to a community as a whole outweigh the individual rights—even though a commercial development is privately owned. The argument is that the jobs created and revenues generated benefit the entire community and the individual could, in fact, relocate to a similar setting.

*Point for Discussion:* Describe a situation in which the interests of the landowner might prevail over the desire of the community to obtain property by eminent domain.

Initially, judges had only to balance individual freedoms against the good of the nation as a whole. But over time, American society became increasingly complex. People from many different cultures, races, and religions came to this country in large numbers. The Industrial Revolution reached full force, followed by the age of advanced technology. The government withstood a civil war, two world wars, and numerous conflicts with other countries of different political structures. The longevity of the U.S. government is largely the result of the willingness of the judiciary and the other branches of government to develop and employ the modern balance in conjunction with the traditional balance.

The modern balance is an especially delicate one. In essence, it is the need to enforce existing legal principles based on the Constitution versus the need to adopt legal principles that are more reflective of current society. To write laws that would envision all the potential situations and changes in society for hundreds of years to come is an impossible task. Thus, the judiciary, with the help of the executive branch and Congress, must be able to recognize those situations where modifications in the existing system are warranted. This balance has been accomplished without ever disturbing the fundamental structure set forth in the Constitution. Indeed, the modern balance is the ability to enforce law consistently while retaining enough flexibility to adapt to changes in societal standards.

## APPLICATION 1.2

Historically, adoption was limited to heterosexual couples. However, as the makeup of the family in the United States began to change, laws were changed to allow single-parent adoptions. Following this, almost every state again amended its legislation to permit adoption of children by homosexual couples. This came on the heels of changes in law that placed the "best interest of the child" as the paramount consideration in determining custody of minor children. The courts and legislatures have determined that, in general, a homosexual couple and a single parent can provide an environment for an adopted child that truly serves the child's best interest over that of temporary placements. Thus, as society changed, so did the laws that reflected the beliefs of the majority.

*(continued)*

## THE MODERN LEGAL SYSTEM

The U.S. government that now enacts and administers federal law in the United States is far more sophisticated and much larger than the first government that took office under the Constitution in 1789. That government was a single Congress of senators and representatives from the thirteen colonies (the Senate with two senators elected by each state legislature and the House of Representatives with members proportionate to the population of each state), a president whose role was still not well defined beyond basic duties listed in Article II of the Constitution, and a single court to serve as the judiciary for an entire nation.

Today, that same Congress includes voting senators and representatives elected by the population of each of the fifty states. The presidency has developed into a complicated office that not only represents this country in foreign affairs but also oversees the administrative agencies of government and approves or rejects all acts of Congress. The federal judiciary has grown to include three separate levels: the Supreme Court, thirteen U.S. circuit courts of appeals, and more than ninety U.S. district courts. Interestingly, all three branches still follow the same basic purposes outlined in the Constitution. The manner in which each of these branches operates today is discussed in greater detail in subsequent chapters.

### The Sources of Law

The primary source of all law in this country is the U.S. Constitution. Added to that are the state constitutions for each of the fifty states. From these flow the other sources of law. A common misconception is that legislatures—either state or federal (i.e., Congress)—are the source of all laws. In reality, legislatures are only one source of law. Law, also known as a **legal standard** or legal principle, comes in different forms and from different sources. It can apply to people in general, a particular group of citizens, or a specific person or entity such as a corporation.

Each branch of government plays an active role in creating the law of the nation. In addition, each state has a system of government that is similar to the federal structure, and law at the state level is created in much the same way as at the federal level. The distinction is that state governments are responsible for dealing with those issues not addressed by the U.S. Constitution. The following discussion examines the sources of law as well as their relationship to one another and the hierarchy of law.

**Statutory Law.** As just noted, the most familiar law is legislative—that is, **statutory law**. Such laws are enacted by a state legislature or by Congress.[4] If a state legislature enacts a law, all persons and entities present in the state must obey it. If Congress enacts a federal law, all persons in the nation are required to follow it. (Chapter 3 addresses the manner in which legislative laws are created.) Once approved by the legislature, a statute will generally continue indefinitely as law until either the legislature repeals (deactivates) it or the high court of the state or federal government rules it unconstitutional. Federal laws must be consistent with the U.S. Constitution, whereas state laws must be in accordance with both the state and the federal constitutions. Similarly, no state constitution can conflict with the U.S. Constitution.[5] The provision of the U.S. Constitution declaring that federal laws take precedence over conflicting state laws is known as the *supremacy clause.*

**legal standard**
Legal principle, point of law. May appear in the form of statutory, judicial, or administrative law.

**statutory law**
A statute. Law created by the legislature.

**Exhibit 1.1**  Sample Legislative Language

---

**West's Ann.Cal.C.C.P. Sec. 128.5**

§ 128.5. Frivolous actions or delaying tactics; order for payment of expenses; punitive damages

(a) Every trial court may order a party, the party's attorney, or both to pay any reasonable expenses, including attorney's fees, incurred by another party as a result of bad-faith actions or tactics that are frivolous or solely intended to cause unnecessary delay. This section also applies to judicial arbitration proceedings under Chapter 2.5 (commencing with Section 1141.10) of Title 3 of Part 3.

(b) For purposes of this section:

(1) "Actions or tactics" include, but are not limited to, the making or opposing of motions or the filing and service of a complaint or cross-complaint only if the actions or tactics arise from a complaint filed, or a proceeding initiated, on or before December 31, 1994. The mere filing of a complaint without service thereof on an opposing party does not constitute "actions or tactics" for purposes of this section.

(2) "Frivolous" means (A) totally and completely without merit or (B) for the sole purpose of harassing an opposing party.

(c) Expenses pursuant to this section shall not be imposed except on notice contained in a party's moving or responding papers; or the court's own motion, after notice and opportunity to be heard. An order imposing expenses shall be in writing and shall recite in detail the conduct or circumstances justifying the order.

(d) In addition to any award pursuant to this section for conduct described in subdivision (a), the court may assess punitive damages against the plaintiff upon a determination by the court that the plaintiff's action was an action maintained by a person convicted of a felony against the person's victim, or the victim's heirs, relatives, estate, or personal representative, for injuries arising from the acts for which the person was convicted of a felony, and that the plaintiff is guilty of fraud, oppression, or malice in maintaining the action.

(e) The liability imposed by this section is in addition to any other liability imposed by law for acts or omissions within the purview of this section.

---

The language of statutes is fairly broad. Such language is necessary because the legislature wants to include as many potential situations as possible when it sets down a legal standard of what is right and what is wrong. However, if a court determines that a law is written so vaguely that citizens cannot determine exactly what is and is not acceptable conduct, the law will not be upheld as valid. The Constitution guarantees the right to fair notice of what is considered illegal conduct. Thus, courts have stricken statutes for being unconstitutional because of overly broad language.[6] The legislature has a particularly difficult but necessary task in establishing laws that apply to all intended persons and situations but that are also specific enough to warn an individual of what is required in a particular situation. Exhibit 1.1 is an example of statutory law.

The case below demonstrates an opinion by the highest court in the United States as it examines the constitutionality of the language of fairly recent legislation. Although the legislatures continue to pass laws that apply to the current needs of society, they must remain consistent with the objectives of the original Constitution. If they do not, they will be invalidated by the courts. Ultimately, for such laws to succeed, the Constitution would require further amendment.

# CASE
### *Ashcroft v. ACLU,*
### 122 S.Ct. 1700, 152 L.Ed.2d. 771 (2002)

---

This case presents the narrow question whether the Child Online Protection Act's (COPA or Act) use of "community standards" to identify "material that is harmful to minors" violates the First Amendment. We hold that this aspect of COPA does not render the statute facially unconstitutional.

*(continued)*

"The Internet . . . offer[s] a forum for a true diversity of political discourse, unique opportunities for cultural development, and myriad avenues for intellectual activity." 47 U.S.C. § 230(a)(3) (1994 ed., Supp. V). While "surfing" the World Wide Web, the primary method of remote information retrieval on the Internet today, individuals can access material about topics ranging from aardvarks to Zoroastrianism. One can use the Web to read thousands of newspapers published around the globe, purchase tickets for a matinee at the neighborhood movie theater, or follow the progress of any Major League Baseball team on a pitch-by-pitch basis.

The Web also contains a wide array of sexually explicit material, including hardcore pornography. See, e.g., *American Civil Liberties Union v. Reno,* 31 F.Supp.2d 473, 484 (E.D.Pa.1999). In 1998, for instance, there were approximately 28,000 adult sites promoting pornography on the Web. Because "[n]avigating the Web is relatively straightforward," *Reno v. American Civil Liberties Union,* 521 U.S. 844, 852, 117 S.Ct. 2329, 138 L.Ed.2d 874 (1997), and access to the Internet is widely available in homes, schools, and libraries across the country, children may discover this pornographic material either by deliberately accessing pornographic Web sites or by stumbling upon them. . . .

When this litigation commenced in 1998, "[a]pproximately 70.2 million people of all ages use[d] the Internet in the United States." App. 171. It is now estimated that 115.2 million Americans use the Internet at least once a month and 176.5 million Americans have Internet access either at home or at work. See More Americans Online, *New York Times,* Nov. 19, 2001, p. C7.

Congress first attempted to protect children from exposure to pornographic material on the Internet by enacting the Communications Decency Act of 1996 (CDA), 110 Stat. 133. The CDA prohibited the knowing transmission over the Internet of obscene or indecent messages to any recipient under 18 years of age. See 47 U.S.C. § 223(a). It also forbade any individual from knowingly sending over or displaying on the Internet certain "patently offensive" material in a manner available to persons under 18 years of age. See § 223(d). The prohibition specifically extended to "any comment, request, suggestion, proposal, image, or other communication that, in context, depict [ed] or describ[ed], in terms patently offensive as measured by contemporary community standards, sexual or excretory activities or organs." § 223(d)(1).

The CDA provided two affirmative defenses to those prosecuted under the statute. The first protected individuals who took "good faith, reasonable, effective, and appropriate actions" to restrict minors from accessing obscene, indecent, and patently offensive material over the Internet. See § 223(e)(5)(A). The second shielded those who restricted minors from accessing such material "by requiring use of a verified credit card, debit account, adult access code, or adult personal identification number." § 223(e)(5)(B).

Notwithstanding these affirmative defenses, in *Reno v. American Civil Liberties Union,* we held that the CDA's regulation of indecent transmissions, see § 223(a), and the display of patently offensive material, see § 223(d), ran afoul of the First Amendment. We concluded that "the CDA lack[ed] the precision that the First Amendment requires when a statute regulates the content of speech" because, "[i]n order to deny minors access to potentially harmful speech, the CDA effectively suppress[ed] a large amount of speech that adults ha[d] a constitutional right to receive and to address to one another." 521 U.S., at 874, 117 S.Ct. 2329.

Our holding was based on three crucial considerations. First, "existing technology did not include any effective method for a sender to prevent minors from obtaining access to its communications on the Internet without also denying access to adults." *Id.,* at 876, 117 S.Ct. 2329. Second, "[t]he breadth of the CDA's coverage [was] wholly unprecedented." *Id.,* at 877, 117 S.Ct. 2329. "Its open-ended prohibitions embrace[d]," not only commercial speech or commercial entities, but also "all nonprofit entities and individuals posting indecent messages or displaying them on their own computers in the presence of minors." *Ibid.* In addition, because the CDA did not define the terms "indecent" and "patently offensive," the statute "cover[ed] large amounts of nonpornographic material with serious educational or other value." *Ibid.* As a result, regulated subject matter under the CDA extended to "discussions about prison rape or safe sexual practices, artistic images that include nude subjects, and arguably the card catalog of the Carnegie Library." *Id.,* at 878, 117 S.Ct. 2329. Third, we found that neither affirmative defense set forth in the CDA "constitute[d] the sort of 'narrow tailoring' that [would] save an otherwise patently invalid unconstitutional provision." *Id.,* at 882, 117 S.Ct. 2329. Consequently, only the CDA's ban on the knowing transmission of obscene messages survived scrutiny because obscene speech enjoys no First Amendment protection. See *id.,* at 883, 117 S.Ct. 2329.

After our decision in *Reno v. American Civil Liberties Union,* Congress explored other avenues for restricting minors' access to pornographic material on the Internet. In particular, Congress passed and the President signed into law the Child Online Protection Act, 112 Stat. 2681-736 (codified in 47 U.S.C. § 231 (1994 ed., Supp. V)). COPA prohibits any person from "knowingly and with knowledge of the character of the material, in interstate or foreign commerce by means of the World Wide Web, mak[ing] any communication for commercial purposes that is available to any minor and that includes any material that is harmful to minors." 47 U.S.C. § 231(a)(1).

. . . Congress limited the scope of COPA's coverage in at least three ways. First, . . . COPA applies only to material displayed on the World Wide Web. Second, . . . COPA covers only communications made "for commercial purposes." And third, . . . COPA restricts only the narrower category of "material that is harmful to minors." *Ibid.*

The statute provides that "[a] person shall be considered to make a communication for commercial purposes only if such person is engaged in the business of making such communications." 47 U.S.C. § 231(e)(2)(A) (1994 ed., Supp. V). COPA then defines the term "engaged in the business" to mean a person:

"who makes a communication, or offers to make a communication, by means of the World Wide Web, that includes any material that is harmful to minors, devotes time, attention, or labor to such activities, as a regular course of such person's trade or business, with the objective of earning a profit as a result of such activities (although it is not necessary that the person make a profit or that the making or offering to make such communications be the person's sole or principal business or source of income)." § 231(e)(2)(B).

Drawing on the three-part test for obscenity set forth in *Miller v. California,* 413 U.S. 15, 93 S.Ct. 2607, 37 L.Ed.2d 419 (1973), COPA defines "material that is harmful to minors" "as any communication, picture, image, graphic image file, article, recording, writing, or other matter of any kind that is obscene or that—

(A) the average person, applying contemporary community standards, would find, taking the material as a whole and with respect to minors, is designed to appeal to, or is designed to pander to, the prurient interest;

(B) depicts, describes, or represents, in a manner patently offensive with respect to minors, an actual or simulated sexual act or sexual contact, an actual or simulated normal or perverted sexual act, or a lewd exhibition of the genitals or post-pubescent female breast; and

(C) taken as a whole, lacks serious literary, artistic, political, or scientific value for minors." 47 U.S.C. § 231(e)(6).

Like the CDA, COPA also provides affirmative defenses to those subject to prosecution under the statute. An individual may qualify for a defense if he, "in good faith, has restricted access by minors to material that is harmful to minors—(A) by requiring the use of a credit card, debit account, adult access code, or adult personal identification number, (B) by accepting a digital certificate that verifies age; or (C) by any other reasonable measures that are feasible under available technology." § 231(c)(1). Persons violating COPA are subject to both civil and criminal sanctions. A civil penalty of up to $50,000 may be imposed for each violation of the statute. Criminal penalties consist of up to six months

in prison and/or a maximum fine of $50,000. An additional fine of $50,000 may be imposed for any intentional violation of the statute. § 231(a).

One month before COPA was scheduled to go into effect, respondents filed a lawsuit challenging the constitutionality of the statute in the United States District Court for the Eastern District of Pennsylvania. . . . While the vast majority of content on their Web sites is available for free, respondents all derive income from their sites. . . . All respondents either post or have members that post sexually oriented material on the Web. *Id.,* at 480. Respondents' Web sites contain "resources on obstetrics, gynecology, and sexual health; visual art and poetry; resources designed for gays and lesbians; information about books and stock photographic images offered for sale; and online magazines." *Id.,* at 484.

In their complaint, respondents alleged that, although they believed that the material on their Web sites was valuable for adults, they feared that they would be prosecuted under COPA because some of that material "could be construed as 'harmful to minors' in some communities." App. 63. Respondents' facial challenge claimed, *inter alia,* that COPA violated adults' rights under the First and Fifth Amendments because it (1) "create[d] an effective ban on constitutionally protected speech by and to adults"; (2) "[was] not the least restrictive means of accomplishing any compelling governmental purpose"; and (3) "[was] substantially overbroad." *Id.,* at 100-101.

The District Court granted respondents' motion for a preliminary injunction, barring the Government from enforcing the Act until the merits of respondents' claims could be adjudicated. 31 F.Supp.2d, at 499. . . . The District Court reasoned that because COPA constitutes content-based regulation of sexual expression protected by the First Amendment, the statute, under this Court's precedents, was "presumptively invalid" and "subject to strict scrutiny." *Id.,* at 493. The District Court then held that respondents were likely to establish at trial that COPA could not withstand such scrutiny because, among other reasons, it was not apparent that COPA was the least restrictive means of preventing minors from accessing "harmful to minors" material. *Id.,* at 497.

The Attorney General of the United States appealed the District Court's ruling. . . . The United States Court of Appeals for the Third Circuit affirmed. . . . The Court of Appeals concluded that COPA's use of "contemporary community standards" to identify material that is harmful to minors rendered the statute substantially overbroad. Because "Web publishers are without any means to limit access to their sites based on the geographic location of particular Internet users," the Court of Appeals reasoned that COPA would require "any material that might be deemed harmful by the most puritan of

*(continued)*

communities in any state" to be placed behind an age or credit card verification system. *American Civil Liberties Union v. Reno,* 217 F.3d 162, 175 (2000) . . .

We granted the Attorney General's petition for certiorari, 532 U.S. 1037, 121 S.Ct. 1997, 149 L.Ed.2d 1001 (2001), to review the Court of Appeals' determination that COPA likely violates the First Amendment because it relies, in part, on community standards to identify material that is harmful to minors, and now vacate the Court of Appeals' judgment.

The First Amendment states that "Congress shall make no law . . . abridging the freedom of speech." This provision embodies "[o]ur profound national commitment to the free exchange of ideas." *Harte-Hanks Communications, Inc. v. Connaughton,* 491 U.S. 657, 686, 109 S.Ct. 2678, 105 L.Ed.2d 562 (1989). "[A]s a general matter, 'the First Amendment means that government has no power to restrict expression because of its message, its ideas, its subject matter, or its content.'" *Bolger v. Youngs Drug Products Corp.,* 463 U.S. 60, 65, 103 S.Ct. 2875, 77 L.Ed.2d 469 (1983). However, this principle, like other First Amendment principles, is not absolute. Cf. *Hustler Magazine v. Falwell,* 485 U.S. 46, 56, 108 S.Ct. 876, 99 L.Ed.2d 41 (1988).

Obscene speech, for example, has long been held to fall outside the purview of the First Amendment. See, e.g., *Roth v. United States,* 354 U.S. 476, 484-485, 77 S.Ct. 1304, 1 L.Ed.2d 1498 (1957). But this Court struggled in the past to define obscenity in a manner that did not impose an impermissible burden on protected speech. See *Interstate Circuit, Inc. v. Dallas,* 390 U.S. 676, 704, 88 S.Ct. 1298, 20 L.Ed.2d 225 (1968). . . . The difficulty resulted from the belief that "in the area of freedom of speech and press the courts must always remain sensitive to any infringement on genuinely serious literary, artistic, political, or scientific expression." 93 S.Ct. 2607.

Ending over a decade of turmoil, this Court in *Miller* set forth the governing three-part test for assessing whether material is obscene and thus unprotected by the First Amendment: "(a) [W]hether 'the average person, applying contemporary community standards' would find that the work, taken as a whole, appeals to the prurient interest; (b) whether the work depicts or describes, in a patently offensive way, sexual conduct specifically defined by the applicable state law; and (c) whether the work, taken as a whole, lacks serious literary, artistic, political, or scientific value." 93 S.Ct. 2607 (internal citations omitted; emphasis added).

*Miller* adopted the use of "community standards" from *Roth,* which repudiated an earlier approach for assessing objectionable material. Beginning in the 19th century, English courts and some American courts allowed material to be evaluated from the perspective of particularly sensitive persons. See, e.g., *Queen v. Hicklin* (1868) L.R. 3 Q.B. 360, 1868 WL 9940; see also *Roth,*

354 U.S., at 488-489, and n. 25, 77 S.Ct. 1304 (listing relevant cases). But in *Roth,* this Court held that this sensitive person standard was "unconstitutionally restrictive of the freedoms of speech and press" and approved a standard requiring that material be judged from the perspective of "the average person, applying contemporary community standards." *Id.,* at 489, 77 S.Ct. 1304. The Court preserved the use of community standards in formulating the *Miller* test, explaining that they furnish a valuable First Amendment safeguard: "[T]he primary concern . . . is to be certain that . . . [material] will be judged by its impact on an average person, rather than a particularly susceptible or sensitive person—or indeed a totally insensitive one." *Miller,* 413 U.S., at 33, 93 S.Ct. 2607. . . .

The Court of Appeals, however, concluded that this Court's prior community standards jurisprudence "has no applicability to the Internet and the Web" because "Web publishers are currently without the ability to control the geographic scope of the recipients of their communications." 217 F.3d, at 180. We therefore must decide whether this technological limitation renders COPA's reliance on community standards constitutionally infirm.

In addressing this question, the parties first dispute the nature of the community standards that jurors will be instructed to apply when assessing, in prosecutions under COPA, whether works appeal to the prurient interest of minors and are patently offensive with respect to minors. Respondents contend that jurors will evaluate material using "local community standards," Brief for Respondents 40, while petitioner maintains that jurors will not consider the community standards of any particular geographic area, but rather will be "instructed to consider the standards of the adult community as a whole, without geographic specification." Brief for Petitioner 38.

In the context of this case, which involves a facial challenge to a statute that has never been enforced, we do not think it prudent to engage in speculation as to whether certain hypothetical jury instructions would or would not be consistent with COPA, and deciding this case does not require us to do so. It is sufficient to note that community standards need not be defined by reference to a precise geographic area. See *Jenkins v. Georgia,* 418 U.S. 153, 157, 94 S.Ct. 2750, 41 L.Ed.2d 642 (1974). . . . Absent geographic specification, a juror applying community standards will inevitably draw upon personal "knowledge of the community or vicinage from which he comes." *Hamling, supra,* at 105, 94 S.Ct. 2887. Petitioner concedes the latter point, see Reply Brief for Petitioner 3-4, and admits that, even if jurors were instructed under COPA to apply the standards of the adult population as a whole, the variance in community standards across the country could still cause juries in different locations to reach inconsistent conclusions as to whether a particular work is "harmful to minors." Brief for Petitioner 39.

Because juries would apply different standards across the country, and Web publishers currently lack the ability to limit access to their sites on a geographic basis, the Court of Appeals feared that COPA's "community standards" component would effectively force all speakers on the Web to abide by the "most puritan" community's standards. 217 F.3d, at 175. And such a requirement, the Court of Appeals concluded, "imposes an overreaching burden and restriction on constitutionally protected speech." *Id.*, at 177.

. . . The CDA's use of community standards to identify patently offensive material, however, was particularly problematic in light of that statute's unprecedented breadth and vagueness. The statute covered communications depicting or describing "sexual or excretory activities or organs" that were "patently offensive as measured by contemporary community standards"—a standard somewhat similar to the second prong of *Miller*'s three-prong test. But the CDA did not include any limiting terms resembling *Miller*'s additional two prongs. See *Reno*, 521 U.S., at 873, 117 S.Ct. 2329. It neither contained any requirement that restricted material appeal to the prurient interest nor excluded from the scope of its coverage works with serious literary, artistic, political, or scientific value. Ibid. The tremendous breadth of the CDA magnified the impact caused by differences in community standards across the country, restricting Web publishers from openly displaying a significant amount of material that would have constituted protected speech in some communities across the country but run afoul of community standards in others.

COPA, by contrast, does not appear to suffer from the same flaw because it applies to significantly less material than did the CDA and defines the harmful-to-minors material restricted by the statute in a manner parallel to the *Miller* definition of obscenity. See *supra*, at 1705, 1707. To fall within the scope of COPA, works must not only "depic[t], describ[e], or represen[t], in a manner patently offensive with respect to minors," particular sexual acts or parts of the anatomy, they must also be designed to appeal to the prurient interest of minors and "taken as a whole, lac[k] serious literary, artistic, political, or scientific value for minors." 47 U.S.C. § 231(e)(6).

These additional two restrictions substantially limit the amount of material covered by the statute. Material appeals to the prurient interest, for instance, only if it is in some sense erotic. Cf. *Erznoznik v. Jacksonville,* 422 U.S. 205, 213, and n. 10, 95 S.Ct. 2268, 45 L.Ed.2d 125 (1975). Of even more significance, however, is COPA's exclusion of material with serious value for minors. See 47 U.S.C. § 231(e)(6)(C). In *Reno,* we emphasized that the serious value "requirement is particularly important because, unlike the 'patently offensive' and 'prurient interest' criteria, it is not judged by contemporary community standards." 521 U.S., at 873, 117 S.Ct. 2329

(citing *Pope v. Illinois,* 481 U.S. 497, 500, 107 S.Ct. 1918, 95 L.Ed.2d 439 [1987]). This is because "the value of [a] work [does not] vary from community to community based on the degree of local acceptance it has won." *Id.,* at 500,107 S.Ct. 1918. Rather, the relevant question is "whether a reasonable person would find . . . value in the material, taken as a whole." *Id.,* at 501, 107 S.Ct. 1918. Thus, the serious value requirement "allows appellate courts to impose some limitations and regularity on the definition by setting, as a matter of law, a national floor for socially redeeming value." *Reno, supra,* at 873, 117 S.Ct. 2329 (emphasis added), a safeguard nowhere present in the CDA.

When the scope of an obscenity statute's coverage is sufficiently narrowed by a "serious value" prong and a "prurient interest" prong, we have held that requiring a speaker disseminating material to a national audience to observe varying community standards does not violate the First Amendment. In *Hamling v. United States,* 418 U.S. 87, 94 S.Ct. 2887, 41 L.Ed.2d 590 (1974), this Court considered the constitutionality of applying community standards to the determination of whether material is obscene under 18 U.S.C. § 1461, the federal statute prohibiting the mailing of obscene material. Although this statute does not define obscenity, the petitioners in *Hamling* were tried and convicted under the definition of obscenity set forth in *Book Named "John Cleland's Memoirs of a Woman of Pleasure" v. Attorney General of Mass.,* 383 U.S. 413, 86 S.Ct. 975, 16 L.Ed.2d 1 (1966), which included both a "prurient interest" requirement and a requirement that prohibited material be "'utterly without redeeming social value.'" *Hamling, supra,* at 99, 94 S.Ct. 2887 (quoting *Memoirs, supra,* at 418, 86 S.Ct. 975).

Like respondents here, the dissenting opinion in *Hamling* argued that it was unconstitutional for a federal statute to rely on community standards to regulate speech. . . . This Court, however, rejected Justice Brennan's argument that the federal mail statute unconstitutionally compelled speakers choosing to distribute materials on a national basis to tailor their messages to the least tolerant community: "The fact that distributors of allegedly obscene materials may be subjected to varying community standards in the various federal judicial districts into which they transmit the materials does not render a federal statute unconstitutional." *Id.,* at 106, 94 S.Ct. 2887.

Fifteen years later, *Hamling*'s holding was reaffirmed in *Sable Communications of Cal., Inc. v. FCC,* 492 U.S. 115, 109 S.Ct. 2829, 106 L.Ed.2d 93 (1989). *Sable* addressed the constitutionality of 47 U.S.C. § 223(b) (1982 ed., Supp. V), a statutory provision prohibiting the use of telephones to make obscene or indecent communications for commercial purposes. The petitioner in that case, a "dial-a-porn" operator, challenged, in part, that

*(continued)*

portion of the statute banning obscene phone messages. Like respondents here, the "dial-a-porn" operator argued that reliance on community standards to identify obscene material impermissibly compelled "message senders . . . to tailor all their messages to the least tolerant community." 492 U.S., at 124, 109 S.Ct. 2829. Relying on *Hamling,* however, this Court once again rebuffed this attack on the use of community standards in a federal statute of national scope: "There is no constitutional barrier under *Miller* to prohibiting communications that are obscene in some communities under local standards even though they are not obscene in others. If *Sable*'s audience is comprised of different communities with different local standards, *Sable* ultimately bears the burden of complying with the prohibition on obscene messages." 492 U.S., at 125-126, 109 S.Ct. 2829 (emphasis added).

The Court of Appeals below concluded that *Hamling* and *Sable* "are easily distinguished from the present case" because in both of those cases "the defendants had the ability to control the distribution of controversial material with respect to the geographic communities into which they released it" whereas "Web publishers have no such comparable control." 217 F.3d, at 175–176. In neither *Hamling* nor *Sable,* however, was the speaker's ability to target the release of material into particular geographic areas integral to the legal analysis. In *Hamling,* the ability to limit the distribution of material to targeted communities was not mentioned, let alone relied upon, and in *Sable,* a dial-a-porn operator's ability to screen incoming calls from particular areas was referenced only as a supplemental point, see 492 U.S., at 125, 109 S.Ct. 2829. In the latter case, this Court made no effort to evaluate how burdensome it would have been for dial-a-porn operators to tailor their messages to callers from thousands of different communities across the Nation, instead concluding that the burden of complying with the statute rested with those companies. See *id.,* at 126, 109 S.Ct. 2829.

. . . If a publisher chooses to send its material into a particular community, this Court's jurisprudence teaches that it is the publisher's responsibility to abide by that community's standards. The publisher's burden does not change simply because it decides to distribute its material to every community in the Nation. See *Sable, supra,* at 125–126, 109 S.Ct. 2829 . . . but nonetheless utilizes a medium that transmits its speech from coast to coast. If a publisher wishes for its material to be judged only by the standards of particular communities, then it need only take the simple step of utilizing a medium that enables it to target the release of its material into those communities.

Respondents offer no other grounds upon which to distinguish this case from *Hamling* and *Sable.* While those cases involved obscenity rather than material that is harmful to minors, we have no reason to believe that the practical effect of varying community standards under COPA, given the statute's definition of "material that is harmful to minors," is significantly greater than the practical effect of varying community standards under federal obscenity statutes. It is noteworthy, for example, that respondents fail to point out even a single exhibit in the record as to which coverage under COPA would depend upon which community in the country evaluated the material. As a result, if we were to hold COPA unconstitutional because of its use of community standards, federal obscenity statutes would likely also be unconstitutional as applied to the Web, a result in substantial tension with our prior suggestion that the application of the CDA to obscene speech was constitutional. See *Reno,* 521 U.S., at 877, n. 44, 882–883, 117 S.Ct. 2329.

Respondents argue that COPA is "unconstitutionally overbroad" because it will require Web publishers to shield some material behind age verification screens that could be displayed openly in many communities across the Nation if Web speakers were able to limit access to their sites on a geographic basis. Brief for Respondents 33-34. "[T]o prevail in a facial challenge," however, "it is not enough for a plaintiff to show 'some' overbreadth." *Reno, supra,* at 896, 117 S.Ct. 2329 . . . Rather, "the overbreadth of a statute must not only be real, but substantial as well." *Broadrick v. Oklahoma,* 413 U.S. 601, 615, 93 S.Ct. 2908, 37 L.Ed.2d 830 (1973). At this stage of the litigation, respondents have failed to satisfy this burden, at least solely as a result of COPA's reliance on community standards. Because Congress has narrowed the range of content restricted by COPA in a manner analogous to *Miller*'s definition of obscenity, we conclude, consistent with our holdings in *Hamling* and *Sable,* that any variance caused by the statute's reliance on community standards is not substantial enough to violate the First Amendment.

The scope of our decision today is quite limited. We hold only that COPA's reliance on community standards to identify "material that is harmful to minors" does not by itself render the statute substantially overbroad for purposes of the First Amendment. We do not express any view as to whether COPA suffers from substantial overbreadth for other reasons, whether the statute is unconstitutionally vague, or whether the District Court correctly concluded that the statute likely will not survive strict scrutiny analysis once adjudication of the case is completed below. While respondents urge us to resolve these questions at this time, prudence dictates allowing the Court of Appeals to first examine these difficult issues.

. . . For the foregoing reasons, we vacate the judgment of the Court of Appeals and remand the case for further proceedings.

It is so ordered.

**Case Review Question**

*Ashcroft v. ACLU*, 122 S.Ct. 1700, 152 L.Ed.2d. 771 (2002).

How is the COPA statute significantly different from the CDA statute?

**Judicial Law.** A second type of law is **judicial law**. The judiciary interprets law from other sources but also on occasion creates legal standards. Judges may consider a statute and determine whether it was meant to apply to the circumstances of a particular case. Persons in similar situations may then look to the judge's decision to guide their own conduct. Furthermore, the legislature cannot possibly enact laws that would apply to every conceivable circumstance. Therefore, when no law exists, judges are responsible for making law or extending decisions of judges in previous similar cases.

The tradition of judges looking to rulings in similar past cases is an integral part of the U.S. system of justice. The continuation of existing legal standards provides the element of stability in the modern balance. This process is commonly referred to as **stare decisis**—literally, "Let the decision stand." The doctrine of stare decisis basically holds that following the same legal principles in similar cases gives our legal system consistency. People can look to the past for guidance in what to expect from the courts in the future. The wisdom of past judges is utilized to achieve fair and consistent treatment of persons involved in similar cases.

When a court applies stare decisis and follows the same type of ruling as issued in a previous similar case, it is following a **precedent**—a previously established legal standard. Courts generally attempt to apply stare decisis with respect to precedents unless the prior case is too dissimilar in facts or issues or unless societal standards have changed since the precedent was established, making the former legal principle of the precedent impractical. In such a case, the court does not employ stare decisis but rules on the case based on new societal standards and establishes a new precedent for future reference. Chapter 2 presents more information on the way in which precedents are created.

In the opinion that follows, the higher court examines whether the lower court property applied precedent in its determination of the case. This reliance on previous judicial opinions and following the legal standards within them is an example of stare decisis.

**judicial law**
Opinions that are issued by members of the judiciary in legal disputes that have the effect of law.

**stare decisis**
"Let the decision stand." Method used by the judiciary when applying precedent to current situations.

**precedent**
Existing legal standards to which courts look for guidance when making a determination of a legal issue.

## CASE
*Duke v. Elmore,*
### 956 So.2d 244 (Miss.App. 2006)

Robert E. Elmore, Jr. ("Robert") moved for modification of custody of his and Heidi Elmore Duke's ("Heidi") minor child. The chancellor granted modification of custody, awarding physical custody, as well as $106.40 per month in child support, to Robert. Aggrieved, Heidi appeals. . . .

Robert and Heidi entered an agreement entitled "Child Custody, Support and Property Settlement Agreement" in 2001, which was eventually incorporated into the final judgment of divorce on May 31, 2001. In the

agreement, Heidi and Robert agreed to give primary physical custody of their minor child, Matthew Swedlund Elmore ("Matthew") to Heidi.

On April 11, 2003, Robert filed a motion for modification of final judgment of divorce and child custody in the Chancery Court of Monroe County. The motion alleged that a material change in circumstances adversely affecting the welfare of Matthew warranted a change of physical custody, in the best interest of the child. The material change in circumstances alleged by

*(continued)*

Robert consisted of allegations that: (a) Heidi was using Matthew's welfare in an attempt to extort money from Robert; (b) Heidi refused to divulge her place of employment and the responsibilities pertaining to such employment; and (c) Heidi was moving Matthew from residence to residence too frequently.

Heidi filed a motion denying the allegations on June 23, 2003. A trial was held on the matter on August 12, 2003, and the chancellor rendered an opinion on the same day. The chancellor found that there had been a material change in circumstances since the entry of the final judgment of divorce, and that, after considering the *Albright* factors, it was in the best interest of Matthew to modify primary physical custody in favor of Robert. The parties maintained joint legal custody, allowing Heidi visitation, and Robert was awarded $106.40 per month in child support.

. . . Heidi asserts that the chancellor erred in modifying the final divorce decree by transferring custody of Matthew to Robert for the following reasons: (1) no material and substantial change in circumstances had occurred since entry of the original divorce decree granting custody to Heidi; (2) the chancellor used an incorrect standard in modifying custody when there existed no adverse effect on the minor child from any actions of Heidi since entry of the original divorce decree; (3) the chancellor used an incorrect legal standard by his application of the *Albright* factors as a substitute for the required finding of substantial and material circumstances adversely affecting the minor child of the parties; (4) the chancellor used an incorrect legal standard by his misapplication of "totality of circumstances" where there was no home environment that was detrimental to the safety of the minor child; and (5) the chancellor committed manifest error in his analysis of the facts that he considered in applying the *Albright* factors in his overemphasis of the "moral" factor where there was no showing that it had adversely affected the minor child.

This Court will not reverse a chancellor's findings concerning modification of custody unless the chancellor was "manifestly wrong, clearly erroneous, or the proper legal standard was not applied." *In re E.C.P.,* 918 So.2d 809, 822(¶ 58) (Miss.Ct.App.2005) . . . "In the ordinary modification proceeding, the non-custodial party must prove: (1) that a substantial change in circumstances has transpired since issuance of the custody decree; (2) that this change adversely affects the child's welfare; and (3) that the child's best interests mandate a change of custody." *In re E.C.P.,* 918 So.2d at 823(¶ 58).

The totality of the circumstances should be considered when considering whether a material change in circumstances has occurred. *In re E.C.P.,* 918 So.2d at 823(¶ 58). . . . If, after examining the totality of the circumstances, a material change in circumstances is found to have occurred, the chancellor "must separately and affirmatively determine that this change is one which adversely affects the children." *Id..* The polestar consideration is, of course, the best interest of the child. *Id.* at 823(¶ 58).

In the case *sub judice,* the chancellor began his bench opinion by citing several cases enunciating the above legal framework. He then continued by noting that the polestar consideration, the best interest of the child, is analyzed through the *Albright* factors, whether dealing with an initial custody decision or a custody modification. The chancellor proceeded to apply the *Albright* factors to the facts as established through testimony. In doing so, the chancellor noted several times that Heidi had moved four times within the two years since the divorce, maintained sporadic employment, and ended up moving into a two-bedroom home with a convicted felon. Heidi testified that she was not sure whether the man was divorced yet at the time, though he subsequently testified that he was, indeed, divorced at the time. Heidi shared a bedroom with the man while her mother shared the second bedroom with Matthew. This went on for approximately ten months until she married the man. In conclusion, the chancellor found that the *Albright* factors came out in favor of the father.

After discussing the *Albright* factors, the chancellor discussed whether there had been a material change in circumstances since the original custody decree, and whether, if such a change had occurred, it was adverse to the best interests of the child. The chancellor stated, after noting that he had considered the totality of the circumstances, the following:

> "Now, the question is, is there a substantial and material change in circumstances here? This child has been exposed to everything from a barn to a felon. I'm not low rating horses. But I'm saying it's not the best place in the world to raise a little boy. It's not the best place in the world to have a stepfather who is a convicted felon. And I know you don't hold this against people for life. At the same time, there is a little child that doesn't even know he is one, by the admission of his own grandmother and his mother that they probably should not tell him that. Now, I'm going to be frank with you. I was not impressed with the testimony of Mr. Duke. I couldn't find him looking me in the eye. My grandfather used to tell me when a man looks you in the eye, you can tell whether or not what he is. Maybe that's not the sole criteria on the custody of children, but it's one of the measuring sticks that I use as a judge. I didn't like his countenance. I don't think it's in the best interests of a child for him to grow up under his leadership as a dad. I find that as one of the circumstances that makes this a substantial change in circumstances relative

to this child. I, secondly, find that his mother, in living with this kind of man for ten months in the presence of this child before she ever married him is likewise a substantial and material change in circumstances. I find that her constant lack of employment, all of those are factors as well as those I have already enumerated in this opinion that give rise to the fact that I contend and so find that there has been a substantial and material change in circumstances."

Heidi argues that the points emphasized by the chancellor as lending to a substantial and material change in circumstances were not supported by the evidence. . . . She argues that the "barn" was actually a nice apartment; that Mark Duke ("Duke"), the convicted felon with whom she lived and shared a bedroom for ten months before marrying, never did drugs and did not have a violent nature; that she had no duty to inform her child of Duke's status as convicted felon; that Duke's failure to look the chancellor in the eye did not indicate that Duke was not telling the truth when he testified; that her cohabitation alone was not sufficient to warrant a change in custody; that, citing *Cheek v. Ricker,* 431 So.2d 1139, 1144 (Miss.1983), a change of residence was not a material change in circumstances justifying a reconsideration of custody; and that she was not "constantly unemployed," but only unemployed for the first three months after the divorce, after which she had a job for eight months until moving to Olive Branch, Mississippi in June of 2002, when she began going to school full-time. Viewing the totality of the circumstances, and giving the findings of the chancellor due deference, we cannot say that he erred by finding that a substantial and material change in circumstances had occurred since the time of the original custody decree. We therefore affirm as to this issue. After finding that, viewing the totality of the circumstances, there was a substantial and material change in circumstances, the chancellor continued by analyzing whether such change adversely affected Matthew's welfare, followed by reiteration of his findings concerning Matthew's best interests. He stated:

> "We can't tell how that does here. I can't read into a crystal ball and say whether it does or not. We don't have that little boy here before us today. He's too young to testify. But what I'm saying is here, when you take the totality of the circumstances . . . that I've looked at here today and analyzed before you, I find that there has been a change that does affect the child's welfare. I find that the environment is not suitable for him to remain in it under the circumstances."

And thirdly, the most important part is that the child's best interests mandate a change of custody. . . . The Court finds that it would be in the best interests of this child that the custody be changed from the mother to the father, and the Court so holds. . . . [T]he case of *Riley v. Doerner,* 677 So.2d 740 . . . states this, that when the environment provided by the custodial parent is found to be adverse to the child's best interest and that the circumstances of the non-custodial parent have changed such that he or she is able to provide an environment more suitable than that of the custodial parent, the chancellor may modify custody accordingly.

Heidi argues that "[a]lthough the Chancellor stated that he found that there had been a change that does affect this child's welfare, the Court failed to cite one fact to show how the custodial parent's conduct had adversely affected the child."

In *Riley,* our supreme court stated that "we further hold that when the environment provided by the custodial parent is found to be adverse to the child's best interest, *and* that the circumstances of the non-custodial parent have changed such that he or she is able to provide an environment more suitable than that of the custodial parent, the chancellor may modify custody accordingly." *Riley,* 677 So.2d at 744. The court went on to state:

> We further hold that where a child living in a custodial environment clearly adverse to the child's best interest, somehow appears to remain unscarred by his or her surroundings, the chancellor is not precluded from removing the child for placement in a healthier environment. Evidence that the home of the custodial parent is the site of dangerous and illegal behavior, such as drug use, may be sufficient to justify a modification of custody, even without a specific finding that such environment has adversely affected the child's welfare. A child's resilience and ability to cope with difficult circumstances should not serve to shackle the child to an unhealthy home, especially when a healthier one beckons. The chancellor clearly found that, considering the totality of the circumstances, Matthew's welfare was adversely affected . . . that . . . Heidi's cohabitation with a convicted felon, when combined with her sporadic employment and frequent moves, constituted an environment adverse to Matthew's welfare. We cannot find that the chancellor was manifestly wrong, in clear error, or that he applied an improper legal standard with regard to this issue. Accordingly, it is without merit. Citing *Sturgis v. Sturgis,* 792 So.2d 1020, 1026(¶ 28) (Miss.Ct.App.2001), Heidi asserts that the chancellor erred because with no identification of the material change in circumstance nor statement of what conduct on the part of Heidi adversely affected the child, the lower court jumped into a weighing of the *Albright* factors. As discussed above, however, the chancellor did consider the totality of the circumstances and find that a substantial and material change in circumstances

(continued)

had occurred. It is obvious from the chancellor's bench opinion that he discussed the *Albright* factors first merely as a means of outlining the totality of the circumstances surrounding the parties. Accordingly, this issue is without merit. Heidi argues, citing *Riley,* 677 So.2d at 744, that there must be evidence that the home of the custodial parent is the site of dangerous and illegal behavior, such as drug use, in order to find that the custody can be changed. She argues that, as there was no evidence that any dangerous or illegal behavior was occurring at her home, the chancellor erred in finding that the environment adversely affected Matthew.

We disagree. *Riley* does not mandate that dangerous or illegal behavior be present in the home in order to allow a chancellor to find that the environment is adverse to the best interests of the child. *Riley* simply stated that such evidence may be sufficient to justify a modification of custody. *Riley,* 677 So.2d at 744. . . . The actual holding of *Riley* was that "where a child living in a custodial environment clearly adverse to the child's best interest, somehow appears to remain unscarred by his or her surroundings, the chancellor is not precluded from removing the child for placement in a healthier environment . . . even without a specific

finding that such environment has adversely affected the child's welfare." *Id.* A chancellor does not have to wait until a child's safety is in question before removing him from an obviously detrimental environment. Heidi's argument with regard to this issue is clearly without merit.

Heidi argues that the chancellor erred by overemphasizing the moral issues of Duke's felony conviction and of Heidi and Duke cohabitating for ten months prior to their marriage. We disagree. As clearly shown from the discussion above, a number of factors contributed to the chancellor's decision. . . . The chancellor also emphasized Heidi's lack of steady employment and frequent moves, which starkly contrasted from Robert's consistent employment and residency. The chancellor was not, therefore, manifestly wrong or in clear error, nor did he apply an improper legal standard. Accordingly, we will not substitute our judgment for that of the chancellor, and we affirm as to this issue.

## Case Review Question

How do you think the result could have changed if the mother had maintained a single residence and job?

Over the years, countless disputes have arisen that required the interpretation of law to achieve resolution. The legal issues involved in such cases are not considered significant or common enough to require a legislative act, and the courts are left to issue rulings to resolve the disputes. In this way, the judiciary frequently serves as a valuable bridge between the people and the legislature when it interprets statutory legal standards in highly specific circumstances or creates legal standards where none exist. For example, José Martinez intends to repair his roof. José is seriously injured when the ladder he is climbing collapses. José wants the ladder company to pay for his injuries, but there is no statute that requires ladder companies to pay for injuries caused by faulty ladders. The court, however, may look to prior cases that require manufacturers to be careful in the design and construction of products. Relying on precedent such as those prior cases, the court can apply stare decisis and require the ladder company to pay for José's injuries.

Judicial law has indirectly provided guidance to the state and federal legislatures as to the type of laws needed to be enacted. A perfect example of this involves the advent of the automobile. At first, many people were skeptical, and certainly most people never envisioned that motor-driven vehicles would become such an essential part of life. However, as increasing numbers of automobiles were placed on the roads, accidents happened, the need for roadways and traffic control developed, an overwhelming source of jobs was discovered, and mass transit became a reality. For the first time in history, the world became highly mobile with unlimited travel that was convenient and fast. Rules were needed so that people could make, sell, and buy vehicles efficiently and travel in them in safety and comfort.

Until the issues of automobile travel and its accompanying disputes became so significant as to warrant legislation, the judiciary handled them. As the number of automobiles and related legal issues increased, however, the legislature stepped in and established broad legal standards for the manufacture, sale, and operation of motor vehicles.

**Administrative Law.** Although the legislature attempts to arrive at legal principles that apply to all persons, the judiciary deals with individual circumstances. Over the years, however, it became increasingly clear that an additional source of law that could tailor rules for specific groups of citizens or subjects was necessary. In many sectors of our society and economy, large numbers of people or areas of commerce need specific guidelines. One such area is the air-transportation industry, which is overseen by the Federal Aviation Administration (FAA). It is impractical for Congress or even state legislatures to attempt to deal with all of the questions raised by this massive industry. At the same time, it would be unduly burdensome and increase the likelihood of inconsistent decisions from different judges in different areas if the judiciary had to handle all cases that arose. The response to dilemmas of this sort has been the advent of **administrative law**.

The Constitution gives the duty to enforce the law to the executive branch, which has the primary responsibility to determine when a law has been violated or whether the law is even applicable to a particular situation. Administrative agencies are overseen by the executive branch with direct influence by the Congress and the judiciary. At the federal level, the president is assisted by administrative agencies in carrying out the law enacted by Congress.

Administrative law primarily consists of two elements: administrative regulations (sometimes called *rules*) and administrative decisions. Administrative agencies issue regulations or rules that more specifically define the broadly written statutes. Administrative decisions issued for specific cases have the same effect of law as judicial or legislative law. These cases usually involve persons or entities that challenge the authority of the agency to issue or enforce a particular regulation.

Administrative law is an extension of statutory law established by Congress. Failure to obey administrative law can result in penalties or even criminal prosecution. Exhibit 1.2 shows an example of administrative law. Administrative law is quite complex and is discussed further in Chapter 4.

**administrative law**
Regulations and decisions that explain and detail statutes. Such regulations and decisions are issued by administrative agencies.

## The Hierarchy of Law

Although the sources of U.S. law are the legislature, the judiciary, and the executive branch, they are all interrelated. If the sources of law were completely independent, then the potential for deadlock would exist if the sources conflicted with regard to the law.

American law is governed by a distinct hierarchy. First in the hierarchy is the U.S. Constitution. Although technically the Constitution and its amendments are statutory law, they are considered superior to all other law because they established the governmental structure and the process for creating all other law. One concept that has remained consistent throughout the legal history of this country is that all branches of state and federal government and all persons in the United States must function within the parameters of the U.S. Constitution. If at any time the will of the people is in conflict with the Constitution, then the Constitution can be amended through the proper process, which is designed to guarantee that the amendment actually does reflect the will of the majority. Chapter 3 discusses further the process for amendment of the Constitution.

Next in the hierarchy of laws are the legislative (statutory) acts of Congress. Statutes have greater weight than judicial or administrative law because they are enacted by Congress and state legislatures, which are composed of people elected by the people. Thus, statutes are most likely to represent the laws intended for and desired by the majority.

**Exhibit 1.2**  4 C.F.R. § 247.3 Entitlement of Tenants to Occupy

---

**Code of Federal Regulations**

**Title 24—Housing and Urban Development**

Subtitle B—Regulations Relating to Housing and Urban Development Chapter II—Office of Assistant Secretary for Housing—Federal Housing Commissioner, Department of Housing and Urban Development Subchapter B—Mortgage and Loan Insurance Programs Under National Housing

Act and Other Authorities Part 247—Evictions from Certain Subsidized and HUD-Owned Projects Subpart A—Subsidized Projects Current through September 17, 2002; 67 FR 58678

§ 247.3 Entitlement of tenants to occupancy.

(a) General. The landlord may not terminate any tenancy in a subsidized project except upon the following grounds:

(1) Material noncompliance with the rental agreement,

(2) Material failure to carry out obligations under any state landlord and tenant act,

(3) Criminal activity by a covered person in accordance with sections 5.858 and 5.859, or alcohol abuse by a covered person in accordance with section 5.860. If necessary, criminal records can be obtained for lease enforcement purposes under section 5.903(d)(3).

(4) Other good cause.

No termination by a landlord under paragraph (a)(1) or (2) of this section shall be valid to the extent it is based upon a rental agreement or a provision of state law permitting termination of a tenancy without good cause. No termination shall be valid unless it is in accordance with the provisions of § 247.4.

(b) Notice of good cause. The conduct of a tenant cannot be deemed other good cause under § 247.3(a)(4) unless the landlord has given the tenant prior notice

that said conduct shall henceforth constitute a basis for termination of occupancy. Said notice shall be served on the tenant in the same manner as that provided for termination notices in § 247.4(b).

(c) Material noncompliance. The term "material noncompliance with the rental agreement" includes:

(1) One or more substantial violations of the rental agreement;

(2) Repeated minor violations of the rental agreement that:

(i) Disrupt the livability of the project,

(ii) Adversely affect the health or safety of any person or the right of any tenant to the quiet enjoyment of the leased premises and related project facilities,

(iii) Interfere with the management of the project, or

(iv) Have an adverse financial effect on the project;

(3) If the tenant:

(i) Fails to supply on time all required information on the income and composition, or eligibility factors, of the tenant household, as provided in 24 CFR part 5; or

(ii) Knowingly provides incomplete or inaccurate information as required under these provisions; and

(4) Non-payment of rent or any other financial obligation due under the rental agreement (including any portion thereof) beyond any grace period permitted under State law, except that the payment of rent or any other financial obligation due under the rental agreement after the due date; but within the grace period permitted under State law, constitutes a minor violation.

---

The judiciary has the authority to interpret legislation and to fill in gray areas where the law is unclear or nonexistent. The judiciary is also obligated to ensure that the law is consistent with the Constitution. We might think of the judiciary as the protectors of the Constitution. In any case that the judiciary determines the law does not meet the requirements of the Constitution, then it has the authority to declare the law invalid and thereby supersede the ordinarily superior statutory law. Constitutionality is the only basis for judicial rather than statutory law controlling an issue. A prime example of this would be a law that is vague or overbroad. Such a law is unconstitutional because it would not provide fair and clear notice to persons of what is illegal conduct. Such notice is a requirement of the Constitution and its amendments. Thus, the court would have the authority to strike down the statute and dismiss charges against anyone who is alleged to have violated the statute.

Last in the hierarchy is administrative law. Administrative agencies assist Congress by issuing regulations and decisions that clarify and aid in the enforcement of statutes. However, Congress has the right to eliminate an agency or regulations that are inconsistent with legislative objectives. The judiciary also has the authority to overrule an agency's actions when they are unconstitutional. The authority of the judiciary to overrule and invalidate law is not exercised lightly or frequently. The courts generally defer to the Congress unless there is a clear constitutional violation.

---

## ASSIGNMENT 1.3

Examine the following situations and determine which source of law would most appropriately deal with each situation.

1. New legal standards need to be created to govern security measures taken by private airports over private planes and pilots.

2. A person charged with driving under the influence on a public thoroughfare claims that she was on private property at the time of the observation by the officer and subsequent arrest.

3. An individual arrested for speeding on a city street says in his situation the law does not apply because he was on horseback.

---

## ETHICAL CONSIDERATIONS

The very heart of the U.S. legal system depends on honor and integrity. It is essential not only that the government work as intended but also that the representatives of that governmental structure act in an ethical manner. Knowing, however, that individuals are fallible and subject to the temptations of power and greed, the framers of the Constitution created a government based on a system of checks and balances that prevents any one person or group of persons from gaining too much power over the government or the population.

---

## ETHICAL CIRCUMSTANCE

In the early part of the twentieth century, the United States suffered through two world wars and an economic depression of epic proportion. Through the end of those Great Depression years and throughout most of World War II, President Franklin D. Roosevelt led the nation. Although the process was complicated and involved the input of many people, Roosevelt was largely credited with ending the Depression and bringing the war near its conclusion. He died shortly before the end of World War II. Before his unexpected death, however, there was a great deal of support for an unprecedented third and then a fourth term of office for Roosevelt as president. So close on the heels of the rise of Hitler to power in Germany, many people feared that the executive branch was gaining far too much power. Thus, in 1951, the Twenty-First Amendment to the Constitution was ratified, precluding any president from seeking a third term of office by election. This effectively defeated the power of any individual—whether pure in intent or unscrupulous—from gaining such a stronghold in the executive branch of government.

---

● | **CHAPTER SUMMARY**

This chapter has introduced the origins and development of the U.S. legal system. The system began as a singular governmental structure under the Articles of

Confederation, which were found to be ineffective and were replaced by the Constitution and the Bill of Rights. Under the Constitution, the government comprises three separate but interrelated branches designed to provide effective government of, by, and for the people: the judiciary, the executive branch, and the legislature (Congress). The Bill of Rights and subsequent constitutional amendments serve as the framework for the protection of individual rights and establish boundaries between areas subject to state and federal law.

The method of law followed in the United States is actually a combination of three theories: naturalist, positivist, and sociological. The naturalist theory believes that people know the difference between right and wrong and should be held accountable for any wrong conduct that results in injuries to another party. The positivist theory is represented by the principle that the supreme authority of a jurisdiction is the final decision in legal matters. Appeals may be made to the highest authority; beyond this, decisions are not subject to challenge or question. The sociological theory tempers U.S. law by providing for changes in the law when they are in the best interest of society as a whole.

The three branches of government are the three sources of law: the legislature (statutes), the executive branch (administrative actions from administrative agencies created by Congress but overseen by the executive branch on a day-to-day basis), and the judiciary (judicial opinions). The legislative body issues broadly written laws that must be adhered to by all persons. Administrative agencies give definition to and enforce statutory law. Judicial law interprets statutory law for specific individual circumstances.

In all law—but most apparent in judicial law—are the balances that enable the American system to function so efficiently. Under the traditional balance, government strives to maintain maximum personal freedom while protecting the interests of society as a whole. The modern balance aims toward following existing legal standards to provide stability to the government and give clear guidance to citizens while responding with flexibility to changes in societal standards.

One constant is that the Constitution is the supreme law of the land. Ordinarily, statutes have priority over judicial opinions and administrative law. However, if the judiciary finds a statute or administrative law to be unconstitutional, then it has the right to invalidate the statute or administrative law and rule on the case based on judicial precedent or other applicable statutory or administrative law. No law, under any circumstance, can be enforced if it is in conflict with the Constitution. If society demands such a law be held valid, then the Constitution must be amended.

The following chapters give much attention to the various branches of government. Each should be fully understood before proceeding to subsequent chapters that refer to the sources commonly responsible for establishing legal standards in particular subjects of law. Further, it is helpful in a more practical sense to understand where law originates as well as the law's place in the hierarchy. Such understanding enables one in a real-life situation to more clearly assess one's position with regard to the law.

## ● | CHAPTER TERMS

| | | |
|---|---|---|
| administrative law | naturalist theory | stare decisis |
| judicial law | positivist theory | statutory law |
| legal standard | precedent | traditional balance |
| modern balance | sociological theory | |

## ● | REVIEW QUESTIONS

1. What was the structure of the U.S. government under the Articles of Confederation?

2. What political theories influenced the structure of the U.S. government?

3. How does the U.S. Constitution guarantee that power will not fall into the hands of one person?

4. Explain how each political theory appears in modern-day government.

5. The flexibility and stability elements of the modern balance express what goals of the judiciary?

6. The individual elements and the elements of the people as a whole of the traditional balance represent what goals of the judiciary?

7. Explain the difference between stare decisis and precedent.

8. Give two characteristics of each type of legal standard: statute, case, and regulation. (An example of a characteristic would be the source of the legal standard.)

9. What is the only situation in which judicial decision is more powerful than a statute?

10. Why does the executive branch have the power to create administrative law through administrative agencies?

## ● | HELPFUL WEB SITES

Government Guide Main (links to local,
  state, federal government offices)      http://www.governmentguide.com

FirstGov (links to branches of
  federal government)      http://www.firstgov.com

## ● | INTERNET ASSIGNMENT 1.1

Locate the official government Web site for each branch of state government where you live.

## ● | INTERNET ASSIGNMENT 1.2

Using the Internet, determine whether the constitution for your state has been amended and, if so, when.

## ● | ENDNOTES

1. *Black's Law Dictionary.*
2. *Id.*
3. *Id.*
4. *Id.*
5. *Gonzalez v. Automatic Emp. Credit Union,* 419 U.S. 90, 95 S.Ct. 289, 42 L.Ed.2d 249 (1974).
6. *Schware v. Board of Bar Examiners,* 353 U.S. 232, 77 S.Ct. 752, 1 L.Ed.2d 796 (1957).

### STUDENT CD-ROM

For additional materials, please go to the CD in this book.

### ONLINE COMPANION™

For additional resources, please go to http://www.paralegal.delmar.cengage.com

# CHAPTER 2

# The Courts

## THE COURT JESTER

Although most people think of American courts as a place they never really want to go, courts are often the first line of defense in the effort to maintain order and fairness in our society. There are those few citizens, however, who are always ready to stretch their civil rights to the maximum, take advantage of all the opportunities the legal system has to offer, and entertain the rest of us in the process. Court isn't just about "getting the bad guy" and "making them pay!" Sometimes it is an opportunity to see more colorful citizens in their element, whether they are parties to a suit or serving their civic duty as jurors. Consider the following actual cases.

A case in New Jersey was filed when a dog owner failed to follow the local ordinance requiring him to seek permission in advance for the dog to defecate on the grassy area claimed as private property by another man.

A California woman was sued for improper election practices when she took snickerdoodle cookies to polling places on election day. The plaintiff in the suit was the political opponent who did not deliver cookies and lost the election by 181 votes—along with the lawsuit.

A West Virginia convenience store worker filed suit, alleging she injured her back while opening a pickle jar. The jury award was nearly $130,066 in damages accompanied by $170,000 for emotional distress and $2.7 million in punitive damages. The defendant appealed the verdict and the appellate court reduced the pickle injury verdict to just $2.2 million.

A suit was filed in Illinois by a male customer at a strip club. The customer claimed that the stripper slammed her breasts into the side of his head as he sat near the stage. He sought damages and claimed he was "bruised, contused, lacerated, and made sore by the breasts."

## CHAPTER OBJECTIVES

After reading this chapter, you should be able to:

- Discuss the characteristics unique to judicial law.

- Explain the twofold purpose of judicial law.

- Discuss the process of legal analysis.

- Apply the process of case analysis to a judicial opinion.

- Describe the structure of the federal court system.

- Describe the role of each primary level of federal courts.

- Describe the modern–day function of the U.S. Supreme Court.

- Describe the two general types of state court structures.

- Discuss the types of cases generally considered by the U.S. Supreme Court.

As explained in Chapter 1, U.S. law comes from one of three sources: the legislative, judicial, or executive (or administrative) branches. This chapter focuses on the law established by the judicial branch of government, giving consideration not only to the manner in which the federal and state court systems are structured but also as to how they function with each other. In addition, the chapter addresses the method of analyzing past judicial law for current and future application.

## THE PURPOSE AND EFFECT OF JUDICIAL LAW

The sampling of more unusual cases in the chapter's opening not only demonstrates the extremes to which people will go to pursue what is considered a legal right but also stands for something much more important. In many systems of government, there is little opportunity for the individual citizen to have personal concerns and issues addressed and legal remedies enforced. A driving force in both the drafting of the Constitution and the establishment of the U.S. legal system was the belief that the government should be responsive to the citizens who were subject to its laws. Although this belief sometimes appears to be tested to its limits, it also reinforces the concept and goal that all citizens are entitled to equal and equitable treatment.

## Characteristics of Judicial Law

All elements of the legal system are equally necessary. The executive branch monitors the conduct of Congress and, through its supervision of administrative agencies, establishes regulations for specific industries and specialized groups. Congress, through legislation, sets down statutory law that guides the conduct of all the people. The judiciary reviews the acts of Congress and the executive branch but, more importantly, serves as a forum for the people. Because every situation is different in some respect, judges are expected to have the knowledge and objectivity to examine individual situations and determine what legal standards are appropriate and how they should apply. Everyone can have access to the governmental system through the judicial branch, which is designed to provide fairness and enforce the rights of all persons.

The judicial branch is the only avenue by which people can seek individual resolution of personal legal issues. The court is the only forum in which a person can present information supporting a legal position and obtain court approval and enforced legal action. Legislatures enact laws to govern all people in a variety of circumstances. The executive branch, through administrative law, further defines and enforces legislative law. But the judiciary considers the situations of individuals on a case-by-case basis and attempts to apply the most appropriate law and reach the result that is most fair under the Constitution. In this way, the courts are the most responsive branch of government to the individual. The judicial branch is the only governmental authority with the power to create law for an individual situation when none exists. The legislative and executive branches are more indirect reflections of the needs of society as a whole. However, these branches are also necessary to establish legal standards that the people can, in most cases, follow without the need for judicial intervention.

## Clarification of the Law

By necessity, statutes are written in general terms that apply to everyone. As a result, it is often unclear whether a statute encompasses a highly specific situation. This is where the assistance of the judiciary becomes essential. Judges are expected to have sufficient knowledge and training to evaluate statutes and determine whether they apply to a particular situation. In the event a judge finds a statute inapplicable, another statute or legal principle from a prior case can be applied. In doing so, the judge is performing one of the primary functions of the judiciary: to clarify the law as it applies to specific circumstances.

These interpretations of statutory or administrative law occur anytime a statute or administrative regulation or decision is an issue in a case. If, for example, someone challenges a speeding ticket, the government must prove that the statute of maximum miles per hour was violated. The judge must review the statute and the facts of the case. The judge must then determine whether under the facts the law applies and whether the law was violated. This is one example of a judicial interpretation of a statute.

As Application 2.1 illustrates, most cases have much more complicated facts than are addressed by the broad language of a statute. There seem always to be specific questions that are not clearly answered by the statute and to which the judge must at this point establish answers. This is done by looking to the purpose of the statute and the intent of the legislature in passing the statute. Judges also look at how past similar cases were treated in the courts. Although no two cases are exactly alike, a judge may apply the same ruling in cases that have striking similarities. Such similarities may be in the facts of the case, in the legal issues involved, or in both. Finally, judges are required to draw on their knowledge and experience to establish what is considered to be a logical and fair interpretation of the statute.

## , APPLICATION 2.1

Sandra Collinise was twenty-three years old when she was involved in a serious accident. Her injuries left her in a persistent vegetative state with no functioning above the brain stem. She had no discernible mental activity. Sandra was kept alive completely through artificial means that included a respirator and a feeding tube. After three years, her condition was unchanged. Her parents and legal guardians wanted to discontinue the medical equipment and allow her to die naturally. However, Sandra did not have a living will, advance directive, or any other documentation to indicate her wishes in the event of such an occurrence. Sandra's medical care providers were under a legal obligation to take the necessary steps to save her life. On filing a petition with the court as her guardians, Sandra's parents would be entitled to present evidence—such as conversations with third parties—as to what Sandra's wishes would be if she could think logically and communicate. The court would then examine the applicable statutes, cases, constitutional right to privacy, and other relevant legal standards to determine whether artificial life support should be discontinued.

*Point for Discussion:* If the Bill of Rights guarantees the right to privacy and, in turn, the right to determine the extent of medical care provided, then how can the state have the right to force artificial life support on an individual?

In cases in which no applicable statute exists, a judge is required to establish the law. This may be done by looking to case law (the precedents of past similar cases) and applying the principle of stare decisis. In a situation in which absolutely no prior judicial precedent exists, a judge must create one. This is known as *common law,* a term that has carried over from medieval times when judges created law for the common man. Technically, common law is defined as a newly established legal principle, whereas *case law* is the application of stare decisis (perpetuating and continuing the application of a prior legal principle). In actual practice, the terms *common law* and *case law* have come to be used interchangeably. The basic concept is that the terms represent judicially created law. In some instances, such law may be a specific interpretation and definition of a statute; in other cases, it refers to the creation or continuation of a legal principle where no statutory language applied. Still another case might call for the creation of a legal standard when no applicable law exists.

Case law significantly benefits the general public. Individuals can look at existing case law in relation to their own situations. By comparing established precedents, persons involved in lawsuits can often predict with some certainty the likely outcome of their case. In so doing, through a process known as *legal analysis,* they can make intelligent decisions about whether to pursue, settle, or dismiss a dispute. Such analysis is also a useful method for determining the best course of action to avoid a dispute. (Legal analysis is discussed in more detail later in the chapter.)

## ASSIGNMENT 2.1

Examine the following situations. Evaluate and determine whether each situation represents a court's application of a statute, creation of common law, or application of stare decisis. Explain your answers.

1. An individual who is regularly taking prescription drugs on a long-term basis misses his medication. He does so deliberately because the medication is not to be taken along with alcohol consumption and

*(continued)*

## ASSIGNMENT 2.1 (Continued)

he plans to attend a party where liquor will be served. Although he is not legally drunk, the effects of the missed dose of medication affect his ability to concentrate. While driving home, he is inattentive and crosses the center line and strikes an oncoming car. The driver of the other car is killed. The family of the victim sues the driver who caused the accident. A judge determines that the knowledge of the driver that failure to take prescribed medication could affect his ability to drive is sufficient to impose responsibility for the death despite no legal precedent for such a circumstance.

2. The owner of a sporting goods store has a large display of live fish. Although some of the fish are carnivorous, the owner has not placed a cover over the tank. A customer's child reaches into the tank and is severely bitten. The customer sues the store owner. The judge holds that failure to take appropriate precautions with known dangers on one's property with regard to invited customers has long been held by the judiciary as a basis for liability in other cases when injuries arise from the danger.

3. A day care provider is licensed to care for up to six children in her home. During an unannounced inspection by a state agency, the provider is found to have fourteen children in her care. The provider's license is revoked for violating the laws of the state government that issued the license.

## Protection of the Law

A second function of the judiciary is to protect and uphold law that is consistent with the Constitution. To provide such protection, the judiciary has the duty to impose legal liability when legal principles are violated. For example, when one person crashes into another person's car, the court would require the driver at fault to accept responsibility and pay for the damage to the innocent driver's vehicle and any other related damages. In a criminal situation, the police may arrest individuals who allegedly commit crimes, but it is up to the judge to determine whether allegations of such violations are true and to see that violators are penalized or make restitution for their actions or both. Essentially, when one person injures the rights, person, or property of another, the court must determine not only whether the law has been violated but also what an appropriate compensation or penalty for the injury would be.

### APPLICATION 2.2

Senior student Casey was a member of a competitive high school marching band. One of the competitions for schools across the state was held at a private university campus's football stadium. The day before the band competition, the stadium was host to a tractor pull put on by a local farmer's association, which rented the field. For the band competition, Casey's band was the first group to take the field. As the band performed, Casey stepped in a depressed area of the field created during the previous day's tractor pull. Casey stumbled and fell with his instrument. As a result, Casey hit his face on the instrument and lost four upper and four lower teeth in the front of his mouth. The missing teeth made it impossible for Casey to ever play his instrument at his prior level of skill. Prior to the accident, Casey had been offered a full scholarship to Julliard and planned a career as a professional musician. Casey sued the university for its failure to properly inspect and maintain the field. The university claimed that the uneven surface is a natural and obvious hazard of walking on an outdoor field and as a result it had no liability. In addition, it claimed that any damage was the responsibility of the farmer's association or Casey's own failure to watch where he was going.

*(continued)*

## APPLICATION 2.2 (Continued)

When reaching its decision, the court must consider the case and answer the following questions:

1. Is the university responsible for the acts of others who pay for the use of the facility and in the process cause damage?
2. Did the university act or fail to act in a way that caused or contributed to the circumstances of the injury?
3. Did any action or nonaction of the facility violate an existing legal principle?
4. Did Casey have an obligation to be aware of possible defects and take appropriate precautions?
5. If the university is found to be at fault, what should be done to compensate Casey?
6. Should any compensation be reduced by any percentage of fault assigned to Casey?

*Point for Discussion:* Why should an accident such as this become the basis for a lawsuit?

## THE STRUCTURE OF THE JUDICIAL SYSTEM

Originally, the U.S. Constitution provided for a single **federal court**. Congress was also given the authority to create new courts as needed.[1] Similarly, each state was responsible for establishing **state courts** to address the needs of its population. In the more than 200 years since the U.S. Supreme Court was created, literally thousands of state and federal courts have been added to the judicial systems to handle the ever-increasing number of legal claims of both individuals and government.

### Trial Versus Appellate Courts

The current federal and state court systems consist of two basic types of courts: trial and appellate. The **trial court** is the court in which the case is presented to the judge or jury. In the trial court, each party follows certain required procedures to prepare the evidence for a fair and complete presentation. The judge and, in many cases, a jury hear the evidence to support the claims of both sides of the dispute. This is the opportunity for both parties in a lawsuit to present their version of what occurred to produce the legal dispute. At the trial court level, testimony is given under oath, other types of evidence such as documents are presented, and each party has the opportunity to address the judge or jury (or both) who is deciding the case. When this is completed, a verdict is then given declaring whether the defendant is at fault for violation of a legal standard. In the event there is a finding of fault, a penalty may be assessed and the defendant may be ordered to compensate those injured by the violation of legal standards.

A court that hears trials is known as a *court of original jurisdiction.*[2] This is where the case is determined for the first time—that is, originates. If a party believes the trial court verdict is the result of failure to properly follow legal requirements for the proceedings, then that party may choose to appeal the verdict. Examples include failure to observe a technical requirement of procedural rules, failure to allow or the improper permission to introduce certain evidence, or anything else that might be considered a flaw in the trial process that affects the outcome of the case. When a case is brought on appeal, the judges of an **appellate court** will review part or all of the trial court's proceedings. An appellate court has authority superior to that of a trial court and has the power to change the trial court's verdict. Appellate courts often consist of several judges who review cases

**federal court**
A court that is part of the U.S. court system, has limited authority, and hears only cases involving the U.S. government, federal laws, or appropriate cases of diversity of citizenship.

**state court**
A court that is a part of the judicial branch in the state in which it is located. Typically, state courts hear cases that involve state law.

**trial court**
A court that has authority to hear the evidence of the parties before it and render a verdict.

**appellate court**
A court that reviews the actions of a trial court and determines whether an error has been committed that requires corrective action.

as a panel. With multiple reviewers, there is less chance that mistakes will be made in the review of an application of law to a particular case. This type of judicial authority is known as *appellate jurisdiction.*[3] Quite often, panels of three judges will review a particular case, but in extremely important cases, the entire group of appellate judges may review a case collectively. In such a situation, the decision the judges render is considered to be *en banc.*[4]

An important distinction between trial and appellate courts is the actual purpose of each court. It is the duty of the trial court to determine the applicable law, hear the evidence, and render a verdict, whereas it is the duty of the appellate court to only review what took place in the trial court and determine whether the law was correctly applied to the evidence presented. Appellate courts generally do not hear new evidence such as the testimony of witnesses. Nor do appellate courts issue new verdicts. Rather, they *affirm* (approve) or *reverse* (reject) the trial (lower) court verdict. If the appellate court reverses the decision of the trial court, then it also generally issues instructions as to the next stage of the proceedings such as ordering a new trial. Whether the court is part of a state system or the federal system, the distinction between trial and appellate court is essentially the same. More information regarding the actual proceedings in trial and appellate courts can be found in the chapters that discuss civil and criminal procedure.

## The Federal Court System

The federal court system started with a single court, now known as the Supreme Court of the United States. Over time, Congress added several courts to the federal judicial branch. Currently, the federal court system comprises three levels (see Exhibit 2.1), each of which functions independently of state court systems, just as each state judicial branch functions independently of the other states.

An easy way to distinguish a federal court from a state court is by the court's name. All federal courts will have the words "United States" or "U.S." in its name. No state court may include this language as part of its name. Of the three levels of federal courts, the trial courts—where the vast majority of federal cases originate—are known as the U.S. district courts. Generally, the U.S. district courts are used as trial courts. However, in limited circumstances, a federal case can be initially heard by an administrative hearing officer with the executive branch and appealed to the U.S. district court. In such an instance, the U.S. district court takes

**Exhibit 2.1** The Three Tiers of the Federal Court System

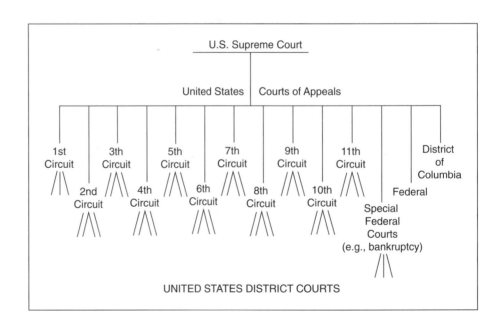

on appellate authority rather than its usual original jurisdiction. Also, certain specific types of cases may be initially filed for trial at the appellate level and bypass the U.S. district court altogether. This is not a common occurrence, however. Typically, the appellate level is reserved for parties who wish to challenge the decision of the U.S. district court. Such an appeal is made to the next level, which is the U.S. court of appeals. Following such an appeal, a party who is still dissatisfied with the result of the case may seek appellate review by the U.S. Supreme Court.

## The U.S. District Courts

Perhaps the busiest courts within the federal court system are the trial courts, known as the U.S. district courts. Currently, there are more than ninety such courts. Congress has increased the number of these courts when warranted by the number of cases filed and tried in the federal system. When the burden becomes too heavy for one court, Congress creates an additional court to handle part of the load.

The various U.S. district courts are separated by geographical boundaries. Legal disputes over federal law that occur or have connections to the court within the court's physical boundaries are subject to the authority of the U.S. district court. For example, if an individual violated a federal law in Montana, the U.S. District Court for the District of Montana would try the case.

For convenience and to facilitate understanding by the population, state lines have been used as district boundary lines. However, there is no connection between state court authority and federal court authority because of the setting of such boundaries. Courts simply use the same imaginary line to separate themselves from other courts. State and federal courts remain distinct even though a state court's or U.S. district court's authority does not exceed the geographical boundaries of the state in which the court is located.

Some states with substantial population and litigation have more than one U.S. district court divided by county lines (for convenience) within the state. For example, the state of Illinois has three U.S. district courts: the Northern District, the Central District, and the Southern District of Illinois. A district that covers a wide geographical area may be subdivided into divisions that operate as branches of a district court, with buildings in each division, to make the court more accessible to the citizens.

## Special Federal Courts

Although the vast majority of cases are brought to and decided through the U.S. district courts and the U.S. courts of appeals, other federal courts are set up for the express purpose of handling specific types of cases. Specified types of claims made against the U.S. government must be filed with the U.S. Court of Federal Claims. Claims involving federal taxation are tried in the U.S. Tax Court. The Court of International Trade hears disputes involving international trade agreements. The U.S. Court of Appeals for the Armed Forces offers a final review of military tribunal actions. These claims involve highly specific and often complex series of legal standards. In addition, the cases are often quite involved and drawn out. Thus, the dedication of specific courts and a judiciary that is specially selected based on experience and training for these types of matters creates a more appropriate environment for the fair disposition of these cases.

## The U.S. Courts of Appeals

A party to a lawsuit who is dissatisfied with a U.S. district court decision may appeal to the U.S. court of appeals designated to hear cases appealed from the particular U.S. district court where the case originated.[5] For example, someone who wanted to appeal a case from a U.S. District Court of Iowa would file the appeal with the U.S. Court of Appeals for the Eighth Circuit. By requiring the appeals from each U.S. district court to go to a specific U.S. court of appeals, parties are prevented from shopping for the appellate court that appears most favorable to their point of view. This system of pairing specific trial courts with a particular appellate court allows the appellate courts to create legal standards to be consistently followed by the designated U.S. district courts subject to each appellate court's authority.

The U.S. courts of appeals in the federal court system are intermediate-level appellate courts. Review at this level resolves cases that would otherwise be appealed to the U.S. Supreme Court, thus lessening the burden on the high court. U.S. courts of appeals were originally established to make appellate review faster, easier, and more accessible to parties in litigation. Over the years, as the number of cases filed has increased, so has the activity of these courts, which today are an essential element of the federal court structure.

Because of the tremendous number of cases filed and appealed in the federal court system, there are now thirteen U.S. courts of appeals known as *circuit courts*. Eleven courts are located across the country and identified by number (e.g., U.S. Circuit Court of Appeals for the First Circuit), and two others: (1) the U.S. Court of Appeals for the District of Columbia Circuit, which hears cases originating in the U.S. District Court for the District of Columbia; and (2) the U.S. Federal Court of Appeals, which hears cases from special federal courts such as the U.S. Court of Claims and the U.S. Court of International Trade.

The U.S. courts of appeals are the courts most responsible for establishing legal standards. These courts publish many more decisions than the U.S. district courts or the U.S. Supreme Court. Whereas the U.S. Supreme Court opinions control in any situation, the limited number of opinions limits the amount of legal standards established by the high court. Thus, when looking for precedent on a federal issue, a likely source would be the published opinions of the U.S. courts of appeals. Furthermore, because these courts are superior authorities to the U.S. district courts, a precedent from such an appellate court would be more persuasive than one from a trial court.

Like the U.S. district court, the physical limits of authority of each U.S. court of appeals are defined by geographical boundaries. For the sake of convenience rather than any connection with the states, the eleven circuits are divided by the boundary lines of several states. These boundaries delineate the area of authority of a particular circuit court of appeals over the U.S. district courts contained within the area. For example, the U.S. Court of Appeals for the Fifth Circuit has authority over all appeals from U.S. district courts located within Texas, Louisiana, and Mississippi. Similarly, the U.S. Court of Appeals for the Eighth Circuit governs U.S. district courts in North Dakota, South Dakota, Nebraska, Minnesota, Iowa, Missouri, and Arkansas.

Each circuit court of appeals is responsible for handling the appeals coming from the federal courts within the circuit's geographical boundaries, which are determined by Congress and altered periodically to adjust the flow of cases more equitably. As with the U.S. district courts, when the burden of cases becomes too heavy for a U.S. circuit court of appeals, Congress has the authority to create a new court or redefine the boundaries of the circuit. Exhibit 2.2 indicates the boundaries of the U.S. circuit courts of appeals and the U.S. district courts.

No U.S. court of Appeals has authority over any other. Each court functions independently and is accountable only to the U.S. Supreme Court. Frequently, different U.S. courts of appeals decide the same issue differently. When this occurs, the Supreme Court may accept one or more of these cases and decide what exactly the legal standard shall be. This eliminates any inconsistency that may arise among the rulings of the various circuits.

**Exhibit 2.2** U.S. Circuit Courts of Appeals and U.S. District Courts

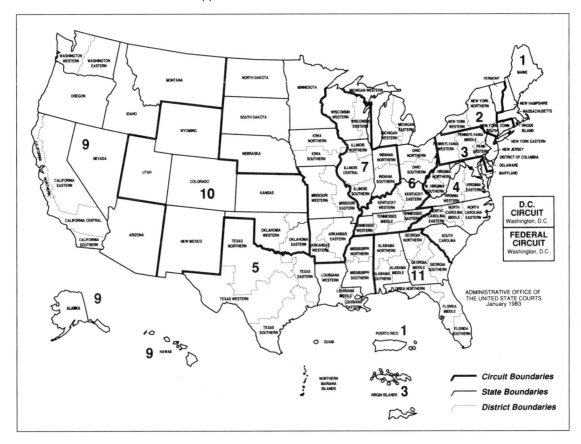

## The U.S. Supreme Court

The U.S. Supreme Court is the final authority on all matters of federal jurisdiction in the U.S. legal system.[6] It has the authority to review actions of Congress, the president, and the state governments. However, this authority is not limitless. Our legal system is based on the Constitution, and if the Court wants to take any action superior to one of the other branches of government, it must do so on constitutional grounds. In other words, the Court cannot overrule Congress or the president unless the legislative or executive branch has in some way violated or exceeded the authority granted to the branch by the Constitution and that action has been challenged in the courts.

The primary function of the Supreme Court is one of review. The Court reviews cases from the federal courts and, in some instances, from the highest state courts that have constitutional issues or that include the government as a party.[7] The key element in the authority of the Supreme Court is that there must be a federal issue at stake either in the form of the parties involved or in the constitutionality of state or federal law.

The Supreme Court has limited original jurisdiction.[8] Cases involving original jurisdiction are not appealed but rather are filed in court for the very first time at the level of the U.S. Supreme Court. Original jurisdiction is limited to only the types of situations listed in Article III of the Constitution.[9]

The U.S. Supreme Court has two common methods of obtaining review.[10] The first is by right. Certain types of cases are automatically entitled to review by the Supreme Court if the party so desires. The Court will review the case as long as the procedural rules for filing the appeal are met.

The second and more common method is known as *certiorari* (pronounced "sir-shore-are-ee"), which describes the authority of the Court to accept a number of cases for review where there is no right but where it would serve the interests of justice to have the Court make a final and ultimate determination of a legal standard. Considerably more than 1,000 petitions for certiorari are filed with the Supreme Court each year. However, because the Court can consider only a limited number within its term, it often selects those cases that contain major issues that have been decided differently in various courts and require a final decision to settle the matter permanently.

Another significant factor in determining to grant certiorari whether a decision offered for review involves constitutional rights. An ultimate goal of the Court is to ensure that the Constitution will be applied fairly for all persons. When the Court declines to accept a petition for certiorari, the practical effect is that it accepts and indirectly affirms the decision of the U.S. court of appeals. Finally, a U.S. court of appeals may "certify a question," in which case the appeals court may specifically request that the Supreme Court resolve a pertinent issue on which the various U.S. courts of appeals are divided.

## THE STATE COURT SYSTEM

Totally independent of the federal courts are the state court systems for each of the fifty states. Each state government has legislative, executive, and judicial branches that in many ways parallel the federal government. Every state has a judicial system to provide a forum for the resolution of disputes among persons and entities within the state. Such disputes must involve acts or occurrences that are controlled by state rather than federal law. The law may be case law or state legislative law. Federal courts and state courts are independent of and not subject to the authority of one another. (The exception is that all courts of the nation are subject to the U.S. Supreme Court.) No state court is bound by the authority of a court from a different state. Nor is a court obligated to follow the rulings of an equivalent court. Like the U.S. courts of appeals, state courts have equal authority. If a state court system has an intermediate appellate level of several courts, then the opinions of these courts would not be binding on one another. Rather, only the lower trial courts within the purview of authority of the particular appellate court would be bound.

The states utilize two basic judicial structures: three-tiered and two-tiered systems. The three-tiered system is comparable to that of the federal system. The three tiers are a *court of last resort* (the highest court of the state), an *intermediate appellate court level,* and a *trial court level.* Heavily populated states may have several appellate courts similar to the numerous U.S. courts of appeals circuits in the federal system. The trial courts include courts for civil and criminal trials, matters of domestic relations disputes, probate, juvenile, small claims, magistrates, and justices of the peace.

Approximately half the states employ the three-tiered system. The other states use a two-tiered system consisting of only one appellate (supreme) court and the various trial courts. However, because of increases in litigation, more states are considering the three-tiered system. In the two-tiered system, appeals from the trial court are taken directly to the high court of the state, placing the total burden on a single group of judges. In the three-tiered system, appeals are first taken to the intermediate appellate court in the same manner as applied in the federal system. A party who wants further review may then appeal to the highest court of the state. However, most appeals end after the first review, as the likelihood of a reversal declines dramatically with each appeal.

The terms *district court* and *circuit court* are used in some states in the same way as in the federal system. Other states reverse these titles. The circuit court is

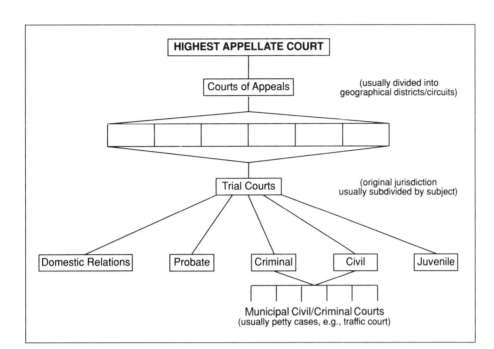

**Exhibit 2.3** Three-Tiered State Court System

the trial court, and the district court is the appellate court. Some states use other names entirely to describe their courts. Persons not trained in the structure of the legal system can be misled as to the importance of a judicial opinion by attaching more weight to the decision than is warranted simply because of the name of the court that rendered the opinion. What matters is that each state has a trial court level and an appellate court level and the decisions carry lesser weight in descending order from the highest appellate level to the lowest trial court.

Because the trial courts of the states handle more cases than any other level of state or federal court in the U.S. legal system, they must be organized to process the multitude of cases filed each year. Most often, state courts will divide the time of the various judges by the type of case filed. For example, certain judges will devote their attention to domestic relations (divorce, custody, support, adoption, etc.), while other judges will hear only criminal cases. These various divisions operate together to create the trial court level. In addition, the trial courts within a particular state (usually, at least one per county) are divided into geographical regions, usually bounded by county borders. Each court is responsible for the legal rights of persons and the legal issues arising from occurrences within the borders of the court's authority. By having a court within each county, the people are guaranteed reasonable access to the courts.

Exhibit 2.3 shows a three-tiered state court system. (A two-tiered system would eliminate the intermediate level of appellate courts.)

## THE PROCESS OF LEGAL ANALYSIS

Analytical ability is present in every fact of life. It is the skill of applying past experiences to current or foreseen circumstances to determine the probable outcome. This skill begins to develop in childhood. For example, if Billy refuses to wear a coat to school on a chilly day and is cold on the way to and from school, in the future he will remember that the experience was unpleasant and on the next cold day will wear a coat to prevent it from happening again. As knowledge accumulates, this ability to examine how situations develop and resolve becomes more refined and guides our present and future conduct. For attorneys, the skill lies in

**legal analysis**
The process of examining precedent in detail in order to predict its effect on future similar circumstances.

the ability to analyze past similar situations handled within the legal system and use them to predict the likely outcome of a current case. Because no two situations are exactly alike and legal issues are not as simplistic as dressing for the weather, **legal analysis** is performed at a much more complex level. It is necessary to identify all of the relevant similarities and differences of facts, the law of the jurisdiction, the parties, and the apparent attitudes of the judge and potential jury. Each of these must be evaluated in terms of their significance and impact on the likelihood of a similar result in the current case. Analytical skill also is directly supported by the training and skill required to locate and identify all relevant facts and law in a particular case.

It is rare that both legal research and investigation and discovery of facts produce little or no result. On the contrary, it is more often the case that attorneys must sift through a great wealth of information and either retain facts as significant or discard them as unimportant or inapplicable. This process in and of itself is legal analysis at the base level. Next, the more complicated task of evaluating (analyzing) the applicability and significance of what remains becomes the focus. Finally comes the crucial point when the lawyer determines the likely outcome of the case by applying the existing legal principles now analyzed in terms of the current case. This determination guides the case in terms of settlement, trial tactics and strategies, and even whether to appeal unsatisfactory results.

Legal analysis is the cornerstone of the U.S. judicial system. Legal professionals, judges, lawyers, and paralegals all use the process in their daily work. Legal analysis allows the judge to resolve a dispute consistent with the modern balance and allows the lawyer to advise the client as to the appropriate course of conduct based on past experiences of similarly situated persons. It enables the paralegal to know what information will be necessary to interview a client and prepare legal documents.

Legal analysis is performed with respect to statutes, administrative law, and cases. The process of analyzing different types of law varies somewhat because the format between law generated for the general public and legal standards applied to specific parties is different. However, the desired effect is the same: to determine the applicability or nonapplicability of the legal standard to the case at hand.

Legal analysis is predominantly the domain of legal professionals and lawyers in particular. The paralegals, legal investigators, and entire support staff of the attorney as well as those professions directly affected by law (e.g., tax law accountants) routinely engage in some level of legal analysis. The nonprofessional also derives significant benefit from the process of legal analysis in the application of legal standards through contact with attorneys and even news media.

By looking to established legal precedents, the paralegal and support staff can develop a sense of how various types of cases typically proceed, which also enables staff members to anticipate and deal with common procedural issues. In knowing what was and was not acceptable when engaged in discovery and investigation based on past cases, the legal support professional can perform these tasks much more efficiently and effectively. Human beings are basically analytical creatures who learn by experience and example. Although traditional methods of education are necessary, lessons are truly learned and then applied in a variety of other circumstances when they are experienced or, at the very least, observed in a realistic setting. It is one thing to read a principle of law such as the definition of negligence, but that principle becomes much more clear when a judicial opinion is read that demonstrates how negligence occurs in a real-life situation. As the legal support professional gains more and more knowledge of legal principles through practice, the skills of the professional can become highly developed.

Of the various methods of legal analysis, case analysis is the specific method of legal analysis of past judicial opinions and their impact on a current situation.

The similarities and differences between past cases and the current situation give insight with regard to whether the outcome should be similar in the current case. Because case analysis is used so extensively, an organized system for publishing and arranging the cases is necessary so that cases on specific topics or from particular courts can be easily accessed.

## APPLICATION 2.3

Mark has worked as a journalist on a small-town newspaper. He wants to make a change and hopes to have a career in law. In the fall he plans to begin college. He is particularly interested in investigative work and plans to become either a paralegal or legal investigator. He wants to sharpen his skills at this type of interviewing and obtains a summer job at a local legal assistance office. Mark is given the task of completing intake interviews. He is provided with a basic questionnaire to use when meeting with clients. However, he does not understand why this document is not just given to clients to fill out on their own. The paralegal in the office explains the importance of fully interviewing clients to gather additional important information that may not be requested on the form due to the uniqueness of every client's situation. Mark sits in on several interviews and concentrates on what types of answers and behaviors of the clients prompt the paralegal to delve more deeply into various parts of the interview. He also learns that, while possibly interesting, information that is not relevant to the case does not need to be further explored, unlike his previous work would have indicated.

*Point for Discussion:* How is a legal interview different from a newspaper interview?

## ASSIGNMENT 2.2

For each of the following situations, explain how legal analysis could help.

1. Darla is seeking legal advice. For many years, her husband was a business partner with his best friend. At one time, the business had a third partner. Ten years ago, when that partner left, Darla's husband and the remaining partner paid the departing partner one-third of the net value of the business as of the last day of the partnership. They did this in a lump sum and borrowed the funds to make the transaction. Darla's husband died approximately five years ago. The sole remaining partner agreed with Darla to pay her along the same terms. The remaining partner does not want to take out another substantial loan. Because of the large amount, Darla and the partner agreed the buyout would occur in equal monthly installments over a period of ten years at 6 percent interest.

Everything had gone as agreed until recently. The partner married a woman who became active in the business. She convinced her husband that because the partner was dead and did not even receive the benefit of the buyout, he should stop paying Darla. Nothing of the agreement was ever put in writing.

2. Chase is hired directly out of school as a paralegal in a law firm. On his first day, he is asked to prepare all of the necessary pretrial motions for an upcoming case based on medical malpractice. Not wanting to appear clueless, he happily takes the assignments and retreats to his desk. He needs to know what types of pretrial motions are typically used in trials of this nature and if there are any relevant questions he should ask the trial attorney with regard to possible additional motions.

## Legal Analysis of Case Law (Judicial Opinions)

Although judicial opinions are discussed in greater detail in subsequent chapters, a brief introduction will be given here for illustration.

Published cases are predominantly appellate for quite practical reasons. First, because trial courts are generally the lowest level of judicial authority, a trial court opinion need not be followed by a judge in a subsequent case. The decisions are applied to a specific case in a particular local. Other trial judges in the same court system or other jurisdictions may or may not interpret the legal standards in the same way. However, when faced with a similar case, trial courts are obligated either to follow a legal standard or interpretation from a higher authority or to make a clear distinction as to why the outcome of the case should be different. Appellate court opinions, on the other hand, must be followed by those trial courts that are subordinate to the authority of the appellate court that issued the opinion. Appellate courts typically hear cases from many different trial courts—for example, the trial courts across a particular region such as the lower part of a state all bring cases for appellate consideration to an appellate court designated to resolve issues within the assigned geographical area. Appellate decisions also are usually rendered by a panel of several appellate judges, rather than a single trial judge, whose collective wisdom is respected by the legal community. Such opinions are infrequently overturned by even higher-level appellate courts and thus provide a stable basis for comparison of the state legal standard to a current situation. A second reason for the limited number of published trial court opinions is cost effectiveness. Literally hundreds of thousands of trials take place annually in this country. It would not be reasonable to publish all of the opinions supporting the outcome of these cases when they are of such limited authority. However, with the advent of computer databases rather than hard-copy published texts, this becomes less and less of an issue.

Judicial opinions are published chronologically in a series of publications as they are handed down by the courts. The published opinions of a jurisdiction, and sometimes more than one, are published in the same series as they are issued. Each new volume in the publication is numbered consecutively and contains the most recently issued opinions. Periodically, format changes are made and a new series of volumes is started to reflect the updates. For example, when there is a change in how the information is presented, such as introductory materials in advance of each published case, the changes may be signaled by a new series of the same publication. A specific example might be the *Pacific Reporter, Pacific Reporter* Second Series, and *Pacific Reporter* Third Series. With each new series, the numbering of volumes starts over. The last book of the first series may be volume 311 (preceded by volumes 1 to 310); the next volume to be issued, if a new series is beginning, would be volume 1 of the second series rather than volume 312. This series and volume renumbering signals a change in the format of the material within. It does not signal a change in the chronological publication of opinions as they come down from the court or courts for whom the reporter is published. In addition, once a particular group of appellate courts is collected for inclusion in a reporter, those courts will continue to have opinions published in that particular publication. In this way, if one is frequently conducting research in a specific jurisdiction, the opinions from the appellate courts for that jurisdiction will be housed together.

The usefulness of published cases is immeasurable. By having access to opinions the courts have issued in the past, the parties can often determine with great accuracy the probable outcome of current disputes. Judges look to published cases to determine the appropriate legal standards and the manner in which the standards should be applied. In addition, it is not uncommon for parties or their lawyers to examine the published cases before taking any action whatsoever. Such examination often guides the conduct of an individual or business in matters that do not involve imminent legal action. Rather, these legal standards may be consulted in an attempt to avoid finding oneself in the same circumstances that have prompted lawsuits in the past.

When judicial opinions are read for the first time, they may appear to be long and drawn out with many difficult terms and obscure references, and they may not seem to make clear sense. However, with some basic skills and practice, reading and analyzing a case may become second nature. It is possible to read an opinion and mentally analyze it simultaneously. Throughout this text, cases are included to illustrate the various legal principles under discussion. Although these cases are edited somewhat to facilitate ease of comprehension, all of the essential elements of the original are represented. Reading the judicial opinions in the text serves two functions. First, they are real-life demonstrations of the subject matter of the various chapters. Second, reading them provides the opportunity to develop basic legal analytical skills. Even those who do not anticipate a career in the legal profession can benefit from learning to read and understand legal principles because law impacts all facets of personal and professional life.

Regardless of the judge or jurisdiction from which an opinion is derived, nearly all complete judicial opinions contain the same essential elements. This consistency allows not only a thorough understanding of the opinion and reasoning behind it but also an easy comparison to other similar legal issues that arise. Because the process of legal analysis allows consistency in the application of legal standards in similar cases, it is necessary that a regular pattern of information and reasoning be included. There are probably as many labels and methods of presenting an analysis of a judicial opinion as there are lawyers. However, regardless of the label or order of information, the content of a judicial opinion analysis is the same. A pair of jeans may be produced under thousands of different labels with countless variations on style, but a pair of jeans is still considered to be a pair of jeans.

The initial step in analyzing the meaning of a case is to know the elements of a judicial opinion. As mentioned above, various methods are available for analyzing a case. And the elements are sometimes broken down differently and given different titles. Below is one method of analyzing a case. The analysis can be renamed or reorganized in any fashion but will still contain the same fundamental elements.

Virtually everyone who performs case analysis consistently uses the term *case briefing*. The legal profession employs many types of briefs. The term *case brief* describes a synopsis of a judicial opinion. A common purpose of a case brief is to facilitate a determination of the effects of a previously issued judicial opinion on a current situation. To accurately make such a determination, one must examine each aspect of the case and decide whether the case is sufficiently similar to the current situation to create a likelihood that the same legal standards would be applied in the same way today.

In the following judicial opinion, which considers a case to terminate life support, the court must consider the actions of the trial court and determine whether legal standards were properly applied. Although the much publicized Schiavo case continued to be addressed through the appellate and even legislative system for four years following this decision, the basis for most of the appeals was procedural in nature and the true legal issues were resolved in the following decision circa 2001.

The following paragraphs describe the elements of a case. Although judicial opinions may be lengthy, the case brief is usually not because a brief's purpose is to identify only those points that were pivotal in the decision and consequently would be considered in a similar case. Therefore, when analyzing a case, no matter what element is being examined, one should focus only on those statements that directly affected the final decision.

# CASE

## In re Guardianship of Schiavo,
### 780 So.2d 176 (Fla. App. 2d Dist. 2001)

Robert and Mary Schindler, the parents of Theresa Marie Schiavo, appeal the trial court's order authorizing the discontinuance of artificial life support to their adult daughter. Michael Schiavo, Theresa's husband and guardian, petitioned the trial court in May 1998 for entry of this order. . . .

Theresa Marie Schindler was born on December 3, 1963, and lived with or near her parents in Pennsylvania until she married Michael Schiavo on November 10, 1984. Michael and Theresa moved to Florida in 1986. They were happily married and both were employed. They had no children. On February 25, 1990, their lives changed. Theresa, age 27, suffered a cardiac arrest as a result of a potassium imbalance. Michael called 911, and Theresa was rushed to the hospital. She never regained consciousness. Since 1990, Theresa has lived in nursing homes with constant care. She is fed and hydrated by tubes. The staff changes her diapers regularly. She has had numerous health problems, but none have been life threatening. The evidence is overwhelming that Theresa is in a permanent or persistent vegetative state. It is important to understand that a persistent vegetative state is not simply a coma. She is not asleep. She has cycles of apparent wakefulness and apparent sleep without any cognition or awareness. As she breathes, she often makes moaning sounds. Theresa has severe contractures of her hands, elbows, knees, and feet. . . .

Over the span of this last decade, Theresa's brain has deteriorated because of the lack of oxygen it suffered at the time of the heart attack. By mid 1996, the CAT scans of her brain showed a severely abnormal structure. At this point, much of her cerebral cortex is simply gone and has been replaced by cerebral spinal fluid. Medicine cannot cure this condition. Unless an act of God, a true miracle, were to recreate her brain, Theresa will always remain in an unconscious, reflexive state, totally dependent upon others to feed her and care for her most private needs. She could remain in this state for many years.

. . . Many patients in this condition would have been abandoned by friends and family within the first year. Michael has continued to care for her and to visit her all these years. He has never divorced her. . . . As a guardian, he has always attempted to provide optimum treatment for his wife. He has been a diligent watch guard of Theresa's care, never hesitating to annoy the nursing staff in order to assure that she receives the proper treatment. Theresa's parents have continued to love her and visit her often. No one questions the sincerity of their prayers for the divine miracle that now is Theresa's only hope to regain any level of normal existence. No one questions that they have filed this appeal out of love for their daughter.

This lawsuit is affected by an earlier lawsuit. In the early 1990s, Michael Schiavo, as Theresa's guardian, filed a medical malpractice lawsuit. That case resulted in a sizable award of money for Theresa. This fund remains sufficient to care for Theresa for many years. If she were to die today, her husband would inherit the money under the laws of intestacy. If Michael eventually divorced Theresa in order to have a more normal family life, the fund remaining at the end of Theresa's life would presumably go to her parents.

Since the resolution of the malpractice lawsuit, both Michael and the Schindlers have become suspicious that the other party is assessing Theresa's wishes based upon their own monetary self-interest. The trial court discounted this concern, and we see no evidence in this record that either Michael or the Schindlers seek monetary gain from their actions. Michael and the Schindlers simply cannot agree on what decision Theresa would make today if she were able to assess her own condition and make her own decision. . . .

This is a case to authorize the termination of life-prolonging procedures under chapter 765, Florida Statutes (1997), and under the constitutional guidelines enunciated in *In re Guardianship of Browning*, 568 So.2d 4 (Fla.1990). First, the Schindlers maintain that the trial court was required to appoint a guardian *ad litem* for this proceeding because Michael stands to inherit under the laws of intestacy. When a living will or other advance directive does not exist, it stands to reason that the surrogate decision-maker will be a person who is close to the patient and thereby likely to inherit from the patient. Thus, the fact that a surrogate decision-maker may ultimately inherit from the patient should not automatically compel the appointment of a guardian. On the other hand, there may be occasions when an inheritance could be a reason to question a surrogate's ability to make an objective decision.

In this case, however, Michael Schiavo has not been allowed to make a decision to disconnect life-support. The Schindlers have not been allowed to make a decision to maintain life-support. Each party in this case, absent their disagreement, might have been a suitable surrogate decision-maker for Theresa. Because

Michael Schiavo and the Schindlers could not agree on the proper decision and the inheritance issue created the appearance of conflict, Michael Schiavo, as the guardian of Theresa, invoked the trial court's jurisdiction to allow the trial court to serve as the surrogate decision-maker.

In this court's decision in *In re Guardianship of Browning,* 543 So.2d 258, 273-74 (Fla. 2d DCA 1989), we described, *in dicta,* a method for judicial review of a surrogate's decision. The supreme court's decision affirming *In re Guardianship of Browning* did not squarely approve or reject the details of our proposed method. However, the supreme court recognized that the circuit court's jurisdiction could be invoked in two manners:

> We emphasize, as did the district court, that courts are always open to adjudicate legitimate questions pertaining to the written or oral instructions. First, the surrogate or proxy may choose to present the question to the court for resolution. Second, interested parties may challenge the decision of the proxy or surrogate. *In re Guardianship of Browning,* 568 So.2d at 16.

In this case, Michael Schiavo used the first approach. Under these circumstances, the two parties, as adversaries, present their evidence to the trial court. The trial court determines whether the evidence is sufficient to allow it to make the decision for the ward to discontinue life support. In this context, the trial court essentially serves as the ward's guardian. Although we do not rule out the occasional need for a guardian in this type of proceeding, a guardian *ad litem* would tend to duplicate the function of the judge, would add little of value to this process, and might cause the process to be influenced by hearsay or matters outside the record. Accordingly, we affirm the trial court's discretionary decision in this case to proceed without a guardian *ad litem*.

Second, the Schindlers argue that the trial court should not have heard evidence from Beverly Tyler, the executive director of Georgia Health Decisions. . . . Ms. Tyler has studied American values, opinions, and attitudes about the decision to discontinue life-support systems. As a result, she has some special expertise concerning the words and expressions that Americans often use in discussing these difficult issues. She also has knowledge about trends within American attitudes on this subject.

We have considerable doubt that Ms. Tyler's testimony provided much in the way of relevant evidence. She testified about some social science surveys. Apparently most people, even those who favor initial life-supporting medical treatment, indicate that they would not wish this treatment to continue indefinitely once their medical condition presented no reasonable basis for a cure. There is some risk that a trial judge could rely upon this type of survey evidence to make a "best interests" decision for the ward. In this case, however, we are convinced that the trial judge did not give undue weight to this evidence and that the court made a proper surrogate decision rather than a best interests decision.

Finally, the Schindlers argue that the testimony, which was conflicting, was insufficient to support the trial court's decision by clear and convincing evidence. We have reviewed that testimony and conclude that the trial court had sufficient evidence to make this decision. The clear and convincing standard of proof, while very high, permits a decision in the face of inconsistent or conflicting evidence. See *In re Guardianship of Browning,* 543 So.2d at 273. In *Browning,* we stated: In making this difficult decision, a surrogate decisionmaker should err on the side of life. . . . In cases of doubt, we must assume that a patient would choose to defend life in exercising his or her right of privacy. *In re Guardianship of Browning,* 543 So.2d at 273. We reconfirm today that a court's default position must favor life.

The testimony in this case establishes that Theresa was very young and very healthy when this tragedy struck. Like many young people without children, she had not prepared a will, much less a living will. She had been raised in the Catholic faith, but did not regularly attend mass or have a religious advisor who could assist the court in weighing her religious attitudes about life-support methods. Her statements to her friends and family about the dying process were few and they were oral. Nevertheless, those statements, along with other evidence about Theresa, gave the trial court a sufficient basis to make this decision for her.

In the final analysis, the difficult question that faced the trial court was whether Theresa Marie Schindler Schiavo, not after a few weeks in a coma, but after ten years in a persistent vegetative state that has robbed her of most of her cerebrum and all but the most instinctive of neurological functions, with no hope of a medical cure but with sufficient money and strength of body to live indefinitely, would choose to continue the constant nursing care and the supporting tubes in hopes that a miracle would somehow recreate her missing brain tissue, or whether she would wish to permit a natural death process to take its course and for her family members and loved ones to be free to continue their lives. After due consideration, we conclude that the trial judge had clear and convincing evidence to answer this question as he did.

Affirmed.

*(continued)*

## Case Review Question

Would the Court have been likely to make a different decision if Michael Schiavo had requested the termination of life support rather than a court determination of whether it should be done?

## Case Brief

*In Re Guardianship of Schiavo,* 780 So. 2d. 176 (Fla.App. 2001).

### Facts

Theresa Schiavo suffered cardiac arrest and subsequent oxygen deprivation in 1990 at age twenty-seven. She never regained consciousness. The husband and guardian of Theresa Schiavo petitioned for the discontinuance of nutrition and hydration support for his wife, who had remained in a persistent vegetative state for approximately ten years. The parents of Theresa Schiavo opposed the petition. Medical reports demonstrated an absence of a large portion of the brain resulting from long-term deterioration. The medical evidence further showed no evidence of independent cognitive functioning. The court found that Theresa would not wish to continue her life in a persistent vegetative state artificially supported. The parents appealed the decision.

### Issue

Whether the trial court erred when it (1) failed to appoint a guardian *ad litem* to represent Theresa Schiavo, (2) admitted evidence regarding societal standards, or (3) granted the petition despite conflicting evidence.

### Law

*In re Guardianship of Browning,* 568 So.2d 4 (Fla.1990): First, the surrogate or proxy may choose to present the question to the court for resolution. . . . In this case, however, we are convinced that the trial judge did not give undue weight to this evidence and that the court made a proper surrogate decision. . . . The clear and convincing standard of proof, while very high, permits a decision in the face of inconsistent or conflicting evidence.

### Rule

Although Michael Schiavo may have had a vested monetary interest in the end of Theresa Schiavo's life, he did not make the determination to end life support but offered the decision to the court as an independent surrogate. As a result, a guardian *ad litem* was not required. Second, the appellate court found that the testimony regarding social standards was not afforded a great deal of weight in reaching a decision by the trial court. Finally, even though there may be evidence presented by the opposition, this does not preclude a finding of clear and convincing evidence when considered in its totality.

## The Facts

Because case law is the application of a prior judicial determination to a similar situation, the first step in preparing a case brief is to identify the key facts. In many situations, such identification will control whether the legal principles of a previous case would be applicable to another situation.

A case brief contains two types of facts: *occurrence facts* and *legal* (sometimes called *procedural*) *facts*. Both are important to the brief for different reasons, generally present in the opinion in full detail, and should be edited in the case brief to include only those facts, either occurrence or legal, that directly affected the result in the case. Facts to be excluded from the case brief include those that provide a backdrop for the case and help to fill in details of the occurrence and legal proceedings but do not directly impact the outcome.

Occurrence facts are the details of the circumstances that initially gave rise to the lawsuit. The amount of such information that is included in the opinion depends largely on the particular writing style of the judge, who is the author. However, most opinions contain a substantial amount of factual information based on what has been disclosed by the parties, which creates a clear representation of the setting of the case, development of legal issues, and circumstances of the various parties to the suit.

Although background information is helpful to thoroughly understand the intricacies of a judicial opinion, it is not necessary to include all factual details in a case brief. When editing an opinion for the composition of a brief, keep in mind that only the most essential facts should be included. Two questions can be asked about each fact when deciding whether to include it in a brief: (1) Will excluding the fact from the brief prevent the reader from understanding the general premise of the case? (2) Was the fact pivotal in the outcome of the case?

The legal facts consist of what took place once litigation began and then a chronicle of the progression of the lawsuit. A number of these facts may be recited in the opinion to show case development, but the only real legal facts usually necessary in a case brief are those that tie directly into the basis for the appeal, which ultimately prompted the ruling and consequent judicial opinion. When one first learns to read and analyze judicial opinions, there is a temptation to assume that the appeal is based on an allegedly improper finding of liability or innocence. Appeals are almost never so simply stated, however. Rather, there must be a legally objectionable basis for how the improper result originated. Examples include exclusion or inclusion of evidence objected to by one of the parties, improper jury instructions, and so forth. When preparing a case brief, the important legal facts to include are those surrounding the alleged error that created the basis for the appeal.

There are, of course, exceptions to the rule as to when less than absolutely vital information should be included. Such cases occur when otherwise ordinary information has an impact because of the particular circumstances of the case. With occurrence facts, an example might be the time of day in a case involving an auto accident, when visibility is an issue, or a date in a contract case. Similarly, a pretrial motion might be a relevant legal fact to include if the subject of that motion ultimately becomes an issue at trial or causes the case to be dismissed before trial. Although such information is more often than not a backdrop for the case, it should be included if it might influence other facts or legal issues.

## APPLICATION 2.4

A lawsuit that ultimately produced an appeal and published judicial opinion arose from the facts reported in the following opinion:

On September 4, 2004, Matt entered ABC University as a freshman student. At the time, Matt was eighteen years old and excited to fully participate in the college experience. Shortly after arriving on campus Matt pledged and began the initiation process for a fraternity. On October 19, Matt and three other pledges were taken to a room in the fraternity house. While there, they were provided with a movie and two kegs of beer. The pledges were told to watch the movie and, in that same amount of time, consume the two kegs of beer in their entirety. At the conclusion of the movie the fraternity brothers returned to the room. The four pledges, including Matt, had consumed the two kegs of beer within approximately two hours. All were intoxicated and Matt appeared to have passed out. The fraternity brothers carried him to another room and placed him on a couch. The next morning Matt was found dead from apparent alcohol poisoning. Matt's family sued the fraternity. The insurance company that held the policy on the fraternity house refused to cover the claim on the basis that the fraternity members had engaged in illegal conduct that ultimately resulted in the death and that this violated the terms of the policy.

*(continued)*

**APPLICATION 2.4** (Continued)

In a case brief, the facts might read something like this: An eighteen-year-old fraternity pledge was required to consume a substantial quantity of alcohol in an initiation ritual. Thereafter, the student died from alcohol poisoning. The insurer for the fraternity declined coverage on the basis that fraternity members had illegally provided the alcohol and engaged in hazing. As a result of the illegal conduct, the insurer claimed the policy did not apply.

*Point for Discussion:* Why is it relevant that the insurance company claimed the policy did not apply?

## The Legal Issue

Identifying the issue in the opinion is quite often one of the most difficult tasks for someone just beginning legal analysis. As with legal facts, the assumption tends to be that the legal issue is the question of guilt or liability of the defendant. In the case of a published judicial opinion, this is almost never the issue. As discussed, the appellate courts that publish the vast majority of judicial opinions do not serve the same function as trial courts. The ultimate legal issue in a trial court is usually one of guilt or innocence, but in the appellate court, and consequently in the published opinion, the issue is almost always whether something inappropriate occurred in the trial court that, in turn, prevented the proper finding on the issue of guilt or innocence. Most often the question turns on whether the trial court judge or jury properly applied one or more legal principles to the evidence before the court.

The authority of a trial court is not one with clearly defined boundaries because the law itself is not black and white. The law instead considers the relevant factors in an individual circumstance. Because no two cases are exactly alike, there must be some room for the court to consider and apply the law it interprets for a given situation. Likewise, no two juries are identical in makeup or in the way they interpret evidence. Because the U.S. legal system places such high value on the ability to have questions decided by one's fellow citizens, a significant respect is also afforded the reasoning by a jury as to why a particular verdict is reached. Consequently, both judges and juries are given a certain degree of discretion in their roles. The appellate court examines whether this grant of discretion has been abused in such a way that the result in the case is clearly and unequivocally contrary to the existing principles of law and whether any justification exists for the deviation. Therefore, when conducting legal analysis of a judicial opinion, the task is to identify what serious breach of discretion is asserted by the *appellant*—that is, the party seeking to have the trial court action reviewed and changed.

The goal of case analysis is to identify why the appellate court ultimately agreed or disagreed with the trial court. This result rests on the question considered by the appellate court. One method that can be helpful to the less experienced in the identification of the legal issue is to read the opinion and then complete the following statement:

The appellant alleges the trial court erred (abused its discretion) when _____.

or

The question before the court is _____.

One of these statements or a similar one frequently appears in the opinion itself. Without exception, the judicial opinion will make some reference to the legal issue either as part of the recitation of the legal facts or in a discussion of the task before the appellate court. For example, it might read, "The defendant sought a new trial and subsequently filed this appeal asserting the jury ignored the manifest weight of the evidence" or "The question that lies before this court is whether the trial court abused its discretion when it granted summary judgment on the finding that no reasonable issue existed as to the defendant's liability."

## The Law

The third step in case analysis is to determine the authority on which the court's decision was based. Because judges always search for guidance from existing legal standards, if there are no such standards, the judge looks to the beliefs of society and the fundamentals of right and wrong as viewed by society. Often the latter are determined by looking to the opinions of legal scholars and other noted authorities on a subject. In any event, the decision in a case will be based on some existing statement of law or wisdom. The court uses such a statement as authority and applies it to the occurrence and legal facts of the case to determine the answer to the issue before the court.

Most often the court will use an established legal standard as authority. However, sometimes the judge applies an opinion of a scholar, but this is private opinion and not law. However, by incorporating such opinion into the judicial opinion, the private opinion becomes the legal standard in that court. Consequently, the use of the term *law* describes the authority adopted and applied by a judge as the guiding legal standard in deciding a case.

In a case brief, one should indicate the source of the "law" (legal principle) used to determine a case. Just as important, the actual principle should be stated. It is not helpful to know one without the other. When analyzing the effects of a case, it is necessary to know not only the source but also the content of the legal standard. When identifying the law for use in a case brief, the student should seek out those principles that address the issue at hand. The following is an excerpt from the part of a judicial opinion that responds to the issue with a legal standard:

> Issue: Can a person be convicted of assisting in a robbery when there is evidence that the person's life was threatened in order to coerce assistance?
>
> Law: "When a party is forced, under threat of serious harm, to perform an illegal act, then that party cannot be held accountable for committing a criminal act."
>
> *Maine v. Jezbera,* 402 A.2d 777 (Maine Sup. Ct. 1980).

The quoted material is the legal standard. The information that follows is the source. Specifically given is the name of the case, the volume number, the name of the reporter series where the opinion is published, and the page number where the case begins. The information in parentheses indicates the court that decided the case and the year of the opinion.

If you looked up *Atlantic Reports,* Second Series, at a library, located volume 402, and opened it to page 777, you would see the case of *Maine v. Jezbera.* You would also find information indicating that this opinion was handed down by the supreme court of Maine in 1980.

## The Rule

Judicial opinions do not merely state the law (both principle and its source) and then follow with a blanket statement of the case's winner. Rather, the court will give some explanation about why or how the legal standard applies to the facts and issue of the case. In a case brief, such information is essential. It is impossible to predict the effects of a case without understanding the reasoning of the court in the judicial opinion. Unless this information is included in the case analysis (brief), one could not determine whether the same legal standards would apply in the current situation and its facts and issue.

Once the facts, issue, law, and rule have been determined, the case brief can be used to compare the case with other situations of similar facts and issue. Similarities and differences should be identified. One should then determine whether the similarities are strong enough to create a likelihood that the same legal standards would be applied in the same way in the other situation. This can be done in large part by examining the rule of the case. One must ask just how and why the previous court applied the particular legal standard to the case. If the case is briefed for purposes of comparison to another situation, then the next issue to explore is the likelihood that the law would be applied in the same way under the facts and issue of the other situation.

What follows are two judicial opinions. A case brief has been provided after the first opinion.

# CASE
## *Iowa v. Leckington,*
### 713 N.W.2d 208 (Iowa 2006)

In the following case, the actions of a trial court in its application of legal standards are reviewed by an appellate court.

. . . On December 17, 2003, Sandra Leckington purchased a half-gallon of vodka to help her eighteen-year-old son, Curtis Jenkins, "celebrate" his impending stint of probation. Jenkins and a group of friends procured more vodka and alcohol so that they could make "jungle juice" for a party at Dominic Major's apartment.

Eleven days later, Sandra allowed her younger son, Shawn Yuille, to have his friend, Travis Talbot, spend the night at their home. The next day, the two thirteen-year-old boys left the Leckington home and went a few houses down the block to Travis's home so that Travis could check in with his mother. . . . After lunch . . . the boys went down the block to the apartment of Dominic Major. Travis and Shawn proceeded to play video games and drink the leftover vodka. Travis consumed three to four glasses of vodka and started to become a problem for Major.

At 2:07 p.m., Major called Sandra and told her to pick up the two boys because Travis was "pretty trashed." On the way to Major's apartment, Sandra picked up her husband, Mark Leckington, from the local convenience store. By the time Sandra arrived at the apartment, Travis was so intoxicated he was having difficulty standing and walking. At one point, he fell and hit his head on one of the pillars of the apartment building. Major carried Travis from the apartment building to the car. Once Travis was placed in the back seat of the car, he immediately slumped over. One witness thought Travis was unconscious when he was placed in the car. Mark asked whether Travis had been drinking, but Sandra, even though she had been told Travis was

"pretty trashed," told Mark that Travis had not been drinking. Mark then asked Shawn what was wrong with Travis. Shawn told him that they had been wrestling around and Travis hit his head. Sandra drove around the block to the Leckington home. According to Sandra, Mark, and Shawn, Travis walked, unaided, out of the car and into the home. After the boys entered the home, Sandra and Mark left to run errands.

Once inside the Leckington home, Travis collapsed on the kitchen floor. Shawn tried to revive Travis by pouring milk down his throat. When this did not work, he went back outside and found some friends to help carry Travis upstairs to the bathtub. The boys then ran cold water on Travis in hopes of reviving him. Travis did not wake up, and he began to foam at the mouth.

Approximately an hour after they left the boys at their home, Sandra and Mark returned home. Mark went to a room in the back of the home. One of the children in the house told Sandra that Travis was "dead" and lying in the bathtub. Sandra "freaked out." She told the boys they had to get Travis out of the bathtub and out of the house. . . . She helped drag Travis down the stairs, but the boys refused to help her put Travis outside in the cold December air. . . . When the paramedics arrived, Travis had a very weak pulse, his mouth was clenched shut, he was extremely cold, his skin had a blue coloring, and his clothing was wet. Travis was . . . placed in pediatric intensive care. Travis regained consciousness fourteen hours later. A doctor testified that his blood alcohol content was approximately 0.3 when he reached the hospital, and that he was at risk of death from the high level of alcohol in his blood.

. . . Sandra Leckington was convicted of child endangerment resulting in serious injury, neglect of a dependent person, and the lesser offense of providing alcohol to a minor. The court sentenced her to consecutive terms of ten years for the child endangerment and neglect charges and a one-year, concurrent term for providing alcohol to a minor.

Sandra challenges the sufficiency of the evidence supporting various elements of her convictions for child endangerment resulting in serious injury and neglect of a dependent person. In regards to the child-endangerment-resulting-in-serious-injury conviction, she claims there was insufficient evidence to prove: (1) she had "control" or "custody" of Travis; (2) she knowingly acted in a manner which created risk to Travis; (3) she willfully deprived Travis of health care or supervision; or (4) her actions resulted in serious injury to Travis. In regards to the neglect-of-a-dependent conviction, she claims there was insufficient evidence to prove she had custody of Travis or that she knowingly or recklessly exposed Travis to a hazard or danger from which he could not reasonably be expected to protect himself. We will discuss each argument in turn.

. . . In order to convict Sandra of child endangerment resulting in serious injury, the jury had to find: (1) Sandra was the parent, guardian, or person having custody or control over Travis; (2) Travis was under the age of fourteen; (3) Sandra knowingly acted in a manner creating a substantial risk to Travis's physical, mental, or emotional health or safety, or Sandra willfully deprived Travis of necessary health care or supervision appropriate to Travis's age when she was reasonably able to make the necessary provisions and which deprivation substantially harmed Travis's physical, mental, or emotional health; and (4) Sandra's act resulted in serious injury to Travis. See *Iowa Code* § 726.6.

Sandra contends she did not have "control" of Travis because she did not have control of the instrumentality creating the risk to Travis (the vodka). She points out that she was not present when Travis consumed the vodka and that the State did not prove she purchased the specific vodka Travis actually consumed.

Sandra's exercise of control over Travis begins with her decision to go to Major's apartment to pick him up after Major told her that Travis was "pretty trashed." When she then chose to move Travis, in his vulnerable condition, to a different location she undertook the supervision of Travis and therefore exhibited the control necessary for the crime of child endangerment. See *id.* § 726.6(3).

Sandra contends there was not sufficient evidence to establish she had conscious awareness, or actual knowledge, that she was acting in a manner that created a substantial risk to Travis's health. The statute at issue prohibits "knowingly act[ing] in a manner that creates a substantial risk to the child or minor's physical, mental, or emotional health or safety." See *id.* § 726.6(1)(a). We interpret the word "knowingly" in this statute to mean "the defendant acted with knowledge that [he or] she was creating substantial risk to the child's safety." *State v. James,* 693 N.W.2d 353, 357 (Iowa 2005). . . . In essence, she argues that knowledge requires more than she "should have known" Travis was in a vulnerable position.

Sandra's argument that she was not cognizant of Travis's condition is not supported by the record. Major specifically told her that Travis had been drinking and was "pretty trashed." She saw Travis stumble and fall and hit his head. She watched Major carry Travis to her car. She also saw Travis slump over in the car. . . . There was abundant evidence to prove Sandra knew Travis was severely intoxicated. Expert testimony, along with a good dose of common sense, would enable a rational trier of fact to conclude Sandra knowingly created a substantial risk to Travis's physical health when she left him at her home without further adult supervision.

Sandra also contends there was not sufficient evidence to establish she willfully deprived Travis of necessary health care. . . . We have also stated willfulness is established by proof of intentional and deliberate conduct undertaken with a bad purpose, in disregard for the rights of another, or contrary to a known duty. In re *Marriage of Jacobo,* 526 N.W.2d 859, 866 (Iowa 1995). Either definition is appropriate for this case. . . .

Sandra knew of Travis's condition when she picked him up from Major's apartment—Major told her Travis was "pretty trashed," she saw Travis fall and hit his head, and she saw him carried to her car. Rather than taking him to the hospital or to his mother or at least monitoring his condition, she decided to move him to an unsupervised location and leave him there. Her decision, to leave the boy in an unsupervised location rather than to provide necessary health care or at least supervision, was intentional and deliberate.

. . . Even after she returned home and found Travis unconscious in her bathtub, she did not immediately call for help. Instead, she tried to move him out of her house. . . . There was substantial evidence to support the conclusion that she tried to move Travis out of her house—rather than call for medical help—because she did not want to be implicated in any potential criminal investigation. The decision to put her own fear of criminal prosecution above the medical needs of a child who was unconscious and foaming at the mouth was an intentional and deliberate decision. Although she

*(continued)*

was unable to completely execute her plan because the other children refused to help her move Travis outside, she nonetheless deprived Travis of medical care until at least the time the other children thwarted her plan. . . . The record contains substantial evidence to support a finding that Sandra willfully deprived Travis of necessary health care.

. . . A rational trier of fact did not have to conclude Sandra made Travis drink the alcohol or that she placed him in the tub full of cold water in order to find her actions resulted in serious injury to Travis. Her action, moving Travis to a private location and leaving him there without adult supervision, allowed a group of minors to make life-threatening choices regarding Travis's physical care. Her actions also were an obstruction to adequate medical assistance. During the time she was gone, Travis's breathing slowed to only five or six breaths per minute and he vomited in his own mouth. Either condition was potentially lethal and subjected Travis to serious injury. See *Iowa Code* § 702.18 ("'Serious injury' means . . . [b]odily injury which . . . [c]reates a substantial risk of death.").

. . . In *State v. Johnson,* 528 N.W.2d 638, 642 (Iowa 1995), we held that the term custody in *section 726.3* is not limited to legal custody. We concluded custody under this statute meant "[t]o be in charge of an individual and to hold the responsibility to care for that individual." *Johnson,* 528 N.W.2d at 641. We also stated that custody implicates not only a power of oversight, but also a responsibility for the care of an individual. *Id.*

Although Travis's parents did not expressly ask Sandra to take custody of their son, Sandra voluntarily undertook this responsibility by taking Travis from Major's apartment and moving him to her home. The key facts in this decision are Travis's helpless condition, Sandra's knowledge of that condition, and Sandra's decision to physically move Travis to a different location. When one chooses to move someone in a helpless condition, they not only take charge of that person, but they also assume responsibility for that person, at least until a third person assumes responsibility for the dependent person. . . . By electing to move Travis to her home while he was in a helpless condition, Sandra assumed custody of Travis for the purpose of this statute. . . .

Sandra argues the district court abused its discretion because it imposed consecutive sentences solely because of the nature of the offense. See *State v. McKeever,* 276 N.W.2d 385, 387 (Iowa 1979). . . . The court's statement at sentencing does indicate the court placed considerable emphasis on the serious nature of the crimes committed. The court stated:

> I note that the defendant does not have a prior criminal history of any serious extent whatsoever;

however the sentence imposed today is imposed because of the very serious nature of the charges [of] which you were convicted, Ms. Leckington. I think that, in hearing the testimony in this case, this was a real disaster in the making, and I think we all feel—I'm sure including you—very thankful that Travis pulled out of this as well as he did. But the fact that your conduct was so serious, in failing to provide this child with the assistance that he required at the time he was transported to your home and in your home, simply causes the Court to find that it's appropriate to impose the serious sentence of consecutive sentences Counts 1 and 2.

However, further analysis of the court's statement shows that the court considered other factors pertinent to sentencing. In the following passage, the court considered Sandra's character and propensities and chances for reform when it stated:

> I note that there are issues that are identified in your presentence investigation as needs, that you need to address, and the first one is to be responsible for your actions, and to work toward a better understanding of your behaviors with respect to responsibility and consequences. You need to be sober and drug free, complete all recommended substance abuse treatment and aftercare, need to obtain mental health treatment, and need to work on health-related issues.

The court went on to state that it believed she would need a long time to address all of the issues before her. The court also stated consecutive periods of incarceration would be needed to "make sure that other young people in the community are safe, because this showed very, very bad judgment on your part, . . . and I frankly would be concerned that if your children weren't in danger, that other children in the community would be."

All of these statements indicate the court considered multiple factors when making its sentencing decision. We find no abuse of discretion. . . . Sufficient evidence supports the verdict. The trial court did not abuse its discretion in imposing consecutive sentences, and Sandra did not prove she received ineffective assistance of counsel. We therefore affirm the judgment of the district court.

## Case Review Question

How relevant is it that the injured child was not the natural child of the defendant? Would the result have been different if the injured child had been twenty-one years of age?

Prepare a case brief for the judicial opinion *Iowa v. Leckington.*

## Statutory and Administrative Analysis

Unlike the case brief, which requires the synopsis of a factual occurrence as well as legal issues, the statutory analysis and administrative legal analysis procedure is much more straightforward. Statutes and administrative regulations are more broadly written and do not generally provide detailed discussions of exact case scenarios. A statute will only be applied when its various conditions or elements are satisfied. Because statutes are written to apply to the entire public rather than specific individuals, the language and description of legal standards is generally quite different from the judicial opinion.

When examining a statute, the first step is to break it down into specific elements. Great care should be used in evaluating the effect of each word in a statute to determine whether all conditions must be met or whether different ones can satisfy the statute alternatively. See Exhibit 2.4.

**Exhibit 2.4** West's Smith-Hurd Illinois Compiled Statutes Annotated

---

**CHAPTER 750. FAMILIES**

ACT 5. ILLINOIS MARRIAGE AND DISSOLUTION OF MARRIAGE ACT

    PART V-PROPERTY, SUPPORT AND ATTORNEY FEES

        5/513. Support for Non-minor Children and Educational Expenses

            § 513. Support for Non-minor Children and Educational Expenses.

            (a) The court may award sums of money out of the property and income of either or both parties or the estate of a deceased parent, as equity may require, for the support of the child or children of the parties who have attained majority in the following instances:

                (1) When the child is mentally or physically disabled and not otherwise emancipated, an application for support may be made before or after the child has attained majority.

                (2) The court may also make provision for the educational expenses of the child or children of the parties, whether of minor or majority age, and an application for educational expenses may be made before or after the child has attained majority, or after the death of either parent. The authority under this Section to make provision for educational expenses extends not only to periods of college education or professional or other training after graduation from high school, but also to any period during which the child of the parties is still attending high school, even though he or she attained the age of 19. The educational expenses may include, but shall not be limited to, room, board, dues, tuition, transportation, books, fees, registration and application costs, medical expenses including medical insurance, dental expenses, and living expenses during the school year and periods of recess, which sums may be ordered payable to the child, to either parent, or to the educational institution, directly or through a special account or trust created for that purpose, as the court sees fit.

                If educational expenses are ordered payable, each parent and the child shall sign any consents necessary for the educational institution to provide the supporting parent with access to the child's academic transcripts, records, and grade reports. The consents shall not apply to any non-academic records. Failure to execute the required consent may be a basis for a modification or termination of any order entered under this Section.

                The authority under this Section to make provision for educational expenses, except where the child is mentally or physically disabled and not otherwise emancipated, terminates when the child receives a baccalaureate degree.

---

*(continued)*

(b) In making awards under paragraph (1) or (2) of subsection (a), or pursuant to a petition or motion to decrease, modify, or terminate any such award, the court shall consider all relevant factors that appear reasonable and necessary, including:

(1) The financial resources of both parents.
(2) The standard of living the child would have enjoyed had the marriage not been dissolved.
(3) The financial resources of the child.
(4) The child's academic performance.

Current through P.A. 94-1054, P.A. 94-1056 to P.A. 94-1068 of the 2006 Reg. Sess.

The specific elements of a statute are rarely given in a laundry list format. Usually, they are written in a narrative form. Often a single sentence includes multiple elements that must be satisfied for the statute to apply and to indicate a result. Consequently, great care must be taken in reading the statute and identifying the exact meaning of each statutory requirement based on the language used.

## ASSIGNMENT 2.4

Examine and evaluate the statute in Exhibit 2.4 and break it into the applicable components.

## Application of Legal Analysis

The evaluation of legal authorities is only one part of the process of legal analysis. Once authorities have been considered and summarized appropriately, the second stage can begin: comparing the legal precedent with the current case. The effective legal professional considers not only those authorities who support the position taken but also those who discount it. The latter can be useful in predicting and preparing for the opposition.

When considering applicable authorities, the key is to compare and distinguish. With respect to judicial opinions, the information contained within the case brief should be closely compared with the current facts and issues. A similarity in legal issues is obviously necessary, but equally important is the fact comparison. A case that is too dissimilar in facts can be easily distinguished as inapplicable. Although no two cases are exactly alike, it is important to seek out those cases involving similar fact patterns with respect to the pivotal facts of the current situation. Any facts that are not present, not mentioned, or dissimilar must be considered in terms of the importance they played or might play in affecting the outcome of the current case. Legal standards should also be compared in terms of their applicability to the current case and the degree of influence the authority, the precedent, and its cited legal standards would have on the court in the current lawsuit if one is pending or anticipated. Ultimately, a decision must be reached as to whether the current case is likely to have a similar or a different outcome.

As mentioned, statutory analysis also requires more than synthesizing the language of the statute. It is important to closely examine all the facts of the current case to determine whether they are addressed in the current statute. If they are not, then the overall applicability of the statute to the case must be determined. If it does apply, then what result does the analysis indicate? If it does not appear to apply because of the absence of facts that satisfy the elements, then be prepared to explain how the statute can be distinguished from the current case.

## ETHICAL CONSIDERATIONS

All legal professionals have an obligation to present all applicable legal standards to the court in a case. As a result, any positive or negative principles determined in the process of legal analysis must be revealed. Although in some instances this might appear to be self-defeating, it is necessary to meet the ultimate goals of the U.S. legal system, which are fairness and consistency to all in the application of laws.

## ETHICAL CIRCUMSTANCE

A paralegal is conducting research for a case that is being considered in court the following day. Toward the end of the day, the paralegal receives a routine e-mail update from the highest appellate court of the state. The update indicates that a decision that day by the high court would severely and negatively impact the case, which until now was quite strong. The paralegal informs the attorney. The attorney is faced with the ethical decision of whether to bring up the recent change in the law at the hearing and almost certainly lose or take the chance that the judge and opposition are unaware of it and win the case for his client.

## ● | CHAPTER SUMMARY

This chapter has explored the judicial branch of the U.S. legal system. The judicial system has several unique characteristics. This branch of government deals with specific cases on an individual and direct basis. It has the authority to overrule an act of the legislature or the executive branch if the act violates the Constitution. When a dispute arises and no statutory law exists, then the judicial branch has power to create law and provide an immediate resolution to the dispute.

The judicial system is set up to clarify and protect the law. The courts must determine whether a broadly written statute or existing precedent applies to an individual circumstance. The courts also have the duty to uphold the U.S. Constitution and see that the other branches of state and federal government honor it as well.

Because state and federal governments operate independently, each has its own judicial system to interpret and apply law. As long as the states establish and apply only law that is consistent with the Constitution of the United States, they are free to enact and enforce any law that is necessary for an orderly society.

The federal judicial system consists of three tiers. The U.S. district courts, where cases are generally filed and trials are held, occupy the lowest tier. The next level is made up of the U.S. courts of appeals, which determine whether errors were committed by U.S. district courts (trial courts) in their determination of disputes. Finally, the U.S. Supreme Court issues the final statement on disputes that claim that the Constitution has been violated. The states follow a similar type of structure, with approximately half incorporating the three-tiered system and the remaining half incorporating a two-tiered system by combining the functions of the court of appeals and the Supreme Court.

Many appellate (and some trial) judicial opinions are published for future reference. They contain certain information that allows an adequate comparison between the opinion and a case currently before a court. This information includes relevant facts, the actual issue in the dispute, the authority used to determine the dispute, and the manner in which the authority was applied.

Chapter 3 examines the legislative system in some detail, then Chapter 4 addresses the functions of the executive branch. It is important to keep in mind that each branch of government has an effect on the law in a distinct way that complements the other two branches.

## CHAPTER TERMS

appellate court        legal analysis        trial court

federal court        state court

## REVIEW QUESTIONS

1. What is a key element in the Supreme Court's authority?
2. What happens when a case has no applicable statute to guide the outcome?
3. What is the difference between common law and case law?
4. What is the significance of common law and case law?
5. How does the judiciary uphold law that is consistent with the Constitution?
6. Why are published cases predominantly from appellate courts?
7. Why is a panel of judges used for appellate cases?
8. What is an easy method to distinguish between a state and federal court?
9. What are the differences between a trial and appellate court?
10. What is the first step in analyzing a statute?

## HELPFUL WEB SITES

Supreme Court of the United States    http://www.supremecourtsus.gov

Federal Courts    http://www.uscourts.gov

## INTERNET ASSIGNMENT 2.1

Identify the Internet address for the U.S. district court and state trial court that would have authority over matters happening where you live.

## INTERNET ASSIGNMENT 2.2

1. What is the Internet address for the highest appellate court in the state where you live?
2. Who are the judges currently sitting on this court?

## ENDNOTES

1. *Black's Law Dictionary* (St. Paul, MN: West, 1979).
2. Opinion of the Justices, 280 Ala. 653, 197 So.2d 456 (1967).
3. William Statsky, *Legal Thesaurus/Dictionary* (St. Paul. MN: West, 1982).
4. *Id.*
5. *Black's Law Dictionary.*
6. 28 U.S.C. Rules of the Supreme Court, Rule 9.
7. *Id.*
8. *Id.,* at Rule 10.
9. 28 U.S.C. Rules of Appellate Procedure, Rule 1,3.
10. *Id.,* at Rules 3 and 4.

## STUDENT CD-ROM

For additional materials, please go to the CD in this book.

## ONLINE COMPANION™

For additional resources, please go to http://www.paralegal.delmar.cengage.com

# Legislation

## LEGISLATURE STRUGGLES WITH DILEMMA OF BEAR WRESTLING

There is, in fact, legislation in place to prohibit anyone from being involved in, profiting from, or associated with bear wrestling for profit. This is just one of many laws that appear to be totally useless and nothing more than a waste of money by the taxpayers who fund the salaries of legislatures. Just how big a problem is bear wrestling? Well, it isn't a problem—at least not any more. In every jurisdiction, laws can be found that appear at best humorous and at worst a waste of time and money by elected members of the legislatures. Did you ever stop to think, though, why bear wrestling is a problem worthy of statutory law? Or why it is not something you even hear of any-more? Legislators don't just sit around thinking of ridiculous situations to address with unnecessary laws. In fact, bear wrestling was becoming a somewhat popular sport at one time in this country. The injuries to the animals and the many people involved were substantially greater than the profits being realized by a limited few. Because those few did glean profit, the practice continued to grow. As a result, the legislature served its function of protection by enacting laws to deal with the situation. The same is true for other laws against driving blindfolded, marrying your brother or sister, flying a plane while drunk, or fishing with a firearm. These things actually occurred to the extent that legislation was required to bring these behaviors under control and prevent injuries to individuals and society. No doubt, 100 years from now people will look back at many of the laws passed today and find them just as entertaining.

## CHAPTER OBJECTIVES

After reading this chapter, you should be able to:

- Distinguish statutory law from judicial law.
- Describe the method of election of members to both houses of Congress.
- Describe the process of legislation.
- Discuss the effect of the presidential veto power on legislation.
- Discuss the publication process of new legislation.
- Describe the role of the lobbyist.
- Describe the role of the judiciary with respect to statutory law.

## THE LEGISLATIVE BRANCH

A primary source of U.S. law is legislation enacted by the federal legislative branch known as Congress. (Because the legislative process at the state level is generally similar to the federal process, this chapter focuses on legislation by the U.S. Congress.) Although the judicial and executive branches make significant contributions to law in the U.S. legal system, often they are responding to actions already taken by the legislature. A primary responsibility of the judicial branch is to interpret and apply the laws. According to the Constitution, the executive branch has the general task to faithfully execute the Constitution and the laws passed by Congress.

The authority of Congress is stated with specificity in Article I of the Constitution. Congress has the power to raise, through taxation, revenues that are used to support governmental functions. Congress also has the authority to determine the manner in which these revenues are to be spent. Another major power of Congress—and the subject of much legislation—is the authority to regulate commerce. This authority generally extends to all aspects of the production, sale, and transfer of interstate commerce. Any commerce that is totally contained within a state and any other subject not addressed in the Constitution are the exclusive subject of state law. Congress also has the authority to raise and support armies and to declare and support wars.

Perhaps the most significant power of the Congress is the authority to establish such law as is necessary and proper to achieve congressional objectives. This broad authority vests in Congress the power to pass virtually any legislation that (1) is constitutional, (2) will facilitate the orderly operation of the government, and (3) will protect the constitutional rights of the citizens in such matters as health, safety, welfare, and personal freedoms. Congress has allowed for the creation of administrative agencies (see Chapter 4) to assist in the delivery of legal rights of the people.

The legislative branch at the federal level is a *bicameral* system (that is, a two-part body), as provided for in Article I of the Constitution. The House of

Representatives consists of persons elected based on the population in geographical districts. This component of the legislature guarantees that all people are represented whether they live in a heavily populated area or a small, rural district. The Senate comprises two senators from each state elected by the voters of the state. The body of the Senate guarantees that all states are represented equally regardless of size, population, or economic strength.

The members of the House of Representatives are elected every two years. A **representative** must be at least twenty-five years old, have been a U.S. citizen for at least seven years, and reside in the state that he or she is representing. The number of representatives for each state is based on the *decennial census* of the population (that is, a census taken every ten years). Invariably, with each census, as population moves and increases, the number of representatives for each state varies. However, the Constitution guarantees that there be at least one representative for each state.

The members of the Senate are elected to six-year terms. The elections of **senators** from the various states are staggered so that one-third of the seats in the Senate come up for election every two years. A U.S. senator must be at least thirty years old, a citizen of the United States for nine years, and a resident of the state that he or she is elected to represent.

The Senate and the House of Representatives function on a separate but related basis. To avoid duplicity of work, joint committees comprising members from both houses work together to draft laws that will meet approval by the entire Congress. Although many laws proceed individually through the houses for passage or defeat, approval is required by a majority of both houses to enact law.

**representative**
A person elected to the U.S. House of Representatives, which is designed to ensure equal representation of all citizens.

**senator**
A person elected to the U.S. Senate, which is designed to ensure equal representation of all states.

## ASSIGNMENT 3.1

Answer the following questions by referring to the U.S. Constitution in Appendix A. Indicate the section of the Constitution in which you find the answer.

1. How were senators for Congress initially chosen?
2. Where must proposed legislation to raise governmental revenue through taxes originate?
3. What is the date of the first session of the U.S. Congress each year?
4. How long is a term in the U.S. House of Representatives?
5. How long is a term in the U.S. Senate?
6. Who supervises the filling of a position in the House of Representatives or Senate when one becomes vacant such as by death?
7. In which house does an impeachment proceeding take place?
8. What is required if one of the houses of Congress wants to conduct business in a location other than the capitol building?
9. How were members of the House of Representatives initially chosen?
10. What was the original term of office for U.S. senators?

## THE PURPOSE OF LEGISLATION

In general, legislation serves three purposes, and the particular purpose a statute serves strongly influences the statute's content and scope. A primary purpose of the U.S. democratic system of government is to provide laws that will protect society from what is unsafe for or unacceptable to the majority of citizens. Generally, statutes serve to protect citizens as a whole from unnecessary physical, social, and financial dangers. Law as a protective measure began with the original ten amendments to the Constitution, known as the *Bill of Rights*. From the very start, specific laws were established to protect the people from unnecessary governmental influence or intrusion into their private lives. The Bill of Rights ensures that people the right to live freely and to comment and produce change when laws are established or enforced unfairly. Unfortunately, it was some time before all races as well as women were identified as persons who were entitled to these basic rights. Also with the passage of time came additional constitutional amendments and statutes designed to provide protection from dangers that would interfere with other fundamental personal rights. In the latter half of the twentieth century, numerous laws were passed to ensure that the rights of all persons are protected regardless of a variety of characteristics that might otherwise be used to differentiate them from the general population.

The protection of fundamental rights as put forth in the amendments to the Constitution is not the only way that legislation protects the public. Many other laws serve another type of protective purpose. Any statute that sets out the type of conduct required of individuals protects the public from improper conduct by others. For example, something as simple as the statutes that govern motor vehicles serves an invaluable protective purpose. Without such laws, persons could drive as they pleased, and untold injuries and deaths could occur.

Many different types of laws serve a *protective* purpose. Laws that make it an offense to manufacture, sell, or distribute illegal drugs attempt to protect our society from an influence that can produce physical, financial, and social harm. Laws that ensure compensation to workers who are injured on the job protect such workers from being left physically disabled and without funds to pay for adequate medical care. These statutes protect citizens not only from invasion of personal rights but also from injury to personal property.

Laws that serve as a protective measure come in a variety of forms and address many subjects that affect members of society and its order. There is, however, a common thread in all laws that serve a protective purpose. Protective laws are designed to set forth what people are entitled to expect as citizens of this country. Protective laws do exactly what their name implies: They protect what are considered to be the rights of the people to have a safe and reasonable environment in which to live and work.

Laws (statutes) passed by the legislature can also serve a remedial purpose. A *remedial statute* is one that creates an alternative action or a means to enforce a right. This type of statute corrects existing law or remedies an existing grievance.[1] As this definition indicates, remedial statutes are designed to cure something that has already gone wrong or caused injury. Occasionally, a remedial statute is one that supersedes a previous statute that was unfair or poorly drafted and resulted in injury or invasion of personal rights or property interests. One example of an extremely important remedial law is the Thirteenth Amendment, which states in part:

> Amendment XIII, Section 1. Neither slavery nor involuntary servitude, except as a punishment for crime whereof the party shall have been duly convicted, shall exist within the United States, or any place subject to their jurisdiction.

With the ratification of this amendment to the Constitution, all previous decisions of courts and state and federal legislatures that permitted slavery were overruled. The amendment was the method of correcting laws that the majority of the people believed were wrong, unfair, and injurious to a large element of our society.

Another example of remedial legislation is the repeal of Prohibition. Congress initially believed that the majority of the people wanted to be protected from the negative effects of alcohol consumption. With the Eighteenth Amendment, intoxicating liquor was outlawed. It soon became apparent, however, that this was not the opinion of the majority. Consequently, Prohibition was repealed, and the sale of intoxicating liquor was legalized again by passage of the Twenty-First Amendment.

Remedial law is not always in the form of a constitutional amendment. More often, remedial laws are federal or state laws that are used to adjust law to the needs of the society. (They would fall under the heading of sociological theory, which was discussed in Chapter 1.) Familiar examples of such statutes are state workers' compensation laws. Every state has enacted laws that provide that an employer will be responsible for costs associated with the injuries of an employee if the injuries occur while the employee is performing duties of employment. Before these laws, many people injured on the job lost their income at the time of the injury. They could not pay their medical bills, and some were forced into poverty. Employees were left with no alternative but to file a formal lawsuit against their employers. Some verdicts were significant enough to put the employer out of business altogether. Those employers who remained in business were rarely willing to allow the employee to return to work after suit was filed.

The burden on individuals and the economy was increasingly great. The response was to pass workers' compensation laws in every state. Under such laws, the employee's medical bills are covered. In addition, if disputes arise between the employee and the employer (or the employer's insurance company) as to how much money is necessary to compensate the employee for the injury, then the law contains a legislative provision for a hearing process. The employee's medical bills can be paid, the employee is entitled to a living allowance while off work, the courts rarely become involved, and usually the employee can return to the job after recovery. With the advent of these laws, many employers took out insurance to cover the costs of medical and financial assistance to injured employees.

Workers' compensation laws are examples of both protective and remedial statutes. On the one hand, a statute may set out the rights that citizens are entitled to enjoy. On the other hand, a statute may also correct a situation that was dealt with ineffectively by the legal system or change a law that is considered unfair by the majority.

A third purpose that legislation serves is to ensure that protective and remedial statutes are available and applied to all citizens in the same way.[2] Such laws are known as *procedural laws*. Subsequent chapters in this text on civil and criminal procedure will discuss the need and actual application of procedural laws. For now, we will deal with procedural laws only in terms of the purpose they serve.

If it were not for procedural laws, citizens would have no effective way of enforcing the rights to which they are entitled. Procedural laws give specific directions on everything from how to initiate a lawsuit to how a trial is to be conducted. They even explain how to get a bill introduced to the legislature for consideration as law. Occasionally, people complain that the procedural laws are too numerous and that the legal system is more concerned with procedures than with resolving issues. In reality, our legal system guarantees all citizens the right to be heard. Consequently, hundreds of thousands of lawsuits are filed every year. All people in the nation have the right to submit their disputes to state and federal legislators, judges, and members of the executive branches of government. Given the size of their task, the procedural laws are extremely efficient.

Procedural laws are not designed solely to deal with great numbers of people. Their true purpose is to ensure that everyone can enjoy the same basic rights in the legal system. All persons are entitled to have their case heard by a judicial officer. All are entitled to voice their opinion to elected delegates in Congress. All persons affected by law are entitled to dispute that law. The procedural laws make it possible for the orderly expression of rights to occur in a fair setting and provide for fair treatment to all parties in a dispute. Without procedural laws, there would be no clear, consistent, and fair method of seeking assistance from or providing input to the legal system.

## ASSIGNMENT 3.2

Examine the statutory language in Exhibits 3.1, 3.2, and 3.3 and determine whether the purpose of each statute is protective, procedural, or remedial. Explain your answer.

**Exhibit 3.1**  Statutory Excerpts

---

**Ala. Code 1975 Sec. 13A-5-59**

§ 13A-5-59. Application of article upon finding of unconstitutionality.

It is the intent of the Legislature that if the death penalty provisions of this article are declared unconstitutional and if the offensive provision or provisions cannot be reinterpreted so as to provide a constitutional death penalty, or if the death penalty is ever declared to be unconstitutional per se, that the defendants who have been sentenced to death under this article shall be re-sentenced to life imprisonment without parole. It is also the intent of the Legislature that in the event that the death penalty provisions of this article are declared unconstitutional and if they cannot be reinterpreted to provide a constitutional death penalty, or if the death penalty is ever declared to be unconstitutional per se, that defendants convicted thereafter for committing crimes specified in Section 13A-5-40(a) shall be sentenced to life imprisonment without parole.

---

**Exhibit 3.2**  Arkansas Code

---

**15-4-502. Articles of incorporation—Contents:**

(a) The articles of incorporation shall state:

(1) The name of the corporation, which name shall include the name of the city, town, or county and the words "industrial development," and the word "corporation," "incorporated," "inc.," or "company." The name shall be such as to distinguish it from any other corporation organized and existing under the laws of this state;

(2) The purpose for which the corporation is formed;

(3) The names and addresses of the incorporators who shall serve as directors and manage the affairs of the corporation until its first annual meeting of members or until their successors are elected and qualified;

(4) The number of directors, not less than three (3), to be elected at the annual meetings of members;

(5) The address of its principal office and the name and address of its agent upon whom process may be served;

(6) The period of duration of the corporation, which may be perpetual;

(7) The terms and conditions upon which persons shall be admitted to membership in the corporation, but if expressly so stated, the determination of such matters may be reserved to the directors by the bylaws;

(8) Any provisions, not inconsistent with law, which the incorporators may choose to insert for the regulation of the business and the conduct of the affairs of the corporation.

(b) It shall not be necessary to set forth in the articles of incorporation any of the corporate powers enumerated in this act.

---

**Exhibit 3.3**  Sample Statutory Language

---

**Nebraska 2006 Session Law Service**

**2nd Session of the 99th Legislature**

NE ST § 60-4,124

60-4,124. (1) A person who is younger than sixteen years of age but is older than fourteen years and two months of age may be issued, by the county treasurer, a school permit if such person lives a distance of one and one-half miles or more from the school he or she attends and either resides outside a city of the metropolitan, primary, or first class or attends a school which is outside a city of the metropolitan, primary, or first class and if such person has held an LPE–learner's permit for two months. A school permit shall not be issued until such person has appeared before an examiner to demonstrate that he or she is capable of successfully operating a motor vehicle, moped, or motorcycle and has in his or her possession an examiner's certificate authorizing the county treasurer to issue a school permit.

---

*(continued)*

**Exhibit 3.3** Continued

In order to obtain an examiner's certificate, the applicant shall present to the examiner (a) proof of successful completion of a department-approved driver safety course which includes behind-the-wheel driving specifically emphasizing (i) the effects of the consumption of alcohol on a person operating a motor vehicle, (ii) occupant protection systems, (iii) risk assessment, and (iv) railroad crossing safety and (b)(i) proof of successful completion of a written examination and driving test administered by a driver safety course instructor or (ii) a certificate in a form prescribed by the department, signed by a parent, guardian, or licensed driver at least twenty-one years of age, verifying that the applicant has completed fifty hours of lawful motor vehicle operation, under conditions that reflect department-approved driver safety course curriculum, with a parent, guardian, or adult at least twenty-one years of age, who has a then current Nebraska operator's license or who is licensed in another state. The Department of Motor Vehicles shall waive the written examination if the applicant surrenders an LPE–learner's permit issued after January 1, 2006, and if such permit is valid or has expired no more than one year prior to application. The written examination shall not be waived if the permit being applied for contains a class or endorsement which is different from the class or endorsement of the LPE–learner's permit.

## THE LEGISLATIVE PROCESS

Each state has a somewhat different method of enacting statutes. With the exception of a few procedural details, the basic legislative process has remained the same in the federal government the U.S. Constitution's 1787 enactment. Article I, Section 7, of the Constitution is quite specific regarding this process (see Appendix A).

### The Path from Concept to Law

When a proposed law is introduced to the legislature, it is called a **bill**. The Constitution requires that revenue-raising bills be initially introduced in the House of Representatives. Other bills may be initiated in either house of Congress. A bill is sponsored by a legislator who introduces it. When a bill is formally proposed as legislation, it is registered and assigned a number. Often, the bill is also known by the name of the legislators who introduce it, for example, the Graham-Rudman Act. Officially, however, the statute is referenced in publications by its assigned number. As the bill progresses through the legislative process, it carries the same number for identification until it is voted into law, defeated, or dies in session. The latter occurs when a bill is introduced but fails to be acted on during Congress's legislative term.

Once a bill has been introduced, it is assigned to the appropriate committee of legislators for consideration of its contents and its potential ramifications as law. Congress has created many such continuing committees to study the need for legislation and proposed laws in specific areas of government, commerce, and other appropriate legislative subjects. At times, the bill will be revised during its time in committee with necessary additions or deletions to make it a complete and effective statute. After committee hearings, the bill is presented to the originating body of Congress (House of Representatives or Senate) for a vote by the legislators. The bill must pass by a majority vote before it can be sent to the corresponding body for consideration. Before a vote, the bill is discussed and debated by Congress. At this time, changes may be made in the language of the bill. Often such changes are necessary to gain the approval of a sufficient number of legislators to pass the bill.

**bill**
Proposed law presented to the legislature for consideration.

If a bill succeeds by a majority vote in the body of Congress where it began, it moves on to the corresponding body. For example, if a bill is introduced in the House of Representatives and passes by a majority vote, the final version is then submitted to the Senate. If the bill passes by a majority in the corresponding body of Congress, it is forwarded to the president for approval or disapproval (either direct or implied).

Once a bill has been submitted to the executive branch, the president's **veto** power may be exercised. The veto is a key element in the system of checks and balances. As mentioned in Chapter 1, each branch of government has a method by which it can influence the other branches. Such a mechanism is designed to prevent one branch from obtaining too much power or acting in a way that is inconsistent with the Constitution. According to Article I of the U.S. Constitution, each bill that has received a majority vote in both houses of Congress shall be presented to the president. After the president receives a bill, under the Constitution, the bill must be acted on within ten days, excluding Sundays.[3] If nothing is done during this time and Congress is still in session, then the bill automatically becomes law. If Congress is not in session, then it becomes a *pocket veto*. If the president signs the bill, it becomes law on the date indicated by Congress. If the president returns the bill with no objections to the house where it originated, the bill is vetoed (rejected). Once a bill has been vetoed, a second vote can be taken. If each body of Congress approves the bill by at least a two-thirds majority (rather than by the originally required simple majority), the bill becomes law regardless of the presidential veto. Exhibit 3.4 illustrates this legislative process. In addition to bills introduced to create law, another type of bill has the sole purpose of repealing an existing law. Nevertheless, even this type of bill is assigned a number and, if passed, is published in place of the law it reverses.

**veto**

Presidential power to invalidate a law passed by a majority of Congress; a two-thirds majority of each house is needed to override a veto.

**Exhibit 3.4** Typical Steps in the Legislative Process

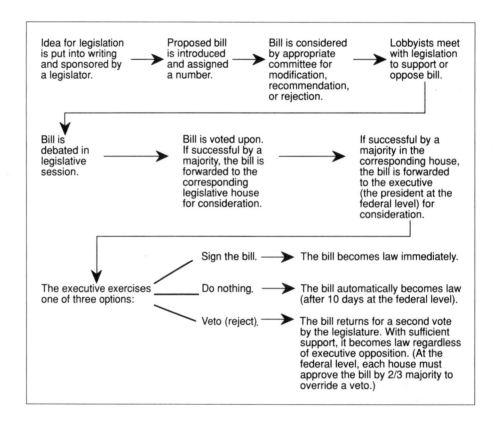

## Constitutional Amendments

The process of passing a constitutional amendment is substantially similar to the process of passing a bill. Because the Constitution is the ultimate law of the land, an amendment must pass both houses by a two-thirds majority rather than the typical simple majority. The amendment must then be approved by three-fourths of the state legislatures before it is ratified and becomes part of the Constitution. By placing such stringent requirements on constitutional amendments, it is extremely difficult to pass law that is not representative of the will of the people.

## The Function of Lobbyists

Throughout the legislative process, **lobbyists** make many contacts with legislators. These individuals represent groups of citizens or industries that have a special interest in certain bills. If a proposed bill is going to substantially affect certain interests, then groups often hire persons to lobby with the legislators to attempt to persuade them to vote in a particular way on the bill. The term originates from the early days of our government when such persons would actually wait in the lobbies of congressional buildings to speak with legislators.

> **lobbyist**
> Individual hired to meet with legislators regarding proposed laws.

Critics of lobbyists say that a few people unduly influence legislators who are supposed to represent the majority of the people. Proponents argue, however, that lobbyists actually represent those people who stand to be directly affected by the legislation and that lobbying is a practical and effective method by which citizens' groups and industry can voice their opinions to legislators.

In general, lobbyists are extremely well educated in the subject of the legislation and the legislation's potential effects on the private sector. The lobbyist can often give insight to legislators about the strengths and weaknesses of proposed legislation. In turn, the legislators receive information with which to amend a bill and make a final decision on whether to support it. Without lobbyists, it would be up to legislators and their support staffs to research and learn about the subject of every bill introduced to Congress. Besides attending sessions of Congress and committee meetings and communicating with their home-state voters, legislators would find it virtually impossible to make informed decisions on all bills presented for a vote.

## Public Hearings and Sessions

Another method by which members of Congress receive information is by attending frequent public hearings at which citizens may appear and voice their opinions and concerns about contemplated or pending actions by Congress. Public hearings enable Congress to hear firsthand the voice of the people it was elected to represent. Although it would not be feasible to allow all interested persons to speak out on every item of proposed legislation, public hearings and direct contact between constituents and their legislators are effective tools to convey the general opinion of the public.

Congress meets several months of each year to consider proposed laws. These meetings are called *sessions*. Each annual session is numbered consecutively (e.g., eighty-fifth Congress). After a full session of Congress has been concluded, all laws passed during the session take on the collective name of **session law**.[4] Session laws are published in the *Statutes at Large*. Each session law is assigned a public law number that represents the session of Congress in which the law was passed and the chronological order of the law in relation to other laws passed during the same session. For example, Public Law 92–397 would be the 397th law proposed during the ninety-second session of Congress. Each session law is identified by its public law number until it can be incorporated into the publication of all statutes (organized by subject) currently in effect. This process of incorporating the public law into the existing law code is known as **codification**.

> **session law**
> Law passed during a particular session of Congress.

> **codification**
> Process of incorporating newly passed legislation into the existing law code.

## Publication of Legislation

All federal laws currently in effect are published in a multivolume set. Because laws are constantly being added, deleted, or modified, it is difficult to keep them organized in a single permanent set of books. Usually these collections of existing laws are known as Revised Statutes or Codes. The U.S. (federal) laws are officially published in the United States Code (commonly referred to as U.S.C.).

The U.S.C. is located in multiple-bound volumes, and the method by which the volumes are organized enables the statutes to remain current in light of constant change. First, all laws are divided by basic subject. For example, virtually all laws pertaining to banking institutions are located in one section in the statutes, known as a *title* (e.g., "Banking"). (This is similar to chapters in the text you are now reading. Each chapter deals with a different subject and bears a name that indicates the subject addressed in that part of the text.) Second, all subjects are arranged in alphabetical order. Third, each law within a title (subject) is assigned a section number, allowing for future revision of the organization of the laws.

If one law exists and is later amended, the amendment is assigned the same number as the previous law. For example, Title 21, Section 1316, can be amended, and the new language of Section 1316 printed where the prior language previously appeared. If an additional law is passed on a general subject (title) and that particular law is new to the subject, it is assigned a new section number that is not assigned to any other law on the subject. For example, assume Section 1316 is the last law to appear in Title 21. If a new law is passed, then it might be assigned Section 1317. Consequently, the subject of law will lead one to the correct title (grouping of laws on a particular topic). Each title contains a table of contents listing specific sections (laws) of the title and descriptive headings for each section. The statutes also have an extensive subject index, making them even more accessible.

As stated previously, the U.S. Code takes up numerous volumes. It would be impractical to publish an entirely new set after every session of Congress to incorporate information from laws that are newly passed, amended, or repealed. For this reason, supplements are used between publications of the bound volumes. After each congressional session, the session laws are codified (given their permanent title and section numbers) and published in supplemental volumes to the Code. Usually, these volumes are paperback books located within the back cover (called *pocket parts*) or next to the hardbound volume where the codified law will eventually appear. Supplements are published annually to incorporate changes from the most recent session of Congress and all past sessions that have occurred since the last bound publication. If an existing law cannot be found in the bound Code, then it is probably located in the corresponding supplement. Periodically, newly bound editions are published that incorporate all prior supplements, and the process of supplementation starts again.

With regard to publication of federal statutes, and in many states, two types of publications are commonly used. The first, just discussed, is the Code. The second is an *annotated statute*. Such collections are no different in terms of the included text of the statutes, supplements, and organization by subject and number. However, an annotated statute has an added feature. Following the text of each statute are *annotations*—brief (usually one-sentence) descriptions of judicial opinions that interpret the particular statute. For the person doing legal research, annotated statutes are especially helpful. Annotated statutes not only give the language of the law but also provide information about any attempts by the judiciary to apply the law. Because statutes are necessarily broad, judicial interpretations often give insight as to the true purpose of the statute.

## LEGISLATION AND JUDICIAL REVIEW

Many times, parties will disagree with a court on one of two common issues relating to statutory interpretation. The first issue is whether a statute should even be applied to the particular situation. The second is how the statute should be applied to the specific circumstances of the case. Because the court system acts as an interpreter of the law, it is up to the court to make these determinations based on legal analysis. Statutes must therefore be analyzed in terms of their effect on a situation in much the same way case law is analyzed. There is, however, a striking difference: Statutes are broadly written and generally do not include discussions of exact case scenarios. Consequently, the process of legal analysis of a statute must be somewhat modified. When examining a statute, one should first break it down into each element that must be satisfied for the statute to apply. Second, one needs to compare each element to the facts of the particular case. If all elements are substantially met, then it is highly likely that the statute would be considered applicable. This method of legal analysis differs in that there are no specific case facts to compare. However, the analysis still requires a close comparison of the statute and current situation as well as a deduction as to the likely outcome of the situation if the statute is applied.

## APPLICATION 3.1

Cathy is a member of a minority race employed in a small local business. Cathy is the only woman employee, and the only minority individual whose work requires her to be in areas where safety equipment is required. Another employee is Hank, a young Caucasian male. On many occasions, Hank has been observed by many other employees violating company policies including refusing to wear required safety equipment such as construction helmets in designated areas. One day on driving home from work, Cathy was in a car accident. She suffered lacerations to her scalp and required several staples to close the wounds. She returned to work four days later on a Friday. She was scheduled to have the weekend off and to have the staples removed the following Monday morning. As a result of the staples in her scalp on Friday, she was unable to tolerate a helmet when she was in an area Friday afternoon that required safety equipment. She removed the helmet and, when questioned, informed her supervisor of the reason. The supervisor summarily fired Cathy for failure to comply with company policies. Cathy filed suit against the employer for discrimination and wrongful discharge on the basis that policies were enforced differently toward her as a minority than other employees such as Hank. The employer defended the decision by noting that during Cathy's four-day absence, a meeting had been held where supervisors were instructed to strictly enforce all safety policies. Employees were not made aware of the meeting, and no one before Cathy had been disciplined.

 The court would have the responsibility to determine if Cathy was treated in a discriminate way because of gender or race. The court would be required to examine not only the facts of the case but also the requirements of state and federal statutes necessary to prevail on a claim of discrimination. The court would then be required to make a finding of whether applicable statutes were violated by the employer.

*Point for Discussion:* Would the case likely be treated differently if Cathy had no injuries and simply chose not to wear the helmet because Hank did not?

## ASSIGNMENT 3.3

Examine the statute in Exhibit 3.3 and break it down into elements that must be satisfied.

## ASSIGNMENT 3.4

Determine whether the statute in Exhibit 3.5 should apply to the following situation. Explain your answer.

*Situation:* Rita was employed by Acme Company. She had been reprimanded several times for violating various company policies. Other employees filed written requests not to have to work with her. On October 9, Rita was injured on the job (three days before her annual performance evaluation). On October 12, she was terminated. Rita claims retaliatory discharge based on her injury and her pending workers' compensation claim.

**Exhibit 3.5** Florida Statute Workers' Comp Law Regarding Retaliatory Discharge

**West's Florida Statutes Annotated**

Title XXXI. Labor

Chapter 440. Workers' Compensation

**440.205. Coercion of employees**

No employer shall discharge, threaten to discharge, intimidate, or coerce any employee by reason of such employee's valid claim for compensation or attempt to claim compensation under the Workers' Compensation Law.

Reprinted with permission by Thomson/West.

In most situations, the job of the court regarding legislation is limited to deciding which laws are relevant to the facts and how the laws apply to a particular situation. On occasion, however, the courts are called on to protect constitutional guarantees from violation by a statute.

Legislatures do not intentionally violate the Constitution when they pass laws. Sometimes it is not apparent until a law is actually put into effect that the law violates a citizen's constitutional rights. If these rights are violated and the citizen brings a claim to the courts, the court has the authority to overrule the statute in favor of protecting the person's constitutional guarantees. This is the only circumstance under which a court can invalidate an action of the legislature. The U.S. Supreme Court has this authority over the Congress, as does the high court of each state over the state's legislative body. Such overruling rarely occurs, but when it does, the law is rendered ineffective and is no longer applied to the citizen.

A final role of the courts with respect to the legislature is a quasi-advisory role. From time to time, the courts will indirectly express an opinion through the language of case law as to what the law should be, but it is not within the court's authority to write laws that will apply as legislation to all of the people. The courts can rule only on situations before them involving particular citizens. Because of its continuous personal contact with the citizens, however, the court is often in a position to assess the needs of the individual. Therefore, the courts will periodically issue opinions on specific cases that include messages to Congress. The courts can thus act as a bridge between the people and the legislators without exceeding their authority or purpose.

# CASE

## Lonsdale v. State,
### 2006 WL 2480342 (Tex. App.)

In the following case, the court examines what is required of a statute to be considered clear and not so vague that it violates constitutional rights to be informed of what constitutes criminal conduct before the fact.

. . . Around 2 A.M. on June 24, 2004, Officer Charlie Foster observed Appellant's vehicle weave from the left lane into the right lane. As the officer followed, Appellant changed lanes three times without signaling his intent to turn. Appellant eventually drove back to his hotel where he was detained by Officer Foster in the parking lot.

Appellant exited his vehicle and Officer Foster asked him three times to stand next to the car. . . . Appellant got back inside the car. As the officer approached, Appellant rolled the window partially down, then up, and then finally down. The officer told him he had failed to signal a turn and asked to see his license and proof of insurance. Appellant first handed him a business card and then his driver's license. By this time, Officer Foster noticed an odor of alcohol coming from the vehicle and asked whether Appellant had had anything to drink. Appellant admitted drinking, but he could not remember how many drinks he had consumed. When he refused to perform field sobriety tests, he was arrested for driving while intoxicated. . . .

We turn first to Appellant's complaint that the traffic offense at issue is unconstitutionally vague. Officer Foster stopped Appellant because he changed lanes three times without signaling his intent to turn. Under the Transportation Code, a driver is required to use a signal to indicate an "intention to turn, change lanes, or start from a parked position." Tex. Transp. Code Ann. § 545.104(a) (*Vernon*, 1999).

A statute is void for vagueness if the conduct it seeks to prohibit is not clearly defined. *State v. Holcombe,* 187 S.W.3d 496, 499 (Tex.Crim.App.2006). . . . In our review, we must determine (1) whether a law-abiding person received sufficient information from the statute that their conduct risks violating the criminal law; and (2) whether the statute provides sufficient notice to law enforcement personnel to prevent arbitrary or discriminating enforcement. *Tanner v. State,* 838 S.W.2d 302, 303 (Tex.App.–El Paso 1992, no pet.), . . . A statute is considered vague if it fails to give a person of ordinary intelligence a reasonable opportunity to know what conduct is prohibited. *Holcombe,* 187 S.W.3d at 499.

Appellant claims Section 545.104 is unconstitutionally vague because it gives officers unfettered discretion to determine when someone has failed to "indicate an intention to turn." Tex. Transp. Code Ann. § 545.104. We disagree. The statute provides sufficient notice to law enforcement that a traffic violation occurs when a driver fails to signal an intent to turn, and a person of ordinary intelligence would understand that failing to signal is a violation of the statute. *Hargrove v. State,* 40 S.W.3d 556, 559 (Tex.App.–Houston [14th Dist.] 2001, pet. ref'd) (plain language of Section 545.104(a) requiring a driver to signal is not unconstitutionally vague). . . .

We now turn to reasonable suspicion and probable cause. An officer has the authority to stop and temporarily detain a driver who commits a traffic violation in his presence. *Lemmons v. State,* 133 S.W.3d 751, 755 (Tex.App.–Fort Worth 2004, pet. ref'd), citing *Armitage v. State,* 637 S.W.2d 936, 939 (Tex.Crim. App.1982). . . . If an officer develops a reasonable suspicion the detainee has engaged in other criminal activity, a continued investigatory detention is justified and an officer may arrest a suspect for the other offense. *Terry v. Ohio,* 392 U.S. 1, 27, 88 S.Ct. 1868, 1883, 20 L.Ed.2d 889 (1968); . . .

Here, Officer Foster observed Appellant fail to signal his intent to turn three times. Having observed the traffic violation, Officer Foster was authorized to stop and detain Appellant. . . . During his investigation of the traffic violation, the officer smelled the odor of alcohol emanating from the vehicle. Appellant appeared dazed, and his hand movements were slow and awkward. . . . Based upon these observations, Officer Foster developed a reasonable suspicion that Appellant was intoxicated, justifying his detention for further investigation. *Terry,* 392 U.S. at 27; *Lemmons,* 133 S.W.3d at 756-57.

Appellant was arrested after Officer Foster concluded he was intoxicated. An officer must have probable cause in order to make a warrantless arrest. *Torres v. State,* 182 S.W.3d 899, 901 (Tex.Crim.App.2005). Probable cause requires an officer to have a reasonable belief, based on the facts and circumstances within the officer's knowledge or which the officer has reasonably trustworthy information, that an offense has or will be committed. *Torres,* 182 S.W.3d at 902; *Sandoval v. State,* 35 S.W.3d 763, 767 (Tex.App.–El Paso 2000, pet. ref'd). . . .

*(continued)*

Officer Foster concluded Appellant was intoxicated based on the following factors: (1) the vehicle smelled like alcohol; (2) Appellant admitted he had been drinking; (3) he refused to submit to field sobriety tests; (4) he looked dazed, his speech was slurred, and his hand movements were slow and awkward; (5) he tendered his business card when asked for his driver's license; (6) he disregarded three requests that he stand by the car; and (7) he had trouble operating the car window. In considering the totality of circumstances, Officer Foster had probable cause to arrest Appellant. . . . Finding no error in the denial of the motion to suppress, we overrule . . . and affirm the judgment of the trial court.

### Case Review Question

Would the result be any different if the word *intent* was not in the statutory language? Would it make the statute more or less vague?

## ETHICAL CONSIDERATIONS

Legislators are particularly concerned with ethical issues. Because an elected official is required to represent the interests of the people, it is important that legislators avoid the appearance of improper influence by private interests. Extensive ethical rules are imposed on all legislators and their staffs. In addition are ethical committees that review alleged violations of ethical rules by legislators. A pronouncement by a committee that a legislator has violated ethical rules can result in formal disciplinary action and irreparable damage to the legislator's political career.

Over the decades, some legislators openly disregarded the rules of ethics, but that trend has largely been reversed. With the advent of mass media, a legislator's constituents are informed almost immediately of any alleged improprieties, which makes the legislator more than ever responsible to act ethically and loyally to the office.

Ethical issues are not new to U.S. government. In the revolutionary era, Thomas Paine made the noted remark, "These are the times that try men's souls." This commentary on the obligation to do what is right demonstrates that ethics are part of the very fabric of the U.S. legal system.

## ETHICAL CIRCUMSTANCE

Congresswoman X is an elected official from an urban population. Although she represents tens of thousands of constituents, she is seldom in contact with individuals. At fund-raisers for election and reelection, however, she becomes extremely familiar with many wealthy business owners who largely provide the necessary financial base for her campaign. They also employ thousands of the citizens she represents. Would it be acceptable for her to then give the majority of her time in Congress to pursue issues of interest to these business owners even if the decisions would result in higher taxes for the individual citizens? Why or why not?

## ● | CHAPTER SUMMARY

As with every branch of government, the legislative branch has a specific and necessary purpose. Like the other branches, the legislature cannot function effectively without the influence of the other branches and the people. With the assistance of these branches, the legislature is able to enact laws that reflect the opinion of the majority regarding what our society should be.

Congress's lawmaking authority includes the power to tax, raise and support armies, declare and support war, regulate interstate commerce, and enact laws that are necessary and proper to carry out its powers and objectives.

The legislature is able to adjust to changing times while keeping sight of those basic guarantees of the Constitution. When the legislature fails in this effort, the judiciary has the authority to act on a statute to prevent the violation of a citizen's constitutional guarantees. Such adaptability helps to serve the various purposes of legislation, such as indicating what will be considered unacceptable conduct, protecting citizens from injury or damage to property, and providing remedies for those citizens when injury or damage does occur. Further, because of the enormous complexity of the legal system and the number of litigants, procedural laws are designed to process claims as efficiently as possible.

A primary reason for the tremendous adaptability of legislation lies in the method in which legislation is created. Citizens elect delegates (senators and representatives) who propose laws (bills) that, when approved by the majority of the delegates, become law. The citizens are thus represented, and laws can be enacted as necessary with little procedural difficulty.

Safeguards exist against the enactment of laws that are not in the best interests of the people or that violate the Constitution. An important safeguard is the president's veto power. Before a vetoed bill can become law, the bill requires approval by a much larger number of members of Congress than initially required. Presumably, this reflects a desire by a significant majority of the people to enact the law. The judicial branch has limited power to override statutory law. The lone exception to the general rule of superiority of statutory over judicial law takes place when the judiciary determines the statutory law to be in violation of the Constitution.

## CHAPTER TERMS

| | | |
|---|---|---|
| bill | representative | session law |
| codification | senator | veto |
| lobbyist | | |

## REVIEW QUESTIONS

1. How do the House of Representatives and the Senate avoid duplicating work?
2. What is the purpose of remedial statutes?
3. What can happen when a bill is passed by Congress and sent to the president?
4. Who are lobbyists and what is their function?
5. What is the purpose of procedural law?
6. What challenges are typically made to the statutes in a particular case?
7. What is the quasi-advisory role?
8. What is the purpose of protective laws?
9. How is a veto overridden?
10. Where do revenue-raising bills originate and why?

## HELPFUL WEB SITES

| | |
|---|---|
| United States Congress | http://www.Congress.com |
| Government Guide to Legislative Branch | http://www.governmentguide.com |

## ● | INTERNET ASSIGNMENT 3.1

Locate the Web site for your representatives in the U.S. Congress, both in the House of Representatives and the Senate.

## ● | INTERNET ASSIGNMENT 3.2

Locate the Internet address for your state legislature and identify at least one bill that is pending before that body. Give the bill number and title.

## ● | ENDNOTES

1. William Statsky, *Legal Thesaurus/Dictionary* (St. Paul, MN: West, 1982).
2. *Litsinger Sign Co. v. American Sign Co.,* 11 Ohio St. 2dl, 227 N.E.2d 609 (1967).
3. Article I, U.S. Constitution.
4. Statsky, *Legal Thesaurus/Dictionary.*

## STUDENT CD-ROM

For additional materials, please go to the CD in this book.

## ONLINE COMPANION™

For additional resources, please go to http://www.paralegal.delmar.cengage.com

# CHAPTER 4

# The Executive Branch and Administrative Authority

## SOMEDAY YOU COULD BE PRESIDENT

At some point when they are children, most Americans are told, "Someday you could be president!" In fact, this is true. Of the relatively few American presidents, fewer than fifty at the time of this writing, there has been a wide array of occupants for the office of president of the United States. The smallest was James Madison, who stood just 5 feet 4 inches and weighed only 100 pounds. Abe Lincoln towered a full two feet taller at 6 feet 4 inches. William Taft weighed in well above 300 pounds and required a custom extra large bathtub to be installed after becoming stuck in the White House tub. Ronald Regan stepped into office after a long career in Hollywood films and California politics. At age sixty-nine, he was the oldest to begin a presidential term. John F. Kennedy was the youngest at just forty-three. No fewer than thirty-one states have claimed a native son as president. Two sets of fathers and sons have served as president. Gerald Ford was never elected but was appointed to the office of vice president and acceded to the presidency when Richard Nixon became the first president to resign in office. Four presidents lost the popular vote but went on to be carried into office on the electoral college ballot. John Quincy Adams kept his pet alligator in the East Room of the White House. Other presidential pets over the last 200-plus years have included birds, horses, cows, tigers, bears, worms, eagle, elephant, goats, turkeys, mice, rabbits, opossum, snakes, rats, fish, geese, sheep, guinea pigs, and the old standards—dogs and cats. Woodrow Wilson was the only president to have achieved a doctorate degree. Many presidents had little or no college education. Careers before the presidency are just as varied. They included schoolteacher, inventor, lawyer, soldier, tailor, sheriff, actor, engineer, rancher, farmer, hatmaker, and newspaper editor. The presidents of the United States have emerged from every economic class from poverty to great wealth. So when someone tells you that "Someday you could be president," agree with them.

## CHAPTER OBJECTIVES

After reading this chapter, you should be able to:

- Describe how members of the electoral college are selected.

- Describe the process of the electoral college and discuss the effect of the Twelfth Amendment on the process.

- List the duties of the president.

- Describe the delegation doctrine.

- Identify the steps in the creation of an administrative agency.

- Discuss the function and purpose of an administrative agency.

- Identify the requirements of an administrative agency when proposing and issuing a new regulation.

- Describe the considerations of a court in the review of an administrative agency action.

- Discuss the purpose and nature of the Administrative Procedure Act.

## THE EXECUTIVE BRANCH

Article II of the U.S. Constitution establishes the executive branch as a fundamental element in our system of government. Consequently, this branch plays an important role in our legal system. Section 1 of Article II specifies the manner in which the president and vice president shall be elected and the term of office of the president and the vice president. Section 1 also contains provisions in case a president does not complete a term, specifies who may run for president, and describes the timing and method of elections. Sections 2 and 3 address the authority and responsibilities of the president. Section 4 lists the offenses for which a president, vice president, or other officer of the U.S. government can be removed from office. To fully appreciate how the executive branch is described, review the text of Article II, Section 1.*

### Changes in the Electoral Process

In 1804, Section 1 of Article II was amended by passage of the Twelfth Amendment, which slightly altered the process of the electoral ballot and election of the president by the House of Representatives in the event no majority was achieved by the electoral college. Perhaps the most significant change was the method of selection of the vice president. Under the original Constitution, the person having the greatest number of votes in the House of Representatives (assuming no majority

*Note that irregularities in spelling, grammar, and punctuation reflect the Constitution's original form and language.

**Exhibit 4.1**  Article II, Section 1

Section 1. The executive Power shall be vested in a President of the United States of America. He shall hold his Office during the Term of four Years, and, together with the Vice-President, chosen for the same Term, be elected, as follows:

Each State shall appoint, in such Manner as the Legislature thereof may direct, a Number of Electors, equal to the whole Number of Senators and Representatives to which the State may be entitled in the Congress: but no Senator or Representative, or Person holding an Office of Trust or Profit under the United States, shall be appointed an Elector.

[From the Twelfth Amendment, which was passed by Congress in December 1803 and ratified in June 1804] The Electors shall meet in their respective States, and vote by Ballot for two Persons, of whom one at least shall not be an Inhabitant of the same State with themselves. And they shall make a List of all the Persons voted for, and of the Number of Votes for each; which List they shall sign and certify, and transmit sealed to the Seat of the Government of the United States, directed to the President of the Senate [who] shall, in the Presence of the Senate and House of Representatives, open all the Certificates, and the Votes shall then be counted. The Person having the greatest Number of Votes shall be the President, if such Number be a Majority of the whole Number of Electors appointed; and if there be more than one who have such Majority, and have an equal Number of Votes, then the House of Representatives shall immediately chuse by Ballot one of them for President; and if no Person have a Majority, then from the five highest on the List the said House shall in like Manner chuse the President. But in chusing the President, the Votes shall be taken by States, the Representation from each State having one Vote; A quorum for this Purpose shall consist of a Member or Members from two-thirds of the States, and a Majority of all the States shall be necessary to

a Choice. In every Case, after the Choice of the President, the Person having the greater Number of Votes of the Electors shall be the Vice President. But if there should remain two or more who have equal Votes, the Senate shall chuse from them by Ballot the Vice-President.

The Congress may determine the Time of chusing the Electors, and the Day on which they shall give their Votes; which Day shall be the same throughout the United States.

No person except a natural born Citizen, or a Citizen of the United States, at the time of the Adoption of this Constitution, shall be eligible to the Office of President; neither shall any Person be eligible to that Office who shall not have attained to the Age of thirty-five Years, and been fourteen Years a Resident within the United States.

In Case of the Removal of the President from Office, or of his Death, Resignation, or Inability to discharge the Powers and Duties of the said Office, the same shall devolve on the Vice President, and the Congress may by Law provide for the Case of Removal, Death, Resignation or Inability, both of the President and Vice President, declaring what Officer shall then act as President, and such Officer shall act accordingly, until the Disability be removed, or a President shall be elected.

The President shall, at stated Times, receive for his Services, a Compensation, which shall neither be encreased nor diminished during the Period for which he shall have been elected, and he shall not receive within that Period any other Emolument from the United States, or any of them.

Before he enter on the Execution of his Office, he shall take the following Oath or Affirmation: — "I do solemnly swear (or affirm) that I will faithfully execute the Office of President of the United States, and will to the best of my Ability, preserve, protect and defend the Constitution of the United States."

was reached in the electorate) would assume the position of president. Following this, the person with the greatest number of votes in the electoral college (other than the person elected president) would be the vice president. If there was no one person with a majority, then the Senate would elect a vice president in a manner similar to the election of the president. Exhibit 4.1 shows the original language and the addition of the Twelfth Amendment.

An obvious difficulty with the original process was that the person with the second greatest number of votes in the electorate would automatically become vice president. This person would probably have been the president's strongest political opponent, which would make administration of government extremely difficult given the opposing views of the two. By having both the president and the vice president go through a second election process (in the event no majority was reached in the electoral college), such a result could be avoided. With the 1804 amendment, the result of a failed majority in the electoral college would be two elections. The House of Representatives would elect the president. However, rather than an automatic appointment of vice president, that person would be elected by the Senate. Although the election of officials with contradictory views remained possible, at least some thought could be given to the most positive combination of personalities.

The 2000 presidential election was the closest test applied in recent history to the constitutional provisions. Because the electoral college is made up of delegates from each of the states, these delegates rely heavily on the popular vote as the indicator of the direction in which their electoral votes should be cast. In 2000, the popular vote was the closest election in history. In addition, the results in some areas, particularly Florida, did not reflect the number of people registered with the various parties. Added to a variety of issues about the actual voting process, recounts, and so forth was a great concern over the accuracy of the numbers reported as the results of the popular vote. Although many people called for a variety of measures to reassess the vote, the U.S. Supreme Court held that the vote would stand. This decision then paved the way for the electoral college, which followed the popular vote. However, doubt remains as to whether President George Walker Bush was the actual winner. This controversy demonstrates in the most powerful way the importance of the vote of each individual and the necessity for the utmost care in the voting process by election officials.

# CASE
## Bush et al. v. Gore, Jr., et al.,
### 148 L.Ed. 2d 388, 121 S.Ct. 525 (2000)

In one of the most famous political cases in the history of the United States, the determination of the presidency came down to a dispute over just a few of the millions of votes cast. The election was ultimately decided in favor of George W. Bush. However, the case prompted sweeping changes in the actual election process in terms of how votes are cast and counted. This opinion demonstrates some of the problems that the election process presented in the highest venue.

On December 8, 2000, the Supreme Court of Florida ordered that the Circuit Court of Leon County tabulate by hand 9,000 ballots in Miami–Dade County. It also ordered the inclusion in the certified vote totals of 215 votes identified in Palm Beach County and 168 votes identified in Miami–Dade County for Vice President Albert Gore, Jr., and Senator Joseph Lieberman, Democratic candidates for President and Vice President. The State Supreme Court noted that petitioner, George W. Bush, asserted that the net gain for Vice President Gore in Palm Beach County was 176 votes, and directed the Circuit Court to resolve that dispute on remand. *Gore v. Harris,* 772 So.2d 1243, 1248, n. 6. The court further held that relief would require manual recounts in all Florida counties where so-called "undervotes" had not been subject to manual tabulation. The court ordered all manual recounts to begin at once. Governor Bush and Richard Cheney, Republican

candidates for President and Vice President, filed an emergency application for a stay of this mandate. On December 9, we granted the application, treated the application as a petition for a writ of certiorari, and granted certiorari.

On November 8, 2000, the day following the Presidential election, the Florida Division of Elections reported that petitioner Bush had received 2,909,135 votes, and respondent Gore had received 2,907,351 votes, a margin of 1,784 for Governor Bush. Because Governor Bush's margin of victory was less than "one-half of a percent . . . of the votes cast," an automatic machine recount was conducted under § 102.141(4) of the election code, the results of which showed Governor Bush still winning the race but by a diminished margin. Vice President Gore then sought manual recounts in Volusia, Palm Beach, Broward, and Miami–Dade Counties, pursuant to Florida's election protest provisions. Fla. Stat. Ann. § 102.166 (Supp.2001). A dispute arose concerning the deadline for local county canvassing boards to submit their returns to the Secretary of State (Secretary). The Secretary declined to waive the November 14 deadline imposed by statute. §§ 102.111, 102.112. The Florida Supreme Court, however, set the deadline at November 26. We granted certiorari and vacated the Florida Supreme Court's decision, finding considerable uncertainty as to the grounds on which it was based.

*Bush I,* 531 U.S., at 78, 121 S.Ct. 471. On December 11, the Florida Supreme Court issued a decision on remand reinstating that date. 772 So.2d at 1273–1290.

On November 26, the Florida Elections Canvassing Commission certified the results of the election and declared Governor Bush the winner of Florida's 25 electoral votes. On November 27, Vice President Gore, pursuant to Florida's contest provisions, filed a complaint in Leon County Circuit Court contesting the certification. Fla. Stat. Ann. § 102.168 (Supp.2001). He sought relief pursuant to § 102.168(3)(c), which provides that "[r]eceipt of a number of illegal votes or rejection of a number of legal votes sufficient to change or place in doubt the result of the election" shall be grounds for a contest. The Circuit Court denied relief, stating that Vice President Gore failed to meet his burden of proof. He appealed to the First District Court of Appeal, which certified the matter to the Florida Supreme Court.

Accepting jurisdiction, the Florida Supreme Court affirmed in part and reversed in part. *Gore v. Harris,* 772 So.2d. 1243 (2000). The court held that the Circuit Court had been correct to reject Vice President Gore's challenge to the results certified in Nassau County and his challenge to the Palm Beach County Canvassing Board's determination that 3,300 ballots cast in that county were not, in the statutory phrase, "legal votes."

The Supreme Court held that Vice President Gore had satisfied his burden of proof under § 102.168(3)(c) with respect to his challenge to Miami–Dade County's failure to tabulate, by manual count, 9,000 ballots on which the machines had failed to detect a vote for President ("undervotes"). *Id.,* at 1256. Noting the closeness of the election, the court explained that "[o]n this record, there can be no question that there are legal votes within the 9,000 uncounted votes sufficient to place the results of this election in doubt." *Id.,* at 1261. A "legal vote," as determined by the Supreme Court, is "one in which there is a 'clear indication of the intent of the voter.'" *Id.,* at 1257. The court therefore ordered a hand recount of the 9,000 ballots in Miami–Dade County. Observing that the contest provisions vest broad discretion in the circuit judge to "provide any relief appropriate under such circumstances," § 102.168(8), the Supreme Court further held that the Circuit Court could order "the Supervisor of Elections and the Canvassing Boards, as well as the necessary public officials, in all counties that have not conducted a manual recount or tabulation of the undervotes . . . to do so forthwith, said tabulation to take place in the individual counties where the ballots are located." *Id.,* at 1262.

The Supreme Court also determined that both Palm Beach County and Miami–Dade County, in their earlier manual recounts, had identified a net gain of 215 and 168 legal votes for Vice President Gore. *Id.,* at 1260. Rejecting the Circuit Court's conclusion that Palm Beach County lacked the authority to include the 215 net votes submitted past the November 26 deadline, the Supreme Court explained that the deadline was not intended to exclude votes identified after that date through ongoing manual recounts. As to Miami–Dade County, the court concluded that although the 168 votes identified were the result of a partial recount, they were "legal votes [that] could change the outcome of the election." *Ibid.* The Supreme Court therefore directed the Circuit Court to include those totals in the certified results, subject to resolution of the actual vote total from the Miami–Dade partial recount.

The petition presents the following questions: whether the Florida Supreme Court established new standards for resolving Presidential election contests, thereby violating Art. II, § 1, cl. 2, of the United States Constitution and failing to comply with 3 U.S.C. § 5, and whether the use of standardless manual recounts violates the Equal Protection and Due Process Clauses. With respect to the equal protection question, we find a violation of the Equal Protection Clause.

The closeness of this election, and the multitude of legal challenges which have followed in its wake, have brought into sharp focus a common, if heretofore unnoticed, phenomenon. Nationwide statistics reveal that an estimated 2% of ballots cast do not register a vote for President for whatever reason, including deliberately choosing no candidate at all or some voter error, such as voting for two candidates or insufficiently marking a ballot. In certifying election results, the votes eligible for inclusion in the certification are the votes meeting the properly established legal requirements.

This case has shown that punchcard balloting machines can produce an unfortunate number of ballots which are not punched in a clean, complete way by the voter. After the current counting, it is likely legislative bodies nationwide will examine ways to improve the mechanisms and machinery for voting.

The individual citizen has no federal constitutional right to vote for electors for the President of the United States unless and until the state legislature chooses a statewide election as the means to implement its power to appoint members of the Electoral College. U.S. Const., Art. II, § 1. This is the source for the statement in *McPherson v. Blacker,* 146 U.S. 1, 35, 13 S.Ct. 3, 36 L.Ed. 869 (1892), that the state legislature's power to select the manner for appointing electors is plenary; it may, if it so chooses, select the electors itself, which indeed was the manner used by state legislatures in several States for many years after the framing of our Constitution. *Id.,* at 28–33, 13 S.Ct. 3.

*(continued)*

History has now favored the voter, and in each of the several States the citizens themselves vote for Presidential electors. When the state legislature vests the right to vote for President in its people, the right to vote as the legislature has prescribed is fundamental; and one source of its fundamental nature lies in the equal weight accorded to each vote and the equal dignity owed to each voter. The State, of course, after granting the franchise in the special context of Article II, can take back the power to appoint electors. See *id.,* at 35, 13 S.Ct. 3 ("'[T]here is no doubt of the right of the legislature to resume the power at any time, for it can neither be taken away nor abdicated'") (quoting S.Rep. No. 395, 43d Cong., 1st Sess. 9 (1874)).

The right to vote is protected in more than the initial allocation of the franchise. Equal protection applies as well to the manner of its exercise. Having once granted the right to vote on equal terms, the State may not, by later arbitrary and disparate treatment, value one person's vote over that of another. See, e.g., *Harper v. Virginia Bd. of Elections,* 383 U.S. 663, 665, 86 S.Ct. 1079, 16 L.Ed.2d 169 (1966) ("[O]nce the franchise is granted to the electorate, lines may not be drawn which are inconsistent with the Equal Protection Clause of the Fourteenth Amendment"). It must be remembered that "the right of suffrage can be denied by a debasement or dilution of the weight of a citizen's vote just as effectively as by wholly prohibiting the free exercise of the franchise." *Reynolds v. Sims,* 377 U.S. 533, 555, 84 S.Ct. 1362, 12 L.Ed.2d 506 (1964).

There is no difference between the two sides of the present controversy on these basic propositions. Respondents say that the very purpose of vindicating the right to vote justifies the recount procedures now at issue. The question before us, however, is whether the recount procedures the Florida Supreme Court has adopted are consistent with its obligation to avoid arbitrary and disparate treatment of the members of its electorate.

Much of the controversy seems to revolve around ballot cards designed to be perforated by a stylus but which, either through error or deliberate omission, have not been perforated with sufficient precision for a machine to register the perforations. In some cases a piece of the card—a chad—is hanging, say, by two corners. In other cases there is no separation at all, just an indentation.

The Florida Supreme Court has ordered that the intent of the voter be discerned from such ballots. For purposes of resolving the equal protection challenge, it is not necessary to decide whether the Florida Supreme Court had the authority under the legislative scheme for resolving election disputes to define what a legal vote is and to mandate a manual recount implementing that definition. The recount mechanisms implemented in response to the decisions of the Florida Supreme Court do not satisfy the minimum requirement for nonarbitrary treatment of voters necessary to secure the fundamental right. Florida's basic command for the count of legally cast votes is to consider the "intent of the voter." 772 So.2d, at 1262. This is unobjectionable as an abstract proposition and a starting principle. The problem inheres in the absence of specific standards to ensure its equal application. The formulation of uniform rules to determine intent based on these recurring circumstances is practicable and, we conclude, necessary.

The law does not refrain from searching for the intent of the actor in a multitude of circumstances; and in some cases the general command to ascertain intent is not susceptible to much further refinement. In this instance, however, the question is not whether to believe a witness but how to interpret the marks or holes or scratches on an inanimate object, a piece of cardboard or paper which, it is said, might not have registered as a vote during the machine count. The factfinder confronts a thing, not a person. The search for intent can be confined by specific rules designed to ensure uniform treatment.

The want of those rules here has led to unequal evaluation of ballots in various respects. See *id.,* at 1267 (Wells, C.J., dissenting) ("Should a county canvassing board count or not count a 'dimpled chad' where the voter is able to successfully dislodge the chad in every other contest on that ballot? Here, the county canvassing boards disagree"). As seems to have been acknowledged at oral argument, the standards for accepting or rejecting contested ballots might vary not only from county to county but indeed within a single county from one recount team to another.

The record provides some examples. A monitor in Miami–Dade County testified at trial that he observed that three members of the county canvassing board applied different standards in defining a legal vote. 3 Tr. 497, 499 (Dec. 3, 2000). And testimony at trial also revealed that at least one county changed its evaluative standards during the counting process. Palm Beach County, for example, began the process with a 1990 guideline which precluded counting completely attached chads, switched to a rule that considered a vote to be legal if any light could be seen through a chad, changed back to the 1990 rule, and then abandoned any pretense of a *per se* rule, only to have a court order that the country consider dimpled chads legal. This is not a process with sufficient guarantees of equal treatment.

An early case in our one-person, one-vote jurisprudence arose when a State accorded arbitrary and disparate treatment to voters in its different counties.

*Gray v. Sanders,* 372 U.S. 368, 83 S.Ct. 801, 9 L.Ed.2d 821 (1963). The Court found a constitutional violation. We relied on these principles in the context of the Presidential selection process in *Moore v. Ogilvie,* 394 U.S. 814, 89 S.Ct. 1493, 23 L.Ed.2d 1 (1969), where we invalidated a county-based procedure that diluted the influence of citizens in larger counties in the nominating process. There we observed that "[t]he idea that one group can be granted greater voting strength than another is hostile to the one man, one vote basis of our representative government." *Id.,* at 819, 89 S.Ct. 1493.

The State Supreme Court ratified this uneven treatment. It mandated that the recount totals from two counties, Miami–Dade and Palm Beach, be included in the certified total. The court also appeared to hold *sub silentio* that the recount totals from Broward Country, which were not completed until after the original November 14 certification by the Secretary, were to be considered part of the new certified vote totals even though the county certification was not contested by Vice President Gore. Yet each of the counties used varying standards to determine what was a legal vote. Broward County used a more forgiving standard than Palm Beach County, and uncovered almost three times as many new votes, a result markedly disproportionate to the difference in population between the counties.

In addition, the recounts in these three counties were not limited to so-called undervotes but extended to all of the ballots. The distinction has real consequences. A manual recount of all ballots identifies not only those ballots which show no vote but also those which contain more than one, the so-called overvotes. Neither category will be counted by the machine. This is not a trivial concern. At oral argument, respondents estimated there are as many as 110,000 overvotes statewide. As a result, the citizen whose ballot was not read by a machine because he failed to vote for a candidate in a way readable by a machine may still have his vote counted in a manual recount; on the other hand, the citizen who marks two candidates in a way discernible by the machine will not have the same opportunity to have his vote count, even if a manual examination of the ballot would reveal the requisite indicia of intent. Furthermore, the citizen who marks two candidates, only one of which is discernible by the machine, will have his vote counted even though it should have been read as an invalid ballot. The State Supreme Court's inclusion of vote counts based on these variant standards exemplifies concerns with the remedial processes that were under way.

That brings the analysis to yet a further equal protection problem. The votes certified by the court included a partial total from one county, Miami–Dade. The Florida Supreme Court's decision thus gives no assurance that the recounts included in a final certification must be complete. Indeed, it is respondents' submission that it would be consistent with the rules of the recount procedures to include whatever partial counts are done by the time of final certification, and we interpret the Florida Supreme Court's decision to permit this. See 772 So.2d, at 1261–1262, n. 21 (noting "practical difficulties" may control outcome of election, but certifying partial Miami–Dade total nonetheless). This accommodation no doubt results from the truncated contest period established by the Florida Supreme Court in *Palm Beach County Canvassing Bd. v. Harris,* at respondents own urging. The press of time does not diminish the constitutional concern. A desire for speed is not a general excuse for ignoring equal protection guarantees.

In addition to these difficulties the actual process by which the votes were to be counted under the Florida Supreme Court's decision raises further concerns. That order did not specify who would recount the ballots. The county canvassing boards were forced to pull together ad hoc teams of judges from various Circuits who had no previous training in handling and interpreting ballots. Furthermore, while others were permitted to observe, they were prohibited from objecting during the recount.

The recount process, in its features here described, is inconsistent with the minimum procedures necessary to protect the fundamental right of each voter in the special instance of a statewide recount under the authority of a single state judicial officer. Our consideration is limited to the present circumstances, for the problem of equal protection in election processes generally presents many complexities.

The question before the Court is not whether local entities, in the exercise of their expertise, may develop different systems for implementing elections. Instead, we are presented with a situation where a state court with the power to assure uniformity has ordered a statewide recount with minimal procedural safeguards. When a court orders a statewide remedy, there must be at least some assurance that the rudimentary requirements of equal treatment and fundamental fairness are satisfied.

Given the Court's assessment that the recount process underway was probably being conducted in an unconstitutional manner, the Court stayed the order directing the recount so it could hear this case and render an expedited decision. The contest provision, as it was mandated by the State Supreme Court, is not well calculated to sustain the confidence that all citizens

*(continued)*

must have in the outcome of elections. The State has not shown that its procedures include the necessary safeguards. The problem, for instance, of the estimated 110,000 overvotes has not been addressed, although Chief Justice Wells called attention to the concern in his dissenting opinion. See 772 So.2d, at 1264, n. 26.

Upon due consideration of the difficulties identified to this point, it is obvious that the recount cannot be conducted in compliance with the requirements of equal protection and due process without substantial additional work. It would require not only the adoption (after opportunity for argument) of adequate statewide standards for determining what is a legal vote, and practicable procedures to implement them, but also orderly judicial review of any disputed matters that might arise. In addition, the Secretary has advised that the recount of only a portion of the ballots requires that the vote tabulation equipment be used to screen out undervotes, a function for which the machines were not designed. If a recount of overvotes were also required, perhaps even a second screening would be necessary. Use of the equipment for this purpose, and any new software developed for it, would have to be evaluated for accuracy by the Secretary, as required by Fla. Stat. Ann. § 101.015 (Supp.2001).

The Supreme Court of Florida has said that the legislature intended the State's electors to "participat[e] fully in the federal electoral process," as provided in 3 U.S.C. § 5.772 So.2d, at 1289; see also *Palm Beach County Canvassing Bd. v. Harris,* 772 So.2d 1220, 1237 (Fla.2000). That statute, in turn, requires that any controversy or contest that is designed to lead to a conclusive selection of electors be completed by December 12. That date is upon us, and there is no recount procedure in place under the State Supreme Court's order that comports with minimal constitutional standards. Because it is evident that any recount seeking to meet the December 12 date will be unconstitutional for the reasons we have

discussed, we reverse the judgment of the Supreme Court of Florida ordering a recount to proceed.

Seven Justices of the Court agree that there are constitutional problems with the recount ordered by the Florida Supreme Court that demand a remedy. The only disagreement is as to the remedy. Because the Florida Supreme Court has said that the Florida Legislature intended to obtain the safe-harbor benefits of 3 U.S.C. § 5, Justice Breyer's proposed remedy—remanding to the Florida Supreme Court for its ordering of a constitutionally proper contest until December 18—contemplates action in violation of the Florida Election Code, and hence could not be part of an "appropriate" order authorized by Fla. Stat. Ann. § 102.168(8) (Supp. 2001).

None are more conscious of the vital limits on judicial authority than are the Members of this Court, and none stand more in admiration of the Constitution's design to leave the selection of the President to the people, through their legislatures, and to the political sphere. When contending parties invoke the process of the courts, however, it becomes our unsought responsibility to resolve the federal and constitutional issues the judicial system has been forced to confront.

The judgment of the Supreme Court of Florida is reversed, and the case is remanded for further proceedings not inconsistent with this opinion.

Pursuant to this Court's Rule 45.2, the Clerk is directed to issue the mandate in this case forthwith.

It is so ordered.

## Case Review Question

Would the result have likely been different if there were no statutory cutoff date for ending election disputes? If so, what would the result have likely been?

## Powers and Authority of the President

Sections 2 and 3 of Article II describe the powers and obligations of the office of the president. Both sections are still influential in the daily operation of government. Frequently, questions arise about the proper use of power by the branches of government and the effectiveness of the system as detailed in the Constitution. A closer look at these two sections may be helpful at this point. See Exhibit 4.2.

The powers described in these sections indicate that the president has the basic authority to negotiate treaties, appoint judges and other government officers, convene the Congress, grant pardons and reprieves, appoint ambassadors and heads of departments (the cabinet), and command the armed forces. Specifically, the president exercises great latitude in establishing, maintaining, and ending foreign relations with other countries. On occasion, this authority covers military actions as well. Under current statutes, however, the president

**Exhibit 4.2**  Article II, Sections 2 and 3

Section 2. The President shall be Commander in Chief of the Army and Navy of the United States, and of the Militia of the several States, when called into the actual Service of the United States; he may require the Opinion in writing, of the principal Officer in each of the executive Departments, upon any subject relating to the Duties of their respective Offices, and he shall have Power to Grant Reprieves and Pardons for Offenses against the United States, except in Cases of Impeachment.

He shall have Power, by and with the Advice and Consent of the Senate, to make Treaties, provided two-thirds of the Senators present concur; and he shall nominate, and by and with the Advice and Consent of the Senate, shall appoint Ambassadors, other public Ministers and Consuls, Judges of the supreme Court, and all other Officers of the United States, whose Appointments are not herein otherwise provided for, and which shall be established by Law; but the Congress may by Law vest the Appointment of such inferior Officers, as they think proper, in the President alone, in the Courts of Law, or in the Heads of Departments.

The President shall have Power to fill up all Vacancies that may happen during the Recess of the Senate, by granting Commissions which shall expire at the End of their next Session.

Section 3. He shall from time to time give to the Congress Information of the State of the Union, and recommend to their Consideration such Measures as he shall judge necessary and expedient; he may, on extraordinary Occasions, convene both Houses, or either of them, and in Case of Disagreement between them, with Respect to the Time of Adjournment, he may adjourn them to such Time as he shall think proper; he shall receive Ambassadors and other public Ministers; he shall take Care that the Laws be faithfully executed, and shall Commission all the Officers of the United States.

must report to the Congress on military actions because the power to declare war is vested in the Congress under the Constitution.

In addition, the president is vested with power to enforce laws. Consequently, federal law-enforcement organizations are overseen by the executive branch. The president also appoints the attorney general, who serves as counsel for the executive branch on matters of enforcement.

The bulk of the powers of the president is derived from one small portion of one sentence near the end of Article II, Section 3: ". . . he shall take Care that the Laws be faithfully executed. . . ." This statement has been expanded to create the executive authority to oversee administrative law, one of the principal sources of law in the United States.

The president cannot create administrative law directly but is responsible for supervising the activities of federal administrative agencies. A similar process occurs at the state level between the state executive branch (the office of governor) and state administrative agencies. The creation and the operation of an administrative agency are discussed in the following sections.

## ASSIGNMENT 4.1

Create a chart that details the two methods of presidential and vice presidential elections before and after the Twelfth Amendment of 1804.

## The Role of the President, Then and Now

Originally, the role of the president was similar to a head of state in other developed nations. Most often in monarchies, the head of state was primarily a ceremonial position. Duties included serving as a physical representative of the nation and thus providing a central exhibit behind which citizens could unite and with whom other nations could identify. One significant duty was the negotiation of treaties with other nations; however, with limited travel capabilities, no form of rapid or mass communication, and a largely rural population separated from other countries by ocean on three sides, the early presidents had few demands placed on them in comparison with presidents in more recent times.

The Civil War tore the very fabric of the nation. A primary postwar objective was to bring the nation together both for the sake of the citizens and as a signal to other nations that the United States was not weakened and subject to intrusion. At about the same time, methods of transportation were advancing with railroads extending throughout the country and maritime travel taking place on both rivers and oceans. Telegraph lines also made communication to most localities possible. These advancements and the need to unify the nation changed the direction of the presidency. The primarily ceremonial role was left behind, and the president became increasingly involved in communicating with and representing the people of the nation with respect to other branches of our own government and other nations.

During the twentieth century, the role of the president changed dramatically. Two world wars and an unprecedented economic depression all within a span of forty-five years put tremendous strains on the nation. The president worked with the other branches of government to keep the nation strong and independent. Technological advancements and immense increases in population through births and immigration required extensive legislation and governmental supervision to protect a largely uneducated public. The result was the creation of numerous administrative agencies within the executive branch of government. It became the responsibility of the president to oversee such agencies in addition to the office's existing duties. The trend continued and, by the end of the twentieth century, the president was as involved with the actual representation of the population as any other element of government.

## ADMINISTRATIVE AGENCIES

### The Role of the Administrative Agency

**administrative agency**
Government office created by the legislature and overseen by the executive branch. The purpose of such an agency is to apply certain specified laws created by the legislature.

An **administrative agency** has a unique and constantly growing place in the role of government in American society. The population of the country is so large, the geographical area so great and varied, and the system of government so complex that it is essential to have government officials who can respond to the specific needs of the many facets of society. When Congress passes a statute, the law must be written broadly enough to encompass all situations it is designed to address. However, that same law must be specific enough to allow people to know whether their actions comply with or violate the law. Hence the need for the administrative agency, whose basic role is to act as liaison between Congress and the people. The administrative agency explains what Congress means in particular statutory language, clarifies and defines terms, and ultimately, under the supervision of the executive branch, enforces the law. (See Exhibit 4.3 for a diagram of the federal government structure and placement of administrative offices.)

The responsibility of the president to carry out and enforce the laws passed by Congress is immense. With the assistance of administrative agencies, individuals can have personal access to government, and they can receive answers about specific situations affected by broadly written statutes. After Congress passes laws that enable the creation of an administrative agency, it then passes additional statutes that must be enforced. The president staffs and oversees the administrative agency as it clarifies, defines, and enforces these congressional statutes. Many of these agencies are controlled by the executive branch's fourteen departments (e.g., the Department of Justice controls the Federal Bureau of Investigation, and the Treasury Department controls the Internal Revenue Service), although some federal agencies are not part of a specific department. The heads of the executive

**Exhibit 4.3** Federal Government Structure

# THE GOVERNMENT OF THE UNITED STATES

## THE CONSTITUTION

### LEGISLATIVE BRANCH

**THE CONGRESS**

**SENATE   HOUSE**

ARCHITECT OF THE CAPITOL
UNITED STATES BOTANIC GARDEN
GENERAL ACCOUNTING OFFICE
GOVERNMENT PRINTING OFFICE
LIBRARY OF CONGRESS
CONGRESSIONAL BUDGET OFFICE

### EXECUTIVE BRANCH

**THE PRESIDENT**

**THE VICE PRESIDENT**

**EXECUTIVE OFFICE OF THE PRESIDENT**

WHITE HOUSE OFFICE
OFFICE OF THE VICE PRESIDENT
COUNCIL OF ECONOMIC ADVISERS
COUNCIL ON ENVIRONMENTAL QUALITY
NATIONAL SECURITY COUNCIL
OFFICE OF ADMINISTRATION

OFFICE OF MANAGEMENT AND BUDGET
OFFICE OF NATIONAL DRUG CONTROL POLICY
OFFICE OF POLICY DEVELOPMENT
OFFICE OF SCIENCE AND TECHNOLOGY POLICY
OFFICE OF THE U.S. TRADE REPRESENTATIVE

### JUDICIAL BRANCH

**THE SUPREME COURT OF THE UNITED STATES**

UNITED STATES COURTS OF APPEALS
UNITED STATES DISTRICT COURTS
TERRITORIAL COURTS
UNITED STATES COURT OF INTERNATIONAL TRADE
UNITED STATES COURT OF FEDERAL CLAIMS
UNITED STATES COURT OF APPEALS FOR THE ARMED FORCES
UNITED STATES TAX COURT
UNITED STATES COURT OF APPEALS FOR VETERANS CLAIMS
ADMINISTRATIVE OFFICE OF THE UNITED STATES COURTS
FEDERAL JUDICIAL CENTER
UNITED STATES SENTENCING COMMISSION

**Departments**

DEPARTMENT OF AGRICULTURE
DEPARTMENT OF COMMERCE
DEPARTMENT OF DEFENSE
DEPARTMENT OF EDUCATION
DEPARTMENT OF ENERGY
DEPARTMENT OF HEALTH AND HUMAN SERVICES
DEPARTMENT OF HOUSING AND URBAN DEVELOPMENT

DEPARTMENT OF THE INTERIOR
DEPARTMENT OF JUSTICE
DEPARTMENT OF LABOR
DEPARTMENT OF STATE
DEPARTMENT OF TRANSPORTATION
DEPARTMENT OF THE TREASURY
DEPARTMENT OF VETERANS AFFAIRS

**INDEPENDENT ESTABLISHMENTS AND GOVERNMENT CORPORATIONS**

AFRICAN DEVELOPMENT FOUNDATION
CENTRAL INTELLIGENCE AGENCY
COMMODITY FUTURES TRADING COMMISSION
CONSUMER PRODUCT SAFETY COMMISSION
CORPORATION FOR NATIONAL AND COMMUNITY SERVICE
DEFENSE NUCLEAR FACILITIES SAFETY BOARD
ENVIRONMENTAL PROTECTION AGENCY
EQUAL EMPLOYMENT OPPORTUNITY COMMISSION
EXPORT-IMPORT BANK OF THE U.S.
FARM CREDIT ADMINISTRATION
FEDERAL COMMUNICATIONS COMMISSION
FEDERAL DEPOSIT INSURANCE CORPORATION
FEDERAL ELECTION COMMISSION
FEDERAL EMERGENCY MANAGEMENT AGENCY
FEDERAL HOUSING FINANCE BOARD

FEDERAL LABOR RELATIONS AUTHORITY
FEDERAL MARITIME COMMISSION
FEDERAL MEDIATION AND CONCILIATION SERVICE
FEDERAL MINE SAFETY AND HEALTH REVIEW COMMISSION
FEDERAL RESERVE SYSTEM
FEDERAL RETIREMENT THRIFT INVESTMENT BOARD
FEDERAL TRADE COMMISSION
GENERAL SERVICES ADMINISTRATION
INTER-AMERICAN FOUNDATION
MERIT SYSTEMS PROTECTION BOARD
NATIONAL AERONAUTICS AND SPACE ADMINISTRATION
NATIONAL ARCHIVES AND RECORDS ADMINISTRATION
NATIONAL CAPITAL PLANNING COMMISSION
NATIONAL CREDIT UNION ADMINISTRATION
NATIONAL FOUNDATION ON THE ARTS AND THE HUMANITIES

NATIONAL LABOR RELATIONS BOARD
NATIONAL MEDIATION BOARD
NATIONAL RAILROAD PASSENGER CORPORATION (AMTRAK)
NATIONAL SCIENCE FOUNDATION
NATIONAL TRANSPORTATION SAFETY BOARD
NUCLEAR REGULATORY COMMISSION
OCCUPATIONAL SAFETY AND HEALTH REVIEW COMMISSION
OFFICE OF GOVERNMENT ETHICS
OFFICE OF PERSONNEL MANAGEMENT
OFFICE OF SPECIAL COUNSEL
OVERSEAS PRIVATE INVESTMENT CORPORATION
PEACE CORPS
PENSION BENEFIT GUARANTY CORPORATION
POSTAL RATE COMMISSION

RAILROAD RETIREMENT BOARD
SECURITIES AND EXCHANGE COMMISSION
SELECTIVE SERVICE SYSTEM
SMALL BUSINESS ADMINISTRATION
SOCIAL SECURITY ADMINISTRATION
TENNESSEE VALLEY AUTHORITY
TRADE AND DEVELOPMENT AGENCY
U.S. AGENCY FOR INTERNATIONAL DEVELOPMENT
U.S. COMMISSION ON CIVIL RIGHTS
U.S. INTERNATIONAL TRADE COMMISSION
U.S. POSTAL SERVICE

Source: *U.S. Government Manual, 1997.* Washington, DC: U.S. Government Printing Office, 1997.

departments serve as members of the president's cabinet (e.g., the secretary of defense and the attorney general).

Although the day-to-day operation of an administrative agency is largely within the executive branch's control, an agency is ultimately created by the Congress. Article I, Section 8, paragraph 18, of the Constitution provides as follows:

> The Congress shall have power . . . To make all Laws which shall be necessary and proper for carrying into Execution the foregoing Powers, and all other Powers vested by this Constitution in the Government of the United States, or in any Department or Officer thereof.

Congress has drawn its authority to make laws from this statement, which has also been interpreted to permit Congress to enact laws that allow government agencies to clarify the laws through regulations and administrative decisions. The president's power to appoint federal officers allows the executive branch to staff the agencies. The executive duty to see that the laws are faithfully executed vests in the president the authority to oversee the agencies as they enforce the laws passed by the Congress.

Administrative agencies have been a part of the U.S. legal system since the 1800s because they can perform many legal functions that Congress, for practical reasons, cannot effectively accomplish. Administrative agencies offer several advantages, including the following:

1. They can deal with large groups of citizens or entire industries.
2. They have the ability to respond quickly to rapidly changing needs of industries or citizens.
3. Their staff members are more knowledgeable about the specifics of an industry or a group of citizens than the legislature or the judiciary.
4. They can provide consistent and fair standards for citizens and industries.

Agencies touch virtually every part of American life. Anyone who is employed is affected by agencies such as the Social Security Administration and Occupational Safety and Health Administration (OSHA), as well as by labor laws and immigration laws. Purchases of property may be affected by the Environmental Protection Agency (EPA), perhaps with the land subject to its rules and regulations. Other areas under agency direction include banking, civil rights, investments, travel, consumer transactions, retirement, and emergency aid for areas hit by natural disaster. See Exhibit 4.4 for a partial list of federal agencies.

An example of an area in which an administrative agency has been particularly effective is social security, which is the administered by the Social Security Administration. All working people in the United States pay into a social security fund, from which payments are made to persons who retire or become disabled. Given the number of persons who have worked in this country since the establishment of this system in 1935, the task of collecting and distributing the funds is incomprehensible. Such a task can be carried out most effectively by an administrative agency such as the Social Security Administration rather than by Congress. This agency establishes rules for eligibility and procedures to receive funds, payment of legally required contributions by workers, cost of living increases, and other matters that are necessary to administer the funds but that do not require an elected body to perform them.

## The Creation of an Administrative Agency

In many areas, an administrative agency is the most effective way to deal knowledgeably, efficiently, and equitably with many legal issues on an individual basis. The following paragraphs examine the basic process for creating an administrative

**Exhibit 4.4**  Sample List of Administrative Agencies

- Advisory Council on Historic Preservation (ACHP)
- American Battle Monuments Commission
- Central Intelligence Agency (CIA)
- Commodity Futures Trading Commission (CFTC)
- Consumer Product Safety Commission (CPSC)
- Corporation for National Service
- Environmental Protection Agency (EPA)
- Equal Employment Opportunity Commission (EEOC)
- Farm Credit Administration (FCA)
- Federal Communications Commission (FCC)
- Federal Deposit Insurance Corporation (FDIC)
- Federal Election Commission (FEC)
- Federal Energy Regulatory Commission (FERC)
- Federal Labor Relations Authority (FLRA)
- Federal Maritime Commission
- Federal Reserve System, Board of Governors of the Federal Reserve System
- Federal Retirement Thrift Investment Board (FRTIB)
- Federal Trade Commission (FTC)
- Federal Consumer Information Center (Pueblo, CO)
- General Services Administration (GSA)
- Institute of Museum and Library Services (IMLS)
- International Boundary and Water Commission
- International Broadcasting Bureau (IBB)
- Merit Systems Protection Board (MSPB)
- National Aeronautics and Space Administration (NASA)
- National Archives and Records Administration (NARA)
- National Capital Planning Commission (NCPC)
- National Commission on Libraries and Information Science (NCLIS)
- National Council on Disability
- National Credit Union Administration (NCUA)
- National Endowment for the Arts (NEA)
- National Endowment for the Humanities (NEH)
- National Indian Gaming Commission (NIGC)
- National Labor Relations Board (NLRB)
- National Mediation Board (NMB)
- National Railroad Passenger Corporation (AMTRAK)
- National Science Foundation (NSF) Board
- National Transportation Safety Board (NTSB)
- Nuclear Regulatory Commission (NRC)
- Nuclear Waste Technical Review Board (NWTRB)
- Occupational Safety and Health Administration (OSHA)
- Office of Federal Housing Enterprise Oversight (OFHEO)
- Office of Personnel Management (OPM)
- Overseas Private Investment Corporation (OPIC)
- Peace Corps
- Pension Benefit Guaranty Corporation
- Postal Rate Commission
- Railroad Retirement Board (RRB)
- Securities and Exchange Commission (SEC)
- Selective Service System (SSS)
- Small Business Administration (SBA)
- Social Security Administration (SSA)
- Tennessee Valley Authority (TVA)
- Thrift Savings Plan (TSP)
- United States Agency for International Development (USAID)
- United States Arms Control and Disarmament Agency (ACDA)
- United States International Trade Commission (USITC) Dataweb (import and export data)
- United States Office of Government Ethics (OGE)
- United States Postal Service (USPS)
- United States Postal Inspection Service (USPIS)
- United States Trade and Development Agency
- Voice of America (VOA)

agency in today's legal system. Be aware that many additional details must be dealt with in the actual agency creation process.

Before an agency comes into existence, Congress must pass a resolution saying that an agency is necessary to carry out the goals of certain legislation. Congress must determine that no more effective way to implement the goals exists and that the goals of the legislation must be enforced. Congress then passes what is commonly referred to as an **enabling act**—a statute that expresses the goals of Congress on a particular subject of legislation.

**enabling act**
Congressional enactment that creates the authority in the executive to organize and oversee an administrative agency by establishing specific legislative goals and objectives.

One example is the enabling act that ultimately provided for the creation of the Environmental Protection Agency, which carries out and enforces legislation passed by Congress to protect, enhance, or correct problems in the environment. When the National Environmental Policy Act (NEPA) was passed as an enabling act in 1969, it was the first major environmental protection law enacted by Congress. Shortly thereafter, President Richard Nixon issued an *executive order* that called for the creation of an agency to carry out the goals set forth in the NEPA. The executive order is a form of procedural law that implements the enabling act. Although executive orders have the weight of law, they are issued by presidents or at their direction and only affect administrative agencies or functions.

The acts that permit the creation of administrative agencies have been a great source of controversy for Congress over the years. In effect, by creating an administrative agency, Congress is relinquishing some of its lawmaking authority. Early on, the delegation of authority to make rules with the effect of law was strictly prohibited by the U.S. Supreme Court.[1] As time passed and the needs of the country grew, however, the Court relaxed its position somewhat to permit administrative agencies to play a larger role in the legislative process. Although they have never been allowed to "create law," agencies are permitted to create regulations to promote efficient, responsive, and effective government.

Through cases that come before them, the courts have continued to closely monitor Congress and the executive branch with respect to the creation and operation of administrative agencies. The courts' chief concern with the creation of administrative agencies is that there be no violation of the **delegation doctrine**, which is based on the premise that Congress cannot be permitted to give away any of its actual lawmaking power.[2] Rather, Congress can only give up or delegate the authority to clarify and enforce laws passed. The delegation of the authority to clarify and enforce laws is permissible even if it means that the agency must enact additional law in the form of rules and regulations as needed to clarify or enforce the original laws of Congress. An agency to which Congress has delegated authority, however, is not free to make original laws of its own. All agency law must serve the functions of clarification and enforcement.

**delegation doctrine**
Principle that Congress may not assign its authority to create statutory law and no other government entity can assume such authority.

Periodically, a person or entity affected adversely by an agency rule or regulation will challenge the agency's authority and charge that it went beyond the objectives of clarification and enforcement of statutory law and created new law. This alleged violation of the delegation doctrine is then reviewed, typically at the agency level first and then in the courts. In some instances, such reviews have proceeded to the U.S. Supreme Court, which has developed certain standards to contain the work of agencies within their purpose.

Through its interpretations of the delegation doctrine, the Supreme Court has established several major criteria that must be followed in the creation and operation of any administrative agency. The authority delegated by Congress does not include the ability of nonlegislative bodies to enact major laws. Therefore, the Court requires any act that enables the creation of an administrative agency to be clear in its purpose with definable limits.[3] In this way, an agency is prevented from enacting regulations in areas other than those it was created to administer.

If it appears from the language of the enabling act that Congress did not clearly state as its purpose an "intelligible principle to which the [agency must] conform," the enabling act can be struck down as being unconstitutionally overbroad.[4] The reasoning is that if a law is so broad that an agency is limitless in the extent of law that it can create, then Congress has delegated its original lawmaking authority rather than the authority to clarify and enforce the laws. This violates the Constitution, which vests the authority to create statutes solely in the Congress.

A second major criterion of the delegation doctrine is that the agency's enforcement of the law must be accomplished fairly and openly.[5] If the enabling act and subsequent statutes enacted by Congress do not give some guidance to the president and the subordinate administrative agencies in the manner of enforcing the law, then the delegation doctrine has been violated. Under the Constitution, the people are entitled to know what the law is and how it will be enforced against persons who do not obey it. Because laws created by Congress must meet this standard, obviously any agency to which Congress gives the power to enforce the laws must also meet it. If an agency fails to create regulations that provide for the fair and open administration of laws, then the president and the agency have not received proper guidance from Congress. Once again, the enabling act will be considered too vague or overbroad and therefore inconsistent with the Constitution.[6]

**Agency Officers.** Finally, Article II of the Constitution states that the president should appoint government officers. With respect to agencies, officers are persons who will be responsible for the enforcement of the law. Agency staff members cannot be employed in any profession or industry that the agency oversees because that would not constitute fair and unbiased administration of the law. Further, according to the Constitution, the laws are to be enforced by the government and not by the private sector. This particular situation came to the attention of the U.S. Supreme Court in 1936. In *Carter v. Carter Coal Company,*[7] many of the regulations for the coal industry were discovered to have been created by committees of persons employed at high levels in the industry. The Court found that this was an improper method of enforcing laws. The president may, however, ask persons who are experts in their field to leave private industry to come to work in the agency.

In summary, the passage of an enabling act and the creation of an agency must be done in a manner that at the very least meets the following criteria:

1. The goals of the statutes must be clear, and the statutes must have definable limits.

2. The methods the agency uses to enforce the statutes must be fair and open to all members of the public.

3. The enforcement of the statutes must be accomplished by officers of the government, not by persons with private interests.

## Agencies Today

During the 1930s, the number of agencies increased dramatically. Agencies were part of the New Deal era, which sought to aid the country in its economic recovery from the Great Depression. Congress increased its use of administrative agencies and cooperated with the president in using them to deal quickly with the nation's problems. Some people believed, however, that the agencies were not acting properly and within the bounds of their authority. In large part, the delegation doctrine was refined during and shortly after this time.

In the years that followed, the courts became more involved in reviewing the efforts of the executive branch to oversee agencies, and the delegation doctrine imposed more stringent requirements on the manner in which agencies could be created and operated. Congress responded in 1946 with the **Administrative Procedure Act (APA)**, which was to be used in addition to each agency's enabling act. The APA included the elements necessary to satisfy the requirements of the

**Administrative Procedure Act (APA)** Congressional enactment that requires all federal administrative agencies to follow certain procedures in the issuance of administrative law.

delegation doctrine. Since that time, the APA has been modified and improved several times to ensure that agencies are in compliance with the criteria the courts have established under the delegation doctrine. Thus, the APA together with the enabling act provides for the creation of an agency as well as for the agency's fair and efficient operation.

## The Operation of an Administrative Agency

Once an agency is staffed, its employees are responsible for organizing its administration and addressing the subject or industry that the statutes affect. An agency is permitted a virtual free rein in its methods of internal operations and management as long as it is well organized and efficient. Such organization and efficiency will vary among agencies. An agency such as the Federal Aviation Administration, which oversees public air travel, does not require the same type of staffing, organization, and procedures as the Internal Revenue Service, which administers the tax laws for both individuals and businesses.

The type of agency that is created influences not only the manner in which the agency is organized but also the agency's basic functions. Some of the more common responsibilities of agencies include:

* enforcing federal statutes through prosecution;
* negotiating settlements of claims made against government entities;
* testing, inspecting, and monitoring industries;
* recalling, seizing, or suspending products or activities that violate federal laws; and
* advising the public of the legal effect of the law.

These various functions are performed through information collection, investigation, issuance of regulations, and administrative hearings.

When an agency must collect information or conduct an investigation to meet its enabling act's goals and purpose, it is permitted to obtain information from the public and industry. However, this information must be voluntary and obtained in a manner that does not infringe on individuals' rights to privacy under the Constitution. In addition, individuals cannot be compelled to testify at agency hearings about any information that might result in criminal prosecution against them, just as they cannot be compelled to incriminate themselves before the judiciary or the legislature.

## Authority of Administrative Agencies

**administrative regulation**
Form of administrative law; a regulation that defines, clarifies, or enforces a statutory objective.

The most prominent function of administrative agencies is their authority to issue regulations. **Administrative regulations** must be required to achieve the goals of the enabling act or any other federal laws that the agency has the responsibility to enforce. Thus, all regulations must be derivative of legislation formerly enacted by Congress. If an agency holds a hearing and determines that a regulation has been violated, then the agency may impose sanctions on the violator.

## ASSIGNMENT 4.2

Determine whether the administrative regulation in Exhibit 4.5 applies to the following situation.

SITUATION: You attended a community college where you received student loans in 1995 and 1996. Three years later, in 1999, you defaulted (stopped payment) on the loan and declared bankruptcy. However, the bankruptcy court would not discharge the student loan debt. In 2000, you resumed payment and completed payment in 2001, you want to resume your education at State U. Are you eligible for a student loan?

*(continued)*

## ASSIGNMENT 4.2 (Continued)

**Exhibit 4.5** Regulation

### 29 CFR 1904.5 Determination of work-relatedness.

(a) Basic requirement. You must consider an injury or illness to be work-related if an event or exposure in the work environment either caused or contributed to the resulting condition or significantly aggravated a pre-existing injury or illness. Work-relatedness is presumed for injuries and illnesses resulting from events or exposures occurring in the work environment, unless an exception in § 1904.5(b)(2) specifically applies.

(b) Implementation.

(1) What is the "work environment"? OSHA defines the work environment as "the establishment and other locations where one or more employees are working or are present as a condition of their employment. The work environment includes not only physical locations, but also the equipment or materials used by the employee during the course of his or her work."

(2) Are there situations where an injury or illness occurs in the work environment and is not considered work-related? Yes, an injury or illness occurring in the work environment that falls under one of the following exceptions is not work-related, and therefore is not recordable.

1904.5(b)(2) You are not required to record injuries and illnesses if . . .

(i) . . . At the time of the injury or illness, the employee was present in the work environment as a member of the general public rather than as an employee.

(ii) . . . The injury or illness involves signs or symptoms that surface at work but result solely from a non–work-related event or exposure that occurs outside the work environment.

(iii) . . . The injury or illness results solely from voluntary participation in a wellness program or in a medical, fitness, or recreational activity such as blood donation, physical examination, flu shot, exercise class, racquetball, or baseball.

(iv) . . . The injury or illness is solely the result of an employee eating, drinking, or preparing food or drink for personal consumption (whether bought on the employer's premises or brought in). For example, if the employee is injured by choking on a sandwich while in the employer's establishment, the case would not be considered work-related.

Note: If the employee is made ill by ingesting food contaminated by workplace contaminants (such as lead), or gets food poisoning from food supplied by the employer, the case would be considered work-related.

(v) . . . The injury or illness is solely the result of an employee doing personal tasks (unrelated to their employment) at the establishment outside of the employee's assigned working hours.

(vi) . . . The injury or illness is solely the result of personal grooming, self medication for a non–work-related condition, or is intentionally self-inflicted.

(vii) . . . The injury or illness is caused by a motor vehicle accident and occurs on a company parking lot or company access road while the employee is commuting to or from work.

(viii) . . . The illness is the common cold or flu (Note: contagious diseases such as tuberculosis, brucellosis, hepatitis A, or plague are considered work-related if the employee is infected at work).

(ix) . . . The illness is a mental illness. Mental illness will not be considered work-related unless the employee voluntarily provides the employer with an opinion from a physician or other licensed health care professional with appropriate training and experience (psychiatrist, psychologist, psychiatric nurse practitioner, etc.) stating that the employee has a mental illness that is work-related.

(3) How do I handle a case if it is not obvious whether the precipitating event or exposure occurred in the work environment or occurred away from work? In these situations, you must evaluate the employee's work duties and environment to decide whether or not one or more events or exposures in the work environment either caused or contributed to the resulting condition or significantly aggravated a pre-existing condition.

(4) How do I know if an event or exposure in the work environment "significantly aggravated" a preexisting injury or illness? A preexisting injury or illness has been significantly aggravated, for purposes of OSHA injury and illness recordkeeping, when an event or exposure in the work environment results in any of the following:

(i) Death, provided that the preexisting injury or illness would likely not have resulted in death but for the occupational event or exposure.

*(continued)*

## ASSIGNMENT 4.2 (Continued)

**Exhibit 4.5** Continued

(ii) Loss of consciousness, provided that the preexisting injury or illness would likely not have resulted in loss of consciousness but for the occupational event or exposure.

(iii) One or more days away from work, or days of restricted work, or days of job transfer that otherwise would not have occurred but for the occupational event or exposure.

(iv) Medical treatment in a case where no medical treatment was needed for the injury or illness before the workplace event or exposure, or a change in medical treatment was necessitated by the workplace event or exposure.

(5) Which injuries and illnesses are considered preexisting conditions? An injury or illness is a preexisting condition if it resulted solely from a non–work-related event or exposure that occurred outside the work environment.

(6) How do I decide whether an injury or illness is work-related if the employee is on travel status at the time the injury or illness occurs? Injuries and illnesses that occur while an employee is on travel status are work-related if, at the time of the injury or illness, the employee was engaged in work activities "in the interest of the employer." Examples of such activities include travel to and from customer contacts, conducting job tasks, and entertaining or being entertained to transact, discuss, or promote business (work-related entertainment includes only entertainment activities being engaged in at the direction of the employer).

Injuries or illnesses that occur when the employee is on travel status do not have to be recorded if they meet one of the exceptions listed below.

**1904.5(b)(6) If the employee has . . . You may use the following to determine if an injury or illness is work-related**

(i) . . . checked into a hotel or motel for one or more days. . . . When a traveling employee checks into a hotel, motel, or into a motel or other temporary residence, he or she establishes a "home away from home." You must evaluate the employee's activities after he or she checks into the hotel, motel, or other temporary residence for their work-relatedness in the same manner as you evaluate the activities of a non-traveling employee. When the employee checks into the temporary residence, he or she is considered to have left the work environment. When the employee begins work each day, he or she re-enters the work environment. If the employee has established a "home away from home" and is reporting to a fixed worksite each day, you also do not consider injuries or illnesses work-related if they occur while the employee is commuting between the temporary residence and the job location.

(ii) . . . taken a detour for personal reasons. . . . Injuries or illnesses are not considered work-related if they occur while the employee is on a personal detour from a reasonably direct route of travel (e.g., has taken a side trip for personal reasons).

(7) How do I decide if a case is work-related when the employee is working at home? Injuries and illnesses that occur while an employee is working at home, including work in a home office, will be considered work-related if the injury or illness occurs while the employee is performing work for pay or compensation in the home, and the injury or illness is directly related to the performance of work rather than to the general home environment or setting. For example, if an employee drops a box of work documents and injures his or her foot, the case is considered work-related. If an employee's fingernail is punctured by a needle from a sewing machine used to perform garment work at home, becomes infected and requires medical treatment, the injury is considered work-related. If an employee is injured because he or she trips on the family dog while rushing to answer a work phone call, the case is not considered work-related. If an employee working at home is electrocuted because of faulty home wiring, the injury is not considered work-related.

Source: 66 FR 6122, Jan. 19, 2001; 66 FR 52034, Oct. 12, 2001, unless otherwise noted.

Authority: 29 U.S.C. 657, 658, 660, 666, 669, 673, Secretary of Labor's Order No. 3-2000 (65 FR 50017), and 5 U.S.C. 533. 29 C. F. R. § 1904.5, 29 CFR § 1904.5. Current through September 5, 2006; 71 FR 52401.

*(continued)*

## ASSIGNMENT 4.2 (Continued)

Determine whether the administrative regulation in Exhibit 4.5 requires the recording of the following incidents to meet OSHA standards.

SITUATION: Manny is a pilot who works as a crop duster for a large corporation involved in commercial farming. While Manny is piloting a plane and spreading chemical over his employer's field, he takes a cell phone call from his wife. During the conversation, Manny and his wife begin to argue and he takes his attention away from the controls of the plane. As a result, he flies into electrical lines and the plane crashes. Manny survives but is severely injured.

Janet is working for a government office as part of a paid internship in her paralegal program of study. The office is planning a retirement party for a fellow employee. Janet is washing out a punchbowl when she accidentally hits it against the sink and the bowl shatters. Janet suffers deep lacerations to her arm that are nearly fatal and require multiple surgeries.

Mija is employed part-time at her job. She comes in on her day off for a scheduling meeting. She is not required to attend and is not paid for the time she is at the meeting. However, she feels it important to have input on the creation of the office work schedule. She eats lunch provided to staff by the employer and, as a direct result, suffers from food poisoning.

Shanda suffers from severe allergies. She takes a prescribed allergy medication. The prescription bottle clearly states that one should not operate heavy equipment while taking the medication. Shanda drives a forklift at her job. As a result of the drowsiness caused by the medication, Shanda drives the forklift into the back of a truck and is seriously injured.

On another day and during a particularly busy time, Shanda agrees to work a double shift at the request of her employer. After being on duty for approximately fifteen hours, she dozes while driving the forklift, crashes into a truck, and is seriously injured.

To issue rules, an agency must follow a specific procedure set forth in the APA. In addition, some enabling acts dictate the precise steps an agency must take when establishing and publishing regulations for the public. These formal rule-making procedures often require public hearings, the opportunity for testimony, and other input from the public before any regulations are put into force. However, most agencies are also allowed to promulgate rules through an informal process governed by a series of detailed requirements set forth in the APA. Most agencies must adhere to the following procedures when passing rules that will have an impact upon the public, an industry, or a subject that the agency regulates:

1. The agency must give advance notice to the public of the basic terms of the rules it proposes to enact. At the federal level, this must be done in the *Federal Register,* a daily publication that includes information about the actions of federal administrative agencies.

2. The agency must give the public the opportunity to participate in the agency decision by submitting comments, ideas, and suggestions regarding the proposed rules.

3. After considering the public comment, the agency must issue a general statement of the basis and purpose of the administrative agency supporting the final rule.[8]

After all the requirements of the APA have been satisfied, the agency issues its formal regulations and publishes them first in the *Federal Register* and then in the **Code of Federal Regulations (CFR)**, where all existing regulations are located. Each agency is assigned a title similar to a title in the code. Each regulation is assigned a specific section number and is placed with the other regulations of that agency under its proper title. Like the code, an index of the regulations within a title is included.

**Code of Federal Regulations (CFR)**
Publication that contains all current administrative regulations.

The APA requires agencies to review their regulations periodically to evaluate their effectiveness and necessity.[9] In addition, the APA gives citizens certain rights with respect to agencies. They have the right to access agency information that pertains to the public and a right to information the agency has about them personally. Business entities or individuals who believe that a regulation has an unfair and adverse effect may have their complaints heard by the agency. If they do not receive satisfaction, then they may have the right to have their issues heard by a judge in the judicial branch of the government.

Frequently, citizens who challenge the authority of an agency to promulgate rules or use a particular method to enforce an agency regulation are required to exhaust their remedies. This means that they must first pursue all opportunities to have the issue resolved by dealing directly with the agency before they can turn to the courts. This may involve formal claims, hearings, or appeals at various levels of the agency structure. Exceptions to this requirement for the **exhaustion of administrative remedies** occur in limited circumstances. For example, an individual may turn to the courts first when it is apparent that there is little or no chance that the matter can be resolved by the agency or if time is an important factor and irreparable damage will be done if the citizen must wait to file a claim in the judicial system. As a general rule, however, a citizen must exhaust any possible remedies at the agency level before bringing the issue before the courts.

If the judicial system does become involved in a dispute between a citizen and an agency, then it will consider several factors. First, the court must determine whether the agency's authority was clearly defined and whether the agency's action exceeded the limits of its authority under the delegation doctrine. Second, the agency must have followed proper statutory procedures according to the enabling act, the APA, and any other relevant statutes. Finally, the court must consider whether the agency's action was conducted fairly and openly and whether it violates any constitutional rights of the citizen. If all of these requirements are satisfied in the agency's favor, then the court will not disturb the action of the agency.

Chapter 1 pointed out that a court will not invalidate laws or substitute its judgment for that of the Congress unless the Constitution has been violated. This is also true with agency law, which, although administered and enforced through the executive branch, is ultimately an extension of the Congress and is entitled to the same protection.

Earlier in this chapter, we focused on the role of the executive branch and its supervision of administrative agencies. Although this role is not always obvious in agency proceedings, the president has a great responsibility and considerable influence with respect to administrative agencies. The president is responsible for keeping the agency appropriately staffed, has influence over the approval of the agency budget, and may exercise authority over the agency through the issuance of an executive order. Such orders specify the manner in which the president wants laws to be executed.

**exhaustion of administrative remedies**
The requirement that anyone having a dispute with an administrative agency must first follow all available procedures to resolve the dispute within the agency before taking the issue before the judiciary.

## ASSIGNMENT 4.3

Which of the following would be more appropriate subjects for law enacted solely by legislature?

a. Licensure provisions for ham radio operators.

b. Requirements that shelters for the homeless must meet to be eligible for state funds.

c. The method by which trials are conducted.

*(continued)*

## ASSIGNMENT 4.3 (Continued)

d. The type of safety equipment employers must provide to workers who use heavy machinery.

e. The creation and administration of retirement plans for state employees.

Which of the following would be more appropriate for legislation and which would be more appropriate for administrative agency supplemental law?

1. The legal limit of permissible blood alcohol to drive.

2. The necessary safety equipment for individuals working in an auto assembly plant.

3. The requirements to open a landfill that accepts biohazardous waste.

4. The steps necessary to obtain a cosmetology license.

5. What is necessary to conduct a prolife demonstration at a government building.

6. The number of days for creditors to make a claim on the assets of someone who files bankruptcy.

7. The information necessary to be submitted in order to collect Social Security benefits.

8. The types of items that can be carried aboard a commercial aircraft.

9. The penalty for attempting to assassinate an elected official.

10. The necessary steps to process meat for public sale.

## ASSIGNMENT 4.4

Which of the items in Assignment 4.3 would be more appropriate for supplemental law from an administrative agency?

## ASSIGNMENT 4.5

Create a flowchart that tracks a concept of law to creation of a regulation used to define the concept.

## ETHICAL CONSIDERATIONS

As the primary elected official in government, the president takes an oath of loyalty to the people of the nation. As the leader of the United States of America, the president is the role model for ethical behavior by all other elected officials. It is the obligation of the president to enforce the laws of the nation fairly and without preference or prejudice.

As representatives of government, agency officials also are obliged to put personal issues aside and to administer the law fairly and equally. This is so significant that an administrative agency, the Human Rights Commission, was created to address this specifically. The very objective of the commission is to see that all persons are afforded equal legal rights and are not treated disparately because of a nonrelevant factor such as race, sex, age, or disability. The very theme of equitable treatment by government as an ethical foundation can be traced to the Declaration of Independence, which sets forth the principle that "all men are created equal."

## ETHICAL CIRCUMSTANCES

In the late 1990s, President Bill Clinton faced impeachment for what amounted to claims of unethical conduct that many people believed to be illegal, conduct. He had engaged in an extramarital relationship. During depositions in a lawsuit, he made statements under oath that implied the relationship had not occurred. He was faced with a moral dilemma of either admitting his conduct publicly and to his family or attempting to cover it with what many considered to be ambiguous but essentially false answers. Ultimately, Clinton made certain admissions about the relationship. The issue before Congress and other disciplinary bodies, such as various bar associations of which he was a member, was not the president's personal conduct, but whether he lied under oath. Although by today's standards this may not seem sufficient to warrant repercussions of such magnitude, the oath to be truthful in matters before the courts is a cornerstone of the U.S. legal system, and the president as much as anyone is obliged to honor this treasure.

## CHAPTER SUMMARY

The executive branch has many important functions such as conducting foreign relations, negotiating treaties, supervising the armed forces, and appointing ambassadors and heads of governmental units. One of the most important functions, and one that has a direct and immediate effect on the citizenry, is to see that the laws are faithfully executed. From this comes the power to oversee administrative agencies and to ensure that the goals of Congress are carried out.

The government operates more effectively by using administrative agencies. Because these agencies are heavily influenced by all branches of government, limits are placed on the potential for abuse of agency power by agency staff or by the executive or legislative branches. In addition, judicially imposed limitations on the areas that are subject to agency regulation also limit such potential for abuse.

An administrative agency can be created only by a legislative enactment. Agency authority is limited to the clarification and enforcement of statutory law. The agency is staffed and overseen by the chief executive (president or governor). In the event the executive fails to properly oversee the agency or the legislative body gives the agency too much authority, the courts have the power to invalidate agency actions.

## CHAPTER TERMS

administrative agency
Administrative Procedure Act (APA)
administrative regulation
Code of Federal Regulations (CFR)

delegation doctrine
enabling act
exhaustion of administrative remedies

## REVIEW QUESTIONS

1. Describe the original role of the president.
2. What are some advantages of administrative agencies?
3. What is an enabling act?
4. Who appoints top federal agency officers?
5. What is meant by exhaustion of remedies?
6. What are the basic responsibilities of the president as outlined by the Constitution?
7. What is the purpose of an administrative agency?
8. In what areas of law are administrative agencies appropriate?
9. What is the delegation doctrine?
10. Describe the minimum criteria for the creation of an administrative agency.

## ⬤ | HELPFUL WEB SITES

Internet Legal Resource Guide      http://www.ilrg.com

U.S. government      http://www.governmentguide.com

http://www.firstgov.gov

Thomas Legislative Information
  at the Library of Congress      http://www.thomas.loc.gov

## ⬤ | INTERNET ASSIGNMENT 4.1

Identify the U.S. senators for your state and the U.S. representatives for your district. Locate the Internet address for each.

## ⬤ | INTERNET ASSIGNMENT 4.2

Consult Exhibit 4.4 and select ten U.S. administrative agencies and identify their primary Internet sites.

## ⬤ | INTERNET ASSIGNMENT 4.3

Locate a list of state administrative agencies. Provide the Web site where the list was found.

## ⬤ | ENDNOTES

1. *Buttfield v. Stranahan,* 192 U.S. 470, 24 S.Ct. 349, 48 L.Ed. 525 (1904).
2. *Id.*
3. *J. W. Hampton, Jr., & Co. v. United States,* 276 U.S. 394, 48 S.Ct. 348, 72 L.Ed. 624 (1928).
4. *Id.*
5. 5 U.S.C.A. § 551 et seq.
6. *Schware v. Board of Bar Examiners,* 353 U.S. 232, 77 S.Ct. 752, IL.Ed.2d 796 (1957).
7. 298 U.S. 238, 56 S.Ct. 855, 80 L.Ed.1160 (1936).
8. 5 U.S.C.A. § 551–§ 1305.
9. 5 U.S.C.A. § 551 et seq.

### STUDENT CD-ROM

For additional materials, please go to the CD in this book.

### ONLINE COMPANION™

For additional resources, please go to www.paralegal.delmar.cengage.com

# CHAPTER 5

# The Legal Professional

The first thing we do, let's kill all the lawyers.

William Shakespeare, *Henry VI*

This commonly used quotation is often employed as a slander against the legal profession. Although it is true that there are many who are disillusioned with the U.S. legal system, there are just as many who make their living working within it. But, like the phrase, the system and the profession are often taken for granted and misunderstood. The line from Shakespeare's play was part of a discussion in the planning of a revolution. It was hypothesized that exterminating all of the lawyers would turn the governmental system to chaos. The same statement probably could be made today, hundreds of years later.

Although in pop culture people are quick to criticize and satirize the government, laws, and legal professionals, and sometimes the jokes really are funny, the reality is quite simple. Without rules there would be anarchy. Without individuals to make the rules, enforce the rules, and assist individuals in protecting their rights under the rules, the United States would be a strikingly different place. Much like children, American citizens cry foul when they do not get their way. But talk to those wrongfully accused of a crime whose freedom was obtained through the effective assistance of counsel and you will hear a different story. Consider the victims of those whose criminal actions would go unpunished if it were not for prosecutors and you will hear a different story. Consider those who have received compensation for injuries suffered as the result of reckless conduct by others who take no responsibility for their actions, and you will hear a different story. It is not a perfect system. Of that, there is no question. Mistakes are made, injustices occur, and there are those who take advantage of the flaws. But these are in the minority. In the end, the current system is much more fair and effective than one based on vigilante justice in which each citizen makes up rules to suit him- or herself regardless of the impact on others. And it is better than a system where the governed have no say in the rules created by the government. So when someone suggests, "Let's kill all the lawyers," remember the effect that statement was originally intended to produce. Lawyers? They are not such an awful lot after all.

## CHAPTER OBJECTIVES

After reading this chapter, you should be able to:

- Describe the special skills expected of a licensed attorney.
- Explain what is necessary to become a licensed attorney.
- Explain the difference between a trial judge and an appellate judge.
- Define the role of an administrative law judge.

- Discuss the evolution of the paralegal profession.
- Describe the skills of a qualified paralegal.
- Discuss the various members of the legal team and their duties.
- Explain why some nonlawyers have a limited license to engage in what would otherwise be considered the unauthorized practice of law.

## WHO ARE TODAY'S LEGAL PROFESSIONALS?

As our society and culture become more complex, so does the legal system designed to maintain order among the population. The growth of the structure of the U.S. legal system has resulted in the evolution of various law-related professions. Initially, the legal professions consisted primarily of judges and lawyers. These professions date back to the earliest beginnings of a civilized society and the imposition of laws to maintain order. Even in ancient Egypt, there were judges and counselors. Often the judges passed orders of punishment and retribution for some violation of laws set down by government leaders such as kings and pharaohs. Counselors were employed by and advised aristocrats on how to remain in favor with the ruling power and with others in positions of power. Eventually, as governments became more sophisticated and the network of legal standards grew, more and more individuals sought out the advice of those who made their living by studying and explaining the law. Over time, a clerical role developed to assist the lawyers and judges in maintaining records of legal events. This was the beginning of the principles we know as precedent and the doctrine of stare decisis. These roles of legal scholars and counselors remained relatively unchanged for hundreds of years. As with all other aspects of society and culture, however, the evolution of the legal professions over the past 200 years has been unparalleled in history. During this time, governments have become extremely complex, populations have soared, and the need for more laws than ever to maintain a sense of order and balance has resulted in a whole new industry of legal professionals. The various roles and opportunities for those who are instrumental to the administration of law in the United States and the world in law-related settings are virtually limitless.

In today's U.S. legal system, those who make their careers in law consist of judges of various types, court clerks and employees, law clerks, court officers, lawyers, paralegals and legal assistants, legal investigators, legal secretaries, and general accounting and clerical staff, among others. Most of these positions developed during the twentieth century as a result of the great increases in population, technology, transportation, and communications systems and the complexity of government. To illustrate some of these changes, take the example of filing a court document. In 1850, a lawyer handwrote a legal document using a quill or fountain pen and bottle of ink. He then carried it to the courthouse and often presented it personally to the judge. Today, more than 150 years later, the same document would probably first be discussed by a lawyer and paralegal, and researched by them or a law clerk. Then a form document might be accessed by computer and completed by simply filling in blanks or dictated by machine or perhaps even spoken directly into a computer. The clerical staff would prepare the final document and format it with such required procedural details as captions (headings) and such attorney identifications as name, address, and license number. The document might be transmitted electronically to the parties to suit and the court or sent or taken in hard-copy form to the court and appropriate parties. At the court, the document is registered, as thousands are annually, recorded into the computerized filing system, and forwarded to an assigned judge. The clerk or an assistant to the judge would then establish a time for hearing and notify all parties of such by telephone, mail, or electronic transmission such as a fax or e-mail.

The technological advances have undoubtedly reduced the amount of labor required for a few people processing a case. Efficiency has certainly improved on a dramatic scale. However, the complexity of the legal system and the sheer volume of cases filed have resulted in new opportunities for all members of professions with their basis in the U.S. legal system. The following discussion gives insight into some of the more common members of the law-related professions and the roles they play.

## Judges

**jurist (judge)**
Judicial officer who presides over cases in litigation within the court system.

**Jurists**, who are commonly called **judges**, are the individuals who resolve disputes between parties who have different interpretations of the law. It is the duty of a judge to objectively evaluate the circumstances of the parties and determine which legal standards are the most appropriate. In the jury trial system, the jury then listens to the evidence presented of the facts as each side views them. The judge presides over the proceedings to ensure that the law is applied properly and that the evidence is presented in accordance with rules of evidence and procedure. Before and often during trial, a judge issues rulings on various procedural issues such as discovery of evidence, motions of parties, selection of a jury, and how the jury is to be instructed about the case in question. The judge must also determine which laws will be applied to the facts of the case presented. The jury has the responsibility to apply the law, as determined by the judge, to the facts and reach a conclusion.

On certain occasions, judges make determinations regarding the outcome of a case without benefit of a jury. In the judicial branch, this occurs in bench trials and appellate reviews. In a bench trial, the parties waive the right to a jury, and the judge makes the determination of law and applies it to the facts for a final conclusion. In an appellate review, a panel of judges reviews the findings at the trial court level and renders a determination of whether the outcome was consistent with the applicable legal principles.

Becoming a trial court or appellate judge is considered an honor and may occur in a variety of ways. Typically, when a judicial position opens, the candidates are considered based on their experience, knowledge of law, and ability to apply the law in a fair and unbiased manner. In the state court systems, some judges are appointed by the executive (governor) with approval of the legislature. Others are appointed by the senior judge or a committee of judges in the particular venue, and still others are elected. Terms of office and methods for retention or removal are just as varied. In the federal judicial system, most appointments are made by the president with approval of Congress; and, with the exception of special courts, federal judicial appointments are for life. This policy has come under fire in recent years, however, as some judges have been found guilty of professional misconduct but technically had the right to retain their position.

The modern-day legal system has various kinds of judges: federal and state appellate judges, trial judges, and magistrates; municipal judges and various levels of hearing officers; and administrative law judges. All have the essential duty to interpret and apply the law within the boundaries of their particular role as officers of the court. However, significant differences in the function and authority of judges lie in the distinctions among trial, appellate, and administrative judges.

**Trial Judges.** To properly perform their duties as described herein, trial judges must always maintain a current knowledge of the law. Because of the large volume of litigation, many courts assign trial judges to specific categories of cases such as domestic relations, probate, or criminal. This not only creates a more organized and efficient court system but also allows trial judges the opportunity to develop expertise in certain areas of law. However, many less-congested courts still have judges in courts of general jurisdiction who hear cases of all types.

Changes in case law begin with the trial judge. At some point, a judge will take the position that an existing legal standard that was relied on in the past as a rule of law is no longer appropriate. The judge may follow new statutory or administrative legal standards or indicate that societal standards dictate a change in the legal standards applicable to a situation. The judge has the option of applying existing precedent. When the case reaches conclusion, and possibly earlier in certain situations, a party dissatisfied with the result may challenge the trial court judgment before an appellate court. In some jurisdictions, including federal, a series of appeals can be taken before increasingly powerful courts. On appeal, the higher court affirms or reverses the position of the trial court and establishes the rule of law to be followed in the future. Consequently, the trial judge plays a crucial role in the establishment of legal standards.

**Appellate Judges.** Appellate judges review cases that have been previously ruled on in a trial court. The goal of an appellate judge is to ensure that the correct law was applied properly, fairly, and consistently. If it is the opinion of the appellate court that the lower court exceeded or improperly used its authority (abuse of discretion), then the court issues a ruling as to what should occur next in the case to correct the error. The case then returns to the lower court for corrective action. If, however, the court finds that the actions in the trial court were appropriate, then the result in the lower court is affirmed. In many cases and in many jurisdictions, there are a series of courts that one can follow with subsequent appeals.

The likelihood of a reversal declines as each subsequent judge or panel of judges considers a case and agrees with those who have previously considered the appeal. Usually, several appellate judges review a case as a panel in an appellate court. This collective wisdom reduces the possibility of error or personal bias on a legal issue. Because it is the duty of appellate judges to ensure proper, fair, and consistent application of law for a jurisdiction, the position of appellate judges requires a great deal of knowledge of legal principles. As with other legal professionals, appellate judges often have the assistance of law clerks, whose jobs are discussed later in the chapter.

Typically, the appellate panel will issue a written opinion after consideration of a case and possibly after hearing a short argument by each party. The opinion will not only give the rationale for the judgment but also indicate the support or nonsupport by each judge. If the entire membership of an appellate court—rather than a panel of a few members—issues a joint decision, such decision is known as an *en banc* opinion. Typically, such collective decisions are reserved for issues of great significance such as a change in precedent. A judge who agrees with the final result in a case but not with the supporting rationale of the other appellate judges may issue a concurring opinion. This explains a different reasoning used to reach the same result. A judge who disagrees with the result but is in the minority may issue a dissenting opinion. Concurring and dissenting opinions are valuable for the light they may shed on future cases or cases that have both significant similarities and differences. The majority opinion, however, is the controlling precedent to which lower courts generally look for guidance in future cases. The majority opinion also dictates the outcome of the particular case on appeal.

**Administrative Law Judges.** The administrative law judge (ALJ) functions in a totally different arena from that of the appellate or trial judge. The duties of ALJs are confined to hearing cases involving the conduct of administrative agencies and the effects of such conduct on the individual or entity who challenges the agency action.

The ALJ is presumed to be an objective judicial authority who rules exclusively on issues of administrative law. The ALJ determines such issues as whether a party is subject to the authority of the agency and whether a party's conduct is in accordance with administrative rules and regulations. Typically, administrative cases are initially filed with the agency rather than in the courts. Appeals of an administrative decision are generally made to the trial court level in the judicial system. This is a limited instance when the trial court exercises appellate rather than original authority.

Each type of judicial officer plays an extremely important role in the U.S. legal system. Whether hearing evidence at trial or reviewing another judge's application of law, the input of a judge as an objective observer with knowledge of legal standards is necessary to the effective operation of the American system of government.

## Lawyers

**The Practice of Law Defined.** Although the definition of the practice of law varies from state to state, certain components of the definition are fairly standard. Most jurisdictions give the lawyer, when licensed to practice law, the generally exclusive privilege to give legal advice and to advocate with third parties on the behalf of a client's legal rights.

**Legal advice and analysis.** Giving legal advice requires a lawyer to have a special analytical ability. A lawyer is responsible for examining the law applicable to a situation, informing a client as to the likely outcome of the case, and often recommending the next course of action. Based on the information received, the client can choose to accept or reject the analysis and recommendation.

A licensed attorney must use analytical ability to locate all relevant legal principles in a given circumstance, recognize the significant facts of the case, and determine the impact of the principles on those facts. To do this, the lawyer must be able to take each applicable legal principle, break it down into the necessary components, and compare it to the specific elements of the client's circumstance. Then based on the similarities and differences identified in this analysis, the lawyer must make a determination of the likely outcome of the client's case if these legal princi-ples were to be applied by a court. Such analytical ability by a lawyer is a valued and respected skill and, because clients often determine future conduct affecting their rights based on the lawyer's recommendation, the process of giving legal advice is li-censed by the state and prohibited for anyone who does not have a proper license.

**Advocacy.** The second function of a licensed attorney is advocacy, or the process of representing the legal rights and interests of another person within the confines of legal proceedings in one branch of government. In business, it is not uncommon to have an agent represent one's interests in such areas as negotiations, sales, and purchases, but a license to practice law is required to represent the interests of another person in court and other legal proceedings. Many times, however, attor-neys delve in nonlegal proceedings if the effect is on the legal rights of the parties, such as in contractual matters, because in the event a dispute arises, a party wishes his or her legal rights to be well protected. Because advocacy frequently has a long-term effect on practice requirements, failure to represent one's client zealously and with the degree of competence required by law can result in an ac-tion for malpractice as well as disciplinary action by a state bar association.

**Becoming a Licensed Attorney.** Because of the increasing complexity of the U.S. legal system, **lawyers (attorneys)** function not only as advocates for clients but also as counselors and liaisons between the lay public and the courts, legislatures, and executive branches of state and federal governments. To become a lawyer, certain graduate-level coursework must be completed and standards for licensure in the state or federal area of practice must be met. Most states require that be-fore licensure, the lawyer must graduate from an accredited law school following completion of an undergraduate bachelor's degree and pass a bar exam in the licensing state or in another state that tests the lawyer's legal knowledge and analytical ability.

> **lawyer (attorney)**
> Individual who has completed the necessary requirements of education and training and who has been licensed to practice law in a jurisdiction.

Typically, the law school component of a lawyer's education consists of study that, if completed in the traditional setting, would consist of three years of full-time study, although today many law schools offer part-time programs so that students may continue full-time employment while preparing for their career in law. The study for a career as an attorney consists almost exclusively of law-related courses in all general subjects of law, some specialized areas, government and court procedures, ethics, and litigation.

Historically, although states often granted licenses to practice to those who demonstrated licensure in another state, a practice known as *reciprocity*, the trend has been to require licensure by examination in each state of practice. At least in part, this is because as laws become more complex in each jurisdiction, the likelihood of variance in legal procedures and standards increases. Consequently, many states require a lawyer to demonstrate a working knowledge of the laws of that particular state before licensure. For example, states with unique elements of their economy, such as states with heavy oil reserves, are likely to be affected dramatically by these qualities, so a knowledge of this area of law is important to provide effective representation to a large element of the population.

Generally, there are three elements to meeting the standard of knowledge for licensure as an attorney. The first is a standardized exam administered to test the knowledge of general areas of law. This is part of the bar exam in so many states that it is referred to as the *multistate*. The second element tests more specific areas of law that tend to have application within the particular state. Often the multistate exam is offered on one day and the state exam on the next or preceding day. In ad-dition, most jurisdictions require that within a period of time before or after the state bar exam, an applicant pass the third element—a separate exam on ethics.

Once an attorney is licensed to practice in a particular state, additional considerations are expected if one is to fully exercise the practice of law. Some states require membership in good standing in a state bar association. Certain federal courts also require specific additional requirements before an attorney is permitted to practice before them. One such example are the U.S. courts of appeals. Before an attorney can appear and represent a client in these courts, the attorney must first be approved. This is accomplished through the submission of an application and the endorsement of several attorneys already licensed to practice therein. As stated, the requirements may vary among jurisdictions, but the objective is the same. Each jurisdiction takes the steps considered reasonably necessary to ensure that one is not permitted to represent, defend, and protect the legal rights of another without first demonstrating a basic level of knowledge of the law, legal analysis, and governmental procedures.

When an individual undertakes the practice of law without a license, a statutory violation occurs and criminal proceedings may be instituted. In recent years, there has been an increasing awareness of this issue as a gray area has developed among lawyers and some other professions. However, the real controversy has been in drawing the line within a lawyer's own office. First, at what point does a subordinate staff member such as a legal assistant, legal secretary, or even law clerk stop providing support and start practicing law? Second, what of the freelance individuals who prepare legal forms, provide legal services, and assist persons in meeting the procedural requirements of the legal system? There has been litigation across the United States in the last decade over issues such as these. Essentially, the courts have maintained their original position: If the conduct of the individual extends in any way to giving advice, thus affecting another person's legal rights or advocacy on behalf of another's legal rights, then the practice of law has occurred. If the individual is not properly licensed, then a criminal prosecution may follow. In addition, if the individual was in the employ of a licensed attorney, a suit for malpractice may be brought and disciplinary action can be taken against the lawyer in some circumstances.

# CASE

## Cincinnati Bar Association v. Bailey,
### 110 Ohio St. 3d. 223, 852 N.E.2d 1180 (Ohio 2006)

The following opinion examines both the type of conduct that is considered to be the unauthorized practice of law and the court's authority to enforce sanctions against those found to be engaged in the unauthorized practice of law even outside the courtroom.

Relator, Cincinnati Bar Association, has charged that respondent, Donald L. Bailey, d.b.a. License Resque, has engaged in the unauthorized practice of law by advising clients and providing instruction on preparing and filing documents with the Ohio Bureau of Motor Vehicles ("BMV") to obtain relief from license suspensions. Respondent is not licensed to practice law and has been the subject of a lengthy investigation and a number of legal skirmishes spanning six years. This case was filed on December 11, 2003, respondent filed an answer on January 30, 2004, and eventually a hearing was held before a panel of the Board on the

Unauthorized Practice of Law on June 9, 2005, where respondent appeared on his own behalf.

A number of exhibits, including case files of License Resque, were entered into evidence, and relator called two witnesses, Christopher McNeil, former lead attorney for the BMV Section of the Attorney General's office, and J. Patrick Foley III, associate legal counsel of the BMV from 1991 to 2000, in addition to respondent. BMV employees Timothy Fisher, assistant chief of the Reinstatement Offices, Annette Pinkerton, chief of the Telecommunications Section, and Julie Simpkins, phone operator, testified on behalf of Bailey.

There was also evidence that in 1996, respondent had entered into a consent agreement with the Columbus Bar Association. Acknowledging that his preparation of a petition and stay order for a client "may have unintentionally violated" Gov.Bar R. VII, he agreed to refrain from engaging in any conduct that violated the Supreme Court Rules for the Government of the Bar of Ohio.

Respondent testified that he has continued to operate in business in nearly the same fashion and has offered the same services since 1989. He provides clients with petitions to modify point suspensions and fills in the name of the court of their residency. He also uses powers of attorney to take actions necessary to restore his clients' driving privileges.

Respondent argued at the hearing that the charges are baseless, claiming that License Resque is simply a courier service that assists people to reinstate suspended licenses and that there is no evidence that any more information was imparted to his customers than that already available from the BMV or a clerk of courts. Respondent asserts that there is no proof of any harm caused by his actions, since relator called none of License Resque's former customers as witnesses. In short, respondent denies that he acted as an attorney and states that he was simply doing business with the BMV in a manner that has already been approved by this court in *Cleveland Bar Assn. v. CompManagement, Inc.,* 104 Ohio St.3d 168, 2004–Ohio-6506, 818 N.E.2d 1181.

A panel of the Board of the Unauthorized Practice of Law heard the cause and made findings of fact, conclusions of law, and a recommendation, all of which the board adopted. The final report concluded that respondent, individually and through others working for License Resque, had engaged in the unauthorized practice of law. Gov.Bar R. VII(7)(E) requires proof by a preponderance of the evidence that respondent has engaged in the unauthorized practice of law. The board specifically found that respondent advised clients regarding time limits for filing requests for administrative hearings and regarding wording and time limits for filing court appeals; he advised them on the requirements for reinstatement of licenses and driving privileges from the 45 to 50 different types of license suspension; he advised clients as to statements to make in court; he interpreted the effect of abeyance letters and advised them on what to do if they missed court deadlines; he prepared requests for appeals, accident reports, affidavits to submit to the BMV, and petitions to modify point suspensions; and he communicated personally and through others working for his business with the BMV and with court employees on behalf of his clients. In summary, the board found that providing legal advice, preparing legal documents, and communicating with administrative and court employees on behalf of others were the types of services that respondent provided to his customers.

The panel and the board recommended an order that respondent be found to have engaged in the unauthorized practice of law, that he be enjoined from continuing to do so both personally and through his business License Resque, and that he be fined $170,000 in civil penalties under Gov.Bar R. VII(8)(B) and costs. Applying the standards in Gov.Bar R. VII(8)(B) for determining the propriety of a civil penalty, the board explained that respondent had committed previous acts of unauthorized practice of law, cited his 1996 consent agreement, his knowledge of the nature of his acts, the substantial financial benefit in gross business revenue, his admitted interactions with numerous clerks of courts and with BMV employees on behalf of clients, and his assistance in preparing forms for many customers. It found that respondent had failed to cooperate over a long time and that no mitigating factors existed and thus recommended "rather harsh and severe" civil penalties.

Respondent presents 38 objections to the board's recommendation. In addition, he argues that nonlawyer representatives participating in actions before the BMV are not engaged in the practice of law, according to *Cleveland Bar Assn. v. CompManagement, Inc.,* 104 Ohio St.3d 168, 2004–Ohio-6506, 818 N.E.2d 1181, . . . and that the imposition of costs and civil penalties is not warranted. . . . In objection . . . respondent argues that the panel erred in admitting the 1996 consent agreement. Although respondent argues that the consent agreement should not have been considered, he himself asked for it to be admitted into evidence. He cannot now complain that it should not be considered.

. . . In objection . . . respondent argues that relator's witnesses were biased. Bias raises an issue of credibility. It does not preclude the admission of the testimony.

. . . Respondent claims Constitutionality of Gov.Bar R. VII in objection . . . yet he cannot show beyond a reasonable doubt that our regulation is clearly incompatible with the constitution. *State v. Smith* (1997), 80 Ohio St.3d 89, 99, 684 N.E.2d 668. With respect to his due process claims, as this is a civil proceeding, respondent's hearing was to comport with general mandates of due process that require notice and meaningful opportunity to be heard. *State v. Hayden,* 96 Ohio St.3d 211, 773 N.E.2d 502, 2002–Ohio-4169, at ¶ 6. The record shows that proper notice of the charges and of the hearing was provided, and the transcript of the one-day hearing shows that these rights were honored. As to the First Amendment, the restrictions on respondent's conduct by prohibiting practicing law without a license do not implicate his right to free speech. See *Ohralik v. Ohio State Bar Assn.* (1978), 436 U.S. 447, 456, 98 S.Ct. 1912, 56 L.Ed.2d 444. . . .

*(continued)*

Finally, respondent objects to the imposition of any penalty as unconstitutional. Respondent maintains that he cannot be fined retroactively because Gov.Bar R. VII did not provide for a $10,000 civil penalty until June 16, 2003. The relator correctly responds, however, that respondent's acts were ongoing in nature. We have previously imposed monetary penalties in a case concerning the unauthorized practice of law when some of the violations predated current Gov.Bar R. VII(8)(B). *Toledo Bar Assn. v. Chelsea Title Agency of Dayton, Inc.*, 100 Ohio St.3d 356, 2003–Ohio-6453, 800 N.E.2d 29. Furthermore, in *Cleveland Bar Assn. v. Sharp Estate Servs., Inc.*, 107 Ohio St.3d 219, 2005–Ohio-6267, 837 N.E.2d 1183, ¶ 16, we noted that Gov.Bar R. VII " 'shall be liberally construed for the protection of the public, the courts, and the legal profession and shall apply to all pending investigations and complaints so far as may be practicable, and to all future investigations and complaints whether the conduct involved occurred prior or subsequent to the enactment or amendment of this rule,'" quoting Gov.Bar R. VII(17). The imposition of monetary sanctions is not prohibited. *Id.*

We reject respondent's factual arguments that he did not engage in the practice of law, for the reasons cited by the board. His misguided attempts to minimize his actions representing individuals before the BMV illustrate why the practice of law must be strictly limited to licensed attorneys. The practice of law is exacting even with the required legal and ethical training, and the legal system cannot adequately safeguard the public's interest unless it ensures a core level of professional competence and integrity. See *Akron Bar Assn. v. Frank* (2000), 88 Ohio St.3d 152, 724 N.E.2d 399 (nonlawyer who "has no idea of judicial procedure, no concept of how to present facts, and [no ability] to interpret case law" was a "living example of why we require character and fitness reviews, examinations of legal ability, and continuing education of those who are permitted to give legal advice and appear in our courts").

Section 2(B)(1)(g), Article IV, Ohio Constitution confers on this court original jurisdiction regarding "[a]dmission to the practice of law, the discipline of persons so admitted, and all other matters relating to the practice of law." A person who is not admitted to the practice of law or certified for limited practice pursuant to the Supreme Court Rules for the Government of the Bar engages in the unauthorized practice of law when he or she provides legal services to another in this state. Gov.Bar R. VII(2)(A); see, also, R.C. 4705.01.

"The practice of law is not limited to the conduct of cases in court. It embraces the preparation of pleadings and other papers incident to actions and special proceedings and the management of such actions and proceedings on behalf of clients before judges and courts, and in addition conveyancing, the preparation of legal instruments of all kinds, and in general all advice to clients and all action taken for them in matters connected with the law." *Land Title Abstract & Trust Co. v. Dworken* (1934), 129 Ohio St. 23, 1 O.O. 313, 193 N.E. 650, paragraph one of the syllabus.

Furthermore, we have already examined the practice of law in connection with the provision of services when drivers' licenses are suspended. In one case, we held that the activities of a company called License Recovery, very similar to those of License Resque's, amounted to the unauthorized practice of law. *Columbus Bar Assn. v. Smith*, 96 Ohio St.3d 156, 2002–Ohio-3607, 772 N.E.2d 637, at ¶ 2 and 3. In *Disciplinary Counsel v. Dylyn*, 95 Ohio St.3d 139, 2002–Ohio-1755, 766 N.E.2d 599, at ¶ 5, we found an unauthorized legal services contract when a nonattorney sought fees for efforts to secure "reinstatement of driving privileges." Respondent's reliance on *Cleveland Bar Assn. v. CompManagement, Inc.*, 104 Ohio St.3d 168, 2004–Ohio-6506, 818 N.E.2d 1181, and *Henize v. Giles* (1986), 22 Ohio St.3d 213, 22 OBR 364, 490 N.E.2d 585, is misplaced, for those cases were expressly limited to workers' compensation and unemployment-compensation matters, respectively.

We therefore adopt the board's findings concerning respondent's unauthorized practice of law. We also agree that a civil penalty is warranted, but we find that the maximum $10,000 penalty for each of "the seventeen (17) specific acts and offenses of the unauthorized practice of law established in the record," as recommended by the board, is excessive here.

The propriety and amount of the civil penalty depend on the factors in Gov.Bar R. VII(8)(B)(1) through (5), including the number of incidents of unauthorized practice, the flagrancy of each incident, and the harm caused to third parties. For example, in *Stark Cty. Bar Assn. v. Bennafield*, 107 Ohio St.3d 29, 2005–Ohio-5832, 836 N.E.2d 562, we did not impose a civil penalty, because the layperson committed only one infraction and did not profit from his efforts. Similarly, in *Cleveland Bar Assn. v. Para-Legals, Inc.*, 106 Ohio St.3d 455, 2005–Ohio-5519, 835 N.E.2d 1240, ¶ 9, two laypersons and their company were not fined, because their illegal acts were relatively few in number, and the company had stopped advertising its unlawful services upon notice that a complaint had been filed. In contrast, the agency in *Toledo Bar Assn. v. Chelsea Title Agency of Dayton, Inc.*, 100 Ohio St.3d 356, 2003–Ohio-6453, 800 N.E.2d 29, was fined $1,000 because it had prepared, through a nonlawyer agent, two deeds for its customers, one after being advised that only a licensed attorney may draft a deed for another.

In respondent's case, there is evidence of noncooperation. Relator's investigation began in 1997. A subpoena was issued to respondent on October 6, 1998, which he failed to comply with until this court ordered that he be incarcerated for ten days for contempt of court. See *Cincinnati Bar Assn. v. Bailey* (2000), 90 Ohio St.3d 136, 735 N.E.2d 428; *Cincinnati Bar Assn. v. Bailey,* 99 Ohio St.3d 1441, 2003–Ohio-3017, 789 N.E.2d 1121. Respondent was on notice at least since 1996, when he signed the consent agreement with the Columbus Bar Association, that his continued actions on behalf of others in providing license-reinstatement services could amount to the unauthorized practice of law. Respondent insists that no evidence of harm exists because individual clients were not called to testify to actual harm done to them. Yet at least six persons had filed consumer complaints with the office of the Attorney General against License Resque. More important, however, Gov.Bar R. VII is designed to prevent harm to unsuspecting individuals who think they have been properly represented.

Based on the foregoing, we accept the board's findings; however, with respect to the number of violations proven with specificity and based on the assertions that respondent made regarding his financial condition during oral argument, we modify the civil penalty recommended. Based upon our view of the evidence, we conclude that a $50,000 civil penalty is more appropriate. . . . Respondent is enjoined from engaging in the unauthorized practice of law, either individually or through others employed by License Resque, including all attempts to appear at the Ohio Bureau of Motor Vehicles or in court or to prepare legal papers on behalf of any person other than himself. We also order respondent to pay a civil penalty of $ 50,000 pursuant to Gov.Bar R. VII(8)(B) and (19)(D)(1)(c). Costs are taxed to respondent.

Judgment accordingly.

## Case Review Question

Would the result be likely to change if the defendant had not previously had an issue with a neighboring bar association in regard to the unauthorized practice of law?

**Places of Employment.** When considering the employment of attorneys, the first thing that comes to mind for most people is an office full of books and large desks and secretaries typing away. However, today, only a percentage of attorneys are employed in the traditional law firm setting. Tens of thousands of attorneys never work in a law firm throughout their careers. Today's opportunities for individuals trained in the law are virtually limitless. Because of the complexity of society, the capability and ease of interstate and even global travel, communication, and commerce, private industry more than ever needs competent legal advice and representation.

Many lawyers still work in the traditional setting and follow a career path that includes representing individuals in matters of civil law. Issues concerning property rights, transfers, and possession are still common. This includes, but is not limited to, transfers of real estate interests, landlord tenant law, property rights among co-owners, and condominium law. The law of domestic relations covers a range of subjects from prenuptial agreements through divorce, custody, support and maintenance, surrogacy, and cohabitation.

Lawyers also work in probate, the law of estates and guardianships, as well as in criminal defense and other areas of general civil law such as personal injury and contracts. In addition to these private party matters, however, are numerous opportunities within the legal setting that have nothing to do with individual disputes. Virtually every type of commercial business is faced with some sort of legal concern. Health care professionals face risk-management issues regarding matters of alleged malpractice. Anyone concerned with transportation of goods, either interstate or international, must consider laws that govern these transactions. Insurance companies must comply with state and federal laws and enter into contractual agreements with providers of health care services or whatever type of business they insure. Banks and investment companies need legal professionals to assist in the management of retirement funds, trusts, and other assets. The explosive growth of e-commerce through the Internet in the past few years has created a new realm of legal issues. As population and technology both continue to increase, so will the potential for problems that must be addressed by those with legal training and expertise.

## Paralegals

**paralegal (legal assistant)**
One who has training and knowledge in legal principles and practices and who supports and assists an attorney in the practice of law.

The concept of the **paralegal** or **legal assistant** has been recognized as a formal profession in this country only during the past few decades, and the development of this career path has been rapid. Although no uniformly accepted definition of a paralegal exists, certain standards have been developed and have gained wide acceptance in the United States. In recent years, many states have issued definitions of paralegals or legal assistants or recognized duties for which services may be billed. Essentially, a paralegal is someone with training and knowledge in the law who should be able to perform all functions historically performed by an attorney with the exception of giving legal advice and advocacy. In some jurisdictions, even limited advocacy may be permitted. Although the typical perception of an attorney is of someone who is in court all of the time, the reality is quite different. Attorneys have traditionally performed many daily functions that are now also within the parameters of the paralegal's job description. The evolving standards of competence of the paralegal clearly identify a growing place of this paraprofessional within the U.S. legal system.

Many paralegals are still employed to conduct, in addition to true paralegal duties, a degree of work that is clerical in nature. This is waning, however, because of the economic benefits of having a trained paralegal perform paralegal functions. Because the tasks performed by a paralegal are traditionally those performed by attorneys, it has been established that a paralegal's services may be billed to clients. This principle was a major achievement in establishing paralegals as legal professionals in their own right. However, a key element that remains in paralegal functions and billing is that billed paralegal work must be performed under the supervision of a licensed attorney. Nevertheless, the paralegal continues to evolve and gain respect as a valuable member of the team comprising those who contribute to the functioning of the U.S. legal system. In addition to the paralegal, many types of support personnel have become recognized as integral parts of today's law office or legal department. Each position represents the performance of duties key to the orderly and efficient progression of legal matters. Although the degree of training and education necessary for the positions may vary dramatically, the role played by each is of equal importance. Much like a team on an assembly line, the legal team works together to move a case or law-related matter from inception to conclusion in such a way as to maximize efficiency, produce the best possible result, and adhere to the necessary parameters, such as procedural rules. Following is a brief description of the personnel often found within law offices and legal departments who provide necessary support services to attorneys.

## CASE
### *Columbus Bar Association v. Thomas,*
### 109 Ohio St.3d 89, 846 N.E.2d 31, 2006–Ohio-1930

The following opinion examines what happens when someone employed in a law firm undertakes the duties that are within the domain of the licensed practice of law.

On February 14, 2005, relator, Columbus Bar Association, filed a two-count complaint alleging that respondent, William Thomas of Columbus, Ohio, had engaged in the unauthorized practice of law by independently representing clients while employed as attorney James E. L. Watson's legal assistant.

Respondent was served with the complaint but did not answer, and relator filed a motion for default pursuant to Gov.Bar R. VII(7)(B). A panel of the Board on the Unauthorized Practice of Law granted the motion and made findings of fact, conclusions of law, and a recommendation, which the board adopted.

. . . Respondent worked for Watson for many years, including several months in 2002 while Watson was recovering at home from a serious injury. Watson relied on respondent—who is not now and never has been licensed to practice law in Ohio—to perform duties subject to Watson's supervision and approval. Respondent, however, exceeded that authority and acted independently on behalf of Richard H. Zahner in his divorce case. For Watson's failure to properly oversee his employee and for aiding in the unauthorized practice of law, we suspended Watson from the practice of law for six months, staying the suspension on conditions. See *Columbus Bar Assn. v. Watson,* 106 Ohio St.3d 298, 2005–Ohio-4983, 834 N.E.2d 809.

Respondent prepared an answer and counterclaim and a motion for a restraining order to file in Zahner's divorce proceedings. Without Watson's review or approval, respondent also signed Watson's name and filed those papers in Franklin County domestic-relations court. Respondent included with the motion for a restraining order a supporting affidavit bearing a signature that he claimed, and Zahner denied, was Zahner's signature. Respondent improperly notarized this signature, using Watson's notary seal and signing Watson's name.

Without Watson's knowledge or authority, respondent also subsequently drafted a letter to Zahner explaining the legal process and giving legal advice relative to his domestic-relations case. Respondent sent the letter, dated December 6, 2002, under Watson's name by again signing for his employer. Upon Watson's instructions, respondent subsequently prepared and filed objections to a magistrate's order in the Zahner case. Respondent did not obtain Watson's approval of this filing or Watson's specific authority to sign on his behalf.

While working for Watson during 1997, respondent agreed to assist his relative, Inez Faulkes, in preparing her will. Respondent signed as a witness to the testator's signature but was not present when Faulkes signed her will, and he did not obtain the required second witness's signature. As a result, Faulkes died without a properly executed will.

Following Faulkes' death, respondent prepared legal documents, including an application for authority to administer the estate, an application to probate will, fiduciary's bond, and an entry admitting the will to probate. Respondent forwarded those documents for filing without Watson's review, and he signed Watson's name on several of them without Watson's knowledge. The Summit County probate court returned the documents unfiled because respondent failed to submit a $200 filing fee and because several of the documents were deficient.

Respondent subsequently sent letters to Faulkes's next of kin providing legal advice about their rights to contest her will. The letters, which Watson did not know of or review, bore Watson's unauthorized signature and falsely represented that Watson had opened the estate.

Respondent also prepared and sent a letter to the Summit County probate judge requesting that Watson be appointed administrator of the Faulkes estate. Watson did not review this letter, which respondent had signed on Watson's behalf and sent without his knowledge. Respondent prepared and sent another letter to Patricia Hollimion providing legal advice relative to her possible appointment as administrator of Faulkes's estate. Watson did not review or sign that letter.

On these facts, the board found that respondent had engaged in the unauthorized practice of law and recommended that we enjoin respondent from such practices in the future. Finding that respondent's victims were unaware that he was acting without professional supervision, that he had forged Watson's signature, and that he had not cooperated in the board proceedings, the board concluded that respondent had violated Gov.Bar R. VII(8)(B)(1), (3), and (4), which allow civil penalties based on lack of cooperation, flagrancy of violations, and harm to third parties. The board recommended a $10,000 civil penalty, representing $5,000 for each count against respondent.

We agree that respondent engaged in the unauthorized practice of law. Section 2(B)(1)(g), Article IV, Ohio Constitution confers on this court original jurisdiction regarding admission to the practice of law, the discipline of persons so admitted, and all other matters relating to the practice of law. A person who is not admitted to the practice of law pursuant to the Supreme Court Rules for the Government of the Bar engages in the unauthorized practice of law when he or she provides legal services to another in this state. Gov.Bar R. VII(2)(A); see, also, R.C. 4705.01.

The practice of law is not limited to appearances in court. It also embraces the preparation of papers that are to be filed in court on another's behalf and that are otherwise incident to a lawsuit. *Cleveland Bar Assn. v. Misch* (1998), 82 Ohio St.3d 256, 259, 695 N.E.2d 244; *Land Title Abstract & Trust Co. v. Dworken* (1934), 129 Ohio St. 23, 28, 1 O.O. 313, 193 N.E. 650.

We have specifically held that a lay employee engages in the unauthorized practice of law by preparing legal documents for another to be filed in domestic-relations court without a licensed attorney's oversight. *Cleveland Bar Assn. v. Para-Legals, Inc.,* 106 Ohio St.3d 455, 2005–Ohio-5519, 835 N.E.2d 1240.

*(continued)*

Providing legal counsel by a layperson in preparing another person's will also constitutes the unauthorized practice of law. *Akron Bar Assn. v. Miller* (1997), 80 Ohio St.3d 6, 684 N.E.2d 288. Further, unauthorized practice occurs when a layperson renders legal advice in the pursuit of managing another person's legal actions and proceedings before courts of law. *Richland Cty. Bar Assn. v. Clapp* (1998), 84 Ohio St.3d 276, 703 N.E.2d 771; *Union Sav. Assn. v. Home Owners Aid, Inc.* (1970), 23 Ohio St.2d 60, 52 O.O.2d 329, 262 N.E.2d 558.

Rules prohibiting the unauthorized practice of law are "intended to protect Ohio citizens from the dangers of faulty legal representation rendered by persons not trained in, examined on, or licensed to practice by the laws of our state." *Disciplinary Counsel v. Pavlik* (2000), 89 Ohio St.3d 458, 461, 732 N.E.2d 985. Thus, although laypersons may assist lawyers in preparing legal papers to be filed in court and managing pending claims, those activities must be carefully supervised and approved by a licensed practitioner. *Cleveland Bar Assn. v. Coats,* 98 Ohio St.3d 413, 2003–Ohio-1496, 786 N.E.2d 449 (paralegal's conduct in appearing as the representative of another at a hearing before the Bureau of Employment Services and in drafting divorce complaints and judgment entries for pro se litigants, without a licensed attorney's supervision, constituted the unauthorized practice of law). Because respondent lacked this professional oversight, his actions with respect to Zahner and Faulkes violated the prohibitions against the unlicensed practice of law.

To discourage such practices, we agree that a civil penalty is warranted, but we find the recommended $10,000 civil penalty to be excessive. Respondent did not appear before the board; however, he did cooperate during relator's investigation by being deposed twice and candidly admitting many of the facts underlying relator's complaint. From this testimony, we are convinced that respondent did not understand, despite his years of experience as a legal assistant, the extent to which he had overstepped the bounds of that role. We find what the panel and board conceded was possible: that respondent believed, although he was seriously mistaken, that he had Watson's permission to prepare and sign documents on his behalf.

Respondent is enjoined from engaging in acts constituting the unauthorized practice of law, including preparing and filing in court papers to determine the legal rights of others and offering legal advice to others about how to protect those rights. We also order respondent to pay a civil penalty of $5,000 pursuant to Gov.Bar R. VII(8)(B) and VII(19)(D)(1)(c). Costs are taxed to respondent.

Judgment accordingly.

## Case Review Question

If the attorney was not in his office during the time the unauthorized conduct took place and was supposedly unaware of them, then why should he be penalized as well?

## Law Office Administrators

A law office administrator manages the day-to-day operations of the law office or legal department as a business entity. Included in a typical administrator's duties are hiring, evaluating, and terminating staff members; scheduling; overseeing billing and accounting issues; delegating work to appropriate personnel; coordinating attorneys and support staff; and supervising risk-management issues such as conflict of interest files, court and deposition schedules, and deadlines.

## Support Personnel

Often a law clerk is a law school student or recent graduate who is awaiting licensure and who performs basic functions such as legal research and drafting documents and correspondence under the supervision of an attorney. In the court system, law clerks usually assist judges by performing legal research and providing synopses of the results in preparations of written judicial opinions.

Another fast-growing field of employment is legal investigation. Originally, legal investigators were most often found in law firms specializing in personal injury. Their primary task was to locate witnesses and evidence in support of the client's case. As the complexity of laws and the basis for lawsuits increase, however, many firms and corporate legal departments now employ legal investigators themselves or contract with legal and private investigation firms. Their primary function is still to collect evidence of all types in support of and opposition to a client's case that will enable the attorney to assess and follow through appropriately on the case.

During the first seventy-five years of the twentieth century, because of the number of legal publications and regular updates, many larger law firms and corporate legal departments had to employ individuals as law librarians to maintain the constantly growing body of information. The publications had to be maintained in an organized fashion, and frequent, sometimes daily, updates had to be incorporated into the existing collection. However, as more and more legal research is performed by computer, the job of the law librarian may change somewhat from manual record keeping to maintaining a current working knowledge of computer programs, updates, and research techniques. The role of the law librarian is still essential in the large firm or corporate legal department to facilitate the work of those who perform legal research.

Historically, the clerical staff in a law firm spent most of its workday typing legal documents. Although such duty is still a fundamental part of the job, the traditional role of the legal secretary has expanded to include having exceptional computer skills, the ability to coordinate the schedules of any number of attorneys from various firms for depositions and hearings, and to act as the primary contact person between the attorney and other staff members as well as clients and professionals outside the firm. The legal secretary may see that documents are properly and timely filed with the courts and provide all forms of general clerical support to the attorney, legal investigator, law clerks, and paralegals.

Even with the advent of the computer transference of information, the legal profession still ultimately relies on hard copies of all pertinent information. The legal documents, correspondence, research, memos, notices, and documentary evidence all must be maintained. Even the smallest law firm processes hundreds, perhaps thousands, of pieces of paper. This must be done in a predictably organized manner and be kept current as well. For this reason, an integral position within any law firm or legal department is an individual who is responsible for managing the documents within the files. Those who have this responsibility must be extremely organized and attentive to detail. It is also important that such individuals and all members of the staff understand the importance of maintaining the confidentiality of all files.

Aside from the practice of law, a law firm or legal department is a business that operates on incoming funds. To do this, it is important to track the time spent by the attorneys and other staff members who bill their time on each client's file. This information must then be integrated into the proper accounts and tracked for billing and collection. The billing clerk may also manage incoming and outgoing funds; in large firms or corporate legal departments, this position may be expanded to a complete accounting department. Smaller firms often coordinate with an independent accountant for monthly accounting statements and tax issues.

The receptionist is one of the most important people in the law firm. Although this person does not have the authority of an attorney or administrator, he or she is often the first and last contact the client has with the law firm. As a result, the attitude, professionalism, and general appearance of the firm may be judged by the presentation of the receptionist. With respect to duties, the receptionist may schedule appointments and screen and route phone calls and appointments with clients and others who come into contact with the firm.

These are a few of the roles necessary to make the legal profession operate in an organized and efficient manner. All work is considered to be done under the attorney's ultimate supervision, and it is the legal responsibility of the lawyer to see that each person works within the constraints of the ethical standards imposed on all licensed attorneys. The failure of any staff member to adhere to appropriate ethical standards can result in liability of the attorney. The absence of any of these individuals also can cause the most organized law firm to falter and even allow for mistakes that might ultimately result in liability for malpractice. Unlike many businesses, the law firm depends on support staff not only for daily operations but also for the practice's continued viability.

## ASSIGNMENT 5.1

Prepare a diagram that shows the placement of each position in a law office's structure.

## Quasi-Legal Professionals

In recent years, as technology and business have developed rapidly, so has the reality that other licensed professionals engage in practices that might be considered as practices of law. For example, a certified professional accountant (CPA) might advise a client on tax matters involving federal, state, and local tax laws. A licensed real estate agent or broker might advise a client about certain laws or regulations relevant to a transfer of property. Thus far, the courts have by and large dealt with such situations on a case-by-case basis. They examine the law involved, the other subject area affected (such as accounting or property), the expectations of the party receiving information, and the extent of the advice given by the professional. Typically, if the conduct of the professional was well within the accepted industry standards of that profession and did not unreasonably affect the legal rights of the individual, then a highly limited ability to practice law is inferred from the individual's professional license.

## THE NEW LEGAL PROFESSIONAL: THE PARALEGAL

In this chapter, we have briefly mentioned the position of paralegal within the law office structure. The entrance of the paralegal as a recognized member of the legal team has been a significant development in the history of the legal profession. The discussion that follows will examine how the position evolved and what changes it has brought to the way law is practiced in the U.S. legal system.

## The Paralegal as a Member of the Legal Team

The most commonly known setting for the paralegal is perhaps the law office, where the paralegal works primarily as an extension of the licensed attorney. The paralegal may assist or even perform many functions independently, albeit ultimately under the attorney's supervision. These functions include interviewing clients and witnesses, scheduling various meetings such as depositions, preparing basic legal documents, and doing legal research and writing. In many offices, especially smaller firms with more limited budgets, the paralegal sometimes also serves in a quasi-clerical role. However, this is not usually the most efficient use of the paralegal's time, skills, or the attorney's resources.

The areas in which the paralegal may be employed are virtually limitless. The position is recognized in the federal government and in most states. Paralegals work in numerous places, from the offices of the legislature to administrative agencies. Many are employed by the courts to assist judges, clerks of court, and other court officers. Administrative agencies make particularly extensive use of paralegals because much of the work performed requires basic legal knowledge but not the advocacy and analytical skills of a licensed attorney. Throughout the various levels of government, the paralegal has come to be viewed as a valuable staff member who carries out the objectives of the legal system. In the past, these roles were largely filled by attorneys, but the training and experience of a qualified paralegal is equally suitable for these positions in the majority of instances. More often than not, a team of attorneys has been replaced by a team of paralegals under the supervision of one or more attorneys.

Paralegals can be part of a team in such government offices as administrative agencies, courts, legislatures, and any other sub-branch that is involved in the creation or enforcement of legal standards. Paralegals in administrative agencies may be used to research or write rules and regulations, prepare cases for litigation, and review applications for agency action. Most of this work can be done by a highly qualified paralegal. The attorney supervises the work, is ultimately responsible for it, and completes any elements of the work that include the actual practice of law. Paralegals in the courts can work on file preparations in the office of the court clerk, assist judges with research and preparing orders and opinions, as well as maintaining records and files. Paralegals can be extremely useful to members of state and federal legislatures with the research and organization of legislative materials and even drafting legislation.

This increasing use of paralegals in what were traditionally attorney roles has not been lost on corporate America. In the past decade, as companies fought to stay current with ever-changing legal standards while keeping costs from escalating, many former corporate attorneys have been replaced with paralegals. The logic is much the same as that used by the government. Much of what is accomplished on a daily basis in a corporate legal department does not require extensive legal analysis or advocacy. Under the supervision of an attorney, corporate paralegals can prepare documents and correspondence, investigate legal issues, and perform legal research. By hiring an individual who has comparable skills in most of the necessary areas but does not have the expertise required for the practice of law, the corporate employer reaps a significant savings in overhead. This translates to the ability to hire more people for less money and thereby increase efficiency while controlling costs.

A myriad of employment opportunities exist for paralegals beyond the law office, government, and large corporations. Virtually every industry in existence encounters legal issues on a daily basis. Manufacturers must comply with environmental and labor regulations; service industries ranging from health care to real estate risk liability for failure to properly follow all the requirements of their profession; banks deal with various legal documents in the form of loans, trusts, and so forth every day; and all entities who have subordinate employees must adhere to applicable labor laws and regulations. As the complexity of the legal system and American society increases, so does the need for individuals who can assist in coping with the interaction of law and society.

## ASSIGNMENT 5.2

Identify five specific types of businesses in which a paralegal might be employed and the type of work this person might perform for each business.

## Development of the Paralegal Profession

The term *paralegal* or *legal assistant* is now firmly entrenched in the vocabulary of the legal profession. Similarly, the general public seems to have a basic awareness of the existence of paralegals, although the profession was still largely unknown to the public as recently as the early 1980s, and their role and function in today's U.S. legal system is often misunderstood. Today, even though great strides have been made, it is still common to find paralegals whose skills are underutilized. As understanding of their abilities increases with demands for competent legal services at a reasonable cost, this situation should improve.

Various changes in American culture during the twentieth century, specifically after 1929, caused a domino effect that kept a steady and astounding pressure on technological development for the remainder of the century and beyond. During the economic depression of the 1930s, the nation was forced to restructure business, banking, employment, and commercial activities. Throughout the 1930s, as the country attempted to recover, the workforce was largely reorganized into areas of mass employment. This was facilitated by the technological development of the business of manufacturing. As more people went to work in large-scale business, many moved away from the more isolated and traditional mom-and-pop operations and farming. Simultaneous with the increase of people in the industrial workforce was the almost explosive dramatic development of the transportation industry. New and improved engines increased the speed, availability, and efficiency of rail and river carriers; the new federal interstate system enabled over-the-road trucking on a wide scale; and the advent of air transportation totally changed the speed of movement of goods and widened the scope of potential customers for businesses nationwide.

On the heels of the depression came World War II. A whole new element entered the workforce in mass. As young healthy men went to war, they were replaced in the factories by women who had almost exclusively worked in the home for all of civilized history. The demand for military supplies and equipment on an immediate and large-scale basis taxed the existing system and required constant development and innovation. Throughout the war, those left behind developed U.S. business and technology and gained a new sense of their ability to contribute their talents outside the home. At the end of the war, the country was optimistic and businesses flourished with new and advancing technology. The predictable increase in population after the war also increased demand for all aspects of a capital-based society. Consequently, the demand for legal services increased dramatically in areas ranging from assistance with the purchase and transfer of real estate to an increase in representation regarding business contracts, estate planning, and, as traditional family roles began to change, an increased demand for legal representation in domestic relations law. These developments in such a relatively short time required more legal expertise than the profession had to give. An additional factor was the need for efficiency and the ability to offer legal services at a cost the general population could afford. By the 1960s, it was dramatically evident that a better way to deliver the services of the legal profession had to be found.

Many other professions found themselves in a similar situation and created paraprofessional positions. This was especially evident with health care providers as educational programs for physician assistants, nurse practitioners, dental hygienists, and dental assistants were developed and flourished. The creation of the role of a paraprofessional seemed to be the perfect answer. Paraprofessionals were not intended to be as extensively trained, but they could deliver many of the less technical and sophisticated services that were previously the responsibility of licensed professionals. Appropriate supervision could be used to ensure the quality of service and contain the scope of service to the appropriate levels.

For attorneys, this paraprofessional role came about in an almost incidental way. The role of paralegal was the natural evolution that merely became more focused and accelerated by the demands on the legal profession. For many years, the legal secretary had performed nonclerical roles to some extent. When clients called or came in and the attorney was not available, it was the legal secretary who answered basic questions about scheduled hearings, status of documents filed with the courts, and so on. Although it was never permissible for a legal secretary to give legal advice or advocate the client's interests with third parties, the rules of conduct were much cloudier for other tasks that were formerly the exclusive domain of the lawyer. As the demand for legal services grew, the need for assistance in routine but time-consuming tasks grew as well: interviewing clients and witnesses, preparing documents, gathering information, organizing collected evidence, and even carrying out basic research assignments. As demands grew, secretaries who had the confidence of their attorney employers were delegated tasks in addition to the basic clerical role of their employment. This had already been in place to some extent, but it became a more formal arrangement for many attorneys in the 1960s. As many legal secretaries began to demonstrate an aptitude for this type of work, attorneys similarly identified the potential value. In addition, even though an attorney could not legally charge for legal services performed by a clerical person, it was conceivable that such services performed by a trained paraprofessional were billable at a rate commensurate with the level of training.

As the use of legal paraprofessionals spread, several developments occurred. The dramatic increase in firms and businesses who employed paralegals demonstrated a broad consensus that there was a valuable role to be served by them within the legal system. The value was both monetary and a support to the profession of attorneys. In terms of serving the public, the concept was popular. The paralegal made the services of the legal profession more accessible and the cost more reasonable. In the relatively short time of thirty or so years, an entirely new profession developed that came to be widely known as paralegal or legal assistant. Today, the U.S. Bureau of Labor Statistics recognizes the paralegal as one of the fastest growing professional opportunities.

## APPLICATION 5.1

Gerard is an attorney who has decided to leave private practice and open a title company. He selected a growing community where there was no competition and most individuals purchasing property used the services of a title company in a nearby town. Gerard prepared and reviewed purchase agreements involving real estate agents and private sales. He also offered the preparation and management of sales that were financed by owners, which are sometimes called "contract for deed." In addition, he conducted title searches on properties that were sold to detect any liens or restrictions against property. Clients typically came to his office to close sales by signing appropriate documents and transferring ownership and purchase money. On a fairly regular basis, additional research was required for issues such as disputed ownership of property.

Shortly after his first year in the title company business, Gerard found himself working long hours to keep up with the growing demands of his business. He decided to evaluate what type of assistance he should hire in the office. Because there is seldom the need to give legal advice or appear in court, another attorney is probably not the most appropriate individual to bring on board. The alternatives are a qualified paralegal or clerical staff. Although a clerical staff member could type the documents, many of these are available in software form and only require minor adjustments before printing. A paralegal with proper supervision could perform legal research, modify form documents, prepare original documents, and conduct title searches. Even though this is not a traditional law office setting, it is one in which paralegal skills are particularly appropriate for the required tasks.

*Point for Discussion:* Why would it be more appropriate to hire a paralegal than an attorney if an attorney is currently performing the required work?

## Current Defining Standards of Competence

By the 1970s, many educational programs were appearing around the United States with the specific objective of providing training for paralegals. Initially, many of these programs were intensified courses of study ranging in duration from several months to a year or so. By the early 1980s, there were accredited academic degree programs throughout the United States. Today, there are any number of alternatives to train paralegals. The original method of the on-the-job training is still applied in many communities, although the trend has been to rely on more formal methods. The intensive and accelerated courses are still considered a successful means to train an entry level position for paralegals, but typically these courses of study are confined to the exclusive field of paralegal training and do not offer other support areas such as English or math that might be useful in a higher-level position. Therefore, paralegals should strive to have adequate skills in these areas before undertaking such a program if future opportunities are to be optimized. There are also many associate and baccalaureate degrees, postbaccalaureate certificates, and even master's degrees available at colleges and universities throughout the United States that focus on paralegal and law office administration. These programs are geared toward a more comprehensive college education with a focus in paralegal and related skills. In the United States, hundreds of training and education programs for paralegals are in place. It is also not uncommon to find individuals who have trained in other fields, or even former lawyers serving in the role of paralegal. The type and extent of training one pursues depends in large part on the background of the paralegal, the kind of support the paralegal wishes to provide in the workplace, and the setting in which the paralegal seeks employment and advancement.

Although the methods and extent of paralegal training and education vary widely, some standards have been established to assist attorneys, paralegals, and the public in developing reasonable expectations of what job skills the qualified paralegal should possess. In reality, many factors have influenced the need for an established set of standards and, even though the standards and tools of measurement are still evolving, there are now widely accepted criteria for a qualified paralegal. Even so, no universally accepted and standardized method of validation exists, and without such standards virtually anyone can be a self-proclaimed paralegal. Thus, the responsibility is on the one who hires a paralegal to fully investigate the true nature and level of education and acquired skill. The strategies used to establish competence vary as widely as the methods of training—from attempts for uniform standards of competence to legal liability for damage caused by malfeasance. It should be noted that many jurisdictions do provide some sort of definition of the term *paralegal* in statute, court rules, or case law, but this varies by state and in some instances is considered on a case-by-case basis.

One natural method of regulation is the extension of the rules used to protect the public from incompetence or malfeasance by attorneys: tort liability. The subject of tort law will be expanded on in a later chapter. At this juncture, it is important only to understand that the law provides a remedy for those who are injured in some way by an attorney's unacceptable acts or omissions. Rules of ethics, standards for licensure as an attorney, and well-established legal principles handed down by the courts present a clear picture of what is expected of attorneys with regard to their levels of skill in the various areas of law and in meeting the duty to serve their clients.

When an attorney accepts an individual as a client, the attorney is obligated to represent that client within the requirements of accepted legal standards of conduct and competence. If the attorney fails to meet any of those standards, a violation of the duty toward the client occurs. If that violation is the primary cause of injury to the client, then the attorney may be held liable for the value associated with the injury. In the event a subordinate of the attorney, such as a paralegal, is actually responsible for the violation, then—as the employer—the attorney may still be held accountable under the theory that he or she did not properly supervise the work of the employee. For example, an attorney has an obligation to keep information provided by a client confidential. This responsibility extends to those employed by the attorney. The employee may also be held personally liable for any damage caused. This is true of a paralegal working under the direction of an attorney. If a paralegal is independently employed or employed on a per job basis by an attorney, such as one employed on a freelance basis, the liability could be directly assigned to the paralegal. In either situation, realistically speaking, the ultimate responsibility for performing work in a competent manner ends with the paralegal. Even if liability is assigned to the supervising attorney, the future career for the paralegal is not too promising if he or she is the ultimate cause of that liability. Although the theory is that the attorney's responsibility is to supervise, the reality is that even the most conscientious attorney cannot be omnipotent with regard to everything a paralegal does and says. There has to be an earned degree of trust between the attorney and the paralegal. That trust must include the paralegal's skills as well as knowledge of the limits between assisting an attorney and the actual practice of law.

Generally speaking, the paralegal cannot give legal advice or advocate a client's legal rights with respect to third parties. Both tasks require a licensed attorney. This is important because legal advice and advocacy can cause a client or third party to act or not act in a way that directly impacts the rights of the client. Therefore, only a licensed attorney—that is, one who has demonstrated comprehensive proficiency at understanding the law and its applicability to given situations—may perform these duties. There is an exception to this rule: Some regulatory agencies permit nonattorneys to represent individuals in agency matters, but this is tightly limited in scope and in the number of agencies that permit it. In the event a paralegal, or anyone else, undertakes to engage in the practice of law, such as by advocating the rights of another or giving legal advice, then two possibilities arise. First, the individual may be prosecuted by the government for practicing law without a license. Second, the individual may be sued for any damage caused by the attempted practice of law. In most jurisdictions, the requirement is that the individual must have acted as a competent attorney would have under the same circumstances. The failure to do so would then result in civil liability. In essence, one who performs the practice of law is held accountable to possess and exercise the skills of a licensed attorney. Because the line drawn between professional services and those that constitute the unauthorized practice of law is not always clearly discernible, it is advisable to use great caution when approaching it.

## APPLICATION 5.2

Norman and Sandy were students in a college paralegal program. After graduation, they accepted jobs with different law firms in the same city. Every Monday they meet at the same restaurant for lunch and discuss their new careers. Norman is satisfied with his employer but would like to be more challenged in his work. Sandy feels almost too challenged and that her assignments are frequently ones that should be done by an attorney. She expresses this to Norman. He asks her exactly what she means. Sandy tells Norman about a recent situation in which her employer asked her to discuss the terms of a settlement offer with clients and to use her influence to persuade the clients to accept the offer. The attorney stated that because Sandy was in

(continued)

## APPLICATION 2.2 (Continued)

much more frequent contact with the clients, they would trust her opinion more. After the clients agreed to the settlement, the attorney commented to Sandy, "That case probably would have been worth a lot more in terms of a verdict. But I promised the wife a cruise for our anniversary next month and I need a chunk of change for that." Sandy is in a dilemma. She feels if she reports the attorney to the ethical and disciplinary commission she would not only lose her job but also likely cause the attorney to be sued. On the other hand, she feels complicit in her actions with regard to clients who trusted her. Norman asks the name of the particular clients Sandy has mentioned. That afternoon he contacted the clients and passed on the information. He also reports the attorney to the bar association. The clients then hired the firm where Norman was employed to sue Sandy's employer and Sandy.

*Point for Discussion:* Despite the conduct of the attorney, has Sandy done anything illegal or unethical?

As a sole means of policing the quality and delivery of services by the paralegal, tort liability's obvious problem is that control is put in place after the harm is done. As a result, although tort liability can be an effective method of compensating the victims of incompetence and misconduct, it does nothing proactively to prevent these behaviors. Thus, early on in the profession of paralegals, the need was clear for some method by which attorneys and the public could identify competent and responsible paralegals.

One method used throughout the United States to address this problem is approval of paralegal programs by the American Bar Association (ABA). Because attorneys are ultimately liable for the work and conduct of the paralegals they employ, the legal profession has a strong interest in creating standards by which paralegals are trained and educated. Consequently, an arm of the ABA was delegated the task of defining standards of education and applying them to the various types of formal paralegal training programs. This group also monitors those programs' adherence to the standards. ABA approval is a voluntary process and not required for any program of education. Programs may also have other types of approval by organizations that survey and rate or approve various types of educational programs and institutions at the postsecondary level. Currently, less than one-half of the existing paralegal programs have ABA approval, although such approval is highly regarded by the legal profession. Approval by the ABA is a rigorous process and is subject to regular review once achieved. Programs must demonstrate comprehensive training by qualified instructors. They must show an established program with definite goals, methods of achievement, and accurate measurement of student progress. The program directors are required to stay abreast of developments in the profession and to incorporate them into the programs when appropriate. Other organizations provide similar credentialization or endorsement of qualified education and training programs. Such approvals offer the legal profession and the aspiring paralegal objective standards by which to measure the quality of education and level of skill to be expected from individuals who graduate from these programs.

The types of subject matter addressed in approved paralegal training and educational programs are those in which the paralegal can expect to be called on in a supportive role to the attorney. This includes a clear understanding of the U.S. legal system, its function, and its form. There is also an expectation of practical knowledge and skills. The ideal paralegal is able to perform all tasks formerly and currently done by attorneys that do not include elements exclusive to the practice

**Table 5.1** Comparison of Duties of Attorneys and Paralegals*

| Duty or Skill | Attorney | Paralegal |
|---|:---:|:---:|
| Legal advice and representation (client contract, settlement negotiation, depositions, trials, and all situations involving advisement or advocacy) | X | |
| Client interviews and subsequent meetings | X | X |
| Legal research | X | X |
| Draft pleadings and motions | X | X |
| Obtaining evidence | X | X |
| Interviewing witnesses | X | X |
| Drafting demand letters and settlement documents | X | X |
| Selecting and preparing jury instructions | X | X |
| Abstracting depositions | X | X |
| Maintaining trial notebook and general case management | X | X |
| Drafting contracts and corporate documents | X | X |

*With proper attorney supervision, the qualified paralegal can perform all of the functions indicated in the table and all other tasks required in the law office that do not involve legal advice or advocacy. Some paralegals also make excellent law office administrators, which is especially helpful in firms that do not employ full-time administrators.

of law. The various supportive tasks in which a qualified paralegal should be trained include legal writing, basic legal research, drafting documents, interviewing clients and witnesses, investigative techniques, and any other routine matters that arise within the procession of a case. Table 5.1 depicts duties traditionally performed by the attorney that a qualified paralegal can do understate within the scope of the profession. Note that there is some variation in the standards and limits from jurisdiction to jurisdiction, and some states permit the paralegal to take an even more active role.

Many legal practices today specialize by confining their practice to particular topics such as real property, estate planning, or tort law (personal injury). A great deal of overlap occurs, though, and the qualified paralegal needs at least an introductory knowledge of most basic subjects of law, including a command of relevant terminology, current legal principles, common procedures, and relevant forms and documents. The paralegal is then in a position to appreciate the potential impact of certain occurrences within a case rather than being limited to a knowledge of how to complete a form and file it with the appropriate court or agency. A fundamental concept supporting paralegal training and education and the profession as a whole is that, to provide a valuable system of support, the paralegal should have the ability not only to perform routine tasks but also to understand the underlying reasons for them and to know when the various tasks are appropriate and why.

In addition to the tort and educational forms of monitoring the quality of skill and service delivered by paralegals—which are retroactive and proactive forms, respectively—methods have developed by which practicing paralegals can measure their ability and achieve a level of acceptance within their profession. As the profession has evolved, paralegal organizations have developed as well, such as the National Association of Legal Assistants (NALA), one of the oldest formalized bodies that supports the paralegal profession. In addition to its local chapters throughout the United States that offer support, continuing education, and communication for paralegals, NALA offers a rigorous and respected examination to test one's paralegal skills. To be eligible for the exam, the candidate must demonstrate a background that would establish a basic knowledge of paralegal skills.

These skills are then measured by the examination, and the successful candidate receives a certificate from NALA that allows the use of the designation *certified legal assistant* (CLA). Throughout the United States, many attorneys consider the exam and certificate authentication of a paralegal's level of skill. The organization and certification are purely voluntary, however, and only a small percentage of the paralegals in the United States have achieved this level. There is a distinction to be made between a person with the CLA designation and one who has received a certificate of completion from a paralegal education or training program. Although both indicate a certain level of demonstrated skill, they are by no means interchangeable titles. Several national, state, and local organizations exist with similar functions for promoting professional standards of competence and acceptance for paralegals. See Helpful Web Sites at the end of the chapter for a partial list of national organizations and their Internet sites.

Another support organization is the National Federation of Paralegal Associations (NFPA), which was formed in 1974. An original objective of NFPA was to bring together various local paralegal organizations and form a cohesive group with a collective ability to advance the paralegal career and professional standards on a national level. The organization has more than sixty paralegal organizations as members throughout the United States and more than 17,500 individual members. In 1994, the organization elected to create a comprehensive exam to validate the skills of paralegals. NFPA recommends a four-year degree, with a minimum two-year degree. The Paralegal Advanced Competency Examination (PACE) is available to paralegals with the title *registered paralegal* (RP). Like NALA, the NFPA organization enjoys a positive reputation in the legal community, and one who has passed the rigorous standards to achieve the title of registered paralegal is considered to have proven skills as a legal professional.

Through the years, many states have sought to establish guidelines and standards for paralegal skills, but as yet no comprehensive legislation is in place to test, regulate, and monitor this profession. However, as most service professions have developed during the last century, the government has identified a strong public interest in regulating such professions to protect an unwitting public from those who would act with less than a necessary degree of competence or integrity. Some states have enacted or modified legislation with respect to the definition of the unauthorized practice of law and placed limitations on law-related services by nonlawyers such as the preparation and sale of generic legal documents, including kits to prepare wills and noncontested divorces. There is no comprehensive legislation at this stage, however, to address licensure or regulation of paralegals. In this respect, the profession is still quite young. Thus, it is highly unlikely that the paralegals will see a great deal of legislation concerning the profession in the near future.

Issues that have arisen with regard to government regulation are serious. Paralegals and attorneys alike recognize the need for some sort of standard by which to measure and monitor paralegal skills and abilities. The problem lies in the wide array of backgrounds that exist in the profession. Universally, an attorney is required to meet minimum educational requirements and demonstrate a basic level of knowledge, but there are no such uniform standards for paralegals. In addition to those who are formally educated, there are thousands of job-trained paralegals and numerous laterally trained paralegals. These are individuals who entered the profession because of their technical knowledge and skill in another field. For example, a medical professional such as a nurse or an engineer can be of invaluable assistance to an attorney involved in complex litigation concerning those subject areas. The legal knowledge of such persons may be limited or nonexistent, yet, along with formally educated and degreed paralegals, they are within the same field of employment. The task of creating a system to evaluate skills relevant to the particular employment of such a wide array of professionals has led to great difficulty for governing bodies. Because of the need for regulation that is clearly identified and generally seen to outweigh the obstacles, it can likely be expected to further develop in the coming years.

## ETHICAL CONSIDERATIONS

The ethics of the legal profession are closely monitored by news media and the public in general. Although other professions have ethical duties, the legal profession is somewhat unique. Most other professionals have a duty with regard to their relationship to the client. The legal profession has this duty as well, but it extends to the representation of that client with third parties, the courts, and other elements of the government. The legal profession is the only one in which the failure to perform the duties undertaken could result in something as serious as the loss of liberty and even the death penalty. The results in almost all circumstances are certainly much less serious, but the degree of responsibility is not.

## ETHICAL CIRCUMSTANCES

Gerry was shot by police during a robbery of a convenience store. His injuries were life threatening, but he received competent medical care and survived. It is the policy of the hospital that information about the actions of anyone brought in under suspicion of criminal conduct be withheld as much as possible from medical personnel until after treatment is provided. This allows the medical staff to offer the best services without influence or emotion about what the individual may or may not have done before the injuries. Gerry was charged with robbery and the murder of the store clerk and two children who had interrupted the robbery when they came in to purchase candy. The children attempted to run, but Gerry shot them in the parking lot to prevent them from identifying him. A local attorney has been appointed to represent Gerry. The attorney and her paralegal are both parents of children of the approximate ages of the children who were murdered. Regardless, the attorney and consequently the paralegal have an ethical duty to represent and defend Gerry to the very best of their ability. Should the attorney ask to be removed from the case?

## ● | CHAPTER SUMMARY

The legal profession is one of the oldest on record. For thousands of years it remained relatively unchanged. During the twentieth century, however, it underwent a dramatic transformation that reflected similar societal and technological advances. Today, the U.S. legal system offers hundreds of different roles for those with legal background and training. In addition, the legal profession has streamed into many other areas of the economy. As a result, legal professionals can be found in an infinite number of settings offering support and insight with regard to the structure and function of all branches of government.

Perhaps the most significant development in the legal profession in recent history has been the advent of the paralegal. This individual bridged a wide gap between the availability of basic legal services for individuals and much needed technical support for attorneys. The paralegal started as a job-trained, highly functioning clerical position. It has grown to one that often involves extensive formal education and duties once considered the exclusive domain of attorneys. The development, however, has happened so rapidly that standards are still lacking to protect the integrity of the profession and to define clear guidelines of competence.

## ● | CHAPTER TERMS

jurist (judge)                  lawyer (attorney)                  paralegal (legal assistant)

## REVIEW QUESTIONS

1. What is the difference between an administrative law judge and an appellate judge?
2. What two skills distinguish a licensed attorney?
3. What is the difference between a certified legal assistant and a registered paralegal?
4. When can someone without a license practice law?
5. Identify five distinct types of settings in which paralegals may be found.
6. How is the function of a qualified paralegal different from that of a legal secretary?
7. What is the role of the law office administrator?
8. Identify and describe two other roles in the law practice other than attorney, paralegal, legal secretary, and law office administrator.

## HELPFUL WEB SITES

| | |
|---|---|
| National Association of Legal Assistants (NALA) | http://www.nala.org |
| National Federation of Paralegal Associations (NFPA) | http://www.paralegals.org |
| American Association for Paralegal Education | http://www.aafpe.org |
| American Bar Association Standing Committee on Paralegals | http://www.abanet.org/legalservices/paralegals/ |
| International Legal Assistant Management Association | http://www.paralegalmanagement.org/ |

## INTERNET ASSIGNMENT 5.1

Using one of the resources listed above, identify a paralegal organization in your state.

## INTERNET ASSIGNMENT 5.2

What constitutes the unauthorized practice of law in your jurisdiction? Provide the citation and relevant statutory language.

## INTERNET ASSIGNMENT 5.3

For what duties are paralegals allowed to bill in your jurisdiction?

### STUDENT CD-ROM

For additional materials, please go to the CD in this book.

### ONLINE COMPANION™

For additional resources, please go to www.paralegal.delmar.cengage.com

# CHAPTER
# 6

# The Law of Ethics

## LEGAL ETHICS: AN OXYMORON?

Webster's dictionary defines *oxymoron* as "a combination of contradictory or incongruous words."

The code of conduct followed by legal professionals has been in place for centuries. Even so, this group of professionals has been derided with such names as "thieves," "bottom feeders," "carpetbaggers," "rats with briefcases," "liyars," and so on. If ethical behavior is that which is considered right and appropriate and good, then lawyers are often tagged with names that imply just the opposite. Why are they the subject of such ridicule? Although some people are quick to sling mud and question a lawyer's motives, those are usually the people on the losing side of a legal controversy. Winners seldom complain. And, even though the court of public opinion frequently makes the legal profession the butt of jokes and slander, the legal profession is actually one of the most heavily monitored and enforced with respect to ethical conduct. Many professions do not even have disciplinary systems for unethical conduct. Punishment for such conduct is left to the courts (and lawyers) for enforcement. And other professions are widely known for codes of secrecy in protecting other members from exposure for inappropriate actions. Not so with lawyers. They are some of the most ethically minded individuals on the planet, a fact that can be seen in everything from licensing eligibility to mandatory prelicensing ethical exams to state organizations that are dedicated solely to investigating and recommending discipline for confirmed unethical behavior. There are lawyers whose entire careers involve dealing with that small minority of attorneys who have, in fact, engaged in unethical behavior.

So how did lawyers get such a bad name? It is quite simple, really. When people find themselves in a difficult legal situation, they often hire lawyers. Quite often the resulting problem partly results from the conduct or lack of conduct by the person hiring the lawyer—and if the individual does not prevail in the legal proceedings, then someone must be blamed. It's always easier to blame someone else than to accept responsibility. Hence, the lawyer must have done something wrong. Legal ethics is not an oxymoron. No, the moronic element more often lies with the disgruntled client. The moral of the story? Hiring an ethical lawyer is not usually the biggest concern or even a difficult task. Rather, hiring a lawyer is much like two people running from a bear. You don't have to run faster than the bear. You just have to run faster than the other guy. Likewise, your lawyer doesn't have to be the best. Your lawyer simply has to be better than the other lawyer in the case who represents the best interests of his or her client within the confines of the law.

## CHAPTER OUTLINE

HOW LAW AND ETHICS INTERRELATE
Legal Ethics and Their Impact on Professionals
Ethical Standards

Ethical Canons and Rules
THE RESULT OF ETHICAL VIOLATIONS

## CHAPTER OBJECTIVES

After reading this chapter, you should be able to:

- Explain the role of ethical standards in the American legal system.
- Discuss the attitude of the legal profession toward ethical standards.
- Describe the ethical standards applicable to various components of the legal profession.
- Distinguish between ethical canons and ethical standards.

- Explain the rationale for holding attorneys accountable for the ethical conduct of subordinates.
- Discuss major ethical requirements that are universal to all legal professionals.

## HOW LAW AND ETHICS INTERRELATE

The Ethical Considerations sections at the end of the preceding chapters have introduced the concept of ethics in law. The concept is not a new one. Throughout history, individuals with economic or governmental power have been subject to the trust of those who are dependent on the wise exercise of such power; and when such individuals violated that trust, the consequences have been severe. Greed, selfishness, and insensitivity to the basic needs of others have toppled many governments. Today, such scenarios still play out in some nations around the globe. In the United States, fortunately, the importance of the trust placed in those with a unique position of power to assist others is recognized and protected.

Ethical considerations are not confined solely to the legal professions. Most professions that require a state authorized license will carry with that license a certain degree of duty to act responsibly with respect to whatever power is given in association with the license. This applies to plumbers and electricians: They have a legal obligation to perform their duties in accordance with approved codes and regulations. It applies to accountants and physicians who have the legal obligation to perform their duties within established standards and to the best of their abilities. In addition, certain professions have increased responsibilities to act with a so-called professional responsibility. This duty carries with it the obligation to act in what the majority of people would consider a morally appropriate manner—one that is appropriate to the high level of trust and the great personal gain or loss associated with that trust by the individual.

## Legal Ethics and Their Impact on Professionals

Legal professionals are quite aware of their responsibility to the public and its seriousness. They know that individuals often place personal legal rights, and possibly tremendous impacts their futures, entirely into the hands of these professionals. This relationship of trust is significant. In some cases, the result has minimal effects; in others, it can mean the difference between prosperity and bankruptcy, freedom and prison, and even the right to a relationship with one's own children. For the client, the personal stakes in a legal dispute are often high. With an increasingly complicated legal system, a plethora of legal standards, a virtual explosion in litigation, and constantly changing technologies, legal professionals face an overwhelming task in effectively representing the best interests of their clients. Rules of ethics help to ensure that this responsibility is met to the highest ability of the legal professional while subject to minimum standards of competence and integrity.

Legal professionals are typically assertive by nature. This is a minimum requirement for success when acting as an advocate for others. Yet, even though the legal professional's objective is to provide the best possible representation for the client, he or she must also be constantly aware of the demanding ethical considerations. The obligation to act in what society would consider a morally correct manner may well affect the method in which representation is given to clients. Certain conduct is strictly prohibited. Other things may be discouraged or, alternately, demanded as part of what would be considered ethical representation. Thus, certain rules have nothing to do with the representation itself but do significantly affect how that representation is delivered.

Established legal ethical standards have a tremendous effect on the legal profession and the public as a whole. Without such standards, legal professionals would have no guideposts for those questionable situations that arise in the ordinary course of business. Each person brings a unique culmination of experience and values to a situation but today's society is far too complex to expect that a uniform and extremely narrow standard of conduct would develop if the entire system were to operate on an honor system. Even in the early development of legal standards in the United States, it became apparent that there were far too many possible interpretations of appropriate behavior, and the need for formally established rules began. In a society such as ours today with its mix of culture and background, it is not surprising that an accepted code of conduct is needed.

## Ethical Standards

Essentially, ethical standards are accepted rules that form the framework of the **fiduciary** (trust-based) relationship between the legal professional and client. Historically, these formalized rules were created for lawyers, but today's paralegal associations have adopted similar rules that correspond to the duties of the paralegal with respect to the client and the supervising attorney.

**fiduciary**
One who is in a position of trust by another with respect to rights, person, or property.

The lawyer–client relationship is entirely based on trust. The client places his or her trust in the lawyer and support staff's ability, commitment to competently perform the required duties, and intention to act in the best interest of the client to the exclusion of all others. Consider the following definitions:

**Ethics**—Principles, moral principles, code of conduct, right and wrong, values, conscience, moral philosophy, mores, criteria.

**Ethical**—Legitimate, proper, aboveboard, correct, unimpeachable, principled, honorable, decent, upright, respectable.

As we can see from these definitions, the foundation for legal ethics is quite similar to the general interpretation of ethical behavior. The U.S. legal system, and society in general, places a high value on behavior that is considered moral, truthful, and concerned about its effects on others. The legal professional's ethical obligations have the same underlying theme. For the legal professional, however, certain acts with respect to the client have been specifically identified and what actually constitutes ethical behavior has been defined. By doing this, the stated ethical rules can provide guidance when a situation occurs that may be somewhat questionable in terms of the legal professional's ethical duty.

## APPLICATION 6.1

Carmen and John are partners in a law practice. The two get along well and complement each other professionally. Their practice consists of generally uncomplicated cases. When they do go to trial, it is rarely for more than a day. However, they do have different personal styles when it comes to running their business. Carmen is quite diligent in maintaining records and substantiating all billing for her clients with proper documentation. John tends to generalize his billing and often does so well after the delivery of services by estimating the time he thinks he probably spent on various assignments.

The two decided to employ a paralegal. In addition to more traditional duties, Kenneth, the paralegal, is also asked to assist with maintaining billing records by checking to see that all work within client files has a corresponding billing charge. Carmen and John hope to increase revenues by catching any missed items. At the end of the first month, Kenneth confirms that all work done by Carmen has been charged and properly billed. Virtually none of John's work is complete. Kenneth produces a list of all of the unbilled activities in the client files attributed to John and asks him for billing charges. The list includes phone calls, correspondence, document preparation, and court appearances. John tells the Kenneth to just look at Carmen's client files and put down amounts similar to Carmen's charges for the same type of activities. For court appearances, he suggests Kenneth adopt a general rule to always put down one-half day unless it was a trial, in which case Kenneth is instructed to record a standard charge of three days' time to include pretrial and post-trial preparation. John further delegates Kenneth to keep up with all of John's billing for the future.

The paralegal is in an ethical dilemma. He is well aware that many of these tasks such as a court appearance may require widely different amounts of time based on the complexity of the particular client's case. He is new on the job and new to the profession. This does not seem right, but he lacks experience in general customs of the private practitioner. He does not know if he should refuse the task and jeopardize his employment or go along with it and hope any ramifications such as charges of unethical conduct would be held solely against John and possibly Carmen.

*Point for Discussion*: Does Kenneth the paralegal have a legally binding ethical obligation as a subordinate of the attorney?

As illustrated in the example, knowing the right thing to do is not always clear. In the application, the paralegal must consider several factors, including the obligation to the firm's clients, how much personal knowledge he or she has about the work performed, and what the ramifications could be if he refused to perform his duties as assigned by his superiors. Often ethical questions fall into a gray area and require close examination and a logical resolution. This can be difficult because ethical standards inherently have an emotional quality. One's sense of right and wrong is based on personal beliefs rather than knowledge of facts. It is not a mathematical or scientific equation that can be answered with absolute certainty, but a qualitative problem that must be transferred somehow into a quantitative sum. This requires a careful balance of all known facts and a disregard of any information that is based in pure emotion.

## ASSIGNMENT 6.1

Consider the following situations and explain whether there appears to be an ethical issue for the legal professional involved.

Tammy and Susanne are business partners who agreed to share equally in the profits and losses of the business. The first year was difficult, and on three occasions they each had to contribute additional monies to keep the business afloat. After that, the business really took off. They now own a successful gift shop and luncheon venue in an affluent community. Susanne is the "people person." She is always at the shop when it is open and visits with customers, ensuring their experience is a pleasant one. She also oversees the sales in the gift shop and the kitchen for the restaurant portion of the business. Tammy handles the ordering of shop inventory, food, and maintains all of the books. On the twenty-first of each month, Tammy issues a net profit check to Susanne for the business concluded the previous month. The two partners use a local accounting firm to prepare the quarterly and annual tax documents for the business. At the end of each year, Tammy provides the firm with necessary accounting information including the amounts distributed to the two partners as profit. Recently, Tammy went through a divorce. She hired a law firm to handle her interests in the divorce, the same firm that prepared the initial partnership agreement for Tammy and Suzanne. Last year, they converted the business to an S-corporation. It did not change the terms of the original agreement, but the law firm is now on retainer to prepare and submit annual corporate documents on behalf of the business.

The paralegal in change of gathering information for the divorce is required to examine the partnership agreement, S-corporation terms, and Tammy's income for the past three years. She was surprised to find that for two years Tammy's income has been exactly double that of Suzanne's, although there was no formal amendment to the partnership agreement. When she asks Tammy if the two had changed the terms, Tammy stated, "Not really, but I put in so many extra hours it only seemed fair. I'm sure Suzanne would agree I am entitled to it. But I'm so stressed over this divorce, I don't think I can handle any more drama right now. So just keep it quiet and I will deal with Suzanne if it ever becomes an issue."

## Ethical Canons and Rules

Rules of ethical conduct were initially established only for attorneys. Today, similar types of rules have been established for other legal professionals, including members of the judiciary and paralegals. Becoming a member of a certain component of a law-related profession, such as licensed attorneys, involves an underlying acceptance to be bound by the formal requirements established for ethical conduct that protect the integrity of the profession and the interests of those who are served by it. Failure to honor these rules can result in a variety of consequences from a formal statement of reprimand to revocation of licensure. For attorneys, the root of ethical considerations is in the form of rules promulgated by the American Bar Association (ABA). Most jurisdictions have adopted these or similar standards as conditions of licensure for attorneys. The ethical standards for attorneys consist of *canons,* or *traits,* that all attorneys should aspire to include in their work when serving clients. These are more or less the qualities of the consummate legal professional with the highest degree of integrity. *Disciplinary rules* are those basic requirements of conduct that, when violated, can result in formal discipline as well as civil actions for damages by parties injured as a result of the conduct. Consequently, the conduct of all legal professionals should fall within a range between the minimum requirements of the disciplinary standards and the ultimate goals of the canons. The professional career of a licensed attorney should reflect a constant compliance with disciplinary rules and evidence of a continuing effort to exemplify the ethical canons. The appendixes of this textbook contain a more complete publication of common standards, although a few of those that are more relevant to the everyday function of lawyers and paralegals will be addressed within the context of this chapter.

---

## APPLICATION 6.2

Sam hired the ABC law firm to represent him in a case against his homeowner's insurer. A few months earlier, Sam's home had caught fire and was destroyed. The insurance company refused to pay on the basis that its investigation showed the fire was intentionally set. The fire marshal concluded the fire was suspicious but could not determine a definitive case of arson. Supposedly, Sam had been camping when the fire occurred. In fact, the day before the fire, he had paid for a camping permit at a large recreational area 100 miles away.

    The paralegal for the law firm was sent to the remains of the house to take photos. Sam came along to describe what the house had been like before the fire. While there, the paralegal commented to Sam that the insurance company was dragging its feet on producing documents. She also commented that she thought things could move much more quickly if his copy of the insurance policy had not burned. To the paralegal's surprise, Sam said he was sure he had a copy of the policy in his camper. The paralegal followed Sam to a storage lot where his camper was located. In the camper, the paralegal saw box upon box of family photos, documents, and what appeared to be a number of valuable collectibles. The camper was virtually full from floor to ceiling of the important things one would ordinarily keep in one's home. Sam noticed her curiosity and told her that he had planned to paint the interior of his house before the fire. In fact, just two days before the fire, he had moved all of his important belongings to the camper for storage while he painted. The paralegal is aware that the attorney handling the case believes the case can be won and Sam will ultimately receive the entire amount of his homeowner's insurance policy. This results would be extremely helpful because Sam's business was in the process of a bankruptcy.

*Point for Discussion:* Should the paralegal's concerns be reported to the attorney who is seeking to compel payment for the fire on the basis that it was an accident? Should the information be reported to the authorities who are conducting the criminal investigation?

---

Four of the most common issues for attorneys and paralegals, as well as support staff, are those involving competency, confidentiality, conflict of interest, and commitment to zealous representation. Each is of extreme importance and has served as the basis for many lawsuits when lawyers or their staff have failed to meet the required standards. There are other standards as well, but these four affect virtually every type of legal professional and every client relationship. While there are numerous publications of extensive ethical standards for legal professionals, a few of the more commonly encountered are discussed within the context of this chapter.

## Competency

### Rule 1.1

A lawyer shall provide competent representation to the client. Competent representation requires the legal knowledge, skill, thoroughness, and preparation reasonably necessary for the representation (ABA Model Rules of Professional Conduct of 2002).

The question of **competence** is more involved than one might first surmise. Every lawyer who is licensed today must pass an examination that tests basic knowledge of legal principles. However, this does not ensure that the attorney will keep abreast of changes in the law and always apply that knowledge when representing clients, but it is an ethical responsibility placed on the attorney as part of the privilege of the license. Many jurisdictions have continuing education requirements to assist in this objective, but this is by no means a guarantee that competence will be exercised in every situation.

To act competently, an attorney should meet one of three basic requirements. He or she must (1) possess an adequate and current knowledge of the subject matter of the representation, (2) obtain such knowledge before undertaking representation, or (3) refer the matter to an attorney who has adequate and current knowledge of the subject matter. Because the law is so varied, complex, and in a constant state of change, maintaining full and current knowledge of one, much less many, areas of law can be a daunting task. Still, this is the requirement imposed on legal professionals to ensure that the client, who places trust in the attorney, is protected.

Although in theory it is quite easy to require competence to be met, in practice it is quite a different thing. After all, the practice of law is a business. A business only profits from serving its customers. If too many clients are referred to other attorneys, then there will not be a practice with enough cases to support the attorney and staff. On the other hand, additional cases that are accepted by an attorney increase the hours needed to properly represent the clients. This may leave scarce time for education and keeping abreast of changes. Then, too, what of the subordinate staff? The attorneys and paralegals who are employed by a firm or legal department are paid to get the work done. Frequent refusals to take on assignments on the ground of lack of competence does not create a promising future for any professional. The obligation is present and serious, but the burden is significant to balance the responsibilities associated with it and client representation in general.

**competence**
Having adequate knowledge, skill, and training to undertake specific legal representation in a matter.

---

# CASE
### *In re Evans,*
### 902 A2d 56 (D.C. C.A. 2006)

---

The following opinion demonstrates how repeated ethical misconduct can result in a cumulative effect with respect to discipline. However, the opinion also clearly discusses the purpose of professional discipline and its relationship to injuries suffered as the result of ethical misconduct.

. . . In this matter, we find the Committee's findings of fact, with one exception noted below, to be amply supported by the record. We have adopted many of them, but have eliminated certain other findings that are unnecessary to the analysis and outcome of this matter. Pursuant to Board Rule 13.7, we have made some additional findings to provide context and further support for our conclusions. Finally, we have revised and reorganized the findings for ease in evaluating the violations at issue.

1. Respondent is a member of the Bar of the District of Columbia Court of Appeals, having been admitted on June 1, 1960. . . . Respondent is also admitted to practice law in Maryland and Kansas. . . .

*(continued)*

2. Respondent's practice has included probate matters in the D.C. Superior Court since that court was formed in 1972. . . .

3. Respondent also has an active real estate settlement practice. In 1997, Respondent owned Delco Title, which he operated out of his law office in Silver Spring, Maryland. (Respondent). Bankers Financial Group, a mortgage lending company, used Respondent and Delco Title repeatedly for mortgage settlements over a three- to four-year period through 1997, sending Delco Title approximately 20 loans per month for handling. . . .

4. Mrs. Zaidee H. Robinson died in 1987. . . . At the time of her death, Zaidee Robinson owned real property located at 716 Ingraham Street in northwest Washington, D.C. (hereinafter the "Ingraham Street property"). As of April 1997, Zaidee Robinson's estate had never been probated. . . .

5. Zaidee Robinson was survived by two sons, Maurice and Clifton. . . .

6. Maurice Robinson died in 1989. He was survived by his wife, Carolyn Robinson and two sons Qawi and Yusef. At the time of his death, Maurice and his family resided at the Ingraham Street property. . . .

7. Following his mother's death, Clifton Robinson was incarcerated. . . .

8. On April 17, 1997, Bankers Financial contacted Delco Title about handling a closing on a real estate loan for Carolyn Robinson. . . . The loan was for $65,000 on the Ingraham Street property, where Carolyn Robinson lived at the time. . . .

9. At some point after the initial referral, Respondent learned that the Ingraham Street property was deeded to Zaidee rather than Carolyn Robinson. . . . Carolyn Robinson subsequently retained Respondent to assist her in becoming personal representative of Zaidee Robinson's estate and in closing the loan on the Ingraham Street property. . . . As described by Respondent, his "office was asked to handle a title closing for Carolyn Robinson and a probate estate was opened to have the appropriate people appointed to sign for the loan.". . . Accordingly, the Board finds that Bar Counsel proved by clear and convincing evidence that Respondent did not himself disclose his conflict to Carolyn Robinson and did not know whether she had knowingly waived the potential conflict prior to representing her in his capacity as an attorney. . . .

11. On April 24, 1997, Respondent filed a Petition for Probate in the Probate Division of the Superior Court of the District of Columbia, on behalf of Qawi S. Robinson, Carolyn Robinson, and Clifton Robinson, as petitioners. Qawi and Carolyn Robinson are listed as personal representatives. The petition bears signatures of all three petitioners and Respondent signed as counsel. . . .

12. The petition listed Maurice Robinson, Carolyn's husband, as "deceased.". . . At the time of the filing, no probate estate had been opened for Maurice Robinson.

13. The petition listed Clifton Robinson as "incarcerated.". . . Respondent was informed by Carolyn Robinson that Clifton would waive his interest in the estate. . . . Respondent made no effort to confirm this purported waiver with Clifton Robinson.

14. Forms entitled "Renunciation, Nomination of Personal Representative and Waiver of Bond" signed by Clifton and Yusef Robinson were filed with the Petition (the "renunciation forms"). . . .

15. On April 29, 1997, a Probate Judge signed an Abbreviated Probate Order appointing Carolyn and Qawi Robinson as co-personal representatives of the estate of Zaidee Robinson. . . .

16. On May 8, 1997, Qawi and Carolyn Robinson, as co-personal representatives of the estate, deeded the Ingraham Street property to Carolyn Robinson. . . .

17. The same day, Carolyn Robinson executed a Deed of Trust mortgaging the Ingraham Street property for $65,000. . . .

18. The interest rate on the mortgage was 12.930%. . . . A broker's fee of $6,500 was paid to Bankers Financial from the settlement funds. . . .

19. Delco Title was paid a settlement fee of $350.

20. Delco Title received a check for $824.20 out of the settlement funds. . . . In addition to the settlement fee listed above, this payment included items 1102 and 1103 on HUD Form 1-A: $325 for "Abstract or title search to Lots and Squares Abstractors" and $160 "Title examination to Spectrum Title Services." . . . In fact, Delco paid only $75 to Spectrum Title Services and $155 to Lots and Squares Abstractors. . . . Accordingly, fees retained by Delco totaled $590.

21. Respondent's law office, Evans & Evans received $1,700.00 in fees from the settlement funds. This included document preparation fees (items and 1104 and 1105 on HUD Form A-1) and $1,300.00 in fees for probate work. . . .

22. In total, Respondent retained $2,290 from this transaction.

23. Respondent did not receive approval from the Probate Court before accepting these payments. . . .

24. Maurice Robinson was an heir to Zaidee Robinson's estate. Bar Counsel's experts testified that, because Maurice Robinson was deceased, it was necessary to open and probate his estate before transferring assets from his mother's estate. . . .

25. Respondent did not open an estate for Maurice Robinson prior to transfer of the Ingraham Street property. . . .

26. It is apparent from the record that the Respondent intended the renunciation forms Clifton and Yusef

Robinson filed with the probate petition to operate as waivers of their interest in the Ingraham Street property. The Committee found it was plain on the face of the document that the signatory only waived the right to act as personal representative of the estate and not the right to estate property. . . . The Board accepts this finding.

27. The Committee noted that Respondent gave inconsistent explanations regarding how he came to make this ineffective filing. Respondent initially claimed that he was acting on advice he received personally from a probate official, Donald Horton. . . . According to Respondent, "the probate official handed this to me and said, instead of having this one signed, sign this one, and have Mr. Clifton Robinson sign this one to renounce his interest in the property."

28. However, the Committee noted that Respondent had made previous statements under oath that his office clerk, not Respondent, received the advice from the probate division regarding what form to use.

29. When confronted at the Hearing with the prior inconsistent testimony, Respondent conceded "I did send Tommy and he went there for me" referring to his assistant Thompkin Hallman. . . . Respondent did not call Mr. Hallman as a witness to this alleged conversation with the probate officer. The probate officer involved, Mr. Horton, now retired from the probate office, was called by Bar Counsel. He had no recollection of a conversation with Tommy Hallman where he suggested they use a "renunciation of personal representation form" to renounce rights to the estate assets. . . .

30. The Committee did not find Respondent's conflicting testimony to be credible. Accordingly, it found that he had not received any advice or suggestion from the probate division that he should use the ineffective form as a release of the signatory's right to estate property. . . .

31. Bar Counsel's expert testified that, in any event, an heir can only renounce a share in an estate within nine months of the date of death. After this time expires, the heir must formally assign his rights to effectively transfer title of estate property. . . .

32. On July 11, 1997, Clifton Robinson filed an affidavit with the Probate Court alleging that his signature had been forged on the Petition for Probate, the Consent and Waiver of Bond, and the Renunciation. . . .

33. In response to this affidavit, the Probate Court entered an Order directing Qawi Robinson and Carolyn Robinson to appear on September 10, 1997 and "show cause why they should not be removed as co-personal representatives" of the estate. . . .

34. At that hearing, the Respondent learned that his client, Carolyn Robinson, had forged Clifton Robinson's signatures. . . . The Committee declined to find that Respondent knew about the forgeries before the hearing and it credited Respondent's testimony that he had no reason to question the signatures obtained by his client. . . .

35. Bar Counsel's probate expert opined that she would write to the other heirs to make sure "they had no interest," and "make certain that theysigned an assignment or something." . . . The Committee concluded, however, that this testimony did not support a finding that a competent probate attorney would have insisted on this course of conduct, i.e., would have spoken to or corresponded with the other heirs personally, rather than accept the statements of Ms. Robinson and the signatures she had supposedly obtained. . . .

36. The show cause hearing was continued until November 13, 1997. Respondent did not attend the November 13 hearing. Respondent later claimed his absence from court was "due to a posting error by new personnel in . . . [my] office." . . .

37. In a written Order issued on November 14, 1997, the Court removed Carolyn and Qawi Robinson as Co-Personal Representatives. The Court noted, "with this loan clouding the status of the [Ingraham Street property] Carolyn Robinson has an obvious conflict of interest of her own that precludes her ability to discharge her fiduciary duty." . . .

38. The Court appointed Benny L. Kass, Esq. to act as personal representative of Zaidee Robinson's estate. . . .

39. The November 14 Order also directed the removed co-personal representatives to file an affidavit detailing the assets and debts of the estate on or before January 5, 1998. . . . Respondent was served with a copy of this Order.

40. The removed co-personal representatives did not file the required affidavit. On the filing deadline, Carolyn Robinson filed a petition for an extension of time, claiming that she needed more time to comply because she was no longer represented by Respondent and that she had expected him to file the affidavit on her behalf. The Court denied this request in a written Order, dated January 28, 1998. . . .

41. In the January 28 Order, the Court expressed concern over (1) Respondent's ownership of the title company used for the loan on the

(continued)

estate property, and (2) Respondent's continued representation of the estate and Ms. Robinson, "knowing that she was using as collateral realty that did not belong to her" and suggested that Bar Counsel should investigate this apparent conflict. . . .

42. The Court also noted that Respondent had made no effort to explain his absence at the November 13 hearing. . . .

43. The January 28 Order was served on both Respondent and Bar Counsel. . . .

44. On February 2, 1998, Respondent moved to withdraw as counsel for the estate, which the Court allowed on March 11, 1998. . . .

45. On May 8, 1998, Mr. Kass filed a civil action against Carolyn Robinson, Qawi Robinson, Respondent and his law firm, and Delco Title over the erroneous probate and property settlement. Respondent settled the claims against him for $37,500. . . .

We agree with the Committee's findings that Respondent violated *Rules 1.1(a), 1.1(b), 1.7(b)(4)* and *8.4(d)* and find no cause to overturn its finding that he did not violate *Rule 3.3(a)* or *8.4(c)*. . . .We find the central factor in Respondent's misconduct was his use of a probate proceeding to facilitate the closing of a questionable real estate transaction in which he had a financial interest. . . . *Rule 1.7* is founded upon the principle that a client is entitled to undivided loyalty and zealous legal representation. Subsection (b)(4) of the Rule, when read in conjunction with subsection (c), prohibits a lawyer from representing a client in a situation where the lawyer's professional judgment may be adversely affected by the lawyer's own financial, business, property, or personal interests in the absence of the informed consent of the client. The Committee found that the record was unclear as to whether "Respondent or a representative of Delco Title or anyone else in Respondent's office" made the required disclosure to Carolyn Robinson. . . . Because it is Respondent's burden to demonstrate his client's waiver of a conflict, the Committee ultimately found that "the consent and disclosure requirements of *Rule 1.7(b)* were not met." . . .

Respondent argues that Bar Counsel did not prove lack of consent and notes that under Delco Title "company policy" the attorney who actually handled the closing, in this case Respondent's associate, was responsible for informing the client of Respondent's interest in Delco prior to settlement. . . . Bar Counsel argues that Respondent's admitted failure to personally ensure that Carolyn Robinson had given her informed consent to the potentially conflicted representation is sufficient support for the Committee's finding of a violation.

We find Bar Counsel's argument persuasive. Our analysis differs from the Committee in that we find that Bar Counsel presented clear and convincing evidence that Respondent did not know whether Ms. Robinson had been informed of and knowingly waived the potential conflict. . . . As the Board has previously explained in a matter involving subsections (2) and (3) of *Rule 1.7(b)* "[w]here a potential conflict of interest exists there is an unqualified obligation to provide 'full disclosure' before accepting the representation of the new client." *In re Boykins,* BDN 375–96 at 20 (BPR June 17, 1999). Although we have found no cases addressing this obligation in a context analogous to the one before us, Comment 25 to *Rule 1.7* ("Business Affiliated with a Lawyer or Law Firm") is instructive. This Comment specifies that both a lawyer recommending the services of an enterprise in which that lawyer has an interest and a lawyer accepting a referral from such an enterprise have an obligation to inform the client of the conflict. In the second situation, "the lawyer should not accept such a referral without full disclosure of the nature and substance of the lawyer's interest in the related enterprise." Cmt. 25 to *Rule 1.7.*

. . . The course of events began when Carolyn Robinson went to a mortgage broker in order to borrow money using the Ingraham Street property as collateral. Respondent's relationship with Carolyn Robinson began when her mortgage broker referred her to Delco Title to close the loan. Upon learning that Carolyn Robinson did not have title to the property and that it was still part of her mother-in-law's estate, Respondent, in his capacity as lawyer, undertook representation of Ms. Robinson with the objective of transferring title of the property to Ms. Robinson so that she could obtain a mortgage loan. Accordingly, as the lawyer accepting the referral, Respondent had an independent duty to make certain that the potential conflict was fully and adequately disclosed to Carolyn Robinson and that she knowingly waived this conflict prior to commencing the representation. He admittedly did not do this. See Tr. II 175–76 (Respondent). We find that Respondent violated *Rule 1.7(b)(4)* by failing to acquire the informed consent of his client regarding the potential conflict arising from his interest in Delco Title. We consider this more than a technical violation of the Rule. As discussed more fully below, Respondent initiated a probate proceeding so that Carolyn Robinson could take title to the Ingraham Street property and then close the mortgage loan. It was in his financial interest for the loan to close, and it did.

Rule 8.4(d) proscribes conduct that "seriously interferes with the administration of justice." *In re Hopkins,* 677 A.2d 55, 61 (D.C.1996), explains that to establish a violation of *Rule 8.4(d)* Bar Counsel must show by clear and convincing evidence that:

1. Respondent's conduct was improper, i.e., that Respondent either acted or failed to act when he should have;
2. Respondent's conduct bore directly upon the judicial process with respect to an identifiable case or tribunal; and
3. Respondent's conduct tainted the judicial process in more than a *de minimis* way, *i.e.,* it must have potentially had an impact upon the process to a serious and adverse degree.

The Committee found that Respondent violated *Rule 8.4(d).* In its analysis, the Committee noted three specific instances of improper conduct in satisfaction of the first element of *Hopkins:* 1) Respondent's failure to attend the November 13 hearing regarding the forged documents; 2) Respondent's failure either to withdraw from the representation or ensure that his client complied with the Probate Court's November 14 Order directing her to file an accounting; and 3) Respondent's acceptance of payment of legal fees from estate assets without prior court approval. HC Report at 21–22. The Committee noted that it might not have found a violation based on any one of these failings alone, but it found a violation because taken together they "impacted adversely on the Probate Division's ability to effectively administer the estate.". . . Respondent argues that this conduct does not establish a violation. First, he argues that missing a single court hearing, which he claims was the result of a new staff member failing to include it on his calendar, cannot provide the basis of a *Rule 8.4(d)* violation. Opposition at 10–12. On the second point, he argues that he had no duty to withdraw from the representation of Carolyn Robinson because her son led him to believe that she would be in contact with him. *Id.* at 12. On the third point Respondent argues that it was not necessary to obtain court approval for his fees.

Although we agree that Bar Counsel has proved a violation of *Rule 8.4(d),* we do not find that the specific instances of misconduct found by the Committee are the only basis for the violation. The record demonstrates that Respondent repeatedly took shortcuts in connection with the Zaidee Robinson probate proceeding and committed numerous other failures in addition to the conduct noted by the Committee. These include:

- Failing to get Carolyn Robinson's waiver of the conflict of interest arising from Respondent's interest in Delco Title (see Section II. A. *supra*);
- Failing to open an estate for Maurice Robinson prior to transfer of the Ingraham Street property. . . . Filing facially defective renunciation forms for Clifton and Yusef Robinson. . . . Failing to even attempt to contact Clifton Robinson regarding his interest in the estate. . . .
- Failing to obtain court approval for the transfer of the Ingraham Street property to Carolyn Robinson, and;
- Ignoring his client's obvious conflict of interest in acting as a fiduciary to the estate. . . .

Although one or two of these individual failings might be attributable to carelessness, collectively they are emblematic of Respondent's misconduct. The totality of circumstances demonstrate that Respondent manipulated the probate proceeding to transfer real estate to his client under questionable circumstances when Respondent's own business interest was to close a mortgage on the property. The first element of *Hopkins*—improper conduct by the Respondent—is met on this record. This improper conduct is different from the typical *Rule 8.4(d)* case involving a failure to appear at a hearing or otherwise cooperate in a judicial proceeding. See *In re Shepherd,* BDNs. 313–98 & 83–89, at 20 (BPR Dec. 10, 2003) . . . . A knowing failure to obey a specific court order is not, however, a required element of a violation.

. . . Here, Respondent both took actions that he should have known had the potential to seriously interfere with the administration of justice and failed to act when necessary to prevent such interference. In Respondent's own words, the "probate estate was opened to have the appropriate people appointed to sign for the loan.". . . Respondent initiated a probate proceeding in order to close a real estate loan on property his client did not own. Given the potential for self-dealing inherent in these circumstances, even if Respondent genuinely believed that Carolyn Robinson would eventually inherit an interest in the Ingraham Street property, he was obligated to use all of his legal skills and knowledge to ensure that she had good title before encumbering the property. He did not. Instead, Respondent took shortcuts and made mistakes without fully considering the propriety of such actions or the effect they might have on the probate proceeding. This allowed his client to encumber improperly the only asset of the estate. We find that this constitutes improper conduct.

Although the Committee did not find that Respondent knowingly participated in fraud, conduct can be "prejudicial to the administration of justice whether it was reckless or somewhat less blameworthy." *Hopkins,* 677 A.2d at 60 (internal citations omitted). In *In re Hallmark,* the Court declined to find a violation where the alleged wrongful conduct—submitting one

*(continued)*

"obviously deficient" CJA voucher—was the result of negligence. 831 A.2d 366, 367 (D.C.2002). The Court contrasted this failing with cases "where there is intentional disregard for the effect that an action may have on judicial proceedings or the client's cause." *Id.* In accordance with *Hallmark,* the Board recently clarified that *Rule 8.4(d)* does not extend to mistakes that are "innocent in character." *In re Agee,* BDN 243–01 (May 14, 2004) at 33. In *Agee,* the respondent failed to properly record or correct a mistake in a court's recitation of a plea agreement. This ultimately resulted in the charges against the defendant being vacated. We declined to find a violation there because the respondent's conduct was a mistake born of momentary inattention. Here, however, Respondent's misconduct did not arise from a passing failure. Respondent's multiple failings reflect an "intentional disregard" for the effect that his actions might have on the probate proceeding. Accordingly, we find that Respondent engaged in improper conduct under the first prong of *Hopkins.*

We further find that Respondent's improper conduct satisfies the final two prongs of *Hopkins.* It bore directly upon the judicial process in connection with an identifiable case by tainting the probate proceeding that Respondent initiated to close the loan. We further conclude that this misconduct had more than a *de minimis* effect on that proceeding. Respondent assisted his client in mortgaging the estate's only asset, the Ingraham Street property. The successor personal representative had to take corrective actions that would not otherwise have been necessary to recapture the value of the estate, including bringing a suit against the Respondent and his former client. Accordingly, we find that Respondent engaged in improper conduct that tainted an identifiable case in more than a *de minimis* way in violation of *Rule 8.4(d).*

*Rule 1.1(a)* obligates every lawyer to "provide competent representation to a client. Competent representation requires the legal knowledge, skill, thoroughness, and preparation reasonably necessary for the representation." An attorney who has the requisite skill and knowledge to provide competent representation, but nonetheless fails to engage in the thoroughness and preparation reasonably necessary in the course of an active representation, violates *Rule 1.1(a). In re Nwadike,* BDN 371–00 (BPR July 30, 2004).

To prove a violation, Bar Counsel must not only show that the attorney failed to apply his or her skill and knowledge, but that this failure constituted a serious deficiency in the representation. *Id; see also In re Ford,* 797 A.2d 1231, 1231 (D.C.2002) (*per curiam*) (*Rule 1.1(a)* violation requires proof of "serious deficiency" in attorney's competence). The determination of what

constitutes a "serious deficiency" is fact specific. It has generally been found in cases where the attorney makes an error that prejudices or could have prejudiced a client and the error was caused by a lack of competence. See *In re Schlemmer,* BDNs 444–99, 66–00 (BPR Dec. 27, 2002), remanded on other grounds, *840 A.2d 657 (D.C.2004).* Mere careless errors do not rise to the level of incompetence. See *Ford,* 797 A.2d at 1231.

The Committee found that Respondent failed to meet the Requirements of *Rule 1.1(a)* in three respects: 1) filing ineffective renunciation statements for Yusef and Clifton Robinson; 2) permitting Carolyn Robinson to distribute estate assets without court approval; and 3) taking his fees out of the estate without court approval. We agree with the Committee that filing the ineffective renunciation form in and of itself establishes a violation of *Rule 1.1(a).* We take a different approach, however, with respect to Respondent's failures to obtain Court approvals. We find that these failings arose from a more general failure by Respondent to apply his skill and knowledge in this matter. We ultimately conclude that this general failure provides the basis for a second, independent violation of *Rule 1.1(a).*

Respondent argues that he reasonably relied on representations from his legal assistant that Mr. Horton, then Deputy Registrar of Wills, told him the renunciation form he filed on behalf of Yusef and Clifton Robinson was sufficient to transfer their interests in the Ingraham Street property. . . . First, we note that Respondent's argument is in effect a challenge to the fact finding of the Committee. We defer to the factual findings made by the Hearing Committee if supported by substantial evidence in the record, viewed as a whole. Board R. 13.7; *In re Micheel,* 610 A.2d 231, 234 (D.C.1992). "Substantial evidence means enough evidence for a reasonable mind to find sufficient to support the conclusion reached." *In re Thompson,* 583 A.2d 1006, 1008 (D.C.1990) (*per curiam*). We find the Committee's determination that Respondent was not relying on the advice of a probate official when he filed the ineffective forms to be supported by substantial record evidence.

. . . . As noted in the comments to *Rule 1.1,* "competent handling of a particular matter includes . . . use of methods and procedures meeting the standards of competent practitioners." On its face the form that Respondent filed only purports to renounce the signatory's right to act as personal representative and waive the requirement of a bond to protect his or her share in the estate. We agree with the Committee that Respondent, as the attorney for Ms. Robinson, was responsible for reading the forms he instructed her to file. HC Report at 16. A competent practitioner would not rely on the advice of non-attorneys to the point of not even reading documents filed on a client's behalf. We further agree with the Committee that, if he had read beyond the title, Respondent would have known that the form was insufficient. Although Respondent had the knowledge and skill to make this determination, he failed to apply it here.

This failing had the potential to prejudice his client. Had Clifton Robinson actually intended to renounce his share of the estate and its sole asset, the Ingraham Street property, the form filed by Respondent would not have accomplished that objective. If, as Respondent believed, his client was the intended beneficiary of the renunciation, then the filing of an ineffective form was directly prejudicial to her interests. The fact that there was no actual prejudice to Ms. Robinson, because Clifton did not intend to renounce his share of the estate, does not remove the potential for prejudice. Accordingly, we find that Respondent's filing of a plainly deficient legal form on his client's behalf violated *Rule 1.1(a)*. . . .

Zaidee Robinson died well before the statutory revision. Respondent argues, however, that the statutory scheme in place when the estate was opened applies to this matter. Opposition at 3–8. Therefore, according to Respondent, it was not necessary to obtain court approval for either his fee or the transfer of the Ingraham Street property. *Id.* He further argues that because this is a reasonable position about an unsettled point of law, his good faith belief that he was acting in accordance with the law protects him from a violation. *Id.* at 8. Bar Counsel argues that the law as it stood at the time of Zaidee Robinson's death, which required court approval, applies and that Respondent's arguments to the contrary "evidence his incompetence." BC Brief at 14.

Although we agree with Bar Counsel that the earlier version of the statute applied to the estate, Respondent's failure to make this distinction may have been no more than a careless error. Moreover, we think that this debate over probate law obscures the gravamen of Respondent's incompetence. Competent handling of a legal matter "*includes inquiring into and analysis of the factual and legal elements of the problem,* and use of methods and procedures meeting the standards of competent practitioners." Cmt. 5 to *Rule 1.1(b)* (emphasis added). Bar Counsel argued to the Committee that "it was incumbent on the Respondent to advise Mrs. Robinson that her apparent desire to obtain legal title to her deceased mother-in-law's property was beset with complications." BC Proposed Findings of Fact and Conclusions of Law at 24. This is true, but it also misses what we find to be the essence of Respondent's incompetence. Respondent failed to make a basic assessment of the factual and legal issues implicated by the proposed transfer of legal title to Carolyn Robinson. As a result, he was unable to properly advise his client.

While actual prejudice to the client need not be shown, potential prejudice is sufficient. Here Ms. Robinson was prejudiced by Respondent's failure to provide competent representation. She was removed as personal representative of the estate and had a legal action filed against her. Although her own dishonesty in connection with the purported forged signature contributed to these consequences, her self-interested transfer and encumbrance of the Ingraham Street property was the primary cause of her removal and the suit against her. See BX F 9 (Complaint in *Kass v. Robinson* and Probate Court Orders attached thereto). Competent probate counsel would have recognized the impropriety of this transaction. Accordingly, we find that Respondent's general failure to provide competent representation to Ms. Robinson was a serious deficiency and violated *Rule 1.1(a)*.

*Rule 1.1(b)* requires a lawyer to "serve a client with the skill and care commensurate with that generally afforded to clients by other lawyers in similar matters." The Committee found that essentially the same conduct that violated *Rule 1.1(a)* also violated subsection (b). In addition, the Committee found that Respondent's failure to open a probate estate for Maurice Robinson was another instance in which Respondent failed to apply the requisite level of skill and care.

. . . Respondent did not differentiate between his defense of the 1.1(a) charge and the 1.1(b) charge. . . . Accordingly, we address here only the additional basis for the Committee's finding a 1.1(b) violation—the failure to open a probate estate for Maurice Robinson. Respondent argues that it was not a legal necessity to open an estate for Maurice, and if he was mistaken in this regard, it was due to excusable inadvertence that does not violate *Rule 1.1(b)*. . . .

Once again, the specific misconduct noted by the Committee is symptomatic of Respondent's greater failing. We find that Respondent failed to act with the skill and care that lawyers would generally use in probating an estate without detaining the specific question of whether he ignored the legal requirement to open an estate for Maurice Robinson. . . . Accordingly, we sustain the Committee's finding that Respondent violated *Rule 1.1(b)*.

*(continued)*

*Rules 3.3(a)(2)* and *8.4(c)* both relate to a lawyer's fundamental duty of honesty. *Rule 8.4(c)* contains a general prohibition against conduct involving dishonesty, fraud, deceit, or misrepresentation. *Rule 3.3* codifies a lawyer's specific duty of candor to a tribunal. The Committee found that Bar Counsel did not establish that Respondent knew or should have known that his client forged Clifton's signature on various probate documents. . . . We agree with the Committee that it was necessary to show either knowing or reckless dishonesty for a violation of either rule to arise from Respondent's submission of the forged probate documents. *In re Schneider,* 553 A.2d 206, 209 (D.C.1989); *In re Shorter,* 570 A.2d 760, 767–68 & n. 12 (D.C.1990). Submitting a document that another person has falsely signed is not obviously wrongful or dishonest. Accordingly, Bar Counsel has the burden of showing intent. *In re Romansky,* 825 A.2d 311, 315 (D.C.2003). The Committee credited Respondent's testimony that he had no reason to doubt the word of his client. Accordingly, the Committee found that Respondent's conduct was neither reckless nor intentional. We will not disturb this finding, which is based on a determination that is within the sphere customarily left to the fact finder. See *In re Arneja,* 790 A.2d 552, 555 (D.C.2002) (citing *Micheel,* 610 A.2d at 234).

. . . The appropriate sanction is what is necessary to protect the public and the courts, to maintain the integrity of the profession and "to deter other attorneys from engaging in similar misconduct." *In re Uchendu,* 812 A.2d 933, 941 (D.C.2002) (internal citations omitted). Recognizing that each case must be evaluated on its facts, the sanction imposed must be consistent with cases involving comparable misconduct. D.C. Bar R. XI, § 9(g)(1); *In re Dunietz,* 687 A.2d 206, 211 (D.C.1996). On the facts before us, we conclude that a longer suspension than recommended by the Committee, with a portion stayed in favor of probation supervised by a practice monitor, is consistent with other cases involving similar misconduct and is necessary to protect the public, the courts, and the integrity of the profession and deter future misconduct on the part of others. . . .

. . . The Committee found that Respondent "engaged in serious misconduct that lead directly to an erroneous transfer of property and erroneous deed being filed with the Recorder of Deeds.". . . The Committee compared this conduct to other cases involving incompetence, conflict of interest, and interference with the administration of justice. The sanctions in the cases it considered ranged from public censure to a ninety-day suspension. . . .

The Committee noted that Respondent's misconduct was more serious . . . because of the multiplicity of violations at issue, and . . . because Respondent, . . . was dealing with a familiar area of law. . . . The Committee found that the Respondent's violations for conflict of interest and interference with the administration of justice were largely the result of incompetence and negligence. . . . We disagree with the Committee's analysis. As discussed above, we find that Respondent's conflict of interest was at the core of his misconduct. Sanctions in matters involving conflict of interest often involve lengthy suspensions, particularly where the conflict served the respondent's self-interest. See *In re McLain,* 671 A.2d 951 (D.C.1996) (90-day suspension for conflict of interest where respondent borrowed money from client); *In re Zelloe,* 686 A.2d 1034 (D.C.1996) (90-day suspension for failure to disclose personal interest and dishonesty in connection with a loan transaction); *In re Hager,* 812 A.2d 904 (D.C.2002) (one-year suspension for conflict of interest and dishonesty in connection with failure to disclose settlement-fee arrangement to clients); *In re James,* 452 A.2d 163 (D.C.1982), *cert denied,* 460 U.S. 1038, 103 S.Ct. 1429, 75 L.Ed.2d 789 (1983). . . Respondent's conflict of interest violation was serious and arose from self-interest. Although his misconduct . . . was not accompanied by dishonesty, it was accompanied by a violation of *Rule 8.4(d),* which is a serious aggravating factor. . . .

Respondent has been subject to discipline on two other occasions. First, he received an informal admonition for failing to supervise the work of an associate attorney in 1982. In 1990, Respondent was suspended for six months for negligent misappropriation for taking a fee from an estate without proper authorization. . . . The conduct at issue in the second proceeding is very similar to that at issue here. . . . As he did here, Respondent failed to make required filings and failed to attend a court hearing addressing these deficiencies. In both cases, Respondent's misconduct had the practical effect of obscuring the finances of an estate from the heirs and the Court. . . . This case suggests that either Respondent learned nothing from his last brush with the Board or that he has lapsed back into unacceptable conduct. We find that Respondent's prior discipline is highly relevant to the issue of sanction. . . .

The Committee concluded that because his client "was the apparent perpetrator of the forged probate documents and the beneficiary of both the resulting probate and erroneous real estate transaction, Respondent's actions cannot be said to have caused her prejudice." . . . Bar Counsel questions this conclusion, noting that Respondent's failure to properly transfer Yusef and Clifton Robinson's interests in the estate and failure to properly open an estate for Maurice Robinson prejudiced his client.... According to Bar Counsel, these failings lead directly to Carolyn Robinson's removal as personal representative and the subsequent civil law suit against her. Although we understand the Committee's reluctance to ascribe prejudice to a client whose own misconduct directly contributed to the adverse results against her, we agree with Bar Counsel that this does not diminish the role Respondent played in the outcome. Had Respondent contacted Clifton Robinson, which he should have done, he would have uncovered Carolyn Robinson's attempted misrepresentation and surely put a stop to it. But Respondent never even tried to make that initial contact. So rather than advising his client not to engage in self-dealing as the personal representative of the estate, Respondent ended up helping her to do so. She was prejudiced by this failure to receive competent legal counsel. Accordingly, we find that Respondent's misconduct ultimately did prejudice his client....

The Committee found that "Respondent remains in denial of any wrongful conduct on his part." ... Lack of remorse does not always weigh in favor of an enhanced sanction. See *In re Kennedy,* 542 A.2d 1225, 1231 (D.C.1988). Under the facts before us, however, where Respondent continues to advance what we consider to be patently erroneous arguments, Respondent's failure to acknowledge any wrongful conduct—or even errors in judgment—is troubling. See *Hager,* 812 A.2d at 915.... Accordingly, we have considered this fact in constructing our sanction as discussed below....

The Board must consider the "total picture" of Respondent's professional conduct. *In re Washington,* 541 A.2d 1276, 1283 (D.C.1988). This matter involves the failure to provide adequate legal services to a single client. Although there was no finding that Respondent acted dishonestly, his neglect of his ethical duties was born of a conflict of interest, coupled with incompetence and serious interference with the administration of justice, that were harmful to both his client and the Court. What is worse, Respondent was subject to previous discipline for similar failings. Under the circumstances, we find that a more substantial sanction than the sixty-day suspension recommended by the Committee is warranted.

A six-month suspension is within the range of sanctions provided for similar conflict of interest cases.... Although Respondent ... failed to obtain a wavier from his client, his misconduct goes far beyond that.... Respondent is an experienced attorney with two prior instances of discipline who has, *inter alia,* seriously interfered with the administration of justice. This weighs in favor of a more stringent sanction.

In *Hager,* the respondent put his own interests ahead of his ethical duties to his client in the course of negotiating a settlement. 812 A.2d at 921. In that action, respondent was suspended for one year for conduct that involved dishonesty in addition to self-serving conflict of interest. *Id.* at 917. The Court found that this conduct "demonstrated at best an ethical numbness to the integrity of the attorney–client relationship, the very core of the active practice of law." *Id.* at 921. Although not found to be dishonest, the instant Respondent's misconduct displays a similar failure to protect the integrity of the relationship at the core of our profession. We find Respondent's misconduct to be less serious than that at issue in *Hager,* but only slightly so. Moreover, the *Hager* Court noted mitigating factors, such as lack of prior discipline and the respondent's record of *pro bono* legal service, which are absent here.

Respondent's prior discipline makes this matter more serious than any of the cases discussed above. His misconduct is also more serious . . . in that it also interfered in the administration of justice and arose from his active legal practice. It is more serious than *Shay* because the conflict of interest was self-serving. However, the fact that Respondent was not found to be dishonest distinguishes this matter from *Hager.* Accordingly, we find that a suspension of more than ninety days, but less than one year is consistent with cases involving comparable misconduct.

. . . Here, there is a strong potential that Respondent, who has demonstrated a serious inattention to the details of his practice, could find himself in a similar situation in the future. Respondent has been sanctioned and suspended for misconduct of a similar character, albeit resulting in different violations, in the past. See generally *Evans,* 578 A.2d 1141. That Respondent is once again before the Board for similar conduct evidences that he has failed to take or maintain the necessary steps to ensure that his conduct meets the required ethical standards.

Our responsibility to the public does not permit us to assume that the Respondent will take these steps of his own accord. He continues to operate both a title company and law practice in the absence of sufficient procedures to protect against potential conflicts. He is willing to assign important tasks, such as responsibility for conflict waivers, court filings and court schedules, to employees, but does not appear to have adequate checks in place to ensure they are performed correctly. Finally, Respondent continues to insist that these procedures are proper and sufficient.

Under these circumstances, we find that the goals of protecting the public and the courts and maintaining

*(continued)*

the integrity of our profession will be best served by appointing a practice monitor to work with the Respondent to reform this practice and his conduct. Accordingly, we recommend that the Court impose a six-month suspension, with ninety days stayed contingent on Respondent's acceptance and successful completion of a one-year probationary period under the supervision of a practice monitor. We have relied on practice monitors in similar cases to help lawyers subject to discipline comply with their ethical obligations.

Accordingly, we recommend that the final ninety days of Respondent's six-month suspension be stayed contingent upon Respondent's agreement to be placed on probation for a period of one year. To ensure that he has sufficient preparation for reinstatement, before his probation begins, Respondent must submit to the Board and Bar Counsel proof that he has completed not less than six hours of continuing legal education courses concerning the proper handling of probate matters and legal ethics during his suspension. During his probation, Respondent will be supervised by a practice monitor to assist him in establishing better office procedures and controls to ensure that each client and matter he handles gets the necessary attention and preparation, and that all conflicts are disclosed, including any that arise out of the interface between Respondent's title company and his law practice. Respondent must meet with the practice monitor as the monitor deems necessary, but not less frequently than

four times a year, to review Respondent's active practice of law. The practice monitor will submit quarterly progress reports to the Board, with a copy to Bar Counsel. If at any point during that year of probation Respondent fails to cooperate with the practice monitor, he will be subject to revocation of probation and the imposition of the stayed ninety days of his suspension.

The Board sustains the Committee's finding that Respondent violated *Rules 1.1(a), 1.1(b), 1.7(b)(4)* and *8.4(d)*. We recommend the following sanction for these violations: (1) that Respondent be suspended for six months; (2) that during his suspension, Respondent be required to complete six hours of continuing education classes in probate law and legal ethics; (3) that the final ninety days of his suspension be stayed on the condition that Respondent agree to be placed on probation for a period of one year; (4) that during the probationary period Respondent be subject to oversight by a practice monitor; and (5) that failure to cooperate with the practice monitor shall constitute a violation of his probation resulting in the imposition of the stayed portion of his suspension.

BOARD ON PROFESSIONAL RESPONSIBILITY

## Case Review Question

Does an attorney owe any ethical obligation toward the opposition in a lawsuit?

## Confidentiality

### Rule 1.6: Confidentiality of Information

(a) A lawyer shall not reveal information relating to representation of a client unless the client consents after consultation, except for disclosures that are impliedly authorized in order to carry out the representation, and except as stated in paragraph (b).

(b) A lawyer may reveal such information to the extent the lawyer reasonably believes necessary:

   (1) to prevent the client from committing a criminal act that the lawyer believes is likely to result in imminent death or substantial bodily harm; or

   (2) to establish a claim or defense on behalf of the lawyer in a controversy between the lawyer and the client, to establish a defense to a criminal charge or civil claim against the lawyer based upon conduct in which the client was involved, or to respond to allegations in any proceeding concerning the lawyer's representation of the client (1999 ABA Model Rules of Professional Conduct).

**client confidentiality**
The obligation to retain all communications of any sort that occur within the attorney–client relationship as private and privileged.

The ethical requirement that is vigorously enforced is the duty to maintain **client confidentiality**. In only a handful of relationships will the courts protect private communications with total commitment. One is the attorney–client relationship. The benefits of protecting the confidentiality of such communications is seen as essential to the protection of the fundamental freedoms associated with the U.S. legal system. Other such relationships include minister–parishioner, physician–patient, and husband–wife. These are relationships that, by their nature, often involve private matters and communications that arise from a bond of trust between the parties. They are also seen as positive relationships that should be supported in and by society and government. The refusal of government to intrude on these relationships and expose their communications to compulsory disclosure is an obvious example of the original intent of the framers of the Constitution to protect individuals from unnecessary or unfair intrusion into private lives. The added benefit is to encourage full disclosure in highly personal relationships that can affect the legal rights of the individual, such as a client who is seeking assistance of legal counsel.

The privilege of confidential communications belongs exclusively to the party who is disclosing private information. In the attorney–client relationship, this party is the client. The privilege cannot be waived or in any way compromised by the attorney. The only exceptions occur when the client personally waives the privilege, when breach of the privilege is necessary to prevent a death or serious bodily harm, or when the client places the substance of the communication in issue or disclosure is necessary pursuant to court order. These exceptions are uncommon and highly scrutinized by the courts.

To qualify as an attorney–client communication, there must be a statement made verbally, nonverbally, or in a documentary form from a party who reasonably believes to be represented by the attorney and further reasonably believes the communication to be subject to the protection of the privilege. For example, the fact that one is a friend of an attorney does not create a professional relationship. Communications that take place as the product of social interaction are usually not considered privileged. Communications that take place before the establishment of a formal legal relationship would not be considered privileged unless those communications were made with the intent that such a relationship be formed as the result—that is, an initial consultation followed by an agreement for representation.

It is not necessary that a statement be made directly to an attorney to receive protected status as confidential. If the relationship exists, then statements made to an employee or other representative of the attorney—such as a paralegal, clerical staff, legal investigator, or another attorney connected with the primary attorney on the case—are also considered privileged. The ethical rules for attorneys require also that the attorneys take reasonable steps to see that their subordinates and associates maintain the same standards with respect to client communications. The failure to do this can have several negative effects. Of course, the attorney can be disciplined for inappropriate conduct that occurred with respect to a matter under his or her supervision. Another significant risk is that of a civil action for malfeasance by the client and against the attorney, the paralegal, or both. In such a case, the client need only prove that confidentiality was breached. In and of itself, this breach is considered to be damaging. There is no requirement to establish that the client suffered some personal or financial harm as the result of the breach.

It is impractical to think an attorney could or should oversee every word spoken and action taken by paralegals and other support staff. Each must monitor his or her own behavior and ensure that it meets the ethical requirements of the attorney. For this reason, it is essential that attorneys educate and impress on their staffs the importance of ethical conduct and make such behavior a key element of continued employment. When it comes to ethical behavior, the law grants little or no tolerance for laziness or neglect.

## APPLICATION 6.3

Mike and China are a married couple. China is a paralegal. Mike refers Salem, a co-worker, to the firm where China works for representation in a worker's compensation claim. China's supervising attorney is handling the case. However, China has been given the responsibility to assemble the necessary documents and research the legal issues. Over dinner, China tells Mike that the case is going to be a difficult one because the individual waited so long to file the claim. She does think they will be successful, but not as much as they could have been if so much time had not elapsed. The next day over lunch, Mike tells several of his co-workers about the conversation. Salem is extremely upset that a staff member from her attorney's office was discussing the case outside the office and that it has now become a topic of conversation at her workplace. She is further concerned that her employer will perceive the gossip as encouraging litigation against the employer and that she will somehow be held accountable.

*Point for Discussion:* Would there be an ethical obligation for China to refrain from discussing the case with her husband because he referred the client to the firm?

## ASSIGNMENT 6.2

With regard to the situation described in Application 6.3, explain why each person listed below would or would not have an ethical obligation to keep information about the case confidential:

1. the supervising attorney
2. China
3. China's husband, Mike
4. Salem
5. Mike's

### Conflict of Interest

#### Rule 1.7: Conflict of Interest: General Rule

(a) A lawyer shall not represent a client if the representation of that client will be directly adverse to another client unless:

   (1) the lawyer reasonably believes the representation will not adversely affect the relationship with the other client; and

   (2) each client consents after consultation.

(b) A lawyer shall not represent a client if the representation of that client may be materially limited by the lawyer's responsibilities to another client or to a third person, or by the lawyer's own interests, unless:

   (1) the lawyer reasonably believes the representation will not be adversely affected; and

   (2) the client consents after consultation. When representation of multiple clients in a single matter is undertaken, the consultation shall include explanation of the implications of the common representation and the advantages and risks involved (ABA Model Rules of Professional Conduct, 1999).

**conflict of interest**
Either the appearance of or actual divided loyalty by one who is a fiduciary.

The issue of **conflict of interest** is a particularly difficult one for attorneys. Unlike other professions, the legal profession is based on an adversarial system. There are conflicting sides to a lawsuit, and each has strategies and information that is not available to the other. Unlike the physician–patient or minister–parishioner relationship, the attorney may also have personal interests that could potentially conflict with those of the client and the duty to put the client's interests first. A wide variety of situations can present conflict-of-interest questions, ranging from a current or former professional relationship with an opposing party to a business opportunity in which both the attorney and the client might be involved.

All professions, including law, have a certain percentage of turnover. It is unusual these days for someone to accept a position and keep that same job for the remainder of his or her career. As opportunities arise, interests change, or personal conflicts develop, people change jobs. Because legal training is relatively specific, the majority of these changes take place within the same employment area both in type of work and geography. The potential for problems is enormous. What happens when a person leaves a job with one local firm and accepts a position with another firm that represents the opposition in several cases? If the first job was of long duration, the individual could have dealt with literally thousands of cases. Working at a firm with clients who are adversaries in any of these cases creates an ethical conflict of interest. The client of the former firm may be at a disadvantage because the legal professional had access to his or her file and is now employed by the opposition. Presumably, the knowledge gained as part of the fiduciary relationship could now be used against the client. To avoid this type of occurrence and unfair treatment of unsuspecting individuals, rules have been established to require certain safeguards to protect the a client's interests.

By definition, a fiduciary relationship is one of trust. The relationship between a lawyer and a client is fiduciary. As a result, the client is entitled to certain expressions of loyalty. This includes not only confidentiality but also that the client's interests will be put first. Thus, when legal professionals change employment, they are not permitted to have any type of contact or to disclose any information with respect to cases that involve either the former client or their adversaries. This is commonly known as *building an ethical wall*. To accomplish this, firms typically maintain a cross-referenced index of clients. Essentially, they maintain an index of all their own clients and a separate index of all opposing parties. It is also helpful to have an index of all opposing counsel in various law firms and the cases they represent. Any new employee should consult this and identify all opposing parties who are or were represented by their former employer. Each of these files should be earmarked in some way to indicate that the new employee is to have no contact with the case in any capacity. Even if the employee (lawyer, paralegal, etc.) did not have contact with the client's case at the former employer, the presumption remains that the accessibility to the file creates a dangerous situation for the client. The best way to avoid problems is to avoid the client's file at the new employer.

Another regularly used safeguard is for a legal professional to maintain an ongoing list of all client files, including names of opposition, with whom there is contact. Clients may change lawyers during the pendency of a lawsuit, and it is unreasonable to expect one to remember the name of every case. A list of client files allows an easier matching of potential conflicts when there is a change in employment. Whatever method is used, the key is to maintain a clear separation from any file with which there has been the opportunity for access to the opposing position's case. Luckily, with the advent of computers, such files and cross indexes are more easily generated than the hand-typed index cards for each client, opposition, and opposing counsel file of just a few years ago.

There are exceptions to the rule on conflicts with regard to client files. For example, a client may have more than one lawsuit pending or completed in the past for which there could be a conflicting interest. However, if there is absolutely no connection with the current case, then it may be permissible for an attorney, paralegal, or other legal personnel to assist on the current case. Even in this situation, there should be a full disclosure to both sides of the case and consent before any action is taken.

## APPLICATION 6.4

Lisa is the first and only paralegal at the small law firm of Smoke and Jolke. She came to the firm quite recently after working for two years in the local court. During college, Lisa worked part-time for the Acme Law Firm to gain experience. Acme is a large law firm that specializes in defense of personal injury lawsuits. One of the biggest cases ever handled by Acme was the defense of a commuter airline company that was sued after a plane crash in which there were no survivors. Lisa did not personally work on that case, but she did share an office with the paralegals that did. Because of unrelated issues, the airline company left Acme and hired the Beetum law firm for defense in the airline disaster case shortly after the case had begun. The case has been going on for some time now and is scheduled for trial in a few weeks unless a settlement is reached. Several of the victim's families were represented by attorney Sirius Shuster. A month ago, Sirius was shot and killed by a disgruntled client in a divorce case. The families of the air disaster victims who were represented by Sirius elected to hire Smoke and Jolke to take over their interests in the case.

The files for the case are extensive and need to be organized and summarized before the attorneys can evaluate them for settlement negotiations. This is exactly the type of work that Lisa was hired to do and the attorneys have asked her to handle this matter, although they are not yet aware that Acme represented the defense early on and have not considered that Lisa worked at Acme part-time in college while Acme was handling the case. Because Lisa once worked at a firm involved in a case with an adverse position, she has a conflict of interest and is ethically disqualified from having any contact with this case whatsoever. However, if the Beetum firm is made aware of the circumstances giving rise to the conflict and provides its consent, Lisa could perform work on the case. However, because the parties are in an adversarial position and the trial date is near, from a strategic standpoint, the Beetum firm would not likely grant their consent.

*Point for Discussion:* Would the matter be handled any differently if Lisa had worked as a file clerk at the other firm? What if she had been working as part of an unpaid internship?

Other issues that can bring about questions of conflict of interest are when a client and lawyer or other legal professional have common business interests. Because it is presumed that the legal professional may have expertise and skills that are superior to those of the client, such relationships are to be avoided. This includes entering into business relationships with clients other than as attorney–client (e.g., co-investors) and entering into competitive business opportunities in which the client would be considered a competitor. If such an opportunity is presented, the legal professional has the obligation to pass on it until such time as it becomes clear that the client has considered but has decided to disregard the opportunity. This approach ensures that the legal professional will not employ his or her professional skill to the detriment of the client. Similarly, a legal professional should generally represent a client in any matter that will result in additional benefits to the legal professional, such as preparing a will for someone in which the legal professional is named as beneficiary. A case such as this would be ripe for attack on the grounds that undue influence was exercised on the client. An exception, however, might be found if the attorney was the only surviving relative of the client and if other facts would make him or her by all indications the most likely beneficiary of the estate regardless of who prepared the will.

There are as many possibilities for conflict of interest as there are clients and attorneys. For this reason, the rules are broadly written, but the basic rule of thumb is that no action should be taken that could in any way be perceived as putting the interests of oneself or another ahead of those of the client or that could be considered as disloyal or a breach of trust in any fashion.

## Commitment to Zealous Representation

### Rule 1.3

A lawyer shall act with reasonable diligence and promptness in representing a client (ABA Model Rules of Professional Conduct, 2001).

Once a professional relationship with a client has been established, there is a duty to represent the client with complete professionalism. This requires that the best efforts of the legal professional be used in all aspects of the case. What constitutes zeal and professionalism is a somewhat open-ended question because every case is unique. However, certain steps can be taken to create and maintain a professional relationship with the client. Important considerations in any professional legal relationship include the following:

1. communicating with clients on a regular basis to keep them abreast of the statute or changes in the matters of representation;

2. meeting all deadlines in a timely manner with respect to communications with the opposition, courts, and all legal proceedings;

3. making sure the client understands the typical steps in the matter of representation and the time frames generally associated with each step;

4. responding promptly and completely to all inquiries of the client, no matter how trivial they seem;

5. providing a thorough explanation of all billing and expenditures made on behalf of the client and for which the client is responsible;

6. consulting the client in advance on all matters that affect the cost or potential outcome of the case;

7. documenting the time, date, and nature of all communications with the client and concerning matters of representation; and

8. demonstrating an ongoing interest in the matters of representation.

These considerations take time—and in the profession of law, time is money. Each item also leads to ethical and effective representation and client relations. The general attitude reflected in the manner and actions of the legal professional has a direct impact on future referrals and client satisfaction. Thus, such behaviors as those listed are not only professional, ethical, and supportive of the duties of the legal professional but also ultimately good public relations and marketing.

## CASE

### *Slovensky v. Friedman et al.,*

### 142 Cal.App.4th 1518, 49 Cal.Rptr.3d 60, 06 Cal. Daily Op. Serv. 8904, 2006

In the following case, although malpractice appears to have been present, the essential element of damages as a result of the malpractice is brought into question.

. . . In March 2000, she [plaintiff] retained defendants to prosecute her toxic mold personal injury action against Sequoia Fairway Apartments (The Fairways).

Defendants said they had about 20 other plaintiffs with claims against The Fairways and would accept no more after her; in fact, they took on further clients and ultimately represented 41 other plaintiffs in 21 similar actions against The Fairways. Defendants did not obtain a waiver from plaintiff of the conflict inherent in the representation of multiple plaintiffs or advise her

*(continued)*

to consult independent counsel on this point before retaining them.

In August 2001, defendants told plaintiff they had scheduled a mediation. She had not known of this or consented to it in advance. She objected that defendants had not adequately analyzed her case and only sought a quick settlement. She demanded that they evaluate and treat her case separately, not as part of a global pool. They assured her they were doing so.

On August 28, 2001, defendants faxed a letter protected by attorney–client privilege to her treating physician's office without plaintiff's knowledge or consent. The letter contained privileged, private facts about plaintiff's case unrelated to and unnecessary for her treatment.

On August 31, 2001, defendant Cutter met with plaintiff and pressured her to sign an agreement to a proposed settlement in a specified sum. Plaintiff gave Cutter the agreement on the condition that he could not use it without further written consent from her. Defendants did not advise plaintiff that she could or should obtain independent legal advice before signing the agreement.

During September 2001, Cutter harassed plaintiff with unannounced home visits and numerous telephone calls, exerting enormous pressure on her to agree to settle her case for the proposed amount. To stop Cutter's harassment, plaintiff agreed to come to his office on September 7, 2001. She told him she could not sign a settlement agreement and release because neither she nor defendants had adequate information about her medical condition and prognosis.

On September 19, 2001, plaintiff's doctor told her that Cutter had informed him plaintiff would be settling her case for the amount specified in defendants' letter to the doctor, which was more than any of defendants' other Fairways clients would receive. This information was within the attorney–client privilege, was not authorized for release to plaintiff's doctor, and was not necessary for his treatment of plaintiff.

As part of defendants' pressure campaign, defendants told plaintiff erroneously that her case was not being treated as part of a global settlement, but was being evaluated individually and independently; that the medical information she had was not reliable; and that she was not as sick from toxic mold exposure as she had been led to believe.

On September 20, 2001, at Cutter's insistence, plaintiff met again with him. He again attempted to pressure her into settling the case. She objected that they did not yet have adequate medical information. He made further erroneous statements to her about her condition and its future course. He also misstated to her that he had negotiated with defendants to win the stated amount for her and that it was a better settlement than those of younger and sicker plaintiffs. When she continued to resist, Cutter brought defendant Friedman into the meeting. Comparing her case to the recent World Trade Center bombings, Friedman told her she was fortunate to be alive and should settle. Plaintiff ultimately signed the pre-printed settlement agreement and release.

On November 10, 2001, Cutter sent plaintiff a limited power of attorney to enable him to endorse the jointly payable settlement check and secure his fee. Plaintiff did not sign the document.

On December 25, 2001, plaintiff received a letter from Cutter stating that The Fairways' attorneys had reissued the check with the Cutter Law Firm as sole payee, at Cutter's request; defendants had cashed the check and taken out their fees and plaintiff's proportionate share of costs. The rest was deposited into a separate account at Wells Fargo Bank in plaintiff's name, where it remains. These actions were done without plaintiff's knowledge or consent.

[Plaintiff brought suit alleging] Defendants failed to exercise the care, skill, knowledge, competence, and diligence required of them by the attorney–client relationship. Their representation of plaintiff violated *California Rules of Professional Conduct 3-310*. They breached their duty of confidentiality in violation of *Business and Professions Code* section 6068. They coerced plaintiff to settle the case and converted the settlement monies. But for defendants' conduct, plaintiff would have obtained a recovery in her case greater than that obtained by defendants, free of the taint of conflict of interest and conversion. . . . Plaintiff prayed for compensatory and punitive damages, costs of suit, and "such other and further relief as the Court may deem proper."

Defendants moved for summary judgment, asserting: (1) Plaintiff's cause of action for legal malpractice lacked merit because plaintiff could not prove causation for damages: she could not have obtained a better result absent the alleged malpractice because her underlying action was barred by the statute of limitations as of the date she retained defendants. (2) Plaintiff's cause of action for breach of fiduciary duty had no existence apart from her malpractice cause of action and failed on the same ground.

Defendants' separate statement of undisputed facts adduced evidence that plaintiff had notice of toxic mold in her apartment and resulting physical ailments well over one year before she retained defendants; she admitted her prior knowledge of the relevant facts to defendant Cutter on July 28, 2001; and her case settled for $340,000. The separate statement did not adduce any evidence as to breach of fiduciary duty. . . .

Plaintiff asserted and offered evidence purporting to show that she did not realize she had suffered toxic mold exposure until shortly before she retained defendants and triable issues of fact existed as to whether she should have known earlier; however, she did not dispute most of defendants' evidence that during the period 1997 to 1999 she was aware of the facts that she later claimed as proof of toxic mold exposure and damage. She also asserted defendants' breaches of fiduciary duty entitled her to fee disgorgement even if she could not prove malpractice damages, and defendants' failure to address her fiduciary breach cause of action was enough to defeat summary judgment. . . .

The trial court issued an order granting summary judgment on the following grounds:

1. Defendants had shown that the one-year statute of limitations for personal injury actions then in effect (Code Civ. Proc., former § 340(3)), raised as an affirmative defense to plaintiff's toxic mold complaint, had expired as of the date plaintiff first consulted defendants. . . . Since her complaint would have been found time-barred had it gone to trial, plaintiff could not have achieved a better outcome than defendants obtained for her; thus she could not prove damages for malpractice. Plaintiff had not raised a triable issue of material fact on this point.
2. Plaintiff's second cause of action for breach of fiduciary duty failed for the same reason. Because it incorporated by reference the damages alleged in the first cause of action, plaintiff's inability to show causation for damages was also fatal to the second cause of action.

. . . The trial court thereafter entered judgment dismissing plaintiff's action.

To prevail on a summary judgment motion that does not request summary adjudication in the alternative, the defendant must show conclusively that all of the plaintiff's causes of action or legal theories fail as a matter of law. (See *Jimenez v. Protective Life Ins. Co.* (1992) 8 Cal.App.4th 528, 534.)

Plaintiff contends defendants are not entitled to summary judgment because she has shown triable issues of fact as to legal malpractice and defendants failed to rebut her claim of fiduciary breach. We disagree. Like the trial court, we conclude that to avoid summary judgment plaintiff must show at least the possibility of proving damages from defendants' conduct and that she cannot do so. Because defendants won her a substantial recovery in a matter where she was not legally entitled to recover anything at all, plaintiff has no cognizable damage claim. . . .

It is undisputed that when plaintiff filed her toxic mold complaint it was subject to a one-year statute of limitations. (Code Civ. Proc., former § 340(3); see now § 335.1, added by Stats.2002, ch. 448, § 2 [extends personal injury limitations period to two years]). Defendants adduced much evidence that plaintiff was on actual or constructive notice of her cause of action well before the spring of 1999, yet did not consult with defendants until March 2000. Plaintiff admits she was aware of those facts, but claims they were insufficient as a matter of law to put her on notice of her cause of action, or at least that triable issues of fact remain on this point. Plaintiff is wrong.

Because plaintiff's claim was time-barred on the day she filed it, she was entitled to no recovery and would inevitably have lost the case had it not settled. Thus, the settlement defendants obtained for her was a windfall. As defendants' alleged malpractice did not damage her, her malpractice claim fails. . . .

"The elements of a cause of action for legal malpractice are (1) the attorney–client relationship or other basis for duty; (2) a negligent act or omission; (3) causation; and (4) damages." (*Kurinij v. Hanna & Morton* (1997) 55 Cal.App.4th 853, 863 (*Kurinij*); italics added.) Summary judgment is appropriate if the defendant negates any of these elements. (*Ibid.*)

. . . To win a legal malpractice action, the plaintiff must prove damages to a legal certainty, not to a mere probability. (*Barnard v. Langer* (2003) 109 Cal.App.4th 1453, 1461–1462.) Thus, a plaintiff who alleges an inadequate settlement in the underlying action must prove that, if not for the malpractice, she would certainly have received more money in settlement or at trial. (*Id.* at p. 1463.) Such claims are likely to be speculative, as even the most skillful attorneys can seldom know whether they obtained the best possible result; thus they are held only to the standard of whether the settlement was within the realm of reasonableness. (*Id.* at pp. 1462–1463, fn. 13, citing 4 Mallen, *Legal Malpractice* (5th ed. 2000) Error-Settlement, § 30.41, pp. 582–585.)

Here, though plaintiff won a substantial settlement, she contends defendants' negligence barred her from proving greater damages at trial. But to recover damages at trial, she would have had to defeat the statute of limitations defense. The undisputed facts reveal she could not have done so.

A cause of action accrues when the claim is complete with all of its elements. (*Norgart v. Upjohn Co.* (1999)

21 Cal.4th 383, 397. Although this ordinarily occurs on the date of the plaintiff's injury, accrual is postponed until the plaintiff either discovers or has reason to discover the existence of a claim, i.e., at least has reason to suspect a factual basis for its elements. (*Id.* at pp. 397–398; *Jolly v. Eli Lilly & Co.* (1988) 44 Cal.3d 1103, 1109 (*Jolly*).) "[P]laintiffs are required to conduct a reasonable investigation after becoming aware of an injury, and are charged with knowledge of the information that would have been revealed by such an investigation." (*Fox v. Ethicon Endo-Surgery, Inc.* (2005) 35 Cal.4th 797, 808.) So long as there is a reasonable ground for suspicion, the plaintiff must go out and find the facts; she cannot wait for the facts to find her. (*Jolly, supra,* 44 Cal.3d at p. 1111.)

Defendants alleged the following facts were undisputed:

1. Beginning no later than the fall of 1997, plaintiff experienced water intrusion into her apartment that was never resolved, making the apartment uninhabitable from around November 1997.

2. A bulletin from The Fairways management went out to tenants on May 8, 1998, stating in part: "We are aware that you have all received a letter from an attorney suggesting that harmful mold may be present in some apartments at The Fairways. . . . IF YOU SEE ANY EVIDENCE OF MOLD, OF ANY KIND, IN YOUR APARTMENT, PLEASE CONTACT THE MANAGEMENT OFFICE . . . SOME EFFECT [sic] FROM THESE TWO MOLDS ARE FLU-LIKE IN NATURE . . . we need to hear from you immediately if you are presently experiencing any water intrusion problem or see any evidence of damage, of any kind, from a prior event."

   Plaintiff admits she wrote and sent a letter dated May 11, 1998, which stated in part: "In response to your letter dated 5–8–98, left on my door on 5–9–98, I spoke with your business office and advised them that I don't have a mold problem[.]" Plaintiff refused to authorize entry into her apartment in her absence, allegedly because she kept firearms there.

3. On or about June 19, 1998, The Fairways' management issued a document to residents citing "[t]he Fairways mold abatement program[,]" stating that water intrusion leads to mold, and requesting entry and inspection. A telephone message slip in The Fairways' business records indicates plaintiff called, acknowledged the notice, and said she did not have a mold problem. Plaintiff neither recalls nor denies leaving this message.

4. Plaintiff and The Fairways did not agree on a mutually acceptable inspection date.

5. Plaintiff did not take air samples or samples from her walls or carpet for testing.

6. Before moving out, plaintiff photographed wall stains where water had leaked in the apartment. She believed that these brownish or black stains (which she described as looking "like mascara—runny mascara") were from leaking roofing paper or mud.

7. Before moving her furnishings out of the apartment no later than March 21, 1999, plaintiff threw out water-soaked clothing, shoes, boxes, and bedding. At times the carpet was also soaked.

8. Plaintiff applied to rent an apartment elsewhere on September 3, 1998, and leased an apartment beginning November 2, 1998.

9. Plaintiff contends she "was extremely sick from exposure to toxic mold which grew in [her] apartment because [her] landlord did not stop water intrusion into the apartment."

10. Plaintiff has suffered from headaches, sinus infections, nosebleeds, hearing loss, dental infections, skin irritations, difficulty in concentrating, chronic fatigue, respiratory distress, and respiratory ailments. Between October 1997 and the date plaintiff moved out of The Fairways, she experienced headaches, shortness of breath, fatigue, and dizziness.

11. Although she does not recall when it started, plaintiff had a "constant cough . . . such a bad cough that it was embarrassing[.]" She attributed it to Vicodin, which she began taking in 1997. A co-worker recalled that plaintiff coughed during the period 1997 to 1999 and had sought medical treatment for the cough.

12. Plaintiff began suffering from head and neck pain in 1997 and her other maladies around 1999. Plaintiff contends that as a result of toxic mold exposure, she suffers from headaches, sinus infections, ear infections, hearing loss, dental infections, skin irritations, difficulty in concentration, and respiratory distress.

13. Plaintiff first sought representation from defendants for a mold claim on March 21, 2000.

14. On or about July 28, 2001, plaintiff told defendant Cutter in a recorded conversation that the "water intrusion problems" in her apartment had begun in 1996 or 1997. Asked if she noticed mold then, she responded, "I didn't notice that there was mold, what I noticed is that . . . looked like soot, brown soot, dark stuff that was seeping through the ceiling."

In her separate statement opposing summary judgment, plaintiff admitted most of these alleged facts were undisputed.

Plaintiff purported to dispute statement No. 1 by asserting: "Defendants cite no evidence to support their assertion that plaintiff claims her apartment was uninhabitable beginning approximately November 1997." However, she did not dispute that she had experienced unresolved water intrusion into the apartment beginning in the fall of 1997.

Plaintiff also purported to dispute statements Nos. 9 and 10. As to statement No. 9, she admitted she had contended in the underlying lawsuit that she was sick from toxic mold exposure, but added: "As shown below in plaintiff's additional disputed facts, plaintiff was not so aware and did not so contend until 2000." As to statement No. 10 (listing her symptoms), she called it, "[u]ndisputed but misleading [because] [p]rior to 2000, plaintiff believed her health problems related to her 1997 auto accident. . . ."

Plaintiff further alleged as undisputed:

She first learned of her toxic mold exposure in January or February 2000. In February or March 2000, plaintiff realized from watching a news program about toxic mold at The Fairways that her apartment had looked worse than the one shown in the program. Although plaintiff had photographed the conditions in her apartment before moving out, she did not know she was photographing evidence of mold. After watching the program, plaintiff met with a city official who examined her photographs and advised her to see a doctor and an attorney right away. Until seeing the program, plaintiff thought what she had observed was leaking or staining of black roofing paper (looking like "runny mascara"); she did not know it was mold, which she believed to be "fuzzy stuff." Plaintiff believes she conveyed that understanding of her wall stains to The Fairways' business office. It took plaintiff six months to move from The Fairways to another complex; she spent time in The Fairways up until she handed in her keys on March 22, 1999, and did not fully vacate the apartment until then. Until early 2000, plaintiff thought her health problems had been caused by her February 1997 automobile accident, and she had so advised the attorney she consulted on March 21, 2000. As of then she did not know which, if any, of her health problems were attributable to toxic mold; therefore she asked defendants to let her drop her case if medical testing was negative. Plaintiff did not consider or discuss filing an action against The Fairways at any time before March 2000.

We conclude as a matter of law (as did the trial court) that plaintiff should have realized she had a cause of action long before March 2000. Beginning in fall 1997 she knew of unresolved water intrusion into her apartment that left black and brown stains on her walls; around the same time she developed a violent

and persistent cough. In May 1998, she received notice from The Fairways' management that apartments could have a mold problem related to water intrusion, that it could cause "flu-like" effects, and that tenants should notify management immediately of "any evidence of damage, of any kind, from a prior event." In June 1998, she received further notice to the same effect, along with a request to enter and inspect her apartment. In response to both notices she denied a mold problem and refused to permit inspection, even as she experienced a battery of physical symptoms—as of 1999 including headaches, sinus infections, chronic fatigue, and respiratory ailments, all reasonably describable as "flu-like"—along with the continuing water intrusion. She refused to believe the stains on her walls could be mold because she clung to the fixed idea—which she did nothing to test—that mold is "fuzzy," not "runny." She refused to investigate whether her physical problems could be mold-related because of her fixed idea that they stemmed from other causes.

When a person knows or believes she is suffering harm and a plausible explanation appears, she cannot reasonably refuse to investigate it merely because other explanations occur to her. A reasonable person in plaintiff's position would not have waited to learn from television news, long after vacating an apartment rendered uninhabitable by water intrusion, that what appeared on her walls could have been mold and could have caused her ailments. She would have put two and two together as soon as she got notice of mold problems from The Fairways and permitted a prompt inspection of her apartment; she also would have discussed the situation with her doctor. Having done those things, she would have discovered she had a cause of action before the statute of limitations expired.

Plaintiff asserts it was reasonable to believe her symptoms (not all of which were "flu-like") stemmed from her automobile accident or the medications prescribed for her afterward. She asserts The Fairways' "ambiguously worded letter" was too "vague" and "general" to give notice that she might have toxic mold in her apartment or that toxic mold could explain any of her health problems. Finally, she quotes dictionary definitions of "mold" and "fungi" to show she could reasonably have believed her wall stains were not mold because they were not "fuzzy." In other words, plaintiff still believes she was entitled to put her head in the sand and ignore all warning signals for years merely because she thought she could explain the facts in some other way. When it comes to statutes of limitations, the law disagrees.

*(continued)*

Plaintiff relies vainly on *Clark v. Baxter Healthcare Corp.* (2000) 83 Cal.App.4th 1048 and *Ward v. Westinghouse Canada, Inc.* (9th Cir.1994) 32 F.3d 1405. In both cases the plaintiffs got the benefit of the delayed-discovery rule on summary judgment because it was unclear whether they reasonably could have known the negligent causes of their injuries before the statute of limitations expired. (*Clark, supra,* 83 Cal.App.4th at pp. 1052–1053, 1057–1059; *Ward, supra,* 32 F.3d at pp. 1406–1408; see *Jolly, supra,* 44 Cal.3d at pp. 1109–1114.) But here plaintiff knew from the fall of 1997 on that The Fairways had wrongfully failed to prevent or remediate water intrusion into her apartment, and learned from The Fairways in mid-1998 that this problem could cause toxic mold. Thus she was fully on notice of the negligent cause of her injury almost two years before she filed suit. The delayed-discovery rule does not help plaintiff.

If a plaintiff has let the limitations period on her cause of action expire because she clung to a mistaken theory until it was too late, she will normally lose her lawsuit. That did not happen to plaintiff here because defendants won her a settlement. If she had fired them so as to proceed apart from the other plaintiffs, The Fairways certainly would have found the fatal flaw in her case. It had no incentive to do so as long as the case was part of a package settlement. . . .

We agree with the trial court that plaintiff cannot show damages from defendants' alleged malpractice as a matter of law.

To the extent plaintiff's fiduciary breach claim alleges the same damages as her malpractice claim, it fails for the same reason. Plaintiff contends, however, that defendants' fiduciary breach entitles her to disgorgement of her fees even if she cannot prove malpractice damages, and defendants' failure to confute her allegations of fiduciary breach compels reversal of the summary judgment. We disagree with both contentions.

Where a defendant moving for summary judgment has failed to controvert factual allegations in the complaint, the trial court must deem the allegations true for purposes of the motion. (*Cox v. State of California* (1970) 3 Cal.App.3d 301, 309.) As noted, defendants did not controvert plaintiff's fiduciary breach allegations on their motion, but attempted to do so for the first time in replying to plaintiff's opposition. That is too late. (*San Diego Watercrafts, Inc. v. Wells Fargo Bank* (2002) 102 Cal .App.4th 308, 316; see *United Community Church v. Garcin* (1991) 231 Cal.App.3d 327, 337.)

Therefore, for purposes of review, we accept as true plaintiff's allegations in her complaint that defendants concealed and misrepresented material facts while dealing with plaintiff, thus violating professional duties spelled out in rule 3-310 of the *California Rules of Professional Conduct* and in *Business and Professions Code* section 6068. Specifically, they misrepresented to plaintiff that they were evaluating and pursuing her case on its own merits, while actually lumping it in with other plaintiffs' cases to seek a global settlement with The Fairways. They failed to advise her of the conflicts arising from this course of action or of her right to seek disinterested advice about whether to waive the conflicts. They concealed from her that the success of the global settlement negotiations turned on her acceptance of the settlement amount worked out by counsel without regard to the merits of her case. They made repeated false statements to plaintiff to pressure her into accepting the settlement. They breached confidentiality to enlist her physician as an agent in their campaign against her. They used pressure tactics to break down her resistance. Finally, after obtaining her consent to the settlement through these improper means, they unilaterally and without notice had her settlement check reissued to themselves so they could deduct their fees.

"[A] breach of fiduciary duty is a species of tort distinct from a cause of action for professional negligence. [Citations.] The elements of a cause of action for breach of fiduciary duty are: (1) existence of a fiduciary duty; (2) breach of the fiduciary duty; and (3) damage proximately caused by the breach. [Citation.]" (*Stanley v. Richmond* (1995) 35 Cal.App.4th 1070, 1086 (*Stanley*).)

"The attorney–client relationship is a fiduciary relation of the very highest character imposing on the attorney a duty to communicate to the client whatever information the attorney has or may acquire in relation to the subject matter of the transaction. [Citations.]" (*Beery v. State Bar* (1987) 43 Cal.3d 802, 813.)

"The scope of an attorney's duty may be determined as a matter of law based on the Rules of Professional Conduct which, 'together with statutes and general principles relating to other fiduciary relationships, all help define the duty component of the fiduciary duty which an attorney owes to his [or her] client.' [Citations.] Whether an attorney has breached a fiduciary duty to his or her client is generally a question of fact. [Citation.]" (*Stanley, supra,* 35 Cal.App.4th at pp. 1086–1087.)

It is undisputed that defendants owed plaintiff a fiduciary duty. Because they failed to controvert plaintiff's factual allegations, their breach of this duty is also undisputed. However, that still leaves unresolved whether plaintiff can establish a triable issue of fact as to damages. We conclude she cannot.

Disgorgement of fees may be an appropriate remedy for an attorney's breach of fiduciary duty. (See, e.g., *In re Fountain* (1977) 74 Cal.App.3d 715, 719 (*Fountain*).) As we shall explain, plaintiff's failure to plead that remedy by name does not prevent her from claiming it.

We recognized in our landmark case, *FPI Development, Inc. v. Nakashima* (1991) 231 Cal.App.3d 367, authored by Justice Blease, that the pleadings delimit the scope of the issues on summary judgment. (*Id.* at p. 381.) However, nothing in FPI suggests that a plaintiff facing summary judgment must adhere to any special rules of pleading. Nor do we know of any other authority so holding. When we apply traditional rules of pleading, we conclude, contrary to the trial court, that plaintiff adequately pled the remedy of disgorgement of fees.

Disgorgement of attorney's fees is a remedy sought by plaintiff. There is a "basic distinction . . . between the cause of action (the primary right and duty, and the violation thereof) and the remedy or relief sought." (4 Witkin, *Cal. Procedure* (4th ed. 1997) Pleading, § 30, p. 92.) "The gravamen, or essential nature . . . of a cause of action is determined by the primary right alleged to have been violated, not by the remedy sought. [Citation.]" (*McDowell v. Watson* (1997) 59 Cal.App.4th 1155, 1159.)

"Since 1872, *Code of Civil Procedure* section 580 has provided that '[t]he relief granted to the plaintiff, if there be no answer, cannot exceed that which he shall have demanded in his complaint; but in any other case, the court may grant him any relief consistent with the case made by the complaint and embraced within the issue.'" (*Castaic Clay Manufacturing Co. v. Dedes* (1987) 195 Cal.App.3d 444, 449.)

"The prayer for relief is no part of the statement of fact, and the fact that too much is asked for does not affect the cause of action stated. Under the prayer for general relief the court can give such judgment as plaintiffs show themselves entitled to, and as may be necessary to effect justice between the parties and protect the rights of both." (*Matteson v. Wagoner* (1905) 147 Cal. 739, 745 (*Matteson*); italics added.) . . .

Plaintiff's claim for disgorgement of fees does not fall on summary judgment merely because she did not use the word "disgorgement" in her complaint. Plaintiff's general prayer for "such other and further relief as the Court may deem proper" was sufficient to plead entitlement to disgorgement as a remedy. (*Matteson, supra,* 147 Cal. at p. 745.) The trial court erred by ruling that plaintiff had to specially plead disgorgement.

Nevertheless, plaintiff's disgorgement claim fails as a matter of law. Where an attorney's misrepresentation or concealment has caused the client no damage, disgorgement of fees is not warranted. (*Frye v. Tenderloin Housing Clinic, Inc.* (2006) 38 Cal.4th 23, 48.) Plaintiff cites *Fountain, supra,* 74 Cal.App.3d 715, and *In re Occidental Financial Group, Inc.* (9th Cir.1994) 40 F.3d 1059 (*Occidental*), but neither creates an exception to the *Frye* rule.

In *Fountain, supra,* 74 Cal.App.3d 715, an attorney accepted a fee to file notice of a criminal appeal, then filed one that was late and inadequate, effectively forfeiting his client's appeal rights. (*Id.* at pp. 717–719.) In *Occidental, supra,* 40 F.3d 1059, an attorney accepted a retainer to file for bankruptcy on behalf of certain firms without disclosing, as required by bankruptcy law, that he also represented the firms' owners, whose interests might be adverse to those of the creditors' committee that had retained him. (*Id.* at pp. 1061–1063.) Thus, in *Fountain* the client had suffered actual damage, and in *Occidental,* the clients stood to suffer potential damage.

Here, by contrast, the only apparent consequence of defendants' fiduciary breach was a substantial settlement plaintiff could not otherwise have obtained. . . . Under these circumstances, the *Frye* rule, *supra,* 38 Cal.4th 34, controls and plaintiff's fiduciary breach claim fails because she cannot establish damages.

The judgment is affirmed. The parties shall bear their own costs on appeal. (Cal. Rules of Court, rule 27(a)(4).)

## Case Review Question

If the statute of limitations had not previously run, would the case have had a different outcome because the amount of damages would have been speculative?

# THE RESULT OF ETHICAL VIOLATIONS

The license to practice law, the certification granted by NALA, and the validation by NFPA are essentially earned privileges. When someone demonstrates the requisite ability and qualifications to receive the license or certification, it is done subject to certain conditions. Failure to abide by these conditions can have a variety of results.

As mentioned, a lawyer can be the subject of disciplinary action by the professional body. A lawyer, paralegal, or other members of the support staff may also be the subject of legal action in the courts initiated by injured parties. These remedies are not mutually exclusive in any way. The professional discipline of an attorney and a lawsuit against a lawyer or paralegal are seen as separate and distinct. The disciplinary action is designed to protect an unwitting public by taking action against the licensure or certification of someone who negligently or deliberately acts unethically in violation of these license or certification requirements. The focus of the lawsuit is to compensate a specifically injured party for damage caused as the result of another's unethical conduct.

In the first circumstance; anyone can lodge a complaint with the appropriate administrative body stating the facts of the alleged unethical behavior. The allegations of the complaint are investigated and a determination made as to whether action is warranted. In some circumstances, a hearing may be held to give the alleged wrongdoer the opportunity to present a response to the complaint in person. Once the merits of the complaint have been evaluated, there are several possible outcomes. Although each state has its own specific rules and disciplinary procedures, common outcomes are often utilized. It is possible that the authoritative body will find the complaint unfounded or the conduct insufficient to constitute a clear violation worthy of disciplinary action. Conversely, if a violation has been found to have occurred, then a variety of forms of discipline may be imposed based on severity, willfulness, previous history of violations, and damage to the client. These include everything from a formal reprimand to suspension or total revocation of licensure. Any negative outcome in a disciplinary action almost always results in negative publicity and a likely increase in the cost of malpractice insurance; and possibly the loss of income as the result of lost business. In some instances, the individual who is the subject of the complaint may be required to attend educational programs to raise his or her level of awareness of ethical duties.

In addition to disciplinary action, the party allegedly injured by the unethical conduct can often file a legal action for malfeasance against the attorney and any involved support staff. The procedure would be the same as for any other type of personal injury lawsuit, including a statement of the allegedly wrongful conduct by the defendant and the consequent injury to the party filing suit (plaintiff). The possible outcome would range from dismissal of the action to a monetary judgment against the defendant and payable to the plaintiff. The party or parties named could include the party who is accused of having acted unethically and, in some instances, the employer if the accused conduct is performed by a subordinate employee of one required by law to conduct business in an ethical manner.

## ETHICAL CONSIDERATIONS

Ethical conduct is expected among the members of the general population, but only a handful of professions condition licensure and the practice of the profession on continued ethical conduct. The legal profession is one such entity. The failure of a lawyer or any other individual working in the legal field to act ethically can have many repercussions ranging from mild to severe, including criminal prosecution in some cases. The duty to act ethically hinges on the fiduciary relationship with the innocent persons who place their trust, and sometimes their personal and financial well-being, in the hands of the legal professionals.

## ETHICAL CIRCUMSTANCES

Simone is the beneficiary of a large inheritance. In a short time she has managed to squander nearly half of the money. In an attempt to preserve the balance, which if properly handled will support her for the rest of her life, Simone hires an attorney to create a trust fund. She trusts the attorney and asks her to manage the trust and distribute the interest earned by the investment of the money on a periodic basis. The attorney agrees. What Simone does not know is that the attorney borrows money from the trust fund now and then. In the past, the money has always been repaid within a year of the "loan." What, if anything, is wrong with the conduct of the attorney?

## ● CHAPTER SUMMARY

The duties and obligations associated with legal ethics are present in every area of law and at every level of the law-related professions. For this reason, it should be a constant presence in the minds of legal professionals and should guide the manner in which they do their work. Keys to ethical behavior consist of acting at all times with honesty, integrity, and the clients' best interest at the forefront. Because the legal relationship to a client is a fiduciary one, the duty to honor a client's trust in matters of confidence is paramount. The privilege of confidentiality belongs to the client and typically can only be waived by the client unless a court order or planned criminal conduct is involved. In addition to confidentiality, all legal professionals, associates, and support staff are required to avoid situations in which a conflict of interest might occur. This requires that the interests of the client come first in matters of business opportunities and in matters involving employment of the legal professional. At no time may an attorney or other legal professional be in a position that might create an occasion for the breach of any other ethical duty, such as confidentiality, or result in benefit to the professional at the expense of the client. In line with this is the obligation to undertake to perform only those duties for which the legal professional has achieved an adequate level of competence. If this cannot be accomplished, then there is an obligation to decline the representation or assistance. This level of competence requires not only training but also current knowledge in the area of concern. Thus, legal professionals are under a continuing obligation to maintain their skills and knowledge of the law. Finally, legal professionals are required to act at all times with a degree of professionalism that constitutes zealous representation of their clients. While attorneys are bound by the ABA code of ethics, the NALA has adopted its own code, which incorporates ABA's code by reference. All subordinate staff members and those associated with the delivery of legal services are similarly bound as a matter of reality even if not as a condition of licensure. The failure to honor legal ethical standards can result in formal disciplinary action, legal action in civil court, and long-term effects on professional employment and advancement.

## ● CHAPTER TERMS

| | | |
|---|---|---|
| competence | conflict of interest | fiduciary |
| client confidentiality | | |

## ● REVIEW QUESTIONS

1. Why are attorney–client communications confidential?
2. What is an ethical wall?
3. What is a conflict of interest?
4. Describe the general ethical responsibilities of a paralegal employed by an attorney.
5. Who in the law office is bound to keep attorney–client communications privileged?
6. Why are ethical codes in place for attorneys and paralegals?

7. What difficulty can arise from continuing representation in a case where there is a conflict of interest?

8. What are the potential consequences of ethical violations?

9. What is the requirement regarding competent representation?

10. When can an attorney represent as the only counsel in a case such as a dissolution of marriage?

## ● | HELPFUL WEB SITES

| | |
|---|---|
| American Bar Association Center for Professional Responsibility | http://www.ABANET.org/cpr/home.html |
| NFPA Model Code of Ethics | http://www.paralegals.org/ |
| NALA Code of Ethics and Professional Responsibility | http://www.nala.org/whatis-Code.htm |
| Legal Ethics Resources | http://www.legalethics.com |

## ● | INTERNET ASSIGNMENT 6.1

Identify the Internet site for your state that contains the ethical requirements for members of the state bar.

## ● | INTERNET ASSIGNMENT 6.2

Where is disciplinary action against attorneys published in your jurisdiction?

### STUDENT CD-ROM

For additional materials, please go to the CD in this book.

### ONLINE COMPANION™

For additional resources, please go to www.paralegal.delmar.cengage.com

# CHAPTER 7

## Substantive and Procedural Issues

### THE THEORY OF FOURS

There are almost as many theories on how certain personality types develop and function as there are people, but the simple theory of fours seems to lend itself to the discussion of substantive and procedural law. Years ago, someone developed a theory that hypothesizes that all of humankind can be placed on a scale of 1 to 7. Those who are in the 1 category are essentially alive and that is all. This would include an individual in a persistent vegetative state with no real cognitive function. At the other end of the scale are the 7s. A 7 is someone with incredible vision for the possibilities in life whether they be motivated by good or evil. Examples include such individuals as the first settlers in America, the founding fathers, Abraham Lincoln, Franklin Roosevelt, John F. Kennedy, and even Adolph Hitler. The rest of us fall somewhere in the middle. The determining factor to one's number is adaptability.

At age eight, this author's parents were called to school because she had announced to her teacher and the second grade class, "Rules are made for people who aren't smart enough to know what to do." This statement was somewhat limited and naive, but it was also fairly insightful for an eight-year-old, and there was some foundation in truth. Our ability to adapt to situations, solve problems, and resolve conflict is directly impacted by our personality. Those who are highly adaptable often accomplish more goals in life, but to do this they must learn to conform when appropriate or necessary.

Most people fall somewhere in the 5 to 6 range. However, there are the 4s. For many people, the 4s frustrate us yet guide us. They confine us and maintain order. The 4s are those who, although not readily adaptable or receptive to change, are masters of organization. They know the rules, sometimes make them, and help others follow the rules for the benefit of the whole population. In law, substance is what will decide a case, but it is the purpose of the rules of procedure, as frustrating as they might sometimes be, to provide a level playing field for all concerned, regardless of their position.

So now the question begs to be asked, where do you fall on the scale?

## CHAPTER OBJECTIVES

After reading this chapter, you should be able to:

- Distinguish substantive and procedural law.

- Explain the difference in procedure between a jury trial and a bench trial.

- Discuss the function and application of an appellate court.

- Explain the purpose and method of applicability of the rules of evidence.

- List and describe each stage of a trial.

- Identify the difference between a motion for judgment NOV and a motion for new trial.

- Explain the purpose of exceptions to hearsay evidence.

- List the two functions of substantive law.

## SUBSTANTIVE AND PROCEDURAL ISSUES

The body of law that has developed in this country can be organized in countless ways. Each method of organization provides a way to distinguish one area of law from another. First, all law can be defined as *substantive* or *procedural*. In addition, law can be divided into *criminal* and *civil law* (of which *contract law* and *tort law* are types). The purpose of this chapter is to clarify the differences between substantive and procedural law and to provide an understanding of the procedural aspects of civil law. Criminal procedure is addressed in Chapter 16. Later chapters will also examine various kinds of civil and criminal substantive as well as procedural law.

### The Difference Between Civil and Criminal Law

**civil law**
Law that governs the private rights of individuals, legal entities, and government.

Let us begin by clarifying the difference between civil and criminal law. **Civil law** governs the issues that arise between parties over private rights. Thus, a citizen who sues another for an invasion of personal rights has grounds for a civil case. Other examples are an individual suing the government for an invasion of private rights and a suit brought by one citizen against another for property damage or

150

physical injury caused by an automobile accident. A civil case is brought by the injured party for damage to his or her personal rights, person, or property. The injured party seeks some sort of compensation (usually monetary) for the injury or damage to the person or property.

A criminal case is a suit that is brought by the government for violation or injury to public rights. Even though a crime may be perpetrated against a single victim, the public as a whole demands safety and certain conduct by all persons. An individual who violates these demands against anyone violates the rights of the public as a whole. The government enforces the rights of the public through prosecution based on criminal law, which ranges from parking violations to murder. Criminal law includes all laws designed by the legislature to maintain order and safety in our society. It carries a penalty of a fine, imprisonment, or community service that is paid to the government rather than to a particular victim. A court may also order restitution (compensation) to the victim. With the exception of an order of restitution, generally any claim for damages by a victim who may have been injured by a crime must be resolved in a civil suit brought by the injured party against the alleged criminal.

In a civil case, the penalties are quite different. First, there is no imprisonment. Second, any judgment that awards money is payable to the individual whose rights were invaded and injured. The award of money should be sufficient to compensate the injured party for the reasonable cost of the injuries, thus the term **compensatory damages**. In addition, in cases where money cannot adequately compensate but some action could, the guilty party may be ordered to act or refrain from acting in a certain way. This is called *injunctive relief* and, more particularly, *specific performance*. This type of relief is quite limited. Some jurisdictions also permit the recovery of punitive damages (also known as *exemplary damages*), which are additional monies that the defendant is ordered to pay as a form of punishment. The reasoning behind punitive damages is that some actions are so grossly improper that the defendant should be punished in a way that will serve as an example to others who might contemplate the same wrongful conduct.

**compensatory damages**
An award of money payable to the injured party for the reasonable cost of the injuries.

In civil cases, procedural law takes effect when citizens bring a dispute to the legal system. In criminal law, the law-enforcement agencies and prosecutors who are part of the legal system initiate a claim against a citizen. Therefore, criminal procedural law begins at the time the law-enforcement personnel anticipate that they will bring a dispute into the legal system. This is addressed at great length in Chapter 16. The remainder of the discussion in this chapter is confined to issues of civil law.

## APPLICATION 7.1

Van left his wife, Riley, for another woman named Kim, whom he soon married. About a year later, Van and Kim were found shot to death. Riley was charged with the murders. However, at trial, the jury did not find beyond a reasonable doubt that Riley had committed the murders. Had the standard been only a preponderance of evidence, it is probable that Riley would have been convicted.

*Point for Discussion:* Why isn't the same standard of evidence used in both civil and criminal cases?

## ASSIGNMENT 7.1

Determine which of the following scenarios would likely give way to a criminal trial, a civil trial, or both. Explain your answers.

Cr 1. Ticket for failing to wear a seatbelt.

Ci 2. Individual A takes legal action against individual B after B's car collides with A's car in a private parking lot.

B 3. In situation 2, add the fact that A watches the incident from a window and then watches B immediately leave the lot.

B 4. Gomez is a police officer on patrol when his car is struck head-on by Jesse, who is found to have a blood alcohol more than double the legal limit.

B 5. Kim is a paralegal who sells so-called how-to kits for do-it-yourself divorces, wills, and real estate transactions. She gave one customer step-by-step instructions on how to fight a custody battle. The customer lost custody of her children and wants Kim to be held accountable.

Ci 6. Jim is a divorce attorney. In one case, his clients lose custody of their children and feel it was the result of Jim's bad performance of legal services.

Ci 7. Genevieve is sitting in a restaurant when her chair gives way. She crashes to the floor and breaks several bones.

B 8. George is in a restaurant and orders the daily special of meatloaf. The waiter screams that meatloaf was yesterday's special. He starts screaming and assaults George. George suffers several broken bones in his face.

B 9. Constance is a nursing student training at a local hospital. When her supervising nurse is not present, Constance attempts to give an injection to a patient. She gives the injection improperly and causes the patient to suffer permanent nerve damage and resulting disability.

B 10. Jordan is a nursing student and is learning to give injections. She feels badly for a particular patient who is terminally ill and in extreme pain. Although Jordan is properly supervised in her administration of medication, the supervising nurse does not know that Jordan altered the medication to cause the patient to die within minutes.

## SUBSTANTIVE VERSUS PROCEDURAL LAW

For hundreds of years, substantive and procedural law have coexisted. Without procedural law, substantive law could never be created. Without substantive law, there would be no need for procedural law. More than ever in today's complex society, substantive law and procedural law clearly play equally important roles in our legal system.

### Substantive Law

**substantive law**
The law that creates and resolves the issue between the parties. Legal standards that guide conduct and that are applied to determine whether conduct was legally appropriate.

**Substantive law** creates, defines, and regulates rights as opposed to *protective, procedural,* or *remedial law,* which provides a method of enforcing rights.[1] It is exactly what its name implies: the body, essence, and substance that guides the conduct of citizens. It encompasses principles of right and wrong as well as the principle that wrong will result in penalty. It includes the rights and duties of citizens, and it provides the basis to resolve issues involving those rights. Every citizen has the right to live and enjoy his or her own property free from intrusion by other citizens. All members of a populous society are obligated to respect and not interfere with the rights of others. Substantive law establishes the extent of this right and obligation to which all persons are subject.

When a person engages in conduct that has an adverse effect on another individual, an injury may occur. An innocent injured party who wants to be compensated for the damage caused by the injury may request assistance from the legal system on the basis that the injuring party acted wrongfully. Such wrongful conduct gives rise to the dispute between the two parties. The court will examine the situation to determine whether the conduct of the party alleged to be at fault was indeed wrongful by society's standards. If it was, then the party will be judged and penalized. If it was not, then the party will be judged innocent. In either situation, the court resolves the issue based on what society has determined to be right and wrong conduct between individuals and entities.

## APPLICATION 7.2

Adam was driving down a busy street near a college campus when Nathan, who was late for class, ran out from between two parked cars. Adam's car struck Nathan and severely injured him. Nathan sued for his injuries, claiming that Adam's negligence caused the injuries when he failed to keep a proper lookout and failed to yield to a pedestrian. These were both items for which Adam was ticketed. Adam claimed the accident was primarily caused by Nathan, who was not in the marked crosswalk just fifty feet away. Nathan was cited for this. Adam also defends that he kept a proper lookout but that any view of Nathan was blocked by the parked vehicle, and Nathan ran into the street without looking. Adam claims his conduct was not the cause of Nathan's injuries.

The court in this case would hear evidence of both parties. If the court determined Adam could have avoided the injuries by keeping a better lookout and yielding to the pedestrian, then Adam would be judged liable and responsible to pay damages for the injuries. However, if the court determined that Nathan's conduct played such a role in the accident that Adam couldn't have avoided it, then there would not be a judgment against him. The existing legal standards of rightful and wrongful conduct of the parties are used to resolve the issue: in this case, not only the generally stated statutes on which the tickets issued were based but also the case law involving similar circumstances.

*Point for Discussion:* In this case, what would happen if the court found that both parties were in violation of the statutes and there was no substantive case law that addressed particular circumstances such as these when both parties appeared to be at fault and there was no clear-cut determination as to who had the superior responsibility to avoid the accident?

## Procedural Law

**Procedural law** prescribes a method of enforcing rights or of obtaining redress for the invasion of rights.[2] The basic function of civil procedural law is to facilitate the movement of a lawsuit through the legal system. Procedural laws are created to ensure that each party will be afforded fair and impartial treatment. Further, procedural law has its goal that judges and juries will receive only evidence that will allow them to make a fair and impartial decision.

Civil procedure can be likened to a large piece of machinery that assembles a product. It does not feel or possess opinions. The function of procedural law is to assemble all of the pieces into a complete product. The parties to the suit provide the pieces to the product at appropriate times and in the appropriate manner. The completed product delivered from the machine is the decision that resolves the dispute. This decision is based on the pieces of information (substantive law and facts of the case) that have been fed into the machine and assembled.

In the lawsuit discussed in Application 7.2, Adam and Nathan became involved in litigation. The principles of law that were applied in their case to determine who should prevail, based on the most reasonable explanation of the facts, is

**procedural law**
Law used to guide parties fairly and efficiently through the legal system.

substantive law. Procedural law also plays a part in the litigation and includes the following:

1. the time limit for bringing a lawsuit,
2. the manner in which the lawsuit is begun (e.g., by filing a complaint or petition),
3. the proper way to inform the defendant that a lawsuit has been filed,
4. the types of information that each party must release to the other party,
5. the procedure at trial,
6. the evidence that can be introduced at trial, and
7. the method for appealing the decision if the losing party feels the decision was unfair.

## The Common Ground

On occasion, substantive rights are affected by procedural law. Most often, when there is a conflict of law (different legal standards apply in different states) or when more than one jurisdiction has contact with the dispute, there is the potential for procedural law to affect the outcome of the suit rather than substantive law. Such a case could arise when the parties bring their action in federal court based on diversity of citizenship (discussed in Chapter 8). Another situation might involve a dispute based on a series of events that occurred in different jurisdictions and ultimately resulted in an injury.

In different jurisdictions, procedural law and conflicting substantive law may be dealt with differently. The general rule is that a court should attempt to apply its own procedural rules regardless of which substantive law applies.[3] The courts, including the U.S. Supreme Court, have addressed issues of this nature for quite some time with no final decision.

The issue of conflicting procedural and substantive standards from varying jurisdictions arises when more than one jurisdiction (area within a court's authority) could serve as the forum for a lawsuit. The party bringing the action will no doubt select the jurisdiction whose laws most favor the claim. An example is a choice between two states based on the statute of limitations laws. The statute of limitations is a procedural law in a jurisdiction that indicates the maximum amount of time in which a lawsuit can be commenced. For example, in some states, a personal injury claim must be brought within three years. In other states, the limit is one year. Thus, if a plaintiff in one of these states with a personal injury claim decides to file a suit two years after the injury, the suit could be brought only in a state with a three-year statute of limitations. In a jurisdiction with a one-year statute of limitations, the suit would be barred after one year had passed. Because the circumstances that produce a lawsuit sometimes occur in more than one jurisdiction, there may be more than one place where suit could be brought.

The conflict of the statute of limitations gave rise to the establishment of the *outcome determinative test* by the U.S. Supreme Court.[4] The test was originally created to be used by federal courts faced with a case based on state laws where more than one state is connected with the case or where either state law or federal law could be applied. Under this test, the court examines what would happen under each law. The goal is that the outcome should be the same whether the case is heard in federal court or state court (under state law). If the outcome of the suit would be different solely because of federal procedural rules (such as a statute of limitations that differs from the state statute of limitations), then the state procedural rule should be applied. The idea is to discourage persons from filing a case in a particular court just because they have a better possibility of winning in that court when they could not win in another court that also had jurisdiction. This practice is referred to as *forum shopping*. Courts encourage parties to select a court because it is the best equipped to hear their claim and consider all the evidence, not because it is the best court strategically. Although in reality part of diligent representation is making the best strategic moves, the courts have tried to place limits on this to the extent that strategy becomes an attempt at manipulation of the outcome, which is supposed to be under fair and impartial terms.

In recent years, the U.S. Supreme Court has formed a blend of the general rule and the outcome determinative test.[5] The accepted rule now is that a court should apply its own procedural rules when possible. However, when the laws of the various jurisdictions involved are so different that it is clear the plaintiff was shopping for the court with the most favorable laws and not for the most appropriate site for the case, the outcome determinative test should be applied.

## ASSIGNMENT 7.2

Consider the following case and explain why the case should or should not be dismissed.

Jeannie and Jim Khamee own a laundromat. One day, Jim was working on a dryer and had to remove the drum. When he replaced it, he accidentally left a small screwdriver inside. That evening Grace, came in and was in a hurry. She used the dryer on the high-heat setting, hoping to speed up the drying of her clothes but did not notice the screwdriver in the dryer. When she reached in to pull out her clothing she wrapped her hand around the screwdriver, suffering third degree burns on her palm. When she burned her hand, she jumped back and fell, striking her head on the floor. As a result of the fall, she suffered a traumatic brain injury.

Grace was a commercial artist, and the injuries prevented her from a full return to work for more than a year. Fifteen months after the accident, Grace was introduced to the laundromat's owners in a social setting. She told them what had happened. They expressed their condolences but offered no more information. They did offer to help with some of the medical bills because the injuries occurred on their property. They told her they would do what they could but that there had been no liability insurance on the property at the time of the accident. A few weeks later, Grace provided them with the remaining unpaid medical bills of $2,500 along with documentation of bills she had paid personally and through health insurance. The amount was more than $37,000. Grace had also lost income and suffered permanent scarring.

Approximately four months after the meeting, the owners sent Grace a check for $2,500 with a letter stating that they were sorry about the accident and felt it only right to help pay her damages. Grace cashed the check. She wrote to the Khamees and asked whether they intended to pay the other $37,000 in bills. They responded that they would like to help but needed time to get the money together. Despite subsequent letters from Grace, she heard no more from them. Grace sought legal counsel approximately one month after the two-year statute of limitations (time to bring a lawsuit after an injury) had expired. An investigation discovered that the laundromat had been closed for equipment repairs and cleaning of all units on the day of the accident until shortly before Grace arrived.

The case was brought against Jim and Jeannie Khamee. Their attorney responded with claims that the statute of limitations had run, and further, that there was no such person as "Jim" Khamee owned the laundromat. Grace's attorney discovered that Mozembiqueno was the real first name of the owner and he only went by the more American name of "Jim." However, only legal documents reflected this, and at all other times he was known publicly as Jim Khamee.

## THE CREATION AND APPLICATION OF CIVIL PROCEDURE LAW

Without procedural law, the legal system could not function in an equitable or efficient manner. As a result, rules of procedure are as important as the substantive law that determines an outcome of the case. Without them, there would be no appropriate and fair manner in which legal disputes could be brought to resolution. It would be akin to attempting to play a game in which there were no rules. If there were no rules, then how would either team ever know it had won?

## Creating Laws of Procedure

Laws of procedure, sometimes referred to as *rules*, are created by the authority of the legislature. Procedural law applies to all people and is created to facilitate an organized court system and to protect the constitutional guarantees to citizens. Because the laws deal with the mechanics of the court system, judges are often better equipped than the legislature to create fair and reasonable rules that provide for an efficient court system. Therefore, in many jurisdictions, the legislatures vest the courts with authority to create such laws. At the very least, the courts have input into what the procedural laws should be.

Even though they are created with the assistance of the judicial branch, procedural laws are adopted by the legislature as statutes. Thus, they can often be found in the published statutes along with the other enactments of the legislature. Although procedural rules are not published with the opinions of the judges on individual cases, interpretations of the rules often appear in judicial opinions.

## Types of Procedural Law

For the sake of convenience, procedural law has been divided into several categories. A person researching the law has a much easier time finding the particular laws or rules that apply to a given case if the law is organized according to subject. Most often, a jurisdiction will divide its procedural law into the following categories:

1. rules of civil procedure
2. rules of criminal procedure
3. rules of evidence
4. rules of appellate procedure

In addition to having the power to create rules that are enacted into law for an entire jurisdiction, courts generally have the power to create local rules that apply only to the court that creates them and to no other court. An example would be a county rules court. Although the procedural laws of a state apply to all of the state courts including county courts, each county court may enact its own local rules as well. Local rules are designed to supplement the state laws of procedure.[6]

---

### APPLICATION 7.3

The federal government has instituted rules of procedure for filing of appeals with the U.S. Supreme Court. In addition, each state has adopted rules for filing of appeals with its own appellate court system. The U.S. Supreme Court is the final court of appeal for the entire United States. If there were not limitations on the types of cases and how appeals were filed, the system would be inundated with claims for appeal, and the Court could not possibly consider all of the cases presented. As a result, many important legal and constitutional issues might be resolved in different ways in various courts and there would be no avenue to establish a consistent and valid precedent that provided equal protection under the law for the entire country.

*Point for Discussion:* Why don't the states all just adopt the same type of procedure for filing appeals that is used by the U.S. Supreme Court?

# RULES OF CIVIL PROCEDURE

The rules of civil procedure include the laws that dictate how a suit will be filed, all pretrial matters, trial proceedings (with the possible exception of rules of evidence), and post-trial issues until the case is concluded or an appeal is initiated. Most state rules of civil procedure follow or are similar to a standard model. Note, however, that each state has the right to create its own procedural rules that are followed and enforced in the state courts and that may vary from the standard rules followed in most jurisdictions.

## Pretrial Proceedings

The rules of civil procedure first become relevant at the time a lawsuit is begun. This occurs by commencing an action with the filing of appropriate initial court documents and fees. In exceptional circumstances, an action may be commenced in some jurisdictions by filing documents that seek immediate court intervention to prevent irreparable damage or harm of some sort. The vast majority of cases, however, are commenced with the filing of a complaint or petition.[7]

**Complaint.** An action (lawsuit) is filed by the plaintiff, who presents the **complaint,** or *petition* (document alleging what the defendant did that was legally wrong), with appropriate filing fees (costs of processing the documents), with the clerk of the court. Traditionally, a complaint sought monetary damages, and a petition sought some sort of equitable relief such as the distribution of assets in a fair manner or specific court-ordered conduct by the defendant for the benefit of the plaintiff. This dates back to a time when courts were divided into two divisions. The courts of chancery dealt with damage claims, and the courts of equity dealt with other matters requiring legal action to achieve a fair result. The latter might be a breach of contract action when the plaintiff wanted the defendant to be ordered to complete the contract terms, or a case of probating and distributing the estate of a decedent. Today, courts usually have several subdivisions in most jurisdictions, but they are more often divided by type of case. Preservation of the terms *complaint* for chancery type actions and *petition* for actions based in equity persists, but some blending has taken place. Each jurisdiction, however, states the appropriate terminology within the procedural rules (local or jurisdiction-wide). The important thing to remember is that either document, regardless of name, achieves the same purpose: to initiate a legal proceeding. For discussion purposes, the term *complaint* will be generally used in this textbook.

The complaint is organized into what are usually single statements numbered and referred to as *paragraphs*. Each statement is either a statement of the existing law or a statement of a fact that the plaintiff alleges has occurred. When read in its entirety, the complaint should state which laws have allegedly been breached and which facts state how the law was allegedly broken. In addition, the complaint will indicate what compensation is necessary to satisfy the plaintiff's injuries (see Exhibit 7.1).

**complaint**
Also known as a *petition*. The document that apprises the court and the defendant of the nature of the cause of action by plaintiff.

**Summons.** Once the lawsuit has been filed, the wheels of the judicial system begin to turn. A *summons* (formal legal notice of suit) is issued to the defendant in the lawsuit, usually accompanied by a copy of the complaint. The method of giving notice of the suit is also prescribed by procedural law. A summons indicates how long a party has to respond to the claims of the complaint. Methods of *service* include personal delivery to the defendant or a suitable representative and publication of the information in a newspaper where the defendant lives or is believed to live. Some states allow other methods, and as technology of communication expands, so most likely will methods of service. If the defendant does not respond to the complaint within the allowed time period, then the court will accept everything alleged in the complaint as true and grant a decision in favor of the plaintiff. This is known as *default judgment*.

**Exhibit 7.1** Complaint

**In the District Court**

45th Judicial District
State of Tucammawa

Buzzy Jamison,
Plaintiff
vs.
Malcolm Smythe,
Defendant.

**COMPLAINT**

Comes now the Plaintiff Buzzy Jamison, by his attorneys Marjoram, Coburn, and McEachern, and for his cause of action against Defendant Malcolm Smythe, complains as follows:

1. On or about March the 17th, 2000, Tucammawa state highway 7098, ran in an east–west direction through Langdon County, State of Tucammawa.

2. On the aforementioned date, at approximately 3:00 A.M., Defendant Malcolm Smythe was operating a motor vehicle in a westerly direction along said highway in the vicinity of highway mile-marker 31.

3. At the aforementioned place and time, Defendant Malcolm Smythe caused his vehicle to cross the median separating east- and westbound traffic, and did then and there enter the eastbound lanes.

4. Immediately following the entry of Malcolm Smythe's westbound vehicle into the eastbound lane, said vehicle collided with the vehicle operated by Plaintiff, in an easterly direction.

5. Said collision was the direct and proximate result of one or more of the following negligent acts or omissions of Defendant Malcolm Smythe:

    a) Driving while under the influence of alcohol and/or other drugs.
    b) Driving too fast for conditions.
    c) Failure to keep a proper lookout.
    d) Failure to properly maintain his vehicle in properly marked lanes.
    e) Westbound entry into lanes limited to eastbound traffic.

6. Said collision was with such force that Plaintiff's vehicle was severely damaged.

7. Said collision further caused serious and permanent injuries to the Plaintiff which include but are not limited to the following:

    a) Injuries to the Plaintiff's head, face, and neck.
    b) Injuries to the Plaintiff's right arm.
    c) Injuries to the Plaintiff's left leg.
    d) Injuries to the Plaintiff's back.
    e) Injuries to the Plaintiff's skeletal, muscle, and nervous system.

8. Said injuries to the Plaintiff have caused great physical and emotional suffering, loss of wages, and medical expenses incurred in an attempt to be cured of said injuries. Said injuries have further caused permanent disability and disfigurement to Plaintiff, and will result in additional future lost wages and expenses in an attempt to be cured of said injuries.

WHEREFORE, the Plaintiff prays that the Court will find the Defendant to be guilty of negligence, and further that the court will grant damages and costs to the Plaintiff as compensation for the above said injuries.

Buzzy Jamison
Attorneys Marjoram, Coburn, & McEachern
7719 Hamilton
Sequoia, Tucammawa 00000

**Response.**  A defendant may respond to the complaint in several ways. *Responsive pleadings* have different names in different states. However, the basic methods of responding to a complaint are the same. One method is through an answer, in which the defendant responds to each item specifically alleged in the complaint. Commonly, the defendant will respond by admitting, denying, or pleading the inability to admit or deny based on lack of information. This latter claim is given in response to an allegation that is vague or cannot be answered with an admission or denial unless more information is provided by the plaintiff. Claiming a lack of knowledge is generally treated as a denial to protect the defendant from having to admit to or deny claims about which too little is known at the time. If an answer is filed, the parties move into pretrial proceedings (see Exhibit 7.2).

Another response to a complaint might be a *motion for a bill of particulars,* a claim by the defendant that the complaint as it is stated cannot be answered. A motion for a bill of particulars requests the court to order the plaintiff to clarify one or more allegations of the complaint by explaining or adding information. If the motion is granted, the plaintiff will be required to provide the defendant with additional information. If the motion is denied, the defendant will be ordered to answer the complaint as it stands.

**Exhibit 7.2**  Answer

---

### In the District Court

45th Judicial District

State of Tucammawa

Buzzy Jamison,
Plaintiff
vs.
Malcolm Smythe,
Defendant.

#### ANSWER

Comes now the Defendant Malcolm Smythe, by his attorneys Cochran, Eastwood, and McQueen, and with respect to the allegations of the Plaintiff's Complaint answers as follows:

1. Admitted.
2. Admitted.
3. Admitted.
4. Admitted.
5. Denied.
6. Denied.
7. Denied.
8. Denied.

#### AFFIRMATIVE DEFENSE

Defendant further states as an affirmative Defense that he was forced into the eastbound lane as the result of a hazard in the westbound lane; and that Plaintiff, seeing the Defendant approach, failed to take any evasive action whatsoever to avoid the collision. The Plaintiff is guilty of gross negligence in failing to take steps to avoid the collision, and as a result should not be permitted to recover against the Defendant.

Malcolm Smythe
Attorneys Cochran, Eastwood, and McQueen
Success Building, Suite I
1700 Pennsylvania Ave
Sequoia, Tucammawa 00000

If the complaint is deficient in some way, a *motion to dismiss* (in some states, a similar document is known as a *demurrer*) may be filed. This simply states that the complaint either does not contain facts that warrant any type of lawsuit or that the complaint is improperly stated according to procedural rules. Every lawsuit brought must be done so under a recognized legal theory also known as a *cause of action*. Each cause of action has specific elements that must be proven. For example, to prove someone was so negligent that he or she is legally responsible for injuries to another person as the result of that negligence, there must be evidence of certain elements that make up the legal definition of negligence. A complaint based on the legal cause of action for negligence must allege sufficient evidence of these elements in the current case. Failure to do so may result in a motion to dismiss for failure to properly state a cause of action against the defendant. In addition, procedural rules specify the type and extent of information to be included in a complaint. Typically, this will include a statement of why the court has jurisdiction over the case, the specific identity of the parties, and the alleged cause of action with sufficient supporting facts to support the elements of the legal theory as well as a claim for the relief sought, such as monetary damages. Some jurisdictions require the complaint to be specific, while others permit more general statements to suffice. It is always important to comply with the procedural rules fully when drafting a complaint. The failure to properly prepare a complaint can result in a delay of months and additional time of the parties as appearances are made in court to argue the sufficiency of the complaint and time spent amending the original document.

If a motion to dismiss or demurrer is granted, the complaint can result in permanent dismissal of the lawsuit or *dismissal without prejudice*. This is the same as *dismissal with leave to amend,* which means that the plaintiff can correct the errors. Often, if this is done within a specified period of time, the suit does not need to be refiled. *Dismissal with prejudice* is a permanent dismissal and is rarely ordered, as the court wants to provide the parties with the full opportunity to pursue their legal rights. An example, however, might be in a case when there is no dispute that the statute of limitations has expired and with it the plaintiff's right to pursue legal remedies.

Whether a request to dismiss on any basis is granted with or without prejudice depends on the reasons supporting the motion or request. If the reason is no basis exists for any type of lawsuit, then the suit may be dismissed with prejudice unless the plaintiff can demonstrate to the court that additional facts could be added to the complaint that would create the foundation for a lawsuit. If the motion is denied and the complaint is found to be proper, then the defendant is ordered to file an answer to the complaint.

Note that the failure to properly serve the summons and complaint on the dismissal on the defendant can result in an action being dismissed. For example, if the summons and complaint were not served on the defendant or an appropriate representative or were served at an inappropriate place or time, then the defendant could file a motion to dismiss. Each jurisdiction has its own procedural rules concerning the service of process that need to be followed closely.

**Arbitration.** A more recent phenomenon to take a firm hold in the justice system is that of **arbitration**. Each year tens of thousands of lawsuits are filed in this country. Statistics show that the large majority end in settlement by the parties at some stage of the proceedings. To this end, the courts in all states favor any measure that relieves the already overcrowded dockets and brings the cases to conclusion sooner than would otherwise occur by the traditional method of litigation. As a result, all states have added a stage of either voluntary or mandatory arbitration.

**arbitration**
Third-party resolution of a legal issue that has arisen between two or more parties. Typically, parties are agreed (arbitration clause) or court ordered (compulsory) to submit evidence to an arbitrator for a binding decision.

At this stage, the parties agree on or accept a court-appointed arbitrator, depending on the jurisdiction. This person is trained not only in law but also in the art of mediating disputes. Often parties will agree that the decision of the arbitrator will be final and not subject to appeal. In some cases, the parties reserve the right to return to the courts for traditional processes in the event the arbitrator's determination is unacceptable to them.

When a case goes through arbitration, the parties submit their accumulated evidence and an objective arbitrator acts as a sort of judge and jury. The evidence is considered in light of applicable law, and the arbitrator renders both what he or she believes a fair result would be and what would be the likely result in the courts. The parties then take this decision, and depending on the terms of their arbitration agreement, either end the case at this stage or go forward in the courts. It is a method by which many less complicated cases can reach conclusion in a fair manner that is far quicker and less expensive than the traditional method of trial in the courts.

Similar to arbitration in this respect is *mediation*. Mediators specialize in working between parties in dispute to reach a settlement that is acceptable and reasonable to both. Mediation is seen frequently in domestic relations cases in which parties are unable to agree about terms of issues such as custody, visitation, support, and other matters that continue to connect the parties after the marriage has ended. Mediation is also effective in other types of cases such as probate of estates and contract disputes. As with arbitration, the goal is to reach an acceptable and fair result without the time and expense associated with processing a case through already overcrowded courts.

**Discovery.** During the period after a suit is filed and before trial or settlement, procedural rules guide the parties in their preparations for the ultimate conclusion of the dispute. The most significant event during this time is known as **discovery**. At this stage, the parties exchange information under strict guidelines and close supervision of the courts. A primary goal of discovery is to foster the fair exchange of information to enable the parties to clearly evaluate their positions.[8] Discovery often results in settlement of the case once the parties become aware of all the information pertinent to the case because the parties may not have been aware of certain facts that would influence the outcome of the case in a trial. Discovery can be considered "show-and-tell" where both parties present their evidence. This practice encourages the objective assessment of the strengths and weaknesses of each side, thereby encouraging settlement. The parties may utilize several different methods of discovery, including interrogatories, requests for production, and depositions.

**discovery**
Court-supervised exchange of evidence and other relevant information between parties to a lawsuit.

**Interrogatories.** Frequently, the first step in discovery is the submission of interrogatories—that is, written questions submitted to the opposing party in the case (see Exhibit 7.3). The party who receives the questions must answer them under oath and in writing. A party may object to answering questions that are irrelevant or immaterial, invade the attorney–client privilege, or violate some other procedural rule. When an objection is raised, the judge will determine whether the party must answer the questions. Many jurisdictions limit the number of interrogatories that may be sent to the opposition.

**Request for production.** Often interrogatories are accompanied by another means of discovery: the *request for production of documents* (see Exhibit 7.4). This is a written request to produce documents or copies of documents. Because many of the functions of our society are dependent on written records, it is often

**Exhibit 7.3**
Interrogatories

---

### In the District Court

45th Judicial District
State of Tucammawa

Buzzy Jamison,
Plaintiff
vs.
Malcolm Smythe,
Defendant.

### INTERROGATORIES

Comes now the Plaintiff Buzzy Jamison by his attorneys Marjoram, Coburn, and McEachern and with respect to the above-named case submit the following interrogatories pursuant to Court Rule 606. Pursuant to said rule, the interrogatories below are to be answered in writing and under oath within 28 days of the date submitted.

1.  With respect to the Defendant please state:
    a)  All names by which the Defendant has been known.
    b)  All addresses at which the Defendant has claimed residence since 1970.
    c)  The names and current address of any current or former spouse.
    d)  The address of Defendant's current employment, position held, and current wage rate.
    e)  The Defendant's social security number.

2.  State the whereabouts of the Defendant between the hours of 3:00 P.M. March 16, 2000, and 3:00 A.M. March 17, 2000.

3.  With respect to the time and dates listed in interrogatory number 2, state the name and address of each person, business, or other entity which provided alcohol or other drugs, by gift or sale, to the Defendant.

4.  State all prescription medications and the prescribing physician's name and address for all drugs the Defendant was taking March 16–17, 2000.

Buzzy Jamison
Attorneys Majoram, Coburn, & McEachern
7719 Hamilton
Sequoia, Tucammawa 00000

Submitted to Defendant by placing the above-stated interrogatories, postage paid, in the United States Mail, on the 31st day of April 2003.

---

**Exhibit 7.4** Request
for Production

---

Comes now the Defendant, in the above-captioned action, and pursuant to applicable rules of civil procedure, request that the plaintiff produce for examination, testing, sampling or copying by the defendant or agents of the following items:

1.  All photographs, recordings, reports, records, documents, videotapes, notes, memoranda, accounts, books, papers, and other recorded, written, photographic or transcribed information that represent, are pertinent or related to in any manner, the allegations of the plaintiff against the defendant. The only exception to such request are the working papers and/or notes of plaintiff's attorney which would be characterized as work product of said attorney.

Marvin Henry, atty.
Winter, Somers and Snow, P.C.
Suite 260 Park Place
Canoga, State 000000

**Exhibit 7.5** Notice of Deposition

Pursuant to the rules of civil procedure applicable to this proceeding, the oral deposition of Defendant shall be taken before a notary public on December 12, 2004, commencing at 1:00 P.M. and continuing thereafter until such time as completed. The aforementioned deposition will be conducted at place of business of the Defendant, 401 East 1st St., Knobbe, IK 030303.

Marvin Henry, atty.
Winter, Somers and Snow, P.C.
Suite 260 Park Place
Canoga, State 000000

helpful to review documents for insight into what actually occurred. These requests are also subject to objection based on a claim that the answers contain privileged or irrelevant information, and a judge may rule whether or not they must be complied with. *Privileged* information is information that was conveyed within the context of a confidential relationship such as the attorney–client, doctor–patient, or clergy–parishioner relationship. Irrelevant information is information that is not probative or likely to produce evidence that is probative of the facts in the case.

**Deposition.** One method of discovery—the deposition—applies not only to the parties in the lawsuit but also to all persons with relevant information about it. In a deposition, the attorneys ask a party or witness in the suit to respond to extensive questions about his or her knowledge of the case. Usually, depositions are taken in person and in the presence of the attorneys for each party. The entire proceeding is taken down by a stenographer court reporter who is also a notary public and asks the person deposed to swear to tell the truth (see Exhibit 7.5).

More often, depositions are taken on videotape. In another type of deposition, the party requesting the deposition sends written questions, and the deposee is asked to answer the questions under oath and to provide a notarized statement that the responses are true and accurate to the best of his or her knowledge.

If it is anticipated that the witness will not be present at trial, then the deposition may be taken for evidentiary purposes. The procedure is basically the same, but in addition to the discovering party asking questions, the other attorneys may ask questions in the same manner as they would in a trial. Both direct examination and cross-examination are conducted. If objections are made, the questions are later presented to a judge. If it is determined that the witness should respond, the answers will be given and presented to the jury.

**Physical evidence.** In some cases, physical evidence is an integral part of the lawsuit. For example, if a person is injured by a tool or on private property, the condition of the tool or the property may become paramount in the lawsuit. When such physical evidence is owned or controlled by another party to the suit, the discovering party may file a request for inspection. This type of discovery allows a party to inspect, photograph, measure, and evaluate a particular item or place. If the party wants custody of an item or wants to subject the item to any procedures that might affect it, court approval may be required. Otherwise, in most cases, plaintiffs and defendants are entitled to reasonable inspection of items that may be produced as evidence in a trial.

**Examination.** A party may also request a physical or mental examination of an opposing party if such examination is relevant to the lawsuit. An example is a

**Exhibit 7.6** Request for Admission

> Comes now the Plaintiff, by and through her attorneys as requests that the Defendant admit the genuineness and truthfulness of content of the attached document for the purposes of the above-captioned action, and further to stipulate the admission of said document into evidence in the above-captioned action.
>
> Marvin Henry, atty.
> Winter, Somers and Snow, P.C.
> Suite 260 Park Place
> Canoga, State 000000

plaintiff who is claiming injuries as the result of alleged negligence by the defendant. In such a case, the defendant may be allowed to select a physician to examine the plaintiff and give an opinion as to the extent of the injuries. Another example is a custody battle by the parents of a child. If the child or one of the parents has a history of abnormal behavior, then the court may allow a mental examination by a qualified specialist to determine whether the behavior has had an adverse effect on the child. However, the court may also enforce limits on the extent or nature of the examination.

**Genuineness of documents.** Finally, if a party discovers information from another party through discovery or through independent investigation and the information is so crucial that it could ruin the other party's case, a *motion to admit genuineness of documents or facts* may be filed. (In some jurisdictions, this is known as a *request for admission*—see Exhibit 7.6). Although this type of motion is not usually considered an official form of discovery, it is directly related to information discovered. It asks the party to review the facts or documents discovered and to either admit or deny the truthfulness of the content. If the truthfulness is admitted or verified, the party who filed the motion may seek an early end to the lawsuit with a *motion for summary judgment* (the effect of which is discussed a little later). Usually, a motion to admit genuineness of documents or facts is not submitted unless the evidence directly contradicts the core basis of the other party's case. Because most parties genuinely believe their case and have evidence to support it, these motions are not seen in the majority of lawsuits.

## CASE
### *Mallard v. Wal-Mart Stores East LP,*
### 2006 WL 2708588 (U.S. S.D. MISS)

In the opinion that follows, the court was required to make a finding of whether a jury could have a question as to whether the defendant had violated a legal duty to the plaintiff. This would be a question of substantive law.

On or about April 19, 2005, the plaintiffs, Betty Mallard and Terri Bullock, were customers at the Wal-Mart store located at 5901 U.S. Highway 49, Hattiesburg, Mississippi. Wal-Mart provides motorized shopping carts, called mart carts, as a convenience to handicapped customers and customers who have trouble getting around the store. As a result of suffering a stroke, Mallard is paralyzed on the right side of her body and uses a wheel chair to move around. On the date in question, upon arriving at Wal-Mart, Mallard exited her wheel chair into one of the motorized shopping carts provided by Wal-Mart.

At some point in the shopping excursion, the plaintiffs decided to use the restroom which was located in the front of the store. According to the pleadings and exhibits on file, this particular restroom is designed without a door. Instead, it uses parallel offset wall panels which create a corridor that causes one entering or exiting the facility to move in a serpentine motion around the panels. When Mallard entered the entrance corridor to the restroom and began maneuvering the mart cart through, the mart cart became stuck as there was not enough room for the cart to make the tight turns necessary to pass through the corridor. Mallard and Bullock were able to free the cart and enter the restroom. However, when they attempted to exit the restroom, the cart again became stuck and while attempting to dislodge the cart from between the walls of the entrance to the restroom, Mallard and Bullock alleges they were both severely injured.

The plaintiffs contend that because there were no signs posted at the entrance of the restroom stating that individuals should not attempt to enter the restroom with a motorized cart, Mallard had no reason to believe that she would encounter any problem entering the restroom as she desired. The defendants contend that there was a sign posted that informed customers not to enter the restrooms with merchandise and that this signage put the plaintiffs on notice that the mart cart, or any other shopping cart, should not be carried into the restroom.

The plaintiffs brought the instant action against Wal-Mart alleging negligent design of he restroom entrance and failure to warn handicapped customers not to drive the mart carts into restrooms. The defendants have moved for summary judgment asserting that the plaintiffs have failed to create any genuine issues of material fact that the restroom was negligently designed or that Wal-Mart had a duty to warn its patrons sufficient to establish liability for the plaintiffs' alleged injuries.

The Federal Rules of Civil Procedure, Rule 56(c) authorizes summary judgment where "the pleadings, depositions, answers to interrogatories and admissions on file, together with affidavits, if any, show that there is no genuine dispute as to any material fact and that the moving party is entitled to judgment as a matter of law." *Celotex Corporation v. Catrett*, 477 U.S. 317, 322, 91 L.Ed.2d 265, 106 S.Ct. 2548 (1986). The existence of a material question of fact is itself a question of law that the district court is bound to consider before granting summary judgment. *John v. State of*

*La.* (Bd. of T. for State C. & U.), 757 F.2d 698, 712 (5th Cir.1985).

A Judge's function at the summary judgment stage is not himself to weigh the evidence and determine the truth of the matter, but to determine whether there is a genuine issue for trial. There is no issue for trial unless there is sufficient evidence favoring the non-moving party for a jury to return a verdict for that party. If the evidence is merely colorable, or is not significantly probative, summary judgment is appropriate. *Anderson v. Liberty Lobby, Inc.*, 477 U.S. 242, 91 L.Ed.2d 202, 106 S.Ct. 2505 (1986).

Although Rule 56 is peculiarly adapted to the disposition of legal questions, it is not limited to that role. *Professional Managers, Inc. v. Fawer, Brian, Hardy & Zatzkis*, 799 F.2d 218, 222 (5th Cir.1986). "The mere existence of a disputed factual issue, therefore, does not foreclose summary judgment. The dispute must be genuine, and the facts must be material." *Id.* "With regard to 'materiality,' only those disputes over facts that might affect the outcome of the lawsuit under the governing substantive law will preclude summary judgment." *Phillips Oil Company v. OKC Corporation*, 812 F.2d 265, 272 (5th Cir.1987). Where "the summary judgment evidence establishes that one of the essential elements of the plaintiff's cause of action does not exist as a matter of law, . . . all other contested issues of fact are rendered immaterial. See *Celotex*, 477 U.S. at 323, 106 S.Ct at 2552." *Topalian v. Ehrman*, 954 F.2d 1125, 1138 (5th Cir.1992).

In making its determinations of fact on a motion for summary judgment, the Court must view the evidence submitted by the parties in a light most favorable to the non-moving party. *McPherson v. Rankin*, 736 F.2d 175, 178 (5th Cir.1984).

The moving party has the duty to demonstrate the lack of a genuine issue of material fact and the appropriateness of judgment as a matter of law to prevail on his motion. *Union Planters Nat. Leasing v. Woods*, 687 F.2d 117 (5th Cir.1982). The movant accomplishes this by informing the court of the basis of its motion, and by identifying portions of the record which highlight the absence of genuine factual issues. *Topalian*, 954 F.2d at 1131.

"Rule 56 contemplates a shifting burden: the non-movant is under no obligation to respond unless the movant discharges [its] initial burden of demonstrating [entitlement to summary judgment]." *John*, 757 F.2d at 708. "Summary judgment cannot be supported solely on the ground that [plaintiff] failed to respond to defendants' motion for summary judgment," even in light of a Local Rule of the court mandating such for failure to respond to an opposed motion. *Id.* at 709.

*(continued)*

However, once a properly supported motion for summary judgment is presented, the nonmoving party must rebut with "significant probative" evidence. *Ferguson v. National Broadcasting Co., Inc.,* 584 F.2d 111, 114 (5th Cir.1978). In other words, "the nonmoving litigant is required to bring forward 'significant probative evidence' demonstrating the existence of a triable issue of fact." *In Re Municipal Bond Reporting Antitrust Lit.,* 672 F.2d 436, 440 (5th Cir.1982). To defend against a proper summary judgment motion, one may not rely on mere denial of material facts nor on unsworn allegations in the pleadings or arguments and assertions in briefs or legal memoranda. The nonmoving party's response, by affidavit or otherwise, must set forth specific facts showing that there is a genuine issue for trial. Rule 56(e), Fed.R.Civ.P. See also *Union Planters Nat. Leasing v. Woods,* 687 F.2d at 119.

While generally "'[t]he burden to discover a genuine issue of fact is not on [the] court,' (*Topalian* 954 F.2d at 1137), 'Rule 56 does not distinguish between documents merely filed and those singled out by counsel for special attention—the court must consider both before granting a summary judgment.'" *John,* 757 F.2d at 712 (quoting *Keiser v. Coliseum Properties, Inc.,* 614 F.2d 406, 410 (5th Cir.1980)).

To prevail on the plaintiffs' negligence claims of negligent design and failure to warn, they must prove by a preponderance of the evidence the following elements:

1. A duty owed by the defendants to the plaintiffs;
2. A breach of that duty;
3. Damages; and
4. A causal connection between the breach and the damages, such that the breach is the proximate cause of the damages.

*Grisham v. John Q. Long V.F.W. Post,* 519 So.2d 413, 416 (Miss.1988).

The defendants' motion has challenged the plaintiffs' negligence claims generally and their ability to prove a breach of duty by the defendant, specifically. The court notes that in order for the plaintiffs to prevail against the defendants' challenge, they must make a showing sufficient to establish the existence of the defendants' breach of duty on which they will bear the burden of proof at trial. See *Celotex Corp. v. Catrett,* 477 U.S. at 322.

There is no dispute about the status of the plaintiffs as business invitees at Wal-Mart on the date of the incident. Under Mississippi law an owner, occupant or person in charge of a premises owes a business invitee the duty to keep the premises in a reasonably safe condition or to warn the invitee of dangerous conditions, not readily apparent, which the owner or occupier knows of or should know of in the exercise of reasonable care. *Waller v. Dixieland Food Stores, Inc.,* 492 So.2d 283 (Miss.1986).

The defendants assert that the restroom at the Wal-Mart store met the design requirements of the Americans with Disabilities Act Accessibilities Guidelines and that its signage complied with those same Guidelines. That signage included a handicapped accessible sign. The plaintiffs counter that they have offered proof of negligent design by virtue of the defendants' expert, Douglas R. Bryant. Bryant has filed a report asserting that the restroom entrance in question met the ADAA Guidelines but acknowledges that the mart cart cannot successfully navigate the entrance.

Whether the signage that no merchandise was allowed in the restroom was sufficient to put the plaintiffs on notice not to carry the mart cart into the restroom is a question for the jury. Further, whether it was negligent to furnish a mart cart that wouldn't fit into the restroom entrance to handicapped individuals is also a question best left to the jury. With those factual questions, summary judgment is not appropriate on the plaintiffs's negligent design and failure to warn claims.

The defendants have also moved for summary judgment on the plaintiffs' punitive damages claims. It is well settled in Mississippi that punitive damages are to be assessed only in extreme cases. See *Gardner v. Jones,* 464 So.2d 1144, 1148 (Miss.1985). "Mississippi law does not favor punitive damages; they are considered an extraordinary remedy and are allowed with caution and within narrow limits." *Life & Cas. Ins. Co. of Tenn. v. Bristow,* 529 So.2d 620, 622 (Miss.1988). Further,

> [a]s a general rule, exemplary or punitive damages are "added damages" and are in addition to the actual or compensatory damages due because of an injury or wrong. The kind of wrongs to which punitive damages are applicable are those which, besides the violation of a right or the actual damages sustained, import insult, fraud, or oppression and not merely injuries, but injuries inflicted in the spirit of wanton disregard for the rights of others.

*Summers ex rel. Dawson v. St. Andrew's Episcopal School, Inc.,* 759 So .2d 1203, 1215 (Miss.2000) (citing *Fowler Butane Gas Co. v. Varner,* 244 Miss. 130, 150–51, 141 So.2d 226, 233 (1962)). See also *Paracelsus Health Care Corp. v. Willard,* 754 So.2d 437, 442 (Miss.1999). "In order to warrant the recovery of punitive damages, there must enter into the injury some element of aggression or some coloring of insult, malice or gross negligence, evincing ruthless disregard for the rights of others, so as to take the case out of the ordinary rule." *Id.* (citing 15 Am. Jur., Damages, Sec. 265, p. 698).

When deciding whether to submit the issue of punitive damages to a trier of fact, the court is required to examine the totality of the circumstances as established by the record, to determine if a reasonable, hypothetical trier of fact could find either malice or gross neglect/reckless disregard in order to justify the imposition of punitive damages. See *Ross-King-Walker, Inc. v. Henson,* 672 So.2d 1188, 1191 (Miss.1996).

Based on the foregoing well settled principles of law, the Mississippi Supreme Court has instructed that "in order for the issue of punitive damages to warrant jury consideration, [the plaintiffs] must show that a question of fact exists as to whether the aggregate of [the defendants'] conduct . . . evidences willful or wanton conduct or the commission of fraud. *Bradfield v. Schwartz,* — So.2d —, 2006 WL 1350051, *5 (Miss.2006).

The court agrees with the defendants that the plaintiffs have failed to create a genuine issue of material fact regarding the imposition of punitive damages and this claim should be dismissed.

*5 IT IS THEREFORE ORDERED AND ADJUDGED that the defendants' Motion for Summary Judgment [# 77] is Denied as to the plaintiffs' negligent design and failure to warn claims and Granted as to the plaintiffs' punitive damages claims. A separate judgment shall be entered herein in accordance with Rule 58, Federal Rules of Civil Procedure.

SO ORDERED AND ADJUDGED this the 20th day of September, 2006.

## Case Review Question

Would the question with regard to punitive damages be considered substantive or procedural?

---

## ASSIGNMENT 7.3

In the following scenario, identify the types of documents and information that would be needed to prepare a defense. Second, state what types of discovery would be most appropriate to obtain the necessary information.

Sixteen-year-old Ken just received his driver's license one month ago. His best friend Julian is fifteen and does not drive. Ken is at Julian's house before the two go to school one evening for play rehearsal in which both boys are involved. Julian's mother, Sonya, also has two toddlers that are both feeling unwell. Sonya suggests Ken should drive her car to take himself and Julian to the rehearsal. Ken and Julian

leave the residence and start off for school in Sonya's car. Ken's parents have not yet added Ken to their own auto insurance policy. On the way to school, Ken strikes three individuals who are crossing the street in a marked crosswalk. Of the three pedestrians, Cody is killed instantly. Marshall suffers extensive injuries but eventually makes a full recovery. However, he will always have significant scarring and a pronounced limp. The third pedestrian, Thad, never recovers consciousness and remains in a persistent vegetative state. Different attorneys represent each of the pedestrians in a lawsuit against Ken and Sonya.

---

**Motion Practice.** Throughout any lawsuit, the parties communicate with the court largely through motions. A **motion** is a request by an attorney whose party seeks assistance—or a ruling—from the court on a particular issue between the parties. Motions can result in something as serious as permanent dismissal of the lawsuit. The following discussion examines some of the more common motions in terms of what they request and the effect they have if granted. We have seen that motions can be used to request dismissal of suit when the complaint is deficient in some way. Motions also have many other uses through pretrial, trial, and even post-trial proceedings. Some of the more commonly sought motions are discussed here.

**motion**
Formal request by a party to a lawsuit for court-ordered action or nonaction.

**Motion to dismiss.** As stated earlier, the motion to dismiss is used when a party believes that the facts of the case do not support a viable legal claim or that the complaint is improperly stated and does not conform to legal requirements as outlined by the rules of procedure (see Exhibit 7.7).

**Exhibit 7.7** Motion to
Dismiss

Comes now the Defendant, Pauline McPaul, by and through her attorneys, Winter, Somers, and Snow, and moves the Court to enter an order dismissing the Complaint of Defendant. In support thereof, the Defendant states as follows:

1. On or about August 19, 2003, the Plaintiff instituted an action against the Defendant in the above-captioned court.
2. The Complaint of Plaintiff fails to state a cause of action upon which relief can be granted.

Further, Plaintiff's allegations are legal conclusions and unsupported by any allegations of fact.

WHEREFORE, the Defendant prays that the Court enter an order dismissing the Plaintiff's complaint, awarding Defendant costs and such other and further relief as the Court deems necessary and proper.

Respectfully submitted,

Marvin Henry, atty.
Winter, Somers and Snow, P.C.
Suite 260 Park Place
Canoga, State 000000

**Exhibit 7.8** Motion to
Make More Definite
and Certain

Comes now the Defendant, Pauline McPaul, by and through her attorneys, Winter, Somers, and Snow, and moves the Court to enter an order requiring Plaintiff to additional facts to support the allegations of his Complaint. In support thereof, the Defendant states as follows:

1. On October 31, 2003, Plaintiff instituted an action against the Defendant alleging breach of contract with respect to an agreement to which both Plaintiff and Defendant were parties.
2. That during the period 2000–2004, Plaintiff and Defendant had an ongoing business relationship, the product of which was no fewer than 70 separate contracts.
3. That Defendant is without information as to the specifics of the alleged breach and as a result is unable to frame a proper answer to the allegations of Plaintiff.

WHEREFORE, the Defendant prays that the Court will enter an order requiring the Plaintiff to more particularly describe the specifics of the facts supporting the allegations of Plaintiff's Complaint.

Respectfully submitted,

Marvin Henry, atty.
Winter, Somers and Snow, P.C.
Suite 260 Park Place
Canoga, State 000000

**Motion to make more definite and certain.** Also called a *bill of particulars,* a motion to make more definite and certain is filed by the defendant and asks that the plaintiff be required to provide more detailed information than that contained in the complaint (see Exhibit 7.8).

**Motion to quash service of process.** A motion to quash service of process is filed when a plaintiff does not follow the rules of procedure for serving a summons and complaint on the defendant. If the rules are violated, the service is quashed, or rejected, and the plaintiff must attempt to serve the defendant properly.

**Motion to inspect.** The motion to inspect is a discovery motion used to gain access to private property. If granted, the party is allowed to inspect the property as it pertains to evidence in the lawsuit. Examples include access to private property that was the scene of an accident and inspection of an item, such as a weapon, that was involved in an injury (see Exhibit 7.9).

Comes now the Plaintiff, Mortimer Vance, by and through his attorneys, Winter, Somers, and Snow, and moves the Court to enter an order permitting Plaintiff to inspect the premises under control of the Defendant. In support thereof, the Plaintiff states as follows:

1. On or about July 5, 2003, Plaintiff instituted an action in this Court against the Defendant alleging injury as the result of negligent conduct of Defendant.
2. Said allegations of neglect arose from an explosion that occurred on Defendant's property in which Plaintiff was seriously injured.
3. It is necessary for Plaintiff to inspect the aforementioned property of Defendant and site of Plaintiff's injuries for the proper preparation of Plaintiff's case.
4. Said inspection is appropriate pursuant to applicable rules of procedure.

WHEREFORE, the Plaintiff prays the Court will enter an order permitting Plaintiff to inspect the aforementioned property of Defendant upon reasonable notice and circumstances for the purposes of discovery in the above-captioned action.

Respectfully submitted,

Marvin Henry, atty.
Winter, Somers and Snow, P.C.
Suite 260 Park Place
Canoga, State 000000

**Exhibit 7.9** Motion to Inspect

Comes now the Defendant, Pauline McPaul, by and through her attorneys, Winter, Somers, and Snow, and moves the Court to enter an order requiring the Plaintiff to submit to a physical exam upon reasonable notice by a physician of Defendant's choice. In support thereof, Defendant states as follows:

1. On or about August 31, 2003, Plaintiff instituted an action against the Defendant alleging negligence and consequent physical injury.
2. That pursuant to applicable rules of civil procedure, when Plaintiff places her physical condition in issue in litigation, the Defendant has the right to reasonable examination of Plaintiff's condition and medical records.
3. To date, Plaintiff has been unwilling to voluntarily undergo physical examination by a physician agent of the Defendant.
4. Said examination is essential to preparation of Defendant's defense to the allegations of the Plaintiff.

WHEREFORE, the Defendant prays that the Court enter an order requiring the Plaintiff, under reasonable notice and circumstances, to submit to a physical examination by a physician of Defendant's choosing and to order such other relief as the Court deems necessary and proper.

Respectfully submitted,

Marvin Henry, atty.
Winter, Somers and Snow, P.C.
Suite 260 Park Place
Canoga, State 000000

**Exhibit 7.10** Motion for Physical Examination

**Motion for mental or physical exam.** The motion for mental or physical exam is used when the mental or physical condition of a party or witness is relevant to the lawsuit. When granted, it allows the party to have the physician of choice examine the other party or witness and to give a report as to the person's mental or physical condition. An example would occur in a personal injury claim. The defendant might want to have his or her own doctor examine the plaintiff to render an opinion as to the extent of the plaintiff's injuries (see Exhibit 7.10).

**Exhibit 7.11** Motion
to Compel

Comes now the Plaintiff, Mortimer Vance, by and through his attorneys, Winter, Somers, and Snow, and moves the Court to enter an order compelling Defendant to respond to Plaintiff's discovery. In support thereof, Plaintiff states as follows:

1. On or about January 13, 2003, Plaintiff submitted interrogations to Defendant in accordance with applicable rules of civil procedure.
2. Response from Defendant to said interrogatories was due on or about February 13, 2003.
3. Said date for response has passed, and Plaintiff has made further written requests to Defendant for compliance with this discovery. As of March 29, 2003, Defendant has failed to respond to the aforementioned interrogatories.
4. Defendant is in violation of the rules of discovery and is thwarting Plaintiff's attempts to proceed with this litigation.

WHEREFORE, the Plaintiff prays the Court to enter an order compelling the Defendant to respond to Plaintiff's interrogatories within 7 days and to order such other further and necessary relief as the Court deems proper.

Respectfully submitted,

Marvin Henry, atty.
Winter, Somers and Snow, P.C.
Suite 260 Park Place
Canoga, State 000000

**Motion to compel.** During discovery, a party has certain time limits to respond to requests for information by the other party. When these time limits are not honored, the party expecting the information may request that the court order compliance immediately (see Exhibit 7.11).

**Motion for sanctions.** A motion for sanctions is used during discovery and at any other time during the proceedings when one party is of the opinion that the other party is willfully disregarding rules of procedure or orders of the court. The motion seeks punishment of the party at fault. If granted by the court, the penalty can range from being held in contempt of court to dismissal of the suit in the aggrieved party's favor.

**Motion for summary judgment.** A motion for summary judgment is not a routinely filed motion. Its basis is that the evidence is so overwhelmingly in favor of one party that no reasonable judge or jury could find in favor of the other party. Consequently, the party seeking the motion contends that there is no basis for a trial and the case should be determined without trial and in favor of the requesting party. The motion for summary judgment is one of the most serious motions that can be filed in any lawsuit. It asks that the judge make a final decision on the issues of the suit without a trial. The decision is made solely on the basis of the evidence that exists at the time of the motion. The effect of such a motion is that the judge removes the case from the hands of the jury before it ever reaches jury members. Because our system of government places so much importance on the jury system, this is a profoundly serious step for any judge to take.

When a motion for summary judgment is sought, the judge must make a serious evaluation of the evidence. If the evidence is so strongly in favor of a party that a jury could only reasonably reach one decision and there is no substantial question left to be determined regarding the facts that occurred, a motion for summary judgment may be granted. However, if there is any way that jurors could reach a different conclusion as to whose version of the story is more probable, a motion for summary judgment must be denied, and the case must be left to the trier of fact.[9]

Because the effect of a successful motion for summary judgment is that there will be no trial in the case, such a motion must be filed before trial begins. Beyond

**Exhibit 7.12** Motion for Summary Judgment

Comes now the Defendant, Pauline McPaul, by and through her attorneys, Winter, Somers, and Snow, and moves the Court to enter an order of Summary Judgment in favor of Defendant and against Plaintiff. In support thereof, the Defendant states as follows:

1. On or about August 31, 2003, Plaintiff filed an Amended Complaint against Defendant alleging that the Defendant negligently caused Plaintiff's financial injury and ultimate bankruptcy as the result of a breach of contract. Defendant filed an answer denying the allegations of the Plaintiff.

2. The parties have subsequently engaged in discovery, and the information discovered indicates that no genuine issue of fact exists to support Plaintiff's allegations.

3. Attached in support of Defendant's motion is the affidavit of Plaintiff's former employee, Alexander Grant. Said affidavit states, inter alia, that as general manager of Plaintiff's business, Mr. Grant had full knowledge of Plaintiff's financial status at the time of the alleged breach of contract.

4. Affiant further states that at the time of the alleged breach of contract by Defendant, the Plaintiff was insolvent and consulting attorneys with respect to filing bankruptcy. Shortly following the alleged breach, Plaintiff did in fact file for bankruptcy.

5. Affiant avers that if called to testify, he would affirmatively state that Plaintiff suffered no financial injury by Defendant's breach and that said breach had no bearing on Plaintiff's subsequent bankruptcy.

WHEREFORE, the Defendant prays that the Court enter a finding that no genuine issue of facts exists with respect to Plaintiff's allegations of damage proximately caused by Defendant, and further that the Court enter an order of Summary Judgment in favor of the Defendant and against the Plaintiff and such other and necessary relief as the Court deems necessary and proper.

Respectfully submitted,

Marvin Henry, atty.
Winter, Somers and Snow, P.C.
Suite 260 Park Place
Canoga, State 000000

that, when or if the motion is filed is up to the moving party. Usually, a motion for summary judgment will not be filed unless there is evidence so strong that the opposing party's case is effectively defeated by the evidence. In most cases, each side has evidence that would tend to prove or disprove the case. Consequently, motions for summary judgment are filed less often than other types of motions and are rarely granted (see Exhibit 7.12).

If a motion for summary judgment by a defendant is granted, the case is dismissed *with prejudice.* This means that the lawsuit brought by the plaintiff will be dismissed and can never be brought again. No amendments to the complaint can be made, and the issue between the parties is permanently settled. If a motion for summary judgment by a plaintiff is granted, the defendant is not entitled to a trial to present evidence in defense to the plaintiff's claims. If the plaintiff asked for a specific dollar amount of damages in the complaint, the defendant is automatically judged liable and must pay the plaintiff an appropriate amount. Sometimes the amount of damages specified in the complaint is appropriate, but other times a trial must be held to determine exactly how much the defendant should pay.

**Motion in limine.** A motion *in limine,* also known as a *motion to limit* or *motion to exclude,* is filed in an attempt to prevent certain evidence from being presented to a jury. It is based on the contention that certain evidence would interfere with an informed and fair decision by the jury. This motion is usually filed when there are graphic depictions of injuries or when information duplicates other evidence. It is granted only when the information would lead a jury to unfair conclusions and when there are other sufficient means of presenting evidence of the facts to the jury (see Exhibit 7.13).

**Exhibit 7.13** Motion
*in Limine*

> Comes now the Defendant, Pauline McPaul, by and through her attorneys, Winter, Somers, and Snow, and moves the Court to enter an order excluding certain evidence that Plaintiff has indicated it intends to submit in the trial of the above-captioned action. In support thereof, the Defendant states as follows:
>
> 1. This action involves allegations of personal injury to the Plaintiff as the result of claimed negligence of the Defendant.
> 2. Through discovery, Defendant has ascertained that Plaintiff intends to submit into evidence certain graphic photographs depicting Plaintiff's injuries.
> 3. Said photographs are immaterial in that they are not necessary to a fair and informed determination by the jury. Further, said photographs are of a nature that could inflame and prejudice the jury and prohibit the jury from making an objective finding.
> 4. Other suitable evidence of Plaintiff's injuries exist that would adequately and accurately depict the injuries for the jury's consideration.
> 5. Attached for the Court's consideration are copies of the aforementioned photographs and the alternative forms of evidence.
>
> WHEREFORE, the Defendant prays that the Court enter an order excluding from evidence the aforementioned photographs and further that the Court order Plaintiff, Plaintiff's attorneys, witnesses, and all others from any direct or indirect reference to said photographs during the proceedings of the above-captioned action.
>
> Respectfully submitted,
>
> Marvin Henry, atty.
> Winter, Somers and Snow, P.C.
> Suite 260 Park Place
> Canoga, State 000000

**Exhibit 7.14** Motion
for Directed Verdict

> Comes now the Defendant, Pauline McPaul, by and through her attorneys, Winter, Somers, and Snow, and moves the Court to enter a Directed Verdict in favor of Defendant and against Plaintiff. In support thereof, the Defendant states as follows:
>
> 1. Plaintiff has concluded the presentation of her case in chief and in doing so has failed to present a *prima facie* case that would reasonably allow a jury to find in Plaintiff's favor based on a preponderance of the evidence.
> 2. "Where the plaintiff fails to present any significant evidence in support of the elements of the alleged cause of action, a directed verdict is appropriate." *Walston v. Dunham,* 111 E.W.2d 444 (CS App. 1987).
>
> WHEREFORE, the Defendant prays that the Court will direct the jury in the above-captioned action to enter a verdict in favor of Defendant and against Plaintiff and such other relief as the Court deems necessary and proper.
>
> Respectfully submitted,
>
> Marvin Henry, atty.
> Winter, Somers and Snow, P.C.
> Suite 260 Park Place
> Canoga, State 000000

**Motion for directed verdict.** Not to be confused with the summary judgment motion, a motion for a directed verdict is filed after evidence has been presented to a jury (rather than before a trial has begun). However, similar to the summary judgment motion, the motion for directed verdict asks that the judge make a determination that there is only one reasonable outcome to the suit and because of this, the jury should be told what its verdict will be (see Exhibit 7.14).

**Motion for judgment notwithstanding the verdict (non obstante verdicto).** Also known as *judgment NOV,* a request for judgment notwithstanding the verdict is made after the verdict has been delivered by the jury and a party contends that the jury misconstrued the evidence and reached a result that is in conflict with the totality of the evidence. If the motion is granted, the judge will substitute his or her own verdict for the jury's verdict. Judges rarely grant this motion, however, because it usurps the jury's function to interpret the evidence.

**Motion for new trial.** The motion for new trial is sought when a party contends that something occurred during the trial that prevented the legally correct result of the lawsuit. Errors can include the wrongful exclusion of certain evidence, improper testimony by a witness, or a procedural error by the judge. Actually, anything to which a party can point that had a significant impact on the case and that the party can convince the judge was irregular or inappropriate can serve as the basis for this motion.

Note that motions such as those for summary judgment, directed verdict, and new trial are rarely granted. When they are, the judge removes the case from the hands of a jury and substitutes his or her own legal opinion for that of several peers of the parties in the suit. Most judges are not willing to take this responsibility without compelling reasons that the jury verdict is or would not be proper under the circumstances of the case.

---

## ASSIGNMENT 7.4

Consider the following motions and the situations that follow. Identify the applicable motion and explain why it would be most appropriate.

1. motion to dismiss
2. motion to quash service
3. motion to compel
4. motion *in limine* (motion to limit)
5. motion for to inspect
6. motion for examination
7. motion to make more definite and certain
8. motion for summary judgment
9. motion for judgment not withstanding the verdict
10. motion for sanctions

After a plane crash, a local news crew obtained video footage that contained sounds of what appeared to be people screaming as the wreckage erupted into a fireball.

Max was at his ex-wife's house to pick up their son for visitation. Someone approached him on the porch and asked if it was his residence. He said yes and was handed a summons. Max did not give the summons to his ex-wife who was inside. In fact, although Max was still on the mortgage and made one-half of the payments, he had not resided at the house for more than one year.

Crystal filed a lawsuit against her former employer for sexual harassment by an immediate supervisor. The only evidence that supported Crystal's claim was her own allegations and the diary she had kept at home. There were no other witnesses, no documentation of complaints, or any other material to support Crystal's allegation that whenever they were alone the supervisor had made continuous suggestive and highly personal remarks about a desire to be intimate with Crystal.

Stephen was sued by a former partner because under the partnership agreement Stephen was entitled to 60 percent of the profits and the partner was entitled to 40 percent. After the partnership suffered two years of losses, the partner voluntarily left the partnership. Stephen continued with the business and in the following year made a substantial profit as the result of a sudden and unexpected business opportunity. The partner thinks Stephen should have told him of the increasing business and given him the chance to rejoin the partnership although there was no evidence of any agreement to do this.

Tom and Carol are attorneys on opposing sides of a lawsuit. During a deposition, Tom makes numerous derogatory remarks about Carol to a witness for Carol's client. On several occasions, Tom instructs the witness not to answer Carol's question because he will object at trial and the objection will be sustained so it is a waste of time to listen to her. He tells the

*(continued)*

## ASSIGNMENT 7.4 (Continued)

witness that Carol is just trying to drag out the deposition and cost the client more money. The witness, not knowing what to do, refuses to answer the questions.

Katarina has filed a lawsuit against her landlord for failure to keep the property in a habitable condition. There was uncontested evidence that the landlord had failed to make roof repairs requested by Katarina. As a result of the neglect, the roof weakened and collapsed in a heavy storm. All of Katarina's personal belongings were destroyed, and Katarina suffered a broken leg and arm in the collapse. Evidence was introduced that Katarina made much of her income through gifts of money she received from men that she dated. The jury found in favor of the landlord.

Mike filed a lawsuit against his neighbor Dale, claiming negligence in the maintenance of his property that, in turn, caused significant damage to Mike's property.

In the lawsuit above involving Dale and Mike, Dale is convinced that Mike is mentally unstable and that if any damage was caused, it was by Mike's own actions. Dale has personally observed Mike on more than one occasion at night up in trees around the neighborhood trimming branches while naked and waving a lit candle.

Barb and Greg are involved in a bitterly contested divorce. Barb is certain that Greg has long been skimming cash from his business in a nearby community. Barb's attorney has requested a list of all of Greg's employees in the past two years. The request has been pending for nearly a year and as of yet has not received a response.

In the divorce above, Greg claims that a mutual friend told him that Barb recently bragged she has long been secreting cash and other liquid assets in their home as she anticipated filing for divorce. The home is old, and a portion of the basement has a dirt floor. It is here that the Greg claims the assets had been buried. If they had, the ground would show evidence of recent activity. Greg's attorney wants to go through Barb's house.

### Stages of Trial

Procedural rules help guide the parties in assembling their evidence and presenting it at trial. Rules of evidence are examined in more detail later in the chapter. At this point, discussion will focus on the actual stages of the trial and the presentation of the evidence.

**Voir Dire.** The first stage of trial is generally the *voir dire*. During this stage, the jury that will hear the case is selected. In what is known as a bench trial, the trier of fact is the judge who hears the evidence and issues a decision. This is one option of the parties regarding the form of trial. In a bench trial, there is no jury and thus no need for the *voir dire* stage. If the case is to receive a jury trial, a fair and impartial jury must be selected.

Voir dire begins with a large pool of potential jurors who are brought into the courtroom. The attorneys for the parties—and sometimes the judge—ask each potential juror a number of questions, the goal of which is to determine whether a potential juror has any biases regarding the parties, attorneys, or circumstances of the case. If an attorney believes that a potential juror has a particular bias that would influence the decision in the case, the attorney has the right to challenge the juror's right to sit on the jury.

An attorney can exercise two types of challenges with regard to potential jurors: *peremptory challenges* and *challenges for cause*. Each party to a lawsuit may use a given amount of peremptory challenges, which vary in number from state to state. An attorney exercising a peremptory challenge does not have to give a reason to the court. A party has an absolute right to have the challenged juror removed from the jury. The only exception is if the removal is based on a person's status within a federally protected class such as race.

In challenge for cause, an attorney asks that a juror be excused on the basis of a particular prejudice that was evident from the juror's answers to the questions previously asked. In challenge for cause, the opposing party can object to the challenge. Usually, the objection will state that the prospective juror did not exhibit a bias so strong that the juror could not fairly consider the case. The judge considers the challenge, any objections, and the statements of the juror and then renders a decision as to whether the juror will be excused.

When the required number of jurors has been reached, *voir dire* is ended. Traditionally, juries are composed of twelve persons and one or two alternates. Some states also have *petit juries,* usually juries of fewer people. Petit juries may be utilized in cases that are less serious but still warrant the right to a trial by a jury of one's peers under state or federal law. Some states do not allow jury trials in the most minor cases, such as traffic violations, where loss of liberty is not at stake.

## CASE
### *Harris v. Kubota Tractor Corporation,*
### 2006 WL 2734460 (U.S. W.D. LA, 2006)

In this case, the court is obligated to determine whether the relevance of evidence outweighs the possibility that evidence of this nature could be given undue weight against a party.

On December 19, 2003, Harris was attempting to remove a rotary tiller from a tractor manufactured by the defendant, Kubota Tractor Corporation ("Kubota"), when his leg became entangled in the tiller. As a result of extensive injuries, Harris's leg had to be amputated. A urinalysis performed after the accident indicated that Harris tested positive for cocaine metabolites and cannabinoids, by-products of the body's use of cocaine and marijuana. During a January 8, 2004, interview with an insurance adjustor for Amicus, Harris was asked whether during the "whole week, Monday to Friday, if [he had] had any drugs, used any medication of any kind," and Harris responded in the negative. Record Document 55, Exhibit 1 at 2. However, in a deposition conducted on May 10, 2005, Harris admitted using cocaine during the "first part of the week before the accident," but was unable to recall specifically on what day the drug use occurred. Record Document 45, Exhibit A at 2. Harris, Amicus and Magnolia Hill Farm and Nursery filed the instant motions in limine to exclude the urinalysis test results and to redact the results from all medical records admitted into evidence. Kubota opposes the motions.

All parties agree that the urinalysis results do not prove Harris was impaired at the time of the accident. Kubota, however, asserts that the results demonstrate that Harris used drugs closer in time to the accident than he admits. Further, Kubota maintains that the results establish that Harris lied when denying his drug use to the Amicus insurance adjustor and when stating during his deposition that he ingested drugs only in the beginning of the accident week. Kubota also argues that Harris's method of detaching the rotary tiller from the Kubota tractor while the tractor was in operation, while the tiller was elevated, and while it was in a raised position was against common sense and can likely be explained by a drug impairment. Therefore, Kubota's position is that Harris's state of mind at the time of the accident, and more specifically, whether he was impaired or not, is at issue in this products liability case. As such, it contends that the extent to which he was impaired at the time of the accident is relevant, probative, and not unfairly prejudicial.

Harris, Amicus, and Magnolia Hill Farm and Nursery contend that the test results should not be admitted into evidence because the probative value of the evidence is substantially outweighed by its prejudicial effect, especially since the presence of metabolites and cannabinoids does not indicate whether a person was impaired at the time in question. Harris further asserts that Louisiana law prohibits impeachment as to a collateral matter, such that evidence of Harris's past drug use should be inadmissible for the purpose of impeaching his credibility and/or veracity.

Both Harris and Kubota have submitted expert opinions as to the significance of the urinalysis results. Harris's expert, Dr. Patrick Harding ("Harding"), states that the urinalysis

> does not provide a quantitative result, but merely show[s] either "positive" or "negative" for [the] presence of the metabolites of the substance being tested for. Metabolites are the by-products produced by the body's processing of these substances. Metabolites remain in the

*(continued)*

body long after any behavioral influence of the drug is gone. . . . No tests were taken to determine the actual presence of marijuana and cocaine in Wesley Harris' body, as opposed to the presence of the metabolites of marijuana and cocaine in Wesley Harris' body.

Record Document 39, Exhibit 1 at 2. Harding further attests that Harris's test results "do not confirm the presence of either marijuana or cocaine," and that this particular type of drug screening is "not a reliable form of testing regarding how recently a substance has been used by the person being tested." *Id.* at 2–3. Harding concludes that Harris's drug use could have been days or even weeks prior to his accident. See *id.* at 3.

On the other hand, Kubota's expert, Dr. William George ("George"), claims that

> the smoking of "one or two" rocks of cocaine at the beginning of the week would not have produced the positive result for cocaine/metabolite on Friday afternoon. . . . The positive test for cocaine/metabolite (Friday PM) is indicative of the use of cocaine nearer to the time of the accident than early in the week (Monday or Tuesday). . . . [I]t is more probable than not that Mr. Harris used cocaine within forty-eight hours or less prior to the time of the accident. . . .[I]f Mr. Harris had used cocaine within twenty-four hours of the test, indirect effects such as fatigue, impaired concentration and apprehension would have been expected.

Record Document 45, Exhibit C at 2–3.

Federal Rule of Evidence 401 provides that relevant evidence is "evidence having any tendency to make the existence of any fact that is of consequence to the determination of the action more probable or less probable than it would be without the evidence." The Supreme Court favors a liberal standard of admissibility. See *Daubert v. Merrell Dow Pharm., Inc.,* 509 U.S. 579, 587, 113 S.Ct. 2786 (1993). Under Federal Rule of Evidence 403, a court may exclude relevant evidence "if its probative value is substantially outweighed by the danger of unfair prejudice. . . ."

The Fifth Circuit Court of Appeals has routinely cautioned that "unfair prejudice as used in Rule 403 is not to be equated with testimony simply adverse to the opposing party. Virtually all evidence is prejudicial or it isn't material. The prejudice must be 'unfair.'" *Ballou*

*v. Henri Studios, Inc.,* 656 F.2d 1147, 1155 (5th Cir.1981) (citing *Dollar v. Long Mfg.,* N.C., Inc., 561 F.2d 613, 618 (5th Cir.1977)). Rule 403 contemplates unfair prejudice to mean "an undue tendency to suggest a decision on an improper basis, commonly, though not necessarily, an emotional one." *Id.* (internal marks omitted). Because Rule 403 allows for the exclusion of relevant evidence, its application "must be cautious and sparing." *Brady v. Fort Bend County,* 145 F.3d 691, 715 (5th Cir.1998). Accordingly, the court must consider the evidence as true when balancing the potential prejudice against the probative force of the evidence. See *Ballou,* 656 F.2d at 1154.

Here, the results of Harris's drug test not only must be relevant; their probative value must also outweigh the prejudicial effect caused by their introduction. Evidence of Harris's use of cocaine and marijuana during the week of his accident is relevant because it may, in the mind of the jury, tend to establish that Harris was impaired at the time of the accident, an issue in this case. See *Bocanegra v. Vicmar Serv. Inc.,* 320 F.3d 581, 587 (5th Cir.2003); see also *Evans v. Toyota Motor Corp.,* No. V-03-09, 2005 WL 3844071, at *1 (S.D.Tx. Sept. 2, 2005). Thus, evidence of drug use during the week of the accident is highly probative of Harris's ability to operate and remove dangerous components from a tractor while the tractor was in operation. This evidence illuminates Harris's "ability to react, perceive and reason." *Evans,* 2005 WL 3844071 at *5. Further, although the urinalysis results will likely have an adverse effect on Harris's case, such prejudice cannot be deemed unfair, as Harris's possible impairment provides a basis for a finding of contributory negligence. See *Ballou,* 656 F.2d at 1155. In short, the probative value of the evidence is not substantially outweighed by the prejudice it may cause. Hence, the test results are relevant, probative, and admissible in this case. Accordingly;

IT IS ORDERED that the motions *in limine* (Record Documents 39 and 43) be and are hereby DENIED.

## Case Review Question

Would evidence that the plaintiff did not consume the drugs within forty-eight hours before the incident have an effect on the court's determination to admit the objected evidence of the presence of drugs in the plaintiff's system?

**Opening Statements.** Following *voir dire,* the final jury is sworn in and the proceedings begin. The first step in most trials is the *opening statement.* Usually, the party who has the burden of proof makes the first opening statement. The responding party has the option of making an opening statement at this time or waiting until the presentation of his or her evidence. Opening statements are not to be argumentative. They are to serve as an opportunity for the attorneys to outline their evidence to the jury. Legal conclusions, arguments, and pleas for verdicts are inappropriate at this time. Opening statements are not evidence. Rather, they serve as an outline of the evidence to be presented.

**Case in Chief.** The *case in chief* is the stage of a trial during which the party with the burden of proof presents evidence to support its claim. The burden of proof previously mentioned refers to the party who must convince the jury of his or her case in order to win the suit. In a civil case, the burden of proof is generally on the plaintiff, who claims injury or damage resulting from the defendant's fault. The party with the burden usually presents evidence first. The standard burden of proof in most civil cases is to prove one's claim by a *preponderance* of the evidence. This means that the party with the burden must establish that the facts alleged in the complaint are more likely than not true. The party who does not have the burden of proof needs only to present enough evidence in opposition to prevent the burden (minimum level of evidence) from being met.

Consider the example discussed earlier in Application 7.2 of the auto accident involving Adam and Nathan. Assume that the suit has commenced. Because Nathan has brought the action against Adam, he is obligated to meet the burden of proof at trial. Nathan claims that Adam was not being observant while driving and struck Nathan. Adam claims that Nathan ran out from between two parked cars without warning and that he could not avoid hitting Nathan. Nathan must prove his case by a preponderance of the evidence. He must establish, with evidence, that his version of the case is more likely than not the way the accident actually occurred. In essence, the burden is on Nathan to produce enough proof to convince the jury that his version is the most plausible.

Evidence for a case of this type might include photographs of the scene and the vehicle as well as expert opinions about skid marks on the road or other indicators of the speed and direction of Adam's vehicle or visibility along the street. The party with the burden of proof must meet an additional step known as presenting a *prima facie* case. Translated literally, *prima facie* means "on the face." In effect, a *prima facie* case is what the party with the burden must prove. The evidence brought at trial must be sufficient to establish each of the facts alleged in the complaint (the face of the claim) and to support the legal claims of the complaint. If no evidence supports each allegation of the complaint, then a *prima facie* case has not been established.

If a *prima facie* case is not established, the claims of the complaint have not been proven. At this point, the party responding to the claims can make a *motion for a directed verdict,* which requests the court to instruct the jury that there is no need to present a defense because the allegations of the complaint have not been proven. If the motion is granted, the judge directs the jury to render a verdict against the party with the burden of proof.

Most parties with the burden of proof attempt to establish a much stronger case than one that is merely *prima facie.* The evidence presented must withstand contradictory evidence presented by the defense and still prevail as the most likely explanation of the circumstances that created the dispute. Realistically, a *prima facie* case is usually not enough to win the case.

**Defense.** After the party (usually the plaintiff) with the burden of proof has presented all of his or her evidence and made a *prima facie* case, that party will rest. At this point, the responding party—usually the defendant—will present his or her case. If the defense did not make an opening statement at the beginning of the trial, the opportunity to make one at this time is available. The opening statement is followed by the presentation of the defendant's evidence.

In the presentation of evidence, the defendant has no initial burden to meet. Rather, a burden occurs only if the plaintiff establishes a *prima facie* case. At this point, the burden shifts, and the defendant must present enough evidence in response to the plaintiff's evidence to create a question in the minds of the jury that the plaintiff's version is not the most likely version of the facts.

After the defendant has concluded the presentation of evidence, the plaintiff may request permission to reopen his or her case. This may be allowed when the plaintiff has evidence that will respond to some evidence introduced by the defendant. However, it is not permissible to present entirely new evidence that the plaintiff may have forgotten or otherwise failed to include in the original presentation of evidence. The plaintiff is permitted only to respond to the evidence of the defendant. The defendant may then be permitted to introduce rebuttal evidence.

**Closing Argument.** After both parties have concluded the presentation of evidence, the attorneys for the plaintiff and the defendant are allowed the opportunity to make *closing arguments,* also known as *summations.* In some jurisdictions, the defense presents its summation first and the plaintiff or prosecution gets the last word. In other jurisdictions, the plaintiff or prosecutor goes first and then gets a few moments of rebuttal to respond to the defendant's summation. At this stage, each attorney summarizes all of the evidence and attempts to persuade the jury of the most plausible explanation for the course of events that led to the lawsuit. Here the attorneys employ their advocacy skills and persuasive tactics to convince the jury in favor of their client.

**Instructions and Deliberation.** After the closing arguments, the judge will read instructions to the jury. These instructions explain the law that applies to the case as well as the burden of proof and indicate what the jury is to consider as evidence. The jury is then *sequestered* for deliberations—that is, the jurors are secluded from all outside influences while they reach a decision. Some courts will allow the jurors to take evidence such as documents and photographs into the jury room during their deliberation. In many jurisdictions, the verdict of the jury must be unanimous in favor of one party. If a jury needs more than one day to reach a verdict, the judge will determine whether the jurors can return home for the night or whether they must be continue to be sequestered, such as put up overnight in a hotel, while they are not deliberating.

---

### APPLICATION 7.4

In 2004 Scott Lee Peterson was put on trial for and convicted of the murder of his wife and unborn child. The case was closely followed by news media after Laci Peterson's disappearance on Christmas Eve 2002. Despite enormous media coverage, the judge found that the jury was able to render an impartial verdict and denied requests to sequester the jury. Sequestration of juries is a substantial issue in an era of mass communication that threatens to flood the senses. However, another substantial consideration is the cost to taxpayers. In 1995, the estimated bill for jury sequestration in the O. J. Simpson case was reported to be as much as $3 million.

*Point for Discussion:* What effects could result from a refusal of a motion to sequester?

**Verdict.** When the jury returns with a verdict, the verdict is read to the parties. If a party requests, the judge may poll the jury. When the jury is polled, the judge asks each juror whether the verdict represents his or her opinion in the case. This is used as a safeguard to assist the court in discovering situations where jurors have been coerced by other members of the jury to change their vote to reach a verdict. If the judge discovers that a juror does not actually support and believe in the verdict, the verdict is not unanimous. This would have the effect of a *hung jury* where the jurors return without a verdict. In a civil suit, when a jury cannot reach a decision that the plaintiff's case is more likely than not true, the burden of proof has not been met, and the defendant prevails.

---

### ASSIGNMENT 7.5

Identify at which stage of pretrial or trial proceedings the following is most likely to occur.

a. motion for summary judgment

b. testimony by the plaintiff in his or her behalf

c. evidence of the defendant's blood alcohol level at the time of the accident that allegedly caused plaintiff's injuries

d. evidence that the plaintiff already suffered from certain injuries at the time of the accident that plaintiff now claims were caused by the accident

e. a description of the evidence by counsel for plaintiff

f. a statement by counsel for the defendant that alleges the plaintiff is a malingerer and not to be believed

g. statement by the judge that the evidence is almost totally in favor of the plaintiff's case and the jury should find as such

h. questions to potential jurors

i. explanation to jurors of the law as it applies to the facts of the case

j. discussion by jurors of the evidence presented

---

## Rules of Evidence

The gathering and introduction of the various types of evidence are subject to many specific rules, but the rules of *relevance* and *materiality* apply to all evidence. Such rules are necessary to ensure that the evidence in any legal action is fair and proper. Evidence that is relevant and material and meets the requirements of more specific rules may be included in the trial and presented to the trier of fact.

**Relevant Evidence.** **Relevant evidence** is that which tends to establish some basic element of the dispute.[10] Each side in a lawsuit are allowed to introduce evidence that will tend to prove that its version of the story is true. For example, in the lawsuit involving Adam and Nathan, evidence Nathan introduced that Adam has been fired from every job he ever held would not be relevant. Such evidence has nothing to do with the accident or one party's driving ability. However, if Nathan introduced evidence that Adam has hit six people in under similar circumstances, the evidence might be highly relevant.

**relevant evidence**
Evidence that tends to establish an essential fact in the dispute.

**Material Evidence.** **Material evidence** is that which is considered necessary to a fair and informed determination of the dispute.[11] The same information from twenty different witnesses may not be material. In most cases, a few of these witnesses could establish the facts just as well as twenty could. In addition, evidence that may inform the court but is so extreme that it might prevent a jury from being fair could be considered immaterial. An example would be grotesque photographs

**material evidence**
Evidence necessary to a fair and informed decision by the trier of fact.

of an injury. Although the jury needs to be informed about the extent of the injuries, often the jurors can be more fair if they consider medical reports rather than extremely graphic photographs. Often the basis for a motion *in limine* will be materiality.

**Hearsay.** A rule of evidence that is employed in nearly every trial is that of *hearsay*. Entire volumes have been written about hearsay, which is defined as follows:

> An out-of-court statement offered to prove the truth of the matter asserted.
>
> Federal Rules of Civil Procedure

Hearsay follows the reasoning that everything said, written, or otherwise communicated in everyday life is not necessarily true. Therefore, such information should usually not be admitted as evidence in a trial where all other evidence is considered to be reliable and true. Hearsay evidence is testimony by a witness who repeats something that was communicated outside the trial by someone not under oath. Further, to be hearsay, the content of the communication must be offered as evidence of the truth. If it is offered only to show the ability to communicate, it would not be considered hearsay.

Because some statements are made under circumstances that are highly reliable and promote only truthful communication, there are exceptions to the hearsay rule. Such information, which would otherwise be considered to be hearsay, is reliable enough in its truthfulness to warrant introduction as evidence in the trial. An example is a person's statement that is directly contrary to the person's own best interest, such as an admission of guilt. Ordinarily, individuals do not confess to acts for which they are not responsible. If there is evidence that a party or a witness made such a statement, the information may be admitted as an exception to hearsay.

When someone has an experience and makes an immediate statement about it, the statement may be considered an exception to hearsay. Statements made in circumstances where there was not time to formulate the best legal answer are highly reliable. Thus, spontaneous statements may be admitted.

Other exceptions include regularly maintained business records, statements made to physicians, and original documents. Although there are many additional exceptions, remember that evidence of communication made out of court must have a high degree of reliability for truth before it will be admitted as an exception to hearsay.

## APPLICATION 7.5

An explosion occurred on a college campus as the result of a chemistry lab experiment gone terribly wrong. One student was killed and several more were severely injured. The students' families brought suit against the instructor and the college. One family claimed its deceased student survived long enough to experience severe pain and suffering, although he was pronounced dead at the scene by authorities. The defense claimed that the death was instantaneous with the explosion and thus there could have been no pain and suffering that would warrant compensation. The family wants to introduce evidence in the form of testimony by the other injured students that they heard the deceased make various unintelligible remarks for several minutes immediately following the explosion. Because there was no actual statement made, and the only evidence is that the individual was alive and had the ability to generate sound, the remarks would not be considered hearsay. However, if the individual had

*(continued)*

---

**APPLICATION 7.5** (Continued)

made a deliberate communication or expression of pain that was considered relevant and material, the hearsay rule would be applied and it would be determined if an exception to the rule applied.

*Point for Discussion:* What if the individual knew he or she was going to die and asked someone on the phone to communicate his or her love to family members? Would this be treated as hearsay? Consider the passengers on United Flight 93 of September 11, 2001, who perished when the hijacked plane crashed into a field in Pennsylvania.

---

**Privilege.** Another important aspect of evidentiary law involves privilege. Generally, a person cannot be required to testify about confidential communications, including communications made in a physician–patient, attorney–client, clergy–parishioner, husband–wife, or any other relationship that the court determines should be protected. With respect to the husband–wife privilege, some exceptions have been made in recent years, especially in the area of criminal law (see Chapter 15). Other exceptions to privilege occur when the party claiming the privilege has placed the very content of the communication in issue. For example, if a person is involved in a personal injury lawsuit, the privilege to withhold confidential medical records about the injury is waived.

**Other Evidence.** Numerous specific rules of evidence exist regarding such areas as opinion, habit, and personal background of a rape victim. Even when evidence is relevant, material, not hearsay, and not privileged, it may still be objected to on the basis of one of the more specific rules. Assembling and presenting admissible evidence is one of the most crucial elements of trial, if not the most crucial element. Consequently, anyone involved in litigation must be fully aware of the rules of evidence.

## Rules of Appellate Procedure

Appellate procedure is largely governed by the appellate system in a jurisdiction. As discussed in Chapter 2, there are two types of appellate jurisdictional structures. One involves appeal directly to the highest court of the jurisdiction, whereas the other involves review by an intermediate court of appeals. If a jurisdiction involves an intermediate court of appeals, such as the federal judicial system's circuit courts of appeals, special rules must be created to guide a case through this level before it reaches the highest court.

The appellate court generally reviews only what has occurred procedurally in the lower court. Such review may encompass what took place before, during, or after the trial. Most often, appellate courts refuse to hear or consider any new evidence in a case. This does not mean that the court will only hear what was admitted at trial. Rather, it will hear all evidence that was offered, irrespective of whether the trial court admitted or refused the evidence. The appellate court will not hear evidence that was available but was not presented to the trial court.[12]

Appellate court decisions are usually confined to the issue of whether an error was made in the trial court. Further, the error must be serious enough to warrant intervention by the appellate court. Consequently, an appellate court will not exchange its opinion of right or wrong or guilt or innocence for that of the trier of fact. It will only consider whether the opinion of the trier of fact was based on a fair presentation of the case according to the requirements of substantive and procedural law.

## APPLICATION 7.6

Vince was a seventy-five-year-old man who has been known all of his life for eccentric behavior. He was a stunt pilot for many years, and those who knew him were well aware of his love of flying. He was also enormously wealthy. Many times, Vince made large anonymous gifts to individuals he encountered. He was recently diagnosed with the earliest stage of Alzheimer's disease. This caused him to have to give up his pilot's license. Because Vince knew his mental status would likely deteriorate progressively over time, he wrote a plan to distribute the vast majority of his estate in the form of gifts to numerous charities. Vince's daughter saw the plan and worried that Vince would not leave what she considered a reasonable amount for her as an inheritance. She filed a case in probate court to have Vince declared mentally incompetent. She introduced several witnesses who testified to unusual behavior such as Vince's frequent recent day trips in which he would board a commercial airplane and fly to and from a distant city just for the ride. She also introduced as evidence Vince's plan to give away virtually all of his assets to organizations with whom he had no previous involvement. The court found that Vince was not exercising judgment in his own best interest and named his daughter as his guardian. Further, she was given complete control over his estate, including all assets. Vince appealed the case on the basis that the court failed to consider his long history of philanthropy and his love of flying, which he could no longer do independently.

The appellate court in this case would not be faced with the decision regarding whether to uphold or set aside the guardianship nor would it be faced with the challenge to determine Vince's competence. Rather, the only function of the court would be to determine whether the evidence was all properly considered and if the manifest weight of the evidence supported the decision. If the court found that it did not, then the case would go back to the trial court for further consideration and a new trial would likely be ordered.

*Point for Discussion:* Why do appellate courts remand cases back to trial courts for further action rather than just correcting the errors based on their own judgment?

---

The appeals process is started by notice to the courts and all other parties from the appealing party (known as the *appellant*), who claims that something improper has taken place. The party who defends against the appeal and claims that the procedure has been proper is the *appellee*.

Once the courts and other parties have been given notice, several events must occur. The order and time for these events may vary from jurisdiction to jurisdiction. Generally, the appellant is responsible for having the trial court records of the case prepared and sent to the appellate court. These records enable the appellate court to review the entire history of the case, including the alleged error by the trial court. The records consist of all legal documents (commonly called *pleadings* and *motions*) filed with the court by the parties. Also included will be court orders in the case and transcribed statements of the parties, attorneys, witnesses, and the judge during court hearings.

In addition to submitting the court records, the appellant as well as the appellee may submit appellate briefs—detailed explanations of the case and the law applicable to the case of the particular party—to the reviewing court. The briefs set forth the facts of the case, the issues that arose in the lower court, and the result of the case. The briefs also suggest applicable law to the appellate court that supports the position of the party with respect to the issue. The appellate court's duty is to select the law that best applies to the situation.

**Exhibit 7.15** Steps in a Civil Suit

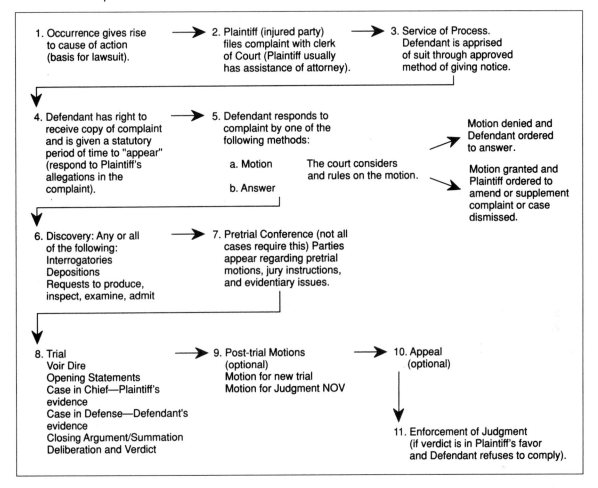

1. Occurrence gives rise to cause of action (basis for lawsuit). → 2. Plaintiff (injured party) files complaint with clerk of Court (Plaintiff usually has assistance of attorney). → 3. Service of Process. Defendant is apprised of suit through approved method of giving notice.

4. Defendant has right to receive copy of complaint and is given a statutory period of time to "appear" (respond to Plaintiff's allegations in the complaint). → 5. Defendant responds to complaint by one of the following methods:

a. Motion     The court considers and rules on the motion.
b. Answer

Motion denied and Defendant ordered to answer.

Motion granted and Plaintiff ordered to amend or supplement complaint or case dismissed.

6. Discovery: Any or all of the following: Interrogatories Depositions Requests to produce, inspect, examine, admit → 7. Pretrial Conference (not all cases require this) Parties appear regarding pretrial motions, jury instructions, and evidentiary issues.

8. Trial
Voir Dire
Opening Statements
Case in Chief—Plaintiff's evidence
Case in Defense—Defendant's evidence
Closing Argument/Summation
Deliberation and Verdict
→ 9. Post-trial Motions (optional) Motion for new trial Motion for Judgment NOV → 10. Appeal (optional)

11. Enforcement of Judgment (if verdict is in Plaintiff's favor and Defendant refuses to comply).

In many appellate cases, the courts permit attorneys for the parties to present oral arguments of the briefs. At this stage, each attorney presents the brief and answers questions by the appellate court about the brief's content. The court may ask the attorneys to explain why they think a particular point of law is applicable to the current case. In addition, the attorneys may respond to the points raised in their adversary's brief.

The appellate court will consider the case and render a written opinion. The court may *affirm* (approve) the proceedings of the lower court or *reverse* the lower court and remand the case to the trial court with an order for new or different proceedings to be conducted. Occasionally, the appellate court will hold that the lower court erred to the point that the proceedings should not even have been held. In such situations, the case is dismissed entirely.

Exhibit 7.15 shows the steps in a civil suit from occurrence of incident giving rise to a lawsuit to appeal and enforcement of judgment.

## ETHICAL CONSIDERATIONS

Discussion frequently takes place about the ethical obligations of legal professionals. Individuals whose ethical duties do not attract much attention, however, are jurors. From the time an individual is selected for a pool of potential jurors, ethical requirements apply. Even potential jurors are asked to take an oath to consider and answer questions of the parties, counsel, and the court in an honest and forthright manner. The duty of a juror is a serious one. The legal rights of total strangers have been entrusted to the juror on the premise that the juror will listen to the evidence objectively and apply only the law and not personal bias to the evidence when reaching a verdict.

Although a somewhat rare occurrence, it is not unheard of for a verdict to be reversed on appeal on the basis of (1) discovered information that a juror considered information not presented as evidence or (2) a juror allowed personal bias to direct the verdict in a lawsuit. Although courts are reluctant to tamper with the sanctity of the jury process, it is necessary to monitor the process as any other aspect of the legal system for unethical conduct by those who are in such a position of trust.

## Question

Can you think of a situation when a juror might act unethically?

### ETHICAL CIRCUMSTANCE

In a rural county, the only physician was sued for malpractice. In the months before trial, the physician let it be well known that if he were found liable, he intended to close his practice and move to a more urban setting. At trial, despite compelling evidence of professional neglect of a patient that ultimately resulted in death, the physician was found not responsible. On interviewing the jurors after trial, it was discovered that three of the jurors had lied during *voir dire* and were, in fact, longtime patients of the physician and that they had harassed and bullied the other jurors into finding the physician not responsible for the death of the patient. In this particular case, the jurors violated their ethical obligations and their oath. Although none were prosecuted, the verdict was overturned and the case was ordered to be retried in a remote community where no patients of the physician resided.

## ● | CHAPTER SUMMARY

Procedural law is never constant. Every jurisdiction creates procedural law to conform to the needs of its particular judicial structure and its population. Then, as society changes, these needs change, and the rules must be altered. In spite of these constant changes, it would be impossible for a legal system as complex and as heavily used as the U.S. legal system to function without some type of procedural standards. In reality, the procedural laws enable any citizen in this country to utilize the court system to obtain answers to legal questions and redress for legal wrongs.

The various types of procedural law address the various stages of litigation. Rules of civil procedure often deal with the pretrial phase of a lawsuit, including the important stage of discovery. Rules of evidence give the court and the parties direction as to what types of information would be appropriate for a jury to reach a fair and intelligent verdict. Rules of appellate procedure guide the parties through the appellate process to have a case properly reviewed by a higher court.

In any lawsuit, once the procedural concerns have been dealt with, the court is free to address the heart of the issue between the parties in dispute. The substantive law guides the judiciary in doing so. The facts are examined, the true issue is identified, and the law is applied to the circumstances to make the determination of which party should prevail. In fact, if more persons would look to these legal standards before taking action, the results would be apparent, and a great number of legal disputes could be avoided. As long as people fail to inquire as to the law or disagree as to its meaning, however, disputes will continue and procedural law will facilitate the application of substantive law in the determination of these disputes.

As a case proceeds through the steps of trial, a jury is selected through a process called *voir dire*. Next, the attorneys make opening statements, which describe the evidence they intend to present. The plaintiff presents evidence first in a stage known as the *case in chief*. The defense responds with evidence that weakens or contradicts the case of the plaintiff. After all the evidence has been introduced, the attorneys summarize the evidence presented in a light most favorable to their client. Following this, the jury is instructed on the law and deliberates until it reaches a verdict.

Throughout the entire litigation process, the attorneys communicate requests to the court in the form of *motions*. These formal requests seek everything from information about the evidence of the opposing party to dismissal of the case against the opposition or even a new trial entirely. The process of motion practice provides an efficient and effective method of resolving issues that arise during litigation and cannot be resolved by the parties.

## CHAPTER TERMS

| | | |
|---|---|---|
| arbitration | discovery | procedural law |
| civil law | material evidence | relevant evidence |
| compensatory damages | motion | substantive law |
| complaint | | |

## REVIEW QUESTIONS

1. When are punitive damages awarded?
2. When is a motion to dismiss usually granted?
3. What is the burden of proof on a plaintiff in a common civil case?
4. How are opening statements different from closing arguments?
5. What is *voir dire* and why is it conducted in jury trials?
6. What is the difference between discovery and investigation?
7. What is the purpose of discovery and investigation?
8. What is the difference between material evidence and relevant evidence?
9. Why is pure hearsay (when not subject to an exception) inadmissible?
10. What is summary judgment and when is it granted?

## HELPFUL WEB SITES

| | |
|---|---|
| Federal Rules of Civil Procedure | http//www.cornell.edu/rules/frcp |
| Substantive Law Research | http//www.law.emory.edu/law/refdesk/country/ |

## INTERNET ASSIGNMENT 7.1

Locate the Web site for your state government that provides access to the procedural rules for state courts.

## INTERNET ASSIGNMENT 7.2

Does your jurisdiction allow punitive damages (damages used to punish the defendant rather than compensate the plaintiff)?

### ● | ENDNOTES

1. William Statsky, *Legal Thesaurus/Dictionary* (St. Paul, MN: West, 1982).
2. *Id.*
3. *Erie R. Co. v. T Tompkins,* 304 U.S. 64, 58 S.Ct. 817, 82 L.Ed. 1188 (1938).
4. *Guaranty Trust Co. of N.Y. v. York,* 326 U.S. 99, 65 S.Ct. 1464, 89 L.Ed. 2079 (1945).
5. *Hanna v. Plumer,* 380 U.S. 460, 85 S.Ct. 1136, 14 L.Ed. 2d 8 (1965).
6. Federal Rules of Civil Procedure, Rule 1.
7. *Id.* at Rule 3.
8. *Stastny v. Tachovsky,* 178 Neb. 109, 132 N.W. 2d 317 (1964).
9. Federal Rules of Civil Procedure, Rule 56.
10. Federal Rules of Evidence, 28 U.S.C.A.
11. *Id.*
12. *In re Edinger's Estate,* 136 N.W.2d 114 (N.D. 1965).

### STUDENT CD-ROM

For additional materials, please go to the CD in this book.

### ONLINE COMPANION™

For additional resources, please go to www.paralegal.delmar.cengage.com

# CHAPTER

## 8

# Jurisdiction

## DO WE NEED A CENTRAL NATIONAL COURT?

Ask anyone on the street and a common response will be that the American legal system is just too complicated for the average citizen to navigate. It's true that the system has developed into an enormous web of elected officials, appointed authorities, levels of state and federal government agencies, offices, and courts. And there are countless rules to direct citizens to the proper destination. Still, even with all of the divisions and subdivisions that have been created to respond to virtually every situation, now and then a circumstance will arise that does not fit into a single definition of how such a case should be handled. Just such an event occurred with the life and death of celebrity Anna Nicole Smith.

In her early life, Smith married and had a son in Texas where much of her family continues to reside. A few years later she met and ultimately married wealthy aristocrat J. Howard Marshall of Texas, who was more than seventy years her senior. Marshall died of natural causes a relatively short time after the marriage. His son from a former marriage and primary heir contested Anna Nicole's right to any part of the estate. Anna, then living in California, instituted legal proceedings there in federal bankruptcy court and took measures to protect her rights as a widow. The Marshall estate was being probated in Texas. The two courts collided as to which court had the greatest authority to rule on the matter. The appellate process began and lumbered through the courts for years. In the meantime, Anna executed a will in her longtime state of residence California, naming her only son as her heir and indicated no other future children or other unnamed individuals should inherit.

Several years later, while the appeals were still climbing the appellate court ladder, Anna, who was pregnant, moved from California to the Bahamas, where she sought citizenship. It is interesting to note that the Bahamas has its own legal system and is not obliged to honor U.S. court orders. She gave birth to a daughter in the Bahamas, and just a few days later her now adult son died unexpectedly while visiting Anna in the hospital in the Bahamas. Anna's longtime companion claimed paternity of the daughter, who was granted dual citizenship of the United States and the Bahamas. Also during this time, Anna became embroiled in a legal battle over her rights to the home in the Bahamas where she was living. Next on the scene was the former boyfriend who claimed paternity and instituted an action in California. Although the California courts were Anna's stronghold in her battle for the Marshall estate, by all accounts she seemed to avoid them when it came to issues of paternity and custody for her daughter. This now left major issues pending in various California courts, Texas courts, and the Bahamas.

In February 2007, during a brief visit, Anna died unexpectedly in Florida without having ever updated or amending her will. At the time of her death, the baby was still in the Bahamas. A battle erupted immediately over the right to Anna's remains The pace also picked up in the child paternity, custody matters, and real estate in the Bahamas, all while the Marshall estate case was still pending after having been handed back by the U.S. Supreme Court with a holding that the California court could proceed with Anna's claims. Enter the Florida courts on the issue of custody of the body.

When all is said and done, the life and death of Anna Nicole Smith at just thirty-nine years old will have been addressed by no fewer than three different states, every level of appellate court, a foreign government, and the U.S. Supreme Court. Despite the fact that Anna is the common denominator in all cases, her movements and actions generated authority on some level in all of these courts. The potential still exists for conflicting court rulings on a variety of matters with regard to the Marshall estate, Anna's estate, and the custody and inheritance rights of the baby who was ultimately found to be the child of Anna's former boyfriend and not the companion whose name appeared on the birth certificate. This case is an example of complex legal situations that are repeated throughout the United States.

The question arises then, is the American legal system adequate? Does it respond appropriately to complex situations? Or, with the extensive amount of interstate movement of citizens, is the system obsolete and should a single central national court be established to address issues of interstate significance? After all, nowadays the rules of "who has authority" are subject to change as often as the members of the bench of the U.S. Supreme Court and legislatures move in and out of office. What would be the objections, however, to such a system that would eliminate courts established by the independent states?

## CHAPTER OUTLINE

## CHAPTER OBJECTIVES

After reading this chapter, you should be able to:

- Distinguish *in personam, in rem,* and *quasi in rem* jurisdiction.

- Describe subject matter jurisdiction.

- Identify the conditions to establish federal jurisdiction.

- Discuss the circumstances of removal and remand of a case based on federal jurisdiction.

- List the possible domiciles of a corporation.

- Explain how the domicile of a corporation is determined.

- Discuss the doctrine of *forum non conveniens.*

- List the factors used to make a *forum non conveniens* determination.

Jurisdiction plays a significant role in the U.S. legal system. It is a necessary element of all lawsuits. Until a court has determined that it has proper jurisdiction, a case will not be allowed to proceed. In essence, jurisdiction is the authority of a court to pass judgment over a specific type of case and each party to the suit. The formal definition is as follows:

1. The power of a court to decide a matter in controversy.

2. The geographic area over which a particular court has authority.[1]

The first definition of jurisdiction can be quite complex. It is based on the principle that a court should not have authority to pass and enforce judgment or sentences over persons or issues with which the court has absolutely no connection. The court has the duty to uphold the rights of those within its boundaries and not to spend time interpreting cases that do not affect the citizens or property within those boundaries. Because the authority of the court is related to all of the parties to the lawsuit and all the incidents that ultimately produced the suit, the decision of exactly which court has jurisdiction can be a complicated process.

The judiciary and the legislatures have created various rules to help courts determine when they have authority over persons and issues associated with a particular lawsuit. Jurisdiction has been broken down into several categories, each of which represents subtypes of the general concept of court authority. Each type of jurisdiction addresses a particular aspect of the court's authority over a case.

## TYPES OF JURISDICTION

Several elements must be considered when determining whether a court has authority to hear a case. The various considerations are represented by the different types of jurisdiction. In any lawsuit, the court must have jurisdiction over the parties as well as over the dispute. This not only allows the court to determine who wins but also gives the court authority to enforce the verdict.

### Subject Matter Jurisdiction

**Subject matter jurisdiction** is just what its name implies. It is the authority of a court over the actual dispute between the parties. This jurisdiction is concerned with the relationship of the court to the dispute.[2]

Persons cannot create this type of jurisdiction by an agreement as to which court will have authority to hear their case. Nor can this type of jurisdiction be created because a party fails to object if a case is improperly brought in a particular court. Rather, subject matter jurisdiction is an issue that each court must identify before any case proceeds.

**subject matter jurisdiction**
Authority of a court to determine the actual issue between the parties.

## APPLICATION 8.1

Kenan operated an Internet retail business. He established his own Web site and wrote all of the terms of agreement for sales to customers. One thing Kenan did not include in the terms of agreement was a requirement that, in the event of a dispute, all customers would be subject to the jurisdiction where Kenan was domiciled. Kenan usually purchased generators from a manufacturer in an adjacent state. Generally, Kenan would receive an order through his online catalog. Once the payment for an order cleared, he made the purchase from the manufacturer. He would have the shipment sent to the customer directly from the manufacturer.

One of the generators was sold by Kenan to a resident of a state 2,000 miles from Kenan and the manufacturer. The customer claimed to have received the generator and operated it properly and according to all instructions. Nevertheless, the generator exploded. The customer's home was burned to the ground and the customer's four children died in the fire. The customer filed suit against Kenan and the manufacturer in the state where the plaintiff resided.

The residents of the state where the explosion occurred had a strong connection to the case. A product was purchased by a consumer and delivered into the state, and its use resulted in the death of several citizens. Even though the defendants would probably prefer to have the case heard in their own jurisdiction, the state where Kenan did business had virtually no connection other than having a resident who processed sales orders over a computer. The state where the manufacturer was located might have an interest, because the product was created there, but it would probably not be considered as strong as where the incident and resulting deaths occurred.

*Points for Discussion:* If the suit was filed in the state where Kenan was located, what state substantive law would be applied?

The citizens of a jurisdiction as a whole must have some interest in a lawsuit before the court will have subject matter jurisdiction to hear the case. Stated another way, the laws of the jurisdiction must be promoted by the determination of the case. A primary obligation of the judiciary is to apply the laws of a jurisdiction for the benefit of the people. Therefore, applying laws of another jurisdiction, when not even one citizen would be affected, would be a misuse of the court's authority. To achieve subject matter jurisdiction, many states require that the circumstances giving rise to the dispute occur in the state or that a party reside in the state. This general rule has exceptions, and the appropriate state law should be consulted when determining the jurisdiction over a particular action.

## ASSIGNMENT 8.1

Examine each of the following situations and determine which court(s) does or does not have subject matter jurisdiction. (At this point, assume there are no other rules regarding jurisdiction and no issue subject to federal jurisdiction.) Be prepared to discuss your answers.

1. Karl is a resident of state A. He drives to state B on a hunting trip. While hunting, Karl is shot by Julian, another hunter.

Julian is a resident of state C. Karl sues Julian for his injuries in state A. Karl later moves to state D, which is known for its high jury awards. He plans to file dismiss the suit in state A and refile it in state D.

2. B.J. is a resident of state M in the northern part of the United States. She is originally from state X, a southern coastal state. The community where she grew up is known for

*(continued)*

## ASSIGNMENT 8.1 (Continued)

its unique handwoven cloth and clothing designed for the tropical climate. She often purchases items from stores there when she visits. On one such occasion, she purchases a nightgown and brings it home. On a winter night, B.J. is wearing the nightgown as she sits near the fireplace. A single spark flies out of the fireplace and instantly ignites the gown. It is later determined that the gown is made from a material that is petroleum based and extremely flammable. The material is not one intended or approved for sleepwear. B.J. files suit against the manufacturer and the store where she bought the gown for the serious injuries she suffered in the combustion of the gown she was wearing.

3. Adam lives in a rural area along the border of states I and G. He orders a musical instrument from a music store in a community located across the border in state G. It is not something the music store typically handles, but it places the order as a favor to Adam because he is a friend of the owner. The store must order the instrument to be shipped in from state C. Adam picks up the instrument at the store and pays for it. The instrument is still in the original shipping carton and appears unopened. When Adam opens it at home, he finds a box full of foam peanuts and a few rocks. The store claims never to have opened the box. The manufacturer in state C claims that the box was inspected before shipment. Both the manufacturer and the store believe Adam opened the box and replaced the instrument with the foam and rocks.

4. Max was a resident of the state of Illinois. He was traveling on his boat along the Mississippi River. After passing along the borders of Missouri, Kentucky, Tennessee, Arkansas, and Louisiana, he stopped on the eastern side of the river where it forms the western border of the state of Mississippi. He docked his boat at a marina and went into a store that was located on the shore. He purchased groceries and supplies there and returned to the boat. As he traveled back up the river toward home, he consumed the groceries. Early on in the trip he began feeling ill. By the time he returned home, he was seriously ill with an *E. coli* infection, and he subsequently died. It was determined he ingested tainted food purchased in Mississippi.

5. Sid lived in New Jersey. He traveled to New York City to attend a sporting event. In the parking lot of the event, Sid was struck by a car driven by the valet driver Keith. The lot was owned and operated by a New York resident. Keith, however, was a resident of New Jersey as well. Sid never fully recovered from the accident and eventually went to live in a nursing home in Connecticut.

In addition to the broad notion of subject matter jurisdiction is a more particular application. State and federal jurisdictions have several judges and, in fact, several courts to hear all of the cases. Chapter 2 discussed the many federal courts. In addition, the states have a court in each county known as a *trial court of general jurisdiction*. These courts can hear at trial any type of case and parties over which they have authority. For matters of convenience and efficiency, many trial courts are divided into subclasses by the type of case or issue being addressed. Trial courts are also often called courts of **original jurisdiction**.

The following is an example of divisions within a trial court. One judge will hear criminal cases, another will hear domestic disputes, and yet another will hear major trials on contract and tort claims. The subject matter authority of the judges within each of these subdivided courts is limited by the type of case the judges are assigned to hear. Consequently, a judge assigned to the domestic relations court would not ordinarily have authority to hear a major breach of contract claim. This type of authority is based on the idea of organization of the courts and is not considered a true form of jurisdiction.

**original jurisdiction**
Authority of a court to determine the rights and obligations of the parties in a lawsuit (e.g., trial court).

## APPLICATION 8.2

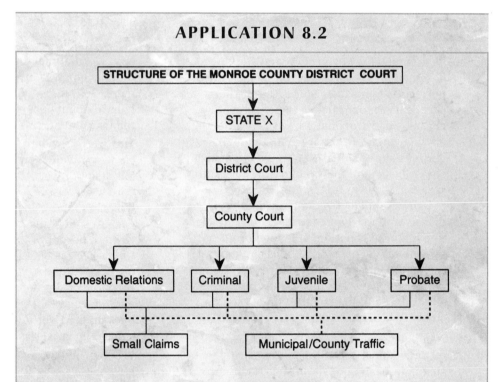

The following is an example of how a court structure as diagrammed here might function.

- District court: Hears all major civil cases with a value assessed at greater than $20,000 and not otherwise assigned to a court by subject matter.
- County court: Hears all civil cases with a value between $2,500.01 and $19,999.99 and not otherwise assigned to a court by subject matter.
- Domestic relations: Hears all matters involving divorce, annulment, alimony (spousal maintenance), child support, child custody, and child visitation, regardless of the dollar value of the case.
- Criminal: Hears all matters involving criminal charges, with the exception of misdemeanor traffic charges and cases involving juveniles as defendants.
- Juvenile: Hears all cases in which juveniles are charged criminally.
- Probate: Hears all cases regarding the estate (property) of decedents, minors, and incompetents (persons legally determined to be incapable of managing their own affairs).
- Small claims: Hears all civil cases of a value of $2,500.00 or less.
- Municipal or county traffic: Hears all cases involving charges of traffic violations of the municipalities of the county or county ordinances that are misdemeanor (penalty of less than one year incarceration or fine of less than $1,000) in nature.

*Point for Discussion:* Why would it be beneficial to have the same judge(s) hear all cases involving a particular area of law such as domestic relations?

**ancillary jurisdiction**
Authority of a court over issues in a case that is subject to the court's authority on other grounds.

**pendent jurisdiction**
Authority of a federal court, presented with a federal claim, to also determine interrelated claims based on state law.

Occasionally, a dispute between two parties is not confined to a single issue. When several claims arise from the same occurrence, a court that has subject matter jurisdiction will also usually have **ancillary jurisdiction**: the authority to hear related claims that the court generally would not have the power to hear if they were in a separate case. Similar to this is **pendent jurisdiction**: the authority of a federal court presented with a federal claim to also hear claims based on state law that arise out of the same set of circumstances that produced the federal claim. Allowing courts to hear such matters prevents duplicity of trials in state and federal courts.

## Jurisdiction *in Personam* (Personal Jurisdiction)

Assume for the purposes of the following discussion that a suit has been filed in a court that has subject matter jurisdiction. The court has the authority to determine who will prevail in the lawsuit. However, the court must still have jurisdiction over the parties to enforce any judgment or ruling it might render in the lawsuit. The court can obtain such authority over the parties in any of three methods.

The first method of authority is *in personam* **jurisdiction**—the authority of the court over the person.[3] This type of authority gives the court the power to compel the person to appear in court and answer questions or claims of a party to the lawsuit. It also includes the power to seize all assets of the person or even to impose a jail sentence.

***in personam*
(personal) jurisdiction**
Authority of a court to render and enforce rulings over a particular individual and the individual's property.

**Domicile.** A court may obtain *in personam* jurisdiction over an individual in several ways. The most common is by *domicile*—that is, the place where one intends to make a permanent residence and has actual residence (even if periodic). A person is presumed to be subject to the authority of a court if that person lives in the geographical jurisdiction. The key to domicile is intent. Although a person may have residences in many states, the domicile is considered to be the primary residence. The domicile may be shown by examples of a strong connection to the jurisdiction, such as paying income taxes in a particular jurisdiction, registering to vote, obtaining a driver's license, or living in that residence more than any other place during the year. The greater the number of elements such as those mentioned, the more likely a certain jurisdiction will be considered one's domicile. A person can have only one domicile.

**Consent (Waiver).** The court may have authority over an individual who is not domiciled in a jurisdiction. Personal jurisdiction can be obtained by consent of the individual either voluntarily or by waiver. If a person agrees to be subjected to the authority of the court, the lawsuit may be filed with that court, assuming, of course, that subject matter jurisdiction exists. An example of this may be two persons who are separated and want to file for divorce. If the parties reside in different states, one may agree to be subject to the *in personam* authority of the state where the other resides and where the parties resided when living together. If a suit is filed against a person over whom the court has no personal jurisdiction and that party does not object at the onset of the lawsuit, the right to object is waived. When a person fails to object to a court's authority over him or her, it is presumed that the person agrees to the exercise of authority. Such authority is *in personam* jurisdiction by waiver.

**Long-Arm Statutes.** Finally, all states have what are known as **long-arm statutes,**[4] which refer to the authority of a court over a nonresident because of contacts within a state. Under these laws, the person or business entity need not live in the jurisdiction or consent to court authority. Rather, one's acts are considered to contain implied consent. The theory is that if one accepts the benefits of a jurisdiction and subsequently injures a party within the jurisdiction, the courts of the jurisdiction have the right to impose responsibility for wrongdoing. Thus, the court has a "long arm" that will reach into other jurisdictions and draw the individual or entity back.

The circumstances that trigger long-arm jurisdiction statutes vary from state to state. One circumstance used in many states concerns the operation of a motor

**long-arm statute**
Authority of a court to impose *in personam* jurisdiction over persons beyond the court's geographical boundaries (allowed only in statutorily specified circumstances).

**INDIANA RULES OF TRIAL PROCEDURE**
**II. COMMENCEMENT OF ACTION; SERVICE OF PROCESS, PLEADINGS, MOTIONS AND ORDERS**
**TRIAL RULE 4.4 SERVICE UPON PERSONS IN ACTIONS FOR ACTS DONE IN THIS STATE OR**
**HAVING AN EFFECT IN THIS STATE**

(A) Acts Serving as a Basis for JURISDICTION. Any person or organization that is a nonresident of this state, a resident of this state who has left the state, or a person whose residence is unknown, submits to the JURISDICTION of the courts of this state as to any action arising from the following acts committed by him or his agent.

(1) doing any business in this state;

(2) causing personal injury or property damage by an act or omission done within this state;

(3) causing personal injury or property damage in this state by an occurrence, act or omission done outside this state if he regularly does or solicits business or engages in any other persistent course of conduct, or derives substantial revenue or benefit from goods, materials, or SERVICES used, consumed, or rendered in this state;

(4) having supplied or contracted to supply SERVICES rendered or to be rendered or goods or materials furnished or to be furnished in this state;

(5) owning, using, or possessing any real property or an interest in real property within this state;

(6) contracting to insure or act as surety for or on behalf of any person, property or risk located within this state at the time the contract was made; or

(7) living in the marital relationship within the state notwithstanding subsequent departure from the state, as to all obligations for alimony, custody, child support, or property settlement, if the other party to the marital relationship continues to reside in the state.

(B) Manner of SERVICE. A person subject to the JURISDICTION of the courts of this state under this RULE may be served with summons:

(1) As provided by RULES 4.1 (SERVICE on individuals), 4.5 (SERVICE upon resident who cannot be found or served within the state), 4.6 (SERVICE upon organizations), 4.9 (*in rem* actions); or

(2) The person shall be deemed to have appointed the Secretary of State as his agent upon whom SERVICE of summons may be made as provided in RULE 4.10. . . .

vehicle. The reasoning is that if a person accepts the benefits of driving on a highway system within a jurisdiction, the person should also accept responsibility for any damage caused while driving. Another example involves persons who do business with parties in a jurisdiction. By accepting the financial benefits of doing business, the persons also must answer to injury claims as a result of doing business. Such claims may cover contract actions or any other type of injury that may occur. Each jurisdiction applies specific considerations to determine whether someone was actually "doing business" within the state (see Exhibit 8.1).

## ASSIGNMENT 8.2

For each of the following situations, state whether there would be *in personam* jurisdiction and, if so, whether it is because of domicile, consent, or long arm.

1. Cody was a lifelong resident of Colorado. He drove to Arizona where he camped for three months in a national park. Disgusted at the amount of money spent by the government on national parks, he then drove to the rim of the Grand Canyon where he tossed in three months' worth of accumulated garbage. On his way out of the park,

*(continued)*

he struck the parked car of a tourist who was a California resident. Cody returned to his home in Colorado.

2. Chrissy was with Cody on the camping trip. However, she enjoyed Arizona so much, she decided to stay. However, in an attempt to help Cody, she put the car that had been struck into neutral and pushed it into the canyon in the hopes it would look like an accident caused by the tourist leaving the car in gear.

3. Judy sold souvenirs at a booth located at the Pennsylvania state fair, which was held near her home. One of the souvenirs was purchased by a patron who was visiting from South Carolina. The patron then mailed the souvenir to a grandchild in Iowa. The child was only two years old and choked to death after putting the toy in her mouth. Judy was sued for failing to warn the patron.

4. Conner and Barb were married in Idaho in December. They set out for a new life together with no particular destination in mind. They worked for a farmer in Nebraska for almost six months and lived in a house provided by the farmer at a modest rent. Then in June they moved on to take jobs in Baltimore, Maryland. They decided to stay in Baltimore permanently and open their

own tattoo parlor and taxidermy service. Approximately one month after they had left, the farmer in Nebraska discovered that Conner and Barbara had virtually destroyed the interior of the house. They had left the house strewn with the carcasses of numerous animals that Conner had killed while hunting and then unsuccessfully attempted to stuff as he practiced his taxidermy skills. The animals had been decomposing in the house during the heat of summer until the farmer noticed the smell from a quarter mile away.

5. Marsha entered a partnership with Jim. Marsha was to create artistic crafts in her home in Ohio. Jim, a resident of Kentucky, agreed to pick up the finished items and sell them at various craft fairs around the Midwest. After six months and the contribution of crafts valued at more than $3,000, Marsha had received no money from Jim. It was only then that she discovered that Jim had never even left his home in Kentucky after collecting the products from her in Ohio. H had made no attempt to sell any of the products. Instead, he had sold all of the crafts at a yard sale for a gross amount of $200. Further, he had spent all of the money on a birthday gift for his son.

# CASE

## Abbott Laboratories v. Mylan Pharmaceuticals, Inc.,
## 2006 WL 850916 (N.D. ILL)

The following case demonstrates how communications and business conducted through mass media can result in a submission to personal jurisdiction. . . .

The following facts are drawn from Abbott's complaint. . . . Abbott holds two patents for Sodium Hydrogen Divalproate Oligomer, . . . each of which is set to expire on January 29, 2008. . . . On August 4, 2000, the Food and Drug Administration ("FDA") approved Abbott's New Drug Application for Depakote, a trademarked product. . . . After the FDA approved Depakote, the FDA listed the drug on the "Approved Drug Products with Therapeutic Equivalence Evaluations" list and associated the two patents with Depakote. . . .

On April 12, 2005, Mylan notified Abbott that it had filed an Abbreviated New Drug Application ("ANDA") with the FDA to make a generic equivalent of Depakote. . . . On October 5, 2005, Mylan notified Abbott that Mylan had modified its ANDA to include a "Paragraph IV" certification, in which Mylan challenged the validity and/or enforceability of Abbott's two patents for Depakote, as permitted by 21 U.S.C. § 355(j)(2)(A)(vii)(IV). . . .

. . . Once a patent holder has received notice that a Paragraph IV certification has been filed that implicates one or more of its patents, the patent holder has 45 days in which to file suit for patent infringement or

(continued)

the ANDA will be approved immediately and the patent protection will be lost. See 35 U.S.C. § 271(e)(5); 21 U.S.C. 355(j)(5)(B)(iii). On November 18, 2005 Abbott filed two suits for patent infringement: one in the Northern District of West Virginia, where Mylan has its corporate headquarters, and one in the Northern District of Illinois, where Abbott has its corporate headquarters. Mylan has moved this Court to dismiss the case before it for lack of personal jurisdiction. . . .

The party seeking to establish jurisdiction bears the burden to make a *prima facie* showing that the forum has personal jurisdiction over the defendant. *Euromarket Designs, Inc. v. Crate & Barrel Ltd.*, 96 F.Supp.2d 824, 833 (N.D.Ill.2000); . . . .

. . . Illinois long-arm statute permits courts to assert personal jurisdiction over a non-resident defendant on any basis permitted by the Illinois and the United States constitutions. See 735 ILCS 5/2-209; *Central States, Southeast and Southwest Areas Pension Fund v. Reimer Express World Corp.*, 230 F.3d 934, 939 (7th Cir.2000). . . .

A plaintiff demonstrates personal jurisdiction over a non-resident defendant through a two-part inquiry: (1) the state's long-arm statute permits personal jurisdiction over the defendant, and (2) that jurisdiction complies with due process. *Inamed Corp. v. Kuzmak*, 249 F.3d 1356, 1359 (Fed.Cir.2001). Illinois' long-arm statute permits jurisdiction over a non-resident defendant in two ways. If the defendant's contacts with the forum state are the same contacts as those at issue in the suit, the defendant may be subject to specific jurisdiction. *Red Wing Shoe Co., Inc. v. Hockerson-Halberstadt, Inc.* 148 F.3d 1355, 1359 (Fed.Cir.1998). . . . If the defendant's contacts with the forum state are not the same contacts as those giving rise to the suit, the plaintiff must meet a higher burden and show that the plaintiff has "continuous, permanent, ongoing and systematic" contact with a forum. See *LSI Indus., Inc. v. Hubbell Lighting, Inc.*, 232 F.3d 1369, 1375 (Fed.Cir.2000); *Milligan v. Soo Line R.R. Co.*, 775 F.Supp. 277, 279 (N.D.Ill.1991). This contact, also known in Illinois as "doing business" in the state of Illinois, will make the defendant amenable to all suits in the state, including suits arising from conduct that did not occur in the forum state. *Milligan*, 775 F.Supp. at 279.

If Illinois has personal jurisdiction over a non-resident defendant, the assertion of jurisdiction must comport with "fair play and substantial justice"—that is, a showing that a suit in the state against the defendant would be fair and reasonable. *Red Wing Shoe*, 148 F.3d at 1358–59. This second stage has also been described as a showing that the defendant's conduct in the forum state is such that the defendant should "reasonably anticipate being haled into court there." *World-Wide*

*Volkswagen Corp. v. Woodson*, 444 U.S. 286, 287, 100 S.Ct. 559, 62 L.Ed.2d 490 (1980).

In this case, Abbott does not allege that Illinois has specific jurisdiction over Mylan. The issue giving rise to this suit is Mylan's Paragraph IV ANDA, the filing of which triggered a statutory right to sue for patent infringement. . . . No part of the preparation of the ANDA or the filing the ANDA took place in Illinois, and there has been no other injury to Abbott, so there is no basis for asserting specific jurisdiction over Mylan.

Abbott instead has sued Mylan in Illinois under principles of general jurisdiction, providing evidence that Mylan is "doing business" in Illinois to the extent that it has such systematic and continuous contact with Illinois that it may be sued in this forum for any activity, including activities that are not connected to Illinois.

There is no all-inclusive test for determining whether a non-resident defendant has such systematic and continuous contact with the forum state as to subject it to general jurisdiction. See *Graco*, 558 F.Supp. at 192. Courts typically have looked to the presence of officers, persons, licenses, or sales activities within Illinois as evidence of systematic contact. See *Milligan*, 775 F.Supp. at 279–80 (discussing test); *Graco*, 558 F.Supp. at 192 (relying on volume of sales). Although courts typically look to these factors, Illinois requires an independent determination in each case of whether, on the basis of all the circumstances, it would be fair to subject the defendant to jurisdiction here. *Alderson v. Southern Co.*, 321 Ill.App.3d 832, 254 Ill.Dec. 514, 747 N.E.2d 926, 941 (Ill.App.Ct.2001).

Abbott concedes that Mylan does not have a physical office or agent in Illinois, as verified via affidavit attached to Mylan's Motion to Dismiss. Abbott relies on five different types of contact that Mylan maintains with Illinois: Mylan's volume of sales and percentage of revenue in Illinois, Mylan's ongoing contracts with companies in Illinois, an Illinois distribution license maintained by Mylan, Mylan's informational website presence, and Mylan's amenability to prior litigation in this district.

Abbott's primary evidence that Mylan has systematic and continuous contact with Illinois are figures obtained from Mylan's documents showing that Mylan distributed substantial quantities of pharmaceuticals to wholesalers and retailers in Illinois, and gained substantial revenues from those sales. Abbott provides information about sales revenue both in absolute monetary terms and as a percentage of the overall revenues of the company and of the company's parent. . . . The revenue from sales in Illinois is substantial and consistent over the five years prior to the suit. Distribution of a defendant company's products in Illinois in sufficient quantities, and with substantial revenues, may subject a non-resident defendant to general jurisdiction. See *Graco*, 558 F.Supp. at 192 (finding that defendant was "doing business" by shipping a large percentage of its equipment through its Illinois subsidiary); see also *Connelly v. Uniroyal, Inc.*, 75 Ill.2d 393, 27 Ill.Dec. 343, 389 N.E.2d 155, 160 (Ill.1979) (directing products to Illinois "on a regular basis and in substantial numbers" sufficient to create general jurisdiction).

Illinois courts have not created a consistent standard as to the necessary showing of volume of sales or revenues before exercising general jurisdiction over a non-resident defendant. Unfortunately, most courts have opted for general descriptions of sufficiency rather than specific data. See *Graco*, 558 F.Supp. at 192 ("large percentage" sufficient to support general jurisdiction); *Connelly*, 329 N.E.2d at 406 (jurisdiction appropriate when product came to Illinois "on a regular basis and in substantial numbers"); *McGill v. Gigantex Technologies Co., Ltd.*, 2005 WL 3436403, *3 (N.D.Ill.Dec.12, 2005) ("small percentage" not sufficient). In those cases that did provide numerical figures, however, Mylan's volume of sales exceeds the volumes that have been sufficient to support general jurisdiction in the past. See, e.g., *Hubbell*, 232 F.3d at 1375 ("millions of dollars of sales" conducted "over the past several years" and "broad distribution network" sufficient for general jurisdiction); *Milligan*, 775 F.Supp. at 280–81 (Illinois sales totaling 3–5% of annual company revenues sufficient for general jurisdiction). The Court finds that Mylan's volume of sales, and the revenues derived from those sales, constitute substantial and continued contact with Illinois supporting a finding of general jurisdiction in this forum.

It is not relevant whether the sales went through a distributor before reaching Illinois; general jurisdiction extends to both direct and indirect sales into the forum state. See *Graco*, 558 F.Supp. at 193 ("Because [defendant] receives substantial economic benefit from its regular activity within the state, it can be said to be 'doing business' here even though its dealings here are indirect."); *Connelly*, 389 N.E.2d at 405 ("A manufacturer's economic relationship with a state does not necessarily differ in substance, nor should its amenability to jurisdiction necessarily differ, depending on whether it deals directly or indirectly with residents of the state"); see also *Giotis v. Apollo of the Ozarks, Inc.*, 800 F.2d 660, 667 (7th Cir.1986) ("A seller at the head of a distribution network thus satisfies the requisite forseeability of due process where it 'delivers its products into the stream of commerce with the expectation that [these products] will be purchased by consumers in the forum state'"). Abbott has shown sufficiently, via Mylan's own documents, that a substantial percentage of Mylan's revenues come from sales to the state of Illinois.

Mylan does not object to the veracity of Abbott's evidence of sales and revenue. Rather, Mylan argues that Abbott's evidence does not support general jurisdiction, because a showing of general jurisdiction in the absence of specific jurisdiction places a higher burden on the plaintiff. In support of its position, Mylan relies on *Bearry v. Beech Aircraft Corporation,* a case from the Fifth Circuit in which the court denied general jurisdiction over an action in which it did not have specific jurisdiction, despite the plaintiffs' evidence of substantial sales into the forum state. 818 F.2d 370, 374–5 (5th Cir.1987). Mylan draws from *Bearry* the notion that general jurisdiction in the absence of specific jurisdiction requires additional evidence besides sales and revenues, such as contract negotiation within the forum or subsidiaries. The Court finds *Bearry* to be unpersuasive, as binding case precedent within this circuit and this state has found general jurisdiction on the basis of sales and revenues in sufficient quantities, and the Court finds that those quantities have been surpassed by Mylan in this case.

Additionally, Abbott has addressed the concerns raised in *Bearry,* and similar concerns raised in cases in this district, by providing supporting evidence of Mylan's other contacts with this forum to supplement its evidence of sales and revenues. Those cases in Illinois that have declined to exercise general jurisdiction in Illinois on the basis of the volume of sales did so because the non-resident defendant had no other contact with the forum state. See *McGill*, 2005 WL 3436403 at *3 (sales totaling less than 3% of defendant's total revenues insufficient to support general jurisdiction without other evidence); *Hot Wax, Inc. v. Stone Soap, Inc.*, 1999 WL 183776, *4 (N.D.Ill. Mar.25, 1999) (where volume of sales small, court will exercise jurisdiction only if defendant also targeted advertisements). As discussed in the following section, Abbott provides additional evidence of other contacts between Mylan and Illinois to bolster its contention that general jurisdiction in this case is appropriate.

Abbott supports the evidence of substantial sales and revenues from Illinois with several additional contacts between Mylan and Illinois. While each of these pieces of evidence standing alone might not subject Mylan to general jurisdiction in Illinois, they support the Court's finding that Mylan has conducted business in Illinois to such an extent that the Court may infer that Mylan has availed itself of the laws of Illinois and that it would be fair to permit them to be sued in this state.

1. License. Mylan holds two current "Licensed Drug Distributor" licenses from the Illinois Department

*(continued)*

of Financial and Professional Regulation. . . . Mylan has held the public licenses since 1999. . . . A license from the Illinois Secretary of State, which may then act as an agent for service of process on a defendant, traditionally establishes a state's jurisdiction over the license holder. See *Polansky v. Anderson,* 2005 WL 3557858 at *4 (N.D.Ill.Dec.29, 2005). Although Mylan's licenses come from an Illinois regulatory agency, and do not automatically establish general jurisdiction, they do represent an ongoing contact with the state of Illinois, and support an inference that Mylan intended to do business within the state.

2. Mylan's Website. Mylan maintains a national website for informational and advertising purposes only. The website does not sell any of Mylan's products or conduct business transactions. However, the website has interactive components, as customers may submit inquiries to Mylan for additional information about Mylan products. Abbott argues that the website should be viewed in conjunction with the other evidence offered in support of jurisdiction, as supporting evidence that jurisdiction over Mylan in Illinois is proper.

The seminal case discussing the Internet and personal jurisdiction, *Zippo Manufacturing Company v. Zippo Dot Com, Inc.,* held that websites should be examined on a "sliding scale" when determining personal jurisdiction. 952 F.Supp. 1119, 1124 (W.D.Pa.1997). In cases where a defendant clearly does business over the Internet, including entering into contracts, personal jurisdiction is proper. Id. On the other side, if the defendant's website is completely passive and allows no interaction with a customer, personal jurisdiction is not proper. Id. The "middle ground" set forth in *Zippo,* which best describes Mylan's website, "is occupied by interactive Web sites where a user can exchange information with the host computer" but cannot purchase products; these sites should be evaluated on a case-by-case basis. Id., see also *Neomedia Techs., Inc. v. AirClic, Inc.,* 2004 WL 848181 at * 4 (N.D.Ill. Apr.16, 2004) (applying the *Zippo* test to personal jurisdiction analysis in Illinois).

A hybrid website alone will not support general jurisdiction over a defendant corporation. *Infosys Inc. v. Billingnetwork.com, Inc.,* 2003 WL 22012687 at *4 (N.D.Ill. Aug.23, 2003). But a website can form part of the basis for general jurisdiction . . . see *Publications Int'l, Ltd. v. Burke/Triolo, Inc.,* 121 F.Supp.2d 1178, 1183 (N.D.Ill.2000). . . . *George S. May Int'l. Co. v. Xcentric Ventures, LLC,* 409 F.Supp.2d 1052, 1059–60 (N.D.Ill.2006). . . . While Mylan's website alone might not support personal jurisdiction, the presence of the website adds weight to the Court's finding that general jurisdiction in this case is proper.

3. Contracts in Illinois. Abbott and Mylan agree that Mylan has pending contracts with approximately twenty separate entities shipping Mylan's products into Illinois, or in some cases repackaging Mylan products at their plants in Illinois. Seven of these companies have their principal places of business in Illinois. Abbott argues that these contracts form an additional basis for finding that Mylan has a continuing relationship with parties in the forum state.

Mylan responds that the contracts do not support personal jurisdiction because defendants are not subject to jurisdiction in a forum based on contracts with out-of-state entities who did business in the forum, citing *Red Wing Shoe,* 148 F.3d 1355. In *Red Wing Shoe,* the state of Minnesota did not have personal jurisdiction over a non-resident defendant that licensed its product to 34 companies doing business in the state. Mylan's reliance on *Red Wing Shoe* is misplaced, however, because the court in *Red Wing Shoe* specifically noted that none of the 34 licensees were incorporated in the forum state or had their principal places of business in the state. Id. at 1357–58. Abbott has alleged, and Mylan has conceded, the seven of the main contracts identified by Abbott for distribution in Illinois are companies that have their principal places of business within the forum state.

4. Prior Litigation within this District. Finally, Abbott raises Mylan's history as a defendant in this court, and its decisions in the past not to contest personal jurisdiction, as further evidence that general jurisdiction over Mylan is proper . . . the fact that Mylan has litigated cases by consent in this forum in the past, including cases of ANDA patent infringement brought by Abbott, weakens Mylan's argument that litigation in this forum is inconvenient.

Once a movant has shown that a non-resident defendant has systematic and continuous contacts with Illinois to support general jurisdiction, the Court must look to whether the decision to exercise jurisdiction comports with due process. Under the Due Process Clause of the Fourteenth Amendment, an Illinois court may exercise jurisdiction over a non-resident defendant if the defendant has "certain minimum contacts with [the state] such that the maintenance of the suit does not offend traditional notions of fair play and substantial justice." *International Shoe Co. v. Washington,* 326 U.S. 310, 316, 66 S.Ct. 154, 90 L.Ed. 95 (1945) (citations omitted). Once a plaintiff has demonstrated that there are minimum contacts, the burden shifts to the defendant to show "a compelling case that the presence of some other considerations would render jurisdiction unreasonable." *Burger King Corp. v. Rudzewicz,* 471 U.S. 462, 477, 105 S.Ct. 2174, 85 L.Ed.2d 528 (1985).

In determining the reasonableness of jurisdiction, the Federal Circuit looks to five factors: (1) the burden on the defendant, (2) the interests of the forum state, (3) the plaintiff's interest in obtaining relief, (4) the interstate judicial system's interest in obtaining the most efficient resolution of controversies, and (5) the shared interest of the several states in furthering fundamental substantive social policies. *Electronics For Imaging,* 340 F.3d at 1352. In this case, Mylan has not demonstrated an unreasonable burden from litigating this case in Illinois. The burden on Mylan to litigate in Chicago is greater than it would be if this case remained in West Virginia, but Mylan has litigated other major cases in this district on prior occasions. Illinois has an interest in protecting its citizens from patent infringement, and Abbott certainly has an interest in obtaining relief from patent infringement. . . .

Abbott has established a *prima facie* case that Mylan maintains systematic and continuous contact with Illinois, through its sales and revenues in Illinois, supported by its contractual connections, Illinois licenses, and interactive website. Mylan has not shown that it would be unreasonable to bring Mylan into court here. . . . Therefore, the Court denies the motion to dismiss for lack of personal jurisdiction. . . .

So ordered.

## Case Review Question

Would a company that operated exclusively through Web site transactions subject itself to personal jurisdiction in any state where there was a customer?

## *In Rem* and *Quasi in Rem* Jurisdictions

*In rem* and *quasi in rem* **jurisdictions** refer to the authority of a court to affect property or a person's rights over property. A suit *in rem* is begun by naming the actual property as a defendant in the court of the state where the property is located. The party claiming ownership defends his or her rights over the property. In fact, if a suit is brought *in rem,* all persons who have an interest in the property must defend that interest. Because the authority is over the actual property, there is no need for personal jurisdiction over persons who claim it.

**in rem jurisdiction**
Authority of a court over a specific item of property regardless of who claims the property or an interest in it.

**quasi in rem jurisdiction**
Authority of a court over a person's interest in certain property.

### APPLICATION 8.3

A group of individuals who were all members of the same church decided to purchase a vacation home together. Fifteen families contributed in exchange for one week per family during summer at the vacation home. Unfortunately, one of the families brought along a guest who fell in the shower and broke her neck. None of the families are well off financially, and they had allowed the insurance on the property to lapse as the result of a miscommunication about who was to send in the payment. The injured guest's only real recourse is to sue for the value of the property. One method would be to sue the property *in rem.* However, assume that the suit was not brought until two years after the incident. In that time, three of the original owners have moved away and their whereabouts are unknown. In that instance, *quasi in rem* would likely be the most appropriate path to follow.

*Point for Discussion:* Would the fact that one of the property owners recently won a large sum of money in the lottery affect the decision of the appropriate method of suit?

The distinction between *in rem* and *quasi in rem* turns on the property owners who are affected. In an action *in rem,* all persons claiming ownership or some other type of interest in the property may be affected and therefore must defend their interest.[5] In an action based on *quasi in rem,* only the interests of the person or persons identified in the suit and who claim rights to the property are affected.[6]

*Quasi in rem* may be a way to obtain jurisdiction over the property interests of a person when *in personam* jurisdiction cannot be achieved. Assume a person is subject to the court's authority but cannot be located. Or perhaps the person appears at trial and a judgment is rendered against the person, but the person seemingly has no assets in that state. In the first instance, the plaintiff can file an action on the basis of *quasi in rem* jurisdiction to attach any of the property of the missing person in the state where the property is located. In the latter situation, a suit that claims *quasi in rem* jurisdiction can be brought in any state where assets exist for the purpose of satisfying the judgment rendered in another jurisdiction.

*In rem* and *quasi in rem* actions are brought much less frequently than actions based on *in personam* jurisdiction. The primary reason is that if a suit is brought *in personam* and is won, virtually all of the assets of the defendant can be used to satisfy the judgment. In an action based on property, no matter how great a judgment, only the value of the property named or the degree of interest in the property can be used to satisfy the judgment. Therefore, if the injuries or rights one seeks to protect are greater than the value of the property, it is wiser to seek *in personam* jurisdiction.

## APPLICATION 8.4

Brian and Ace are college roommates. After college, they accept jobs in the same city and rent a house together. Eventually, they purchase the house in Brian's name and make many improvements. Ace contributes one half of all expenses. Together they take out a personal loan to cover the costs of a new roof, furnace, air conditioner, and kitchen remodel. The loan is due to be repaid in a balloon note in two years. Ace and Brian even signed an agreement they wrote themselves in which Ace acknowledged his responsibility for one-half of the personal loan and one-half of the monthly mortgage payment as rent for a minimum term of five years. After that, Ace can extend the agreement under the same terms on a year-to-year basis with Brian's consent. Shortly after the work is completed, Ace decides to give up his job and follow his dream to be a roadie for touring rock bands. Brian is unable to find Ace. Without Ace's contributions, Brian stands to default on the personal loan and the mortgage and possibly lose his home.

Brian is aware that Ace and his sister Diamond are the equal owners of a house that was left to them on their parent's death a few years earlier. Diamond currently resides in the house and just happens to be dating Brian. By filing suit against the house *in rem*, Brian can seek a judgment against the house to the extent of the value of the house. By filing *quasi in rem*, Brian can seek a judgment against the house to the extent of Ace's interest. If the judgment is awarded, Brian can ultimately petition to have Ace and Diamond's house sold.

*Point for Discussion:* What method would be the least detrimental to Diamond's interest?

## ASSIGNMENT 8.3

Examine the following situations and determine whether each suit was brought *in personam, in rem,* or *quasi in rem.*

1. Partners Joy, Bob, and Bud were equal owners of a golf driving range. In his divorce settlement, Bob was ordered to pay $10,000 to his ex-wife, Shirley. When Bob refused to pay, Shirley filed another suit to collect and was awarded the entire driving range.

2. Same situation as question 1, except Shirley is now equal partners with Joy and Bud.

3. Maxine sued Vince for damages he allegedly caused in a car accident. Maxine prevails and collects her judgment by seizing Vince's vacation cabin, boat, and gun collection.

## FEDERAL JURISDICTION

As pointed out in earlier chapters, the federal and state court systems operate independently. Although similar in many respects, each system has its own substantive and procedural law, and each has its own system of appeals. The opportunity to present a case in a federal court is most often the result of those situations where (1) a federal law or the Constitution is involved, (2) the United States is a party, or (3) there is complete diversity of citizenship and a controversy valued in excess of $75,000. The following sections describe each of these situations.

As always, the federal court where the case is filed must have subject matter jurisdiction. If it does not, then the case must be transferred to the federal court or the state court where such jurisdiction exists. If the suit is brought against a citizen of the United States, automatic *in personam* jurisdiction exists because citizenship implies domicile in this country.

Subject matter jurisdiction in the federal courts can be established only in specific circumstances. The courts are careful to avoid unnecessary interference with the authority of state court systems and simultaneously burden federal courts with the time and expense of processing claims related to a state's own laws and citizens.

### Federal Question

One type of federal jurisdiction known as a **federal question** occurs when a primary issue in the dispute is based on federal law. Such law can include regulations of federal administrative agencies, federal laws, or elements of the Constitution or its amendments. For this type of jurisdiction to exist, the issue that arises out of federal law must be considered by the court to be a substantial issue in the case, for example, a claim that a police officer violated the civil rights of a minority citizen by using unnecessary force.

If it appears that a party has created a federal question by adding an issue of federal law to the suit when it was unnecessary or when it was not an inherent part of the claim, the court will not take the case.[7] The conspiring in such a tactic by a plaintiff and a defendant is referred to as *collusion*. As a result, no federal jurisdiction will exist. Similarly, a defendant cannot create a federal question in a countersuit—and thereby create federal jurisdiction by simply alleging application of a federal law in the answer to the plaintiff's lawsuit—unless the lawsuit is actually based on or affected by a federal law.

**federal question**
Authority of a federal court to hear a case on the basis of the Constitution and other federal law.

### APPLICATION 8.5

Jim was employed by ACME corporation. After many years, ACME began losing its place in the market, and the business slowly faded. Jim saw this development and planned to seek employment elsewhere. However, before he found another job, he was terminated by ACME as part of an employee cutback. Jim was fifty-seven years old at the time he was terminated and unable to find other comparable employment. Over lunch with a former co-worker and friend, Jim confided his plans to file a lawsuit against ACME claiming that he was discriminated against because of his age and fired for that reason. He mentioned that he had already created several memos he planned to claim he sent to his superiors complaining about his treatment at work in the weeks before the termination. He stated his case would include allegations that the memos were destroyed and he was fired for sending them instead of the reason actually given as lack of available work. Jim told his friend that he hoped to gain enough money from the suit to avoid ever having to work again and go to live on a beach somewhere.

*(continued)*

## APPLICATION 8.5 (Continued)

Jim's attorney is well aware that the CEO of ACME has a high profile in the community and a large judgment could cause the company to fold, putting hundreds of citizens out of work. As a result, he plans to file suit in the federal court which is located two counties away. He will claim a violation of federal antidiscrimination statutes. Unfortunately, Jim's friend is still employed at ACME and in his own self-interest informed the employer of Jim's plan.

*Point for Discussion:* If Jim really had sent the memos claiming discrimination and was subsequently terminated, would there be federal jurisdiction?

A pendent claim exists when there are separate issues based on federal and state law filed in the same lawsuit in federal court. In such a situation, the federal court has pendent jurisdiction. The federal court will usually not order that the case be split into two cases but it may exercise pendent jurisdiction and hear the federal and state issues. When this is done, the federal court will follow principles of state law in determining the state issues and will apply federal law when determining the federal issues.

The case of pendent jurisdiction occurs frequently in federal courts. As legal disputes in our society become more and more complex and many issues must be decided, the likelihood increases that some of the issues will arise out of state law and others will arise from federal law. It would be far too expensive and time consuming for the parties and the courts to try all of the issues separately. Exercising pendent jurisdiction has become the solution to this problem. However, if the state and federal issues are totally distinct, the judge may order that the claims be severed and tried in separate courts. This prevents parties from combining claims for the sole purpose of having them heard in a court that may be perceived as more favorable to the case.

**concurrent jurisdiction**
Situation in which more than one court has authority to hear a particular case.

Distinguished from pendent authority is **concurrent jurisdiction**, which occurs when more than one federal court or federal and state courts have subject matter jurisdiction over a case. The case may have solely federal or state issues, but because of the domicile of the parties or the occurrence of several parts of the claim in different jurisdictions, more than one court finds itself with the authority to determine the issues. In such a situation, the case may be filed by the plaintiff in any court with subject matter jurisdiction. However, the case may be subject to transfer under *forum non conveniens* (see subsequent discussion).

### The United States as a Party

An obvious type of federal jurisdiction exists when the United States has been named as a party to the suit. Because the federal courts are a branch of the federal government, when the U.S. government is sued, the suit must be filed in federal court. Such a suit might involve an employee, officer, or elected official of the federal government or a federal agency.

The U.S. government traditionally followed the English doctrine of sovereign immunity: The sovereign (the government entity) is immune from claims by the citizens—that is, the government may not be sued. The United States has made some exceptions to this rule. A handful of statutes have set forth specific instances in which the government may be liable for physical or financial injuries to a citizen. If a suit is brought against the United States, it must be done in accordance with these statutes.[8] Each requirement of the statutes must be met. Often this includes first making a claim to the appropriate administrative agency. If no satisfaction is received, a claim may then be filed in the courts. If there is no statutory provision for the type of claim an individual wishes to make, no suit can be filed against the United States.

## Diversity of Citizenship

A much-used method of achieving federal jurisdiction is through diversity of citizenship. This basis for jurisdiction was developed because juries and judges in a state court system are drawn from that particular state. As a consequence, it is possible that a party to the suit who is from another state will not receive fair or adequate treatment. In today's mobile society, this possibility is less of a threat than 200 years ago when there were great rivalries among the states. However, as a safeguard, the federal courts still accept cases of substantial value that involve parties from different states. From time to time, Congress amends the amount in controversy between parties that serves as the minimum for a case involving diversity of citizenship. The basis for this is to prevent use of the federal courts for matters that are not considered substantial in terms of dollar value.

Diversity of citizenship means that all parties to the lawsuit must have citizenship in different states than an opposing party. Thus, all plaintiffs must reside in different states than all defendants. It is acceptable if the plaintiff resides in one state or several states; the same is true of defendants. No state, however, can be common between any plaintiff and any defendant. Diversity among parties must be complete.

---

### APPLICATION 8.6

1. Jeff, the plaintiff, is domiciled in South Carolina, while Jack, the defendant, is domiciled in North Carolina. Thus, there is complete diversity of the state citizenship between the plaintiff and the defendant, and Jeff may sue Jack in federal court.

2. Jeff sues Jack and Molly in federal court. Jeff and Molly are domiciled in South Carolina, while Jack is domiciled in North Carolina. There would be no federal jurisdiction in this situation because a plaintiff and one of the defendants are domiciled in the same state. Thus, diversity is not complete.

A simple method to determine whether diversity exists is to make a table with two columns. In one column, list the states of domicile of all the plaintiffs; in the second column, list the states of domicile of each defendant (see accompanying diagram). If any state appears in both columns, there is no diversity. Conversely, if no state appears in both columns, the first condition of diversity jurisdiction is satisfied. Like federal question jurisdiction, diversity cannot be created by collusion of the parties. Simply put, a party cannot represent domicile in a state different from the defendant for the purpose of creating jurisdiction. Domicile must be the intended permanent residence.

| Situation 1 | | Situation 2 | |
|---|---|---|---|
| Plaintiff | Defendant | Plaintiff | Defendants |
| SC | NC | SC | SC |
| | NC | | |

*Point for Discussion:*

1. Regarding situation 1, assume Jeff has all relevant connections, including longest annual residence in North Carolina, except that he claims South Carolina as his domicile for purposes of paying federal income tax. Is the result different? Explain your answer.

2. Regarding situation 2, what if Jack and Molly were domiciled in South Carolina and Jeff was domiciled in North Carolina? Would the result be different?

A second aspect of citizenship diversity is required for federal jurisdiction to apply. The claim must allege damages of more than the statutorily required amount. It does not matter whether a single claim or several claims in the same suit exceed the minimum amount. It is necessary only that the claim be valued at more than the minimum. Generally, this is not a problem. However, if it is discovered that the claim could never be considered as reasonably worth the statutory minimum, then the federal court will dismiss the case. If a jury should return a verdict of less than the statutory minimum, federal jurisdiction is not defeated. It must only be shown that the claim could reasonably have been considered as worth that much. Thus, it is important that a party claiming jurisdiction by diversity of citizenship be able to establish not only that the diversity is complete but also that the claim is reasonably worth more than the statutory minimum.

Two exceptions exist to a claim of federal jurisdiction based on diversity of citizenship: domestic relations and probate cases. The law governing domestic relations (divorce, adoption, custody, support, alimony, and other related issues) is so specific from state to state that the federal courts will not generally become involved in these issues. The same applies to the law of probate, which includes the distribution of estates of deceased persons and the management of estates of minors and adults who are legally disabled. The federal government will not determine the rights of parties in these actions. The only exception is that if the requirements of diversity are met after the case has been determined, then the federal court may exercise jurisdiction to interpret or enforce the decrees of the state court.

## ASSIGNMENT 8.4

Examine the following situations and determine whether federal jurisdiction applies to each and, if so, what type.

1. Kyle and Cindy were both driving when their cars collided. Both suffered serious injuries. Each claims the accident was the fault of the other driver. Kyle and Cindy were both domiciled in state F at the time of the accident, which occurred in state O.

2. Kyle and Cindy were both driving when their cars collided. Both suffered serious injuries. Each claims the accident was the fault of the other driver. Kyle and Cindy were both domiciled in state F at the time of the accident, which occurred in state O. Alicia was a passenger in Kyle's car and was also injured in the accident. Alicia is a resident of state O.

3. Kyle and Cindy were both driving when their cars collided. Both suffered serious injuries. Each claims the accident was the fault of the other driver. Kyle was domiciled in state F at the time of the accident, which occurred in state O where Cindy was domiciled.

4. Kyle and Cindy were both driving when their cars collided. Both suffered serious injuries. Each claims the accident was the fault of the other driver. Kyle and Cindy were both domiciled in state F at the time of the accident, which occurred in state O. Also destroyed in the accident was a U.S. interstate sign valued at $2,000. The government plans to join the suit to seek damages for the sign.

5. Kyle and Cindy were both driving when their cars collided. Both suffered serious injuries. Each claims the accident was the fault of the other driver. Kyle and Cindy were both domiciled in state F at the time of the accident, which occurred in state O. The basis for Cindy's suit is that Kyle was driving a home-crafted electric car he made himself that does not meet the legal requirements for operation on an interstate highway. Kyle claims that the law is an unconstitutional violation of his right to travel freely.

### Removal and Remand

What happens when there is concurrent jurisdiction between the state and federal courts but the plaintiff brings the action in state court? Or if there is no federal jurisdiction at the outset of the lawsuit but developments cause it to arise? Examples include amendments of claims to add federal question issues and change of domicile of a party, thereby creating diversity. The defendant is not totally at the mercy of the plaintiff's choice of forum. When federal jurisdiction exists or arises in a state court action, the defendant may seek to have the case brought before the federal courts.

The Congress has passed the following law:

Title 28 United States Code Section 1441: Actions Removable Generally.

(a) Except as otherwise expressly provided by Act of Congress, any civil action brought in a State court of which the district courts of the United States have original jurisdiction, may be removed by the defendant or the defendants, to the district court of the United States for the district and division embracing the place where such action is pending.

(b) Any civil action of which the district courts have original jurisdiction founded on a claim or right arising under the Constitution, treaties or laws of the United States shall be removable without regard to the citizenship or residence of the parties. Any other such action shall be removable only if none of the parties in interest properly joined and served as defendants is a citizen of the State in which such action is brought.

(c) Whenever a separate and independent claim or cause of action which would be removable if sued upon alone, is joined with one or more otherwise nonremovable claims or causes of action, the entire case may be removed and the district court may determine all issues therein, or, in its discretion, may remand all matters not otherwise within its original jurisdiction.

Translated, the basic thrust of this statute is that if the federal court would also have jurisdiction to hear a case, the defendant can remove the case from the state and into federal court (see Exhibit 8.2). When this occurs, the case is actually transferred from the state to the federal system. The procedure for removal is quite specific:

(a) A defendant has only thirty days from the date the defendant should be aware there is federal jurisdiction to file for removal. If federal jurisdiction exists from the outset, the suit must be filed within thirty days of the defendant being served with the suit. If something occurs during the suit that establishes federal jurisdiction, the defendant has thirty days from knowledge of that event to seek removal. An example of the latter would be if a party moved his or her domicile and there was diversity of citizenship.

(b) To start the removal proceedings the defendant must file a petition for removal in the federal court. The petition must be filed in the federal court whose geographical boundaries include the location of the state court. The petition must state all of the facts of the case that indicate there is federal jurisdiction. The petition must be verified. This means that the defendant must swear in writing that all of the information in the petition is true and accurate. Also, all pleadings (legal documents) that have been filed in the case in state court must be attached to the petition. A copy of the petition must be sent to all parties.

(c) In addition to the petition, the defendant must file a bond with the federal court. This is a sort of insurance policy that the removal is properly based on actual federal jurisdiction over the case. A fee or promise of a fee is given to the court as bond. If the case remains in the federal court, then the defendant is entitled to have the bond returned. If it turns out that the case was removed improperly, then the defendant forfeits the amount of the bond to the court.

(d) Once the petition for removal is filed, all proceedings in the state court stop. All future hearings, motions, and the trial will be conducted in the federal court. The state court loses authority over the case. Removal is automatic, and it cannot be prevented from happening by objections from the plaintiff.

**Exhibit 8.2** Petition to Remove

---

**IN THE UNITED STATES DISTRICT COURT**
**DISTRICT OF MONTE VISTA**

MATHIAS SNYDER,   ]
Plaintiff       ]
vs.          ]     Docket No. 94-321
            ]     Judge David Madde
BILL BOON,     ]
Defendant      ]

**PETITION TO REMOVE**

Comes now the Defendant, Bill Boon, by and through his attorneys, Smart, Steel, and Harper, and petitions this court to remove the above-captioned case from the state court where it is pending and to accept said case into this court for further proceedings. In support of his petition, the Defendant states as follows:

1.  On or about June 1, 2003, the Plaintiff instituted an action against Defendant in the District Court of Diamond County, State A, which case is assigned state Docket number 03-1010.

2.  Since the commencement of Plaintiff's action against Defendant, diversity of citizenship has occurred when Plaintiff's domicile changed on or about August 31, 2003, from State A to State B.

3.  Plaintiff's complaint alleges damages due from Defendant in an amount in excess of $50,000.

4.  The current circumstances of the pending case satisfy all requirements of diversity of citizenship, and consequently, this court is vested with the authority to remove said case pursuant to the Federal Rules of Civil Procedure.

WHEREFORE, Defendant prays that this court will grant said petition and cause the aforementioned case to be removed from the state court where it is currently pending and to be filed in this court for further proceedings.

Respectfully submitted,

Sam Harper
Attorney for Defendant Bill Boon
Smart, Steel, and Harper
# 1 Empire Drive
Union City, UN 11190

---

A plaintiff who believes that a case was improperly removed may file a motion to remand—that is, a motion filed with the federal court that asks the court to review the case and determine whether federal jurisdiction actually exists (see Exhibit 8.3). If the court finds that it does not, then the case will be *remanded,* or sent back to the state court. The federal court will take no further action in a case after it is remanded. If a motion to remand fails, the case remains in the federal court.

Regardless of whether a case is filed in federal court by a plaintiff or removed by a defendant, the court will not entertain a case where federal jurisdiction is based on collusion. (Recall that collusion occurs when one or more of the parties to the lawsuit conspire to create the appearance of federal jurisdiction.) For example, if a party changes domicile for the sole purpose of creating diversity of citizenship, such action is treated as an attempt to falsely allege the existence of federal jurisdiction, and the action will be remanded. Thus, the reason for federal jurisdiction must be a sincere and real part of the dispute.

```
                    IN THE UNITED STATES DISTRICT COURT
                          DISTRICT OF MONTE VISTA

MATHIAS SNYDER,              ]
Plaintiff                    ]
vs.                          ]            Docket No. 94-321
                             ]            Judge David Madden
BILL BOON,                   ]
Defendant                    ]


                            PETITION TO REMAND
```

Comes now the Plaintiff, Mathias Snyder, by and through his attorneys, Hayford, Stanley, and Jackson and petitions this court to remand the above-captioned case to the state court where it was originally filed, for all further proceedings. In support of his petition, the Plaintiff states as follows:

1. On or about September 30, 2003, the Defendant filed a Petition to Remove the above-captioned case on the basis of diversity of citizenship and subject to the Federal Rules of Civil Procedure.

2. In said petition, the Defendant represented to this Court that the Plaintiff's domicile had changed to State B.

3. The Plaintiff has a temporary residence in State B for the purpose of attending State University during the months of August through May 2004.

4. At no time has the Plaintiff had the intent to adopt State B as his domicile and further has maintained all domiciliary ties with State A.

5. Defendant's petition is unfounded as both Plaintiff and Defendant continue to reside in State A. Therefore, diversity of citizenship does not exist between the parties to this action.

WHEREFORE, the Plaintiff prays that his petition to Remand be granted and that the above-captioned action be permitted to resume proceedings in the District Court where it originated.

Respectfully submitted,

Michael J. George
Attorney for Plaintiff Mathias Snyder
Firm of Hayford, Stanley, and Jackson
311 Lagoon Lane
Harristown, UN 11115

**Exhibit 8.3** Petition to Remand

## OTHER JURISDICTIONAL CONSIDERATIONS

### Corporations

As discussed, the domicile of an individual is important for purposes of determining proper state jurisdiction, the existence of federal jurisdiction cases, and venue. Ordinarily, the law treats a corporation as a person (recall that a person can have only one domicile). This can create a particular problem when a corporation has a continuing business in several states. As a result, special rules have been developed to determine the domicile of a corporation.

The state in which a corporation has filed its articles of incorporation is presumed to be the corporation's domicile. A corporation that does regular business in a state other than where it was incorporated is required to register as a foreign corporation. In doing so, the corporation must appoint someone in that state who will accept notice on behalf of the corporation of lawsuits filed in the state courts. This person is known as the *registered agent* and may be someone in an office of the corporation or some other individual, so long as it is clearly designated who will accept legal documents. Many states designate or require their secretary of state to accept legal documents on behalf of any corporation registered to conduct business within the state.

For purposes of federal jurisdiction, a problem arises in determining diversity of citizenship. A corporation is not considered to be domiciled in every state where it does business. If this were so, it would be virtually impossible for large corporations to ever be subject to federal jurisdiction by way of diversity. In a determination of diversity, a corporation is considered to have dual citizenship, or domiciles. A corporation is considered to be domiciled in the state of incorporation as well as in the state where the corporation's central business is conducted. If the operations are diffuse, the court will apply the *nerve center test,* which examines the location of the administration of the corporation. An example is the corporate headquarters. Once the domiciles of a corporation have been identified, a determination can be made as to whether diversity exists with opposing parties.

# CASE

## *Smith v. Ross Dress for Less Inc., et al.,*

### 2006 WL 3702194 (W.D. LA)

The following opinion discusses how diversity of citizenship is established and the result of a case in which diversity of citizenship is improperly pled in an attempt to gain federal jurisdiction.

. . . Plaintiff filed suit against defendants on May 4, 2006, in the Fourth Judicial District Court for the Parish of Ouachita, State of Louisiana, seeking damages for injuries allegedly sustained in a slip and fall accident at the Ross Dress for Less store on November 17, 2005.

On June 7, 2006, Defendants removed the case to this Court, basing jurisdiction on claims that the amount in controversy exceeded the federal jurisdictional amount and that there was complete diversity of citizenship because Defendants, Monique D. Brumfield ("Brumfield") and Clara Williams ("Williams"), had been fraudulently joined. Plaintiff filed the instant motion claiming that there is no diversity of citizenship, that removal was premature, and that the amount in controversy does not exceed the federal jurisdictional amount. Defendants oppose the motion.

Subject matter jurisdiction in this case is premised on 28 U.S.C. § 1332(a)(1), "(a) The district courts shall have original jurisdiction of all civil actions where the matter in controversy exceeds the sum or value of $75,000, exclusive of interest and costs, and is between—(1) citizens of different States."

"A case falls within the federal district court's 'original' diversity 'jurisdiction' only if diversity of citizenship among the parties is complete, i.e., only if there is no plaintiff and no defendant who are citizens of the same State." *Wisconsin Dept. of Corrections v. Schacht,* 524 U.S. 381, 388, 118 S.Ct. 2047, 2052, 141 L.Ed.2d 364 (1998). When removing a case to federal court, the removing party bears the burden of showing that federal jurisdiction exists and that removal is proper. *De Aguilar v. Boeing Co.,* 47 F.3d 1404, 1408 (5th Cir.1995). Any jurisdictional determination is based on the claims in the state court petition as they existed at the time of removal. *Cavallini v. State Farm Mut. Auto Ins. Co.,* 44 F.3d 256, 264 (5th Cir.1995).

Defendants argue that Brumfield and Williams were improperly joined as defendants in order to defeat diversity jurisdiction. Congress has provided a statutory framework for removal of certain cases where there is diversity of citizenship. Those statutes have been interpreted by the courts to require complete diversity; jurisdiction is lacking if any defendant is a citizen of the same state as any plaintiff. That strict requirement would, on its face, permit a plaintiff to name as a defendant any citizen of his home state and defeat removal. To prevent such shams, the "judge-imported concept of fraudulent joinder" has developed. *Bobby Jones Garden Apartments, Inc. v. Suleski,* 391 F.2d 172, 176 (5th Cir.1968). The Fifth Circuit has recently adopted the term "improper joinder" to describe the doctrine, though it took care to note that there is no substantive difference between the two terms. *Smallwood v. Illinois Central R.R. Co.,* 385 F.3d 568 n. 1 (5th Cir.2004) (en banc).

There are two ways to establish improper joinder: (1) actual fraud in the pleading of jurisdictional facts, or (2) inability of the plaintiff to establish a cause of action against the non-diverse party in state court. Only the second way is at issue in this case. That second test asks whether the defendant has demonstrated there is no reasonable basis for the district court to predict the plaintiff might be able to recover against the in-state defendants. *Smallwood,* 385 F.3d at 573; *Travis v. Irby,* 326 F.3d 644, 646–47 (5th Cir.2003).

The "no reasonable basis" determination may take place in two different settings. In the first, the defendant challenges the adequacy of the plaintiff's pleadings, without the submission of evidence. The court conducts a Rule 12(b)(6)-type analysis to determine whether the complaint states a claim under state law against the in-state defendant. *Smallwood,* 385 F.3d at 573. Any ambiguities in state law must be resolved in favor of the plaintiff. *Gray v. Beverly Enterprises-Mississippi, Inc.,* 390 F .3d 400, 405 (5th Cir.2004).

But merely pleading a valid state law claim, or one whose validity is reasonably arguable, against the resident defendant does not necessarily mean that the joinder of the resident defendant is proper. The second setting for the "no reasonable basis" contest permits the defendant to challenge the plaintiff's allegations and attempt to demonstrate by summary judgment-type evidence that the plaintiff is unable to prove all of the facts necessary to prevail. The court has discretion in those circumstances to pierce the pleadings and analyze the improper joinder claim based on that evidence. *Hornbuckle v. State Farm Lloyds,* 385 F.3d 538, 542 (5th Cir.2004).

On the date of the accident, Brumfield was the manager of the Ross store in Monroe and Williams was an area supervisor for Ross. Smith alleges that Brumfield and Williams, while acting within the course and scope of their employment, were negligent in

A.  Failing to properly maintain walkways;
B.  Failing to have adequate warning signs of debris in walkway;
C.  Failing to do all things necessary and proper to avoid an accident such as this one;
D.  Failing to instruct the store employees;
E.  Failing to train store employees; and
F.  Failing to follow up with store employees.

(Plaintiff's Amended Petition, Doc. # 2-pg. 2).

In Louisiana, Courts use a four-part test to determine whether an individual employee working in the course and scope of her employment can be held liable for a patron's injury. See *Canter v. Koehring Co.,* 283 So.2d 716 (La.1973). The Court must find that

1.  The principal or employer owes a duty of care to the third person . . . breach of which has caused the damage for which recovery is sought.
2.  This duty is delegated by the principal or employer to the defendant.
3.  The defendant officer, agent, or employee has breached this duty through personal (as contrasted with technical or vicarious) fault. . . .
4.  With regard to the personal . . . fault, personal liability cannot be imposed upon the officer,

agent, or employee simply because of his general administrative responsibility for performance of some function of the employment. He must have a personal duty towards the injured plaintiff, breach of which specifically has caused the plaintiff's damages. If the defendant's general responsibility has been delegated with due care to some responsible subordinate or subordinates, he is not himself personally at fault and liable for the negligent performance of this responsibility unless he personally knows or personally should know of its nonperformance or mal-performance and has nevertheless failed to cure the risk of harm. Id. at 721.

The original petition in this matter fails to allege a cause of action against the non-diverse managers. In addition, the unrefuted affidavits of Monique Brumfield and Clara Williams show that neither had a personal duty to the plaintiff which could have been breached. The two non-divers defendants were clearly joined in this action in order to defeat diversity jurisdiction. Such joinder is improper, and remand on the basis of lack of diversity of citizenship is therefore also improper.

As for the amount in controversy, the complaint clearly does not support jurisdictional amount on its face. The allegations of injury are general and non-specific and are simply not sufficient to allow the undersigned to discern the actual extent and seriousness of the injuries. In addition, a review of the medical records supplied by the defendant in opposition to the motion to remand do not support a claim that the amount in controversy in these proceedings exceeds $75,000.00. The MRI reports showed minimal bulges in the cervical and lumbar areas; there is no indication that surgery will be needed; and there is no proof that anything but conservative treatment will be necessary or that the plaintiff will suffer from any permanent injury. Therefore, the undersigned finds that the defendant has not met its burden of proving that the amount in controversy exceeds $75,000.00. Should additional information become available to allow the defendant to establish that amount in controversy does exist, then removal would be proper at that time. At this time, however, the plaintiff's motion to remand is GRANTED and this case remanded to the Fourth Judicial District Court, Ouachita Parish, Louisiana, for further proceedings. Remand of this matter is to be STAYED for 15 days in order to allow the parties an opportunity to appeal this decision. Should no appeal be filed within the applicable delays, this matter is to be remanded forthwith.

## Case Review Question

Why would a plaintiff add defendants to a case for the sole purpose of avoiding federal jurisdiction

## Venue

If jurisdiction exists, all courts within a system, such as all federal district courts, have authority to hear a case. An additional requirement, however, is that the case must be brought in the proper *venue:* the specific court within a judicial system where a case is brought. Venue is the court where the case should be tried according to the law of procedure. Although each type of federal jurisdiction has its own rules regarding what constitutes proper venue, it can be safely said that proper venue will always have some relationship to the domicile of the parties or the subject of the lawsuit.

Typically, the proper venue is the court within whose geographical boundaries all defendants (or sometimes all plaintiffs) are domiciled or where the lawsuit arose. In state systems, the proper venue would be the trial court at the county level. In the federal system, it would be the particular district court within whose boundaries one of the jurisdictional elements exists.

Frequently, the media will feature a news story about a request for a change of venue in a much-publicized case. Although the courts have the authority to hear cases over which there is proper jurisdiction and venue, they also have discretion to decline venue when a case could not be fairly heard. This discretion also extends to cases where there is concurrent jurisdiction with other courts and another court would be more suitable. The process of declining jurisdiction in such a case is known as *forum non conveniens* (discussed in the following section).

---

### APPLICATION 8.7

A bookkeeper for a large church is arrested after some twenty years of allegedly embezzling funds from the church. She is charged criminally. However, the religious organization also files suit against her for repayment of more than one-half million dollars she allegedly stole. The civil suit claimed the bookkeeper had secretly stolen funds in small amounts over the many years, purchased numerous parcels of property in and around her community, and put all of the property in her mother's and husband's names. Because the alleged theft was that of money donated by local citizens to a religious group, the media attention has been relentless. The bookkeeper vigorously denies the allegations, claiming it was the pastoral staff that stole the money and named her as a scapegoat when the thefts came to light. She defends the allegations against her on the basis that her parents had always lived frugally and accumulated land. Further, the properties she owned with her husband were nothing more than a continuation of that pattern. She has requested that the civil trial be conducted in a rural area in another part of the state where cable television is not available and few citizens have satellite dishes. It is possible in this situation that the court would allow the trial to be conducted in a location where the pool of jurors would not likely include individuals who had personally donated money to the church or who knew persons who had. Even if the juror pool could be cleansed of affected persons, the media attention would still be considered as a potential threat to the juror impartiality.

*Point for Discussion:* How is venue different from jurisdiction?

---

### Forum Non Conveniens

When more than one jurisdiction has authority to hear a case, the plaintiff is usually given the choice of where the lawsuit will be conducted. Literally translated, the term *forum non conveniens* means "an inconvenient forum" and refers to the situation in which a court, for all practical purposes, is nonconvenient when compared with other courts that also have jurisdiction to hear a case. In such a situation, the court has the discretion to use its own judgment and determine whether the case should be dismissed with permission granted to the plaintiff to file suit in another jurisdiction.

The courts are hesitant to disturb the right of the plaintiff to choose the forum. However, if it appears that another court is in a much better position to decide the case, the first court may decline to exercise its jurisdiction based on *forum non conveniens*.

The issue of *forum non conveniens* is usually brought to the attention of the court by the defendant. The most common scenario is a defendant who believes that the plaintiff filed a suit in a particular jurisdiction for no other reason than to obtain the most favorable result. For example, such motions often appear in jurisdictions where jury verdicts are reported to be unusually high in certain types of cases. Whatever the plaintiff's reason for filing suit in a jurisdiction, the court will not question it—that is, until a motion is made to the court based on *forum non conveniens*. When such a motion is filed, the court compares all courts with jurisdiction over the case.

The consideration of the court in such an issue is commonly referred to as an *unequal balancing test.*[9] The court presumes that the plaintiff's right to choose the forum will be honored unless the defendant shows that another court would be a far more appropriate place to have the trial. In making this determination, the court considers several factors:

1. the residence of the parties,
2. the location of the witnesses,
3. the location of the evidence,
4. the site of the occurrence (in cases when a judge wants a jury to see the site and when the site is accessible),
5. the docket of the two courts (where could the trial be held sooner?),
6. the interest of the citizens of the current jurisdiction in having the case heard (will the case help settle an issue of undecided law in the state?), and
7. the state law to be applied.

If the balance of these facts strongly favors the defendant's suggested forum, it will be considered to outweigh the important right of the plaintiff to choose the forum. Although it occurs less frequently, the court may also invoke *forum non conveniens* on its own motion. In either situation, the same test is applied. If the test establishes a significantly more appropriate forum, the case will be dismissed in the original court, and the order of dismissal will indicate where the case should be filed.

## ESTABLISHING JURISDICTION

To summarize, in establishing the appropriate jurisdiction, the court would ask the following questions:

1. Where did the actual basis for a lawsuit occur? What state? What county? What federal district?
2. Who are the plaintiffs?
3. Who are the defendants?
4. Are any of the parties corporations? If so, what is the state of incorporation? What is the nerve center of the corporation?
5. Does the suit involve federal law? If so, is the law subject to the authority of a special federal district court (e.g., a U.S. district court of claims)?
6. Will any officer or branch of the U.S. government be named as a party?

7. Does any plaintiff share a common state of domicile with any party? If not, is the amount in controversy greater than the statutory minimum?

8. Is property the basis for jurisdiction? If so, where is it located?

9. Does any one court have **exclusive jurisdiction**?

10. What are the possible venues?

11. If there is concurrent jurisdiction, is there one court with significantly more contacts to the case than another?

**exclusive jurisdiction**
Authority of a court to hear a case, that authority being superior to the authority of all other courts.

---

## APPLICATION 8.8

An accident occurs between a truck and a family vehicle. The truck is owned by a corporation with businesses in Ohio and Pennsylvania. The truck driver is from Ohio. The corporation is incorporated in Delaware but is headquartered in Pennsylvania. The family members in the vehicle include a grandmother domiciled in New Jersey and a mother and daughter domiciled in Connecticut. The accident occurs in New York. The family sues the corporation.

*Point for Discussion:*

1. Is there federal jurisdiction?
2. What states have jurisdiction? (Assume subject matter jurisdiction requires the incident or the residents of all defendants to be in the state of suit.)

---

## ETHICAL CONSIDERATIONS

Jurisdictional issues are often raised in response to questions about the truthfulness of parties regarding domicile, place of injury, and so on. The very doctrine that disallows collusion was developed in response to parties who conspired to circumvent the purpose of procedural laws. It is extremely important that parties to suit understand that their ethical obligations are not limited to telling the truth when on the stand, but that these obligations commence with the very first representations to the court about matters as seemingly trivial as one's intended place of permanent residence. The procedural laws pertaining to jurisdiction are firmly embedded and well founded in the rationale of procedural law, and all those who take advantage of the benefits of the legal system are commensurately obligated to follow the system's standards.

## Question

What might a person seek to gain by misrepresenting his or her domicile to obtain jurisdiction in a particular court?

## ETHICAL CIRCUMSTANCE

Joe works for a boat company that hauls barges up and down the Mississippi River. While at work, he is seriously injured. A federal law allows maritime workers to file suit in state or federal court and not be subject to workers' compensation laws. Joe's lawyer plans to file a lawsuit against his employer for providing faulty equipment to the employees. The jury verdicts in county X have a history of averaging three times as much from those in county Y just 100 miles downstream. One choice for jurisdiction is to file where the accident occurred. Joe has told his lawyer that he is almost certain the boats had passed into county Y when the accident occurred. The lawyer knows that if the accident is claimed to have occurred in county X and the case is filed there, the outcome for Joe and his lawyer is likely to be much greater. The boat was in constant motion, so there is little evidence beyond Joe's own recollection as to where the accident occurred. To file the suit in county X would effectively result in Joe's lying under oath.

## CHAPTER SUMMARY

Jurisdiction truly opens the doors of the legal system to those persons who have need of the system's benefits. Jurisdiction should always be the first consideration of persons who consider seeking judicial review of an issue and of the court to whom the issue is brought. Parties should be aware that even though a court has jurisdiction, it may decline to hear the case entirely. The ultimate function of the courts with respect to jurisdiction is to have the dispute between parties decided by the most appropriate law and in the appropriate court.

Jurisdiction must exist over the issue (subject matter) and the litigants (*in personam*) or their property or property interests (*in rem, quasi in rem*). In federal courts, the jurisdiction must be based on either a federal law, the fact that the United States is a party to the suit, or diversity of citizenship and a controversy valued at more than the statutory minimum. With regard to diversity, corporations may have residence in more than one state.

Clearly, no lawsuit can proceed until all jurisdictional questions have been addressed.

## CHAPTER TERMS

ancillary jurisdiction
concurrent jurisdiction
exclusive jurisdiction
federal question

*in personam* (personal) jurisdiction
*in rem* jurisdiction
long-arm statute

original jurisdiction
pendent jurisdiction
*quasi in rem* jurisdiction
subject matter jurisdiction

## REVIEW QUESTIONS

1. Why are courts required to have subject matter jurisdiction?
2. What is personal jurisdiction?
3. Why do states have long-arm jurisdiction statutes?
4. What are the most common bases for federal jurisdiction?
5. What process is used to move a case from state to federal court? (Describe the steps involved.)
6. What process is used to move a case from federal to state court? (Describe the steps involved.)
7. What is concurrent jurisdiction?
8. What is collusion?
9. Where is a corporation considered to be domiciled for purposes of jurisdiction?
10. What determines domicile for an individual?

## HELPFUL WEB SITES

Law and Borders: The Rise of Law in Cyberspace, 48 *Stanford Law Review* 1367 (1996).   http://www.temple.edu/lawschool/dpost/Borders.html

Chicago: Kent College of Law Cyber Jurisdiction   http://www.kentlaw.edu/cyber

LII—Law—About Jurisdiction   http://www.law.cornell.edu/topics/jurisdictio

## ● │ INTERNET ASSIGNMENT 8.1

Locate an article (other than the one listed in Helpful Web Sites) that discusses jurisdictional issues in cyberspace.

## ● │ INTERNET ASSIGNMENT 8.2

Locate the statute in your jurisdiction that describes the circumstances in which long-arm jurisdiction can be applied to a defendant.

## ● │ ENDNOTES

1. William Statsky, *Legal Thesaurus/Dictionary* (St. Paul, MN: West, 1982).
2. *Lowry v. Semke,* 571 P.2d 858 (1977).
3. *Estate of Portnoy v. Cessna Aircraft Co.,* 603 F.Supp. 285 (S.D.Miss. 1985).
4. *Black's Law Dictionary,* 5th ed. (St. Paul, MN: West, 1979).
5. *T.J.K. v. N.B.,* 237 So.2d 592 (Fla.App. 1970).
6. *Atlas Garage & Custom Builders Inc. v. Hurley,* 167 Conn. 248, 355 A.2d 286 (1974).
7. Federal Rules of Civil Procedure, 28 U.S.C.A.
8. *Id.*
9. 10 A.L.R. Fed. 352.

### STUDENT CD-ROM

For additional materials, please go to the CD in this book.

### ONLINE COMPANION™

For additional resources, please go to www.paralegal.delmar.cengage.com

# Torts

## A TORT BY ANY OTHER NAME

In 2007, a Washington, D.C., man became notorious when he sued a dry cleaner who lost his favorite pair of pants. Alone, this would not be considered that unusual of a case, but the man was so distressed at the loss of his favorite item of raiment that he sued for $54 million over an alleged violation of the dry cleaner's posted policy of "satisfaction guaranteed." Ultimately, he lost. However, in the 1980s, a man did win a verdict for tens of thousands of dollars because a paper cut on his lip interfered with his favorite pastime of whistling. Although these alleged violations of personal rights at the hands of another are some of the more extreme cases, they are actually the signs of a healthy legal system.

Under American principles, anyone who feels they have been legally wronged in a compensable manner by another can bring an action in court where an objective third party can review the case. Yes, there are frivolous suits and sometimes the real injury to society is the stupidity of some individuals who are allowed to roam freely. Yes, there is some basis to the advocated position that there should be an early warning system about such people. The vast majority of claims, however, are well founded and sincere. The openness of our court system to all citizens is the ultimate sign of a free and responsive society. It is up to the rest of us as that objective third party of judges and juries not only to honestly evaluate and not perpetuate claims based on greed or stupidity but also to ensure that those who are responsible for actual injuries are held accountable. In doing so, we must keep in mind that what is of no importance to one person may be devastating to another.

## CHAPTER OBJECTIVES

After reading this chapter, you should be able to:

- Distinguish negligence from intentional torts.
- Distinguish negligence from strict liability.
- Explain the applicability of respondent superior in tort cases.
- List the defenses to claims of negligence.
- Discuss the applicability of the doctrine of last clear chance.

- List the types of action for defamation.
- List the elements of negligence.
- List the requirements for application of *res ipsa loquitur.*
- Distinguish the torts of assault and battery.
- Describe employment discrimination.

Tort law encompasses a wide range of subjects, including most subjects of law not directly related to contract principles (see Chapter 13) or criminal law (see Chapter 15). An exploration of some of these subjects may be the best way to explain or define the place of torts in the U.S. legal system.

## WHAT IS A TORT?

Legal authorities have been unable to agree on a single definition of a tort, although most would accept the following:

> An injury to an individual or property (not related to a breach of contract) that may or may not encompass criminal acts.

This definition cannot begin to encompass everything that constitutes the law of torts in this country. Fittingly, it concentrates on what is *not* a tort.

By definition, tort law involves only civil matters, including disputes between individual citizens and businesses or governments (state or federal) over private or proprietary rights. In other words, the parties in a tort case are involved in a dispute over rights of an individual's person or property or the property of the government. Tort law does not include criminal matters (matters in which the government acts against a party charged with a crime that injures the public good and, in many cases, specific citizens). Criminal law encompasses cases ranging from speeding in a vehicle to murder in the first degree. Tort claims that involve the government are actions regarding the value of property owned by the government or actions involving disputes between government officials and private citizens over private rights—for example, a car accident involving a government official driving a government vehicle and a private citizen driving his or her private vehicle. Dependent on fault for the accident, one party might sue the other for personal injuries and property damage to the vehicle. This particular action would not encompass any criminal charges that might arise from the accident. Such charges would be dealt with in a separate criminal case.

A tort does not include breach of contract. Although contract actions are included in the definition of civil law, the elements of a lawsuit in tort are different from the elements of a case in contract. Contract actions occur when two or more parties voluntarily enter into a legal relationship with certain rights and obligations and subsequently a dispute arises as to the nature or extent of those rights or obligations. In contrast, a tort arises when a party infringes on the rights of another person (or government) when there was no permission or agreement to do so and causes harm as a result of that infringement. This does not mean, however, that the parties were never involved in a relationship. Rather, it means that the action (tort) committed by one party was without permission or approval of the other party irrespective of the parties' relationship.

The formal definition of a tort indicates that some harm must occur. This is an important element of the definition. No matter how seriously one party may infringe on the rights of another party, there is no action in tort unless there is a verifiable harm that requires some form of compensation to repair it.

The individual circumstances of a situation have a great influence on the viability of a lawsuit. In an attempt to provide a better understanding of tort law and the role circumstances play in it, the following sections explore the development of tort law and some specific types of torts that are commonly litigated in this country.

## THE DEVELOPMENT OF TORT LAW

Like much of the law in the majority of U.S. jurisdictions, the American concept of tort law began in England. During the Middle Ages, the royal government instituted what came to be known as *forms of action*.[1] These forms were similar to modern laws that state the types of lawsuits that can and cannot be brought by a citizen. When someone had a grievance against another, the injured party was required to file a complaint stating the facts and, specifically, which form of action (law) allowed him or her to bring the lawsuit. The forms were extremely limited and vague as to the types of conduct allowed as the basis for a lawsuit. Thus, it was often difficult to know whether one had a successful legal claim against another.

### Trespass and Trespass on the Case

Two of the most commonly employed forms of action were *trespass* and *trespass on the case*.[2] To avoid confusion, note that during the Middle Ages the word *trespass* meant "wrong" rather than its current meaning of intrusion into another's property. The difference between trespass and trespass on the case was at first quite simple. A lawsuit based on trespass meant that the alleged guilty party had acted in such a way that the party bringing the lawsuit was directly injured because of the wrongful conduct. Trespass on the case, on the other hand, was appropriate when the injury was indirect. Consider the following scenarios:

1. A farmer is building a new fence for his pasture. He takes the old fence posts and throws them alongside the adjacent road. Just as he throws a large post, a horse and rider round the bend and are struck and injured by the post.

2. A farmer is building a new fence for his pasture. He takes the old fence posts and throws them alongside the adjacent road. Some of the posts actually land in the road. That night as a neighbor is returning home in the dark, he trips over a fence post and lands unconscious in the ditch by the road.

Scenario 1 illustrates an action of trespass, whereas scenario 2 is an action of trespass on the case. The difference is that the injury in the second example did not result directly from the farmer's throwing the post. Rather, the injury occurred as an indirect result. The direct result of the farmer's action was the post landing in the road creating a dangerous condition; as a further (or indirect) result of that, the neighbor was injured.

Through the years, lawsuits were filed on this type of basis in both England and the United States. It became increasingly difficult, however, to distinguish between trespass and trespass on the case. In addition, insufficient attention was being paid to whether the act was intentional. In response, the courts and lawmaking authorities attempted to define the terms, but the confusion continued.

## Liability of Parties

In the early 1800s, several things happened that led to the development of tort law as it exists in the United States today. At that time, the law in effect made certain persons dealing with the public liable (responsible) for injuries caused by them.[3] For example, doctors and smiths (metal workers) were automatically considered to be liable as a matter of contract with their customers. Others such as innkeepers and carriers (stagecoaches and the like) were liable by legislative statutes for failure to provide adequately for the safety of their customers. As the populations of urban areas increased, carriage accidents among private citizens rose dramatically, as did injuries from employment as the Industrial Revolution got under way. These developments led U.S. courts in the 1820s to accept the action of *negligence* as a basis for liability.[4] Negligence applied to all persons, including parties not previously included by contract or law, in disputes over injuries received as the result of a person's failure to act carefully in the interest of others.

Shortly after the emergence of negligence as a legal concept, the courts began to develop and refine related bases for liability such as the actions for intentional torts and, later, strict liability. Hand in hand with these came the creation of legal defenses for conduct that would otherwise be considered improper.

## Increase in Tort Claims

In recent years, the term *litigation explosion* has become commonplace. With the increase in technology, industry, and population, the number of lawsuits has increased dramatically. Although property and contract suits are prevalent, much of the focus of law has been on the increasingly large number of tort claims filed each year. A primary reason for the attention given to these claims are the effects of such claims on the economy as a whole. Many actions in tort are defended by insurance companies that insure the defendant—for example, automobile insurance that covers claims that the insured person caused damage with the insured automobile.

Claims of professional liability, premises liability (home or business owners), and so on all contribute to the suits in which the cost of defending a lawsuit is borne by the insurance company. The chain reaction comes when costs for insurance companies increase, forcing up the costs of insurance premiums. As these increases are passed on in costs to consumers, they contribute to overall inflation.

In response to this so-called explosion, many legislatures have adopted laws that place restrictions on the amounts that can be awarded in certain types of tort claims and sometimes even on the circumstances under which certain tort claims can be filed. With the increased amount of litigation in tort law has come a refinement of many tort concepts into well-established doctrines. Although many of these doctrines are examined later in the chapter, keep in mind that as society changes and evolves, so does its law.

## TERMINOLOGY IN TORTS

It is helpful at this point to examine certain essential terms frequently encountered in the law of torts. Although not exhaustive, the following list provides an initial explanation of some of the more commonly employed terminology in torts.

- Negligence. The term **negligence** is the basis for those causes of action among parties who claim (1) that a legal duty was owed by another; (2) that by failing to engage in reasonable conduct (of a standard that would prevent the harm), that duty was violated or breached; and (3) that as a proximate result of that breach, the complaining party was significantly injured. Specifically, the elements that must be proven by facts introduced to the court to sustain a cause of action in negligence are (1) duty, (2) the standard of care, (3) breach of the standard, and (4) damage proximately caused by the breach.

- Reasonable conduct. Throughout the law of negligence, conduct of the alleged wrongdoer is measured against the standard of reasonableness (what would have been proper). Most often, the actions or omissions of a party accused of negligence are measured against what the conduct of a reasonable person would have been. The conduct of a reasonable person varies with the circumstances of each case. However, this person is always presumed to be one who would act with care and attention to all details that affect the situation. **Reasonable conduct** requires the actor to evaluate the surroundings, all benefits, and all risks and to respond in the most careful manner. This measurement of the reasonableness of the alleged liable person does not usually take into account the mental state of the actor. It does, however, take into account the intelligence, age, experience, and physical conditions over which the actor has no control.

- Foreseeability. In negligence, one cannot be held responsible for an injury caused as a result of one's conduct unless the risk of that injury was apparent (foreseeable). Foreseeability is determined by a finding of whether the risk of harm was known to the actor by constructive knowledge. This finding is generally based on what the actor knew or, by reasonable examination of the situation, should have known. Foreseeability plays a key role in determining what the reasonable standard of care should have been. A person must be able to foresee an occurrence before he or she can be held responsible for it.

- Proximate cause. The necessary relationship between a breach of a duty and claimed damage in a negligence action is **proximate cause**. To sustain an action for negligence, the injured party must prove that the injuries occurred as a consequence of the breach of the duty by the actor both as a matter of fact and as a matter of law.

- Intentional tort. This category of torts differs from negligence in several respects. The primary distinguishing factor is the element of intent. In an **intentional tort**, it is necessary for the actor to have the intent to engage in conduct that will,

**negligence**
An act or failure to act toward another when (1) a duty was owed to the other person; (2) the act or failure to act was less than a reasonable person would have done under the circumstances; (3) the act or failure to act was the direct cause of injury to the other person; and (4) the injury resulted in measurable financial, physical, or emotional damage to the other person.

**reasonable conduct**
That action or nonaction that is appropriate under the circumstances when all risks and benefits are taken into account.

**proximate cause**
The direct cause that is sufficient to produce a result. There can be no other intervening force that occurs independently and before the result that is also sufficient to produce the result.

**intentional tort**
An act that the actor knows or should know with substantial certainty will cause harm to another.

with near certainty, produce a result that invades the rights of or injures another. It is necessary not that the intent be to invade or injure but that the actor know or should know that the action will in all probability produce such an invasion or injury.

**strict liability**
Liability without fault. Applied in situations where the intention or neglect of the party is immaterial. The mere performance of the act will result in liability.

- Strict liability. A narrower (but steadily growing) area of tort law in the United States is **strict liability**. It is not concerned with fault or intent to cause injury. Rather, it is applied in situations where the actor derives some benefit from an activity that is extremely dangerous to other parties who have no control over the situation. The reasoning behind strict liability is that one who benefits from such a dangerous activity should shoulder the responsibility for injuries to innocent persons or property caused by it regardless of how carefully the actor conducts the activity.

Throughout the remainder of the chapter, additional peripheral terms will be introduced that play an important role in the various aspects of tort law. Note that although these terms have general meanings accepted by most, some states have employed variations of these definitions when developing their own tort law.

## NEGLIGENCE

In an action for negligence, the injured party must plead and ultimately prove at trial the facts of an occurrence, showing that each of the necessary elements existed. Only after such proof will the defendant (the party who is alleged to be at fault) be required to compensate the plaintiff for the injuries. The following elements[5] must be proven:

1. The actor (defendant) owed a duty to the injured party (plaintiff) to refrain from conduct that would cause injury.
2. By failing to exercise a care of a reasonable standard, the actor breached his or her duty.
3. The breach of the duty proximately caused an injury to the plaintiff.
4. The plaintiff's injuries are significant enough to be measurable and warrant compensation from the actor.

### The Concept of Duty

The first element that must be proven in any negligence action is that of duty. Specifically, the injured party (plaintiff) must demonstrate that the actor (defendant) owed a duty of acting with care for the plaintiff's safety or well-being. It is commonly accepted that all persons have a general duty not to act negligently and thereby harm others around them. This general duty also includes the responsibility to act carefully for one's own safety under the circumstances. It should be noted that there are occasions when the duty is to act rather than to refrain from acting. Therefore, failing to act—an omission—can also be a violation of a person's duty. An example of such an omission is a situation where danger to another is within a person's control and the person fails to exercise that control even though he or she has the opportunity to do so.

### APPLICATION 9.1

Floyd is employed by a college. He is driving a college-owned vehicle on campus while talking on his cell phone to a friend. The vehicle is equipped with an alarm that beeps loudly outside when the vehicle is in reverse. As he backs up out of a parking

*(continued)*

## APPLICATION 9.1 (Continued)

place, he runs over a student. He has a duty to drive safely in an area known to have many pedestrians. He has a further duty to drive without distraction such as talking on a cell phone.

*Point for Discussion:* What duty, if any, did the student have?

## Range of Possible Injury

To prove the element of duty in a negligence action, several things must be shown. The first is that the defendant owed a duty to the plaintiff who was injured. It is not necessary to show that the defendant owed a duty to this particular individual. Rather, it must be shown that the defendant knew or should have known that others within a certain range (which included the plaintiff) could be affected by his or her actions.

Two primary schools of thought have developed as to the area this range should include. One theory is often called the *zone of danger,*[6] which refers to the area that the defendant should reasonably expect or foresee his or her actions to affect. Consequently, no duty is owed, and no negligence can be shown for injuries that occur beyond the zone of danger. This means that usually there can be no recovery for injuries that are the result of remote or bizarre chain reaction events. Whether something is remote or not is generally determined by whether the defendant's conduct proximately caused the plaintiff's injuries. (Proximate cause is addressed in greater detail later.)

The second theory is the *world-at-large* approach,[7] which takes into account a much wider range. It requires the defendant to foresee more remote possibilities of harm to persons not in the immediate area and of injuries not as readily foreseeable to occur from his or her conduct. The defendant is expected to identify all persons in the surroundings who could reasonably be subjected to danger of injury as the result of the defendant's actions. The extent of this range also turns on a question of whether the conduct proximately caused the injury, but it allows a more indirect chain of events to be included as to what composes proximate cause.

## Degree of Duty

Once it has been shown that the plaintiff was within the area that the defendant should have expected to be affected by his or her conduct, it is necessary to establish the degree of duty that is relative to the degree of risk of injury. The defendant's actions will expose the plaintiff to certain potential dangers in the range where risk exists. The defendant is responsible for those risks that foreseeably could cause significant harm. What this means is that when a party engages in conduct that may affect others in the surrounding area, that actor must act carefully so as not to allow that conduct to injure those persons in ways that can be reasonably foreseen. Thus, the lower the risk of significant injury, the less the degree of duty owed to others to protect them. An example is the floor of a grocery store. Although the store would have a duty to keep its floor reasonably clean from spills and debris, it would not be required to post a guard in each aisle to warn customers of recently mopped areas. A cautionary sign would be sufficient.

In some instances, a specific duty is imposed by statute or common law. The legislature and judiciary have identified particular situations as those in which a duty is always warranted. An example is traffic laws. With the establishment of these laws came the duty to obey the laws for the safety of others as well as oneself.

## The Standard of Care

Once it has been established that a duty existed between the defendant and the plaintiff, it must then be established that the defendant violated the duty. This is accomplished by first establishing the appropriate standard of care to which the defendant should have adhered to meet the duty.

The usual test applied in negligence actions is whether the defendant, under all the circumstances, exercised ordinary (reasonable) care.[8] Whether the defendant acted with ordinary care is determined by measuring his or her conduct against what a reasonable person would have done in a similar situation. On the one hand, no two situations are alike, and each must be judged in light of its own unique circumstances. On the other hand, there are generally enough similarities to other commonly encountered situations that a determination can be made of what a reasonable person would have done.

Note that the reasonable person in each case is generally presumed to have the same characteristics of age, intelligence, experience, and physical ability (or disability) as the defendant.[9] Also to be considered are (1) the underlying reason or necessity of the defendant's conduct (was it an act of great social value such as saving a life?), (2) the surrounding physical environment, (3) any activities that were taking place, and (4) the types of people in the area (was it an area, for example, where children with disabilities were playing?).[10]

The particular mental ability or disability in matters of judgment of the defendant is generally not considered.[11] The mental ability of an intoxicated defendant is no doubt impaired, but intoxication is a voluntary condition, and liability for one's actions cannot be escaped through this method. In addition, one cannot possibly identify degrees of mental ability in all those possible negligent persons who surround him or her and then take appropriate measures of protection. Consequently, most courts have determined that the actor is in the best position to determine what is and is not safe conduct given his or her mental ability. Keep in mind that the courts can moderate this rule by considering the age, experience, intelligence, and physical condition of the defendant, which may affect the mental ability consideration. An example is a defendant who is mentally impaired. In some cases, this impairment so affects a person's intelligence that mental ability to evaluate circumstances is altered. Conversely, someone certified or serving in the capacity of a specialist or an expert in some field (e.g., a brain surgeon or bankruptcy lawyer) can be held to a higher standard of care than the average member of his or her respective profession.

After determining who the reasonable person is in a situation, the court must determine how the reasonable person would have acted. This is done while keeping in mind that the reasonable person takes into account all details of the surroundings, appreciates all foreseeable risks, and acts in the most prudent and careful manner. Once this is determined, the standard of care is established.

In some cases, standards other than ordinary care are applied. Two other standards sometimes applied are *extraordinary* (great) care and *slight* care. The standard of extraordinary care is usually applied in situations identified by the lawmaking authorities where the plaintiff is not capable of protecting him- or herself from the defendant's actions.[12] An example is common carriers such as buses, trains, and airplanes. Many jurisdictions require common carriers to act with extraordinary care for the safety of their passengers who have virtually entrusted their lives to the carrier.

Slight care is the most basic of all duties to take even the most minimal action to prevent injuries to those in the surrounding area.[13] When this most basic and minimal duty is violated, many jurisdictions permit an action in addition or as an alternative to one for negligence. If there is a standard of ordinary care in place, the plaintiff may also be permitted to sue for punitive damages for the failure to exercise even slight care. *Punitive damages* are used in some jurisdictions in addition to compensatory damages. Punitives—or *exemplary damages,* as they are sometimes called—punish the defendant and are designed to deter others from such gross carelessness. Circumstances that impose only a duty of slight care include situations such as the duty of a landowner to trespassers. Although there is not a duty to obey a standard of ordinary care to persons invading another person's property, neither can a person willingly expose others to substantial risks of danger.

## Proximate Cause

Regardless of the degree of duty (standard of care), a duty must be shown in each case of negligence. The plaintiff must also establish that the defendant in some respect breached or failed to meet the standard of care that accompanied the duty to the plaintiff. Following this, the plaintiff has the further burden of establishing a legally recognized causal link between the breach and the plaintiff's injury.

Proximate cause is a major element of any negligence action. The plaintiff must demonstrate that the defendant's conduct proximately caused the plaintiff's injuries.[14] The issue is decided in two parts. First, it must be shown that the injuries were the result of the conduct as a matter of factual occurrence (known as *cause in fact*). Second, it must be shown that the injuries were caused by the conduct as a matter of law (commonly called the *legal cause*).

William Prosser, a well-known and respected authority on tort law, has said that proximate cause is the "reasonable connection between the act or omission of the defendant and the damage which the plaintiff has suffered. . . . Legal responsibility must be limited to those causes which are so closely connected with the result and of such significance that the law is justified in imposing liability."[15]

In the test of proximate cause, the cause in fact is generally the simplest factor to establish. The plaintiff needs only to trace a chain of events, short or long, that leads directly from the defendant's conduct to the plaintiff's injuries. This is influenced somewhat by the extent of the duty of the defendant as discussed earlier. In simple situations, where there are no intervening forces or remote circumstances, cause in fact and legal cause may be established by the same evidence.

**Tests for Determining Proximate Cause.**  Two tests are commonly employed when deciding whether there has been proximate cause. Both are used in determining cause in fact. The first is often called the *but for test.*[16] Simply put, the question is asked, "But for the defendant's actions, would the plaintiff's injuries still have occurred?" This test is rarely applied because a multitude of variables can contribute to the severity of an injury. Thus, the but for test is not appropriate for many situations.

The decline in the application of the but for test has been matched by the increasing use of *substantial factor* analysis,[17] which examines whether the defendant's conduct was a substantial factor in producing the plaintiff's injury.[18] If it was, irrespective of other factors that may have contributed, then cause in fact has been established. Overall, substantial factor analysis seems to be a fairer method of determining cause in fact than the but for test.

---

### ✗ APPLICATION 9.2

Kamisha was a passenger in her friend Ronnie's car when an accident occurred as the result of Ronnie driving too fast around a curved entrance ramp on an interstate highway. Kamisha was not seriously injured, but Ronnie was unconscious in the overturned

*(continued)*

## APPLICATION 9.2  (Continued)

car. Kamisha left the car and ran up the ramp and onto the overpass of the highway to get to help at a nearby gas station. At the same time, Mike was driving along the same road. Unfortunately, he was loading a new CD into the dash of his vehicle and did not see Kamisha. As he looked down to the dash, his car veered onto the shoulder. His car grazed Kamisha—although it did not seriously injure her, she was struck with enough force to cause her to fall over the railing of the overpass and onto the road below. There several cars struck her and she was killed. Although Ronnie's negligent driving caused the initial accident that prompted Kamisha to exit the vehicle, her death was caused by the actions of Mike and the cars that ultimately caused her death—even though, as a matter of cause in fact, Kamisha's presence on the road was the result of the accident caused by Ronnie.

*Point for Discussion:*  Would there be legal causation if Mike's car had struck Ronnie's car and resulted in Kamisha's death?

**Proving Proximate Cause.**  When proximate cause becomes an issue, it can be the most disputed point in the case. Proximate cause is heavily influenced by the extent of the duty imposed by the court: the larger the area to which a defendant owes a duty, the greater the chance of a remote occurrence causing an injury to someone within that area. Consequently, such situations present a greater likelihood for an issue of proximate cause.

Sometimes an injury occurs and the cause is not easily foreseeable. In such a situation, proximate cause is not easily proven. Proximate cause is more than a chain of events from the act to the injury. It is a chain of events in which the actor should have reasonably foreseen the likelihood of injury. Proximate cause can be established in fairly remote situations, even when other forces come into play in producing the injury. However, when these remote situations are so removed that the occurrence is bizarre or considered a freak accident, then proximate cause will be difficult to establish. Similarly, when an intervening force capable of producing the injury independently occurs between the moment of conduct by the defendant and the moment of injury, the proximate cause is extremely difficult to prove in terms of the original defendant. Again, the courts often apply the but for test or substantial factor analysis to determine legal cause.

## APPLICATION 9.3

Ziggy was roller-blading down the street on the sidewalk when Cosmo approached from the other direction on a skateboard. Cosmo attempted to pass Ziggy. In response, Ziggy swerved and fell into Antony, who was playing in his own yard adjacent to the sidewalk. When Ziggy landed on Antony, the fall caused Antony to suffer a broken arm. Under the but for test, Cosmo may or not be considered the cause of Antony's injury. Under the substantial factor test, Cosmo's presence and Ziggy's response to that presence would be considered substantial factors in bringing about Antony's injuries.

*Point for Discussion:*  Would the outcome be changed if Ziggy fell immediately after Cosmo had passed?

## Damage

A key element in any action for negligence is that of damage. The plaintiff must prove that he or she suffered some type of compensable injury—that is, that something happened to the plaintiff or the plaintiff's property as the proximate result of the defendant's breach of the standard of care that warrants compensation by the defendant to the plaintiff. For example, the fact that the plaintiff was delayed by the defendant's actions in and of itself is probably not sufficient. However, if the defendant's negligent conduct is the cause of a delay to the plaintiff that causes the plaintiff to suffer monetary loss (e.g., miss a flight for an important business trip), then the defendant may be required to compensate the plaintiff.

Damage comes in many forms: monetary, physical, or mental or emotional. It may affect the person or the person's property. However, in a negligence action, it must be significant enough under the circumstances to warrant a monetary award as compensation.

# CASE

### *Stowers v. Clinton Central School Corporation,* —N.E.2d—, 2006
### WL 3026304 (Ind.App.)

The following judicial opinion demonstrates the reluctance of the courts to make findings with regard to the elements of negligence and instead entrust such determinations to the finders of fact—typically, a jury.

On July 31, 2001, Travis was seventeen years old . . . at Clinton Central High School, where he was a member of the football team. Travis had played organized football . . . , and he had played the two previous years on the high school football team. . . . July 30, 2001, was the first day of football practice for the 2001–2002 season. The first two days of practice were "no contact" days, which meant that there was to be no physical contact between the players. The players only wore helmets, shoulder pads, mesh jerseys, and shorts. Coach Gilbert had used the same practice schedule for many years, and it was provided to parents in advance and posted on the internet. . . .

Prior to the start of the football season, Travis spent time during the summer doing chores around the family farm, which included taking care of the family's livestock, baling hay, and mending fences. He also baled hay for other farmers. Travis had no trouble participating in these chores in the summer and was encouraged by his parents to take breaks and drink lots of water while working outside. Additionally, in the summer of 2001, Travis had attended a football lineman's camp at DePauw University, which was held outdoors and consisted of three practices a day, with drills that were very similar to the ones used by Coach Gilbert. Travis also participated in Clinton Central's summer weightlifting and conditioning program and ran on his family's treadmill. He had no problems performing any of these activities. One week prior to the

beginning of football practice, Travis traveled to Washington, D.C. to attend a Future Farmers of America leadership conference. Therefore, he missed a week of pre-season conditioning and returned home on the day before practices were to begin.

On the first day of football practice, which was hot and humid, Travis did not experience any adverse reaction to the heat. That night, Travis told his parents that some players had vomited during that first day of practice. The Stowers told Travis that the next day was going to be equally hot and that he should be sure to drink lots of water.

On July 31, 2001, Coach Gilbert checked the weather reports . . . before beginning practice. The day was hot and humid, but no heat advisories had been issued by the National Weather Service. Although at that time, Clinton Central did not have any means of measuring the on-field temperature and humidity to determine the heat index, it had been given charts by the IHSAA and the Indiana Department of Education that could be used for that purpose. Clinton Central did not use these charts on July 31. Coach Gilbert had posted information disseminated by the IHSAA on heat-related illnesses near the scales in the locker room. The players were to monitor their water weight loss by weighing in every morning and weighing out every afternoon and documenting their weights on a chart. They were to report to the coaches if there was any abnormal weight loss. Travis weighed in on July 30 at 256 pounds and weighed out at 254 pounds; on July 31, he weighed in at 254 pounds.

The football coaches and the team athletic trainer, Ericka Daniels, stressed the importance of hydration

*(continued)*

to the players. During practice, water was supplied by a water tree, which consisted of a PVC pipe several yards in length attached to a hose. Water would shoot continuously out of holes in the pipe. The players could leave practice and get water any time they felt they needed it. The coaches and trainer repeatedly told the players that if they felt ill in any way, they were to tell one of the coaches or Daniels.

Morning practice on July 31 began at 7:30 A.M. and ran until 10:00 A.M., followed by a ninety-minute rest period and a twenty-minute team meeting. Afternoon practice ran from 12:00 P.M. until 2:00 P.M. At the time of this incident, IHSAA Rule 54-4 stated in pertinent part:

> The first two days [of football practice] shall be non-contact practices limited to two 90-minute sessions per day or less with a two-hour break between sessions. There shall be no live contact between participants and protective equipment is limited to helmet, shoes, shoulder pads and mouthpieces. Footballs may be used. The two days are to be used primarily for physical conditioning, sprints, agility drills, etc.

The morning practice consisted of activities such as "stretch," "crash," and "offensive drills." "Stretch" included actual stretching, touching toes, and jumping jacks. "Crash" was physical conditioning where players would go to different stations and perform activities such as push-ups, sit-ups, and running drills. On the morning of July 31, the time allotted for "crash" was shortened by half. For the rest of the morning, offensive linemen, like Travis, were taught several different blocking techniques, which was done by putting the players in the correct stance and working on their steps. Players were given water breaks every fifteen to twenty minutes. Players were to keep their helmets on when they were on the football field, which included wearing them on water breaks until they reached the water tree area.

During morning practice, at approximately 7:50 A.M., Coach Gilbert observed Travis having "dry heaves" during the "crash" portion of practice and Travis stopped his activity for a minute. When he resumed his activity, Coach Gilbert continued to monitor him. After morning practice ended, the offensive line coach, Coach Marvin Boswell, saw Travis vomit. Coach Boswell asked Travis if he felt better, and Travis responded that he did. Coach Boswell also told Travis to make sure he replenished his fluids, and Travis agreed to do so. Another coach, Coach Jamie Bolinger, also saw Travis vomit after the morning practice and asked if he was okay, and Travis answered affirmatively.

During the rest period, Travis ate some lunch and kept it down. He also spent time lying on the floor of the locker room. Right before the team meeting, Coach Boswell saw Travis and asked him how he was feeling. Coach Boswell thought that Travis looked pretty good and had color in his face. Over the lunch break, the coaches discussed Travis's vomiting and another player's light-headedness and agreed they would watch these players during the afternoon practice. At the team meeting, Coach Gilbert lightheartedly mentioned that Travis had gotten sick in the morning and asked him if he was okay, to which Travis smiled and responded that he was.

Afternoon practice again consisted of "stretch" and "crash," the latter of which was shortened. It was also decided that water breaks would be given every ten minutes that afternoon, and that sprints would be cut from practice. After "crash," the players worked on defensive techniques, which included a lot of repetition of stances. Although Travis's brother, Jared, testified that Travis "seemed a little dizzy" during these drills, Coach Boswell did not notice Travis having any trouble with them. Approximately ten or fifteen minutes before practice was to end, Travis went to Coach Jeffrey Parker and told him that he did not feel well. . . . Coach Parker asked Travis what was wrong, and Travis said he did not know. Travis then asked if they were going to run sprints that afternoon, and when Coach Parker told him they were not, Travis smiled. The water whistle blew, and Coach Parker told Travis to go get some water.

While Coach Parker spoke to Travis, he did not notice any indication that Travis was ill or suffering from any heat-related problems. During the water break, at approximately 1:45 P.M., several players yelled for the coach because Travis had collapsed near the water tree. Daniels and Coach Gilbert assisted Travis in removing his helmet and shoulder pads and in loading him on a golf cart to take him to the locker room. In the locker room, Daniels placed Travis in a cool shower and placed ice around him. Coach Gilbert called 911, and Travis was taken away by ambulance. Travis lost consciousness in the locker room, which he never regained, and he died around 4:00 A.M. the following day.

. . . the Stowers filed a complaint against Clinton Central alleging that Clinton Central had acted negligently and proximately caused Travis's death. . . . The Stowers filed a motion for summary judgment as to the negligence of Clinton Central and as to Clinton Central's affirmative defenses. Both of these motions were denied. Clinton Central also filed a motion for summary judgment, raising the affirmative defenses of incurred risk and contributory negligence, which was denied by the trial court. A jury trial was held, and at its conclusion, the jury returned a verdict in favor of Clinton

Central. The Stowers filed a motion to correct errors and for judgment on the evidence, which was denied by the trial court. The Stowers now appeal. . . .

The Stowers argue that the trial court erred when it denied their motions for summary judgment regarding Clinton Central's negligence as a matter of law and as to Clinton Central's ability to raise contributory negligence and incurred risk as affirmative defenses. . . .

The Stowers specifically argue that the trial court erred when it denied their summary judgment motion as to the negligence of Clinton Central because they believe that Clinton Central was negligent as a matter of law. Negligence consists of three elements: (1) a duty on the part of the defendant owed to the plaintiff; (2) a breach of that duty; and (3) an injury to the plaintiff that was proximately caused by that breach. *Dennis v. Greyhound Lines, Inc.*, 831 N.E.2d 171, 173 (Ind.Ct. App.2005), *trans. denied*. Our Supreme Court has recognized that a duty exists on the part of school personnel to exercise ordinary and reasonable care for the safety of the children under their authority. *Mark v. Moser,* 746 N.E.2d 410, 414 (Ind.Ct.App.2001). Summary judgment is generally inappropriate in negligence cases because they "are particularly fact sensitive and are governed by a standard of the objective reasonable person-one best applied by a jury after hearing all of the evidence." *Rhodes v. Wright*, 805 N.E.2d 382, 385 (Ind.2004).

The Stowers claim that the undisputed facts support a conclusion that Clinton Central breached its duty to Travis. First, they argue that Clinton Central was obligated to comply with IHSAA Rule 54-4 and the practice exceeded the time limits set forth under that rule. Second, they assert that although the IHSAA supplied materials regarding heat-related illness to Clinton Central, Clinton Central did not recognize that Travis was suffering from heat stroke, and returned Travis to practice without having Daniels examine him, despite the "high risk" of heat-related illness and the fact that Travis had vomited earlier in the day. We disagree.

Although Clinton Central's practice on July 31, 2001, may have exceeded the stated limits of Rule 54-4, the designated evidence showed that Coach Gilbert responded to the heat and modified the practice schedule by shortening the "crash" portions, eliminating sprints, and adding more frequent water breaks. The coaches emphasized the importance of drinking fluids, which were available at any time during practice in the end zone, and told the players to contact one of them or Daniels if they did not feel well. During the lunch break, several coaches approached Travis to inquire as to how he was feeling, and he responded that he was fine. During the afternoon practice session, the coaches saw no indication that Travis was feeling ill until he collapsed. After Travis collapsed, Daniels and Coach Gilbert took him by golf cart to the locker room where he was placed in a cool shower and they called 911. Based on this evidence, we conclude that a genuine issue of material fact exists as to whether Clinton Central was negligent as a matter of law, and the trial court did not err when it denied summary judgment on this issue.

The Stowers also claim that the trial court erred when it denied their motion for summary judgment as to Clinton Central's affirmative defense of contributory negligence. Contributory negligence is conduct on the part of the plaintiff, contributing as a legal cause to the harm he has suffered, which falls below the standard to which he should conform for his own protection and safety. *Carter v. Indianapolis Power & Light Co.*, 837 N.E.2d 509, 523 (Ind.Ct.App.2005). A plaintiff must exercise that degree of care which an ordinary reasonable person would exercise in like or similar circumstances. However, contributory negligence must be the proximate cause of the plaintiff's injury in order to constitute a complete bar to recovery.

The Stowers specifically rely on two findings by the trial court for their contention that summary judgment should have been granted as to contributory negligence. First, the trial court found that Travis acted reasonably by performing the conditioning and practice drills during football practice and second, that he acted reasonably by being willing to endure physical hardship to better himself and the team. . . . Although in these findings, the trial court states that Travis acted reasonably, we do not believe that they foreclosed the issue of whether Travis was contributorily negligent. The findings only determine that Travis was not unreasonable in actually participating in football practice on July 31, 2001; the findings do not establish that every action he took on that date was reasonable.

The designated evidence showed that Travis was repeatedly told by the coaches, Daniels, and his parents the importance of drinking the appropriate amounts of fluids while being in the heat. Coach Gilbert also instructed the players that if they were not feeling well they had the right to stop what they were doing and to notify one of the coaches or Daniels. Travis had the opportunity to go see Daniels when he was not feeling well, but chose not to do so. Further, when members of the coaching staff inquired as to Travis's well-being during the lunch break, Travis reported to each of them that he was fine. We therefore conclude that a

*(continued)*

genuine issue of material fact existed as to whether Travis was contributorily negligent as a matter of law, and the trial court did not err in denying summary judgment as to this issue.

The Stowers next contend that there was no genuine issue of material fact as to incurred risk by signing the release forms or by Travis participating in football practice on July 31, 2001. The affirmative defense of incurred risk requires evidence of a plaintiff's actual knowledge and appreciation of the specific risk involved and voluntary acceptance of that risk. *Kostidis v. Gen. Cinema Corp. of Indiana,* 754 N.E.2d 563, 571 (Ind.Ct.App.2001), *trans. denied.* A plaintiff must have more than just a general awareness of a potential for injury. *Id.* Incurred risk also involves a mental state of "venturousness" and has been described as negating a duty and therefore precluding negligence. *Carter,* 837 N.E.2d at 522.

Here, the trial court made a specific finding that Travis did not have actual knowledge of the specific risk of heat stroke. . . . We note that this finding by the trial court would have been sufficient to grant summary judgment, but no designated evidence was shown to support this finding. The designated evidence showed that the coaches and the trainer repeatedly stressed the importance of proper fluid intake and information disseminated by the IHSAA regarding heat-related illnesses was posted in the locker room. The Stowers had discussions with Travis about drinking fluids when in the heat, and after Travis had reported that other players had gotten sick at practice on July 30, they reenforced the necessity to drink fluids often and not to overdo it in the heat. We conclude that a question of fact existed as to whether Travis had actual knowledge of the specific risk and incurred the risk. The trial court did not err in denying summary judgment as to incurred risk.

. . . Where all or some of the issues in a case tried before a jury or an advisory jury are not supported by sufficient evidence or a verdict thereon is clearly erroneous as contrary to the evidence because the evidence is insufficient to support it, the court shall withdraw such issues from the jury and enter judgment thereon or shall enter judgment thereon notwithstanding a verdict.

Ind. Trial Rule 50(A). When reviewing a trial court's ruling on a motion for judgment on the evidence, we use the same standard as the trial court. *Faulk v. Nw. Radiologists, P.C.,* 751 N.E.2d 233, 238 (Ind.Ct.App. 2001). The evidence is considered in the light most favorable to the non-moving party. *Id.* . . . We determine only: (1) whether there exists any reasonable evidence supporting the claim; and (2) if such evidence does exist, whether the inference supporting the claim can be drawn without undue speculation. *Id.*

The Stowers argue that the trial court abused its discretion when it denied their motion for judgment on the evidence. They contend that the jury's verdict was contrary to the evidence presented at trial because the evidence was overwhelmingly in their favor and insufficient to support the jury's verdict. . . . We conclude that the trial court did not abuse its discretion in denying the Stowers' motion for judgment on the evidence because there were issues of fact and evidence presented to the jury, . . . which supported the jury's verdict. We will not reverse the trial court's admission of evidence absent a showing of prejudice.

The Stowers argue that the trial court erred by allowing the IHSAA Acknowledgement and Release Form and the Clinton Central Athletic Department's Acknowledgment and Release Forms (collectively "the Release Forms") into evidence during the trial. They specifically contend that the Release Forms should not have been admitted because they did not contain the word negligence and were therefore not relevant evidence. Ind. Evidence Rule 401, states:

"Relevant evidence" means evidence having any tendency to make the existence of any fact that is of consequence to the determination of the action more probable or less probable than it would be without the evidence.

Prior to the beginning of football season, Travis's mother, Sherry, signed Clinton Central's release form, which gave permission for Travis to participate in organized athletics and acknowledged that in such activities the potential for injuries is inherent and may be a possibility. Additionally, both Sherry and Travis signed the IHSAA release form, which acknowledged that there was a risk of serious injury and even death from athletic participation and showed that they accepted all responsibility for Travis's safety It also contained language holding the school and the IHSAA harmless of any responsibility and liability for any injury or claim resulting from athletic participation. *Id.* Clinton Central moved to admit the Release Forms at trial, the Stowers objected, and the trial court admitted them over this objection.

At issue at the trial was whether Clinton Central was negligent in conducting football practice and whether Travis was either contributorily negligent or had incurred the risk involved. We conclude that the Release Forms were relevant as to the defense of incurred risk and were therefore admissible. "The affirmative defense of incurred risk requires evidence of a plaintiff's actual knowledge and appreciation of the specific risk involved and voluntary acceptance of that risk."

*Kostidis,* 754 N.E.2d at 571. . . . The Release Forms outlined the risks involved in athletic participation and stated that serious injury and even death were possible in such participation. They were relevant as to the affirmative defense of incurred risk, and the admission of them into evidence for that limited purpose was not an abuse of discretion.

We review a trial court's refusal to tender a requested jury instruction for an abuse of discretion. *America's Directories Inc., Inc. v. Stellhorn One Hour Photo, Inc.,* 833 N.E.2d 1059, 1066 (Ind.Ct.App.2005). The trial court's refusal to give a tendered instruction will be reversed if: (1) the instruction is a correct statement of law; (2) it is supported by the evidence; (3) it does not repeat material adequately covered by other instructions; and (4) the substantial rights of the tendering party would be prejudiced by the failure to give the instruction. *Id.*

The Stowers contend that the trial court erred when it refused to give their proposed jury instruction regarding the Release Forms. At the close of evidence, the Stowers offered a final instruction, which they asserted set forth the applicable standard of law to be applied when considering the Release Forms. The instruction stated:

> As a matter of law, the Plaintiffs Alan and Sherry Stowers have not released the Defendant Clinton Central from any alleged negligent acts when the release forms at issue contain language expressly addressing the risks inherent in the sport of football and other vigorous physical activity, but nowhere expressly state the release of Clinton Central or its agents from their own negligence. The trial court refused to give the proposed instruction. The Stowers argue that this instruction should have been given because it would have defined the scope of the Release Forms and provided guidance to the jury on how to consider the documents.

It is well established in Indiana that exculpatory agreements are not against public policy. *Marsh v. Dixon,* 707 N.E.2d 998, 1000 (Ind.Ct.App.1999). "Generally, parties are permitted to agree that a party owes no obligation of care for the benefit of another, and thus, shall not be liable for consequences that would otherwise be considered negligent." *Id.* However, this court has held that an exculpatory clause will not act to absolve a party from liability unless it "'specifically and explicitly refer[s] to the negligence of the party seeking release from liability.'" *Id.*

The Stowers' proposed instruction set out that the Release Forms did not absolve Clinton Central of liability for negligent acts if they did not contain language specifically referring to negligence; thus, it was a correct statement of the law. Because the Release Forms did not contain any specific or explicit reference to the negligence of Clinton Central or the IHSAA, the proposed instruction was supported by the evidence. No other instructions were given that adequately covered the information in the Stowers' instruction. The substantial rights of the Stowers were prejudiced by the failure to give the instruction because the admission of the Release Forms without the redaction of the language regarding release could have been exceptionally prejudicial to the Stowers. A jury reading the Release Forms without a limiting instruction might conclude that the Stowers released Clinton Central of liability when the trial court had already determined that they had not as a matter of law in the summary judgment order. We conclude that the trial court abused its discretion when it refused to give the Stowers' proposed instruction regarding the Release Forms. We therefore reverse and remand for a new trial and instruct the trial court to give an instruction stating the correct law regarding the Release Forms.

Instructing the jury lies within the sound discretion of the trial court, and we will reverse only for an abuse of that discretion. *St. Margaret Mercy Healthcare Ctrs. v. Poland,* 828 N.E.2d 396, 404 (Ind.Ct.App.2005). . . . The Stowers argue that the trial court abused its discretion when it gave Final Instruction 22(A) on incurred risk. They contend that the instruction was an incomplete and incorrect statement of the incurred risk doctrine and was given in error. Final Instruction 22(A) stated:

> When a person knows of a danger, understands the risk involved and voluntarily exposes himself to such danger, that person is said to have "incurred the risk" of injury. In determining whether a person incurred the risk you may consider the experience and understanding of a person, whether a person had reasonable opportunity to abandon the course of action, and whether a person of ordinary prudence, under the circumstances, would have refused to continue and would have abandoned the course of conduct.

The Stowers claim that Final Instruction 22(A) failed to instruct the jury on two essential elements of incurred risk: (1) that the plaintiff must have actual knowledge and appreciation of the specific risk; and (2) that the knowledge must be more than a general awareness. They point to Indiana's pattern jury instruction regarding incurred risk, which states:

> The plaintiff incurs the risk of injury if [he] actually knew of a specific danger, understood the risk involved, and voluntarily exposed [himself] to that danger. Incurred risk requires much more than the general awareness of a potential for mishap. Determining whether the plaintiff had incurred

*(continued)*

the risk of injury requires a subjective analysis focusing upon:

1. The plaintiff's actual knowledge and appreciation of the specific risk, and
2. The plaintiff's voluntary acceptance of that risk.

Ind. Pattern Jury Instruction (Civil) 5.41 (2d ed.2003).

In *Kostidis,* the trial court, over objection, gave a jury instruction on incurred risk with language almost identical to Final Instruction 22(A). 754 N.E.2d at 570. . . . On appeal, this court found that although the proposed instruction was a correct statement of the law and would have provided a fuller explanation of the law regarding awareness of risk, the instruction that was given covered the same issue and was not incorrect, and the trial court did not abuse its discretion in giving the instruction. *Id.*

Although the instruction given in *Kostidis* was found not to be in error, that case was factually different from the present case. There, the specific risk at issue was the danger of slipping on ice or snow in the parking lot where a movie theater was located. The plaintiff testified that he knew that there was ice and snow on the ground, assumed that there would be ice and snow in the parking lot, and knew he should be watchful for icy conditions. *Id.* While not deciding whether the trial court erred in the present case by giving Final Instruction 22(A), we believe that in its exercise of discretion on remand, the trial court should give the pattern jury instruction to provide the jury with the fullest explanation of the law on incurred risk.

Affirmed in part, reversed in part, and remanded.

## Case Review Question

If the court found that summary judgment should have been granted with regard to negligence, what would have been left to determine at trial?

### Res Ipsa Loquitur

"The thing speaks for itself" is the traditional translation of the Latin term *res ipsa loquitur.*[19] This doctrine has been applied for many years in cases of negligence involving special circumstances. A plaintiff may claim the doctrine to ease the burden of proof in a case of negligence only when he or she can prove that (1) the occurrence was of a type that would not happen without negligence, (2) the instrument producing the injury during the occurrence was exclusively in the defendant's control, and (3) the plaintiff did not contribute to the injury.[20]

*Res ipsa loquitur* is used in cases where the evidence that would disclose how the defendant was negligent is not available to the plaintiff. Such cases arise where the plaintiff or his or her witnesses have no opportunity to determine precisely which conduct produced the injury. To prevent unwarranted claims of negligence, however, the plaintiff must prove the three elements noted previously.

Although the doctrine of *res ipsa loquitur* is limited in its application, in appropriate cases the plaintiff can use it to prove negligence where a cause of action might not otherwise be available for the simple reason that the plaintiff does not have access to information in the defendant's control or because there were no witnesses to the injury. It should be realized, however, that with broadening rules of discovery of information by parties, the doctrine is declining steadily.

## APPLICATION 9.4

Cecilia went to a busy tanning salon to get a head start on her tan before spring break. She honestly filled out the questionnaire and went to the tanning bed. The timer was programmed by an employee. Cecilia was extremely warm and uncomfortable but, as it was her first experience, she did not leave the tanning bed until the timer stopped. Cecilia suffered severe burns and required hospitalization. She was left with disfiguring scars. Shortly after Cecilia was injured, the tanning salon closed and the equipment was sold. The owners moved back to their native country in Southeast Asia and

*(continued)*

## APPLICATION 9.4 (Continued)

took all business records with them. Cecilia brought a lawsuit based on *res ipsa loquitur*. She had no access to evidence or witnesses concerning the actual cause of negligence. In a *res ipsa loquitur* case such as this, she would only need to prove that the injuries would not ordinarily have occurred without negligence, that the instrument causing the injury (the tanning bed) was under the exclusive control of the owner and its employees, and that she did not contribute to the cause of her injuries.

*Point for Discussion:*  If the salon was still in business and the identity of the employee was known, would this case still be appropriate for *res ipsa loquitur?* Why or why not?

# CASE
### *Holzauer v. Saks & Co.*, 346 MD 328,
### 697 A.2d 89 (1997)

The following case demonstrates the application of the theory of *res ipsa loquitur* in modern case law.

CHASANOW, Judge.

The United States District Court for the District of Maryland has certified the following three questions to this Court pursuant to the Maryland Uniform Certification of Questions of Law Act, Maryland Code (1974, 1995 Repl.Vol., 1996 Supp.), Courts & Judicial Proceedings Article, ss 12-601 through 12-613, and Maryland Rule 8-305.

1. Do Appellant's allegations with respect to negligence amount to a waiver of RES IPSA LOQUITUR, as in *Dover Elevator Co. v. Swann*, 334 Md. 231, 638 A.2d 762(1994)?

2. If not, does the doctrine of RES IPSA LOQUITUR apply under the facts thus far alleged in the instant case?

3. If the doctrine of RES IPSA LOQUITUR does apply, is there any reason, including the views expressed by the Court of Appeals in *Dover*, why the facts of this case require a different approach than that in *Beach v. Woodward & Lothrop, Inc.*, 18 Md.App. 645, 308 A.2d 439 (1973) (Where the escalator "stop[ped]and start[ed]up with a jerk")? . . .

The facts of the case are not disputed. On February 24, 1994, Appellant, Eugene Holzhauer, was shopping in the Saks Fifth Avenue department store in Owings Mills Mall. Appellant injured his right shoulder when the escalator upon which he was riding, with his hand on the railing, came to a sudden stop, causing him to stumble down ten to twelve steps in a twisting motion. Appellant filed suit in the United States District Court for the District of Maryland against Saks & Co., the owner of the escalator, and Montgomery Elevator Company, the organization hired to service and maintain the escalator

(collectively "Appellees"). Appellant alleged that Appellees were negligent in:

The suit was originally instituted in the Circuit Court for Baltimore County, but it was removed to the United States District Court for the District of Maryland based on the parties' diversity of citizenship. 28 U.S.C. s 1441.

a. "[M]aintain[ing] as a part of such escalator and the operating mechanism thereof, old, loose, worn, frayed, and antiquated parts, apparatus and equipment;

b. [F]ail[ing] to install in such escalator as a part of the operating mechanism thereof, a proper device to prevent said escalator from suddenly stopping when in use . . . ;

c. [P]ermitt[ing]such escalator and the working parts thereof to be and remain in a condition of disrepair for an unreasonable length of time;

d. [F]ail[ing]to inspect such escalator in a proper manner and at proper intervals;

e. [F]ail[ing]to warn plaintiff of the dangers connected with the escalator and to provide to plaintiff any protection from such dangers."

Appellant alleged, additionally, that Montgomery Elevator Company "negligently installed and maintained the escalator and failed to properly maintain, inspect and repair the escalator."

The following additional information was revealed during discovery. The parties do not know what caused the escalator to stop on February 24, 1994. The escalator had been inspected by the Maryland Department of Licensing and Regulation, Division of Labor and Industry Safety Inspection Unit in June of 1993. The escalator had not malfunctioned between the time of the inspection and the time of Appellant's injury, and it has not

*(continued)*

malfunctioned since Appellant's injury. On the day of the incident, the escalator remained stopped until a store employee restarted it with a key, at which time the escalator immediately began to run properly. Upon restarting, the escalator made no unusual movements or noises, and it did not require any repairs. Montgomery Elevator Company, in fact, was not informed of the events that occurred on February 24 until this suit was instituted.

The escalator was turned on and off daily, using a key, at the opening and closing of business by Saks & Co.'s Building Engineer or by a member of its Security Department. Any individual can also cause the escalator to stop by pushing one of the emergency stop buttons located at the top and bottom of the escalator, respectively. Once stopped, the escalator will not run again until it is started with a key.

Appellant has offered no additional evidence to support the allegations of negligence in his complaint, and it appears that he does not intend to offer expert testimony in the field of escalator maintenance, operations, or repair. The only expert witness listed on Appellant's Designation of Expert Witnesses is Dr. Steven Friedman, a medical doctor. Furthermore, in his Response to [Saks & Co's] Motion for Summary Judgment, Appellant states that "[he] is not offering any direct evidence or expert testimony, other than evidence of the event itself. He is not attempting to prove how or why the escalator stopped suddenly, only that it did."

Appellees filed Motions for Summary Judgment at the close of discovery, arguing that Appellant failed to produce evidence sufficient to sustain his burden of proof at trial. The Honorable Frank A. Kaufman initially granted the Appellees' Motions for Summary Judgment in a one sentence memorandum stating: "For reasons which this Court will shortly set forth in a more detailed document, to be filed in this case, this Court will enter summary judgment for defendants." When Judge Kaufman began to write the opinion in support of his ruling, however, he concluded that he could not continue without the answers to the three questions certified to this Court. Judge Kaufman has denied Appellees' Motions for Summary Judgment, and he will reconsider them once this Court has announced its decision.

The United States District Court seems to suggest by its phrasing of question number one that *Dover Elevator Co. v. Swann,* 334 Md. 231, 638 A.2d 762 (1994), stands for the proposition that the pleading of specific acts of negligence will preclude a plaintiff from relying on the doctrine of RES IPSA LOQUITUR. This is not so. *Dover* did not concern the mere pleading of acts of negligence; rather it dealt with a plaintiff's attempt to establish specific grounds of negligence at trial. We

held, in that case, that one of the reasons why the plaintiff was prohibited from relying on *res ipsa* was because he proffered direct evidence of negligence at trial. *Dover,* 334 Md. at 237, 638 A.2d at 765 ("[N]umerous Maryland cases have explained that a plaintiff's 'attempt to establish specific grounds of alleged negligence precludes recourse to the doctrine of RES IPSA LOQUITUR.'") (quoting *Smith v. Bernfeld,* 226 Md. 400, 409, 174 A.2d 53, 57 (1961)).

In *Dover,* David Swann was injured when he entered an elevator car, the floor of which was approximately one foot below the floor outside of the elevator. 334 Md. at 234, 638 A.2d at 764. He sued three defendants, one of which was *Dover,* the company that manufactured, installed, and maintained the elevator at issue. *Id.* Swann alleged in his Complaint that the defendants negligently designed, manufactured, installed, and maintained the elevator. *Dover,* 334 Md. at 234–35, 638 A.2d at 764. These pleadings, however, were not the reason that Swann was precluded from relying on *res ipsa.* Rather than ask the jury to draw an inference of defendant's negligence from the mere fact that the elevator misleveled, Swann had an engineer/elevator consultant testify at trial that the elevator misleveled because the elevator's contacts were "burned" and that *Dover* was negligent in, *inter alia,* cleaning rather than replacing the burned contacts. *Dover,* 334 Md. at 244, 638 A.2d at 769.

We held that, under the circumstances," the doctrine of RES IPSA LOQUITUR was inapplicable to the evidence before the jury. . . ." *Dover,* 334 Md. at 262, 638 A.2d at 777. The purpose of *res ipsa,* we explained, is to afford a plaintiff the opportunity to present a *prima facie* case when direct evidence of the cause of an accident is not available or is available solely to the defendant. *Dover,* 334 Md. at 237, 638 A.2d at 765. Direct evidence of the specific cause of his injuries was available to Swann, however, and he proffered that direct evidence to the jury in the form of an expert opinion. Thus, one of the reasons we held *res ipsa* to be inapplicable was because the expert "purport[ed] to furnish a sufficiently complete explanation of the specific causes of [the elevator's] misleveling, which . . . preclude[d] plaintiff's reliance on RES IPSA LOQUITUR." *Dover,* 334 Md. at 239, 638 A.2d at 766.

Unlike the petitioner in *Dover,* Appellant in the present case has not had the chance to proffer direct evidence as to the specific cause of his injuries. Thus far, he has only pleaded specific acts of negligence. This Court discussed the impact that pleading specific acts of negligence has on a claim of RES IPSA LOQUITUR in *Joffre v. Canada Dry Ginger Ale, Inc.,* 222 Md. 1, 158 A.2d 631(1960). In that case, a woman in a delicatessen was cut in the leg by a piece of glass when a Canada Dry soda bottle shattered. *Joffre*, 222 Md. at 3, 158 A.2d at 632. Appellant sued the Canada Dry bottler and the delicatessen. *Id.* Appellant alleged that the bottler "was negligent in" placing on the market . . . a product designed for purchase in the original package without making that package safe against reasonably-to-be-anticipated variations in temperature and hazards of handling, and that the bottle was defective or the pressure within it excessive." *Id.* She alleged that the delicatessen "was negligent in failing to so locate and guard the bottle as to prevent injury to customers, knowing it might explode." *Id.* The judge directed a verdict for both defendants at the close of the plaintiff's evidence, and Appellant argued on appeal that summary judgment was improper and that she was entitled to submit her claim to the jury under the theory of RES IPSA LOQUITUR. *Id.* The delicatessen argued that Appellant was precluded from relying on that theory because she had pleaded specific acts of negligence. *Joffre*, 222 Md. at 3–4, 158 A.2d at 632.

This Court stated that the delicatessen's argument had previously been rejected in Maryland. *Id.* (citing State for Use of *Parr v. Board of County Com'rs of Prince George's County*, 207 Md. 91, 103–04, 113 A.2d 397, 402–03 (1955)). We explained that "'[t]he doctrine RES IPSA LOQUITUR is not a rule of pleading. It relates to burden of proof and sufficiency of evidence.'" *Joffre*, 222 Md. at 6, 158 A.2d at 634 whether a party will be precluded from relying on the doctrine of RES IPSA LOQUITUR turns upon the evidence produced by the party and whether that evidence satisfies the three essential components of RES IPSA LOQUITUR; whether specific allegations of negligence have been pleaded is of no moment. We answer the first certified question in the negative.

Appellant cannot satisfy the three essential components of RES IPSA LOQUITUR, however, and, for that reason, he may not rely on the doctrine in the present case. Three elements must be proven in order to create an inference of negligence on the part of a defendant: (1) a casualty of a kind that does not ordinarily occur absent negligence, (2) that was caused by an instrumentality exclusively in the defendant's control, and (3) that was not caused by an act or omission of the plaintiff. *Dover*, 334 Md. at 236–37, 638 A.2d at 765. Appellant cannot satisfy the first two criteria.

In order to rely on RES IPSA LOQUITUR, Appellant must first prove that the accident would not have occurred in the absence of Appellees' negligence.

"[T]he doctrine of RES IPSA LOQUITUR is applicable only when the facts and surrounding circumstances tend to show that the injury was the result of some condition or act which ordinarily does not happen if those who have the control or management thereof exercise proper care. It does not apply where it can be said from ordinary experience that the accident might have happened without the fault of the defendant."

*Greeley v. Baltimore Transit Co.*, 180 Md. 10, 12–13, 22 A.2d 460, 461(1941). Appellant cannot satisfy this requirement because the evidence and inferences fairly deducible from the evidence indicate that, in addition to the possibility that Appellees were negligent, there is an equally likely explanation for the escalator's abrupt stop.

For safety reasons, the escalator in question was equipped with two emergency stop buttons, located at the top and bottom of the escalator, respectively. When either button is pushed, if the escalator is functioning as intended, the escalator will stop. The buttons are safety devices designed to stop the escalator quickly should a hand, foot, or article of clothing become caught; thus, ready accessibility to the buttons is only sensible. We cannot say that the escalator would not stop in the absence of Appellees' negligence because the escalator would also stop whenever any person pushed one of the emergency stop buttons.

The record is silent as to whether anyone did, in fact, push one of the stop buttons, but this is of little concern. The facts need not show that a stop button definitely was pushed to preclude reliance on *res ipsa;* they need only show that something other than Appellees' negligence was just as likely to cause the escalator to stop. The fact that the escalator had never malfunctioned before the day in question, and has not malfunctioned since, makes it equally likely, if not slightly more likely, that the escalator did not malfunction on the day in question but, rather, that it stopped because somebody intentionally or unintentionally pushed an emergency stop button.

Appellant also cannot rely on RES IPSA LOQUITUR in the present case because he cannot satisfy the second essential component of the doctrine, that the injury-causing instrumentality be in the exclusive control of the defendant.

"The element of control has an important bearing as negativing the hypothesis of an intervening cause beyond the defendant's control, and also as tending to show affirmatively that the cause was one within the power of the defendant to prevent by the exercise of care. Thus it has been held that the inference is not permissible where . . . the opportunity for interference by others weakens the probability that the injury is attributable to the defendant's act or omission." (Citations omitted).

*(continued)*

*Lee v. Housing Auth. of Baltimore,* 203 Md. 453, 462, 101 A.2d 832, 836 (1954). This Court has often held *res ipsa* to be inapplicable when the opportunity for third-party interference prevented a finding that the defendant maintained exclusive control of the injury-causing instrumentality. See, e.g., *Joffre,* 222 Md. at 8–10, 158 A.2d at 635–36 (holding defendant's control not exclusive where customers had access to soda bottles for approximately two months before one bottle inexplicably shattered); *Williams v. McCrory's Stores Corp.,* 203 Md. 598, 604–05, 102 A.2d 253, 256 (1954) (holding defendant's control not exclusive where thousands of customers had access to revolving stools every week).

In the present case, we must necessarily conclude that Appellant is unable to satisfy the second essential component of *res ipsa.* Hundreds of Saks & Co.'s customers have unlimited access to the emergency stop buttons each day. If the escalator's two emergency stop buttons are readily accessible to all persons in the vicinity and any customer can cause the escalator to stop simply by pressing one of the buttons, then it is impossible to establish that the escalator was in Appellee's exclusive control.

In *Trigg v. J.C. Penney Company,* 307 F.Supp. 1092 (D.N.M.1969), the United States District Court for the District of New Mexico held *res ipsa* inapplicable to facts very similar to those in the present case. In that case, the plaintiff was injured when the escalator upon which he was riding, in a department store, stopped suddenly. *Trigg,* 307 F.Supp. at 1092. The escalator was equipped with emergency stop buttons. *Trigg,* 307 F.Supp. at 1093. Although there was no evidence that anyone had pushed the button on the day that the plaintiff was injured, the court concluded that the "plaintiffs failed to prove . . . two crucial elements of the doctrine of RES IPSA LOQUITUR. There is no showing that the instrumentality was within the exclusive control of the defendant. Anyone could push one of [the emergency stop buttons] causing the escalator to stop. This conclusion necessarily leads the court to find that the second element has also not been proved. If anyone could stop the escalator by pressing the button, either intentionally or unintentionally, the accident is not one that ordinarily would not have happened in the absence of negligence on the part of the defendant."

*Id.*

There is yet a third reason that *res ipsa* is inapplicable to the case *sub judice.* We have, for many years, held that *res ipsa* is only applicable when "the circumstances attendant upon an accident are themselves of such a character as to justify a jury in inferring negligence as the cause of that accident." *Benedick v. Potts,* 88 Md. 52, 55, 40 A. 1067, 1068 (1898). This is the case when "the common knowledge of jurors [is] sufficient to support an inference or finding of negligence on the part of" a defendant. *Meda v. Brown,* 318 Md.

418, 428, 569 A.2d 202, 207 (1990); any person who regularly uses stairs knows that they rarely collapse beneath one's feet. See *Blankenship v. Wagner,* 261 Md. 37, 273 A.2d 412 (1971). The plaintiffs were permitted to rely on *res ipsa* because lay jurors possess the background knowledge necessary to decide whether these events ordinarily occur in the absence of someone's negligence. See also *Strasburger v. Vogel,* 103 Md. 85, 63 A. 202 (1906) (explaining that *res ipsa* would be proper where brick from defendant's chimney fell onto the head of an infant on the sidewalk below if defendant had not presented evidence of an intervening cause).

In some cases, however, "because of the complexity of the subject matter, expert testimony is required to establish negligence and causation." *Meda,* 318 Md. at 428, 569 A.2d at 207. For example, *Orkin, supra,* addressed the applicability of *res ipsa* in a medical malpractice case. In that case, the plaintiff sustained an injury to her median, ulnar, and radial nerves on her right side during surgery to repair a perforated ulcer. The plaintiff was under general anesthesia while her surgery was being performed, and she "could not 'ascribe a particular negligent act to any defendant.'" *Orkin,* 318 Md. at 432, 569 A.2d at 209. She proffered proof that her injury was one that usually does not occur absent negligence through the testimony of a neurologist.

The trial court granted summary judgment in favor of the defendants, and the plaintiff appealed, arguing that she should have been permitted to present her case to a jury under the theory of RES IPSA LOQUITUR.

Although this Court held that the trial court erred in granting the defendants' motion for summary judgment, and, therefore, remanded the case to the circuit court, we explained that the plaintiff should not be permitted to rely on RES IPSA LOQUITUR on remand. We stated that a case involving complex issues of fact, for which expert testimony is required, is not a proper case for RES IPSA LOQUITUR.

"This is not an 'obvious injury' case. Resolution of the issues of negligence and causation involved in a case of this kind necessarily requires knowledge of complicated matters, including human anatomy, medical science, operative procedures, areas of patient responsibility, and standards of care. Complex issues of the type generated by a case of this kind should not be resolved by laymen without expert assistance. RES IPSA LOQUITUR does not apply under these circumstances. *Meda v. Brown,* [318 Md. 418, 569 A.2d 202]."

We quoted this language with approval in *Dover,* where we held RES IPSA LOQUITUR to be inapplicable in a case involving the misleveling of an elevator, in part, because the common knowledge of jurors was insufficient to support an inference that the misleveling was caused by the defendant's negligence. *Dover,* 334

Md. at 254, 256, 638 A.2d at 773–74. An elevator "may experience problems absent anyone's negligence," and, thus, we explained that "[w]ithout [an expert's] opinion that the misleveling was [most likely] caused by negligence, an inference that this elevator did not mislevel or experience other problems absent someone's negligence may be unjustified." *Dover*, 334 Md. at 255, 638 A.2d at 774.

"'Mechanical, electrical, and electronic devices fail or malfunction routinely—some more routinely than others. A speck of dust, a change in temperature, misuse, an accidental unforeseen trauma—many things can cause these devices to malfunction. To allow an inference that the malfunction is due to someone's negligence when the precise cause cannot be satisfactorily established appears . . . to be unwarranted.'"

*Dover*, 334 Md. at 255, 638 A.2d at 774. Thus, in cases concerning the malfunction of complex machinery, an expert is required to testify that the malfunction is of a sort that would not occur absent some negligence.

When an expert raises an inference of a defendant's negligence, however, a plaintiff must necessarily be precluded from relying on RES IPSA LOQUITUR. "If expert testimony is used to raise an inference that the accident could not happen had there been no negligence, then it is the expert witness, not an application of the traditional RES IPSA LOQUITUR doctrine, that raises the inference." *Dover*, 334 Md. at 254, 638 A.2d at 773. In such a case, the jury is not asked or permitted to draw an inference unaided by expert testimony. *Meda*, 318 Md. at 425, 428, 569 A.2d at 205, 207. Instead, the jury's function is to decide whether the expert's inference that a defendant was negligent is credible.

In the present case, Appellant has declined to present expert testimony. In doing so he has, perhaps, "confused the question of whether an inference may be drawn by an expert with that of whether an inference may be drawn by a layman." *Meda,* 318 Md. at 428, 569 A.2d at 206. It is not the presence of expert testimony that, if presented, would prevent a jury in the present case from drawing an inference of Appellees' negligence, rather, it is the complex and technical issue presented by the facts of this case. Like the elevator in *Dover,* an escalator is a complex machine. Leaving aside the presence of any emergency stop buttons, whether an escalator is likely to stop abruptly in the absence of someone's negligence is a question that laymen cannot answer based on common knowledge. The answer requires knowledge of "complicated matters" such as mechanics, electricity, circuits, engineering, and metallurgy. RES IPSA LOQUITUR does not apply under these circumstances.

For all of the foregoing reasons, we answer the second certified question in the negative. We are called upon to answer the third certified question only if the doctrine of RES IPSA LOQUITUR applies to the present case. We have stated that the doctrine does not apply.

In sum, we answer the first certified question in the negative; the allegations in Appellant's Complaint with respect to negligence do not amount to a waiver of RES IPSA LOQUITUR. We also answer the second certified question in the negative; *res ipsa* does not apply to the facts of the instant case because Appellant cannot prove that the event would not occur in the absence of Appellees' negligence. In addition, Appellant cannot prove that the escalator was in Appellees' exclusive control. Finally, because of the complex and technical nature of the issue presented in this case, lay jurors would not be permitted to draw an inference of negligence without the aid of expert testimony, negating the very definition of RES IPSA LOQUITUR.

## Case Review Question

What are the factual elements of *res ipsa loquitur* in this case?

## ASSIGNMENT 9.1

With regard to the fact situation below, answer the following questions.

Who owes the duty?

To whom is the duty owed?

What is the duty?

How is the duty breached?

What is the reasonable foreseeable result of a breach of the duty?

How does the breach cause injury in fact and in law?

What is the damage?

Perry is driving his friend Katrina home from school. The roads are icy. Perry drives a few miles per hour above the posted speed limit. Suddenly, a deer jumps in front of Perry's car. Perry swerves to avoid the deer and loses control of the car, crashing it into a ditch. Perry and Katrina are uninjured. They get out of the car and start walking toward home. On the way, Katrina falls on the ice and breaks her leg.

## STRICT LIABILITY

Strict liability is a much narrower area of tort law, but it is also one of the fastest-growing areas of civil law. Traditionally, strict liability was applied in cases of extremely dangerous activities. This area of law grew out of the law of negligence for use in special circumstances. Specifically, strict liability was developed for use in cases of persons who obtained some personal or financial benefit from an activity that could not be made safe and from which the innocent public could not protect itself. Originally, strict liability was applied in cases where a person dealt with dangerous animals or was involved in other activities that could greatly injure members of the public who were in no position to protect themselves—for example, persons who used explosives, such as construction or demolition crews.

Fault, carelessness, or intent is not an issue in actions for strict liability because no matter how carefully an activity might be conducted or an animal might be guarded, it is a near certainty that if the danger escapes into a public area, innocent bystanders will be harmed. It is further reasoned that the persons in control of the activity or animal benefit from it and it is only reasonable that they should bear the costs of harm.

More recently, strict liability has been the primary basis of litigation against manufacturers of products. Consumers (users) of products have no means of knowing how the product was designed and what aspects of it could cause injury. The manufacturer who designed the product, however, is well aware of the product's defects or dangerous aspects, and if the defect is not corrected or if a proper warning of the dangers is not given, then the manufacturer has placed in commerce a dangerous instrument that is likely to injure innocent persons. This is a basis for liability of the manufacturer who ultimately benefits most from the sale of such products.

## CASE
### *Irvine v. Rare Feline Breeding Center Inc.*
### 685 N.E.2d 120, (Ind.App. 1997)

### Issues

The parties raise various issues which we restate as:
I.   Whether STRICT LIABILITY is the law in Indiana WILD animal cases;
II.  Whether any exceptions or defenses to STRICT LIABILITY should be recognized; and,
III. Whether a genuine issue of material fact exists regarding either Irvine's status or any available defenses.

### Facts and Procedural History

For the past thirty years, Mosella Schaffer ("Schaffer") has lived on a fifty-acre farm in Hamilton County, Indiana where she has raised and maintained exotic ANIMALS. These ANIMALS have included zebras, llamas, camels, kangaroos, and, beginning in 1970, Siberian tigers. Although her original intent was to breed and sell the ANIMALS, she soon found it difficult to part with many of them.

In 1993, Scott Bullington ("Bullington") was renting a room in the garage area of Schaffer's house. Aware of his friend Irvine's interest in WILD ANIMALS, Bullington informed Irvine of Schaffer's farm and the ANIMALS she kept there. Irvine, then in his late twenties, began to stop by and see the ANIMALS as per Schaffer's open invitation. Over the next two years, Irvine visited Schaffer's farm several dozen times. During these visits, people would occasionally pet the tigers through a fence.

On the afternoon of December 2, 1995, Irvine arrived at Schaffer's home to see Bullington. The two men drank alcohol and watched television until early evening when Bullington announced that he had to leave to attend his employer's Christmas party. Because Irvine had consumed a substantial amount of alcohol, Bullington told Irvine he could stay over night on the couch. Some time after Bullington had left, Irvine exited Bullington's apartment, walked to the front of Schaffer's property and visited with the llamas and zebras. As he was doing so, Schaffer drove up, stopped her car, had a brief, friendly conversation with Irvine, and went into her house.

Around 8:00 P.M., Irvine decided to visit the tigers before going to sleep. Thus, he went through Schaffer's garage, proceeded through the utility room, continued through the sun room, and ended up in the back yard. Irvine then approached the wire caging, as he and others had done in the past, placed a couple fingers inside the enclosure, and attempted to pet a male tiger. As he was scratching the male tiger, a female tiger made some commotion, which caused Irvine to look away from the male tiger. At that moment, the male tiger pulled Irvine's arm through the two inch by six inch opening of the wire fence.

Upon hearing Irvine's shouts, Schaffer came out of her house, banged an object against the fence, and freed Irvine. Schaffer immediately drove Irvine to the hospital. Irvine was treated and admitted to the hospital. Later, he was transferred to another hospital, and underwent six surgeries during a thirteen-day hospital stay. Further surgeries are indicated though Irvine is uninsured.

On May 30, 1996, Irvine filed a complaint against Schaffer containing four counts: negligence, STRICT LIABILITY, nuisance, and punitives. On September 6, 1996, Irvine filed his motion for partial summary judgment on the basis that incurred risk and assumption of risk are not valid defenses to a STRICT LIABILITY WILD animal claim, on the basis that assumption of risk is not available in a non-contract case, and on the basis that the defense of open and obvious is not available in an animal liability case. Schaffer filed a response on January 14, 1997. Irvine filed a reply on January 21, 1997. The trial court denied Irvine's motion for summary judgment on the STRICT LIABILITY count, denied summary judgment on the issue of assumption of risk, and granted summary judgment on the issue of open and obvious. The trial court granted Irvine's petition to certify three issues for interlocutory appeal: (1) whether incurred risk or other defenses are available in a STRICT LIABILITY animal case; (2) whether Irvine was an invitee as a matter of law; and (3) whether the defense of assumption of risk is available in a noncontractual case. We accepted jurisdiction of the interlocutory appeal.

## Discussion and Decision

Irvine first argues that Indiana has historically adhered to strict tort liability in WILD animal cases. He further argues that when the Indiana Comparative Fault Act (Ind.Codes 34–4–33–1 et seq., the "Act") was adopted, it did not change the law in WILD animal cases. Moreover, he claims that no exceptions to STRICT LIABILITY in WILD animal cases have ever been applied in Indiana. He also argues that even if

his status is somehow relevant, he was clearly an invitee. Thus, he asserts that the trial court should not have denied his summary judgment on the STRICT LIABILITY issue. In contrast, Schaffer argues that Indiana has not adopted, and should not adopt, STRICT LIABILITY animal cases. . . .

Upon review of the grant or denial of a summary judgment motion, we apply the same legal judgment is appropriate only when there are no genuine issues of material fact and the moving party is entitled to judgment as a matter of law. Ind.Trial Rule 56(C); *North Snow Bay, Inc. v. Hamilton*, 657 N.E.2d 420, 422 (IND.CT.APP.1995). On review, we may not search the entire record to support the judgment, but may only consider that which had been specifically designated to the trial court. *Id.* The party appealing the trial court's grant or denial of summary judgment has the burden of persuading this court that the trial court's decision was erroneous. *Id.*

### I. Liability in a WILD Animal Case

We first address whether STRICT LIABILITY is the common law rule for WILD animal cases in Indiana. The parties have not cited and we have not found a case specifically applying STRICT LIABILITY to a true WILD animal case in Indiana. However, the basic rule has been frequently stated in various contexts. *Holt v. Myers*, 93 N.E. 31 (Ind.Ct.App.1910) (mentioning WILD animal STRICT LIABILITY rule although case dealt with vicious dog). Accordingly, we have little difficulty concluding that Indiana's common law recognized the STRICT LIABILITY rule for WILD animal cases—despite the fact that previously, Indiana courts have not had the opportunity to apply the rule.

We next address the issue of whether the adoption of the Act changed the common law rule of STRICT LIABILITY in WILD animal cases. "We presume the legislature does not intend by the enactment of a statute to make any change in the common law beyond what it declares, either in express terms or by unmistakable implication." An abrogation of the common law will be implied (1) where a statute is enacted which undertakes to cover the entire subject treated and was clearly designed as a substitute for the common law; or, (2) where the two laws are so repugnant that both in reason may not stand. *Id.* "As a statute in derogation of the existing common law, the Act must be strictly construed." *Indianapolis Power & Light Co. v. Brad Snodgrass, Inc.*, 578 N.E.2d 669, 673 (Ind.1991).

The Act, enacted in 1983 and effective in 1985, "governs any action based on fault [.]" Ind.Code s 34–4–33–1. STRICT LIABILITY, by definition, is liability without fault. Thus, the Act would seem to be inapplicable to a

*(continued)*

STRICT LIABILITY action. The legislative history lends further support for this conclusion. The original version of Ind.Code s 34–4–33–2 provided that "Fault," for purposes of the Act, "include[d] any act or omission that [was] negligent, willful, wanton, reckless, or intentional toward the person or property of others, or that subject[ed] a person to strict tort liability, but [did] not include an intentional act. The term also include[d] breach of warranty, unreasonable assumption of risk not constituting an enforceable express consent, incurred risk, misuse of a product for which the defendant otherwise would be liable, and unreasonable failure to avoid injury or to mitigate damages." (Emphasis added).

By the time of its effective date, that same section had been changed to its current form: "'[f]ault' includes any act or omission that is negligent, willful, wanton, reckless, or intentional toward the person or property of others. The term also includes unreasonable assumption of risk not constituting an enforceable express consent, incurred risk, and unreasonable failure to avoid injury or to mitigate damages." Ind.Code s 34–4–33–2. The current form includes no reference to STRICT LIABILITY. Narrowly construing the Act, we conclude that it does not explicitly apply to a STRICT LIABILITY claim. See *Templin v. Fobes,* 617 N.E.2d 541, 544 n. 1 (Ind.1993) (products liability case in which our Supreme Court noted, "practical problems arise, at least in part, because of the operation of Indiana's Comparative Fault Act, which would apply in Templins' negligence claims against Fobes but not in the Templins' STRICT LIABILITY claim against Rockwood.").

## II. Exceptions or Defenses

Having concluded that the Act has not changed common law STRICT LIABILITY in WILD animal cases, we next address Irvine's contention that no exceptions to STRICT LIABILITY in WILD animal cases have ever been applied in this state. While we agree with Irvine's contention, this fact is of no surprise in view of the lack of any true WILD animal cases in Indiana. As this is an issue of first impression, we look to the reason behind the STRICT LIABILITY WILD animal rule and consult other sources as necessary.

We have previously set out the rationale for imposing STRICT LIABILITY against owners for injuries caused by an attack by a naturally ferocious or DANGEROUS animal. See *Hardin v. Christy,* 462 N.E.2d 256, 259, 262 (Ind.Ct.App.1984). STRICT LIABILITY is appropriately placed:

upon those who, even with proper care, expose the community to the risk of a very DANGEROUS thing. . . . The kind of "DANGEROUS animal" that will subject the keeper to STRICT LIABILITY . . . must pose some kind of an abnormal risk to the particular community where the animal is kept; hence, the keeper is engaged in an activity that subjects those in the vicinity, including those who come onto his property, to an abnormal risk. . . . The possessor of a WILD animal is strictly liable for physical harm done to the person of another . . . if that harm results from a DANGEROUS propensity that is characteristic of WILD ANIMALS of that class. Thus, STRICT LIABILITY has been imposed on keepers of lions and tigers, bears, elephants, wolves, monkeys, and other similar ANIMALS. No member of such a species, however domesticated, can ever be regarded as safe, and liability does not rest upon any experience with the particular animal.

Although having done so in an asbestos case and using slightly different terms, Judge Posner concisely set out the rationale for the WILD animal STRICT LIABILITY rule using the following hypothetical:

[k]eeping a tiger in one's backyard would be an example of an abnormally hazardous activity. The hazard is such, relative to the value of the activity, that we desire not just that the owner take all due care that the tiger not escape, but that he consider seriously the possibility of getting rid of the tiger altogether; and we give him an incentive to consider this course of action by declining to make the exercise of due care a defense to a suit based on an injury caused by the tiger—in other words, by making him strictly liable for any such injury.

*G.J. Leasing Co. v. Union Electric Co.,* 54 F.3d 379, 386 (7th CIR.1995).

With the rationale for the rule in mind, we analyze whether any exceptions or defenses to the STRICT LIABILITY WILD animal rule are appropriate. Like the sources previously cited, the *Restatement* provides:

(1) A possessor of a WILD animal is subject to liability to another for harm done by the animal to the other, his person, land or chattels, although the possessor has exercised the utmost care to confine the animal, or otherwise prevent it from doing harm.

(2) This liability is limited to harm that results from a DANGEROUS propensity that is characteristic of WILD ANIMALS of the particular class, or of which the possessor knows or has reason to know.

*Restatement (Second) of Torts* s 507 (1977). However, because the general rule in s 507 is "subject to a number of exceptions and qualifications, which are too numerous to state in a single Section," s 507 should be read together with s 508, s 510, s 511, s 512, s 515, and s 517. *Restatement, supra* cmt. a, s 507. Thus, we look to those other sections to help flesh out the *Restatement's* rule.

Section 510(a) provides: "The possessor of a WILD animal . . . is subject to STRICT LIABILITY for the resulting harm, although it would not have occurred but for the unexpectable . . . innocent, negligent or reckless conduct of a third person." However, "[a] possessor of land is not subject to STRICT LIABILITY to one who intentionally or negligently trespasses upon the land, for harm done to him by a WILD animal . . . that the possessor keeps on the land, even though the trespasser has no reason to know that the animal is kept there." *Restatement, supra* s 511. Invitees and licensees are dealt with in s 513, which states: "The possessor of a WILD animal . . . who keeps it upon land in his possession, is subject to STRICT LIABILITY to persons coming upon the land in the exercise of a privilege whether derived from his consent to their entry or otherwise." Yet, if the invitee or licensee "knows that the DANGEROUS animal is permitted to run at large or has escaped from control they may be barred from recovery if they choose to act upon the possessor's consent or to exercise any other privilege and thus expose themselves to the risk of being harmed by the animal. (See s 515)." *Restatement, supra,* cmt. a, s 513.

Section 515(2), in turn, provides: "The plaintiff's contributory negligence in knowingly and unreasonably subjecting himself to the risk that a WILD animal . . . will do harm to his person . . . is a defense to the STRICT LIABILITY." Comment c. to s 515(2) explains:

Although one harmed by a WILD . . . animal that has escaped from control of its possessor or harborer is not barred from recovery because he has not exercised ordinary care to observe the presence of the animal or to escape from its attack, he is barred if he intentionally and unreasonably subjects himself to the risk of harm by the animal. Thus one who without any necessity for so doing that is commensurate with the risk involved knowingly puts himself in reach of an animal that is effectively chained or otherwise confined cannot recover against the possessor or harborer of the animal. So, too, although a licensee or an invitee upon land of another upon which he knows that WILD . . . ANIMALS are kept under the possessor's control does not take the risk that they will escape and harm him, he does nonetheless take the risk of harm by the ANIMALS that he knows are roaming at large, so that he will to a reasonable certainty encounter them if he avails himself of the invitation or permission held out to him by the possessor of the land. (Emphasis added).

Comment d. to s 515(2) states: "This kind of contributory negligence, which consists of voluntarily and unreasonably encountering a known danger, is frequently called either contributory negligence or assumption of risk, or both."

Section 515(3) provides: "The plaintiff's assumption of the risk of harm from the animal is a defense to the STRICT LIABILITY." The comment to s 515(3) states that "one employed as a lion tamer in a circus may be barred from recovery by his assumption of the risk when he is clawed by a lion. In the same manner, one who voluntarily teases and provokes a chained bear, or goes within reach of a vicious dog, is barred from recovery if he does so with knowledge of the danger." (Emphases added).

As indicated by the extensive quotations above, the *Restatement* clearly recognizes exceptions or defenses to WILD animal STRICT LIABILITY. Prosser and Keeton also agree that defenses are available to a STRICT LIABILITY WILD animal claim. "[C]ontributory negligence by way of knowingly and unreasonably subjecting oneself to a risk of harm from an abnormally DANGEROUS animal will constitute a defense" to a STRICT LIABILITY claim. Prosser and Keeton, *supra* s 79, at 565. "Thus, a plaintiff who voluntarily and unreasonably comes within reach of an animal which he knows to be DANGEROUS, . . . has no cause of action when it attacks him." *Id.* at 566.

Because we agree with the rationale of the exceptions and/or defenses set out in the *Restatement,* and because we find it to be in keeping with Indiana's recent policy regarding allocation of fault, we adopt the *Restatement*'s approach in WILD animal cases.

## B. Defenses

In adopting the *Restatement*'s view that incurred risk/assumed risk may be a defense to a STRICT LIABILITY WILD animal claim, we must next examine whether genuine issues of material fact exist regarding a defense in Irvine's case. Incurred risk requires a mental state of venturousness and a conscious, deliberate and intentional embarkation upon the course of conduct with knowledge of the circumstances. *Perdue Farms, Inc. v. Pryor,* —N.E.2d—, 63S01–9509–CV–172, (Ind. July 22, 1997), slip op. at 7. In other contexts, we have stated that the defense of incurred risk is generally a question of fact, and the party asserting it bears the burden of proving it by a preponderance of evidence. *Schooley v. Ingersoll Rand Inc.,* 631 N.E.2d 932, 939 (Ind.Ct.App.1994).

Here, the parties designated conflicting evidence regarding whether Irvine knowingly and unreasonably put himself within reach of a WILD animal that was effectively chained or otherwise confined. There was evidence that around the time of the accident, Irvine had been volunteering at the Indianapolis Zoo and had been told not to have contact with tigers. Moreover,

*(continued)*

there was evidence that Irvine was aware of a prior incident wherein the tiger which injured him grabbed another man's thumb. However, there was other evidence tending to indicate that Schaffer and others had petted the tiger safely in the past. Also, there was evidence that Irvine may have been rather intoxicated on the night in question. In view of the conflicting evidence and inferences, summary judgment was properly denied on the issue of whether a defense was appropriate in this case.

Affirmed.

## Case Review Question

Why is strict liability allegedly applicable in this case as opposed to a case of gross negligence?

## INTENTIONAL TORTS

The third major category of torts is a tort in which the primary element is intent. This is an action in which the defendant has manifested an intent to bring about a particular result and, as a consequence, the plaintiff was injured. It must be shown that the defendant acted voluntarily, even with the knowledge that the act would almost certainly bring about the injury. In some instances, the injury itself is the desired result, but it need not be to constitute an intentional tort. It must only be shown that the defendant knew or should have known with substantial certainty that his or her action would bring about the injury.[21]

Intentional tort differs from the concept of degree of duty in negligence because, in an intentional tort, the risk is so great that it can be counted on to produce the injury. If the actor commits the action anyway, such action constitutes an intentional tort against the injured party. A major distinction between gross negligence and intentional tort is that in an intentional tort, mere knowledge and appreciation of a danger are insufficient. As stated, there must be evidence of voluntary conduct in light of the knowledge and appreciation of the danger. In addition, the risk of harm must be a near certainty rather than a likelihood.

Several types of intentional torts provide a basis for liability. Some of the more common types are discussed here to demonstrate the basis for the more commonly litigated actions. (Table 9.1 lists the elements of these and other torts.)

## Assault

Assault is commonly considered to be a physical attack of some sort, but its meaning is quite different in tort law. To prove an act of assault, it must be shown that the actor engaged in physical conduct, which may or may not have been accompanied by words, that placed the plaintiff in apprehension of immediate and harmful contact.[22] By definition, the tort of assault involves no physical contact, only the threat of such contact. A plaintiff cannot claim assault when the threatening act consisted only of words unless under circumstances that could create a reasonable perception of imminent harm. Nor is an assault committed when a threat is made for some future point in time. The basis for an assault action is that the threat of immediate physical harm produces such fear or a reaction or both that it actually injures the plaintiff. For example, if I threaten to beat you up at the park the next time I see you there, no assault has occurred because you have no realistic fear. You can avoid the attack by avoiding the park. However, if I am in the park with you and tell you that I am going to beat you up, your response may be such fear of an imminent harmful contact that the fear causes injury (e.g., heart attack) and, consequently, an assault has occurred.

**Table 9.1** Torts and Related Causes of Action: The Elements

| The Cause of Action | Its Elements |
| --- | --- |
| 1. Abuse of Process | i. Use of civil or criminal proceedings<br>ii. Improper or ulterior purpose |
| 2. Alienation of Affections | i. Intent to diminish the material relationship between spouses<br>ii. Affirmative conduct<br>iii. Affections between spouses are in fact alienated<br>iv. Causation |
| 3. Assault (Civil) | i. Act<br>ii. Intent to cause either:<br>   a. an imminent harmful or offensive contact or<br>   b. an apprehension of an imminent harmful or offensive contact<br>iii. Apprehension of an imminent harmful or offensive contact to the plaintiff's person<br>iv. Causation |
| 4. Battery (Civil) | i. Act<br>ii. Intent to cause either:<br>   a. an imminent harmful or offensive contact or<br>   b. an apprehension of an imminent harmful or offensive contact<br>iii. Harmful or offensive contact with the plaintiff's person<br>iv. Causation |
| 5. Civil Rights Violation | i. A person acting under color of state law<br>ii. Deprives someone of a federal right |
| 6. Conversion | i. Personal property (chattel)<br>ii. Plaintiff is in possession of the chattel or is entitled to immediate possession<br>iii. Intent to exercise dominion or control over the chattel<br>iv. Serious interference with plaintiff's possession<br>v. Causation |
| 7. Criminal Conversation | Defendant has sexual relations with the plaintiff's spouse (adultery) |
| **Defamation (Two Torts)** | |
| 8. Libel | i. Written defamatory statement by the defendant<br>ii. Of and concerning the plaintiff<br>iii. Publication of the statement<br>iv. Damages<br>   a. In some state, special damages never have to be proven in a libel case<br>   b. In other states, only libel on its face does not require special damages. in these states, *libel per quod* requires special damages<br>v. Causation |
| 9. Slander | i. Oral defamatory statement by the defendant<br>ii. Of and concerning the plaintiff<br>iii. Publication of the statement<br>iv. Damages:<br>   a. Special damages are not required if the slander is slander *per se*<br>   b. Special damages must be proven if the slander is not slander *per se*<br>v. Causation |

*(continued)*

**Table 9.1** (*Continued*)

| | |
|---|---|
| 10. Disparagement | i. False statement of fact |
| | ii. Disparaging the plaintiff's business or property |
| | iii. Publication |
| | iv. Intent |
| | v. Special damages |
| | vi. Causation |
| 11. Enticement of a Child or Abduction of a Child | i. Intent to interfere with a parent's custody over his or her child |
| | ii. Affirmative conduct by the defendant: |
| | a. to abduct or force the child from the parent's custody, or |
| | b. to entice or encourage the child to leave the parent, or |
| | c. to harbor the child and encourage him or her to stay away from the parent's custody |
| | iii. The child leaves the custody of the parent |
| | iv. Causation |
| 12. Enticement of Spouse | i. Intent to diminish the marital relationship between the spouses |
| | ii. Affirmative conduct by the defendant: |
| | a. to entice or encourage the spouse to leave the plaintiff's home, or |
| | b. to harbor the spouse and encourage him or her to stay away from the plaintiff's home |
| | iii. The spouse leaves the plaintiff's home |
| | iv. Causation |
| 13. False Imprisonment | i. An act that completely confines the plaintiff within fixed boundaries set by the defendant |
| | ii. Intent to confine plaintiff or a third person |
| | iii. Causation of the confinement |
| | iv. Plaintiff was either conscious of the confinement or suffered actual harm by it |
| 14. Intentional Infliction of Emotional Distress | i. An act of extreme or outrageous conduct |
| | ii. Intent to cause severe emotional distress |
| | iii. Severe emotional distress is suffered |
| | iv. Causation |
| 15. Interference with Contract Relations | i. An existing contract |
| | i. Interference with the contract by defendant |
| | iii. Intent |
| | iv. Damages |
| | v. Causation |
| 16. Interference with Prospective Advantage | i. Reasonable expectation of an economic advantage |
| | ii. Interference with this expectation |
| | iii. Intent |
| | iv. Damages |
| | v. Causation |
| **Invasion of Privacy (Four Torts)** | |
| 17. Appropriation | i. The use of the plaintiff's name, likeness, or personality |
| | ii. For the benefit of the defendant |
| 18. False Light | i. Publicity |
| | ii. Placing the plaintiff in a false light |
| | iii. Highly offensive to a reasonable person |

**Table 9.1** (*Continued*)

| | |
|---|---|
| 19. Intrusion | i. An act of intrusion into a person's private affairs or concerns |
| | ii. Highly offensive to a reasonable person |
| 20. Public Disclosure of Private Fact | i. Publicity |
| | ii. Concerning the private life of the plaintiff |
| | iii. Highly offensive to a reasonable person |
| 21. Malicious Prosecution | i. Initiation or procurement of the initiation of criminal proceedings |
| | ii. Without probable cause |
| | iii. With malice |
| | iv. The criminal proceedings terminate in favor of the accused |
| 22. Misrepresentation | i. Statement of fact |
| | ii. Statement is false |
| | iii. *Scienter* (intent to mislead) |
| | iv. Justifiable reliance |
| | v. Actual damages |
| 23. Negligence | i. Duty |
| | ii. Breach of duty |
| | iii. Proximate cause |
| | iv. Damage |
| **Nuisance (Two Torts)** | |
| 24. Private Nuisance | An unreasonable interference with the use and enjoyment of private land |
| 25. Public Nuisance | An unreasonable interference with a right that is common to the general public |
| 26. *Prima Facie* Tort | i. Infliction of harm |
| | ii. Intent to do harm (malice) |
| | iii. Special damages |
| | iv. Causation |
| 27. Seduction | The defendant has sexual relations with the plaintiff's daughter, with or without consent. |
| 28. Strict Liability for Harm Caused by Animals | Domestic Animals: |
| | i. Owner has reason to know the animal has a specific propensity to cause harm. |
| | ii. Harm caused by the animal was due to that specific propensity |
| | Wild Animals: |
| | i. Keeping a wild animal |
| | ii. Causes harm |
| 29. Strict Liability for Abnormally Dangerous Conditions or Activities | i. Existence of an abnormally dangerous condition or activity |
| | ii. Knowledge of the condition or activity |
| | iii. Damages |
| | iv. Causation |
| 30. Strict Liability in Tort | i. Seller |
| | ii. A defective product that is unreasonably dangerous to person or property |
| | iii. User or consumer |
| | iv. Physical harm (damages) |
| | v. Causation |
| 31. Trespass to Chattels | i. Personal property (chattel) |
| | ii. Plaintiff is in possession of the chattel or is entitled to immediate possession |

(continued)

**Table 9.1** (*Continued*)

| | | |
|---|---|---|
| | iii. | Intent to dispossess or to intermeddle with the chattel |
| | iv. | Dispossession or intermeddling |
| | v. | Causation |
| 32. Trespass to Land | i. | An act |
| | ii. | Intrusion on land |
| | iii. | In possession of another |
| | iv. | Intent to intrude |
| | v. | Causation of the intrusion |
| **Warranty (Three Causes of Action)** | | |
| 33. Breach of Express Warranty | i. | A statement of fact that is false |
| | ii. | Made with the intent or expectation that the statement will reach the plaintiff |
| | iii. | Reliance on the statement by the plaintiff |
| | iv. | Damage |
| | v. | Causation |
| 34. Breach of Implied Warranty of Fitness for a Particular Purpose | i. | Sale of goods |
| | ii. | Seller has reason to know the buyer's particular purpose in buying the goods |
| | iii. | Seller has reason to know that the buyer is relying on the seller's skill or judgment in buying the goods |
| | iv. | The goods are not fit for the particular purpose |
| | v. | Damage |
| | vi | Causation |
| 35. Breach of Implied Warranty of Merchantability | i. | Sale of goods |
| | ii. | By a merchant of goods of that kind |
| | iii. | The goods are not merchantable |
| | iv. | Damage |
| | v. | Causation |

Note: Adapted from W. Statsky, *Torts: Personal Injury Litigation* (New York: Delmar, 2001).

## Battery

The tort of battery is perhaps the most litigated intentional tort, because it includes all unpermitted physical contact that results in harm. Battery encompasses physical attacks, medical treatment without consent, and every other conceivable act that results in physical contact between two parties as long as (1) there is the intent to make physical contact, (2) there is no consent to such contact, (3) the contact occurs to the person or to anything that is so closely attached that it is considered part of the person (e.g., clothing), and (4) the contact results in injury to the person.[23]

Battery encompasses much more than a physical fight between two persons. In fact, in recent years, battery has been the basis for medical malpractice claims, including such actions as leaving foreign objects (sponges or instruments) in a patient's body or performing a procedure to which the patient had not previously consented.

The *emergency rule* is an exception or defense to actions for battery.[24] The rule states that unpermitted physical contact (including medical treatment) may be allowed if a medical or other emergency exists that prevents the person from making a decision as to whether to permit the contact. For example, if an unconscious patient suffers heart failure during an operation, doctors are permitted to perform additional measures to save the patient's life even though the patient never consented to such procedures.

# CASE
## Denman v. Sanders, 2006
## WL 452018 (S.D.N.Y.)

This case examines the necessary elements to recover for the commission of an intentional tort.

Denman, a former actor, is the manager of the Grand Havana Room, an exclusive private club in Manhattan. Sanders is the president of two companies, and his primary work is in finance, mergers, and acquisitions. At the time in question, Sanders was a member of the Grand Havana Room and regularly attended the club's California and New York locations. The parties' first conflict arose several months before the night of the incident leading to this case. Sanders and some guests were visiting the club late one night. The club's bartender, Walter Osorio ("Osorio"), who testified at trial, told Sanders the club was closing, and asked them for their "last call" drink orders. *Id.* Osorio testified that Sanders told his guests, "Watch this," and made a call on his cell phone. Sanders testified that he called the club's owner, Stan Schuster ("Schuster"), asked if he and his guests could stay later at the club, and that Schuster gave him permission. Denman then received a call from Schuster, who told him to tell Osorio that he would be fired if he "does that again."

On October 14, 2004, Sanders and two friends came to the Grand Havana Room at approximately 12:30 A.M. The security guard told him the club had closed. *Id.* Sanders called Schuster, and told him he wanted to enter the club.. Schuster called Denman and told him to let Sanders into the club, which Denman did.. Denman told the remaining staff to serve Sanders as usual, with "no attitude.". . . Sanders and his friends bought drinks and champagne. Eventually, Denman sent the rest of the staff home, including Osorio. He also suggested to Sanders that the club would be closing soon. Sanders responded that he wasn't finished, and ordered more drinks.. Sanders testified that he was drunk..

At about 2:30 A.M., Denman gave Sanders his check, and Sanders signed it around 3:00 A.M. Denman went into the kitchen to wash his hands. Sanders came into the kitchen and complained about Denman's lack of respect. Denman argued with Sanders, questioning his own lack of respect demonstrated by staying at the club for hours after it had closed. *Id.* The two continued to argue until Denman walked away and called Sanders an "asshole" under his breath. Sanders demanded that Denman come back and then punched him in the head. *Id.* Both parties left the kitchen. Denman, who was disoriented and in pain, began to clean up Sanders's table while holding his head. As Sanders

left, he made another derogatory comment to Denman and told him he was fired. Sanders called Schuster, who called Denman. Denman reported there was a problem, was put on hold, waited for a while, and then went home without speaking further to Schuster that night.

At home, Denman felt sick. He took a shower and found that his head was bleeding badly. *Id.* He went to the hospital, was given a tetanus shot and a bandage, and paid $50 for the emergency room visit. The jury saw photos of the lacerations on his face and the emergency room medical report containing Denman's report that he was assaulted by a customer. . . . He returned to work the next day, with the bandage on his face, but did not tell co-workers what happened because he was embarrassed that he had been hit by a customer. He has a one-quarter inch scar above his eye and a lasting uneasiness when tall people stand in front of him because he is afraid he will get hit again. Denman also reported the incident to the police. Sanders was charged with a misdemeanor. He surrendered himself to the police and spent half a day in jail. The criminal case was later dismissed for failure to prosecute on a timely basis.

Sanders first moves to overturn the jury's verdict pursuant to FRCP 50(b). He argues that the jury's verdict was rendered against the weight of the evidence. As a threshold issue, Sanders has failed to meet the procedural requirements of FRCP 50(b). To invoke the rule, a party must have made an initial motion under FRCP 50(a) at trial, at the close of all evidence, before seeking to renew the motion under FRCP 50(b). *Phillips v. Bowen,* 189 F.R.D. 50, 52–53 (N.D.N.Y.1999). Furthermore, "even when a pre-verdict motion for judgment as a matter of law has been made, the movant may not add new grounds after trial. The post-trial motion is limited to those grounds that were 'specifically raised in the prior [Rule 50(a)] motion.'" *Id.* Sanders's counsel made a motion at the close of the plaintiff's presentation of evidence, but not at the close of all evidence.

Judgment as a matter of law may only be granted where there is a complete absence of evidence supporting the jury's verdict, or if the evidence in favor of the moving party is so overwhelming that no reasonable person could arrive at a verdict against it. *Galdieri-Ambrosini v. Nat'l Realty & Dev. Corp.,* 136 F.3d 276, 289 (2d Cir.1998). In assessing the record, the Court must view the evidence in the light most favorable to the nonmoving party and must draw all

*(continued)*

reasonable inferences in favor of that party. *Galdieri-Ambrosini*, . . . 136 F.3d at 289. Further, the Court may not weigh the testimony of the witnesses, but must defer to the jury's credibility determinations. *Galdieri-Ambrosini*, 136 F.3d at 289. . . . Under this standard, Sanders's motion for judgment as a matter of law must be denied.

"Under New York law, punitive damages are permitted for tortious conduct in cases involving 'gross, wanton, or willful fraud or other morally culpable conduct.'" *Cohen v. Davis*, 926 F.Supp. 399, 405 (S.D.N.Y.1996). Such damages are particularly appropriate in the case of intentional torts where "'elements of fraud, malice, gross negligence, cruelty, or oppression are involved. . . .'" *Pepe v. Maklansky*, 67 F.Supp.2d 186, 187–88 (S.D.N.Y.1999).

Sanders argues that the facts as presented at trial do not demonstrate the required element of "malice or insult" necessary to sustain the jury's award of punitive damages. He states that he was intoxicated and entered the kitchen of the Grand Havana Room to register a complaint about the quality of service. Denman became upset and raised his voice to argue with him. According to Denman, only when he called Sanders an "asshole," did Sanders demand that he return, and then punch him. Sanders argues that this kind of behavior, particularly his intoxication, does not constitute the kind of reckless conduct that merits punitive damages, while Denman argues Sanders's intoxication alone supports the punitive damages award.

Neither party is correct on this point. Denman cites *Rinaldo v. Mashayekhi*, 585 N.Y.S.2d 615, 616 (App. Div.3d Dep't 1992), where the court upheld a punitive damage award in a drunk driving accident, but in that case the court considered additional factors besides the defendant's drunk driving, including the speed at which he was driving and the location, a populated place. . . . The courts generally require a case by case analysis of the act of driving while intoxicated as well as the surrounding circumstances. See *Finlay v. Simonovich*, 1997 WL 746460, at 5 (S.D.N.Y. Dec. 2, 1997). In any case, this line of cases involves driving while intoxicated, and here the case involves an assault. Rather than support Denman's contention that intoxication alone supports punitive damages, the cases merely demonstrate the courts' willingness to consider intoxication as a factor when reviewing a punitive damages award.

Sanders cites *Thompson v. Corbett*, 787 N.Y.S.2d 563, 565 (App. Div. 4th Dep't 2004), in support of his contention that intoxication does not support a punitive damages award. In that case, the court dismissed the punitive damages award against corporate defendants,

owners of a bar where an individual defendant had been served despite his apparent intoxication, and later stabbed the plaintiff. *Id.* Moreover, punitive damages have been allowed for assaults where the defendant was intoxicated. See, e.g., *Comeau v. Lucas*, 455 N.Y.S.2d 871, 872 (App. Div. 4th Dep't 1982). . . . As there was testimony about the words exchanged between the parties, the jury has already had an opportunity to consider this in their deliberations. The Court, of course, must defer to the jury's credibility determinations, which were key to the outcome of this case. Given that Sanders failed to follow the procedural requirements of FRCP 50(b) and has not demonstrated that there was a complete absence of evidence supporting the jury's verdict, or that no reasonable person could arrive at the verdict the jury gave, his 50(b) motion to vacate the punitive damages award is DENIED.

A new trial may be granted under FRCP 59 if the jury verdict constitutes a "miscarriage of justice" or a "seriously erroneous result." *Smith v. Lightning Bolt Prod., Inc.*, 861 F.2d 363, 370 (2d Cir.1988). Sanders argues that double recovery is not allowed and therefore the jury's two awards of $125,000 for the "exact same injury" represent a serious miscarriage of justice and must be vacated. Denman first argues that Sanders waived this argument as he failed to object to the special verdict form allowing the jury to divide its award between the two claims and, in fact, presented separate proposed jury instructions on each of the claims. Second, Denman points out that assault and battery are separate claims, with separate elements, and it was allowable for the jury to allocate damages between the two claims.

Assault and battery do have separate elements: "An 'assault' is an intentional placing of another person in fear of imminent harmful or offensive contact. A 'battery' is an intentional wrongful physical contact with another person without consent." *United Nat. Ins. Co. v. Waterfront New York Realty Corp.*, 994 F.2d 105, 108 (2d Cir.1993). The two torts result in separate injuries: "fear" and "contact." However, the conduct involved in causing those injuries, at least in this case, is exactly the same. The Second Circuit has recognized that where a *prima facie* tort and a traditional tort are involved, the New York courts do not allow recovery for both. *Hughes v. Patrolmen's Benevolent Ass'n of New York, Inc.*, 850 F.2d 876, 882 (2d Cir.1988). . . . What New York law prohibits is recovery of damages for both a traditional tort such as the intentional infliction of emotional distress and for a *prima facie* tort. . . . However, where two traditional torts are involved, the law is much less clear-cut than Sanders contends . . . "seemingly duplicative awards made separately for overlapping causes of action . . . [will be] sustained where it appeared that the jury intended to award the aggregate sum." *Bender v. City of New York,* 78 F.3d 787, 794 (2d Cir.1996).

In *King v. Macri,* 993 F.2d 294, 298 (2d Cir.1993), the Court addressed separate punitive damage awards for three causes of action involving overlapping forms of conduct: excessive force, false arrest, and malicious prosecution. While expressing "some concern that the verdict form invited the jury to make a separate award for punitive damages," the Court emphasized that "district judges retain discretion in determining whether to permit a jury to make separate punitive awards or one aggregate award, but they should bear in mind the risk that separate awards for each component of misconduct might unduly increase the amount of the total award." *Id.* at 299. . . . The possible duplication did not result in the entire award being vacated, as Sanders has suggested is appropriate here, but instead contributed to the Court's analysis of whether the award should be reduced. *Id.*

. . . in *Bender,* 78 F.3d at 793, the Court focused on the plaintiff's resulting injury. The Court found that a jury's separate awards for false arrest, malicious prosecution, and intentional infliction of emotional distress were substantially duplicative because the torts resulted in overlapping injuries. Id . The Court indicated that

> [a] proper verdict form and jury charge would have focused the jury's attention on the extent to which the injuries resulting from the various torts alleged were separate, and the extent to which they were not. As to the latter, the jurors should have been instructed that they can award additional damages, beyond what they award for an overlapping tort, only to the extent that they find some aspect of injury that has not been already compensated for by the award of damages for the related tort.

*Id.* at 794. It found plain error despite defendants' failure to object to the jury charge or verdict form. *Id.* at 795. The Court then considered the likelihood of "impermissible duplication" in its decision to reduce the verdict. *Id.*

As mentioned above, Sanders did not object to the verdict form at trial, and submitted separate proposed jury instructions for assault and battery. While aggregate awards may be preferred, a verdict form allowing the jury to allocate damages under each cause of action is permissible. . . . The jury here may have meant to award the aggregate sum and merely allocated the damages under each cause of action. . . . While overlapping conduct is definitely at issue in this case, assault and battery result in distinct injuries, which is the

determinative factor in this kind of analysis. *Bender,* 78 F.3d at 793. Denman testified not only to his physical injuries (the contact required for battery), but the emotional effect of the incident (the fear required for assault). He testified that he suffered lacerations on his face and a permanent scar. . . . He also testified that he felt stupid and embarrassed the next day, working with a bandage on his face.. Finally, Denman testified he has a lasting uneasiness when tall people stand in front of him because he is afraid he will get hit again. The jury could have considered these as separate injuries resulting from one act of misconduct for which there are two forms of liability, and sought to compensate Denman accordingly. . . . The possible duplication here does not merit vacating the entire assault award . . .

. . . in considering a motion for a new trial, a court "is free to weigh the evidence . . . and need not view it in the light most favorable to the verdict winner." *Id.* Sanders argues that both the compensatory and punitive damage awards are against the weight of evidence and represent a serious miscarriage of justice. In alternative to a new trial, Sanders seeks a *remittitur* of the compensatory damage award to not more than $5,000, and of the punitive damage award to not more than $20,000. . . . The Supreme Court has held that in New York the district court is to apply *New York Civil Practice Law and Rules* § 5501(c) (McKinney 1995), because, although § 5501(c) contains a procedural instruction assigning decision-making authority to the New York Appellate Division, the State's statutory objective is manifestly substantive. Although § 5501(c) is phrased as an instruction to the Appellate Division, it applies to trial judges. . . . The standard under § 5501(c) provides that a judge may alter a jury award where he determines that the award "deviates materially from what would be reasonable compensation." . . . This test replaces the common law "shock the conscience" test, requiring the court to apply more probing scrutiny of jury awards. See *Kukla,* 928 F.Supp. at 1336 "[T]he 'deviates materially' standard . . . influences outcomes by tightening the range of tolerable awards." *Gasperini,* 518 U.S. at 425. To determine whether a jury award deviates materially from what would be reasonable compensation, New York courts compare the award . . . to verdicts approved in similar cases. *Gasperini,* 518 U.S. at 425.

Sanders argues the compensatory damages award of $250,000 is excessive, particularly in light of the minimal injury Denman incurred. "[W]hile a jury has broad discretion to award damages as it feels appropriate . . . a jury verdict cannot stand if it is the result of a miscarriage of justice and represents a windfall to the

*(continued)*

plaintiff without regard for the actual injury." *Carter v. Rosenberg & Estis, P.C.,* 1998 WL 150491, at 5 (S.D.N.Y. Mar. 31, 1998).

In comparison to other similar cases, and in light of the "deviates materially" standard, the total compensatory damages award is excessive, especially in consideration of the types of injuries Denman related at trial, and in light of the possible duplication of damages. However, Sanders's suggestion that the award be reduced to $5,000 is not required by the case law. Instead, a total compensatory award of $50,000 would be more in line with awards upheld in cases of assault and/or battery. . . .

In assessing the validity of a punitive damages award, three factors are considered: a) the degree of reprehensibility of the defendant's conduct, b) the ratio of punitive damages to the actual or potential harm inflicted on plaintiff, and c) the difference between the remedy at issue and those authorized for comparable misconduct. *BMW of North Am., Inc. v. Gore,* 517 U.S. 559, 575, 580, 583 (1996). . . . The purpose of punitive damages is "'to punish the defendant and to deter him and others from similar conduct in the future.'" *Lee v. Edwards,* 101 F.3d 805, 809 (2d Cir.1996). . . . As with the compensatory award, the $600,000 punitive damages award given here deviates materially from those given in similar cases and must, therefore, be reduced or a new trial ordered. As outlined below, an award of $200,000 would be more appropriate.

An evaluation of the reprehensibility of a defendant's acts requires a consideration of three aggravating factors: the presence of violence, deceit or malice as opposed to negligence, and repeated misconduct. *Id.* at 809. Here, Sanders's conduct involved violence and his intoxication demonstrates recklessness rather than negligence. Provocation can be considered to mitigate damages, *Levine,* 512 N.Y.S.2d at 220, but Sanders began the heated argument, and Denman's single insult is hardly commensurate with a blow to the head. As for malice, in deciding its punitive damages award, the jury likely considered not only Sanders's final act of violence, but his repeated exercise of influence over

Denman and other staff at the Grand Havana Room. However, the fact that an on-going conflict erupted into a one-time incident of violence which escalated no further does mitigate the reprehensibility of Sanders's actions.

For this factor, "the proper inquiry is whether there is a reasonable relationship between the punitive damages award and the harm likely to result from the defendant's conduct as well as the harm that actually has occurred." *Gore,* 517 U.S. at 581. . . . The jury's award constituted less than a four-to-one ratio. Ratios of ten-to-one have recently been upheld, but with the remark that this ratio constitutes the upper-limit provided for by due process principles. *Rosenberg v. Mallilo & Grossman,* 798 N.Y.S.2d 322, 331 (Sup.Ct.2005). The *remittitur* I order here would reduce the compensatory award to $50,000 and the punitive award to $200,000, which constitutes a four-to-one ratio.

This final factor requires a comparison to awards authorized in similar cases. Considering the same cases outlined above, the punitive damages awarded here obviously exceed those approved in cases involving forms of misconduct beyond that demonstrated by Sanders. An award of $200,000 would better comport with these cases, constitute a reasonable ratio to the amount suggested for compensatory damages, and still adequately reflect the jury's intention to punish Sanders for his resort to violence in the context of his wealth and abuse of influence.

In light of the foregoing analysis. Sanders's motion is DENIED in part and GRANTED in part. I will order a new trial unless Denman accepts the *remittitur* suggested above by March 10, 2006: a reduction to a total compensatory damages award of $50,000 and a total punitive damages award of $200,000.

SO ORDERED

## Case Review Question

If the plaintiff was compensated appropriately for his injuries, why should he also receive punitive damages?

## False Imprisonment

False imprisonment occurs when a party (not necessarily a law-enforcement agency) creates boundaries for another party with the intent that the other party be confined within those boundaries. It requires also that the second party is aware of the confinement, does not consent to it, and perceives no reasonable means of escape.[25] False imprisonment has been the basis for lawsuits ranging from false arrests by law-enforcement officers to kidnapping and even unwarranted detention in stores by store security and personnel.

The boundaries in a false imprisonment action need not be actual walls. It is only necessary to show that through physical barriers, conduct, or words, the injured party reasonably believed his or her liberty was restricted.[26] There is also no requirement of actual damages. The loss of liberty is considered to be an injury in and of itself, although there are often other, more tangible injuries as well.

Note that an action for false imprisonment cannot be brought if the defendant was exercising a privilege when detaining the plaintiff. For example, security officers and law-enforcement agencies are given a wide latitude in detaining persons suspected of criminal activity. Even if the persons are innocent, public policy requires that investigation of reasonable suspicions be allowed. If the suspicions are wholly unfounded, however, or if the investigation or detention is for an unreasonable period of time, then the privilege may not apply. This most often becomes an issue in cases when store security guards detain customers on suspicion of shoplifting. If the suspicion, the detainment, and treatment of the customer are reasonable, then there probably would be no grounds for an action of false imprisonment.

## CASE
### *Jury v. Giant of Maryland, Inc., et al.,* 254 Va.235, 491 S.E.2d 718 (1997)

The following opinion examines what constitutes false imprisonment and when detention is legally justifiable.

In this appeal we consider whether Code § 18.2-105 provides a merchant absolute immunity from civil liability for assault and battery, negligence, and intentional infliction of emotional distress alleged to have occurred during the detention of a customer suspected of shoplifting.

On January 23, 1993, 46-year-old Carlotta Jury went to a Giant Food store in Annandale, Virginia, to exchange a prescription for her niece and purchase some other items. She left two of her children, ages three and ten, in her car. After exchanging the prescription and selecting some batteries and hair ties, she returned to the front of the store, ready to check out. At that point, a man who did not identify himself approached her, grabbed her arm, and told her to accompany him. When she refused, he hit her in the chest, causing her to fall backward into the aisle between the cash registers. As Jury attempted to catch her breath, the man continued to lean over her and tried to jerk her up by pulling on her arm. Another unidentified man approached and, along with the first man, took Jury to a storage area in the back of the store. The first man twisted Jury's arm behind her back and shoved her while walking her to the back of the store. Jury later discovered that the first man who approached her was Arthur Bridcott, a security guard for the Giant Food store, and the second man was James Parker, manager of the store.

As the three reached the back of the store, one of the men kicked Jury in the back of the leg, knocking her to the floor. Her face fell in a pile of dirt, and the men were "scrounging" her face in the dirt. Jury tried to ask what was going on, but they told her to "[s]hut up," "[y]ou're a thief," and "[w]e're taking care of this and we're going to take care of you." The men called Jury crude and obscene names and subjected her to similarly crude and obscene remarks and gestures. Parker, the manager, picked Jury up off the floor by her hair, pulling some of it out of her head, and "stomped" on her foot. The men refused to allow her to use the restroom, and when she tried to tell them that her children were in the car and she was worried about them, the men responded "we'll take care of that or Social Services will."

Jury was detained in the back of the store for approximately one hour. The security guard, Bridcott, told Jury that they would let her go if she provided a written confession and if she would not come back to the store. She refused, stating that she had done nothing wrong. Parker asked Bridcott what merchandise Jury had concealed, and Bridcott responded that Jury had taken possession of batteries and hair ties. The men handcuffed Jury and summoned the police. Jury was arrested and escorted to the police station. She was released later that evening and went to the hospital the next day. At the hospital, Jury was treated, x-rayed, bandaged, given medication and a neck collar, and advised to see an orthopedic doctor.

Jury was subsequently convicted of concealment of merchandise in the general district court. That conviction was reversed on appeal to the circuit court.

*(continued)*

Jury filed a motion for judgment alleging assault and battery, negligence, and intentional infliction of emotional distress, against Giant of Maryland, Inc. and its employees involved in Jury's detention at the Giant Food store (collectively "Giant"). She sought recovery for injuries she sustained during her detention. Prior to trial, Giant's motion for summary judgment on the assault and battery and negligence claims was granted and the claims were dismissed based on the trial court's determination that §18.2-105 granted Giant immunity from civil liability for these claims.

Following Jury's presentation of evidence on her intentional infliction of emotional distress claim, the trial court granted Giant's motion to strike, holding that § 18.2-105 also provided Giant with immunity from civil liability base on this claim. We awarded Jury an appeal and, because we concur with Jury's assertion that §18.2-105 does not provide a merchant with absolute immunity, we will reverse the judgment of the trial court and remand the case for further proceedings.

Code § 18.2-105 provides in pertinent part that: [a] merchant, agent or employee of the merchant, who causes the arrest or detention of any person . . . shall not be held civilly liable for unlawful detention, if such detention does not exceed one hour, slander, malicious prosecution, false imprisonment, false arrest, or assault and battery of the person so arrested or detained . . . provided that . . . the merchant, agent or employee . . . had at the time of such arrest or detention probable cause to believe that the person had shoplifted or committed willful concealment of goods or merchandise.

We construed this statute in *F.B.C. Stores, Inc. v. Duncan,* 214 Va. 246, 198 S.E.2d 595 (1973), as encompassing "virtually all of the intentional torts to person recognized at common law" and determined that the "scope" of the immunity "intended by the General Assembly was very broad." *Id.* at 249, 198 S.E.2d at 598. We also, however, reaffirmed the principle that, in construing statutes, "courts presume that the legislature never intends application of the statute to work irrational consequences." *Id.* at 249–50, 198 S.E.2d at 598.

Construing this statute to provide absolute immunity as the trial court has done, and as Giant urges here, requires the conclusion that the General Assembly intended to shield a merchant, its agents or employees, from any and all types of assaults and batteries. Under

this construction, a merchant would not be civilly liable for breaking a suspected shoplifter's legs or for other extreme assaultive actions taken to detain a suspected shoplifter. We cannot ascribe such an intent to the General Assembly.

Because we have concluded that the immunity granted by § 18.2-105 is not absolute, we must determine the scope of that immunity. We are again guided by *Duncan.* In that case, we stated that the statute represented the General Assembly's attempt to "strike a balance between one man's property rights and another man's personal rights." *Id.* at 251, 198 S.E.2d at 599. The statute "enlarged" a merchant's rights to protect his property, but did not enlarge them "infinitely," and diminished, but did not extinguish, "the litigable rights of the public."

As applied to the issue in this case, we conclude that the balance between personal and property rights in § 18.2-105 is achieved by providing immunity from civil liability based on a wide range of torts, but not extending such immunity in circumstances in which the tort is committed in a willful, wanton or otherwise unreasonable or excessive manner. Under our construction, merchants, their agents or employees are shielded from civil liability for actions reasonably necessary to protect the owners' property rights by detaining suspected shoplifters. But, individuals retain their "litigable rights" in the circumstances just noted. This construction of the statute is also consistent with the limitations imposed on other legislative grants of immunity from civil liability. See e.g., §§ 8.01-220.1:1, -225, -225.1, -226.2, -226.3; 22.1-303.1; 54.1-2502, -2907, -2908, -2922, -2923, -2924.

In light of our construction of the statute, we conclude that dismissing Jury's motion for judgment on the basis that § 18.2-105 provided Giant with absolute immunity from the claims asserted by Jury was error. Accordingly, we will reverse the judgment of the trial court and remand the case for further proceedings, consistent with this opinion.

Reversed and remanded.

## Case Review Question

Under the statute, was the detention proper other than the physical assault—including leaving the suspect's children unattended in the parking lot? Why or why not?

## Trespass

Trespass is the intentional invasion of property rights. It occurs when someone personally or through his or her property enters the land of another or permits such an invasion to continue when another takes control of the property.[27] An example of the latter occurs if you sell your house to someone but leave your car parked in the backyard. This is an invasion of the purchaser's right to the property.

The actor is not required to have the intent to commit a trespass or even the knowledge that he or she is doing so. It is enough that the actor intends to commit the invasive act: As a result of the commission of that act, a trespass occurs. Such a case often occurs when hunters are on publicly owned land and unknowingly enter onto private property. Even though they believe they are still on public land, they have violated a property interest. Violation of this right of landowners to quiet enjoyment free from intrusion is enough to bring an action for trespass. If the trespasser causes damage to persons or property, then he or she is liable for that as well.

## Fraud

The intentional tort of fraud is perhaps the most commonly claimed tort in business and financial dealings. Fraud is not easily proven, however, because the injured party must be able to show that he or she did not have the opportunity to detect any misdealing. The elements required to prove an action for fraud are numerous. It must be shown that (1) the defendant made a material (significant) representation to the plaintiff that was untrue, (2) the defendant knew the statement was untrue or that his or her failure to ascertain its truth was reckless, (3) some affirmative conduct by the defendant indicates the intent to have the plaintiff rely on the statement, and (4) the plaintiff reasonably relied on the statement and as a proximate result was injured by it.[28]

### APPLICATION 9.5

Carnie meets Colin at a local business owners' association meeting. Carnie is new to town and plans to go into business for herself. Colin finds this interesting as he plans to sell his small retail business and roam the southern United States in an RV. Colin offers to sell his business as a turnkey operation to Carnie. Colin explains to Carnie that the only liabilities are those listed on the books of the business such as current utility bills, a few invoices for inventory, and some minor miscellaneous items. Carnie asks if there are any liabilities of which Colin is aware but that are not on the books. Colin emphatically tells her there are not. Carnie agrees in writing to buy the business including all assets and liabilities. The hard assets are valued at $153,000, including a small building where the business is operated. The liabilities add up to $23,000. Carnie also pays some for the established business name and agrees to the purchase for the amount of $200,000. The deal is closed and Colin is off to see the country.

Six months after Carnie takes over the business, a lawsuit is filed for injuries received when a customer fell on a wet floor in the business and broke her neck two weeks before Carnie met Colin. The customer was rendered a total quadriplegic. Carnie in turn files a suit for fraud against Colin on the basis that he withheld material information about the fall and the fact that he had allowed the insurance on the property to lapse before the customer's injuries and had only reinstated it after the incident.

*Point for Discussion:* Would there be a case for fraud if Carnie had not inquired as to liabilities other than those on the books?

## Defamation

Defamation is the combined name for two types of intentional torts: libel and slander. *Libel* is an action for injuries that occur as the result of a written communication to a third party.[29] *Slander* is the appropriate action when the injuries occur as the result of an oral communication.[30]

In both types of actions, it is necessary to show that the defendant actor made a communication to a third party about the plaintiff that caused other third persons to have a lowered opinion of the plaintiff or be discouraged from associating with him or her.[31] This communication must be made by the speaker with the intent that the receiving party perceive it as directed to him- or herself. For example, giving a written statement about someone to a secretary for the sole purpose of having it typed is not a communication of libel. Communicating the statement to the secretary with the intent that he or she believe it or giving the message to another party would constitute a communication of libel.

A different standard of defamation requirements exists with respect to public figures. Persons who place themselves in the public light are inviting comment or publicity under the constitutional rights of free speech. Nevertheless, there are limits to what can be said publicly about another. If it can be shown that a statement was made with actual malice (knowledge that the statement was false or reckless disregard for its truth or falsity), even a public figure can maintain an action for defamation.[32]

Some defenses are peculiar to actions based on defamation. First, the truth is always a defense. If a truthful statement is made about another, no matter how damaging, no action for defamation can be brought. Another defense is known as *privilege*. Because certain communications are deemed to serve the public interest, someone's opinion may be exempt from an action for defamation. For example, an employer who fires an employee for suspected drug use is privileged with respect to reporting this information to such government agencies as unemployment departments. Generally, if a terminated employee seeks unemployment compensation, the employer will be asked the reasons for termination. The employer may not be able to prove the absolute truth of this statement about a former employee. If the suspicions were reasonable, however, the employer is permitted to give the information to government agencies, which will keep the information confidential. Privilege applies whenever public policy requires communication between the private sector and the government.

## Emotional Distress

Emotional distress is often called the *catchall* tort. A plaintiff can plead it as a negligence action or as an intentional tort. Frequently, when it is difficult to prove the necessary elements of a specific intentional tort, emotional distress is used as the cause of action. It can also accompany an intentional tort as a separate and independent action.

Jurisdictions are divided on the issue of whether an actual physical contact must accompany the emotional injury. To prove an action for intentional infliction of emotional distress, however, it must be shown that the actor intentionally engaged in conduct so outrageous that the actor knew or should have known that its likely result would be a mental or emotional disturbance to the plaintiff of such a magnitude that it could produce a resulting physical injury—for example, falsely or mistakenly informing a new mother that her baby was stillborn. Such a severe blow to one in an already weakened condition could likely have physical effects.

Emotional distress can also be brought as the basis of negligence. This generally occurs when the conduct was unquestionably unreasonable, but proving the intent (under the definition of an intentional tort) of the actor is difficult. This type of action is based on conduct so extremely reckless that it is considered unreasonable.

Some jurisdictions also acknowledge a separate action for negligent infliction of emotional distress. The requirements are those of an action in negligence with a damage requirement of emotional distress as previously defined.

## Special Damages Awarded for Intentional Torts

Many of the intentional torts discussed here may also be the basis for a separate criminal prosecution. However, the action for an intentional tort is a dispute that is purely between the private parties, and no imprisonment or fines are imposed. If proven, however, because of the element of intent, civil actions for intentional torts often result in more severe money judgments than in cases of negligence based on careless conduct. In addition, when a jurisdiction permits, punitive damages are often awarded to the plaintiff in addition to the ordinary compensatory damages. This occurs because the courts want to send a message that conduct intentionally resulting in harm to another will be dealt with severely.

### ASSIGNMENT 9.2

Examine the following situations and identify the intentional tort, if any, that was committed.

1. Rita was chasing Ben in a game of touch football when Ben fell and struck his head on a piece of metal lying in the grass on the field.

2. Rita was chasing Ben and threatening to beat him up for something he said about her when Ben fell and struck his head on a piece of metal lying in the grass on the field.

3. Ben told Rita's teacher's that the reason Rita did so well in school was because she had hacked into the school Web site and obtained access to tests before they were given. Actually, Rita had not hacked into the computers, but she had stolen the tests from the school office where they were printed the day before they were administered.

4. Ben told Rita's teacher's that the reason Rita did so well in school was because she had hacked into the school Web site and obtained access to tests before they were given. Rita did not hack into the computers.

5. Rita found Ben in an empty classroom. She told him that if he left before she told him to, she would claim he assaulted her and have him not only expelled from school but also arrested. Ben has a history of getting into trouble in school while Rita is known as the star student. Ben believes Rita and stays in the room overnight.

## PRODUCT LIABILITY

Product liability is not a specific body of tort law such as negligence, strict liability, or intentional torts. Rather, it describes a subject of a tort action that may be based on any one of the major tort theories. The common denominator is that the action involves a product that has been placed in commerce. The number and variety of commercial products has grown to such proportions that an entire area of law has been developed to establish precedent for disputes that arise out of the sale and use of products. Each year, several million injuries result from use of manufactured products. It is not surprising that the number of lawsuits in this area has grown accordingly.

## Causes of Action

Some of the legal standards that have been established include standards of care and causes of action in product liability cases. For example, the commonly encountered causes of action in the latter cases include:

- breach of express warranty,
- breach of implied warranty of fitness for a particular purpose,
- breach of implied warranty of merchantability,
- negligence,

- deceit, and
- strict liability.

It is apparent that many of the causes of action resemble ordinary tort actions. In reality, product liability actions are derived from basic tort law. However, to accommodate the unique position of the consumer or injured party and manufacturer, certain modifications have been made. Also note that *res ipsa loquitur* is commonly employed in product liability cases because the plaintiff frequently has no opportunity to discover the exact action of the defendant that produced the danger in the product.

Specific legal standards regarding the standard of care in product liability cases include the idea that a manufacturer is presumed to be an expert on the product and therefore must manufacture the product with the same care as someone with extensive knowledge about the product and its potential dangers. A manufacturer who does not have such knowledge or does not utilize it to make reasonably sure that the product is safe can be held accountable for injuries caused by the product.

## Defenses

Defenses in product liability cases are similar to those found in other areas of negligence. In addition, a manufacturer may also claim as a defense extreme misuse of the product. It is established that manufacturers must foresee a certain degree of misuse of a product. If, however, the consumer significantly modifies the product or uses it in a manner that the manufacturer could not have been reasonably expected to foresee, the manufacturer will not be held liable for any injuries.

---

### APPLICATION 9.6

Chris is a Boy Scout leader. He also works as a pipefitter making specially designed pipe for commercial building construction projects. He decides to bring his scout troop to his work and show them how the machinery works. He is especially anxious to show off his brand new AARGHHH 9000, which puts threading on pipe pieces, allowing them to be screwed together. He brings the scouts down to the shop and gathers them all around the AARGHHH 9000. He removes a large plastic shield to provide a better view of how the machine works, turns it on, and begins a demonstration. As he is grinding the threads into the pipe surface, several shards of metal fly off and hit the boys. One boy's eye is pierced and he permanently loses his sight in that eye. Chris did not provide the boys with safety glasses because they were not the ones operating the machine. The instructions for the AARGH 9000 (still unopened and in the packing crate at the time of the accident) clearly stated that anyone within 20 feet of the machine should wear protective eye gear. As a result, any action against the manufacturer will probably fail on the defense that the product was misused in terms of having an audience present without protective gear. In addition, removal of the plastic shield could be considered a significant modification.

*Point for Discussion:* What if the instructions did not address bystanders?

---

## Statute of Limitations

One area of difficulty in product liability law involves the statute of limitations. Typically, the statute of limitations begins to run at the time the plaintiff knows or should know he or she has a cause of action. This was found to create a problem in the area of product liability because injuries often did not occur until many years after products were manufactured. Consequently, the defendant manufacturer was at a tremendous disadvantage. Much of the evidence and many of the witnesses with knowledge about a product's design and creation were no longer available. In response, many state legislatures enacted what are known as *statutes of repose* that place an absolute limit from the time of manufacture in which an action can be brought. For example, in a state with a statute of repose of fifteen years, no product liability action can be brought more than fifteen years after the manufacture of the product or when the statute of limitations runs out, whichever is first.

The unique characteristics of commercial products that are distributed (often in mass quantities) and that remain in use for many years have necessitated the development of special rules of law. With these precedents, manufacturers and consumers alike have a better awareness of their rights with respect to the sale, purchase, and use of products.

## CASE
### Calles v. Scripto-Tokai Corp., et al.,
### —N.E.2d —, 2007 WL 495315 (Ill.)

This edited case provides insight into the heavily litigated area of the applicability of the strict liability doctrine in modern product manufacture.

On March 31, 1998, plaintiff Susan Calles resided with her four daughters, Amanda, age nine, Victoria, age five, and Jenna and Jillian, age three. At some point that night, Calles left her home with Victoria to get videos for Amanda. When she left, the twins were in bed and Amanda was watching television. Calles returned to find fire trucks and emergency vehicles around her home. It was subsequently determined by a fire investigator, Robert Finn, that Jenna had started a fire using an Aim N Flame utility lighter Calles had purchased approximately one week earlier. The Aim N Flame was ignited by pulling a trigger after an "ON/OFF" switch was slid to the "on" position. As a result of the fire, Jillian suffered smoke inhalation. She was hospitalized and died on April 21.

Calles, individually and as administrator of Jillian's estate, filed suit in the circuit court of Cook County against Tokai, designer and manufacturer of the Aim N Flame, and Scripto-Tokai, distributor (collectively Scripto), alleging that the Aim N Flame was defectively designed and unreasonably dangerous because it did not contain a child-resistant safety device. According to the complaint, a safety device was available, inexpensive, and would have reduced the risk that children could ignite the lighter. Calles' claims sounded in strict liability, negligence, and breach of the implied warranties of merchantability and fitness for a particular purpose. Calles further alleged that Scripto was negligent and strictly liable because of a failure to give adequate warnings.

Calles also filed a medical malpractice claim against Dr. Richard Fox and Loyola University Medical Center (collectively Loyola) in connection with their treatment of Jillian following the fire. Scripto filed counterclaims against Calles and Loyola. Loyola then filed a countercomplaint for contribution against Scripto.

Thereafter, Scripto filed a motion for summary judgment on the claims brought by Calles and Loyola. Scripto argued that: (1) the Aim N Flame was not defective or unreasonably dangerous because it worked as expected; (2) Scripto had no duty to make an adult product child resistant; (3) Scripto had no duty to warn because the dangers of the Aim N Flame were open and obvious; and (4) there was no breach of warranties because the Aim N Flame operated as intended and expected.

In support of its motion for summary judgment, Scripto offered the deposition testimony of Calles and Robert Finn, the fire inspector. In her deposition, Calles admitted she was aware of the risks and dangers presented by lighters in the hands of children, and, for this reason, she stored the Aim N Flames on the top shelf of her kitchen cabinet. Calles further admitted that the Aim N Flame operated as intended and expected.

In opposition to Scripto's motion for summary judgment, Calles offered affidavits from several experts including John Geremia, a chemical and mechanical engineer; Tarald Kvlseth, a mechanical and industrial engineer; William Kitzes, a board-certified product safety manager; Richard Dahlquist, an electrical engineer; and Carol Pollack-Nelson, an engineering psychologist. All

*(continued)*

of these experts opined that the Aim N Flame was defective and unreasonably dangerous because it lacked a child-resistant design. They also opined that a technologically and economically feasible alternative design, which included a child-resistant safety device, existed at the time the Aim N Flame was manufactured. Several of the experts averred that Scripto was aware of the desirability of a child-safety device because it knew children could operate the Aim N Flame. Further, according to these experts, Scripto owned the technology to make the Aim N Flame child resistant in 1994 and 1995.

With respect to the cost of an alternative design, Kvlseth noted that the Consumer Product Safety Commission, the regulatory body for lighters, in a proposed rule dated September 30, 1998, estimated the increased cost of adding a safety device to the lighter would be $0.40 per unit. However, it was Kvlseth's opinion that, had the feature been incorporated into the original design, the cost would have been negligible.

Calles also offered evidence of the dangerousness of lighters in the hands of children and Scripto's awareness of such dangers. She introduced into evidence statistics showing the number of previous fires started by children with lighters (both utility and cigarette), the number of deaths and injuries that had occurred each year as a result of fires started by children, and the reduction in cost to society that would be derived from the addition of child-resistant safety devices on the lighters. Calles further pointed to Scripto's answers to interrogatories, in which Scripto admitted they had been named as defendants in 25 lawsuits filed between 1996 and 2000 for injuries that occurred between 1992 and 1999 under circumstances similar to this case.

The trial court granted summary judgment in favor of Scripto on both Calles' complaint and Loyola's counter-complaint. The trial court found that all claims "must fall because these defendants neither owed nor breached any duty imposed upon them by law" under any of the causes of action raised. On appeal, the appellate court affirmed in part and reversed in part. 358 Ill.App.3d 975. With respect to strict liability, the appellate court held that the Aim N Flame "does not qualify as the kind of especially simple device for which the result of the risk-utility balancing is too obvious for trial." 358 Ill.App.3d at 983. Accordingly, the appellate court reversed the trial court's grant of summary judgment in favor of Scripto. 358 Ill.App.3d at 984. The appellate court also reversed summary judgment on the negligent-design claims and remanded for further proceedings. 358 Ill.App.3d at 984. We granted Scripto's petition for leave to appeal. 210 Ill.2d R. 315.

In *Suvada v. White Motor Co.*, 32 Ill.2d 612, 622–23 (1965), this court adopted the strict liability doctrine set forth in section 402A of the *Second Restatement of Torts.* Under this doctrine, strict liability is imposed upon a seller of "any product in a defective condition unreasonably dangerous to the user or consumer or to his property." *Restatement (Second) of Torts* § 402A, at 347–48 (1965). The test outlined in section 402A for determining whether a product is "unreasonably dangerous" is known as the consumer-expectation or consumer-contemplation test. This test provides that a product is "unreasonably dangerous" when it is "dangerous to an extent beyond that which would be contemplated by the ordinary consumer who purchases it, with the ordinary knowledge common to the community as to its characteristics." *Restatement (Second) of Torts* § 402A (1965).

Under the consumer-expectation test, a plaintiff must establish what an ordinary consumer purchasing the product would expect about the product and its safety. This is an objective standard based on the average, normal, or ordinary expectations of the reasonable person; it is not dependent upon the subjective expectation of a particular consumer or user. See *American Law of Products Liability* 3d § 17:24, at 17–44 (1997); L. Bass, *Products Liability: Design & Manufacturing Defects* § 4:1 (2d ed.2001). . . .

The consumer-expectation test was originally applied to manufacturing defects, but soon came to be applied to design-defect issues as well. Over time, the applicability of the consumer-expectation test to design-defect cases was questioned, primarily because it became apparent that consumers might not be aware of what to expect regarding the safety of certain products. See *Barker v. Lull Engineering Co.*, 20 Cal.3d 413, 427–28, 573 P.2d 443, 452–53, 143 Cal.Rptr. 225, 234–35 (1978). Accordingly, this court in *Lamkin v. Towner,* 138 Ill.2d 510, 528 (1990), adopted a second, alternative test for design defect cases known as the risk-utility, or risk-benefit, test. See *Blue v. Environmental Engineering, Inc.*, 215 Ill.2d 78, 91 (2005). . . . In *Lamkin,* this court held that a plaintiff may demonstrate a product has been defectively designed "in one of two ways." One way a plaintiff may demonstrate a design defect is to present evidence that the product fails to satisfy the consumer-expectation test. Alternatively, a plaintiff may demonstrate a design defect by presenting evidence that the risk of danger inherent in the challenged design outweighs the benefits of such design. *Lamkin,* 138 Ill.2d at 529; *Blue,* 215 Ill.2d at 98–99.

The rationale for employing two tests was explained in *Barker.* There, the court noted that "at a minimum a product must meet ordinary consumer expectations as to safety to avoid being found defective." *Barker,* 20 Cal.3d at 426 n. 7, 573 P.2d at 451 n. 7, 143 Cal.Rptr. at 233 n. 7. However, "the expectations of the ordinary consumer cannot be viewed as the exclusive yardstick for evaluating design defectiveness because '[i]n many situations . . . the consumer would not know what to expect, because he would have no idea how safe the product could be made.' [Citation.]" *Barker,* 20 Cal.3d at 430, 573 P.2d at 454, 143 Cal.Rptr. at 236. Thus, even if a product satisfies ordinary consumer expectations, "if through hindsight the jury determines that the product's design embodies 'excessive preventable danger,' or, in other words, if the jury finds that the risk of danger inherent in the challenged design outweighs the benefits of such design," a product may be found defective in design. *Barker,* 20 Cal.3d at 430, 573 P.2d at 454, 143 Cal.Rptr. at 236. . . . Since *Lamkin,* this court has continued to employ these two tests when determining whether a product is unreasonably dangerous. See *Blue,* 215 Ill.2d at 91–92; *Hansen v. Baxter Healthcare Corp.,* 198 Ill.2d 420, 433–38 (2002). We now turn to them.

. . . under the consumer–expectation test, a plaintiff may prevail if he or she demonstrates that the product failed to perform as an ordinary consumer would expect when used in an intended or reasonably foreseeable manner. In the case at bar, there is a threshold question. Whose expectations control, i.e., the adult purchaser or the child user? Calles argues we must apply the consumer–expectation test from the point of view of a child. We disagree.

For purposes of the consumer–expectation test, "ordinary" modifies consumer. Ordinary means "[r]egular; usual; normal; common." *Black's Law Dictionary* 989 (5th ed.1979). See also 1 Madden & Owen on *Products Liability* § 8:3, at 71 (Supp.2006). Several courts in other jurisdictions have held that the "ordinary consumer" of a lighter is an adult, not a child. See, e.g., *Talkington v. Atria Reclamelucifers Fabrieken BV,* 152 F.3d 254, 263 (4th Cir.1998); *Curtis v. Universal Match Corp.,* 966 F.2d 1451 (6th Cir.1992); *Kelley v. Rival Manufacturing Co.,* 704 F.Supp. 1039, 1043 (W.D.Okla. 1989); *Welch v. Scripto-Tokai Corp.,* 651 N.E.2d 810, 814 (Ind.App.1995); *Bellotte v. Zayre Corp.,* 116 N.H. 52, 54, 352 A.2d 723, 725 (1976). In light of these cases, we hold that the ordinary consumer of a lighter, such as the Aim N Flame here, is an adult—the typical user and purchaser. Therefore, the expectations regarding the Aim N Flame's use and safety must be viewed from the point of view of the adult consumer.

We now consider whether the Aim N Flame meets the consumer-expectation test. The purpose of a lighter,

such as the Aim N Flame, is to produce a flame. See T. Peters & H. Carroll, *Playing with Fire: Assessing Lighter Manufacturers' Duties Regarding Child Play Lighter Fires,* 9 Loy. Consumer L. Rep. 339, 340 (1997). Clearly then, the ordinary consumer would expect that, when the trigger is pulled, a flame would be produced. Here, the Aim N Flame was not used in its intended manner, i.e., by an adult. Thus, the question is whether it was used in a reasonably foreseeable manner. We find that it was.

An ordinary consumer would expect that a child could obtain possession of the Aim N Flame and attempt to use it. Thus, a child is a reasonably foreseeable user. Likewise, an ordinary consumer would appreciate the consequences that would naturally flow when a child obtains possession of a lighter. See M. Madden, *Products Liability, Products for Use by Adults, And Injured Children: Back to the Future,* 61 Tenn. L.Rev. 1205, 1222 (Summer 1994). Specifically, an ordinary consumer would expect that the Aim N Flame, in the hands of a child, could cause the result that occurred here—the starting of a fire that led to injury to a child. *Flock v. Scripto-Tokai Corp.,* 319 F.3d 231, 242 (5th Cir.2003) (Texas law); *Curtis,* 778 F.Supp. at 1430 (Tennessee); *Bondie v. BIC Corp.,* 739 F.Supp. 346, 349 (E.D.Mich.1990); *Williams v. BIC Corp.,* 771 So.2d 441, 449–50 (Ala.2000); *Welch,* 651 N.E.2d at 814; *Price v. BIC Corp.,* 142 N.H. 386, 390, 702 A.2d 330, 333 (1997); *Campbell v. BIC Corp.,* 154 Misc.2d 976, 978, 586 N.Y.S.2d 871, 873 (1992); *Perkins v. Wilkinson Sword, Inc.,* 83 Ohio St.3d 507, 513, 700 N.E.2d 1247, 1252 (1998); *Hernandez v. Tokai Corp.,* 2 S.W.3d 251, 258 (Tex.1999).

Under the facts of this case, the Aim N Flame performed as an ordinary consumer would expect—it produced a flame when used in a reasonably foreseeable manner, i.e., by a child. This leads to the inescapable conclusion that the ordinary consumer's expectations were fulfilled. In other words, the Aim N Flame did not fail to perform as an ordinary consumer would expect when used in a reasonably foreseeable manner. Thus, as a matter of law, no fact finder could conclude that the Aim N Flame was unreasonably dangerous under the consumer-expectation test. Therefore, Calles cannot prevail under this theory. This does not end our analysis however. Though the Aim N Flame satisfies the consumer-expectation test, it may, nonetheless, be deemed unreasonably dangerous under the risk-utility test.

Under the risk-utility test, a plaintiff may prevail in a strict liability design-defect case if he or she demonstrates that the magnitude of the danger outweighs the utility of the product, as designed. *Lamkin,* 138 Ill.2d

*(continued)*

at 529. Stated differently, "[t]he utility of the design must therefore be weighed against the risk of harm created" and "[i]f the likelihood and gravity of the harm outweigh the benefits and utilities of the product, the product is unreasonably dangerous." 63A Am.Jur. 2d *Products Liability* § 978, at 146–47 (1997).

Relying on *Scoby v. Vulcan-Hart Corp.*, 211 Ill.App.3d 106 (1991), Scripto argues there is a "simple product" exception to the application of the risk-utility test. In other words, Scripto contends that, when a product is deemed "simple," the risk-utility test need not be employed. We disagree. In *Scoby,* an individual was injured while working in a restaurant kitchen when he slipped and fell and his arm became submerged in hot oil contained in an open deep-fat fryer. *Scoby,* 211 Ill.App.3d at 107. The plaintiff sued the . . . manufacturer, alleging a design defect, and argued liability under the risk-utility test. *Scoby,* 211 Ill.App.3d at 109. Relying on *Lamkin,* the manufacturer argued that, because the danger at issue was not "excessive," the risk-utility test should not be utilized. *Scoby,* 211 Ill.App. 3 d at 111–12.

The *Scoby* court agreed with the defendant. *Scoby,* 211 Ill.App.3d at 112. Noting that hot oil in a fryer was an open and obvious danger and that, for efficient kitchen operation, it was often necessary to keep a lid off the fryer, the *Scoby* court concluded:

"We do not deem that *Lamkin* or other cases applying aspects of the danger-utility test intend that all manufacturers . . . should be subject to liability depending upon a trier of fact's balancing under that test. . . . Somewhere, a line must be drawn beyond which the danger-utility test cannot be applied. Considering not only the obvious nature of any danger here but, also, the simple nature of the mechanism involved, we conclude the circuit court properly applied only the consumer-user contemplation test." *Scoby,* 211 Ill.App.3d at 112.

Several appellate court decisions have followed *Scoby* in various situations giving rise to the so called "simple product" exception to the application of the risk-utility test. *Miller v. Rinker Boat Co.,* 352 Ill.App.3d 648, 664 (2004); *Mele v. Howmedica, Inc.,* 348 Ill.App.3d 1, 19 (2004); *Bates v. Richland Sales Corp.,* 346 Ill.App.3d 223, 234 (2004); *Wortel v. Somerset Industries, Inc.,* 331 Ill.App.3d 895, 908 (2002). . . . In support of their position that summary judgment was properly granted in their favor, Scripto also cites to *Todd v. Societe Bic, S.A.,* 21 F.3d 1402 (7th Cir.1994), wherein the court applied the *Scoby* exception to facts very similar to those in the case at bar. In *Todd,* a two-year-old child died when a four-year-old child used a Bic lighter to start a fire in the two-year-old's bedroom. *Todd,* 21 F.3d at

1403. The plaintiff filed a strict liability design-defect claim against the manufacturer, alleging the lighter was unreasonably dangerous because it did not contain a child-resistant safety device. *Todd,* 21 F.3d at 1404. The district court granted summary judgment in favor of the manufacturer and the plaintiff appealed. *Todd,* 21 F.3d at 1405. The Seventh Circuit Court of Appeals affirmed, concluding that the lighter was not unreasonably dangerous under the consumer-expectation test because it performed exactly as a consumer would expect—it produced a flame when activated. *Todd,* 21 F.3d at 1407.

The *Todd* court then observed that this court had adopted a second test in strict liability design-defect cases, the risk-utility test. The court also observed, however, that in *Scoby,* a simple-product exception to application of this test had been adopted. *Todd,* 21 F.3d at 1410–11. Noting that this court had not yet addressed the *Scoby* exception, the *Todd* court opined that this court "would not apply the risk-utility test to simple but obviously dangerous products." *Todd,* 21 F.3d at 1412. The *Todd* court then concluded the lighter was a simple product and, for that reason, the risk-utility test was not applicable. *Todd,* 21 F.3d at 1412.

While this court has made reference to *Scoby* in past decisions, we have never had occasion to squarely address the simple-product exception it adopted. See *Blue,* 215 Ill.2d at 108; *Hansen,* 198 Ill.2d at 437. We do so now.

Upon close examination of *Scoby,* we find that it uses "simple" and "open and obvious" as separate components. However, in our view, the dangers associated with a product that is deemed "simple" are, by their very nature, open and obvious. See, e.g., *Swix,* 373 F.3d at 684–85 (finding "that the fact that a product may be a 'simple tool' is not dispositive in a design defect case—the obviousness of a danger is merely one factor in the analysis of whether the risks are unreasonable in light of the foreseeable injuries"). We conclude, then, that *Scoby*'s adoption of a "simple product" exception is nothing more than the adoption of a general rule that a manufacturer will not be liable for open and obvious dangers.

A majority of courts have rejected the notion that the open and obvious danger of a product is an absolute defense to a defective-design claim in strict liability. *Restatement (Third) of Torts: Products Liability* § 2, Reporters' Note, Comment d, at 84–85 (1998) (identifying 25 jurisdictions that have rejected a *per se* rule). See also *American Law of Products Liability* 3d § 28:82, at 28–108 (1997); 61 Tenn. L.Rev. at 1227–28. We, too, recognized this principle in *Blue,* when this court stated:

"In strict products liability cases, the open and obvious nature of the risk is just one factor to be considered in the range of considerations required by the risk-utility test, and it will only serve to bar the liability of the manufacturer where it outweighs all other factors to be considered in weighing the inherent design risks against the utility of the product as manufactured." *Blue,* 215 Ill.2d at 103. Moreover, this court noted that such a ruling appeared to be consistent with Illinois law. *Blue,* 215 Ill.2d at 103, citing *Coney v. J.L.G. Industries, Inc.,* 97 Ill.2d 104, 119 (1983) (assumption of risk is not a bar to recovery in strict liability). See also *Miller,* 352 Ill.App.3d at 661; *Wortel,* 331 Ill.App.3d at 902. As one case has held, the obviousness of a risk inherent in a product, simple or nonsimple, does not by itself obviate a manufacturer's liability. *Cacevic v. Simplimatic Engineering Co.,* 241 Mich.App. 717, 725, 617 N.W.2d 386, 390 (2000), vacated in part, 463 Mich. 997, 625 N.W.2d 784 (2001).

Policy reasons also support rejection of a *per se* rule excepting simple products with open and obvious dangers from analysis under the risk-utility test. Adoption of such a rule would essentially absolve manufacturers from liability in certain situations even though there may be a reasonable and feasible alternative design available that would make a product safer, but which the manufacturer declines to incorporate because it knows it will not be held liable. This would discourage product improvements that could easily and cost-effectively alleviate the dangers of a product. A *per se* rule would also frustrate the policy of preventing future harm which is at the heart of strict liability law. See 1 Madden & Owens on *Product Liability* § 8:3, at 447; *Restatement (Third) of Torts: Products Liability* § 2, Comment a, at 16 (1998); *Restatement (Third) of Torts: Products Liability* § 2 (1998) .

Accordingly, we hold that the open and obvious danger of a product does not create a *per se* bar to a manufacturer's liability, nor does it preclude application of the risk-utility test. Rather, the open and obvious nature of a danger is one factor that may be weighed in the risk-utility test. *Blue,* 215 Ill.2d at 103. See also *Restatement (Third) of Torts: Products Liability* § 2, Reporters' Note, Comment d, at 85 (1998). We reject *Scoby's* adoption of a *per se* rule excepting simple products with open and obvious dangers from analysis under the risk-utility test. Accordingly, we reject Scripto's assertion that only the consumer-expectation test applies here. We now consider whether Calles presented sufficient evidence under the risk-utility test to withstand summary judgment.

Under the risk-utility test, a court may take into consideration numerous factors. In past decisions, this court has held that a plaintiff may prove a design defect by presenting evidence of "the availability and feasability of alternate designs at the time of its manufacture, or that the design used did not conform with the design standards of the industry, design guidelines provided by an authoritative voluntary association, or design criteria set by legislation or governmental regulation." *Anderson v. Hyster Co.,* 74 Ill.2d 364, 368 (1979). . . . We find the factors set forth in . . . cases are relevant when engaging in risk-utility analysis. See *Blue,* 215 Ill.2d at 92.

John W. Wade, dean and professor of law, emeritus, Vanderbilt University School of Law, has also identified several factors relevant when engaging in risk-utility analysis. These factors include:

"(1) The usefulness and desirability of the product—its utility to the user and to the public as a whole.

(2) The safety aspects of the product—the likelihood that it will cause injury, and the probable seriousness of the injury.

(3) The availability of a substitute product which would meet the same need and not be as unsafe.

(4) The manufacturer's ability to eliminate the unsafe character of the product without impairing its usefulness or making it too expensive to maintain its utility.

(5) The user's ability to avoid danger by the exercise of care in the use of the product.

(6) The user's anticipated awareness of the dangers inherent in the product and their availability, because of general public knowledge of the obvious condition of the product, or of the existence of suitable warnings or instructions.

(7) The feasibility, on the part of the manufacturer, of spreading the loss by setting the price of the product or carrying liability insurance." J. Wade, *On The Nature of Strict Tort Liability for Products,* 44 Miss. L.J. 825, 837–38 (1973).

Wade's factors have been adopted and relied upon by numerous jurisdictions, including our own appellate court. See *LaBelle v. Philip Morris, Inc.,* 243 F.Supp.2d 508, 515 n. 4 (D.S.C.2001). . . .

Lastly, we find that when assessing the utility of a product, the following factors may also be relevant: "(1) the appearance and aesthetic attractiveness of the product; (2) its utility for multiple uses; (3) the convenience and extent of its use, especially in light of the period of time it could be used without harm resulting from the product; and (4) the collateral safety of a feature other than the one that harmed the plaintiff." *American Law of Products Liability* 3d § 28:19, at 28–30 through 28–31 (1997).

*(continued)*

Although we have listed a number of factors which courts may consider when assessing risk-utility, we do not mean to imply that the list is exclusive. The factors cited merely illustrate those that may assist a court and jury in evaluating whether a design is unreasonably dangerous. A plaintiff need not present proof on each of the factors. In the first instance, the court must balance factors it finds relevant to determine if the case is a proper one to submit to the jury. *Restatement (Third) of Torts: Products Liability* § 2, Reporters' Notes, Comment e, at 94 (1998). Once this threshold determination has been met, it is up to the fact finder to determine the importance of any particular factor, and its "relevance, and the relevance of other factors, will vary from case to case." See *Restatement (Third) of Torts: Products Liability* § 2, Comment f, at 23 (1998). We now apply those factors identified above to the evidence presented in the case at bar.

After reviewing the evidence presented, we find the only factor which favors Calles and a finding of unreasonably dangerous is the second Wade factor-safety aspects. Calles presented specific and detailed evidence as to the likelihood of injury and the seriousness of injury from lighters which do not have child-safety devices.

Factors which would favor Scripto and a finding that the product is not unreasonably dangerous are the first and sixth Wade factors—the utility of the Aim N Flame and the user's awareness of the dangers. As to the utility of the Aim N Flame, it is both useful and desirable to society as a whole—it serves as an inexpensive alternative source of fire. Moreover, compared to other sources of fire, such as matches, it is more convenient and longer lasting since it is a multiuse product. The lighter may also be safer since it will extinguish if dropped on the floor while lit, unlike a match. With respect to the user's awareness of the dangers, there is no question, based on Calles' deposition testimony, that it was obvious to her that the lighter could come into the hands of a child and the dangers and risks that situation would pose.

In connection with the remaining relevant factors, we find that these neither weigh for nor against a finding of unreasonably dangerous. Calles claims that a substitute product was available, but the only evidence she relies upon is the fact Bic introduced a child-resistant utility lighter in March 1998, the very same month of the incident here. This is insufficient to demonstrate that a substitute product was available at the time of the manufacture of the Aim N Flame. Calles offered expert affidavits regarding the availability and feasibility of an alternative design, including product impairment and cost factors, along with industry standards. Each expert opined, in a conclusory fashion,

that a feasible alternative design existed. Kvlseth identified three alternative designs.

Scripto argues that, although Kvlseth set forth these alternative designs, he failed to give a basis for his feasability determination, nor did he show that these alternative designs met regulatory standards. In this regard, Scripto notes that the Consumer Product Safety Commission (CPSC), the regulatory body for these products, required safety devices on cigarette lighters beginning in 1994, but exempted utility lighters. It was not until 1999 that CPSC required safety devices on utility lighters. See, e.g., *Bartholic v. Scripto-Tokai Corp.,* 140 F.Supp.2d 1098, 1117 (D.Colo.2000). CPSC exempted utility lighters because it was concerned about "flashbacks" (the build up of gas and resultant sudden flash when a lighter was not ignited properly). Specifically, CPSC feared that if a child-resistant device on a utility lighter needed to be reset between attempts, this could cause a delay in ignition, resulting in the increased risk of flashback. Scripto maintains that this concern shows that some of the child-resistant options proffered by Kvlseth in his affidavit were not, in fact, feasible. Scripto also disputes Calles' claim that there would be no impairment to the Aim N Flame from modification with a child-resistant safety device since she cites no evidence in support of her argument.

With respect to the cost feasability, Calles offered evidence through Kvlseth's affidavit. According to Kvlseth, "the CPSC [Consumer Product Safety Commission] in the Proposed Rule dated September 20, 1998, has estimated that the rule will likely increase the cost of manufacturing utility lighters by about $0.40 per unit. The defendants have indicated that such a cost increase would only be a few cents per lighter. However, had a utility lighter . . . been originally designed to be effectively child resistant, . . . then the incremental cost due to an effective child-resistancy feature would have been negligible."

There is nothing in our record showing Scripto provided any amount as to the increase in cost of incorporating a safety device. Apparently, according to Loyola, this information was offered into evidence in *Flock,* 319 F.3d 231, where an internal Scripto memorandum authored in 1996 estimated cost increase would be $0.03 per unit. In light of the foregoing, we conclude that a material issue of fact exists on the question of whether there was a feasible alternative design available, which cannot be determined on the basis of the record as it currently stands.

Lastly, with respect to the user's ability to avoid the danger, Calles testified she put the Aim N Flames on the top shelf of her kitchen cabinet. However, she also acknowledged she could have left them on the counter. As Scripto maintains, the appellate court embraced the former testimony, despite contradictory evidence. This is a factual determination we cannot make. Based on a review of the foregoing factors, reasonable persons could differ on the weight to be given the relevant factors, particularly where additional proofs are necessary, and thus could differ on whether the risks of the Aim N Flame outweigh its utility. Therefore, reasonable persons could differ as to whether the Aim N Flame is unreasonably dangerous, and we cannot say that Scripto was entitled to judgment as a matter of law. As such, we affirm the appellate court's decision reversing the trial court's decision granting summary judgment in favor of Scripto on the strict liability claims.

The next question we must decide is whether Scripto was entitled to summary judgment on the negligent-product-design claims.

. . . There was no majority opinion in *Blue* holding that the risk—utility test was not applicable to negligent-product-design cases. Rather, as Justice Freeman pointed out, only three Justices concurred. *Blue,* 215 Ill.2d at 115 (Freeman, J., specially concurring). As such, the conclusion that the risk-utility test is not applicable in negligent-product-design cases is not binding precedent. Accordingly, we conclude that the appellate court erred in reversing summary judgment based on *Blue* and we must review anew the trial court's order that Scripto owed no duty, nor breached any duty owed.

A product liability action asserting a claim based on negligence, such as negligent design, falls within the framework of common law negligence. *Flaugher v. Sears, Roebuck & Co.,* 61 Ill.App.3d 671, 675 (1978). Thus, a plaintiff must establish the existence of a duty of care owed by the defendant, a breach of that duty, an injury that was proximately caused by that breach, and damages. *Ward v. K mart Corp.,* 136 Ill.2d 132, 140 (1990). The key distinction between a negligence claim and a strict liability claim lies in the concept of fault. *Coney v. J.L.G. Industries, Inc.,* 97 Ill.2d 104, 117 (1983). In a strict liability claim, the focus is on the condition of the product. *Coney,* 97 Ill.2d at 117–18. However, in a negligence claim, a defendant's fault is at issue in addition to the condition of the product. *Coney,* 97 Ill.2d at 117–18.

A manufacturer has a nondelegable duty to design reasonably safe products. *Doser v. Savage Manufacturing & Sales, Inc.,* 142 Ill.2d 176, 188 (1990), quoting *Savage Manufacturing & Sales, Inc. v. Doser,* 184 Ill.App.3d 405, 410–11 (1989) (Jiganti, P.J., dissenting); *Coney,* 97 Ill.2d at 117. The crucial question in a negligent-design case is whether the manufacturer exercised reasonable care in the design of the product. *American Law of Products Liability* 3d § 28:46, at 28–64 (1997); 63A Am.Jur.2d *Products Liability* § 953, at 130 (1997). See also *Restatement (Second) of Torts* § 398, at 336 (1965) ("A manufacturer of a chattel made under a plan or design which makes it dangerous for the uses for which it is manufactured is subject to liability to others whom he should expect to use the chattel or to be endangered by its probable use for physical harm caused by his failure to exercise reasonable care").

In determining whether the manufacturer's conduct was reasonable, the question is "whether in the exercise of ordinary care the manufacturer should have foreseen that the design would be hazardous to someone." *American Law of Products Liability* 3d § 28:48, at 28–66 (1997). See also 63A Am.Jur.2d *Products Liability* § 953, at 129 (1997) (a manufacturer has a "duty to design against reasonably foreseeable hazards"). To show that the manufacturer acted unreasonably based on the foreseeability of harm, the plaintiff must show the manufacturer knew or should have known of the risk posed by the product design at the time of manufacture. 63A Am.Jur.2d *Products Liability* § 942, at 120 (1997).

Scripto argues that if the Aim N Flame is not unreasonably dangerous for purposes of strict liability because of the open and obvious nature of the dangers associated with it, then the Aim N Flame is not unreasonably dangerous for purposes of negligent product design. Stated differently, Scripto maintains that, because of the patent nature of the danger, no duty exists on their part as a matter of law, and they are entitled to summary judgment.

We disagree with Scripto's argument for many of the reasons stated in connection with our discussion of the strict liability claim. The open and obvious nature of a danger is just one factor in evaluating whether a manufacturer acted reasonably in designing its product. It is not dispositive.

After reviewing the evidence presented here, we find that conflicting evidentiary facts were presented with respect to whether the design of the Aim N Flame was defective. We further find that conflicting evidentiary facts were presented in connection with foreseeability, i.e., Scripto's knowledge of the potential risks posed by the Aim N Flame's design. Accordingly, we conclude that questions of fact exist as to whether Scripto exercised reasonable care in the design and manufacture of the Aim N Flame, precluding summary judgment. For the reasons stated, we affirm the appellate court's reversal of summary judgment in

*(continued)*

favor of Scripto on the negligent product design claims.

We find there is no *per se* rule excepting application of the risk-utility test where a product is deemed simple and its dangers are open and obvious. We also find that there are material questions of law and fact that preclude us from finding, as a matter of law, that the Aim N Flame was not unreasonably dangerous under the risk-utility test. For the reasons set forth above, we affirm the appellate court's reversal of summary judg-

ment in favor of Scripto on the strict liability claims and on the negligent-product-design claims.

Appellate court judgment affirmed.

## Case Review Question

If the consumer willingly purchases a product as a voluntary act, then why are individuals allowed to recover against manufacturers on a basis of strict liability?

## EMPLOYMENT AND TORTS

Tort law has had a significant influence in the area of employment. It concerns not only the actions by or against third parties but also the relationship between the employer and the employee. All states have certain statutes and case law governing the employment relationship and indicating when actions for tort based on it are permitted. Certain exceptions to these statutes also give rise to actions in tort.

### Employer–Employee Relationship

Under a long-established rule of law in this country commonly known as *respondeat superior* (literally, "let the master answer"),[33] a superior may be held responsible for injuries caused by his or her employee. Generally, an injured third party has the right to elect to sue the employer if the third party can demonstrate that the employee was a regular employee and not an independent contractor (someone who works on a per-job basis such as a plumber who goes to someone's office to repair a leaky faucet) and that the injury was caused by the employee while acting within the scope of his or her employment. Simply stated, the latter means that the employee is acting subject to the ultimate supervision of the employer. The employee does not need to be engaged in a regular job duty as long as he or she is engaged in a task that benefits the employer in some direct manner. Generally, employers are not responsible for occurrences while the employee is going to or from work. However, a different rule would apply if the employee were running an errand for the employer (even though it may not be a part of his or her regular duties to do so).

Ordinarily, employers will not be held responsible for intentional torts committed by an employee. An intentional tort requires that the actor knew or should have known with substantial certainty that the act would produce the injury. An employer cannot be held responsible for such intentional acts over which he or she has no control. If this were permitted, then employees could escape responsibility for acts that the employer neither benefited from nor condoned. The exception to this rule takes place when the intentional tort is considered to be within the scope of the employee's duties. Security guards are a common example. Such personnel often are required to restrain customers physically or compel them to leave the premises. In such a situation, the actions of the employee are presumed to be directed by the employer. Therefore, any injuries resulting from the guard's conduct could result in liability of the employer.

## Statutes Governing the Employment Relationships That Govern Tort Actions

The federal government and every state have enacted a variety of legal standards pertaining to the workplace. These include statutes, case law, and administrative regulations regarding the physical environment of the workplace; discrimination laws to place all qualified applicants and employees on an equal footing; laws designed to prevent superiors from using their authority to wrongfully manipulate the conduct of workers on nonwork-related matters; and laws to protect those injured in the performance of job duties.

The federal Occupational Safety and Health Administration (OSHA) is a branch of the U.S. Department of Labor. Each state has a similar agency. The purpose of these agencies is to establish and enforce standards that provide a safe work environment regardless of the type of industry. Given the infinite number of variables in the workplace, however, it is impossible to anticipate every conceivable danger. As a result, other laws are in place to deal with employee injuries. In fact, this is one of the most heavily legislated and regulated aspects of employment law.

In the late eighteenth and early nineteenth centuries, mass production and the growth of machinery in the workplace resulted in large numbers of individuals going to work in factories rather than in the traditional small craftsman shops and farming. Many of these individuals were untrained, and working conditions were sometimes brutal. The result was a significant number of injuries in the workplace. With disabling injuries, many workers had little alternative but to file tort actions against their own employers for damages. The length of time for such a process was often significant, and the hardship on these employees' families was immense. At the same time, employers were suffering the blows of large jury awards for employee injuries when cases finally did come to trial. Insurance was usually available but often cost-prohibitive. Also, once an employee sued the employer, the animosity created by that suit effectively ended any chance of returning to work. Both sides were losing, and legislatures responded with workers' compensation laws during the mid-1900s.

Although the details of workers' compensation laws vary from state to state, the underlying principle is the same.[34] The statutes provide a basis for compensation to employees who are injured while performing job-related duties, although they also place limitations on the extent to which an employer may be held financially liable. Workers' compensation laws in each state have fairly well-defined methods to calculate limits of compensation for various injuries. This in turn enables employers to predict with some degree of certainty what their liability will be in the event of injury. With such limits, insurers are then able to provide insurance to employers at a more reasonable cost without risking huge monetary awards by juries.

A second and major benefit of workers' compensation laws is that they typically are not based on findings of fault or negligence by the employer. This aids the injured employee who could not recover without proof of tortious conduct of the employer. The employer is presumed to have the benefit of the employee's presence on the job and contribution toward the making of profits. Having the employer bear the cost of injuries on the job, even accidental ones, seemed only fair.

One major development in the latter half of the twentieth century with respect to workers' compensation statutes had to do with job security. Employers quickly discovered that the fewer claims against them, the lower the cost of workers' compensation insurance. Many employers subsequently engaged in a kind of subversive tactic to inhibit injured employees from filing actions for workers' compensation benefits. Some employers fired employees who filed claims; others simply did not have a job available for the injured employees when they were ready to return to work. This practice quickly gained the attention of the courts and legislatures and was rightly condemned. The employers were found to be chilling the rights of employees to pursue the rights given to them as a matter of law. As a matter of public policy, the right to pursue statutory rights has always been protected. Now states have statutes that make it illegal to fire an injured employee for filing a workers' compensation claim.[35] If such an employee is in fact terminated, the employer must be able to establish totally independent grounds for the termination or be subject to a tort action by the employee for wrongful discharge. This provides the injured employees the opportunity to seek reasonable compensation for their injuries and for wages lost from time not working without fear of losing employment. Ultimately, the workers' compensation laws have reduced the number and expense of lawsuits between employers and employees, encouraged employers to provide a safer working environment, and directly contributed to the flow of industry and commerce in this country.

## Employer Liability Laws

Certain circumstances, however, are exempt from otherwise applicable workers' compensation laws. For example, if an employer places an employee in a position of great danger and this action demonstrates a clear disregard for the safety of the employee, many states permit an avoidance of the workers' compensation laws in favor of an unlimited action for tort. In addition, certain types of employment that have been historically considered extremely dangerous with a high probability of serious injury or death of one's work life are subject to federal employer liability laws. These laws preceded workers' compensation laws and are limited primarily to the railroad and maritime industries.

Although each law has specific provisions, an employer liability law will generally permit a civil action by an employee against an employer for injuries received within the scope of employment. It must be shown, however, that both parties are subject to the statute and that the employer was somehow negligent. This differs from the no-fault standard of workers' compensation laws. In addition to federal employer liability laws, a number of states also have state employer liability laws for specified areas of employment. The federal laws do not necessarily apply to employees of the federal government. Rather, they are laws passed by the national government that apply to an entire industry that operates on an interstate basis.

Originally, employer liability laws were enacted to provide protection to a class of workers who were engaged in a hazardous occupation where serious injuries or fatalities were frequent, and where the workers were often disadvantaged economically and educationally. The reasoning behind such laws was to provide protection to employees whose education and ability to seek other types of employment were frequently limited—even more so after a serious injury. The injuries that commonly occurred in these industries were so serious that the employees were often prevented, through this combination of factors, from ever working again, thus leaving them and their families with no means of support other than government assistance. Consequently, legislatures enacted statutes to ease somewhat the burden of proving civil suits against employers while removing the limitations of recovery under the workers' compensation statutes. Although the statutes usually require the proof of negligence, they make the proof easier to establish.

## Discrimination Issues

It has only been during the past 100 years that employers have been charged with the responsibility to be fair to all persons in the manner in which they are hired, supervised, and terminated. Employers have long been subject to liability for injuries to employees or third parties that arose during employment. In the more recent past, the focus has been just as great on the injuries that affect the psychosocial and economic aspects of employment. Today, state and federal government legislatures and agencies have established minimum legal standards for employers regarding hiring, termination, and providing a suitable work environment. Although some common law liability remains, the majority of actions are based in alleged statutory violations of legislation designed to make the workplace more fair and appropriate to all employees.

A few major strides from 1850 to 1950 for minorities and women laid the foundation for the sweeping changes that were to come in the second half of the twentieth century. The social movements of the 1960s brought about a greater awareness of the rights of minorities, women, individuals with physical impairments, and other Americans who received disparate treatment in the workplace. Case after case established that many employers would not hire individuals with certain characteristics or would treat them differently from other employees. As a result, legislation and regulations were passed to protect various classes of people. These laws were designed to keep employers from discriminating against employees for possessing characteristics that had nothing to do with their ability to adequately perform the duties of employment. Such characteristics include gender, race, religion, and age. Similar restrictions apply for individuals who are physically impaired. If an employer is found to treat an employee differently, refuse to hire someone, or use as a cause for termination one or more of the characteristics of the protected classes, the employer is subject to scrutiny under federal law. If it is determined that the employer violated the legal standards by using improper reasons for hiring, termination, or discipline, then the employer may be subject to a variety of penalties.

Another area of employment law that has grown tremendously is the psychological safety of the work environment. Just as federal agencies such as OSHA strive to protect the employee from physical dangers on the job, the branches of state and federal government are now focused on protecting the employee from unnecessary psychological and emotional dangers on the job as well. One such example is sexual harassment. If an employee can demonstrate that an employer participated or acquiesced in a course of conduct that subjected the employee to an environment that was reasonably perceived as hostile because of differential treatment based on the gender or sexual preference of the employee, the employee may have a basis for legal action against the employer. This imposes on the employer the responsibility to monitor the conduct of all employees and to be responsive to complaints in a continuing effort to maintain a workplace that encourages fair and professional treatment of each employee by the employer and co-workers alike.

Although all states have workers' compensation laws in effect, some injuries or, actually, *causes* of injury are exempt from these statutes. Such a case may occur when an employer willfully or deliberately places an employee in great danger and that danger results in injury to the employee. Such willful or deliberate misconduct is often an exception to workers' compensation laws, and the employee has the opportunity to file a civil action for damages against the employer.[36] Although this action imposes the requirement of proving the wrongful conduct, there is no limitation on the amount of damages that can be claimed.

## MEDICAL MALPRACTICE

In the latter half of the twentieth century, a new term was coined: *litigation explosion.* This phrase came to represent the large number of cases, often based in tort, that were being brought in courts across the United States. Although the reason and timing of the event was largely predictable as a result of a growing mobile population and advancements in technology, it nonetheless gained a great deal of attention from news media. Many bar associations and legislatures took action to ensure frivolous lawsuits would not be encouraged or tolerated. Even so, the number of cases filed continued to grow. As time progressed and we entered the latter part of the twentieth century, a large number of these cases involved allegations of professional malfeasance by health care professionals. Although news media might insinuate that this is because of the greed of the legal profession, the "deep pockets" of medical providers, and their insurance companies, the reality is much less sinister.

The dramatic increase in cases with regard to the delivery of health care services can be attributed to several causes including but not limited to the following:

1. an aging population that is rapidly increasing in size and its needs for advanced health care,

2. dramatic advances in medical science,

3. a shortage of health care providers in relation to the number of individuals who require health care, and

4. the mass manufacturing of products that are untested in a large market in terms of safety.

Proponents who desire legislation that limits both awards and the prosecution of cases alleging medical malpractice often assert that the problem lies with an overzealous legal profession and juries that are too free with their damage awards. However, it cannot be ignored that studies of health care providers show an overwhelming number have personally witnessed instances of professional malfeasance in the delivery of health care. Regardless of the causes, the reality remains that the causes listed above are likely to continue in the foreseeable future. This in turn will produce circumstances of malfeasance whether through accident or sheer recklessness. Because, however, of the need to contain costs of health care that are directly impacted by rising malpractice insurance rates following judgments against insurers of health care providers, certain measures must be followed. Specifically, allegations of malpractice should be thoroughly investigated at the earliest opportunity. Health care providers and those in charge of risk management in health care facilities must be vigilant when providing health care services and products.

## TORT DEFENSES

In response to the many theories of liability in tort, defenses for conduct have been developed that are used to justify the defendant's actions or expose the plaintiff's own part in the occurrence that produced the injury. Even today, these defenses are developing and changing. Although they vary slightly among jurisdictions, the underlying principles are substantially the same.

### Contributory and Comparative Negligence

**contributory negligence**
The doctrine that maintains a plaintiff who contributes in any way to his or her injury cannot recover from a negligent defendant.

**Contributory negligence** is a well-known defense in this country. At one time, it was highly popular but is now experiencing a decline in popularity. In the past, the courts applied this defense when a defendant could prove that the plaintiff contributed to his or her own injury by some form of negligent conduct. For example, in a car accident, although the defendant was driving under the influence of alcohol, the plaintiff may have been speeding on a dark and rainy night. The plaintiff was also acting negligently and contributed to the cause of the accident. When a court applies the defense of contributory negligence, the plaintiff cannot recover any damages from the defendant. The rationale for this defense is that one should not ultimately receive compensation for injuries caused by one's own wrongdoing.[37]

The defense of contributory negligence has become less popular for several reasons. As society has become increasingly complex, so have the causes of injuries. No longer are causes of injuries simply determined. In addition, a growing body of thought reasons that although plaintiffs should not recover for their own misconduct, neither should defendants be relieved of liability for theirs. Accordingly, the theory of **comparative negligence** has been developed. In comparative negligence, each party's degree of negligence is assigned a percentage of the fault for the occurrence.[38] The jury arrives at such a calculation and reduces the judgment for the plaintiff by the percentage that the plaintiff contributed to his or her own injury.

**comparative negligence**
Degree of plaintiff's own negligent conduct that was responsible for plaintiff's injury.

Some jurisdictions apply pure comparative negligence in which a plaintiff who is found by the jury to be 99 percent at fault recovers only 1 percent of the damages. However, many jurisdictions apply modified comparative negligence, which prevents any recovery if a plaintiff was the significant cause of the injury—that is, was more than 50 percent at fault. In some states, a combination of contributory and comparative negligence applies. If a plaintiff is grossly negligent, contributory negligence will apply. Otherwise, comparative negligence will apply.[39]

Comparative negligence responds to the plaintiff's negligence without relieving the defendant of liability for his or her own misconduct. A steady trend by jurisdictions in this country has been to adopt the theory of comparative negligence in some form and abandon the traditional theory of contributory negligence.

## Assumption of Risk

The defense of **assumption of risk** is also seeing some decline in response to the growth of comparative negligence. Traditionally, a defendant could prevent recovery by a plaintiff if the defendant could prove that the plaintiff was aware of the risk of danger, appreciated the seriousness of the risk, and voluntarily exposed him- or herself to the risk.[40] As with the application of comparative negligence, the recovery would not be barred but would be modified.

**assumption of risk**
Defense to negligence on the basis that the plaintiff knew of, appreciated, and voluntarily encountered the danger of defendant's conduct.

Many jurisdictions still accept assumption of risk as a defense to establish the degree to which the plaintiff was responsible for his or her own injury. An example of assumption of risk is a person attending a car race who sits at the edge of the racetrack. It is easily foreseeable that a car traveling at high speed could lose control and strike the onlooker. If the onlooker nevertheless remains in this position of danger, it may well be held that he or she assumed the risk of the danger.

## Last Clear Chance

Another still widely used defense is the doctrine of **last clear chance**, which, in reality, is a defense to a defense. When a defendant claims a defense such as contributory negligence that would bar recovery by a plaintiff, the plaintiff may respond with a claim of last clear chance. The doctrine states that even though a plaintiff contributed to endangering him- or herself, the defendant had the last clear opportunity to avoid the occurrence and prevent the plaintiff's injury but failed to do so.[41] An example is the preceding driving case. Even though the plaintiff was speeding in bad weather, if the defendant could have swerved at the last second and did not, then the plaintiff could still recover for the defendant's failure to take advantage of the last clear chance to avoid the occurrence.

**last clear chance**
Defense of plaintiff responding to defenses of allegedly negligent defendant, in which plaintiff claims defendant had the last opportunity to avoid plaintiff's injury irrespective of plaintiff's own negligence.

## Intentional Tort Defenses

Defenses raised in response to claims of intentional tort include the charge that not all of the elements were satisfied as well as consent, privilege, immunity, and various procedural defenses.

Although the first defense—that not all elements were satisfied—may be raised as a defense in any type of tort action, it is especially appropriate in an intentional tort case. By definition, the elements of intentional torts tend to be quite specific. Thus, it is usually much easier to establish the absence of a specific event than it is to establish that the defendant's conduct met the reasonable standard of care under the circumstances in a negligence action.

Similarly, the defenses of consent, privilege, immunity, and involuntary conduct are seen most often in intentional tort suits. The defense of consent consists of proof by the defendant that the plaintiff in fact consented to or agreed overtly or by implication to the defendant's action. For example, a plaintiff might sue a defendant for battery that allegedly occurred when the defendant physician operated on the plaintiff. The defendant could claim that the plaintiff, by subjecting himself to the surgery, consented to procedures that the defendant deemed appropriate during surgery.

The defense of privilege is quite different from that of consent. In consent, the focus is on the conduct of the plaintiff toward the defendant; in privilege, the view is taken that regardless of the plaintiff's agreement or protestations, the defendant had a special legal right to act. For example, a plaintiff attempts to collect unemployment and is denied because the defendant (plaintiff's former employer) informed the labor department that the plaintiff was fired for drug use on the job. The plaintiff cannot successfully sue the defendant for defamation because the employer has a privileged relationship with the government. By protecting employers, the government has the benefit of full disclosure and can therefore deny benefits to someone who is guilty of criminal activity. A variety of situations exist in which a party has a privileged relationship, and any tortious activity resulting from that privileged relationship cannot be prosecuted by a plaintiff.

Another common privilege is that of self-defense. Depending on the circumstances, a person has the right to use reasonable or necessary force to defend him- or herself and can even use force to defend someone else if that person was entitled to use self-defense. Limited force can also be used to defend property, but not if it would result in a breach of the peace, and the privilege never extends to the use of deadly force to defend property.

Like privilege, immunity gives protection to otherwise guilty defendants. The most common example is that of sovereign immunity. Historically, no lawsuit could be brought against the government for the torts committed by government servants. This was inherently unfair. However, to totally lift this ban could result in enough lawsuits against the government to bankrupt it. Consequently, federal and state legislatures have enacted laws that allow suits against the government in limited circumstances and in accordance with strict procedural rules. In this way, the government is accountable for its torts but is not at risk of being victimized by a litigation explosion of its own.

## ASSIGNMENT 9.3

Examine each of the following circumstances and identify any major tort defenses that would apply.

1. John sued Corey after a car and pedestrian accident. Corey was found guilty of speeding immediately before the accident. At the time of the accident, John was on foot crossing the street midblock rather than in a designated crosswalk. The jury found each of the parties 50 percent at fault.

2. John sued Corey after a car and pedestrian accident. Corey was found guilty of speeding immediately before the accident. At the time of the accident, John was on foot

(continued)

## ASSIGNMENT 9.3 (Continued)

crossing the street midblock rather than in a designated crosswalk. The jury found each of the parties 50 percent at fault and prevented John from recovering for his injuries.

3. John sued Corey after a car and pedestrian accident. At the time of the accident, John was on foot crossing the street midblock rather than in a designated crosswalk. The jury found John was the predominant cause of the accident.

4. John sued Corey after a car and pedestrian accident. At the time of the accident, John was on foot crossing the street midblock rather than in a designated crosswalk.

Corey claimed that traffic conditions prevented him from swerving and avoiding John and that John could have stepped out of the way of the vehicle if he had been paying attention to the street traffic.

5. John sued Corey after a car and pedestrian accident. Corey was found guilty of speeding immediately before the accident. At the time of the accident, John was on foot crossing the street midblock rather than in a designated crosswalk. The jury found that John, by entering a heavily trafficked street outside the designated area, should have known that he was subjecting himself to danger.

## DAMAGES IN TORT ACTIONS

In the successful tort action, the trier of fact is faced with the task of awarding damages. In all actions at law, damages are monetary. The amount depends on a myriad of factors as well as the law of the jurisdiction. Some legislatures have enacted law that precludes anything but strictly compensatory damages; others allow punitive damages, prejudgment interest, and attorney's fees. The purpose here is to distinguish the types of damage that are possible if permitted legally by law of the jurisdiction.

| Damage | Purpose |
|---|---|
| Compensatory | To compensate the plaintiff for injury. |
| Specials | Those items of compensatory damage that can be specifically calculated—for example, medical bills. |
| Generals | Those items of compensatory damage that must be estimated as to monetary value—for example, pain and suffering, loss of reputation. |
| Punitive (also known as exemplary damages) | To punish defendant and to deter defendant and others from future similar conduct. |
| Nominal | Allowed in cases other than negligence (in which actual damage is an element that must be proven) for commission of a tort by defendant but for which no actual loss by plaintiff is proven. |

Typically, the award to the plaintiff will consist of compensatory damages. The types of damage that support an award of compensatory damage include property damage, physical injury, lost wages, and more abstract notions such as pain and suffering, shortened life expectancy, loss of consortium (elements of the marital relationship), and emotional distress. If proven, all are acceptable bases for compensation. In those jurisdictions where punitives are permitted, they may be awarded in especially egregious cases where the defendant's conduct was particularly reckless.

## ETHICAL CONSIDERATIONS

The importance of ethics is obvious in such areas of law as contract, property, and business. At first glance, it is not so obvious in tort law. However, the requirement for ethical conduct is especially important in torts because juries in these cases are required to consider intangible factors such as pain, suffering, lost future wages, disability, and disfigurement. All of these factors contain built-in emotional triggers. For the unethical person, such cases provide an opportunity to manipulate and take advantage of a situation to the detriment of another. Early in the chapter, the litigation explosion was mentioned. In addition to this so-called explosion, a great deal of publicity has focused on some lawyers and plaintiffs who file frivolous claims in the hope of monetary gain. The response of many legislatures has been to enact statutes that penalize anyone found guilty of filing an unfounded claim. In turn, lawyers and their clients alike have been put on notice to carefully evaluate a situation before proceeding with a formal lawsuit.

## Question

Assume you are a lawyer and a client comes to you with what appears to be an attempt to obtain money from a proposed defendant through an obviously unfounded claim of injury. What should you do?

## ETHICAL CIRCUMSTANCE

You are a paralegal working in a civil litigation firm. During your collection of evidence in the investigation of a pending case, you discover the client has filed the exact type of suit with the same facts and injuries filed by another firm in a neighboring jurisdiction. Even the dates of the alleged injuries are similar. The client claims to have fallen and been injured in a retail store, with no alleged witnesses to either instance. Should the client be confronted about the situation or should it be assumed the client is just accident-prone?

## ● | CHAPTER SUMMARY

The law of torts is growing and changing on a daily basis. The courts are constantly being presented with variations on the basic principles. Legislatures in every state are considering additional statutes that will affect tort law. As a result, it is a challenge to keep current on these changes and the way that they affect our lives both personally and professionally.

Some constants remain in tort law, especially the recognized areas of tort. Negligence is the appropriate claim when one party has a duty to act with a certain degree of care toward another party and that duty is breached. For a negligence claim to succeed, it must be shown that the breach was the legal and factual cause of an injury and that the injury is of a type and extent that is compensable.

When a party's conduct goes beyond mere disregard for potentially dangerous circumstances and involves actions that are nearly certain to result in significant injury to another, an intentional tort has been committed. Although the knowledge of the actor may be more difficult to prove in such cases, when it is accomplished, the penalties are often more severe.

Finally, there are certain extremely dangerous situations in which no amount of care can prevent injury to innocent bystanders. In such instances, the party that produces the situation and benefits from it will be held responsible for the injuries. This is totally irrespective of whether that party knew of or took steps to avoid the injury. The cost of the benefit is responsibility for the injury as a matter of strict liability.

These principles have remained basically constant, although the manner and circumstances in which they are applied have changed. In addition, defenses to tort law continue to evolve and develop into principles that will produce the fairest result for all concerned. This is evidenced by the shift from the absolute defense of contributory negligence to the defense of comparative negligence, which apportions fault between the parties.

## ● CHAPTER TERMS

| | | |
|---|---|---|
| assumption of risk | intentional tort | proximate cause |
| comparative negligence | last clear chance | reasonable conduct |
| contributory negligence | negligence | strict liability |

## ● REVIEW QUESTIONS

1. How does negligence differ from an intentional tort?
2. When is an employer liable for the acts of an employee?
3. Under what circumstances is assumption of risk applied?
4. Which party claims last clear chance?
5. What are the types of defamation actions?
6. How have workers' compensation laws affected tort actions?
7. When can *res ipsa loquitur* be applied?
8. What types of claims involve strict liability?
9. How do the torts of assault and battery differ?
10. How does a claim of strict liability differ from a claim for negligence?

## ● HELPFUL WEB SITES

| | |
|---|---|
| American Tort Reform Association | http://www.atra.org |
| Tort Law at Megalaw.com | http://www.megalaw.com |
| A Guide to Tort Law | http://www.hg.org/torts.html |

## ● INTERNET ASSIGNMENT 9.1

Using Internet resources, identify whether your state has a statute that disallows frivolous lawsuits (claims determined to be unfounded).

## ● INTERNET ASSIGNMENT 9.2

Does your jurisdiction have limitations on recovery in medical malpractice suits?

## ● ENDNOTES

1. Prosser, *Handbook on Torts* (St. Paul. MN: West, 1971), Chapter 2, Section 7.
2. *Id.*
3. *Id.*
4. *Id.*
5. *Id.* at Chapter 5, Section 30.
6. *Palsgraf v. Long Island R. R. Co.,* 248 N.Y. 339, 162 N.E. 99 (N.Y. 1928).
7. *Id.,* see dissent of Justice Andrews.
8. 65 C.J.S., Negligence, Section 10 (1955); (1987 supp.).
9. 65 C.J.S., Negligence, Section 11 (1955); (1987 supp.).

10. See note 9, *supra.*
11. See note 10, *supra.*
12. *Id.*
13. *Id.*
14. *Id.*
15. Prosser, *Handbook on Torts,* Chapter 7, Section 41.
16. *Id.*
17. *Id.*
18. William Statsky, *Torts: Personal Injury Litigation* (St. Paul, MN: West, 1982), p. 364.
19. *Id.*
20. Annot., 23 A.L.R.3rd 1083.
21. Prosser, *Handbook on Torts,* Chapter 5, Section 31.
22. American Law Institute, *Restatement of the Law on Torts II,* Section 21(1), 1976.
23. *Id.,* Section 13; *Mason v. Cohn,* 108 Misc.2d 674, 438 N.Y.S.2d 462 (1981).
24. Statsky, *Torts: Personal Injury Litigation,* p. 415.
25. See note 23, Section 35; *Cimino v. Rosen,* 193 Neb. 162, 225 N.W.2d 567 (1975).
26. *Id.*
27. See note 23, Section 217; *Guin v. City of Riviera Beach, Fla.,* 388 So.2d 604 (Fla.App. 1980).
28. See note 23, Sections 525–552.
29. See note 23, Sections 558–559.
30. *Id.*
31. *Id.*
32. *Id.; New York Times v. Sullivan,* 376 U.S. 254, 84 S.Ct. 710, 11 L.Ed.2d 686 (1964).
33. See note 23, Section 46.
34. 81 Am.Jur., Workers' Compensation, Section 1; 315.
35. Annot., 32 A.L.R.4th 1221.
36. Annot., 96 A.L.R.3rd 1064.
37. *Id.*
38. *Id.*
39. See note 23, Section 479; *Ortego v. State Farm Mutual Auto Ins. Co.,* 295 So.2d 593 (La.App. 1974).
40. See note 23, Section 496; *Parr v. Hamnes,* 303 Minn. 333, 228 N.W.2d 234 (1975).
41. Prosser, *Handbook on Torts.*

## STUDENT CD-ROM

For additional materials, please go to the CD in this book.

## ONLINE COMPANION™

For additional resources, please go to www.paralegal.delmar.cengage.com

## CHAPTER 10

# Family Law

## HAS THE AMERICAN FAMILY BECOME A GAME OF CHANCE?

For thousands of years, the term *family* was well defined and confined. A family meant that a woman served as wife and mother, a man served as husband and father, and in most instances children were born to the couple or came in the form of adopted relatives. Then came the Industrial Revolution, wars that paved the way for women to enter the workforce en masse to replace the men who were off fighting, and all of the other societal and cultural developments that led to the evolution of the notion of family.

Today families come in quite literally every configuration. Like popular word games in which random letters are gathered together to form cohesive terms, families are now created by the lifestyle choices of the individuals involved. Marriage may or may not be a factor. It is no longer assumed that the two members of a couple will be members of opposite sexes. Children may be born "the old-fashioned way," adopted from across the world, or even engineered through scientific advances that include the DNA of one or both parents or even total strangers. Certainly many people oppose what they consider to be the "breakdown" of the American family, but if individuals come together in unity and provide a nurturing supportive environment for each other and for children, then the question begs to be asked: Is it a breakdown or is it an expansion? Or is it a sort of hi-tech return to societies thousands of years old where the village worked as a complete unit to ensure the survival of all?

## CHAPTER OBJECTIVES

After reading this chapter, you should be able to:

- Explain the requirements for a valid antenuptial agreement.
- List the requirements for marriage.
- Explain the purpose of legal annulment.
- Discuss the rights of parties who cohabit without marriage.

- Discuss the function of temporary orders.
- Explain how courts determine custody issues.
- Discuss the disadvantages of joint custody.
- Explain the concept of no-fault divorce.

Family law is an area of U.S. law that experienced phenomenal growth in the twentieth century. Before the latter half of that century, divorce was a rare occurrence. In addition, a woman's role was perceived to be primarily that of a caretaker of home and children, not of a worker in the public workplace. In the event of divorce, there was no question but that the husband would be solely responsible for the material needs of his wife and children. The relatively few divorces, social pressures, and the fact that the public was largely uneducated in matters of law resulted in few challenges to the fairness of court-ordered divorce settlements.

Over the years, the role of women changed in large part because of technological developments, the opening of the job market to women, and the growth of educational opportunities for women. Gradually, women began to live independently. This trend increased markedly during World War II, when large numbers of women entered the nation's workforce for the first time. In addition, our society became more mobile as families relocated away from the traditional extended family to find jobs. These societal changes were accompanied by an increased awareness of legal rights. And for the first time, specific laws were put into place that protected the rights of victims of domestic violence. As a consequence of these developments, the option of dissolving a marriage became a more realistic choice for many people. Multiple marriages in one lifetime became more likely; as a result, more detailed laws on the total marriage relationship became necessary.

The changes in family law have ranged from defining and, in many states, abolishing common law marriage to regulating custody and visitation rights when parents live in different states. Aside from the fact that virtually everyone has some contact with family law during his or her lifetime, this area of law is having an increasing effect on the workplace. For example, some employers have the duty to report and withhold wages for payment of child support or maintenance (alimony), and job transfers or changes may be delayed while a divorced parent seeks changes in the visitation schedule or obtains court permission to remove a child from the state.

This chapter addresses the creation and dissolution of marriages and the relationships that result from terminated marriages. Its emphasis will be on the dissolution of marriages and the resulting relationships because the parties are generally in accord with respect to marital concerns such as child care and education during a marriage. It is when discord occurs and cannot be resolved that the parties seek intermediary help from the legal system.

## MARRIAGE AND ANNULMENT

As long as there has been marriage, there has always been a sort of "buyer's remorse" when one or both parties or members of their families look up and ask, "What was I . . ." or "What were you thinking?" Whether by misguided intentions or a failure to observe appropriate legal standards, there are circumstances in which a marriage should not have occurred or never really took effect as a matter of law. This section examines what may occur to create or void a legal marriage.

### Antenuptial (Prenuptial) Agreements

**Antenuptial agreements** (sometimes referred to as **prenuptial agreements**) are contracts entered into by parties who are going to be married. Such contracts provide for the division of property rights at the time the marital relationship between the parties ends. Originally, antenuptial agreements dealt only with property division on the death of a spouse. Ordinarily, one spouse cannot entirely disinherit the other. If no provisions are made by will, then the surviving spouse can elect under a special statute (one exists in each state) to receive a percentage of the estate. In a traditional antenuptial agreement, however, each spouse may agree by contract not to challenge the provisions of the other spouse's will. This is often done when one spouse possesses a great deal more wealth or when one spouse has children from a previous marriage and seeks to protect the children's inheritance.

More recently, antenuptial agreements have taken on an entirely new meaning. In a time in which dissolution occurs frequently, some parties attempt to arrange in advance for an orderly distribution of debts and assets should the marriage be dissolved. These agreements are no longer reserved only for the wealthy. Now they are often a reasonable alternative for spouses who each have a career and the ability to contribute financially to the relationship. Many such couples have minor children from previous relationships whose interests must be protected. For these and other reasons, an antenuptial agreement often resolves the concerns that may prevent parties from getting married at all. The agreement allows the parties to continue their relationship with one less concern. Perhaps the agreement will never be utilized—but if and when it is, there is some reassurance in knowing that reasonable terms were arranged when each of the parties was acting logically with fairness to the other in mind.

**antenuptial agreement (prenuptial agreement)**
Agreement between parties who intend to marry that typically provides for the disposition of the property rights of the parties in the event the marriage ends by death or divorce.

**Requirements for an Enforceable Agreement.** It has taken some time for the courts and legislature to determine the requirements for an enforceable antenuptial agreement with provisions for a dissolution of the marriage. The agreement is essentially a contract and must contain the necessary elements of any contract.[1] Most states also require the agreement to be in writing pursuant to the statute of frauds. An exception to the requirement of writing occurs when one party can demonstrate that he or she has significantly altered his or her position in a detrimental manner as a direct result of reliance on the other party's promises in an oral antenuptial agreement.[2]

---

## APPLICATION 10.1

Leslie and Stuart decide to marry. Leslie lives in the southwest United States and Stuart lives in New York. The two agree that Stuart will quit his lucrative job and sell his Manhattan apartment to move to Los Angeles, where they will be married and live. Because she wants to get married as soon as possible and before the impending birth of their first child, Leslie agrees that if Stuart will start over financially, everything that is hers will be his. Stuart leaves a job in which he would have been vested in the company retirement plan in just a few months. He also takes a loss on his apartment, which he had owned for less than a year.

Stuart moves to California and the two are married. Leslie wanted to take advantage of the time together before they became parents, so she planned a six-week honeymoon in Europe. Approximately eight weeks after they return, Stuart has not found a job. Leslie decides he was not the dreamboat she once thought and kicks him out. She files for divorce. Stuart claims the existence of an antenuptial agreement that would entitle him to one-half of everything Leslie owns.

Even though the agreement was never reduced to writing, Stuart took significant steps detrimental to his own interests as a result of Leslie's promises. This would likely create an enforceable contract.

*Point for Discussion:* Would the result be likely to be different if it were Stuart who filed for divorce?

---

In addition to the requirement of writing, consideration must be given for the promises of each party in the antenuptial agreement. Consideration is given by each party in exchange for the promises made in the terms of the contract and is easily satisfied. Traditionally, the promise of marriage by each party has served as consideration for the other party's agreement to the terms of the antenuptial contract. Finally, a valid antenuptial agreement must be made with the free will of both parties without duress or coercion, conditional on divorce, and not be unconscionable either when made or implemented.

**Challenging an Agreement.** Mutual assent to the terms of the contract has been carefully examined in most cases in which such a contract has been challenged. The court is concerned that unscrupulous persons would take advantage of the position of another and persuade the other person to enter an agreement that, in the event of divorce, would be inherently unfair (known as *overreaching*). Examples include parties who do not disclose the full measure of their assets and liabilities and parties who accumulate assets directly from the support of their spouse but in a dissolution action allege that the support did not occur or was not substantial.

## APPLICATION 10.2

A wealthy elderly man married a 20-year-old exotic dancer who had virtually no assets at the time of the marriage. After full disclosure, the parties entered a written agreement stating that if the marriage came to an end for any reason within five years, the young woman would receive a $20,000 settlement and no further rights either through divorce or inheritance. The man would be entitled to 90 percent of any assets accumulated by the woman from the man by any means during the marriage. During the next three years, the woman asked for and received numerous pieces of jewelry from the man as gifts. The value of the jewelry was estimated to be $4 million.

During the fourth year of the marriage, the man decided to divorce the woman. She claimed that gifts are not considered part of the settlement because contracts for gifts are unenforceable. However, the written agreement did not require the man to make the gifts and thus they did not defeat the agreement. Furthermore, the agreement clearly stated that he was entitled to a return of 90 percent of the value of items obtained by any means. It is likely the agreement would be enforced and the woman would be required to turn over 90 percent of the value of the jewelry less $20,000.

*Point for Discussion:* Would the result be different if the woman had not asked for the gifts?

As the preceding example illustrates, it is crucial that any antenuptial agreement fully disclose assets and liabilities.[3] In addition, the agreement should contain provisions for some fair and reasonable economic settlement. The parties do not usually anticipate divorce and cannot anticipate what their accumulation of wealth will be at the time of a divorce. However, they can anticipate that each will contribute to the marriage, and assets should be divided in a manner fair to each based on that contribution.

**Upholding an Agreement.** A difficulty in dealing with the settlement provision is that courts will often not recognize an agreement that provides for a specific financial award because such an agreement is seen as encouraging dissolution of the marriage in an attempt to obtain a monetary settlement.[4] The courts will, however, uphold agreements that provide for a fair distribution of assets to be determined by an objective third party, such as a court, in the event the parties should cease to share marital assets. This reassures the parties that they are not being taken advantage of. Such an agreement also does not include any anticipation of divorce that the court might see as encouraging the end of a marriage. To ensure an enforceable and fair agreement, each party should seek independent legal counsel before entering into an antenuptial agreement.

## ASSIGNMENT 10.1

Consider the following facts and identify those that would be necessary to (1) disclose or (2) include in an antenuptial agreement.

1. Kim has two children from a former marriage. Mike has no children.

2. Kylar has an annual salary of $37,000. Corrine has an annual salary of $34,000.

3. Georgia has investments worth $1,400. Salvador has no investments.

4. Francine has an annual salary of $350,000 and receives annual bonuses that average $200,000. Corey has an annual salary of $42,000.

5. As the result of a trust set up by his grandfather, 21-year-old Dominic will receive approximately $2.1 million on his twenty-fifth birthday. He is a freshman in college with no job. Denise is twenty-one years old and works as a nurse earning $45,000 per year.

## Requirements for Marriage

The process of getting married has become quite complex in the legal sense. In many states, two people who wish to marry cannot simply obtain a license at the justice of the peace and be married at the same time. Because marriage so deeply affects the lives of those involved and because many marriages do not succeed, laws have been created to establish the best possible environment for the marriage. These laws also address issues of public health and various other concerns linked to citizen welfare. Every state has enacted laws that set forth certain requirements that must be met before a recognized marriage will exist.

**Capacity and Consent.** For a marriage to be valid, there must be capacity and consent.[5] As previously noted, capacity requires that each party be of legal age and not be declared legally incompetent. Each party must be capable of making the decision to enter into such an agreement. Many states also have provisions for parental or court consent in the event a party to the marriage is not of legal age or has been legally determined to be incapable of appreciating the consequences and responsibilities of marriage. If there is capacity, it is also necessary that each party openly and voluntarily consent to the marriage.

**Marriage License.** Each state has a licensure provision for marriages.[6] Before a legal marriage exists, the parties are directed to make application for a marriage license. The license is generally granted unless some factor exists that would prevent the marriage from being legal under state law. Examples of such factors include (1) the parties are family members who have a close blood relationship (each state indicates the degree of kinship that will prevent a valid marriage), (2) the parties are persons of the same sex (although this is a highly volatile subject of law at state and federal levels and some states give basic rights as domestic partners), (3) one or both parties lack legal capacity, and (4) one of the parties is already in an existing marriage.

Blood tests and a waiting period are also often required to obtain a marriage license. The purpose behind blood tests is twofold. First, it is presumed that each party to the marriage has the right to know whether the other carries any sexually transmitted disease that could place the party at risk. In light of the AIDS crisis in the United States, some states have amended their statutes to require an additional blood test or disclosure that would provide information regarding the presence of HIV. The second reason for blood tests is that the parties should be informed if there is a conflict between their particular blood types that may make it difficult for them to have healthy children. Although medicine and medical technologies have advanced to the point that most problems can be treated effectively, the parties are still presumed to be entitled to this information.

The statutes that require a waiting period (usually a matter of a few days) seek to discourage marriages that are entered into without sufficient thought to the consequences. Thus, requiring a brief delay between issuance of the license and the time when it can be validated by a judge or minister encourages the parties to consider the ramifications of their action.

**Marriage Vows.** Finally, the parties are ordinarily required to solemnize the marriage. This involves the exchange of vows (an agreement to marry) in the presence of one who is permitted to legally acknowledge the marriage.[7] Usually, this is a minister or a judge, who will then validate the license by certifying that the parties have indeed agreed to be married. At that time, the minister or judge and the parties will sign the license. Additional witnesses to the marriage also are often required to sign the license. If citizens of one state wish to marry but would not be permitted to do so in their own state, they may not simply go to another state for the purpose of marrying. Many states now have laws that declare a marriage invalid if it was entered into in another state for the purpose of avoiding the first state's laws. Thus, in some states, parties otherwise unable to legally marry can no longer cross a state line to be married. They must be able to show that they had valid reasons for conducting the marriage ceremony in another state.

## Annulment

A legal **annulment** is a judicial declaration that a marriage never actually existed because the legal requirements for a valid marriage were not met.[8] This is to be distinguished from a religious annulment. The latter is granted by a church authority for reasons of, and in accordance with, religious procedures. A religious annulment has no legal meaning or effect. Accordingly, a legal annulment has no religious significance.

Legal annulments can be obtained for a variety of reasons. Whatever the basis for the annulment, one requirement is common to all. The reason that the marriage should be declared invalid must have existed at the time the parties entered into the marriage.[9] Therefore, if an annulment is sought on the basis that one or both of the parties was under the legal age or without sufficient mental capacity, the incapacity must have existed at the time the parties attempted a marriage. Other common reasons for annulment include close blood relationships, incest, or bigamy. The general rule is that an annulment may be granted if the reason for the annulment would have legally prevented the parties from marrying if it had been previously disclosed.

If the party seeking the annulment has taken any steps toward accepting and acknowledging the marriage relationship, his or her request may be denied. The theory is that one who attempts to solemnize a marriage cannot then take the position that the marriage never existed.[10] This is especially similar to the contractual defense of unclean hands, which holds that a party who helped create the circumstances for a breach of contract cannot then turn and allege that he or she has been injured because of the breach. Nevertheless, the courts may still grant an annulment if the reason is a serious one such as bigamy or incest.

Less frequently encountered actions for annulment include actions based on frolic, duress, or fraud. If the parties married as some sort of joke or game and never truly intended a binding marriage, the court will grant an annulment. As with most contractual agreements, intent is required for a valid marriage to exist. For example, a marriage by parties who were intoxicated at the time of the marriage and did not intend to actually marry would be invalid.

If a party believes that he or she has no choice but to marry or alternatively suffer serious physical, financial, or other harm, a marriage of duress has taken place. Effectively, the party had no real choice in the matter, and the courts will likely find no real intent to marry. As a result, annulment is a decidedly real possibility in such situations.

Annulment on the basis of fraud is one of the most difficult to establish. The party seeking the annulment must prove all of the necessary elements of fraud. In the case of marriage, the elements are that (1) a misrepresentation of a fact essential to the marriage relationship must have been made and (2) the party claiming fraud must have reasonably relied on the misrepresentation as truth when making the decision to marry. Examples of misrepresentations sufficient for an annulment based on fraud include religious beliefs or ability to biologically parent children.

Although an annulment is a declaration that the marriage relationship never existed in the eyes of the law, it does not mean that no relationship existed. Therefore, the courts may apportion rights and duties regarding property, assets, debts, and even children as if the annulment were an action for dissolution of marriage

**annulment**
Court order that restores the parties to their positions before the marriage. The marriage of the parties is void and treated as if it never existed. It is permissible in situations in which a particular legal disability prevented the marriage from becoming valid.

(divorce).[11] The purpose is to return the parties to their original position before the marriage. If the parties have contributed anything to the relationship or if there are children, then the court will consider the rights under the same equitable grounds used in dissolving a marital relationship. Exhibit 10.1 is an example of an annulment law.

## Common Law Marriage

A minority of states still allow marriages created by common law. Such marital relationships are created by agreement of the parties. However, the formal requisites of license and legal solemnization by vows are not observed. Even states that do not permit the creation of common law marriages will recognize a common law marriage validly established in another state.

Generally, no public record of a common law marriage is made. Contrary to popular belief, a common law marriage is not based on the length of time two parties live together. Rather, the courts usually examine the following in determining whether such a marriage exists:

1. Did the parties hold themselves out to the public as married?
2. Did the parties cohabit?
3. Did the parties file joint tax returns?
4. Does the conduct of the parties indicate an intent to be married?

If the evidence is insufficient to establish a common law marriage or the relationship was created in a state that does not recognize common law marriage, the parties still may have legal rights under principles that deal with cohabitation (which is discussed in greater detail in the section that addresses nonmarital relationships).

## The Marriage Relationship

Today, most states have statutes that impose an equal duty on each spouse to aid and financially support the other spouse during the marriage. Thus, it is no longer the sole duty of the husband to provide financial support for the wife. The practical result is that in the event of a dissolution, the husband may also be entitled to financial support and, in most cases, maintenance (alimony) is no longer awarded for life unless special circumstances exist. (These specifics are discussed later in the section that deals with the question of maintenance.)

During the marriage, the spouses have an ongoing duty to provide support of at least that which is necessary to meet the needs of the parties.[12] Such necessities include food, shelter, and clothing. If one party has agreed to work outside the home while the other remains at home, then that party also has a duty to provide items necessary to the couple's existence. Often what is considered necessary is largely influenced by the income of the spouses and what that income enables the parties to provide.

During the marriage, most states recognize the theory of marital debt. Thus, if one spouse assumes a debt, the other spouse is equally bound. This becomes particularly important if the parties subsequently terminate their relationship. The marital debts must be apportioned fairly while taking into account the ability of each party to satisfy the claims of outside creditors. (The subject of apportionment is addressed later in the section that deals with property and debt division.)

The primary rule regarding existing marriages is the policy of nonintervention. The courts generally refuse to become involved in settling marital disputes regarding the duties of the parties.[13] When third parties such as creditors become involved and debts are not being paid, the court may declare that both parties are

**Exhibit 10.1** McKinney's Consolidated Laws of New York Annotated Domestic Relations Law Chapter 14 of the Consolidated Laws Article 9—Action to Annul a Marriage or Declare It Void

§ 140. Action for judgment declaring nullity of void marriages or annulling voidable marriage

(a) Former husband or wife living. An action to declare the nullity of a void marriage upon the ground that the former husband or wife of one of the parties was living, the former marriage being in force, may be maintained by either of the parties during the life-time of the other, or by the former husband or wife.

(b) Party under age of consent. An action to annul a marriage on the ground that one or both of the parties had not attained the age of legal consent may be maintained by the infant, or by either parent of the infant, or by the guardian of the infant's person; or the court may allow the action to be maintained by any person as the next friend of the infant. But a marriage shall not be annulled under this subdivision at the suit of a party who was of the age of legal consent when it was contracted, or by a party who for any time after he or she attained that age freely cohabited with the other party as husband or wife.

(c) Party a mentally retarded person or mentally ill person. An action to annul a marriage on the ground that one of the parties thereto was a mentally retarded person may be maintained at any time during the life-time of either party by any relative of a mentally retarded person, who has an interest to avoid the marriage. An action to annul a marriage on the ground that one of the parties thereto was a mentally ill person may be maintained at any time during the continuance of the mental illness, or, after the death of the mentally ill person in that condition, and during the life of the other party to the marriage, by any relative of the mentally ill person who has an interest to avoid the marriage. Such an action may also be maintained by the mentally ill person at any time after restoration to a sound mind; but in that case, the marriage should not be annulled if it appears that the parties freely cohabited as husband and wife after the mentally ill person was restored to a sound mind. Where one of the parties to a marriage was a mentally ill person at the time of the marriage, an action may also be maintained by the other party at any time during the continuance of the mental illness, provided the plaintiff did not know of the mental illness at the time of the marriage. Where no relative of the mentally retarded person or mentally ill person brings an action to annul the marriage and the mentally ill person is not restored to sound mind, the court may allow an action for that purpose to be maintained at any time during the life-time of both the parties to the marriage, by any person as the next friend of the mentally retarded person or mentally ill person.

(d) Physical incapacity. An action to annul a marriage on the ground that one of the parties was physically incapable of entering into the marriage state may be maintained by the injured party against the party whose incapacity is alleged; or such an action may be maintained by the party who was incapable against the other party, provided the incapable party was unaware of the incapacity at the time of marriage, or if aware of such incapacity, did not know it was incurable. Such an action can be maintained only where an incapacity continues and is incurable, and must be commenced before five years have expired since the marriage.

(e) Consent by force, duress or fraud. An action to annul a marriage on the ground that the consent of one of the parties thereto was obtained by force or duress may be maintained at any time by the party, whose consent was so obtained. An action to annul a marriage on the ground that the consent of one of the parties thereto was obtained by fraud may be maintained by the party whose consent was so obtained within the limitations of time for enforcing a civil remedy of the civil practice law and rules. Any such action may also be maintained during the life-time of the other party by the parent, or the guardian of the person of the party whose consent was so obtained, or by any relative of that party who has an interest to avoid the marriage, provided that in an action to annul a marriage on the ground of fraud the limitation prescribed in the civil practice law and rules has not run. But a marriage shall not be annulled on the ground of force or duress if it appears that, at any time before the commencement of the action, the parties thereto voluntarily cohabited as husband and wife; or on the ground of fraud, if it appears that, at any time before the commencement thereof, the parties voluntarily cohabited as husband and wife, with a full knowledge of the facts constituting the fraud.

(f) Incurable mental illness for five years. An action to annul a marriage upon the ground that one of the parties has been incurably mentally ill for a period of five years or more may be maintained by or on behalf of either of the parties to such marriage.

jointly liable. Beyond this, the courts presume that the parties are meeting their obligations of support for one another as long as they continue to live together and maintain a marital residence.

If the parties cease living together and abandon the marital relationship, then the courts may become involved in dictating the legal rights of each party before and after a formal dissolution of the marriage. Most states have enacted statutes that permit awards of support during a legal separation or while a divorce is pending. Because divorces can sometimes become quite drawn out, it may be necessary to provide for the well-being of the parties (and possibly any children) during the interim.

## Effects of Tort and Criminal Law on Domestic Relations

An additional factor to be considered regarding the marital relationship is the effect of a marriage on tort and criminal law. Historically, one spouse was not permitted to bring a legal action against the other spouse for injuries inflicted during the marriage. The reasoning was that marital harmony would be disturbed if the courts entertained lawsuits by spouses against one another. Slowly, the realization came about that if injuries by one spouse to another were so serious as to warrant a lawsuit, then marital disharmony more than likely already existed. Further, it seemed unfair that gross negligence or intentional misconduct would be excused if it only injured a family member. Thus, most states have now abolished the doctrine of interspousal tort immunity.[14] Parties who cause injury to their spouses are no longer immune from legal action.

**Third-Party Actions against the Marriage.** Other torts that affect the marital relationship include actions of third parties against the marriage. Such actions are generally quite difficult to prove, and most persons are reluctant to raise the issue. Two such torts are *criminal conversation* (an action by one spouse against a third party for adulterous conduct with the other spouse) and *alienation of affection* (an action by a spouse against a third party who has induced the other spouse to transfer his or her affections to that party).[15] Because these actions have been used as a means to threaten and as virtual extortion (blackmail), some states have abolished the statutes that permit them. In addition, as noted previously, the very nature of the actions inhibits a significant amount of actual prosecution of claims by the injured party.

**domestic violence**
Violence perpetrated by one member of a household onto another.

**Domestic Violence.** Unfortunately, the occurrence of **domestic violence** (violence perpetrated by one member of a household onto another) is all too prevalent in American society and law. In 1998, the U.S. Department of Justice conducted a study and concluded that between partners alone (not including children and other family members) there were between 1 million and 4 million estimated annual incidents of domestic violence in the United States. In 1996, the Federal Bureau of Investigation reported that one in three female murder victims was killed by a husband or boyfriend. In 1998, another government study reported that one in five female high school students had suffered physical or sexual abuse by a partner. This does not include the number of males abused by females, child abuse, or elder abuse cases. Worse yet, it does not include the immeasurable number of cases that go unreported.

One benefit of the growing knowledge by individuals regarding their personal legal rights and the desensitization of society regarding the former shame associated with domestic violence is the increased willingness of individuals to step forward in such matters. As a result, a body of law has been developed and continues to evolve in the area of domestic violence. As recently as the mid-twentieth century, many persons aware of domestic violence in another household did not report it because the privacy of each family was considered superior to the rights of the individuals being abused. The old saying, "A man's home is his castle," was very much a reality in many communities urban and rural. However, as society became increasingly open and the awareness of the enormity of the problem became more obvious, people began to report violence, organizations formed to assist victims, and communities came together to support those men, women, and children who found themselves in violent circumstances. As a result, state and federal government began to collect data and enact legislation to respond to the growing problem.

Many people consider the actions of legislatures, courts, and law—enforcement agencies to still be in the formative stages, but there is no doubt the move is on to create legal standards designed to protect individuals against domestic violence (see Exhibit 10.2). Although in the past such matters dealt at best with things such as temporary restraining orders, the supporting laws were vague enough that these orders were difficult to enforce. Today, those laws have been elaborated and better defined to give law-enforcement officials real authority to intervene in cases of domestic violence even when a restraining order is not in place.

**Exhibit 10.2** Family Violence Statute Connecticut General Statutes Annotated Title 46B. Family Law Chapter 815E. Marriage

---

### § 46b-38a. Family violence prevention and response: Definitions

For the purposes of sections 46b-38a to 46b-38f, inclusive:

(1) "Family violence" means an incident resulting in physical harm, bodily injury or assault, or an act of threatened violence that constitutes fear of imminent physical harm, bodily injury or assault between family or household members. Verbal abuse or argument shall not constitute family violence unless there is present danger and the likelihood that physical violence will occur.

(2) "Family or household member" means (A) spouses, former spouses; (B) parents and their children; (C) persons eighteen years of age or older related by blood or marriage; (D) persons sixteen years of age or older other than those persons in subparagraph (C) presently residing together or who have resided together; and (E) persons who have a child in common regardless of whether they are or have been married or have lived together at any time.

(3) "Family violence crime" means a crime as defined in section 53a-24 which, in addition to its other elements, contains as an element thereof an act of family violence to a family member and shall not include acts by parents or guardians disciplining minor children unless such acts constitute abuse.

(4) "Institutions and services" means peace officers, service providers, mandated reporters of abuse, agencies and departments that provide services to victims and families and services designed to assist victims and families. § 46b-38b. Investigation of family violence crime by peace officer. Arrest,

when. Assistance to victim. Guidelines. Education and training program

(a) Whenever a peace officer determines upon speedy information that a family violence crime, as defined in subdivision (3) of section 46b-38a, has been committed within his jurisdiction, he shall arrest the person or persons suspected of its commission and charge such person or persons with the appropriate crime. The decision to arrest and charge shall not (1) be dependent on the specific consent of the victim, (2) consider the relationship of the parties or (3) be based solely on a request by the victim.

(b) No peace officer investigating an incident of family violence shall threaten, suggest or otherwise indicate the arrest of all parties for the purpose of discouraging requests for law enforcement intervention by any party. Where complaints are received from two or more opposing parties, the officer shall evaluate each complaint separately to determine whether he should seek a warrant for an arrest.

(c) No peace officer shall be held liable in any civil action regarding personal injury or injury to property brought by any party to a family violence incident for an arrest based on probable cause.

(d) It shall be the responsibility of the peace officer at the scene of a family violence incident to provide immediate assistance to the victim. Such assistance shall include but not be limited to; (1) Assisting the victim to obtain medical treatment if such is required; (2) notifying the victim of the

*(continued)*

**Exhibit 10.2** Continued

right to file an affidavit or warrant for arrest; and (3) informing the victim of services available and referring the victim to the commission on victim services. In cases where the officer has determined that no cause exists for an arrest, assistance shall include: (A) Assistance included in subdivisions (1) to (3), inclusive, of this subsection; and (B) remaining at the scene for a reasonable time until in the reasonable judgment of the officer the likelihood of further imminent violence has been eliminated.

(e) On or before October 1, 1986, each law enforcement agency shall develop, in conjunction with the division of criminal justice, and implement specific operational guidelines for arrest policies in family violence incidents. Such guidelines shall include but not be limited to: (1) Procedures for the conduct of a criminal investigation; (2) procedures for arrest and for victim assistance by peace officers; (3) education as to what constitutes speedy information in a family violence incident; (4) procedures with respect to the provision of services to victims; and (5) such other criteria or guidelines as may be applicable to carry out the

purposes of subsection (e) of section 17-38a and sections 17-38g, 46b-1, 46b-15, 46b-38a to 46b-38f, inclusive, and 54-1g.

(f) The municipal police training council, in conjunction with the division of criminal justice, shall establish an education and training program for law enforcement officers, supervisors and state's attorneys on the handling of family violence incidents. Such training shall: (1) Stress the enforcement of criminal law in family violence cases and the use of community resources and include training for peace officers at both recruit and in-service levels; (2) include: (A) The nature, extent and causes of family violence; (B) legal rights of and remedies available to victims of family violence and persons accused of family violence; (C) services and facilities available to victims and batterers; (D) legal duties imposed on police officers to make arrests and to offer protection and assistance; (E) techniques for handling incidents of family violence that minimize the likelihood of injury to the officer and promote safety of the victim.

**Marital Violence.** A rapidly changing area of criminal law that affects the family involves marital violence. More than one-half the states have now enacted statutes that permit an action by a wife for marital rape by her husband. However, many of these statutes require the parties to have been living apart at the time of the incident.[16] In addition, because of the doctrine of nonintervention in the marital relationship, there has been little if any alternative for the spouse who has been violently abused by the other spouse. States do have statutes, however, that permit special intervention by police and subsequently by the courts where a reasonable belief exists that a spouse has committed a felony against his or her partner.

The statute in Exhibit 10.2 is just one example of an attempt to deal with the domestic violence issue through the legal system. In addition, many community and charitable organizations have established shelters, crisis intervention centers, hotlines, counseling services, and other methods to effectively deal with the domestic violence that occurs in our society. As more cases are reported and the guilt often felt by victims of domestic violence is exposed as unfounded, this area of law and community support can be expected to grow dramatically in coming years.

In criminal law, certain principles affect the marriage relationship. A primary example is the *testimonial privilege*. Traditionally, a spouse could not testify against the other spouse during a criminal prosecution. Over time, however, the law has been modified, and most states now permit but cannot compel a spouse to testify against his or her partner. Because the spouse has the right to protect the confidentiality of the marriage relationship, testimony cannot be forced or ordered.

## ENDING THE MARITAL RELATIONSHIP

Even when a legal marriage has occurred and existed for a period of time, there are circumstances that can arise to cause one or both parties to make the decision to end the relationship. When this happens, legal standards have been developed to provide what will hopefully be a fair distribution of assets and liabilities and to make provision for any minor children whose responsibility is shared by the parties involved. There are also attempts by the states to create similar standards for decisions affecting minor children who may reside in a different state than one of their parents.

## Jurisdiction

When one or both of the parties to a marital relationship decide to end the marriage, a judicial declaration must be made before the marriage and its associated rights and duties will be terminated. The declaration must come from a court that has jurisdiction over the parties to the suit. Procedural rules in each state specify when the courts will accept jurisdiction over a marital dissolution action.

Many of the requirements in these statutes are similar throughout the states. Perhaps the most common is the requirement of residency. Although the length of residence varies, generally the states require the party commencing the action to have been a resident of the state for a specified period of time before initiating the action for dissolution. Parties may also obtain jurisdiction in a court if the marriage was formalized there or if the grounds for divorce occurred while the parties maintained their residence in the state (regardless of whether the time requirement has been met).[17]

When a party obtains a decree but the court does not have jurisdiction to decide matters involving the settlement of the marital estate (e.g., assets are located in another jurisdiction), the decree may be registered with a court that has jurisdiction over both of the parties and their property. That court may then proceed to determine the rights and obligations of each party. Under the U.S. Constitution, each state is obligated to give full faith and credit to the judgment of another state's decree. This means that a state should honor and enforce the judgments of a court from another state.

A major jurisdictional issue in dissolution actions pertains to the authority of a court over the rights and duties concerning children of a marriage. Initially, the court that has jurisdiction to determine the rights, duties, and division of the assets of the marital estate also has authority to make findings regarding custody, visitation, and support of minor children. However, later adjustments to these findings, commonly termed *modifications,* may raise serious issues as to which court has authority. Fortunately, these issues have been settled in large part by a number of uniform acts including the Uniform Reciprocal Enforcement of Support Act (URESA), the Uniform Child Custody Jurisdiction Act (UCCJA), and the more recent Uniform Child Custody Jurisdiction and Enforcement Act (UCCJEA). A majority of states adhere to the acts, which state quite specifically what courts have jurisdiction over matters concerning children of divorced parties.

## Grounds for Dissolution of a Marriage

Although requirements of jurisdiction vary, the acceptable grounds for a divorce set forth by state statute are typically quite similar. Although slight variations may exist, the basic premise for **dissolution of marriage** remains the same in most states. There must be sufficient evidence of some type that will establish that the marital bond is irreparably broken.

The grounds most commonly set forth in state statutes as sufficient to establish the end of the marriage relationship include, but are not limited to, the following:[18]

1. habitual drunkenness or drug abuse,

2. adultery,

3. physical cruelty,

**dissolution of marriage**
The end of the marriage relationship (also known as *divorce*).

4. mental cruelty,

5. abandonment, and

6. insanity.

Traditionally, the party who suffered because of the existence of one or more of these grounds brought an action for divorce. He or she would be required to give evidence of the grounds, and on that basis the divorce would be granted.

More recently adopted has been the concept of no-fault divorce, the grounds for which are called *irreconcilable differences*. It has been recognized for many years that parties would agree to a specific grounds for a divorce as a means to expedite the end of the legal relationship when the marriage itself had come to an end sometime before. Many times, parties who no longer wish to be married have various reasons other than the statutorily stated grounds. In addition, the time and expense associated with divorce to the individuals and courts alike have increased significantly. As a result, in the past several years, every state has adopted a no-fault statute in some form. Although the requirements of proof of a broken marriage differ from state to state, the premise remains the same. It is unnecessary to claim that one party unilaterally caused the break in the marital bond. Rather, the parties have reached a point where they are no longer interested in maintaining the marital relationship.[19] For this reason, the bond is broken, and the legality of the relationship can be dissolved.

In an attempt to prevent parties from entering into a no-fault divorce when conciliation could still be achieved, many statutes impose requirements of proof that the marital bond is irreparably broken. Such requirements include lengthy separations before a no-fault divorce will be granted. Parties should be given every opportunity to evaluate the situation carefully and be sure of their decision. However, those parties who have firmly made a decision to end the marriage evade these requirements by returning to the former method of privately agreeing to one or more grounds based on fault of a party so that the divorce may be granted immediately. Thus, although the statutes have assisted many people in obtaining a divorce without laying blame, abuse of statutes by giving grounds of fault continues in some states where it is much more time consuming to obtain a divorce on grounds of no-fault than on fault of a party.

## Legal Separation

As previously mentioned, many times a divorce is a long and complicated process. Also, many parties do not file for divorce immediately on separation. This may be for religious reasons, or the parties may want time to consider the possibility of reconciliation or at least the potential for agreement to the terms of the divorce. During this period, the parties remain legally obligated to each other as well as for the support of their children. As a consequence, a special area of law has developed by statute and by judicial decision that governs the rights of the parties during this period of **legal separation**.

**legal separation**
Legal document that establishes the property rights of the parties without effecting a dissolution of the actual marriage relationship.

Courts are reluctant to recognize antenuptial agreements that provide specifically for divorce. However, when a physical separation has occurred or is about to occur, the courts will consider an antenuptial or separation agreement between the parties that discusses the parties' rights and duties before the divorce when the marriage still exists legally but marital assets and liabilities are no longer shared. The courts will generally examine the agreement for fairness, full disclosure, and availability of legal counsel to each party.[20]

Separation agreements include such issues as custody, visitation, and support of minor children; possession of the marital residence; responsibility for payments due on marital debts; and maintenance (alimony) where appropriate. If the terms are agreeable to the parties, then they may also serve as the basis for the terms in the final divorce decree for matters of convenience to the parties. However, it is important to note that legal separations have no direct connection to dissolution proceedings, and each may take place without the other.

## ASSIGNMENT 10.2

Prepare a chart that details the differences between dissolution, annulment, common law divorce, and legal separation.

## Temporary Orders

Unfortunately, not all parties are willing to reach an agreement regarding property and other rights. In such instances, state statutes give a court authority to make temporary provisions during the period after commencement of a divorce but before a final decree is issued. These temporary orders provide terms that the parties must follow with respect to the marital obligations previously discussed.

In addition to issuing temporary orders, courts are often requested to issue **temporary restraining orders** and **preliminary injunctions**. These are granted in circumstances where the court is convinced that one spouse will injure the partner or harm, destroy, or dispose of marital property.[21] If the threat of injury or harm is immediate to the spouse or property, the spouse in danger can appear in court *ex parte*. An *ex parte* proceeding is conducted without giving the other party to the action the opportunity to be present and voice his or her position. Because these orders are based on one person's version of the story, the court will usually issue the order only in compelling circumstances, and such an order is usually effective for only a short period of time as an emergency measure.

**temporary restraining order**
Court order that temporarily orders a party to act or refrain from acting in a particular manner until such time as the court has the opportunity to consider a more permanent ruling on an issue.

**preliminary injunction**
Court order that orders a party to act or refrain from acting in a particular manner for a specified period of time (often during the pendency of a legal proceeding).

## APPLICATION 10.3

Ramona and Baron were married for several years. They decided to divorce. Ramona immediately went to court and petitioned for temporary restraining orders based on her testimony that Baron was addicted to drugs and would be likely to dispose of the parties' liquid assets. She also claimed that he was a physical risk to the couple's children because of his drug use. She stated in her petition that she did not know of Baron's whereabouts. The court granted a ten-day temporary order to freeze all assets, at which time a hearing would be scheduled to hear Baron's side of the story.

Baron left the home at the time of the split and stayed with his parents. He told friends of his location but had not yet told Ramona. Unaware of the restraining order, on day 6 he arrived at Ramona's home while she was gone and asked their teenage children if they would like to come with him to see the apartment he had just rented. They agreed to go with him. Ramona came home to find the children had left a note stating they were with their father. She called the police and had Baron arrested for violation of the restraining order. In addition, the check he wrote from their joint account to pay the deposit on the apartment was refused by the bank. In turn, Baron had to post bail to obtain release from custody and was immediately locked out of the apartment he had not yet moved into.

Baron had never been served with notice of the orders. Unless he could demonstrate that Ramona obtained the orders based on false testimony, including drug use or knowledge of his whereabouts or both, the bank and police would be appropriate in their actions.

*Point for Discussion:* Should Ramona have been required to attempt to locate Baron before seeking the temporary restraining orders?

After a temporary restraining order has been issued, it is served on the party who is restrained. Even if the restrained party cannot be located, the order is effective; if it is violated, the party can be arrested.[22] Without such a rule, a party could simply avoid being served and in the interim destroy marital property or perhaps seriously injure his or her spouse. Given the alternatives, the safer course seems to be to give the order effect from the time it is issued.

Temporary restraining orders are usually issued for short periods of time. Thus, a party who can show evidence that such an order was improperly issued can have the order revoked at the earliest opportunity. When a hearing is held, however, if sufficient evidence is presented to warrant continuance of the order, then a preliminary injunction will be issued that remains in effect during the pendency of the dissolution proceedings.

A preliminary injunction contains virtually the same provisions as a temporary restraining order. However, the injunction will be effective until the final divorce decree is entered. At that time, if marital property will continue to be held jointly or if the physical danger still exists, a **permanent injunction** may be issued that will remain effective until an order of the court removes it. Many times, these orders are left in force forever.

**permanent injunction**
An injunction that remains effective until an order of the court removes it; sometimes such orders are left in force forever.

---

## APPLICATION 10.4

Tyra and Thomas were at the final hearing on their divorce. During the proceedings, Thomas petitioned for permanent injunctions. He testified that Tyra had approached him and his fiancé on numerous occasions in public places. He claimed she threatened them both, and on one occasion they left a restaurant to find the tires on his fiancé's car had been slashed. A note was left on the windshield that stated, "Next time it will be your throats." He testified Tyra had claimed she was not the one to slash the tires but had left the note. A permanent injunction was granted to Thomas that required Tyra to remain 150 yards from him at all times. She was also prohibited from contacting him for any reason. The order stated it was to continue until such time as one or both of the parties approached the court to evaluate the situation.

*Point for Discussion:* Why is the order not issued to include Thomas's fiancé?

---

## CUSTODY

**custody (parental rights)**
The rights to oversee the care, education, and rearing of a child.

**Custody** over minor children is perhaps one of the most litigated areas of family law, and the term is used to describe the care, control, and education of a minor child. It is effective as long as the child is a minor or is still in high school. A synonymous term used in some jurisdictions is **parental rights**. For purposes of this discussion, the term *custody* will be used. When the child reaches the age of majority under statute in the state where the child resides, custody ends and the child is considered to be an adult.[23] Residence is determined by the child's permanent dwelling, not by where the child attends school or where the other parent whom the child visits may live. Generally, the custodial parent's state of residence is the child's state of residence.

Custody may not end at the age of majority for a child with mental disabilities. In cases when the child is unable to accept responsibility for his or her actions, the parent may be appointed as permanent custodian.[24]

In the event of the death of the custodial parent, the presumption is that custody will be transferred to the other parent. The exception to this is if the surviving parent is not able to provide an acceptable environment for the child. In such circumstances, stepparents, grandparents, or other interested parties who can provide a suitable environment for the child may be appointed guardian.

Fortunately, the courts rarely have to deal with such cases. However, there are quite often decisions to be made by the courts when both parents are living and willing to provide a home for the child or children. Formerly, the mother almost always received custody of the children. No longer is this the case. Courts consider numerous factors to determine who is best able to care for and attend to the children's needs.[25]

Under what is known as the *tender years doctrine,* which was followed for many years but is rapidly declining in this country, the mother was presumed to be the best alternative for custody of young children of "tender years"[26] (usually children who had not reached their teens). The only way a father could overcome this presumption and have a chance for custody was to prove that the mother was unfit or, at the very least, far less able than the father to care for the children.

In recent times, many fathers have taken an increasingly active role in the upbringing of their children. In addition, various movements throughout the country for equal rights for men have supported fathers in their quest for custody. Furthermore, it is no longer the general rule that mothers stay at home to care for the children. Many mothers work and are away from the home just as much as a father would be. For all of these reasons, many courts have struck down the tender years doctrine in favor of a case-by-case evaluation of who will best serve the interests and needs of the child.[27]

## Who Gets Custody?

What is the standard that must be proven to obtain custody of a child? Contrary to popular belief, it is not necessary to prove that the other party is unfit as a parent. Although the evidence may establish this in some cases, it is not the standard used by most courts. Rather, the courts look at what will be in the child's best interests. Divorce is extremely difficult for children of all ages. That is not to say it may not be a better alternative than the continuation of a marriage, but divorce does mean that a child's world goes through dramatic changes that require adjustment. Consequently, the court examines several areas that affect the child's life and looks to the child's particular needs. The court then looks at the environment that each parent will offer the child. The environment that is most compatible with the child's needs is the one that is in the child's best interests. Thus, each parent may offer a suitable environment, but the parent who is better suited to meet the needs of the child should prevail.

As this suggests, the standard that a parent must prove is that the child's best interests are served if that parent is awarded custody. The factors that a court considers in making this determination may include, but are not limited to, the following:[28]

1. the ability of the parent to care for the child personally (as opposed to extensive child care services),

2. the religion of the parent,

3. the ability of the parent to attend to any special needs of the child because of young age or disability,

4. immoral conduct that would have a direct effect on the child (otherwise, this is considered irrelevant),

5. the ability to give continuity to the child's current environment (such as home, school, and friends), and

6. available contact with members of the child's extended family.

None of the preceding factors is individually controlling, and the court will usually consider factors that are peculiar to each case when making its determination.

The U.S. Supreme Court has determined that race or ethnic background cannot be used as the only determining factor in a custody case, although a court may consider race or ethnicity along with the other factors in a custody decision when it is relevant.[29]

An additional factor that is not controlling but may be given some weight is the desire of the child. The general rule is that a child may not be able to determine objectively what is in his or her best interests. However, as a child matures, courts are often more willing to consider the child's opinion. Many states have statutory provisions that expressly permit the judge to give weight to this factor after a child reaches a certain age.[30] Because the child is still a minor and is deemed legally incompetent to make such significant decisions, a court will rarely accept the child's wishes as the sole determining factor.

## Joint Custody

Thus far, the discussion has been confined to the issue of single-parent custody, in which one parent has the primary responsibility for the care, control, and education of the child. The noncustodial parent has visitation rights but no legal right to take an active part in the decisions regarding the child's rearing.

Because the limitation on such input was unacceptable to many parents, the concept of *joint custody* was developed. A common misconception is that joint custody involves only shared physical custody of the child or children. Although this sometimes occurs in joint custody, it is not the primary purpose. The child may very well live permanently with one parent. Joint custody gives each parent the right to take an active part in the rearing of the child. The parents will discuss and agree on matters of education, religion, and, in general, all major decisions that affect the child's life.[31]

A majority of states have enacted statutes that permit the courts to award joint custody. It is left to the discretion of the judges to determine on a case-by-case basis whether the circumstances are appropriate for joint custody or whether the child's interests would be better served by an award of individual custody to one parent and significant contact with the other parent.

In the best of circumstances, joint custody allows both parents to have input into all aspects of a child's upbringing. As a practical matter, however, it is often an untenable situation. Because of this, judges are often reluctant to grant joint custody unless the circumstances appear overwhelmingly in favor of it.

The problem that arises with joint custody is that in many situations it is contradictory to the divorce itself. The parties have sought a dissolution of their marriage because their relationship was one involving irreconcilable differences. Yet, in joint custody, the parties seek permission of the court to have the legal right to determine important matters, with each having an equal voice in the decision. Often the parties are so opposed to each other they are not willing to work together, even in the best interests of the child. The result is that the parties return to the same judge for mediation of their disputes on matters concerning the child. The purpose of joint custody is not achieved, the parents incur additional legal expenses, and the child is subjected to more disruption than ever. Thus, unless the parties seem to be genuinely interested and capable of working with each other, many courts are hesitant to grant joint custody.

## Enforcement of Custody Orders

An increasingly common issue in child custody cases is that of court jurisdiction. With the expanding mobility of American society, it is no longer uncommon for parents to live in different states. Consequently, enforcement of child custody orders can rapidly develop into a costly and time-consuming battle for parents in conflict. In response, the Uniform Child Custody Jurisdiction Act—and, in some states, the more recent Uniform Child Custody Jurisdiction and Enforcement Act—has been adopted, setting up guidelines for determining jurisdiction and establishing cooperation among the states in the enforcement of custody orders. Although not a cure, this uniform law has eliminated a great many of the problems and concerns that parents might face when they live in separate jurisdictions. Exhibit 10.3 gives the text of the UCCJA and relevant excerpts of the UCCJEA. Note that, as with any proposed uniform law, the final legislation in any given state may be a variation of the proposed language.

**Exhibit 10.3** Uniform Child Custody Jurisdiction Act

§ 1. Purposes of Act; Construction of Provisions.—

(a) The general purposes of this Act are to:

(1) avoid jurisdictional competition and conflict with courts of other states in matters of child custody which have in the past resulted in the shifting of children from state to state with harmful effects on their well-being;

(2) promote cooperation with the courts of other states to the end that a custody decree is rendered in that state which can best decide the case in the interest of the child;

(3) assure that litigation concerning the custody of a child take place ordinarily in the state with which the child and his family have the closest connection and where significant evidence concerning his care, protection, training, and personal relationships is most readily available, and that courts of this state decline the exercise of jurisdiction when the child and his family have a closer connection with another state;

(4) discourage continuing controversies over child custody in the interest of greater stability of home environment and of secure family relationships for the child;

(5) deter abductions and other unilateral removals of children undertaken to obtain custody awards;

(6) avoid re-litigation of custody decisions of other states in this state insofar as feasible;

(7) facilitate the enforcement of custody decrees of other states;

(8) promote and expand the exchange of information and other forms of mutual assistance between the courts of this state and those of other states concerned with the same child; and

(9) make uniform the law of those states which enact it.

(b) This Act shall be construed to promote the general purposes stated in this section.

§ 2. Definitions.—As used in this Act:

(1) "contestant" means a person, including a parent, who claims a right to custody or visitation rights with respect to a child;

(2) "custody determination" means a court decision and court orders and instructions providing for the custody of a child, including visitation rights; it does not include a decision relating to child support or any other monetary obligation of any person;

(3) "custody proceeding" includes proceedings in which a custody determination is one of several issues, such as an action for divorce or separation, and includes child neglect and dependency proceedings;

(4) "decree" or "custody decree" means a custody determination contained in a judicial decree or order made in a custody proceeding, and includes an initial decree and a modification decree;

(5) "home state" means the state in which the child immediately preceding the time involved lived with his parents, a parent, or a person acting as parent, for at least 6 consecutive months, and in the case of a child less than 6 months old the state in which the child lived from birth with any of the persons mentioned. Periods of temporary absence of any of the named persons are counted as part of the 6-month or other period;

(6) "initial decree" means the first custody decree concerning a particular child;

(7) "modification decree" means a custody decree which modifies or replaces a prior decree, whether made by the court which rendered the prior decree or by another court;

(8) "physical custody" means actual possession and control of a child;

(9) "person acting as parent" means a person, other than a parent, who has physical custody of a child and who has either been awarded custody by a court or claims a right to custody; and

(10) "state" means any state, territory, or possession of the United States, the Commonwealth of Puerto Rico, and the District of Columbia.

§ 3. Jurisdiction.—

(a) A court of this State which is competent to decide child custody matters has jurisdiction to make a child custody determination by initial or modification decree if:

(1) this State (i) is the home state of the child at the time of commencement of the proceeding, or (ii) had been

(continued)

**Exhibit 10.3** Continued

the child's home state within 6 months before commencement of the proceeding and the child is absent from this State because of his removal or retention by a person claiming his custody or for other reasons, and a parent or person acting as parent continues to live in this State; or

(2) it is in the best interest of the child that a court of this State assume jurisdiction because (i) the child and his parents, or the child and at least one contestant, have a significant connection with this State, and (ii) there is available in this State substantial evidence concerning the child's present or future care, protection, training, and personal relationships; or

(3) the child is physically present in this State and (i) the child has been abandoned or (ii) it is necessary in an emergency to protect the child because he has been subjected to or threatened with mistreatment or abuse or is otherwise neglected [or dependent]; or

(4) (i) it appears that no other state would have jurisdiction under prerequisites substantially in accordance with paragraphs (1), (2), or (3), or another state has declined to exercise jurisdiction on the ground that this State is the more appropriate forum to determine the custody of the child, and (ii) it is in the best interest of the child that this court assume jurisdiction.

(b) Except under paragraphs (3) and (4) of subsection (a), physical presence in this State of the child, or of the child and one of the contestants, is not alone sufficient to confer jurisdiction on a court of this State to make a child custody determination.

(c) Physical presence of the child, while desirable, is not a prerequisite for jurisdiction to determine his custody.

§ 4. Notice and Opportunity to be Heard.—Before making a decree under this Act, reasonable notice and opportunity to be heard shall be given to the contestants, any parent whose parental rights have not been previously terminated, and any person who has physical custody of the child. If any of these persons is outside this State, notice and opportunity to be heard shall be given pursuant to section 5.

§ 5. Notice to Persons Outside this State; Submission to Jurisdiction.—

(a) Notice required for the exercise of jurisdiction over a person outside this State shall be given in a manner reasonably calculated to give actual notice, and may be:

(1) by personal delivery outside this State in the manner prescribed for service of process within this State;

(2) in the manner prescribed by the law of the place in which the service is made for service of process in that place in an action in any of its courts of general jurisdiction;

(3) by any form of mail addressed to the person to be served and requesting a receipt; or

(4) as directed by the court [including publication, if other means of notification are ineffective].

(b) Notice under this section shall be served, mailed, or delivered, [or last published] at least [10, 20] days before any hearing in this State.

(c) Proof of service outside this State may be made by affidavit of the individual who made the service, or in the manner prescribed by the law of this State, the order pursuant to which the service is made, or the law of the place in which the service is made. If service is made by mail, proof may be a receipt signed by the addressee or other evidence of delivery to the addressee.

(d) Notice is not required if a person submits to the jurisdiction of the court.

§ 6. Simultaneous Proceedings in Other States.—

(a) A court of this State shall not exercise its jurisdiction under this Act if at the time of filing the petition a proceeding concerning the custody of the child was pending in a court of another state exercising jurisdiction substantially in conformity with this Act, unless the proceeding is stayed by the court of the other state because this State is a more appropriate forum or for other reasons.

(b) Before hearing the petition in a custody proceeding the court shall examine the pleadings and other information supplied by the parties under section 9 and shall consult the child custody registry established under section 16 concerning the pendency of proceedings with respect to the child in other states. If the court has reason to believe that proceedings may be pending in another state it shall direct an inquiry to the state court administrator or other appropriate official of the other state.

(c) If the court is informed during the course of the proceeding that a proceeding concerning the custody of the child was pending in another state before the court assumed jurisdiction it shall stay the proceeding and communicate with the court in which the other proceeding is pending to the end that the issue may be litigated in the more appropriate forum and that information be exchanged in accordance with sections 19 through 22. If a court of this State has made a custody decree before being informed of a pending proceeding in a court of another state it shall

**Exhibit 10.3** Continued

immediately inform that court of the fact. If the court is informed that a proceeding was commenced in another state after it assumed jurisdiction it shall likewise inform the other court to the end that the issues may be litigated in the more appropriate forum.

§ 7. Inconvenient Forum.—

(a) A court which has jurisdiction under this Act to make an initial or modification decree may decline to exercise its jurisdiction any time before making a decree if it finds that it is an inconvenient forum to make a custody determination under the circumstances of the case and that a court of another state is a more appropriate forum.

(b) A finding of inconvenient forum may be made upon the court's own motion or upon motion of a party or a guardian *ad litem* or other representative of the child.

(c) In determining if it is an inconvenient forum, the court shall consider if it is in the interest of the child that another state assume jurisdiction. For this purpose it may take into account the following factors, among others:

   (1) if another state is or recently was the child's home state;

   (2) if another state has a closer connection with the child and his family or with the child and one or more of the contestants;

   (3) if substantial evidence concerning the child's present or future care, protection, training, and personal relationships is more readily available in another state;

   (4) if the parties have agreed on another forum which is no less appropriate; and

   (5) if the exercise of jurisdiction by a court of this State would contravene any of the purposes stated in section 1.

(d) Before determining whether to decline or retain jurisdiction the court may communicate with a court of another state and exchange information pertinent to the assumption of jurisdiction by either court with a view to assuring that jurisdiction will be exercised by the more appropriate court and that a forum will be available to the parties.

(e) If the court finds that it is an inconvenient forum and that a court of another state is a more appropriate forum, it may dismiss the proceedings, or it may stay the proceedings upon condition that a custody proceeding be promptly commenced in another named state or upon any other conditions which may be just and proper, including the condition that a moving party stipulate his consent and submission to the jurisdiction of the other forum.

(f) The court may decline to exercise its jurisdiction under this Act if a custody determination is incidental to an action for divorce or another proceeding while retaining jurisdiction over the divorce or other proceeding.

(g) If it appears to the court that it is clearly an inappropriate forum it may require the party who commenced the proceedings to pay, in addition to the costs of the proceedings in this State, necessary travel and other expenses, including attorneys' fees, incurred by other parties or their witnesses. Payment is to be made to the clerk of the court for remittance to the proper party.

(h) Upon dismissal or stay of proceedings under this section the court shall inform the court found to be the more appropriate forum of this fact, or if the court which would have jurisdiction in the other state is not certainly known, shall transmit the information to the court administrator or other appropriate official for forwarding to the appropriate court.

(i) Any communication received from another state informing this State of a finding of inconvenient forum because a court of this State is the more appropriate forum shall be filed in the custody registry of the appropriate court. Upon assuming jurisdiction the court of this State shall inform the original court of this fact.

§ 8. Jurisdiction Declined by Reason of Conduct.—

(a) If the petitioner for an initial decree has wrongfully taken the child from another state or has engaged in similar reprehensible conduct the court may decline to exercise jurisdiction if this is just and proper under the circumstances.

(b) Unless required in the interest of the child, the court shall not exercise its jurisdiction to modify a custody decree of another state if the petitioner, without consent of the person entitled to custody, has improperly removed the child from the physical custody of the person entitled to custody or has improperly retained the child after a visit or other temporary relinquishment of physical custody. If the petitioner has violated any other provision of a custody decree of another state the court may decline to exercise its jurisdiction if this is just and proper under the circumstances.

(c) In appropriate cases a court dismissing a petition under this section may charge the petitioner with necessary travel and other expenses, including attorneys' fees, incurred by other parties or their witnesses.

§ 9. Information under Oath to be Submitted to the Court.—

(a) Every party in a custody proceeding in his first pleading or in an affidavit attached to that pleading shall give information under oath as to the child's present address, the

*(continued)*

**Exhibit 10.3** Continued

places where the child has lived within the last 5 years, and the names and present addresses of the persons with whom the child has lived during that period. In this pleading or affidavit every party shall further declare under oath whether:

(1) he has participated (as a party, witness, or in any other capacity) in any other litigation concerning the custody of the same child in this or any other state;

(2) he has information of any custody proceeding concerning the child pending in a court of this or any other state; and

(3) he knows of any person not a party to the proceedings who has physical custody of the child or claims to have custody or visitation rights with respect to the child.

(b) If the declaration as to any of the above items is in the affirmative the declarant shall give additional information under oath as required by the court. The court may examine the parties under oath as to details of the information furnished and as to other matters pertinent to the court's jurisdiction and the disposition of the case.

(c) Each party has a continuing duty to inform the court of any custody proceeding concerning the child in this or any other state of which he obtained information during this proceeding.

§ 10. Additional Parties.—If the court learns from information furnished by the parties pursuant to section 9 or from other sources that a person not a party to the custody proceeding has physical custody of the child or claims to have custody or visitation rights with respect to the child, it shall order that person to be joined as a party and to be duly notified of the pendency of the proceeding and of his joinder as a party. If the person joined as a party is outside this State he shall be served with process or otherwise notified in accordance with section 5.

§ 11. Appearance of Parties and the Child.—

[(a) The court may order any party to the proceeding who is in this State to appear personally before the court. If that party has physical custody of the child the court may order that he appear personally with the child.]

(b) If a party to the proceeding whose presence is desired by the court is outside this State with or without the child the court may order that the notice given under section 5 include a statement directing that party to appear personally with or without the child and declaring that failure to appear may result in a decision adverse to that party.

(c) If a party to the proceeding who is outside this State is directed to appear under subsection (b) or desires to appear

personally before the court with or without the child, the court may require another party to pay to the clerk of the court travel and other necessary expenses of the party so appearing and of the child if this is just and proper under the circumstances.

§ 12. Binding Force and *Res Judicata* Effect of Custody Decree.—A custody decree rendered by a court of this State which had jurisdiction under section 3 binds all parties who have been served in this State or notified in accordance with section 5 or who have submitted to the jurisdiction of the court, and who have been given an opportunity to be heard. As to these parties the custody decree is conclusive as to all issues of law and fact decided and as to the custody determination made unless and until that determination is modified pursuant to law, including the provisions of this Act.

§ 13. Recognition of Out-of-State Custody Decrees.—The courts of this State shall recognize and enforce an initial or modification decree of a court of another state which had assumed jurisdiction under statutory provisions substantially in accordance with this Act or which was made under factual circumstances meeting the jurisdictional standards of the Act, so long as this decree has not been modified in accordance with jurisdictional standards substantially similar to those of this Act.

§ 14. Modification of Custody Decree of Another State.—

(a) If a court of another state has made a custody decree, a court of this State shall not modify that decree unless (1) it appears to the court of this State that the court which rendered the decree does not now have jurisdiction under jurisdictional prerequisites substantially in accordance with this Act or has declined to assume jurisdiction to modify the decree and (2) the court of this State has jurisdiction.

(b) If a court of this State is authorized under subsection (a) and section 8 to modify a custody decree of another state it shall give due consideration to the transcript of the record and other documents of all previous proceedings submitted to it in accordance with section 22.

§ 15. Filing and Enforcement of Custody Decree of Another State.—

(a) A certified copy of a custody decree of another state may be filed in the office of the clerk of any [District Court, Family Court] of this State. The clerk shall treat the decree in the same manner as a custody decree of the [District Court, Family Court] of this State. A custody decree so filed has the same effect and shall be enforced in like manner as a custody decree rendered by a court of this State.

(b) A person violating a custody decree of another state which makes it necessary to enforce the decree in this

**Exhibit 10.3** Continued

State may be required to pay necessary travel and other expenses, including attorneys' fees, incurred by the party entitled to the custody or his witnesses.

§ 16. Registry of Out-of-State Custody Decrees and Proceedings.—The clerk of each [District Court, Family Court] shall maintain a registry in which he shall enter the following:

(1) certified copies of custody decrees of other states received for filing;

(2) communications as to the pendency of custody proceedings in other states;

(3) communications concerning a finding of inconvenient forum by a court of another state; and

(4) other communications or documents concerning custody proceedings in another state which may affect the jurisdiction of a court of this State or the disposition to be made by it in a custody proceeding.

§ 17. Certified Copies of Custody Decree.—The Clerk of the [District Court, Family Court] of this State, at the request of the court of another state or at the request of any person who is affected by or has a legitimate interest in a custody decree, shall certify and forward a copy of the decree to that court or person.

§ 18. Taking Testimony in Another State.—In addition to other procedural devices available to a party, any party to the proceeding or a guardian *ad litem* or other representative of the child may adduce testimony of witnesses, including parties and the child, by deposition or otherwise in another state. The court on its own motion may direct that the testimony of a person be taken in another state and may prescribe the manner in which and the terms upon which the testimony shall be taken.

§ 19. Hearings and Studies in Another State; Orders to Appear.—

(a) A court of this State may request the appropriate court of another state to hold a hearing to adduce evidence, to order a party to produce or give evidence under other procedures of that state, or to have social studies made with respect to the custody of a child involved in proceedings pending in the court of this State; and to forward to the court of this State certified copies of the transcript of the record of the hearing, the evidence otherwise adduced, or any social studies prepared in compliance with the request. The cost of the services may be assessed against the parties or, if necessary, ordered paid by the [County, State].

(b) A court of this State may request the appropriate court of another state to order a party to custody proceedings pending in the court of this State to appear in the proceedings, and if that party has physical custody of the child, to appear with the child. The request may state that travel and

other necessary expenses of the party and of the child whose appearance is desired will be assessed against another party or will otherwise be paid.

§ 20. Assistance to Courts of Other States.—

(a) Upon request of the court of another state the courts of this State which are competent to hear custody matters may order a person in this State to appear at a hearing to adduce evidence or to produce or give evidence under other procedures available in this State [or may order social studies to be made for use in a custody proceeding in another state]. A certified copy of the transcript of the record of the hearing or the evidence otherwise adduced [and any social studies prepared] shall be forwarded by the clerk of the court to the requesting court.

(b) A person within this State may voluntarily give his testimony or statement in this State for use in a custody proceeding outside this State.

(c) Upon request of the court of another state a competent court of this State may order a person in this State to appear alone or with the child in a custody proceeding in another state. The court may condition compliance with the request upon assurance by the other state that state travel and other necessary expenses will be advanced or reimbursed.

§ 21. Preservation of Documents for Use in Other States.—In any custody proceeding in this State the court shall preserve the pleadings, orders and decrees, any record that has been made of its hearings, social studies, and other pertinent documents until the child reaches [18, 21] years of age. Upon appropriate request of the court of another state the court shall forward to the other court certified copies of any or all such documents.

§ 22. Request for Court Records of Another State.—If a custody decree has been rendered in another state concerning a child involved in a custody proceeding pending in a court of this State, the court of this State upon taking jurisdiction of the case shall request of the court of the other state a certified copy of the transcript of any court record and other documents mentioned in section 21.

§ 23. International Application.—The general policies of this Act extend to the international area. The provisions of this Act relating to the recognition and enforcement of custody decrees of other states apply to custody decrees and decrees involving legal institutions similar in nature to custody institutions rendered by appropriate authorities of other nations if reasonable notice and opportunity to be heard were given to all affected persons.

*(continued)*

**Exhibit 10.3** Continued

[§ 24. Priority.—Upon the request of a party to a custody proceeding which raises a question of existence or exercise of jurisdiction under this Act the case shall be given calendar priority and handled expeditiously.]

§ 25. Severability.—If any provision of this Act or the application thereof to any person or circumstance is held invalid, its invalidity does not affect other provisions or applications of the Act which can be given effect without the invalid provision or application, and to this end the provisions of this Act are several.

## UNIFORM CHILD CUSTODY JURISDICTION AND ENFORCEMENT ACT

[ARTICLE] 1

SECTION 102. DEFINITIONS. In this [Act]:

(1) "Abandoned" means left without provision for reasonable and necessary care or supervision.

(2) "Child" means an individual who has not attained 18 years of age.

(3) "Child-custody determination" means a judgment, decree, or other order of a court providing for the legal custody, physical custody, or visitation with respect to a child. The term includes a permanent, temporary, initial, and modification order. The term does not include an order relating to child support or other monetary obligation of an individual.

(4) "Child-custody proceeding" means a proceeding in which legal custody, physical custody, or visitation with respect to a child is an issue. The term includes a proceeding for divorce, separation, neglect, abuse, dependency, guardianship, paternity, termination of parental rights, and protection from domestic violence, in which the issue may appear. The term does not include a proceeding involving juvenile delinquency, contractual emancipation, or enforcement under [Article] 3.

(5) "Commencement" means the filing of the first pleading in a proceeding.

(6) "Court" means an entity authorized under the law of a State to establish, enforce, or modify a child-custody determination.

(7) "Home State" means the State in which a child lived with a parent or a person acting as a parent for at least six consecutive months immediately before the commencement of a child-custody proceeding. In the case of a child less than six months of age, the term means the State in which the child lived from birth with any of the persons mentioned. A period of temporary absence of any of the mentioned persons is part of the period.

(8) "Initial determination" means the first child-custody determination concerning a particular child.

(9) "Issuing court" means the court that makes a child-custody determination for which enforcement is sought under this [Act].

(10) "Issuing State" means the State in which a child-custody determination is made.

(11) "Modification" means a child-custody determination that changes, replaces, supersedes, or is otherwise made after a previous determination concerning the same child, whether or not it is made by the court that made the previous determination.

(12) "Person" means an individual, corporation, business trust, estate, trust, partnership, limited liability company, association, joint venture, government; governmental subdivision, agency, or instrumentality; public corporation; or any other legal or commercial entity.

(13) "Person acting as a parent" means a person, other than a parent, who:

(A) has physical custody of the child or has had physical custody for a period of six consecutive months, including any temporary absence, within one year immediately before the commencement of a child-custody proceeding; and

(B) has been awarded legal custody by a court or claims a right to legal custody under the law of this State.

(14) "Physical custody" means the physical care and supervision of a child.

(15) "State" means a State of the United States, the District of Columbia, Puerto Rico, the United States Virgin Islands, or any territory or insular possession subject to the jurisdiction of the United States.

[(16) "Tribe" means an Indian tribe or band, or Alaskan Native village, which is recognized by federal law or formally acknowledged by a State.]

(17) "Warrant" means an order issued by a court authorizing law enforcement officers to take physical custody of a child . . .

UNIFORM CHILD CUSTODY JURISDICTION AND ENFORCEMENT ACT (Continued)

SECTION 106. EFFECT OF CHILD-CUSTODY DETERMINATION. A child-custody determination made by a court of this State that had jurisdiction under this [Act] binds all persons who have been served in accordance with the laws of this State or notified in accordance with Section 108 or who have submitted to the jurisdiction of the court, and who have been given an opportunity to be heard. As to those persons, the determination is conclusive as to all decided issues of law and fact except to the extent the determination is modified.

SECTION 107. PRIORITY. If a question of existence or exercise of jurisdiction under this [Act] is raised in a child-custody proceeding, the question, upon request of a party, must be given priority on the calendar and handled expeditiously.

The language change from "case" to "question" is intended to clarify that it is the jurisdictional issue which must be expedited and not the entire custody case. Whether the entire custody case should be given priority is a matter of local law.

SECTION 108. NOTICE TO PERSONS OUTSIDE STATE.

(a) Notice required for the exercise of jurisdiction when a person is outside this State may be given in a manner prescribed by the law of this State for service of process or by the law of the State in which the service is made. Notice must be given in a manner reasonably calculated to give actual notice but may be by publication if other means are not effective.

(b) Proof of service may be made in the manner prescribed by the law of this State or by the law of the State in which the service is made.

(c) Notice is not required for the exercise of jurisdiction with respect to a person who submits to the jurisdiction of the court.

SECTION 109. APPEARANCE AND LIMITED IMMUNITY.

(a) A party to a child-custody proceeding, including a modification proceeding, or a petitioner or respondent in a proceeding to enforce or register a child—custody determination, is not subject to personal jurisdiction in this State for another proceeding or purpose solely by reason of having participated, or of having been physically present for the purpose of participating, in the proceeding.

(b) A person who is subject to personal jurisdiction in this State on a basis other than physical presence is not immune from service of process in this State. A party present in this State who is subject to the jurisdiction of another State is not immune from service of process allowable under the laws of that State.

(c) The immunity granted by subsection (a) does not extend to civil litigation based on acts unrelated to the participation in a proceeding under this [Act] committed by an individual while present in this State.

SECTION 110. COMMUNICATION BETWEEN COURTS.

(a) A court of this State may communicate with a court in another State concerning a proceeding arising under this [Act].

(b) The court may allow the parties to participate in the communication. If the parties are not able to participate in the communication, they must be given the opportunity to present facts and legal arguments before a decision on jurisdiction is made.

(c) Communication between courts on schedules, calendars, court records, and similar matters may occur without informing the parties. A record need not be made of the communication.

(d) Except as otherwise provided in subsection (c), a record must be made of a communication under this section. The parties must be informed promptly of the communication and granted access to the record.

(e) For the purposes of this section, "record" means information that is inscribed on a tangible medium or that is stored in an electronic or other medium and is retrievable in perceivable form.

SECTION 111. TAKING TESTIMONY IN ANOTHER STATE.

(a) In addition to other procedures available to a party, a party to a child-custody proceeding may offer testimony of witnesses who are located in another State, including testimony of the parties and the child, by deposition or other means allowable in this State for testimony taken in another State. The court on its own motion may order that the testimony of a person be taken in another State and may prescribe the manner in which and the terms upon which the testimony is taken.

(b) A court of this State may permit an individual residing in another State to be deposed or to testify by telephone, audiovisual means, or other electronic means before a designated court or at another location in that State. A court of this State shall

*(continued)*

UNIFORM CHILD CUSTODY JURISDICTION AND ENFORCEMENT ACT (Continued)

cooperate with courts of other States in designating an appropriate location for the deposition or testimony.

(c) Documentary evidence transmitted from another State to a court of this State by technological means that do not produce an original writing may not be excluded from evidence on an objection based on the means of transmission.

SECTION 112. COOPERATION BETWEEN COURTS; PRESERVATION OF RECORDS.

(a) A court of this State may request the appropriate court of another State to:

(1) hold an evidentiary hearing;

(2) order a person to produce or give evidence pursuant to procedures of that State;

(3) order that an evaluation be made with respect to the custody of a child involved in a pending proceeding;

(4) forward to the court of this State a certified copy of the transcript of the record of the hearing, the evidence otherwise presented, and any evaluation prepared in compliance with the request; and

(5) order a party to a child-custody proceeding or any person having physical custody of the child to appear in the proceeding with or without the child.

(b) Upon request of a court of another State, a court of this State may hold a hearing or enter an order described in subsection (a).

(c) Travel and other necessary and reasonable expenses incurred under subsections (a) and (b) may be assessed against the parties according to the law of this State.

(d) A court of this State shall preserve the pleadings, orders, decrees, records of hearings, evaluations, and other pertinent records with respect to a child-custody proceeding until the child attains 18 years of age. Upon appropriate request by a court or law enforcement official of another State, the court shall forward a certified copy of those records.

[ARTICLE] 2

SECTION 201. INITIAL CHILD-CUSTODY JURISDICTION.

(a) Except as otherwise provided in Section 204, a court of this State has jurisdiction to make an initial child-custody determination only if:

(1) this State is the home State of the child on the date of the commencement of the proceeding, or was the home State of the child within six months before the commencement of the proceeding and the child is absent from this State but a parent or person acting as a parent continues to live in this State;

(2) a court of another State does not have jurisdiction under paragraph (1), or a court of the home State of the child has declined to exercise jurisdiction on the ground that this State is the more appropriate forum under Section 207 or 208, and:

(A) the child and the child's parents, or the child and at least one parent or a person acting as a parent, have a significant connection with this State other than mere physical presence; and

(B) substantial evidence is available in this State concerning the child's care, protection, training, and personal relationships;

(3) all courts having jurisdiction under paragraph (1) or (2) have declined to exercise jurisdiction on the ground that a court of this State is the more appropriate forum to determine the custody of the child under Section 207 or 208; or

(4) no court of any other State would have jurisdiction under the criteria specified in paragraph (1), (2), or (3).

(b) Subsection (a) is the exclusive jurisdictional basis for making a child-custody determination by a court of this State.

(c) Physical presence of, or personal jurisdiction over, a party or a child is not necessary or sufficient to make a child-custody determination.

SECTION 202. EXCLUSIVE, CONTINUING JURISDICTION.

(a) Except as otherwise provided in Section 204, a court of this State which has made a child-custody determination consistent with Section 201 or 203 has exclusive, continuing jurisdiction over the determination until:

(1) a court of this State determines that neither the child, the child's parents, and any person acting as a parent do not have a significant connection with this State and that substantial evidence is no longer available in this State concerning the child's care, protection, training, and personal relationships; or

(2) a court of this State or a court of another State determines that the child, the child's parents, and any person acting as a parent do not presently reside in this State.

(b) A court of this State which has made a child-custody determination and does not have exclusive, continuing jurisdiction under this section may

UNIFORM CHILD CUSTODY JURISDICTION AND ENFORCEMENT ACT (Continued)

modify that determination only if it has jurisdiction to make an initial determination under Section 201.

SECTION 203. JURISDICTION TO MODIFY DETERMINATION. Except as otherwise provided in Section 204, a court of this State may not modify a child-custody determination made by a court of another State unless a court of this State has jurisdiction to make an initial determination under Section 201(a)(1) or (2) and:

(1) the court of the other State determines it no longer has exclusive, continuing jurisdiction under Section 202 or that a court of this State would be a more convenient forum under Section 207; or

(2) a court of this State or a court of the other State determines that the child, the child's parents, and any person acting as a parent do not presently reside in the other State.

SECTION 204. TEMPORARY EMERGENCY JURISDICTION.

(a) A court of this State has temporary emergency jurisdiction if the child is present in this State and the child has been abandoned or it is necessary in an emergency to protect the child because the child, or a sibling or parent of the child, is subjected to or threatened with mistreatment or abuse.

(b) If there is no previous child-custody determination that is entitled to be enforced under this [Act] and a child-custody proceeding has not been commenced in a court of a State having jurisdiction under Sections 201 through 203, a child-custody determination made under this section remains in effect until an order is obtained from a court of a State having jurisdiction under Sections 201 through 203. If a child-custody proceeding has not been or is not commenced in a court of a State having jurisdiction under Sections 201 through 203, a child-custody determination made under this section becomes a final determination, if it so provides and this State becomes the home State of the child.

(c) If there is a previous child-custody determination that is entitled to be enforced under this [Act], or a child-custody proceeding has been commenced in a court of a State having jurisdiction under Sections 201 through 203, any order issued by a court of this State under this section must specify in the order a period that the court considers adequate to allow the person seeking an order to obtain an order from the State having jurisdiction under Sections 201 through

203. The order issued in this State remains in effect until an order is obtained from the other State within the period specified or the period expires.

(d) A court of this State which has been asked to make a child-custody determination under this section, upon being informed that a child-custody proceeding has been commenced in, or a child-custody determination has been made by, a court of a State having jurisdiction under Sections 201 through 203, shall immediately communicate with the other court. A court of this State which is exercising jurisdiction pursuant to Sections 201 through 203, upon being informed that a child-custody proceeding has been commenced in, or a child-custody determination has been made by, a court of another State under a statute similar to this section shall immediately communicate with the court of that State to resolve the emergency, protect the safety of the parties and the child, and determine a period for the duration of the temporary order.

SECTION 205. NOTICE; OPPORTUNITY TO BE HEARD; JOINDER.

(a) Before a child-custody determination is made under this [Act], notice and an opportunity to be heard in accordance with the standards of Section 108 must be given to all persons entitled to notice under the law of this State as in child-custody proceedings between residents of this State, any parent whose parental rights have not been previously terminated, and any person having physical custody of the child.

(b) This [Act] does not govern the enforceability of a child-custody determination made without notice or an opportunity to be heard.

(c) The obligation to join a party and the right to intervene as a party in a child-custody proceeding under this [Act] are governed by the law of this State as in child-custody proceedings between residents of this State.

SECTION 206. SIMULTANEOUS PROCEEDINGS.

(a) Except as otherwise provided in Section 204, a court of this State may not exercise its jurisdiction under this [article] if, at the time of the commencement of the proceeding, a proceeding concerning the custody of the child has been commenced in a court of another State having jurisdiction substantially

*(continued)*

UNIFORM CHILD CUSTODY JURISDICTION AND ENFORCEMENT ACT (Continued)

in conformity with this [Act], unless the proceeding has been terminated or is stayed by the court of the other State because a court of this State is a more convenient forum under Section 207.

(b) Except as otherwise provided in Section 204, a court of this State, before hearing a child-custody proceeding, shall examine the court documents and other information supplied by the parties pursuant to Section 209. If the court determines that a child-custody proceeding has been commenced in a court in another State having jurisdiction substantially in accordance with this [Act], the court of this State shall stay its proceeding and communicate with the court of the other State. If the court of the State having jurisdiction substantially in accordance with this [Act] does not determine that the court of this State is a more appropriate forum, the court of this State shall dismiss the proceeding.

(c) In a proceeding to modify a child-custody determination, a court of this State shall determine whether a proceeding to enforce the determination has been commenced in another State. If a proceeding to enforce a child-custody determination has been commenced in another State, the court may:

(1) stay the proceeding for modification pending the entry of an order of a court of the other State enforcing, staying, denying, or dismissing the proceeding for enforcement;

(2) enjoin the parties from continuing with the proceeding for enforcement; or

(3) proceed with the modification under conditions it considers appropriate.

### SECTION 207. INCONVENIENT FORUM.

(a) A court of this State which has jurisdiction under this [Act] to make a child-custody determination may decline to exercise its jurisdiction at any time if it determines that it is an inconvenient forum under the circumstances and that a court of another State is a more appropriate forum. The issue of inconvenient forum may be raised upon motion of a party, the court's own motion, or request of another court.

(b) Before determining whether it is an inconvenient forum, a court of this State shall consider whether it is appropriate for a court of another State to exercise jurisdiction. For this purpose, the court shall allow the parties to submit information and shall consider all relevant factors, including:

(1) whether domestic violence has occurred and is likely to continue in the future and which State could best protect the parties and the child;

(2) the length of time the child has resided outside this State;

(3) the distance between the court in this State and the court in the State that would assume jurisdiction;

(4) the relative financial circumstances of the parties;

(5) any agreement of the parties as to which State should assume jurisdiction;

(6) the nature and location of the evidence required to resolve the pending litigation, including testimony of the child;

(7) the ability of the court of each State to decide the issue expeditiously and the procedures necessary to present the evidence; and

(8) the familiarity of the court of each State with the facts and issues in the pending litigation.

(c) If a court of this State determines that it is an inconvenient forum and that a court of another State is a more appropriate forum, it shall stay the proceedings upon condition that a child-custody proceeding be promptly commenced in another designated State and may impose any other condition the court considers just and proper.

(d) A court of this State may decline to exercise its jurisdiction under this [Act] if a child-custody determination is incidental to an action for divorce or another proceeding while still retaining jurisdiction over the divorce or other proceeding.

### SECTION 208. JURISDICTION DECLINED BY REASON OF CONDUCT.

(a) Except as otherwise provided in Section 204 [or by other law of this State], if a court of this State has jurisdiction under this [Act] because a person seeking to invoke its jurisdiction has engaged in unjustifiable conduct, the court shall decline to exercise its jurisdiction unless:

(1) the parents and all persons acting as parents have acquiesced in the exercise of jurisdiction;

(2) a court of the State otherwise having jurisdiction under Sections 201 through 203 determines that this State is a more appropriate forum under Section 207; or

(3) no court of any other State would have jurisdiction under the criteria specified in Sections 201 through 203.

(b) If a court of this State declines to exercise its jurisdiction pursuant to subsection (a), it may fashion

UNIFORM CHILD CUSTODY JURISDICTION AND ENFORCEMENT ACT (Continued)

an appropriate remedy to ensure the safety of the child and prevent a repetition of the unjustifiable conduct, including staying the proceeding until a child-custody proceeding is commenced in a court having jurisdiction under Sections 201 through 203.

(c) If a court dismisses a petition or stays a proceeding because it declines to exercise its jurisdiction pursuant to subsection (a), it shall assess against the party seeking to invoke its jurisdiction necessary and reasonable expenses including costs, communication expenses, attorney's fees, investigative fees, expenses for witnesses, travel expenses, and child care during the course of the proceedings, unless the party from whom fees are sought establishes that the assessment would be clearly inappropriate. The court may not assess fees, costs, or expenses against this State unless authorized by law other than this [Act].

SECTION 209. INFORMATION TO BE SUBMITTED TO COURT.

(a) [Subject to [local law providing for the confidentiality of procedures, addresses, and other identifying information], in] [In] a child-custody proceeding, each party, in its first pleading or in an attached affidavit, shall give information, if reasonably ascertainable, under oath as to the child's present address or whereabouts, the places where the child has lived during the last five years, and the names and present addresses of the persons with whom the child has lived during that period. The pleading or affidavit must state whether the party:

(1) has participated, as a party or witness or in any other capacity, in any other proceeding concerning the custody of or visitation with the child and, if so, identify the court, the case number, and the date of the child-custody determination, if any;

(2) knows of any proceeding that could affect the current proceeding, including proceedings for enforcement and proceedings relating to domestic violence, protective orders, termination of parental rights, and adoptions and, if so, identify the court, the case number, and the nature of the proceeding; and

(3) knows the names and addresses of any person not a party to the proceeding who has physical custody of the child or claims rights of legal custody or physical custody of, or visitation with, the child and, if so, the names and addresses of those persons.

(b) If the information required by subsection (a) is not furnished, the court, upon motion of a party or its own motion, may stay the proceeding until the information is furnished.

(c) If the declaration as to any of the items described in subsection (a)(1) through (3) is in the affirmative, the declarant shall give additional information under oath as required by the court. The court may examine the parties under oath as to details of the information furnished and other matters pertinent to the court's jurisdiction and the disposition of the case.

(d) Each party has a continuing duty to inform the court of any proceeding in this or any other State that could affect the current proceeding.

[(e) If a party alleges in an affidavit or a pleading under oath that the health, safety, or liberty of a party or child would be jeopardized by disclosure of identifying information, the information must be sealed and may not be disclosed to the other party or the public unless the court orders the disclosure to be made after a hearing in which the court takes into consideration the health, safety, or liberty of the party or child and determines that the disclosure is in the interest of justice.]

SECTION 210. APPEARANCE OF PARTIES AND CHILD.

(a) In a child-custody proceeding in this State, the court may order a party to the proceeding who is in this State to appear before the court in person with or without the child. The court may order any person who is in this State and who has physical custody or control of the child to appear in person with the child.

(b) If a party to a child-custody proceeding whose presence is desired by the court is outside this State, the court may order that a notice given pursuant to Section 108 include a statement directing the party to appear in person with or without the child and informing the party that failure to appear may result in a decision adverse to the party.

(c) The court may enter any orders necessary to ensure the safety of the child and of any person ordered to appear under this section.

(d) If a party to a child-custody proceeding who is outside this State is directed to appear under subsection (b) or desires to appear personally before the court with or without the child, the court may require another party to pay reasonable and necessary travel and other expenses of the party so appearing and of the child.

*(continued)*

UNIFORM CHILD CUSTODY JURISDICTION AND ENFORCEMENT ACT (Continued)

[ARTICLE]  3 ENFORCEMENT

SECTION 301. DEFINITIONS. In this [article]:

(1) "Petitioner" means a person who seeks enforcement of an order for return of a child under the Hague Convention on the Civil Aspects of International Child Abduction or enforcement of a child-custody determination.

(2) "Respondent" means a person against whom a proceeding has been commenced for enforcement of an order for return of a child under the Hague Convention on the Civil Aspects of International Child Abduction or enforcement of a child-custody determination.

SECTION 302. ENFORCEMENT UNDER HAGUE CONVENTION. Under this [article] a court of this State may enforce an order for the return of the child made under the Hague Convention on the Civil Aspects of International Child Abduction as if it were a child—custody determination.

SECTION 303. DUTY TO ENFORCE.

(a) A court of this State shall recognize and enforce a child-custody determination of a court of another State if the latter court exercised jurisdiction in substantial conformity with this [Act] or the determination was made under factual circumstances meeting the jurisdictional standards of this [Act] and the determination has not been modified in accordance with this [Act].

(b) A court of this State may utilize any remedy available under other law of this State to enforce a child-custody determination made by a court of another State. The remedies provided in this [article] are cumulative and do not affect the availability of other remedies to enforce a child-custody determination.

SECTION 304. TEMPORARY VISITATION.

(a) A court of this State which does not have jurisdiction to modify a child-custody determination, may issue a temporary order enforcing:

(1) a visitation schedule made by a court of another State; or

(2) the visitation provisions of a child-custody determination of another State that does not provide for a specific visitation schedule.

(b) If a court of this State makes an order under subsection (a)(2), it shall specify in the order a period that it considers adequate to allow the petitioner to obtain an order from a court having jurisdiction under the criteria specified in [Article] 2. The order

remains in effect until an order is obtained from the other court or the period expires.

SECTION 305. REGISTRATION OF CHILD-CUSTODY DETERMINATION.

(a) A child-custody determination issued by a court of another State may be registered in this State, with or without a simultaneous request for enforcement, by sending to [the appropriate court] in this State:

(1) a letter or other document requesting registration;

(2) two copies, including one certified copy, of the determination sought to be registered, and a statement under penalty of perjury that to the best of the knowledge and belief of the person seeking registration the order has not been modified; and

(3) except as otherwise provided in Section 209, the name and address of the person seeking registration and any parent or person acting as a parent who has been awarded custody or visitation in the child-custody determination sought to be registered.

(b) On receipt of the documents required by subsection (a), the registering court shall:

(1) cause the determination to be filed as a foreign judgment, together with one copy of any accompanying documents and information, regardless of their form; and

(2) serve notice upon the persons named pursuant to subsection (a)(3) and provide them with an opportunity to contest the registration in accordance with this section.

(c) The notice required by subsection (b)(2) must state that:

(1) a registered determination is enforceable as of the date of the registration in the same manner as a determination issued by a court of this State;

(2) a hearing to contest the validity of the registered determination must be requested within 20 days after service of notice; and

(3) failure to contest the registration will result in confirmation of the child-custody determination and preclude further contest of that determination with respect to any matter that could have been asserted.

(d) A person seeking to contest the validity of a registered order must request a hearing within 20 days after service of the notice. At that hearing, the court shall confirm the registered order unless the person contesting registration establishes that:

UNIFORM CHILD CUSTODY JURISDICTION AND ENFORCEMENT ACT (Continued)

(1) the issuing court did not have jurisdiction under [Article] 2;

(2) the child-custody determination sought to be registered has been vacated, stayed, or modified by a court having jurisdiction to do so under [Article] 2; or

(3) the person contesting registration was entitled to notice, but notice was not given in accordance with the standards of Section 108, in the proceedings before the court that issued the order for which registration is sought.

(e) If a timely request for a hearing to contest the validity of the registration is not made, the registration is confirmed as a matter of law and the person requesting registration and all persons served must be notified of the confirmation.

(f) Confirmation of a registered order, whether by operation of law or after notice and hearing, precludes further contest of the order with respect to any matter that could have been asserted at the time of registration.

SECTION 306. ENFORCEMENT OF REGISTERED DETERMINATION.

(a) A court of this State may grant any relief normally available under the law of this State to enforce a registered child-custody determination made by a court of another State.

(b) A court of this State shall recognize and enforce, but may not modify, except in accordance with [Article] 2, a registered child-custody determination of a court of another State.

SECTION 307. SIMULTANEOUS PROCEEDINGS. If a proceeding for enforcement under this [article] is commenced in a court of this State and the court determines that a proceeding to modify the determination is pending in a court of another State having jurisdiction to modify the determination under [Article] 2, the enforcing court shall immediately communicate with the modifying court. The proceeding for enforcement continues unless the enforcing court, after consultation with the modifying court, stays or dismisses the proceeding.

SECTION 308. EXPEDITED ENFORCEMENT OF CHILD-CUSTODY DETERMINATION.

(a) A petition under this [article] must be verified. Certified copies of all orders sought to be enforced and of any order confirming registration must be attached to the petition. A copy of a certified copy of an order may be attached instead of the original.

(b) A petition for enforcement of a child-custody determination must state:

(1) whether the court that issued the determination identified the jurisdictional basis it relied upon in exercising jurisdiction and, if so, what the basis was;

(2) whether the determination for which enforcement is sought has been vacated, stayed, or modified by a court whose decision must be enforced under this [Act] and, if so, identify the court, the case number, and the nature of the proceeding;

(3) whether any proceeding has been commenced that could affect the current proceeding, including proceedings relating to domestic violence, protective orders, termination of parental rights, and adoptions and, if so, identify the court, the case number, and the nature of the proceeding;

(4) the present physical address of the child and the respondent, if known;

(5) whether relief in addition to the immediate physical custody of the child and attorney's fees is sought, including a request for assistance from [law enforcement officials] and, if so, the relief sought; and

(6) if the child-custody determination has been registered and confirmed under Section 305, the date and place of registration.

(c) Upon the filing of a petition, the court shall issue an order directing the respondent to appear in person with or without the child at a hearing and may enter any order necessary to ensure the safety of the parties and the child. The hearing must be held on the next judicial day after service of the order unless that date is impossible. In that event, the court shall hold the hearing on the first judicial day possible. The court may extend the date of hearing at the request of the petitioner.

(d) An order issued under subsection (c) must state the time and place of the hearing and advise the respondent that at the hearing the court will order that the petitioner may take immediate physical custody of the child and the payment of fees, costs, and expenses under Section 312, and may schedule a hearing to determine whether further relief is appropriate, unless the respondent appears and establishes that:

*(continued)*

UNIFORM CHILD CUSTODY JURISDICTION AND ENFORCEMENT ACT (Continued)

(1) the child-custody determination has not been registered and confirmed under Section 305 and that:

(A) the issuing court did not have jurisdiction under [Article] 2;

(B) the child-custody determination for which enforcement is sought has been vacated, stayed, or modified by a court having jurisdiction to do so under [Article] 2;

(C) the respondent was entitled to notice, but notice was not given in accordance with the standards of Section 108, in the proceedings before the court that issued the order for which enforcement is sought; or

(2) the child-custody determination for which enforcement is sought was registered and confirmed under Section 304, but has been vacated, stayed, or modified by a court of a State having jurisdiction to do so under [Article] 2.

SECTION 309. SERVICE OF PETITION AND ORDER. Except as otherwise provided in Section 311, the petition and order must be served, by any method authorized [by the law of this State], upon respondent and any person who has physical custody of the child.

SECTION 310. HEARING AND ORDER.

(a) Unless the court issues a temporary emergency order pursuant to Section 204, upon a finding that a petitioner is entitled to immediate physical custody of the child, the court shall order that the petitioner may take immediate physical custody of the child unless the respondent establishes that:

(1) the child-custody determination has not been registered and confirmed under Section 305 and that:

(A) the issuing court did not have jurisdiction under [Article] 2;

(B) the child-custody determination for which enforcement is sought has been vacated, stayed, or modified by a court of a State having jurisdiction to do so under [Article] 2; or

(C) the respondent was entitled to notice, but notice was not given in accordance with the standards of Section 108, in the proceedings before the court that issued the order for which enforcement is sought; or

(2) the child-custody determination for which enforcement is sought was registered and confirmed under Section 305 but has been vacated, stayed, or modified by a court of a State having jurisdiction to do so under [Article] 2.

(b) The court shall award the fees, costs, and expenses authorized under Section 312 and may grant additional relief, including a request for the assistance of [law enforcement officials], and set a further hearing to determine whether additional relief is appropriate.

(c) If a party called to testify refuses to answer on the ground that the testimony may be self-incriminating, the court may draw an adverse inference from the refusal.

(d) A privilege against disclosure of communications between spouses and a defense of immunity based on the relationship of husband and wife or parent and child may not be invoked in a proceeding under this [article].

SECTION 311. WARRANT TO TAKE PHYSICAL CUSTODY OF CHILD.

(a) Upon the filing of a petition seeking enforcement of a child-custody determination, the petitioner may file a verified application for the issuance of a warrant to take physical custody of the child if the child is immediately likely to suffer serious physical harm or be removed from this State.

(b) If the court, upon the testimony of the petitioner or other witness, finds that the child is imminently likely to suffer serious physical harm or be removed from this State, it may issue a warrant to take physical custody of the child. The petition must be heard on the next judicial day after the warrant is executed unless that date is impossible. In that event, the court shall hold the hearing on the first judicial day possible. The application for the warrant must include the statements required by Section 308(b).

(c) A warrant to take physical custody of a child must:

(1) recite the facts upon which a conclusion of imminent serious physical harm or removal from the jurisdiction is based;

(2) direct law enforcement officers to take physical custody of the child immediately; and

(3) provide for the placement of the child pending final relief.

(d) The respondent must be served with the petition, warrant, and order immediately after the child is taken into physical custody.

UNIFORM CHILD CUSTODY JURISDICTION AND ENFORCEMENT ACT (Continued)

(e) A warrant to take physical custody of a child is enforceable throughout this State. If the court finds on the basis of the testimony of the petitioner or other witness that a less intrusive remedy is not effective, it may authorize law enforcement officers to enter private property to take physical custody of the child. If required by exigent circumstances of the case, the court may authorize law enforcement officers to make a forcible entry at any hour.

(f) The court may impose conditions upon placement of a child to ensure the appearance of the child and the child's custodian. . . .

SECTION 313. RECOGNITION AND ENFORCEMENT. A court of this State shall accord full faith and credit to an order issued by another State and consistent with this [Act] which enforces a child—custody determination by a court of another State unless the order has been vacated, stayed, or modified by a court having jurisdiction to do so under [Article] 2.

The enforcement order, to be effective, must also be enforced by other States. This section requires courts of this State to enforce and not modify enforcement orders issued by other States when made consistently with the provisions of this Act. . . .

## ASSIGNMENT 10.3

Examine the UCCJA and UCCJEA excerpts in Exhibit 10.3. Based on those excerpts, answer the following questions and include the relevant citation.

1. How long must a child live in a state that is not the child's home state before a court obtains jurisdiction as the result of residency?
2. When can a court with jurisdiction in a child-custody matter decline to exercise its jurisdiction?
3. When is a party to a custody hearing not required to be given notice?
4. Who may be a contestant in a child-custody proceeding?
5. Can a court decline jurisdiction in the custody proceeding and still hear the related proceeding for divorce or dissolution of marriage?

6. How can a party seek enforcement of a custody decree rendered in another state?
7. Can a court in one state ask the court of another state to take action in a custody determination?
8. What is a "home state" in a custody proceeding?
9. If a person files a custody petition and the court dismisses the petition as an inconvenient forum and identifies a more appropriate forum, is the person liable for any costs of the other party?
10. If custody proceedings are pending simultaneously in different states, when can the proceeding initiated in the second state continue?

# CHILD SUPPORT

Although the obligation to provide support to a spouse may end with the dissolution of the marital relationship, support of the marriage's children continues as long as the court determines it is necessary. Generally, this is for the remainder of the child's minority or until high school graduation.[32] However, judges are increasingly coming to the view that parents, when able, should also contribute toward a child's college education.[33] The theory is that the child of divorced parents should be in a position similar to the child of nondivorced parents who has the benefit of family support. In addition, support may be extended beyond a child's majority if the child has some physical or mental incapacity that prevents the child from becoming responsible for filling his or her own needs. Many states now have statutes that address issues of support during postsecondary education or incapacity.

If a child marries or becomes legally emancipated before the age of majority, the child will become fully independent. As a result, the parents will no longer be legally responsible for providing support for the child. On the other hand, if a parent dies and leaves no provision for the support of the child, the child is still entitled to a share of the parent's estate for support. The exception to this occurs when the parent leaves a will in which he or she specifically disinherits the child. If this occurs, the support may, in some states, be terminated, and the child becomes the sole responsibility of the surviving parent. However, as with matters of domestic law, the particular state's law should be examined in a situation before reaching any conclusions.

There is usually little contest over the obligation to provide support. Most parties accept that they are obligated to support their natural or adopted children. The real turmoil begins when the parties attempt to determine the amount of support to be contributed. If financially able, the noncustodial parent—whether the mother or the father—is responsible for periodically paying a specified amount to the custodial parent. The money is to be used for such needs of the child as food, shelter, clothing, and medical and educational expenses.

Unless the parties agree to an amount for support, a hearing will be held to determine the child's financial needs based on information provided by the parties and the noncustodial parent's ability to contribute to the child's financial needs. With this information, the court will make a decision as to what an appropriate amount would be and how often the amount should be paid.[34]

## Child-Support Guidelines

When determining the amount of child support, the court considers many independent factors that influence the amount of support that it will actually order. Many states have guidelines that provide formulas for calculation or factors that should be considered, including, but not limited to, the following:

1. the number of children (of this marriage or others) for whom the parent is obligated to provide support,
2. whether one of the parents provides health insurance for the child,
3. the net income of each parent,
4. any special medical or educational needs of the child, and
5. the standard of living the child would have enjoyed had the divorce not occurred.[35]

It is assumed that an equitable share is contributed by the custodial parent who physically provides the food, shelter, clothing, and attention to other needs of the child.

A particularly helpful statute has been adopted in recent years that establishes child support guidelines (see Exhibit 10.4). These guidelines have been adopted in most states and provide a formula that courts can employ to determine the appropriate amount of child support, given the financial circumstances of the parties. However, these are only guidelines, and typically a court has the authority to override them in cases involving special considerations.

**Exhibit 10.4** Nevada Revised Statutes Title 11. Domestic Relations. Chapter 125B. Obligation of Support. General Provisions

125B.070. Amount of payment: Definitions; review of formula by State Bar of Nevada.

1. As used in this section and NRS 125B.080, unless the context otherwise requires:

(a) "Gross monthly income" means the total amount of income from any source of a wage-earning employee or the gross income from any source of a self-employed person, after deduction of all legitimate business expenses, but without deduction for personal income taxes, contributions for retirement benefits, contributions to a pension or for any other personal expenses.

(b) "Obligation for support" means the amount determined according to the following schedule:

(1) For one child, 18 percent;

(2) For two children, 25 percent;

(3) For three children, 29 percent;

(4) For four children, 31 percent; and

(5) For each additional child, an additional 2 percent, of a parent's gross monthly income, but not more than $500 per month per child for an1 obligation for support determined pursuant to subparagraphs (1) to (4), inclusive, unless the court sets forth findings of fact as to the basis for a different amount pursuant to subsection 5 of NRS 125B.080.

2. On or before January 18, 1993, and on or before the third Monday in January every 4 years thereafter, the State Bar of Nevada shall review the formulas set forth in this section to determine whether any modifications are advisable and report to the legislature their findings and any proposed amendments.

125B.080. Formula for determining amount of support.

1. A court shall apply the appropriate formula set forth in paragraph (b) of subsection 1 of NRS 125B.070 to:

(a) Determine the required support in any case involving the support of children.

(b) Any request filed after July 1, 1987, to change the amount of the required support of children.

2. If the parties agree as to the amount of support required, the parties shall certify that the amount of support is consistent with the appropriate formula set forth in paragraph (b) of subsection 1 of NRS 125B.070. If the amount of support deviates from the formula, the parties must stipulate sufficient facts in accordance with subsection 9 which justify the deviation to the court, and the court shall make a written finding thereon. Any inaccuracy or falsification of financial information which results in an inappropriate award of support is grounds for a motion to modify or adjust the award.

3. If the parties disagree as to the amount of the gross monthly income of either party, the court shall determine the amount and may direct either party to furnish financial information or other records, including income tax returns for the preceding 3 years. Once a court has established an obligation for support by reference to a formula set forth in paragraph (b) of subsection 1 of NRS 125B.070, any subsequent modification or adjustment of that support must be based upon changed circumstances or as a result of a review conducted pursuant to NRS 125B.145.

4. Notwithstanding the formulas set forth in paragraph (b) of subsection 1 of NRS 125B.070, the minimum amount of support that may be awarded by a court in any case is $100 per month per child, unless the court makes a written finding that the obligor is unable to pay the minimum amount. Willful underemployment or unemployment is not a sufficient cause to deviate from the awarding of at least the minimum amount.

5. It is presumed that the basic needs of a child are met by the formulas set forth in paragraph (b) of subsection 1 of NRS 125B.070. This presumption may be rebutted by evidence proving that the needs of a particular child are not met by the applicable formula.

6. If the amount of the awarded support for a child is greater or less than the amount which would be established under the applicable formula, the court shall set forth findings of fact as to the basis for the deviation from the formula.

7. Expenses for health care which are not reimbursed, including expenses for medical, surgical, dental, orthodontic and optical expenses, must be borne equally by both parents in the absence of extraordinary circumstances.

8. If a parent who has an obligation for support is willfully underemployed or unemployed, to avoid an obligation for support of a child, that obligation must be based upon the parent's true potential earning capacity.

9. The court shall consider the following factors when adjusting the amount of support of a child upon specific findings of fact:

(a) The cost of health insurance;

(b) The cost of child care;

(c) Any special educational needs of the child;

(d) The age of the child;

(e) The responsibility of the parents for the support of others;

*(continued)*

**Exhibit 10.4** (Continued)

---

(f) The value of services contributed by either parent;

(g) Any public assistance paid to support the child;

(h) Any expenses reasonably related to the mother's pregnancy and confinement;

(i) The cost of transportation of the child to and from visitation if the custodial parent moved with the child

from the jurisdiction of the court which ordered the support and the noncustodial parent remained;

(j) The amount of time the child spends with each parent;

(k) Any other necessary expenses for the benefit of the child; and

(l) The relative income of both parents.

---

## Modification of Support

Once support has been awarded, it is due and payable until the child reaches the age of majority or the court orders a change in the amount of support payable. If support is being paid to a custodial parent for the care of more than one child, the noncustodial parent cannot automatically reduce the support when one of the children reaches the age of majority. Usually, a party is required to petition the court to review the original support order and modify it accordingly.

Modification of support may be granted in circumstances other than a child's reaching majority. Courts will periodically entertain petitions to modify support when there has been a substantial change in the general cost of supporting the child. If a divorce occurs when a child is very young, it may be necessary for the custodial parent to seek an increase in support at some time during the child's minority. After several years, as the child enters school, inflation and other factors may increase the cost of meeting the child's needs. The custodial parent may need to seek an upward modification of the original order of support.

The status of the parents may change dramatically over a longer period of time. If one parent meets with long-term financial difficulty, a downward or upward modification may be in order. If the custodial parent enjoys tremendous financial gain, it may serve no purpose for the noncustodial parent to continue contributing to the child's support. The point is that many circumstances could occur that necessitate a change in the original order of support. However, most states limit the frequency with which such changes may be made and require that the circumstances that warrant such a change be substantial and long-term.

## Failure to Pay

If a party fails to adhere to an order of support, several things may take place. Usually, the first to occur is a legal action by the custodial parent against the parent obligated to pay support. The action is generally a request to hold the noncustodial parent in contempt of court for deliberately disobeying a court order to provide support for the minor child. In addition, many states have enacted or are considering procedures by which the licenses (drivers, business, professional, liquor, etc.) of parents failing to pay child support can be revoked. A parent who is unable to pay support on the date ordered should always attempt to modify rather than ignore the court order. In the eyes of the court, if the parent is able to pay the support but does not or is habitually late in paying, then the court may enter an order of contempt.[36]

The results of a finding of contempt of court may be many and varied. The wages of the party may be garnished. The party may be fined. In extreme cases—usually where there has been ongoing contemptuous conduct—the party may be jailed for a period of time. Contrary to popular belief, a court will not deny visitation on the sole basis of failure to pay child support. Nor should a custodial parent ever expect a court to approve of deliberate denial of visitation rights based on a failure to pay support. The two issues are treated as totally separate. The reasoning of the court is that although failure to support may adversely affect a child, denial of visitation has no positive effect on the child but only increases the adversity that the child must deal with. If a court does deny visitation, then it is usually on the basis that the parent has abandoned all parental responsibility.

In the past, many actions to recover support were rendered virtually impossible because the noncustodial parent lived in another state. This made it extremely difficult for the court to exercise any control over the parent in terms of compelling payment of support. However, all states have now adopted the Uniform Reciprocal Enforcement of Support Act, a pact among all states to assist one another in enforcing support orders. An action may be filed in the state where the dependent resides. However, a public prosecutor in the state where the noncustodial parent resides may try the case there and enforce any orders of support or contempt. No longer can a noncustodial parent avoid support simply by moving beyond the custodial parent's jurisdictional and financial reach.

## ASSIGNMENT 10.4

Consider the following situation and determine what would likely be considered when making a determination about support.

Teri and Tom were married for four years. Teri has custody of the children. Tonya, who was age three at the time of the divorce, is now eighteen and attending college. Tim was one year old at the time of the divorce and is now sixteen. The child support originally ordered was 45 percent of Tom's net pay. Teri agreed to this in lieu of a combination of child support and maintenance. Fourteen years later, the award remains unmodified. Tom now wishes to reduce the amount of child support because Tonya is a legal adult. Teri wishes to increase the amount of child support to correspond to Tom's current income. Teri was not employed during the marriage or at the time of the divorce but now earns an income comparable to that of Tom. However, she claims that Tonya still lives at home and thus the expenses have not decreased. She further claims that Tim is a gifted violinist, and she needs additional income to afford the various lessons and supplies necessary to support his training. Tonya works part-time when in school and full-time during the summer but does not contribute to the household expenses.

## VISITATION

When one parent is awarded custody of the child, the noncustodial parent is usually given specific visitation rights. In some cases, the rights are characterized as *reasonable visitation*. However, this tends to leave the visitation to the discretion of the custodial parent in determining what is reasonable. Often the parents will dispute over this term because what is reasonable visitation to one may be unreasonable to the other. Ultimately, many parties return to court to have a judge make the determination. Therefore, the preferred choice is to set forth specific times and sometimes arrangements (when travel is involved) for visitation.

Every parent is deemed to possess a constitutional right to share the companionship of his or her child.[37] Unless the parent's conduct would endanger the child, this right cannot be abridged. However, if the parent's conduct might endanger the child, the court may limit or place conditions on the visitation. Common conditions include requiring visitation to be confined to a specific place or requiring visitation to be supervised by a third party to ensure the child's safety and well-being. Extreme situations may result in a court's denial of visitation for a period of time to protect the child's welfare.

Many states have statutory guidelines that judges attempt to follow to ensure each parent time and the opportunity to share special holidays and other occasions with the child. It must be understood that a visitation schedule sets forth the minimum rights of the noncustodial parent. If the two parents agree to additional or different times for visitation, this is entirely appropriate. If problems arise, however, the court will generally not enforce such agreements but will usually follow only the scheduled visitation plan.

Penalties may result in cases where a visitation schedule is set forth in a court order and the custodial parent interferes with visitation. Interference includes such things as refusing visitation, not having the children available for visitation when the noncustodial parent arrives, directly influencing the children to avoid visitation, or engaging in other conduct that interferes with the noncustodial parent's constitutional right to share companionship with the children.

When such conduct occurs, the noncustodial parent has the right to bring an action against the custodial parent for contempt of court. The allegation is generally that the custodial parent willfully ignored or interfered with a court order of visitation. A court is not likely to be tolerant of such conduct. Penalties range from monetary fines to jail sentences. In continuing and extreme cases, the court may view the conduct as adverse to the best interests of the child and order a change of custody.

## PROPERTY AND DEBT DIVISION

**property settlement**
Agreement as to the property rights and obligations of co-owners or co-debtors such as parties to a marriage.

The states follow two schools of thought with respect to **property settlement** in the case of divorce. Some states are separate property states; others are community property states. The theory that a state follows will dictate the rights of the parties seeking a divorce. In cases where the parties were formally married, lived, or divorced in different states, the court will usually look to the law of the state where the parties resided when the property was acquired.

### Separate Property

Separate property states take the position that all property individually owned before the marriage is individual property and not jointly owned marital property.[38] In addition, property acquired during the marriage through gift, inheritance, or personal earnings without contribution by the other spouse is individual property. In a divorce action, parties are awarded their individual property respectively, and the court determines how marital property should be distributed.

In a complete application of the separate property theory, a nonemployed spouse may be entitled to virtually nothing at the conclusion of the divorce. Because this effect is not fair, based on each spouse's contribution to the marital relationship, many courts have modified the rule to result in a more equitable application. Although a state may still adhere to the theory of separate property, the court has a duty to equitably distribute property obtained during the marriage. Such property may have been purchased solely with the earnings of one spouse. If, however, the other spouse cared for the home and otherwise supported and enabled the first spouse to earn the money to purchase the property, then such property is considered the result of a joint effort. In this way, the court can fairly consider certain property to be marital property and distribute it equally.

### Community Property

Community property states take a different approach to the disposition of the property of spouses. In such states, property acquired during the marriage through personal earnings is presumed to be marital property.[39] Also included is property individually owned before the marriage that a party contributed to the marriage. When a spouse can establish that certain property was never comingled or otherwise shared with the other spouse as marital property would be, then such property is not included as community property.

After the court has determined what, if any, separate property exists, it attempts to equitably divide the community property. The court considers the contribution of each partner to the marriage and then attempts to make a fairly equal division of the property. Circumstances must be rather compelling before a court is permitted to make a significantly unbalanced distribution of the parties' assets.

## Pensions and Employee Benefit Programs

Under either type of property state, if a spouse was employed and received an interest in a pension or benefit plan during the marriage, the other spouse may have a claim to a portion of the amount to be received under the plan. Determination of what is equitable is a perplexing problem for most courts. In many cases, the divorce occurs many years before the benefits are to be received. In addition, it is difficult to determine what an equitable share of an earned pension or benefit program would be because the spouse has not earned the maximum pension or benefit possible. A final problem is that the parties remain somewhat bound to each other even through retirement. Many courts prefer to make a valuation of each party's interest and have one party buy out the other party's interest at the time of the dissolution. In this way, the parties' ties to each other can be completely and permanently severed, thus lessening the possibilities for future legal disputes.

Note that to establish division of pension and retirement funds in a way that will be recognized by the Internal Revenue Service, a qualified domestic relations order (QDRO) must be issued (in addition to other documents such as a property settlement agreement and a decree of dissolution of marriage) that details the rights and obligations of the parties with respect to these matters.

## Marital Debts

The manner in which individual and marital debts are determined and distributed is substantially the same as with property. The same tests are applied to determine whether debts were incurred as part of the marital relationship or on behalf of the individual. Similarly, the courts attempt an equitable distribution of responsibility for such debts. However, debts incurred during a marriage have an additional aspect that property usually does not: the claims of third parties.

While parties may agree—or a court may determine—that certain debts are individual rather than marital, great legal expense can arise from claims of third parties that the debt is joint. For example, as long as the parties are joint owners of a credit card, any property purchased with the credit card is a joint debt. Even if a debt is taken on individually, if it is done during the marriage then there is a presumption that the debt benefited both parties.

Another facet of this problem arises when the divorce is final and responsibility for debts has been distributed equitably between the two spouses. If one spouse fails to honor the responsibility, the third party can claim and collect the debt from the other spouse. Although this may appear unfair at first, it should be remembered that the creditor was not even involved in the distribution of the debts. Therefore, the creditor is not bound by any court order as to who should bear responsibility. Because this situation arises fairly often, it is critical that all decrees contain a provision that entitles a spouse to collect reimbursement when he or she pays a debt that was to have been the responsibility of the other spouse.

# CASE

### *Moses v. King,*
### 281 Ga.App. 687, 637 S.E.2d 97 (Ga.App. 2006)

This judicial opinion examines the issue of a change in custody based on differing views of natural parents with respect to lifestyle choices.

When reviewing a child custody decision, this court views the evidence presented in the light most favorable to upholding the trial court's order. *Gibson v. Pierce,* 176 Ga.App. 287, 288, 335 S.E.2d 658 (1985). As ever, we are "mindful that the Solomonic task of assigning the custody of children lies squarely upon the shoulders of the judge who can see and hear the parties and their witnesses, observe their demeanor and attitudes, and assess their credibility." (Citation and punctuation omitted.) *Gordy v. Gordy,* 246 Ga.App. 802, 803(1), 542 S.E.2d 536 (2000). Thus, if the record contains any reasonable evidence to support the trial court's decision on a petition to modify custody, it will be affirmed on appeal. *Durham v. Gipson,* 261 Ga.App. 602, 605(1), 583 S.E.2d 254 (2003).

So viewed, the record demonstrates that Moses and King are parents of a 12-year-old daughter. The couple lived together for a time, but, apparently, were never married. In December 2002, the child was legitimated by King, Moses and King were awarded joint legal custody, Moses was appointed the primary physical custodian, and King was ordered to pay $850 per month in child support.

After Moses filed an action for contempt in 2004 for King's failure to pay child support, on December 7, 2004, the court found King to be $16,500 in arrears in child support payments, ordered him incarcerated pending a payment of $5,000, set up a payment schedule for him to pay off the amount in arrears, and ordered King to continue future child support payments. The following day, King, *pro se,* filed a complaint for modification of child support and change of custody. In the change of custody complaint, King alleged certain circumstances had changed in that:

> [Moses] has become irresponsible and has failed to provide adequate care for child. [Moses] has had several (4) same sex domestic partners of which the most recent resides in the household with the child. [The] Department of Family and Children Services has been contacted by Gwinnett County School regarding marks on child by Defendant involving same sex partner. Child is in continuous company of gay and lesbian adults. Child's grades have dropped since [Moses] was awarded primary physical custodian and changed her school. [Moses] has left minor child alone with other adults for long periods of time. [Moses] has failed to provide basic physical

needs. The minor child has expressed to [King] the desire to reside with him and it is in the child's best interest to reside with [King], who has prepared to give her proper care.

Following a hearing, the trial court granted the petition, awarded primary physical custody to King, and ordered Moses to pay child support. The court expressed that,

> My decision was not made on your [Moses'] sexual preference, and I don't want you to think that it was. I do find that there has been a change of circumstance, one of those changes in circumstance is not the nature of those relationships but the number of relationships that I believe that you've had and the number of women that you've brought into the home and the fact that you are in fact living with a partner now outside of marriage. And I understand that you can't marry a woman in the State of Georgia. But I did-and I think the evidence is clear that you and your partner are living together, and that's pretty standard for me in any heterosexual relationship. And when I have heterosexual parents who have divorced, it has always been the order of this Court that there will be no cohabitation, no meretricious relationships outside the presence of marriage. I don't allow women and men to live together in the presence of the child. And that's the situation I've got now. I don't know whether you will believe me or not, but I do want to be clear that it has nothing to do with the fact that the person living with you is female; it has to do with the fact that you are in what I view as a meretricious relationship in front of your child. And I do find that to be a significant change in circumstance.

The court had interviewed the minor child in private, and by agreement, neither the parties nor a court reporter was present. The trial court indicated at the hearing that it was persuaded by the child's comments. In the corresponding order, the court granted Moses visitation and ordered that she pay $416 per month in child support with such payments being offset by the amount of King's arrearage.

Moses filed a motion for new trial from this order, which the trial court granted in part and denied in part. In its order, the trial court essentially restated the terms of its earlier order, but granted Moses' motion for new trial "for the limited purpose of allowing the parties' minor child to either testify in open court or speak privately with the Court in the presence of a court reporter so that the child's testimony may be recorded." The trial court's findings of fact included that:

[Moses] has had at least two partners within the last few years, one of which currently resides in the home with [Moses] and the parties' minor child. [Moses] and her partner are involved in a meretricious relationship. [Moses] testified that on prior occasions she did have her previous partner spend the night while the child was in the residence. . . . [King] is married and has children with his current wife. [King] and his wife have been married since July, 2001. [King], his wife and two children, and his mother live in a four bedroom home. [King's] home provides a more stable environment for the minor child.

Moses, thereafter, filed an application for discretionary appeal which was dismissed because Moses did not comply with the procedures for seeking an interlocutory appeal, which were required as the order was not a final judgment. Subsequently, the trial court held a transcribed hearing at which the child testified, and then entered a "final judgment" in the case, incorporating the findings of facts from the previous orders, and also finding that the child "indicated that she wanted to spend equal time with each of her parents." The court awarded joint legal and physical custody of the child to the parties. The court also held that because the parties are to share physical custody, neither party would be obliged to pay child support to the other. The court did not address, however, the issue of King's repayment of his past due child support obligation. Moses again filed an application for discretionary appeal, challenging the modification of custody and child support and the issue of King's repayment of his past due child support obligation. Again, because the trial court had scheduled a hearing on the support issue, no final judgment had in fact been entered, and the application was dismissed. The trial court, subsequently, entered an order requiring that King pay $200 a month to satisfy the arrearage. Moses, thereafter filed an application for discretionary appeal which this court granted, and this appeal ensued.

1. Because Moses' first two enumerations are related, we will consider them together. She argues that the trial court erred in modifying custody on the basis of her partner living with her because there was no showing that her living relationship had any adverse effect on the child, and that there was no showing of new and material conditions arising subsequent to the initial award of custody.

A trial court is authorized to modify [a] custody award upon a showing of new and material changes in the conditions and circumstances substantially affecting the interest and welfare of the child. The proof must show both a change in conditions and an adverse effect on the child or children. *Todd v. Casciano,* 256 Ga.App. 631, 632(1), 569 S.E.2d 566 (2002). If the trial court finds that there has been a material change of conditions, it is authorized to modify custody if it is in the best interests of the children. *Bodne v. Bodne,* 277 Ga. 445, 446, 588 S.E.2d 728 (2003).

"Though the trial judge is given a discretion [in modifying custody, it] is restricted to the evidence and is unauthorized to change the custody where there is no evidence to show new and material conditions that affect the welfare of the child." *Mahan v. McRae,* 241 Ga.App. 109, 110, 522 S.E.2d 772 (1999). This court will not interfere with that discretion absent abuse. *Daniel v. Daniel,* 250 Ga.App. 482, 484(2), 552 S.E.2d 479 (2001). Here, the trial court concluded that "there has been a substantial change in conditions and circumstances with respect to the parties' minor child," and apparently based on its findings of facts discussed earlier, including that, "[Moses] has had at least two partners within the last few years, one of which currently resides in the home with [Moses] and the parties' minor child. [Moses] and her partner are involved in a meretricious relationship," and that King is married and lives in a four bedroom home which provides a more stable environment for the minor child.

There is no evidence in the record, however, that these facts are new or that they demonstrate a material change in circumstances. King, who married his present wife in 2001, was already married when Moses was granted primary physical custody in 2002, and at the modification hearing, there was evidence that the mother's relationship with other women was the primary issue at the original custody hearing. In fact, the mother appears to be in a more stable relationship than when she was originally awarded custody, in that she and her partner have been together for two years and have lived together for one year.

With respect to the mother's cohabitation, the trial court reasoned that it does not allow unmarried men and women to cohabitate in the presence of the child and therefore Moses' relationship with her partner is meretricious per se. However, Georgia's appellate courts have held that a parent's cohabitation with someone, regardless of that person's gender, is not a basis for denying custody or visitation absent evidence that the child was harmed or exposed to inappropriate conduct. See, e.g., *Hayes v. Hayes,* 199 Ga.App. 132, 133, 404 S.E.2d 276 (1991); *Livesay v. Hilley,* 190 Ga.App. 655, 656-657(2), 379 S.E.2d 557 (1989).

Pretermitting the legal merit of the trial court's apparent bright line rule regarding cohabitation, the trial court subsequently abandoned that rationale entirely. In its original modification order the court granted King primary physical custody, with Moses receiving only periodic visitation. Moreover, the trial court also

*(continued)*

ordered Moses to "refrain from having sexual partners, other than a spouse, spend the night in [her] home when the child is present." But in its subsequent award after hearing the child's testimony on the record, the court granted the child's wish to spend equal time with each parent. Furthermore, there is no requirement in the subsequent order that Moses change her current lifestyle. It necessarily follows that the trial court implicitly reversed itself on the very finding that justified a change in custody in the first instance, since the new custody arrangement does nothing other than to reduce the amount of time the child spends with Moses and her partner.

Moreover, contrary to the requirement that the material changes adversely affect the welfare of the child, the trial court found only that the "welfare and happiness of said child would be substantially improved by modifying custody." There was no finding that the changed circumstances in any way adversely affected the child. In fact, the evidence suggests that the child was doing well in school, loved the mother's partner, and was happy and well-balanced. We note that, to the credit of both Moses and King, it is evident that both parents care deeply for their daughter, and it appears that both parents provided loving environments for her. Regardless of whether she was in the custody of Moses or King, the child appears happy and outgoing, and has strong attachments to both parents and her extended family.

No evidence in the record supports the trial court's conclusion that there was a new and material change of condition subsequent to the custody modification which adversely affected the child. Thus, the trial court's order is reversed, and this case is remanded to the trial court for entry of an order consistent with this opinion.

2. Because we have so decided, we need not address Moses' arguments regarding the implications of the trial court's ruling on the broader issues of same-sex cohabitation, partnerships, and parenting.

Judgment reversed and case remanded with direction.

## Case Review Question

Based on the court's discussion, would the case have likely turned out differently had the mother not been in a monogamous relationship but instead been living as a single parent?

## MAINTENANCE (ALIMONY OR SPOUSAL SUPPORT)

Awards of maintenance or spousal support (formerly called *alimony*) are becoming an increasingly rare occurrence. The reasons are numerous. Previously, in a pure application of separate property, the wife often did not receive a significant share of marital assets. Today, all states (whether they are community property or separate states) attempt to provide a more equitable distribution. In addition, women now activity participate in the workforce and have greater opportunities than ever before to become self-sufficient.

Currently, a court might award maintenance to a spouse who is unable to secure employment sufficient to meet reasonable necessary expenses or to a child for whom care by one other than the parent during working hours would not be appropriate.[40] An example of the former is a spouse who has not worked for many years and, for all practical purposes, would not be able to reenter the workforce at a level that would provide independent financial support. An example of the latter is a child who suffers from physical or emotional conditions that necessitate skilled care at a cost greater than what the parent could earn if he or she were required to work full time outside the home.

As these examples suggest, the trend of the courts is to award maintenance only in compelling circumstances. Although many situations are not as clearly defined as those described, often a spouse requires some form of assistance before he or she can be restored to an independent earning capacity. For example, a spouse may have been away from the workforce but would be capable of reentering with some retraining, or the parties may have several young children who will be entering school in the reasonably near future. In such situations, short-term maintenance would be appropriate. The court may award maintenance for a specified period of time to supplement the income of the other spouse.

Today, the goal of the court is to give a spouse sufficient time and resources to prepare for financial independence. Thus, the spouse required to pay maintenance is not burdened with lifetime support of a former spouse, and the spouse receiving maintenance is not suddenly thrust into the world unequipped to provide for such basic expenses as food and shelter. Maintenance is awarded only for a period of time that is deemed reasonably sufficient to enable the receiving spouse to achieve independence.

The amount and duration of maintenance are generally left to the discretion of the court, which will consider such factors as each party's earning power and reasonable needs. Also considered is the amount of time necessary to prepare the spouse receiving maintenance to successfully return to the workforce.[41] If the age and educational level of this spouse effectively prevent a return to the workforce, then permanent maintenance may be considered. The same is true of a situation in which the parties have an incapacitated child.

If either party dies, maintenance automatically terminates. If the intent is that the receiving party should continue to be entitled in the event of death of the payor, it should be so stipulated in the court order approving maintenance.

If the financial status of either party changes significantly during the period of maintenance payments, a modification may be requested. A formal petition must be filed with the court setting forth the reasons that would justify adjustment of the maintenance order. It is then within the discretion of the court to determine whether the modification is warranted. Significant changes in circumstances include a substantial decrease in the earning power of the payor spouse or a substantial increase in the earning power of the recipient spouse. Remarriage or cohabitation of the recipient spouse also may be considered sufficient grounds to terminate maintenance.

Failure to pay maintenance is remedied by a request to hold the wrongful party in contempt of court. The procedure and penalties are basically the same. The court will hear the petition, and penalties will ensue if grounds exist to find that a party has willfully ignored the order of maintenance.

## ASSIGNMENT 10.5

Examine the following situations and indicate whether a court would be likely to grant maintenance and, if so, whether maintenance would be permanent or temporary. Give reasons to support your answers.

Situation 1: Jamie and John have been married for eighteen years. Jamie is now thirty-eight. At the time of the marriage, she was a professional model who gave up her career to travel with and assist John, who was a professional golfer. Jamie did not finish high school and has few if any prospects for resuming her modeling career at this age. John has been moderately successful and has had an income for the past several years in excess of $500,000 annually. Jamie has requested permanent maintenance.

Situation 2: Beverly is sixty-two and a college professor. Her husband John is fifty-three and previously had a business buying real estate, rehabilitating the property, and then selling it. His income was always intermittent and considered supplemental by the parties during the thirty-year marriage and used for things such as vacations. Beverly's income has always been the parties' primary income. At age fifty-two, John suffered a serious heart attack; although he is able to do some things, he cannot return to his former occupation. The parties want to divorce, and John has requested maintenance. Beverly wants to retire, but if she does so before age sixty-seven, her income would be insufficient to support two households.

## NONMARITAL RELATIONSHIPS

As previously indicated, most states do not recognize the creation of a common law marriage. Nevertheless, many couples cohabit without the formal requisites of marriage. Although they share in the acquisition of property and debts, when they decide to terminate their relationship, they do not have the specific legal rights of persons who are dissolving a legal marriage.

Although previous courts had issued decisions addressing various aspects of this particular situation, the landmark opinion was issued in *Marvin v. Marvin*.[42] In that case, the court fully addressed the issues associated with the dissolution of nonmarital cohabitation. Courts in several other states have cited the decision with approval and have used it as persuasive authority to adopt the position taken by the court in the *Marvin* decision.[43]

## CASE
### *Marvin v. Marvin,*
### 18 Cal. 3d 660, 134 Cal.Rptr. 815, 557 P.2d 106 (1976)

This case presents . . .

### *En banc*

1. The factual setting of this appeal.

. . . Plaintiff avers that in October of 1964 she and defendant "entered into an oral agreement" that while "that parties lived together they would combine their efforts and earnings and would share equally any and all property accumulated as a result of their efforts whether individual or combined." Furthermore, they agreed to "hold themselves out to the general public as husband and wife" and that "plaintiff would further render her services as a companion, homemaker, housekeeper and cook to . . . defendant."

Shortly thereafter, plaintiff agreed to "give up her lucrative career as an entertainer [and] singer in order to "devote her full time to defendant . . . as a companion, homemaker, housekeeper and cook"; in return defendant agreed to "provide for all of plaintiff's financial support and needs for the rest of her life."

Plaintiff alleges that she lived with defendant from October of 1964 through May of 1970 and fulfilled her obligations under the agreement. During this period the parties as a result of their efforts and earnings acquired in defendant's name substantial real and personal property, including motion picture rights worth over $1 million. In May of 1970, however, defendant compelled plaintiff to leave his household. He continued to support plaintiff until November of 1971, but thereafter refused to provide further support.

On the basis of these allegations plaintiff asserts two causes of action. The first, for declaratory relief, asks the court to determine her contract and property rights; the second seeks to impose a constructive trust upon one half of the property acquired during the course of the relationship.

Defendant demurred unsuccessfully, and then answered the complaint. Following extensive discovery and pretrial proceedings, the case came to trial. Defendant renewed his attack on the complaint by a motion to dismiss. . . .

After hearing argument the court granted defendant's motion and entered judgment for the defendant. Plaintiff moved to set aside the judgment and asked leave to amend her complaint to allege that she and defendant reaffirmed their agreement after defendant's divorce was final. The trial court denied plaintiff's motion, and she appealed from the judgment.

2. Plaintiff's complaint states a cause of action for breach of an express contract.

In *Trutalli v. Meraviglia* (1932) 215 Cal. 698, 12 P.2d. 430, we established the principle that nonmarital partners may lawfully contract concerning the ownership of property acquired during the relationship. We reaffirmed this principle in *Vallera v. Vallera* (1943) 21 Cal.2d 681, 685, 134 P.2d 761, 763, stating that "If a man and woman [who are not married] live together as husband and wife under an agreement to pool their earnings and share equally in their joint accumulations, equity will protect the interests of each in such property."

In the case before us plaintiff, basing here cause of action in contract upon these precedents, maintains that the trial court erred in denying her a trial on the merits of her contention. . . .

Numerous . . . cases have upheld enforcement of agreements between nonmarital partners in factual settings essentially indistinguishable from the present case. *In re Marriage of Foster* (1947) 42 Cal.App.3d 577, 117 Cal.Rptr. 49; . . . *Ferguson v. Schuenemann* (1959) 167 Cal.App.2d 413, 334 P.2d. 668; . . . *Ferraro v. Ferraro* (1956) 146 Cal.App.2d 849, 304 P.2d 168.

We conclude that the judicial barriers that may stand in the way of a policy based upon the fulfillment of the reasonable expectations of the parties to a nonmarital relationship should be removed. As we have explained, the courts now hold that express agreements will be enforced unless they rest on an unlawful meretricious consideration. We add that in the absence of an express agreement, the courts may look to a variety of other remedies in order to protect the parties' lawful expectations.

We do not seek to resurrect the doctrine of common law marriage, which was abolished in California by statute in 1895. (See *Norman v. Thomson* (1898) 121 Cal. 620, 628, 54 P. 143; *Estate of Abate* (1958) 166 Cal.App.2d 282, 292, 333 P.2d 200.) Thus we do not hold that plaintiff and defendant were 'married,' nor do we extend to plaintiff the rights which the Family Law Act grants valid or putative spouses; we hold only that she has the same rights to enforce contracts and to assert her equitable interest in property acquired through her effort as does any other unmarried person.

The courts may inquire into the conduct of the parties to determine whether that conduct demonstrates an implied contract, implied agreement of partnership or joint venture (see *Estate of Thornton* (1972) 81 Wash.2d 72, 499 P.2d 864), or some other tacit understanding between the parties. . . . Finally, a nonmarital partner may recover *in quantum meruit* for the reasonable value of household services rendered less the reasonable value of support received if he can show that he rendered services with the expectation of monetary reward. (See *Hill v. Estate of Westbrook, supra,* 39 Cal.2d 458, 462, 247 P.2d 19.)

Our opinion does not preclude the evolution of additional equitable remedies to protect the expectations of the parties to a nonmarital relationship in cases in which existing remedies prove inadequate; the suitability of such remedies may be determined in later cases in light of the factual setting in which they arise.

Since we have determined that plaintiff's complaint states a cause of action for breach of an express contract, and, as we have explained, can be amended to state a cause of action independent of allegations of express contract, we must conclude that the trial court erred in granting defendant a judgment on the pleadings.

## Case Review Question

What if infertility had been the reason the relationship ended?

Some courts have rejected the Marvin decision on the basis that it too closely resembles recognition of common law marriage, and they are not willing to adopt a position that so closely parallels it. In a time when cohabitation is a frequent occurrence, however, methods may have to be developed to determine the legal rights of the parties involved.

A major issue that has arisen in recent years is that of same-sex marriages and the rights of same-sex partners who are not married. This topic continues to be a lightning rod of controversy as state and federal legislatures and the court systems attempt to reach a consensus on the rights of individuals in what most would consider a nontraditional committed relationship. Currently only three countries and three Canadian provinces outside the United States legally permit gay marriages. In the United States, it is a widely contested issue. Some states, and even local jurisdictions, have attempted to provide a means to create a legal relationship of marriage or something with similar rights such as civil unions and domestic partnerships. These laws have been consistently challenged in the home state legislatures, state courts, and federal courts. Also, partners who created a legal union in one state and then moved to another have frequently had to challenge the constitutionality of the second state's failure to recognize the union even when that state has a history of honoring the laws of sister states. However, the ability to marry is not the only consideration. Rather, most proponents of same-sex marriages will agree that the legal ramifications of marriage are what the gay community is most concerned with.

Although individuals in a long-term committed relationship may desire to solemnize that relationship through an exchange of vows similar to those of heterosexual couples, this is not the only objective. If parties have no blood relationship and no relationship by marriage or adoption, then their rights may be severely limited. Although estate planning can be done to provide for an unrelated person, wills may in fact be subject to challenge in any case, and cases involving same-sex partners are no exception. Just as important, as long as same-sex marriages are not legally recognized by the federal government, the parties cannot file joint tax returns, collect government disability and retirement benefits as a spouse of their deceased or disabled partner, or obtain many other government benefits. Issues may arise with respect to adoption, custody of children the couple has co-parented in the event of a split, and so on. Quite often employer-provided health insurance will not allow an employee to include an individual to whom the employee is not related or married on the health insurance plan. Even plans that do allow nonmarried partners to be included on the return may require proof of dependency in the form of inclusion of the dependent individual on the employee's tax return. This is not generally an option for same-sex couples. In addition, many company-funded pension plans will not allow a nonspouse to collect benefits in the same manner as a spouse on the employee's death. In many jurisdictions, a life partner may have fewer rights than a blood relative with whom an incapacitated individual has little or no contact when it comes to making important health care decisions, including issues as extreme as the continuation of life support.

To address this concern, a minority of states have enacted legislation that allows persons to create civil unions or register as domestic partners. Although it provides no federal rights in terms of federal income tax laws, estate taxes, and so on, such registration may provided limited benefits to those who cannot marry for whatever reason but who are in committed relationships. In addition, until these issues are resolved, it is imperative that anyone engaged in a committed relationship but who is unmarried for whatever reason have as many of these issues as possible resolved through proper documentation such as estate planning, wills, trusts, advanced directives for health care, durable power of attorney, and so forth. Because this is an area of law that is so volatile, any legal work performed in this venue should be thoroughly researched for the most current legal standards in the relevant jurisdiction.

# CASE

### *Sutton v. Valois,*

### 66 Mass.App.Ct.258, 846 N.E.2d 1171, Mass.App.Ct., (2006)

This case examines the nature of legal rights and status for individuals who cohabitate and accumulate assets but do not marry.

We recite the facts as found by the trial judge, undisputed in the record, or in conformity with the judge's findings, *Bruno v. Bruno,* 384 Mass. 31, 35, 422 N.E.2d 1369 (1981), generally reserving detail for discussion of the issues. Sutton, a nurse earning approximately $32,000 a year, and Valois, an electrical engineer earning approximately $65,000 a year, met in October of 1999 and began dating. Valois moved in with Sutton and her roommate in April of 2000. While the parties lived there Valois paid one third of the rent.

In July, 2000, Valois purchased, in his name alone, a home at 16 Logan Path in Grafton for $143,500, financed entirely through withdrawals from his investment accounts. The parties lived together at the Logan Path home until the end of October, 2002. During this period, Sutton asked Valois to loan her $20,000 so that she could pay off a car loan. Valois loaned her the money, and Sutton agreed to pay him back at the rate of approximately $500 per month. She made seven payments, amounting to $3,500. The parties then began to discuss the possibility of marriage. After . . . Valois indicated that Sutton need not repay the debt. In their discussions about marriage, the parties talked of having children and buying a bigger house, which would include space for Sutton to operate a planned massage business. In May or June of 2001, the parties became engaged.

In October of 2002, based on the proposed marriage, the parties bought a house . . . for $274,000. Both signed the purchase and sale agreement, the mortgage application, and the mortgage and promissory note. The deposit and the cash paid at closing, however, including the down payment, totaling in excess of $80,000, were, in effect, paid by Valois. Although the money paid came from checks drawn on a joint checking account, all of the funds for the down payment were deposited in that joint account by Valois, who had emptied his retirement account to do so. While Sutton had made some contributions to the joint account, her withdrawals for her personal and credit card expenses exceeded her contributions. The property was deeded to Sutton and Valois; as the deed does not specify the manner in which the parties took title, they are presumed to have taken title as tenants in common. . . .

The parties moved to their new home on November 1, 2002; Valois rented out the house at Logan Path. During the time they lived in the new home, Sutton collected four rent checks from the tenant who was now occupying the house at Logan Path. Valois maintained at trial that these checks, totaling $2,500, were to be deposited in the joint account; they were in fact retained by Sutton and deposited in her personal account. Sutton maintained that she did this with Valois's knowledge and approval and that Valois had told her to keep the checks. The probate judge made an explicit finding on this issue that Valois was credible and Sutton was not, and ruled that Sutton had been unjustly enriched in part by "the four rent checks [s]he obtained from Mr. Valois'[s] tenant." Sutton maintained that Valois had told her to keep the checks.

. . . [I]n December of 2002, the relationship soured. In February, 2003, approximately three years after they began living together, and eighteen months after becoming engaged, Sutton told Valois that she was never going to marry him or have children with him. She declined to go to counseling and began to contact other men on the Internet and to remain away from the

house for extended periods. When she left for the weekend of March 7 and 8, Valois packed her personal belongings and put them in the garage. Sutton retrieved her belongings thereafter and withdrew $4,000 from the couple's joint account, and the relationship terminated.

In April of 2003, Sutton filed a complaint in equity in the Probate Court, seeking equitable division of personal property and a one-half interest in the house 4 Hill Road. She also filed a petition for partition of the property. Valois filed a cross complaint, which he later amended. In six counts, he sought reformation of the deed based on fraud, on mutual mistake and intent, and on misrepresentation of material fact. He also claimed equitable distribution of personal property, unjust enrichment, and a resulting trust. As relief, Valois sought to be declared the sole owner of the house, repayment of the balance of Sutton's debt to him, payment of the rent checks retained by Sutton, and repayment of the $4,000 withdrawn from the joint account.

While the case was pending, and against a background of declining interest rates, the judge ordered Sutton to convey her interest in the property to Valois, so that he could refinance the home at a lower rate of interest. Without objection, Sutton conveyed her interest to Valois, the reduced interest mortgage was obtained, a court-ordered notice of *lis pendens* concerning the property was immediately placed on the record, and a motion to dismiss the petition for partition was filed.

Prior to trial, the parties resolved all differences with respect to the personal property. At trial the only issues before the judge were the ownership of the house and the money, if any, owed by Sutton to Valois. The judge provided what she styled a "brief rationale" in support of her judgment, which declared Valois to be the sole owner of 4 Hill Road, and ordered Sutton to repay Valois the balance of the loan, the four rent checks, and the $4,000 withdrawn from their joint checking account, totaling $23,000.

. . . [T]he judge first concluded that the value of the property as of March 1, 2003, was $270,000, some $4,000 less than had been paid. She based the value on a real estate appraisal performed for Valois by Thomas Walsh, whom she found credible. She found Sutton's appraiser, who valued the property at $307,000, not credible. The judge ruled that, since Valois had paid the entire down payment for the real estate and there was no equity increase in the property, it was "equitable to award him sole ownership." She also concluded that Sutton had been unjustly enriched in the amount of $23,000, "when she knew that the relationship was irretrievably broken down, yet continued to avail herself of funds of, or belonging to[,] Charles Valois."

*(continued)*

The amount included $16,500 as the remaining balance of the $20,000 loan, the four rent checks totaling $2,500 obtained from the tenant, and $4,000 withdrawn from the joint checking account on March 10, 2003, after the relationship had ended.

Remedies available to cohabitants. "Cohabitation in Massachusetts does not create the relationship of husband and wife in the absence of a formal solemnization of marriage, . . . [and] the incidents of the marital relationship [do not] attach to an arrangement of cohabitation." *Collins v. Guggenheim,* 417 Mass. 615, 617, 631 N.E.2d 1016 (1994). Common-law marriage is not recognized in Massachusetts. *Id.* at 618, 631 N.E.2d 1016.

The Supreme Judicial Court has, however, held valid oral promises between unmarried cohabitants, so long as "illicit sexual relations were [not] an inherent aspect of the agreement or a 'serious and not merely an incidental part of the performance of the agreement.'" *Margolies v. Hopkins,* 401 Mass. 88, 92, 514 N.E.2d 1079 (1987). . . . More recently, in *Wilcox v. Trautz,* 427 Mass. 326, 693 N.E.2d 141 (1998), in adjudicating a claim with respect to the disposition of property between unmarried cohabitants, the court held that "unmarried cohabitants may lawfully contract concerning property, financial, and other matters relevant to their relationship." *Id.* at 332, 693 N.E.2d 141. In so doing, the court recognized that "[s]ocial mores regarding cohabitation between unmarried parties have changed dramatically in recent years and living arrangements that were once criticized are now relatively common and accepted." *Id.* at 330, 693 N.E.2d 141. "Such . . . contract[s are] subject to the rules of contract law, and [are] valid even if expressly made in contemplation of a common living arrangement, except to the extent that sexual services constitutes the only, or dominant, consideration for the agreement, or that enforcement should be denied on some other public policy ground." *Id.* at 332, 693 N.E.2d 141. Cases to the contrary in Massachusetts were expressly overruled. *Ibid.* The court in *Wilcox, supra* at 335, 693 N.E.2d 141, also acknowledged that, in the circumstances, the Probate and Family Court had jurisdiction over the plaintiff's *quantum meruit* claim. *Wilcox, supra* at 331 n. 3, 693 N.E.2d 141, however, limits the grant of property rights to cases where there is an express contract and does not provide for an equitable distribution of property. See *Northrup v. Brigham,* 63 Mass.App.Ct. 362, 369–370, 826 N.E.2d 239 (2005). Equitable remedies are, however, available to cohabitants. See *Collins v. Guggenheim,* 417 Mass. at 617–618, 631 N.E.2d 1016. . . .

Other states permit equitable claims by, and grant equitable remedies to, unmarried cohabitants as they seek resolution of property issues, where the claims are not specifically predicated either on sexual relations or, in some cases, on the status of being an unmarried cohabitant; these courts generally conclude that equitable remedies will not contravene a public policy recognizing the importance of marriage. See, e.g., *Salzman v. Bachrach,* 996 P.2d 1263, 1267–1269 (Colo.2000). . . . Here we proceed to address the plaintiff's equitable claims.

The Hill Road property. Sutton first argues that the judge erred when she ruled that Valois should retain sole ownership of the 4 Hill Road property "by virtue of a resulting trust." As Valois observes, however, the judge did not state, either in the judgment or in her brief rationale, that the judgment with respect to the ownership of the property rested on a theory of resulting trust. She simply stated, "Mr. Valois contributed all the money for the acquisition . . . [and] there is no equity to be divided between the parties. Since Mr. Valois paid the entire down payment . . . the Court finds it equitable to award him sole ownership." While this language might seem to indicate a judgment based on the judge's personal notions of fairness and equity, see, e.g., *Raymond Leasing Corp. v. Callico Distribs., Inc.,* 62 Mass.App.Ct. 747, 749 n. 3, 820 N.E.2d 267 (2005), when considered in the context of the judge's factual findings, it is clear that the judgment is founded in recognized equitable doctrine. Though not stating as much, the judgment in effect denied any claim, based on either legal or equitable grounds, that Sutton made for a share in the property.

From the judge's findings, it is clear that Sutton's claims are not predicated either solely or predominantly on sexual services. Sutton's original claim, and any later equitable claim arising after her transfer of title to Valois, was predicated on her holding legal title to the property together with Valois, along with her signing the note and mortgage. Sutton yielded any legal claim when, in compliance with court order, and without any written agreement or reservation with respect to her claim of title, she transferred her legal interest in the property to Valois, so that the property might be remortgaged.

Upon the voluntary transfer of her interest in the property, albeit at the order of the probate judge, Sutton moved to dismiss her separate petition for partition, and her claim became an equitable one, based on equitable theories of unjust enrichment, constructive trust, or resulting trust. See *Fortin v. Roman Catholic Bishop of Worcester,* 416 Mass. 781, 789–790, 625 N.E.2d 1352, *cert. denied,* 511 U.S. 1142, 114 S.Ct. 2164, 128 L.Ed.2d 887 (1994). Sutton's original pleadings suffice to permit consideration of her claims on the equitable theories of unjust enrichment, were Valois to retain sole ownership without payment to her, or that, after her conveyance of the property to him, Valois then held title in a constructive or resulting trust for Sutton's benefit.

We conclude, on the grounds apparent in the record, as outlined below, that there was no error in the determination that Valois should have sole ownership of the property. We consider each of Sutton's equitable claims in turn.

In advancing her claim, Sutton first challenges the judge's finding that Valois contributed the entire down payment for the property, but as Valois argues, the judge's finding is supported by uncontroverted testimony that Valois was, by a mathematical necessity, the financial source for the entire down payment. Sutton withdrew for her own use monies in excess of all deposits she made to the joint account, and Valois contributed not only monies sufficient for the down payment, but to make up for Sutton's excess withdrawals. Further, it is also uncontroverted, and the judge found, that (1) the parties were engaged to be married when they purchased the house in October, 2002; (2) a principal reason for purchasing the house was that it was big enough so that the parties could begin a family together; (3) in December, 2002, the couple began to have problems with their relationship; (4) in February, 2003, Sutton told Valois that she would never marry him or have children with him; and (5) she departed permanently from the residence in early March, 2003. These findings would support an ultimate finding that Valois advanced the monies for the purchase and that he agreed to the tenancy in common predicated on Sutton's promise to marry and to have a family with him.

A determination that a party would be unjustly enriched "require[s], generally, . . . that [the] party [would] hold property under such circumstances that in equity and good conscience he ought not retain it." *Stevens v. Nagel,* 64 Mass.App.Ct. 136, 141, 831 N.E.2d 935 (2005), quoting from *Simonds v. Simonds,* 45 N.Y.2d 233, 242, 408 N.Y.S.2d 359, 380 N.E.2d 189 (1978). "The fundamental question in the present case[, therefore,] is whether [Valois] . . . received [a property interest that] in equity and good conscience belongs to [Sutton]." *National Shawmut Bank of Boston v. Fidelity Mut. Life Ins. Co.,* 318 Mass. 142, 150, 61 N.E.2d 18 (1945). A determination on the unjust enrichment here hinges on "the reasonable expectations of the parties." *Community Builders, Inc. v. Indian Motorcycle Assocs.,* 44 Mass.App.Ct. 537, 560, 692 N.E.2d 964 (1998). We conclude that it would be unreasonable for Sutton to expect to gain an ownership interest in the property where its purchase was predicated on her promise to marry and have a family, a promise that she broke soon after the purchase.

While the promise to marry and have a family obviously connotes a promise with a sexual dimension, this vastly complex relationship and undertaking cannot be said to be solely, or even predominantly, sexual in a way offensive to public mores. If Sutton were to receive "one-half of the property's fair market value less the original outstanding mortgage obligation" that she suggests should be hers, she would receive a windfall of half of Valois's approximately $80,000 deposit, having contributed no funds toward that deposit. It would contravene any notions of equity and good conscience to conclude that Valois must face the possible loss of some $40,000, given the fact that he expended the funds and agreed to accept the property in his and Sutton's name in anticipation of marriage and a family with Sutton, plans that began to fall apart less than two months after the purchase of the property. This is particularly so given the dearth of evidence as to any monetary contribution Sutton made to the relationship. In sum, Sutton would be unjustly enriched if she were found to possess an interest in the property such that she could recover any of Valois's deposit, and the probate judge crafted a proper equitable solution on this issue. See, in this regard, *De Cicco v. Barker,* 339 Mass. 457, 159 N.E.2d 534 (1959).

Nor could Sutton prevail on a theory that Valois held a share of the property for Sutton in constructive or resulting trust. A constructive or resulting trust may be imposed to prevent injustice, unjust enrichment, or fraud. See *State Street Bank & Trust Co. v. Beale,* 353 Mass. 103, 105, 227 N.E.2d 924 (1967); *Fortin v. Roman Catholic Bishop of Worcester,* 416 Mass. at 789–790, 625 N.E.2d 1352. They are equitable remedies, applied where there is no stated intention to create a trust and where legal title to property is obtained by fraud, in violation of a fiduciary relationship, where confidential information was misused, or where there was "significant wrongdoing" by the party claiming title. See *Barry v. Covich,* 332 Mass. 338, 342, 124 N.E.2d 921 (1955). Nothing in the record here suggests that Valois obtained legal title by fraudulent means or by "significant wrongdoing." He obtained his legal title by providing all of the cash consideration for the purchase and by his agreement to pay the note secured by the mortgage to the property. Full title to the property came to rest in Valois as the result of a court order made in the course of the present proceedings. All obligations that Sutton had to pay under the original note were extinguished by the new mortgage and note on which Valois alone was obligated. Nothing in the record suggests that Sutton contributed to any of the initial mortgage payments. There is no suggestion in the record that Valois engaged in fraud, either on Sutton or on the court, with respect to obtaining full title to the property or by refinancing the existing mortgage

*(continued)*

at more favorable rates. Sutton conveyed her interest in the premises to Valois without contesting or appealing the court order and voluntarily dismissed her claim for partition.

As there was no fraud or other wrongdoing with respect to Valois's obtaining full title to the property, and no enforceable agreement, Sutton's claim for a constructive or resulting trust could only be based on unjust enrichment. Compare *Lewis v. Mills,* 32 Mass.App.Ct. 660, 593 N.E.2d 1312 (1992). As set out *supra,* any such claim must fail. Recovery on a theory of Valois's being unjustly enriched would be appropriate "only if the circumstances of [his] retention are such that, as between [Sutton and Valois,] it is unjust for [Valois] to retain [it]." Restatement of Restitution § 1 comment c (1937). Valois's retaining the entire premises does not have the characteristics of a "windfall." *J. A. Sullivan Corp. v. Commonwealth,* 397 Mass. 789, 794, 494 N.E.2d 374 (1986). Sutton's claim in this regard must fail.

Propriety of order that Sutton repay Valois $23,000. Sutton challenges the probate judge's determination that Sutton was required to repay the $16,500 balance on Valois's $20,000 loan to her, claiming "the evidence raised the inference" that Valois waived repayment. Sutton relies on testimony in which Valois acknowledged that he made the loan to Sutton because he loved her, but ignores Valois's direct denial—found in the same section of testimony cited by Sutton—that he ever told Sutton that he forgave the debt. It was for the probate judge to evaluate and weigh the witness on this point, including her determination of the credibility of the testimony, see *Adoption of Daniel,* 58 Mass.App.Ct. 195, 200, 788 N.E.2d 998 (2003). Nothing in the record directs us to a conclusion that the judge committed clear error in holding Sutton to the legal obligation created by the $20,000 loan. The evidence, rather, suggests that any waiver of the original loan payments was predicated on Sutton's promise to marry.

Regarding the $2,500 in rent money that Sutton was ordered to return, Sutton relies on her testimony—contradicted by Valois's testimony—that Valois knew that she was depositing the checks into a separate account. Here again, it was the probate judge's province to resolve conflicts in testimony and to evaluate the parties' credibility as witnesses. The testimony permitted the judge to conclude that the rent checks at issue were wrongfully diverted by Sutton and that, as Sutton lacked any reasonable expectation that she had permission to retain the funds for her own use, equity and good conscience required that the rent be remitted to Valois.

Finally, as regards the $4,000 that Sutton withdrew from the parties' joint checking account when the couple's relationship reached its end, Sutton argues that she justifiably emptied the account "in order to help pay the expenses of reestablishing herself as a single person living in an apartment." As Valois observes, however, at the time of the parties' parting, Sutton had taken out of the account for personal expenses more than she had contributed to it, leaving in the account only money contributed by Valois. The probate judge did not err in concluding that, if Sutton were permitted to take the $4,000 with her, she would receive a windfall that she could not have reasonably expected was hers to keep, and that, on principles of unjust enrichment set forth *supra,* Valois was entitled to the funds.

Judgment affirmed.

## Case Review Question

What could the plaintiff have done to protect her property rights without marrying the defendant?

## REPRODUCTIVE LAW

As technology advances, so does the need for legal standards for issues that invariably arise when the technology creates new opportunities to either resolve legal issues or create new situations for which no law exists. Reproductive medicine is a prime example of technological advancement that is impacted by both situations.

## Paternity

An entirely new area of law that emerged in the U.S. legal system during the latter part of the twentieth century and continues to develop is the result of tremendous scientific advancements and a relaxation of cultural standards. Initially, this area developed when the shame that had been historically associated with children born out of wedlock was overshadowed by an increasing social view that men take responsibility for children they fathered. This was also advanced by the development of scientific means of testing for paternity. The latter developed so significantly in recent years through DNA testing that it is possible to trace ancestral lines back hundreds of years as was publicized in the case of the connections among descendants of Sally Hemmings and U.S. President Thomas Jefferson. Today, paternity testing can virtually eliminate all but the true father of a child and, consequently, parental responsibilities can be placed on both mother and father.

Historically, there was no presumptive father for a child born out of wedlock. If a woman had the courage to initiate an action for paternity despite strong social pressures not to do so, the case often became focused on an issue of the credibility of both the mother and the alleged father. The cases were frequently notarized in newspapers as the two parties battled a finding that they were telling the truth. Even if an individual is named on the birth certificate as the father, there is no legal presumption of this fact unless the man is married to the mother at the time of the birth or openly acknowledges his paternity of the child. Any other circumstance ultimately requires a court finding of paternity.

A paternity action is initiated in the same essential manner as any other civil suit. However, many states have statutes that require specific methods of notice to the alleged father of the action. Although it is rare that a court has authority to order invasive physical procedures such as blood tests, this is one instance where, unless a man admits to paternity or accepts a finding of paternity by default, a court may order blood tests to definitively determine whether the alleged father is the biological parent of the child in question. These actions are most often filed when the mother or guardian of the child is seeking financial assistance in the form of child support. An action may also be filed by the state if the child or its mother is receiving government financial assistance such as welfare benefits. In turn, the state seeks reimbursement from the father. However, it is no longer uncommon for the action to be filed by a man who wants to resolve whether he is the father of a child because fathers have assumed an increasingly active role in the lives of their children in recent years. By establishing parenthood, the father not only accepts the responsibilities but also gains the rights associated with parenthood, such as a right of companionship of the child and the right to oppose adoption of the child by another man or by parents who wish to adopt the child from the natural mother. In accordance with this, many states now even have registries created by statute that allow a man who believes himself to be a father to register his name and the pertinent information about the child and mother. This in turn prevents the mother from placing the child for adoption without consent until paternity is established.

More recently, a variety of issues have resulted in litigation with respect to children who are as yet unborn. Scientific advancements have created the real possibility that the cellular material necessary to create life can be preserved. This includes the collection of sperm, eggs, and even fertilized embryos. These materials are collected from potential parents for many reasons. However, because life is not a static state, circumstances change and so do the needs or desires of those with legal claim to these potential lives. Courts continue to deal with such issues as individuals come forward to claim adverse interests. An example might be prospective parents who contribute and finance frozen embryos and those parents then divorce. Who, if anyone, has the right to control the fate of the embryos? If a child from such a source is born to a mother against the father's wishes, does the father have a legal obligation toward the child? What if the father wants control of the embryos to destroy them? What if he wants to have them implanted in another woman for gestation? All of these concerns currently face courts in many states. And overshadowing all of this is the very real possibility of human cloning and the legal issues that will produce. History has shown that scientific advancements often outpace the legal system. Until these issues are resolved in a majority of jurisdictions or by the Supreme Court, it is likely that there will be inconsistent results across the states.

## APPLICATION 10.5

Amy is an extremely wealthy unmarried woman. She gave birth to a child. Two weeks later, she married her longtime friend Mitchell, who both claimed to be the father of the child. However, a petition was filed by Brandon to have the paternity of the child established because he also claimed to be the father. Because Amy and Mitchell were not married at the time of the child's birth, there would be no presumption of Mitchell's paternity. In this case, the petition would likely be granted because there is a lack of presumption of paternity. Even if the two had been married before the baby's birth, Brandon's petition may well be granted if he could present evidence to rebut the presumption of Mitchell's paternity. This is especially true because the tests to establish paternity are relatively simple and noninvasive.

*Point for Discussion:*  Referring to the chapter on probate, what could be the result for Brandon if he established paternity and Amy subsequently died while the baby was still a minor?

## Adoption

Another area of law that has seen immense growth in terms of statutory legal standards is adoption. There was a time when a child could essentially be handed over to another person or to a child care facility such as an orphanage with little or no formality. However, the exposure of baby-selling practices and other activities that did not place the best interest of the child first and ahead of any personal interests led to nationwide legislation by the states to carefully monitor the placement and adoption process. It is common now to require counseling and waiting periods for the natural parent or parents who seek to place their child for adoption. Adoptive parents are often required to go through a series of evaluations and even trial periods with the child before the adoption will be finalized regardless of whether the parties unanimously consent to the adoption.

Historically, the vast majority of adoptions were private in that the adoptive and natural parents did not know one another's identity. A trend emerged in the latter part of the twentieth century toward open adoptions. In this situation, the parents know of one another and sometimes communicate, and in some cases the adoptive parents allow the natural parents to visit with the adopted child and develop some sort of relationship. Obviously, the open adoption is not something that is acceptable to all parties and the majority of adoptions are still private.

Historically, when an adoption occurred, all records with respect to the child before the adoption were sealed. The rationale was that an adopted child should be raised in the belief that the adoptive parents were the family, and when one placed a child for adoption he or she relinquished all rights to further contact with the child. Many times as well, because of emotional and societal pressures, the natural parent did not want to be identified. Even if an adoptive child or natural parent wanted this access, state statute prohibited such from occurring. However, with the other changes in domestic relations law in the latter twentieth century, this too has seen dramatic revision.

For a variety of reasons, adopted children and natural parents began seeking records with respect to the other party in great numbers in the 1990s. As they encountered great difficulty because of statutory prohibitions, movements began to change the laws. These movements were often supported by the medical profession as science produced more evidence of the importance of knowing one's genetic background and parental medical histories. As a result, in adoptions today, much more medical information is required at the time of an adoption. In addition, natural parents may indicate whether they are willing to have their identities released to the adoptive child. Adoptive parents have the option of revealing their own identity and that of the adopted child to the natural parents. Once the adopted child has reached the age of majority, this decision becomes his or her own. Thus, even though statutes still attempt to protect privacy and many individuals who were party to adoptions before statutory changes still meet with the frustration of not being able to locate their natural relatives, the laws today are much more flexible in meeting individuals' needs and desires with respect to continued contact among natural relatives after an adoption has occurred.

## CASE

### In re Adoption of R.B.F. and R.C.F. Appeal of B.A.F. and C.H.F.
### In re Adoption of C.C.G. and Z.C.G. Appeal of J.C.G. and J.J.G.
### 2002 WL 1906000 (Pa. 2002)

These consolidated appeals raise the issue of whether the Adoption Act requires a legal parent to relinquish his or her parental rights in cases where a same-sex partner seeks to adopt the legal parent's child. We hold that Section 2901 of the Adoption Act, 23 Pa.C.S. § 2901, affords the trail court discretion to determine whether, under the circumstances of a particular case, cause has been shown to demonstrate why a particular statutory requirement has not been met. As Appellants' adoption petitions were summarily dismissed, they did not have the opportunity to demonstrate cause why the relinquishment provision need not be met here. Accordingly, we vacate the orders of the Superior Court and remand to the trial courts for evidentiary hearings.

The appellants in the case of In re: Adoption of C.C.G. and Z.C.G., both male, are involved in an intimate relationship and have been domestic partners since 1982. On October 24, 1991, Appellant J.J.G. adopted C.C.G. He adopted his second child, Z.C.G. on April 21, 1999. After the children were adopted, Appellant J.J.G. and his partner, Appellant J.C.G., lived together with the children as a family. On May 9, 1999, Appellants filed a petition wherein J.C.G. sought to adopt both children. The Erie County Common Pleas Court denied the adoption petition on June 18, 1999, and subsequently affirmed that order upon Appellants' request for rescission.

The *en banc* Superior Court affirmed the denial of the adoption petition, nothing that the court cannot create judicial exceptions to the requirements of the Adoption Act. *In re Adoption of C.C.G. and Z.C.G.*, 762 A.2d 724 (Pa.Super.2000). The court held that the clear and unambiguous provisions of the Adoption Act do not permit a non-spouse to adopt a child where the legal

parents have not relinquished their respective parental rights. It relied on Section 2711(d) of the Adoption Act, which states that the consenting parent of an adoptee under the age of eighteen must provide a statement relinquishing parental rights to his or her child. Appellant J.J.G., the legal parent, had attached a consent form to the adoption petition, but the phrase indicating that he intended to permanently give up his rights to his children was intentionally omitted from the form. The court held that this omission rendered the consent invalid, as it did not meet the requirements of Section 2711. It concluded that Appellant J.C.G. therefore had no legally ascertainable interest, notwithstanding the equal protection clause.

The Superior Court noted that the only exception to the unqualified consent requirement was Section 2903 of the Adoption Act, which provides that "[w]henever a parent consent to the adoption of his child by his spouse, the parent–child relationship between him and his child remain whether . . . he is one of the petitioners in the adoption proceeding." 23 Pa. C.S. § 2903. It relied on our decision in *In re Adoption of E.M.A.*, 487 Pa. 152, 409 A 2d 10 (1979), for the proposition that Section 2903 applies solely to "stepparent" situations and has no application to unmarried persons. The court concluded that because our Commonwealth only recognizes marriages "between one man one woman," 23 Pa.C.S. § 1704, Appellant J.C.G. does not qualify as a "spouse" under Section 2903.

The Superior Court rejected Appellants' claim that the trial court was afforded when "cause has been shown" under Section 2901. The court held that "for cause shown" relates to reasons why the statutory requirements of adoption need not be met. It concluded that until the statutory requirements have been met, or

*(continued)*

cause shown as to why they need not be met, an analysis of the best interest and general welfare of the children cannot be considered. *Id.* at 729. The court further held that Appellants had failed to demonstrate cause in the instant cases and therefore their adoption petitions were properly denied.

Judge Johnson filed a dissenting statement, in which Judges Kelly and Todd joined. Judge Johnson opined that the Adoption Act permits an adoption when the children's only legal parent advocates the adoption, has joined in the petition for adoption and has retained his parental rights. He found that the majority's strict construction of Section 2711 contravenes the mandate of the Statutory Construction Act, 1 Pa.C.S. §§ 1501–1991, and is inconsistent with the Legislature's purpose in enacting Section 2711. Judge Johnson stated that the principles relied upon by the majority applied only to the involuntary termination of parental rights and that the majority failed to recognize that Section 2901 granted the trail courts discretion to grant the adoptions in the instant cases. Finally, he found that the majority's analysis erroneously focused upon the relationship between the appellants rather than the parent–child relationship.

Judge Todd filed a separate dissenting opinion, which was joined by Judges Kelly and Johnson. Judge Todd emphasized the impact of the majority's decision on the children at issue. She noted that children will not be afforded the benefits of adoption, which include: the legal protection of the children's existing familial bonds; the right to financial support from two parents; the right to inherit from two parents; and the right to obtain other available dependent benefits, such as health care insurance and Social Security benefits, from either parents. Recognizing that there have been over one hundred "second-parent" adoptions granted in this Commonwealth in at least fourteen counties, Judge Todd opined that the majority's decision would deny many children the legal benefits of parenthood.

The appellants in the case of *In re Adoption of R.B.F. and R.C.F.*, both female, are also engaged in an intimate relationship and have been domestic partners since 1983. When the couple decided to raise a family, Appellant C.H.F. conceived through in vitro fertilization with the sperm of an anonymous donor, who retains no parental rights. C.H.F. gave to twin boys on March 11, 1997. On April 24, 1998, C.H.F. and her partner, B.A.F., filed a petition, wherein B.A.F. sought to adopt the boys. As in the companion case, C.H.F. attached a consent form to the adoption petition, which intentionally omitted the phrase indicating that she intended to permanently give up rights to the children. The Lancaster County Common Pleas Court dismissed the petition with prejudice on October 22, 1998.

A panel of the Superior Court affirmed the denial of the adoption petition. On January 21, 2000, Appellants filed an application for reargument/reconsideration, which was granted. The matter proceeded for oral argument before the *en banc* Superior Court. In a decision filed the same day as *In re Adoption of C.C.G. and Z.C.G.*, the court affirmed the denial of the adoption petition. The analysis was nearly identical to that set forth in C.C.G., and similar concurring and dissenting opinions were filed. This Court subsequently granted allowance of appeal in both case. We begin by recognizing that adoption is purely a statutory right, unknown at common law. *In re Adoption of E.M.A.*, 487 Pa. 152, 409 A.2d 10,11 (1979). To effect an adoption, the legislative provisions of the Adoption Act must be strictly complied with *Id.* Thus, our analysis is focused entirely on the relevant statutory provisions.

The Adoption Act provides that "[a]ny individual may be adopted, regardless of his age or residence." 23 Pa.C.S. § 2311. Similarly, "[a]ny individual may become an adopting parent." *Id.* at § 2312. Section 2701 sets forth the requisite contents of a petition for adoption filed by a prospective adoptive parent. The requirement at issue here first appears at Section 2701(7), which mandates that "all consents required by section 2711 (relating to consents necessary to adoption) are attached or the basis upon which such consents are not required." *Id.* at § 2701(7). Section 2711(a)(3) provides that consent to an adoption shall be required of the following: "The parents or surviving parent of an adoptee who has not reached the age of 18 years." *Id.* at § 2711(a)(3). Subsection (d) of Section 2711 sets forth the contents of consent and mandates, inter alia, that the consent of a parent of an adoptee under 18 years of age include the following statement:

> I understand that by signing this consent I indicate my intent to permanently give up all rights to this child *Id.* at § 2711(d)(1).

An exception to this relinquishment provision appears at Section 2903, entitled "Retention of parental status," which provides as follows:

> Whenever a parent consents to the adoption of his child by his spouse, the parent-child relationship between him and his child shall remain whether or not he is one of the petitioners in the adoption proceeding.

*Id.* at § 2903.

Thus, absent a qualifying provision appearing elsewhere in the Adoption Act, it is clear from a plain reading of these sections that a legal parent must relinquish his parental rights in order to consent to the adoption of his child by a non-spouse. The lower courts properly found that the spousal exception provision in Section 2903 is inapplicable to the instant cases. As noted, 23 Pa.C.S. § 1704 provides that the Commonwealth only recognizes marriage "between one man and one woman." Thus, a same-sex partner cannot be the "spouse" of the legal parent and therefore cannot attain the benefits of the spousal exception to relinquishment of parental rights necessary for a valid consent to adoption.

We addressed the aforementioned provisions in our decision in *In re Adoption of E.M.A.* There, the issue was whether a non-spouse may become an adopting parent of a biological father's child, when the biological father gives only "qualified" consent, retaining his parental rights. Our Court affirmed the denial of the adoption petition on the grounds that the consent given by the biological father did not meet the statutory requirements for adoption by a non-spouse.

### We stated:

> By its express terms, section 503 [the predecessor to Section 2903] is clearly limited to adoption by the spouse of a natural parent. This statutory provision is available only in private or family adoptions, upon the marriage or remarriage of the natural father or mother. Only in such intra-family adoption may a natural parent execute a valid consent retaining parental rights. And only in such a husband-wife relationship is the qualified consent legally sufficient for the spouse seeking to become an adopting parent.

We went on to hold that our Court has no authority to decree an adoption in the absence of the statutorily required consents. We ruled that to construe the spousal exception as applying to a non-spouse "would be unwarranted and impermissible judicial intrusion into the exclusive legislative prerogative." *Id.* Our Court rejected the appellant's contention that the spousal exception to relinquishment of parental rights is unconstitutional as applied because it discriminates against unmarried persons who wish to adopt. We held that because the Adoption Act did not preclude an unmarried person from adopting a child, it withstood constitutional scrutiny. We concluded "[i]t is appropriate and entirely reasonable for the Legislature to provide, as section [2903] does, a special type of consent available only where there is a husband–wife relationship." *Id.* at 12.

Appellants contend that *E.M.A.* is distinguishable on three grounds. First, they argue that *E.M.A.* involved only Section 2903, which they concede is not applicable in cases involving same-sex partners. Second they argue that *E.M.A.* did not involved an "intra-family adoption" and the prospective adoptive parent did not reside with the legal parent. Finally, Appellants allege that *E.M.A.* predated the Legislature's amendment of Section 2901, which they argue affords the trial court discretion to waive the statutory requirements necessary for an adoption petition upon a showing of cause.

We shall address these claims seriatim. Initially, we find that although *E.M.A.* focused upon the spousal exception to the relinquishment of parental rights provision, the decision also reinforced the proposition that the judiciary may not engraft exceptions to the statutory consent requirements of an adoption petition. Further, we discount Appellant's characterization of the opinion as relying upon the residence of the prospective adoptive parent or the fact that the prospective adoptive parent was not part of the nuclear family. Rather, the decision was based upon the fact that the prospective adoptive parent was not the spouse of the biological parent. Thus, the Court concluded that she could not adopt the child absent relinquishment of the father's parental rights.

Appellants' final contention as to why *E.M.A.* is distinguishable, however is persuasive. It is based upon the subsequent 1982 amendment to Section 2901 of the Adoption Act. Section 2901 states in its entirely:

> § 2901. Time of entry of decree of adoption
> Unless the court for cause shown determines otherwise, no decree of adoption shall be entered unless the natural parent of parents' rights have been terminated, the investigation required by section 2535 (relating to investigating) has been completed the report of the intermediary has been filed pursuant to section 2533 (relating to report of intermediary) and all other legal requirements have been met. If all legal requirements have been met, the court may enter a decree of adoption at any time.

23. Pa. C.S. § 2901.

Appellants argue that the Legislature's amendment of this provision after we decided *E.M.A.* was intended to alter that decision by affording the trial court discretion, upon cause shown, to waive a particular statutory requirement. Appellants clarify that they agree with the lower court's finding that "cause shown" is essentially an explanation as to why the statutory requirements are not met. They submit that the court can exercise its discretion in this regard by first determining the underlying purpose of the statutory requirement that the prospective adoptive parent seeks to excuse. According to Appellants, the court would then determine, upon examination of a factual showing by the petitioner, whether the purpose of the statutory requirement will otherwise be met or is irrelevant to the particular circumstances of the case.

Appellants contend that the Superior Court erred in holding that they failed to demonstrate "cause" when they were never given an opportunity to do so. They urge our Court to remand the matter so that they may set forth a factual basis for finding that the purpose of the relinquishment provision would be fulfilled by maintaining the children's relationship with their

*(continued)*

existing parent. They assert that cause can be demonstrated in the instant cases because, "[h]ere, as in a stepparent adoption, the only means to guarantee family integrity ordinarily achieved through termination of existing legal parent's rights would be through preservation of that parent's rights." Appellants' Brief at 30.

After careful consideration, we agree with Appellants that there is no reasonable construction of the Section 2901 "cause shown" language other than to conclude that it permits a petitioner to demonstrate why, in a particular case, he or she cannot meet the statutory requirements. Upon a showing of cause, the trial court is afforded discretion to determine whether the adoption petition should, nevertheless, be granted. The exercise of such discretion does not open the door to unlimited adoptions by legally unrelated adults. Such decisions will always be confined by a finding of cause and a determination of the best interests of the child in each individual case. Moreover, like other trial court decisions, findings of cause will be reviewed on appeal for an abuse of discretion.

We note that our decision is not creating a judicial exception to the requirements of the Adoption Act, but rather is applying the plain meaning of the terms employed by the Legislature. When the requisite cause is demonstrated, Section 2901 affords the trial court discretion to decree the adoption without termination of the legal parent's right pursuant to Section 2711(d). An examination of Section 2701(7), which was also amended after *E.M.A.* was decided, comports with our decision as it requires that the necessary consents under Section 2711 be attached to the adoption petition "or the basis upon which such consents are not required." 23 Pa.C.S. § 2701(7). Thus, contrary to our holding in *E.M.A.*, the Legislature contemplated limited circumstances where the requisite consents may not be necessary.

Furthermore, a contrary interpretation of the "cause shown" language would command an absurd result as the Adoption Act does not expressly preclude same-sex partners from adopting. See I Pa.C.S. § 1922(1) (General Assembly does not intend a result that is absurd, impossible of execution or unreasonable). See also 23 Pa.C.S. § 2312 (stating that "any individual" can adopt). For example, the denial of Appellants' adoption petitions is premised solely upon the lack of unqualified consent by the existing legal parent. There is no language in the Adoption Act precluding two unmarried same-sex partners (or unmarried heterosexual partners) from adopting a child who had no legal parents. It is therefore absurd to prohibit their adoptions merely because their children were either the biological or adopted children of one of the partners prior to the filing of the adoption petition. It is a settled rule

that in the construction of statutes an interpretation is never to be adopted that would defeat the purpose of the enactment, if any other reasonable construction can found which its language will fairly bear. *McQuiston's Adoption,* 86A.2d 205, 206 (Pa.1913).

Another example rendering absurd a contrary interpretation of Section 2901 is Appellants' and supporting amici's suggestion that Appellants could have filed their adoption petitions with the requisite unqualified consent of the legal parent, including the relinquishment of parental rights, and then seek to adopt their children jointly. In view of the fact that there appears to be no statutory bar to such approach, our interpretation of Section 2901 avoids such a convoluted procedure that would serve no valid purpose.

Although not directly on point, we also find support for our decision in *In re Long,* 745 A.2d 673 (Pa.Super.2000), where the Superior Court was called upon to interpret similar "cause shown" language. There, an adoptee sought to recover information regarding her biological parents. At issue was "cause shown" language in another provision of the Adoption Act, Section 2905. Section 2905 provides that all adoption records "shall be kept in the files of the court as a permanent record thereof and withheld from inspection except on an order of court granted upon cause shown. . . ." 23 Pa.C.S. § 2905(a).

On the record presented, the Superior Court could not determine whether the trial court made a factual finding as to whether the appellant demonstrated cause for disclosure of the adoption records as set forth in the statute. The court recognized the lack of guidance as to the meaning of the language employed in Section 2905, as well as the overriding privacy concerns of the adoption process and the Adoption Act. The court described "cause" for disclosure as a demonstration, by clear and convincing evidence, that the adoptee's need for adoption information clearly outweighed the considerations behind the statute. *Id.* at 675. Accordingly, the court remanded for an evidentiary hearing at which such a determination could be made.

Presented with a similar dilemma here, we vacate the orders of the Superior Court and remand to the respective trial courts for evidentiary hearings to determine whether Appellants can demonstrate, by clear and convincing evidence, cause as to whether the purpose of Section 2711(d)'s relinquishment of parental rights requirement will be otherwise fulfilled or is unnecessary under the particular circumstances of each case.

## Case Review Question

Why did the appellate court not grant the right to adopt instead of remanding the case back to the trial court?

## Fertility and Surrogacy

A relatively new area of medicine and subsequently law is that regarding reproductive medicine. Substantial technological advances in the last half of the twentieth century led to increase methods of conception as well. The development of various procedures resulted in the ability to conceive children outside the womb, the insemination and fertilization of an egg by anonymous donors, and even the implantation of embryos from one woman into another for the gestational period before birth. These procedures ultimately produced legal questions too numerous to mention. The most publicized cases, however, have dealt with parental rights when more than two individuals are involved with the conception and gestation of the child, such as when a surrogate mother gives birth and then decides she wants to keep the child. In some instances, the egg is provided by the mother and the sperm provided by the man in a married couple who wish to rear the child. In that case, the wife of the man would be an adoptive parent. Other cases involving implantation of an embryo raise the issue of whether the maternal legal rights are attached to the egg or to the woman who carries it within her body through gestation and gives birth. Questions remain as to the anonymous sperm donor. Does he have any legal paternal rights with respect to a child produced? What of parties who have embryos frozen and then divorce, and the wife proceeds to have the embryo implanted and subsequently delivers a child? Does the natural father have obligations or rights with respect to this child he never intended to be produced? Is it even a question for courts in matters of divorce as to who should have custody of such frozen embryos because they are truly the product and part of the physical being of both parties?

As can be seen, the legal questions arise as quickly as medical technology advances. This area of law will continue to experience explosive growth in the coming decades.

# CASE
### *Roman v. Roman,*
### 193 S.W.3d 40 (2006)

The following decision considers the area of law evolving out of the technological capability to create embryos and suspend maturity through cryopreservation.

In a case of first impression in Texas, appellant, Randy M. Roman, appeals the judgment of the trial court that awarded three frozen embryos to appellee, Augusta N. Roman, in the couple's final decree of divorce. In five issues, Randy argues that the trial court (1) failed to declare the rights of the parties pursuant to a contract; (2) erred in awarding the three frozen embryos to Augusta; (3) erred in failing to make findings of fact and conclusions of law concerning constitutional issues; (4) violated his constitutional rights by awarding the frozen embryos to Augusta; and (5) erred in awarding frozen embryos to Augusta when Randy had withdrawn his consent.

Augusta and Randy married on July 5, 1997. After a few years of marriage, the parties began trying to have children. When the traditional avenues of childbirth proved unsuccessful, the parties tried artificial insemination. Several attempts at artificial insemination likewise proved unsuccessful.

In August 2001, the parties met with Dr. Vicki Schnell, the Medical Director at the Center for Reproductive Medicine (the "Center"). Augusta had laparoscopic surgery and three more attempts at artificial insemination, but was still unsuccessful at getting pregnant.

Dr. Schnell then recommended that the parties try in vitro fertilization ("IVF"). The process of IVF "involves the aspiration of ova or oocytes from the follicles of a woman's ovaries and fertilization of these ova in a laboratory procedure using the husband's or donor's sperm. The resulting [embryos] are transferred to the uterus of the potential mother, whereupon a viable pregnancy may occur. Because the IVF procedure frequently produces more [embryos] than safely may be transferred at one time, the extra [embryos] may be frozen for future use through a process called

*(continued)*

cryopreservation." *In the Interest of O.G.M.*, 988 S.W.2d 473, 474 (Tex.App.–Houston [1st Dist.] 1999, pet. dism'd).

On March 27, 2002, the parties signed a number of documents at the Center, including one entitled "Informed Consent for Cryopreservation of Embryos" ("embryo agreement"). In this document, the parties authorized the storage of the embryos in a frozen state until the Center determined that appropriate conditions existed for transfer of the embryos to the woman's uterus and both husband and wife agreed to the transfer. In addition, the parties chose to discard the embryos in case of divorce. The document also contained a provision that allowed the parties to withdraw their consent to the disposition of the embryos and to discontinue their participation in the program.

On April 17, 2002, thirteen eggs were extracted from Augusta. Six of these eggs were successfully fertilized with Randy's sperm, resulting in six embryos. Of the six embryos that were fertilized, only three reached a stage of development to warrant the cryopreservation process. Dr. Schnell scheduled Augusta's implantation for April 20. On the night before the implantation, Randy expressed feelings to Augusta that led him to withdraw his consent to the implantation scheduled for the next day. The next day, the parties told Dr. Schnell that Augusta would not undergo the implantation procedure. A month after they decided to wait, the parties signed an agreement to unfreeze three embryos and implant them. The agreement was contingent on the parties' obtaining approval from a counselor. That agreement never took effect because Randy and Augusta did not progress through counseling.

On December 10, 2002, Randy filed for divorce and Augusta filed a counterclaim for divorce that included claims for fraud and intentional infliction of emotional distress. The parties reached a final binding agreement during mediation as to the division of the marital property, except for the frozen embryos. At trial, Randy asked the trial court to uphold their written agreement, which specified that the embryos be discarded. Augusta wanted the opportunity to have the embryos implanted so that she could have a biological child. If any children were born from the embryos, Augusta stated that Randy would not have parental rights or responsibilities. The day after the trial ended, the trial court ordered that Augusta take possession of the remaining three embryos. After the trial court awarded the embryos to Augusta, Randy complied with section 160.706(a) of the Texas Family Code, which allows him to seek parental rights to any child born from the embryos. See Tex. Fam.Code Ann. § 160.706(a) (*Vernon*, 2002).

On March 29, 2004, Randy filed a motion for new trial and a request for findings of fact and conclusions of law regarding the award of the frozen embryos to Augusta. The trial court signed its first set of findings on April 26, 2004. The trial court's pertinent findings of fact provide as follows:

1. Three embryos, now frozen, were created during the marriage using the sperm of Randy Roman and the eggs of Augusta Roman.

2. The parties signed a mediation agreement addressing all issues involving the division of community property except for the three frozen embryos.

3. The three frozen embryos are community property.

The trial court's conclusions of law state:

1. The division of the community property agreed to by Petitioner and Respondent in their mediation agreement and the award to Respondent of the three frozen embryos as set forth in the Modified Final Decree of Divorce is just and right and a fair and equitable division of the community property.

On May 13, 2004, the trial court signed a second and more thorough set of findings submitted by Augusta. The record reflects that Randy never filed a request for additional findings.

The trial court's second set of findings of fact state, in relevant part the following:

13. The Court considered all evidence and testimony in balancing the constitutional rights of both parties in making the award of the three (3) frozen embryos to AUGUSTA N. ROMAN.

14. The Court considered all evidence and testimony regarding documents 44 the parties signed with the Center of Reproductive Medicine. . . .

The second set of conclusions of law states,

7. The award of three (3) embryos to [Augusta] is part of a just and right division of the community estate having due regard for the constitutional rights of each party.

8. The order for the Center of Reproductive Medicine to surrender the three (3) frozen embryos to [Augusta] is necessary to effect a just and right division of the community estate.

In this case of first impression in Texas, we consider the merits of the trial court's award of frozen embryos to Augusta as part of a "just and right" division of community property in light of the parties' prior written agreement to discard the embryos. We answer the issue with which we are presented as narrowly as possible in anticipation that the issue will ultimately be resolved by the Texas Legislature.

In his second issue on appeal, Randy argues that the trial court erred when it awarded the three frozen embryos to Augusta because the award violated the parties' embryo agreement. Randy contends that the agreement clearly provided for disposal of the frozen embryos in the case of divorce and that the trial court erred by not enforcing the agreement. Randy points to the following specific provisions in the embryo agreement:

> . . . We consent and authorize the embryo(s) to be stored in a frozen state until Dr. Schnell and the IVF Laboratory determine that appropriate conditions exist for transfer of the embryo(s) to the wife's uterus and both husband and wife agree to the transfer. . . . If we are divorced or either of us files for divorce while any of our frozen embryos are still in the program, we hereby authorize and direct, jointly and individually, that one of the following actions be taken:

> The frozen embryo(s) shall be . . . Discarded.

Randy argues that these provisions of the embryo agreement allow transfer of the embryos only if both parties agree and that the trial court erred by not enforcing the agreement and ordering the embryos destroyed. Randy also argues that no evidence or insufficient evidence supports a finding that the embryo agreement was not enforceable or invalid. Although no Texas case has ruled on whether these types of agreements are enforceable, Randy contends that other jurisdictions have held that similar agreements are enforceable.

> . . . We understand that legal principles and requirements regarding IVF and embryo freezing have not been firmly established. There is presently no state legislation dealing specifically with these issues. We have been advised that each embryo resulting from the fertilization of the wife's oocytes by the husband's sperm shall be the joint property of both partners based on currently accepted principles regarding legal ownership of human sperm and oocytes. We are aware that these regulations may change at any time. This section acknowledges that Texas laws regarding legal ownership of frozen embryos could change and that this area of the law continues to develop. Because it is not necessary to the disposition of this appeal, we do not address the parties' characterization of the frozen embryos as "joint property."

Augusta does not dispute that she signed and initialed the embryo agreement. She does dispute, however, the agreement's validity and the interpretation of the agreement. Specifically, Augusta argues that the trial court could have chosen not to enforce the agreement because other state supreme courts have found agreements similar to the one at issue here invalid. Because this issue has not been decided by any court in Texas, we will review the scant case law on the issue.

All but one of the cases surveyed involved an oral or written agreement regarding disposition of frozen embryos. In *Davis v. Davis,* the earliest case, the husband and wife did not have an agreement for the disposition of the embryos. 842 S.W.2d 588, 589 (Tenn.1992), *cert. denied sub nom, Stowe v. Davis,* 507 U.S. 911, 113 S.Ct. 1259, 122 L.Ed.2d 657 (1993). The trial court awarded custody of the frozen embryos to the wife, but the court of appeals reversed on the ground that the husband had a constitutional right not to beget a child. *Id.* at 589. In affirming the judgment of the court of appeals, the Supreme Court of Tennessee ultimately chose to weigh the interests of each party and concluded that the husband's interest in avoiding parenthood was more significant than the wife's interest in donating the embryos to another couple for implantation. *Id.* at 604.

Although the parties did not have an agreement concerning disposition of the frozen embryos, the court discussed the enforceability of a contract in this situation. The court stated, "an agreement regarding disposition of any untransferred preembryos in the event of contingencies (such as the death of one or more of the parties, divorce, financial reversals, or abandonment of the program) should be presumed valid and should be enforced as between the progenitors." *Id.* at 597. The court further stated that,

> [W]e recognize that life is not static, and that human emotions run particularly high when a married couple is attempting to overcome infertility problems. It follows that the parties' initial "informed consent" to IVF procedures will often not be truly informed because of the near impossibility of anticipating, emotionally and psychologically, all the turns that events may take as the IVF process unfolds. Providing that the initial agreements may later be modified by agreement will, we think, protect the parties against some of the risks they face in this regard. But, in the absence of such agreed modification, we conclude that their prior agreements should be considered binding.

*Id.* at 597.

In *Kass v. Kass,* prior to implantation, the parties signed a consent form which stated that the frozen embryos would not be released from storage without the written consent of both parties. 91 N.Y.2d 554, 673 N.Y.S.2d 350, 696 N.E.2d 174, 176 (1998). Another part of the consent agreement provided that if the parties could not reach a mutual decision on the frozen embryos, the embryos would be donated to research. *Id.* at 177. Before filing suit, the wife decided that she

*(continued)*

opposed the destruction of the embryos. *Id.* The trial court awarded custody of the embryos to the wife and directed her to implant them within a medically reasonable time. *Id.* The appellate division reversed. It unanimously agreed that the consent agreement regarding the disposition of unused fertilized eggs should control. *Id.* A two-justice plurality found that the parties' consent agreement indicated their desire to donate the embryos for research purposes if they could not both consent to the embryos' disposition. *Id.*

The highest court of New York affirmed the lower court's holding that the parties' consent agreement should control. The court noted that the parties had expressed their intent that if they could not agree on the embryos' disposition, they would be donated for research purposes. *Id.* at 178. It stated, "[P]arties should be encouraged in advance, before embarking on IVF and cryopreservation, to think through possible contingencies and carefully specify their wishes in writing. Explicit agreements avoid costly litigation in business transactions." *Id.* at 180. The court further stated,

> Advance directives, subject to mutual change of mind that must be jointly expressed, both minimize misunderstandings and maximize procreative liberty by reserving to the progenitors the authority to make what is in the first instance a quintessentially personal, private decision. Written agreements also provide the certainty needed for effective operation of IVF programs. *Id.*

A New Jersey appellate court, by contrast, rejected an alleged oral agreement to procreate as against public policy. See *J.B. v. M.B.,* 331 N.J.Super. 223, 751 A.2d 613, 615 (2000). In *J.B. v. M.B.,* the husband wanted to preserve the frozen embryos for his use or that of an infertile couple. 751 A.2d at 615. The wife wanted the frozen embryos destroyed, and she did not want her former husband to retain them for his own use or to donate them to anyone else. *Id.* at 616. The trial court ruled in favor of the wife, who wanted the embryos destroyed, because the family unit was no longer intact. *Id.* The appellate court balanced the wife's right not to become a parent with the husband's right to procreate using the embryos under the Fourteenth Amendment and concluded that the husband's right would not be impaired if the embryos were destroyed because he still would be able to father children. *Id.* at 618–19. Thus, even if the Fourteenth Amendment applied, the court rejected the husband's argument that his constitutional rights would be violated if the embryos were destroyed. *Id.* at 619. The appellate court further held that a contract to procreate is contrary to New Jersey public policy and is unenforceable. *Id.* The court thus affirmed the trial court's order that the frozen embryos be destroyed. *Id.* at 620.

The Supreme Court of New Jersey affirmed, but modified the court of appeals' holding, recognizing "that persuasive reasons exist for enforcing preembryo disposition agreements." *J.B. v. M.B.,* 170 N.J. 9, 783 A.2d 707, 719 (2001). The supreme court held that the parties' consent agreement did not "manifest a clear intent by [the parties] regarding disposition of the preembryos in the event of a dissolution of their marriage." *Id.* at 713. In reaching its ultimate holding, the court considered the constitutional rights of the parties and stated that, "[w]e will not force [the wife] to become a biological parent against her will." *Id.* at 717. The court held that it will "enforce agreements entered into at the time in vitro fertilization [has] begun, subject to the right of either party to change his or her mind about disposition up to the point of use or destruction of any stored preembryos." *Id.* at 719. If the parties disagree about disposition because one party has reconsidered their decision, the court stated, "the interests of both parties must be evaluated." *Id.*

In *A.Z. v. B.Z.,* before the eggs were retrieved from the wife, the parties signed consent forms. 431 Mass. 150, 725 N.E.2d 1051, 1053–54 (2000). The wife filled out the form, which stated that if they "[s]hould become separated, [they] both agree[d] to have the embryo(s) . . . return[ed] to [the] wife for implant." *Id.* at 1054. The court noted that the husband always signed a blank consent form. *Id.* After the husband signed the consent form, the wife would fill in the disposition and sign the form herself. *Id.*

The trial court permanently enjoined the wife from utilizing the frozen embryos held in cryopreservation. The supreme judicial court stated that "in view of the purpose of the form (drafted by and to give assistance to the clinic) and the circumstances of execution, we are dubious at best that it represents the intent of the husband and the wife regarding disposition of the preembryos in the case of a dispute between them." *Id.* at 1056.

Specifically, the court stated that neither the form nor the record indicated that the parties intended the form to be a binding agreement. *Id.* Instead, the court interpreted the form only to "define the donors' relationship as a unit with the clinic." *Id.* In reaching its decision, the court also noted that the consent form did not contain a duration provision and that it could not assume that the donors intended their consent form to govern a disposition of frozen preembryos four years after it was executed. *Id.* at 1056–57.

The court also looked to the donors' conduct in connection with the execution of the consent forms and determined that their conduct created doubt that the consent form represented the intentions of both donors. *Id.* at 1057. Because the husband signed a blank form and the wife later filled in her choice regarding disposition of the frozen embryos, the court concluded that the consent form did not represent the true intentions of the husband. *Id.*

In *Litowitz v. Litowitz,* the husband and wife contracted with an egg donor and an IVF clinic. See 146 Wash.2d 514, 48 P.3d 261, 263 (2002), *cert. denied,* 537 U.S. 1191, 123 S.Ct. 1271, 154 L.Ed.2d 1025 (2003). After the husband's sperm fertilized three of the donor's eggs, the eggs were implanted, resulting in the birth of a child. Before the birth, however, the parties separated, and sued for divorce. At trial, the wife asked to be awarded the remaining embryos to implant in a surrogate. The trial court awarded the embryos to the husband, who wanted to donate them to an out-of-state couple. The appeals court, in reviewing the egg donor contract, noted that it did not provide what would be done with the embryos if the parties could not agree or if they dissolved their marriage. The court concluded that the husband's right not to procreate compelled an award of the embryos to him. *Id.* at 265. The Supreme Court of Washington reversed, holding the parties to their preembryo cryopreservation contract, which provided that the remaining embryos would be thawed out, but not allowed to undergo further development, and that they would be disposed of after they had been maintained in cryopreservation for five years. *Id.* at 271.

The most recent case to consider the issue, *In re Marriage of Witten,* 672 N.W.2d 768, 771–72 (Iowa 2003), likewise focused on the embryo agreement. In *Witten,* the parties signed an embryo storage agreement with the IVF clinic prior to undergoing the IVF process. *Id.* at 772. The consent form provided that frozen embryos would be released only with the approval of both the husband and the wife. *Id.* The trial court concluded that the embryo storage agreement governed the dispute over the frozen embryos. *Id.* at 773. The parties were thus enjoined from taking any actions with the embryos unless both parties consented. *Id.*

The Iowa Supreme Court noted that the embryo agreement did not specifically address what would happen to the embryos upon divorce. *Id.* The court reviewed the three approaches that courts have used in resolving these types of disputes and adopted the contemporaneous mutual consent model. *Id.* at 783. In adopting this model, the court found that it would be against Iowa public policy "to enforce a prior agreement between the parties in this highly personal area of reproductive choice when one of the parties has changed his or her mind concerning the disposition or use of the embryos." *Id.* at 781. Nevertheless, the court recognized that an embryo agreement between embryo donor and fertility clinics "serves an important purpose . . . ensuring that all parties understand their

respective rights and obligations." *Id.* Given these different considerations, the court stated, "[W]e reject the contractual approach and hold that agreements entered into at the time in vitro fertilization is commenced are enforceable and binding on the parties, 'subject to the right of either party to change his or her mind about disposition up to the point of use or destruction of any stored embryo,'" providing that any change of intention is communicated in writing to all parties. *Id.* at 782–83 (quoting *J.B.,* 783 A.2d at 719). Because the agreement did not address disposition of the embryos upon divorce and neither party could agree on the embryos' disposition, the court enjoined both parties from utilizing the embryos without the other's written consent. *Id.* at 783.

We are mindful of the cases that have addressed this issue and particularly what we see as an emerging majority view that written embryo agreements between embryo donors and fertility clinics to which all parties have consented are valid and enforceable so long as the parties have the opportunity to withdraw their consent to the terms of the agreement. Because we are not bound by state law from other jurisdictions, however, we will also review our own statutes to determine the public policy of this State in the context of embryo agreements.

Currently, the State of Texas has laws regarding children of assisted reproduction and gestational agreements, both contained within the Uniform Parentage Act. See Tex. Fam.Code Ann. § 160.701–.707 (*Vernon,* 2002), § § 160.751–.763 (*Vernon,* Supp.2005). Assisted reproduction means a method of causing pregnancy other than sexual intercourse, including IVF and transfer of embryos. *Id.* § 160.102(2)(D) (*Vernon,* 2002). The statute requires that both husband and wife consent to assisted reproduction. *Id.* § 160.704(a). However, section 160.704(b) acknowledges that a child may be born without the husband's consent. *Id.* § 160.704(b). Section 160.706 addresses paternity in the event of divorce as follows: "if a marriage is dissolved before the placement of eggs, sperm, or embryos, the former spouse is not a parent of the resulting child unless the former spouse consented in a record that if assisted reproduction were to occur after a divorce the former spouse would be a parent of the child." *Id.* § 160.706(a). This section also provides that consent of the former spouse may be withdrawn at any time before the placement of eggs, sperm, or embryos. *Id.* § 160.706(b). Noticeably absent from these sections is any legislative directive on how to determine the disposition of the embryos in case of a contingency such as death or divorce. Nor is there anything in the case law that is incompatible with the recognition of the parties' agreement as controlling.

*(continued)*

We also look to new legislation concerning gestational agreements. A gestational agreement is an agreement between a woman and the intended parents of a child in which the woman relinquishes all rights as a parent of a child conceived by means of assisted reproduction and which provides that the intended parents become the parents of the child. See *id.* § 160.752(a) (*Vernon,* Supp.2005). The statute specifically authorizes a gestational mother, her husband if she is married, each donor, and each intended parent to enter into a written agreement that relinquishes all parental rights of the gestational mother and provides that the intended parents become the parents of the child. See *id.* § 160.754(a). The statute also requires that the parties to a gestational agreement must enter into the agreement before the 14th day preceding the date of transfer of eggs, sperm, or embryos to the gestational mother. See *id.* § 160.754(e). Parental rights are transferred when a court validates the gestational agreement. See *id.* § 160.753(a), (b). To validate a gestational agreement, the court must find, in relevance to our issue, that each party to the agreement voluntarily entered into and understood the terms of the agreement. *Id.* § 160.756(b)(4). The statute also provides that "[b]efore a prospective gestational mother becomes pregnant by means of assisted reproduction, the prospective gestational mother, her husband if she is married, or either intended parent may terminate a gestational agreement. . . ." *Id.* § 160.759(a).

We glean from these statutes that the public policy of this State would permit a husband and wife to enter voluntarily into an agreement, before implantation, that would provide for an embryo's disposition in the event of a contingency, such as divorce, death, or changed circumstances. We agree with the New York Court of Appeals that "[a]dvance directives, subject to mutual change of mind that must be jointly expressed, both minimize misunderstandings and maximize procreative liberty by reserving to the progenitors the authority to make what is in the first instance a quintessentially personal, private decision." *Kass,* 673 N.Y.S.2d 350, 696 N.E.2d at 180. These agreements should thus be "presumed valid and should be enforced as between the progenitors." *Davis,* 842 S.W.2d at 597; *Kass,* 673 N.Y.S.2d 350, 696 N.E.2d at 180–181.

We believe that allowing the parties voluntarily to decide the disposition of frozen embryos in advance of cryopreservation, subject to mutual change of mind, jointly expressed, best serves the existing public policy of this State and the interests of the parties. We hold, therefore, that an embryo agreement that satisfies these criteria does not violate the public policy of the State of Texas.

We now determine whether the embryo agreement in this case manifests a voluntary unchanged mutual intention of the parties regarding disposition of the embryos upon divorce. Absent ambiguity, we interpret a contract as a matter of law. *DeWitt County Elec. Co-op., Inc. v. Parks,* 1 S.W.3d 96, 100 (Tex.1999). "Whether a contract is ambiguous is a question of law that must be decided by examining the contract as a whole in light of the circumstances present when the contract was entered." *Columbia Gas Transmission Corp. v. New Ulm Gas, Ltd.,* 940 S.W.2d 587, 589 (Tex.1996). "If the written instrument is so worded that it can be given a certain or definite legal meaning or interpretation, then it is not ambiguous and the court will construe the contract as a matter of law." *Coker v. Coker,* 650 S.W.2d 391, 393 (Tex.1983). "An ambiguity exists only if the contract language is susceptible to two or more reasonable interpretations." *Am. Mfrs. Mut. Ins. Co. v. Schaefer,* 124 S.W.3d 154, 157 (Tex.2003). The language in a contract is to be given its plain grammatical meaning unless doing so would defeat the parties' intent. *DeWitt County Elec. Coop.,* 1 S.W.3d at 101. We presume that the parties intended every clause to have an effect. *Heritage Res., Inc. v. NationsBank,* 939 S.W.2d 118, 121 (Tex.1996).

The following elements are required for the formation of a valid and binding contract: 1) an offer, 2) acceptance in strict compliance with the terms of the offer, 3) a meeting of the minds, 4) each party's consent to the terms, and 5) execution and delivery of the contract with the intent that it be mutual and binding. *Wal-Mart Stores, Inc. v. Lopez,* 93 S.W.3d 548, 555–56 (Tex. App.–Houston [14th Dist.] 2002, no pet.). Consideration is also a fundamental element of every valid contract. *Turner-Bass Assocs. of Tyler v. Williamson,* 932 S.W.2d 219, 222 (Tex.App.–Tyler 1996, *writ denied*).

The evidence shows that the parties came to the Center on March 27, 2002 to sign a variety of forms. The parties received a cover page along with nine forms. The cover page stated, "Many forms require careful thought regarding decisions you and your spouse will be asked to make." We focus our discussion on one of the documents entitled, "Informed Consent for Cryopreservation of Embryo." On page two, under the sub-heading "Consent for Cryopreservation," the document states,

> 1. We, Augusta Roman (wife) and Randy Roman (husband), the undersigned, hereby authorize and consent to the freezing of some or all of the remaining embryos that result from our participating in the IVF process.

> 2. We consent and authorize the embryo(s) to be stored in a frozen state until Dr. Schnell and the IVF Laboratory determine that appropriate conditions exist for transfer of the embryo(s) to the wife's uterus and both husband and wife agree to the transfer.

On page three, the document states,

7. We understand that legal principles and requirements regarding IVF and embryo freezing have not been firmly established. There is presently no state legislation dealing specifically with these issues. We have been advised that each embryo resulting from the fertilization of the wife's oocytes by the husband's sperm shall be the joint property of both partners based on currently accepted principles regarding legal ownership of human sperm and oocytes. We are aware that these regulations may change at any time.

8. We hereby authorize and require that the actions we have marked below be taken if either or both of us should die while any of our frozen embryos are still in possession of the Center of Reproductive Medicine IVF Program. We consent to the following: If only one of us survives, the surviving spouse shall have full authority to decide what is to be done with the embryo(s).

9. We understand that if both of us die, the frozen embryo(s) will be discarded.

On page four, the document states,

10. If we are divorced or either of us files for divorce while any of our frozen embryos are still in the program, we hereby authorize and direct, jointly and individually, that one of the following actions be taken:

The frozen embryo(s) shall be . . . Discarded.

. . . If other circumstances arise whereby embryos remain which are not used for the purpose of attempting to initiate a pregnancy in the wife or if the husband and wife are not able to agree on disposition of remaining embryos for any reason, we hereby authorize and direct that the unused frozen embryo(s) will be discarded.

On page five, the document states,

We agree and acknowledge that we are voluntary participants, but we understand that we are free to withdraw our consent as to the disposition of our embryo(s) and to discontinue participation by requesting relocation of our embryo(s) to another suitable location at any time without prejudice.

20. Our questions regarding these procedures have been answered to our satisfaction. Our participation is voluntary. We understand that we may withdraw our consent at any time prior to the procedure. We have read and understand this form. We have received a copy of this form.

Neither party disputes that he or she signed the agreement or initialed the bottom of each page of this agreement. They also do not dispute that each one of them specifically initialed section 8 (embryo disposition in the event of a death) and section 10 (embryo disposition

in the event of divorce). They also do not dispute that their frozen embryos were still in the program or that, when they filed for divorce, they had not withdrawn consent as to the disposition of the embryos and discontinued in the participation in the program.

Rather, Augusta argues that she understood the embryo agreement to apply to remaining embryos only after implantation had occurred. She testified that she never agreed to destroy all the embryos without an opportunity to get pregnant. Although she does not refer specifically to it in her brief, Augusta is apparently relying on the first section of the embryo agreement, entitled Consent for Cryopreservation. This section provides, "[The parties] hereby authorize and consent to the freezing of some or all of the remaining embryos that result from our participation in the IVF process." We disagree with Augusta's interpretation of the embryo agreement.

For this Court to follow Augusta's interpretation, we would necessarily have to impute language to the contract that is not present and disregard language that is. Specifically, Augusta would have us read the clause as stating that "the parties hereby authorize and consent to the freezing of some or all of the remaining embryos [after an initial set of embryos is implanted] that result from our participating in the IVF process." In an unambiguous contract, we will not imply language, add to language, or interpret it other than pursuant to its plain meaning. See *Schaefer,* 124 S.W.3d at 162; *Natural Gas Clearinghouse v. Midgard Energy Co.,* 113 S.W.3d 400, 407 (Tex.App.—Amarillo 2003, pet. denied).

Section 10 of the agreement specifically states, "If we are divorced or either of us files for divorce while any of our frozen embryos are still in the program, we hereby authorize and direct, jointly and individually, that one of the following actions be taken: The frozen embryo(s) shall be . . . Discarded." Although the parties could have chosen to release the frozen embryos either to Randy or Augusta, they chose the option to discard the frozen embryos in the event of divorce.

The embryo agreement's language could not be clearer. Section 10 specifically addresses the disposition of the frozen embryos in the event of a divorce. It is undisputed that Augusta and Randy both signed the entire embryo agreement, and they both initialed section 10. The evidence shows that the parties considered this section and did not sign it without thought.

Randy testified that before signing the embryo agreement, he and Augusta discussed their options about what would happen to the embryos upon divorce. Randy stated that they were both excited about taking the next step forward, but also nervous. Randy did not notice that Augusta was too emotionally upset to give consent. He also testified that they did not disagree as

*(continued)*

what to do in the event of a divorce. He further testified that no coercion, threats, bribery, or promises were used to make them sign the embryo agreement.

Dr. Schnell testified that the purpose of the cryopreservation form was to determine the parties' desires for the disposition of their embryos upon certain events such as divorce or death. Dr. Schnell testified that the couple had chosen to have the embryos discarded in the event that they divorced. On the day the parties signed the consent forms, Dr. Schnell testified that Augusta "was able to participate in the consult, and that she was able to understand the questions that I asked her, and she was able to state that she did initial those and that she understood the consents and that all her questions were answered concerning the process." At that time, Dr. Schnell did not notice any outward signs of an emotional problem that would prevent Augusta from understanding and making an informed consent.

Augusta testified that she would have signed anything to move forward because her goal was to have a child. She testified that it was possible that because she was taking birth control pills she was not in the right mental state to understand the agreement. Augusta further stated that she understood the agreement, "but I wasn't focusing on much on the [inaudible] to the outcome of the whole process of having a child." She also stated that no one was putting any force, coercion or threats on either of the parties to sign the agreement. She understood that one of the options she had been offered was to give the embryos to herself in the event of divorce. Augusta testified that she signed the agreement with the Center. When asked whether she and Randy had had a meeting of their minds as to what would happen in the unlikely event that they ever divorced, Augusta responded, "We didn't talk about divorce. I mean, it wasn't even a remote—it wasn't a conversation that we had. He signed and I signed—and I initialed it." She was also asked, "So you and Randy Roman never had an agreement on what would happen if you divorce, what would happen to the embryos if you divorced." She responded, "No, we didn't have a discussion." Augusta clarified that they did not have an agreement, other than that expressed in the consent form with the center.

"[P]arties strike the deal they choose to strike and, thus, voluntarily bind themselves in the manner they choose." *Natural Gas,* 113 S.W.3d at 407. Although Augusta's choice may not have been fully considered, the evidence shows that she was aware of and understood the significance of her decision. The parties' embryo agreement clearly indicates their wishes in the event of divorce. We conclude that the parties' embryo agreement was not ambiguous so as to preclude a meeting of the minds.

Our conclusion that section 10 shows a meeting of the minds is bolstered by section 8 of the embryo agreement, which provides that in the event that one or both of the parties should die, they agree to give the embryos to the surviving spouse even though they could have chosen to discard the embryos. The parties' choice to give the surviving spouse full authority over the embryos indicates that the parties were aware of other options in the agreement. The agreement shows that when the parties wanted to discard the embryos, they made that choice. When the parties wanted to give the embryos to one party, they made that choice. In fact, the embryo agreement shows that at some point in signing section 8, Augusta's initials were on the option that would have discarded the embryos. Her initials were subsequently crossed out and re-entered on the choice giving the surviving spouse full authority for the embryos.

We also note that section 11 is applicable to this dispute. Section 11 states, "[I]f the husband and wife are not able to agree on disposition of remaining embryos for any reason, we hereby authorize and direct that the unused frozen embryo(s) will be discarded." Even without section 10, which clearly provides the course of action in the event of divorce, section 11 would also inform the trial court of what to do in the event of a contingency when the parties could not agree.

Texas statutory law and section 16 of the embryo agreement allow a party to withdraw consent to assisted reproduction procedures. See Tex. Fam.Code Ann. § 160.706(b) (*Vernon, 2002*) (stating that consent may be withdrawn at any time before the placement of eggs, sperm, or embryos). Neither Randy nor Augusta withdrew consent to the provision in the embryo agreement that the frozen embryos were to be discarded in the event of divorce. Nor did they withdraw consent to the provision within section 11 of the embryo agreement—that if the parties could not agree on the disposition of the embryos, the frozen embryos were to be discarded. Rather, their embryos were still in the program, and the embryo agreement was still in effect when the parties divorced.

Augusta also argues that Randy "breached the intent and purpose of the IVF agreements, thereby invalidating any decisions made by Mrs. Roman based upon her belief that the entire agreement would be honored." Augusta does not cite any argument or authority for this proposition. Therefore, we will not consider it on appeal. See Tex.R.App. P. 38.1(h).

Augusta also argues that the embryo agreement did not reflect a meeting of the minds and was not a valid agreement concerning the disposition of the embryos. She reasons that because Randy deceived her as to his true state of mind, there could be no meeting of the minds. Although there was evidence that Randy had been upset with Augusta in the two years prior to the scheduled implantation, we cannot see how this precludes a meeting of the minds in regard to their mutual decision for the disposition of their embryos in the event of a divorce. See *CU Lloyd's of Texas v. Hatfield*, 126 S.W.3d 679, 682 (Tex.App.–Houston [14th Dist.] 2004, pet. denied) ("If a written contract is so worded that it can be given a definite or certain legal meaning, then it is unambiguous, and [we] may not consider parol evidence as to the parties' intent."). Randy's deceit may have been relevant for proving fraud, but the trial court found against Augusta on that issue.

Augusta additionally argues that because the Center agreed to do whatever the Court ordered it to do, the Center's actions supersede the Center's cryopreservation document and render it moot. Augusta does not state why the embryo agreement is rendered moot, nor does she cite any authority for the proposition. We decline to address her argument. See Tex.R.App. P. 38.1(h).

We hold that the embryo agreement provides that the frozen embryos are to be discarded in the event of divorce. By awarding the frozen embryos to Augusta, the trial court improperly rewrote the parties' agreement instead of enforcing what the parties had voluntarily decided in the event of divorce. Accordingly, the trial court abused its discretion in not enforcing the embryo agreement.

We sustain Randy's second issue. Because Randy's second issue is dispositive, we decline to address Randy's remaining issues. See Tex.R.App. P. 47.1.

We reverse the judgment and remand the cause to the trial court to enter an order consistent with this opinion and with the parties' agreement that the frozen embryos be discarded. All pending motions are denied.

## Case Review Question

If someone contributes egg or sperm to an embryo and then gives up all parental rights, should that person be required to pay child support once the child is born?

## ETHICAL CONSIDERATIONS

Legal ethics plays an important role in the law of domestic relations. It is not uncommon for only one party to retain counsel in situations involving dissolution, marital property, or interests regarding children. In such situations, the attorney is under an ethical obligation to make it clear to the other party that a lawyer cannot represent both sides of a legal issue. To do so would constitute a conflict of interest. Consequently, it is quite common that a property settlement or other document of settlement of legal issues contain a clause that identifies who is represented by the attorney.

In an uncontested dissolution of marriage in which there are few matters to be determined such as division of property, the parties may elect to use one attorney to minimize the cost. However, this does not change the position of the attorney. Ethically, the attorney can represent only one of the parties. The other party who chooses to agree to the terms presented must do so independently and without the advice or counsel of the attorney. Further, that party must always retain the right to seek legal advice on the matter from another attorney. In this way, the initial attorney cannot be considered to be attempting to represent the best interest of two parties on opposite sides of a conflict.

## ETHICAL CIRCUMSTANCE

Joann and Tyrell have decided to end their marriage of fifteen years. They have limited financial resources and barely generate enough income to support themselves and their three children. They have approached legal assistance organizations, but most have a waiting list for services that are not considered emergencies. They contact an attorney for representation. It is clear that both have different ideas of how the issues of property rights and responsibilities, visitation, and custody should be resolved. The attorney wants to help them but knows the cost to counsel will be unaffordable. The attorney must inform them that only one can be represented by the firm.

A much less expensive alternative to suggest is arbitration: They would agree to present both sides to an arbitrator and be bound by the arbitrator's final recommendation. Such a situation takes business away from the attorney but provides an ethical resolution. For the attorney to represent one side, knowing the other cannot afford counsel and will thus be at a disadvantage, may be legal but certainly would not be ethical.

## Question

Could the attorney provide any other alternative?

## ● | CHAPTER SUMMARY

The law of domestic relations in this country has undergone radical changes in the last century. This area of law is also probably the most different from its origins, unlike areas such as contract and property law that retain many foundations in the original principles brought from England. Since the middle of the twentieth century, divorce has gone from a rare and socially unacceptable occurrence to a certainty in almost half of all marriages. Dissolution of marriage and the consequent issues comprise the majority of legal principles in domestic relations law.

Assuming a marriage is legally accomplished through meeting of formal and statutory requisites, it can be ended by annulment in limited circumstances. Specifically, a condition of marriage must not have existed at the time the marriage occurred that, in turn, prevented it from having ever become valid. The other and much more common alternative is dissolution of marriage in which a valid marriage relationship is dissolved and the assets, debts, maintenance, and other joint issues of the parties such as child custody, support, and visitation are resolved.

Some parties elect to legally separate rather than divorce, although this is in the minority of cases. In the event of a legal separation, the marital relationship is left intact. The parties remain married for legal purposes; however, they separate their property, assets, debts, and responsibilities with respect to minor children. Historically, this was often done for parties who did not wish to continue living together but remained married because of social, cultural, and religious pressures and issues. Dissolution today is more accepted, and parties most often opt for it to bring the relationship to an end and allow them to move forward in their lives independently of one another.

Parties who cohabit as if they are married are no longer considered common law spouses in the vast majority of jurisdictions. Rather, in the event the cohabitation and relationship end, the parties are left to resolve matters themselves or to pursue the issues in the courts under contract and partnership principles. This assumes, however, that the relationship was not contingent on sexual services, in which case the purpose is considered illegal and the courts will not enforce rights as if a contract or partnership existed.

## ● | CHAPTER TERMS

| | | |
|---|---|---|
| annulment | dissolution of marriage | preliminary injunction |
| antenuptial agreement | domestic violence | property settlement |
|   (prenuptial agreement) | legal separation | temporary restraining |
| custody (parental rights) | permanent injunction |   order |

## ● | REVIEW QUESTIONS

1. Are antenuptial agreements legally enforceable?
2. What is necessary for a valid marriage?

3. When can a marriage be legally annulled?

4. What rights are available to persons who cohabit but do not marry in the event the relationship ends?

5. How does a legal separation differ from the dissolution of a marriage?

6. What relief is available to the parties after dissolution is sought but before it is granted?

7. What standard do the courts apply when determining custody?

8. What is joint custody?

9. What is the difficulty with joint custody?

10. What are no-fault grounds for dissolution?

## ● | HELPFUL WEB SITES

Family law          http://legalcareers.about.com/od/legalspecialties/a/familylaw.htm
                    http://en.wikipedia.org/wiki/Family_law

## ● | INTERNET ASSIGNMENT 10.1

Using Internet resources, identify the requirements for marriage in your jurisdiction including waiting period, blood tests, prohibited relationships, and licensure. Trace your steps.

## ● | INTERNET ASSIGNMENT 10.2

Does your jurisdiction allow for the creation of domestic partnerships?

## ● | INTERNET ASSIGNMENT 10.3

Has your jurisdiction adopted all or part of the UCCJEA?

## ● | ENDNOTES

1. *In re Estate of Cummings,* 493 Pa. 11, 425 A.2d 340 (1981).
2. 81 A.L.R.3d. 453.
3. *Id.*
4. Mobilia, "Ante-nuptial agreements anticipating divorce: How effective are they?" 70 *Massachusetts Law Review* 82 10 (June 1985).
5. 55 C.J.S., Marriage, Section 10.
6. *Id.*, Sections 24, 25.
7. *Id.*, Sections 28–31.
8. *Id.*, Section 48.
9. *McDonald v. McDonald,* 6 Cal.2d 457, 58 P.2d 163 (1936).
10. *Wirth v. Wirth,* 175 Misc. 342, 23 N.Y.S.2d 289 (1940).
11. 81 A.L.R.3d. 281.
12. *Jackson v. Jackson,* 276 F.2d 501 (D.C.Cir. 1960).
13. *Maschauer v. Downs,* 53 App.D.C. 142, 289 Fed. 540 (1923).
14. 41 Am.Jur.2d., Husband and Wife, Section 522.
15. Federal Rules of Evidence, 28 U.S.C.A. Rule 501.
16. 23 *Journal of Family Law* 454 (April 1985).
17. 51 A.L.R.3d 223.
18. *Id.*
19. 24 Am.Jur.2d, Divorce and Separation, Section 29.
20. *Glendening v. Glendening,* 206 A.2d 824 (D.C. App. 1965).
21. Uniform Marriage and Divorce Act, Section 304(b) (2).
22. 24 Am.Jur.2d., Divorce and Separation, Section 328.
23. 75 A.L.R.3d.

24. 48 A.L.R.4th 919.
25. *Id.*
26. *Id.*
27. 70 A.L.R.3d 262.
28. 24 Am.Jur.2d., Divorce and Separation, Sections 974, 975.
29. *Id.*
30. *Id.*
31. 17 A.L.R.4th 1013.
32. *Perla v. Perla,* 58 So.2d 689 (Fla. 1952).
33. Smith, "Education support obligations of noncustodial parents," 36 *Rutgers Law Review* 588 (September 1984).
34. Comment, "Battling inconsistency and inadequacy: Child support guidelines in the states," *Harvard Women's Law Journal* 197 (Spring 1988).
35. See note 21, Section 102(5); 309.
36. 23 Am.Jur.2d, Desertion and Non-support, Section 128, et seq.
37. *In re J. S. & C.,* 129 N.J.Super. 486, 324 A.2d 90 (1974).
38. 24 Am.Jur.2d., Divorce and Separation, Section 866.
39. *Id.*; 20 Am.Jur. 2d, Sections 321–370.
40. 97 A.L.R.3d 740.
41. See note 38, Section 584.
42. Monroe, "Marvin v. Marvin: Five years later," 65 *Marquette Law Review* 389 (Spring 1982).
43. *Marvin v. Marvin,* 18 Cal.3d 660, 134 Cal.Rptr. 815, 557 P.2d 106 (1976).

## STUDENT CD-ROM

For additional materials, please go to the CD in this book.

## ONLINE COMPANION™

For additional resources, please go to www.paralegal.delmar.cengage.com

# Estates and Probate

## THE IMPORTANCE OF PLAN B

The saga over the estate of Anna Nicole Smith continues like a daytime drama, begging the question, Who gets the money? Although Smith had limited financial resources at the time of her death, she had the legal potential for hundreds of millions of dollars in her battle over the estate of her deceased husband, J. Howard Marshall. At the time that Smith's will was executed, years before her own death, it named her only child as the sole heir entitled to her entire estate.

The will contained some rather unusual language to disinherit any future heirs. If the will were found to be otherwise valid, ordinarily the entire estate would pass to whoever is identified as the heir to the residual portion of the estate. This person controls bequests that could not be distributed or those assets that were not specifically bequested or obtained after the execution of the will. In this case, the entire estate would normally pass to the residuary because Smith's only named beneficiary predeceased her and the bequest could not be filled. However, the will does not contain an alternative beneficiary or residual clause. This is also quite unusual. In addition, the will stated that anyone who challenged the will would not be entitled to any portion of the estate. In this case, under general legal principles, even if the will were found to be valid it would not matter because there is no one named under the will still alive to inherit. If the will fails because it cannot be probated for distribution to the named heir, the estate would likely pass by intestate succession. Under these rules and in this situation, the daughter would receive the entire estate. The twist is this. Smith expressly disinherited future children. However, by failing to have an alternative beneficiary or updating the will after the death of her son and only named heir, she executed a will that contained language that could not be enforced with regard to future heirs. Ultimately, it appears that the daughter will be the primary beneficiary of the estate regardless of what Smith did or did not desire at the time of her death. With hundreds of millions of dollars at stake and an entire team of lawyers at her disposal, it is a mystery that no one impressed on Smith the importance of an alternative solution. Although this case has received enormous media attention because of the celebrities in-volved and the size of the estate, this scenario is repeated throughout the United States almost daily. As Benjamin Franklin mused, the only things certain are death and taxes. In probate law, both come into play. Consequently, proper estate planning, and amendment when necessary, should be on every American's "to do" list.

## CHAPTER OBJECTIVES

After reading this chapter, you should be able to:

- Distinguish *per stirpes* and per capita distribution.
- List the requirements for a valid will.
- List the grounds to contest a will.
- List the steps of probate.
- Describe the obligations of the personal representative.

- Discuss the rights of a surviving spouse.
- Distinguish testate from intestate distribution.
- Describe the process of dealing with the inheritance of one who is alleged to be responsible for a decedent's death.
- Discuss the requirements for a valid oral will.

## WHAT IS PROBATE AND ESTATE LAW?

**probate**
Process of paying creditors and distributing the estate of one who is deceased.

One area of law that affects many lives is that of **probate** and estates. At some point, many people are involved in the law of domestic relations, property, and business, as well as other subject areas. In today's society, few citizens die with no assets, no debt, and no legal heirs. Those who die without debt incur costs for burial or cremation unless they donate their body to science. Rarely does a person die without a final medical expense, even if it is confined to ambulance transportation of the body. Persons who are heirs or wish to dictate how their estate will be handled after their death will be affected by the law of probate. This area of law affects every facet of society. In addition to those who stand to inherit, nearly every person or entity with whom the deceased was in some form of financial contact before death is affected. Popular misconceptions are that when someone dies, the person's possessions are immediately divided among the surviving family. In reality, the legal process is more complicated. Similarly, anyone involved in some way with **guardianship** of one who is incapacitated as an adult or a minor in need of the supervision of an adult will likely encounter the probate division of the courts as well. When an adult is unable to manage his or her own affairs for any reason that severely limits mental capacity, there is a need to take

**guardianship**
One who has legal and fiduciary responsibility to care for the welfare of another as court ordered.

proper legal steps to appoint someone to manage the disabled individual's affairs. The following discussion addresses such topics as the distribution of an estate when there is no will and when there is a valid will. The probate process is also explained. Although probate administration of estates is governed by state law, many of the procedures are similar in most states. This discussion is limited to those general procedures observed in most jurisdictions.

## THE FUNCTION OF THE PROBATE COURTS

The probate division of the legal system is assigned the task of administrating the estates of those who are deceased and those who are under legal guardianship. In either instance, the party can no longer be responsible for his or her own legal issues; as a result, the probate courts oversee these matters. The probate courts follow specific rules of procedure and well-established substantive law with respect to the processing of these cases. Unlike the typical civil litigation, a case in the probate court may or may not have adversarial parties represented by attorneys. Indeed, a case may be entirely handled by one attorney or a large number of attorneys.

The processing of the estate of someone who is deceased typically involves an attorney for the estate. Any parties who wish to contest the manner in which the estate is considered and depleted also may be represented by counsel. This might include potential heirs, creditors, or persons who wish to contest the validity of a will or the jurisdiction of the court to process the estate. In short, anyone who stands to be affected by the final accounting and distribution of the estate of someone who is deceased may elect to have an attorney enter an appearance in the case to protect his or her interests.

### APPLICATION 11.1

Emily was a 34-year-old single mother of two young children when she suffered a cerebral hemorrhage and died. The older child, Kyra, age six, has no father or paternal relatives of record. The younger child, Camen, age four, is the son of Emily and her former husband, Ricco. Ricco is deployed overseas in the military. However, his parents have been extremely active in maintaining a relationship with both children through regular visitation. Emily is also survived by her sister Kelly and brother-in-law James. A petition was filed by Kelly and James to seek custody of both children. Camen's grandparents have also filed a counterpetition to seek custody of Camen until his father returns and to adopt Kyra. Outside parties will be appointed to represent the best interests of the children and a hearing will be conducted to evaluate who could serve in the best interests of the children as guardians while the matter is under consideration by the courts.

*Point for Discussion:* Why should the court not conduct just one hearing to make a final determination?

The probate courts are also responsible for acting in a supervisory role for incapacitated adults and minors without parents who have full parental rights and responsibilities. At first, one might think of this as being confined primarily to orphans and persons in a physical condition so severe as to constitute a vegetative state. This makes up only a tiny percentage of the persons for whom the probate court appoints and oversees guardianships. There are countless situations in modern society that render an individual legally or physically unable to make a legally binding decision in a manner consistent with the individual's best interest. In many such cases, the courts will assume a supervisory role for the individual through the guardianship (conservator) process. Although some jurisdictions use different terminology, the fundamental concept of helping those not in a position to help themselves remains the same.

In the case of minors, quite often the courts will intervene on a temporary or permanent basis to protect the interests of minors. Obviously, when someone is orphaned while still a minor, the courts are obliged to step in until such time as an adoption or the age of majority or legal emancipation occurs. The same situation arises when the parental rights over a minor are superseded by the courts either temporarily or permanently. This most often occurs when a child is removed from the home by a government agency for reasons such as abuse or neglect. In any event, when the government intervenes on behalf of a minor, it may supersede the rights of the parent or parents and assume responsibility for making decisions in the best interest of the minor child.

In the case of incapacitated adults, guardianship may occur in a wide variety of situations. One such example is when a youth who is mentally disabled reaches the age of majority. If the young person is not declared legally incompetent and then proceeds to enter into legally binding agreements or situations, it may be that the young person is considered liable for the terms of the agreement.

## APPLICATION 11.2

Robbie is a challenged adult. He lives with his parents and works at a part-time job. One day after an argument with his adult sister at her home, Robbie grabs the keys to his sister's boyfriend's car and attempts to run away. Robbie has never been taught how to drive and a short distance from home manages to cause a major accident involving several vehicles. Robbie's parents are sued for the damages. However, because Robbie is a legal adult who has never been adjudicated as incompetent, he is responsible alone for his actions. The action against the parents would likely be unsuccessful.

*Point for Discussion:* How would the situation differ if Robbie had been adjudicated as legally incompetent before the accident and his parents were his legal guardians?

Another situation that may occur when an adult requires assistance from the courts is when a person is temporarily or permanently incapacitated because of illness or injury and did not have adequate documents in place before the occurrence to authorize such help in the event of incapacitation.

When the court is presented with a minor or an adult in need of legal supervision because of physical or mental condition or both, a petition is filed and the court establishes a form of guardianship for the individual. The terms and extent of this guardianship depend largely on the circumstances of the incapacitated individual. The court appoints a person or entity such as a bank to act on behalf of the incapacitated person. In addition, if any dispute arises as to who the guardian should be or as to the terms of the guardianship, then an attorney may be appointed as a guardian *ad litem*. The guardian *ad litem* should be objective to the dispute and review the circumstance in terms of the best interest of the individual at issue. The guardian *ad litem* then makes recommendations to the court on what he or she considers to be in the best interest of the disabled person. Issues may involve physical custody and living arrangements, health care alternatives, and management of the assets of the one who is incapacitated.

Once a guardianship has been established, the guardian is required to periodically report to the courts with respect to the guardianship and the status of the incapacitated person. The frequency of reports often depends on the age and condition of the individual as well as the size of any estate that is being overseen. In some instances the disability may resolve, or in the case of a minor returned to the full care and custody of the parents, the guardianship is discontinued. In other circumstances, the guardianship may continue under the court's supervision for the remainder of the disabled person's natural life.

## CASE
### In re Guardianship of E.L.,
### 154 N.H. 292, 911 A.2d 35 (N.H. 2006)

The following opinion discusses the function of the probate court with respect to living individuals who are subject to guardianship proceedings.

The following facts could be found from the record. In 1994, E.L. was convicted of sexually assaulting his wife. He was deemed incompetent to be sentenced and confined to the Secure Psychiatric Unit (SPU) at the New Hampshire State Prison. While at SPU, his behavior fluctuated. At times, he was transferred to the most restricted unit because he verbally abused the staff, failed to follow rules, displayed inappropriate behavior, lacked self control and refused medication. By November 1995, his behavior was reported to be increasingly aggressive. He was diagnosed with bipolar disorder, and a guardian was appointed to ensure that he took prescribed medication and followed medical advice. He cooperated in taking lithium carbonate (lithium), a mood-stabilizing medication, and his condition improved. By June 1996, E.L. was deemed competent and was sentenced to seven and one-half to fifteen years in prison. He was transferred to the prison's general population in August 1996. . . .

E.L.'s current treatment team consists of Catherine Fontaine, an advanced registered nurse practitioner who is primarily responsible for prescribing and monitoring E.L.'s medication, Laura Magzis, E.L.'s therapist at the prison, and Bonnie Ham, E.L.'s designated staff guardian, who works for Tri-County Community Action Program, Inc. In 2003, E.L. exhibited psychotic behavior and made delusional statements. Specifically, he reportedly was unkempt and disheveled, would not bathe, spoke "legal mumbo jumbo" and during therapy sessions related provocative language he used with fellow inmates that in his therapist's view had the potential to incite arguments. According to his therapist, E.L. suspected she was reading his mail, recording therapy sessions and interfering with his transfer to a prison in Maine. E.L. also related memories of events in prison that could not have happened and

displayed an inability to appreciate the possibility that his memory was imprecise. He was diagnosed as suffering from psychotic features of his bipolar disorder, and in July 2003, an anti-psychotic medication, Risperidone, was prescribed for him. While E.L. did not agree that he suffered any psychosis, he agreed to take the prescribed medication. His behavior reportedly improved, and he continued to be compliant with taking his prescribed medications.

At some point, E.L. complained that he was suffering side effects from Risperidone. He grew concerned that it could cause diabetes. According to E.L., his son suffers from diabetes, as did his late father. He expressed a desire to stop taking Risperidone, or at least reduce the dosage or switch to a substitute drug. His treatment team agreed to a dosage reduction and to explore other medications should the side effects continue. In 2004, E.L. requested the probate court to terminate his nearly ten-year guardianship. His guardian opposed the motion. In February 2005, psychiatrist Gerald Lazar conducted an independent evaluation of E.L. and reported that in his judgment, the limited guardianship should continue. In April 2005, after an evidentiary hearing, the probate court denied E.L.'s motion, and this appeal followed.

Any interested person may file a petition with the probate court seeking a finding of incapacity with respect to a proposed ward and the appointment of a guardian. RSA 464-A:4, I (2004). By statute, there is a legal presumption of capacity, and the party seeking guardianship bears the heavy burden of proving with "competent evidence [and] beyond reasonable doubt that the proposed ward is incapacitated and in need of a guardian." RSA 464-A:8, IV (2004). At a hearing convened on such a petition, the probate court must "(a) [i]nquire into the nature and extent of the functional limitations of the proposed ward; and (b) [a]scertain his or her capacity to care for himself or herself or his or her estate." RSA 464-A:9, I (2004).

*(continued)*

Guardianship may be imposed over a person only after finding in the record based upon evidence beyond a reasonable doubt that:

    (a) The person for whom a guardian is to be appointed is incapacitated; and

    (b) The guardianship is necessary as a means of providing continuing care, supervision, and rehabilitation of the individual, or the management of the property and financial affairs of the incapacitated person; and

    (c) There are no available alternative resources which are suitable with respect to the incapacitated person's welfare, safety, and rehabilitation or the prudent management of his or her property and financial affairs; and

    (d) The guardianship is appropriate as the least restrictive form of intervention consistent with the preservation of the civil rights and liberties of the proposed ward.

RSA 464-A:9, III (2004).

When a ward seeks to terminate guardianship, "[u]nless the motion [to terminate] is without merit, the court shall hold a hearing similar to that provided for in RSA 464-A:8 and RSA 464-A:9 at which the guardian shall be required to prove . . . the grounds for appointment of a guardian provided in RSA 464-A:9." RSA 464-A:40, II(c). Accordingly, the guardian must prove beyond a reasonable doubt the existence of each factor delineated by RSA 464-A:9, II; namely, that: (1) the ward remains incapacitated; (2) guardianship is necessary; (3) no suitable alternative resources exist; and (4) guardianship is the least restrictive form of intervention.

In this case, the probate court concluded that "the reasons that the guardianship was granted remain." The probate court's decision explained:

    [E.L.] suffers a mental illness. His diagnosis is Antisocial Personality Disorder and either Bipolar Affective Disorder, Manic with Psychotic Features or Schizoaffective Disorder. His illness has been effectively treated with medications which [have] been administered because of the existence of the guardianship and the consent of his guardian.

    [E.L.] would like to terminate his guardianship which is limited to medical issues. He thinks that he is capable of making his own medical decisions. However, he has repeatedly stated his desire to stop taking Risperidone because of its side effects. In the opinion of Gerald Lazar, M.D., an independent psychiatrist, this would not reflect an informed decision. [E.L.] has limited insight into his illness.

The court finds that the reasons that the guardianship was granted remain. [E.L.] remains incapacitated

with respect to making medical decisions. The court further finds that the limited guardianship is the least restrictive alternative. A power of attorney would not be sufficient because [E.L.] could cancel it. A springing guardianship would not meet [E.L.'s] needs because it would require [E.L.] to decompensate before it could be implemented. This would make further treatment more difficult and could result in an injury to [E.L.] or some other person during the time he decompensated.

The petition to terminate the guardianship is denied.

By statute, "[t]he findings of fact of the [probate court] are final unless they are so plainly erroneous that [they] could not be reasonably made." RSA 567-A:4 (1997); see RSA 464-A:47 (2004) (providing that appeals from probate court decisions are governed by RSA chapter 567-A). Thus, we do not reweigh the evidence to determine whether we would have ruled differently. Rather, we review the record of the probate proceedings to determine if the probate court's findings could be reasonably made given the testimony and the evidence before it. *In re Buttrick*, 134 N.H. 675, 676, 597 A.2d 74 (1991). We defer to the judgment of the probate court to resolve "conflicts in testimony, measur[e] the credibility of witnesses, and determin [e] the weight to be given to testimony," *In re Guardianship of Kapitula*, 153 N.H. 492, 497 (2006), recognizing that as the trier of fact, it is in the best position to "measure the persuasiveness and credibility of evidence," *In re Estate of King*, 151 N.H. 425, 429, 857 A.2d 1257 (2004). It lies "within the province of the trial court to accept or reject, in whole or in part, whatever evidence was presented." *In re Guardianship of Kapitula*, 153 N.H. at 497–98, 897 A.2d 977.

On appeal, E.L. argues that the probate court erred in finding that the evidence demonstrates beyond a reasonable doubt that he remains incapacitated and that no less restrictive alternative to guardianship exists, both necessary statutory components for the continuation of guardianship, see RSA 464-A:9, III(a), (c), (d). Our task is to review the record to determine whether it supports the probate court's finding that the guardian proved these statutory components beyond a reasonable doubt. See RSA 464-A:8, IV. Because E.L. challenges the sufficiency of the evidence, we examine whether the probate court's actual or implicit factual findings on the statutory components required for guardianship are reasonably supported by competent evidence. See *id.*; *In the Matter of B.T.*, 153 N.H. 255, 259, 891 A.2d 1193 (2006)."We will not disturb the probate court's decree unless it is unsupported by the evidence or plainly erroneous as a matter of law." *In re William A.*, 142 N.H. 598, 600, 705 A.2d 1196 (1998).

We first turn to whether the evidence supports the probate court's finding beyond a reasonable doubt that E.L. remains incapacitated to make his own medical decisions. E.L. argues that no evidence of recent acts or occurrences demonstrates beyond a reasonable doubt that he is incapacitated. According to him, substantial evidence establishes his competency, including his ten-year history of full compliance with taking his prescribed medications, his consent to continued consultation with medical providers and the soundness of his reasons for wanting to stop or reduce his intake of Risperidone. The New Hampshire Department of Corrections (State) contends that while the symptoms of E.L.'s mental illness have abated due to the success of the guardianship, he has limited insight and judgment about his illness and the consequences of stopping his medications. According to the State, the evidence establishes that E.L.'s sole motivation for terminating guardianship is to discontinue the very medications which have dramatically helped him, thereby causing him to decompensate and pose a danger to himself and others.

Incapacity is "a legal, not a medical, disability." RSA 464-A:2, XI (2004). To be deemed incapacitated, a person must have "suffered, [be] suffering or [be] likely to suffer substantial harm due to an inability to provide for his personal needs for food, clothing, shelter, health care or safety or an inability to manage his or her property or financial affairs." *Id.* Further, incapacity is measured by a person's "functional limitations," *id.;* that is, behavior or conditions in an individual which impair his or her ability to participate in and perform minimal activities of daily living that secure and maintain proper food, clothing, shelter, health care or safety for himself or herself.

RSA 464-A:2, VII (2004). Therefore, to overturn the probate court's finding that he continues to have an incapacity for making sound medical decisions, E.L. must demonstrate that no reasonable fact finder could find beyond a reasonable doubt that: (1) he is unable to provide for his personal needs for health care or safety; and (2) this inability has caused him to have suffered, be currently suffering or be likely to suffer "substantial harm." See RSA 464-A:2, XI. We particularly examine the record for evidence of "behavior or conditions" that impair E.L.'s "ability to participate in and perform minimal activities of daily living that secure and maintain proper . . . health care or safety . . . for himself." See RSA 464-A:2, VII.

The record contains competent evidence to support the conclusion that E.L. has limited insight into his mental illness, intends to stop taking his prescribed

medications, is unable to exercise sound judgment about the potential consequences of ceasing or modifying his current medication regime and is likely to decompensate without medication, thus posing a danger to himself and others. Considered as a whole, this evidence supports a finding beyond a reasonable doubt that E.L. is unable to participate in and perform the minimal activities necessary for his health care such that substantial harm will likely occur without the medical guardianship.

With respect to E.L.'s understanding of his mental illness, both Lazar and Fontaine testified that he does not believe that he suffers psychotic features from his bipolar condition. While E.L. may acknowledge that he suffers from bipolar disorder, there is evidence that he does not appreciate the gravity of the symptoms he displays when not taking proper medication. Lazar testified that E.L.'s sexual assault of his wife, the crime for which he is incarcerated, is likely connected to his mental illness. Yet, E.L. denied to Lazar that he committed the assault, stating that his wife fabricated the charge. Further, E.L. told Lazar that he believes that he is "not mentally ill to the degree people say." Indeed, in his motion to terminate guardianship he stated: "My illness is not severe and I do as well off meds as on them."

In addition, evidence in the record permits a reasonable person to conclude that upon termination of the guardianship, E.L. intends to stop taking his prescribed medications either because he does not believe they are necessary or because he is concerned about their side effects. E.L. informed his guardian that he wanted a "medication holiday" to see how he feels. Again, in his motion to terminate guardianship, E.L. asserted: "I do as well off meds as on them." While portions of the record suggest that E.L. may be amenable to continuing lithium and maintaining a reduced dosage of Risperidone or another anti-psychotic medication, it was within the probate court's discretion, having assessed witness credibility, to conclude that E.L. was intent upon ceasing his medications. See *In re Estate of King,* 151 N.H. at 429, 857 A.2d 1257.

No one disputes that E.L. has been compliant with his prescribed medications since his guardianship was imposed in 1995. Evidence supports the conclusion, however, that his compliance has been the direct result of the guardianship. Although requested to do so, E.L. refused to take any medications before the guardianship was ordered. Further, Fontaine testified that "[p]art of why he [maintains consistency with his medication] is the fact that he knows that he has someone else who has control over his need to stay on medication." Lazar's report refers to a January 2000

*(continued)*

treatment plan review which noted that E.L. remained compliant with taking prescribed medications because he believed that refusing to do so would cause him difficulties. E.L. himself testified that he would continue to take Risperidone and lithium because he is "[told] to do it." Therefore, the probate court could have reasonably found that E.L. has been compliant with prescribed medications due to the compulsory nature of the guardianship and not because he appreciates the need for them.

The record also would support a finding that E.L. is unable to exercise sound judgment in assessing the risk of interrupting his current medication regime. While Lazar noted that it is possible for someone to have an illness and refuse treatment in a sound manner for reasons the medical professional may disagree with, he testified that E.L. is unable to exercise sound judgment in deciding upon a particular course of medical treatment. Lazar explained that while E.L. can understand all the factual information concerning his illness and the efficacy of medication, he lacks the ability to rationally and reasonably weigh the competing risks involved with accepting or rejecting a particular treatment plan.

Although E.L.'s treatment team affirmed his concerns about the side effects of his medications, evidence would support a finding that E.L. has focused exclusively upon the side effects. E.L. testified that he initially denied suffering from bipolar disorder because he did not want to be labeled a "freak," but that over time he has grown to accept that he is afflicted with a mental illness and needs lithium. His testimony, as well as the remaining record, however, is devoid of evidence that reveals his consideration of and appreciation for the symptoms that would likely arise in the event he stopped or altered his medications and decompensated. E.L.'s limited understanding of his mental illness, as well as his failure to appreciate and consider the risks of interrupting a medication regime that has effectively treated it, supports the finding that his ability to exercise sound judgment about his medical treatment remains meaningfully impaired. As Lazar testified, "It's hard to make an informed decision about your medications if you don't have an appreciation for the fact that you have a particular illness and that there are consequences to not treat as well as to treating and make a decision based on the most favorable outcome."

Finally, there is evidence of E.L.'s prior dangerousness when not adequately medicated. The record refers to his prior convictions for willful cruelty towards children, and he currently is incarcerated for sexually assaulting his wife. Further, there is evidence in the record that E.L.'s wife reported that he beat her over a five-year period. Once transferred to SPU after his conviction, he was at times confined in the most restrictive unit because he verbally abused the staff, failed to follow rules, displayed inappropriate behavior and lacked self control. He also refused to take medications and displayed obsessive behavior. Once guardianship was imposed, however, he began to take prescribed medication, and his behavior substantially improved.

While incarcerated and medicated only with lithium, E.L. was in two prison fights. The second fight, in 2002, was so significant that his facial injuries required reconstructive surgery. Although E.L. denies that he provoked the altercation in any manner, evidence shows that this fight occurred about one year prior to the diagnosis of the psychotic component to his bipolar disorder and prescription for Risperidone. According to his treatment team, before E.L. began taking Risperidone, he would report interactions with other inmates where he used provocative language that the treatment team concluded could trigger arguments. Moreover, the probate court could have reasonably questioned the credibility of E.L.'s account of the prison fight considering that he denied to Lazar that he sexually assaulted his wife and blamed her for fabricating the charge.

Lazar testified that E.L.'s crimes involving children and his wife likely were connected to his mental illness. E.L.'s treatment team and Lazar himself expressed concern about his history of violence and testified that should he refuse to take his medications, he will likely decompensate and become a danger to himself and others. Lazar and members of the treatment team also expressed concern that should E.L. decompensate, his relationship with others and the quality of his life would likely suffer, that he might not be able to live in the prison's general population, that his opportunity for parole in 2008 could be diminished and that restoring his current good functioning could be a lengthy process, if not impossible.

E.L. argues that the acts which gave rise to guardianship in 1995 are not relevant, and that the guardian failed to present sufficient recent evidence to support continuation of the guardianship. See RSA 464-A:40. E.L. appears to contend that by statute, to prove that he remains incapacitated, the guardian could only rely upon evidence of acts that occurred within six months of the date of the filing of the termination motion. See RSA 464-A:2, XI. The State argues, however, that application of this specific time requirement is relevant only to initial petitions for guardianship.

In matters of statutory interpretation, we are the final arbiter of the intent of the legislature as expressed in the words of a statute considered as a whole. *Snedeker v. Snedeker,* 145 N.H. 19, 20, 749 A.2d 315 (2000). We first examine the language found in the statute, and where possible, we ascribe the plain and ordinary meanings to words used. *Id.* at 20–21, 749 A.2d 315. However, we will not interpret statutory language in a literal manner when such a reading would lead to an absurd result. See *State v. Warren,* 147 N.H. 567, 568, 794 A.2d 790 (2002).

As noted earlier, "incapacity" is defined to mean or refer to any person who has suffered, is suffering or is likely to suffer substantial harm due to an inability to provide for his personal needs for food, clothing, shelter, health care or safety or an inability to manage his or her property or financial affairs.

RSA 464-A:2, XI. The statute requires that such "[i]nability . . . be evidenced by acts or occurrences, or statements which strongly indicate imminent acts or occurrences." *Id.* Moreover, [a]ll evidence of inability must have occurred within 6 months prior to the filing of the petition and at least one incidence of such behavior must have occurred within 20 days of the filing of the petition for guardianship. *Id.* This specific time requirement, however, does not apply to proceedings for termination of guardianship.

When a ward seeks to terminate guardianship, the probate court conducts "a hearing similar to that provided for in RSA 464-A:8 and RSA 464-A:9." RSA 464-A:40, II(c). By utilizing the phrase "similar to," the legislature understood that not all aspects of a guardianship termination proceeding would be identical to an initial proceeding seeking the appointment of a guardian. At the termination proceeding, "the guardian [must] prove that the grounds for appointment of a guardian provided in RSA 464-A:9 continue to exist," *id.*, including, necessarily, that the ward remains incapacitated, see RSA 464-A:9, III(a). For a ward who has been deemed incapacitated and is under guardianship care, the outward manifestations of incapacity may have decreased, if not completely dissipated, as a result of the proper attention and care provided through the guardian. While having secured some ability to provide for his personal needs, the ward may not have necessarily regained capacity to the degree that obviates the need for a guardianship. In such a case, requiring the guardian to prove the continuation of the ward's incapacity based exclusively upon evidence of acts, occurrences or statements that happened within six months of the termination motion would lead to an absurd result. Accordingly, we conclude that while a guardian's burden to prove the continuation of incapacity under RSA 464-A:40, II(c) requires proof of the ward's present inability to provide for his personal care as defined under RSA 464-A:2, XI, the guardian is not restricted to

presenting evidence of acts, occurrences or statements that occurred within the specific time period provided under RSA 464-A:2, XI.

In sum, we conclude that evidence in the record supports the probate court's finding beyond a reasonable doubt that E.L. is presently unable to participate in or perform minimal activities of daily living with respect to his health care and that he is likely to suffer substantial harm if the guardianship is terminated. See RSA 464-A:2, VII, XI. Accordingly, we uphold the probate court's finding that E.L. continues to have an incapacity for making his own health care decisions.

We next address E.L.'s argument that the probate court erred in finding that the guardian sustained its burden of proving beyond a reasonable doubt that no less restrictive alternative to guardianship exists. In addition to establishing E.L.'s continuing incapacity in order for the guardianship to continue, the record must support beyond a reasonable doubt that, among other things, no available alternative resources exist that are suitable to E.L.'s needs, RSA 464-A:9, II(c), and guardianship is the least restrictive form of intervention, RSA 464-A:9, II(d). Specifically, with respect to available resources, chapter 464-A requires that no available alternative resources [exist] which are suitable with respect to the incapacitated person's welfare, safety, and rehabilitation or the prudent management of his or her property and financial affairs.

RSA 464-A:9, II(c)."Available alternative resource" is defined to mean "alternatives to guardianship including, but not limited to, . . . powers of attorney. . . ." RSA 464-A:2, II (2004).

Concerning the least restrictive form of intervention, chapter 464-A provides that guardianship must be:

> appropriate as the least restrictive form of intervention consistent with the preservation of civil rights and liberties of the proposed ward. RSA 464-A:9, II(d). "Least restrictive form of intervention" is defined to mean that the guardianship imposed on the ward represents only those limitations necessary to provide him or her with needed care and rehabilitative services, and that the ward shall enjoy the greatest amount of personal freedom and civil liberties consistent with his or her mental and physical limitations. RSA 464-A:2, XIV (2004).

Evidence was presented on two alternatives to guardianship at the evidentiary hearing: medical power of attorney and springing guardianship. Under these alternatives, a power of attorney would be invoked or a guardianship would "spring" into effect

*(continued)*

should certain prescribed events occur or symptoms arise. The probate court found:

> A power of attorney would not be sufficient because [E.L.] could cancel it. A springing guardianship would not meet [E.L.'s] needs because it would require [E.L.] to decompensate before it could be implemented. This would make further treatment more difficult and could result in an injury to [E.L.] or some other person during the time he decompensated.

We conclude that there is sufficient evidence to support the probate court's rejection of the alternatives to continued guardianship.

As discussed earlier, the evidence supports a finding that E.L. intends to change or discontinue his current medication regime. While E.L.'s incarceration would permit prison officials and medical personnel to closely monitor E.L.'s behavior, Lazar testified that if guardianship were terminated and E.L. went off his medications, his deterioration could be slow and not immediately visible to others, including his treatment team. Lazar also explained that "[t]here would be a lag time" between the moment E.L.'s decompensation is detected, a decision is made to trigger guardianship and guardianship is actually reinstated. The medical professionals expressed concern that if E.L. decompensated, he might not be able to be stabilized again because in some cases medicine that was once effective may be ineffective when taken again after an interruption.

Fontaine testified that the structure of guardianship itself is significant to E.L.'s clinical treatment because he consistently maintains his medication due to the fact that another person controls his decision to take it. She explained that a springing guardianship may be appropriate for an individual who understands his mental illness as well as the need for continuing his medication, and who would remain compliant with medication with or without a guardian. Given E.L.'s limited insight into his illness and his impaired judgment concerning his current medication regime, evidence supports the probate court's finding that E.L. is not an appropriate candidate for a springing guardianship or a health care power of attorney. In sum, taking the evidence as a whole, we conclude that it was not unreasonable for the probate court to find beyond a reasonable doubt that no less restrictive alternative other than guardianship exists. See RSA 464-A:9, II(c), (d). Accordingly, we hold that the evidence in the record is sufficient as a matter of law to support the probate court's denial of E.L.'s motion to terminate guardianship. Affirmed.

## Case Review Question

What could an individual do to avoid guardianship if he or she suffers from mental illness but understands this and wishes not to engage in treatment?

---

The law of estates affects every facet of society. Of course, there are those persons who stand to inherit when another person dies. But just as important, virtually every entity with whom the deceased was in financial contact before death is affected.

## INTESTATE SUCCESSION

**intestate**
Dying without a valid will.

Someone who dies **intestate** has left no known valid will. Often persons with substantial assets do not make provisions for the distribution of those assets after death. The obvious disadvantage to not leaving a valid will is that distribution by the state may not be at all what the deceased would have wished. Nevertheless, it is such a frequent occurrence that the states have designed several methods to distribute the assets of a deceased person. The manner in which this is done is called *intestate succession* (see Exhibit 11.1). Literally, this means that the state decides who will succeed to the assets of a person who dies without a valid will.

**per capita distribution**
Distribution of an estate in equal shares, with each person representing one share.

One method that is now seldom applied in laws on the distribution of estates is called **per capita distribution,** which is discussed here for purposes of comparison. Per capita is a rather simple method. The initial task is to identify all living relatives of the deceased. The assets of the deceased that remain after probate of the estate are divided equally among the number of survivors.[1] For

**Exhibit 11.1** Wisconsin Statutes Annotated Chapter 852—Intestate Succession

---

### 852.01. Basic rules for intestate succession

(1) Who are heirs. The net estate of a decedent which he has not disposed of by will, whether he dies without a will, or with a will which does not completely dispose of his estate, passes to his surviving heirs as follows:

(a) To the spouse:

1. If there are no surviving issue of the decedent, or if the surviving issue are all issue of the surviving spouse and the decedent, the entire estate.

2. If there are surviving issue one or more of whom are not issue of the surviving spouse, one-half of that portion of the decedent's net estate not disposed of by will consisting of decedent's property other than marital property and other than property described under 861.02(1).

(b) To the issue, the share of the estate not passing to the spouse under part (a), or the entire estate if there is no surviving spouse; if the issue are all in the same degree of kinship to the decedent they take equally, but if they are of unequal degree then those of more remote degrees take by representation.

(c) If there is no surviving spouse or issue, to the parents.

(d) If there is no surviving spouse, issue or parent, to the brothers and sisters and the issue of any deceased brother or sister by representation.

(e) If there is no surviving spouse, issue, parent or brother or sister, to the issue of brothers and sisters; if such issue are all in the same degree of kinship to the decedent they take equally, but if they are of unequal degree then those of more remote degrees take by representation.

(f) If there is no surviving spouse, issue, parent or issue of a parent, to the grandparents.

(g) If there is no surviving spouse, issue, parent, issue of a parent, or grandparent, to the intestate's next of kin in equal degree.

(2) Requirement that heir survive decedent for a certain time. If any person who would otherwise be an heir under sub. (1) dies within 72 hours of the time of death of the decedent, the net estate not disposed of by will passes under this section as if that person had predeceased the decedent. If the time of death of the decedent or of the person who would otherwise be an heir, or the times of death of both, cannot be determined, and it cannot be established that the person who would otherwise be an heir has survived the decedent by at least 72 hours, it is presumed that the person died within 72 hours of the decedent's death. In computing time for purposes of this subsection, local standard time at the place of death of the decedent is used.

(2m) Requirement that heir not have intentionally killed the deceased.

(a) If any person who would otherwise be an heir under sub. (1) has unlawfully and intentionally killed the decedent, the net estate not disposed of by will passes as if the killer had predeceased the decedent.

(b) A final judgment of conviction of unlawful and intentional killing is conclusive for purposes of this subsection.

(bg) A final adjudication of delinquency on the basis of unlawfully and intentionally killing the decedent is conclusive for purposes of this subsection.

(br) In the absence of a conviction under par. (b) or an adjudication under par. (bg), the court, on the basis of clear and convincing evidence, may determine whether the killing was unlawful and intentional for purposes of this subsection.

(c) This subsection does not affect the rights of any person who, before rights under this subsection have been adjudicated, purchases for value and without notice from the killer property that the killer would have acquired except for this subsection; but the killer is liable for the amount of the proceeds. No insurance company, bank or other obligor paying according to the terms of its policy or obligation is liable because of this subsection unless before payment it has received at its home office or principal address written notice of a claim under this subsection.

(3) Escheat. If there are no heirs of the decedent under subs. (1) and (2), the net estate escheats to the state to be added to the capital of the school fund.

---

**per stirpes distribution**
Distribution of an estate in equal shares to one level or class of persons. If a member of this level or class is deceased, then his or her heirs divide the share.

example, assume that two children, one grandchild, three aunts, and four cousins were left as survivors of the deceased. The entire estate would be distributed into ten equal shares (the total number of survivors).

The second method, and the one employed by the majority of states, is known as **per stirpes** distribution (*stirpes* meaning "branch"). Under this method, as with per capita, all surviving relatives are identified. However, entitlement to receive any of the estate and the percentage received depend on the proximity of the relationship.[2] For example, if children of the deceased are living but no spouse survives, the children would be entitled to the entire estate even if many cousins and siblings of the deceased may still be living because the children are direct descendants of the deceased. If the previous example for per capita distribution were modified to leave no surviving descendants, then the ascendants (aunts and possibly cousins) would receive portions of the estate. Another reason why a majority of states use *per stirpes* distribution is its equitable nature. In a *per stirpes* jurisdiction, members of a certain degree of relationship or generation will inherit equally so that, for example, a grandchild would not inherit more than a child or other grandchild.

## ASSIGNMENT 11.1

Based on the statute in Exhibit 11.1, identify how your own estate would proceed by intestate succession.

Each state that utilizes the *per stirpes* method has particular methods for determining exactly how the estate will be distributed. The common thread is that whether a person inherits depends on the person's relationship to the deceased and how many other persons have the same relationship. Generally, the estate is distributed to descendants. If there are none, then it is distributed to ascendants such as parents and across to siblings (brothers and sisters) and then to the descendants of the siblings. If there are no living relatives at these levels, then it proceeds to ascendants such as aunts and uncles and their descendants (i.e., cousins). Depending on the limit set by the state statute, this may continue on for several degrees of family relation. The following are some of the more common rules employed based on the survivors.

1. If there are a surviving spouse and children all born to the surviving spouse and the deceased, then the spouse receives a lump sum of money and an additional percentage of the estate. The children receive the entire remaining percentage to be distributed equally.

2. If there are a surviving spouse and children, some or all of whom are not the children of the surviving spouse, then the spouse and children receive one-half of the estate each. If there is more than one child, then the second one-half will be divided equally among the number of children.

3. If there are a surviving spouse, no children, surviving parents, or siblings or children of siblings, then the surviving spouse is entitled to a lump sum of cash and one-half of the estate. Parents and siblings each take an equal share of the remaining one-half of the estate. If a sibling is deceased but leaves children, then the children each take an equal share of what would have been the sibling's share.

4. If there are surviving parents, siblings, and children of siblings, then the entire estate would be distributed on the same basis as indicated in item 3.

As indicated, the shares under *per stirpes* are divided based on categories of living relatives. Thus, if siblings are alive, the shares are divided among the number of living siblings, and the siblings' children are entitled only to split a deceased sibling's share. This is different from per capita, which gives no attention to the level of the relationship but rather distributes according to the number of relations.

## APPLICATION 11.3

Melba died and was survived by her live-in boyfriend of eighteen years, one grand-daughter whom she had not seen since birth, and a sister who took full responsibility for Melba's care during a lengthy illness. Without a will that identified her boyfriend, he would receive nothing of the estate. In addition, anything he owned jointly with Melba would either have to be sold and the portion of Melba's interest given over to the estate or he would have to buy out Melba's interest. Under intestate per capita distribution, Melba's sister and granddaughter would split the estate equally. Under *per stirpes* distribution in most jurisdictions, Melba's granddaughter would receive the entire estate.

*Point for Discussion:* Would the distribution change if the granddaughter was a minor in the custody of Melba's detested former son-in-law, who was the ex-husband of the child's mother (Melba's daughter) who predeceased Melba?

The *per stirpes* method does not search out relatives to an infinite degree to receive the estate. Rather, most states have a maximum level of relationship, such as a fifth cousin, who can inherit the estate.[3] If there are no sufficiently close relatives left surviving, the estate of the deceased goes into what is called *escheat,* the process by which the assets are taken over by the state. The assets become the property of the state, and no individuals are entitled to inherit them.[4]

What of persons who have a partial blood relationship or relationship created by law to the deceased? As previously indicated, a spouse is considered to be a blood relative for purposes of inheritance, even though the relationship is a legal one. But what is the status of adopted children? The relationship is recognized by law. Generally, when a parent adopts a child, the child is treated as a natural child of the parent for all purposes of intestate succession.[5] The states are divided on the status of any remaining testamentary relationship between the adopted child and the biological parents. Many states permit the child to claim inheritance from the biological parents. Other states consider the bond severed at the time of adoption and do not permit such claims. However, most states do not permit the biological parent to inherit from the adopted child in the event the parent survives the child. Any permitted inheritance in such a situation would, of course, require knowledge of the identity of the parties involved.

Siblings of half-blood relationships share only one parent with the deceased. In most states, a half-blood sibling is entitled to inherit at least some portion of the estate.[6] These states vary from a percentage inheritance to a full entitlement, which a full-blood brother or sister would receive.

If a child is born out of wedlock and subsequently makes a claim of inheritance against the father's estate, the father is usually required to make some formal acknowledgment of the child during the father's lifetime.[7] This can be demonstrated by a legal finding of paternity or by actions of the father that would indicate he believed the child to be his. However, with the advancement of scientific technology, it may soon be the general rule that proof of paternity as evidence to claim inheritance can be produced after the father's death.

A child who is born within ten months of the death of a parent can make a claim as a posthumous heir to the estate.[8] Otherwise, all persons claiming against the estate must be alive at the time of, and for a specified period of time after, the decedent's death.[9] Consider how this latter situation could create a question.

A husband and wife are killed in an accident. The wife had two children by a previous marriage. The husband had some distant relatives (but still close enough to inherit under *per stirpes*). If it can be proven that the wife outlived the husband by a sufficient period of time, the wife's estate would be entitled to the entire estate of the husband. Consequently, the wife's two children (from a former marriage) would be entitled to the entire estate of their mother. If the wife did not survive the husband for a requisite period of time, the children would inherit only their mother's estate and none of their stepfather's. Ultimately, the distant relatives of the husband would inherit his entire estate by *per stirpes*.

Another matter that affects both intestate succession and testate succession (distribution by will) arises when the deceased has been murdered. Anyone who is found by the probate court to be responsible for the death of the decedent as the result of foul play cannot inherit.[10] Many states do not even require a criminal conviction but only establish in probate court that the person was accused of and prosecuted for the murder. Some states have a hearing in the probate court to determine whether by probate standards a murder occurred (these standards are generally less stringent than what is required for a conviction of first-degree murder in a criminal prosecution).

In addition, certain acts by a spouse before the death of the deceased may cause the spouse to lose rights of inheritance in some states. Examples include adulterous conduct, abandonment for a long period of time, and other acts that indicate the spouse discarded the marital relationship. Further, a spouse who is divorced from the decedent cannot inherit by intestate succession.[11]

As this discussion has shown, intestate succession is a well developed area of the law because of the numerous cases of death without a will. Although the law prefers creation of a will, many rules govern this process to ensure that the *testator* (deceased who left a will) created the will intentionally, without improper influences, and with a clear mind.

## ASSIGNMENT 11.2

In the following situations, assume the individuals listed are the only survivors of the decedent. Determine who would inherit and to what percentage of the estate the heirs would be entitled.

1. A surviving spouse and two children who are the children of the surviving spouse and the decedent.

2. A surviving spouse, two children who are the natural children of the decedent and not the surviving spouse, and one child who is the stepchild of the decedent and natural child of the surviving spouse.

3. Two stepchildren and one natural child of the decedent.

4. One parent and one grandchild of the decedent.

5. Three brothers, one sister, and one parent of the decedent.

6. Two children and two grandchildren who were the issue of a child who predeceased the decedent.

7. One parent, two siblings, and a surviving spouse.

8. Two adopted children of the decedent who are not the adopted or natural children of the surviving spouse, four stepchildren, and a surviving spouse.

9. A grandparent and two parents who are divorced.

10. Two parents, two siblings, an adult child, and a surviving spouse (not the parent of the adult child).

# TESTATE SUCCESSION

Clearly, the courts and population at large prefer that an individual be allowed to dispose of his or her estate according to personal wishes. Upon death, this is accomplished with a legally recognized document that was executed during the individual's lifetime and that expresses these wishes. When an estate is distributed based on the terms of such a document, it is referred to as *testate succession*.

## Requirements of a Valid Will

Before a will can be used as the instrument to distribute an estate, it must be declared a valid will. Contrary to what may be depicted in old movies, notes written on a slip of paper immediately before death rarely meet the requisites of a valid will. Every state has statutes that dictate the exact procedure for the preparation of a will. If the procedure is not followed or if any significant irregularities are present, then the will may be declared invalid and the estate distributed by intestate succession.

A majority of states now require that a will be in writing. Although oral wills are permitted in some states, it generally must be shown that at the time of the oral will (1) the deceased believed death to be imminent and (2) the terms of the will were declared to witnesses who would not stand to inherit.[12] The rationale for upholding oral wills by states that still honor them is that such circumstances would lend credence to the terms of the testator's oral will and thus would be truly indicative of the deceased's intent.

---

## APPLICATION 11.4

Christian and Leah lived together for five years. Christian was totally financially dependent on Leah, who was independently wealthy. She always told Christian that she would take care of him for the rest of his life. However, she had no valid will. The two were involved in a car accident in which Leah was seriously injured. As she was being extricated from the vehicle by emergency technicians, she told Christian, "It's all yours now, baby. Make the most of it." Leah then lost consciousness and died a short while later. Even though Leah's remark was made in front of witnesses when death was imminent, it is unlikely that the remark would be construed as a will. The remark was somewhat general in nature and did not directly or even indirectly refer to Leah's estate.

*Point for Discussion:* Would the result likely be different if Christian produced a love letter from Leah in which she declared she would " take care" of him for the rest of his life?

---

Oral wills are an increasingly rare occurrence. The bulk of the statutes instead now pertain to the requirements for a valid written will. It is required that a testator sign the will with knowledge that the instrument being signed is a declaration of intent for distribution of assets on death. Thus, if it is established that someone was tricked into signing a document without knowledge that it was a will, then the document will be invalid. If the testator knows the document is a will but because of some limitation is unable to sign it, then the testator can direct another person to affix the signature so long as it is accomplished in the testator's presence.[13]

The testator is also required to have capacity to issue the will. This does not mean that the testator must have legal capacity as required in contract law, only that it must be shown that the testator understood the extent and value of the estate and the effect of a will—that is, giving the estate to specified others on death.[14]

If it is established that the testator prepared the will under some mental impairment that would prevent a full comprehension of the will's effects, then the testator may be considered to not have had the requisite capacity. In addition, if the testator prepares the terms of the will under false information, undue influence, fraud, or some other factor that would impede the ability to exercise a voluntary testamentary document, then the testator would be considered to have lacked capacity. Either circumstance will result in an invalid will, and the estate will be distributed by the law of intestate succession.

Witnesses are a necessary element to any valid will.[15] It is not required that they know the contents of what they are signing. The purpose of witnesses instead is to establish that the document was voluntarily signed by the testator. If the testator signs the document in the presence of the witnesses and the witnesses then affix their signatures, the requirement has been met. Witnesses generally do not have to sign in the presence of one another, so long as they each were present when the testator signed the document or acknowledged the testator's signature. Thus, witnesses could sign the document at a later point in time, and the requirement of witnesses to the signature would still be met.

A significant issue that arises in many will contests is the intention of the actual terms of the will. A will often cannot be entirely stated on one page. Thus, when there are several pages, there is the opportunity for unscrupulous individuals to insert additional terms in the will. Therefore, any will of multiple pages should indicate on each page the page number and the total number of pages, thus decreasing the chances of alterations. Also, many courts prefer that the testator and witnesses initial each page of the will and affix their signatures to the final page of the document.

Some wills mention other documents and incorporate the terms of those documents. This is done by reference to the document and by indicating the intent that the document become part of the will. An example is a parent who, as part of the will, wants to create a trust fund for a child. The will would make reference to the documents used to create a trust fund. This type of reference to other documents is *incorporation by reference.*[16] The documents to which the will makes reference are incorporated into the terms of the will as if they were actually a physical part of the will. To incorporate another document by reference, it is required by statute that the document already existed at the time the will was created and that it referred to the will within its contents. This prevents persons from creating the document to serve their own purposes after the will is executed and the testator is deceased.

A testator may also place conditions on bequests received under a will. The testator may indicate an intent to grant the bequest only if the person receiving the bequest performs certain conditions. If these conditions are not met, then that portion of the will is considered ineffective, and the inheritance will not occur.[17]

It is permissible for a testator to disinherit anyone but a spouse.[18] Testators can direct almost without limitation who will receive under the will as well as detailed and specific bequests of property or money. However, by state law, a spouse is entitled to a portion of the estate unless one of the circumstances of misconduct mentioned previously exists at the time of the testator's death.

## Will Codicils and Will Revocation

Many times, a person continues to live for many years after the will has been executed. During such time, circumstances may take place that alter the intent of the person with respect to the person's estate after death. Such factors as the deaths of other family members, divorce, birth, marriage, and changed financial status influence testamentary intent. At some point, the contents of one's will may need to be altered. This can be accomplished through a codicil or the execution of a new will and the revocation of the old one. Which is more appropriate depends on the extent and type of changes to be made.

A *codicil* is an addition to an existing will.[19] Any codicil must incorporate by reference the preexisting will or the codicil may be considered a complete and new will. All of the requirements necessary for a valid will are also required of a codicil because the terms in the codicil actually become part of the will for all legal purposes. When a codicil is executed and signed, the incorporation by reference serves as a sort of reaffirmation of the terms of the original will. As a result, the date of the will is considered to be that of the codicil.[20] This is important when several wills are presented to the court: The most recent is presumed to be the valid will reflecting the final intent of the testator.

A codicil should not contradict the terms of a previous will. If this is necessary to accomplish the objective of the testator, then an entirely new will should be prepared. Often codicils are included to make new provisions for bequests when a party who would have inherited dies before the testator. Codicils also can be used to distribute assets acquired after the original will was executed.

Will revocation becomes necessary when the intent of the testator changes with respect to the distribution of assets on death. When a new will is executed, all previous wills are considered to be revoked and invalid because they no longer reflect the intent of the testator.[21] Even if a testator does not execute a new will, the old will can still be revoked. If not revoked by a written document, it is often required that the testator take some steps to physically destroy or obliterate the existing will. It is not usually required that the will be destroyed, only that the damaged condition of the will and acts of the testator show that destruction was intended.

In some instances, after revocation a testator will seek to have the previous will made valid again. This can occur in one of several ways. When a new will is executed, it can contain a statement that if it is declared invalid, the old will should be reinstated. This prevents automatic intestate succession if the new will is defective. Another method is for the testator to say and do acts in the presence of witnesses that clearly establish the intent that the former will be revived. A condition of this method is usually that the original will still exists. Assuming that a will is located and presented to the court for probate (the process of the distribution of the estate), parties still have the opportunity to challenge the contents of the will. This occurs during probate and can be based on several different grounds, as discussed in the next section.

## APPLICATION 11.5

Bryce and Lauren were married. Each had one adult children from a previous relationship. Bryce and Lauren each had a valid will in which they left their personal estates to their respective children and their marital estates to their spouses. They were on a camping trip and were attacked by bears. The autopsy showed that Bryce died almost instantly in the attack. Lauren had less serious injuries but died of exposure several days after the attack. The best estimate of the medical examiner is that Lauren survived three to four days. In the probate of the estate, if Lauren survived beyond Bryce by the statutory requirement of three days, his child would inherit the entire marital estate as well as Bryce's personal estate.

*Point for Discussion:* How would the result change if it could be proven that Lauren died fewer than three days after the death of Bryce?

# CASE
## Gray, v. Gray III.,
## 947 So.2d 1045 (Ala. 2006)

The following judicial opinion shows the importance of maintaining a current and clear will as well as using personal identification of all parties affected rather than descriptive terms.

In 1981, John executed his will. At that time, John was married to Mary Rose Gray and had two children from a prior marriage, Robert B. Gray and Monica L. Muncher. John's will devised all of his estate to his wife Mary and did not include his two children. In 1984, John and Mary gave birth to John Merrill "Jack" Gray III. In 1989, John and Mary divorced. John and Mary's divorce judgment and property settlement included a provision creating a trust for Jack, which states that "[o]ne-half of all assets, inheritance or disbursements of any kind received by the Husband from his mother's estate shall be placed in trust for his son, Jack." Pursuant to Ala.Code § 43-8-137, even though John's will devised all of his estate to Mary, Mary would not inherit under John's will upon his death because John and Mary divorced. In 2004, John died without having changed his will.

William Terry Gray, the executor of John's estate, petitioned the Jefferson County Probate Court to probate John's will. Jack petitioned the probate court for an order finding that he is entitled to a share of John's estate under Ala.Code 1975, § 43-8-91, which provides in full:

(a) If a testator fails to provide in his will for any of his children born or adopted after the execution of his will, the omitted child receives a share in the estate equal in value to that which he would have received if the testator had died intestate unless:

(1) It appears from the will that the omission was intentional;

(2) When the will was executed the testator had one or more children and devised substantially all his estate to the other parent of the omitted child; or

(3) The testator provided for the child by transfer outside the will and the intent that the transfer be in lieu of a testamentary provision be reasonably proven.

The executor moved the probate court to dismiss Jack's petition. The executor argued that Ala.Code 1975, § 43-8-91(a)(2), applies because John had two children when he executed his will and devised substantially all of his estate to Jack's mother, Mary. Therefore, the executor argued, Jack was not entitled to his intestate share of John's estate. The executor also argued that Ala.Code 1975, § 43-8-91(a)(3), applies because, he

argued, John provided for Jack in a non-testamentary transfer in lieu of a testamentary transfer when he established a trust in Jack's favor upon his divorce from Jack's mother. Robert and Monica, John's children from his previous marriage, also moved the probate court to dismiss Jack's petition under Ala.Code 1975, § 43-8-91(a)(3). The probate court granted Jack's petition, holding that Jack is entitled to a distribution from John's estate equal in value to the share he would have received had John died intestate. The executor appeals the order of the probate court. The parties do not dispute the facts of this case. Therefore, we are presented only with questions of law. Questions of law are reviewed *de novo. Alabama Republican Party v. McGinley,* 893 So.2d 337, 342 (Ala.2004).

The executor argues that the probate court erred in holding that Jack is entitled to a share of John's estate. He argues that Ala.Code 1975, § 43-8-91, excludes Jack from taking a share because of the exception set forth in subparagraph (a)(2): "When the will was executed the testator had one or more children and devised substantially all his estate to the other parent of the omitted child." Specifically, he notes that when John executed his will, John had two children from a prior marriage and John devised all of his estate to Mary, the mother of Jack, the omitted child.

Jack argues that the holding in *Boackle v. Bloom,* 272 Ala. 490, 132 So.2d 586 (1961), applies in this case. In *Boackle,* we held that where a testator's will did not provide for any of his eight children who were living when he executed his will and the will was devoid of any indication that he had contemplated having children after he executed his will, a child born after the making of the will was entitled to take a child's part the same as if the father had died intestate. 272 Ala. at 494, 132 So.2d at 590. Jack's argument is unpersuasive because *Boackle* is based on a former version of the pretermitted child statute; the current version became effective on January 1, 1983. In determining whether Jack may benefit from § 43-8-91, we give the words of the applicable statute their plain, ordinary, and commonly understood meaning, and we interpret the language to mean what it says. See *Ex parte Gadsden Reg'l Med. Ctr.,* 904 So.2d 234, 236 (Ala.2004) ("'[W]e must give the words in a statute their plain, ordinary, and commonly understood meaning, and where plain language is used we must interpret it to mean exactly what it says.'" (quoting Bean Dredging, *L.L.C. v. Alabama Dep't of Revenue,* 855 So.2d 513, 517 (Ala.2003).

We recognize the instruction of Ala.Code 1975, § 43-8-2, that the Probate Code be "liberally construed" to promote its underlying purposes, one of which is to "make effective the intent of a decedent in the distribution of his property." § 43-8-2(b)(2). However, § 43-8-91(a)(2) does not place before the courts the issue of the decedent's intent, in contrast with § 43-8-91(a)(1) and (a)(3). Those provisions preclude the omitted child's inheritance under the will when "[i]t appears from the will that the omission was intentional" or "[t]he testator provided for the child by transfer outside the will and the intent that the transfer be in lieu of a testamentary provision be reasonably proven." In § 43-8-91(a)(2), the legislature has made assumptions regarding the testator's intent where the two stated factors are present. The courts are not invited to make further inquiry, as we are in § 43-8-91(a)(1) and (a)(3). In *Foster v. Martin,* 286 Ala. 709, 246 So.2d 435 (1971), this Court stated:

> "[T]he pretermission statute is one of substance rather than remedial. It creates and confers upon natural born and adopted children a right to property which would not be theirs without the statute. It is in derogation of the common law, and must therefore be strictly construed, and it will not be extended further than is required by the letter of the statute. *Pappas v. City of Eufaula,* 282 Ala. 242, 210 So.2d 802 [(1968)]; *Mobile Battle House, Inc. v. Wolf,* 271 Ala. 632, 126 So.2d 486 [(1961)]." 286 Ala. at 712, 246 So.2d at 438.

Section 43-8-91 states that, if a child is born subsequent to the execution of a will and the will fails to provide for the child, the omitted child is entitled to a share of the testator's estate, except in certain circumstances. One of those exceptions is that an omitted child is not entitled to a share of the estate if "[w]hen the will was executed the testator had one or more children and devised substantially all his estate to the other parent of the omitted child." In 1981, when John executed his will, he had two children by a prior marriage, and his will devised all of his estate to Jack's mother Mary. Therefore, § 43-8-91(a)(2) applies, and Jack may not receive a share of John's estate.

Jack argues that the exception in § 43-8-91(a)(2) should not apply to him because, he says, § 43-8-91(a)(2) "does not appear to contemplate a situation wherein the testator has children, divorces their mother, remarries, executes a will that makes no provision for any children whatsoever, than [sic] has a child with that second wife." Jack's brief, pp. 8–9. However, § 43-8-91(a)(2) states only two conditions for excluding an omitted child from an intestate share of the testator's estate: (1) the testator had one or more children at the time he executed his will, and (2) the testator's will devised substantially all of the testator's estate to the other parent of the omitted child. Because the statute is one of substance and is in derogation of the common law, we must construe it strictly and not extend its reach beyond its terms. See *Foster, supra.* Jack's argument, therefore, fails. The fact that John's other children were from a prior marriage is immaterial under § 43-8-91. Thus, Jack does not escape the exclusion found in § 43-8-91(a)(2). Accordingly, Jack is not entitled to receive a share of John's estate under § 43-8-91. . . . Because, as § 43-8-91(a) makes clear, the entire provision is dealing only with omitted children who are "born or adopted after the execution of [the testator's] will," to adopt the construction that it is intended to apply only to a child "then in being" is to give to the statute a meaning opposite of what it says. We will leave such rewriting to the legislature, whose job it is to amend or repeal statutes." If a statute is not ambiguous or unclear, the courts are not authorized to indulge in conjecture as to the intent of the Legislature or to look to consequences of the interpretation of the law as written." *Ex parte Presse,* 554 So.2d 406, 411 (Ala.1989). Section 43-8-91(a)(2) is not ambiguous. Thus, we are not at liberty to ponder whether and how the legislature might have written the statute differently to further its intention in the case now before us, nor may we read into the statute additional language the legislature might have included to facilitate the result it might desire in this case. We are not prepared to revise a statute to have it do what the legislature did not provide for it to do, simply because there is no evidence indicating that the decedent would not have done what we might decide he should have done. Choosing a course of action based on the absence of evidence is always treacherous. In addition, the testator in this case chose to omit his older, then living children from his will, and at the same time devised his estate to someone other than to their mother; we might assume that he would similarly have wanted to omit Jack and not to have Jack's mother inherit from his estate. . . . Before this Court sets about revising a statute, we must find not simply a desirable reason for doing so, but an absolutely compelling reason. This case does not meet the test enunciated in *Abramson v. Hard,* 229 Ala. 2, 155 So. 590 (1934). There is no ambiguity in this statute, and that fact disposes of the justification offered. However, even if there were ambiguity, while the result provided by the legislature may or may not be the one that those of us on this Court would have provided, it certainly does not reach the level of absurdity required before this Court is compelled to

*(continued)*

conclude that the legislature meant something other than what its words convey.

We reverse the probate court's order and remand the case to the probate court for further proceedings consistent with this opinion. Because we are reversing the probate court's order based on Ala.Code 1975, § 43-8-91(a)(2), and remanding the case to the probate court for further proceedings, we pretermit consideration of the executor's remaining arguments.

## Case Review Question

How can a testator avoid intestate distribution to a child he or she wishes to disinherit?

---

### ASSIGNMENT 11.3

In the following situations, identify the problem with the current will and explain how it should be corrected.

1. Bart is seriously ill. He executes a will and leaves one-half of his estate to his daughter Clementine and one-half of his estate to his daughter Jewel. He makes no mention of his daughter Marie, who is also his primary caretaker.

2. On January 1, 2007, Corey married Rachael. On January 2, 2007, he executed a will that leaves his entire estate to his "wife" but gives no name. Shortly thereafter, he discovered Rachael was having multiple affairs and divorced her. On August 1, 2007 Corey married Candace. On September 2, 2007, Corey was diagnosed with a well-advanced terminal illness and given only a few weeks to live.

3. Jacob executes a will leaving one-half of his estate to his mom and one-half of his estate to his dad. Jacob's parents are divorced, and his father has remarried. A few months after the will is executed, Jacob's dad suffers a serious stroke and is in a persistent vegetative state and not

expected to survive for more than a few months at best.

4. Kim has an estate valued at approximately $30,000. She executes a will leaving her entire estate to a local humane society and leaves nothing to her two grown brothers. They are close but both have steady employment and Kim feels that her relatively small estate would do more good as a charitable gift. Kim wins the lottery and after taxes receives approximately $28 million. She is so thrilled she immediately makes plans to go on a "thrill seeker's world tour" in which she will attempt ultradangerous activities at a variety of locations around the globe.

5. Bonnie owns her own house. She executes a will leaving "my home" to her children. The residual of her estate is left to her boyfriend, Sam, and consists of a few thousand dollars in a bank account. The house is the only bequest to Bonnie's children because it is her most valuable asset. Bonnie then marries Sam. Within about a year, Bonnie sells the house and moves to another house that she and Sam purchase together.

---

## Will Contests

Most publicity regarding probate cases concerns *will contests*—that is, when a person challenges the validity of a will. The three common grounds for will contests are mistake, duress or improper influence, and fraud. Generally, one who contests a will has the burden of proof to establish that the will is not a valid testamentary instrument properly executed by the deceased by clear and convincing evidence (less than the standard of beyond a reasonable doubt but more than a mere preponderance of the evidence).

When a will is challenged on the basis of *mistake,* the challenger must allege that the testator either did not know a final will was being signed or was not aware of all of the terms and the effects of what had been included in the will.[22] When mistake is proven as to any part of a will, most courts will declare the entire instrument invalid. The reasoning is sound: If it can be shown that the testator made a significant mistake with respect to one part of the will, then who is to say that other mistakes were not made as well? When the entire will is declared invalid, the estate passes by intestate succession.

The second method used to challenge a will is that of *duress* or *improper influence.* The thrust of this type of challenge is that the testator did not execute the will independently and voluntarily. In most cases, it must be shown by the contestant that the testator was convinced that there was no real intent to execute the will. The testator instead was so impaired that the contents of the will reflect the desires of another and that the testator would not have executed the terms of the will but for the existence of improper influences.[23]

As stated, it is the general rule that the person challenging the will has the burden of proving the duress or improper influence. There is, however, an exception to this rule. When the will is drawn up or witnessed by someone who is a fiduciary (one who is in a position of personal trust to the testator) or who stands to receive under the will, then many states will presume that there was undue influence.[24] Thus, a will should always be drawn and witnessed by disinterested parties. Otherwise, no matter how sincere the testator could have been, the burden is shifted against the parties alleging the will is valid. The presumption is that there was undue influence, and the will is considered ineffective unless it can be shown by clear and convincing evidence that there was no improper influence. Because attorneys are fiduciaries, they should avoid drafting or witnessing wills in which they are beneficiaries (although most states will make an exception if the will is for a close or immediate family member).

Persons who may not draft or witness a will without the presumption of improper influence are specified in the statutes of each state. Similarly, the burden of proof (amount of evidence) needed to show that the will was properly executed is also dictated by statute. The preceding are common rules, but variations may exist in some states. Consequently, before relying on these propositions, always consult existing statutes in the particular state of interest.

The final reason for challenging a will is an allegation of *fraud.* The contestant must prove several elements before a will is considered to be ineffective on the grounds of fraud. Specifically, it must be demonstrated that (1) an identifiable person made false statements to the testator, (2) such person did so with the intent of misleading the testator by the statements, (3) the testator was in fact misled and executed a will based on the false statements, and (4) the testator would not have executed the terms of the will in the absence of reliance on the false allegations.[25]

An example of fraud is the case whereby a child (presumably an adult child) convinces a parent that another child of the parent is dead. The parent then executes a will leaving the entire estate to the child who made the false allegations. If the parent would not have executed the same will with the knowledge that the second child was living and there is no reasonable basis of determining whether the parent would have executed the will, the will was created under circumstances of fraud.

# CASE
## *In re Probate of the Will Ryan,*
### 34 A.D.3d 212, 824 N.Y.S.2d 20 (N.Y.A.D. 1 Dept), 2006

This opinion demonstrates how circumstances occurring around the execution of a will can be contested as fraud and undue influence as well as the importance of clearly explained intent within the testamentary documents.

Order, Surrogate's Court, New York County (Renee R. Roth, S.), entered March 1, 2005, which, insofar as appealed from as limited by the briefs, denied that branch of petitioner-appellant's motion for summary judgment dismissing the third objection to probate of

*(continued)*

the will premised, *inter alia,* on fraud and undue influence, and further denied objectant-respondent-appellant's cross motion for summary judgment denying probate based on the objection and on violation of public policy, modified, on the law, the objections to probate based on fraud, undue influence and violation of public policy dismissed, and otherwise affirmed, without costs, and the matter remanded for further probate proceedings consistent herewith.

Decedent died on February 26, 1995, at the age of 92, leaving an estate valued at approximately $450,000. In her last will, dated June 24, 1992, decedent specifically disinherited three of her children, Juan, Ricardo and Catalina, the objectants to the will, leaving the bulk of her estate equally to four of her five remaining children and the wife of her eldest son, Tomas. As explained in the propounded will, objectants were disinherited, albeit regretfully, because, over decedent's objection, they had refused to call off a proceeding they had initiated in California to remove Tomas and his wife, Viviane, as co-fiduciaries of the estate of decedent's brother-in-law. The propounded will stated that objectants knew "from the beginning that [decedent] disapproved of what they were doing" and were warned on numerous occasions that they would be disinherited unless they called off the lawsuit against Tomas. Attached to the will was a handwritten statement, signed and dated by decedent on June 24, 1992, which reiterated her reason for disinheriting Juan, Catalina and Ricardo.

In November 1995, the disinherited children filed objections to the probate of the will, which alleged, *inter alia,* that the will was obtained by fraud and undue influence and violated public policy. Party depositions were taken and in August 1999, petitioner, a daughter of decedent and the preliminary executrix, moved for summary judgment dismissing the objections. Objectants, in turn, cross-moved for summary judgment denying probate. As pertinent to this appeal, the Surrogate denied summary judgment on the third objection, finding sufficient factual dispute as to whether the propounded instrument was procured by undue influence. We disagree. Although summary judgment in a contested probate proceeding must be exercised cautiously, it is appropriate where, as here, the petitioner establishes a *prima facie* case for probate and the moving objectant's evidence does not raise a genuine triable issue of fact as to undue influence (*Matter of Minervini,* 297 A.D.2d 423, 424 [2002]; see also *Matter of Wilson,* 266 A.D.2d 164 [1999]; *Matter of Tully,* 227 A.D.2d 288 [1996]).

"To be 'undue,' the influence exerted must amount to mental coercion that led the testator to carry out the wishes of another, instead of her own wishes, because the testator was unable to refuse or too weak to resist" (PJI 7:55; see also *Matter of Burke,* 82 A.D.2d 260, 269 [1981]). In order to justify a submission of undue influence to the jury, objectant must make a showing of motive and opportunity to exert undue influence as well as that such influence was actually utilized (*Matter of Walther,* 6 N.Y.2d 49, 55 [1959]; see also *Matter of Bustanoby,* 262 A.D.2d 407, 408 [1999]). Circumstantial evidence, demonstrated, *inter alia,* "by all the facts and circumstances surrounding the testator, the nature of the will, [her] family relations, the condition of [her] health and mind, [her] dependency upon and subjection to the control of the person supposed to have wielded the influences, the opportunity and disposition of the person to wield it, and the acts and declarations of such person" (*Matter of Camac,* 300 A.D.2d 11, 12 [2002], may be used to prove undue influence; however, this evidence must be of a substantial nature (*Walther,* 6 N.Y.2d at 54).

Objectant's claim that decedent's relationship with Tomas, which allegedly consisted of her always being willing to take his side in all disputes, unduly influenced her to disinherit three children to appease Tomas is insufficient to support a finding of undue influence. While the evidence may be consistent with objectant's hypothesis that decedent's act of disinheriting objectants was based upon a misbelief, instigated by Tomas, that objectants had wronged Tomas in the California lawsuit, the evidence is equally consistent with the assumption that decedent cared not about whether objectants' suit had any merit but that three of her children had rejected her plea to cease their public airing of their family laundry. As such, "'an inference of undue influence cannot be reasonably drawn from circumstances when they are not inconsistent with a contrary inference'" (*Walther,* 6 N.Y.2d at 54, 223 N.Y. 582 [1918].

Additionally, "[g]ratitude, love, esteem or friendship which induces another to make testamentary dispositions of property cannot ordinarily be considered as arising from undue influence, and all these motives are allowed to have full scope, without in any way affecting the validity of the act" (*Children's Aid Socy. v. Loveridge,* 70 N.Y. 387, 394–395 [1877]; see also *Burke,* 82 A.D.2d at 269). Here, decedent had a very close relationship with Tomas, her firstborn, that predated the execution of any of the eight wills she executed. As reflected by numerous letters written by decedent to various of her children both before and after the execution of the propounded will, objectants' lawsuit against Tomas was "killing" her. She could not sleep and felt the need to seek advice from her priest. When her pleas to objectants were ignored, decedent concluded that she had no other alternative but to disinherit them. According to decedent's January 1, 1993 letter to petitioner, to ignore what objectants tried to do to Tomas would be "more or less giving [her] silent approval," which she could not do.

Nor is there any evidence that Tomas actually compelled decedent to do something she did not want to do. Such influence is not demonstrated by the mere fact that the will favored Tomas over objectants (see *Matter of Fiumara,* 47 N.Y.2d 845, 846 [1979]). "[U]ndue influence to avoid a will must be a present constraint, operating upon the mind of the testator at the time of the testamentary act" (*Matter of Kaufmann,* 14 A.D.2d 411, 412 [1961] . . . ). Here, given Tomas's testimony that he was not even aware of the existence of the fourth and fifth wills, let alone the propounded will, and evidence showing that at the time the propounded will was executed, decedent was living with her daughter in Mexico while Tomas resided in New York, objectant is entitled to no inference of undue influence in the absence of evidence demonstrating Tomas's direct involvement in the preparation or execution of the will (see *Matter of Bartel,* 214 A.D.2d 476, 477 [1995]).

Additional factors that suggest a lack of undue influence are decedent's physical and mental condition (cf. *Matter of Callahan,* 155 A.D.2d 454 [1989]), which are not in dispute, and the fact that the propounded instrument did not materially deviate from decedent's prior testamentary pattern (cf. *Matter of Kruszelnicki,* 23 A.D.2d 622 [1965]).

As this Court observed recently, the evidence must permit an inference that "the decedent was so dependent upon and subject to [the alleged influencer's] control that she could not resist the wielding of his influence" (*Matter of Korn,* 25 AD3d 379, 380 [2006]). This is a very heavy burden of proof, which objectant does not meet. The mere fact that the attorney who drafted the propounded will was a close friend of Tomas is, on these facts, insufficient to show a triable issue of fact on undue influence.

To state a claim for fraud, objectant was required to demonstrate that Tomas "knowingly made a false statement to the testator which caused [her] to execute a will that disposed of [her] property in a manner differently than [s]he would have in the absence of that statement" (*Matter of Evanchuk,* 145 A.D.2d 559, 560 [1988]). Here, objectant submitted only conclusory and speculative evidence that Tomas made such a false statement, and as such, he failed to raise a triable issue of fact regarding the fraud claim (*Matter of Clapper,* 279 A.D.2d 730, 732 [2001]; *Bustanoby,* 262 A.D.2d at 408). The claim that the propounded will violates public policy is likewise unpersuasive.

## Case Review Question

What could have been done by the testator to avoid the will contest?

## PROBATE OF ESTATES

Probate describes the process of distributing the estate of a person who is deceased. Whether the person dies intestate or **testate,** the court determines what creditors are entitled to funds from the estate and what persons are entitled to receive a share of that which remains after debts of the estate are paid.

**testate**
Dying with a valid will.

Originally, each state developed laws of probate. These laws established formal procedures for handling assets, evaluating and paying persons claiming to be creditors of the deceased, and distributing the remaining assets to heirs and persons named in wills. With the increasing mobility of our society, it is no longer unusual for a decedent's assets to be scattered throughout several states. Laws of property generally require that real property be governed by the law where it is located. However, the law of estates often requires the probate to take place in the jurisdiction where the decedent was domiciled at the time of death. In response to these and similar potential conflicts, the Uniform Probate Code was adopted. A majority of states have adopted the code, which establishes identical probate procedures and standards in each adopting state. In the past, it was possible that under differing state laws the rights of inheritance could vary dramatically. With the uniform code, however, the inheritance rights are determined in the same manner irrespective of where the property of the estate is located.

Regardless of whether a state has adopted the Uniform Probate Code, the procedure for probating an estate follows some common basic steps (see Table 11.1).

**Table 11.1** Typical Steps in Probate

| Testate | Intestate |
|---|---|
| 1. Filing of petition* (to admit will and for appointment of personal representative) | 1. Filing of petition (to open estate and for appointment of personal representative) |
| 2. Notification of heirs and beneficiaries | 2. Notification of heirs |
| 3. Notice to creditors | 3. Notice to creditors |
| 4. Inventory of estate | 4. Inventory of estate |
| 5. Hearing on creditors' claims and payments | 5. Hearing on creditors' claims and payments |
| 6. Final accounting of estate | 6. Final accounting of estate |
| 7. Distribution of estate to beneficiaries in accordance with terms of the will** | 7. Distribution of estate in accordance with the laws of intestate succession |
| 8. Hearing on creditors' claims and payment | |

* Law varies by state regarding when a hearing on a will contest occurs.

** In some cases, bequests cannot be honored because the property did not exist in the estate or the property was sold or otherwise used to satisfy creditors or the spouse's statutory rights.

When an individual dies, state law often requires that all assets be frozen (although businesses owned by the person may continue). All bank accounts, stocks, bonds, and other financial transactions in the name of the deceased must stop. These assets are frozen until such a time as the court has finally determined the status of the deceased's estate (assets and liabilities).

The first step in probate is to file with the court the appropriate documents, which generally include the original copy of the will and affidavits by the witnesses that they signed the will after witnessing the signature of the testator.[26] If there is no will, a petition is presented to the court for probate of an intestate estate.

Before going any further, challenges to the validity of the will are made and decided. Once determined, the court decides whether to probate the estate testate (with a will) or intestate (without a will), according to procedures of state law. For all practical purposes, the estates are probated in the same manner until such time as it becomes necessary to distribute the assets of the estate.

The next step in probate is to appoint someone to oversee the assets of the estate during probate. In many states, such persons are called *administrators* (in the case of an intestate estate) or *executors* (in testate cases). These persons are responsible for overseeing the estate. They must inventory the assets, pay creditors (when approved by the court), and generally protect the estate until it is finally distributed. The administrator or executor is a fiduciary of the estate[27] and is under an obligation to care for the assets of the estate and not to convert them to personal use or waste them. Any breach of the duty as a fiduciary can result in criminal charges.

If the deceased is survived by a spouse or minor children, then claims can be made for living allowances—that is, sums of money that the spouse or children or both can use for daily living expenses until such time as the estate is probated.[28] Statutes give some direction and judges have discretion as to what is a suitable allowance based on the size of the estate and the needs of the spouse and children.

In addition to allowances, certain property in which the deceased may have had an interest is exempt from probate.[29] Generally, such property includes the primary residence of the deceased (if the surviving spouses or minor children reside there), an automobile, apparel, home furnishings, and other personal items specified by statute. The idea is to protect the family from claims against the property by creditors. Again, these allowances are generally effective only when there is a surviving spouse or minor children, and state statutes list exactly what may be considered exempt from the estate of the deceased.

After an executor or administrator is appointed, the inventory of the estate has been completed, and allowances to the spouse and children have been handled, it is necessary to process the claims of creditors. Seldom these days does a person die totally free of obligations. Thus, each state has procedures for notifying creditors of the deceased person. Often such procedures include publication in the legal section of the classified ads of local papers and other methods designed to reasonably alert potential creditors of the pending probate of the deceased's estate.[30]

Creditors are generally given a specific amount of time to come forward with claims against the estate—often several months to provide every opportunity for claims. Creditors who seek to have obligations paid by the estate must file the appropriate forms with the court that document the amount and nature of the claim. If the administrator or executor challenges the validity of the claim, a hearing is needed to determine whether it should be paid by the estate in whole or in part.

After the deadline has passed for making claims, the court considers all requests by creditors. Arrangements are made for the payment of the claims from the assets of the estate. Occasionally items of property must be sold to obtain enough money to pay all of the creditors. This is so even if the sale of assets depletes items that were bequeathed in a will.

Following the payment of creditors, many states give the surviving spouse in a testate estate the option of accepting what he or she is entitled to under the will or claiming what is known as a **forced share.** This law grants an absolute minimum to a surviving spouse, which is generally a significant portion of the estate. The only exception to such a case might be if the spouse had previously waived the right to claim a forced share by signing an antenuptial agreement.

Once all creditor claims and the claim by the spouse have been addressed, the court can proceed to distribute the estate. If there is a will, the estate will be distributed according to its terms so long as the assets bequeathed (granted in the will) are still in the estate. Each state has provisions that indicate how situations are to be dealt with when a bequeathed asset is no longer part of the estate (known as *ademption*) either because the testator disposed of it before death or because sale was necessary to satisfy the claims of creditors.

Most wills also have what is known as a *residuary clause* that identifies a beneficiary to receive all remaining assets in the estate after bequests have been satisfied. This can cover a major portion of the estate if a person entitled to receive property died before the testator. Another possibility that could greatly increase the residuary clause is if additional assets were acquired after the execution of the will and no codicil was prepared to distribute them.

In the case of intestate estates, the common procedure is to reduce the assets to cash or appraise their value and distribute them according to the intestate method of distribution recognized by the state. As stated, this is generally going to be by *per stirpes*.

**forced (elected) share**
Right of a spouse to receive a statutorily designated percentage of a deceased spouse's estate.

## ETHICAL CONSIDERATIONS

As demonstrated in the discussion of will contests, ethics plays a significant role in probate law. A person's inheritance can be directly affected by the propriety of conduct exercised with respect to the testator. Probate courts are required to consider everything from an allegedly greedy family member or friend to cases of murder. Lawyers who prepare wills are under an obligation to take the necessary steps to eliminate doubts about the capacity of the testator, and personal representatives have the responsibility to care for and protect the inventory of the estate until it can be distributed. All of the preceding responsibilities inherently require ethical conduct, including both objectivity and fiduciary duty. The failure to undertake such conduct could result in a distribution of an estate that has no resemblance to the intent of the testator.

If you are a paralegal and are asked to sign as a witness to a will of a client of your firm whom you have never met, what should you ask to ethically undertake the responsibility of witness?

## ETHICAL CIRCUMSTANCE

Samantha is a probate lawyer who has been in practice for twenty-five years. She has one sister who has not been in touch with her family in more than a decade and who has virtually no relationship with any of them. Samantha has cared diligently for her parents and took her mother in to live with her after the death of her father. Samantha's mother wishes to execute a new will leaving her entire estate to Samantha. She asks Samantha to prepare the will. If she were to do so, she would open the door to Samantha's sister for a will contest. First, it would be unethical to prepare a will in which the preparer is the only heir. This is compounded by the fact that the only other surviving heir is being disinherited in the document. Regardless of the circumstances of the relationship with the disinherited child, it would be inappropriate for Samantha to prepare the will in which she doubles her inheritance. Even while the information provided would give a slanted view against the sister, no information has been given about Samantha, the condition of her mother, or any other relevant factors.

## ● | CHAPTER SUMMARY

It is hoped that this chapter has produced a better understanding of some of the complexities of estate law. From the discussion in the chapter, it should be clear that the death of someone affects not only the family, employers, and insurance companies but also banks and all persons or entities with whom the deceased had any financial dealings if they are drawn into the probate process. Consequently, in any aspect of business or industry, it is important to understand the legal consequences of a person's death.

When a person leaves a will, the document must have been properly written and under fair and reliable circumstances. When irregularities exist in a will or when no will was left by the deceased, the law of intestate succession takes effect. Although this does not always account for all of the wishes of the deceased, it does provide an equitable distribution of the property to the heirs who are presumed to be the most likely candidates for devise had the testator left a valid will. If one wants control over the distribution of the estate, the solution is quite simple. A proper will should be executed and kept current as changes occur in the estate or the people selected to inherit.

Regardless of whether a person dies testate or intestate, the probate courts serve the function of ensuring that the debts of the estate are paid and that the remaining assets of the estate are properly distributed. This is also accomplished with the assistance of an administrator in an intestate case and an executor in a testate estate. In either case, this party keeps the estate organized and intact until the final order of the probate court is issued to dissolve and close the estate.

## ● | CHAPTER TERMS

| | | |
|---|---|---|
| forced (elected) share | per capita distribution | probate |
| guardianship | *per stirpes* distribution | testate |
| intestate | | |

## REVIEW QUESTIONS

1. How is *per stirpes* different from per capita distribution?

2. What is required for a valid will?

3. On what grounds can a will be contested?

4. What are the major steps in probate of an estate?

5. Define the term *estate.*

6. What are the duties of an administrator or an executor?

7. Who can be disinherited in a will?

8. Who can inherit by intestate succession?

9. Who determines the inheritance of a person charged with murdering the testator?

10. Explain the common requirements of an oral will in states where such a will is permitted.

## HELPFUL WEB SITES

| | |
|---|---|
| Estate planning page | http://www.estateattorney.com |
| Estate planning basics | http://www.estateplanningbasics.com |
| Estate planning | http://www.estateplanning.com |

## INTERNET ASSIGNMENT 11.1

Consult the law of your jurisdiction using Internet resources and locate the *per stirpes* distribution statute.

## INTERNET ASSIGNMENT 11.2

Pick two jurisdictions and answer the following question for each: What is the inheritance right of a half-blood sibling (i.e., shares one parent) compared to a sibling who was adopted.

## ENDNOTES

1. *Martin v. Beatty,* 253 Iowa 1237, 115 N.W.2d 706 (1962).
2. *Id.*
3. *Richard Trust Co. v. Becvar,* 440 Ohio St.2d 219, 339 N.E.2d 830 (1975).
4. *United States v. Board of Com'rs of Public Schools of Baltimore City,* 432 F.Supp. 629 (D. Md. 1977).
5. 1a C.J.S., Adoption of Children, Sections 63–65.
6. 26A C.J.S., Descent and Distribution, Section 25.
7. 3 C.J.S., Bastards, Sections 24–29.
8. *Id.*
9. *Debus v. Cook,* 198 Ind. 675, 154 N.E. 484 (1926).
10. *Lofton v. Lofton,* 26 N.C. App. 203, 215 S.E.2d 861 (1975).
11. *McLendon v. McLendon,* 277 Ala. 323, 169 So.2d 767 (1964).
12. 79 Am.Jur.2d., Wills, Section 289.
13. *Id.,* at Section 321.
14. *In re Bernatzki's Estate,* 204 Kan. 131, 460 P.2d 527 (1969).
15. 71 A.L.R.3d. 877.
16. *In re Erbach's Estate,* 41 Wis.2d 335, 164 N.W.2d 238 (1969).
17. *Wright v. Benttinen,* 352 Mass. 495, 226 N.E.2d 194 (1967).
18. *Solomon v. Dunlap,* 372 So.2d 218 (Fla.App. 1st Dist. 1979).
19. *Remon v. American Sec. & Trust Co.,* 110 U.S.App. D.C. 37, 288 F.2d 849 (1961).
20. *Estate of Krukenberg,* 77 Nev. 226, 361 P.2d 537 (1961).

21.  *Crosby v. Alton Ochsner Medical Foundation*, 276 So.2d 661 (Miss. 1973).
22.  79 Am.Jur.2d, Wills, Sections 415–418.
23.  36 Am.Jr.2d, Proof of Facts, Section 109.
24.  *Id.*
25.  92 A.L.R. 784.
26.  79 Am.Jur.2d, Wills, Section 407.
27.  C.J.S. Wills, Section 1262.
28.  *Id.*
29.  *Id.,* at Section 1311.
30.  *Id.,* at Section 1288.

### STUDENT CD-ROM

For additional materials, please go to the CD in this book.

### ONLINE COMPANION™

For additional resources, please go to www.paralegal.delmar.cengage.com

# Property Law

## POSSESSION IS NINE-TENTHS OF THE LAW

In a common law court in England in 1774, Lord Mansfield coined the phrase, "property is nine points of the law." The more common American rendition is that "possession is nine-tenths of the law." What does this mean and how does it affect the law of property? The phrase does not mean that if you obtain physical possession of something that you have a 90 percent chance of keeping it from someone else, including the rightful owner. What it does mean is that someone in possession of property may have an advantage over someone who wants it and deems it properly theirs. In most property cases based on U.S. civil law, a case needs to be proven "by a preponderance." This means the person seeking recovery or compensation must prove that, more likely than not, his or her evidence supports the true and proper result when legal standards are applied. If percentages were applied to the evidence, the plaintiff must show entitlement to a favorable verdict by at least 51 percent. Because having possession of the property in question would be evidence of the individual's right to keep it, he or she would have that much more evidence in his or her favor. When added to other evidence, the person in possession often has the mathematical advantage. However, this can also be used to charge an individual with ownership as well. Consider the person caught by authorities in possession of stolen property or illegal drugs. The person is now saddled with a presumption of ownership. In this event, even though the standard for criminal prosecution is much higher than the civil preponderance standard, it is still a hurdle to overcome the perception in the mind of a judge or jury. The moral of this story? Be careful what you hold on to, and be sure that you want it!

## CHAPTER OBJECTIVES

After reading this chapter, you should be able to:

- Distinguish real property, personal property, and intellectual property.

- Explain the concept of undivided interest.

- Distinguish tenancy in common, joint tenancy, and tenancy by the entirety.

- List the elements of adverse possession.

- Discuss the remedies to retrieve wrongfully taken or held personal property.

- Distinguish habitability and quiet enjoyment.

- Explain the concept of constructive eviction.

- Discuss the basic obligations of landlord and tenant.

The law of property in this country stems in large part from the common law principles of English property law. During the Middle Ages, the English court system created general rules for the possession, transfer, and disposition of property on the owner's death. Although many of these principles continue in the U.S. legal system in some ways, the states have altered, modified, and, in some cases, even abolished certain rules over time to develop the statutory and common law of property in our country today. These legal changes have been the result of an effort to adapt to the changes that have occurred in society and in the types of land interests in this country that did not exist in feudal England. This chapter defines and examines the current law of property, including personal property, real property, and associated interests.

Before discussing the types of property and the rights related to the purchase, conveyance (transfer), ownership, possession, or alteration of property, we clarify the legal definition of the term *property,* which generally means the right to possess or control.[1] This meaning is different from the everyday language used to interpret property as an actual physical thing such as a parcel of land. Consequently, in legal terms, when discussing an interest in property, the focus is on the type of right to possess, control, or own the item in question rather than on the item itself. This chapter is organized by type of area subject to property law, and the rights associated with them within those areas are discussed.

**real property**
Land or anything permanently affixed to land and no longer movable.

## REAL PROPERTY

**Real property** is land or that which is attached to the land in such a way that it is permanent, fixed, and immovable.[2] The law of real property governs all that is part of the land naturally or as a result of being artificially incorporated into the land in a permanent way. Real property includes houses, buildings, and other structures that are affixed to the property by some permanent means. An example of something that would not ordinarily be considered real property is a mobile home that has not been permanently affixed to the ground. This type of structure is considered movable and falls into the category of personal property (discussed at the end of the chapter).

The following sections discuss the types of interest or rights to real property. These interests and rights can be affected by ownership, inheritance, marital status, and terms of possession. The right to control or own property can be obtained in many ways; as they are explored, it should become clear that property law is one of the most well developed areas of law in our country.

## Freehold Estates

Traditionally, **freehold estate** has been the term used to describe ownership and interests in land.[3] This is to be distinguished from nonfreehold estates such as lease or rental agreements (discussed later in the chapter). Freehold estates involve the rights of a property owner and the conditions or limitations that might be imposed on that ownership. Several types of freehold estates exist, including single ownership, ownership by two or more persons, and certain rights of uninterfered possession without actual ownership.

**freehold estate**
An interest in real property that involves certain rights of ownership.

**Fee Simple.** The most common type of ownership in the United States is **fee simple**.[4] Under English common law, when a man obtained property in fee simple, it meant that the man owned the property for the duration of his lifetime.[5] In other words, the man possessed a life estate (discussed next). At the end of the owner's life, the property automatically reverted back to the original owner.

To own property outright on a permanent basis, the property had to be owned in fee simple *absolute,* which required special language in the document used to transfer the property (deed) that prevented it from reverting to the original owner. In the United States today, fee simple has an interpretation of fee simple absolute. All transfers of ownership of property are by fee simple unless otherwise stated. Such transfers are considered to be a sale of total and absolute rights over the property. In most jurisdictions, a limited term of possession or ownership must be granted by express language in the transferring document.

**fee simple**
In U.S. law, this involves absolute ownership of real property.

**Life Estates.** A **life estate** gives the holder the right to totally control the property for the holder's lifetime without interference. Such an estate includes the right to do all things an owner in fee simple could do with one exception: The property cannot be disposed of (sold or given away) or treated in such a way as to ruin it for its usual purpose[6] (known as *wasting*). An example of wasting property would be one who had a life estate in farmland and put toxic chemicals on the land that prevented the land from being used in the future as farmland. If a life estate holder is found to be wasting the property, the life estate can be legally terminated. When the life estate ends by legal termination of the estate or death of the holder, ownership goes to the party who originally owned the property or to the person designated by the original owner to receive the property.

A life estate is considered to be a type of freehold estate in and of itself, even though it does not contain the basic element of transferability. A person with a life estate cannot transfer ownership to someone else but can transfer part or all of his or her interest in the property, if allowed by the grantor. This means that a life tenant could lease the property during the course of his or her lifetime, but such a lease would expire when the life tenant died. Thus, with the exception of limitations on transferability and the condition of not wasting the property, the life

**life estate**
The right to possess and use real property for the duration of one's life with limited ownership rights.

estate holder has all the rights otherwise associated with ownership. One common situation of the creation of a life estate occurs when a spouse leaves a life estate in solely owned real property to the surviving party who may not otherwise have rights of inheritance over the property. When the surviving spouse dies, the estate passes completely and automatically to an heir named in the will of the spouse who originally owned the property.

---

## APPLICATION 12.1

Nicky and Noelle are sisters. They were both widowed with adult children. The entire family resided in upstate New York. Two years ago, they decided to make the most of their retirement years. They sold most of their belongings and together purchased an oceanfront home in Florida. Nicky was financially in a position to buy the home. Noelle did not have as much in the way of assets, but she had a regular income from her late husband's pension. Noelle contributed the money for the upkeep, all of the new furniture they purchased for the home, as well as redecorating costs. The only concern the sisters had was if Nicky predeceased Noelle. Both sisters wanted their estates to pass to their respective children. However, Nicky did not want Noelle to be forced from their home; she assumed the children would want to sell the house and divide the proceeds. To protect Noelle, Nicky created a life estate for Noelle in the property that would allow her the right of possession the home for the remainder of her life. On Noelle's death or surrender of the property, possession would revert to Nicky's children, who would have inherited the other rights of ownership. However, without further discussion in Nicky's will, the money invested by Noelle on redecorating, and likely increasing the value of the property, would probably not be considered as any sort of offset for Noelle's estate.

*Point for Discussion:* What rights would Nicky's children have after her death and during the term of Noelle's life estate?

---

**Other Estates.** Various other types of *conveyances in fee* (transfers of property interest) exist. *Conveyances subject to reversion* require that, under certain conditions, the property revert back to its original owner. The effect of such estates is similar to the old definition of fee simple but occurred under different circumstances. An example is a person who is buying land by paying rent along with a payment toward ownership each month. The agreement might provide that if the lessor or buyer dies before the property is paid for, all interests in the property will revert to the original owner.

*Defeasible fees* are those that end ownership on the occurrence of a certain event, at which time the property would pass to another named person. Although the various fee estates had great influence historically in property rights, today they rarely become an issue. Land is owned predominantly in fee simple or fee simple subject to a life estate.

The *remainder interest* is one type of interest that has survived the changes in property law. This interest is created automatically on the end of another. Giving one's surviving spouse a life estate is one type of remainder interest. Unless the remainder interest is indicated on the document used to transfer title (e.g., the deed), a conveyance of property ownership is presumed to be in fee simple absolute, with total control and ownership vested in the receiving party.

Today, the law is much more equal to spouses in the distribution of property than under old English law. Under original property law, women could not own property. Even property inheritances were passed on to the woman's spouse and male children. Currently, there is no distinction between men and women on the issue of property ownership and inheritance. In the event that a spouse does not provide adequately for the surviving spouse by will, a statutory provision for what is commonly known as a **forced** (or elected) **share**[7] permits a surviving spouse to claim or elect a certain percentage of the property (real and personal) of the deceased. This claim is superior to all other heirs and prevails even if it decreases the amount received by persons designated in a will. One can generally disinherit children or anyone else by will except for a spouse. The law makes no distinction whether the surviving spouse is husband or wife. The interest received is in fee simple (rather than a life estate), and surviving children are not necessary for the interest to be received. (The rights of surviving spouses are discussed in greater detail in Chapter 11, "Estates and Probate.")

**forced share**
The legal right of a surviving spouse to receive a certain percentage of the estate of a deceased spouse that is superior to the terms of a will or other rights of inheritance of heirs.

## ASSIGNMENT 12.1

For each of the following occurrences, identify the ownership interest of the parties or their action in terms of its effect on the property (or both where appropriate).

1. Dennis leaves his house to his children. However, they will not receive title or possession until the death of Dennis's life partner, Ralph, who has the right to control the property for the rest of his life.
2. Jennifer was married to James. When James died, his will left everything in his estate to his church, including the residence occupied by him and Jennifer valued at $80,000 and James's personal property valued at $2,000. The real property was in James's name only. Jennifer goes to court to claim one-half of the estate.
3. Assume Jennifer and James were not married.
4. Assume Jennifer and James owned the property as joint tenants.
5. Max and Joe own property for forty years as tenants in common. They rent out the property for income. Max married Susan and was killed while on their honeymoon.

## Types of Ownership Between Multiple Parties

Today it is common for more than one party to hold the title to (i.e., own) real property. The relationships of these persons and reasons for multiple ownership vary. As a result, certain types of ownership have evolved that govern the rights of these various multiple ownership arrangements. Such arrangements may be for business or personal reasons. The different types of multiple ownership of property clarify such issues as what portion of the property is possessed by each person, who has the right to sell or dispose of the property, and what should happen in the event one of the owners dies. The most commonly employed types of multiple ownership are tenancy in common, joint tenancy, and tenancy by the entirety.

**Tenancy in Common.** Unless otherwise stated in the purchase agreement, the type of tenancy of multiple owners is presumed to be **tenancy in common**. With this type of ownership, each owner has an undivided interest in the property,[8] meaning that each owner has an equal share in every part of the property. The undivided interest guarantees that no one owner has a better portion of the property. Each owner has a balanced interest in both the positive and negative aspects of the property as a whole. The percentage of undivided interest is equal to the percentage of ownership. For example, if one tenant owns 50 percent of the property and two remaining partners each own 25 percent of the property, then the first partner is entitled to a one-half undivided interest in all the property and the other partners are each entitled to an undivided 25 percent share in the total property.

**tenancy in common**
A form of multiple ownership of property whereby each tenant (owner) shares with the other(s) an undivided interest in the property.

In addition to their undivided interest, tenants in common may do all things with their interest as if they owned the property entirely. The only limitation is that they cannot act in such a way as to interfere with the rights of the other tenants in common. A tenant in common can neither make use of the property in a way that is inconsistent with the other tenants nor waste the property. A tenant who does either of these things with any part of the property is doing it with a portion of the property controlled by the other tenants.

## APPLICATION 12.2

A group of seven individuals who are avid hunters decide to purchase a large parcel of hunting land. By pooling their resources, they are able to afford a much larger acreage and in turn provide more opportunity for hunting. They purchase the property as tenants in common. For some fifteen years they work together to create a general habitat that will attract the types of animals they hunt. They designate specific portions of the property for each of the individual hunters as a means of avoiding any one hunter gaining an unfair advantage over the others in terms of the number of animals taken from the property.

A portion of their property overlooks the Mississippi River in an area north of a large city. As the city grows, the land surrounding it becomes increasingly valuable. A wealthy individual approaches the hunter that has designated control over approximately 50 acres overlooking the river. The individual wants to purchase the property and develop it as a majestic homesite. The hunter agrees to the purchase. However, during the process of the sale it is discovered that the entire property is owned as tenants in common with the other hunters. Thus, according to the title of ownership, all of the hunters own an equal and undivided interest in all parts of the property as a whole. Consequently, all of the hunters would need to consent to the sale and share in the profits.

*Point for Discussion:* If all of the hunters agreed to the sale, would the hunter designated for that portion of the property sold lose his tenancy in common in the property as a whole?

When tenants in common (or other types of multiple ownership tenants) cannot agree on the rights and use of the property, then a legal action for partition may be brought by one or more of the tenants. In a *partition action,* the court divides the land into individual portions and creates an individually owned portion of land for each party. The effect of this is to equitably extinguish the tenancy in common and create two or more fee simple tenancies. Another possible result in such a situation would be for a tenant to buy the interest of another tenant and thus convert the tenancy in common to a single tenancy in fee simple.

## APPLICATION 12.3

In Application 12.2, a decision had to be made by all of the owners about what to do with the property. If no agreement could be reached and the individual hunter wanted to sell the property interest, it would be necessary to determine whether the group had any form of written partnership agreement. Assuming there was no such agreement, the hunter could ask that his interest be purchased by the other partners for an

*(continued)*

## APPLICATION 12.3  (Continued)

amount comparable to what he would have received in a sale to the proposed buyer. If the parties could not agree on a sale price, an action for partition could be filed. In this type of situation, a court would make a determination of how to equitably (fairly) split the property into equal shares for each of the hunters. At the conclusion of the partition action, each hunter would be granted a specific parcel of land as sole owners. If the hunter received the portion of land sought by the outsider, he could then sell it.

*Point for Discussion:* If the matter is resolved through a partition action, how could the offer of the private buyer who initially sought to purchase the property be affected?

When one tenant in common voluntarily sells or conveys his or her interest in the property, the new owner becomes a tenant in common with the other tenants in common. Similarly, when one tenant in common dies, the heirs of the estate become tenants in common with the other tenants in common. Tenants in common have no rights of survivorship. The exception to this rule is when the property is owned by a partnership—in this case, when a tenant in common dies, the ownership of that tenant goes to the surviving partners rather than the tenant's heirs.

In a tenancy in common, the individual's ownership interest can be conveyed during that person's lifetime, but no more than the tenancy in common interest can be transferred. In other words, one cannot convey a type of tenancy not possessed such as joint tenancy. The rights are those of tenancy in common, so that is all that can be transferred. This will become clearer as the other types of tenancy are explored.

**Joint Tenancy.** Joint tenancy must be specified in the instrument that transfers the property: the deed. It is generally accepted that **joint tenancy** includes the **right of survivorship**[9]—that is, when one joint tenant dies, the remaining joint tenants automatically take ownership of the property. The heirs of the deceased owner have no claim or inheritance.

Simply stated, the right of survivorship means that when a party to joint tenancy dies, the interest automatically vests by operation of law in the other tenant or tenants. In this way, the joint tenancy among surviving tenants is preserved. However, technically, a new joint tenancy is created when each surviving tenant simultaneously receives an undivided right of possession from the deceased party. The previous rights of the parties remain the same, and there is usually no requirement to formally create a new joint tenancy through a new deed.

The right of survivorship restricts a party's interest from flowing naturally to the descendants. Because of this, it is necessary for a party involved in a joint tenancy to formally agree from the outset that there is the intent to create such an interest. In this way, the heirs are protected from losing an interest in property when it was not the desire of the deceased to do so.

For joint tenancy to exist, the joint tenants must establish four common points of ownership called *unities:*

1. Each tenant must have received his or her interest in the property at the same moment (unity of time).

2. The interest for each must come from the same source—namely, the previous owner (unity of title).

**joint tenancy**
A form of multiple property ownership whereby the property owners have fee simple and share four unities, and each owner shares in the right of survivorship.

**right of survivorship**
A characteristic associated with multiple property ownership in which the ownership interest transfers automatically to surviving co-owners on death of an owner rather than passing by will or intestate succession.

3. Each tenant must have identical rights regarding the property such as an equal share (unity of interest).

4. Each party must have an undivided interest in the land itself (unity of possession).

Thus, the only way to have a joint tenancy is when the multiple owners agree to it with the intent of right of survivorship among themselves and they purchase the entire property at the same time, from the same owner, in equal shares, and with an undivided right of possession. If all of the preceding occur and a state statute does not indicate otherwise, the parties also receive the right of survivorship. In some states, the statute requires that the intent for a right of survivorship be specified in the conveying instrument (usually the deed). If no such statute exists, then the right is usually presumed from the words *joint tenancy* in the deed.

It should be recognized that a joint tenancy exists only so long as the four unities exist. When one party conveys his or her interest in the property to an outsider, only the remaining original joint tenants remain as joint tenants. The new owner is a tenant in common. The important effect of this is that the new tenant does not have a right of survivorship should one of the original joint tenants die.[10] Consequently, if any party conveys any right to title or interest or possession in the property, then the joint tenancy as to that party is destroyed. Any conveyance to another would violate the unity of time and title because the new recipient would obtain an interest at a different time and from a different source than the other owners. Joint tenancy is also severed when a party conveys his or her interest to other members of the original joint tenancy.

## APPLICATION 12.4

Kirk, Janice, Patrice, and Yolanda are siblings. They want to purchase a retirement home for their mother and father. The four siblings purchase a home as joint tenants and move their parents into the property. Three years later, Kirk and Janice are traveling together when they are killed in an accident. Patrice and Yolanda would inherit Kirk and Janice's interest through right of survivorship. Shaken by the unexpected turn of events, Patrice is extremely concerned that if something happened to her and Yolanda, the property would fall through the estates to their children. This would not be so bad except Yolanda is divorced with small children. Her ex-husband would likely have some control over the assets of the children. Her ex-husband and her parents have such bitter feelings that all are subject to restraining orders to keep them from being around one another. Yolanda and Patrice sell one-half of the property interest to their parents. The parents would receive tenant in common interest and Yolanda and Patrice would remain as joint tenants.

*Point for Discussion:* Does the sale of the property interest as tenants in common ensure that the parents would receive the entire property interest on the deaths of Yolanda and Patrice?

The basic rights of joint tenants are similar to those of tenancy in common. The joint tenant can use and possess the property in any way that does not waste the property or interfere with the rights of the other joint tenants. However, a joint tenant cannot successfully devise (give) his or her interest to heirs in a will. Such conveyance would take place after the owner's death, which would violate the right of survivorship. Therefore, a bequest in a will does not sever the joint tenancy and will not be honored if a right of survivorship exists in the joint tenancy.

When the right of survivorship does exist, it occurs by operation of law—that is, it is automatic on the death of a joint tenant as a matter of law, and the wishes of the tenant expressed in a subsequently probated will are not considered. Consequently, if a joint tenant wants to sever the joint tenancy, then such severing must be done before death by legal conveyance of one or more of the unity interests to another.

# CASE
## *Morgan v. Cornell,*
### 939 So.2d 344 (Fla.App. 2nd 2006)

This opinion examines the importance of clear language in transference of real property interests such as a life estate.

The specific devises of the will at issue state:

"(E) If I own the home [in] New Hampshire at my death, I leave said home and real estate together with the contents therein to Julia H. Morgan for the term of her life, subject to the obligation to pay all real estate taxes, upkeep, insurance and ordinary costs of ownership, with a remainder interest in fee simple as Tenants in Common to her children . . . , *per stirpes.*

(F) If I own the home [in] Naples, Florida at my death, I leave said home and real estate together with the contents therein which were purchased by Julia and myself to Julia H. Morgan for the term of her life, subject to the obligation to pay all real estate taxes, upkeep, insurance and ordinary costs of ownership, with a remainder interest in fee simple to my children . . . , as Tenants in Common. . . ."

The personal representative of Mr. Cornell's estate, his daughter Elizabeth L. Cornell, filed a petition seeking construction of these conditional devises, alleging that the condition—"If I own the home"—is unclear in extent, nature, and meaning. On one hand, the word "own" could be read to mean "to the extent I own the home," so that the specific devises would be effective for whatever interest the testator possessed at his death. On the other hand, the word "own" could be interpreted more strictly, so that the condition would be fulfilled only if the testator were the sole owner of each home at the time of his death. If the second interpretation were operative, the condition would fail and the testator's interest in the homes would become part of the residuary estate and pass to his three children.

In their motion for summary judgment, Mr. Cornell's two sons contended that the language was unambiguous and could be construed in only one way: the devise would be effective only if their father owned one hundred percent of the property at the time of his death.

The trial court agreed with the sons and made the following ruling:

There is no genuine issue of material fact. The language in the will regarding the specific devises of real property is not ambiguous. If Mr. Cornell is not the 100% owner of the specified properties, then the specific devises will fail and Mr. Cornell's interests in the properties will pass through the residuary clause.

An appellate court, like the trial court, must examine the language of the will to ascertain the testator's intent." The intention of the testator as expressed in his or her will controls the legal effect of the testator's dispositions. "§ 732.6005(1), Fla. Stat. (2005); *In re Estate of Budny,* 815 So.2d 781, 782 (Fla. 2d DCA 2002). Ascertaining intent is a court's paramount objective in construction of a will. *Wilson v. First Fla. Bank,* 498 So.2d 1289, 1291 (Fla. 2d DCA 1986).

In construing the key language of these devises—"If I own the home"—we must assume the testator meant what he said, see *Filkins v. Gurney,* 108 So.2d 57, 58 (Fla. 2d DCA 1959), and give the words their usual meaning, see *Estate of Martin,* 110 So.2d 421, 422 (Fla. 2d DCA 1959). We agree with the trial court that the language contains no ambiguity. However, the trial court erred when it read into the plain language of the devise a limitation on the kind of ownership required to trigger the condition.

The Cornell sons assert that *Elmore v. Elmore,* 99 So.2d 265 (Fla.1957), is exactly on point and controls this case. In *Elmore,* the testatrix sought to devise one particular acre of a ten-acre parcel to a Mrs. Turner. The testatrix, however, owned an undivided one-half interest in the land as a tenant in common with her son. Because she did not have fee simple title to the parcel and had not partitioned the acreage before her death, as a tenant in common she could not convey a specific portion of the whole property to a third person, and the third person could not become the sole owner of the conveyed property.

*(continued)*

The *Elmore* court noted that an "attempt to alienate a specific, located portion of the interest of a tenant in common is voidable at the election of the grantor's co-tenants. . . . Obviously, the plaintiff [the testatrix's son] in this case has elected to avoid the devise of one acre to Mrs. Turner." *Id.* at 266. The court concluded that the testatrix had misconceived "the character and extent of her estate," *id.* at 267, and the devise to Ms. Turner failed.

In contrast, Mr. Cornell did not attempt to devise a particular portion of the real estate to a third party; instead, he devised his entire interest to Ms. Morgan, the co-owner. And there is no question that Mr. Cornell knew that he owned these properties as a tenant in common with Ms. Morgan.

As did the court in *Elmore,* we attribute to the word "own" its usual meaning in the context of the disposition of real property. To "own" means to "rightfully have or possess as property; to have legal title to." *Black's Law Dictionary* 1137 (8th ed.2004). Land ownership, in particular, encompasses the dual concepts of actual physical control and the right to use and enjoy the land:

> While it is usual to speak of ownership of land, what one owns is properly not the land, but rather the rights of possession and approximately unlimited use, present or future. In other words, one owns not the land, but rather an estate in the land. This is, in some degree, true of any material thing. One owns not the thing, but the right of possession and enjoyment of the thing.

Bryan A. Garner, *A Dictionary of Modern Legal Usage* 633 (2d ed.1995) (quoting 1 H.T. Tiffany, *The Law of Real Property* § 2, at 4 (B. Jones ed., 3d ed.1939)).

The parties in this case agree that Mr. Cornell and Ms. Morgan owned the real properties as tenants in common. When two persons own property as tenants in common,

A and B each owns in his own name, and of his own right, one-half of Blackacre. . . . It means that each owns separately one-half of the total ownership. . . . Each is entitled to share with the other the possession of the whole parcel of land. Each may transfer his undivided one-half interest as he wishes so long as the transfer does not impair the possessory rights of the other tenant in common. Each may transfer his undivided one-half interest by will. . . . The central characteristic of a tenancy in common is simply that each tenant is deemed to own by himself, with most of the attributes of independent ownership, a physically undivided part of the entire parcel.

Thomas F. Bergin & Paul G. Haskell, Preface to *Estates in Land & Future Interests* 58–59 (1966). The estate of a tenant in common is both inheritable and devisable. *Tyler v. Johnson,* 61 Fla. 730, 55 So. 870 (Fla.1911).

As a tenant in common, Mr. Cornell owned a physically undivided part of each entire parcel in New Hampshire and in Naples. Without question, Mr. Cornell did "own" the property at the time of his death; the ownership condition was fulfilled; and each devise validly passed a life estate in his undivided half interest to Ms. Morgan—just as he intended.

Our construction of this unambiguous language is further bolstered by Mr. Cornell's significant omission of any language limiting his ownership in the devise; he did not say "if I solely own the property."

Reversed and remanded for further proceedings consistent with this opinion.

## Case Review Question

What could have been done by the testator to prevent this type of dispute over the terms of his will?

---

**tenancy by the entirety**
A form of multiple ownership of property between spouses that includes the characteristics of joint tenancy, including the right of survivorship.

**Tenancy by the Entirety.** The last and least common type of tenancy is **tenancy by the entirety,** which is held by husband and wife. Many states no longer recognize this tenancy as different from joint tenancy; those that do often require it to be specified in the deed. This type of tenancy includes the presence of the four unities. In addition, the unity of person (that the tenants be husband and wife) is necessary. Tenancy by the entirety also has the right of survivorship: When one spouse dies, the other receives the property as the sole owner in fee simple.

Tenancy by the entirety cannot be conveyed because of the unity of person requirement. Any conveyance by one spouse would result in a tenancy in common between the remaining spouse and the new purchaser. The interest of a tenant by the entirety also cannot be conveyed by a will to another person. Nor is the interest of one of the tenants subject to claims of nonjoint creditors. By operation of law, when one spouse dies and there is a tenancy by the entirety, the surviving spouse automatically receives the entire share of the property. Thus, because the property has already been transferred, there is nothing to pass under the terms of the will.

## ASSIGNMENT 12.2

Consider the following chain of ownership of a particular tract of land. For each owner, identify the type of tenancy.

In 1934, Sid and Zelda purchased 12 acres of land at the edge of the city. Because they were married, each had a right of survivorship in the property interest. During the years 1934 and 1940, Sid built twelve houses (one per acre) and installed a common street for access to the houses. They lived in one house and rented the others. During the years 1940 and 1945, Sid and Zelda gave each of their six children a house as a wedding gift. In 1950, Sid and Zelda divorced. They did not address the ownership of the property in the divorce. Sid simply moved into one of the rental houses. During the years 1962 and 1966, each of the first four grandchildren of Sid and Zelda who married were given houses as a gift on college graduation. In 1968, Zelda married Alan, and at that time she and Sid each took sole possession of one of the houses. In her will, Zelda gave Alan the right to live in the house she occupied until he relinquished possession or died. Sid and Zelda each willed all of their property interests in the land to their first great-grandchild. In 1980, Zelda died. Sid and Alan both died in 1982.

## Air and Subsurface Rights

Since the early days of property principles in common law, it has been held that the ownership of property extends below the property to the center of the Earth and above the property to the top of the sky.[11] With respect to moving waters, when a nonnavigable stream flows on property, the owner possesses the bed of the stream but not the water flowing on it because that water is not a permanent part of the land. Navigable streams are part of the public domain, and ownership of property adjacent to them generally extends to the shore.[12]

As population and technology have grown, these concepts have been altered slightly but, remarkably, the basic principle still holds true. Although an owner possesses all of the property to the very heights, the public necessity of flight cannot be abridged, and it overrides the right to control the entire sky above one's property. Similarly, although an owner is entitled to control a streambed on the property, the course of the bed cannot be changed so as to substantially alter the flow of water across another's property because such change could flood the adjacent land or deprive downstream owners of the use of the water.

The owner has the right, consistent with these rights above and below the land, to sell or lease these portions of property (except that which is controlled for public use). For example, the owner of a condominium on the twelfth floor of a high rise actually owns the air space occupied by that condominium. However, the owner is not entitled to alter the construction of the air space because—as with moving land or water—such change would invade another's right over his or her own property. Similarly, one who owns the land can sell the rights to property below the land's surface—for example, sell mineral rights to another and allow the person to set up a drill to obtain oil or other deposits from beneath the land.

## Incorporeal Interests

In the law of property, the term *incorporeal interests* describes rights or privileges associated with ownership of real property. One such right that is highly protected is the right of quiet enjoyment. It is presumed that the right to possess real property automatically includes the right to such possession and use free from interference by others. When someone invades another's property, in effect, he or she is invading the right of quiet enjoyment. A corresponding area of incorporeal interests deals with the law of *easements*—that is, the legal rights of nonowners to affect the use of the owner's real property. Essentially, this area of law permits the holder of the easement a limited right of interference with the property otherwise protected by the right of quiet enjoyment. The law of easements is fairly complex and is only briefly introduced here.

**Easements.** An *easement* is a right of one other than the owner to affect the property owned. In simpler terms, it is a limited legal right to invade the right of possession and quiet enjoyment of a property owner.[13] The property that is affected is sometimes referred to as the *servient tenement* (it serves someone other than its owner). The party with the right to affect use of someone else's property is known as the *dominant tenement* (it dominates the servient owner). An easement is not a right to possess part or all of the servient tenement, rather the limited right to use or control the use of the servient tenement. This is often only a portion of the property. If an easement is *in gross,* the dominant tenement is the right of a specific person or group to use the servient tenement, and this right cannot usually be transferred (although some commercial or business easements in gross are transferable). If an easement is *appurtenant,* the dominant tenement is a specific parcel of land whose owner has the right to use the servient tenement, and this right passes to each new owner of the dominant tenement.

An easement is an interest associated with real property and is therefore subject to the statute of frauds, which, as will be discussed in Chapter 13, requires that certain legal transactions be in writing before a court will enforce them. Among them is the transfer of any interest in real property. If real property or an easement affecting it is conveyed, conveyance must be done in writing to be effective. Therefore, the voluntary creation or continuation of an easement must be in writing before a court will enforce it.

An easement can be created in several ways. Three common methods are easement by *prescription, easement by necessity* (or *implication*), and *easement by conveyance* (or *grant*). An easement by prescription is when the right to control a portion of property is developed over time through open and consistent use and control over the property. This is similar to the adverse possession method of gaining title to real property discussed later in this chapter. An easement of necessity (implication by circumstances) can be created when no other reasonable alternative exists to satisfy the rights of others. Because all property is adjacent to other property, it is somewhat common for the use of one's property to interfere with another's. An easement created by necessity may be without the consent of the owner but, unless agreed to by the owner, must be recognized by a court before it can be enforced. Easement by conveyance occurs when a party voluntarily grants an easement affecting his or her property. Often this is an easement in gross and done in exchange for compensation of some type, such as the right to drill for oil on another's land. Finally, an easement can be created by prescription when a landowner acquiesces to someone else's use of his or her land without permission for a certain period of time. A prescriptive easement is similar to adverse possession, which is discussed later in the chapter.

Easements are classified in two ways. The first is known as an *affirmative easement* and occurs when the party holding the dominant tenement has the right to enter onto the servient tenement for a particular purpose.[14] This could be having the right to cross the land of another party to reach one's own property when no other reasonable means of reaching it exists.

## APPLICATION 12.5

Maurice purchased an acreage in the mountains on which he planned to build a dude ranch. Most months of the year, he would be able to drive directly onto the property by using a dirt road that winds back and forth along the side of a steep hill. Because the property is so far away from any commercial development, the cost to pave the road would cost more than the property itself. However, during at least two months during winter and often in the typical wet weather of May and June, the road is often to muddy or slippery to navigate safely. The adjoining property has a much more level access road and ends just at the boundary line. Maurice wanted to create a road on his property that would lead to the road of the adjoining landowner. The landowner refused. Without the access, Maurice stood to lose a large portion of his seasonal business. Maurice estimated approximately fifteen weekly guests would bring vehicles onto the property and leave seven days later. In addition, Maurice needed access approximately two times per week to go into town for supplies. It is likely with this limited use a court would allow the average of seventeen travelers per week, eight weeks per year, to use the road when balanced with the development of Maurice's property versus nondevelopment because of a lack of access.

*Point for Discussion:* What argument could the adjacent landowner advance to try to prevent granting of the easement?

The other type of easement is known as a *negative easement*: the right to prevent certain uses of property by the owner of the servient tenement because these uses would adversely affect the rights of the dominant tenement.[15]

## APPLICATION 12.6

Candice, a homeowner, decided to erect a shed at the back of her property to store lawn equipment and other items. She dug down about 6 inches and poured a 10-foot by 20-foot concrete slab 12 inches thick. She erected a brick building on the foundation that matched the exterior of her home. Two years after the storage building was completed, she arrived home from a two-week vacation to see the contents of the building on her lawn, the building demolished, and the foundation jackhammered into gravel. Where the building once stood, a hole had been dug and then filled. Candice was in a rage. It only grew when the utility company stated that the building was on its easement and it had no obligation to make repairs beyond covering up the hole in the ground.

*Point for Discussion:* Why would the utility company not have to replace the shed and foundation it destroyed?

## ASSIGNMENT 12.3

Examine the following situation, determine what easements, if any exist. Then identify the dominant and servient tenements and whether the easements are affirmative or negative.

Three cattle ranches adjoin one another. Ranches A and B have a natural waterway that flows through them. Ranch C has no natural water source, and the rocky soil is such that it would not be feasible to drill a private well. Rancher C wants the right to cross the property of Ranch B to obtain water for his cattle. Rancher B needs to cross Ranch A to gain access to the public roadway. The only other access is by boat. Rancher A purchased the right to mine for silver on the property of Rancher C, but the only way to reach the mine is to cross the property of Rancher B. Rancher A cannot erect buildings or graze cattle within a 2,000-foot perimeter of the mine.

## CASE

### *The Arrechea Family Trust v. Adams,*
### 2006 WL 3008158 (Miss.App.)

The following case discusses not only easements but also the value of an easement transformed by adverse possession into what is essentially ownership.

This case commenced upon John Palmer Adams' filing of a petition for easement naming the Arrechea Family Trust and David and Katherine Reed (Trust) as parties. By way of a warranty deed executed on March 31, 2004, Adams acquired his landlocked property, the dominant estate, from the Estate of Johnnie Jackson, which Johnnie Jackson initially purchased on June 9, 1959. In his petition, Adams asserted that for at least thirty years Jackson continuously used for ingress and egress a fifteen-foot-wide easement, running north to south, over the servient property presently owned by the Trust. The current record title owner of the servient estate, the Trust, received the property by virtue of a quitclaim deed executed on October 5, 1996, and recorded shortly thereafter on October 18, 1996. Prior to the Trust's ownership of the property, John and Lois Arrechea owned the servient estate since January 5, 1992. Earlier record title ownership was held by Lambert and Dorothy Hill from October 17, 1973 until January 5, 1992. The record also reflects that both the dominant and servient parcels of land were carved and derived from the same tract of land, Original City of Oxford Lot Number 601.

Adams contends that while his predecessor, Jackson, held title to the dominant estate, he accessed the public street, University Avenue, by crossing the Trust's servient estate from 1959 until Jackson's death in 1999. Adams further contends that for more than three decades, Jackson traversed this property under claim of ownership, with actual possession, openly and notoriously, continuously and uninterrupted, which far exceeds the statutory requirement of ten years. Miss.Code Ann. § 15-1-13 (Rev.2003). However, the Trust contended that Jackson had used the easement by permission and consent of the Hills from 1973 and the Arrecheas since 1992.

The chancellor granted Adam's motion for summary judgment, finding that upon review of the pleadings, taken together with numerous affidavits, plats, photographs and other evidence, there existed no genuine issue of material fact disputing whether a prescriptive easement existed across the Trust real property to the landlocked property of Adams. Jackson had fulfilled the ten year requirement for prescription from 1959 through 1969. Therefore, although the Trust presented evidence regarding consent to the use of the driveway in the years of 1973 and 1992, this consent was inconsequential to the easement already vested with Jackson prior to these years.

. . . There exists three methods of creating easements: by prescription, by implication, or by grant. *Simcox v. Hunt,* 874 So.2d 1010, 1017(¶ 32) (Miss.Ct.App.2004). An easement may be acquired by ten years possession, just as may a fee simple title. *Rutland v. Stewart,* 630 So.2d 996, 999 (Miss.1994). A prescriptive easement is created when there has been ten years of use that is (1) open, notorious, and visible; (2) hostile; (3) under a claim of ownership; (4) exclusive; (5) peaceful; and (6) continuous and uninterrupted. *Myers v. Blair,* 611 So.2d 969, 971 (Miss.1992). Each of these aforementioned elements are discussed below. Consent for use of property from the record title owner will make the use permissive and not adverse, as required for a prescriptive easement. *Id.*

### (1) Open, notorious and visible

Neither Adams nor his predecessor in title, Jackson, attempted to hide the use of the driveway as a means of ingress and egress to the property. Jackson used the easement from 1959 until his death in 1999, and most importantly between the years of 1959 and 1969 without consent from the record title owner. Several affidavits attested that the owners of the servient property, including the Arrecheas' predecessors in title, the Hills, were aware of Jackson's open and visible use of the drive. Additionally, an excerpt from the Minute Book of the City of Oxford confirms the city's recognition of the easement to both the Hills and Jackson for access to University Avenue, therefore establishing that Jackson's use was notorious. The evidence shows that Jackson's use was sufficiently open, notorious and visible.

### (2) Hostile

"[U]se by express or implied permission or license, no matter how long continued, cannot ripen into an easement by prescription since adverse [or hostile] use is lacking." *Myers v. Blair,* 611 So.2d 969, 971 (Miss.1992). The Trust claims that there is no proof that Adams' or Jackson's use of the driveway was adverse or hostile to the Trust's predecessor in title. Adams maintains that neither he nor his predecessor, Jackson, requested permission from the Trust or their predecessors in title. Case law mandates that Adams is not required to prove the negative: that his predecessor, Jackson, was not given permission to use the easement, but that the Trust was to prove that Jackson was given permission for use. Morris, 792 So.2d at (¶ 9). The Trust was unable to prove that consent was given to Jackson during the years between 1959 and 1969. No evidence was presented that demonstrated that Jackson or Adams made a request for permission to use the easement for ingress and egress to the property during the applicable periods of time for prescription. Hostility is further evinced by proof that an antiquated chain-link fence is positioned between the dominant and servient estates crossing the easement.

"Where . . . a use of the lands of another for roadway purposes has been open, visible, continuous, and unmolested since some point in time anterior to the memory of the aged inhabitants of the community, such use will be presumed to have originated adversely.'" *McCain v. Turnage,* 117 So.2d 454, 455 (Miss.1960). Reviewing the record, we find that the Trust offered no evidence which would rebut this presumption that the easement was created hostilely. The parties do not dispute any material fact concerning a request for permission for use of the property during the significant period of time, 1959 until 1969, when the possession ripened into title. Thus, because the Trust has not alleged that permission for use of the property was granted during the applicable time periods for prescription, the Trust cannot divest Adams' of title which had already ripened during the period of time necessary to create a prescriptive easement.

### (3) Under claim of ownership

At trial, the evidence showed that Jackson had used the easement as his own by giving permission to others to use the easement in order to reach his home. This use by Jackson gave a reasonable inference to the community that the driveway was owned by him. The Trust presented no evidence to the contrary. Therefore, we find the evidence sufficient to support a claim of ownership.

### (4) Exclusive

The evidence presented through testimony, survey plats, and other observations to the lower court concerning the use of the easement support the conclusion that the easement was used strictly by Adam's predecessor, Jackson, and presently by Adams as a driveway and not for public use. There is no other purpose for the easement than to enter and leave the property of Adams. Therefore, the evidence presented is sufficient to support a finding of exclusive use.

### (5) Peaceful

The mere existence of a dispute over the use of land does not present an obstacle to satisfy the element of peaceful use. Simple disputes often arise between neighboring landowners, but do not rise to the level of destroying the peaceful existence between them. *Dieck v. Landry,* 796 So.2d 1004, 1009(¶ 15) (Miss.2001). No evidence is presented establishing a non-peaceful existence between the Trust and Adams and their respective predecessors in title. Therefore, this element of prescription is satisfied.

### (6) Continuous and uninterrupted use for ten years

The evidence clearly demonstrated that the easement had been in use for a ten-year period. Jackson began to use the easement in 1959 when he purchased the property. This use continued well in excess of the statutorily proscribed time period. Although the record reflects that permission for use was granted in the years of 1973 and 1992, the prescriptive time period

*(continued)*

had already been satisfied and the easement had vested in 1969.

## CONCLUSION

We agree that the lower court was correct in finding that a prescriptive easement existed prior to 1992 when the Arrecheas purchased the property now titled to the Trust. Adams presented adequate proof that the use of the easement was open, notorious and visible; hostile; under claim of ownership; exclusive; peaceful; and continuous and uninterrupted for ten years. Although Adams, himself, only owned the property for approximately one year before filing his petition, his use is tacked onto the use of his predecessor, Jackson. In reviewing this case in the light most favorable to the Trust, taking together admissions in pleadings,

answers to interrogatories, depositions, affidavits, testimony presented at trial, etc., we find that no genuine issue of material fact exists. We, therefore, affirm the grant of summary judgment by the Chancery Court of Lafayette County in holding that a fifteen foot wide prescriptive easement exists over the Trust property for ingress and egress to the Adams property.

THE JUDGMENT OF THE CHANCERY COURT OF LAFAYETTE COUNTY IS AFFIRMED. ALL COSTS OF THIS APPEAL ARE TAXED TO THE APPELLANT.

### Case Review Question

What is the difference between an easement by consent and one obtained through prescription? How did this one change in nature?

## Buyers' and Sellers' Rights

Persons who have not previously been involved in the sale of real property are not aware of the many issues that must be addressed before such a sale is completed. The sale generally includes not only the buyer and the seller but also a broker, a mortgagor, a financier, and an attorney, as well as others who play a necessary role in completing the transaction.

Documents associated with the sale of property include the following:

1. purchase agreement (seller agrees not to sell to another; buyer pays earnest money as a deposit) (see Exhibit 12.1);

2. mortgage or financing agreement (agreement between buyer and party financing the sale for repayment);

3. deed (used to record the transfer of title);

4. required government forms (used to make necessary records of property transfers within a state);

5. required inspections (often required by government and also customary for parties to produce certificates of inspection of the property, such as a termite certificate, and to ensure the property is structurally sound);

6. escrow agreement (written agreement between buyer and seller as to who— usually an independent party—will hold the earnest money deposit during the completion of the transaction);

7. buyer and seller agreements (often called *contract for deed,* used when the seller finances the sale and turns over the deed to the property when the buyer has completed payment); and

8. title policy (an insurance policy from a title company that guarantees that it has searched the chain of title to the property, that no other claims to the property are superior to the prospective buyer, and that the seller has the right to convey the title).

Although it is generally true that conveyances of title to real property must be in writing under the statute of frauds, an exception is recognized in some jurisdictions. Under the doctrine of part performance, if a substantial portion of the purchase price has been paid and actual possession of the property has been turned over, the transaction will be enforced.[16] The court infers from the actions

**Exhibit 12.1** Purchase Agreement

**THIS IS A BINDING CONTRACT, IF NOT UNDERSTOOD SEEK COMPETENT LEGAL ADVICE.**

The undersigned BUYERS agree to purchase and the undersigned OWNERS agree to sell the real estate and all improvements located at _____

Upon the following terms:

$_____ shall be Earnest Money evidenced by personal check to be deposited upon acceptance of this offer as deposit on the purchase price. Said Earnest Money shall be deposited in escrow in an interest-bearing account at _____ Bank and shall not be subject to withdrawal prior to closing unless this Contract should become null and void and for failure of one or more of the conditions of sale set forth in this Agreement. Upon closing, said Earnest Money shall be paid directly to OWNERS. In the event this contract fails due to any fault, neglect, or intentional breach by BUYERS, said _____ Earnest Money and all interest accrued thereon shall be paid directly to OWNERS. In the event this contract fails due to any fault, neglect, or intentional breach by OWNERS, said Earnest Money and all interest accrued thereon shall be paid directly to BUYERS.

$_____ Balance due on the specified date of closing, upon delivery of Warranty Deed conveying merchantable title free and clear of liens and encumbrances except easements, restrictions, and covenants of record, and which have been made known to BUYERS.

$_____ :Purchase Price.

This sale is contingent upon BUYERS obtaining a home mortgage at a fixed rate of _____% plus one point or less, for a term of no less than 3 years amortized over 30 years. Loan to be applied for within 10 days and approved within 30 days. Appraisal to be equal to or greater than the purchase price. BUYERS and OWNERS agree to pay in equal shares costs of closing, including but not limited to title insurance and recording fees. Closing to be on or before 90 days from the date of this contract.

Upon acceptance of the terms by OWNERS, the Earnest Money shall be applied as part payment on the purchase price but shall be held in escrow prior to closing as stated above. If this offer is rejected by the OWNERS, or if title to said premises is not merchantable or cannot be made so within sixty (60) days after written notice is delivered to OWNERS stating the defects, or if no effort is made to make the said property merchantable by OWNERS, this contract shall be null and void and all earnest money shall be refunded to BUYERS who shall have no further

claim against the OWNERS. If this sale is not consummated within 30 days of the closing date stated above, time being of the essence, because of neglect or failure on the part of the BUYERS to comply with the terms and conditions herein agreed to, then all Earnest Money shall be forfeited and this Contract shall be of no further binding effect. But such forfeiture shall not release BUYERS from any liability for the fulfillment of this Contract of sale if OWNERS shall, within 30 days after BUYERS have defaulted, give BUYERS written notice by certified mail of their intention to sue.

The property is to be conveyed by good and sufficient Warranty Deed and insured Title Policy, in an amount equal to the purchase price, showing merchantable title free and clear of all liens and encumbrances except easements, or restrictions of record, or those which the purchaser agrees to assume as part of the purchase price as herein set forth. OWNERS shall pay all costs and expenses necessary to convey title in fee simple.

OWNERS shall maintain fire and extended coverage insurance on the premises until the date of closing. In the event the premises shall be destroyed or damaged prior to closing, BUYERS shall have the option to accept the insurance settlement and complete the transaction or to declare this Contract void, and thereupon all deposits made hereunder shall be refunded to the BUYERS. BUYERS shall make said election within seven (7) days after receipt of written notice of the injury to the property.

Real estate taxes, utilities, and sewer charges due, if any, shall be prorated as of the date of closing or the date of possession, whichever is later, taxes to be prorated on the last known tax bill which buyers agree to assume and pay accordingly.

BUYERS have personally inspected the property and are accepting it in its present condition, with the exception of any contingencies listed. OWNERS agree to maintain the heating, sewer, plumbing, and electrical systems and any built-in appliances and equipment in normal working order and to maintain the grounds and to deliver the property in the same condition as at the time of inspection by BUYERS.

OWNERS hereby warrant that prior to the execution of this instrument, neither they nor their agent has received any notice issued by any city, village, or other governmental authority, of a dwelling code violation upon the premises herein described.

It is understood and agreed that only the personal property listed below is included in the sale: all built-in appliances, water softener, all ceiling fans, computerized temperature monitor and sensors, custom-made draperies, 2 garage door openers with remote controls, retractable clothesline.

*(continued)*

**Exhibit 12.1** Continued

OWNERS agree that any personal property left upon the premises after delivery of possession has been abandoned by OWNERS and becomes the property of BUYERS. OWNERS agree to leave premises in a clean condition, free of all litter and debris.

In the event OWNERS shall remove any personal property included in this Contract, or any improvements, OWNER(s) shall pay BUYERS in an amount equal to the replacement or repair cost of the item or items so removed or damaged.

OWNERS agree to vacate the premises prior to closing and shall pay a rent from the date of closing the sum of $_____ per month in advance for each month or portion thereof OWNERS remain in possession of the premises.

OWNERS to provide a termite certificate showing no active infestation.

This agreement shall be binding upon the parties hereto, their heirs, executors, administrators, and assigns.

This sale is subject to the terms and conditions set forth in this agreement.

We, the BUYERS, hereby agree to purchase the above-described property on the terms above and agree to pay the price of $176,000 for said property.

Dated: _____

Buyer: _____

Buyer: _____

We, the OWNERS, hereby approve the above sales agreement and agree to sell the above described real estate for $ _____

Dated: _____

Accepted by Owner _____

Accepted by Owner _____

Dated: _____

Accepted by Buyer _____

Accepted by Buyer _____

of the parties that the parties intended the conveyance of the property, and the court will require the parties to complete the transaction. The courts are divided on this issue, and many states require a written agreement to enforce completion of a real property transaction.

Even when a written agreement exists, the problem often arises as to responsibility for the property during the completion of the purchase requirements. The numerous documents and other transactions associated with the purchase of property are not prepared overnight. A sale of property often takes two to six months to complete. During this time, what happens if the property is damaged or destroyed? What if the property is discovered to have a claim on it? What if the seller wastes the property? These are all issues that have arisen in the past.

Although there is some variation among the courts, general principles have been established. Generally, if something occurs during a pending sale that damages or destroys the property through no fault of the seller, the liability for the loss is on the buyer.[17] An example is a house that is destroyed by fire and the house is the only real asset of the property. The seller may require the buyer to complete the sale. If the property is only damaged and repair is feasible, the seller is given a reasonable amount of time to adequately repair it, and the buyer may be held to the purchase agreement. Because the buyer bears some risk of loss, the buyer may also insure the property to the extent of the risk, even though title has not yet passed.

A minority of jurisdictions place the cost of loss from a casualty on the seller. However, the most common occurrence is that the purchase agreement will specify who bears the risk of loss. If it is the buyer, then the buyer has a valid interest that can be insured even though title to the land has not yet been formally passed.

If some defect or irregularity in the title is discovered, the seller is given a reasonable amount of time to cure the defect and is generally allowed to use part of the purchase price to do so.[18] If, for example, there is a government lien on the property for back taxes, the seller would be allowed a reasonable amount of time to raise the money to satisfy the tax debt or would be allowed to accept the purchase price and pay the debt before conveying title. Ordinarily, the purchase price and title are conveyed simultaneously.

All sellers are under a general duty to care for the property and prevent it from waste during the time necessary to complete the sale. In the sale of real property with dwellings on it, a seller is also under a duty to convey the property in habitable condition (generally interpreted to mean safe for occupancy and having access to utilities).

Not all duties, however, are on the seller. The courts do apply the theory of *caveat emptor:* "Let the buyer beware."[19] Under this theory, a purchaser of property has the limited duty to reasonably investigate and discover defects in the property. Failure to do so can result in the court's refusal to rescind the purchase agreement or require the owner to repair the defect. If, for example, a buyer notices an air-conditioning unit outside the house, he or she should not assume that the unit works properly. Questions regarding the working order and age of all appliances and portions of the house that might require replacement or repair should be asked. Then, if the seller makes representations that turn out to be false, the buyer may have recourse in actions for breach of an express warranty or fraud.[20] Any of the generally accepted duties of buyer and seller can be altered by agreement.

## CASE
### *Nicosia v. Mayzler,*
### 2006 WL 2934077 (N.J.Super.A.D.)

The following opinion demonstrates the old adage "Buyer Beware," which has its roots in the law of real property.

We incorporate by reference the judge's findings of fact contained in his oral opinion of June 8, 2005, summarizing them briefly as follows. The parties entered into a contract for the sale of defendants' house, grounds and swimming pool. The contract contained the customary inspection clause, and plaintiff had the premises inspected in a timely fashion with the exception of the pool. After the contract had been signed, plaintiff asked defendants to allow him to have a company fully open and inspect the pool. When defendants refused, plaintiff did not tell his lawyer about the dispute and proceeded to attend the closing and accept the deed. In pertinent part, the deed provided as follows:

ALL REPRESENTATIONS AND/OR STATEMENTS MADE BY SELLER . . . SHALL NOT SURVIVE CLOSING OF TITLE. This means that the Seller DOES NOT GUARANTEE the condition of the premises AFTER the deed and affidavit of title have been delivered to the Buyer at the "Closing."

When plaintiff had the pool opened the next day the defects were discovered. Defendants did not know of the defects and had no reason to know of them.

The trial judge applied the covenant of good faith and fair dealing, but it is inapplicable here. The governing principle was expressed in *Dieckman v. Walser,* 114 N.J. Eq. 382, 385 (E. & A.1933): It is the general rule that the acceptance of a deed for land is to be deemed *prima facie* full execution of an executory agreement to convey, and thenceforth the agreement becomes void, and the rights of the parties are to be determined by the deed, not by the agreement. In *Levy v. C. Young Construction Co., Inc.,* 46 N.J.Super. 293 (App.Div.1957), aff'd 26 N.J. 330 (1958), that principle, taking into account the exception for a seller's fraud or concealment, was applied to deny recovery to a purchaser who had closed title in a case involving a sale by a builder. *Id.* at 297. Although the Supreme Court affirmed, it did not do so for the reasons expressed by the majority opinion below, noting that it did not have to decide "[w]hether the widely established rule followed below is harsh and inequitable and should be rejected, or whether it is sound and workable. . . ." *Levy, supra,* 26 N.J. at 334. In *T & E Industries, Inc. v. Safety Light Corp.,* 123 N.J. 371, 388 (1991), however, the Court described this doctrine as the law of New Jersey, to be applied except when the seller "conceals or fails to disclose" a condition that he "knew or should have known" existed and that the buyer was not likely to discover. Since the trial judge correctly found that the exceptions were not applicable here, defendants were entitled to judgment.

Reversed and remanded for entry of judgment for defendants with costs.

### Case Review Question

What could the buyer have done to avoid this suit and still close on the sale of the property?

## Adverse Possession

Not all real property is obtained by purchase or gift. The law has created a method by which a party can gain good title to land simply by using the land. The theory of *adverse possession* is recognized as a means of obtaining title to property without consent or voluntary transfer by the owner when certain conditions are met. The reasoning behind adverse possession is that the government encourages the productive use of land, and if the owner does not productively use the land and does not protect the right to possess owned property, then the law will recognize ownership in one who will.

Although every state has a statute setting the requirements, the following elements are usually needed to prove title by adverse possession:[21]

* open and notorious possession,
* continuous possession,
* exclusive possession, and
* adequate duration of possession.

*Open possession* requires that the person seeking title by adverse possession actually possess the property. This does not mean that the person must spend the days walking the boundaries. However, the adverse possessor must act in such a way that others, including an alert property owner, would perceive such actions as those of one exercising control over the entire property. An example is farming a large acreage or building a permanent home on the property.

*Continuous possession* is designed to prevent transients and squatters from claiming title to the property. The law does not propose to vest title in anyone who wants the property. Rather, it gives title to persons who show an ongoing concern for the property. Therefore, it is necessary to exercise control or possession of the property in a way that is perceived as continuous. Abandonment for a significant time will prevent this element from being proven.

*Exclusive possession* is necessary to show that the person claiming title by adverse possession acted in a way to exclude others from possessing the property. Until all the elements are sufficiently met, this does not apply to the original owner. The true owner of the property who becomes aware of someone else possessing the property can retrieve it. However, after the statutory period, the adverse possessor has the right to exclude others from the property, for example, by erecting "No Trespassing" signs.

The final element requires the adverse possessor to do all of the preceding for a specified period of time—that is, for an *adequate duration*. Statutes vary on the length of time, but generally, the provision requires possession for a period of five to twenty years. The reasoning is that possession should be for a period of time that not only demonstrates a continuing intent to utilize the land but also gives the true owner every opportunity to reclaim his or her property.

Many states as well as the federal government do not permit claims of adverse possession over their land. Those that allow such claims do so only in specified areas. For example, national parks are not subject to claims of adverse possession. Preservation of these large areas of protected wilderness takes precedence over any needs or rights of private individuals.

Adverse possession can be established even though a series of different persons actually possessed the property during the specified period of time. When this occurs, it is called *tacking* and is allowed only under certain circumstances. When a statute permits tacking, it usually requires succeeding owners to be descendants or heirs, a spouse, or someone who was voluntarily granted possession during the life of the first adverse possessor.[22]

The law gives every chance to the original owner to retain the rights of title to the property. However, when there is a total failure to utilize property for a significant period of time and there is a party who would make beneficial use of the property, adverse possession takes effect.

# CASE
## *Stokes v. Kummer,*
### 85 Wash. App. 682, 936 P.2d 4 (1997)

The following opinion demonstrates the development of a successful claim of property through adverse possession despite knowledge by the property owners who purchased title of the use of the property by the adverse possessors.

SCHULTHEIS,

JUDGE.

The court denied Duane Stokes, Sandra Baker, Terry Johnson and B. G. Knight's claim for ejectment and quieted title to three parcels of land used by brothers Terril Kummer, Arlan Kummer and Kevin Kummer for dry land wheat farming, based on their adverse possession of the fields for more than 10 years. The court also granted the brothers a 75-foot easement across Mr. Stokes's and Ms. Baker's property, for access between two of the fields. On appeal, Mr. Stokes, Ms. Baker and Mr. Knight contend the Kummers' use of field 2 was permissive at its inception, negating the element of hostility required to demonstrate adverse possession. Mr. Johnson contends the Kummers conceded his superior title in 1982 by not contesting an easement he granted to others and did not prove adverse possession for a sufficient period thereafter. All of the appellants contend biennial cropping of agricultural land is insufficient use to establish title by adverse possession. We affirm.

The property at issue in this case is in a fairly desolate part of Kittitas County, accessible only by a gravel county road. The region is rocky and arid, covered mostly with sagebrush and tumbleweeds. There are pockets or hummocks of soil, however, that are suitable for dry land wheat farming. Aerial photographs show the three fields at issue have been cultivated since at least 1954. Sometime during or before October 1971 the quarter section where these fields are located, the northeast one-quarter of Section 33, Township 17 North, Range 18 East, Willamette Meridian, and the quarter section immediately west, the northwest one-quarter of Section 33, Township 17 North, Range 18 East, Willamette Meridian, were divided into tracts of roughly 20 acres each. The platted subdivision, known as the Valley View Ranch tracts, was not recorded. Nor was it surveyed, permanently staked or fenced. The appellants each own a Valley View Ranch tract underlying the three wheat fields that the Kummer brothers have been farming since 1976. See the field survey map attached as an appendix.

It is unclear from the record when Lawrence Hall began growing winter wheat in the area, but in 1953 he leased from Agnes C. Meagher "all that certain crop land owned by [her] and lying within a certain fenced area" in the northeast one-quarter of Section 33 to grow wheat. The lease was for four years, from October 1, 1953, to October 1, 1957. Mary Hall married Lawrence Hall in 1956, and in 1957 moved to the old homestead house on his property south of Umptanum Road and west of Durr Road. Mrs. Hall said that when she moved out to the property, Mr. Hall was farming the same fields across the road (Umptanum Road) that the Kummer brothers later farmed. Mr. Hall originally farmed some of the property north of the road for Estil Wright under a crop share agreement, but later bought that property.

On January 28, 1976, the Kummer brothers bought out the Halls. They acquired title to 2,540 acres, including that part of the northeast one-quarter of Section 33 lying south and east of Umptanum Road, and most of the northwest one-quarter of Section 34, which borders the Valley View Ranch tracts on the east. Mr. Hall drove them around the various fields on the property and also gave the Kummers a 1954 aerial photograph of the area. It shows numerous wheat fields, which are irregularly spaced and shaped due to uneven topography and soil.

In March 1976 the Kummers moved onto the property and began farming the same areas Mr. Hall had farmed, including the three fields just north of Umptanum Road. There were no fences, posts or other markers suggesting the northeast one-quarter of Section 33 had been divided into parcels. The Kummers have continuously harvested wheat from all their fields every other year, beginning in 1976—except one year in the early 1980s when they participated in a federal program and ended up harvesting in an odd year, 1981. During crop years they reseed the fields if necessary early in the season, spray later for weeds, harvest the wheat with a combine, and, when soil moisture permits, plow the stubble under in the fall. During the intervening fallow years, they plow, cultivate, fertilize and seed the fields. Every year the Kummers post the perimeters of their wheat fields against trespassing and hunting, and they regularly tell people to get off the land during hunting season.

Meanwhile, S & S Enterprises, Inc., was selling Valley View Ranch tracts. Duane Stokes acquired tract 40 in

*(continued)*

August 1988 by quitclaim deed from his parents, who had bought it in approximately 1972. When Mr. Stokes first visited the property in fall 1973, he observed most of it was sagebrush, but there was evidence the northern part had been farmed. It looked substantially the same when he next visited in fall 1980—he saw wheat stubble on the northern end. When he last visited in fall 1991 it looked the same, "like somebody had plowed the field."

Sandra Baker (nee Burchfield) acquired tract 41 in June 1973 by deed from S & S Enterprises, after her brother assigned her his interest under a 1971 purchase contract. She first visited the property shortly after she acquired it and was thoroughly unimpressed. It was dry, arid and rocky, covered with sagebrush and tumbleweeds. She visited the property again in the early 1980s, twice in one year, but she only looked at the tract from the road. She did not walk the property and could not see the northern part of it. She did the same thing once more later in the 1980s. Every visit was during winter. Until the lawsuit, she had never seen the north end of the property where the wheat fields extend onto it.

B.G. Knight acquired tract 36 in the 1970s from Melvin and Emma Orness, who deeded the tract to him in January 1980 in fulfillment of his contract with them and their 1971 purchase contract. He saw only a picture of the property when he bought it and it was apparent from the picture that it had been farmed. He learned about the Valley View Ranch tracts from Alex Varunok, a close friend and fellow Boeing employee, who had bought tracts 34 and 35.

In 1978, Mr. Varunok approached the Kummer brothers and told them they were farming on property north of Umptanum Road that did not belong to them. He showed them a deed and a map. After some discussion and correspondence between Terril Kummer and Mr. Varunok, they reached a lease agreement. On May 7, 1978, Mr. Varunok signed a handwritten "farm lease/share agreement," apparently drafted by him, in which Kevin Kummer agrees to farm tracts 35 and 36, belonging to Mr. Knight and Mr. Varunok, and to provide 25 percent of the gross proceeds of the 1978 and 1979 crops and thereafter 33 1/3 percent. Mr. Knight signed on May 8 and Kevin Kummer signed on May 17 at the request of his brother Terril. Terril Kummer then returned the signed lease agreement to Mr. Varunok with a note advising him that they normally harvest wheat every other year, so the next crop after 1978 would likely be 1980.

On November 20, 1978, Terril Kummer sent Mr. Varunok a note and a check for $1,035. In August 1979 Terril Kummer sent Mr. Varunok a letter and newspaper article explaining they had had serious crop damage from grasshoppers. On November 1, 1981, Terril Kummer sent Mr. Varunok a note and a check for $1,810.90. In June 1983, the Kummers bought tracts 34 and 35 from Mr. Varunok. They continued farming field 2 as they always had, believing they now owned the tracts underlying it.

Mr. Knight received his share of the 1978 and 1981 lease payments from Mr. Varunok. He never met or talked with any of the Kummer brothers. Though he did not receive any payments after 1981, he did not ask Mr. Varunok about it. When Mr. Knight visited his property in winter 1982 or 1983, he noticed it had obviously been farmed in wheat because there was wheat stubble on part of it and sagebrush on part. Mr. Knight visited his property probably once more in the 1980s and again in about 1991, both times in the winter. He said he assumed somebody would send him money if the Kummers farmed his property, and since he was not receiving any money, he concluded they must not be farming it. Mr. Knight did not try to contact the Kummers until approximately 1991 or 1992, when he learned from a Realtor that his property was being farmed. At that time, he was unable to locate a telephone number for the Kummer brothers and did not pursue the matter further.

Finally, Mr. Johnson acquired tract 39 in December 1990 by quitclaim deed from his parents, who had bought it in September 1975 from the original purchasers, Derwin and Avis Lisk. Mr. Johnson first saw the property in 1975 just before the Lisks transferred it to his parents, and at that time, part of it was a wheat field, early fallow or stubble. Tract 39 is divided roughly into western and eastern halves by a road that provides access from Umptanum Road to the north. The road was not shown on the unrecorded plat map, but it was there when the Johnsons bought the tract and Milo England had been using it to get to his property ever since he bought his acreage in summer 1976.

Mr. England remembered the fields on either side of the road had been farmed when he moved there, and that the Kummers had farmed both fields since 1976. In fact, they crossed the road to get from one field to the other and when they did not raise their tractor attachments high enough they disturbed the already rough road surface. In October 1982, Mr. England contacted the Johnsons, after determining from county records that they owned tract 39, and asked if they knew their property was being farmed. They apparently did not. Terry Johnson visited the property and ascertained it was being farmed by the Kummers. He met with Mr. England and Earl and Lorna Lyon, who also used the road to get to their property, and on behalf of his parents gave them a recorded, handwritten easement to use the road.

Mr. Johnson also met with at least two of the Kummer brothers. He advised them he was giving the Englands and the Lyons an easement and discussed the Kummers' farming of his property. According to Mr. Johnson, he insisted the Kummers sign a written lease with him and agree to pay something for the crops they had taken in previous years, or he would not give them permission to continue farming. No agreement was reached, but the Kummers continued farming as they always had. Mr. Johnson returned in January or February 1987, and once again in winter 1990. Both times the property was just as it was when he first saw it in 1975. He did not contact Mr. England or the Kummers after October 1982.

The tract owners, all of whom live west of the Cascade Mountains, joined in this ejectment suit. The Kummers were served on January 12, 1994, and the summons and complaint were filed on March 18. They answered, and counterclaimed to quiet title in themselves under the doctrine of adverse possession. After a two-day bench trial in February 1995, the court quieted title to the three wheat fields in the Kummers and granted them a 75-foot easement across tracts 40 and 41 for access between fields 1 and 2. The tract owners appeal.

## Adverse Possession

In order to establish a claim of adverse possession, there must be possession that is (1) open and notorious, (2) actual and uninterrupted, (3) exclusive, and (4) hostile, all for a period of 10 years. *ITT Rayonier, Inc. v. Bell*, 112 Wash.2d 754, 757, 774 P.2d 6 (1989); RCW 4.16.020. Because the presumption of possession is in the holder of legal title, the party claiming adverse possession has the burden of establishing each element. *ITT Rayonier*, 112 Wash.2d at 757, 774 P.2d 6. Adverse possession is a mixed question of law and fact. Whether essential facts exist is for the trier of fact; but whether the facts, as found, constitute adverse possession is for the court to determine as a matter of law.

## Field 2

Tract owners Mr. Stokes, Mr. Knight and Ms. Baker contend the Kummers farmed field 2, covering much of the Knight tract and a small portion of the Baker and Stokes tracts, after they received permission to do so under the May 1978 lease agreement. They assert permissive use is not hostile and does not commence the running of the prescriptive period. They argue the permissive use of this wheat field could not ripen into a prescriptive right unless the Kummers made a distinct and positive assertion of a right hostile to the owners.

As the Kummers point out, and the court found, Mr. Stokes and Ms. Baker were not privy to the lease and could not gain any benefit from it. The Kummers established they adversely possessed those parts of tracts 40 (Stokes) and 41 (Baker) that they and their predecessor Mr. Hall had farmed continuously from the 1950s into the 1990s, including the prescriptive easement granted by the court.

With respect to Mr. Knight, use of his property was not permissive at its inception, though it may have been from mid-1978 to mid-1983. The lease does not make it clear that Mr. Knight was the Kummers' landlord for any specific property, or that he owned one of the tracts outright. The court found the statutory period began running at the latest in June 1983, when the Kummers bought tracts 34 and 35 from Mr. Varunok.

The tract owners assign error to the finding that the Kummers thought they were buying the 40 acres covered by the Varunok and Knight lease. The finding is supported by the evidence, although it is not necessary for a determination of adverse possession since it is irrelevant whether they appropriated the land knowingly or by mistake. *Chaplin*, 100 Wash.2d at 860, 676 P.2d 431.

As the court pointed out in its memorandum decision, the assertion that the Kummers never repudiated the lease is without merit. Apart from questions whether it was ever valid or whether it terminated with Mr. Varunok's sale of his tracts, the sale itself signaled a significant change in the parties' relationship. Mr. Varunok had handled all aspects of the lease arrangement, including paying Mr. Knight his share; Mr. Knight had never even spoken with any of the Kummer brothers. When Mr. Varunok advised Mr. Knight he was selling out, Mr. Knight was put on notice he would have to make different arrangements regarding the lease, which, as previously noted, did not specify his interest in any event. He did nothing. That fall, when he did not receive a lease payment, he again did nothing. He did nothing until this suit was commenced in January 1994 by service on the Kummers, and by then it was too late.

Possession is hostile when one holds property as his own, whether under mistaken belief or willfully. Here, after they bought the two tracts upon which they thought their wheat field was located, the Kummers no longer made lease payments because they held the property as their own. They continued to farm it openly and they kept the proceeds from the crops. The Kummers' actions were of such open, notorious and hostile character that Mr. Knight would have known they were farming his land, had he looked or inquired.

## Fields 1 and 3

Mr. Johnson contends the Kummers did not prove adverse possession for the requisite 10 years. First, he

*(continued)*

argues they did not establish tacking because Mr. Hall farmed the property under a 1953 lease and Mrs. Hall recalled he farmed some property north of Umptanum Road under a verbal agreement with another landowner. There was no evidence that Mr. Hall's occupancy was anything other than permissive; thus, if there was adverse possession it could not have begun before 1976.

The evidence establishes Mr. Hall farmed both fields from 1957 to 1976, but it does not establish he did so under a lease or with other permission. The property descriptions in the 1953 lease and Mrs. Hall's deposition testimony are too vague to determine what property was covered. The evidence also does not establish Mr. Hall possessed the property adversely, except that the Johnsons never gave anyone permission to farm tract 39. Under these circumstances, the earliest the prescriptive period could begin was September 1975, when the Johnsons acquired their interest.

Second, Mr. Johnson argues the Kummers deferred to and acknowledged the superior title of Mr. Johnson to the tract 39 wheat fields in October 1982 when they permitted him to grant and record an easement to Mr. England and the Lyons.

From 1976 when they acquired their property from the Halls, the Kummers' use of fields 1 and 3 was open, notorious and hostile. By at least October 1982, Mr. Johnson had actual notice they were farming his land. He confronted them and told them he owned the property, wanted payment for crops already harvested, and would not allow them to continue farming his land unless they executed a written lease. Had the Kummers stopped farming, Mr. Johnson's actions would have interrupted their possession and restarted the prescriptive period. But they did not. They continued farming the fields just as if they owned them, not in a manner indicating recognition of or subordination to Mr. Johnson.

Mr. Johnson's grant of the easement was nothing more than permission for the Englands and the Lyons to use an existing road to access their properties. That did not interfere with or interrupt the Kummers' use of the fields on either side of the road. The Kummers' possession of the fields was (1) exclusive, (2) actual and uninterrupted, (3) open and notorious, and (4) hostile. Because he failed to effectively assert his own ownership over the fields (as opposed to the road) for more than 10 years after acquiring actual knowledge of the Kummers' adverse possession, Mr. Johnson lost his title.

Finally, the tract owners contend adverse possession cannot occur by cultivation of open farm land for crops harvested on a biennial basis when the land lies fallow in the intervening years.

The contention is completely without merit. The use and occupancy of the property need only be of the character that a true owner would assert in view of its nature and location. *Chaplin,* 100 Wash.2d at 863, 676 P.2d 431. That requirement is easily met by the Kummers' dry land farming of these fields in precisely the same manner they farm the rest of their acreage in the area. Ample evidence, including the aerial maps and the testimony of some of these tract owners, demonstrates just how visible is the Kummers' use of the property. As the surveyor put it, when asked if he had any difficulty discerning the difference between the fields and the surrounding property: "It's either field or sagebrush."

The decision of the superior court is affirmed.

SWEENEY, C.J., and BROWN, J., concur.

## Case Review Question

What is meant by the term *quiet title?* Why is it used in adverse possession proceedings?

---

## ASSIGNMENT 12.4

Situation: Steve owns property on which he has a quick shop. He erects a large, lighted sign next to the driveway on land that actually belongs to the adjoining property owner, a fundamentalist church. The owner does not object because Steve often advertises "Church Specials" for persons who attend services at the church. After twenty years, Steve dies and his son moves into town and converts the shop into a nude dancing establishment, which he advertises on the sign. The church demands the sign be removed.

Question: Does the church meet the requirements of adverse possession?

# Rights and Duties of Ownership

As stated previously, ownership of property generally includes the right of possession and control free from interference of third parties. Often called the *right of quiet enjoyment,* this right protects the right of one to do with one's own property as one pleases. Although this right is strongly protected by the law, certain obligations accompany it.

**Public or Private Nuisance.** The first obligation is not to use one's property in such a way that it becomes a public or private nuisance to surrounding areas. A *private nuisance* is a use that has a direct adverse effect on specific persons[23] such as unreasonable noise or noxious fumes emitted from the property or any continuing conduct that is harmful or poses a danger in some way to certain persons in the area. If this conduct continues, these persons have a right of action for private nuisance. They can sue in equity to have the conduct cease, and they can sue at law for damages as a result of the nuisance.

A *public nuisance* is one that generally has a continuing adverse effect on the public good, welfare, or safety.[24] Even though entirely done on one's own property, conduct can be considered a public nuisance if its effects extend beyond the property. An example is a manufacturing plant that pollutes a waterway or emits noxious fumes over a broad area. If such harmful conduct becomes a continuing problem, then public authorities may bring an action for public nuisance (1) at equity to stop the conduct and (2) at law to seek compensation for damages already incurred. Generally, a private party cannot bring an action for public nuisance unless the party's injury is different from that to the general public.

**Condition of Property.** Basic obligations also exist regarding the condition of one's property for persons entering it. This includes trespassers, licensees, and invitees. Some states treat licensees as invitees. In other states, the obligations toward each are different. However, all are owed some degree of protection from harm even if trespassing on the property.

*Trespassers.* A trespasser is one who enters onto another's property without consent of any kind by the owner. The law does not offer any special protections to persons who violate the right of quiet enjoyment belonging to a landowner. However, the landowner does owe a duty to keep the property free from unreasonable dangers that a trespasser could not be expected to discover. There is no general duty to warn or take action to protect, only the duty to correct conditions that would cause injury or to give notice of these conditions.[25] (The owner's rights against a trespasser are discussed in Chapter 15.)

*Licensees.* Licensees are persons who enter with the permission of the landowner but are not associated with the landowner's business. For example, a person hunting on property with permission free of charge and a person attending a party are common types of licensees. In states that distinguish between licensees and invitees, the obligation of a landowner toward these persons may be slightly greater than that owed trespassers. With respect to licensees, a landowner owes a general duty to warn of dangers present on the property. The reasoning is that because they are there by consent or invitation, the landowner owes a greater duty to see to their safety. This duty is somewhat broader than the duty toward trespassers and requires additional action on the part of the landowner.[26]

*Invitees.* The invitee is invited (expressly or impliedly) to the property of the owner for business purposes—for the purpose of obtaining benefit for a business or for reasons of employment. Consequently, shopkeepers and landowners have a duty to actively inspect their premises to protect their invitees from harm.[27] For example, a grocery store owner has a duty to clean up a spill in one of the aisles and to restore the aisle to a safe condition in a reasonable time. An owner who does not do so could be held liable for injuries to anyone who steps on the area, slips and falls, and is injured.

Although the privilege of quiet enjoyment is protected, the law recognizes that there are those who would abuse the privilege, and there are always occasions of persons entering on the property of others for various reasons. Consequently, the imposing of these basic duties on the landowner places the landowner under minimal obligation in return for virtually unlimited use of the property.

## Condominiums

A somewhat specialized area of law is that regarding condominiums. The concept of owning property that has both freehold and nonfreehold interests is not new. Records dating to medieval Europe indicate that this type of land interest existed even then. It was not unusual at that time for a person to purchase a room, apartment, or floor of a building. The owner of the building would maintain any hallways or surrounding yard. This type of ownership occurred primarily in crowded cities, where land and entire buildings were too expensive for the majority of the population. For many reasons, including the lack of established principles setting forth responsibilities of the parties to such an arrangement, this type of property ownership saw a decline. In recent times, however, with the problem of crowded cities, fast-paced lifestyles, and rising costs of purchasing and building homes, the concept of condominiums has dramatically increased in popularity, especially in the United States.

A condominium is a freehold interest. It is an absolute ownership in the property described. The property is real in that it is inextricably attached to the land. However, it may be located far above the actual soil and has specific dimensions without traditional air and subsurface rights. A condominium, however, has some nonfreehold characteristics as well. Condominium ownership usually involves collateral obligations to abide by certain rules regarding the use of the property, payment of fees for the maintenance of surrounding areas, and restrictions on the sale of the property. Consequently, condominiums are a hybrid of landlord–tenant (nonfreehold) estates (discussed in the following section) and ownership in fee (freehold) estates.

The owners of adjoining condominiums are considered to be owners by tenancy in common over the air and subsurface rights. They are owners in fee simple over their own particular building or portion of a building. Because of this individual–multiple ownership between persons who do not have common interests and are usually strangers, all fifty states have enacted laws to govern the establishment and running of condominium complexes.[28]

Usually, a condominium complex is established by developers, who create a document known as a *declaration* to dedicate its use to that type of ownership. A plan created to provide for the ongoing needs of the complex allows for a committee to make decisions regarding upkeep of the property, collection of fees from the owners for standard maintenance, and enforcement of any restrictions regarding purchase or sale of the property.

Although it is permissible to impose restrictions on owners regarding the sale and purchase of their condominiums, these restrictions cannot be unconstitutional or even unreasonable. The law has been clear that restrictions based on race, religion, sex, or nationality are not permitted.[29] Furthermore, a restriction that is so enforced that it effectively prevents the owner of disposing of the property may be considered unreasonable.

---

## APPLICATION 12.7

The Humane Homes Condiminium complex was developed by a group of retired pet lovers who found it difficult to find condominiums that allowed pets. Joy was just such an individual and the owner of a tiny poodle. She purchased a condominium at the Humane Homes and promptly moved in, happy to be among other animal lovers. She purchased the retirement property through an online real estate firm. Her particular property had been for sale for quite some time, and she felt she got a great deal. She never visited the property because she lived several thousand miles away. She retired and a few weeks later arrived to move in. What she did not realize was that her adjacent condominium neighbor owned several primates. The smell was overwhelming, not to mention the noise created by the animals as they romped through the condominium. She approached the condominium board about changing the restrictions to disallow animals that affected the overall property value. The board members agreed but stated the owner of the primates was an attorney and threatened a prolonged legal battle at great expense to the condominium association if it attempted to remove him. Many of the current owners were descendants and heirs of previous owners who had been unable to sell their condominiums because of the primates' noise and smell. In this case, if the bylaws were amended to restrict the number and types of pets allowed, it would likely be upheld because of the effects on the rights of the tenants as a whole in terms of property value. In essence, continuing to allow such animals would have the same effect as a restriction on the property that prevented owners from disposing of their portion of the property.

*Point for Discussion:* If a restriction against primates was enforced as a reasonable restriction, then why would a restriction against either men or women as owners not be considered reasonable?

---

Because the owners of the individual units are tenants in common over the air and subsurface rights and common areas, their obligations are equal as landowners. Therefore, if a trespasser, licensee, or invitee is injured on a common area through negligence, the owners are equally liable for the injuries. Consequently, the courts do allow some restrictions so that owners can ensure that they will become tenants in common with reasonable persons.

As more people become property owners and consider that property to be their most significant asset, they have an interest in protecting the property value. For this reason, many areas now have homeowners' associations. These groups of homeowners in a particular area create an organization in which all homeowners consent to certain restrictions on their property to maintain certain standards within the community. Restrictions range from colors used on the exterior of homes to the presence of outbuildings, types of fences, types of exterior construction, and number and types of vehicles parked on or adjacent to the property. The rationale is that by giving up some degree of the right of quiet enjoyment, the value of the property will not be reduced by other property owners who might not otherwise maintain their property in a similar manner.

## Nonfreehold Estates

**nonfreehold estate**
An interest in real property that is limited in duration and involves the right of possession but not ownership.

In addition to interests associated with freehold estates of ownership, numerous nonfreehold estate interests are present in U.S. property law. **Nonfreehold estates** are those that include specific rights to possess property, control it, and even exclude the true owner. However, these estates generally are by agreement, are for a fixed time, and do not include any rights of ownership. One who possesses a nonfreehold estate cannot convey ownership, the party in possession does not have the right to waste the property, and the possessor must return the property to the true owner at the agreed time or on proper eviction proceedings. Most often, this relationship between owner and possessor is that of landlord and tenant and is governed in part by property law and in part by contract law.

Nonfreehold estates are commonly called *leaseholds*. The parties are generally referred to as *landlord* and *tenant*. Leaseholds may or may not be in writing, depending on the specific nature of the agreement. Generally, agreements that will extend beyond one year must be in writing under state law according to a statute of frauds because the agreement involves real property. Basic elements should be present for an oral or written leasehold agreement to be valid. Each party must have contractual capacity—that is, each party must have reached the age of majority or be considered legally competent or both. A clear agreement to give and accept possession of the property on specified terms must exist. A description of the property must be included that adequately describes the exact premises of which the tenant will have possession.[30]

The terms of the agreement should be clearly understood. If the agreement contains an option to renew and the option is not formally exercised but the tenant remains in possession beyond the original term, then the leasehold becomes one at will. This and other types of leaseholds and tenancies are discussed subsequently. It is important, however, to first understand the rights and obligations of a landlord and tenant.

**Rights and Obligations of Landlord and Tenant.** The landlord and tenant each have basic rights and obligations associated with nonfreehold property interests (see Exhibit 12.2). The landlord has the duty to turn over the property free from latent (not reasonably discoverable) defects or dangers and to ensure that the property is habitable.[31] Although the definition of habitability varies from state to state, it is presumed to be that which is absolutely necessary to make a premises one on which persons can reasonably be expected to live. Typically, habitable property has access to electricity, hot water, shelter from the elements, and, in some states, heat. If the landlord fails to provide these things or fails to continue them during the term of the agreement, then the warranty of habitability is violated and the landlord is presumed to have breached the terms of the lease agreement.

In contrast, the tenant is responsible to prevent waste from occurring on the property, to discover patent (reasonably obvious) defects or dangers, and to make ordinary repairs.[32] If a significant patent defect exists or occurs, the tenant is obligated to notify the landlord and to give the landlord a reasonable opportunity to repair it. If the defect does not affect habitability, such as a clogged sink, the tenant is generally responsible for the repair; in many states, any costs of having the sink cleared would be the responsibility of the tenant.

### APPLICATION 12.8

Stephen rented an apartment in the back of a house that was occupied by the landlord. When he moved into the apartment on August 1, Stephen signed a one-year lease agreement to pay $400 per month for rent and utilities combined. The only thermostat

*(continued)*

## APPLICATION 12.8 (Continued)

in the house was in the part occupied by the landlord. The landlord spent a good deal of his time staying with a girlfriend. As a result, when the furnace was turned on in early October, the thermostat was set at 54 degrees by the landlord to save on the cost of utilities. As the winter became colder, Stephen became increasingly uncomfortable. His requests to the landlord to raise the thermostat were ignored. On January 1, when the outside temperature was a chilly 12 degrees, Stephen had enough and told the landlord he would be moving out at the end of the week. The landlord sued Stephen for the balance of the rent. In such a case, the landlord would likely prevail. Although utilities were guaranteed, there was no definition provided with respect to the amount of heat. The property was in a habitable, albeit chilly, condition. As long as the property had some heat, shelter from the elements, and water, it would likely be considered habitable.

*Point for Discussion:* What would be the obligation of the landlord after Stephen moved out with regard to the apartment? If the landlord failed to meet the obligation, how would it affect the case against Stephen?

**Exhibit 12.2** Landlord and Tenant Law

**Excerpts from VERMONT STATUTES ANNOTATED**

**TITLE NINE. COMMERCE AND TRADE**

**PART 7. LANDLORD AND TENANT**

**CHAPTER 137. RESIDENTIAL RENTAL AGREEMENTS**

**§ 4455. Tenant obligations; payment of rent**

(a) Rent is payable without demand or notice at the time and place agreed upon by the parties.

(b) An increase in rent shall take effect on the first day of the rental period following no less than 60 days' actual notice to the tenant.

**§ 4456. Tenant obligations; use and maintenance of dwelling unit**

(a) The tenant shall not create or contribute to the noncompliance of the dwelling unit with applicable provisions of building, housing and health regulations.

(b) The tenant shall conduct himself or herself and require other persons on the premises with the tenant's consent to conduct themselves in a manner that will not disturb other tenants' peaceful enjoyment of the premises.

(c) The tenant shall not deliberately or negligently destroy, deface, damage or remove any part of the premises or its fixtures, mechanical systems or furnishings or deliberately or negligently permit any person to do so.

(d) Unless inconsistent with a written rental agreement or otherwise provided by law, a tenant may terminate a tenancy by actual notice given to the landlord at least one rental payment period prior to the termination date specified in the notice.

(e) If a tenant acts in violation of this section, the landlord is entitled to recover damages, costs and reasonable attorney's fees, and the violation shall be grounds for termination under section 4467(b) of this title.

**§ 4457. Landlord obligations; habitability**

(a) Warranty of habitability. In any residential rental agreement, the landlord shall be deemed to covenant and warrant to deliver over and maintain, throughout the period of the tenancy, premises that are safe, clean and fit for human habitation and which comply with the requirements of applicable building, housing and health regulations.

(b) Waiver. No rental agreement shall contain any provision by which the tenant waives the protections of the implied warranty of habitability. Any such waiver shall be deemed contrary to public policy and shall be unenforceable and void.

(c) Heat and water. As part of the implied warranty of habitability, the landlord shall ensure that the dwelling unit has heating facilities which are capable of safely providing a reasonable amount of heat. Every landlord who provides heat as part of the rental agreement shall at all times supply a reasonable amount of heat to the dwelling unit. The landlord shall provide an adequate amount of water to each dwelling unit properly connected with hot and cold water lines. The hot water lines shall be connected with supplied water-heating facilities which are capable of heating sufficient water to permit an adequate amount to be drawn. This subsection shall not apply to a dwelling unit intended and rented for summer occupancy or as a hunting camp.

The tenant is bound by the terms of the agreement and is expected to pay the rent and to give reasonable notice when vacating the property, commonly referred to as *quitting the property*. The tenant has the right to quiet enjoyment.

If either party substantially fails to meet his or her responsibilities, then such failure may be treated as a breach, and the innocent party has the right to terminate the agreement. A landlord's failure to meet the required obligations is termed *constructive eviction*.[33] In other words, the tenant is left in a position where he or she has no reasonable choice but to vacate the premises.

The landlord does not necessarily have to intentionally fail to meet his or her legal responsibilities. In cases where the property is so damaged by fire or otherwise damaged that it becomes uninhabitable, the tenant is constructively evicted. Many times, the lease agreement will allow the landlord a reasonable time to repair the premises before the lease agreement will be terminated. It is important to carefully read the lease—as all legal documents should be read!—to determine just what the obligations of the parties are with respect to damage to the property and continuation of the agreement. If the lease is effectively terminated by a constructive eviction, then the question of whether the tenant is able to recover any advance deposits depends on the terms of the agreement between the parties and whether the damage was the fault of the tenant.

Regardless of who initially breached the agreement, many states impose on both parties a duty to mitigate any damage caused by the premature end of the landlord–tenant relationship. *Mitigation of damages* is the term used when one is required to lessen or minimize the damage when possible. This prevents persons from adding to their damages to increase the amount of monetary recovery in a lawsuit. In the event the property is significantly damaged, the landlord is often required to make every reasonable effort to repair the premises and restore habitability. Further, if a tenant vacates or abandons the property, the landlord must make reasonable attempts to rent the property. The landlord cannot merely let the property stand empty and seek to collect the balance of the rent from the tenant.

The tenant also is responsible for mitigating damages. A tenant who is forced to move on grounds of constructive eviction must make reasonable efforts to minimize the cost of the move and damage to any personal property before recovering compensation from the landlord. The tenant who played a role in creating the condition that forced the constructive eviction probably has no recourse against the landlord.

**Types of Leasehold.** The type of leasehold is determined by the length of the lease, which will dictate whether the lease must be in writing under the statute of frauds. Generally, leases that are intended to extend beyond the period of one year and those that contain the option to purchase the leased property are required to be in writing. Shorter and less restrictive leases may be based on an oral agreement. However, it is always best to have the agreement in writing and signed by the parties to avoid future disputes as to the exact original terms of the agreement. (Exhibit 12.3 shows a sample lease.)

# CASE

## *Aris Vision Institute Inc. v. Wasatch Property Management Inc., et al.,*
## 143 P.3d 278, 558 Utah Adv. Rep. 29, 2006 UT 45 (Utah 2006)

The case which follows demonstrates that difficulties and expense that can arise out of a landlord failing to follow the proper steps with regard to the property occupied by a tenant who is not honoring the original lease agreement.

After Respondent Aris Vision Institute, Inc. (Aris) fell behind on its rent payment, Petitioners JDJ Properties, Inc. (JDJ) and Wasatch Property Management, Inc. (Wasatch) retaliated by refusing to allow Aris to remove its personal property from the premises for a period of five months. Aris brought a claim for wrongful eviction, conversion, and forcible detainer. The district court concluded that JDJ and Wasatch were liable and awarded treble damages to Aris for loss, damage, and depreciation of personal property pursuant to Utah Code section 78-36-10(3). The court of appeals affirmed. JDJ and Wasatch have asked us to review the decision of the court of appeals.

Aris operated a laser eye surgery clinic on premises leased from JDJ and managed by Wasatch. Aris owned the furniture and equipment in the clinic and contracted with four physicians who performed the surgeries. Following an industry downturn, Aris informed employees and vendors that it planned to terminate its business. When Aris failed to make its January rent payment, and Wasatch learned of Aris's financial difficulties, Wasatch indicated that it would not allow Aris to remove its furniture and equipment from the premises.

Aris attempted to negotiate with the physicians for the sale of the equipment and the assumption of the lease. During negotiations, the physicians were permitted to remain on the premises and continue performing surgeries. Unbeknownst to Aris, Wasatch was also negotiating with the physicians to move them into a separate space in the same complex under a more favorable lease. As a result, negotiations between Aris and the physicians failed and the physicians moved out of the premises.

In late January, Aris attempted to remove its personal property, but Wasatch forbade it from doing so, saying that Aris had abandoned the premises and defaulted on the lease. On multiple occasions, Wasatch refused to allow Aris to enter the building or to remove equipment, despite Aris's repeated offers to pay the outstanding rent. Twice Wasatch changed the locks and refused to provide Aris with keys. Eventually, Aris was allowed to enter the building to inventory the equipment under Wasatch's supervision. During one of these inventories, Aris discovered that several pieces of equipment were missing and that two of the lasers had been damaged while in Wasatch's custody. Aris attempted to sell the equipment to a third party, but Wasatch 280 refused to release the equipment unless it was given all of the proceeds of the sale. In late June 2002, after Aris initiated litigation, Wasatch finally allowed Aris to remove its personal property. Because of rapid advances in eye surgery technology, Aris's equipment had depreciated considerably, and Aris was able to sell it for only approximately one-third of what the value of the equipment would have been when Aris initially asked for its release in January 2002.

The district court found that Wasatch and JDJ were liable for wrongful eviction, conversion, and forcible detainer and awarded Aris damages for the depreciation of the property, for the value of the missing property, and for the damage to the lasers. The court then trebled damages pursuant to Utah Code section 78-36-10(3). The appellate court affirmed, and we granted *certiorari*.

On *certiorari*, we review the of the court of appeals, not the trial court. . . . Whether damages for loss, damage, and depreciation to personal property may be trebled pursuant to Utah Code section 78-36-10(3) is an issue of statutory construction, which we review for correctness. . . .

The only issue presented in this petition is whether the lower court correctly interpreted and applied the forcible detainer statute. We conclude that it did. We will first address the meaning of the statute as evidenced by the statutory language and then the scope of damages available.

When interpreting statutes, "our primary role is to give effect to the legislature's intent as set forth in the statute's plain language." *State v. McCoy*, 2000 UT 39, ¶ 9, 999 P.2d 572 In addition, "'we determine the statute's meaning by first looking to the statute's plain language, and [by] giving effect to the plain language[,] unless the language is ambiguous.'" *Dick Simon Trucking, Inc. v. Utah State Tax Comm'n*, 2004 UT 11, ¶ 17, 84 P.3d 1197.

Title 78, chapter 36 of the Utah Code deals with disputes between landlords and tenants. Section 10 addresses the remedies available in such disputes and states:

(2) The jury or court . . . shall also assess the damages resulting to the plaintiff from any of the following:
  (a) forcible entry;
  (b) forcible or unlawful detainer;
  (c) waste of the premises during the defendant's tenancy, if the waste is alleged in the complaint and proved at trial;
  (d) the amount of rent due, if the unlawful detainer is after default in the payment of rent; and
  (e) the abatement of nuisance by eviction as provided in Sections 78-38-9 through 78-38-16.

(3) The judgment shall be entered against the defendant for the rent, for three times the amount of the damages assessed under Subsections 2(a) through 2(c), and for reasonable attorney's fees, if they are provided for in the lease or agreement.

(4) If the proceeding is for unlawful detainer after default in the payment of rent, execution upon the judgment may be issued and enforced immediately.

*(continued)*

The plain language of the statute contains no apparent ambiguities. It clearly states that damages for forcible entry, forcible or unlawful detainer, and waste shall be trebled. However, because of the highly penal nature of the trebling of damages, this provision is subject to strict construction. It must be interpreted carefully and narrowly." While the statute provides for recovery of rents, damages, and waste, it is 281 damages only that are to be trebled." Thus, the issue becomes whether the term "damages" in the statute is intended to include damages to personal property. If so, then a plain reading of section 78-3-10(3) would require that damages to personal property be trebled.

Relying primarily on Judge Orme's dissent at the court of appeals, Wasatch contends that the award of treble damages is a severe remedy limited to a possessory interest in real property and that therefore damages for forcible detainer are limited to the reasonable rental value of the premises during the time for which they were detained. We disagree. Such a reading would deprive subsections of the statute of much of their meaning. This court has held that "[s]tatutory enactments are to be construed as to render all parts thereof relevant and meaningful. . . . We will avoid an interpretation which renders portions of, or words in, a statute superfluous or inoperative." *Labelle v. McKay Dee Hosp. Ctr.,* 2004 UT 15, ¶ 16, 89 P.3d 113 If the "damages resulting to the plaintiff" were intended to be limited only to reasonable rental value, the specification in subsection 2(d) that damages be assessed for "the amount of rent due" is rendered superfluous. Utah Code Ann. § 78-36-10(2) Additionally, subsection (3) makes a clear distinction between damages assessed for rent and damages which may be trebled: "The judgment shall be entered against the defendant for the rent, for three times the amount of the damages assessed under subsections (2)(a) through (2)(c), and for reasonable attorney's fees." *Id.* § 78-36-10(3).

An interpretation limiting damages to reasonable rental value would eliminate the need for this distinction. To the contrary, the specific references to "rent" indicate a legislative intent to include damages beyond those pertaining to a possessory interest in real property.

Wasatch further argues that there is no such thing as forcible detainer of personal property and that, consequently, no damages may be awarded for the loss, damage, and depreciation of personal property. While it is possible that the statutory definition of forcible detainer may not be applicable to personal property, the distinction, in this case, is irrelevant since Utah Code section 78-36-10(2) requires only that the jury or court "assess the damages resulting "from the forcible

detainer of the real property. We see no legal or logical reason why resulting damages may not include damages to personal property.

The language of the statute is clear and unambiguous. It contains no exceptions or limitations modifying the term "damages," therefore indicating that in "assessing the damage resulting to the plaintiff," the jury or the court should assess all damages resulting to the plaintiff as a result of any of the circumstances listed in subsections 2(a) through 2(c).

Absent any ambiguity, we "give effect to each term according to its ordinary and accepted meaning." *C.T. v. Johnson,* 1999 UT 35, ¶ 9, 977 P.2d 479 "Damages" is commonly defined as "the estimated money equivalent for detriment or injury sustained." Random House Webster's Unabridged Dictionary 504 (2nd ed.2001). Additionally, *Black's Law Dictionary* defines "damages" as "[m]oney claimed by or ordered to be paid to, a person as compensation for loss or injury." *Black's Law Dictionary* 393 (7th ed.1999). This court has previously said that the term "damages" is synonymous with the term "compensation." *Fuller v. Dir. of Fin.,* 694 P.2d 1045, 1047 (Utah 1985) Further, "[d]amages are based on fault [and] are generally limited only by the findings and conscience of the jury." *Id.*

Utah Code section 78-32-10 employs only the general term "damages" without any specification as to the types of damages that may be awarded under the statute. Courts are bound by the plain language of the statute. The sole qualifier that the statute places on damages which may be trebled is one of causation. The statute specifies only that the damages must be "resulting" from (a) forcible entry, (b) forcible or unlawful detainer, or (c) waste of the premises. Utah Code Ann. § 78-36-10(2)–(3) As a consequence, we now turn to the question of what types of damages qualify as "resulting" damages.

This court has held that "damages . . . are measured by the rule that they must be the natural and proximate consequences of the acts complained of and nothing more." *Forrester v. Cook,* 77 Utah 137, 292 P. 206, 211 (1930) In other words, the damages must be directly traceable to the forcible entry, forcible or unlawful detainer, or the waste committed by the defendants. A causal connection that is too attenuated, such as an unlawful detainer which allegedly results in loss of consortium, would not justify an award for damages. There must be a common sense relationship. Whether the damages claimed are the natural and proximate cause of the forcible detainer is a question of fact to be determined in the trial court.

In this case, the trial court was acting within its permitted discretion when it found that the loss, damage, and decrease in resale value to Aris's personal property was proximately caused by Wasatch's forcible detainer of the premises. Wasatch denied Aris access to its personal property for a period of five months. During the time that the personal property was exclusively in Wasatch's custody, several pieces of equipment were lost, and two lasers were damaged. Also, due to rapidly changing technology, Aris was forced to sell its equipment at a substantially lower price than it would have been able to command five months earlier.

In all three instances, the damages awarded represent the difference between the value of the personal property in January 2002, when Aris originally tried to recover the equipment, and the value of the property in June 2002, when Wasatch finally released the equipment. Pursuant to Utah Code section 78-36-10(3), the trial court was required to treble these damages. As the party successful on appeal, Aris is also entitled to

attorneys fees and costs incurred on appeal. The plain language of Utah Code section 78-36-10 clearly requires that damages resulting to the plaintiff from forcible entry, forcible or unlawful detainer, or waste shall be trebled. As the statute contains no language limiting the scope of damages, we hold that all damages directly and proximately resulting from the forcible detainer are subject to the requirement that they be trebled. We affirm the decision of the court of appeals, and remand to the trial court for the determination of the amount of attorneys fees and costs awarded to Aris.

## Case Review Question

What should a landlord do if he or she believes in good faith that a tenant is going to breach the lease agreement?

## ASSIGNMENT 12.5

In the following scenario, identify the facts relevant to the following items and to whom it applied:

duty to mitigate

duty to provide a habitable property

duty to make ordinary repairs

duty to disclose latent defects

duty to discover patent defects

construction eviction

Brad and Doug decide to move in together to save expenses. As they look around town, they see a new apartment complex going up. It is just what they want and close enough to their places of work that they could walk. They are in a large city where transportation and parking can cost as much as one's rent. They make arrangements to move into the first apartment to be completed. It is located on the second floor of a four-unit building. On January 31, they go to the complex's business office, which is located across town. They pay the first month's rent and are given the keys. They go to their respective apartments (which must be vacated by midnight) and load their moving trucks. Brad and Doug both arrive at the new apartment within minutes of each other. They enter the apartment and find that the kitchen has no sink or counters, just topless cabinets. The laundry room has not been plumbed. The bathroom has a working bathtub, but neither

the shower nor the sink is plumbed. The carpet for the apartment is still on the roll and lying in one of the bedrooms. There are no light bulbs in any of the light fixtures. They contact the landlord, who claims to have been promised by the contractor that the apartment was ready. Having nowhere to go and limited funds, Doug and Brad move in. They travel to their parent's homes each day for three weeks to shower while the apartment is being finished. They decide after one day they do not want to wash dishes in the bathtub when they cook. After that, they eat out every evening at an upscale restaurant. Finally, after three weeks, the apartment is finished. As they stand in the kitchen, Brad (an average-sized individual) jumps into the air and yells, "Yes! Finally!" As he lands on the floor, there is a tearing sound and the vinyl floor beneath him gives way. It appears that in an effort to save money, no subfloor was laid and the vinyl has been stretched across the rafters for the ceiling below. Brad fell through to the apartment below but was not seriously injured. When the next month's rent is due, instead of money, they submit to the landlord the receipts for the meals out in the amount of $1,800 (they were generous tippers) and a bill for the $500 emergency room visit for Brad to be checked out after the fall through the kitchen floor.

**Exhibit 12.3** Sample
Lease

---

# RESIDENCE LIFE
# CONTRACT

NAME _____ SOCIAL SECURITY NUMBER _____

HOME (mailing) ADDRESS _____ DATE OF BIRTH _____

STATUS _____ 1st year _____ 2nd year _____

3rd year _____ 4th year _____

HOME TELEPHONE NUMBER _____

PARENT'S NAMES FATHER _____ MOTHER _____

_____

Resident hall occupancy shall be subject to all rules and regulations of the College, including those stated in the Student Handbook. A copy of the Student Handbook is available from the Student Services Office.

**GENERAL REGULATIONS**

The same obedience to the laws of the land and the conduct rules of the College expected of students generally is also expected of students as residence hall residents, visitors or guests. Therefore, acts contrary to federal, state or local laws constitute violations of residence hall rules. Recognition of the personal and property rights of others is expected of residence hall occupants, visitors and guests. Interference with the rights of other occupants to the use of their rooms for study or sleep constitutes violation of residence hall rules. Room-to-room canvassing and unauthorized defacing or permanently altering residence hall facilities is prohibited. Only these electrical devices may be used: coffee pots, self-contained popcorn poppers, hair dryers and electric blankets. See Handbook for further information on residence hall regulations.

Date _____        _____

Signature of Student

_____

Dean of Students

---

*Month-to-month tenancy.* Also called *periodic tenancies,* month-to-month tenancies are the least restrictive. The agreement between the parties is effective for one month. Unless otherwise stated, the month is presumed to begin on the first day and end on the last day of the calendar month following the date of the agreement. This type of lease automatically renews each month thereafter until one of the parties chooses to terminate it by giving the other party reasonable notice. The states have statutes indicating what reasonable notice is. In most cases, it is the equivalent of a one-month term and would therefore be one month. Generally, notice must be given on or before the first day of a term.

## APPLICATION 12.9

Don rented a commercial building for his new business. He rented the property on a month-to-month basis because he was unsure how well the business would fare. He paid rent on April 1 and opened his business. He opened a gourmet condiment shop selling specialty ketchup, mustard, and mayonnaise. By the end of the summer, Don

*(continued)*

## APPLICATION 12.9 (Continued)

had yet to see a single month in which he was anywhere near a profit. He decided to pack it in and go back to school. He made his decision on August 2 and notified his landlord. The landlord responded that rent would be due through the end of September because August 1 had passed.

*Point for Discussion:* Why do you think the tenancy would not end on August 31 because it is thirty days from the date of notice?

*Year-to-year tenancy.* The law is basically the same for agreements to lease on a year-to-year basis. Such agreements that will extend for more than one year are required to be in writing under the statute of frauds. This type of lease may renew each year unless otherwise stated, or it may require formal renewal, depending on the terms of the agreement by the parties. The reasonable time to end a year-to-year lease is often specified in a state statute or in the agreement between the parties. A common number is three or six months. Many states have laws that limit the length of extended leases. Usually, this is not a problem for landlords and tenants because the limitation is often 100 years.

A tenant who remains in possession of the property beyond the agreed term without exercising an option to do so or without automatic renewal has no legal right to remain on the premises. Such persons are considered tenants at sufferance and can be evicted without notice. However, state statutes generally prescribe the procedure for eviction. The law does not permit "self- help." In other words, a person cannot be physically, forcibly removed from the premises by the property owner. The eviction must go through a court, and when physical eviction is ordered often is overseen by law enforcement officers.

*Tenancy at will.* An additional type of tenant is a tenant at will—one who enters or remains on the property with no certain terms of agreement. Consent of the owner is sufficient. Tenancy at will continues indefinitely and has no fixed term on which it will end. The amount of notice to end such a tenancy is usually set by statute. Often reasonable notice is considered to be one month. This type of tenancy and tenancy at sufferance are the least desirable for the tenant because he or she may be required to vacate with very little or no notice.

## ASSIGNMENT 12.6

Based on the following lease terms, answer the questions stated below.

This contract is between tenant and landlord. Said tenant and landlord agree to all terms of the contract as stated herein. The term of the tenancy shall be defined as April 1, 20— to March 31. The rent for this tenancy shall be $6,000 payable in twelve equal monthly installments due on the first of each month. The tenancy may be renewed for a period of one year at the current rent if the tenant indicates the intent and promise to renew in writing no less than ninety days before the end of the tenancy. If the agreement is not renewed, the landlord can modify the rent or end the agreement at any time upon thirty days notice to the tenant. If the agreement is not renewed as stated above, the tenant is required to provide no fewer than thirty days notice of the intent to vacate the property. Any rent remaining due on the agreement shall be due and payable at the time the property is vacated.

1. What type of tenancy exists during year one?

*(continued)*

## ASSIGNMENT 12.6 (Continued)

2. If the agreement is not renewed, what type of tenancy exists during year two?

3. If the tenant wants to renew the agreement to lock in the rent, what is the last day the written notice can be given?

4. If the tenant gives thirty days notice and moves out on December 31 of year one, what is owed to the landlord?

5. If the tenant does not renew the agreement and the landlord wants to raise the rent by

$100 more per month, what is the earliest date the rent can be raised?

6. If the tenant does not renew the agreement and decides to vacate the property on February 1 of year two, how much rent is due on the date the property is vacated?

7. If the tenant does not renew the agreement, does there need to be notice of the intent to vacate the property at the end of year one?

## Fixtures

**fixture**
An item of personal property that has been affixed to real property for a specific purpose and in a semipermanent manner.

**Fixtures** are articles of personal property that have become firmly attached to real property; they do not include houses and buildings. Fixtures are actually considered to be part of the real property in some respects because they have none of the characteristics of personal property such as being ordinarily movable. Fixtures are those items of personal property that are affixed to the real property in such a way that they cannot be easily moved without damage to the real property but are capable of being moved. Common examples of fixtures are items that have been physically incorporated into the structure but are removable such as lighting and bathroom fixtures. Typically, fixtures are conveyed when the property is conveyed.

Disputes have arisen in the past as to what is and is not a fixture when the buyer and seller both want the personal property that is claimed to be a fixture. Generally, to determine whether something is a fixture, four things are considered: (1) intent, (2) mode of annexation, (3) adaptation, and (4) damage that will result if the object is removed (significant damage to the building indicates a fixture). *Intent* means the original intent of the party who attached the personal property to the real property.[34] If intent was to make the item a permanent attachment, the law would tend to consider the property to be a fixture. The *mode of annexation* is the actual method of attaching the fixture to the real property. Personal property that was attached in such a way that it cannot be removed without altering or damaging the real property has taken on the characteristic of a fixture. Finally, *adaptation* involves the function of the personal property. If the property has become attached in a way that it serves to benefit the real property in some functional way, then it would be considered a fixture. The function need not be necessary, but it must directly enhance or benefit the property in some way other than its mere presence.

A special type of fixture is known as a *trade fixture*—an item of personal property attached to the real property for the purpose of benefiting the particular trade or business of the party who is responsible for attachment of the fixture.[35] For example, a man opening a dry-cleaning business would buy or lease property and install very specialized equipment. When he terminates ownership or possession, the presumption would be that the equipment he installed is a trade fixture and would not be conveyed with the real property but would be removed by the owner of the trade fixture. Often it is necessary to attach such items to the real property for practical purposes. In this example, however, because the equipment is necessary for the owner's livelihood, the owner is allowed to remove it when leaving the property. The owner of trade fixtures, however, has a duty to restore the real property substantially to the condition it was in before the trade fixtures were installed.

## ASSIGNMENT 12.7

In the following fact situation, identify and categorize the property as real property, personal property, fixture, or trade fixture.

Cassie owns a hair styling shop located on the ground level of a two-story building at 222 Grand Avenue. She lives in an apartment above the shop. As her business grows, she decides to move to a larger location and sell her current property. In addition to the land and building, she agrees to sell the portable stove and refrigerator in the apartment. In the sales agreement, there is no mention of the cabinets she had built in the shop that are recessed into the wall. She plans to take these with her. She also plans to take the three sinks used in her business for washing hair.

## PERSONAL PROPERTY

**Personal property** includes money, goods, and movable, tangible items.[36] Legally, personal property can be sold, lent, given, lost, stolen, abandoned, or altered. Personal property does not include land or, generally, items permanently attached to land such as permanent buildings, known as *real property*. Nor does it ordinarily include personal rights to certain intangible interests, such as the right to bring an action at law or equity (commonly called a *chose in action*). For example, if a person's car was damaged in an accident, the person could not sell the right to sue the person who caused the damage. Examples of intangible items that are considered to be personal property are patents and goodwill of a business, which are rights that are indirectly associated with movables.

**personal property**
Movable items that are not land or items permanently affixed to land. Personal property includes tangible (physical) and intangible items such as rights of ownership in property held by others (e.g., bank accounts or ownership in legal entities such as stock). It does not include the rights to bring legal action against others, commonly known as a *chose in action.*

### Bailment

Bailment takes place when one party having possession of personal property (the *bailor*) temporarily delivers possession of the property to another party (the *bailee*). The delivery is made for a specific purpose or as part of a contract (or both) with the understanding that the property will be cared for and returned to the original party on demand.[37]

Specifically, the elements of a bailment are as follows:

1. personal property,
2. transferred by a party with the right to possession,
3. to a second party for a specific purpose or as part of the terms of a contract or both,
4. that the property will be protected, and
5. that the original party has the right to reclaim the property.
6. In some cases, an additional element requires compensation in return for some act pertaining to the property.

States often have statutes that address bailment. Examples are safe deposit boxes and vehicle parking services (garages or valet parking). In the absence of statutes, general principles of common law principles of bailment apply.

**Types of Bailment.** Bailments generally fall into one of two categories. The type of bailment depends on the rights and duties of the bailee.

*Gratuitous bailment.* Gratuitous bailment occurs when one party is benefited by the bailment without obligation or benefit to the other.[38] An example of sole benefit of bailor is free storage of winter clothing by a dry cleaning establishment. Allowing the use of one's property by another without expecting compensation, such as lending a lawnmower, is an example of bailment that benefits only the bailee. In either situation, the bailee (party receiving the property) has the duty to exercise ordinary care to protect the bailed property. Ordinary care includes reasonable precautions under the circumstances.

*Mutual benefit bailment.* A *bailment for hire* or *compensation* (payment of some type) is the most frequent kind of bailment. Such bailment encompasses all occurrences of a temporary nature in which one party promises to pay some sort of compensation in return for a second party's safekeeping of personal property that belongs to the first party. In turn, the receiving party will return the property on demand or at a time provided for by contract in exchange for the compensation.[39] Additional terms of the bailment may require the performance of some duty other than safekeeping of the property. Bailments often include the duty to clean or repair property for compensation. An example is giving one's watch to a jeweler for repair. The jeweler is responsible for the care as well as the repair of the watch in exchange for compensation by the owner.

Whether property has been bailed is based on the giving party's demonstrated intent to divide the rights of possession and ownership.[40] For example, leaving a vehicle in someone else's care is not considered a bailment unless the keys are turned over because, without keys to a vehicle, the receiving party cannot exercise the control over the car associated with the right of possession. If the car is parked but the owner retains the keys, the relationship is one of a lease or license dependent on the terms and duration. The owner leases or has a license to use the space in which to park the car but retains possession of the car at all times through the car's keys. In bailment, the owner retains the title and right to ownership of the property but temporarily gives up the right to exercise possession.

When faced with a decision of whether a bailment exists and, if so, what type of bailment exists, a court will examine the relationship of the parties and determine the reasonable expectations under the circumstances. For example, if the court finds, based on the circumstances, that the two parties are close friends and often exchange property with each other, it is likely the court will find the reasonable expectation to be a gratuitous bailment, with no duty beyond ordinary care and no requirement of compensation.

Generally, the duty of a bailee is only to possess and protect the bailment from damage unless other conditions are specified by an agreement between the parties. Such an agreement can be inferred from the circumstances; in cases of a bailment for mutual benefit, the duty to care for the bailed property is greater than in a gratuitous bailment. For example, taking a coat to a dry cleaners implies that the bailor wants the coat cleaned and that the bailee will clean it in addition to holding it in safekeeping for the bailor. A compensated bailor is expected to take greater steps than mere ordinary care to protect the property. The compensation is, at least in part, for the ensured well-being of the property.

## Lost and Mislaid Property

*Lost property* is property that is separated from its owner involuntarily and accidentally,[41] whereas *mislaid property* is property that is intentionally left in a place and later forgotten.[42] Most states have statutes as well as common law principles that govern the rights and obligations of the finder of lost or mislaid property. Regarding the statutory law, some jurisdictions treat the finder of lost or mislaid property as a constructive bailee for benefit of bailor.[43] In such cases, it is implied that the finder is holding the property for its true owner. The bailee has a duty to care for the property until it is recovered and, depending on the statute, may or may not have the right to receive compensation for costs of the care of the property. If a statute permits recovery of compensation, the duties will be those of a bailee for hire, which are somewhat greater than those of a gratuitous bailee.

Other jurisdictions do not consider lost or mislaid property to be a bailment. In such states, the finder has the right to claim possession and ownership. In the case of lost property, claims to the property may be made by the finder wherever the property is found.[44] In contrast, mislaid property belongs to the owner of the premises where it is located (this party is not always the finder of the property[45] because the mislaid property was intentionally left on the premises belonging to the owner). The exception to this is the concept of *treasure trove*.[46] When items of great monetary value are found, they may be claimed by the finder regardless of whether they were lost or mislaid. For treasure trove to apply, the item must usually be cash or its equivalent (e.g., coins, gold, or bullion). In any event, a person who finds personal property having value should always consult the law of his or her jurisdiction to determine rights and obligations with respect to the property.

## Abandoned Property

If property has been abandoned, it must be shown that the owner gave up possession with the intent to give up dominion, control, and title to the property.[47] If so, the finder can take over possession and be declared its owner so long as the intent to dominate, control, and exercise title is continuously shown. For example, one cannot come across an item such as a piece of jewelry on the beach and ignore it and later try to claim ownership as the first finder with rights superior to another who also found it and identified it as valuable. It must be apparent to others that one intends to make the property one's own.

## Confused Property

An additional aspect of property whose ownership is unclear deals with items that become confused with other similar items. An example is money. If several persons put their money in the same place and a party alleges that a certain portion of a sum of money is actually that person's property alone and that party is responsible for its becoming confused with the other money, then the burden of proof is on the party claiming right to a specific portion to establish what amount of money actually belongs to that party. In cases where the items become confused and the proof cannot be established as to particular rights, the value of the confused items is shared equally by those who can establish that they are entitled to any share.[48]

## Actions to Recover Property or Its Value

Many legal disputes over property arise when there is disagreement over the rights of possession or ownership. In cases dealing with persons who claim to have somehow lost possession of their property, there are several legal alternatives to regain the property. Of course, if the property was stolen, then criminal laws apply. If a contract existed between the original and subsequent possessor regarding the property, then an action for breach of contract may exist. In addition, other civil actions provide methods to regain wrongfully obtained property or at least its value.

**Conversion.** Conversion is the basis for an action when one party receives possession of the property of another and wrongfully holds the property.[49] This can occur in one of two ways. In the first instance, a party may seize control of property without permission. In the second and more common instance, a party may refuse to return property that was previously bailed.

In the case of a bailment that becomes a conversion, there may also be a cause of action for the tort of negligence or for breach of contract if either element can be proven. (A further discussion of negligence and breach of contract is presented in Chapters 9 and 13, respectively.) The owner is also permitted to allege a lawsuit based on conversion that requires only proof of wrongful possession of the property by another and that the intent of the other party is to exercise control and to exclude the owner from rightful possession and ownership of the property. If the owner proves conversion, then the property may be recovered; if the property has been altered or disposed of, then its value may be recovered. If the property is returned, then the owner may also recover the fair market value of the use of the property during the time he or she was deprived of it. In many cases where conversion is applicable, there may also be a criminal action available to punish the party responsible for taking the property.

**Trespass to Chattels (Personal Property).** This type of action for return of property occurs when a party substantially interferes with another's possession or ownership of property. The primary difference between conversion and trespass to chattels is that in the latter, there is no need to show intent of the second party to exercise control of the property. It is only necessary to show that the second party dispossessed the first party of his or her property permanently or for a substantial period of time.[50]

As in the action for conversion, the party claiming trespass can claim the fair market value of the property. If the property was ultimately returned, then a claim can still be made for the fair market value of its use during the period the true owner was denied access to the property.

## ASSIGNMENT 12.8

Read the following information and identify the nature of the property in the possession of Virgil and what, if any, action might be taken by the housemates to retrieve the property or its value.

Virgil is a member of a college fraternity. He resides in a house shared by several members of the fraternity. Virgil and two other housemates stay in the house through the summer. Four other students graduate and move out. Four additional students leave for the summer with the intent to return in the fall. Throughout the summer, Virgil finds many personal items around the house. He takes a stereo left by one of the students gone for the summer to a girlfriend's house and installs it with the intent to leave it there. He uses the house petty cash fund to pay for food for a party. This fund was something all housemates contributed to in equal shares each month to cover the costs of household supplies for cleaning, paper products, and condiments. He takes the sheets from the bed of one of the graduating students and a poster from another and puts them in his own room. While cleaning out the house and garage, he locates an electric scooter that one of the graduating students had been unable to locate before moving. He also finds $10 or so in change in the couches in the house.

**Replevin.** Some jurisdictions still provide for the common law action of *replevin,* which was developed in England and remains a recognized cause of action in many states. The purpose of an action in replevin is to regain possession of the actual property that was wrongfully taken, not its value. This type of equity action is based on a claim that money damages are insufficient to remedy the wrong.[51]

To bring an action for replevin, it is necessary to prove the following:

1. Plaintiff has right to immediate possession, providing plaintiff and defendant do not both have right to immediate possession.

2. Property in issue must be personal property.

3. Property must be unlawfully possessed and detained by defendant at the time the action is commenced. (The defendant need not have unlawfully taken the property.)

---

## APPLICATION 12.10

Ben lives next door to a man who raises championship rabbits. Ben is appalled that that rabbits are kept in small cages in the backyard without the ability to move about. They are also frequently exposed to the elements. When the neighbor takes some of the bunnies to a show, or for a breeding appointment, he pays Ben to care for those bunnies left behind. Unable to stand it any longer, Ben decides to liberate the bunnies.

1. If Ben intends to make himself the owner of the bunnies and all the benefits associated with ownership, then his neighbor would have an action for conversion against him.

2. If Ben deliberately sets the bunnies free and allows them to run away, then the neighbor would have an action against him for trespass to chattels.

3. If Ben absconds with the bunnies without knowing that they are the last surviving descendants of a championship bloodline, then the neighbor could have an action for replevin on the theory that money could not adequately compensate the loss.

*Point for Discussion:* What would happen if Ben incorporated the bunnies into a larger herd of bunnies and was unable to differentiate them from the larger group?

---

## ASSIGNMENT 12.9

In the situation below, identify whether the property in question is one of the following:

  a. gratuitous bailment

  b. lost property

  c. mislaid property

  d. confused property

  e. property subject to an action for conversion

  f. property subject to an action for trespass to chattels

  g. property subject to an action for replevin.

Jim and Marshall own a private resort that leases out camping sites by the year. Throughout the year, the various tenants maintain their own site. Tenant B needs to get on the roof of his RV regularly to birdwatch. Jim allows him to keep a ladder belonging to the campground at B's RV. As Jim is working in and around the campground, he drives a tractor pulling a trailer with tools and supplies. A set of socket wrenches bounces off the trailer and lands alongside the road in some tall grass. Tenant M knows that tenant B keeps Jim's ladder at his campsite. Tenant M feels he has been overcharged for various items he has purchased in the store. To even things up, he goes to the storage shed of the campground and helps himself to an empty propane tank and marks it with his own name. While he is at it, he fills the tank with the intent to use the propane to heat his RV in cool weather. Jim stops by the site of Tenant B to get the ladder for a project on a roof of the beachhouse. He discovers that Tenant B has taken the ladder to his home some 100 miles away. Tenant B says the ladder is not worth the amount of gas it would take to retrieve it and refuses to go and get it. He offers his house key to Jim if Jim wants to go after the ladder. Jim is so frustrated that he does not realize he left several of his tools at the campsite next to Tenant B, when Jim was there working on the electric meter. Later, when Jim retraces his steps and goes to the campsite to retrieve his tools, he finds that the tenant at that site has put them

*(continued)*

in a toolbox with his own tools. There are several duplicates in the type and manufacture of the tools located in the box. However, among the tools is a handmade knife that was handed down in Marsha's family for generations. In its handle, the knife has the initials of each family member who ever possessed the knife, including Marsha's. However, having found the knife among the other tools on his campsite, the tenant claims "finder's, keeper's" and refuses to return it.

## INTELLECTUAL PROPERTY

An area of law that has experienced exponential growth in recent years is the field of Intellectual Property. Unlike tangible real and personal property, intellectual property is something that is literally created. For centuries, individuals have sought to protect their ownership interests over inventions such as various types of equipment. Today this is accomplished through patents. Individuals also have similarly sought to protect and control use of artistic creations through copyright law. However, with the advent of mass media, global advertising, and communication systems such as the Internet, the definitions and rules applied to intellectual property have been in a continuous state of development.

Intellectual property can most easily be categorized in one of two ways. First, there is that which is represented by a physical item such as an invention of equipment, machinery, or other type of object that is used in industry and commerce. The second type of intellectual property consists of purely artistic creations such as music, works of art, literature, and so on. The issues that commonly arise with regard to intellectual property often relate to preemptive strikes by third parties and individuals who attempt to closely mimic intellectual property and thereby gain the benefits of the advertising and reputation of the original item.

Preemptive strikes occur when a party identifies a potentially successful item of intellectual property and attempts to legally establish possession. For example, if someone creates a Web site that has a great deal of potential but does not take appropriate steps to protect the domain of the Web site, then a third party could essentially clone the site and register it to itself. The process of appropriating someone else's Web site is commonly referred to as *cyber-squatting*. As more and more people and companies do business through the Internet, it becomes increasingly important to protect one's rights and remain vigilant for those who would for all intents and purposes steal the work product of another.

The act of mimicking intellectual property is nothing new. It is simply acquiring the legally protected creative notions of someone else and making only the most minor adjustments to create an almost identical item. Although the rights to intellectual property may be legally protected, the advent of mass communications make concepts readily accessible to anyone who wants to search for them. However, identifying a nearly identical product and proving that the intellectual property rights have been infringed upon is a much more difficult and costly process. Nevertheless, if someone can establish that an interloper has appropriated protected intellectual property that is identical to the original product for all intents and purposes, then the courts will enforce the rights of the original artist or inventor. Because the Internet is a worldwide system of communication, it is virtually impossible to protect oneself completely. This is especially true with respect to persons or entities located in other countries who are, for most practical purposes, immune from prosecution in the U.S. courts. There are organizations that assist in the protection of Web domains and take steps to remove those who infringe on the legal rights of others, but clearly this is an area of law that will continue to evolve both in the United States and around the world.

## ETHICAL CONSIDERATIONS

Pervasive throughout property law are ethical principles. Because most property agreements are contractual in nature, the same ethical concepts of honesty and fair dealing apply to property transactions as to other types of contracts. In addition, some aspects of property lease or ownership involve long-term relationships between the interested parties. As a result, the parties have an ongoing duty to consider the legal and ethical expectations of the other when taking action with respect to the property. A landlord should make defects in rental property known to a tenant. In addition, the landlord has the obligation not only legally but also as a matter of business ethics to keep the property habitable. One who sells property to another makes certain representations about the condition of the property. Failure to do this in an honest manner not only can have legal implications but also reflects on the seller's ethical standards and may, in fact, affect future transactions. Ethics in property—and in all activities, for that matter—not only involve moral standards of the individual but also have a direct effect on professional interactions in society.

## Question

If a property seller knows of a significant defect in property but the buyer does not ask about it, does the property seller (owner) have an ethical (not necessarily legal) obligation to tell the buyer about the defect?

## ETHICAL CIRCUMSTANCE

Max Broader is a jeweler. A woman comes into his business with a diamond bracelet and asks that Max repair it. He originally sold the bracelet to the woman and knows it to be worth far more than $2,500. He has done much business with the woman over the years and does not issue her a receipt for the bracelet. He simply tells her the bracelet will be ready the following week. The next day, Max reads in the newspaper that the woman suffered a stroke, causing a car accident shortly after leaving his store. The article reports that the woman recalls nothing of the entire day of the accident. He waits, and no one from the family comes to claim the bracelet. He assumes they are unaware she left it with him. Consider Max's legal and ethical obligations.

## ● | CHAPTER SUMMARY

Property law is an extremely complex area and continues to change. Remember that principles of property law may vary somewhat from state to state, so the laws of a particular state must be examined before evaluating the rights or obligations with respect to personal or real property. This chapter has discussed basic principles as they have developed until now. However, as changes continue to occur, it is necessary to keep abreast of modifications of the law of property.

A final note to remember in all property transactions is that each area discussed in the text, when relevant, should be thoroughly addressed in clear and written terms in any document that represents the property interests of owners and others with an interest or rights in the property. Most legal disputes occur as the result of misunderstandings at the time of the transactions. Such misunderstandings can be avoided through prudent consideration of all pertinent issues by each party.

The basic tenets of property law are that real property involves all land and items that are immovably attached to the land. Personal property includes those movable items in which ownership can be readily transferred and actual possession exchanged. Fixtures are those items of personal property that have been affixed to real property in such a way that they cannot be removed without damage to the real property.

Interests in personal property can be affected by bailment or by losing, mislaying, or abandoning the property by the owner. Nonowners can obtain the property by sale, conversion, or trespass or by finding it. Real property interests can be affected by sale, inheritance, devise, easements, trespass, or adverse possession. The remedy for one whose property or interest in it has been altered depends on the type of property and the manner in which the property was affected. In some cases, the original owner may actually lose his or her interest in the property if care is not taken to protect it.

## CHAPTER TERMS

| | | |
|---|---|---|
| fee simple | joint tenancy | real property |
| fixture | life estate | right of survivorship |
| forced share | nonfreehold estate | tenancy by the entirety |
| freehold estate | personal property | tenancy in common |

## REVIEW QUESTIONS

1. How is real property different from personal property?
2. What is a fixture?
3. Describe an easement.
4. What is the right of survivorship?
5. Distinguish abandoned property from lost property.
6. What is a warranty of habitability?
7. What is adverse possession and why is it permitted?
8. What is constructive eviction?
9. Distinguish a mutual benefit bailment from a gratuitous benefit in terms of legal rights and responsibilities.
10. What is a nonfreehold estate?

## HELPFUL WEB SITES

| | |
|---|---|
| Real Property, Probate and Trust Law Journal | http://www.abanet.org/rppt.html |
| RentLaw.com | http://www.rentlaw.com |
| Personal Property Law | http://www.hg.org/perprop.html |
| Findlaw for Students | http://www.stu.findlaw.com/ |

● | **INTERNET ASSIGNMENT 12.1**

Using the Internet, locate a form lease agreement.

● | **INTERNET ASSIGNMENT 12.2**

Locate an organization that polices the use of registered domain names.

● | **ENDNOTES**

1. William Statsky, *Legal Thesaurus/Dictionary* (St. Paul, MN: West, 1982).
2. *Id.*
3. Boyer, *Survey of the Law of Property,* 3rd ed. (St. Paul, MN: West, 1981), p. 12.
4. *Id.*
5. *Id.*
6. *Id.*
7. *Id.*
8. *Wagman v. Carmel,* 601 F.Supp 1012, 1015 (E.D.Pa. 1985).
9. *Bouska v. Bouska,* 159 Kan. 276, 153 P.2d 923 (1944).
10. *Daniel v. Wright,* 352 F.Supp. 1, 3 (D.D.C. 1972).
11. 63 Am.Jur.2d, Property.
12. *Sneed v. Weber,* 307 S.W.2d 681, 690 (Mo.App. 1958).
13. Powell & Rohan, *Powell on Property:* Matthew Bender (1968); Restatement of the Law of Property Sec. 404, American Law Institute.
14. *Putnam v. Dickinson,* 142 N.W.2d 111, 124 (N.D. 1966).
15. *Huggins v. Castle Estates, Inc.* 36 N.Y.2d 427, 369 N.Y.S. 2d 80, 330 N.E.2d 48, 51 (1975).
16. 40 Annot., 27 A.L.R. 2d 444.
17. Annot., 36 A.L.R.4th 544.
18. 8 American Jurisprudence Sec. 2, Bailments.
19. Ch. 12, Torts, Infra.
20. Annot. A.L.R. 3d 1294.
21. See note 18.
22. *Carpenter v. Coles,* 75 Minn. 9, 77 N.W. 424 (1898); *Thomas v. Mrkonich,* 247 Minn. 481, 78 N.W.2d 386 (1956).
23. See note 34, Sec. 1014[2] Annot. 96 A.L.R.3d Sec. 1014[2].
24. See note 23, Sec. 865.6[4][c][ii][B].
25. *Id.*
26. *Thacker v. J.C. Penney Co.,* 254 F.2d 672, 676 (8th Cir. 1958).
27. *Id.*
28. *Paul v. Traders & General Ins. Co.,* 127 So.2d 801, 802, (La.App. 1961).
29. See note 23, Sec. 633.33.
30. *Id.;* 42 U.S.C.A. § 2000a et seq.
31. Rose, *Landlord & Tenants*: Transactions Books (1973), p. 14.
32. *Id.,* pp. 38–41.
33. *Id.*
34. Annot. 96 A.L.R.3d 1155.
35. See note 16, page 512.
36. *Id.*
37. *Ralston Steel Car Co. v. Ralston,* 112 Ohio St. 306, 147 N.E. 513 (1925).
38. See note 18.
39. *Id.* See note 18.
40. *Id.*
41. *United States Fire Ins. Co. v. Paramount Fur Services, Inc.,* 168 Ohio St. 431, 156 N.E.2d 121 (1959).
42. *Favorite v. Miller,* 176 Conn. 310, 407 A.2d 974 (1978).
43. *Paset v. Old Orchard Bank & Trust Co.,* 62 Ill.App.3d 534, 19 Ill.Dec. 389, 393, 378, N.E.2d 1264, 1268 (1978).
44. 8 American Jurisprudence, Sec. 62, Bailments.
45. See note 8.
46. See note 8.
47. *Schley v. Couch,* 155 Tex. 195, 284 S.W.d 2d 333, 335 (1955).

48. See note 7.
49. Annot., 39 A.L.R. 553.
50. 63 American Jurisprudence Sec. 14, Property.
51. *Ready-Mix Concrete Co. v. Rape,* 98 Ga.App. 503, 106 S.E.2d 429, 435 (1958).

## STUDENT CD-ROM

For additional materials, please go to the CD in this book.

## ONLINE COMPANION™

For additional resources, please go to www.paralegal.delmar.cengage.com

# The Law of Contracts

## THE TELEPHONE GAME

It should not be a difficult proposition for parties to follow through with their agreements. Nevertheless, the courts are kept busy throughout the United States, day after day, week after week, month after month, and year after year with cases involving disputes over agreements. Although the law of contracts has been refined and competent professionals can draft an agreement to cover just about every conceivable circumstance, still there are conflicts. Most often it is not the terms but the interpretation of the terms that generate litigation based on contracts. A game most of us are familiar with as children is the telephone game. One person whispers something into the ear of another. The second person then whispers what was heard into the ear of a third person and so on until everyone in the circle has heard the message. The last person announces the message to the group. The first person states what the original message was. It is usually hilarious to see how the message changed in transit. This is not because our hearing is so poor that we cannot clearly understand what is being said. Rather, our perceptions are influenced by our own memories and experiences. Often we hear what we expect to hear. The same is true with a contract. Although a term might be crystal clear to one person, the term may have an entirely different meaning to another person. As a result, contracts often require explanations of terms and expectations in a manner that is so clear as to be virtually incapable of misinterpretation. Even then, discrepancies occur, unforeseen circumstances arise, and sometimes people simply do not live up to their end of the agreement. At this point, the parties may seek court intervention. A majority of disputes, however, can be avoided if a contract is well planned and executed instead of being thrown together like a hurried game of telephone.

After reading this chapter, you should be able to:

- Identify the elements of a valid offer to contract.

- Differentiate between a unilateral and bilateral contract.

- Distinguish fraud in fact and fraud in the inducement.

- List the defenses to alleged breach of contract.

- Distinguish compensatory damages, liquidated damages, and specific performance.

- Explain the purpose of the statute of frauds.

- Discuss the application of assignment and delegation in a contract.

- Discuss the remedies available to one who has entered a contract with a mistaken understanding of the terms of the agreement.

Contract law is based on the principle established in most societies that people should be secure in the knowledge that promises will be honored and are legally enforceable when made between persons in order to provide each party with some type of benefit. This principle has evolved and developed over the years into one of the most precise areas of the law. Because so many of the transactions among individuals involve some type of reliance on one another, contract law has pervaded virtually all aspects of society. Consequently, other areas of law are frequently affected by principles of contract law.

Because each situation is unique, the law of contracts continues to change. Rarely does anyone go through a day of his or her life without becoming involved in or receiving benefits from a **contract.** The food we eat is usually produced, shipped, bought, and sold through contractual agreements. The same applies to clothing. Even the utilities in our homes such as heat, water, and cooling are received through contractual agreements to provide and pay.

As technology grows and society changes, the potential for contractual agreements (and disputes) grows. This chapter discusses the basic and settled principles of contract law. Apart from slight variations or modifications in each state, these principles continue to be the accepted standards by which persons who enter contractual agreements should guide their conduct. Typically, when new situations arise, the essential principles of contract law are modified or adapted to reach a result that is fair and consistent with precedent when possible.

**contract**
A legally binding agreement that obligates two or more parties to do something they were not already obligated to do or refrain from doing something to which they were legally entitled.

416

The leading authorities on contract law have defined a **contractual agreement** as a legally enforceable and voluntary promise exchanged by two or more parties to provide the terms of the promise in exchange for something of value known as consideration.[1] In essence, this means that if parties make a promise or promises to one another, those parties are obligated to perform (complete) the terms of the promise(s). Consequently, in the event a party fails to complete the obligations of a promise, the party who is injured by not receiving that to which he or she is entitled by the promise will have recourse in the courts against the party who broke the promise. For example, a person who borrows money from a bank promises to repay the money. If that person fails to repay the money, the bank can go to court and attempt to collect the money that is owed.

**contractual agreement**
A promise or set of promises for the breach of which the law provides a remedy and the performance of which the law recognizes a duty.

## ELEMENTS OF A VALID CONTRACT

Every valid contract has certain characteristics. If any of them are absent, the enforceability of the agreement comes into question. Essentially, every contract must have parties who provide some act or benefit that the other party does not otherwise have the legal right to receive. Specifically, all contracts must involve (1) at least two parties, (2) parties who have legal capacity, (3) a manifestation of assent by all parties to the contract, and (4) consideration that supports a legal and enforceable promise.[2] The following discussion addresses each of these elements in greater detail.

### At Least Two Parties

No one can enter into a contractual agreement with oneself. This issue has generally arisen in situations when a person who has a partial ownership interest in a business also attempts to make an agreement with the business to provide it with certain benefits. An example is a lawyer who is also a CPA who contracts with his or her own incorporated law firm to provide accounting services to the firm.

The rule traditionally has been that a person with an ownership interest in a business cannot contract to render services that are part of the primary purpose of the business. Generally, such services are deemed part of the responsibility of the owner. In recent times, however, exceptions to this rule have been made, especially when the services contracted for are not ordinary duties of an owner.[3] The preceding example would be such a case. Although the attorney–CPA would ordinarily be required to render the skills of an attorney, maintenance of accounting records for the firm probably would not be considered part of the duties of an attorney for the firm. Such services would not be within the ordinary expectations of the business toward any particular owner. Thus, the attorney likely could contract as an individual to provide these services to the law firm as separate entity. Consequently, two distinct legal entities—the attorney–CPA as (1) an individual and as (2) a member of the total firm—are parties to the contract.

Typically, the contractual requirement of at least two parties is the most easily met when establishing the elements of a contract in a given circumstance. However, this remains a basic element of contract law.

### Parties Who Have Legal Capacity

In contract law, *legal capacity* means that a person is an adult (based on the age defined by state statute) and has mental competence (which simply means that the person has not been declared by any court to be incapable of managing his or her own affairs). The law is relatively settled that only competent adults can be bound by the terms of contracts. An issue arises, then, when a party without **contractual capacity** enters into a contract.

**contractual capacity**
The ability to enter into and be bound by a legal contract; the ability is not diminished by age of minority or adjudicated incompetence.

**Age.** The age requirement is forthright. The parties to the contract must be of the age of majority according to the law of the state governing the contract at the time the agreement is entered. A simple determination of the beginning of the agreement and the date of birth of the parties is the only information necessary. However, a question may arise if there is a dispute as to the state whose law will govern the contract. This comes into question when the parties or the subject of the agreement involve more than one state. For example, an 18-year-old goes into state X where the age of majority is 18 and contracts to purchase a car. However, the state of domicile of the 18-year-old (state Y) considers the age of majority as 20. If the 18-year-old buyer defaults on the payments, does the law of state X or state Y control? If the applicable state law is that of X, then there is an enforceable contract. If the law of State Y is applied, then there was no capacity and thus no valid contract between the parties.

To avoid such issues, usually a written contract will indicate by agreement the law of the state that will apply in the event of a contractual dispute. When there is no written agreement, the court will determine the law of the state to be applied. As you can see, this determination can substantially affect the suit. This is why most written contracts include an agreement as to the state law to be applied in the event of a dispute.

**Mental Capacity.** The issue of mental capacity is somewhat more complicated. Technically, lack of mental capacity only considers persons who have been legally adjudicated (by order of the court) to be without the ability to manage their own affairs. However, what of the case when someone is quite obviously severely mentally challenged? Generally, the law that only adjudicated incompetents lack capacity will be upheld. Most individuals are given a minimal amount of responsibility to avoid contracting with someone who is obviously mentally challenged to the degree this person's ability to complete a contract is in question.

Many people may appear to be outside the normal range of behavior. This does not mean they are without the ability to manage their own affairs. Many famous and wealthy individuals have been notorious for "odd" behavior, but that behavior did not prevent them from amassing great fortunes. Conversely, some of the most notorious and vicious criminals of our time functioned in society relatively unnoticed for years. The law cannot be based on subjective individual perceptions of sane or insane behavior. Thus, anyone who has not been declared incompetent by a court is responsible for any contractual agreements to which he or she is a party regardless of his or her actual mental abilities.

## APPLICATION 13.1

Victor is a well-educated 74-year-old man. He is widowed and lives alone. His two children live in distant states and only see him periodically when he visits them for holidays and other family gatherings. Neither of the children has been to Victor's home for several years. Recently, both children notice that Victor's conversations do not reflect the clear-minded and highly intelligent man they always knew. Over a period of several months, Victor's mental ability seems to deteriorate. When the children discuss this with each other, they decide a visit is in order. When they arrive at Victor's home unannounced, they find him mowing the backyard—completely naked and seemingly unaware of the strangeness of this behavior. When they enter the house, they are shocked to find thousands of music CDs. All have been opened and many are either nailed to the walls or used as trivets, hot pads, coasters, and so on, rendering them worthless. On further investigation, it appears that over time Victor had

*(continued)*

**APPLICATION 13.1** (Continued)

joined virtually every music subscription company he could find and had ordered the entire catalog of selections for each. When the children look at Victor's various credit cards, the find he has accumulated tens of thousands of dollars in bills for the CDs. All told, his debts far exceed his net worth. A physician's exam reveals that Victor suffers from a progressive mental disability. Because Victor was never legally adjudicated incompetent, the contracted agreement with the credit card companies to pay for charges incurred will be valid and enforceable. It is entirely possible that Victor could be forced into bankruptcy.

*Point for Discussion:* Would the outcome be any different if Victor had been adjudicated after he took out the credit cards but before he purchased all of the CDs?

**Contracts with Persons without Capacity.** Traditionally, if a person with capacity entered a contract with a person without legal capacity, the person without capacity could choose whether to complete the terms of the contract. The other party to the contract was virtually at the mercy of the person without capacity. The party without capacity could disaffirm or withdraw from the contract at any time. It did not matter that the party with capacity had already performed all obligations under the contract. The minor or incapacitated person could accept the benefits of that performance without further obligation. The reasoning behind this was that because the party was legally incapable of being a party to a contract, a contract could not be enforced against the person.

The inherent unfairness of this situation caused the courts and some legislatures to set forth legal standards that would protect parties with capacity who entered in good faith into a contract with a minor or incapacitated person. This was done under the theory of restitution,[4] which is based on the principle of fairness. With respect to contracts, the theory basically states that if one person accepts or takes a benefit from another who was not obligated to provide that benefit, then some sort of payment should be made.

In addition to enacting the law of contracts, many states have enacted statutes, and many courts have issued decisions that follow the theory of restitution. Such legal standards provide a remedy to those who have entered contractual agreements with parties who do not have capacity. However, these legal standards often limit the recovery from the minor or incapacitated person. Commonly, such limitations involve the amount of liability of the minor or incapacitated person. Such amount will be the reasonable value of the goods or services received rather than the amount contracted for. An example is a contract between a minor and a competent adult to purchase a car. Although the minor enters a contract to purchase a car for $8,000, if the minor fails to complete payment, the car owner may be able to recover only the actual value of the car under the theory of restitution. If a court determines that the car is worth only $4,000, that amount is all that could be recovered from the minor. In addition, the law of several states regarding the liability of minors and incompetents is that restitution can be claimed only for items considered to be necessary to life such as food and shelter.[5]

As a consequence of the law of contracts and the law of restitution, the person with capacity usually requires the minor or incompetent to have an additional party enter the contract in his or her behalf. For example, a competent adult might cosign a loan with a minor. Then, if the minor breaches the contract, the contract can be enforced against the adult who cosigned. (Note that competent persons may also be required to have a cosigner as a condition of the contract for other reasons, such as to guarantee good credit.)

## ASSIGNMENT 13.1

Which of the following have capacity to enter a contract based on the information given? Assume no other facts.

1. Zach is 19 years old and heavily addicted to heroin.
2. Maurice is 19 years old and a ward of the state because he suffers from schizophrenia. However, with medication he is often lucid and highly intelligent.
3. Alicia is 15 years old and intellectually gifted. She has received a Bachelor's degree and is working on a Master's degree. She still resides with her parents who support her.
4. Carmen is 21 years old and developmentally delayed. She left high school at age 16 and works as a dishwasher at a small diner. She lives with her parents, who provide most of her support.
5. Ben is a 78-year-old retired physician who suffers from Alzheimer's. He still resides at home with his wife, who for several years has handled all decisions including when he should sleep and eat because he is unclear about such matters.

### Manifestation of Assent by All Parties

In all contracts, each party to the agreement must signify acceptance of the terms in some way. This requirement to manifest or demonstrate a willingness to be bound by the contract is essential. Otherwise, it would be possible for persons to claim a contract existed where one party did not even have notice of a contract or the intention to enter one. The following discussion explores several issues relevant to the manifestation of assent: (1) the objective standard that must be met to prove there was assent, (2) circumstances that may affect the termination of whether there was assent, and (3) methods of creating a situation for assent to a contract by the parties.

**Objective Standard.** Whether someone has manifested assent to a contract is measured by an objective standard. There is a great difference between objectivity and subjectivity. When one is objective, no personal bias plays a role in one's perceptions; when one is subjective, personal bias greatly influences one's perceptions. For example, if an individual were named as a defendant in a lawsuit, he or she would probably have strong feelings about his or her innocence. This view of the lawsuit would be quite subjective. However, if a person were to stop others on the street and tell them about the lawsuit, the perceptions would be objective if the listeners knew none those involved in the suit and was unfamiliar with the suit's details.

As discussed in Chapter 7, during the *voir dire* stage, the parties in a suit attempt to select jurors who have no personal experience or beliefs that would prevent an objective consideration of the evidence as it applies to the parties. Similarly, in contract law, as a fundamental part of determining whether all the elements of a contract were present, the judge and jury have the duty to determine whether there was mutual assent by all parties to the agreement.

The objective standard requires that a third person observing the transaction would perceive that the parties agreed to the terms of the contract and intended to be legally bound by those terms. The parties do not need to say or do any particular thing. Only their conduct needs to indicate agreement to the terms of the contract.[6] The existence of subjective intent claimed or denied by a party is not relevant for the purposes of determining whether a contract existed. For example, the jury will not consider the claim of a party that the party's conduct, even though it may appear to indicate intent, was not what the party meant.

## APPLICATION 13.2

Brian lives next door to John. One morning Brian notices that John has hired a man to paint the fence that adjoins Brian's fenced yard. Brian introduces himself and asks the man how much he is charging John to paint the fence. The man replies, " I usually charge $10 per yard of fence, so I guess it will be about $300." Brian comments, " Really? I think I'd pay someone $8 per yard but not $10." Brian then gets in his car and drives away. When he returns that evening, his fence has been painted. Brian's fence is much longer because of the size of his yard. He finds a bill for $720 attached to his door with the notation "90 yards × $8." In this circumstance, a bystander would probably not perceive that Brian's comment constituted an offer to contract. It was a general statement made in conversation and not even directed specifically to the painter.

*Point for Discussion:* What if Brian had said, "I would be willing to pay you $8 per yard"?

**Circumstances.** The following situations will not give rise to the creation of a valid and enforceable contract:

1. agreements made in jest or as jokes,

2. negotiations prior to the creation of an actual contract,

3. promises or indications of future gifts in exchange for another's promise or performance, or

4. promises for what a person is already legally obligated to do.

*Agreements made in jest.* Persons cannot be held to agreements that have been made in jest. If such agreements were enforced, then everyone would have to be on guard against saying things in conversations that could later be construed as a contractual promise. An example is an individual who says in idle conversation that he or she would sell a second person a house for 50 cents. However, cases of this type are usually more realistic. Often a very real offer and acceptance will be made. One party, however. will claim that the other party should have known that there was no real intent and that the discussion was just that and not the establishment of contractual terms.

A primary legal obstacle to enforcing contracts when there are circumstances indicating jest is the inability to prove that the party meant to be bound by the agreement. Normally, persons talking in jest have no real intent to form a contract. Therefore, when attempting to enforce a contract under such circumstances, it would be necessary to show that an objective observer would conclude that the parties actually intended to be bound by their statements or conduct regardless of the jovial manner of their discussion. In the preceding example, it would be necessary to show that the seller really intended to convey the house for only 50 cents. In nearly all cases, this would be quite difficult to prove. Suppose that someone at a party says to another guest, "I've always loved your house. If you ever wanted to sell it, I'd pay you $100,000—no questions asked" and the guest responds, "It's yours for $100,000." If the seller declined and attempted to avoid the purchase, then the jury would have to determine whether there was real contractual intent given the general value of the house and circumstances of the conversation.

*Negotiations.* For much the same reason, negotiations do not constitute contractual agreements. During negotiation, there is no real intent to make a firm commitment.

The intent of parties during negotiation is to explore whether the parties can meet on a common ground. If they cannot, then no contract will have been entered, and both parties are left as they started. If this were not the case, then little business would ever be accomplished because parties who engaged in an initial discussion about a contract could later be bound by that discussion.

*Future gifts or performance.* With respect to the third circumstance, it may at first seem illogical to refuse enforcement of contracts for future gifts. It is certainly possible to contract for a future performance of some act. It is also necessary in every contract that a person promise something he or she is not otherwise legally obligated to do. So why is it not legal to contract for a future gift? The answer is quite simple. In legal terms, a gift has the quality of something that one is never *required* to grant. In a contract, however, if something becomes the basis of a contractual agreement, it loses its gift quality and is required to be delivered. If not delivered, there are legal consequences. Thus, it is a contradiction in terms to promise a gift (something one is not required to do) as part of a contract, where performance of the "gift" becomes a legal obligation.

*Legal obligation.* Another situation of interest occurs when someone contracts to do what is already legally required. The basis of any contractual agreement must be voluntary acts by the parties. If persons promised what they were already legally obligated to do, then the receiving party would not be getting anything to which he or she was not already entitled. Thus, there would be no basis for a mutual agreement. For example, Bridget and Larry enter into a contractual agreement. Under the terms of the agreement, Bridget promises to buy Larry a new car if Larry will promise not to drive above the speed limit. Under current laws, Larry already has the obligation to drive at or below the speed limit. Therefore, Bridget is receiving nothing that she would not receive in the absence of her promise, so there is no basis to support her promise in the agreement.

**Elements of Assent.** Before there can be assent to a contract, the parties must have come to some meeting of the minds about the terms of the contract. Frequently, an offer to enter a contract does not occur until after various types of negotiation have taken place. When one party has actually made an offer, the other party can accept or reject the offer for as long as it is in effect. The following discussion examines the stages of offer and acceptance and some particular situations that affect these stages.

*Offer.* The terms *offer* and *acceptance* are commonly employed in reference to the assent by each party. The party who creates the opportunity to be bound by a contract (as opposed to negotiation) is the *offeror.* The party who accepts the offer is the *offeree.* The acceptance is the last step in the formation of a valid contract, assuming the subject of the contract constitutes appropriate consideration. (Acceptance is discussed more specifically a little later in this section.) An integral part of any offer and acceptance to contract is *consideration.* Simply stated, consideration is the value each party gives in exchange for the benefit he or she expects to receive. Consideration is examined later in the chapter in greater detail, not only as an element of assent but also as a necessary and integral part of any contract.

**bilateral contract**
An agreement between two or more persons in which each party promises to deliver a performance in exchange for the performance of the other.

An offer can be made to enter a bilateral contract or a unilateral contract. If the offeror makes a promise and by that promise induces the offeree to make a return promise, then a **bilateral contract** has been created.[7] Each party gives a promise in exchange for the other party's promise. Completion of what is promised by each party will complete the contract. An example is the promise of a car salesperson to give title to a car to a customer who promises to make monthly payments for twenty-four months. At this point, the two parties have entered into the contract. The purchaser must make the payments, and the salesperson must deliver title to the vehicle. When these steps are accomplished, the contract and the obligations of the parties have been satisfied, and the agreement has reached its logical end.

A **unilateral contract** is created when a promise is made in exchange for actual performance (without first making a promise of that performance).[8] Using a scenario similar to the previous example, a unilateral contract would occur if the following took place: A car salesperson promises to give title to a car to a customer in exchange for payment of $5,000 (the promise). The customer gives the salesperson $5,000 (the performance). The salesperson gives title to the car to the customer (completion of the promise). At this point, all terms of the contract have been satisfied.

When negotiations precede the contract, it is sometimes difficult to distinguish the offeror from the offeree. Usually, both parties will suggest terms for the contract. When negotiations take place, the point at which they cease to be mere negotiations—the point at which one party makes an offer that can become the basis for a contract—must be determined.[9] Identifying when negotiations end as well as the identity of the offeror and the offeree is necessary to separate the terms of the contract from the terms of the negotiations. Only the terms of the contract will be enforceable. In the law of contracts, the following definition of an offer has been developed for use in making the determination of when the offer is made and by whom: the demonstration of conduct perceived as one who desires to enter a contractual agreement with sufficiently specific terms to enable an informed acceptance to be legally bound.

The question to be asked is, would a reasonable objective observer perceive the actions of a person to be those of one who is creating the opportunity for a second person to enter into a contractual relationship by doing nothing more than accepting the terms that are already clearly set forth by the first person? If so, then the last person to have offered terms during the negotiations would be the offeror. The offeror is the person who identifies all significant terms of the actual contract and then promises or performs. All that needs to follow is the assent by promise or performance of the second person, who is the offeree. In addition, the time for acceptance by the offeree must be reasonably ascertainable.[10]

*Advertisements.* Much of the general public shares the belief that all advertisements are offers to enter contractual agreements for the sale of goods or services. Conversely, much of the legal community believes that such advertisements do not create an offer because certain terms of the agreement are lacking. In reality, both are partially correct and partially incorrect. Whether an advertisement is an offer must be judged on an individual basis.

As a consequence of the requirements of identity of the offeror, time for acceptance, and clearly defined consideration, most advertisements do not contain sufficient specificity to constitute an offer. Rather, they are an invitation to a buyer to make an offer after selecting specific goods or services. If, however, an advertisement indicates a particular good or service whose value can be reasonably ascertained by one who sees or hears the advertisement, then the time for the contract to be accepted is clear and the offeree is clearly identified (e.g., the first ten customers), so the advertisement may be treated as an offer, and offerees have the opportunity to accept it and form a contract.

**unilateral contract**
A contractual agreement in which one party makes a promise to perform on the actual performance of another.

---

## APPLICATION 13.3

The following newspaper advertisements illustrate the differences between nonoffers and offers:

Nonoffer: "All shoes on sale! Available to the public at one low price of $19.99 while supplies last."

Offer: "All genuine snakeskin shoes on sale! Available to first twenty customers, Saturday March 18, at one low price of $19.99 per pair. One pair per customer."

*Point for Discussion:* What is the significant difference between the two examples?

---

*Indefinite promises.* Similar to the advertisement is the indefinite promise. Even if all the terms necessary to a contract are technically present, an indefinite promise is not an offer and cannot lead to a valid and enforceable contract. A promise is indefinite if the benefit offered by the promise (the consideration) is vague or incapable of having its value reasonably determined.[11] For example, the promise by a cat breeder of simply "a cat" in exchange for $400 would probably not be a contract. However, if the breeder promises a registered kitten from a litter of Burmese cats, the value of such a kitten is much more easily discovered than a vague description such as "a cat." If the vague language in contracts were enforceable, then persons could take advantage of others who had different expectations. Much of the determination of whether a promise is indefinite is based on the circumstances and whether the other party could, in fact, identify with specificity the value of the consideration to be received.

*Auctions.* When identifying the offeror and offeree in an auction, the key term is *reserve.* In an auction, all elements of the offer are usually present. The item is specific, it can be inspected and valued, and the time for acceptance is set (while the item is being bid upon). The only thing that will affect the identity of the party who makes the offer is a sale with or without reserve. If an auction is conducted with reserve, the auctioneer can reserve in advance the right to refuse a bid before the final sale of the particular item. In effect, this makes the auctioneer an offeree with the right to refuse an offer (bid). Therefore, until an auctioneer announces whether a bid will be accepted, the contract is not formed. In an auction without reserve, the auctioneer is an offeror on calling for bids (acceptance) of the promise of any amount on an item. When a bid is received, the contract is established.[12] As noted earlier, the amount of the bid (promise to pay) is not a matter of legal concern.

*Illusory promises.* An illusory promise is one in which the promisor retains the ability to negate the promise[13]—for example, "I may sell you my house if you promise to pay me $50,000." In reality, the owner of the house has promised nothing at all. Therefore, the person promising to pay $50,000 is receiving no consideration for that promise. There is nothing real to induce the promise.

*Termination of the offer.* Until acceptance occurs, the offeror has the opportunity to retract the offer at any time. The only exception to this is when the offeree has purchased an option—a type of contract in and of itself. Generally, an offeror and offeree will enter into an agreement where the offeree has the exclusive right to accept the offer during a specific period of time. The offeree gives consideration of some type in exchange for the offeror's consideration of promising not to accept an offer from another offeree or cancel the offer during the specified time. Otherwise, the offeror may withdraw the offer at any time before acceptance. However, if the offer is for a unilateral contract and the offeree begins performance, then the law will imply an option contract that prevents the offeror from revoking the offer during the performance by the offeree.[14]

## APPLICATION 13.4

Richard and Nicole have been renting the same house for two years. Their rent is $600. The landlord informs them of his plans to sell all of his rental properties and retire. The house Richard and Nicole live in is going to be sold for $75,000. Richard and Nicole need a down payment of $15,000 to purchase the house and qualify for a low-interest mortgage. They currently have $11,000 in savings. They offer $5,000 to the landlord as an option contract to purchase the contract at the end of the year. They plan to work two jobs each and accumulate the additional $9,000 they would need to buy the house. The landlord accepts the option contract and the $5,000 in addition to the regular rent. He agrees to allow Richard and Nicole exclusive rights to purchase the house for $75,000 for one year. Throughout the year, Richard and Nicole are plagued with unexpected expenses. At the end of the year, they have saved only $10,000 of the $15,000 needed. The landlord puts the house up for sale, and someone buys it the first week it is on the market. Richard and Nicole have lost their $5,000 because it was the consideration in exchange for the exclusive right to purchase the house during the one-year period. Their failure to do so or the reasons behind the failure are irrelevant.

*Point for Discussion:* Would the result be any different if the landlord decided to sell the house at the end of the one-year period for $70,000? What if the landlord was offered $100,000 for the house before the one-year period?

*Implied option contract.* Cindy contracts with Kelley to paint her house. Cindy promises to pay Kelley $500 after the house has been painted. Kelley accepts the offer by starting to paint Cindy's house. Two weeks later, when Kelley is approximately halfway finished, Cindy says she has changed her mind: She does not want the house painted and will not pay Kelley. Ordinarily, performance must be complete to accept a contract. However, in situations such as this, the law will imply an option on Kelley's part. Thus, the offer must remain open until Kelley has had the opportunity to complete the performance. The implied option contract prevents unfair results for someone who has entered into performance in a contract in good faith. When the circumstances show that a party has entered into performance in a unilateral contract and taken substantial steps toward completion, then the party has the option to complete the performance regardless of the desire of the other party to withdraw or cancel the offer. This places responsibility on the offeror to be certain he or she desires the contract terms before making the promise.

In addition to cancellation by the offeror, an offer may terminate before acceptance in other ways. An offer that is open for a specified time and is not accepted during that time will cease to be an offer. If no time is specified, then the law will imply a reasonable time for that type of offer. If the offeree rejects the offer, then the offer is no longer effective; to contract, a new offer must be made. A counteroffer by an offeree is considered a rejection of the offeror's offer and is treated as a new and different offer, thereby making the initial offeree the offeror. Finally, if the offeror or the offeree should die or lose legal capacity before acceptance, the offer will be terminated automatically.[15]

*Acceptance.* The ultimate step in creating any contract is an acceptance of the terms by the offeree. What constitutes an acceptance is at least in part dictated by the type of contract. In a bilateral contract (a promise for a promise), before the contract becomes binding, the offeree must give a promise in exchange and as consideration for the offeror's promise. At that point, both parties are obligated to fulfill their promises according to their terms.

To solidify a unilateral contract, the offeree must begin performance in response to the offeror's promise. The contract is not actually accepted until the offeree has substantially performed what was asked by the offeror. At that time, however, the offeror cannot withdraw the offer that induced the offeree to perform and is obligated to allow the offeree to finish the job. This prevents an offeror from accepting the benefits of a performance and withdrawing the offer before the performance is complete. If the offeree completes the task, then the offeror must provide the promised consideration. When an offeree does not complete performance of a unilateral contract, the offeror may have to pay partial consideration for the work done if the offeree substantially performed.

The offeree must have knowledge of an offer. Acceptance cannot be the result of coincidence. If by chance or for some other reason the offeree promises or performs what the offeror seeks, then there will be no contract. For a contract to exist, the offeree must be induced by the offeror's promise to give a specific promise or performance in exchange. Similarly, the consideration for each party must be something the party would not otherwise be entitled to receive. If it is not, then consideration would not act as an inducement to enter the contract.

As a general rule but subject to the following exception (discussed below under "Methods of acceptance"), an offeree cannot alter, delete, or add terms to the contract when accepting. The contract must be accepted or rejected "as is." If such changes were allowed, then there would really be no offer at all. In bilateral contracts (where acceptance is by making a promise), the altered or additional terms would actually be nothing more than another offer or additional negotiations of what the offeree's promise should be. More important, in unilateral contracts (where acceptance is by performance), allowing changes in the terms could cause the offeror to receive something very different from what he or she sought. The offeror might not want the different type of consideration. Thus, performance by the offeree would no longer be of consideration that would encourage the offeror to honor the original promise.[16] An example of the latter situation would be if someone offered to pay $15,000 for the immediate delivery of an Arabian horse. In response, an offeree ships a Shetland pony. The offeror should not be bound in this situation, because a Shetland pony was not what the offeror contracted to receive.

The exceptions to this general rule are commercial transactions between persons engaged in the sale of goods. Merchants are governed by the laws of the state designed especially for commercial transactions and commercial contractual agreements. The Uniform Commercial Code (commonly referred to as the UCC) is a series of laws regarding commercial transactions that have been adopted, at least in part, by all the states. The UCC governs the various practices of sales and financing by commercial businesses with one another and the general public. A variety of other subjects, such as banking and bulk transfers, are included in the code. Each subject is addressed in a separate article, similar in organization to a book chapter. Article 2 of the UCC sets forth provisions for commercial transactions involving the public sale of goods by merchants. Under Article 2, it is permissible for an offeree to include additional or varied terms when accepting a written contract. However, if the offer in the contract states that such changes must be expressly approved by the original offeror, no acceptance is valid, and no contract exists until the offeror has approved of the offeree's added or varied terms.[17] Article 2 also has provisions that guide the conduct of parties who are involved in a contract and the breach of that contract occurs or is imminent. (Breach of contract pertaining to financing agreements is discussed near the end of the chapter.)

*Methods of acceptance.* Generally, acceptance is effective at the time it is tendered. The exception, of course, occurs in a unilateral contract. Acceptance by the tender of performance is sufficient to create an option to continue until the performance and consequent acceptance are complete. If the offer is made to a specific individual or type of individual (e.g., the first ten customers), then no one else may respond. If it is made to the general public, then all who become aware of the offer are offerees and have the right to accept the contract. This is also subject to rules regarding advertisements.

In face-to-face confrontations, usually little doubt exists as to when an acceptance becomes effective. At the moment an objective observer would perceive the offeree as tendering an acceptance of the contract terms, the contract would take effect. Often the situation is much different, however, and acceptance is communicated through a medium other than a face-to-face meeting.

A common situation occurs when an offeree accepts the terms of an offer by mail, telegraph, or electronically. As a general rule, in such cases the acceptance is effective when posted. However, it is necessary for the offeree to do everything that is required to ensure delivery. For an offer accepted by mail, the proper address must be included, the postage prepaid, and the acceptance deposited in a valid postal receptacle or post office. In the case of telegrams, the communication must be delivered to the telegraph office and paid for in advance. More recently, the Internet has become a new arena for contracts and contract law. Although the same basic rules of contract law apply, the use of electronic communications to offer, accept or reject, and create contracts has benefits and disadvantages when it comes to acceptance or cancellation of an offer. On the one hand, e-mail communications provide data that include the exact moment of the transmission. This eliminates most questions about whether an acceptance or cancellation took place first. However, electronic data are always subject to damage or loss by a variety of occurrences. For this reason it remains essential to maintain actual documents showing the communications and transmissions to support any claim regarding a contract. In the case of unilateral contracts, the offeror must have a reasonable basis to discover that performance has begun.[18]

At any time before acceptance, the offeror may revoke the offer. If this is done by mail, then the offeror's revocation will generally be considered valid when received by the offeree. If an offeree mails an acceptance at approximately the same time an offeror sends a revocation, then the court can use the mail carrier's date stamp to ascertain whether acceptance or revocation occurred first. If the rule was that acceptance was effective on receipt, then it would be up to the parties to convince the court when actual receipt occurred. In addition, in the case of unilateral contracts, if acceptance by performance begins and a communication is sent to inform the offeror of this, then it would be unfair to require the offeree to perform at his or her own risk until such time as the acceptance reached the offeror. After all, in local transactions, the start of performance binds the offeror, and the rule should be no different for long-distance transactions.

An exception to the rules regarding acceptance conveyed by mail, telegraph, or electronic communications is the *reasonableness* of mail or telegraph as a means of communication. If the circumstances indicate that another method of acceptance such as personal delivery or face-to-face acceptance would be more reasonable, then the court may find that it was improper to accept by mail, and it will be ineffective to create a contract.

## ASSIGNMENT 13.2

Which of the following situations describe an offer and acceptance sufficient to create a valid contract? If no contract exists, explain why.

1. Forty-year-old Carolyn drives a delivery truck locally. She is self-employed and contracts with various businesses. If she takes any time off, she loses income. Carolyn decides to go on a cruise, so she makes an offer to 16-year-old Cecilia to drive the truck for two weeks. In exchange, Cecilia will receive $10 per hour for each hour she drives the truck. Cecilia accepts the keys and a copy of the delivery route.

2. Moses needs a new roof on his house. He knows that next door is a sheltered care home with several disabled adults living there as part of a state program to reintroduce these individuals into the community after several years of living in an institutional setting. Moses offers several of the disabled adults $10 each if they spend the day on his roof tearing off shingles. They immediately climb up on the roof and start tearing off shingles.

3. Denali fancies himself an entrepreneur. He invents a product he thinks will sweep the nation. He attends a college job fair and offers a graduating senior the opportunity to set up a store and sell the product. The senior will pay Denali the cost of the product plus 10 percent in exchange for the exclusive right to sell the product in a 10-mile radius for two years. The student shakes hands with Denali and says he will start immediately upon graduation in one month.

4. On Joseph's eighteenth birthday, his dad offers him $50 for each month Joseph does not receive a traffic ticket. At the end of one year, Joseph submits a bill for $600 to his father.

5. Brenda offers Colleen $200 if she does not run for homecoming queen at their college. Both girls are graduating seniors, and Brenda wants the position as she anticipates a career in beauty pageants. Colleen says she will not do it for less than $500. Brenda leaves $500 cash for Colleen in her mailbox.

## Consideration That Supports a Legal and Enforceable Promise

As stated, to constitute an offer to contract, all material terms must be present. One of these terms is consideration: the benefit received by a party in exchange for the party's promise or performance. Essentially, consideration is the element that induces a person to enter a contract.[19] The person promises or does something he or she is not obligated to do in exchange for a promise or performance he or she is not otherwise entitled to receive.

The value of the consideration for the specific contract must be determinable. This is merely to ensure that a party is getting something of value in exchange for the promise or performance. Essentially, such determination is required to prevent deception of innocent parties. The courts will not recognize a contract where the description of the consideration is vague or where the consideration's value is incapable of being measured. The courts are not usually concerned with the amount of value of a consideration or whether one party benefits more than another. That is a matter left for the parties to negotiate. The law does require, however, that a party to a contract be able to reasonably determine the value, quantity, and quality of the consideration to be received. This allows the party to make an informed decision of whether to enter the contract.

For consideration to be legally enforceable, it must be something that the law will recognize as a proper basis for a contract. Generally, this means that the consideration cannot be something that would be illegal or that would force the party to engage in illegal conduct. If, for example, one party promised another party $50 in exchange for stealing a typewriter, then there would not be a valid contract. Because one party's consideration is an illegal act, the fourth element necessary to establish a contract—consideration that supports a legally enforceable promise—is not met.

In addition, the consideration must be something that is genuine. It does not matter that one party's consideration is seemingly inadequate when compared with the other party's offered consideration. The law does not concern itself with the adequacy of consideration.[20] The only exception to this would be if the consideration was represented as the real article and was actually a fake. If the consideration is a promise that turns out to be a sham in an attempt to deceive another party, then it may not be treated as valid consideration, and the contract will not be enforced.

## APPLICATION 13.5

Ken is an auctioneer. He frequently visits the homes of customers to discuss the details of a planned auction. On one such visit, he is touring a barn with the customer to discuss the auction of farm equipment. The farmer has died, and with no one to assist her, the elderly and physically ill widow plans to sell everything and move into a nursing home. Ken notices a tarp over something large in a corner and asks about it. The widow removes the tarp. Ken is shocked to find a mint condition car some eighty years old. The vehicle has just 100 miles on the odometer. Ken asks the widow if she would be willing to sell. She says certainly because she has no need of the vehicle. For as long as she can remember, her husband started the car once each month and drove it up and down the driveway. The couple had adopted an Amish lifestyle decades before and given up all motorized transportation. On further examination, the original bill of sale is found in the car. When purchased, it cost $450. Ken offers the widow $400 because it is a used car. She agrees. Ken subsequently sells the car for $25,000. Because the law does not concern itself with the adequacy of consideration, the sale would be considered valid without further evidence of attempted deception by Ken.

*Point for Discussion:* Would the result be different if the widow were entering the nursing home as a result of decreased mental ability even though she had not been adjudicated as incompetent?

## CASE
### *Smith v. Solo Watersports, Inc.,*
### 112 Wash.App. 1051 (Wash. App. Div. 1 2002)

In the following opinion, the court considers what must occur for a contract to be modified.

On October 4, 2000, William Smith loaned $100,000 to Solo Watersports Inc. and Ski-Free Watersports Development Inc. (collectively Solo). Solo signed a promissory note providing a due date of October 25, 2000, for repayment of the loan. As additional consideration for the loan, Smith received 100,000 shares of Ski-Free common stock. Robin Sells, the president of both Ski-Free and Solo, also executed a personal guarantee on the loan.

The due date on the note passed without payment and Smith began informal efforts to collect on the loan. After assuring Smith several times that payment was forthcoming, Sells wrote a check for the amount due on November 4, 2000. After Smith learned that there were insufficient funds to honor the check, he served a notice of default on Sells on November 21, 2000. Under the terms of the note, Solo had five days to cure the default.

Still receiving no payment, Smith visited Sells' office on December 15, 2000, to collect on the loan. Although the

*(continued)*

parties disagree over what was said, it is undisputed that at that meeting, Sells issued Smith an additional 100,000 shares of Ski-Free stock.

Smith later received information on the excessive debt and the lack of financial health of Solo and Ski-Free. He also learned that since the fall of 2000, the state had been in the process of issuing a "cease and desist" order forbidding Solo and Free Ski Inc. from distributing shares, based on numerous violations of state security laws.

On February 1, 2001, Smith sued Sells, Solo, and Ski-Free seeking to collect on the note. Smith moved for summary judgment on May 23, 2000, asserting that no genuine issues of material fact existed and that he was entitled to judgment as a matter of law.

Solo opposed summary judgment, asserting that on December 15, 2000, Sells and Smith had agreed to extend the due date for repayment. In a declaration submitted to the trial court, Sells stated that during the December 15th meeting, Smith:

> extended the due date on the Note by agreeing to forego any type of legal proceedings against [Solo] or myself to collect on the Note, with the understanding that the principal together with the interest due on the Note would be paid to William Smith upon completion of our next phase of funding. At that time, we anticipated that funding would be available to us within three to six months. As consideration for this agreement, William Smith was issued 100,000 additional shares of stock in Ski-Free Watersports Development, Inc.

Solo also submitted a copy of a letter that Sells claims was sent to Smith memorializing this agreement. The letter, dated December 15th, states in part:

> Further to our conversations in connection with your past due loan in the amount of $100,000, we are pleased to issue you share certificate #00672 as additional consideration for our outstanding indebtedness to you. We acknowledge that the loan has entered into default status, but with this additional consideration we appreciate your willingness to forgo any type of legal proceedings against, Ski-Free, SOLO or me, personally, with the understanding that the principal together with all accrued interest will be paid to you upon the completion of our next phase of funding. As discussed, this funding may be derived from either the injection of capital from private source funding, venture capital, the offering processes that have been described in the shareholders meetings and investor newsletters or other sources that may present themselves. When this funding has been received with a minimum advance to us of at least $750,000 we will

then be in a position to retire our obligation to you in full. . . . As we are continually working on the funding process and with the interest that we have garnered thus far, we anticipate and hope that funding in at least one of these categories will be available to us within the next three to six months, if not sooner.

Smith replied with his own affidavit denying there was any agreement to extend the due date on the note, and asserting that Sells paid him the 100,000 additional shares as consideration for the forbearance he had already granted. Smith also denied ever receiving the above-quoted letter. Smith also submitted the declaration of a Ski-Free employee who was present at the December 15th meeting. She stated that Sells told Smith "I promise I'll get you some of the money in a few days," but that Smith never agreed not to sue on the note. According to the employee, Sells gave Smith a certificate for additional Ski-Free shares, stating something to the effect of "this is for your patience."

The trial court granted summary judgment in Smith's favor. As to Solo's claim that the note was modified on December 15th, the trial court noted that "the subsequent agreement, as alleged, does not include all of the essential elements of a contract," because Sells' promise to pay was illusory. Solo now appeals.

## Analysis

When reviewing summary judgment, we engage in the same inquiry as the trial court. We affirm if there is no genuine issue of material fact and the moving party is entitled to judgment as a matter of law.

The central issue in this case is whether Smith was entitled to payment under the promissory note as of the time of summary judgment or whether, as Solo contends, the due date was extended by agreement. A promissory note is a simple contract to pay money. *Reid v. Cramer*, 24 Wn.App. 742, 744–45, 603 P.2d 851 (1979). Written contracts, including those that purport to forbid such modification, may be orally modified by the contracting parties. *Pacific N.W. Group A v. Pizza Blends, Inc.*, 90 Wn.App. 273, 277–78, 951 P.2d 826 (1998). Contract modification requires mutual assent in the form of an offer and acceptance on the essential terms of the modification, as well as additional consideration over and above that which supported the original contract. *Bulman v. Safeway, Inc.*, 144 Wn.2d 335, 351–52, 27 P.3d 1172 (2001): *Saluteen-Machersky v. Countrywide Funding Corp.*, 105 Wn.App. 846, 851–52, 22 P.3d 804 (2001).

Solo contends that genuine issues of fact remain over whether the parties orally modified the promissory note on December 15, 2000, to extend the time for repayment. Solo points out that additional Ski-Free shares were given to Smith on that date as consideration, and refers to Sells' affidavit and the letter that Sells purportedly sent to Smith. Based on those documents, Solo contends the note was modified so that the due date was extended until such time that Solo and Ski-Free achieved the next "phase of funding" from investors to the level of $750,000. We disagree.

Parties may modify executory contracts, including promissory notes, to extend the time for performance. But to be binding, an extension of time "must be for a definite and certain time or be capable of being made so by some future event which is sure to happen." 17A. Am.Jur.2d Contracts § 531 (2001): *Pavey v. Collins,* 31 Wn.2d 864, 870–71, 199 P.2d 571 (1948). Absent sufficient definiteness, a contractual promise is essentially illusory and unenforceable. An illusory promise is one that is so indefinite that it cannot be enforced, or by its terms makes performance optional or entirely discretionary on the part of the promisor. Such a promise is insufficient consideration to support enforcement of a return promise.

The time-tested case of *Stickler v. Giles* (*Stickler v. Giles,* 9 Wash. 147, 37 P. 293 [1894]) demonstrates this need for definiteness with regard to promissory notes. In that case, a borrower, who was a contractor, defaulted on a loan debt because he had fallen on hard times and did not have the funds to repay the lender. During the default period, the debtor notified the lender that he had been awarded a contract with the county, that he expected to receive his first estimate for the work between August 12th and 15th, and that he would repay the loan with agreed interest when he was paid on the contract. The lender replied that "he would wait." Our Supreme Court held that this was not a valid modification of the contract for repayment. In so holding, the Court reasoned that the time for repayment was indefinite and that the contingency for repayment—that the debtor would perform under the expected contract with the county—was entirely uncertain and dependent upon conditions which might or might not result. The Court noted that if "for any reason the work was not done to the satisfaction of the county it might refuse the estimate; or the work might be entirely abandoned and any right to payment therefore forfeited by the [lender]." *Stickler,* 9 Wash. at 149.

Here, Solo's alleged promise to pay Smith upon achieving the "next phase of funding" was similar to *Stickler* in its indefiniteness. It was entirely possible that the purported influx of funding would never occur due to any number of contingencies, including the lack of investors or their refusal to provide sufficient capital. Additionally, it was speculative whether Solo or Ski-Free would ever reach the required level of $750,000 in funding mentioned in the letter as a contingency for repayment. And as the trial court noted, achieving this level of funds was an event that was dependent upon and was largely within the control of the debtors, who could simply choose not to pursue the funding in a timely fashion. Thus, the language of the letter and Sells' affidavit reveal that the occurrence of the condition precedent to repayment was entirely uncertain and dependent upon conditions "which might or might not result." *Stickler,* 9 Wash at 149. The trial court properly granted summary judgment.

Solo also points out the general rule that where a contract is unclear as to the time for performance, a court can impose a "reasonable time." See *Smith v. Smith,* 4 Wn.App. 608, 612, 484 P.2d 409 (1971) (where contract is silent as to the time of duration, court may imply that performance was intended to take place within a reasonable time). Solo argues that the trial court should have imposed a three to six month extension for repayment, based on Sells' statement in the December 15th letter that this was the anticipated time frame for achieving the "next phase of funding." We disagree that this was sufficient to cure the illusory promise to repay. Solo fails to cite a single case where, as here, the reasonable time proposed was based on the mere "anticipation and hope" that the contingency for performance would occur. As discussed above, Sells' proposed three-to-six-month time frame was built upon factors that were entirely speculative and largely within the borrowers' control. Because the alleged promise to pay is illusory, the letter cannot reasonably be construed as imposing a six-month extension of the note.

We affirm.

## Case Review Question

Would the result change if the respondent had applied for a specific bank loan to pay the debt?

# THIRD-PARTY INVOLVEMENT IN CONTRACTS

Sometimes parties will enter a contract with the intent to benefit persons who are not directly involved in the contract. Such an agreement is known as a *third-party contract,* and the person entitled to the contractual benefits is known as a **third-party beneficiary.** Another situation occurs when a party enters into a contract

**third-party beneficiary**
One who, as the result of gift or collateral agreement, is entitled to the contractual performance owed another.

and later turns his or her contractual interest over to a third party. This latter occurrence is called *assignment and delegation*. Specific rules govern the rights and duties of all concerned in such situations.

## Third-Party Contracts

Three types of third-party contracts exist. The third parties in these types of contracts are known as *donee beneficiaries*, *creditor beneficiaries*, and *incidental beneficiaries*. The donee beneficiary receives benefit from the contract as a gift from one of the promisors. The creditor beneficiary receives benefit from one promisor as satisfaction of an existing debt from the other promisor. The incidental beneficiary is not intended by the parties to benefit directly from the contract but receives the benefit as a side effect of the contract.

The various beneficiaries are distinguished in terms of their rights in satisfaction of the contract. A donee or creditor beneficiary can enforce the contract against the party obligated to provide the benefit. The creditor beneficiary can enforce the contract against the party who owes the benefit or against the party who has contracted to provide it.[21]

---

### APPLICATION 13.6

Henry planned to attend college in the fall. His grandmother agreed to pay his tuition directly to the college because this would qualify her for a tax credit. Henry wanted to show his appreciation for his grandmother's help. Henry knew that his grandmother had offered her best friend, Laura, a vegetable garden on a one-acre lot as a birthday gift. He waited until his grandmother left on vacation with Laura. He went to the Humpty Dumpty hardware store and bought all of the necessary supplies for his plan. While his grandmother and Laura were gone, he put in a one-acre vegetable garden.

In this situation, the college is the creditor beneficiary. It was a creditor of Henry and received the benefit of the payment by Henry's grandmother. Laura was a donee beneficiary as she received the benefit of a gift to Henry's grandmother in the form of the cost of the garden supplies and labor. The Humpty Dumpty store was an incidental beneficiary in that it profited from the sale of goods to Henry.

*Point for Discussion:* Would Laura's status change if she annually paid Henry's grandmother to plant her garden?

---

The incidental beneficiary has no rights against either party to the contract, because there was never any intent to make the contract for the purpose of benefiting this party. If the contract can be satisfied without involvement of the particular beneficiary, then the parties are not obligated in any way to make compensation for failure to provide the benefit.

## Assignment and Delegation

Assignment or delegation takes place when one or more parties to a contract assign rights or delegate duties under the contract to a third party. Generally, assignment or delegation is acceptable unless (1) the parties have stipulated in the contract that it is not permissible or (2) the assignment or delegation would significantly alter the duty or rights of the other party to the contract.[22]

In assignment, a party assigns the rights or benefits he or she is entitled to receive under the terms of the contract. The party to the contract is the *assignor,* and the party receiving these rights is the *assignee*. If there is a complete assignment, then the assignee steps into the shoes of the assignor and can enforce the contract against the remaining party to the contract. In a partial assignment, the enforcement would come from the assignor.

The following is an example of an impermissible assignment. Pak has purchased and paid for a three-year maintenance agreement for his computer with a local office supply business. After one year, Pak closes his business and assigns his rights to maintenance of his computer to another business with two computers. This would significantly increase the obligations of the remaining party to the contract (the office supply store), and the assignment would probably not be considered valid.

To delegate one's duties under a contract, the person accepting the duties (delegatee) must be able to provide an equivalent performance. In addition, the party delegating the duties (delegator) remains responsible under the contract until the duties are performed satisfactorily by the delegate.[23]

The following is an example of delegation. Pak owns a fleet of taxi cabs. He has an agreement with a local service station for routine maintenance and major repairs at a specified rate. The owner of the station in turn delegates the duties of maintenance and repair to the local high school shop class. If the class does not perform the repairs satisfactorily, then the station owner, in addition to the high school class, may be held responsible.

# CASE

## *Motorists Mutual Insurance Co. v. Columbus Finance, Inc.,*
## 68 Ohio App.3d 691, 861 N.E.2d 605 (Ohio App. 10 Dist. 2006)

This opinion discusses the necessary elements of a contractual agreement and the result when a mistake occurs with regard to the creation of the agreement.

Columbus Finance, Inc. ("CFI"), defendant-appellant, appeals the judgment of the Franklin County Municipal Court, in which the court found Motorists Mutual Insurance Co. ("Motorists"), plaintiff-appellee, was entitled to recover an automobile liability insurance payout made by Motorists to CFI.

CFI financed a vehicle purchased by Monica Randall and obtained a security interest on the vehicle. On July 17, 2003, Randall was a passenger in the vehicle she owned, while the vehicle was being operated on Interstate 71 in Columbus, Ohio, by Shirley Simons. Simons and Randall were involved in an accident caused by the negligence of the driver of another vehicle owned by Bessie Simpkins and operated by Brian Hatfield. Randall's car was a total loss.

Motorists contacted CFI and indicated Motorists' insured was at fault in the Randall accident. On July 25, 2003, Motorists and CFI executed a Lienholder's Agreement to Furnish Title ("lienholder's agreement"), in which they agreed that Motorists would pay CFI $4,568.81 if CFI would cancel its lien on Randall's

certificate of title, surrender the title, and deliver the vehicle to Motorists. Motorists received the vehicle on July 27, 2003. On July 29, 2003, CFI cancelled its lien on the vehicle title and delivered the title to Motorists, after which Motorists paid CFI $4,568.81. CFI deposited the check on the same day, stamped Randall's note "Paid," and surrendered the note to Randall. CFI paid Randall an overage on her payoff, and Randall deposited the check the same day, July 29, 2003.

On August 4, 2003, Motorists contacted CFI and informed CFI that Motorists had misidentified the parties involved in the Randall accident, and, thus, the payment was in error. Apparently, on the same date and the same highway as the Randall accident, Lisa Barnick, who was Motorists' insured, negligently caused an accident involving Douglas Simmons. Motorists claimed it had confused the names of the parties involved in the Randall and Barnick accidents and mistakenly linked the two claims as being the same. CFI refused to return the payment to Motorists.

On August 23, 2004, Motorists filed an action against CFI seeking repayment of the insurance proceeds paid by Motorists to CFI. . . . On September 21, 2005, the trial court issued a judgment in favor of Motorists,

*(continued)*

finding that CFI must return the payment to Motorists. CFI has appealed the court's order, asserting the following assignments of error:

ASSIGNMENT OF ERROR NO. I: THE LOWER COURT ERRED AS A MATTER OF LAW AND FACT AND ABUSED ITS DISCRETION IN FAILING TO ENFORCE THE CONTRACT BETWEEN THE PARTIES.

ASSIGNMENT OF ERROR NO. II: THE LOWER COURT ERRED AS A MATTER OF LAW AND FACT AND ABUSED ITS DISCRETION IN HOLDING THAT THERE WAS AN ALLEGED MISTAKE WHICH PERMITTED MOTORISTS TO RECOVER ITS PAYMENT, INCLUDING FAILING [TO] HOLD THAT EVEN IF THERE WAS A MISTAKE, A) CFI DETRIMENTALLY CHANGED ITS POSITION IN RELIANCE UPON MOTORISTS' CONDUCT AND PAYMENT, AND B) MOTORISTS WAS UNDER A LEGAL DUTY TO DETERMINE THE CORRECT FACTS REGARDING THE CLAIM IT PAID, BOTH OF WHICH PRECLUDE RECOVERY BASED UPON AN ALLEGED MISTAKE.

ASSIGNMENT OF ERROR NO. III: THE LOWER COURT ERRED IN FAILING TO ACCEPT THE STIPULATIONS OF THE PARTIES, AND IN ADDING FACTS NOT STIPULATED TO BY THE PARTIES.

ASSIGNMENT OF ERROR NO. IV: THE LOWER COURT ERRED AS A MATTER OF LAW, ABUSED ITS DISCRETION, AND ENTERED A DECISION CONTRARY TO THE MANIFEST WEIGHT OF THE EVIDENCE IN HOLDING THAT MOTORISTS WAS NOT NEGLIGENT AND EXERCISED DUE DILIGENCE IN MAKING THE PAYMENT AT ISSUE.

ASSIGNMENT OF ERROR NO. V: THE LOWER COURT ERRED IN FAILING TO HOLD THAT MOTORISTS' NEGLIGENCE OR FAILURE TO EXERCISE DUE DILIGENCE BARRED RECOVERY OF AN ALLEGED MISTAKEN PAYMENT[.]

ASSIGNMENT OF ERROR NO. VI: THE LOWER COURT ERRED IN FAILING TO HOLD MOTORISTS' CLAIM WAS BARRED BY ESTOPPEL.

ASSIGNMENT OF ERROR NO. VII: THE LOWER COURT ABUSED ITS DISCRETION AND ITS DECISION IS AGAINST THE MANIFEST WEIGHT OF THE EVIDENCE AND OTHERWISE CONTRARY TO THE FACTS.

We will address CFI's first, second, fourth, and fifth assignments of error together, as they are related. CFI argues in its first assignment of error that the trial court erred in failing to contractually enforce the lienholder's agreement between the parties. CFI argues in its second assignment of error that the trial court erred when it held there was a mistake that permitted Motorists to recover its payment. CFI argues in its fourth and fifth assignments of error that the trial court erred when it failed to find that Motorists was barred from recovery because Motorists was negligent in making the payment to CFI.

The existence of a contract is a question of law. *Zelina v. Hillyer,* 165 Ohio App.3d 255, 2005–Ohio-5803, at ¶ 12, citing *Telxon Corp. v. Smart Media of Delaware, Inc.,* Summit App. No. 22098, 2005–Ohio-4931, at ¶ 40. This court reviews questions of law regarding the existence of contracts de novo. *Continental W. Condominium Unit Owners Assn. v. Howard E. Ferguson, Inc.* (1996), 74 Ohio St.3d 501, 502. A valid contract consists of an offer, acceptance, and consideration. *Tersigni v. Gen. Tire, Inc.* (1993), 91 Ohio App.3d 757, 760. A meeting of the minds as to the essential terms of the agreement is a requirement to enforcing the contract. *Episcopal Retirement Homes, Inc. v. Ohio Dept. of Indus. Relations* (1991), 61 Ohio St.3d 366, 369.

In the present case, the trial court found the lienholder's agreement did not create a contract, although it provided no explanation. However, after a review of the record and the lienholder's agreement, we find an enforceable contract was formed. The contract complied with the three requirements of proper contract formation: offer, acceptance, and consideration. An offer is defined as "the manifestation of willingness to enter into a bargain, so made as to justify another person in understanding that his assent to that bargain is invited and will conclude it." *Reedy v. Cincinnati Bengals, Inc.* (2001), 143 Ohio App.3d 516, 521. Here, the lienholder's agreement memorialized Motorists' definite offer of $4,568.81 in settlement of Randall's vehicle damage. Further, conduct sufficient to show agreement, including performance, constitutes acceptance. *Nagle Heating & Air Conditioning Co. v. Heskett* (1990), 66 Ohio App.3d 547, 550. In the current case, the lienholder's agreement indicates CFI's acceptance of Motorists' payment to satisfy the settlement. As to consideration, such may consist of either a detriment to the promisee or a benefit to the promisor. A benefit may consist of some right, interest, or profit accruing to the promisor, while a detriment may consist of some forbearance, loss, or responsibility given, suffered, or undertaken by the promisee. *Lake Land Emp. Group of Akron, LLC v. Columber,* 101 Ohio St.3d 242, 2004–Ohio-786, at ¶ 16. Here, Motorists agreed to pay CFI $4,568.81 in settlement of any claim CFI may have against Motorists, thereby constituting sufficient consideration.

However, that the basic elements for contract formation existed, does not end the inquiry. To constitute a valid contract, there must also be a meeting of the minds of the parties. *Noroski v. Fallet* (1982), 2 Ohio St.3d 77. Although, in the present case, there was a meeting of the minds insofar as the contents of the agreement and the parties' duties, there must also exist a meeting of the minds with regard to the underlying formation of the contract. A mutual mistake of fact results in a lack of "meeting of the minds." See *Robert's Auto Center, Inc. v. Helmick*, Summit App. No. 21073, 2003–Ohio640, fn. 1, and "calls into question the very existence of the contract." *Reitz v. West* (Aug. 30, 2000), Summit App. No. 19865. Thus, a mutual mistake as to a material part of a contract can be grounds for the rescission of the contract and renders the contract voidable. *Reilley v. Richards* (1994), 69 Ohio St.3d 352.

In the present case, the parties executed the lienholder's agreement and performed their respective duties thereunder, based upon a mutual mistake of fact. A mutual mistake of fact is present where a mistake by both parties as to a basic assumption on which the contract was made has a material effect on the agreed exchange of performances. *Reilley*, at 353, citing 1 Restatement of the Law 2d, Contracts (1981), 385, Mistake, Section 152(1). The rule of mutual mistake is applicable in those situations where the parties are mistaken as to a vital existing fact at the time of contracting. *Mollenkopf v. Weller*, Franklin App. No. 03AP-1267, 2004–Ohio-5539, citing Calamari & Perillo, *Law of Contracts* (2 Ed.1977) 498, Section 13-13. Here, the parties executed the lienholder's agreement under the mistaken belief that the vehicle for which CFI was a lienholder was in an accident caused by a vehicle insured by Motorists. Both parties performed their respective duties under the contract based upon this mistaken belief, and neither would have entered into the agreement had they known it was not Barnick, Motorists' true insured, who was responsible for the Randall accident. That it had not been Barnick who was at fault in the accident with Randall was a vital fact and basic assumption underlying the parties' formation of a contract and had a material effect on the agreed exchange of performances. Therefore, a mutual mistake of fact existed, and the contract was voidable.

However, where there has been a mutual mistake, the contract is voidable by the adversely affected party only if that party did not bear the risk of the mistake under the rule stated in 1 Restatement of the Law 2d, Contracts (1981), 385, Mistake, Section 154. Section 154 provides that a party bears the risk of a mistake when: (a) the risk is allocated to him by agreement of the parties; (b) he is aware, at the time the contract is made, that he has only limited knowledge with respect to the facts to which the mistake relates but treats his limited knowledge as sufficient; or (c) the risk is allocated to him by the court on the ground that it is reasonable in the circumstances to do so. . . . Here, we find the risk of mistake must be allocated to Motorists because it is reasonable under the circumstances to do so. Motorists is responsible for the error at hand. Motorists failed to adequately investigate the Barnick accident. Motorists claims it confused the names involved in the two accidents, but a review of the accident reports or further communications with its insured would have revealed the proper parties. It is apparent Motorists also did not review the accident reports or adequately communicate with its insured before executing the lienholder's agreement and paying CFI. Reasonable standards of practice in the insurance industry demand that an insurer investigate an accident involving its insured and determine the proper parties involved prior to binding itself under contract to make a settlement payment. Thus, Motorists not only was responsible for the initial error in misidentifying the parties involved, but it also failed to properly oversee the matter throughout the full period of the settlement process.

Further, as merely the lienholder of a customer involved in an accident, CFI was an innocent party and bore no responsibility to discover the proper insureds involved. CFI is not a processor of insurance claims and was responsible only for obtaining a satisfaction in settlement of the loss of the vehicle for which they possessed a lien. Motorists represented itself as the proper party to pay such settlement, and CFI accepted the payment via Motorists' lienholder's agreement. Motorists, as an insurer, had the ability and the responsibility to determine its own liability. CFI had no reason to scrutinize the matter as long as it had Motorists' promise to pay, and CFI reasonably proceeded with its usual course of business in handling the matter after Motorists executed the lienholder's agreement. We also note the record contains no allegations that CFI knew of Motorists' error, misled Motorists, or committed any fraud in accepting the payment. Therefore, given Motorists had access to the facts upon which the mistake was founded, but failed to properly investigate the matter both immediately after the accidents and prior to payment to CFI, Motorists should bear the costs of the mistake over CFI.

Furthermore, the Ohio Supreme Court has recognized the doctrine of mutual mistake as a ground for rescission only where the complainant is not "negligent" in failing to discover the mistake. See *Reilley*, at 352–353, citing *Irwin v. Wilson* (1887), 45 Ohio St. 426 . . . , we find Motorists' failure to discover the mistake constituted negligence. Motorists was a sophisticated party

*(continued)*

and was experienced in insurance matters. . . . Specifically, Motorists, through its automobile insurance business, was in the daily practice of insuring motor vehicles, identifying parties involved in motor vehicle accidents involving its insureds, and entering settlements with those claiming damages as a result of the negligence of its insureds. Further, there is no evidence that Motorists was peculiarly or involuntarily rushed or pressured to enter the lienholder's agreement and settle the matter. In these respects, Motorists' negligence was not merely inadvertence or excusable neglect. . . . Motorists had a duty to investigate the facts but breached such duty and wholly failed to investigate with whom it was making the contract. Motorists' fault herein amounts to a failure to conform to the fair and reasonable standards of practice within the insurance industry. . . . Therefore, even if we were to consider whether Motorists was negligent in making the mistake, we find that it was so.

We also note that the trial court relied heavily upon *Firestone Tire & Rubber Co. v. Central Natl. Bank of Cleveland* (1953), 159 Ohio St. 423, for several propositions. In one regard, the trial court cited *Firestone* for the notion that the general test for recovery of a mistaken payment is if the payee, in equity and good conscience, is entitled to retain the money. *Id.* at 431. However, paragraph five of the *Firestone* syllabus refines this concept and provides that the test of the right of recovery of money paid under mistake of fact is whether "the payee has a right to retain the money . . . . If the money belongs to the payer and the payee can show no legal or equitable right to retain it he must refund it." In the present case, our determination above is grounded upon a binding agreement between the parties that satisfied the essential elements of a contract; thus, CFI has shown a "legal" contractual right to retain the monies, thereby taking the present circumstances out of the purview of the purely equitable remedies upon which *Firestone* is based.

The trial court also cited *Firestone* for the proposition that a mistaken payment made under a mistake of fact may be recovered by the payor unless the payment has caused such a detrimental change in the position of the payee that it would be unjust to require a refund. The trial court in the present case found CFI did not detrimentally change its position. However, even if we were to consider the notion of detrimental reliance discussed in *Firestone,* we find CFI did, in good faith, change its position to its detriment after receiving the payment from Motorists. Although certain parts of the transaction could be undone without any detriment to either party, such as the return of the damaged vehicle, CFI cancelled Randall's original note as being "Paid," surrendered the note to Randall, and cancelled the lien on the original title. As CFI no longer has the note and the note is marked "paid," it cannot reinstate the cancelled lien on a new title. Further, even though the title is still in Motorists' possession and was never filed with the Bureau of Motor Vehicles, the fact remains that it is the original title, is stamped "Paid," and represents a valid cancellation of the lien. Also, even if it were theoretically possible to overcome these hurdles through further legal avenues, CFI would incur legal fees and other associated expenses in attempting to undo these matters. Therefore, we find that, even if we were to analyze the present case under the equitable principles enunciated in *Firestone*, CFI would still be entitled to retain the monies.

For the above reasons, we find the mutual mistake made by the parties did not render the contract voidable by Motorists, and Motorists cannot escape the terms of the lienholder's agreement. As a matter of law, the trial court erred when it found the contract to be invalid and failed to enforce the contract between the parties . . . the judgment of the Franklin County Municipal Court is reversed, and this matter is remanded to that court for further proceedings in accordance with law, consistent with this opinion.

Judgment reversed and cause remanded.

## Case Review Question

Do you think the result would have been different if Motorist's had discovered its mistake and requested return of the funds before the checks had been deposited and the lien had been marked paid?

## PROBLEMS IN CREATING OR ENFORCING THE CONTRACT

### Terms of the Contract

On occasion, both parties intend to enter, and believe they have entered, into a valid contractual agreement, but as they begin to fulfill their contractual obligations, it becomes apparent that they have understood and agreed to different terms. When this situation occurs, the law has developed methods of determining whose expectations will be enforced.

Generally, in the case of an innocent mistake, the court will examine each side of the contract and make a determination as to what a reasonable person would perceive the terms to be under the circumstances (use of objective standard to determine intent). If it appears that a reasonable person would have understood what the offeror intended, then the offeree will be bound by the offeror's original terms. Similarly, if it is apparent that the offeror should have understood the intentions of the offeree and the terms that supported the offeree's consideration, then the offeror will be bound by the offeree's interpretation of the terms of the contract.

In making this interpretation of the terms of the contract, the court will apply the *plain meaning rule*.[24] Simply stated, this means that in most cases the court will assume that the offeror or offeree should have used ordinary meanings and definitions when interpreting the terms of the contract. The court will, however, deviate from this rule when *terms of art* (terms of technical terminology or terms used in a particular trade) are used. If all parties to the contract are members of the profession or trade that utilizes this type of terminology, then the common meaning of the term by members of the profession or trade will be used to determine what the offeror and offeree should have interpreted the term to mean.[25]

---

## ASSIGNMENT 13.3

Which of the following items could constitute valid consideration?

1. A promise not to use profane language.

2. A promise by a woman to bear three children in the next five years and sell all of her future offspring to an adoption agency.

3. A man who acts as a donor to a sperm bank is promised $100 per donation.

4. A promise to raise a child in the Muslim religion.

5. A promise to not murder one's spouse in his or her sleep no matter how vile he or she behaves when awake.

6. A promise to maintain a B+ grade point average in medical school.

7. A promise to work in an inner-city homeless shelter for two years after graduation from college.

8. A promise to write a book that is named to the *New York Times* bestseller list.

9. A promise to not burn down a neighbor's house.

10. A promise to be kind and friendly to a neighbor one despises.

---

## Unconscionable Contracts

There are two basic types of unconscionable contracts. The first is the *classic* unconscionable contract in which the innocent party had no real bargaining power or opportunity to decline. This is often based on a lack of knowledge of the true terms of the contract. The innocent party is given the terms of the contract without an opportunity to discover their real meaning and extent. For example, an unqualified person goes to the sight of a natural disaster such as a hurricane and takes contracts for home repairs for elderly persons at exorbitant rates. Because the homeowners are in need of immediate shelter, they have little choice but to pay the price regardless of how high it may be. Effectively, the homeowners are in an untenable position. They have nowhere to go and no shelter if they do not seize the opportunity. They do so only to find that the work is unsatisfactory and greatly overpriced. In such cases, the contract may be considered unconscionable.

The second type of unconscionable contract is an *adhesion* contract, which is induced by duress. The innocent party enters the contract under the threat of some type of force.[26] The threat may include physical injury, financial injury, injury to reputation, or anything else that might cause significant harm to the innocent party. A perfect example is a promise to pay money in exchange for a promise not to publish information that would be damaging to a person's reputation. If a court finds that in reality a reasonable person would have no choice but to agree to the terms of the contract as a means of protecting him- or herself, then the contract will be unconscionable because it is an adhesion contract. Sometimes the circumstances may also support criminal charges of extortion.

Unconscionability is extremely difficult to prove for several reasons. First, the courts are reluctant to judge a party's real motivation for entering a contract. Second, there is a presumption that every party should investigate the terms of a contract before agreeing to it. Finally, if the terms are for an illegal purpose, then the party has the option of calling the appropriate law-enforcement agencies rather than succumbing to the other party's demands. Nevertheless, occasions do occur in which a party believes there is no alternative but to enter into a contract that is unconscionable. In such instances, the court will declare the contract to be invalid.

## Fraud in Contracts

Fraud is an action that can be brought in a variety of situations, one of which is contract. Specifically, two types of actions for fraud can be brought to invalidate a contract: *fraud in fact* and *fraud in the inducement.* They occur under different circumstances and, if proven, have different results.

Fraud in fact occurs when one party tricks another into signing a contract by leading the other party to believe the contract is something entirely different[27]—for example, asking for a party's signature on a receipt for merchandise when, in fact, the "receipt" not only acknowledges receipt of that merchandise but also includes a purchase contract for additional merchandise.

Fraud is difficult to prove because parties generally have a duty to examine a document before affixing their signature. However, if it can be shown that the terms were not obvious or were added later, or that some other circumstance existed that prevented the party from ascertaining that he or she was actually signing a contract, the court may find fraud in fact.

When fraud in fact is proven, the result is *recision*—that is, the contract is treated as if it never existed. The court will take necessary steps to restore the parties to the condition they were in before the contract. For example, if an innocent party has incurred obligations because of the contract, the party responsible for the fraud may be forced to pay or to do whatever is necessary to satisfy or eliminate these obligations.

The elements of fraud in the inducement are as follows:

1. A misrepresentation of a present or past fact that is false must exist.
2. The party making the misrepresentation must know that what he or she is presenting is false and also must intend for it to operate as an inducement to another to enter a contractual agreement.
3. The innocent party must be reasonable both in the belief that the representation is true and in the reliance on the term as an inducement to enter the contract.
4. The misrepresentation must be a material element of the contract.[28]
5. The innocent party must suffer measurable damages as a result of its reasonable reliance on the misrepresentation.

Fraud in the inducement generally occurs when one party intentionally misrepresents the amount or quality of the consideration the opposing party is to receive under the contract. For example, a party takes reasonable steps to determine the value of the consideration he or she will receive in exchange for the promise or performance and relies on the value of the consideration in making the decision to enter the contract. In reality, the consideration is worth considerably less, and fraud in the inducement has occurred.

---

## APPLICATION 13.7

An urban couple who has always lived in New York in a rented apartment accepts a job opportunity more than 2,000 miles from where the couple's current residence. They attempt to search for a home to purchase through advertisements in the local paper. An individual contacts them about a historic home with seven bedrooms and four baths. The seller claims application has been made to place the home on the national registry of historic properties. Photos of the home show it as a magnificent Victorian mansion. The seller also sends photos of several lovely rooms such as the living room, library, and dining room and tells the couple that the house could be considered in "move-in" condition. The couple makes an offer based on research as to what such a home should be worth. The offer is accepted and the couple takes possession on arrival. The couple arrives at the house, which has been freshly painted and looks wonderful from the street. They enter the home and are stunned to find that there is no furnace, no hot water, no air conditioning, and the kitchen sink does not have running water. Water for the sink and bathtubs must be carried in from a pump approximately 50 feet behind the house. The "four baths" consist of four old bathtubs lined up in a second-story room. The "seven bedrooms" consisted of a large attic with six curtains placed at 8-foot intervals. There is no sewer connection, and the only usable toilet consists of a 100-year-old outhouse that has never been moved or cleaned and is located next to the water pump in the backyard. Further investigation shows that the application was made for placing the home on a registry, but that the application had been denied years earlier. The home was infested with rodents to the extent that rats and mice were visibly moving about in every room. Large rugs are used to cover areas where the floor has completely rotted away.

On the one hand, the buyer had an obligation to investigate before entering the contract. However, because there were significant misrepresentations as to the condition of the property, and what an objective bystander would perceive from the statements of the seller, as well as the habitability of the property, an argument could be made for fraud in the inducement.

*Point for Discussion:* Would the result be any different if the couple lived 100 miles from the house instead of 2,000?

---

When an action for fraud in the inducement succeeds, a court will allow a party to disaffirm the contract. This means that each party walks away from the contract. An attempt may be made to achieve fairness based on the true value of the consideration, but the parties will not be restored to their original condition.

## Statute of Frauds

Although all states recognize oral and written contracts, it has long been established that certain types of contracts must be in writing before they are considered valid and enforceable. The concept of a **statute of frauds** originated in England. Historically, the courts established certain important matters of agreement that should be in writing to minimize doubt or difficulty in completing the agreement.

**statute of frauds**
Statutory law that specifies what contracts must be in writing before they will be enforced.

Today, this theory has been followed in each state with the enactment of a similar statute that states what types of contracts must be in writing before a court will enforce them. Generally, these are substantial contracts whose terms should be clearly stated to minimize the opportunity for mistake or misinterpretation.[29] There are some variations from state to state, but most jurisdictions require the following types of contracts to be written before they become effective:

1. a promise by the executor or administrator of an estate to answer personally for the debts or obligations of the deceased;

2. a promise by one party to answer for the debts or obligations of another;

3. a promise given in exchange for a promise of marriage;

4. a promise to sell, transfer, or convey an interest in land (this may include ownership, possession, control, or any other interest);

5. a promise for the sale of goods by a merchant in which the price exceeds $500; and

6. an agreement that, by its terms, cannot be completed within one year.

If a contract is not required to be written and is in fact oral, the existence of a contract will be judged objectively by what the conduct of the parties would indicate they meant the terms of the agreement to be. If, however, the contract falls within one of the situations covered by the state statute of frauds, then it must be in writing before a court will even recognize that a contract exists.

## ASSIGNMENT 13.4

In the following situations, determine whether the contract should be in writing to be enforceable.

1. Maya and Ella agree to split the money equally from a bank robbery in which Maya plans to demand (and receive) $10,000 and Ella agrees to drive the getaway car.

2. George promises to pay Sam $5,000 to marry George's daughter Maggie.

3. Jesse and Kenneth agree that Jesse will give Kenneth haircuts for one year in exchange for a one-time fee of $150.

4. Olivia is the 23-year-old daughter of Martin. Olivia is being threatened with a lawsuit to collect on a debt she owes a local department store. Martin phones the department store and offers to pay the amount of the debt plus an extra $100 if the store will refrain from suing Olivia. The store agrees.

5. Beau offers to sublet the house Jack is renting for the amount of the regular rent plus $25 per month. Jack agrees.

## DEFENSES TO AN ALLEGATION OF BREACH OF CONTRACT

When an action for breach of contract is brought, several defenses are available that may prevent a judgment against the defendant. Many were discussed previously as defects or irregularities in the steps of creating a contract. The following discussion covers these and other defenses in the context of defenses.

Some of the more common defenses include the following:

1. absence of one or more essential elements to create a contract,

2. unconscionable contract,

3. fraud,

4. statute of frauds,

5. accord and satisfaction,

6. justifiable breach,

7. impossibility or impracticability, and

8. frustration of purpose or terminated duty.

A party may allege one, several, or all of the defenses alternatively. Thus, even though a jury may not find sufficient evidence to support one defense, it might be persuaded that another applies, and the plaintiff's case will fail.

One defense is known commonly as *accord and satisfaction*. Under this defense, the defendant claims to have performed by completing a new and different performance on which the parties agree in place of the original consideration. The "accord" amends the original agreement by substituting a new performance for the original, and the "satisfaction" is the fulfillment of the original contract by the substituted performance. For example, the defendant would claim to have satisfied the contract by painting the plaintiff's house instead of fixing the plaintiff's car as promised in the original contract. If the defendant fails to complete the satisfaction, however, the plaintiff can sue on either of the defendant's promises.

A second type of defense is a *justified breach of contract*. When one party breaches a contract, the second party is excused from the completion of performance. The reasoning is that the second party did not receive the consideration that originally induced his or her own promise or performance. Therefore, if consideration fails, there is no basis for requiring the contractual agreement to continue.

In addition, some circumstances force involuntary breach of contract. When this occurs, the party who fails to perform as required by the contract will not be held liable. Most commonly, such situations are referred to as impossibility or impracticability of performance and include situations where the contract cannot be completed through no fault of the parties.[30]

## APPLICATION 13.8

Jenny owns a large pet boarding and grooming business. She plans to expand her current facility and erects a large building next to the existing kennel. On January 1, she contracts with next door neighbor Burt to manufacture twelve additional runs for the new building at a cost of $6,000. She pays $2,000 on the contract. The contract is to be completed and the new runs installed by April 1 with the balance of payment due on delivery. The runs consist of a portable fenced wall system that is adjustable to create larger or smaller spaces. On January 3, a fire breaks out and the new building burns to the ground. On April 1, Burt arrives with the completed runs and demands payment. Jenny refuses and Burt sues for breach. In all likelihood, Jenny's breach would be considered justifiable. Burt clearly had notice of the fire as he lived next door. Because it occurred so soon after the contract was created, he had not had time to invest a great deal of money and labor in the project.

*Point for Discussion:* Would the result be different had Burt lived many miles away from Jenny and been unaware of the fire? If so why?

Similar to the impossibility or impracticability rule are the defenses of frustration of performance and terminated duty. Frustration of performance occurs when, through no action by the parties, the purpose of the contract is destroyed. Consequently, the duty to perform ends.[31] For example, a distributor contracts to sell liquor to a grocery store with delivery seven days per week. If the legislature passes a law prohibiting the sale of liquor on Sundays, the distributor is frustrated in performance of his or her obligations under the contract. When this occurs, the duty to perform is terminated, and there can be no action for breach of contract.

## REMEDIES FOR BREACH OF CONTRACT

As the preceding examples illustrate, numerous defenses can be offered against the charge of breach of contract, but it is up to the trier of fact to determine whether these defenses warrant a finding in favor of the defendant. When the finding is that a breach did occur and is not justified in any way, then the plaintiff will be entitled to some type of remedy for the damage incurred as a result of the breach.

Breach of contract has three common remedies: compensatory damages, liquidated damages, and specific performance. Each is distinct and applies only in particular situations of breach.

The most common remedy is compensatory damages to a plaintiff who has suffered from a breach of contract. The purpose of compensatory damages is to award a sufficient amount of money to place the plaintiff in the same position he or she would be in if the contract had been fulfilled. In this way, the plaintiff is compensated for any loss or injury. Even if the injury or loss did not actually involve money, the purpose of the remedy is to enable the plaintiff to repair the damage.

Parties use a liquidated damage clause when they know that a court will have difficulty estimating actual damages in the event of breach. In a true liquidated damage clause, the parties will arrive at a fair compensation to be paid by a party in the event that party breaches the agreement. This clause will then be included in the terms of the contract (see Exhibit 13.1).

Liquidated damages are an alternative to compensatory damages. The court has the duty to determine whether a breach occurred and, if so, whether the liquidated damage clause of the contract was, in fact, for liquidated damages or merely a prestated penalty for breach. If the court finds that the clause is a penalty, then the clause will not be enforced. The courts do not generally impose penalties set by the parties. Rather, the court will determine whether a penalty is appropriate in addition to the compensatory damages. The reasoning behind the refusal to enforce penalty clauses is quite simple. In some situations, a party does not have a defense to the breach but, for unforeseen reasons, must cease performance under the contract. Many times there are circumstances in which a party had no prior intent to breach but finds it necessary to do so. In such instances, it would not be fair to allow parties to penalize one another in excess of what would be reasonable compensation for the breach. The courts prefer to retain authority to determine appropriate circumstances for penalizing persons who breach a contract.

In a very limited number of circumstances, a court will award specific performance in cases of breach. When specific performance is awarded, the party who has breached is ordered to continue performance under the contract to the best of his or her ability. Cases in equity are based on the principle that money is an insufficient remedy and fairness warrants the imposition of performance. The

**Exhibit 13.1** Liquidated Damage Clause

In the event that the seller fails to tender the property in satisfactory condition pursuant to the terms of this agreement, on the date heretofore agreed upon, the seller shall be in default of the terms of this agreement and shall pay to the buyer as liquidated damages the amount of $200 per day for each day the seller remains in default. Said liquidated damages shall serve as reasonable compensation for costs incurred as the direct and proximate result of seller's default. Provided, if seller should remain in default of this agreement for a period greater than 60 days, the buyer shall have the option of retaining liquidated damages for said period and further buyer may elect to be released from all obligations and liability associated with this agreement. In the latter event, the seller shall be similarly released from all further obligations to buyer with respect to this agreement.

key to obtaining compelled performance is that the performance is so unique that the only way it can be satisfied is through the actual performance. In contract law, this equitable remedy is called *specific performance.* Before the court will award specific performance, the plaintiff must show that he or she has fully satisfied all obligations under the contract and that he or she has *clean hands* (meaning that the plaintiff has not acted in such a way as to cause the breach by the defendant such as through frustration or lack of cooperation). Another common requirement, known as "laches," is that the plaintiff must not have waited so long to raise the claim that the defendant is impaired in the ability to render performance.

## CASE
### Wilson v. Mike Steven Motors, Inc., et al.,
### 111 P.3d 1076 (Kan.App 2005)

In the following judicial opinion, the court examines what is necessary to constitute an unconscionable circumstances that would prevent enforcement of a contract.

Mike Steven Motors, Inc. (Dealer) appeals the denial of its motion to stay the district court proceedings and to compel arbitration of its dispute with Cornelia Wilson, arising out of the negotiation and sale of an automobile. We reverse and remand with instructions to grant the motion to compel arbitration.

In July 2003, Wilson purchased a new Toyota Camry from Dealer, allegedly based in part upon the salesperson's representation that she would receive a $500 rebate. The purchase was financed through Toyota Motor Credit Corporation (Toyota Credit). A few days after the sale, Wilson reviewed the sales paperwork and discovered the documentation did not reflect the rebate. When Wilson made inquiry of Dealer, she was stalled at first and then directed to resolve her dispute with Toyota Credit. Wilson returned the vehicle to Dealer. In August, Toyota Credit notified Wilson that her account was past due. In December 2003, the vehicle was sold at auction, even though it purportedly had only 58 miles on the odometer, with the consequence that Wilson owed a deficiency of over $7,000.

In March 2004, Wilson sued Dealer and Toyota Credit. . . . Wilson's first cause of action against Dealer alleged a deceptive act and practice under the Kansas Consumer Protection Act, K.S.A. 50-623 et seq. (KCPA). The second cause of action alleged negligent misrepresentation. Both were based on the false statement that Wilson would receive a $500 rebate.

Before filing an answer to the petition, Dealer filed a motion to stay proceedings and compel arbitration. The motion alleged that the sales contract included an arbitration agreement which applied to every claim arising out of the negotiation and sale of the vehicle. Dealer further alleged that the transaction involved interstate commerce, making the Federal Arbitration Act, 9 U.S.C. § 1 et seq. (2000) (FAA) controlling.

Wilson responded to the motion, contending that Dealer's deceptive and unconscionable acts rescinded the contract, making the arbitration agreement moot. The argument is that the entire contract was effectively rescinded by Dealer's fraudulent inducement of Wilson's vehicle purchase.

In the alternative, the response also argued that the contracts were executed in a procedurally unconscionable manner, thereby rendering the arbitration agreement unenforceable. Wilson claims that Dealer was in a superior bargaining position; that Dealer gave Wilson a large stack of forms to sign without allowing her adequate time to review all of the documents, including the arbitration agreement; and that Dealer induced the sale by making a false promise of a rebate.

The district court heard arguments on the motions. The only evidence submitted was the sales contract. After taking the matter under advisement, the district court filed a journal entry denying the motion. All of the court's findings are set forth below in their entirety:

"(1) The Court adopts as its own the facts set out and the conclusions of law in the 'Plaintiff's Response to Defendant's Mike Steven Motors' Motion to Compel Arbitration';

(2) The Defendant's motion should be denied;

(3) The case shall proceed with discovery in Sedgwick County District Court." . . .

Wilson chose to restate the issues necessary to the disposition of the appeal, which is permissible under

*(continued)*

Supreme Court Rule 6.03(b) (2004 Kan. Ct. R. Annot. 37). Wilson's restated issues are:

"I. Whether the arbitration agreement between Ms. Wilson and MSM–Eddy's Toyota [Dealer] is unenforceable because it is contrary to the public policy of this state.

"II. Whether the arbitration agreement between Ms. Wilson and MSM–Eddy's Toyota is enforceable under the facts presented.

"III. Whether the matter should be remanded for trial before the district court on the issue of whether the arbitration agreement is enforceable."

In addition, two associations submitted amicus curiae briefs, with their own characterization of the issues presented. The Wichita Auto Dealers Association made the following statements as the issues presented: (1) The FAA applies to the arbitration agreement; (2) Wilson's fraud inducement claim is referable to arbitration; and (3) Wilson's unconscionability claim is referable to arbitration, and even if it is not, the arbitration agreement was not unconscionable. The Kansas Automobile Dealers Association recited under the statement of issues that it would rely on the issues outlined in the appellant's brief but then presented arguments under the following headings:

"I. The Federal Arbitration Act completely occupies the field relating to arbitration agreements, and such agreements are subject to dissolution only upon finding fraud specific to the arbitration agreement itself.

A. Refusal to Honor an Uncoerced and Otherwise Valid Arbitration Agreement Based upon the Kansas Consumer Protection Act Cannot Be Reconciled with the Federal Arbitration Act and the Supremacy Clause of the United States Constitution as Interpreted by the United States Supreme Court.

B. When Parties to a Contract Freely Agree to Arbitrate All Potential Disputes, including Contract Formation, one Party May Not Thereafter Evade the Agreement Merely by the Couching of a Clever Draftsperson; Otherwise, the Bare-Bones Allegation of Fraud in the Inducement Would Be Sufficient to Defeat Every Arbitration Agreement.

. . . 3 "II. Plaintiff's arguments of unconscionableness are hypothetical, and lack the substantiality required by the United States Supreme Court to invalidate the arbitration agreement.

A. The United States Supreme Court Has Invariably Refused to Eviscerate Arbitration Agreements Based upon Hypothetical Arguments of Inadequacy or Excessive Arbitration Costs.

B. Enforcement of the Arbitration Agreement as Against the Plaintiff Does Not Forestall the Kansas Attorney General from Enforcing the KCPA Either for the Benefit of a Single Consumer, or on a Class-wide Basis."

The arbitration agreement provided that "[n]o class action arbitration may be ordered and there shall be no joinder of parties except for joinder of parties to the same Contract." At oral argument, Wilson's counsel stated that the sole question for this court to decide was whether the waiver of a class action in the arbitration agreement violated the KCPA's provision that prohibits a consumer's waiver of rights, thus rendering the arbitration agreement unenforceable. . . .

. . . "[W]henever a motion to compel arbitration comes on for hearing, the threshold determination to be made by the court is whether an agreement to arbitrate exists and whether this agreement includes arbitration of the specific point at issue. [Citation omitted.]" *City of Wamego v. L.R. Foy Constr. Co.,* 9 Kan.App.2d 168, 171, 675 P.2d 912, rev. denied 234 Kan. 1076 (1984). . . . If the plaintiff demonstrates a genuine issue of material fact as to the agreement to arbitrate, then a trial on the issue is necessary. See *In Re Universal Serv. Fund Tele. Billing Practices,* 300 F.Supp.2d 1107, 1117 (D.Kan.2003). . . .

The federal courts employ a separability doctrine when a party challenges the enforceability of an arbitration agreement. An allegation of fraud in the inducement of a contract as a whole is subject to arbitration, if the agreement to arbitrate was not alleged to have been fraudulently induced. *Prima Paint v. Flood & Conklin,* 388 U.S. 395, 403–04, 18 L.Ed.2d 1270, 87 S.Ct. 1801 (1967). The Supreme Court relied on § 3 of the FAA, saying that when considering a stay under this section, "a federal court may consider only issues relating to the making and performance of the agreement to arbitrate." 388 U.S. at 404. Sections 3 and 4 apply to the federal courts. See 9 U.S.C. § § 3–4; Southland Corp, 465 U.S. at 16 n. 10. . . .

The distinction between void and voidable contracts makes sense. If a party is claiming that the contract containing an arbitration agreement never had a legal existence, then, if true, there could never have been a legal agreement to submit the dispute to an arbitrator. Therefore, the courts should make the determination whether the whole contract was void *ab initio*. On the other hand, by definition a voidable contract does have legal effect, including any provision requiring arbitration, until the allegedly aggrieved party chooses to seek rescission. Therefore, on voidable contracts, the courts should permit the arbitration of the question of the rescission of the contract as a whole, unless the court decides the arbitration agreement is separately infirm.

Therefore, we restrict our analysis to whether the arbitration agreement, standing alone, is enforceable. To that end, we will consider whether the arbitration agreement was unenforceable because: (1) it was fraudulently induced; (2) it violated Kansas public policy by contravening a consumer's rights under the KCPA; or (3) it was unconscionable. . . .

Dealer presented the court with a written, signed arbitration agreement. . . . Under the separability doctrine, it was incumbent on Wilson to come forward with evidence of some material disputed fact which would establish that the arbitration agreement was fraudulently induced. However, Wilson's response to the motion, ostensibly adopted by the district court, attacked the contract as a whole. The response contended "that the entire contract was a result of the misrepresentations and unconscionable conduct of [Dealer]" because the Dealer falsely "promised a rebate to the plaintiff to induce her to purchase the Camry." The response then declared that "Wilson's notice of recission [sic] nullified the contract and without a valid contract there can be no resulting agreement requiring the parties to arbitrate." Other than tying the arbitration agreement's validity directly to that of the purchase agreement, Wilson does not effectively establish a material dispute as to the validity of the separate, written, and signed Arbitration Agreement.

Wilson provides no authority for the proposition that the notice of rescission rendered the entire contract a nullity. Indeed, whether the purchase contract could be rescinded is the question to be decided, either by the court or the arbitrator. Because the district court simply adopted Wilson's response as its findings, we must declare that the court erred in finding that Wilson's agreement to arbitrate was nullified by her notice of rescission. To the extent the district court's motion denial was based on fraudulent inducement, it is reversed.

. . . "Unconscionability is a doctrine under which courts may deny enforcement of unfair or oppressive contracts because of procedural abuses arising out of the contract formation, or because of substantive abuses relating to the terms of the contract, such as terms which violate reasonable expectations of parties or which involve gross disparities in price. [Citation omitted.] Either abuse can be the basis for a finding of unconscionability." *Remco Enterprises, Inc. v. Houston,* 9 Kan.App.2d 296, 301, 677 P.2d 567, rev. denied 235 Kan. 1042 (1984).

The district court's adoption of Wilson's response to Dealer's motion as its findings leaves us with the impression that the court did not make a specific finding of unconscionability of the arbitration agreement, but rather found the entire contract unconscionable. . . . In considering whether the arbitration agreement was unconscionable, we apply general contract law principles. See *Doctor's Associates, Inc. v. Casarotto,* 517 U.S. 681, 686–89, 134 L.Ed.2d 902, 116 S.Ct. 1652 (1996). In *Wille v. Southwestern Bell Tel. Co.,* 219 Kan. 755, 758–59, 549 P.2d 903 (1976), our Supreme Court identified the following factors to aid in the determination of unconscionability.

> "(1) The use of printed form or boilerplate contracts drawn skillfully by the party in the strongest economic position, which establish industry wide standards offered on a take it or leave it basis to the party in a weaker economic position [citation omitted]; (2) a significant cost-price disparity or excessive price; (3) a denial of basic rights and remedies to a buyer of consumer goods [citation omitted]; (4) the inclusion of penalty clauses; (5) the circumstances surrounding the execution of the contract, including its commercial setting, its purpose and actual effect [citation omitted]; (6) the hiding of clauses which are disadvantageous to one party in a mass of fine print trivia or in places which are inconspicuous to the party signing the contract [citation omitted]; (7) phrasing clauses in language that is incomprehensible to a layman or that divert his attention from the problems raised by them or the rights given up through them; (8) an overall imbalance in the obligations and rights imposed by the bargain; (9) exploitation of the underprivileged, unsophisticated, uneducated and the illiterate [citation omitted]; and (10) inequality of bargaining or economic power." Furthermore, "there must be additional factors such as deceptive bargaining conduct as well as unequal bargaining power to render the contract between the parties unconscionable." 219 Kan. at 759.

Wilson argued to the district court that Dealer was in a superior bargaining position as the only Toyota dealer in Wichita, that she had been given a large stack of forms to sign without adequate time to review the arbitration agreement, and that Dealer used deceptive tactics by promising a rebate in order to induce Wilson into purchasing the vehicle. On appeal, Wilson adds that the Amicus Wichita Auto Dealers Association admitted its members regularly use the preprinted form arbitration agreement, that the agreement denies her basic rights and remedies, that Wilson would not have purchased the vehicle except for the promise of the rebate, and that Wilson is not as sophisticated as Dealer.

Our review of the arbitration agreement fails to disclose unconscionability on its face. The arbitration provision

*(continued)*

is not hidden in fine print, but rather it is contained in a separate, one-page document, clearly entitled "ARBITRATION AGREEMENT," in an adequately sized typeface. The last paragraph of the agreement is in large type, all capital and bold-faced letters, stating:

> "THE PARTIES ACKNOWLEDGE THAT THEY HAD A RIGHT TO LITIGATE CLAIMS THROUGH A COURT BEFORE A JUDGE OR JURY, BUT WILL NOT HAVE THAT RIGHT IF EITHER PARTY ELECTS ARBITRATION. THE PARTIES FURTHER ACKNOWLEDGE THAT DISCOVERY IS MORE LIMITED IN ARBITRATION. THE PARTIES HEREBY KNOWINGLY AND VOLUNTARILY WAIVE THEIR RIGHTS TO LITIGATE SUCH CLAIMS IN A COURT BEFORE A JUDGE OR JURY UPON ELECTION OF ARBITRATION BY EITHER PARTY."

The document was signed by both parties on lines situated immediately below the bold-faced paragraph, making it difficult to miss the warning. Wilson had a legal obligation to make some effort to read the agreement before signing. See, e.g., *Rosenbaum v. Texas Energies, Inc.*, 241 Kan. 295, 299, 736 P.2d 888 (1987). The remaining language of the agreement is not unduly difficult to understand.

While automobile dealers may routinely use the form provided by their trade associations, the record does not reflect that Dealer would have missed the sale if Wilson had balked at signing the separate arbitration agreement. We also question whether there existed an inequality of bargaining or economic power. One would not expect to be inundated with media advertisements proclaiming sales, rebates, and low to no interest financing if vehicle purchasers have no bargaining power. Granted, Wilson may have been at a distinct disadvantage with respect to sales techniques, but we do not perceive that her lack of sophistication warrants a finding that the arbitration agreement was unconscionable. . . . The district court should have granted Dealer's motion to stay the proceedings and to compel arbitration. We reverse and remand with directions for the district court to grant the motion.

Reversed and remanded with directions.

## Case Review Question

Would the outcome be affected if the arbitration agreement were located on the back of one of the forms, in fine print, and did not require a separate signature?

---

## APPLICATION 13.9

A wealthy couple is building a custom home using wood harvested entirely from the large property on which the house is built. They contract with a general carpenter to mill the wood and install hardwood floors, an outdoor deck, and woodwork around the windows. They also contract with the carpenter's brother, a master craftsman, to hand carve banisters on staircases, a buffet table in the dining room, mantles for all of the fireplaces, and a custom door for the entryway. Each item is to be intricately carved with a repeating pattern throughout the house. After a few months, the craftsman brother is offered a higher-paying job. His work is only one-third completed. The general carpenter brother decides to take over the entire project. He thinks he can come pretty close to the pattern his brother started, although he has no experience in this type of work. The couple sues the master craftsman for specific performance. Because the work has unique and artistic characteristics, it is probable that specific performance would be granted.

*Point for Discussion:* Would the result be different if the general carpenter had accepted a higher-paying job and the craftsman wanted to undertake his brother's responsibilities under the contract?

---

## ETHICAL CONSIDERATIONS

An obligation underlying all contractual agreements is the duty to act ethically. This includes fair dealing and honesty. As seen in the preceding discussion, dishonesty regarding the terms of the contract, misrepresentations as to the consideration, and taking unfair advantage of the vulnerabilities of the other party can result in legal action against the wrongdoer. Consequently, anyone who is engaged in a contractual agreement has made an unspoken additional commitment to act in a manner that would be considered by an objective observer to be ethical. This is not to say that one who is contracting must put the interests of the co-contractor above one's own interests. Rather, the duty is to act in such a way that the co-contractor is not the victim of unfair advantage or dishonesty.

## Questions

If you were selling your car and knew that the tires (which are obviously worn) do not handle well in snow, do you have an ethical obligation to tell this to all prospective buyers? What if the defect were instead a loose electrical connection that had caught fire in the past but is not readily noticeable?

### ETHICAL CIRCUMSTANCE

Nick is a paralegal working for a law firm. He is asked by the attorney to have a client on an existing case come in and sign a contract for representation. The file does not contain a contract from the initial meeting with the client, and the attorney claims that this was somehow missed at the initial meeting. Among other things, the contract waives responsibility on the part of the lawyer for any loss of evidence left in her possession. Nick knows for a fact that the lawyer recently left her briefcase in a bar and lost several client files including that of this client. Nick also remembers the lawyer telling him that she was concerned because several Polaroid photos to be used as evidence in the case had been in the file and could not be reproduced. Should Nick ask the client to sign the contract without divulging this information?

## ● | CHAPTER SUMMARY

The law of contracts is complex and contains many intricacies not addressed here. It is also an area of law that continues to change and adapt to new situations, so it is important to remember that beyond the basic principles set forth here are many, many variations of these themes that should be explored when confronted with a contractual dispute. The best approach is always to prepare a contract with the fullest expectation that it will be litigated someday. By using this approach, many of the grounds for dispute can be prevented through clear and appropriate language and good faith compliance by the parties.

When preparing or interpreting a contract, be mindful that there must be two or more parties, legal capacity, assent, and consideration. Each element is determined by objectively looking at the situation surrounding the creation of the contract. Further, the terms of the contract—such as time of performance, price, quantity, and identity of the offeror and offeree—must be definite. Many contracts must be in writing before a court will enforce them. Enforcement may also be denied on the basis of irregularities in the circumstances surrounding the contract such as mistake, fraud, illusory promises, frustration of purpose, or unconscionable terms. Persons with a third-party relationship to a contract such as beneficiaries, assignees, or delegatees may also have certain rights or obligations with respect to the contract that must always be addressed.

Finally, the remedies for a broken or breached contract include money damages, recision, reformation, and, in limited cases, specific performance. How appropriate each of these remedies may be depends entirely on the nature of the contract and the circumstances under which the contract was created. Therefore, when evaluating or creating a contract, be particularly aware of the situation that surrounds it.

## ● CHAPTER TERMS

bilateral contract             contractual capacity          third-party beneficiary
contract                       statute of frauds             unilateral contract
contractual agreement

## ● REVIEW QUESTIONS

1. Describe capacity to contract.
2. What is the difference between an objective and subjective standard in determining the effectiveness of a contract?
3. Why are contracts for gifts unenforceable?
4. What is assignment?
5. What is delegation?
6. What is fraud in fact?
7. Why are adhesion contracts unenforceable?
8. Why are advertisements generally not considered contracts?
9. When can an offer be terminated?
10. What is the difference between a bilateral and unilateral contract?

## ● HELPFUL WEB SITES

General contract law principles        http://www.freeadvice.com/law/518us.htm
Contract forms                         http://www.contractsonline.net

## ● INTERNET ASSIGNMENT 13.1

Using Internet resources, locate a form contract to use for the following:
1. purchase of an automobile
2. legal representation
3. agreement to provide a personal service (e.g., home repair or remodeling).

## ● INTERNET ASSIGNMENT 13.2

What is the statute of limitations to file suit for breach of (1) written contracts and (2) oral contracts in your jurisdiction?

## ● ENDNOTES

1. William Statsky, *Legal Thesaurus/Dictionary* (St. Paul, MN: West, 1982).
2. 17 Am.Jur.2d., Contracts, Section 10.
3. *Id.,* Section 15.
4. Restatement (Second) of Contracts, Section 12.
5. *Id.;* Childres and Spritz, *Status in the Law of Contracts,* 47 New York Law Review 1 (April 1972).
6. *Kilroe v. Troast,* 117 N.H. 598, 376 A.2d 131 (1977).
7. 1 Williston on Contracts 3d ed., Section 13.
8. *Flemington National Bank & Trust Co. (N.A.) v. Domler Leasing Corp.,* 65 A.D.2d 29, 410 N.Y.S.2d 75 (1978).

9. Restatement (Second) of Contracts, Section 24.
10. 17 Am.Jur.2d, Contracts, Section 31.
11. *European-American Banking Corp. v. Chock Full O'Nuts Corp.,* 109 Misc.2d 615, 442 N.Y.S.2d 715 (1981).
12. 7A C.J.S., Auctions and Auctioneers, Section 11.
13. *Schmidt v. Foster,* 380 P.2d 124 (Wyo. 1963).
14. *Mobil Oil Corp. v. Wroten,* 303 A.2d 698, aff'd 315 A.2d 728 (Del. 1973).
15. *Taylor v. Roberts,* 307 F.2d 776 (10th Cir. 1962).
16. *Honolulu Rapid Transit Co. v. Paschoal,* 51 Hawaii 19, 449 P.2d 123 (1968).
17. 17 C.J.S., Contracts, Section 43.
18. *Reserve Insurance Co. v. Duckett,* 249 Md. 108, 238 A.2d 536 (1968).
19. *Clausen & Sons Inc. v. Theo. Hamm Brewing Co.,* 395 F.2d 388 (8th Cir. 1968).
20. *Wavetek Indiana, Inc. v. K. H. Gatewood Steel Co., Inc.,* 458 N.E.2d 265 (Ind. App. 1984).
21. *Id.*
22. Restatement (Second) of Contracts, Section 302, et seq.
23. *Id.*
24. 17A C.J.S., Contracts, Section 586.
25. *Damora v. Christ-Janer,* 184 Conn. 109, 441 A.2d 61 (1981).
26. *Mitchell v. Aetna Casualty & Surety Co.,* 579 F.2d 342 (5th Cir. 1978).
27. *Christian v. Christian,* 42 N.Y.2d 63, 396 N.Y.S.2d 817, 365 N.E.2d 849 (1977).
28. See note 21. Sections 151, 152.
29. *Id.*
30. 17 Am.Jur.2d. Contracts, Section 400, et seq.
31. *Id.*

## STUDENT CD-ROM

For additional materials, please go to the CD in this book.

## ONLINE COMPANION™

For additional resources, please go to www.paralegal.delmar.cengage.com

# The Law of Business

## IS IT A DONKEY OR A HORSE?

It is an interesting thing about donkeys and horses. When donkeys feel threatened, they act individually to rear and kick in all directions. Ultimately, they may end up kicking each other to death. Horses, their close relatives, have an entirely different reaction to trouble. They will form a circle with all heads pointing inward together. They then proceed to kick out at anything that might intrude on or threaten the group. The same is true of those engaged in business together. If the business gets into trouble and those involved in the business do not work together, they can often be the greatest contributors to its demise. However, if the owners and employees of the business work together to address the issues, quite often the problems can be overcome and the business can succeed. For donkeys or horses, the choice to randomly kick or circle together is largely by instinct. For people, it is a matter of conscious choice. Playing the blame game will increase the degree of difficulty for the business and create weaknesses that are perceived as opportunities for predators. By accepting responsibility and being actively involved, however, the resolution for people can result in a win for everyone involved and a business whose health is stronger than ever.

## CHAPTER OBJECTIVES

After reading this chapter, you should be able to:

- Discuss the role of agency in partnerships and corporations.
- Distinguish actual and apparent authority.
- Distinguish by characteristic the business forms of partnership, corporation, and sole proprietorship.
- List the determining factors for the existence of a partnership.

- Discuss limited partnerships' unique characteristics and describe the steps to create a corporation.
- Discuss a corporate promoter's role.
- Explain the rationale behind the doctrine of piercing the corporate veil.
- Describe the process of dissolution of a corporation.

This chapter focuses on the major categories of business entities: sole proprietorships, general and limited partnerships, and corporations (see Exhibit 14.1). In addition, the law of agency is discussed within the context of business organizations.

The way a business entity is organized will dictate who receives the income of the business, who is liable for debts or judgments against the business, and who in the business has the authority to make decisions regarding its operation. In addition, the law of agency governs such issues as who is permitted to represent the business in dealings with other entities and the methods and procedures for such dealings.

This chapter contains references to certain model laws that have been adopted by all or a majority of the states. These laws, often known as *uniform acts,*

**Exhibit 14.1.** Business Organizations

| Characteristic | Sole Proprietorship | General Partnership | Limited Partnership | Corporation |
|---|---|---|---|---|
| Number of owners | 1 | 2+ | 2+ | 1+ |
| Life | Limited | Limited | Limited | Unlimited |
| Liability | Unlimited personal | Unlimited personal | General: unlimited personal<br>Limited: limited personal | Limited personal |
| Control | Complete | Shared | General: shared<br>Limited: none of day-to-day | Limited to policy changes |
| Income | All personal | All personal | All personal | Only dividends personal |
| Legal status | None | Very limited | Very limited | Separate entity |

are precisely what the name implies. They are designed for adoption by all the states so that every state will treat a particular business entity or transaction in substantially the same way. With interstate transactions becoming more frequent, these laws provide for fair and consistent treatment of business no matter where it is transacted. In the law of business, one of the most frequently employed uniform laws is the Uniform Commercial Code (UCC).

The UCC has been adopted, at least in part, by every state. It contains a series of laws that detail the legal rights and obligations of parties to formal business transactions. The adoption of this code has eliminated many of the inconsistencies in the way legal disputes over common transactions were dealt with in the various state courts.

## AGENCY

**agent**
A person authorized, requested, permitted, by another to act on his or her behalf.

**agency**
When one party known as the *agent* acts on behalf of another party known as the *principal*. In a valid agency relationship, the agent can legally bind the principal.

An **agent** is formally defined as:

> A person authorized (requested or permitted) by another person to act for him; a person entrusted with another's business.[1]

The person who gives authority to another to act in his or her behalf is the *principal;* the person who receives authority to act on behalf of another is the *agent*. An example of a typical **agency** relationship is a retail company and its sales force. As agents, these salespersons have the authority to act on behalf of the retail company (which is their principal) to sell the company's products.

## APPLICATION 14.1

Kim is employed by the Romano Pizza restaurant as a delivery driver. Kim picks up the pizzas from the restaurant and delivers them. She also collects payments for the pizzas on behalf of her employer. The owner of the Romano restaurant is the principal, and Kim is the agent. Kim's actions while working are entirely on behalf of and in place of the owner of the restaurant.

*Point for Discussion:* Assume Kim also sells handmade pizza cooking stones when she delivers. Is she still an agent of Romano Pizza during this activity?

## Creation of the Agency Relationship

Before an agency can be created, the principal must have the legal capacity to authorize such a relationship[2]—that is, the principal must have the ability to enter into a contract. Specifically, the principal must be over the age of majority in the jurisdiction (usually eighteen or twenty-one) and must be legally competent. A declaration of *legal incompetence* means that the court has found that a person is not capable of managing his or her own affairs. If the principal is a business entity such as a corporation or partnership, then it should be organized in such a way that it is recognized as that type of business entity by the laws of the state.

Conversely, it is not necessary for an agent to have contractual authority.[3] Conceivably, a principal could appoint a minor or a person who has been declared legally incompetent to act as an agent. In agency, it is still possible for such a person to have authority to deal in the affairs of a principal. Most jurisdictions, however, do impose minimum levels of competence for an agent. Generally, persons who are virtually totally deficient in mental ability (insane) will not be considered part of a valid principal–agent relationship.

---

### APPLICATION 14.2

Gino makes and sells gourmet foods. He allows schools and churches to sell the foods on his behalf as part of a fund-raising program whereby the school or church will receive a percentage of the profits for the foods it sells. The schools and churches take orders, collect money, and deliver food. This is often done by young people well under the age of majority. Gino is the principal. The individuals associated with the schools and churches are agents. They are not required to have contractual capacity to enter into the principal agent relationship because they have no responsibility with regard to the product they assist Gino in selling. If it were discovered that some of the food was tainted and caused illness, then the responsibility would lie with Gino.

*Point for Discussion:* How would the results be different if the schools and churches bought the food, stored it, and then resold it?

---

### ASSIGNMENT 14.1

In the following situation, identify each principal, agent, and act of agency. Also identify whether the agency is employment related.

Stan and Terrell are business partners. They also hire Terrell's brother Xavier to work in the business. On Monday morning, Stan picks up Xavier and gives him a ride to work. On the way, Stan says he will run to the donut shop and get everyone some breakfast. Before doing this, he drops Xavier off at the post office to pick up mail for the business and to go next door and get Stan's suit from the dry cleaners. Stan gets the donuts and picks Xavier up. They go on to work, where Stan passes out the donuts to the rest of the staff.

Terrell has been in the office already that morning. He has negotiated a new service contract for the office equipment in the business. Xavier is asked to meet a delivery truck at the warehouse next to the office and supervise the unloading of new inventory. Xavier approves the delivery and signs for the products. The delivery company is a nationwide delivery service. The driver also gives a box to Xavier and asks him to sign for it. The box contains an expensive piece of jewelry that Terrell ordered for his wife as an anniversary gift. Terrell had already told Xavier the box was coming and asked him to keep it as his house until Terrell's anniversary.

## Agent's Duties

The agent has several duties toward the principal. First is the duty of a fiduciary. The agent owes complete loyalty to the interests of the principal, including protecting those interests and any confidential communications regarding them.[4] If the agent acts on behalf of another or even on his or her own behalf in a way that is in conflict with the principal's interest, then the agent has violated the fiduciary duty.

Second, every agent owes the principal a duty to act with reasonable care to protect the assets and interests of the principal. An agent who is in possession of property belonging to the principal must take reasonable steps to protect it. An agent with confidential knowledge regarding the interests of the principal must act reasonably not to allow this information to be exploited. Failure to do either of these things would constitute a breach of the agent's duty of reasonable care.[5]

Finally, the agent owes the principal a certain degree of obedience. Within the principal–agent relationship, the principal can, to a reasonable extent, direct the actions of the agent in accomplishing the purpose of the agency.[6] For example, if the agency involves the sale of the principal's product, the principal may, to a reasonable extent, dictate the sales methods used by the agents. If an agent deviates substantially from the directions of the principal, then the agent has breached the duty of obedience.

If an agent does breach one of the duties owed to a principal, then several things may occur. First, the responsibility of the principal to be bound to third parties by the agent's acts may be affected. The principal may also have an action at law against the agent to recover any damage suffered as a result of the breach. If the agent was paid for the services rendered, then the principal may sue for damages incurred directly as a result of the breach of one or more of the duties.

Whether an agent is paid for services rendered or performs the services as a gratuitous gesture, the principal may sue the agent in tort for the breach of reasonable care of property or the failure to make reasonable efforts to accomplish the purpose of the agency. Specifically, the principal could sue the agent for negligently or intentionally failing to perform the duties of an agent.

If the agent breaches the fiduciary duty and profits from dealing on his or her own behalf rather than on behalf of the principal, then the principal may recover all of the profits accumulated through the agent's self-dealing. This is allowed to prevent agents from profiting at the expense of the principal.

## Principal's Duties

Just as binding are the duties of the principal toward the agent. Unless the agent has agreed to act gratuitously, every principal owes an agent a duty of reasonable compensation for the services performed on behalf of the principal.[7] In addition, an agent is entitled to reimbursement by the principal for reasonable expenses incurred in achieving the agency's objective.[8] This duty of reimbursement also extends to losses the agent may suffer while engaged in the agency relationship. Finally, a principal has the duty to cooperate in allowing the agent to complete his or her assigned tasks.

An exception to the duty of compensation and reimbursement occurs when the loss is incurred through the fault of the agent. For example, if an agent traveling on behalf of the principal's business is in an automobile accident, the principal could be held responsible for the agent's property loss, such as damage to the car, as well as for the agent's medical costs for treatment of injuries. If, however, the accident is caused by the agent's careless driving, the principal would have no liability for the agent's losses. (Note that this does not relieve the principal of liability for injuries caused to third persons by the agent's conduct.)

If the principal fails or refuses to honor any of these duties, then the agent is entitled to bring an action at law against the principal for breach of contract. In addition, the agent may be entitled to impose a possessory lien on property of the principal that the agent holds. For example, if an agent is in possession of property of the principal and the principal does not pay the agent due compensation for work performed, then the agent often has the option of holding the property until the principal complies with the duty of compensation or reimbursement.

## Types of Authority

Assuming that both parties have the requisite capacity and are aware of the duties of each, four general types of authority can be exercised: *actual authority, apparent authority, inherent authority,* and *authority by ratification.* They are distinguished by the kind of authority given to the agent and the manner in which it is given. Each is created in a different way and imposes different degrees of responsibility on the parties.

**Actual Authority.** For actual authority to exist, the element of consent must be present.[9] The principal and the agent must both speak or act in a way that manifests agreement to the relationship. In addition, the principal must have legal capacity. The agency is not required to serve a purpose that will benefit both the principal and the agent. It is entirely possible for an agency to exist in which the agent receives no consideration for representing the principal.

Usually, a written agreement regarding the agency relationship is not required. Words or actions of the two parties are enough to establish that an agency exists between them. Some states, however, have an exception to this—that is, if a purpose of the agency is to grant authority to the agent to enter into written contracts on behalf of the principal. In this situation, the agent must have written evidence of authority from the principal. This is known as the *equal dignities rule.*[10] If a contract must be in writing under the statute of frauds (the statute in each jurisdiction that states which contracts must be in writing to be valid), it is only logical that the grant of authority to enter into the contract on behalf of another should also be in writing.

An agency based on actual authority is created solely by the principal and agent through agreement and is not based on what a third party perceives as the relationship between the principal and the agent. Actual authority includes two subcategories that indicate the way in which the agency was created and, to some degree, the extent of the agent's authority.

*Actual express authority.* Actual express authority occurs when the principal gives to the agent an overt verbal or written communication stating the nature of the authority.[11] The principal need not put specific limits on the authority, such as time or degree, although this is desirable. If no limits are placed on the agent and a question arises as to whether the agent exceeded the authority, the court will limit the authority to what would be usual and customary under the circumstances.[12]

An example of express authority is the relationship between the owner and the sales staff at an automobile dealership. The owner (principal) gives actual express authority to the sales personnel to negotiate for the sale of cars in the inventory of the business. The authority of the agents would not ordinarily extend to the point of giving the cars away or selling the property where the business is located.

*Actual implied authority.* Actual implied authority takes effect when the principal acts in such a way that the agent reasonably believes that the authority to act for the principal has been granted.[13] In limited situations, implied authority can occur in conjunction with express authority. The agent who has express authority to accomplish certain objectives for the principal also has the principal's implied authority to do whatever is reasonably necessary to accomplish the objectives. For example, a housekeeper who is authorized to manage a household, clean the house, and prepare meals would generally also have implied authority to purchase necessary cleaning supplies and groceries on behalf of the principal.

It is also considered reasonable for an agent with express authority in a particular type of business to employ customs and methods generally used in that type of business. For example, a construction company (principal) gives express authority to an agent to submit bids for building contracts. If the customs or methods used in the bidding include negotiating first with subcontractors, then it is implied that the agent has the authority to engage in such negotiations to be competitive and to obtain contracts for the principal.

A type of actual implied authority that is independent from actual express authority is called *implied authority by acquiescence*. It takes place when the principal has not given an agent the express authority to do certain acts on behalf of the principal.[14] Nevertheless, the agent does act, and the principal does not interfere or object and accepts any benefit that results from the agent's actions. When this type of conduct occurs, the agent is presumed to have implied authority to continue acting on behalf of the principal, and the principal will be bound by the acts of the agent that are consistent with previous actions agreed to or acquiesced to by the principal.

## APPLICATION 14.3

Paralegal Leeza has created a document service. She drafts basic fill-in-the-blank type legal documents and sells them in a do-it-yourself package. Leeza is located in a large city and needs help to get her product out. She plans to visit all of the potential outlets for her product that have departments devoted to reference materials, such as bookstores and office supply stores. She hires Cain to deliver completed products to existing customers with whom Leeza has a contract for her kits. During his working time, Cain also talks with the customers and takes orders for requested documents, including those that are not currently in Leeza's inventory. Cain negotiates the price for the latter. He purchases the necessary supplies for the kits such as large envelopes, tab dividers, and so on and charges them against Leeza's sales to the business. If Leeza poses no objection, then Cain has implied authority to take the additional orders and charge items against her sales.

*Point for Discussion:* Could Leeza avoid the obligation to generate and sell new documents at the price set by Cain on the basis that she had told Cain previously not to take orders for documents not in inventory?

Actual authority (express or implied) can be terminated. The simplest means of terminating an agency is to make the termination part of the original agency agreement. When the agency is created, the principal states when it will end. Often this is based on a certain date or the happening of a specified event. For example, if the agent is hired to obtain a certain construction contract, then the agency will end when the contract is awarded to a construction company.

More complicated are agencies that end because of unforeseen circumstances. If something occurs that effectively prevents the purpose of the agency from being accomplished, a court will often find that the agency terminated at that point. If the agent continues on after the occurrence, then a court may hold the agent entirely responsible for any contracts or obligations incurred. Examples of circumstances that would automatically terminate an agency include the loss or destruction of items necessary to the purpose of the agency (a fire that destroys the equipment of the construction company), a drastic change in business conditions (the opening of a new highway that diverts all traffic away from the dairy), a change in relevant laws, potential bankruptcy of the principal or agent if it is relevant to the purpose of the agency, death of the principal or agent, total loss of capacity of the agent, loss of capacity by the principal, or, if the principal is a business entity, dissolution of the entity. In addition, if an agent takes action that is adverse to the principal or the principal's purpose in hiring the agent, then the agency will automatically terminate. With respect to the last method, however, if a contract is involved, there may still be liability for breach of contract.

**Apparent Authority.** Apparent authority, also known as *ostensible authority,* is created through the acts of the principal and the perception of these acts by third parties.[15] Generally, a third party cannot conclude that an agency agreement exists based solely on the acts and assertions of the agent. The general rule regarding apparent authority is that if a principal acts in such a way that third parties would reasonably believe an agency relationship exists, then those third parties can rely on and deal with the agent, and the principal will be bound by such dealings.[16]

First, assume an agent represents to a third party that he or she has the authority to act for the principal. If the principal knows of this and does not tell the third party differently, then the third party is justified in believing the agent has the authority. Apparent authority can also be created if the principal acts in such a way or makes statements that would reasonably lead the third party to believe the agent has authority. In such a case, if the third party and the agent make an agreement, regardless of whether the agent in fact has authority, then the principal will be bound to the terms of the agreement.

## APPLICATION 14.4

Rob has worked at a local college for several years. In his duties, he regularly ordered office equipment, including computers. He was the only person on campus with this authority. The school typically ordered eight to ten basic computers each July for use in classrooms and as upgrades for employee offices. Rob planed to retire on January 21. In early January, he ordered an elaborate and state-of-the-art computer system unlike any previous purchase and arranged for it to be delivered to the college. He confirmed a delivery date of January 21. That day, the computer arrived, and as he carried his various belongings out of his office on a cart, he included the computer and took it home. When the bill arrived the following month at the college, the purchase order number could not be tracked to any approved purchase. The college did not send out any communication to its suppliers with regard to Rob's retirement. Based on Rob's previously established authority to make purchases, the supplier would probably be considered reasonable in believing that Rob had apparent authority to make the purchase. Even though the computer was of a different type and ordered at a different time, Rob was the only person the company did business with on behalf of the college and had no basis to suspect he did not have authority to order it.

*Point for Discussion:* Would the result be likely to change if Rob had the computer delivered directly to his home address?

A principal can be held responsible for an agent whose authority has previously been terminated if the principal does not make the termination known to parties who previously did business with the agent. This is known as *lingering apparent authority*.[17] If the principal does not make such notification, then third parties are reasonable in believing that the agency still exists. As a consequence, the principal will continue to be held responsible for the agent's actions. An exception to this rule is the death or incompetency of the principal, in which case no notice need be given to third parties. The agent's authority automatically ceases, and the principal's estate will not be bound to any agreements entered into after the death or declaration of incompetence of the principal.

**Inherent Authority.** In certain limited situations, a principal will be held responsible for the acts of an agent even though nothing has occurred to give the agent actual or apparent authority. This is called *inherent authority*, and it is based on a balance of the interests of the principal and innocent third parties. Inherent authority is often imposed when an agent has actual or apparent authority to do one thing and does another.

Two circumstances in which the courts will impose inherent authority are *respondeat superior* and *similar conduct*.[18] Under *respondeat superior*, a principal is held liable for the acts of an employee even when the specific act complained of was not authorized. For example, a delivery truck driver crashes the truck into another vehicle. The employer (principal) authorized deliveries, not automobile accidents. Nevertheless, the principal is liable because the accident took place while the driver (agent) was performing an authorized act.

The theory of similar conduct is based on the concept that a principal should be held responsible for actions that are so similar to the authorized acts that third parties would not be expected to know the difference. Refer to the earlier example of a construction company that hires an agent to submit bids for building contracts. If the agent is represented to have authority to bid and then modifies the bid slightly, a third party would be justified in believing the agent had this type of authority. Consequently, if a principal wants to place precise limits on the authority of an agent, then such limitations should be clearly conveyed to any third parties.

**Ratification.** Ordinarily, if no agency relationship exists but someone represents agency authority to a third party, who then relies on the representation and deals with the agent, then the principal will not be bound. However, if the principal becomes aware of the representation after the fact and agrees to it, then *agency by ratification* exists. In essence, the principal agrees to the agency after the agent has already acted on behalf of the principal.[19] If the principal does not agree, then no agency exists, and the principal is not bound by the acts of the agent.

This theory is distinct from the other possible theories of agency that may apply in similar situations such as actual implied authority or *respondeat superior* if the agent's acts were similar or closely related to those for which authority had been granted. If the principal ratifies the actions of the agent, then normally that ratification is retroactive. For example, if the purported agent enters into a contract on behalf of the purported principal, then the contract will be in effect from the day it was entered, not the day the principal ratified it. If the contract is one that must be completed in a certain period of time, this may be quite significant.

An exception to the time element of ratification occurs when the principal did not have legal capacity at the time of the agent's actions. Thus, if the principal gains capacity (e.g., reaches the age of majority) on or before the date of ratification, then the agency and acts of the agent become effective as of the date of ratification.

A principal cannot ratify only part of the agent's actions. If the principal accepts any part of the agent's actions, then all of the agent's actions must be accepted.[20] To do otherwise would be unfair to the third party, who is already in peril because of reliance on the agent who did not really have authority.

A final requirement of the entire agreement is knowledge of material facts. The principal must have access to knowledge of all facts that affect the transaction entered into by the agent before the principal ratifies them. To do otherwise would be to lead a principal blindly into an agreement that may not serve his or her best interest.

## Respondeat Superior

The requirements for an action of *respondeat superior* based on an agency are generally the same as those based on employment. First, it must be shown that there was a master–servant relationship[21]—that is, a relationship that had a clearly defined authority exhibit and a person to carry out the directions from the authority. This may be either an employer–employee or a principal–agent relationship. A partner in a partnership is an example of a principal–agent relationship that does not involve an employer and an employee. The partnership as a business entity has authority to give direction. The partners as individuals carry out these directions. Thus, the partnership would be the principal, and the partners would be the agents. Partners are not considered employees of the partnership, however.

The second requirement of *respondeat superior* is that the agent acts within the scope of the agency. Specifically, this means that the act of the agent who injured the third party must have been committed while the agent was engaged in performance of the purpose of the agency.[22] An example is an agent who is running an errand for a principal and causes an auto accident on the way. A third person who is injured in the accident could have an action against the principal as well as the agent because the agent was involved in carrying out the purpose of the agency at the time of the accident.

It is not relevant that the principal did not authorize the specific act of the agent that precipitated the injury to a third person. It is only necessary that the action be reasonably required for the completion of the agency or be of the same general nature as the conduct authorized or both. Thus, an agent who takes a slightly different route from that directed by the principal would still be considered to be acting within the scope of the agency.

An exception to a principal's responsibility for an agent under *respondeat superior* occurs when the agent deviates substantially from the instructions of the principal or when the agent is engaged in conduct that ultimately serves the agent rather than the principal.[23] In most jurisdictions, the doctrine does not apply to incidents that result from the agent's smoking while driving. For example, assume an agent who is a smoker is driving to a certain location for a principal. While handling, lighting, or disposing of a cigarette, the agent is inattentive to the road and causes an accident. The agent—not the principal—would be responsible for injuries to any third parties. Examples of deviation from the purpose include picking up hitchhikers, making personal stops, changing routes for personal purposes, and driving while intoxicated. Generally, any activity that substantially departs from the purpose of the agency and benefits the agent more than the principal will be considered sufficient to relieve the principal of liability.

An additional exception to a principal's liability for the acts of an agent is an intentional tort. A principal will not be responsible for injuries to third parties if the injuries were caused intentionally by the agent.[24] The reasoning behind this is that all persons should be responsible for their own intentional acts. A principal may be held responsible for intentional acts, however, if it is the general nature of the principal's business to engage in such acts and the agent's intentional acts further the purpose of the agency. A commonly used example is a bouncer in a bar. It is customary for bouncers to employ physical force against unruly patrons. Because this serves the purpose of the principal and is done with the principal's consent, the principal can be held liable for injuries caused by the agent.

# CASE

## State v. ABC Towing,

### 954 P.2d 575 (Alaska 2006)

The following opinion demonstrates the extent to which a principal's responsibility may extend to the acts of an agent.

Rodney E. Lewis does business as "ABC Towing." When one of Lewis's employees discharged gasoline on the ground, the State brought criminal charges against both the employee and ABC Towing; both defendants were charged with violating an anti-pollution statute, AS 46.03.710.

Under Alaska law, organizations face broader vicarious criminal responsibility than do individuals. Generally speaking, an individual can be held criminally responsible for the conduct of another only if the individual asks or encourages the other person to commit the offense or if the individual helps to plan or commit the offense. See AS 11.16.110(2). The State presented no evidence that Lewis asked his employee to discharge the gasoline, or that Lewis aided or abetted the employee's act. However, an organization can be held accountable for criminal conduct that its owners, members, officers, or directors did not know about until afterwards. Under AS 11.16.130(a)(1), an organization is criminally responsible for an offense committed by one of its agents if the agent was acting in behalf of the organization and within the scope of the agent's employment, or if the organization subsequently ratified or adopted the agent's conduct. The State charged ABC Towing with the pollution violation, alleging that Lewis's employee had been acting within the scope of his employment, and in behalf of ABC Towing, when he discharged the gasoline on the ground.

The case against ABC Towing was tried to District Court Judge Natalie K. Finn on stipulated facts. The parties agreed that ABC Towing's employee had violated the anti-pollution statute and that the employee had been acting within the scope of his employment and in behalf of ABC Towing when he committed this violation. There was only one disputed issue, and that was an issue of law: was ABC Towing an "organization" for purposes of AS 11.16.130(a), so that it could be held liable for its employee's discharge of gasoline?

AS 11.81.900(b)(39) defines the term "organization" for purposes of Title 11. Under that definition, "organization" means:

> a legal entity, including a corporation, company, association, firm, partnership, joint stock company, foundation, institution, government, society, union, club, church, or any other group of persons organized for any purpose.

Lewis's attorney contended that ABC Towing was not an "organization" because it was a sole proprietorship—an unincorporated business owned solely by Lewis. In a well-reasoned opinion, Judge Finn concluded that this contention was correct—that sole proprietorships are not "organizations" under the statutory definition. Judge Finn wrote:

> [A] sole proprietorship is not a legal entity. [It] has no legal significance apart from its sole proprietor. It cannot incur debts, conduct business, sue or be sued, or incur or pay taxes apart from its sole proprietor. Legally, it makes no difference whether the business is named ABC Towing or Rodney E. Lewis. The accountability of ABC Towing is therefore no different from that of an individual. . . . This court finds that ABC Towing, a sole proprietorship, is not an organization within the meaning of AS 11.81.900(b)(39) and is therefore not legally accountable [for acts of its agents under] AS 11.16.130.

Judge Finn therefore dismissed the complaint against ABC Towing, and the State now appeals Judge Finn's decision.

Under AS 11.81.900(b)(39), "organization" (for purposes of Title 11) "means a legal entity." The statute does not define "legal entity" except by example, and the term "legal entity" is not further defined in Title 11 or, indeed, anywhere else in the Alaska statutes. However, the term "legal entity" does have a common-law meaning, and that meaning presumptively governs our interpretation of AS 11.81.900(b)(39). See AS 01.10.010 (the common law remains the rule of decision in this state unless it is inconsistent with the laws passed by the Alaska legislature or inconsistent with the federal or Alaska constitutions).

The concept of "legal entity" is a useful fiction employed by the law to distinguish an ongoing human endeavor from the people who presently own or control that endeavor. As Judge Finn correctly pointed out in her decision, the defining characteristic of a "legal entity" is its separate legal existence apart from its owners, officers, and directors.

At common law, sole proprietorships are not "legal entities." Neither are partnerships (for most purposes: compare *Pratt v. Kirkpatrick,* 718 P.2d 962, 967–68 (Alaska 1986)). Rather, sole proprietorships and partnerships are deemed to be merely the alter egos of the proprietor or the partners (as individuals). In a sole proprietorship, all of the proprietor's assets are completely at risk, and the sole proprietorship ceases to exist upon the proprietor's death. Harry J. Haynsworth, *Selecting the Form of a Small Business Entity* (1985), § 1.02, pp. 2–3; see also Harry G. Hehn and John R. Alexander, *Laws of Corporations and Other Business Entities* (3rd ed.1985), § 18, p. 58. Similarly, a partnership is not a separate legal entity (for most purposes). Haynsworth, § 1.03 pp. 4, 7; Hehn & Alexander, § 19, pp. 63–64.

The common law adopted a strict view [of partnership] and accorded no recognition to the partnership as an entity for the purposes of ownership of real property, contract, suit, etc[,] although many of these disabilities have been abolished or altered by statute.

Hehn & Alexander, § 19, p. 64. Alaska law recognizes the common-law rule. See *Williams v. Mammoth of Alaska, Inc.,* 890 P.2d 581, 584 (Alaska 1995) ("The nearly universal rule is that if the employer is a partnership, then each partner is an employer of the partnership's employees. This is because a partnership is not a legal entity separate from its partners."); *Berger v. Ohlson,* 120 F.2d 56, 60, 10 Alaska 84, 93 (9th Cir.1941) ("[T]he Alaska Railroad is not a corporate or any other legal entity. It is a name only. The sole owner of the railroad and its terminals . . . is the United States.")

With regard to a sole proprietorship, Alaska law deems the "company" to be simply an alter ego of the proprietor, who is engaged in commerce under a nom d'affaires—an assumed name adopted for business purposes. See *Roeckl v. Federal Deposit Insurance Corp.,* 885 P.2d 1067 (Alaska 1994), which contains a lengthy discussion of an individual's legal ability to conduct business or business transactions under an assumed name. *Roeckl* notes that, unless a person uses a fictitious business name in order to facilitate a fraud, it has always been legal for a person to transact business in the name of a fictitious entity that has no legal existence apart from the individual(s) running the business. *Roeckl,* 885 P.2d at 1073 (citations omitted). This practice is, in fact, normal for sole proprietorships and partnerships. *Roeckl,* 885 P.2d at 1074, quoting *United States v. Dunn,* 564 F.2d 348, 354 n. 12 (9th Cir.1977). (*Roeckl* answers the State's contention that ABC Towing should be considered a separate legal entity because a business license has been issued in the name of ABC Towing.)

With this background, we return to our definitional statute, AS 11.81.900(b)(39), and we find that it contains troublesome ambiguities. The statute declares that the term "organization" means a "legal entity." If the legislature had stopped there, then neither a sole proprietorship nor a partnership would be considered an "organization," because neither form of business is a legal entity. However, the statute then adds that the term "legal entity" includes "partnerships" as well as "associations," "societies," "clubs," and "any other group of persons organized for any purpose." This is a marked expansion of what the common law would recognize as a "legal entity" for other purposes (suing or being sued, holding title to property, employing workers, etc.).

The legislature undoubtedly has the authority to enlarge the definition of "legal entity" beyond its common-law boundaries. See *State v. Erickson,* 574 P.2d 1, 15 (Alaska 1978) (in statutes regulating drugs, the legislature can define "narcotic" differently from its normal pharmacological meaning). It appears that AS 11.81.900(b)(39) was intended to modify the common-law definition of "legal entity" by broadening it to include partnerships, informal associations and clubs, and (in general) "any other group of persons organized for any purpose." However, the statutory roster of "legal entities" does not specifically include sole proprietorships.

The State argues that a sole proprietorship becomes a "firm" or an "association" or a "group" under AS 11.81.900(b)(39) whenever the sole proprietor hires other people to assist in the conduct of the business. We think that this is a strained interpretation of the statute. Under the State's reading of the statute, an ice cream vendor or a house painter who employed a part-time helper during the summer would suddenly become a "firm," an "association," or a "group." In fact, under the State's wide-ranging construction of the phrase "group of persons organized for any purpose," home owners would seemingly become "organizations" whenever they hired someone to clean their house or maintain their lawn. Such a construction of the statute conflicts with the fact that employees generally do not direct the conduct of a business. Their contract of employment does not make them partners of the persons or entities who hire them, and they do not have the same legal rights and responsibilities as their employers. Based on the wording of AS 11.81.900(b)(39) and its legislative history, we doubt that the legislature intended the results advocated by the State.

Moreover, two rules of statutory construction counsel us to uphold the trial court's decision in this case. The first rule is that statutes in derogation of the common law should be construed strictly. That is, when courts are presented with a question involving the proper construction of a statute that modifies the common law, the normal rule of interpretation is that such statutes are construed so as to preserve the pre-existing common law unless the legislature has clearly indicated its purpose to change that law. See *Roeckl,* 885 P.2d at 1074;

*(continued)*

*University of Alaska v. Shanti*, 835 P.2d 1225, 1228 n. 5 (Alaska 1992). The second rule is that statutes imposing criminal liability should be construed narrowly. When the scope of a criminal statute is unclear, courts should normally construe the statute against the government—that is, construe it so as to limit the scope of criminal liability. See *Magnuson v. State*, 843 P.2d 1251, 1253 (Alaska App.1992).

The question in this appeal is whether sole proprietorships are to be treated as legal entities apart from their proprietors, so that the government can prosecute sole proprietorships for the acts of their agents under the theory of vicarious responsibility codified in AS 11.16.130(a). Under the common law, sole proprietorships are not legal entities. The expanded definition of legal entities in AS 11.81.900(b)(39) does not include a specific reference to sole proprietorships. The State has presented some inventive arguments as to why sole proprietorships should be viewed as "associations" or "firms" for purposes of Title 11, but in the end those arguments are only colorable, not convincing. On this point, the statute remains, at best, ambiguous.

This being so, we construe AS 11.81.900(b)(39) to preserve the pre-existing common law rule that sole proprietorships are not legal entities, and to narrowly construe the scope of vicarious criminal responsibility imposed by AS 11.16.130(a). We conclude that sole proprietorships are not "organizations" for purposes of AS 11.16.130(a). The district court therefore correctly granted the defendant's motion to dismiss.

The judgement of the district court is AFFIRMED.

## Case Review Question

Would the result change if the employer was aware and did not object to the employee's conduct?

## ASSIGNMENT 14.2

In each of the following circumstances, determine whether there is an agency relationship and, if so, whether it involves (1) actual express authority, (2) actual implied authority, (3) apparent authority, (4) inherent authority, or (5) authority by ratification. Explain your answer.

Cosmo and Janine have their own law practice. They employ an associate attorney, Miguel, and a paralegal, Tom. In the course of business over a period of one month, the following situations occur:

Cosmo renewed the annual lease on the office space he and Janine have occupied for ten years. They agreed at the quarterly partner's meeting several months before that they would renew the lease. Janine was involved in a car accident and seriously injured. She gave Cosmo a written power of attorney to deal with her financial and professional responsibilities. Janine commented to Miguel that she hoped the case could be settled quickly and that she would rely on his expertise in that matter. Miguel perceived this as an assignment of authority and asked Tom to prepare the documents necessary to seek a settlement. Miguel then negotiated a settlement on behalf of Janine with the owner and driver of the car that struck her. Miguel handled most of the personal injury cases for clients of the practice, and as a result was on a first-name basis with the representative of the insurance company for the owner and driver of the other car. Janine was furious with Miguel for settling the case without consulting her, but she ultimately signed the release papers and accepted the settlement. Cosmo deposited Janine's paycheck and settlement check into her bank account. He then paid her personal monthly bills from the same account.

## SOLE PROPRIETORSHIPS

The sole proprietorship is the simplest of all forms of business entities. The entire ownership of the business is vested in one individual. Consequently, it is unnecessary to have an agreement that indicates who has authority in the business, how profits and losses will be shared, or who is responsible for debts or judgments against the business. A sole proprietorship may employ any number of employees, but as long as the employees do not take part in ownership decisions or have the right or obligation to share in profits and losses, the business remains individually owned.

Sole proprietorships were once the most common form of business. Although they are still popular, many sole proprietorships are changing their legal status, usually to that of a corporation even if it is a corporation with only one shareholder. The reasons for this vary, but two reasons in particular are making the sole proprietorship less and less attractive to entrepreneurs. First, an individual operating a sole proprietorship must claim all profits of the business as personal income. A corporation, however, pays taxes on its own income, and the shareholders pay taxes only on the actual income they receive from the business. Often the tax liability for the individual is much less as a shareholder than as a sole proprietor. For example, if nearly all profits are reinvested in a corporation, the shareholders would not pay personal income tax on these profits; and if an individual has several sources of income, then heavy profits from a sole proprietorship could increase personal income so that the owner is placed in a much higher tax bracket.

A second reason for the decline of sole proprietorships is judgment liability. When an outside party sues a sole proprietorship and wins, the judgment can be enforced against the individual owner, including all of the owner's personal assets. For example, if a person who is injured while in the shop of a sole proprietor sues and wins, then the judgment can be collected from both the business and the individual owner's personal assets such as houses, cars, and bank accounts. Although businesses often have insurance and business assets, these may be insufficient to satisfy the judgment. Consequently, personal assets are pursued. In the case of corporations, the shareholders are vulnerable only to the amount of their previous investment in the business. With the increasing number of lawsuits against and among businesses, many sole proprietors are left with no choice but to incorporate to protect their own personal and real property.

## PARTNERSHIPS

Unlike the sole proprietorship, partnerships are designed to share the wealth— and the risk. In some cases, circumstances arise in which the partners disagree on a variety of subjects including whether a partnership ever really existed. The following section examines the legal standards that have been developed to resolve issues unique to the partnership form of business.

### The Nature of Partnerships

A **partnership** is defined as follows:

> An unincorporated business organization owned by two or more persons. Partnerships are usually owned and managed according to a partnership agreement and each partner usually have full liability for all partnership debts. Partnership income and losses are usually allocated among the partners according to their shares, with taxes paid by the partners individually.[25]

**partnership**
An agreement of two or more parties to engage in business or enterprise with profits and losses shared among all parties.

Most often an issue in partnership is resolved through the law of contracts and agency. Over time, however, some rules specific to partnership law have been developed. In addition, the Uniform Partnership Act, a model law adopted by a majority of the states, outlines procedures for the creation, operation, and termination of a partnership. Because the Uniform Partnership Act has been adopted as law by a majority of the states, the principles discussed here are consistent with the act's principles.

### Characteristics of a Partnership

In a partnership, each partner is the agent of the partnership and represents the other partners. This authority allows one partner to legally bind the partnership and, ultimately, the personal assets of the partners in contractual agreements.

Generally, a partner's personal assets are not protected from being applied to pay debts of the business. The liability for debts of the partnership is joint and several among the partners.[26] If there is a determination that the partnership owes a debt that exceeds the worth of the partnership assets, then any individual partner (as several individuals) or all partners (as joint individuals) together may be forced to pay the debt. An obligation does not have to be divided among the partners equally. Thus, a partner who is particularly wealthy has the greatest risk of being forced to pay partnership debts after the business assets have been applied. If, however, one partner is required to satisfy a large portion of the debt, the act permits that partner to require the other partners to reimburse a share of the payment that was made, assuming that the other partners have the financial ability to reimburse that share of debt. Therefore, a major concern before one enters a partnership is the personal financial stability of the other partners.

Generally, in a partnership, the partners share profits and losses equally. The exception would be if the partners had a written agreement that provided for a different distribution, such as 70:30, which could be the case if one partner had more invested in the business. The partnership is required to file tax returns for record-keeping purposes only because any actual taxes are paid personally by the partners based on the income they receive from the partnership. Similarly, if the partnership has an annual financial loss, then the partners can claim their proportionate share of the loss against their total annual income on their personal returns in accordance with federal and state tax laws.

Each state has its own rules of procedure that indicate the manner in which a partnership is sued. Some states require that the name of the partnership as well as the names of the partners be included in the suit. Other states require only that one or the other be named.

## Limited Partnerships

**limited partnership**
Partnership of two or more persons in which the limited partners can be held liable for partnership debts only to the extent of their investment and cannot take part in the general management and operation of the partnership business.

A special type of partnership known as a **limited partnership** can be used to protect the personal assets of a partner from liability and to provide other benefits with respect to investments and taxes. The Revised Uniform Limited Partnership Act and the more recently revised Uniform Partnership Act are other model laws adopted by a majority of the states as statute and that set forth the specific rights, liabilities, and means of creating and dissolving a limited partnership. Generally, in a limited partnership, a limited partner is held liable only for the amount of his or her investment or promised investment in the partnership.[27] In this sense, a limited partner is similar to a corporate shareholder. The cost to a limited partner, however, is the loss of all control or influence in the operation of the partnership.

A limited partner can have no input into the operation of the business of the partnership and cannot work for the partnership. Finally, the limited partner's name cannot be used in the partnership name. If any of these rules are broken, then a limited partner may be treated as a general partner and be subject to joint and several liability.[28] Because limited partners cannot contribute services to the partnership, as a practical necessity the partnership also must have general partners who operate the business of the partnership. Although these general partners manage the continuing business of the partnership, their personal assets are at risk as well.

## The Relationship of Partners

Partners have a fiduciary obligation to each other. A fiduciary relationship is one in which there is a particular trust between the parties. In a partnership, each partner is trusted to place the interest of the partnership above personal interest. Therefore, any partner who makes a profit in a business venture of the type the partnership would ordinarily be involved in owes that profit to the partnership.

The partnership should decide in advance whether a partner is to be compensated for work done in the partnership. A partner is not entitled to payment for services rendered as an employee but only to a share of the profits or losses, as are the other partners. The exception is when a partner or partners are winding up the partnership business after the death of another partner. In that case, it is proper to provide reasonable compensation to the survivors for their services in closing the partnership accounts.

Partners are entitled to receive payment for monies they have expended in the ordinary business of the partnership.[29] Thus, it is not necessary to have partnership approval for payment of every expense. If the expense is one that would reasonably be incurred in the operation of the business, then a partner generally has the right either to obligate the partnership for payment or to receive reimbursement if he or she makes payment personally on the partnership's behalf.

If a dispute arises among parties to a partnership, then certain legal actions are permitted. Specifically, a partner may sue the partnership for an accounting of partnership assets and liabilities when one or more of the following instances[30] occur:

1. The partnership is winding up business,

2. a partner has been improperly excluded from activity in the partnership, or

3. there is a reasonable basis to suspect a partner has made personal profit at the expense of the partnership.

Other than in these instances, a partner is generally not permitted to sue a partnership because as an individual, the partner would be the plaintiff; but as a member of the partnership, he or she would be the defendant. The law does not permit persons to sue themselves, even in different capacities.

## Partnership Property

Partnerships are generally allowed to own personal property or real property in the name of the partnership. Financing for such purchases, however, is still sometimes required to be in the names of the partners because if it becomes necessary to sue the partners for repayment, the original loan documents clearly state who the partners were.

Although partners have individual rights to the partnership's income, they cannot claim an individual interest in the partnership's assets (such as vehicles or office supplies) unless otherwise agreed. Occasionally, a conflict arises regarding whether property belongs to the partnership or to a particular partner individually. When this happens, a court will look to the answers to the following questions[31] before making a finding as to true ownership:

1. Was the property acquired with partnership funds?

2. Has the partnership made use of the property?

3. Does the partnership have legal title to the property?

4. Is the property of a type that would be used in the business of the partnership?

5. Has the partnership taken any steps to maintain or improve the condition of the property?

6. Is the property recorded in the books of the partnership as an asset?

If the answers to these questions strongly indicate that the partnership was the rightful owner of the property, then all partners will be held responsible for any obligations with respect to the property. Likewise, if the property should suddenly increase in value, then the partners will be joint owners of the property for that purpose as well.

## The Life of a Partnership

**Creation.** A partnership is an entity that must be created by agreement of those who will be responsible for its existence. The agreement is covered by the law of contracts. An example is the contractual requirement of capacity. If a person without capacity attempts to enter a partnership agreement, then the law would not recognize the person's role as partner, and the person would have no liability for partnership debts. Thus, it is in the best interest of potential partners to ascertain in advance the legal capacity of one another.

In some states, the statute of frauds does not require that a partnership contract be in writing. Oral agreements are permissible as long as the conduct of the parties is clear enough to permit inference of the agreement.

**Recognition.** Several factors must be considered to determine whether a partnership actually exists and should be legally recognized as such. The following questions are most often considered:

1. Do the alleged partners have some type of joint title to real or personal property?
2. Do the alleged partners operate under a single name?
3. Do the alleged partners all share in the profits and losses of the business?
4. How much money and time does each alleged partner invest in the business?

Because none of these factors independently establishes a partnership, all of them are considered jointly. If it is determined that most of them indicate an agreement between the parties to act as a partnership, then the likely result is that the law will recognize a partnership.[32]

A partnership may also be established under the principle of partnership by *estoppel*. This occurs when one party allows a second party to represent himself or herself as a partnership to outsiders. If the outsider relies on the representation, then the original party may be held responsible for the acts of the second party. The first party is precluded from denying the existence of a partnership after allowing another to represent to outsiders that such a relationship, in fact, existed.[33]

## Partnership Dealings with Third Parties

Generally, every partner in a partnership has authority to act as an agent of the partnership. The partnership entity acts as the principal. A general principle of partnership is that a partner has apparent authority.[34] A partner may transfer title to property held in the partnership name or obligate the partnership in business agreements or purchases that relate to the business of the partnership. If, however, the transaction is one that would not ordinarily be encountered in the business of the partnership, then a partner must have actual authority from the partnership before he or she can make a binding agreement with third parties.

In addition to having joint and several liability for contract obligations, a partnership may also be held responsible to third parties for wrongful acts of the partners or partnership employees. For example, if a partner or partnership employee negligently injures another while engaged in the business of the partnership, then the partnership may be held liable for the injuries.[35]

The liability of partners in such a situation can be claimed in one of two ways. Some jurisdictions take the position that liability is joint and that every partner must be sued for the injuries. Many other jurisdictions have made the liability joint and several, which means that all the partners or an individual partner may be sued. As in contract situations, however, if an individual partner must satisfy the entire debt of the partnership, then that partner may require the other partners to contribute toward reimbursement for payment of the judgment.[36]

# CASE
## *Mardanlou v. Ghaffarian, et al.,*
### 135 P.3d 904, 550 Utah Adv. Rep. 16, 2006 UT App 165 (2006)

In this case, the court examines what is necessary to establish a legally enforceable partnership.

On November 5, 1991, M & M Motors, Inc. and Access Auto, Inc., owned by Mardanlou and Ghaffarian respectively, executed a lease agreement to rent property located at 3960 South State Street in Salt Lake City, Utah. The lease agreement was for a one-year term, with an option to renew the lease for one additional year and an option to purchase the property at the end of the lease term. After the parties signed the lease, Ghaffarian shook hands with Mardanlou and said "we are in this together, partner." Shortly thereafter, Ghaffarian added Mardanlou to Access Auto's insurance policy so that it listed both Mardanlou and Ghaffarian as insureds.

Mardanlou purchased business cards for Access Auto with his and Ghaffarian's names equally placed on the cards. Mardanlou purchased furniture used by Access Auto, while Ghaffarian paid $6,000 for the first and last month's rent on the leased property. There was a division of labor between Mardanlou and Ghaffarian, with Ghaffarian in charge of the bookkeeping as well as purchasing vehicles to sell at Access Auto. Mardanlou sold vehicles and managed the other sales associates. At no time did Mardanlou have access to Access Auto's books or any of the financial aspects of the business, although he did write checks on Access Auto's account.

Mardanlou worked at Access Auto from 1992 through 1997, receiving a salary while the other sales personnel in the office were paid on commission. Mardanlou was not aware of how much Ghaffarian was paid or received as income from the business. In March 1993, Ghaffarian gave Mardanlou $10,000 that Mardanlou believed was his share of the profits of Access Auto. Although Mardanlou was not in charge of paying employees, he did pay the salaries for two of Access Auto's employees on one occasion.

In November 1993, Ghaffarian unilaterally exercised the option to purchase the property contained in the lease, placing the property in his own name. However, Ghaffarian made the mortgage payments on the property with proceeds from the business, Access Auto. Ghaffarian did not inform Mardanlou of his actions and Mardanlou did not discover the purchase until late 1994 or early 1995. Hashem Farr, Ghaffarian's good friend, was present when Mardanlou confronted Ghaffarian regarding the purchase. Farr heard Ghaffarian tell Mardanlou, "Don't worry, we're partners."

From 1991 to 1997, Ghaffarian filed the tax returns for Access Auto in his name only. Although Mardanlou repeatedly approached Ghaffarian about the need for partnership tax statements, Ghaffarian failed to prepare any such statements. Mardanlou filed his tax returns for those years as an employee of Access Auto. In 1997, Mardanlou left Access Auto. In November 1998, he initiated this action requesting a share of the profits based upon the dissolution of the partnership.

The trial court determined that Ghaffarian and Mardanlou had entered a partnership agreement by the time they executed the initial lease agreement. The court also found that Ghaffarian had appropriated the partnership's real property by placing it solely in his name. As a result, the court awarded Mardanlou a one-half interest in the real property of Access Auto, subject to various offsets. Further, the court ordered Ghaffarian to pay Mardanlou one-half of the $83,500 annual rental value of the property, plus interest, from November 7, 1997, to the date of final judgment. Ghaffarian appeals.

Ghaffarian challenges the trial court's finding that Mardanlou and Ghaffarian intended to create a partnership. "On review, [an appellate court] is obliged to view the evidence and all inferences that may be drawn therefrom in a light most supportive of the findings of the trier of fact. The findings and judgment of the trial court will not be disturbed when they are based on substantial, competent, admissible evidence." *Nupetco Assocs. v. Jenkins,* 669 P.2d 877, 881 (Utah 1983) (quoting *Car Doctor, Inc. v. Belmont,* 635 P.2d 82, 83–84 (Utah 1981)); see also *Cutler v. Bowen,* 543 P.2d 1349, 1350–51 (Utah 1975). Further, Ghaffarian contends that the trial court's partnership finding was erroneous, as a matter of law, because the trial court did not specifically find profit sharing and mutual control. "Questions about the legal adequacy of findings of fact and the legal accuracy of the trial court's statements present issues of law, which we review for correctness, according no deference to the trial court." *Shar's Cars, L.L.C. v. Elder,* 2004 UT App 258,¶ 12, 97 P.3d 724. Ghaffarian also argues that Mardanlou's claims are barred by a four-year statute of limitations. See Utah Code Ann. § 78-12-25 (2002). "'The applicability of a statute of limitations and the applicability of the discovery rule are questions of law, which we review for correctness.'" *Russell Packard Dev. Inc. v. Carson,* 2005 UT 14,¶ 18, 108 P.3d 741 (quoting *Spears v. Warr,* 2002 UT 24,¶ 32, 44 P.3d 742). Finally, Ghaffarian argues

*(continued)*

that the trial court erred in awarding rental value and interest as part of its valuation of Mardanlou's partnership interest. See Utah Code Ann. § 48-1-39 (2002). "'We review the trial court's decision to award damages under a standard which gives the court considerable discretion, and will not disturb its ruling absent an abuse of discretion.'" *Shar's Cars, L.L.C.*, 2004 UT App 258 at ¶ 13, 97 P.3d 724 (quoting *Lysenko v. Sawaya*, 1999 UT App 31,¶ 6, 973 P.2d 445).

Ghaffarian's first contention is that the trial court erred because "the undisputed facts establish that the relationship between Mr. Mardanlou and Mr. Ghaffarian did not satisfy the elements of a partnership." The "basic principle of partnership law is set forth in our Uniform Partnership Act, Title 48 of U.C.A.1953." *Cutler v. Bowen*, 543 P.2d 1349, 1351 (Utah 1975). "'Partnership' is defined as 'an association of two or more persons to carry on a business for profit.'" *Parduhn v. Bennett*, 2002 UT 93,¶ 14, 61 P.3d 982.

> are not exactly defined, but certain elements are essential: The parties must combine their property, money, effects, skill, labor and knowledge. As a general rule, there must be a community of interest in the performance of the common purpose, a joint propriety interest in the subject matter, a mutual right to control, a right to share profits, and unless there is an agreement to the contrary, a duty to share in any losses which may be sustained. *Bassett v. Baker*, 530 P.2d 1, 2 (Utah 1974).

In this case, the trial court determined that there were sufficient facts to demonstrate that the parties intended to create a partnership. Specifically, the court's findings of fact stated that:

1. The lease/purchase agreement establishes that plaintiff [Hassan Mardanlou] and defendant Ali Ghaffarian entered into this agreement with lessor/seller Cline's Investments as either a partnership agreement or joint venture.
2. The insurance document contains both plaintiff and defendant Ali Ghaffarian as insureds under the policy inferring a partnership.
3. The insurance agent believed that the plaintiff and defendant Ali Ghaffarian were partners.
4. The Access Auto business cards contain both names equally on the card.
5. Defendant Ali Ghaffarian represented to his friend, Hashem Farr, that plaintiff and he were partners.
6. Hashem Farr was present when defendant Ali Ghaffarian was confronted by plaintiff regarding that the Access Auto real property was purchased only in defendant Ali Ghaffarian's name and Hashem Farr heard defendant Ali Ghaffarian state to plaintiff, "Don't worry, we're partners."
7. There was a division of labor between plaintiff and defendant Ali Ghaffarian.
8. Plaintiff purchased the furniture used in the business of Access Auto, indicating he viewed Access Auto, the business, as a partnership.
9. Plaintiff purchased the business cards for the business, indicating he viewed Access Auto, the business, as a partnership.
10. The salaries for two of Access Auto's employees were paid by plaintiff, indicating he viewed Access Auto, the business, as a partnership.
11. Defendant Ali Ghaffarian represented to plaintiff that he was the only other member of Access Auto besides plaintiff.
12. Defendant Ali Ghaffarian signed the doing business as Access Auto prior to the association of plaintiff in only his name.
13. Defendant Ali Ghaffarian filed the tax returns for Access Auto only in his name.
14. The mortgage on his property was paid for by the proceeds from the business, Access Auto, run by plaintiff and defendant Ali Ghaffarian.

Viewing these findings and all the inferences that can be drawn therefrom in the light most favorable to the trial court, we cannot say that the trial court's partnership determination was not supported by the evidence. Ghaffarian has not pointed to a single factual finding that he believes was wrongly decided, instead arguing that the above facts do not support a finding of intent to create a partnership. We disagree. The trial court's findings, although not dispositive by any means, provide a sufficient basis upon which to infer that the parties intended to carry on a business for profit as co-owners. Thus, Ghaffarian's attack on the trial court's finding fails. See *Koesling v. Basamakis*, 539 P.2d 1043, 1046 (Utah 1975)

Ghaffarian also challenges the trial court's legal determination of partnership in the absence of what he sees as two key elements: an express finding of shared control of Access Auto and an express finding of the sharing of profits. Contrary to Ghaffarian's assertions, Utah statutes governing partnerships do not set out any mandatory requirements for the finding of a partnership. See Utah Code Ann. § 48-1-1 to -40 (2002). Caselaw suggests that, [a]s a general rule, there must be a community of interest in the performance of the common purpose, a joint propriety interest in the subject matter, a mutual right to control, a right to share in the profits, and unless there is an agreement to the contrary, a duty to share in any losses which may be sustained.

*Bassett v. Baker*, 530 P.2d 1, 2 (Utah 1974). But even this definition does not demand absolute proof of each factor in every case, indicating that the necessity of each factor will be based largely on the facts of the case. Similarly, the *Bassett* court did not demand proof that profits were actually shared, but only that there was a right to share in any profits. See *id.*

To the extent that profit sharing and control can be deemed requirements, the trial court did implicitly determine that these factors had been met by reaching the ultimate conclusion that "[a]s a matter of law, plaintiff and defendant Ali Ghaffarian were partners." In reviewing the record, we determine that there is enough evidence to support the trial court's partnership conclusion. The trial court specifically found that Mardanlou and Ghaffarian divided the labor between them and that Mardanlou contributed assets to the partnership. It appears that Mardanlou was in charge of the other salesman at Access Auto and the day-to-day operation of the business, thus illustrating mutual control of the business.

Regarding profits, an agreement to share profits need not be formal and "may be proven by the actions taken by the parties." *Rogers v. M.O. Bitner Co.*, 738 P.2d 1029, 1032 (Utah 1987). In 1993, Mardanlou received a check for $10,000, which he claimed was his share of the profits. Given the lack of evidence to the contrary, we find that this $10,000 payment supports a finding of profit sharing. The fact that this is the only time Mardanlou received a large lump sum of money does not defeat his claim, as the partnership may have chosen not to distribute any profits for the remaining years and instead to invest any profits back into the business. Additionally, Ghaffarian never submitted any evidence to indicate that there were profits for the other years that were withheld from Mardanlou or that Ghaffarian was withdrawing additional profits himself. Mardanlou received ongoing payments each month for his work in the partnership. Although Ghaffarian labeled these funds as a salary, they may instead have represented Mardanlou's share of the profits and the court did not have to accept Ghaffarian's characterization.

We conclude that there was evidence to support the trial court's determination that a partnership existed, and therefore Ghaffarian's argument to the contrary fails.

Ghaffarian argues that Mardanlou's claims fell outside the applicable statute of limitations period and were therefore barred. "As a general rule, a statute of limitations begins to run 'upon the happening of the last event necessary to complete the cause of action.' Once a statute has begun to run, a plaintiff must file his or her claim before the limitations period expires or the claim will be barred." *Russell Packard Dev., Inc. v. Carson*, 2005 UT 14,¶ 20, 108 P.3d 741 A contract "not

founded upon an instrument in writing" may be brought within four years. Utah Code Ann. § 78-12-25 (2002). "In certain instances, however, the discovery rule tolls the limitations period until facts forming the basis for the cause of action are discovered." *Spears v. Warr*, 2002 UT 24,¶ 33, 44 P.3d 742. The "equitable discovery rule may operate to toll an otherwise fixed statute of limitations period" in two situations:

(1) where a plaintiff does not become aware of the cause of action because of the defendant's concealment or misleading conduct, and

(2) where the case presents exceptional circumstances and the application of the general rule would be irrational or unjust, regardless of any showing that the defendant has prevented the discovery of the cause of action. *Russell Packard Dev., Inc.*, 2005 UT 14 at ¶ 25, 108 P.3d 741 (quotations and citation omitted).

The trial court determined that Ghaffarian breached the oral partnership agreement when he "appropriated the partnership real property by placing it solely in his name." Ghaffarian exercised the option in November 1993, and the statute of limitations period on this claim would ordinarily have expired in November 1997. However, the limitations period did not begin to run until Mardanlou discovered that Ghaffarian had unilaterally exercised the option to purchase. See *Cheves v. Williams*, 1999 UT 86,¶ 22, 993 P.2d 191). The record suggests that Mardanlou did not discover the details of the purchase until late 1994 or early 1995, pushing the limitations date to late 1998 or early 1999.

Regardless of the exact date of Mardanlou's discovery, the trial court found that, whenever Mardanlou discovered the purchase, he approached Ghaffarian and Ghaffarian specifically told him, "Don't worry, we're partners." Under the circumstances, a reasonable person in Mardanlou's position would be justified in concluding that Ghaffarian's statement indicated that they were in a partnership, and that the Access Auto property belonged to the partnership. Mardanlou's reliance on Ghaffarian's representation of a partnership tolled the statute of limitations until 1997, when it became clear to Mardanlou that Ghaffarian no longer recognized him as a partner. See *Charlesworth v. Reyns,* The complaint was filed on November 6, 1998, one year after Mardanlou discovered that Ghaffarian had misled him about the status of the partnership and the property ownership. Accordingly, Mardanlou filed his complaint within the statute of limitations period and Ghaffarian's argument on this point fails.

Finally, Ghaffarian argues that the district court erred in awarding post-dissolution rental damages. "In the absence of an agreement to the contrary . . . the rules

*(continued)*

for distribution of partnership assets upon dissolution are provided for by statute." *Knutson v. Lauer*, 627 P.2d 66, 68 (Utah 1981). Utah Code section 48-1-39 allows a retiring partner to "choose between 'the value of his interest at the date of dissolution' or 'in lieu of interest, the profits attributable to the use of his right in the property of the dissolved partnership.'" *Wanlass v. D Land Title*, 790 P.2d 568, 572 (Utah Ct.App.1990) (quoting Utah Code Ann. § 48-1-39 (1989)). This court "must affirm the award of damages if evidence in the record supports the award." *Shar's Cars, L.L.C. v. Elder*, 2004 UT App 258,¶ 28, 97 P.3d 724.

The trial court awarded Mardanlou a one-half interest in the property as of the date of dissolution, subject to set-offs, plus one-half the annual rental value of the property until the date judgment was entered. Ghaffarian does not contest the property award, only the reasonable rental value award. The trial court's award of rental value from 1997 to judgment was to compensate Mardanlou for his rights in the property during that time period. Mardanlou is entitled to compensation for Ghaffarian's continuing exclusive use of the property, and this award represented that compensation.

Ghaffarian provided the court with no alternative evidence of profits for those years, no alternative way to compensate Mardanlou for the property use, and no evidence that the actual value of the use in the property was less. While there may be multiple ways to determine the appropriate damages award, the trial court's reliance on the reasonable rental value of the property, the major partnership asset, was appropriate. Because there is evidence in the record to support this award, we determine that the trial court did not exceed its permitted range of discretion in awarding reasonable rental value. See *Morgan v. Morgan*, 854 P.2d 559, 566 (Utah Ct.App.1993) (affirming the trial court's valuation of partnership property when the valuation was "'within the range of values established by all the evidence'" (alteration and citation omitted)).

We affirm the trial court's finding of a partnership agreement because the evidence and accompanying inferences, viewed in the light most favorable to the decision, support the partnership finding. Additionally, there is no statute of limitations bar in this case because Ghaffarian concealed his appropriation of the partnership property and confirmed the existence of a partnership with Mardanlou until 1997. Finally, the trial court's damage award is an appropriate remedy under the circumstances and will not be reversed on appeal. For the foregoing reasons, we affirm.

## Case Review Question

What separates this case from a situation in which a part-time employee can claim ownership after a lengthy period of employment?

## CASE

### *Hilme v. Chastain and C & H Custom Cabinets, Inc.,*
### 75 S.W.3d 315 (MO 2002)

This next case examines the slightly different approach by another court to determine the existence of a partnership.

Appellant, Brent Chastain, ("Chastain") appeals from the First Amended Judgment and Order Appointing Special Master rendered by the Circuit Court of Laclede County after a bench trial. The trial court found that a partnership existed between Chastain and Respondent, Douglas Hillme ("Hillme"), ordered an accounting and appointed a special master to assist in the process. In his sole point on appeal, Chastain maintains there was insufficient evidence supporting the trial court's judgment finding that a partnership existed between himself and Hillme.

The trial court found that that part of its judgment, as amended, with respect to the finding of the existence of a partnership, was final for purposes of appeal per Rule 74.01(b). See Rule 74.01(b), Missouri Court Rules (2001). Appellant, C & H Custom Cabinets, Inc., originally brought a third-party action against Hillme alleging that Hillme was indebted to the corporation. However, C & H Custom Cabinets, Inc., is not involved in the appeal of this particular claim.

"Appellate review of a judgment in a court-tried case is that established in *Murphy v. Carron*, 536 S.W.2d 30, 32 (Mo. *banc* 1976)." *Eul v. Beard*, 47 S.W.3d 424, 425 (Mo.App.2001) We must affirm the trial court's judgment unless there is no substantial evidence to support it, it is against the weight of the evidence, or it erroneously declares or applies the law. *Id.* at 426, *Murphy*, 536 S.W.2d 30 at 32. "The appellate court reviews the evidence in the light most favorable to the prevailing party, giving it the benefit of all reasonable inferences and disregarding the other party's evidence except as it supports the judgment." *Meyer v. Lofgren,* 949 S.W.2d 80, 82 (Mo.App.1997). "It does not weigh the evidence and must give due deference to the trial judge in determining the credibility of witnesses." *Id.*

A partnership is statutorily defined as "an association of two or more persons to carry on as co-owners a business for profit." § 358.060.1. Statutory rules applicable in determining the existence of a partnership are set forth in § 358.070. Statutory references are to RSMo 1994.

A partnership has also been judicially defined, as "a contract of two or more competent persons to place their money, effects, labor and skill, or some or all of them, in lawful commerce of business and to divide the profits and bear the loss in certain proportions." *Meyer,* 949 S.W.2d at 82 (quoting *Kielhafner v. Kielhafner,* 639 S.W.2d 288, 289 (Mo.App.1982)).

The partnership agreement may be written, expressed orally, or implied from the acts and conduct of the parties. *Morrison v. Labor & Indus. Relations Comm'n.,* 23 S.W.3d 902, 908 (Mo.App. 2000). The intent of the parties is the primary factor for determining whether such a relationship exists. *Binkley v. Palmer,* 10 S.W.3d 166, 169 (Mo.App.1999). The required intent necessary to find a partnership existed "is not the intent to form a partnership, but the intent to enter a relationship which in law constitutes a partnership." *Meyer,* 949 S.W.2d at 82.

At trial, Hillme had the burden of proving the existence of a partnership by clear, cogent, and convincing evidence. *Morrison,* 23 S.W.3d at 907–08. The "clear, cogent, and convincing" evidentiary standard simply means that the trial court should be "clearly convinced of the affirmative of the proposition to be proved." *Grissum v. Ressman,* 505 S.W.2d 81, 86 (Mo.1974). "This does not mean that there may not be contrary evidence." *Id.*

A partnership agreement may be implied from conduct and circumstances of the parties and the parties are not required to know all the legal implications of a partnership. *Grissum,* 505 S.W.2d at 86. Partnership property that is held only in an individual name does not affect the partnership status. *Id.* at 87. The filing or non-filing of a partnership income tax return is not sufficient alone to prove or disprove the existence of a partnership. *Brotherton v. Kissinger,* 550 S.W.2d 904, 907–08 (Mo.App.1977). A voice in the management of the partnership business, a share of the profits of the partnership business, and a corresponding risk of loss and liability to partnership creditors are all indications of a partnership. *Arnold v. Erkmann,* 934 S.W.2d 621, 630 (Mo.App.1996).

Viewed in a light most favorable to the judgment of the trial court as we must, *Meyer,* 949 S.W.2d at 82, the record shows that Chastain and Hillme had each worked for a period of time at Classic Cabinets, a cabinet making shop. Hillme had worked there for about four years and had eight or nine years experience in cabinet making. He was in charge of the "specialty items, the mantles, the bookcases [and] gun cabinets." Chastain had also worked for the same concern and for the most part performed staining, finishing and installation work. Chastain testified that he had built cabinets on his own several years before and had worked in construction for ten years. Early in 1997, Hillme and Chastain discussed going into business together as cabinetmakers. They also had similar discussions with Chastain's spouse and Hillme's fiance at Chastain's home.

Classic Cabinets later changed its name to Classic Woodworks.

In April of 1997, Chastain and Hillme made the decision to go into business together. Hillme testified that they both agreed to divide the workload, profit, expenses, and losses equally, that is on a "50/50" basis. No written partnership agreement was executed. Each drew a flat and equal amount of pay each week. According to Hillme, any money left over they agreed to let accumulate in the partnership account.

Chastain quit his job prior to Hillme terminating his employment. Hillme wrote a check for the purchase of plywood and Chastain also contributed monies for the venture. Chastain rented a building and purchased some woodworking equipment. He also negotiated the rent for the building. Both spent time cleaning the building and prepared to move into the building. Hillme purchased furnace parts to heat the building. Both contributed tools and equipment to the business. A business insurance policy was obtained. The parties named the business "C & H Custom Cabinets." The "C" stood for Chastain's last name and the "H" stood for Hillme's last name. Both had input as to the layout of the business cards, the building sign, and Yellow Pages advertisement. Each advertisement, including the business cards, set out each one's full name and home telephone number.

The record further shows that Chastain holds a bachelor's degree in accounting. They agreed that Chastain would handle the accounting and bookkeeping matters for their business. During the day-to-day operation, Chastain ran errands and applied stain and finish to cabinets. Hillme's time was generally spent building the

*(continued)*

cabinets. Chastain was also in charge of paying bills and scheduling installations. Neither one worked any set hours and the order in which work was to be done and by whom was settled by them as the need arose.

A checking account for the business was opened at "Central Bank." The name shown on their checks was "C & H Cabinets." It was Hillme's understanding that as business partners, they were both owners of the jointly-held account at the bank. Both issued checks from the account and each carried the concern's checkbook on occasion.

Title to the checking account went through several changes while they were working together during the period of mid-1997 through mid-1999. As best we glean, initially and unbeknownst to Hillme, the checking account was titled in Chastain's name doing business as C & H Custom Cabinets. Nevertheless, Hillme and Chastain's wife were given authorization to sign checks on the account. A year and a half later, again unbeknownst to Hillme, the account was changed to reflect that owners of the account were Chastain and his spouse. Hillme was not named as an account owner. Then in 1998 the account was made "payable on death" to Hillme. In time, Hillme was removed all together from the concern's checking account. Hillme testified that he remembered signing a "different" account card from the bank, but recalled Chastain telling him that the bank had made a mistake.

In 1997, Chastain and Hillme decided their business required a cargo trailer for hauling cabinets to the installation site. They discussed the purchase and both went to a vehicle dealer to select one. According to Hillme, it was his understanding that the cargo trailer was to be paid out of the partnership account. A bank loan was initially obtained for the purchase of the cargo trailer. Both Chastain and Hillme personally signed the note for the loan. Unbeknownst to Hillme title to the cargo trailer was placed in Chastain's name only. To the question, "Did you agree with Mr. Chastain that the title of this trailer would be issued in his own name, rather [than]the two of you as partners?," Hillme answered, "No." Hillme also stated that it was not until after his lawsuit had commenced that he had found out how the title to the cargo trailer was held.

Hillme further testified that in October 1998, a 1994 Dodge pickup truck was purchased. Hillme related that funds generated by the partnership were used for this purpose and be understood that the vehicle was to be a partnership vehicle. According to Hillme, Chastain informed him that once the 1994 pickup truck was paid for, the partnership would buy Hillme a pickup truck. However, the pickup truck was not titled in the name of the business. Rather, it was titled in Chastain's name. Once again, Hillme testified it was only after the lawsuit was filed that he first learned that the pickup truck was titled solely in Chastain's name.

According to Hillme, Chastain showed him the business records for 1997 and gave Hillme tax documents for the 1997 tax year so that Hillme could file his individual return. Each of the parties claimed half of the business expenses, such as utilities, and each claimed half of the gross income. Neither one filed an IRS partnership Form K-1.

At trial, Chastain variously claimed that Hillme was a subcontractor and then an employee Chastain's lawyer described Hillme as an independent contractor. Significantly, Chastain's 1997 tax return did not show that he had paid Hillme either as an employee or as contract laborer. Indeed, as previously set out, for the tax year involved, Chastain split the expenses of the business with Hillme. Later, Hillme received Form 1099s from Chastain for the tax years 1998 and 1999. Hillme testified, however, that the Form 1099s held no particular significance to him.

According to Hillme, in early 1999 Chastain informed him that he would incorporate the business for tax purposes, but assured him that it would not affect their agreement. They had a limited discussion regarding the incorporation. Hillme testified that Chastain informed him that they needed to incorporate their business because of possible tax savings.

In time, the parties disagreed over Chastain's plans to build a new shop building at a cost of twenty to twenty-five thousand dollars. Hillme felt it was unwise to borrow the money for the building at that time. Because of this disagreement, Chastain built the building himself out of his personal funds.

Eventually, further disagreements over management caused Hillme to open his own cabinetmaking business some time in 1999. By then Hillme had become aware of Chastain's claims that they were not partners.

In his sole point on appeal, Chastain maintains the trial court erred in finding that a partnership existed between himself and Hillme because there was insufficient evidence to support the trial court's ruling. Chastain asserts that Hillme failed to demonstrate the necessary elements of partnership, such as co-ownership of business assets, mutual rights of control of the business, an agreement in fact, and the right to share in profits and duty to share in losses. We disagree.

As previously related, the intent of the parties is the primary factor in determining whether a partnership exists. *Binkley*, 10 S.W.3d at 169. It is apparent that the trial court found Hillme's testimony to be more credible that that of Chastain. *Meyer*, 949 S.W.2d at 82.

While each evidentiary factor standing alone may not evince a partnership, it is clear that the combination of the following probative factors is supportive of the trial court's conclusion that a partnership was created by Chastain and Hillme in 1997.

The factors we note are the following: The name of the business was based on each party's last name. All of the advertising included each party's name and home telephone number. The day-to-day operation of the business relied on each one's specialized skills—Hillme's greater experience in cabinet making and Chastain's accounting and management skills. Each party co-signed the note for the cargo trailer. A joint checking account was originally established using the name of the business. Both parties were authorized to issue checks on the account. At one point Hillme was named a "payable at death" beneficiary of the business checking account. Additionally, Hillme had a voice in the management of the partnership. This is evidenced by his "veto" of using partnership assets for the construction of an additional shop building. Furthermore, during the first year of the partnership in 1997, each divided equally the income and expenses generated through the business. Although Chastain testified that this sharing of expenses for tax year 1997 was a "gift," it is apparent the trial court was not persuaded of the efficacy of this assertion.

We cannot say that the trial court erred in finding that a partnership existed between Chastain and Hillme. Sufficient evidence in the record supports the trial court's judgment. *Grissum*, 505 S.W.2d at 88. Point denied.

The trial court's judgment is affirmed.

## Case Review Question

Would the outcome have been different if there were evidence that the plaintiff was aware assets and bank accounts were in the name of the defendant and that he should have filed a partnership tax return?

## Termination or Dissolution

Any change in the partners of a partnership will result in the dissolution of that partnership.[37] Thus, when a partner dies, declares bankruptcy, sells his or her interest in the partnership, or withdraws, the partnership is dissolved. This does not mean that the partnership will cease to do business. The business of the partnership may be terminated or a new partnership begun. In addition, if the previously lawful business of the partnership becomes illegal, the partnership is dissolved and business must cease.

When a partnership is dissolved, third parties who have done business with the partnership are entitled to notice. This prevents partners from wrongfully representing apparent authority and binding the members of a dissolved partnership to third parties. All partners have the right to act as agents of the partnership and perform such duties as are required to conclude existing business obligations and concerns. However, a partner who has declared bankruptcy is no longer considered to be an active partner and cannot act on behalf of the partnership. The dissolving partnership is not allowed to engage in any new business such as entering contracts or taking new orders.

Any partnership assets that remain after all creditors have been paid in full are distributed according to a specific procedure. First, any partner who has loaned money to the partnership, over and above investment in the partnership, will be repaid. Second, all partners are repaid the amount of their contribution or investment in the partnership. Any cash that still remains is distributed among the partners on a *pro rata* basis. If one partner contributed 50 percent and two other partners contributed 25 percent each of the capital for the partnership, the funds would be distributed in a 2:1:1 ratio. The first partner would receive 50 percent of the remaining funds, and the other two would each receive 25 percent of the funds.

More often, after paying the creditors, a partnership's assets are insufficient to repay all the partners for their investment. In such cases, the shortage is also distributed on a *pro rata* basis. To follow the preceding example, the 50 percent contributor would absorb 50 percent of the shortage, and the other two partners would each be responsible for 25 percent of the shortage.

Create a plan to dissolve the partnership described below. Establish each step that would be necessary and determine how the partnership assets would be distributed. What issue could develop to create a problem between the partners?

Gill and Evangel have operated a partnership together for many years as an office supply store. They never reduced their agreement to writing, but they put equal amounts of cash into the partnership as needed. Because Gill worked approximately twice as many hours in the business as Evangel, he typically took 60 percent of the net profits and Evangel took 40 percent.

Gill and his family plan to move cross-country for a new opportunity. Evangel does not want to run the business alone, and so they decide to retire. They have four employees working within the business and four employees who conduct outside sales with area businesses. They do not know how much the building and land they own is worth, but a realtor said it should list for approximately $112,000 and to expect to get $95,000 after realtor's fees and closing costs are paid. This does not include the mortgage, which still has $12,000 owed. They have accounts receivable (money owed the business) in the amount of $32,000. They have an average collection rate of 95 percent. They have outstanding expenses in the amount of $18,000. They have just closed the books for the year and distributed profits. As a result, any excess after the business closes would be considered a return of capital (investment).

## CORPORATIONS

**corporation**
Entity legally recognized as independent of its owners, who are known as *shareholders*. A corporation can sue or be sued in its own name regarding its own rights and liabilities.

Legal advantages make the **corporation** one of the most common forms of business. In addition, because a corporation is created purely by statute, the legislatures have been free to create different subtypes of corporations to suit the needs of different types of businesses. Nevertheless, most corporations share standard characteristics, many of which have been embodied in the Model Business Corporation Act (MBCA).

### Corporate Characteristics

The following are some of the more common considerations when examining the traits of a business organization for the purpose of establishing corporate existence.

**A Legal Person.** Under the law, a corporation is recognized as a person. It can be taxed and held responsible for its acts for the purposes of lawsuits. Generally in the past, however, a corporation was not considered to be capable of committing crimes. When criminal conduct occurred, the individuals who actually committed the crime were held responsible.[38] This outlook has been changing. More and more statutes permit corporations and their agents to be convicted of criminal acts. Although a corporation cannot be imprisoned, it can be fined or dissolved as a penalty for illegal conduct. In addition, the acting individual can be held criminally responsible.

**Life.** Generally, the life of a corporation goes on indefinitely as long as the requirements of the statutes that permitted its creation are met. The statutes that set forth the ways in which a corporation must be created often establish annual obligations that must be met for the corporation to continue to exist. Often these obligations include such things as payment of an annual fee for continued registration with the state as a recognized corporation and annual reports describing the activities of the corporation during the preceding year.

**Limited Liability.** Perhaps the greatest advantage of a corporation is that individuals who invest in it have limited exposure for losses. Ordinarily, a person who invests in a corporation is called a *shareholder*. In return for the investment, a shareholder is given shares of stock in the corporation. The shares represent a percentage of ownership. The greater the investment, the greater the percentage of ownership. If the corporation does well, the shareholder's ownership becomes more valuable in terms of the price of the shares or the distribution of profits. If the corporation does badly or a large monetary judgment is rendered against it as the result of a lawsuit, the shareholders usually stand to lose only the amount of their original investment.[39] Thus, the corporation differs from most other types of business entities in which the owners are responsible for the entire judgment irrespective of whether it exceeds their investment.

---

## APPLICATION 14.5

Kendall is independently wealthy. Ten years ago, his financial holdings were valued at approximately $1 million. Through savvy investments and business dealings, he has acquired a net worth of more than $200 million. Ten years ago, Kendall invested in several companies. One of the companies was Startrektech. He purchased 100 shares at $100 per share. This was the par value (company stated value) of the shares. Six months later, the company was doing so well that Kendall decided to buy more shares. He bought another fifty shares of the same type of stock at the going rate of $200 per share. Over time, the company began to fail, and Kendall received a notice that the company was going to liquidate its holdings and close. The company had debts that exceeded its worth by more than $40 million dollars. Essentially, Kendall's stock was worthless, but he was not liable for the debts of the corporation because of the limited liability of corporate stockholders.

*Point for Discussion:* If the company had assets sufficient to cover its debts and buy the stock back from the stockholders, how much would Kendall receive?

---

**Ownership Versus Control.** A corporation may have many thousands of shareholders. Often the persons who are in a position to invest are not the persons who are best qualified to run the corporation. Therefore, for this and other practical reasons, another characteristic common only to corporations is that management of the business is separate from ownership. When a corporation is created, a board of directors is appointed that oversees the general operation of the corporation and the officers of the corporation who supervise day-to-day activities. This method of separating the management from ownership protects the interests of shareholders who do not wish to be involved in management. It is not necessary for members of the board of directors or the officers to have any ownership interest in the corporation.

**Sale of Ownership.** Unlike other types of businesses, ownership (represented by shares of stock) in a corporation can be freely transferred by sale or gift with virtually no effect on the corporation. This allows the investors the opportunity to profit from their investments, and because management and ownership are separated, the corporation can continue operating uninterrupted.

**Limits on Operation.** When a corporation is formed, the reasons for the corporation and other information are set forth in a document called the **articles of incorporation** or *charter*. These documents generally contain the name and purpose of

**articles of incorporation**
Document filed with the state at the time of incorporation that states the purpose of the corporation and defines the corporate structure.

the corporation, the number of shares to be issued and their value per share to the corporation, the voting rights of shareholders, and provisions for the election, removal, or appointment of board members or officers. The basic rules of operation and the methods to be used in carrying out the corporate purpose and in governing the corporation are set forth in **bylaws.** These charter documents can generally be changed only with the consent of the shareholders. The officers and board of a corporation cannot depart from what is set forth in the bylaws and articles of incorporation in any substantial manner without prior approval.

## Creating a Corporation

**Promoters.** For some businesses, a corporation is formed by **promoters**—persons who are often initial incorporators and shareholders. A promoter's primary duty is to obtain sufficient funding (*capitalization*) for the corporation and ensure that all the formalities required by the statute for incorporation are satisfied. In some jurisdictions, promoters are personally liable for the contracts they make on behalf of the corporation unless and until the corporation agrees to substitute itself for the promoter in the contract (known as a *novation*). If more than one promoter is involved in forming a corporation, then each has a fiduciary duty to the other and cannot act in his or her own self-interest if it will harm the interests of the other promoters.

The promoters also have a fiduciary duty to the corporation and its shareholders.[40] They cannot use secret corporate information for their personal benefit or gain. If a promoter does use secret information for self-profit, then the corporation and its shareholders can file suit to reclaim that profit. If, however, the promoter fully discloses the information to the corporation and the corporation or interested shareholders who would be affected approve, then the promoter may use the information to obtain all possible profits.

---

### APPLICATION 14.6

Corey and Conner plan to open a new restaurant and eventually chain it throughout the United States. The restaurant incorporates free child care with fully interactive entertainment and food for kids along with an adjacent upscale restaurant for parents. They incorporate as "CareFree" and hire Max as a promoter to locate investors. As Max travels around the country, he encounters a successful restaurant exactly like that which Corey and Conner plan to open, and it is in one of the three key cities that Corey and Conner want to target their first year. Max decides to buy the restaurant and run it himself. He incorporates as "KidsFree" and offers the opportunity to invest in his corporation to potential investors as well. Max's conduct is a clear violation of his fiduciary duty to Corey and Conner. He would be liable for any profits he obtained through the investments and probably the restaurant as well.

*Point for Discussion:* What if Max completed his job for Corey and Conner on May 1 and then on May 2 decided to incorporate and open an identical business?

---

**Statutory Requirements.** All states have some type of statutory law to govern the creation, operation, and dissolution of corporate entities. A majority of the states have enacted the Model Business Corporation Act, a series of laws that address all legal aspects of corporate existence. The act includes provisions for everything from establishing a corporate name to the proper procedures for dissolution. By establishing the same basic statutory provisions in most states, the process of handling legal disputes over corporate statutes is much easier to accomplish. The following is an example of a provision of the MBCA:

---

**bylaws**
Document of a corporation that details the methods of operation such as officers and duties, chain of command, and general corporate procedures.

**promoter**
One who is hired as a fiduciary to recruit investors in a proposed corporation.

### Sec. 32 Quorum of Shareholders

Unless otherwise provided in the articles of incorporation, a majority of the shares entitled to vote, represented in person or by proxy, shall constitute a quorum at a meeting of shareholders, but in no event shall a quorum consist of less than one-third of the shares entitled to vote at the meeting. If a quorum is present, the affirmative vote of the majority of the shares represented at the meeting and entitled to vote on the subject matter shall be the act of the shareholders, unless the vote of a greater number or voting by classes is required by this act or the articles of incorporation or bylaws.

## ASSIGNMENT 14.4

You are the officer of a corporation. Several important issues are on the agenda for the upcoming shareholders' meeting. You are concerned that insufficient numbers of shareholders will vote to legally pass on any of the issues. Analyze the language in "Sec. 32 Quorum of Shareholders." Break it down into the basic components and outline the exact requirements to bind the corporation on any of the issues voted on at the meeting.

Some of the most important statutory requirements of the MBCA or any statutory law with respect to corporations are those that provide for the creation of a corporation. Typically, this is accomplished through several steps, including the drafting of certain documents. The articles of incorporation and bylaws must be drafted and signed by the incorporators. Necessary documents and fees must be submitted to the secretary of state or other designated person where the business is incorporated. When the incorporators have complied properly with these formalities, the secretary of state will grant a certificate of incorporation.

The mere drafting of these documents does not establish a corporation. All other statutory requirements of the particular state must be met for the corporation to be recognized by the state as a corporation doing business in that state. Until these requirements are met, the corporation will not be entitled to the benefits generally afforded to corporations such as limited liability. When an outside party makes a claim against an alleged corporation in court, however, the court may find that a corporation exists for the purposes of the dispute even though the state has not previously recognized it.

Each state also has statutes that explain the procedure for the formation of a *professional corporation* (sometimes referred to as a PC). The states use various names for this entity, but the concept is basically the same. A professional corporation allows a member or members of a certain profession such as law, medicine, dentistry, or accounting to form a business that has many of the legal advantages of a corporation.[41] These corporations often do not have actual shares of stock; when they do, the shares are usually held entirely by the professional members.

## Types of Corporate Status

A de jure corporation (corporation by law) is created by meeting each requirement of relevant statutes that provide for corporation formation and maintenance. These statutes usually require that incorporators have legal capacity and submit articles of incorporation and bylaws. When all of the provisions for incorporation have been satisfied, the state issues a certificate of incorporation that is generally valid as long as the corporation continues to satisfy the statutes.

On occasion, incorporators attempt to satisfy the statutes but are not successful. In some cases, the law will recognize the organization as a de facto corporation

(corporation by fact or actions). The shareholders of a business that is recognized as a de facto corporation are protected in liability the same as de jure corporation shareholders would be.

To establish a de facto corporation, there must be evidence that the incorporators made a good faith attempt to comply with the state laws regarding incorporation and continuance of corporations and that the business has been conducted as if it were a corporation. It must also be shown that the corporation was represented as such and not as another type of business entity and that outside persons dealt with the business as if it were a corporation.[42] When all such evidence exists, the court may recognize the entity as a de facto corporation and allow it to claim all of the privileges of a de jure corporation.

Corporation by estoppel (preclusion from denial of corporate existence) comes into play in one of two ways. In the first, a person or persons hold a business out as a corporation to the public and deal with the public as a corporation but later attempt to deny that the corporation ever existed.[43] The second occurs when outsiders deal with a business as a corporation with knowledge that it is not a proper corporation. Then, when a dispute arises between the two, the outsiders attempt to deny that a corporation exists and claim that the owners should be personally liable.[44] In either instance, the courts will often treat the business as a corporation by estoppel and apply the law as if it were a real corporation. The rationale is that people should not be able to derive all of the benefits from acting as or dealing with a corporation while avoiding the obligations of one.

## Personal, Close Corporations, and Limited Liability Companies

The Internal Revenue Service (IRS) designates the common general corporation as a C corporation, which includes certain subtypes. The most common forms of small corporations are the S corporations, professional corporations, and limited liability companies. Each provides some degree of limitation on personal liability for corporate acts, but each allows the income of the corporation to flow through directly to the owners for tax purposes. With a general corporation, profits are taxed at a corporate rate and separate from the owners. Any distribution of profits to the owner shareholders is in the form of dividends. These are then considered personal income of the recipient for the purpose of income tax. The smaller personal corporations pay tax only once because all of the income of the corporation is considered income of the owners. Depending on the nature of the business, its size, its profitability, the number of owners, and their own personal tax status, the most attractive corporate form may be general or personal.

Personal and close corporations are totally created and overseen through statutory law just as the general corporation. Specific statutes prescribe the necessary steps to create, maintain, and dissolve such corporations. Historically, the S corporations were used for small operations of several individuals in virtually any type of legal business who sought to limit the exposure to liability they might have in a partnership. The professional corporation was created for licensed professionals whose business was to provide services rather than ordinary types of commercial business. This corporate form continues to be common among licensed professionals such as physicians, attorneys, accountants, and other similarly situated independent service providers. However, the limitation of liability will not protect the professional for his or her own personal malfeasance in the delivery of professional services.

The newest corporate form, the *limited liability company* (LLC), is rapidly growing in acceptance and has been recognized by statute in a majority of jurisdictions. Typically, the professional corporation statutes require all shareholders to be members of a common profession. Under the LLC, individuals who are not members of the profession that is the basis for the business may be owners. For example, a physician may enter into an LLC with an attorney in which the physician provides medical services as the primary business of the corporation, and the attorney is responsible for other issues such as the management of the business. In this type of company, most often the shareholders are subject to personal liability only for their own personal conduct. Thus, in this example, the attorney would not ordinarily be held accountable for the medical malpractice of the physician. Therefore, if an action were brought against the LLC for matters related to property ownership or business dealings, any judgment could only be recovered from assets of the business and not the owners. However, if a judgment for malfeasance were obtained against the business for the professional actions of an owner engaged in the primary focus of the business, then the professional found culpable would also be subject to personal liability.

## Piercing the Corporate Veil

A court will sometimes ignore the corporate structure of a de jure corporation and hold all or some of the shareholders, officers, and directors responsible for the acts of the corporation. Thus, the court ignores the wall of protection from exposure to liability that shareholders usually enjoy as owners of a corporation. This is called *piercing the corporate veil* and happens when a court finds that the members of a corporation have improperly used corporate status.

Generally, a corporation may be subject to piercing of the corporate veil in three instances: (1) when it is necessary to prevent fraud, (2) when there is inadequate capitalization, and (3) when the corporation refuses to recognize the formalities necessary to a de jure corporation.

**Prevention of Fraud.** In the case of the prevention of attempted fraud, the veil will be pierced only when it can be shown that a person or persons formed the corporation in a direct attempt to avoid legal obligations to creditors or others with legal rights. Usually, such debts were incurred through the corporation, but the funds were used in ways to benefit the shareholders personally. This is not the same as protecting the shareholders from obligations incurred as the result of the ordinary business of the corporation. If the obligations were originally intended to benefit the business of the corporation or were the result of doing business of the corporation, then the corporation will be responsible for the obligations, and the shareholders will continue to be protected.

**Inadequate Capitalization.** In the case of inadequate capitalization, the point at which the corporate veil will be pierced is not as clear. Although it is true that shareholders are generally responsible only for the amount invested in the corporation, it is also true that the original corporate structure must provide for investment that is adequate to allow the corporate purpose to be achieved. For example, a family that wanted to form a corporation to operate a shoe store would have to invest enough money to purchase inventory, fixtures, and a place for the store to operate. In addition, a sufficient amount of the profits of an ongoing corporation must be reinvested to enable the corporation to continue until such time as the shareholders agree to dissolve it. If this is not done, then the corporation is destined for failure, and the evidence indicates there was never a true intent to form a legal corporation for the purpose of doing legitimate business.[45]

**Refusal to Recognize Corporate Formalities.** Finally, the corporate status of a corporation that refuses to recognize corporate formalities will be ignored, and the shareholders will be held individually responsible as if they were partners in an ordinary business venture. One basis for piercing the corporate veil because of lack of corporate formality is to claim alter ego. Specifically, this means that the corporation has no true purpose of its own but is simply a tool of another organization. Although a corporation may be properly created and actually engage in the business stated as its purpose, a close examination will reveal that the business is merely a front for another business. In determining whether a business is an alter ego corporation, a court may consider whether the business shares employees, funds, equipment, and any other element usually used exclusively by a business entity.

One type of alter ego corporation involves very small or close corporations, which generally consist of only a few shareholders, all of whom are often active in the business of the corporation. The problem arises when the shareholders begin to treat the property of the corporation as personal property. For example, the shareholders may use corporate funds to pay private debts, fail to keep separate corporate accounting records, or take or use corporate funds or property without following proper procedures. If the shareholders are engaging in such activities, a court is likely to find that the corporation has not had a true corporate existence.[46]

Another situation in which the alter ego theory may be applied involves parent and subsidiary corporations. It is entirely legal for one corporation to totally own and control another corporation. However, unless both corporations operate independently, comply separately with the legal corporate formalities, and represent themselves to the public as separate and distinct, the courts may consider them to be a single corporation, with one corporation acting as the alter ego of the other.[47] In that event, the parent or owning company, which usually has the greater assets, can be held liable for the debts of the subsidiary.

A situation that is encountered less frequently but is nevertheless a basis for the alter ego theory is that of joint ownership. If a shareholder has a major interest in more than one corporation and strongly influences the policies and actions of the various corporations so that they become mere common tools for the manipulation of the business of this shareholder, then the corporations may be considered alter ego corporations and be held liable for the actions of one another.

**Liability of Parties.** When a corporation, large or small, consistently engages in any such conduct, the court is likely to find that the intent of the parties was not to carry on the business as a corporation. In addition, if it is found that the conduct of the shareholders, officers, or directors has resulted in injustice to outside persons, then the court may refuse to recognize the corporate status. This forces the shareholders to be individually responsible to injured outsiders for the damage that resulted from the injuries.

When the court does ignore the corporate structure and holds the shareholders liable, it does not necessarily follow that all shareholders will have to bear the business's losses. If a corporation consists of many shareholders, only those who have actively engaged in the wrongful conduct will be held responsible.[48] Innocent shareholders who did not take part in the management of the corporation will not ordinarily be held responsible for the acts of the persons in control.

**Claims Resulting in Piercing of the Veil.** Certain types of claims most commonly result in piercing of the corporate veil. One type is tort claims made by persons whose person or property has been injured by some negligent or intentional act of the corporation. Usually, such persons had no business dealings with the corporation. If the corporate veil could not be pierced, then those who have been unjustly injured could be placed in a position of suing a corporation that is nothing more than a shell with no assets against which to file a claim. For example, assume that a person is involved in a car accident with a bus. Assume also that the bus company has no assets and does no business other than renting three old buses for charters. Assume further that the bus company carries no insurance on the buses. If it can be shown that the owners of the bus company acted in one of the ways previously discussed, it would be unfair to force the injured person to bear the total cost of the injuries while the owners continued to profit from the bus company's business.

A second instance of piercing the corporate veil occurs in contract claims. In such situations, a party has business dealings with the corporation, only to find out later that the corporation was a sham. In most cases, the courts will find that the outsider had an opportunity to investigate the credibility of the corporation before doing business with it. If the situation did not lend itself to this, however, and would have appeared proper to reasonable persons, then the corporate veil will be pierced. For example, if a seemingly credible advertisement appears in the media and persons respond to it only to find later that they have been swindled, then the corporate veil might be pierced.

## ASSIGNMENT 14.5

Consider the following situations and explain what basis could be used to challenge and pierce the corporate veil.

1. Pete, his brother Phil, and their father, Paul, own a construction company known as "P. Smith." For many years, the company has been incorporated as a general corporation. Each owner has an equal share in the corporation, and the three split their profits equally. However, each of the men functions totally independent of the others in the work that is done. Pete does the foundation work such as digging and pouring concrete for basements, drives, and so on. Phil then comes in and frames the homes and completes the interior construction such as walls, ceilings, and so forth. Paul is exclusively responsible for installing the exterior siding or brick. Subcontractors are used for plumbing, electrical, and other work.

   Among the assets owned by the corporation are the homes of the three men, their respective vehicles, and three boats used by each of them for recreation. The corporation claims that the homes are display homes that they use to attract customers. In reality, each year on the Fourth of July and New Year's Day, the homes are opened to the public as the three men hold large parties. It is maintained that the vehicles are used predominantly in the business and the boats are used to entertain potential clients and existing customers. The men generally pay most personal bills through the business. Unknown to most people,

when any of the men need cash, they simply deposit checks made out to the corporation "P. Smith" into their personal accounts.

   Pete's wife, Sarah, has an interior decorating business. She frequently buys supplies and materials on account and then pays for the supplies when she receives payment from her customer. Pete and Sarah decide to divorce. During the proceedings, Pete cuts Sarah off financially. She uses the payments from her current customers for living expenses. Because the personal assets are all held within the corporation, Pete and Sarah own virtually nothing in their own names. There is a lengthy legal battle ahead for Sarah. In the meantime, Sarah's creditors for her business are demanding payment and sue her for collection.

2. Pete, his brother Phil, and their father, Paul, own a construction company known as "P. Smith." For many years, the company has been incorporated as a general corporation. Each owner has an equal share in the corporation. The corporation itself claims no significant assets other than enough money in the bank account to pay the rent and utilities on the office. When construction supplies are needed, the three men collect partial advance payments from customers in amounts just sufficient to make the purchases. Each man owns his own tools. In addition, the father, Paul, personally owns various items of larger equipment and tools necessary in the business.

(continued)

## ASSIGNMENT 14.5 (Continued)

Paul donates the use of these items whenever needed.

Unknown to most people, when payments are received that are not necessary for purchases and consist of profit, Paul deposits the check made out to the corporation "P. Smith" into his personal account. An amount for two-thirds is then withdrawn from the account and distributed to the other two owners. Recently, a home built by the corporation P. Smith was subjected to a heavy rainfall. As a result, the ground became saturated and the house slid off the side of the hill on which it was built. The owners sue the P. Smith corporation for negligent construction. However, the corporation claims to have no assets to cover the costs of the damage.

## CASE

### *Lock Realty Corp. v. U.S. Health, L.P., et al.,*
### 2006 WL 2788590 (N.D.Ind.)

This case demonstrates the examination made by a court when determining whether to pierce the corporate veil.

While trying to enforce its judgments against U.S. Health, Lock Realty received a check from "AmeriCare Living Centers." When that check bounced, Lock Realty discovered that U.S. Health had assigned its interest in the lease agreement to AmeriCare III on July 1, 2003; Mr. New signed the agreement on behalf of both the assignor and assignee. Lock Realty maintains that U.S. Health's assignment violates the lease agreement which provides, "[t]he Tenant shall not transfer, assign, mortgage this Lease, or the Tenant's interest in and to the Leased Premises, without first procuring the written consent of the Landlord."

Lock Realty moves to amend the court's judgments under Fed.R.Civ.P. 60(b), claiming the assignment from U.S. Health to AmeriCare III constitutes newly discovered evidence which by due diligence could not have been discovered, as well as fraud and misrepresentation by an adverse party. The court agrees there is sufficient evidence of misrepresentation given that AmeriCare III's failure to disclose the assignment throughout this litigation has prevented Lock Realty from fully and fairly presenting its meritorious claim. *Lonsdorf v. Seefeldt,* 47 F.3d 893, 897 (7th Cir.1995). AmeriCare III says an amendment to the judgments would violate its due process rights and is contrary to *Nelson v. Adams USA,* 529 U.S. 460 (2000) since AmeriCare III hasn't had an opportunity to defendant itself against the imposition of liability. The court doesn't agree.

In *Nelson v. Adams,* the Supreme Court held that due process requires a prospective party, even one on notice of the lawsuit, be afforded the opportunity to respond to claims against it. *Nelson v. Adams,* 529 U.S. at 465–467 ("due process does not countenance such swift passage from pleading to judgment in the pleader's favor"). Our case is different from *Nelson v. Adams* because *Nelson* included no finding that the party added to the judgment was an alter-ego of the party already named in the judgment. See, e.g., *William H. Morris Co. v. Group W, Inc.,* 234 F.3d 1279 (9th Cir.2000). Lock Realty says the named defendants and AmeriCare III are the "same," and service upon AmeriCare III would mechanically be the equivalent as service on the defendants. As counsel for Lock Realty explained in open court: "[w]e would mail all the same things to all the same places that we did the first case. All the same people would be involved." It appears Lock Realty asks that the court disregard AmeriCare III's corporate structure for purposes of finding it to be party to this litigation, and so bound by the court's judgment.

The court's jurisdiction over this case is based on diversity of citizenship, so Indiana law governs the corporate structure's penetrability. "Where one corporation so controls another corporation that, as a practical matter, the two entities function as one, service on one corporation is effective as to both." *Bally Export Corp. v. Balicar, Ltd.,* 804 F.2d 398, 405 (7th Cir.1986); . . . The corporate form should be disregarded in limited circumstances, but may ignored to prevent fraud or unfairness to third parties. *Winkler v. V.G. Reed & Sons, Inc.,* 638 N.E.2d 1228, 1232 (Ind.1994). "When a court exercises its equitable power to pierce a corporate veil, it engages in a highly fact-sensitive inquiry," *Id.,* and "while no one talismanic fact will justify with impunity piercing the corporate veil, a careful review of the entire relationship between various corporate entities, their directors and officers may reveal that such an equitable action is warranted." *Stacey-Rand, Inc. v. J.J. Holman, Inc.,* 527 N.E.2d 726, 728 (Ind. Ct.App.1988).

Several factors guide the court in determining whether U.S. Health and AmeriCare can be considered a single business enterprise, including whether (1) similar corporate names were used; (2) the corporations shared common principal corporate officers, directors, and employees; (3) the business purposes of the corporations were similar; and (4) the corporations were located in the same offices and used the same telephone numbers and business cards. *Oliver v. Pinnacle Homes, Inc.,* 769 N.E.2d at 1192. The court also may disregard the separateness of affiliated corporations when the corporations are not operated as separate entities but are manipulated or controlled as one enterprise through their interrelationship to cause illegality, fraud, or injustice or to permit one economic entity to escape liability arising out of an operation conducted by one corporation for the benefit of the whole enterprise. *Id.*

U.S. Health and AmeriCare III meet virtually all these indicia. First, U.S. Health and AmeriCare III share the same business address and have the same registered office. In fact, a party seeking to serve U.S. Health and AmeriCare III could do so via the same entity—Heritage Medical Group, Inc.—which is a general partner of U.S. Health and the registered agent of AmeriCare III. Ind. Trial Rule 4.6. Second, U.S. Health and AmeriCare III share common corporate officers, directors, and employees: (1) Mr. New is an officer of both AmeriCare III and Heritage Medical Group, a limited partner of U.S. Health, and the registered agent for U.S. Health and Heritage Medical Group; (2) attorney Jeffery Robbins has represented U.S. Health, Mr. New, and the Bartles throughout this litigation, while also serving as corporate counsel for AmeriCare III; and (3) the Bartles are limited partners of U.S. Health and serve as officers for AmeriCare III. Third, U.S. Health and AmeriCare III have been or are engaged in virtually identical lines of business; both have been the operator and tenant of the AmeriCare Living Center of Goshen.

Even more indicative of their common identity is the way the use by Mr. New and the Bartles of these entities as one enterprise would permit AmeriCare III to escape liability arising out of an operation U.S. Health conducted for the benefit of the whole enterprise. Not only did Mr. New covertly assign U.S. Health's interest in violation of the lease agreement, he and the Bartles concealed the assignment from Lock Realty and the court throughout this litigation. Moreover, it appears from the record that the majority of funding for the operation of the nursing home is paid from Medicaid, Medicare, and the Indiana Department of Health to AmeriCare III. When combined with Mr. Bartle's email explaining to Lock Realty's president that seizing the defendants' assets is a collection "strategy that will not work," this strongly suggests that Mr. New and the Bartles are using U.S. Health, along with 83 other active entities, as a means of sheltering the overall enterprise from liability.

There is adequate evidence to conclude U.S. Health and AmeriCare III are both instrumentalities of an single enterprise controlled by the defendants. As such, service of U.S. Health, Mr. New, and the Bartles is sufficient for service of AmeriCare III and the court may exercise jurisdiction over AmeriCare III. See *Swaim v. Moltan Co.,* 73 F.3d 711, 719 (7th Cir.1996) ("Valid service of process is a prerequisite to a district court's assertion of personal jurisdiction . . . more than actual notice; it requires a legal basis for holding the defendant susceptible to service of the summons and complaint."). The due process concern expressed in *Nelson v. Adams*—an adequate opportunity to defend against the imposition of liability—isn't implicated since AmeriCare III was more than a prospective party on notice; it was a party to the litigation per its common identity with the named defendants.

For the foregoing reasons, Lock Realty's motion to amend judgment [Doc. No 51] is GRANTED and its motion to modify the time limits for filing [Doc. No. 52] is DENIED AS MOOT. The clerk shall enter judgment accordingly. SO ORDERED.

## Case Review Question

What steps could a wholly owned subsidiary take to legally separate itself from its parent corporation?

## Corporate Stock

As stated earlier, a person who invests in a corporation owns a percentage of the corporation. This ownership is evidenced by shares of stock. The articles of incorporation state specifically how many shares will be issued. The total number of shares represents the total ownership of the corporation. The corporation will also usually give the shares a stated or par value—that is, the amount the corporation considers the shares to be worth.

Normally, the greater the investment, the greater the number of shares one possesses; and the greater the number of shares, the greater the percentage of ownership or control. As the corporation's profitability increases, however, so does the public value of having an ownership interest. Therefore, in times of great earnings by the corporation, the shares increase in public value, and an investor may have to spend large amounts to obtain only a few shares. The investor hopes, of course, that the shares will increase even more in value so they can be sold to the next investor at a profit. The corporation continues to value the shares at the stated value.

**Types of Stock.** Corporations have different classes of stock. All corporations have *common stock*. Corporations may also choose to issue *preferred stock,* which is usually entitled to higher and more frequent dividends and thus may be more marketable.

Some corporations issue what is called *cumulative preferred stock*. This type of stock accumulates rights to dividends. In the event there is not enough money in one year to declare a dividend, the dividend right of the preferred stock is added to the next year. When a dividend is finally declared, the preferred shareholders are entitled to payment of back dividends before any dividend can be declared on common stock.

**Stock Rights.** Certain rights are acquired along with some types of stock. If, for example, a shareholder purchases *voting stock,* the shareholder receives the right to cast one vote for each share of stock in addition to having ownership interest. Voting is usually done annually to elect new directors and to approve major changes such as an amendment to the articles of incorporation.

Some shares also have certain provisions regarding dividends. When the board of directors determines that a corporation is profitable, it may declare a dividend after reinvesting a reasonable amount of the profits. When a dividend is declared, the money assigned to the dividend is split among the shareholders, based on the type and number of shares owned. Preferred stock usually has a higher value than common stock and is entitled to dividends first. If sufficient funds are left, then a dividend for common stock may then be paid. Ordinarily, dividends are paid in cash, but some may be given in the form of additional stock or some product of the corporation.

Also to be considered are *liquidation rights*—that is, the rights of shareholders to receive the value of assets of the corporation in the event of dissolution. Preferred shareholders may have the first right to receive these assets up to the value of their stock. Common shareholders are apportioned remaining assets toward their investment. Regardless of how much a shareholder may have paid for stock, only the par or stated value is paid. This is what the corporation originally indicated each share of preferred and common stock would be worth.

Some corporations will sell stock with *preemptive rights*. This means that when a corporation decides to issue additional stock, the shareholders with preemptive rights are given an opportunity to purchase the shares of new stock based on their percentage of ownership before the shares are offered for sale to the public. Such rights are a sort of reward for investors who have previously contributed to the corporation. In addition, they allow an investor to maintain the same percentage of ownership.

**Stock Subscriptions.** A corporation may sell subscriptions to stock when it is formed or after its formation when approved by the directors. Generally, a stock subscription is an agreement between the corporation and a subscriber for the stock to purchase a certain number of shares at a certain price. A corporation that has not yet been formed accepts such agreements at the time of incorporation when shares are authorized and issued. Generally, persons who offer to purchase subscriptions do not have a contract with the corporation until the board of directors accepts the subscription; instead, the subscribers have an option that the board may accept or reject.[49]

If a corporation accepts a stock subscription and the subscriber defaults and does not pay for the stock, then the corporation has all of the remedies that are available in the case of a breached contract, including an action against the subscriber for the value of the stock under the subscription agreement.[50]

Stock subscriptions are especially helpful to promising new corporations. The corporation receives adequate capitalization from the investors; in return, the investors obtain the opportunity to purchase large amounts of stock at a price that is usually lower than the cost on the open market. Thus, if the prospects for a new corporation are hopeful, subscribers have an opportunity to buy more shares.

**The Securities and Exchange Commission.** The courts have addressed issues such as improper profits and other illegal behavior by corporations, but significant issues with respect to the buying, selling, and trading of stock resulted in the creation of the Securities and Exchange Commission (SEC). Following the stock market crash of 1929, the Securities and Exchange Act of 1934 established the SEC to oversee the stock market system in the United States. The SEC administers laws of Congress and issues regulations with respect to major transactions of stock, corporate ownership, and management. The goal of the SEC is to see that corporations and major corporate shareholders do not take advantage of unwary minor shareholders or vulnerable corporations.

As mentioned earlier, a person who owns a controlling interest in a corporation has certain influence in corporate operations and opportunities. Under SEC rules, a shareholder who possesses 10 percent or more of the corporate stock is considered to have certain responsibilities.[51] The SEC further considers a 10 percent shareholder to owe a fiduciary duty to the corporation and its shareholders. Officers and directors have an even greater fiduciary duty to the shareholders.[52]

When a controlling shareholder sells the controlling interest in a corporation, the fiduciary duty requires that the stock not be transferred to someone who would injure the corporation. Therefore, before selling a controlling interest, the shareholder has the duty to investigate the interested purchaser. If this is not done or if the interest is sold to someone the shareholder should know will injure the corporation to obtain personal gain (sometimes called "looting"), the shareholder may be personally liable for any damage to the corporation or other shareholders.[53]

In addition, a controlling shareholder, officer, or director who purchases controlling stock and sells that stock within a six-month period must disclose and return any profits to the corporation. This prevents the use of inside information for personal gain that will injure the corporation. The minority shareholders and the public are thus not at a disadvantage. It would be unfair to allow persons with access to information that may affect the value of the stock to avoid losses or to obtain huge profits while other shareholders or the public who lack the information lose or at least do not have the same opportunity to improve their investment. The key to legal stock transactions is disclosure. If major shareholders fully disclose their actions and adhere to the other requirements of the SEC, then the corporation, its shareholders, and the public are protected.

## The Corporate Existence

As stated earlier, the first board of directors of a corporation is responsible for complying with all of the statutory formalities, including preparation of the articles of incorporation and bylaws. Generally, the officers of the corporation will be responsible for daily management and administrative decisions, while long-range decisions about the policies of the corporation are made by the board.

Shareholders also have limited input into the operations of the corporation. They usually vote on major changes in the direction of the corporation and elect new board members when a term ends or a vacancy occurs. Shareholders also generally have the right to remove a director with or without reason. Examples of justifications for removal include mismanagement of the corporation or negligent risking of the shareholders' investments.

In smaller corporations, the officers, board of directors, and shareholders are often all the same people. In large corporations, however, many shareholders never even meet the board or the officers. Voting at annual meetings may be conducted by mail, and the shareholders make decisions on the basis of annual reports of the progress of the business and other printed materials provided by the corporation.

Shareholders who are dissatisfied with the job a particular director is doing may vote against the reelection of the director or vote to remove the director during a term of office. Each state has statutes that indicate when and how this may be accomplished. Each state's statutes also contain provisions that dictate the minimum number of meetings each corporation must have with shareholders annually. Statutes also provide for the type, timing, and method of notice that must be given to each shareholder before a meeting and the procedure for voting by mail if a shareholder cannot attend a meeting.

## Voting by Shareholders

Fixed rules exist with regard to which shareholders are entitled to vote on a corporate matter. Because stocks are continually sold and transferred on the stock market, a corporation's shareholders may change every day. Statutes specify a *record date,* the date by which one must own stock in a corporation before a shareholders' meeting to be eligible to vote on corporate changes. The board of directors then includes this time frame, or an even longer one, in the bylaws of the corporation when stating the amount of notice of a meeting that will be given to shareholders. Only persons whose names appear as shareholders in corporate records on the record date are entitled to vote at the annual meeting.[54]

If a shareholder cannot attend a meeting or does not vote by mail, then the vote may be made by proxy, the written consent of one person to vote on behalf of another. It is also legal for a group of persons to request other shareholders to give their proxies so that votes can be accumulated on a certain issue. With respect to public corporations, this is strictly controlled by the SEC and must follow specific guidelines. A proxy can be solicited only if the shareholders are given an accurate description of the matter to be voted on and are allowed to vote for or against the issue on appropriate proxy forms. This enables the persons soliciting the proxies to determine in advance how many votes they have secured in favor of a given issue. Statutes require that at least a majority of the issued shares be voted. An amendment to the articles of incorporation may require more than a mere majority. Generally, every share is entitled to at least one vote. However, the articles of incorporation may allow for the issuance of shares without the right to vote, such as some preferred shares.

In a corporation with an extremely large number of shareholders, persons owning only one or a few shares would not have the opportunity to have much influence over decisions because others own a great many shares. Under the method of cumulative voting, each share is entitled to one vote, and when several different issues are to be decided, each shareholder will cast one vote for every share on every issue. For example, if three new directors are to be elected and a person owns one share, then that person will cast three votes total (one share vote for each issue). If a shareholder has five shares and three issues are up for vote, then the shareholder has the right to cast a total of fifteen votes (5 × 3). If cumulative voting is permitted, then the shareholder can apportion the votes in any way he or she wants. Shareholders can also add their votes together to increase voting power.

Some states allow what are commonly called *voting trusts* and *pooling agreements*. In a voting trust, several shareholders give their proxies to one person who is known as the *trustee,* who votes on the issues. The advantage of a voting trust is that the weight of shares on a single issue is greater.[55] The disadvantage is that the trustee votes on all issues in the manner most advantageous to the group. This may not always be perceived as what is most advantageous to an individual.

A pooling agreement is somewhat similar to a voting trust. The goal here is to concentrate the votes on an issue. In a pooling agreement, the members of the pool agree that they each will vote in the way that the majority of the members of the pool indicate.[56] Generally, in a pooling agreement, a vote per share will be cast for or against each issue. Also, a written contract states which persons are involved in the agreement.

## Rights of Shareholders

In most states, all shareholders, by virtue of their ownership interest in the corporation incorporated there, are entitled to certain rights in the corporation in addition to voting rights. Shareholders ordinarily have the right to inspect the corporate records on reasonable notice and at a reasonable time.[57] Although shareholders do not ordinarily have input into the day-to-day management and operations of the corporation, they are entitled to observe them to some extent. The rationale is that they will be better informed about their investment and will be able to make intelligent decisions when voting on corporate issues or selling their stock. In addition, limited inspection is not seen as unnecessary interference with the business of the corporation. Historically, shareholders were given the right to inspect only if they could show a *proper purpose.* In response, most states have now enacted statutes that do away with the requirement of proper purpose.

The right to inspect corporate records is subject to limitation. Generally, inspection must be done during a time and subject to conditions set out in the corporate bylaws. This permits shareholders to inspect and also allows the corporation to avoid unreasonable interruptions of its operations. If a state statute permits such inspections and a corporation refuses or through its bylaws makes it virtually impossible to inspect, then the corporation and the officers who refuse inspection may be subject to legal penalties in the event the shareholder sues the corporation. In addition, a shareholder has the alternative of bringing an action against the corporation.

In addition to having the right of inspection, shareholders have privileges that are specified in the articles of incorporation for the particular type of stock they own. As stated earlier, these privileges may be liquidation, voting, and dividends. Finally, shareholders have the right to sue persons involved with the corporation when they have mismanaged the corporation.

## Corporate Actions

Two types of actions can be brought against persons who have a fiduciary relationship to the corporation. The first is a direct action by shareholders, generally brought against officers of the corporation. If it becomes apparent that an officer has placed self-interest or the interest of a third party above the interest of the corporation in business dealings, then the fiduciary duty has been breached. If this breach results in direct injury to the shareholders, such as the loss of their investment, the shareholders may maintain a direct suit against the officers.[58] It is only necessary for the shareholders who bring the suit to have been damaged and not for them to have been shareholders at the time of the wrongful conduct. If the shareholders are successful in such a suit, they may be awarded damages.

The second type of action is called a *derivative action.* This can be brought only by persons who were shareholders at the time of the wrongdoing and throughout the duration of the suit. Such shareholders act on behalf of the corporation against officers or others who owed a fiduciary duty to the corporation. It must be shown that the duty was breached and, as a result, the business of the corporation was damaged.[59] Any damages that are awarded are payable to the corporation.

---

## ASSIGNMENT 14.6

Based on the information provided below, identify the type of business entity described.

Max receives a percentage of profits each year from a business in which he is a part owner but has absolutely no involvement. Income tax on the profits are paid by both the business and Max.

Usually Max receives a percentage of profits each year from a business in which he is a part owner. This year the business operated at a loss, but Max was not required to assist in the payment. The business did not claim the loss on a tax return.

Max owns a business in which his wife and members of his family work but are not owners. Max sold the business to his brother, who started it as a new business.

Max owns a business in which members of his family work and share equally in the profits and losses.

Max, his brother, and his sister own a business in which they provide health care in exchange for money. The brother is sued for the manner in which he provided health care. A judgment is rendered, but Max, his brother, and his sister are not responsible for paying the amount of the judgment from their personal assets.

---

## Dissolution of the Corporation

As stated at the outset of this discussion, the life of a corporation is created by statute. It ends in the same manner. As long as the corporation complies with statutory requirements, the secretary of state will continue to recognize the business as a corporate entity. A corporation may dissolve, however, on grounds that include failure to comply with legal requirements or the action of shareholders or creditors. It may also dissolve by voluntary assent of the board of directors and, when necessary, of the shareholders. Although each state has specific requirements for dissolution, the items discussed in the following paragraphs are generally common to all state statutes.

When a corporation decides to dissolve voluntarily, several things must be accomplished before the dissolution. Before a formal voluntary dissolution takes effect, the following[60] are generally required.

1. The shareholders consent to the dissolution.

2. Notice is given to creditors.

3. All assets are sold.

4. No suits are pending against the corporation.

5. Debts are paid, and the remaining cash is distributed to shareholders.

Although court proceedings are usually not required in a voluntary dissolution, the corporation is usually required by statute to file documents that indicate the intent to dissolve the corporation. With the exception of what is required for the sale of assets and payment of debts, the corporation must stop doing business. After all business is completed, articles of liquidation are filed with the secretary of state. If all requirements have been complied with, then a certificate of dissolution is issued.[61]

Involuntary dissolution of a corporation may come about in one of several ways. Persons who have legal authority to request an involuntary dissolution in court are the attorney general of the state, shareholders, and creditors. When an outside party is attempting to force the cessation of business, the grounds for involuntary dissolution are limited and specific.

The attorney general of the state may bring an action to dissolve a corporation when the corporation fails to appoint a registered agent to accept service (delivery) of legal documents, when the corporation exceeds or abuses its authority as stated in the articles of incorporation, or when the corporation was created through fraud.[62] Frequently, statutes provide that the attorney general must file a complaint in the courts requesting an order of involuntary dissolution. The corporation may respond to the complaint, and the court will make a determination as to the validity of the allegations.

Shareholders are entitled to bring an action to dissolve the corporation when the conduct of the directors seriously threatens the shareholders' well-being. Examples of such activities include mismanagement, fraud, deadlock on corporate decisions, wasting of corporate assets, and illegal conduct. Generally, the courts will look to the actions of the directors and, in some cases, the controlling shareholders to determine whether the directors' conduct is likely to cause irreparable injury to the shareholders.[63]

Creditors are the most limited in their ability to cause the involuntary dissolution of a corporation. In most cases, this can be accomplished only when the creditor has an actual legal judgment against the corporation and the corporation is unable to pay the debt, or when the debt has not been declared by a court but the corporation admits the existence of the debt and its inability to pay.[64]

## Bankruptcy

Every business venture is not a success. Neither is every personal financial situation. In some instances, the debt-to-profit or debt-to-income ratio becomes so extreme that the only reasonable alternative is to abandon the current endeavor. Bankruptcy laws have been developed over the years to provide a variety of options and protections to both debtors and creditors.

A common misconception is that when bankruptcy is declared, the creditors lose all hope of collection. In reality, the effect of bankruptcy in many respects can be a positive result. Several different forms of bankruptcy will be discussed in this section. The forms of bankruptcy depend on either the nature of the entity or the person seeking relief, as well as on the type of relief sought. However, a few characteristics are common to all forms.

Initially, when a petition is made to the bankruptcy courts, an immediate *stay* is granted. The stay prohibits further attempts at collection and effectively freezes the financial activity of the debtor. To ensure fairness, the debtor is required to list all creditors with the court and provide notice of the filing of the bankruptcy petition to those creditors. By doing so, not only is the debtor protected from further collection attempts but also the creditors are protected because they are advised of the financial situation of the debtor and have the opportunity to discontinue further extensions of credit.

Generally, following the filing of a bankruptcy petition, a series of hearings are conducted to allow input by the debtor and creditors so that the court may make an informed finding regarding whether the bankruptcy petition filed is an appropriate form of relief for the debtor and creditors. Ultimately, an order is rendered by the court that details the rights of the debtor and creditors with respect to repayment or discharge of debts.

The two primary forms of bankruptcy are *reorganization* and *liquidation*. Reorganization provides an entity or person protection from collection while a plan for repayment of all debts is developed and implemented. Sometimes, the amount and time of payment is different from that originally agreed on by the debtor and creditor. However, the creditor does receive repayment of either the total debt or an accepted amount. The law also imposes limits as to how long repayment under the plan may take.

Liquidation is the absolute discharge of debt. In this type of bankruptcy, the assets of the debtor (subject to some exceptions) are liquidated or converted to cash. The court prioritizes the debts and begins the process of repayment. What are known as *secured debts*—those for which there is a written pledge of collateral such as a car or house—have the highest priority. If the amount of liquidated assets is not sufficient to cover the total amount of debt, then those at the bottom of the priority list are discharged, meaning that these creditors must accept that they will never receive payment for the amount owed and thus write it off as a bad debt. Just as certain assets cannot be seized and liquidated in a bankruptcy, certain debts also cannot ordinarily be discharged. These are listed in the statutes and are only included in the discharged debts in extreme circumstances—and in some cases not at all.

When discussing the different types of bankruptcy, various references are made to the term *chapter*. The term in this case refers to the chapter in the bankruptcy statutes that deals with the particular type of entity or person in bankruptcy or the specific type of relief sought. For example, Chapter 7 of the federal bankruptcy statutes is the chapter that provides for the liquidation of assets and discharge of debts. Chapter 13 provides for a reorganization plan by the individual, and Chapter 11 provides for reorganization by most corporations and partnerships. Various other chapters provide for relief to farmers and highly regulated industries such as insurance companies.

When the individual or company wants to continue attempting repayment, there is a form of relief sometimes used by creditors known as *involuntary bankruptcy*. This type of bankruptcy occurs when a number of creditors of a single debtor cooperatively file a petition asking the court to declare a stay and impose bankruptcy. At first the question may arise, why would a creditor seek bankruptcy and possibly foreclose the chance of full repayment? The answer is quite simple: If the debtor shows an established pattern of accumulating debt beyond the value of assets, then the creditors may want to put a halt to the increasing debt and thereby protect their chances of at least a partial repayment.

Bankruptcy has been a part of U.S. law for more than 100 years. The laws continue to evolve in an attempt to provide fairness to both creditors and debtors. Consequently, bankruptcy is an area of law that is subject to frequent changes and variations. For most of bankruptcy law's history in the United States, the core policies and procedures stayed essentially the same. From time to time amendments would be made to avoid abuse. An example is the exclusion of student loan debt from bankruptcy. As more and more individuals attended college and the expenses began to climb, student loans became an option that made college available to students who could not otherwise afford it. However, it became apparent in the latter part of the twentieth century that many individuals were completing college educations on student loan funds and then declaring bankruptcy to avoid payment. Because many of these individuals did not have an established credit history, they stood to lose very little. Thus, an amendment was made to the Code to eliminate most instances of discharging student loan debt as an option in a bankruptcy proceeding. Similarly, throughout the 1990s it became apparent that some debtors were running up high amounts of consumer debt such as through purchases on multiple credit cards. These individuals did not have the means to pay the cards, which often carried a high-interest commitment. Creditors were losing tens of millions of dollars in discharged debts, and consumers were obtaining the goods and money, which they had no intention of repaying. In 2005, the largest changes to the bankruptcy code in history were passed to prevent abuse of the system.

Some of the more significant changes to the Code include, but are not limited to, the following:

- Individuals can no longer elect to file Chapter 7 or 13. They must pass or prove the right to file Chapter 7, which allows a total discharge of debt rather than Chapter 13, which creates a payment plan. A *means* (income) test must be passed or challenged and overruled by the court before an individual can file Chapter 7.

- Debtors must receive credit counseling from an approved source before they can file bankruptcy, and any tax returns due must be completed and filed within weeks of filing bankruptcy.

- No longer are debts in a Chapter 13 filing subject to dramatic reductions. There are precise conditions that must be satisfied and circumstances that must exist before certain debts such as auto loans will be reduced.

- Debts that survive a Chapter 7 bankruptcy and liquidation could previously be submitted for a Chapter 13 bankruptcy to establish a long-term payment plan. Today, a two-year interval is required between the end of a Chapter 7 bankruptcy and the initiation of a Chapter 13 bankruptcy.

- Limitations have been placed on the debts subject to the automatic stay upon the filing of a bankruptcy petition. For example, there is no stay applicable in actions to collect back child support or completion of pending eviction proceedings.

- In addition to student loans, recent tax obligations, and back support, many additional items have been added to the list of debts that cannot be discharged in bankruptcy such as purchases of luxury goods valued at more than $500 made within seventy days of filing.

Although these changes have the intended effect of reducing fraud and abuse in the bankruptcy system, another very real result is the impact they have had on honest individuals who have encountered unexpected and catastrophic financial circumstances. Anyone contemplating bankruptcy should consult with competent legal counsel in this area as soon as the possibility of a bankruptcy filing is known. Failure to follow the proper procedures and timelines can significantly affect a debtor who is attempting to obtain relief through the bankruptcy code.

## NEGOTIABLE INSTRUMENTS

In all aspects of commerce, both business and personal, the exchange of money is a fundamental part of life in today's society. Although the bartering of goods and services was commonplace early on in this country, today it is much more of a rarity. Rather, goods and services are provided in exchange for a much more liquid asset—money. However, because the danger of carrying sums of cash around on one's person is a constant risk, a variety of methods have been developed to transfer monetary funds without the physical transfer of cash or even gold or silver. As these methods have evolved over time, many laws were developed to ensure that the parties conducting the exchange were protected.

Parts of the Uniform Commercial Code that deal with the transfer of funds have been adopted in all states. However, each state has the right to make some changes to integrate the uniform code with the existing laws of its particular jurisdiction. Nevertheless, there are essentially standardized rules throughout the fifty states with respect to the manner in which funds are legally transferred via documents. These documents, when they meet the required standards, are referred to as *negotiable instruments*. A negotiable instrument is something that can be offered in lieu of actual money and can then be redeemed for money.

Originally, most negotiable instruments were individually issued documents from banks for specific transactions, but today negotiable instruments are most often seen in the form of bank checks. Other examples include traveler's checks, certificates of deposit, and money orders, among other forms. A negotiable instrument will typically identify the person or entity to be paid, the amount, the person from whose accounts the money is to be taken, and the date on or after which the money is to be made available to the payee.

With the advent of electronic technology, scanning devices have largely eliminated the individual review of the most commonly used negotiable instrument: bank checks. As a result, the date may or may not have significance in some jurisdictions. Many banks will attempt to process the check when presented regardless of the date. Also, checks today typically have identifying symbols that are electronically read to identify the particular bank and account from which the money is to be paid. Because of the rapid transfer of information via computers, negotiable instruments are presented for payment much more quickly than when they were processed by hand and delivered to the bank on which they were drawn. As a result, individuals are at risk for civil and criminal prosecution if they offer negotiable instruments that are not supported at that time by actual funds in the bank on which the instrument is drawn. Although it has always been a requirement that the account contain adequate funds, it was not unusual that a check would be written and the person issuing the check would have a period of several days to get the funds into the account before the check was presented for payment. Today, that is no longer the case. In some cases, an additional security measure may be obtained in the form of a check or draft specially issued by the bank for a particular amount that guarantees that the amount will be available when the draft is presented. An example of this type of document is a cashier's check. This is often used in high-dollar transactions such as the sale of an automobile.

Even bank checks are declining in use. Not so long ago in the 1960s, school children were told of a fascinating time in the future when something known as an *electronic funds transfer* (EFT) would be commonplace. With EFT, a consumer would possess a card that would pass through a machine. In turn, the machine would communicate via phone lines with machines at the bank, and money for purchases would be instantly transferred from the consumer's account to that of the seller of goods. At the time, this was an incredible thought for these now-middle-aged Americans who use bank cards and ATMs as if they had always been available. In addition, with the advent of EFT, negotiable instruments are less and less commonplace. As a result, there are fewer opportunities for unscrupulous individuals to pass off worthless documents as negotiable instruments. However, negotiable instruments are still in wide use and subject to laws with respect to the requirements necessary for what is otherwise a scrap of paper to become a document that has a monetary value equal to the amount stated.

### Excerpted from Uniform Commercial Code § 3-104. NEGOTIABLE INSTRUMENT.

- "(a) Except as provided in subsections (c) and (d), "negotiable instrument" means an unconditional promise or order to pay a fixed amount of money, with or without interest or other charges described in the promise or order, if it:
  (1) is payable to bearer or to order at the time it is issued or first comes into possession of a holder;
  (2) is payable on demand or at a definite time; and
  (3) does not state any other undertaking or instruction by the person promising or ordering payment to do any act in addition to the payment of money, but the promise or order may contain (i) an undertaking or power to give, maintain, or protect collateral to secure payment, (ii) an authorization or power to the holder to confess judgment or realize on or dispose of collateral, or (iii) a waiver of the benefit of any law intended for the advantage or protection of an obligor."

If a negotiable instrument is transferred without an identified recipient, it is considered to be payable to the *bearer* or person in possession. This means that if something such as a bank check is written and the person to be paid is not identified, then anyone who possesses the check can cash it. Even in situations where the negotiable instrument is payable on demand (when it is presented for payment), it has a shelf life. Also, if an instrument is presented and the funds it purports to guarantee are no longer available, then there must be some method for the payee to seek payment from the person who initially provided the negotiable instrument in exchange for goods or services. Finally, it is not uncommon for one person to issue a negotiable instrument to another and for that second person to pass the negotiable instrument on to yet another party. All of these and many more circumstances that have been known to arise with some regularity are addressed in the Uniform Commercial Code. The laws adopted in the code lay a clear framework for the issuance and redemption of negotiable instruments. They also provide distinct remedies for individuals who accept negotiable instruments in good faith and then are not able to redeem them. In addition to these basic statutory rules, many individuals and businesses have established their own policies and procedures to further ensure that any document they issue or receive is, in fact, backed up by real funds in an account.

## APPLICATION 14.7

Kyra went away to college several hundred miles from her home. Her parents gave her a check when she left home to cover the deposit and first month's rent for an apartment and living expenses. She opened a checking account at a local bank on Friday when she arrived. Later that same day she rented an apartment. She wrote a check on the new bank account for the rent and deposit. On Tuesday, the landlord appeared at Kyra's door demanding that she leave. He had presented her check for payment and the bank where it was drawn and had been refused payment based on insufficient funds. Kyra went to the bank to ask why it had not paid on the check because she had deposited a much larger amount in her new account. The bank teller pointed to several posted signs around the bank that stated funds deposited by check would not be available for as many as four business days. This was not a statutory requirement but rather a bank policy to protect itself from loss. If the bank had paid on the check to the apartment manager and then found later that the check Kyra had deposited from her parents was not good, then the bank would have suffered a financial loss and would have to pursue Kyra for payment.

*Point for Discussion:* What are alternatives, other than carrying large sums of cash, to avoid a bank hold on Kyra's money?

## ETHICAL CONSIDERATIONS

Members of the business community are required to honor a code of proprietary behavior in addition to the required ethical behavior of all legal professionals. The core of any business is the relationship of the business with customers, whether they be other businesses or members of the general public. To maintain an ongoing customer relationship—or, for that matter, to encourage new customers—it is essential that a business follow certain practices that incorporate fairness and honesty. The failure to do so results in bad customer relations and often bad publicity.

Although some transactions are open to scrutiny—thus making unethical conduct easy to detect—other activities are not so visible. Many times, such situations are dealt with through administrative agencies such as the Securities and Exchange Commission to protect an unwary public from unethical persons. However, the ultimate responsibility for enforcing ethics is within the business arena. Companies do not want to be known for unethical practices or be associated with companies committing such practices. Consequently, ethical behavior in the workplace is an increasing concern, not only at an academic level but also in the real world of work.

## Question

If you are one of four partners in a business and have knowledge that the other three partners routinely engage in unethical conduct that could result in injury to an unwary customer, realistically, what are your options?

### ETHICAL CIRCUMSTANCE

Sharon is a recent business school graduate and is hired as an assistant to the head of a large stock brokerage firm. She undergoes several background checks and is subject to intense security clearance before being hired. She begins her new position and quickly finds that she has access to highly sensitive materials regarding business mergers and acquisitions. She quietly feeds this information to her stepsister, who buys and sells small quantities of stocks over a period of time. After ten years, Sharon and her sister have amassed some $20 million as the result of her use of confidential information. Sharon's conduct is unethical even though the information is not stolen or gained through illegal means because she uses a position of trust between her employer and clients to her own advantage and places herself in a highly advantageous position not available to the general public.

## ● | CHAPTER SUMMARY

This chapter has discussed the unique characteristics and similarities of various types of businesses. Sole proprietorships involve a single owner, with all profits considered personal income of that owner. The life of the business is limited to the time in which the individual owner operates the sole proprietorship. Similarly, partnership profits are considered to be the personal income of the partners, and the life of the partnership is limited in much the same way as that of the sole proprietorship. The liability of a sole proprietorship and of a partnership is personal, subject to the exception of limited partnerships. In exchange for liability limited to the extent of investment, the limited partner gives up the privilege of input in management decisions for the business. The corporation has unlimited life, regardless of any change in the owners. Liability is limited to the investment. Management decisions are made by the officers and directors, who may or may not be shareholders.

All of the forms of business typically involve the use of agency in which persons (agents) represent the fiduciary interests of other individuals or businesses (principals) for a specific purpose. Under the law of agency, the principal may be bound by the acts of the agent. Under the theory of *respondeat superior,* the principal may be held legally responsible for any actions by the agent that injure other parties so long as the actions are within the scope of the agency relationship.

## ● | CHAPTER TERMS

| | | |
|---|---|---|
| agency | bylaws | partnership |
| agent | corporation | promoter |
| articles of incorporation | limited partnership | |

# REVIEW QUESTIONS

1. What role does agency play in a partnership? In a corporation?
2. How does actual authority differ from apparent authority?
3. When is *respondeat superior* applicable? When is it inapplicable?
4. How does a partnership differ from a sole proprietorship?
5. How does a partnership differ from a corporation?
6. What elements are examined to determine whether a partnership exists?
7. What must be done to create a corporation?
8. When can the personal assets of shareholders in a corporation be reached by someone suing the corporation?
9. What is a promoter?
10. How is a corporation dissolved?

# HELPFUL WEB SITES

| | |
|---|---|
| Newsletter for Securities and Exchange Commission | http://www.SEClaw.com |
| General questions on business law | http://www.njbizlawyer.com/CM/FSDP/PracticeCenter/ |
| Business law, legal research | http://www.findlaw.com |
| Uniform laws | http://www.abanet.org/buslaw/library |
| National Conference of Commissioners on Uniform Laws | http://www.nccusl.org/Update/ |

# INTERNET ASSIGNMENT 14.1

Using Internet resources, identify the contact source in state government to register the name of a new corporation.

# INTERNET ASSIGNMENT 14.2

What uniform laws with regard to business organizations has your jurisdiction adopted?

# ENDNOTES

1. *Oran's Dictionary of the Law,* 3d ed. (Clifton Park, NY: Thomson Delmar Learning, 2000).
2. 3 Am.Jur.2d, Agency, Sections 9–16.
3. *Id.*
4. *Sim v. Edenborn,* 242 U.S. 131, 37 S.Ct. 36, 61 L.Ed. 199 (1916).
5. 3 Am.Jur.2d, Agency, Sections 222–224.
6. *Id.,* Section 218.
7. *Consolidated Oil & Gas, Inc. v. Roberts,* 162 Colo. 149, 425 P.2d 282.
8. *Lauderdale v. Peace Baptist Church,* 246 Ala. 178, 19 So.2d 538 (1944).
9. 3 Am.Jur.2d, Agency, Section 73.
10. *McGirr v. Gulf Oil Corp.,* 41 Cal.App.3d 246, 115 Cal.Rptr. 902 (2d. Dist. 1974).
11. *Elliott v. Mutual Life Insurance Co.,* 185 Okl. 289, 91 P.2d 746 (1939).
12. 3 Am.Jur.2d, Agency, Section 77.
13. *Bronson's Ex'r v. Chappell,* 79 U.S. (12 Wall.) 681, 20 L.Ed. 436 (1871).
14. 3 Am.Jur.2d, Agency, Section 75.
15. *Cavic v. Grand Bahama Dev. Co.,* 701 F.2d 879 (11th Cir. 1983).
16. *Id.*

17. *Pfliger v. Peavey Co.,* 310 N.W.2d 742 (N.D. 1981).
18. *Shafer v. Bull,* 233 Md. 68, 194 A.2d 788 (1963).
19. 3 Am.Jur.2d, Agency, Section 185.
20. *Id.,* Section 280.
21. *Id.*
22. *Pacific Tel. & Tel. Co. v. White,* 104 F.2d 923 (9th Cir. 1939).
23. 3 Am.Jur.2d, Agency, Section 280.
24. *Friedman v. New York Telephone Co.,* 256 N.Y. 392, 176 N.E. 543 (1931).
25. *Oran's Dictionary of the Law,* 3d ed. (Clifton Park, NY: Thomson Delmar Learning, 2000).
26. *Id.,* Section 15.
27. Uniform Limited Partnership Act, Section 7.
28. *Id.,* Section 4, 5, 7.
29. *Id.,* Section 18(b).
30. *Id.,* Section 22.
31. *In re Belle Isle Farm,* 76 B.R. 85, 88 (Bkrtcy. Va. 1987).
32. Uniform Limited Partnership Act, Section 7.
33. Uniform Partnership Act, Section 16.
34. *Id.,* Section 9.
35. *Id.,* Section 13.
36. C.J.S., Partnership, Section 95.
37. Uniform Partnership Act, Section 29.
38. Model Business Corporation Act, Section 4.
39. *Id.,* Section 25.
40. 18 Am.Jur.2d, Corporations, Section 104.
41. Model Business Corporation Act, Section 37.
42. *Lamkin v. Baldwin & Lamkin Mfg. Co.,* 72 Conn. 57, 43 A. 593 (1899).
43. *Lettinga v. Agristor Credit Corp.,* 686 F.2d 442 (6th Cir. 1982).
44. *Fitzpatrick v. Rutter,* 160 Ill. 282, 43 N.E. 392 (1896).
45. 18 Am.Jur.2d., Corporations, Section 2804.
46. *Id.,* Sections 45, 51.
47. *Id.,* Section 49.
48. *Id.,* Sections 55, 61.
49. Model Business Corporation Act, Section 17.
50. *Id.,* Section 25.
51. *Id.*
52. *Id.*
53. *Id.,* Section 48.
54. *Id.,* Section 30.
55. *Id.,* Section 34.
56. *Id.*
57. *Guthrie v. Harkness,* 199 U.S. 148, 26 S.Ct. 4, 50 L.Ed. 130 (1905).
58. 18 Am.Jur., Corporations, Sections 2245, 2246, 2249.
59. *Id.,* Section 2260.
60. *Id.,* Sections 82–93.
61. *Id.*
62. *Id.,* Sections 94–98, 102.
63. *Id.*
64. *Id.*

## STUDENT CD-ROM

For additional materials, please go to the CD in this book.

## ONLINE COMPANION™

For additional resources, please go to www.paralegal.delmar.cengage.com

## CHAPTER 15

# Criminal Law

## A GLAMOROUS DAY IN THE LIFE OF A CRIMINAL LAWYER?

Whether prosecutor or defense attorney, in most instances, television depictions of criminal law are about as realistic and true to life as Saturday morning cartoons. Realistically speaking, most defendants charged with heinous crimes are not innocent. They are not generally intelligent, articulate, and well-groomed individuals who had the tragic misfortune to be in the wrong place at the wrong time. Rather, they are quite often criminals and act like them. Many have no more difficulty lying to their own attorney than they do to anyone else. And if they would commit a violent crime such as murder, are they really going to be intimidated by the threat of charges of perjury for lying under oath? As for prosecutors, they rarely have immediate access to crime scenes and oversee the collection of evidence that might later be needed. Witnesses do not often come forward voluntarily and offer to publicly testify in open court against someone who has been accused of a violent crime. In many cases, the witnesses also have a criminal history, which affects their credibility with a jury. Evidence may be scarce, lost, or nonexistent. Backlogged courts and overloaded attorneys who generally work for less money than just about any other area of legal specialty cause trials to be delayed for months and, in some cases, years. Although television law may be entertaining, it is important to remember its real purpose: to entertain. It provides a thumbnail sketch of how the process would work in a perfect world. Consider such portrayals to be like so many of the diet supplement ads with before and after photos. At least those infomercials have a fine-print disclaimer, "Not a typical result." Perhaps something similar should be credited in television shows about the law.

## CHAPTER OBJECTIVES

After reading this chapter, you should be able to:

- Distinguish *actus reus* and *mens rea.*
- Identify the parties to crime under common law principles.
- Identify the parties to crime under the Model Penal Code.
- Explain the distinction between theft and robbery.

- Define and distinguish the types of homicide.
- Discuss the concept of corporate criminal liability.
- Distinguish justifiable and excusable conduct.

**criminal law**
Law created and enforced by the legislature for the health, welfare, safety, and general good of the public.

As discussed in earlier chapters, **criminal law** applies to those situations wherein public standards are violated and the public welfare is thus injured. Consequently, the government prosecutes on behalf of the people, and penalties (with the exception of restitution) are paid or served to the public. Although many crimes result in injury to specific victims, such injuries are personal and are typically dealt with in civil actions, such as those for tort or breach of contract. In addition, the government may prosecute for violation of the criminal law.

In the United States today, criminal law is statutory—that is, the legislature determines what will be criminal conduct. All crimes must be stated as such by statute before the conduct described will be considered criminal. When presented with the prosecution of a defendant based on a criminal statute, the judiciary examines the particular situation to determine whether it falls within the definition of the crime specifically charged. The legislature cannot enact a statute making certain conduct criminal and provide for punishment of persons who performed the conduct before it was declared illegal.

The process of punishing someone for conduct that occurred before it was made illegal is known as an *ex post facto law* and is prohibited by Article I, Section 9, of the U.S. Constitution. In the United States, a primary element of all criminal laws is the concept of *fair warning.* Under the Constitution, this means that one must be capable of determining that conduct would be considered criminal before the fact. Allowing persons to perform some act and then making that act a criminal offense and prosecuting them for it would not be fair. This does not mean that persons must actually be aware of the criminality of their conduct but only that they could have discovered it in advance and altered their course of action had they so chosen. Thus comes the saying, "Ignorance of the law is no excuse."[1] All persons are presumed to be responsible for ascertaining the rightfulness of their actions in advance. Generally, this is not a problem because in everyday life, right and wrong are quite apparent to persons who act in accordance with the established societal standards.

The discussion that follows examines the basic principles of criminal law that exist today in the United States. Although criminal law encompasses offenses from the most minor traffic violation to capital murder, the focus will be on the elements of more serious crimes. Further, because a majority of the states have adopted the Model Penal Code as the basis of their criminal statutes, reference will be made to the code when appropriate. States that have not adopted the code rely on principles and definitions created in common law as the basis for criminal statutes. Accordingly, reference will be made to the basics of common law as well. States that are described as common law jurisdictions here are states that have established their statutes on the basis of common law principles developed and adopted by the courts. Jurisdictions identified as Model Penal Code states are those that follow the principles of the code in their criminal law.

## DEFINITIONS AND CATEGORIES OF CRIME

When attempting to comprehend any subject with a large amount of material, it is easier to understand and apply criminal law when it is broken down into smaller subdivisions. Definitions of crime are used to distinguish different types of criminal conduct. Categories of crime are used to group similar crimes together for purposes of prosecutory and sentencing rules.

### Categories of Crime

The two basic categories of crimes are felony and misdemeanor. A **felony** is any offense punishable by death or by imprisonment exceeding one year. A **misdemeanor** is a crime punishable by fine or by detention of one year or less in a jail or an institution other than a penitentiary.[2] Many states have further divided felonies and misdemeanors into subclasses, usually for the purpose of sentencing. For example, crimes that are considered Class 1 misdemeanors may carry a heavier penalty than crimes considered Class 2 misdemeanors. Once the classes are established, the various crimes are placed within a class. The definition of the criminal offense itself will indicate the elements necessary for someone to be convicted of the crime. The category and subclass will indicate to the court what sentence should be imposed.

In some cases, a mandatory sentence is required. This means that the judge has no discretion to impose or suspend a sentence. The statute prescribes exactly what the sentence must be. In the absence of a mandatory sentence, the judge is usually given a range of punishment. The judge is responsible for imposing a sentence within this range that will adequately punish the defendant for the crime committed. This range allows the judge to take the circumstances of each case into account.

**felony**
Serious crime punishable by imprisonment in excess of one year or by death.

**misdemeanor**
Criminal offense punishable by a fine or by imprisonment of less than one year.

### Definition of Crime and the Elements of Criminal Conduct

Crime has been defined as follows:

> Conduct in violation of the criminal laws of a state, the federal government, or a local jurisdiction, for which there is no legally acceptable justification or excuse.[3]

In more general terms, *criminal conduct* refers to acts that may be injurious not only to an individual but also, and more important, to society. All persons in society should have the right to expect and enjoy certain basic privileges, including privacy, ownership of property, and physical safety. When one person invades the basic rights of another, the basic rights of society are also invaded. Therefore, criminal laws have been set up to punish and deter individuals from such actions.

Criminal law differs from civil law in several respects. Perhaps the most significant is that in criminal law, the government protects and upholds society's rights. In a civil case, individuals bring lawsuits to seek remedy for their personal injuries. In criminal law, the government prosecutes the offender to punish the person who caused the injuries. Thus, the purpose and goals of the two are distinct, although civil and criminal issues may arise from the same situation.

Included in all crimes are two basic elements: the physical conduct and the mental conduct of the perpetrator necessary for violation of a penal law. The physical conduct is called the **actus reus**, a Latin term meaning "the wrongful act."[4] All crimes require an *actus reus,* although in some circumstances, the wrongful conduct can be a failure to act. The mental conduct of the person is known as the **mens rea,** which means "a guilty mind or guilty purpose."[5] The state-of-mind element requires a certain degree of intent to commit the wrongful act or omission.

**Actus Reus.** Under the Model Penal Code, three steps are followed in establishing the *actus reus.*[6] First, it must be shown that actual conduct—either affirmative or by omission (failing to act when one should have acted)—took place. If the criminal conduct is an omission, then it must be shown that the accused was capable of acting and was obligated directly or indirectly by law to act. Second, if the definition of the particular crime requires a result from the criminal conduct, then that result must occur to prove *actus reus.* For example, to charge a person with battery, the victim must have suffered some actual physical injury as the result of unpermitted physical contact. This would satisfy the requirements of prohibited conduct and a result that is necessary to prove an offense of physical battery. Finally, under some statutes, certain circumstances must exist for conduct to constitute a crime. For example, by definition, the crime of burglary involves an unlawful or unpermitted entrance onto one's property. Thus, this is a required circumstance. If someone entered the property with permission, then burglary could not be established.

---

**actus reus**
Element of physical conduct necessary for someone to commit a criminal act.

**mens rea**
Mental state required on the part of the accused as an element to convict him or her of criminal conduct.

---

## APPLICATION 15.1

Amanda owned a small retail store that specialized in extremely expensive custom jewelry. When sales were paid in cash, Amanda did not record them. Instead, she deposited the money into a separate drawer and left the item sold on the inventory list. She then did not report the money as income on her financial statements or tax returns. Amanda's mother worked part-time in the store. She was aware of Amanda's conduct but did not take any steps to stop Amanda or report her actions to the Internal Revenue Service.

Amanda's conduct was a deliberate criminal act with regard to her legal obligation to report all income and accept any associated tax liability. Her mother's failure to act constitutes a criminal omission in her failure to report known criminal activity.

*Point for Discussion:* Why would the conduct be considered criminal if there was no individual victim? What should Amanda's mother have done?

**Mens Rea.** The definition of each crime in the statutes requires a *mens rea,* which means "guilty purpose, wrongful purpose, criminal intent, guilty knowledge, willfulness."[7] *Mens rea* describes the state of mind or the degree of intent that the actor has toward accomplishing a criminal goal. Under common law, the two basic subtypes of *mens rea* are known as *specific intent* and *general intent.* More serious crimes often require specific intent on the part of the actor to produce the result of the crime, whereas general intent crimes require a basic awareness of the likely consequences of one's actions.[8] Under the Model Penal Code, the state of mind required for the commission of a crime is based on degrees of knowledge that range from criminal negligence to recklessness to knowledge, with the most serious crimes requiring a criminal purpose. Exhibit 15.1 shows examples of intent and act under both common law and the Model Penal Code.

In common law jurisdictions, the statute for a particular crime or group of crimes will generally indicate only whether the intent required is specific or general. Specific intent requires that the actor form the actual intent to achieve the result of the crime,[9] whereas general intent only requires knowledge of the likelihood of the result of the act.[10] Similarly, a Model Penal Code jurisdiction will indicate the degree of awareness in the language of the statute.[11] Statutes with a *mens rea* standard of *criminal negligence* require only that the actor knew or should have been aware of the probability that the action would produce a criminal result.[12] The standard of *recklessness* requires, in addition to a general awareness, that the actor demonstrate a disregard for the consequence of the action. *Criminal knowledge* requires an awareness that the conduct would undoubtedly produce a criminal result. Finally, *criminal purpose* requires premeditated intent to act in a manner consistent with criminal activity.

Criminal law follows a theory similar to tort law regarding transferred intent. In criminal law, although an individual may intend to injure or kill one person but, in fact, injures or kills an entirely different person, the intent is transferred to the person actually injured or killed. The intent and act were present. It need not be shown that the intent and act were meant for a particular person or object.

A few excepted crimes have no requirement of *mens rea.* Commission of such crimes can result in conviction irrespective of general or specific intent. These are known as *crimes of strict liability.* Strict liability crimes have none of the ordinary intent requirements. Under criminal statute that imposes strict liability, an individual can be prosecuted on the basis of the act irrespective of the presence of general or specific intent.

Strict liability laws are often established to protect the general good of society. Crimes of strict liability generally do not require a preconceived intent to do or

**Exhibit 15.1** Examples of Intent and Act Under Common Law and Under the Model Penal Code

| Common Law | |
| --- | --- |
| General intent | Driving above the speed limit |
| Specific intent | Deliberately running down a pedestrian |

| Model Penal Code | |
| --- | --- |
| Negligence | Driving above the speed limit |
| Recklessness | Driving while intoxicated |
| Knowledge | Driving a car that is known to have unsafe tires (pieces of tread frequently tear away at speeds above 50 mph) |
| Purpose | Deliberately running down a pedestrian |

not do a particular act.[13] Rather, they are usually applied when someone's preventive measures could greatly reduce social or public harm.

An example of a strict liability crime is a violation of the statutory duty of persons selling liquor to sell it only to persons over the age of twenty-one. Such persons may not intend to break the law, but when they allow minors to be served liquor, they are endangering both the minors and the public at large. Simple monitoring of the persons served could totally prevent the harm that is presumed by law to result from the sale of liquor to minors. Therefore, if the duty to take preventive measures is minimal when compared to the social value of these measures, then strict liability may be imposed. In other words, failure to take the preventive measures may result in conviction regardless of whether there was general or specific intent to cause the harm. Rather, the guilt is based on the failure to prevent the harm.

## ASSIGNMENT 15.1

For each of the following circumstances indicate whether the situation includes criminal conduct.

1. Driving ten miles per hour above the speed limit.
2. Cheating on a test in college.
3. Failing to include income on a tax return from various jobs that were paid in cash and not reported to the IRS by the employer. The total amount of all income (taxable and nontaxable) is sufficient to meet the requirement to file a federal tax return.
4. Having no part in a crime but witnessing a relative commit a crime, and, when questioned by the police, claiming to have no knowledge.
5. Going into a bar at age eighteen and purchasing alcoholic drinks, with no identification being requested.
6. Working in a bar and serving alcohol to someone believed to be over age twenty-one without checking identification.
7. Serving alcohol to someone aged twenty-three who subsequently drives drunk and drives into a ditch, wrecking his car but injuring no one else.
8. The driver in number 7.
9. Borrowing $1,000 from a friend with a promise to repay the loan as soon as possible but then failing to ever pay it back.
10. Calling a telethon and pledging to donate $25 per month for one year. The donor's name is flashed across the television screen along with the donation commitment, but no money is ever actually sent.

## CASE

### State of Missouri v. Hicks,
### 203 S.W.3d 241 (MO 2006)

In this opinion, the court examines the roles associated with criminal conduct that are subject to criminal prosecution.

Viewed in the light most favorable to the verdict, the evidence adduced at trial revealed the following. On the night of July 3, 2004, Curtis M. Rowden ("Victim") attended a house party in Springfield, Missouri, where he met and talked with Shane Chesher ("Chesher") and Defendant. Victim remained at the party until 2:45 A.M. the next morning, when he left to go home. Shortly after Victim got into his car, Chesher let himself in the

vehicle and asked Victim if he would drive Chesher and Defendant to Chesher's car. Victim told them "sure" and Defendant proceeded to get into the back seat. As Victim drove, both Chesher and Defendant provided directions. Victim was led to a cul-de-sac where Defendant and Chesher told him to pull into a driveway. Victim noticed that a van was parked in the driveway and he asked Chesher where his car was. Chesher told him it was in the garage.

As Victim was unlocking his door, Chesher pointed a gun at his face and said, "Give me all you got." Defendant had his fist in the air and told Victim, "Just do what he says." Victim gave Chesher the following items: a watch, a class ring, his wallet with $20 in it, his checkbook, a ring with black and white stones, and his car keys. Defendant then told Victim to get out of the car, get on the ground and count to 200. As he was lying on the ground, Defendant began digging through his pockets, taking Victim's cell phone. He then pulled out Victim's asthma inhaler, laid it on his back, and told him he could keep it. Defendant and Chesher told Victim to stay on the ground and to keep counting. Defendant and Chesher left in a green and tan Isuzu Trooper owned by Defendant's sister, which Victim had seen at the party earlier that morning. After they left, Victim went to a neighboring house and called the police. Later that same day, a woman found a checkbook belonging to Victim in the driveway of Defendant's parents' house. The woman knocked on the door, asked Defendant about the checkbook and left it with him. Later that day, the police came to the home to investigate the checkbook that had been stolen in the robbery. They spoke to Defendant's Mother, Patricia Hicks ("Patricia"), who was unaware that a checkbook had been found earlier in her driveway. In the presence of the police, Patricia telephoned Defendant, who admitted to her that a woman had given him a checkbook earlier that day.

Defendant was charged with the class A felony of robbery in the first degree and after waiving his right to a jury trial he was tried before the court. The trial court found Defendant guilty and sentenced him to eighteen years in the department of corrections. This appeal followed.

Defendant was tried and convicted under a theory of accomplice liability. Both points raised by Defendant challenge the sufficiency of the evidence supporting his conviction. Appellate review of the sufficiency of the evidence in a court-tried criminal case is the same as the standard employed in a jury-tried case. Rule 27.01(b); *State v. Niederstadt,* 66 S.W.3d 12, 13 (Mo. *banc* 2002). "The appellate court's role is limited to a determination of whether the state presented sufficient evidence from which a trier of fact could have reasonably found the defendant guilty." *Id.* at 13–14. "[A]ll evidence and inferences reasonably drawn from the evidence are viewed in the light most favorable to the verdict, and contrary evidence and inferences are disregarded." *State v. May,* 71 S.W.3d 177, 183 (Mo.App. W.D.2002). The credibility of witnesses and inconsistencies in testimony are for the trier of fact to consider. *Id.*

"The law of accessory liability emanates from statute, as construed by the courts." *State v. Barnum,* 14 S.W.3d 587, 590 (Mo. *banc* 2000). Section 562.041.1(2) provides that "[a] person is criminally responsible for the conduct of another when . . . [e]ither before or during the commission of an offense, with the purpose of promoting the commission of an offense he aids or agrees to aid or attempts to aid such other person in planning, committing or attempting to commit the offense." Missouri no longer recognizes a distinction between principals and accessories. *State v. Wurtzberger,* 40 S.W.3d 893, 895 (Mo. *banc* 2001). Therefore, all persons who act in concert to commit a crime are equally guilty. *Id.*

Defendant was charged with first-degree robbery under Section 569.020.1, which provides:

> A person commits the crime of robbery in the first degree when he forcibly steals property and in the course thereof he, or another participant in the crime,
>
> (1) Causes serious physical injury to any person; or
>
> (2) Is armed with a deadly weapon; or
>
> (3) Uses or threatens the immediate use of a dangerous instrument against any person; or
>
> (4) Displays or threatens the use of what appears to be a deadly weapon or instrument.

Under accomplice liability, the evidence need not show that Defendant personally committed every element of a crime. *State v. Shockley,* 98 S.W.3d 885, 890 (Mo.App. S.D.2003). "[A]ny evidence that shows affirmative participation in aiding the principal to commit the crime is sufficient to support a conviction." *Id.* Affirmative participation may be proven by circumstantial evidence. *Id.*

Defendant first argues that his conviction cannot stand because the State presented no evidence as to the intent of the principal actor, Chesher. We disagree. Again, in Missouri, there is no distinction between principals and accessories. *Wurtzberger,* 40 S.W.3d at 895. "The central tenet of accomplice liability is the notion that all who act together with a common intent and purpose in committing a crime are equally guilty." *State v. Biggs,* 170 S.W.3d 498, 504 (Mo.App. W.D.2005). "Intent may be established by circumstantial evidence or may be inferred from surrounding facts." *State v. Durant,* 156 S.W.3d 524, 527 (Mo.App. W.D.2005). In addition, one's mental state may be reasonably inferred from the act itself. *Id.*

The testimony at trial revealed that after Chesher pointed a gun at Victim's face and said, "Give me all you got," Defendant had his fist in the air and said, "Just do what he says." After Victim had given his belongings to Chesher, Defendant told Victim to get on the ground and count to 200. Victim complied, and as he was lying

*(continued)*

on the ground, Defendant went through his pockets and took his cell phone. Victim saw Defendant and Chesher get into a green and tan Isuzu Trooper similar in kind to one owned by Defendant's sister. Victim's checkbook was later found in the driveway of Defendant's parents' home. There was substantial evidence from which the trial court could reasonably draw the inference that Chesher and Defendant acted with a common intent and purpose in committing first degree robbery. While Defendant did not personally commit every element of the crime, the evidence shows his affirmative participation in aiding Chesher to commit the crime. *Shockley,* 98 S.W.3d at 890. Such evidence is sufficient to support a conviction. *Id.* Defendant's first point is denied.

In his second point, Defendant maintains that the State failed to prove that he was guilty of first degree robbery in that there was no evidence that he "knowingly intended or encouraged" Chesher to be armed with a deadly weapon in the commission of the robbery. We disagree.

Defendant is correct that in order to establish accomplice liability the State is required to prove that Defendant: 1) purposely promoted the offense, and 2) had the culpable mental state for the charged offense. *England v. State,* 85 S.W.3d 103, 110 (Mo.App. W.D.2002); see also § 562.036. However, "[c]riminal responsibility for the acts of another does not require a common intent other than the promotion of the commission of an offense." *State v. Forister,* 823 S.W.2d 504, 507 (Mo.App. E.D.1992). In order to be convicted as an accomplice, a defendant need not possess the intent to commit the underlying felony. *Id.* A defendant who embarks upon a course of criminal conduct with others is responsible for those crimes which he could reasonably anticipate would be part of that conduct. *Id.* at 508. "Proof of any form of participation by [D]efendant in the crime is sufficient to support a conviction." *Id.*

A nearly identical argument as that posited by Defendant was rejected by the court in *Forister.* In that case, the defendant appealed a conviction for attempted robbery, arguing that the trial court erred in denying his motion for judgment of acquittal, because while "he believed that a burglary would take place . . . he did not know that [his accomplice] was armed and capable of robbery." *Id.* at 507. In rejecting this argument, the court noted that the defendant planned the burglary; drove his accomplices to the site of the burglary; and when his accomplice returned to the car, he drove away. *Id.* at 508. The court found that "this proof was sufficient to make defendant responsible for the attempted robbery." *Id.* Here, the State was not required to prove that Defendant intended for Chesher to display a deadly weapon. The State only needed to show that Defendant and Chesher acted together with the purpose to commit a criminal offense. The law of accomplice liability imputes the criminal agency of Chesher to Defendant. *State v. Neel,* 81 S.W.3d 86, 91 (Mo.App. W.D.2002). A defendant who embarks upon a course of criminal conduct with others is responsible for those crimes which he could reasonably anticipate would be part of that conduct. *Forister,* 823 S.W.2d at 508. In this case, it would have been reasonable for Defendant to anticipate that Chesher would display a deadly weapon considering the particular course of their criminal conduct. Defendant's second point is denied.

The State presented sufficient evidence from which the trial court could have reasonably found Defendant guilty of first degree robbery, under a theory of accomplice liability. The judgment and sentence of the trial court is affirmed.

BATES, C.J., and BARNEY, J., concur.

## Case Review Question

Why is it appropriate to convict the accomplice of the same crime as the primary perpetrator?

## PARTIES TO CRIME

Usually, one thinks of a criminal as the person who actually committed the criminal act that caused injury or damage. Many times, however, persons act together to commit a crime. This may involve cooperation in the criminal act or assistance before or after the crime. In criminal law, one who assists in a crime can also be accused and convicted of criminal conduct. Because common law principles and the Model Penal Code are somewhat different on this point, they are discussed separately. The issue of cooperation in a joint enterprise, commonly referred to as *conspiracy,* is discussed later.

Under common law, there are four basic categories of participants in criminal conduct. Specific terms describe the various types of involvement by the *principals*—persons who are actually involved in the primary criminal conduct[14]—

and the *accessories*—persons who aid the principals before or after the crime.[15] Common law defines two types of principals and two types of accessories.

## Principal in the First Degree

Principals in the first degree are the parties who actually take part in a criminal act. It is necessary that they perform the *actus reus* and that they have adequate *mens rea* at the time they commit their crimes. Under a variation of the definition, persons who can be charged as principals in the first degree include those who possess the *mens rea* but convince another to perform the actual physical conduct. This would include situations of coercement, threat, and trickery or that involve trained animals.

## Principal in the Second Degree

Principals in the second degree are persons who actually assist in the physical commission of a crime or persons whose conduct enables the principal in the first degree to commit the crime. If the conduct of a party is required to complete the crime successfully, either at the moment of the crime or immediately before or after, then that person would be considered a principal in the second degree—for example, someone who makes deliveries for a dealer of illegal drugs. The person does not obtain, sell, or perhaps even use the drugs, but by assisting in the delivery of the drugs, he or she is enabling the crime to be completed.

## Accessory Before the Fact

Accessories before the fact are those persons who enable or aid the principal to prepare for a crime. Their conduct may consist of providing the principal a place to plan or wait until the time has arrived for the actual commission of the crime. One of the most famous examples involved the owners of a boarding house in Washington, D.C., who supposedly knew the assassination of President Abraham Lincoln was being planned. These persons were convicted and subsequently hanged for their participation in the assassination.

## Accessory After the Fact

Persons who assist in a successful escape or concealment of criminal activity are accessories after the fact. This category includes anyone who is aware of the criminal activity and aids the principal in successfully avoiding prosecution. Conduct of this type ranges from giving the principal a place to hide to rendering medical care or misleading authorities about the principal or the facts of the crime. Persons who are closely related to the principal are an exception to the rule. Under common law, it was considered detrimental to family unity to prosecute someone for aiding his or her spouse or children. Therefore, these persons could not be charged as accessories. This exception is still recognized in most states. In addition, a person charged as a principal cannot also be charged as an accessory.

Usually, the division into principals and accessories applies to felonies. In the commission of misdemeanors, all those who are involved are considered equally guilty. Common law also held that accessories could not be prosecuted, convicted, and sentenced unless the principal was convicted. Today, most of the jurisdictions that apply common law rather than the Model Penal Code no longer require the conviction of the principal before the conviction of the accessory.

Another modern change in these jurisdictions is that principals in the first and second degree and accessories before the fact are generally considered principals. Conduct that aids the preparations for a crime or enables a crime to be committed

**Exhibit 15.2** Basic Concepts of Modern Common Law and Model Penal Code

|  | Common Law | Model Penal Code |
|---|---|---|
| *Actus reus* | Physical conduct | Physical conduct or encouragement of physical conduct |
| *Mens rea* | General intent | Negligence |
|  | Specific intent | Recklessness |
|  |  | Purpose |
| Parties | Principal first degree | Knowledge |
|  | Principal second degree | Principal |
|  | Accessory before fact | Accessory |
|  | Accessory after fact | Obstructing governmental operations |

Under modern common law, these are also considered equal principals.

is considered as serious as the actual commission of the crime. Modern laws tend to grade the involvement of the principals and accessories as a way of determining the severity of punishment to be imposed. Thus, one who actually committed the crime may be graded more seriously than an assistant.

## Parties to Crime Under the Model Penal Code

The Model Penal Code recognizes principals, accessories, and persons who commit offenses of obstructing governmental operations.[16] The code defines principals as persons who actually possess the *mens rea* and who either commit the required *actus reus* or control the commission of the *actus reus* by such means as coercion, trickery, or manipulation. Accessories are persons who agree to aid or actually aid in the completion of the crime, including actual physical assistance or mere encouragement. Persons who commit offenses of obstructing governmental operations can be prosecuted for assisting in the escape of the principal or the accessory or the concealment of the crime.

Under the Model Penal Code, it is not necessary that the principal be convicted before the accessory or the person who has obstructed governmental operations. Instead, each is judged on his or her own criminal conduct, although the seriousness of the penalty may be adjusted to reflect the amount of criminal involvement of the individual. This is done in much the same way as the trend toward grading the severity of each person's involvement under modern common law.

The primary difference between modern common law jurisdictions and Model Penal Code jurisdictions lies in terminology. With a few adjustments, the basic concepts are the same, as shown in Exhibit 15.2.

## ASSIGNMENT 15.2

**"Parties to Crime"**
In the following situation, identify (1) whether each party mentioned committed a criminal act; if so, (2) whether that party's intent was general or specific under common law standards; and (3) whether the intent would be considered purpose, knowledge, recklessness, or negligence under the Model Penal Code.

Cameron, Connelly, Rheatta, and Shanda shared an apartment during college. One night they decided to go out clubbing. They drove Shanda's car. All had been drinking heavily for several hours when they headed for home. Cameron spotted a young man on a sidewalk whom Cameron had never liked. He suspected the young man was responsible for Cameron's

*(continued)*

ASSIGNMENT 15.2 (Continued)

having been caught cheating on a test. As a result of being caught, Cameron had to repeat the course and would not graduate on time. Connelly saw the young man and suggested they scare him by driving up onto the curb. Rheatta and Shanda said nothing. Cameron accelerated the car and headed directly at the young man, whose back was to the car. Cameron struck the young man at a speed of more than 40 miles per hour. Rheatta said they should go back, but Shanda urged Cameron to keep going. Connelly told Cameron to pull over. Cameron did, and Connelly got into the driver's seat and drove the car home. No one in the group ever stopped or called for help. The young man bled to death as he laid in the street; it was several hours before he was found. Shanda parked the car in a rented storage garage for several months and then drove it out of state to Shanda's home, where she filed an insurance claim alleging she had struck a deer.

## ELEMENTS OF SERIOUS CRIMES

The following discussion explains basic elements that must be present before an individual can be convicted of some of the more common crimes in our society. In addition to submitting the required proof of criminal conduct by the accused, the legal system must follow the criminal procedures outlined in Chapter 16. The laws and procedures are designed to avoid conviction of innocent persons based on improper or unfair evidence of criminal conduct.

### Inchoate Offenses

*Inchoate offenses*[17] are crimes that occur before but facilitate or enable other crimes. Inchoate crimes include conspiracy to commit, attempts to commit, and solicitation to commit criminal acts. Each is addressed individually.

**Conspiracy to Commit Criminal Acts.** The crime of conspiracy involves the cooperation of two or more people in planning and completing a crime as a joint undertaking.[18] Conspiracy in itself is a crime distinct from the additional criminal act that is the common goal of the parties. As a result, conspiracy has its own *mens rea* and *actus reus,* and a defendant can be charged with both the completed criminal act and conspiracy to commit that act (as opposed to attempt and solicitation, which "merge" with the criminal act if it is completed).

The *mens rea* of conspiracy under common law requires specific intent. Each party to the conspiracy must have intent to agree with the other parties. Further, the agreement must be to accomplish something that is illegal. Regardless of whether the crime is actually committed, persons who have agreed to work toward a common goal that is illegal are guilty of conspiracy.

The *actus reus* is perhaps the most difficult element to establish in a prosecution for conspiracy. There is seldom any concrete evidence, such as a contract, that will establish that the persons have taken steps to agree to a common criminal goal. Generally, the jury must rely on evidence of the actions of the parties to the conspiracy. The prosecution's description of the acts of these parties must convince the jury beyond a reasonable doubt that the parties had no other purpose than to conspire to commit a criminal act. Many statutes today have extended this burden of proving *actus reus* beyond the common law. Today, most statutes require at least one of the parties to perform some physical act that demonstrates his or her intent to be part of a conspiracy.

Under the Model Penal Code, the elements of conspiracy are much more specific. Proof of the *actus reus* can be shown in one of three ways. There must be evidence that the conspirators assisted in planning, soliciting, attempting, or committing the actual criminal offense that is the goal of the conspiracy. In contrast, the *mens rea* of conspiracy required in the Model Penal Code is much less stringent. There need only be evidence that each person accused entered the agreement with the purpose of promoting or facilitating a goal of criminal conduct.[19]

**The Crime of Attempt.** Under statutes in all states, an attempt to commit a crime is considered criminal. An attempt takes place when the person has the *mens rea* (state of mind) to commit a particular crime and indicates a willingness to complete the crime. For some reason, however, the *actus reus* is never completed.[20] As a consequence, the person cannot be convicted of that particular crime. It is not in the interest of society's goals, however, to condone even attempts at crime. Moreover, sometimes injuries result from a failed attempt—for example, in attempted murder. A would-be murderer should not go free simply because the victim was fortunate enough to live through a violent crime designed to produce death. Consequently, if someone takes material steps toward such a crime, then attempt can be charged.

The question the courts must determine in cases of attempt is, How far must an individual go toward the commission of a crime before the individual is considered guilty of actually attempting the crime? Several tests have been employed in common law. Perhaps the most frequently applied today is that of *proximity*. The court considers how close the defendant was to completing the crime. The closer a defendant was, the less likely he or she would have turned away before completion. Adequate proximity to completion of the crime means that it is highly likely that the defendant would have completed the crime if given the opportunity. This is the point at which an attempt can be said to occur.

In a variation on this rule, the court examines the individual and determines whether that particular individual would be likely to commit the particular crime. The court may also examine whether the defendant had control over all of the necessary elements to commit the crime. Whatever specific questions are applied, the basic issue remains the same. Given sufficient opportunity, is it likely beyond a reasonable doubt that the person would have completed the crime?

Unquestionably, a person cannot be convicted of attempt if his or her actual goal was not criminal. Even if the individual believes that his or her conduct will constitute a crime, if it actually does not, then there can be no conviction of attempt. Similarly, if a person attempts to commit a crime but his or her actions in reality do not constitute a crime, then there can be no conviction of attempt. However, a defendant who takes steps toward the commission of the crime and would have committed the crime except for some intervening fact or force can be convicted of attempt.

## APPLICATION 15.2

Jamal decides to kill his former girlfriend. He invites her over to talk about things and offers her a drink. Jamal has laced the drink with his mother's window cleaner. He is certain this will poison the girl. The cleaner consists of vinegar and water. The girl doesn't like the taste, doesn't finish the drink, or even become sick. In this instance, no crime is committed. The conduct could not have resulted in the death of the girl because vinegar is not toxic.

*(continued)*

## APPLICATION 15.2 (Continued)

Assume, however, that Jamal put another household cleaner in the drink, and the girl again did not like the taste and did not finish the drink. In this instance, Jamal attempted and completed the necessary steps to adequately poison his former girl-friend to death. However, his crime was incomplete. In this situation, he could, in fact, be convicted of attempting the crime of murder. (An alternative charge might be assault and battery—which, in fact, was completed.)

*Point for Discussion:* Would either outcome have changed if the girl had become very ill?

If the intended crime is completed, a person cannot be convicted of the offense of attempt as well as of the actual crime. It is considered that an attempt becomes part of the actual crime when it is complete.[21] Thus, the two are merged into one crime. The usual terminology is that the attempt is a "lesser included offense"—that is, it is included in the greater and more serious offense of the crime. If the crime cannot be proven for some reason, then a person may still be charged with and, in many cases, convicted of attempt.

For the crime of attempt, the Model Penal Code requires that the actor do much more than simply prepare for criminal conduct. The actor must take what would be considered a "substantial step" toward completion of the crime. This substantial step is something that makes the crime more than a contemplation. At this point, the elements of the crime are within the control of the defendant and can be completed with the defendant's further actions.

The *mens rea* required of attempt under the Model Penal Code is more complex. The prosecution must show that the defendant had the intent to attempt the crime and must also prove any requirements of *mens rea* for commission of the crime itself. Thus, in a trial, the jury must look to the *mens rea* of the crime that the defendant attempted and determine whether all of the *mens rea* requirements were met. Then the jury must determine whether the defendant had the specific intent to actually commit the criminal act. In some situations, this may be redundant.

The Model Penal Code is somewhat more liberal than the common law regarding charges and conviction. In common law, one must be charged with attempt or the actual crime or both. If convicted of the crime, however, one cannot be convicted of attempt, and vice versa. Although the result under the Model Penal Code is the same, the required procedure is slightly different. The code permits a person to be charged with only the crime. However, if the jury finds that the person did not complete the crime but did attempt it, the person can be convicted of attempt. There is no requirement that the individual be formally charged with attempt in addition to the charge for the actual crime.

**The Crime of Solicitation.** Solicitation has been defined as the act of enticing, inviting, requesting, urging, or ordering someone to commit a crime.[22] It differs from conspiracy or attempt. In conspiracy, two or more persons work together to achieve a common goal of criminal conduct. The crime of attempt describes the acts under the control of an individual toward completion of a crime. Solicitation is a crime wherein an individual seeks to persuade another individual to commit a crime. The trend in common law states is to adopt the Model Penal Code view of solicitation. The code allows conviction and punishment of one who solicits any criminal offense, no matter how minor. The traditional common law approach was to punish only solicitation of more serious offenses against society.

At common law, conviction can be had for anyone who attempts to communicate with another in such a way that the other person will be encouraged to commit a crime. It is not necessary that the other person receive the communication or commit the crime. Solicitation is based on the premise that it is wrong in and of itself to willfully encourage criminal conduct. The *actus reus* is any conduct that would demonstrate such encouragement.

Solicitation is considered a specific intent offense in common law. The person who solicits a crime by another must intend that the crime actually be committed. It is not required that the person who solicits understand that solicitation itself is considered criminal conduct. Rather, it need only be shown that the person knows that the conduct that is being encouraged is criminal.

The Model Penal Code definition of *actus reus* in solicitation is quite similar to the common law interpretation. The primary difference is that under the Model Penal Code, a person needs to intend and demonstrate the intent to communicate the encouragement. As with common law, it is not required that the intent actually be communicated to the other person.

The *mens rea* for solicitation in the Model Penal Code requires that the person be aware that the encouragement is for a criminal act. Further, to prosecute for solicitation, it must be proven that a person has the intent that would be required to actually commit the offense that is encouraged.

In addition to conviction for solicitation, in common law states, the accused may also be convicted of being an accessory before the fact. Under the Model Penal Code, a person cannot be convicted as an accessory or as a conspirator in addition to being convicted for solicitation.

## Miscellaneous Offenses

Some crimes, although categorized in some states as felonies, by definition are distinctly inchoate in characteristics. Such acts directly enable a person to commit a crime. Like the crimes previously discussed, these acts are such an integral part of creating the opportunity for other criminal conduct that they become crimes in and of themselves. Common examples include the illegal possession of weapons or the possession of such large quantities of drugs that it is probable that the drugs will be distributed illegally. Another example of such an offense is burglary. Traditionally, burglary was an offense that consisted of forcibly entering the home of another at night with the intent of committing a felony within the residence. This definition has been somewhat modified in many states under modern statutes. Today, definitions of burglary are much more general and often include any unpermitted entry (regardless of whether it requires force) into the property of another (regardless of whether it is the home, automobile, or other property) at any time of day with the intent to commit a felony within the property.[23] This sounds remarkably inchoate in its definition. Burglary is an act that creates the opportunity for felonious conduct.

In cases of burglary, it is no longer required that the intended felony actually occur. Society wants to discourage unpermitted entry into the property of another with additional criminal intent. Such unpermitted entry is a necessary precursor to the commission of a felony on the property. Thus, if burglary is punished, perhaps persons will be deterred from entering private property to commit felonies. In any event, such persons can be punished for any actions they take that would enable the felonious conduct.

The Model Penal Code also recognizes these offenses and punishes them. Generally, punishment for all inchoate offenses under the Model Penal Code includes a range of severity that approaches the penalty for the actual commission of the more serious offense that might follow a conspiracy, attempt, solicitation, burglary, or other inchoate offense. Consequently, the Model Penal Code does not recognize any offenses that are perhaps beyond the inchoate offense but are not quite completion of the more serious offense. Some common law states have such intermediate stages. Under the Model Penal Code, the definition of an inchoate offense includes all conduct leading to the moment the subsequent offense is actually completed.

Under common law, categories of homicide might include attempted murder, assault with intent to kill, and murder. Assault with intent to kill might describe a situation wherein a person actually inflicts deadly force on an individual but the individual survives. It is more than a mere attempt even though the actual murder was not achieved.

Under the Model Penal Code, a person may be charged with attempted murder or murder. The definition of *attempt* is broad enough—and the penalties allowed are severe enough—to include the situation where the accused comes within a breath of murder.

## Felony Crimes

As the preceding discussion indicates, the common law jurisdictions and Model Penal Code jurisdictions regard the same basic types of conduct as criminal. The distinction between the two is generally in the way the crimes are formally defined. The following sections discuss additional felony crimes that occur with some frequency. The definitions are based on basic principles of law, with the understanding that each state may have its own definitions and penalties.

**Assault.** In a civil case, assault is considered to be action threatening an unpermitted physical contact. However, in the criminal sense, assault often includes actual physical contact and is synonymous with civil battery. Depending on the nature of the particular offense, assault is often a felony crime. Generally, an assault that is committed with a weapon or with the intent to do dangerous bodily harm or that results in serious bodily harm will be treated as a felony. When criminal laws differentiate assault from battery, assault is generally considered to be more consistent with the civil definition. Thus, criminal assault would be an act that causes fear of immediate physical harm through unpermitted physical contact.[24]

**Battery.** Many times in criminal law, the terms *assault* and *battery* are interchangeable. When a distinction is made, battery is considered to be the unlawful contact with another person. Such contact can be direct or through an instrument such as a weapon.[25] Like assault, the extent of the contact and the actor's intent will often dictate whether the crime will be prosecuted as a felony or a misdemeanor.

Usually, the *mens rea* required for assault or battery is one of general intent. A person need only be aware that his or her conduct is likely to result in an unpermitted physical contact. Of course, if a more specific intent is present, then that would also be sufficient, but the minimum requirement would be only a reasonable awareness.

**Theft, Robbery, and Larceny.** In ordinary usage, many laypersons interchange the terms *burglary, theft,* and *robbery.* However, as previously indicated, burglary does not include the taking of another person's property, only the invasion of it. Similarly, *theft* and *robbery* are distinct terms, whereas *theft* and *larceny* are often synonymous in criminal law.

*Theft.* Theft occurs when a party unlawfully obtains the property of another with the intent to dispossess that person of the property.[26] The intent required can be merely to dispossess, to convert the property to one's own uses, or to convey the property to another. As long as the intent is to deprive an owner of the use, possession, or ownership of property, the *mens rea* requirement is satisfied.

In many jurisdictions, the value of the property influences the severity of the punishment. The theft of more valuable property, usually in excess of a stated dollar amount, is considered *grand larceny* and is a felony. The theft of property that is valued below the stated dollar amount is considered to be *petty* (also known as *petit*) *larceny* and is usually considered to be a misdemeanor.

*Robbery.* The most serious offense involving unlawfully taking property is robbery. To commit a robbery, one must deprive an owner of property by the use of force or threats of force. The robber must either use physical violence or demonstrate to the owner that unless the property is turned over, physical violence will be used to obtain the property.[27] Thus, robbery must be committed in the presence of the owner. If the owner were not present to perceive the force or threats, then there would be no necessity for their use. Robbery includes situations in which physical force or weapons are used or threatened against victims. Because robbery is considered to be a crime of violence, the penalties are generally more severe than those for larceny.

**Homicide.** When a person is killed as the result of conduct or omission by another person, then a homicide has been committed. If there is no legal justification or excuse for such conduct, then a criminal homicide has been committed. Only criminal homicide can result in conviction and punishment. Legal justification or excuse includes situations in which the actor's conduct is considered noncriminal, generally because the required *mens rea* for a criminal homicide is not present.

There are various types of homicide. Most often they are described as *manslaughter* and *murder.* Manslaughter is usually considered a less serious offense than murder because it is death caused without malice aforethought—a mental state that includes the intent to inflict deadly force. Manslaughter is further broken down into two categories: *voluntary* and *involuntary.*

*Voluntary manslaughter.* Voluntary manslaughter is applicable in situations where the death of another was intentional but where special circumstances existed.[28] An example of such a case is a crime of passion in which a person loses all ability to reason as a result of extreme provocation by the deceased. It must be established that the deceased did something so outrageous to provoke the defendant that it is understandable that the defendant lost the ability to reason and, in the heat of the moment, attacked the deceased. Common situations include injury to one's family or to the marital relationship. One point is clear. The provocation must have been of a type so extraordinary that a jury could consider the defendant's conduct reasonable. This does not mean that the charges against the defendant will be dropped. Rather, it explains why the defendant is not charged with murder.

If the defendant has time to consider the action before it is taken, then a charge of voluntary manslaughter would be inappropriate. The key element that separates murder from voluntary manslaughter is that, in the latter case, the defendant did not have time to consider the ramifications of the actions about to be taken. In murder, there is time for someone to consider and plan the death or injury that ultimately produces death of another. Thus, the longer the period of time that elapses between the provocation and the act of killing, the more likely the charge will be murder.

*Involuntary manslaughter.* Involuntary manslaughter occurs when one person is responsible for the death of another because of gross and extreme negligence or recklessness and without the intent to kill or inflict bodily harm.[29] Such conduct is considered to show total disregard for the safety or well-being of others. In some states, death caused as the result of driving while intoxicated is considered to be involuntary manslaughter. However, many states have a separate statute for this, such as *vehicular* or *motor vehicle homicide*. Another example of involuntary manslaughter is hunting in or around a populated area. When negligence and recklessness are differentiated by statute, negligence is treated as extreme carelessness, whereas recklessness involves a total disregard for others. Although both are types of involuntary manslaughter, generally the penalties are more severe for reckless homicide than for negligent homicide.

*Reckless* or *negligent homicide* may occur during the commission of another crime that is a misdemeanor (e.g., death caused by a drunk driver or as the result of reckless driving), or it may occur as the result of some careless act not intended to be criminal. The latter often includes situations that are the result of circumstance, although created by negligence (e.g., a person who target shoots in his or her backyard in a suburban area). Assume in such a case that a neighbor is hit and killed by a stray bullet. There was never any intent to commit a crime, and certainly no intent to kill the neighbor. Nevertheless, discharging deadly weapons in a populated area would be considered extremely careless.

*Manslaughter under the Model Penal Code.* The Model Penal Code recognizes the same basic principles regarding manslaughter. Although it does not use the terms *voluntary* and *involuntary*, it grades the degree of the offense and the severity of the penalty in accordance with situations that are reckless or negligent. The code places emphasis not on the actual provocation but on the actual emotional condition of the defendant at the time death was caused. If the defendant was in a mental state such that control was impossible, then the death could be considered voluntary manslaughter. Under this application, there is no need to examine whether the defendant had time to cool off after the provocation. The entire question turns on the defendant's actual mental state at the time of the killing.

*Murder.* As indicated previously, murder is a premeditated act committed with specific malicious intent. Contrary to what the community-used term *with malice aforethought* would suggest, the actor need not have thought out a careful plan to kill with hatred. Rather, the term describes the state of mind of a person who is aware of what he or she is doing and who can make the choice not to act. Many states that apply this common law theory of murder break up the definition by varying states of mind.

The term *degree* is often used to indicate various categories of murder. *Murder in the first degree* is usually the most serious felony. It often requires that the actor have the preconceived intent to kill and carry out that intent to fruition. This differs from *murder in the second degree,* which often describes a situation in which a person intends to inflict serious physical harm on the victim and death follows. Finally, there is murder as the result of recklessness that is so great that the actor had no reasonable basis to believe that the death of another would not result from the action. The risk of death is more than substantial: It is a near certainty that a person will die from the actor's conduct.

*Felony murder rule.* Some states employ an additional category of murder known as the *felony murder rule*. This rule has two basic requirements: (1) The actor must be engaged in the commission of a dangerous felony, and (2) the acts pertaining to the felony must proximately cause the death of another.[30] Further, in some states, if the victim is injured but dies as a proximate result of those injuries within one year, the actor can be charged with murder, even though other circumstances may have contributed to the death.

## APPLICATION 15.3

Jim had a history of violence, and his wife took out a restraining order to keep him away. Angered, he decided to kill his wife and went to the home of his wife's parents, where his wife had been staying. He murdered his in-laws, but his wife escaped in a car. Jim was chasing his wife through traffic and firing a gun at her. He was being chased himself by police when he hit another car in a head-on collision. The driver of the other car was critically injured and left paralyzed and on a ventilator. As a result, she was placed permanently in a long-term care facility. Ten months after the accident, the injured driver contracted a bacterial infection while hospitalized and died within a matter of days. The felonious criminal action of Jim caused the injury, which ultimately resulted in the physical condition that contributed to the other driver's death. As a result, in recognizing jurisdictions, Jim would be subject to charges of felony murder.

*Point for Discussion:* Would the result for Jim be different if the accident had occurred while he was on his way to kill his wife but had done nothing legally wrong yet other than speeding?

## ASSIGNMENT 15.3

Refer back to the situation described in Assignment 15.2. In what category would the individuals be placed under (1) common law? (2) modern common law? (3) the Model Penal Code? Or would there be no criminal liability?

*Murder under the Model Penal Code.* The Model Penal Code follows the same basic premise as common law when determining guilt in cases of murder. Murder that results from the intent to inflict fatal injuries is defined in much the same way as murder in the first degree under common law.[31] The Model Penal Code also provides for situations of serious bodily harm or great recklessness that produces death, although these two situations are considered an offense of the same severity under the code. The primary difference is that the Model Penal Code contains no provision for the felony murder rule. The reasoning is that the person should be charged with murder or manslaughter in addition to the felony rather than be charged with a combined single charge of felony and murder. It is reasoned that the actual guilt and *mens rea* can be more easily and fairly determined by this method.

**Rape.** In recent years, the crime of rape has received a great deal of notoriety for a variety of reasons. Although the crime of rape went largely unreported in the past, changes in the roles of women in our society along with rape shield statutes have contributed to an increasing number of reports of sexual assault. Previously, it was not uncommon for the entire sexual history of the victim to be disclosed at the trial of the defendant in an attempt to show that the victim somehow encouraged the defendant's conduct. However, a majority of states have enacted rape shield statutes that prevent such information from being introduced as evidence. Women also are now coming forward with charges of *acquaintance rape* (*date rape*), which was virtually unheard of in the past. The government now recognizes that rape need not, and usually does not, occur between total strangers.

Rape (also known as a type of *sexual assault* in some jurisdictions) is the forcible act of sexual intercourse by a male against a female without consent of the female. It is a crime in all jurisdictions, and penalties range from a few years to life in prison, depending on the circumstances. The act of rape or even consensual intercourse with a minor typically carries even heavier penalties. When consensual intercourse occurs between an adult and a minor (to whom the adult is not married), the crime of *statutory rape* has been committed. The presumption is that the minor is incapable of making a proper decision as to whether to consent to intercourse, and therefore intercourse with a minor is criminal per se. The age at which a minor is presumed to have sufficient capacity to consent to intercourse varies among jurisdictions. In some jurisdictions, the fact that the minor lied about his or her age also is an adequate defense to the charge of statutory rape.

## PUNISHMENT

Common law and the Model Penal Code have similar concepts of punishment. Under each, the general rule is that a greater degree of specific intent will result in a more severe range of punishment for the convicted defendant. With respect to the most extreme punishment—death—the Model Penal Code includes it but neither advocates nor discourages it. The provision for the death penalty is included as an acknowledgment that the death penalty is part of U.S. criminal law at this time. The position of common law has varied on the issue of capital punishment. At this time, it is considered an acceptable form of punishment by the government for certain types of crime.

Other punishments typically include imprisonment, monetary fines, community service (time spent doing activities that benefit the community at large), and restitution (repayment to a victim for injury to his or her person or property). Whatever the punishment, one constant remains: The punishment must not be cruel or unusual for the crime committed, according to the Eighth Amendment. For example, the death penalty has been determined to be cruel and unusual punishment for the crime of rape, although it is still permissible for other crimes such as murder.

## CASE
### *State of Kansas v. Neff,*
### 145 P.3d 75 (Table) (Kan.App.2006)

The following case illustrates that a person's conduct, location, and acquaintances are more than adequate to support a charge of conspiracy.

When authorities investigated a report of unusual traffic in a rural area, they discovered an abandoned farm containing a methamphetamine lab and two unoccupied vehicles. Further investigation revealed Neff and his girlfriend, Rhonda Hart, hiding in a ditch about 600 feet from the lab. Neff was charged with unlawful manufacture and conspiracy to unlawfully manufacture methamphetamine. Before Neff's trial, Hart pled guilty to manufacture of methamphetamine.

At Neff's trial, Hart was called to testify against him and provided damning evidence of Neff's involvement in the manufacturing of methamphetamine. Neff's theory of defense was that he and Hart were in the ditch to have sex, but got caught in the wrong place at the wrong time. The jury found Neff guilty as charged and he was sentenced to 49 months' imprisonment.

Neff first challenges the sufficiency of the evidence to support his conviction of conspiracy to unlawfully manufacture methamphetamine. When the sufficiency of the evidence is challenged in a criminal case, the standard of review is whether, after review of all the

*(continued)*

evidence, viewed in the light most favorable to the prosecution, the appellate court is convinced that a rational factfinder could have found the defendant guilty beyond a reasonable doubt. *State v. Kesselring,* 279 Kan. 671, 679, 112 P.3d 175 (2005).

In order for the State to prove Neff was guilty of conspiracy to manufacture methamphetamine beyond a reasonable doubt, it was required to establish:

> "1. That the Defendant agreed with another person to commit or to assist in the commission of the crime of manufacturing methamphetamine;
>
> "2. That the Defendant did so agree with the intent that the crime of manufacturing methamphetamine be committed;
>
> "3. That the Defendant or any party to the agreement acted in furtherance of the agreement by obtaining ingredients, supplies and manufacturing materials; transporting ingredients, supplies and manufacturing materials; and meeting at the manufacturing site;
>
> "4. That this act occurred on or about the 21st day of January, 2003 in Rush County, Kansas." See PIK Crim.3d 55.03.

Our review of the evidence reveals that Hart and Neff drove her vehicles with her following him the majority of the way, with manufacturing supplies in the vehicle he was driving, to the location where he "cooked" methamphetamine. She had supplied the candles needed in the process and had bought Heet that morning. Additionally, the two of them had stopped together to pick up Neff's black bag, which Hart stated had been hidden 2 months earlier. Any one of these acts could be viewed as an overt act in furtherance of an agreement to manufacture methamphetamine given the remainder of testimony and physical evidence admitted during the trial, which included the testimony of the arresting officer and a KBI scientist describing the means, methods, supplies, and ingredients used to manufacture methamphetamine. Viewing this evidence in the light most favorable to the prosecution, we are convinced that a rational factfinder could have found Neff guilty beyond a reasonable doubt of conspiracy to unlawfully manufacture methamphetamine.

Neff next challenges the district court's giving of the accomplice instruction, PIK Crim 3d 52.18. We note, however, that Neff included this instruction in his proposed instructions filed with the court and made no objection when it was included. A litigant may not invite a trial court into error and then complain of the trial court's action on appeal. *Kesselring,* 279 Kan. at 693; See *State v. Borman,* 264 Kan. 476, 480, 956 P.2d 1325 (1998). We reject Neff's challenge to this instruction.

Finally, Neff argues that he was denied a fair trial due to the prosecutor's elicitation of Hart's fear of Neff. Appellate review of an allegation of prosecutorial misconduct requires a two-step analysis. First, the appellate court decides whether the comments were outside the wide latitude that the prosecutor is allowed in discussing the evidence. Second, the appellate court decides whether those comments constitute plain error; that is, whether the statements prejudiced the jury against the defendant and denied the defendant a fair trial. *State v. Swinney,* 280 Kan. 768, 779, 127 P.3d 261 (2006).

The challenged exchange was as follows:

> State: "Mrs. Hart, first of all how do you feel about testifying today?
>
> A: "I'm a little scared.
>
> Q: "Who or what are you scared of?
>
> A: "Of Dennis.
>
> . . .
>
> Q: "I can't hear? I'm sorry?
>
> A: "I'm scared of Dennis.
>
> Q: "Okay. And Dennis, what [is] his last name?
>
> A: "Neff.
>
> Q: "And is he in the courtroom today?
>
> A: "Yes."

Hart was then asked to identify Neff. There does not seem to be any material reason for this line of questioning except that it led into Hart's identification of the defendant and may have served to explain later testimony from Hart regarding her initial refusal to speak to law enforcement officers. There was no objection to this line of questioning. Additionally, later Hart described Neff's attempt to choke her when they were hiding in the ditch. There were also no objections to this testimony.

Although Hart's fear of Neff might have been irrelevant, we perceive no substantial prejudice to Neff by reason of these statements and the associated in-court identification. We conclude that the exchange was not outside the wide latitude allowed the prosecutor and certainly did not deny Neff a fair trial. See *State v. Tosh,* 278 Kan. 83, 85, 91 P.3d 1204 (2004). We reject Neff's suggestion that prosecutorial misconduct requires a reversal of his convictions and a new trial.

Affirmed.

## Case Review Question

Based on the decision above, how could someone who literally was "in the wrong place at the wrong time" avoid a conspiracy conviction?

## WHITE-COLLAR CRIME

Crime also exists in the workplace, and criminal responsibility for such crime has received increased attention in recent years. Although corporations generally are not specifically liable for criminal acts, it does not mean that liability is nonexistent. Although the corporation is considered a person under the law in terms of equality of rights, it is still a legal fiction. Because the corporation does not possess a mind, it is incapable of formulating the adequate *mens rea* to commit a criminal act. Only those who represent the corporation can do that. The law has come to recognize that the persons who represent the corporation are, in fact, the mind of the corporation, and through them the corporation can be convicted of most criminal acts.

If a person is employed by a corporation and acts on its behalf, then the corporation can be held responsible for those acts under the theory of *respondeat superior.* As long as the act was performed within the scope of the person's employment and related directly to the corporation, the entity as well as the individual can be held responsible. Although a corporation cannot be imprisoned, it can be heavily fined or dissolved involuntarily.

Crimes frequently committed on behalf of corporations include tax law violations, securities law violations, burglary and theft (in the case of trade secrets), and damage to the property of competitors. All of these actions require some actual mental and physical conduct by an individual, but they directly or indirectly benefit the corporation. If it can be shown that the corporate representatives acted, encouraged these acts, or accepted the benefits of these acts, then the corporation may be charged for the crime as well. In addition, the individuals may be held responsible as principals.

The Model Penal Code recognizes liability of business entities in much the same manner as the common law. The only real difference is that the Model Penal Code has a fairly narrow definition of the types of offenses for which a business entity may be held responsible. Specifically, for a business entity to be held responsible under the code, the offense must be one that the legislature clearly intended to apply to corporations or one in which the criminal actions can be proven to be consistent with the purpose of the corporation.[32] In other cases, only the individual will be held responsible for the criminal acts.

In addition to those crimes for which a corporation or business entity might be held criminally liable, crimes can be committed against the entity by its fiduciaries. For example, a bank employee who extracts funds from the bank for personal use over a period of time has committed *embezzlement,* which is essentially theft of property. Other crimes include violation of securities laws to injure or destroy a competitor's business or to take unfair advantage of investors. In the 1980s, much publicity centered around Wall Street figures Michael Milken and Ivan Boesky, who were convicted of obtaining huge profits in the securities market by violating securities laws designed to promote fairness among investors.

Although white-collar crime often appears to be victimless because no clearly identifiable and individual injury is caused by the act, it is nevertheless a violation of law and is dealt with in much the same manner as other criminal conduct.

## CASE
### *Karr v. State of Alaska,*
### 660 P.2d 450 (Alaska 1983)

Diana Karr embezzled $356,000 from Meyeres' Real Estate, Inc. between November 1979 and December 1981. Karr was charged with one count of embezzlement by an employee for the money she took prior to January 1, 1980. (Former AS 11.20.280 reads: Embezzlement by employee or servant. An officer, agent, clerk, employee,

*(continued)*

or servant who embezzles or fraudulently converts to his own use, or takes or secretes with intent to embezzle or fraudulently convert to his own use, money, property, or thing of another which may be the subject of larceny, and which has come into his possession or is under his care by virtue of his employment is guilty of embezzlement. If the property embezzled exceeds $100 in value, a person guilty of embezzlement is punishable by imprisonment in the penitentiary for not less than one year nor more than 10 years. If the property embezzled does not exceed the value of $100, a person guilty of embezzlement is punishable by imprisonment in a jail for not less than one month nor more than one year, or by a fine of not less than $25 nor more than $100.) [Karr] was charged with theft in the first degree, AS 11.46.120, for money she took after January 1, 1980, the effective date for the revised criminal code.

(AS 11.46.120 reads: Theft in the first degree. (a) A person commits the crime of theft in the first degree if he commits theft as defined in § 100 of this chapter and the value of the property or services is $25,000 or more. (b) Theft in the first degree is a class B felony.) After Karr pled nolo contendere to these charges, Judge James R. Blair sentenced her to serve ten years with five suspended and to pay $300,000 restitution. Karr was sentenced to five years on each count, and the sentences were made consecutive to each other. The five-year sentence for embezzlement by employee was suspended, resulting in a sentence of ten years with five suspended.

Karr appeals her sentence to this court. We affirm.

Karr first contends that the sentence imposed was excessive. Karr is thirty-four years old and has no prior criminal record. She points to *Austin v. State*, 627 P.2D 657, 658 (Alaska App.1981), where we said, '[n]ormally a first offender should receive a more favorable sentence than the presumptive sentence for a second offender. It is clear this rule should be violated only in an exceptional case. Karr also argues that we should consider her offense as one crime, since her crime was charged as two offenses only because the new criminal code came into effect on January 1, 1980. Karr argues that an offender who embezzled only after January 1, 1980, would have been charged only with one count, theft in the first degree. She contends she should not be treated differently merely because she embezzled both before and after January 1, 1980.

The record is clear that Judge Blair did not treat Karr differently because she was convicted of two counts. Essentially Karr was sentenced to ten years with five years suspended for theft in the first degree for a number of different acts of embezzlement committed over a period of over two years. Karr's sentence is not excessive under *Austin* because this is an exceptional case. Judge Blair classified Karr's offense as a particularly serious offense for an embezzlement. See AS 12.55.155(c)(10). Karr embezzled $356,000. The record establishes that Karr had earned a position of trust with Bud Meyeres, who owned Meyeres' Real Estate, and then used that position to embezzle. This amount was taken over a period of two years and involved numerous individual acts of embezzlement. In Karr's position she had to be aware of the effects of her embezzlement: at the time of Karr's sentencing, Meyeres was sixty-seven years old, and his real estate business was in serious financial trouble due to the embezzlement. Meyeres indicated that for the foreseeable future he will have to work hard to try to salvage his real estate business. It is unlikely that he will ever be able to retire. This is clearly an aggravated case. The presumptive sentence for a second class B felony offender is four years. Karr's actual sentence of imprisonment exceeds that by one year. In reviewing a sentence to determine whether it exceeds the presumptive sentence for a second offender under *Austin,* our primary focus is on the amount of imprisonment actually imposed. See *Tazruk v. State,* 655 P.2D 788 (Alaska App.1982). Judge Blair imposed the consecutive five-year suspended sentence primarily to enforce the restitution order. Karr's probation cannot be revoked for failure to make restitution if she makes a good faith effort to pay restitution but is unable to do so. See AS 12.55.051. In the event it is revoked she is entitled to another sentence appeal. Due to the seriousness of the offense, we conclude that this is an exceptional case, and the sentence of ten years with five suspended is not excessive.

The amount of money which Karr embezzled is the major distinguishing factor which separates this case from former Alaska cases in which lesser sentences were imposed for similar offenses. See *Fields v. State,* 629 P.2D 46 (Alaska 1981); *Huff v. State,* 598 P.2D 928 (Alaska 1979); *Amidon v. State,* 565 P.2D 1248 (Alaska 1977).

Karr also argues that the trial judge should not have imposed a consecutive sentence. However, Karr's total sentence did not exceed the sentence which she could have received for one count of theft in the first degree. Where a consecutive sentence is imposed but the total sentence does not exceed the sentence which could be imposed on one count, a consecutive sentence is not improper. See *Mutschler v. State,* 560 P.2D 377, 381 (Alaska 1977).

Karr next argues that the amount of restitution which Judge Blair ordered was excessive. Judge Blair acknowledged that it would be impossible for Karr to pay such a large amount of restitution. Karr argues that AS 12.55.045(a) is violated when a trial judge orders an amount of restitution which cannot be paid. AS 12.55.045(a) provides:

The court may order a defendant convicted of an offense to make restitution as provided in this section or as otherwise authorized by law. In determining the amount and method of payment of restitution, the court shall take into account the financial resources of the defendant and the nature of the burden its payment will impose.

It is clear that it will be difficult for Karr to pay the whole $300,000 in restitution. She appears to have some assets and therefore may be able to pay some restitution now. During her period of incarceration it is unlikely that she will be able to make any restitution. It appears Judge Blair considered these factors, as well as the fact that Karr will probably have difficulty in obtaining future employment similar to her previous employment, when he predicted that full restitution would be impossible.

Due to the difficulty in predicting from this point in time what amount of restitution is reasonable for Karr to pay, we conclude that it was reasonable for Judge Blair to order a large amount of restitution. In so doing he did not violate AS 12.55.045(a). Karr does not argue that she did not steal at least this amount from Meyeres. By ordering restitution, Judge Blair can require Karr to attempt to undo some of the damage caused by her criminal acts. The court can only enforce the order to the extent that it is reasonable for Karr to make restitution. We conclude that the court did not err in ordering $300,000 restitution.

The sentence is AFFIRMED.

### Case Review Question

What purpose is served by imposing a fine that can never be paid?

## DEFENSES TO CHARGES OF CRIMINAL CONDUCT

For every act committed, there are explanations for why the act occurred. In cases of criminal acts, some explanations are sufficient to prevent conviction and punishment of the actor. Such explanations are known as *defenses,* and they are wide and varied. The following sections examine a number of defenses that accused persons frequently assert.

### Common Defenses

What follows below are some of the more frequently employed defenses to charges of criminal conduct. If established through sufficient evidence, then each defense can be used to defeat a conviction.

**Justifiable or Excusable Conduct.** Traditionally, justifiable or excusable conduct was a defense that could be applied in criminal cases. In modern-day law, conduct that is justifiable or excusable is not considered criminal conduct and thus does not provide a basis for arrest or prosecution. **Justifiable conduct** is an act that takes place under special circumstances such as defense of oneself or others.[33] **Excusable conduct** refers to acts that would be considered criminal except for the actor's status at the time of the act.[34] For example, when law-enforcement officers or military personnel intrude onto another's property or perhaps even kill in the line of duty, their conduct—which would otherwise be considered criminal—is excused because they are supposedly doing so in the interest of the public welfare. Of course, this may not apply if such persons abuse their authority and commit these acts without basis.

**Involuntary Conduct.** A defense to charges of criminal conduct always exists in situations where the actor's conduct was not voluntary. Obviously, involuntary conduct includes acts over which the actor has no physical control.[35] Examples

**justifiable conduct**
Conduct by one who, under the circumstances, is considered to be innocent of otherwise criminal behavior.

**excusable conduct**
Conduct by one who, under the color of authority, is considered to be innocent of otherwise criminal behavior.

would include acts performed while sleeping, during seizures, or as the result of a reflex. Whether acts performed while under the influence of hypnosis or prescribed medication are voluntary is still questionable.

The key to the defense of involuntary conduct is proving that the defendant was physically incapable of forming the required *mens rea* before committing the crime. The lower the degree of requirement, such as general intent or awareness, the more difficult it is to prove the act was involuntary. (With respect to strict liability, because intent is not a consideration, involuntariness would not be a defense.)

**Duress.** A similar defense is duress, in which a third party causes another person to act by exerting influence over that person. The actor has a mental choice between following or refusing the commands of the third person. If the situation is extreme, duress may be used as a defense on the basis that, in reality, only one choice could be made. For example, if the actor is told to act or his or her children will be killed, then duress would apply. Although the actor has technically been given an option, he or she has no choice in practical terms. The court will examine the circumstances to determine just how reasonable a refusal to act would have been.

**Mistake.** Mistake is a common defense to accusations of criminal acts. Two types of mistake can be alleged. *Mistake of fact* occurs when the person commits the act while reasonably believing something that was not true.[36] Many cases have been reported of persons who leave a store or other public building and drive away in what they think is their car—but, in fact, their key fits an identical car belonging to someone else. Although such persons did indeed steal the automobile, they are not guilty of auto theft. They reasonably believed they were driving their own car. Thus, they made a mistake of fact. Any mistake of fact must bear directly on the intent required for the particular crime.

*Mistake of law* is applied much more rarely. It is appropriate only where a person actually believed that his or her conduct was lawful under one statute, despite the existence of another statute that might indicate such conduct was unlawful. An example is persons who exercise their right to avoid a search of their property by police without a proper warrant when another law gives police the right to search property in emergencies. If such persons are not aware of the emergency and deny the police entry, they are exercising a legal right. If, for example, unbeknownst to these persons, a criminal is hiding in their basement, these persons have made an honest mistake of law in protecting their rights and cannot be prosecuted for something such as obstruction of justice.

The Model Penal Code acknowledges both mistakes of fact and mistakes of law. In cases of mistake of fact, the mistake must be something that is believed and is part of the state of mind of the actor.[37] The code, in line with common law, generally holds that ignorance of the law is no excuse. It does, however, allow certain exceptions that are similar to the common law exceptions that create a valid defense. Examples of these exceptions include: (1) the actor did not have reasonable access to the law, (2) the actor reasonably believed the conduct was lawful (as in the common law example above), and (3) the actor was relying on the statement of the government or a government official. A person's lawyer's advice that conduct was permissible is not a defense. Such a statement must come from someone in a government capacity.

**Entrapment.** A defense that has gained some notoriety in recent years is entrapment, which alleges that law-enforcement personnel created a situation that would lead a law-abiding citizen with no prior criminal intent into criminal activity. The police must plant the idea and lead a person into criminal conduct that the person would not otherwise be predisposed to commit. This is often used in cases of prostitution and drug dealing. It is absolutely necessary for the police to do no more than accept or enhance the criminal conduct. The opportunity and intent to complete the crime must be developed by the criminal without any significant influence by the police.

## The Insanity Defense

Probably the most publicized defense in criminal law is the insanity defense. Although substantive as well as procedural law varies on this defense among the jurisdictions, the defense has common denominators. In all cases where insanity is raised as a defense to charges of criminal conduct, the issues are ultimately reduced to whether a mental impairment existed and whether the impairment played a role in the defendant's conduct at the time of the crime.

The insanity defense standards applied in approximately one-third of the states is the *M'Naughten Rule,* which in its original form dates back to 1843.[38] Although the rule has been modified in some states, the basic tenet of the M'Naughten decision is that the mental impairment either (1) prevented the defendant from understanding the criminal nature and quality of the criminal act or (2) prevented the defendant from determining whether the act was legal or illegal. The difficulty with the M'Naughten Rule is that it requires a determination that the defendant was sane or insane, with no middle ground. Consequently, a majority of states have chosen other methods to determine the question of insanity as an influence on one charged with criminal conduct.

In place of or in addition to the M'Naughten Rule, some jurisdictions allow the *irresistible impulse theory.* Under this premise, the defendant claims to have been unable to control his or her behavior as the result of mental impairment at the time of the alleged criminal conduct. The irresistible impulse theory rests on the basis that the defendant at the time of the crime was subjected to a sudden impulse that he or she did not have the capacity to control.

Finally, several states have adopted a defense standard similar to that used in federal prosecutions. In 1984, this defense was embodied in a statutory definition by the Congress:

> (a) Affirmative Defense: It is an affirmative defense to a prosecution under any Federal statute that, at the time of the commission of the acts constituting the offense, the defendant, as a result of a severe mental disease or defect, was unable to appreciate the nature and quality or the wrongfulness of his acts. Mental disease or defect does not otherwise constitute a defense.
> (b) Burden of Proof: The defendant has the burden of proving the defense of insanity by clear and convincing evidence.[39]

This statute made it more difficult to prove insanity as a defense. In the past, insanity was seen as a way to avoid prosecution for the acts of an otherwise reasonable individual. This statute requires extensive proof of mental disability. It must be shown that the disability was severe and that it prevented any ability to appreciate or understand the act itself and its consequences. An additional hurdle is that the burden is placed on the defendant. Usually, the burden is on the prosecution to show guilt beyond a reasonable doubt. Thus, any doubt created in the minds of the jury by the defense is sufficient to prevent conviction. Under the new insanity statute, however, the defendant must present clear and convincing evidence of the required elements.

The Model Penal Code is the approach the majority of the states take with regard to the insanity defense. The code permits a defendant to raise the insanity defense, but the defense must prove that the defendant did not have the ability to "appreciate the criminality of his conduct" or "conform his conduct to the requirements of law."[40] This requirement parallels and strengthens the reasoning of the common law approach. Under this rule, the defendant has the burden of establishing that he or she had some cognitive inability to understand right from wrong and was unable to control his or her actions within legal bounds. The rule's significance is that although the prosecution ordinarily has the burden of proving the defendant guilty, the burden is switched when the insanity defense is raised, and the defendant has the burden to present proof to meet the jurisdiction's insanity defense standard.

## ASSIGNMENT 15.4

Go to the subject index of the statutes for your particular state. Examine the statutes pertaining to homicide and determine whether the statute follows common law or the Model Penal Code. Then determine whether a statute or rule of evidence sets forth the requirements for pleading insanity as a defense to a crime.

## ETHICAL CONSIDERATIONS

Most persons consider themselves neither to be criminals nor to be unethical. However, the same type of conduct that many people frequently engage in on a daily basis could be technically considered unethical, perhaps even criminal. For example, if you drive through a fast-food restaurant and arrive home to discover that the clerk gave you 35 cents more in change than you were due, how likely is it that you will get back in your car and return the money to the restaurant? Most people would probably not return the money because of the amount of time required for such a small figure. But keeping the money is no more ethical or legal just because the amount is considered by most people as insignificant. Much of the reason why criminal laws mirror ethical standards of society is the belief that violations of the standards should not be tolerated.

## Question

Can you identify three situations that are not ethical but are entirely legal?

## ETHICAL CIRCUMSTANCE

Caesar often traveled on company business. It was the policy of the company that anyone who also used company benefits for personal use report it and pay a portion of the expenses. Caesar was scheduled to attend a conference in Orlando, Florida. He traded his full-coach airline ticket in for a refund and used it to purchase four lower-fare tickets. He also had his wife and two children stay in the hotel room reserved for him by the company. Each day, they would drop him off at the conference and use the company rental car to go to nearby Disney World. He did pay for the meals of his family members and admission to Disney World. The cost of the airfare, hotel room, and car did not change as the result of having his family along. However, he violated company policy to the extent it was not only unethical but also could be considered theft because it amounted to using company funds for personal benefits.

## ● | CHAPTER SUMMARY

This chapter has briefly examined some of the more frequently encountered crimes. The common thread that pervades all criminal conduct is that the defendant must be aware of the decision to act or not to act. This awareness may be merely that, or it may be a general intent, a specific intent, or awareness as defined by the Model Penal Code. Each statute that defines criminal conduct indicates expressly or by implication the level of awareness required. Further, the statute sets forth with some certainty the acts or omissions that constitute criminal conduct. In contrast, defenses are created largely by judicial law. In most cases, the courts have formulated what is an acceptable or unacceptable reason for what would otherwise be criminal conduct. This generally includes not only the core criminal act but also all acts that enable the crime to be committed or prevent the discovery of the crime or the actor. These ideas are present in both the common law and the Model Penal Code. The primary difference between the two is the manner in which they are applied.

Note that simply because criminal conduct occurs, conviction is not always in order. The circumstances of the crime and the motivation of the parties involved may excuse or justify the conduct, or they may defeat the necessary elements for commission of the crime, such as the absence of specific intent or insanity.

Further research into the criminal law of a particular jurisdiction should always involve an initial determination of whether the jurisdiction applies common law principles or the Model Penal Code. Once this determination has been made, the appropriate principles of *mens rea* and *actus reus* will apply. Thus, it is necessary to determine only the specifics of *mens rea* and *actus reus* that are required for the particular crime in question.

## ● | CHAPTER TERMS

| | | |
|---|---|---|
| *actus reus* | felony | *mens rea* |
| criminal law | justifiable conduct | misdemeanor |
| excusable conduct | | |

## ● | REVIEW QUESTIONS

1. What is a felony?
2. Explain the difference between *actus reus* and *mens rea*.
3. What types of acts are subject to strict criminal liability?
4. Identify the parties to crime under the Model Penal Code and under common law.
5. What is an inchoate offense?
6. What is the difference between theft and robbery?
7. What are the types of homicide, and how are they differentiated?
8. When can a corporation be held criminally liable?
9. How does justifiable conduct differ from excusable conduct?

## ● | HELPFUL WEB SITES

Criminal law

http://www/criminal.findlaw.com/
http://www.ncjrs.org

## ● | INTERNET ASSIGNMENT 15.1

Using Internet resources, identify whether your jurisdiction has adopted a felony murder statute and give the location of your source of information.

## INTERNET ASSIGNMENT 15.2

Go to the subject index of the statutes for your particular state. Examine the statutes pertaining to homicide and determine whether the statute follows common law or the Model Penal Code. Then determine whether a statute or rule of evidence sets forth the requirements for pleading insanity as a defense to a crime.

## ENDNOTES

1. *Lord Fitzgerald Seaton v. Seaton, L.R.* 13 Ap.Ca. 78 (1888).
2. William Statsky, *Legal Thesaurus/Dictionary* (St. Paul, MN: West, 1982).
3. Frank Schmalleger, *Criminal Justice Today,* 8th ed. (Upper Saddle River, NJ: Prentice Hall, 2007).
4. *Id.*
5. *Id.*
6. Model Penal Code, Section 1.13(9).
7. *In re Michael,* 423 A.2d 1180 (R.I. 1981).
8. *United States v. Sterley,* 764 F.2d 530 (8th Cir. 1985).
9. *People v. Love,* 11 Cal.App. 3d Supp.1, 168 Cal. Rptr. 591 (1980).
10. *Id.*
11. 95 A.L.R.3d 248.
12. *People v. Levitt,* 156 Cal.App. 3d 500, 156 Cal. Rptr. 276 (1984).
13. Model Penal Code, Section 1.13; 2.02.
14. *People v. Bargy,* 71 Mich.App. 609, 248 N.W.3d 636 (1976); *State v. Furr,* 292 N.C. 711, 235 S.E.2d 193 (1977).
15. *Id.*
16. Model Penal Code, Section 242.3; 2.06.
17. Statsky, *Legal Thesaurus.*
18. *Manner v. State,* 387 So.2d 1014 (Fla. App. 4th Dist. 1980).
19. Model Penal Code, Section 5.03.
20. *State v. Stewart,* 537 S.W.2d 579 (Mo.App. 1976).
21. *Pinkett v. State,* 30 Md.App. 458, 352 A.2d 358 (1976).
22. Statsky, *Legal Thesaurus.*
23. *State v. Lora,* 213 Kan. 184, 515 P.2d 1086 (1973).
24. *Anderson v. State,* 61 Md.App. 436, 487 A.2d 294 (1985).
25. *Id.*
26. *Wilcox v. State,* 401 So.2d 789 (Ala.Crim.App.1980).
27. *Dunn v. State,* 161 Ind.App. 586, 316 N.E.2d 834 (1974).
28. *State v. Beach,* 329 S.W.2d 712 (Mo. 1959).
29. *Callahan v. State,* 343 So.2d 551 (Ala.Crim.App. 1977).
30. *Goldsby v. State,* 226 Miss. 1, 78 So.2d 762 (1955).
31. *Wooden v. Commonwealth,* 222 Va. 758, 284 S.E.2d 811 (1981).
32. Model Penal Code, Section 210.2.
33. Model Penal Code, Section 2.07.
34. *State v. Williams,* 545 S.W.2d 342 (Mo.App. 1976).
35. *Law v. State,* 21 Md.App. 13, 318 A.2d 859 (1974).
36. Model Penal Code, Section 3.09.
37. Model Penal Code, Section 3.04.
38. Daniel M'Naughten's Case, 10 Cl. & F.200, 8 Eng.Rep. 718 (H.L. 1843).
39. 18 U.S.C.A. Section 20.
40. Model Penal Code, Section 402.

### STUDENT CD-ROM

For additional materials, please go to the CD in this book.

### ONLINE COMPANION™

For additional resources, please go to www.paralegal.delmar.cengage.com

## CHAPTER 16

# Criminal Procedure

## GETTING AWAY WITH MURDER

How often do we hear about someone who "got away" with committing a crime or who "got off on a technicality"? This type of comment is common in our society when discussions arise about the shortcomings of the U.S. legal system. In truth, this does not really happen at all. Certainly, there are individuals who commit crimes and are not caught or punished. There are also those who are charged and prosecuted only to have the charges dropped later despite a near certainty that these individuals committed crimes. So how can it be said that people do not get away with crime or get off on technicalities? Because it simply is not true. The constitutionally based U.S. legal system, with all of its flaws, does not fail us on this. Rather, people fail us and technology fails us—but not the Constitution. Before our constitutional rights were established, individuals had little or no protection of their basic human rights. If someone in authority and with the skill of persuasion had the preconception that another person was guilty of a crime, then a prosecution and conviction generally followed.

In the summer of 1692, less than 100 years before the enactment of the U.S. Constitution, some twenty individuals in Salem, Massachusetts, were tried and executed and another four died in prison as the result of accusations of witchcraft that had developed in the preceding few months. The entire circumstance spread like wildfire when the illness of a child who became sick and delusional could not be explained. There were many contributing factors, but the illness of a small child appears to have been the catalyst. These defendants were given little chance of fair treatment. In fact, the twentieth individual was an octogenarian who saw the process of a trial so futile that he refused to attend and was summarily sentenced to death by "pressing." Subsequently, the 80-year-old man was slowly and excruciatingly crushed until he died. Today, the attitude is much different. An individual cannot be convicted and forced to carry out a sentence unless he or she has been treated fairly by law enforcement. This is a right guaranteed to all because we are presumed innocent until proven guilty. There are protections against evidence based on emotions or preconceptions rather than fact. The homes and other areas where all citizens have a reasonable expectation of privacy cannot be summarily searched or seized based on no more than suspicion by a government official. Individuals without legal training or knowledge cannot be forced to defend themselves or testify in the presence of legal experts who would have the clear advantage. These and other safeguards protect the citizenship as a whole from the recurrence of something as heinous as the Salem witch trials in which lives were lost as the result of no more than innuendo by individuals who sought to avoid their own possible role in deteriorating conditions in the community and a mass hysteria based on nothing more than ignorance and superstition.

It is true that individuals who have probably committed crimes have been released and, in some cases, gone on to commit additional terrible crimes. The fault lies, however, not with the system, the courts, inept prosecutors, or even clever defense attorneys. The fault lies with the inadequacy of a less than perfect system. Without omnipotent knowledge, we cannot always be sure of who is truly responsible for a crime. So we do the best we can. We follow a Constitution put in play by individuals who designed it to prevent the innocent lives of hundreds of millions of people from being in constant danger of destruction by a handful of less than honorable government officials who would succeed in their own careers by disrespecting and abusing human rights and wrongfully convicting and punishing the accused on cases based in conjecture rather than fact.

## CHAPTER OUTLINE

## CHAPTER OBJECTIVES

After reading this chapter, you should be able to:

- Explain the purpose of selective incorporation and list the rights adopted into the definition of due process through selective incorporation.

- Explain the concept of double jeopardy and when it does not apply, even though the defendant has gone to trial.

- Discuss when a defendant has the right to counsel.

- Discuss the determination of bail.

- Discuss when an arrest warrant is not required.

- Compare grand jury proceedings and preliminary hearings.

- Explain the process of arraignment.

Criminal procedure is one of the most rapidly changing areas of law in the United States today. It differs significantly from civil procedure. Of course, the obvious difference is that rules of civil procedure govern civil actions and rules of criminal procedure govern criminal prosecutions. In addition, criminal procedure comes into play long before the action is formally commenced against a defendant. Criminal procedure affects the prosecution from the moment a crime is suspected.

Criminal prosecutions take place in both the federal and state judicial systems, each of which has its own rules of procedure. However, all are ultimately governed by certain constitutional requirements. Through its various amendments, the U.S. Constitution protects all persons from unfair and unequal treatment during criminal prosecutions. The courts vigorously enforce the Constitution and require that all persons be treated fairly and equally. Therefore, although the rules may differ somewhat from jurisdiction to jurisdiction, the effect of the rules must be constitutionally permissible or the rules may be invalidated by the courts.

This chapter provides a limited introduction to the constitutional limitations on criminal procedure, the current status of criminal procedure, and the stages of a criminal prosecution. Keep in mind that because the law is subject to radical changes as the courts review various procedural rules and judge their constitutionality, only basic principles are discussed here—and even they may be subject to change.

## CRIMINAL PROCEDURE AND THE CONSTITUTION

The first ten amendments of the United States Constitution are amazing texts when examined closely. Individuals who did not even have the benefit of electricity, motorized travel, or even steam-generated power nevertheless had the wisdom and foresight to identify the basic rights necessary to create a fair system of government that would last for centuries. Although the system certainly falls short of perfection, it is nothing short of amazing how these individuals summarized in a few sentences what would become the most important safeguards to ensure a stable government that could carry out the goals of the Declaration of Independence in a free society.

### The Approach of the U.S. Supreme Court

Various amendments to the U.S. Constitution affect criminal rights. The Bill of Rights was adopted, in part, to protect individuals from being unfairly or unnecessarily penalized by the justice system.

The Fourth, Fifth, Eighth, and Fourteenth Amendments address virtually every aspect of criminal procedure, including but not being limited to invasion of one's property for the purpose of searching for and seizing criminal evidence, self-incrimination, and the grounds for capital offenses (where punishment can be death). The effects of these amendments on criminal procedure are discussed in subsequent sections.

### The Fourteenth Amendment: Due Process

In recent years, the Fourteenth Amendment, which was passed in 1868, has played a controversial role in criminal procedure. The obvious interpretation is that all citizens are subject to federal law and, further, that no state may pass or interpret laws that would conflict with federal law or the specific rights listed in the amendment. For many years, this was the interpretation given by the U.S. Supreme Court.[1] In various decisions, the Court maintained that the Fourteenth Amendment guaranteed only fundamental rights necessary to justice and order. It did not interpret the amendment to mean that all states must follow with absolute certainty all other constitutional amendments when creating law. Rather, as long as their laws did not conflict with constitutional guarantees, the states were permitted to create laws in any manner they chose.

During the 1950s and 1960s, the Court's approach to the Fourteenth Amendment changed. At that time, the justices who had been appointed to the Court were more liberal as a group than at any time in the Court's history. In addition, there was a great deal of unrest in the United States. Many people believed that the constitutional guarantees in the Bill of Rights were being ignored or violated at the state level. The result was a great many alleged discrimination claims against the state governments as well as civil disobedience by the citizens. In various parts of the country, individuals protesting against the alleged inequities of state laws engaged in riots and other actions. Protest marches were held, sit-ins were conducted, and various other measures were taken by individuals to protect what they perceived to be fundamental rights. In the South, civil rights volunteers came from various other parts of the country to help secure the freedom of blacks to vote, assemble, and be treated with equality in the way laws were applied. All around the United States, people began to stand up against local and state governments that they believed operated with indifference to the fundamental protections that were so important in the creation of the original Constitution and Bill of Rights.

Although the Supreme Court of the 1950s and 1960s was quite liberal in its thinking, it was unwilling to utilize the total integration approach.[2] This approach follows the theory that the Fourteenth Amendment effectively integrates the entire Constitution and its amendments into each state's laws. The actual result would be to replace the state constitutions with the federal Constitution or at least to add the federal Constitution and its amendments to all state constitutions. The states would have virtually no say in what rights would be afforded their citizens or how those citizens would be governed. All state laws would be virtually identical to federal laws.

**selective incorporation**
Process of expansion of the definition of due process to include certain guarantees enumerated in the Bill of Rights.

**due process**
That which is necessary to fundamental fairness in the U.S. system of justice.

**Selective Incorporation.** Because the Court believed total integration invaded too much on the ability of state citizens to govern themselves without unnecessary federal government interference, it engaged in **selective incorporation**.[3] Previously, the Court had followed the rule that only the rights specifically stated in the Fourteenth Amendment were required to be followed explicitly by the states, including the right to **due process** (fundamental fairness) in the application of law before a person's life, liberty, or property could be taken, denied, or seized. In simpler terms, an individual could not be sentenced to death or prison or have real or personal property taken by any state or federal government unless the person was treated fairly by the government. In addition, all persons were to be treated equally in the way laws were applied. For a time, this was sufficient; however, it became increasingly apparent that state and local governments did not always take a liberal view as to what constituted fundamental fairness in the way accused persons were treated and prosecuted.

To remedy this, the Court decided to more thoroughly and clearly define the term *due process*. In the past, it had been interpreted to mean essentially that which was fundamentally fair in a system of justice. However, the Court took the position that the states needed further clarification of the term. Because the Congress passed the Fourteenth Amendment, which required the states to give all citizens due process, the U.S. Supreme Court had the authority to interpret the amendment and, specifically, its language of due process. As noted earlier, the Court could do this by simply stating that all rights in the Bill of Rights were included in the definition of due process. Because this was seen as too invasive, however, the Court opted instead to review cases one by one and determine whether a certain right in the Bill of Rights should be included in the definition of due process. If the Court determined that right was included, then it would state with specificity how the right was to be protected at the state level.

Over the years, the process of selective incorporation has expanded the definition of due process to include the Fourth, Fifth, Sixth, and Eighth Amendments. One by one, cases have come to the Supreme Court, which determined that the circumstances of treatment of the accused did not afford the accused the fundamental of fairness during investigation, arrest, and prosecution.[4]

The ultimate effect of selective incorporation is quite simple. Once the Supreme Court finds that a particular right is incorporated into the Fourteenth Amendment, any state laws that would affect this right must be fair and reasonable. The Court will invalidate state laws that affect protected federal constitutional rights.

Selective incorporation has been especially relevant to laws of criminal procedure, which guide criminal prosecutions and set forth what is considered fundamental to the criminal process. These laws ultimately affect the American theory of innocence until guilt is proven beyond any reasonable doubt by controlling the manner in which the accused is treated and evidence is obtained.

The following sections discuss the amendments to the U.S. Constitution that have been selectively incorporated into the Fourteenth Amendment. The reasoning behind the incorporation of each particular amendment and the effect of the amendment's incorporation on state laws are included. It is especially helpful to examine the cases in which the Court made these decisions because the cases provide examples that actually occurred.

## The Fourth Amendment: Search and Seizure

As early as 1914, the U.S. Supreme Court first held that evidence in a federal criminal prosecution that was obtained without a proper search warrant or probable cause would be inadmissible in court.[5] This was the beginning of the *exclusionary rule,* under which improperly obtained evidence is excluded from trial. Consequently, no matter how damaging, such evidence cannot be used to convict someone of a crime. The Supreme Court adopted this position with regard to the federal court system's criminal prosecutions.

The idea that the Fourth Amendment should be incorporated into the Fourteenth, thereby requiring states to apply the exclusionary rule, was first addressed in 1949 in *Wolf v. Colorado*[6] (338 U.S. 25,69 S.Ct. 1359, 93 L. Ed. 1782). At that time, the Court examined what the states had done on their own and found that some thirty states had considered the exclusionary rule used in federal cases but had chosen not to follow the rule in state criminal prosecutions. These states instead decided to develop their own methods to discourage police from unreasonable practices in obtaining evidence. In *Wolf,* the Court decided that because a majority of the states had rejected the exclusionary rule and were using means other than the exclusion of evidence to prevent unlawful searches and seizures, it should not forcibly impose the requirement on the states. Thus, the Court held that the states could adequately protect the rights of their citizens without a forced application of the exclusionary rule to guarantee rights under the Fourth Amendment. Therefore, the Fourth Amendment was not at this time incorporated into the Fourteenth Amendment definition of due process. Consequently, the states were not yet required to adopt the federal position on the exclusionary rule. The effect was that as long as the state law was followed, a person's property could be searched and seized and any evidence of criminal activity used against the individual in a prosecution.

## APPLICATION 16.1

Stella was walking home from work one night when it started to rain heavily. A co-worker, Jonah, came by and offered Stella a ride. She accepted. As they drove on the rain-slicked streets, they were involved in a car accident in front of Stella's home when they ran over several mailboxes and a stop sign. They went inside to call the police. When the police arrived, Jonah and Stella met them at the door but did not invite the police in. As the police officers questioned the two, they noticed some unusual items on Stella's table behind her. They walked into the house uninvited and began to walk through the rooms over Stella's objections. When the officers went to the basement, they found a fully functional methamphetamine lab. Stella and Jonah were both placed under arrest and charged with multiple felonies. Stella claimed that Jonah was her boyfriend and she had no idea he had been producing illicit drugs in the basement. Astonished, Jonah claimed he had never been to Stella's residence before the night of the arrest. At trial, it was found that the search was illegal and all evidence obtained during the search was excluded from evidence under the exclusionary rule. The charges were dropped against both Stella and Jonah. However, because of the initial arrest, the two were fired from their jobs.

*Point for Discussion:* Would the result be different if Stella invited the police officers inside the front door to fill out the accident report?

Just twelve years after *Wolf v. Colorado,* the Supreme Court reconsidered the incorporation of the Fourth Amendment into the Fourteenth Amendment. In *Mapp v. Ohio*[7] [367 U.S. 649, 81 S. Ct. 1684, 6 L.Ed. 2d 1081 (1961)], the Court reversed its previous holding (an extremely rare occurrence) and held that the federally developed exclusionary rule is the most appropriate way of protecting citizens from unreasonable searches and seizures. The Court further held that for a citizen to be afforded due process in a criminal prosecution (a right guaranteed in the Fourteenth Amendment), then the Fourth Amendment protections must be adhered to—including the federal method of using the exclusionary rule. Consequently, the Fourth Amendment protections should be incorporated into the definition of the Fourteenth Amendment. Further, the states should be required to follow the exclusionary rule, which is the method of choice to enforce the Fourth Amendment rule of no unreasonable search and seizure.

A large part of the reason for the Court's reversal of its position was the fact that after the *Wolf* decision many states had tried methods other than the exclusionary rule and had failed. Many of these states then turned to the exclusionary rule on their own. The Court in *Mapp v. Ohio* affirmed this as an acceptable method of protecting citizens' rights.

**Exclusionary Rule.** With this decision, the Fourteenth Amendment began to be expanded to include the rights enunciated in other amendments. The results of the decision in *Mapp v. Ohio* are continuing even today. Since that time, the Court has reviewed many state laws to determine what is a reasonable or an unreasonable search or seizure. Evidence obtained through the latter is prohibited under the exclusionary rule from being used as evidence at a trial.

Over the years, a great deal of concern has been expressed about the exclusionary rule, which was intended to deter or prevent law-enforcement personnel from obtaining evidence by means that violate Fourth Amendment rights. The rationale was that individuals were not in a position to protect their rights against law-enforcement agencies. Further, if these agencies were not encouraged in some way to honor the constitutional amendment against unreasonable search and seizure, then our society could be reduced to a police state, which, in its most extreme form, might include random invasions of people's homes and property in search of evidence that might incriminate them.

However noble the intent of the exclusionary rule, the actual result is indisputable. When evidence is obtained in a questionable manner, the person who benefits is the accused. Although our government follows the doctrine that an accused is innocent until proven guilty, in many such cases, the evidence excluded is so strong that it would undoubtedly result in a verdict of guilty by a jury. As a consequence of applying the exclusionary rule to protect a defendant's Fourth Amendment rights, many criminals have gone free or plea bargained for greatly reduced charges.

The Supreme Court has been faced with a double bind. Without the exclusionary rule, improper searches and seizures of innocent people's property can occur. With the exclusionary rule, known criminals can go free because of a technical, minor, or innocent violation of the rule. In 1984, the Court considered this dilemma in *United States v. Leon* (468 U.S. 817, 104 S. Ct. 3405, 82 L.Ed. 2d. 677).[8] In the *Leon* decision, the Supreme Court addressed at length the difficulty with enforcing a broad application of the exclusionary rule. The Court recognized that excluding evidence because of an improper search or seizure, no matter how small the infraction that caused it to be improper, resulted in preventing the jury from accurately determining innocence or guilt at a trial. When the exclusionary rule is applied, often the case is dismissed because little admissible evidence is available to support a conviction. At the very least, the jury is given only limited information with which to make its decision. The jurors are allowed to consider only properly obtained evidence. In fact, they generally do not know that additional evidence exists and has been excluded.

In *Leon,* the Court was faced with a situation where the police properly requested a search warrant. The judge properly reviewed the information to support the warrant and then issued the warrant. The police exercised the search warrant and found incriminating evidence. Only after the search occurred was it discovered that the warrant was improper. The police had requested a warrant on the basis of limited surveillance and the information of a person who had never before acted as an informant. Unless informants have a history of providing accurate information to law-enforcement agencies, their testimony usually requires much additional evidence before a judge will believe there is probable cause to suspect a crime and issue a search warrant. In this case, the defendant challenged the validity of the search warrant, and a higher judge found that it should never have been issued on such limited information.

The Supreme Court used the *Leon* decision to make a major exception to the exclusionary rule. Observing that the police had made every effort to follow the requirements to protect the defendant's Fourth Amendment rights, the Court reasoned that because this was the entire goal of the exclusionary rule, the rule had been satisfied. The police had gone so far as to request permission of a judge to search for criminal evidence. Therefore, the goal of the rule had been met, and the citizen's rights had been protected. The Court refused to exclude the evidence (a large amount of illegal drugs), and the defendant was prosecuted. The Court stated that the exclusionary rule is designed to deter unreasonable practices by law-enforcement personnel, not to remedy poor exercises of authority by judges.

The *Leon* decision is of vital importance in the law of criminal procedure. It signals that the Court has shifted toward a more conservative view of what is necessary to protect the rights of citizens. The Court currently regards certain areas as private and subject to the protection of a citizen's Fourteenth Amendment rights by requiring satisfaction of the guarantees under the Fourth Amendment.

**probable cause**
More than mere suspicion of criminal activity but less than evidence adequate to justify conviction.

**Probable Cause.** What a person considers to be private is that which cannot be searched or seized without **probable cause**. The Court has established a two-step test to be used in determining what is private property. First, it must be decided whether the person acted in such a way as to keep the property private from others. Second, it must be determined whether the person was reasonable in believing such property should be allowed to be kept private.[9]

Before law-enforcement personnel can search or seize private property, they must have probable cause to believe a crime has been committed or that the owner of the property has been involved in criminal activity (or both). There must also be probable cause to believe that a search of the property will result in evidence that will assist in proving this. Further, when possible, the law-enforcement agency must seek approval of the search and seizure by obtaining a warrant from a judicial officer. The basis for the warrant must be probable cause. Although it is much debated, no absolute formula has ever been developed to determine what constitutes probable cause. Rather, probable cause falls within a range that, when examined by a neutral observer, would be considered more than basic suspicion but less than evidence adequate to justify conviction.[10]

If law-enforcement personnel can support their suspicions and allegation of probable cause with outside information or other evidence that would create this degree of probability that the person or property is connected with criminal activity, then a search warrant may be issued by a judge. If there is not time to request a search warrant, the officers may proceed with the search if there is probable cause to conduct it.[11] Because the officers are not considered to be as objective as a judicial officer, they are under a particularly heavy burden to show that their search was made with probable cause. To qualify as an exception to the warrant requirement, there must be an immediate danger that the property or person associated with the criminal activity will be lost unless an immediate search is conducted.

**Warrants.** The type of property that may be searched has also been discussed by the courts. Generally, before a private residence can be searched, a warrant must be issued. If the property has been abandoned, then a citizen has no expectation of privacy and thus no warrant is needed.[12] In addition, if the criminal activity or evidence can be observed by persons around or above the property, then the property is considered to be in view of the public, and thus there is no expectation of privacy.[13] If an officer is lawfully on another person's property for any reason and discovers criminal evidence in plain view, then the property may be seized immediately (known as the *plain view rule*). Finally, if someone other than the resident has access to the residence and voluntarily allows officers entrance to the property, such entrance is treated as if permission had been given by the resident. Therefore, landlords, roommates, or guests have the power to admit police officers voluntarily to a residence for the purpose of searching for evidence of criminal activity.[14] In such situations, no warrant is necessary.

Police do need a warrant to invade private property by other than ordinary means. If, for example, a wiretap is going to be used to obtain the content of conversations in a residence or on a telephone line from a residence, then a search warrant must be obtained because the public would perceive a reasonable expectation of privacy in such a situation. However, devices that merely record the numbers called from a residence are not considered private because the telephone company has access to this information at all times. Further, tracking devices on vehicles are permissible because the purpose is to track the vehicle in public. There can be no expectation of privacy about where one goes in public.

**Vehicles.** Vehicles have created a whole new arena for questions about search and seizure. They are a form of private property that is capable of concealing a great deal of other property. At the same time, they are transported in public, which means that the expectation of privacy is lower than that in a residence. The courts have held that looking into the vehicle from the outside is not a search; if evidence of criminal activity is seen, then there is no need for a warrant.[15]

If a car has been abandoned, then there is no expectation of privacy. Therefore, no warrant is needed to examine the interior of the vehicle. The courts have also given officers the ability to search those areas of a car that are within reasonable reach of the owner when a stop is made.[16] The rationale is that the owner may be within reach of a weapon that could be used to assault the officers or to effect escape. The recent trend has been to approve searches of vehicles even when the suspect is no longer in the car or the car has been impounded. The basic requirement seems to be not that an emergency must exist but rather that the officer must have probable cause to believe that evidence or dangerous items may be in the car, its compartments, or containers within it or that the car is not in the possession of the police and is subject to removal from the jurisdiction. The regulation of police searches of automobiles is a rapidly evolving area of the law with many distinctions between states and federal government. Accordingly, it is important to know the law specific to your jurisdiction.

This is a brief examination of some of the areas that have been addressed by the courts in determining what constitutes a search under the Fourth Amendment. Because the amendment has been applied to the states, these rules must be followed by state as well as federal law-enforcement officers. The theory is that these rules will afford citizens due process and fairness before their privacy is invaded or their property is searched or seized by the state government. The rules also help to ensure fairer criminal prosecutions by reducing the chances of improper convictions.

**Arrest.** The same basic warrant requirements that apply to search and seizure of property apply to arrest. In essence, an arrest is a search and seizure of a person. Thus, the person is entitled to the same fair treatment as his or her property would be afforded. Consequently, the courts prefer that arrest warrants be obtained on a showing of probable cause before the arrest is made. Often criminal activity is discovered while it is occurring or immediately after it has occurred. In such cases, it is usually unreasonable to expect that the criminal will remain until a warrant is obtained. Therefore, most arrests are made on the basis of a probable cause determination by law-enforcement officers. This determination is subject to judicial review, just as a search made without a warrant would be.

When an arrest based on probable cause has been made, the officer may search the arrested person and all areas within his or her reach.[17] The reason for this is that the arrestee may be carrying a weapon that could be used to harm the officer. If the officer recovers other evidence of criminal activity during the search, then the evidence may also be seized. Even though it is not what the officer may have been searching for, it is considered to be the fruits of crime. A suspect who carries evidence of criminal activity on his or her person and is subsequently lawfully arrested does not have a reasonable expectation of privacy regarding that property.

Even when a full-fledged arrest is not made, the officers are entitled to take minimum steps to protect their own safety. Occasionally, an officer will stop an individual on suspicion of some criminal activity, perhaps even a minor infraction, such as a traffic violation. Even on stopping such an individual, the officer has the right to frisk the individual for a concealed weapon if the officer has a reasonable suspicion that the suspect is armed or otherwise dangerous.[18] This is permitted to avoid disastrous circumstances that have occurred and still occur when an individual stopped for a minor infraction pulls out a weapon and kills an officer of the law.

As this far from exhaustive discussion illustrates, the law of search and seizure is quite complex. Further, this area of law changes continually as the Supreme Court seeks to mold specific rules regarding the expectation of privacy by individuals for themselves and their property. The Court must balance these expectations against what is necessary to promote law enforcement and the safety of the people as a whole. As long as this balancing continues, this area of criminal procedure will grow.

## ASSIGNMENT 16.1

Consider the following situations and explain why you think the evidence should or should not be suppressed under the exclusionary rule.

1. Mike broke up with his girlfriend, Kimberly, in order to date Tara. On an Internet chat room, Kimberly indicated she intended to "make Tara bleed for stealing Mike." Approximately two days later, Tara was found laying dead in a pool of blood after suffering a stab wound. Mike told police of Kimberly's Internet post a few days before. The investigating officer went to Kimberly's house and asked if he could ask her a few questions about a neighbor suspected of drug activity. Kimberly agreed and allowed the officer to enter her home. Once inside, the officer immediately began conducting a full search of the residence over Kimberly's objections. Under a stack of clothes in a night stand next to Kimberly's bed, he found a knife similar to the one suspected to have been used in the attack on Tara. Kimberly claimed she always kept the knife in her nightstand for protection because she lived alone. The officer arrested Kimberly. There was no other evidence with which to support the charges.

2. Sam entered a men's room at a nightclub. Acting quite normally, he took out a prescription medication bottle and placed it on the edge of the sink. He then took one of the pills while commenting that the smoke in the club caused his allergies to flare up. He then placed the bottle back in his pocket. Unknown to Sam, the man next to him was an off-duty rookie police officer. Earlier in the club he had overheard Sam comment, "Some X would make the evening a lot more fun." The officer ordered Sam against the wall and retrieved the bottle from his pocket. He looked in the bottle and found not only the prescription medication, but also the illegal drug ecstasy. Sam was placed under arrest and charged with possession of illegal drugs.

3. After Sam's arrest, he was taken to a local hospital and forced to submit a blood sample. Although no evidence of ecstasy was found in his system, there was evidence of a fairly large amount of cocaine. The officer returned to the club and searched Sam's car in the parking lot. There police found an enormous amount of cocaine that appeared to have been prepackaged in small amounts suitable for sale. Sam was charged with possession of cocaine and the intent to distribute.

## The Fifth Amendment: Double Jeopardy and Self-Incrimination

Practically speaking, the role of the Fifth Amendment in criminal procedure has been primarily confined to the issues of double jeopardy and self-incrimination, which are addressed individually because they are wholly separate rights.

**Double Jeopardy.** Every citizen has the right not to be tried more than once for a specific crime charged. The theory of **double jeopardy** is that the government should prove guilt beyond a reasonable doubt at trial. If this cannot be accomplished, then the presumption of innocence is sustained and questions of guilt are dismissed. Citizens cannot be subjected to multiple trials for

**double jeopardy**
Being placed on trial for the same crime twice.

the same crime each time the government believes it can produce new evidence or select a more critical jury.

The rule of double jeopardy was rather easily incorporated into the Fourteenth Amendment and applied to the states. The Fourteenth Amendment clearly states that there can be no deprivation of life or liberty without due process of law. It seems quite logical that to force someone to be tried over and over again for the same crime would not be an exercise of due process of law. The very notion of fair treatment to all citizens is contrary to the thought that a citizen could be singled out and charged repeatedly with the same crime until the prosecution was successful.

The courts have clearly defined the point at which double jeopardy becomes an issue. A person is not considered to be in jeopardy of loss of life or limb (in modern terms, *penalty, liberty,* or *life*) until it is a real possibility that such a result will occur. After a person is charged with a crime and until the time of trial, there is a possibility that the charges will be dropped. After the trial begins, however, it is assumed that a verdict will be reached and a penalty may ensue. Therefore, a person is not in jeopardy until such time as the jury has been sworn in.[19] In a bench trial before a judge without a jury, double jeopardy attaches when the first witness is sworn. At either point, the defendant can be subjected to a second trial for the charge only if the first trial results in a mistrial.

Once the verdict is reached, it is considered final. Following this, if the accused person is acquitted (found not guilty), then he or she cannot be charged and tried again for the identical crime. In addition, the person generally cannot later be charged for other possible charges arising out of the same incident.[20] Thus, if the prosecution is unsuccessful in trying a person for murder, it cannot then charge the person with manslaughter or assault. If the judge dismisses the case because of a lack of evidence that would support a finding of guilty, then ordinarily there can be no second prosecution.[21]

Once a trial has commenced and jeopardy has attached, the person cannot be charged and tried again with a crime, with a few exceptions. If there is a dismissal or a mistrial is called for any reason other than a lack of evidence or if the defendant appeals a guilty verdict, then the charges may be reinstated and the case tried again. The Supreme Court has refused to adopt the double jeopardy right as a means of escaping conviction on technicalities. Thus, if the prosecution has sufficient evidence to uphold a conviction, then the case may be retried. Further, if the defendant appealed a conviction and is granted a new trial, there is a second chance for sentencing as well. As long as the sentence is justified by the crime, a judge in a second trial may impose a stricter sentence than was given in the first trial.

The double jeopardy rule puts a burden on the prosecution to be relatively sure of its case before presenting it to a jury. However, the defendant is faced with the decision of accepting a guilty verdict or taking a chance on a potentially more severe sentence in a new trial.

**Self-Incrimination.** Interpretations regarding what constitutes self-incrimination are much more pervasive than interpretations of double jeopardy. The primary question has been, at what point does the right to refuse to give information that may be incriminating originate? Under the Fifth Amendment, no person may be forced to give information that may then be used to convict that person of a crime. For nearly the first 200 years of the amendment's history, the courts merely examined whether information had been given voluntarily. During the past few decades, however, the courts have begun to give more attention to the circumstances surrounding communications with persons suspected or accused of a crime. The courts began to recognize that, in some cases, suspects or defendants might be influenced by the circumstances and in this way be compelled to give information that they would ordinarily withhold as their right not to take part in self-prosecution.

A landmark decision in this area of the law came in *Miranda v. Arizona* [384 U.S. 497, 98 S.Ct.824, 54 L. Ed 2d 717 (1966)].[22] In that decision, the Supreme Court firmly stated that every person accused of a crime must be informed at the very outset that all further communications might be used in a prosecution. The result of that decision was the adoption of the *Miranda rights,* which are now read to all persons in this country at the time of interrogation or arrest. All accused individuals are advised that (1) they have the right to remain silent, (2) anything they say may be used against them in a court of law, (3) they have the right to an attorney, and (4) they may have an attorney appointed if they cannot afford one.

As with double jeopardy, it was a logical step to incorporate this aspect of the Fifth Amendment into the Fourteenth Amendment and thus require the states to adhere to it in their own laws. Because it would be impossible to provide due process of law to any individuals who are forced to testify against themselves at any stage of a criminal proceeding, such individuals must be allowed the opportunity to remain silent.

At first this may appear to be contrary to the purpose of criminal justice, which is to catch and punish persons committing crimes against society. However, the Constitution is designed to protect all of the people, including those persons who may be innocent but lack the ability to act in their own best interest. Persons who are not adept at giving testimony and for whom the circumstances would imply guilt should have the right to protect their innocence with silence and not be penalized for it.

The *Miranda* decision clearly established that the right against self-incrimination originates at the moment an individual is held for interrogation or is placed under arrest, whichever occurs first. Therefore, all persons detained are placed on notice that any utterance can be used against them. Anything a suspected criminal says while in custody, even if it is not said to a police officer, may be used against him or her in a prosecution. The right against self-incrimination is the right to remain silent. It is not the right to make statements to some persons and not to others. A statement made to officers or within the confines of a police facility are considered to be voluntary statements with the exception of confidential communication to one's attorney.

If the police wish to interrogate a prisoner, then the questioning must be done in the fairest of circumstances. The police must either allow an attorney to be present on behalf of the accused or demonstrate that the prisoner waived the right to have an attorney present.[23] Evidence of this waiver must be documented. It must be clear that the prisoner knew and understood the reasons for having an attorney present and intelligently chose not to have an attorney present. Further, the police cannot set up circumstances that play on the weaknesses of the accused to the point that there is no voluntary waiver. For example, if a prisoner is known to suffer from some mental incapacity, then the police may not take advantage of this to further impair the prisoner's ability to make a decision regarding counsel.

A prisoner who is willing to answer questions or give a statement or confession may do so without the presence or advice of legal counsel, although the courts will scrutinize the record to make sure such information was given voluntarily. Therefore, the police will generally ask prisoners to sign a written statement that they know and understand their rights. A prisoner will acknowledge in the statement that he or she waives the right to remain silent and the right to counsel. Subsequently, the Supreme Court has held that if a prisoner knows of the right to counsel (following Miranda warnings) and does not request counsel, then the police may interrogate. Once a prisoner requests counsel, however, the police are under a heavier burden to show that any communications outside the presence of counsel were indeed voluntary.

## APPLICATION 16.2

Kim is romantically involved with Emilio. She is also married to Duane. Kim has a drug habit and is arrested when her name is given to the police as a dealer who provided drugs to elementary children on a date when one of the children overdosed and died. Kim has been charged in association with the drugs and the child's death. In reality, Kim was with Emilio on the date of the incident. They had gone to a town some fifty miles away where no one knew them and stayed the entire day. Kim refuses to testify because she knows if she draws Emilio into the case, he will break off her relationship. She has no other explanation as to where she was on the day of the incident. The only evidence presented that connects Kim to the case is the testimony of a police inform- ant who is himself a twice-convicted felon and who recently enrolled in a drug rehabilitation program at the time of trial.

*Point for Discussion:* What can the jury legally infer from Kim's failure to testify on her own behalf?

The *Miranda* decision was actually one of several similar cases. The Court was presented with numerous appeals on the same issue, although the facts differed somewhat from case to case. However, the Court applied its opinion in *Miranda* to each of the cases individually.

## CASE
### *Miranda v. State of Arizona,*
### 384 U.S. 436, 86. S.Ct. 1602, 16 L.Ed.2d 694 (1966)

The following edited version of the *Miranda* decision demonstrates how the court came to identify the rights so crucial to a fair prosecution.

Mr. Chief Justice WARREN delivered the opinion of the Court.

The cases before us raise questions which go to the roots of our concepts of American criminal jurispru- dence: the restraints society must observe consistent with the federal Constitution in prosecuting individuals for crime. More specifically, we deal with the admissi- bility of statements obtained from an individual who is subjected to custodial police interrogation and the ne- cessity for procedures which assure that the individual is accorded his privilege under the Fifth Amendment to the Constitution not to be compelled to incriminate himself.

We dealt with certain phases of this problem recently in *Escobedo v. State of Illinois,* 378 U.S. 478, 84 S.Ct. 1758, 12 L.Ed.2d 977 (1964). There, as in the four cases before us, law enforcement officials took the defendant into custody and interrogated him in a po- lice station for the purpose of obtaining a confession. The police did not effectively advise him of his right to

remain silent or of his right to consult with his attor- ney. Rather, they confronted him with an alleged ac- complice who accused him of having perpetrated a murder. When the defendant denied the accusation and said "I didn't shoot Manuel, you did it," they hand- cuffed him and took him to an interrogation room. There, while handcuffed and standing, he was ques- tioned for four hours until he confessed. During this interrogation, the police denied his request to speak to his attorney, and they prevented his retained attorney, who had come to the police station, from consulting with him. At his trial, the State, over his objection, introduced the confession against him. We held that the statements thus made were constitutionally inadmissible.

This case has been the subject of judicial interpretation and spirited legal debate since it was decided two years ago. Both state and federal courts, in assessing its im- plications, have arrived at varying conclusions. . . . A wealth of scholarly material has been written tracing its ramifications and underpinnings. . . . Police and prosecutor have speculated on its range and desirabil- ity. . . . We granted certiorari in these cases, 382 U.S. 924, 925, 937, 86 S.Ct. 318, 320, 395, 15 L.Ed.2d 338,

*(continued)*

339, 348, in order further to explore some facets of the problems, thus exposed, of applying the privilege against self-incrimination to in-custody interrogation, and to give concrete constitutional guidelines for law enforcement agencies and courts to follow.

We start here, as we did in *Escobedo,* with the premise that our holding is not an innovation in our jurisprudence, but is an application of principles long recognized and applied in other settings. We have undertaken a thorough re-examination of the *Escobedo* decision and the principles it announced, and we reaffirm it. That case was but an explication of basic rights that are enshrined in our Constitution—that "No person shall be compelled in any criminal case to be a witness against himself," and that "the accused shall have the Assistance of Counsel"—rights which were put in jeopardy in that case through official overbearing. These precious rights were fixed in our Constitution only after centuries of persecution and struggle. And in the words of Chief Justice Marshall, they were secured "for ages to come, and designed to approach immortality as nearly as human institutions can approach it," *Cohens v. Commonwealth of Virginia,* 6 Wheat. 264, 387, 5 L.Ed. 257 (1821).

\* \* \*

Our holding will be spelled out with some specificity in the pages which follow but briefly stated it is this: the prosecution may not use statements, whether exculpatory or inculpatory, stemming from custodial interrogation of the defendant unless it demonstrates the use of procedural safeguards effective to secure the privilege against self-incrimination. By custodial interrogation, we mean questioning initiated by law enforcement officers after a person has been taken into custody or otherwise deprived of his freedom of action in any significant way. (This is what we meant in *Escobedo* when we spoke of an investigation which had focused on an accused.) As for the procedural safeguards to be employed, unless other fully effective means are devised to inform accused persons of their right of silence and to assure a continuous opportunity to exercise it, the following measures are required. Prior to any questioning, the person must be warned that he has a right to remain silent, that any statement he does make may be used as evidence against him, and that he has a right to the presence of an attorney, either retained or appointed. The defendant may waive effectuation of these rights, provided the waiver is made voluntarily, knowingly and intelligently. If, however, he indicates in any manner and at any stage of the process that he wishes to consult with an attorney before speaking there can be no questioning. Likewise, if the individual is alone and indicates in any manner that he does not wish to be interrogated, the police may not question him. The mere fact that he may have answered some questions or volunteered some statements on his own does not deprive him of the right to refrain from answering any further inquiries until he has consulted with an attorney and thereafter consents to be questioned.

1.

The constitutional issue we decide in each of these cases is the admissibility of statements obtained from a defendant questioned while in custody or otherwise deprived of his freedom of action in any significant way. In each, the defendant was questioned by police officers, detectives, or a prosecuting attorney in a room in which he was cut off from the outside world. In none of these cases was the defendant given a full and effective warning of his rights at the outset of the interrogation process. In all the cases, the questioning elicited oral admissions, and in three of them, signed statements as well which were admitted at their trials. They all thus share salient features—incommunicado interrogation of individuals in a police-dominated atmosphere, resulting in self-incriminating statements without full warnings of constitutional rights.

An understanding of the nature and setting of this in-custody interrogation is essential to our decisions today. The difficulty in depicting what transpires at such interrogations stems from the fact that in this country they have largely taken place incommunicado. From extensive factual studies undertaken in the early 1930s, including the famous Wickersham Report to Congress by a Presidential Commission, it is clear that police violence and the "third degree" flourished at that time. . . . In a series of cases decided by this Court long after these studies, the police resorted to physical brutality—beatings, hanging, whipping—and to sustained and protracted questioning incommunicado in order to extort confessions. . . . The Commission on Civil Rights in 1961 found much evidence to indicate that "some policemen still resort to physical force to obtain confessions," 1961 Comm'n on Civil Rights Rep., Justice, pt. 5, 17. The use of physical brutality and violence is not, unfortunately, relegated to the past or to any part of the country. Only recently in Kings County, New York, the police brutally beat, kicked and placed lighted cigarette butts on the back of a potential witness under interrogation for the purpose of securing a statement incriminating a third party. *People v. Portelli,* 15 N.Y.2d 235, 257 N.Y.S.2d 931, 205 N.E.2d 857 (1965).

\* \* \*

Again we stress that the modern practice of in-custody interrogation is psychologically rather than physically oriented. As we have stated before, "Since *Chambers v. State of Florida,* 309 U.S. 227, 60 S.Ct. 472, 84 L.Ed. 716, this Court has recognized that coercion can be mental as well as physical, and that the blood of the accused is not the only hallmark of an unconstitutional inquisition." *Blackburn v. State of Alabama*, 361 U.S. 199, 206, 80 S.Ct. 274, 279, 4 L.Ed.2d 242 (1960). Interrogation still takes place in privacy. Privacy results in secrecy and this in turn results in a gap in our knowledge as to what in fact goes on in the interrogation rooms. A valuable source of information about present police practices, however, may be found in various police manuals and texts which document procedures employed with success in the past, and which recommend various other effective tactics.

Even without employing brutality . . . the very fact of custodial interrogation exacts a heavy toll on individual liberty and trades on the weakness of individuals. . . . Interrogation procedures may even give rise to a false confession. The most recent conspicuous example occurred in New York, in 1964, when a Negro of limited intelligence confessed to two brutal murders and a rape which he had not committed. When this was discovered, the prosecutor was reported as saying: "Call it what you want—brainwashing, hypnosis, fright. They made him give an untrue confession. The only thing I don't believe is that Whitmore was beaten." N.Y. Times, Jan. 28, 1965, p. 1, col. 5. In two other instances, similar events had occurred. N.Y. Times, Oct. 20, 1964, p. 22, col. 1; N.Y. Times, Aug. 25, 1965, p. 1, col. 1. In general, see Borchard, Convicting the Innocent (1932); Frank & Frank, Not Guilty (1957).

\* \* \*

In the cases before us today, given this background, we concern ourselves primarily with this interrogation atmosphere and the evils it can bring. In No. 759, *Miranda v. Arizona,* the police arrested the defendant and took him to a special interrogation room where they secured a confession. In No. 760, *Vignera v. New York,* the defendant made oral admissions to the police after interrogation in the afternoon, and then signed an inculpatory statement upon being questioned by an assistant district attorney later the same evening. In No. 761, *Westover v. United States,* the defendant was handed over to the Federal Bureau of Investigation by local authorities after they had detained and interrogated him for a lengthy period, both at night and the following morning. After some two hours of questioning, the federal officers had obtained signed statements from the defendant. Lastly, in No. 584, *California v. Stewart,* the local police held the defendant five days in the station and interrogated him on nine separate occasions before they secured his inculpatory statement.

In these cases, we might not find the defendants' statements to have been involuntary in traditional terms.

Our concern for adequate safeguards to protect precious Fifth Amendment rights is, of course, not lessened in the slightest. In each of the cases, the defendant was thrust into an unfamiliar atmosphere and run through menacing police interrogation procedures. The potentiality for compulsion is forcefully apparent, for example, in *Miranda,* where the indigent Mexican defendant was a seriously disturbed individual with pronounced sexual fantasies, and in *Stewart,* in which the defendant was an indigent Los Angeles Negro who had dropped out of school in the sixth grade. To be sure, the records do not evince overt physical coercion or patent psychological ploys. The fact remains that in none of these cases did the officers undertake to afford appropriate safeguards at the outset of the interrogation to insure that the statements were truly the product of free choice.

It is obvious that such an interrogation environment is created for no purpose other than to subjugate the individual to the will of his examiner. This atmosphere carries its own badge of intimidation. To be sure, this is not physical intimidation, but it is equally destructive of human dignity. . . . The current practice of incommunicado interrogation is at odds with one of our Nation's most cherished principles—that the individual may not be compelled to incriminate himself. Unless adequate protective devices are employed to dispel the compulsion inherent in custodial surroundings, no statement obtained from the defendant can truly be the product of his free choice.

The question in these cases is whether the privilege is fully applicable during a period of custodial interrogation. In this Court, the privilege has consistently been accorded a liberal construction. *Albertson v. Subversive Activities Control Board,* 382 U.S. 70, 81, 86 S.Ct. 194, 200, 15 L.Ed.2d 165 (1965); *Hoffman v. United States,* 341 U.S. 479, 486, 71 S.Ct. 814, 818, 95 L.Ed.2d 1118 (1951); *Arnstein v. McCarthy,* 254 U.S. 71, 72–73, 41 S.Ct. 26, 65 L.Ed. 138 (1920); *Counselman v. Hitchcock,* 142 U.S. 547, 562, 12 S.Ct. 195, 197, 35 L.Ed. 1110 (1892). We are satisfied that all the principles embodied in the privilege apply to informal compulsion exerted by law-enforcement officers during in-custody questioning. An individual swept from familiar surroundings into police custody, surrounded by antagonistic forces, and subjected to the techniques of persuasion described above cannot be otherwise than under compulsion to speak. As a practical matter, the compulsion to speak in the isolated setting of the police station may well be greater than in courts or other official investigations, where there are often impartial observers to guard against intimidation or trickery. . . .

*(continued)*

This question, in fact, could have been taken as settled in federal courts almost 70 years ago, when, in *Bram v. United States,* 168 U.S. 532, 542, 18 S.Ct. 183, 187, 42 L.Ed. 568 (1897), this Court held:

"In criminal trials, in the courts of the United States, wherever a question arises whether a confession is incompetent because not voluntary, the issue is controlled by that portion of the fifth amendment commanding that no person 'shall be compelled in any criminal case to be a witness against himself.'"

In *Bram,* the Court reviewed the British and American history and case law and set down the Fifth Amendment standard for compulsion which we implement today:

"Much of the confusion which has resulted from the effort to deduce from the adjudged cases what would be a sufficient quantum of proof to show that a confession was or was not voluntary has arisen from a misconception of the subject to which the proof must address itself. The rule is not that, in order to render a statement admissible, the proof must be adequate to establish that the particular communications contained in a statement were voluntarily made, but it must be sufficient to establish that the making of the statement was voluntary; that is to say, that, from the causes which the law treats as legally sufficient to engender in the mind of the accused hope or fear in respect to the crime charged, the accused was not involuntarily impelled to make a statement when but for the improper influences he would have remained silent." 168 U.S., at 549, 18 S.Ct. at 189. And see, *id.,* at 542, 18 S.Ct. at 186.

\* \* \*

The decisions of this Court have guaranteed the same procedural protection for the defendant whether his confession was used in a federal or state court. It is now axiomatic that the defendant's constitutional rights have been violated if his conviction is based, in whole or in part, on an involuntary confession, regardless of its truth or falsity. *Rogers v. Richmond,* 365 U.S. 534, 544, 81 S.Ct. 735, 741, 5 L.Ed.2d 760 (1961); *Siang Sung Wan v. United States,* 266 U.S. 1, 45 S.Ct. 1, 69 L.Ed. 131 (1924). This is so even if there is ample evidence aside from the confession to support the conviction, e.g., *Malinski v. People of State of New York,* 324 U.S. 401, 404, 65 S.Ct. 781, 783, 89 L.Ed. 1029 (1945); *Bram v. United States,* 168 U.S. 532, 540–542, 18 S.Ct. 183, 185–186 (1897).

Today, . . . there can be no doubt that the Fifth Amendment privilege is available outside of criminal court proceedings and serves to protect persons in all settings in which their freedom of action is curtailed in any significant way from being compelled to incriminate themselves. We have concluded that without proper safeguards the process of in-custody interrogation of persons suspected or accused of crime contains inherently compelling pressures which work to undermine the individual's will to resist and to compel him to speak where he would not otherwise do so freely. In order to combat these pressures and to permit a full opportunity to exercise the privilege against self-incrimination, the accused must be adequately and effectively apprised of his rights and the exercise of those rights must be fully honored.

\* \* \*

At the outset, if a person in custody is to be subjected to interrogation, he must first be informed in clear and unequivocal terms that he has the right to remain silent. For those unaware of the privilege, the warning is needed simply to make them aware of it—the threshold requirement for an intelligent decision as to its exercise. More important, such a warning is an absolute prerequisite in overcoming the inherent pressures of the interrogation atmosphere. It is not just the subnormal or woefully ignorant who succumb to an interrogator's imprecations, whether implied or expressly stated, that the interrogation will continue until a confession is obtained or that silence in the face of accusation is itself damning and will bode ill when presented to a jury. . . . Further, the warning will show the individual that his interrogators are prepared to recognize his privilege should he choose to exercise it.

The Fifth Amendment privilege is so fundamental to our system of constitutional rule and the expedient of giving an adequate warning as to the availability of the privilege so simple, we will not pause to inquire in individual cases whether the defendant was aware of his rights without a warning being given. Assessments of the knowledge the defendant possessed, based on information as to his age, education, intelligence, or prior contact with authorities, can never be more than speculation; . . . a warning is a clearcut fact. More important, whatever the background of the person interrogated, a warning at the time of the interrogation is indispensable to overcome its pressures and to insure that the individual knows he is free to exercise the privilege at that point in time.

The warning of the right to remain silent must be accompanied by the explanation that anything said can and will be used against the individual in court. This warning is needed in order to make him aware not only of the privilege, but also of the consequences of foregoing it. It is only through an awareness of these consequences that there can be any assurance of real understanding and intelligent exercise of the privilege.

Moreover, this warning may serve to make the individual more acutely aware that he is faced with a phase of the adversary system—that he is not in the presence of persons acting solely in his interest.

The circumstances surrounding in-custody interrogation can operate very quickly to overbear the will of one merely made aware of his privilege by his interrogators. Therefore, the right to have counsel present at the interrogation is indispensable to the protection of the Fifth Amendment privilege under the system we delineate today. Our aim is to assure that the individual's right to choose between silence and speech remains unfettered throughout the interrogation process. A once-stated warning, delivered by those who will conduct the interrogation, cannot itself suffice to that end among those who most require knowledge of their rights. A mere warning given by the interrogators is not alone sufficient to accomplish that end. Prosecutors themselves claim that the admonishment of the right to remain silent without more "will benefit only the recidivist and the professional." Brief for the National District Attorneys Association as amicus curiae, p. 14. Even preliminary advice given to the accused by his own attorney can be swiftly overcome by the secret interrogation process. Cf. *Escobedo v. State of Illinois,* 378 U.S. 478, 485, n. 5, 84 S.Ct. 1758, 1762. Thus, the need for counsel to protect the Fifth Amendment privilege comprehends not merely a right to consult with counsel prior to questioning, but also to have counsel present during any questioning if the defendant so desires. The accused who does not know his rights and therefore does not make a request may be the person who most needs counsel. As the California Supreme Court has aptly put it:

> "Finally, we must recognize that the imposition of the requirement for the request would discriminate against the defendant who does not know his rights. The defendant who does not ask for counsel is the very defendant who most needs counsel. We cannot penalize a defendant who, not understanding his constitutional rights, does not make the formal request and by such failure demonstrates his helplessness. To require the request would be to favor the defendant whose sophistication or status had fortuitously prompted him to make it." *People v. Dorado,* 62 Cal.2d 338, 351, 42 Cal.Rptr. 169, 177–178, 398 P.2d 361, 369–370, (1965) (Tobriner, J.).

In *Carnley v. Cochran,* 369 U.S. 506, 513, 82 S.Ct. 884, 889, 8 L.Ed.2d 70 (1962), we stated: "(I)t is settled that where the assistance of counsel is a constitutional requisite, the right to be furnished counsel does not depend on a request." This proposition applies with equal force in the context of providing counsel to protect an accused's Fifth Amendment privilege in the face of interrogation. See Herman, The Supreme Court and Restrictions on Police Interrogation, 25 Ohio St.L.J. 449, 480 (1964). Although the role of counsel at trial differs from the role during interrogation, the differences are not relevant to the question whether a request is a prerequisite.

Accordingly we hold that an individual held for interrogation must be clearly informed that he has the right to consult with a lawyer and to have the lawyer with him during interrogation under the system for protecting the privilege we delineate today. As with the warnings of the right to remain silent and that anything stated can be used in evidence against him, this warning is an absolute prerequisite to interrogation. No amount of circumstantial evidence that the person may have been aware of this right will suffice to stand in its stead. Only through such a warning is there ascertainable assurance that the accused was aware of this right.

If an individual indicates that he wishes the assistance of counsel before any interrogation occurs, the authorities cannot rationally ignore or deny his request on the basis that the individual does not have or cannot afford a retained attorney. The financial ability of the individual has no relationship to the scope of the rights involved here. The privilege against self-incrimination secured by the Constitution applies to all individuals. The need for counsel in order to protect the privilege exists for the indigent as well as the affluent. In fact, were we to limit these constitutional rights to those who can retain an attorney, our decisions today would be of little significance. The cases before us as well as the vast majority of confession cases with which we have dealt in the past involve those unable to retain counsel. . . . While authorities are not required to relieve the accused of his poverty, they have the obligation not to take advantage of indigence in the administration of justice. . . . Denial of counsel to the indigent at the time of interrogation while allowing an attorney to those who can afford one would be no more supportable by reason or logic than the similar situation at trial and on appeal struck down in *Gideon v. Wainwright,* 372 U.S. 335, 83 S.Ct. 792, 9 L.Ed.2d 799 (1963), and *Douglas v. People of State of California,* 372 U.S. 353, 83 S.Ct. 814, 9 L.Ed.2d 811 (1963).

In order fully to apprise a person interrogated of the extent of his rights under this system then, it is necessary to warn him not only that he has the right to consult with an attorney, but also that if he is indigent, a lawyer will be appointed to represent him. Without this additional warning, the admonition of the right to consult with counsel would often be understood as

*(continued)*

meaning only that he can consult with a lawyer if he has one or has the funds to obtain one. The warning of a right to counsel would be hollow if not couched in terms that would convey to the indigent—the person most often subjected to interrogation—the knowledge that he too has a right to have counsel present. . . . As with the warnings of the right to remain silent and of the general right to counsel, only by effective and express explanation to the indigent of this right can there

be assurance that he was truly in a position to exercise it. . . .

## Case Review Question

Even though mass media have long communicated to the public the "right to remain silent" in criminal situations, why are police officers still required to give this warning?

## CASE
### *Kirk v. Louisiana,*
### 122 S. Ct. 2458 (2002)

In the case below, the Supreme Court elaborated on what constituted a circumstance so critical that a warrant based on evidence was not necessary before a search and seizure in the privacy of a citizen's home.

Police officers entered petitioner's home, where they arrested and searched him. The officers had neither an arrest warrant nor a search warrant. Without deciding whether exigent circumstances had been present, the Louisiana Court of Appeal concluded that the warrantless entry, arrest, and search did not violate the Fourth Amendment of the Federal Constitution because there had been probable cause to arrest petitioner. 00-0190 (La. App.11/15/00), 773 So. 2d 259. The court's reasoning plainly violates our holding in *Payton v. New York,* 445 U.S. 573, 590, 100 S.Ct. 1371, 63 L.Ed.2d 639 (1980), that "[a]bsent exigent circumstances," the "firm line at the entrance to the house . . . may not reasonably be crossed without a warrant." We thus grant the petition for a writ of certiorari and reverse the Court of Appeal's conclusion that the officers' actions were lawful, absent exigent circumstances. We also grant petitioner's motion for leave to proceed *in forma pauperis.*

On an evening in March 1998, police officers observed petitioner's apartment based on an anonymous citizen complaint that drug sales were occurring there. After witnessing what appeared to be several drug purchases and allowing the buyers to leave the scene, the officers stopped one of the buyers on the street outside petitioner's residence. The officers later testified that "[b]ecause the stop took place within a block of the apartment, [they] feared that evidence would be destroyed and ordered that the apartment be entered." 773 So. 2d, at 261. Thus, "[t]hey immediately knocked on the door of the apartment, arrested the defendant, searched him thereto and discovered the cocaine and the money." *Id.,* at 263. Although the officers sought

and obtained a search warrant while they detained petitioner in his home, they only obtained this warrant after they had entered his home, arrested him, frisked him, found a drug vial in his underwear, and observed contraband in plain view in the apartment.

Based on these events, petitioner was charged in a Louisiana court with possession of cocaine with intent to distribute. He filed a pretrial motion to suppress evidence obtained by the police as a result of their warrantless entry, arrest, and search. After holding a suppression hearing, the trial court denied this motion. Petitioner was convicted and sentenced to 15 years at hard labor.

On direct review to the Louisiana Court of Appeal, petitioner challenged the trial court's suppression ruling. He argued that the police were not justified in entering his home without a warrant absent exigent circumstances. The Court of Appeal acknowledged petitioner's argument: "[Petitioner] makes a long argument that there were not exigent circumstances for entering the apartment without a warrant." *Id.,* at 261. The court, however, declined to decide whether exigent circumstances had been present, because "the evidence required to prove that the defendant possessed cocaine with the intent to distribute, namely the cocaine and the money, was not found in the apartment, but on his person." *Ibid.* The court concluded that because" [t]he officers had probable cause to arrest and properly searched the defendant incident thereto . . . [, t]he trial court properly denied the motion to suppress." *Id.,* at 263.

The Louisiana Supreme Court denied review by a vote of 4 to 3. In a written dissent, Chief Justice Calogero Explained:

"The Fourth Amendment to the United States constitution has drawn a firm line at the entrance to the home, and thus, the police need both probable cause to either arrest or search and exigent circumstances to justify a nonconsensual warrantless intrusion into private premises.... Here, the defendant was arrested inside an apartment, without a warrant, and the state has not demonstrated that exigent circumstances were present. Consequently, defendant's arrest was unconstitutional, and his motion to suppress should have been granted." App. to Pet. for Cert. 1–2.

We agree with Chief Justice Calogero that the Court of Appeal clearly erred by concluding that petitioner's arrest and the search "incident thereto," 773 So. 2d, at 263, were constitutionally permissible. In *Payton,* we examined whether the Fourth Amendment was violated by a state statute that authorized officers to "enter a private residence without a warrant and with force, if necessary, to make a routine felony arrest." 445 U.S., at 574, 100 S.Ct. 1371. We determined that "the reasons for upholding warrantless arrests in a public place do not apply to warrantless invasions of the privacy of the home." *Id.,* at 576, 100 S. Ct. 1371. We held that because "the Fourth Amendment has drawn a firm line at the entrance to the house . . . [, a]bsent exigent circumstances, that threshold may not reasonably be crossed without a warrant." *Id.,* at 590, 100 S. Ct. 1371. And we noted that an arrest warrant founded on probable cause, as well as a search warrant, would suffice for entry. *Id.,* at 603, 100 S. Ct. 1371.

Here, the police had neither an arrest warrant for petitioner, nor a search warrant for petitioner's apartment, when they entered his home, arrested him, and searched him. The officers testified at the suppression hearing that the reason for their actions was a fear that evidence would be destroyed, but the Louisiana Court of Appeal did not determine that such exigent circumstances were present. Rather, the court, in respondent's own words, determined "that the defendant's argument that there were no exigent circumstances to justify the warrantless entry of the apartment was irrelevant" to the constitutionality of the officers' actions. Brief in Opposition 2–3. As *Payton* makes plain, police officers need either a warrant or probable cause plus exigent circumstances in order to make a lawful entry into a home. The Court of Appeal's ruling to the contrary, and consequent failure to assess whether exigent circumstances were present in this case, violated *Payton.*

Petitioner and respondent both dispute at length whether exigent circumstances were, in fact, present. We express no opinion on that question, nor on respondent's argument that any Fourth Amendment violation was cured because the police had an "independent source" for the recovered evidence. Brief in Opposition 8. Rather, we reverse the Court of Appeal's judgement that exigent circumstances were not required to justify the officers' conduct, and remand for further proceedings not inconsistent with this decision.

*It is so ordered.*

## Case Review Question

Why is allowing a known drug dealer to go free a better result than permitting a warrantless search of his property after drug activity was observed?

## The Sixth Amendment: Speedy Trial, Impartial Jury, and Confrontation

**Speedy Trial by an Impartial Jury.** In the past, the Supreme Court has determined that a speedy trial is absolutely necessary to due process.[24] Therefore, a speedy trial must be included in the due process definition of the Fourteenth Amendment. However, the Court has just as adamantly refused to consider a standard test to determine whether a trial has or has not been provided quickly enough. The Court recognizes that different types of criminal cases require different amounts of preparation and investigation. Therefore, as long as the time for preparation is reasonable and trial is available, the Sixth Amendment right will have been honored.

The Court has established certain criteria for determining whether the Sixth Amendment right has been honored. When it is alleged that the right to a speedy trial has been violated, the Supreme Court has provided a four-factor test that judges may employ to determine whether the allegation is true. Judges should examine (1) the actual time of the delay from arrest to trial, (2) the reasons the government has cited as a basis for the delay, (3) whether the defendant requested a speedy trial at any time before trial, and (4) whether the delay caused any harm to the defendant. The harm can include problems for the defense such as unavailability of witnesses after a long period of time, lengthened detention if no bail was granted, or any other detriment to the defendant that would have been avoided by a speedy trial.

The guarantee of a speedy trial takes effect only on the actual indictment for a crime. Before the formal charge, the prosecution is free to investigate at length before determining that there is sufficient evidence to charge a defendant. Once this evidence has been accumulated, the prosecution is obligated to make the decision of whether to prosecute. If the decision is made not to prosecute, then the investigation may continue and charges may be brought later. It is required only that there be reason for the delay other than to impair the defendant's ability to obtain evidence to be used in defense.

## ASSIGNMENT 16.2

Consider the following facts and explain whether the case satisfies the requirement of a speedy trial or whether charges should be dropped because of a failure to provide this constitutional right.

Darren was arrested for drug possession with intent to distribute. The initial arrest occurred on August 1, 2002. At first, Darren attempted to hire counsel. However, after thirty days and twelve interviews with various attorneys, he was unable to come up with a sufficient retainer to hire any of them. He requested a public defender. On September 18, a public defender was assigned to his case and began preparations to defend Darren. Trial was set for November 1, 2002. On October 31, 2002, the child of the public defender was killed in an accident, and the attorney took an indefinite leave of absence. The case was rescheduled for January 1, 2003. A new public defender was assigned the case on December 1, 2002. On January 1, the public defender requested an extension over Darren's objections because of a

sudden and unusually large caseload as the result of the loss of the previous attorney from the public defender's office. The case was rescheduled for March 1, 2003.

In February, the judge assigned to the case suffered a stroke. All trials were postponed for sixty days to enable the court to shift cases and replace the judge. The case was reset for May 1, 2003. The trial began as scheduled on that date—but after approximately two hours, the judge (newly appointed to the bench) announced that she was totally inexperienced in criminal matters and did not believe she was adequately prepared to provide a fair trial to Darren. The case was reassigned to a judge with experience adjudicating criminal cases and scheduled for August 1, 2003. During the preceding twelve months, Darren was unable to come up with sufficient bail to secure his release, and as a result lost his job, home, personal property, car, and even visitation rights with his children from a previous marriage.

**critical stage**
Stage of a criminal proceeding in which the presumed innocence of the accused is in jeopardy, and therefore the accused is entitled to the representation of counsel.

**Right of Confrontation.** Also included in the Sixth Amendment (and in the definition of what constitutes due process under the Fourteenth Amendment) is the right to confront one's accusers. It is inherent in U.S. law that before a person can be convicted on the basis of statements made by others, he or she must be given the opportunity to face and challenge the statements of accusers. Because not every person accused of a crime can adequately confront his or her accuser, this has been determined to be a **critical stage** in the prosecution that requires the assistance of counsel. This includes pretrial procedures such as identification and confrontation on testimony at trial. The rationale is that the defendant should be given every opportunity to expose errors or irregularities in the testimony of witnesses for the prosecution.

## APPLICATION 16.3

Edwin was a clergyman with a sexual penchant for children and young adolescents. On several occasions he molested two young girls named Rita and Mandy along with other unidentified children. Mandy died as the result of what was ruled a suicide. Shortly after the funeral, Rita told Mandy's parents of the molestation, and the police were contacted. Rita was interviewed extensively by the police. Edwin, who had been a pillar of the small community where they had all lived, was charged with molestation. Before trial, Edwin contacted Rita and told her that if she or any of the others testified, she would "end up just like Mandy." Despite Rita's fears, Edwin has the right through counsel (or as his own counsel) to confront Rita and challenge her accusations in court.

*Point for Discussion:* Why could Rita's videotaped interview with the police not be used? In the alternative, why could Rita's testimony not be given from another location with her voice electronically altered and her appearance hidden behind a screen?

**Right to Counsel.** Subsequent to *Miranda,* the Court held that for the protection of several necessary rights (such as the right to not incriminate or assist in the prosecution against oneself), counsel must be available at all points in a prosecution where there is opportunity for unfairness or where untrustworthy evidence may be obtained. Later decisions have identified these stages of prosecution as interrogation or questioning, identification procedures, first court appearance where action may be taken against the defendant, preliminary hearing or grand jury, arraignment, trial, sentencing, and probation revocation hearings. Various rights in addition to those in the Fifth Amendment have been interpreted to require this as part of the due process guarantee in the Fourteenth Amendment. The result has been that each state must follow these requirements in its own state laws and prosecutions.

Unless there are compelling circumstances, any accused person is entitled to have an attorney present at the time a witness is asked to identify the accused as the one who committed a crime. Compelling circumstances would include situations that make it unreasonable to wait for an attorney to be present. In addition, if a witness is shown only photographs of potential defendants, neither the defendant nor defendant's counsel has the right to be present. The right to assistance of counsel is considered to be necessary to aid the defendant in adequately responding to charges of a witness. Because there is little room for unfairness or prejudice in identifying a photograph, disallowing the presence of the defendant or counsel at this procedure is considered to do no harm to due process.

## APPLICATION 16.4

The police were called to a residence with a report of domestic disturbance. The residence was located in an area with an extremely high crime rate. When officers arrived, they found a man lying in a yard suffering from a gunshot wound. He claimed that his neighbor shot him after an argument about the property line. The neighbor was immediately taken into custody. The man continued to communicate and accurately provided his name and other basic information such the current date and his wife's place of work, including the exact address. He then asked why his grandparents were

*(continued)*

## APPLICATION 16.4 (Continued)

there and began to speak incoherently. The man died a few minutes later. It was subsequently determined that his grandparents had been deceased for some thirty years before the incident. Even though the man ultimately began to lose clear thought, at the time he provided the identity of the assailant and other details he was giving accurate information. The neighbor was charged with the murder. He claimed to have been in his home watching television at the time of the shooting. He further alleged the victim had previously said he owed money to people who had threatened to kill him if he did not pay it back. In this type of situation, the identification by the victim of his assailant at the scene would be admissible. The rationale is that the circumstances make it unlikely the victim or anyone else would manipulate the identification process and thereby compromise the rights of the defendant.

*Point for Discussion:* Would the result be different if the accurate information were intermingled with the incoherent and nonsensical remarks?

The Supreme Court has also found that the right to assistance of counsel occurs only after the defendant has been charged with a crime and the prosecution has commenced.[25] Therefore, if a person is asked to take part in a lineup or other form of identification procedure before arrest, then no right to assistance of counsel attaches. The point has been raised that most law-enforcement agencies are encouraged to conduct identification procedures before charging the defendant and thus avoid the necessity of counsel. This is not seen as a particularly significant issue, however. First, the individual has the right to refuse to appear voluntarily in the lineup. Second, if the procedure is conducted in an unfair manner that unduly suggests the suspect to witnesses as the criminal, then the suspect (subsequently the defendant) has the opportunity to allege this at trial. If proven, the evidence of the identification of the defendant will be inadmissible. Without a witness to identify the defendant as the one who committed the crime, a prosecution is often unsuccessful. Therefore, police have the incentive to ensure that lineups are fairly conducted even before a defendant is formally charged with a crime.

### The Eighth Amendment: Bail and Cruel and Unusual Punishment

The Eighth Amendment has also been clearly drawn into the Fourteenth Amendment definition of due process. The issues involve that of bail and freedom from cruel and unusual punishment.

**Bail.** The Supreme Court has specifically addressed the issue of *bail*, the term used to describe release from custody during the time between arrest and conviction. Generally, the court asks for some guarantee or assurance that the defendant will not flee or commit other crimes if released. This assurance is the type or amount of bail that is required.[26] The Eighth Amendment guarantee against excessive bail has been integrated into the Fourteenth Amendment and applied to the states in an attempt to prevent the unwarranted detention and deprivation of liberty of accused persons before trial.

Many jurisdictions have specified amounts of bail that are predetermined for misdemeanors. In many states, if a person is charged with a traffic violation, then his or her permanent driver's license will be accepted as bail. The license is then returned if the accused is found innocent or is given another penalty on conviction. If the charges are minor, a specific dollar amount may be posted with the police to obtain release until a hearing is conducted. In other cases, the persons charged must remain in custody until they have an opportunity to appear before a judge or magistrate. Usually, this is within a matter of hours or, at most, a few days. The judge will determine what is an appropriate assurance or, in some instances, may even release the persons on their word that they will reappear at the formal hearing on the charges against them. The latter is known as being *released on one's own recognizance,* or O.R. In serious cases, and when there is reason to believe the accused will commit other crimes or flee the jurisdiction, the court may deny bail entirely and detain the person until trial.

The Eighth Amendment states that bail will not be excessive. A person is considered innocent until proven guilty in this country. Therefore, until proven guilty at a trial, the rationale is that accused persons should be allowed to continue their lives, earn a living, and reside with their families. Just as the circumstances vary with every case, however, so do the considerations of what would be excessive bail. For minor offenses, it is relatively assured that most persons will appear at trial. Therefore, bail may be a predetermined amount for all persons charged with those offenses. For serious crimes where the penalty on a finding of guilt may be severe, the temptation to avoid a trial and possible sentencing by fleeing the jurisdiction is much greater. In addition, many of the accused in these cases have criminal backgrounds. Thus, the likelihood that they will continue to commit crime while on bail is much greater.

The Eighth Amendment has been drawn into the definition of the Fourteenth Amendment on the basis of the general concept of due process.[27] The Supreme Court has reasoned that pretrial detention because bail is not allowed or is so excessive that it effectively prevents an accused person from posting it, could be a deprivation of liberty without due process of law (essentially, a sentence of imprisonment before a trial). Thus, the factors that are considered in determining bail and the amount of bail that is required should be directly related.

The function of the courts in determining bail is to set an amount that will reasonably assure the appearance of the accused at trial.[28] If the judge determines that this cannot be assured by a sum of money and that a person should not be released on bail, then the judge must make a clear statement in the court record of reasons that support this decision.[29] The presumption is that all persons should have an opportunity to be released on bail. Therefore, this can be denied only in compelling circumstances.

The courts must consider several factors when determining bail, including but not limited to the following:

1. past criminal history of the accused,
2. past bail history of the accused,
3. the accused's connections to the community (such as job, family, and home),
4. danger posed to the community by the accused, and
5. likelihood the accused will flee from the jurisdiction.

If enough of these factors or other considerations convince the court that the accused is likely to commit crimes or flee the jurisdiction, then the court is justified in denying bail entirely. This does not constitute an improper violation of the individual right to due process because the government interest in protecting the public is considered to be greater. This goes back to the traditional balance that courts try to achieve: the good of the individual versus the good of the people.

More often, the court is faced with a case that falls into a gray area. Although some factors are present that raise concern about the accused's conduct on bail release, the evidence is not sufficient to warrant holding the accused in custody until trial. In such cases, the judicial officer must make a determination of what amount of bail is reasonable to ensure that the accused will not commit crimes or flee the jurisdiction. The court must also consider what amount the accused can reasonably be expected to post as assurance that he or she will appear for trial.

In questions of bail, there is a wide berth for judicial discretion. The decision must be made on a case-by-case basis, and every individual accused presents a unique situation to the court. Therefore, for more serious crimes, there is generally no set rule for the amount of bail a court will require. The court must consider all the evidence before it on this question and exercise its best judgment. As long as a higher court can find that a determination of bail falls somewhere within a range of reasonableness, the initial determination of bail will not be altered.

## ASSIGNMENT 16.3

Which of the following situations, in which the defendant is charged, will likely result in (1) a hearing to determine the proper bail or (2) an automatic predetermined amount of bail? Explain your answer.

1. driving under the influence
2. hitchhiking on an interstate highway
3. murder
4. larceny for a theft of less than $500
5. arson and conspiracy to commit insurance fraud
6. driving on an expired license
7. trespassing
8. assault resulting from a bar fight
9. driving too fast for conditions
10. attempted murder and using a weapon to commit a felony

**Cruel and Unusual Punishment.** This guarantee of the Eighth Amendment protects all citizens from punishment deemed to be excessive or inappropriate for the crime committed, according to societal standards. What defines cruel and unusual has gone through dramatic change in our nation's history that have been consistent with the changes in our society.

Essentially, the Supreme Court has defined due process to include the protection of the Eighth Amendment with regard to the imposition of sentence. However, the Court has been somewhat reluctant to state specifics with regard to what constitutes such punishment. The Court has gone so far as to prohibit "barbaric" punishment or punishment that is excessive for the crime. Further, it has upheld the death penalty, refusing to categorize it as cruel and unusual. Part of the Court's rationale for its position on the death penalty is that the penalty is approved by a significant majority of the states. This, in turn, supposedly reflects the belief of a majority of people that capital punishment is acceptable and appropriate. Although the death penalty continues to be a topic of debate at the state level and the subject of many protests, until these laws are changed to reflect a changing society, it is unlikely that the Court will reverse its position.

Exhibit 16.1 lists the constitutional guarantees in the Bill of Rights and highlights those guarantees that have been included in the definition of due process.

**Exhibit 16.1** Bill of Rights Constitutional Guarantees*

---

I. Establishment of religion.

Free exercise of speech.

Free exercise of press.

Peaceable assembly.

Petition of government for redress of grievances.

II. Well-regulated militia.

III. To exclude soldiers from homes in times of peace and in times of war except as prescribed by law.

IV. To be secure against unreasonable search and seizure and that no warrants shall be issued without probable cause.

V. No civilian shall be tried for capital crimes except upon grand jury indictment.

No one shall be subjected to double jeopardy.

No one shall be compelled to be a witness against himself.

No one shall be deprived of life, liberty or property without due process of law.

No private property shall be taken for public use without just compensation.

VI. Right to a speedy and public trial by an impartial jury.

To be informed of the nature and cause of the accusation.

To confront witnesses for the prosecution.

To have compulsory process to obtain witnesses in one's favor.

To have assistance of counsel in one's defense.

VII. Right to jury trial in common law actions valued greater than $20.

Jury determinations of fact are subject only to appeal in accordance with rules of common law.

VIII. No excessive bail.

No excessive fines.

No cruel and unusual punishments.

IX. No rights in the Constitution shall be used to deny other rights.

X. Powers not delegated to the U.S. or prohibited by the Constitution are reserved to the states.

---

*Rights affecting criminal procedure are underlined. Rights that have been integrated into the definition of due process through selective incorporation are in bold-face type.

# CASE
## *Morales v. Tilton,*
### 465 F.Supp.2d 972 (N.D.Cal.2006)

The following judicial opinion discusses the impact of the prohibition against cruel and unusual punishment and its effect on a sentence of death by lethal injection.

Few issues in American society have generated as much impassioned debate as the death penalty. At one end of the spectrum, abolitionists condemn the intentional taking of human life by the State as barbaric and profoundly immoral. At the other, proponents see death, even a painful death, as the only just punishment for crimes that inflict unimaginable suffering on victims and their surviving loved ones. Even among those with less absolute positions, there are vigorous arguments about the social, penological, and economic costs and benefits of capital punishment.

Any legal proceeding arising in this context thus acts as a powerful magnet, an opportunity for people who care about this divisive issue to express their opinions and vent their frustrations. However, because courts (and particularly trial courts) exist not to resolve broad questions of social policy but to decide specific legal and factual disputes, it is important at the outset for this Court to make very clear what this case is not about.

This case is not about whether the death penalty makes sense morally or as a matter of policy: the former inquiry is a matter not of law but of conscience; the latter is a question not for the judiciary but for the legislature and the voters. Nor is it about whether California's primary method of execution—lethal injection—is constitutional in the abstract: the arguments and evidence presented by the parties address the specific manner in which California has implemented that method and proposes to do so in the future. Nor is it about whether the Constitution requires that executions be painless: binding precedent holds that the Eighth Amendment prohibits only "the unnecessary and wanton infliction of pain," *Gregg v. Georgia,* 428 U.S. 153, 173, 96 S.Ct. 2909, 49 L.Ed.2d 859 (1976) (plurality opinion), and procedures that create an "unnecessary risk" that such pain will be inflicted, *Cooper v. Rimmer,* 379 F.3d 1029, 1033 (9th Cir.2004).

*(continued)*

Nor, finally, does it somehow involve a comparison of the pain that Plaintiff, a condemned inmate at California's San Quentin State Prison, might suffer when he is executed with the horrific suffering of the young woman he raped and murdered. The Court has considered seriously the constitutional issues raised by this case not because of some imagined personal sympathy for Plaintiff but because it is its fundamental duty to do so. As a practical matter, there is no way for a court to address Eighth Amendment issues in the capital context other than in a case raised by a death-row inmate; by definition, the acts of which such an inmate stands convicted are viewed by the law and a majority of the community as so abhorrent as to warrant the ultimate penalty. Lest there be any doubt, this Court has the most profound sympathy for the family and loved ones of Plaintiff's victim.

In fact, this case presents a very narrow question: does California's lethal-injection protocol—as actually administered in practice—create an undue and unnecessary risk that an inmate will suffer pain so extreme that it offends the Eighth Amendment? Because this question has arisen in the context of previous executions, see *Beardslee v. Woodford,* 395 F.3d 1064 (9th Cir.2005); *Cooper,* 379 F.3d 1029, and is likely to recur with frequency in the future, the Court has undertaken a thorough review of every aspect of the protocol, including the composition and training of the execution team, the equipment and apparatus used in executions, the pharmacology and pharmacokinetics of the drugs involved, and the available documentary and anecdotal evidence concerning every execution in California since lethal injection was adopted as the State's preferred means of execution in 1992, see 1992 Cal. Stat. 558. The Court has reviewed a mountain of documents, including hundreds of pages of legal briefs, expert declarations, and deposition testimony, and it has conducted five days of formal hearings, including a day at San Quentin State Prison that involved a detailed examination of the execution chamber and related facilities. The Court concludes that absent effective remedial action by Defendants—the nature of which is discussed in Part IV of this memorandum—this exhaustive review will compel it to answer the question presented in the affirmative. Defendants' implementation of lethal injection is broken, but it can be fixed.

Plaintiff Michael Angelo Morales raped and murdered Terri Winchell. A jury convicted Plaintiff of murder, found special circumstances, and sentenced him to death. See generally *Morales v. Woodford,* 388 F.3d 1159, 1163–67 (9th Cir.2004).

In California, "[i]f a person under sentence of death does not choose either lethal gas or lethal injection within 10 days after the warden's service upon the inmate of an execution warrant [then] the penalty of death shall be imposed by lethal injection." Cal.Penal Code § 3604(b) (West 2006). More specifically, "[t]he punishment of death shall be inflicted . . . by an intravenous injection of a substance or substances in a lethal quantity sufficient to cause death, by standards established under the direction of the Department of Corrections." *Id.* § 3604(a). Defendants have adopted San Quentin Operational Procedure No. 0-770 ("OP 770") as California's protocol governing executions by lethal injection. This protocol, like those used by the federal government and most other states, provides for the injection of three drugs into a person being executed: sodium thiopental, a barbiturate sedative, to induce unconsciousness; pancuronium bromide, a neuromuscular blocking agent, to induce paralysis; and potassium chloride, to induce cardiac arrest.

Plaintiff filed the present action on January 13, 2006, contending that OP 770 and the manner in which Defendants implement it would subject him to an unnecessary risk of excessive pain, thus violating the Eighth Amendment's command that "cruel and unusual punishments [not be] inflicted." U.S. Const. amend. VIII. Five days later, the Superior Court of California for the County of Ventura issued a death warrant, setting Plaintiff's execution for February 21, 2006. This Court then ordered briefing and limited discovery and held two hearings on Plaintiff's application for a preliminary injunction to stay his execution so that the Court could conduct a full evidentiary hearing to consider his claims.

On February 14, 2006, the Court issued an order conditionally denying Plaintiff's request for a stay of execution. *Morales v. Hickman,* 415 F.Supp.2d 1037 (N.D.Cal.2006). The Court reviewed in detail evidence from execution logs, which indicated that "inmates' breathing may not have ceased as expected in at least six out of thirteen executions by lethal injection in California." *Id.* at 1045. This and other evidence raised concerns that inmates may have been conscious when they were injected with pancuronium bromide and potassium chloride, drugs that the parties agreed would cause an unconstitutional level of pain if injected into a conscious person. Given this evidence, the Court fashioned a remedy that was intended to permit Defendants to proceed with Plaintiff's execution as scheduled by executing him with only barbiturates or by retaining the services of a qualified expert to ensure that Plaintiff would be unconscious when exposed to the painful drugs. *Id.* at 1047. In so holding, the Court stated,

> Whether or not Defendants implement the remedy and thus proceed to execute Plaintiff as scheduled, the Court respectfully suggests that

Defendants conduct a thorough review of the lethal-injection protocol, including, *inter alia,* the manner in which the drugs are injected, the means used to determine when the person being executed has lost consciousness, and the quality of contemporaneous records of executions, such as execution logs and electrocardiograms. Given the number of condemned inmates on California's Death Row, the issues presented by this case are likely to recur with considerable frequency. Because California's next execution is unlikely to occur until the latter part of this year, the State presently is in a particularly good position to address these issues and put them to rest. It is hoped that the remedy ordered by this Federal Court in this case will be a one-time event; under the doctrines of comity and separation of powers, the particulars of California's lethal-injection protocol are and should remain the province of the State's executive branch. A proactive approach by Defendants would go a long way toward maintaining judicial and public confidence in the integrity and effectiveness of the protocol.

*Id.* at 1046–47.

The day after the Court issued its order, Defendants responded that they had retained the services of two anesthesiologists who would attend Plaintiff's execution pursuant to the terms of the order. Based upon Defendants' written submissions, and over Plaintiff's strenuous objections, the Court stated that it was satisfied that the anesthesiologists would "take all medically appropriate steps to ensure that Plaintiff is and remains unconscious" when injected with pancuronium bromide and potassium chloride. (Final Order Re Defendants' Compliance with Conditions, Doc. No. 67 at 4 n. 3.; *id.* at 5 (finding that "the anesthesiologists designated by Defendants are qualified professionals who will use their professional judgment not merely to observe the execution but to ensure that Plaintiff is and remains unconscious").)

On February 19, 2006, the United States Court of Appeals for the Ninth Circuit affirmed. 438 F.3d 926 (9th Cir.2006). The Ninth Circuit construed this Court's order as

> clearly contemplating that [the anesthesiologists] have the authority to take "all medically appropriate steps"—either alone or in conjunction with the injection team—to immediately place or return Morales into an unconscious state or to otherwise alleviate the painful effects of either or both the pancuronium bromide or potassium chloride.

*Id.* at 931.

However, for reasons that remain somewhat unclear, there was a "disconnect between the expectations articulated in the orders of this Court and the Court of Appeals and the expectations of the anesthesiologists" regarding how they would participate in Plaintiff's execution. (Order on Defendants' Motion to Proceed with Execution, Doc. No. 78 at 3.) Defendants apparently had told the anesthesiologists that the anesthesiologists merely would have to observe the execution, while Defendants' counsel represented to the Court that the anesthesiologists would ensure that Plaintiff would remain unconscious after he was injected with sodium thiopental. This disconnect became apparent on the evening of February 20, 2006, approximately three or four hours before Plaintiff's scheduled execution (which Defendants had set for 12:01 A.M. on February 21), when Defendants provided copies of the Ninth Circuit's opinion to the anesthesiologists. Almost immediately, the anesthesiologists stated that they could not proceed for reasons of medical ethics. Several hours of tense discussions (including what Warden Ornoski described as "training" of the anesthesiologists) and telephonic hearings followed, during which Defendants postponed the execution. At approximately 2:45 A.M. on February 21, Defendants stated that they would seek approval from the Court to execute Plaintiff using only sodium thiopental (and without the participation of the anesthesiologists); the execution was rescheduled for 7:30 P.M.

The parties submitted briefing on Defendants' request, and the Court heard approximately one hour of telephonic argument during the morning of February 21. Because Defendants had indicated their desire to proceed using only sodium thiopental only hours earlier, the record contained virtually no evidence as to the details of how such an execution would be carried out, and Plaintiff had no meaningful opportunity for appellate review. Accordingly, shortly before 3:00 P.M., the Court issued an order in which it held that, in light of the unique circumstances then presented,

> due process requires that . . . Defendants' obligations be set forth in a way that leaves no room for reasonable doubt. Accordingly, while Defendants may proceed with the execution this evening using only sodium thiopental, they may do so only if the sodium thiopental is injected in the execution chamber directly into the intravenous cannula by a person or persons licensed by the State of California to inject medications intravenously.

(*Id.*) Defendants were unwilling or unable to execute Plaintiff in accordance with these requirements, and a stay of execution to permit an evidentiary hearing

*(continued)*

issued automatically pursuant to the Court's order of February 14. 415 F.Supp.2d at 1048.

The Court then set an expedited schedule for an evidentiary hearing to be held in May 2006. Thereafter, at the joint request of the parties, the evidentiary hearing was deferred until September 2006 to enable the parties to complete discovery. On February 28, 2006, the Governor's Office hosted a meeting lasting approximately an hour and a half at which potential changes to OP 770 were discussed. Although more significant modifications were proposed by some of the participants, the Governor's Legal Affairs Secretary concluded that the only change that would be undertaken at that time was what was described as a "tweak" of the chemical aspects of the protocol. It was decided that the dosages of the three drugs would be adjusted and that a continuous infusion of sodium thiopental during the administration of pancuronium bromide and potassium chloride would be added. There is no indication from the record that the participants in the meeting addressed or considered issues related to the selection and training of the execution team, the administration of the drugs, the monitoring of executions, or the quality of execution logs and other pertinent records. Defendants issued the revised version of OP 770 on March 6, 2006; this version remains current and is the version that Defendants intend to follow in executing Plaintiff.

The Pacific News Service ("PNS") thereafter filed a related lawsuit, *Pacific News Service v. Tilton,* No. C 06 1793 JF RS (N.D. Cal. filed Mar. 8, 2006), challenging Defendants' use of pancuronium bromide during executions. PNS moved to consolidate its action with this one. The Court noted that "despite the fact that not consolidating the actions may leave an unresolved First Amendment challenge to California's lethal-injection protocol pending even after the conclusion of the proceedings in *Morales,* Defendants urge the Court to take a deliberate approach to managing these cases, with PNS being addressed after *Morales.*" The Court declined to consolidate the cases, stating, "While the Court is committed to resolving all aspects of the present litigation expeditiously, it will defer to the State's expressed concerns." (Order Denying Motion to Consolidate without Prejudice, Doc. No. 110 at 2.) In reaching this conclusion, the Court observed,

> At the hearing, counsel for *Morales* expressed the concern that an appeal of the Court's judgment in *Morales* might be pending while the PNS action was still unresolved. Because of the closely related nature of these actions, as well as the Court's inherent authority to determine the timing of its decisions, the Court considers this scenario unlikely. On March 30, 2006, the Court convened at San Quentin State Prison for what

the parties agreed would be a preliminary session of the evidentiary hearing. At San Quentin, the Court examined the equipment and facilities used during executions, and it heard partial testimony from the then-leader of Defendants' execution team.

In preparation for the remainder of the evidentiary hearing, the parties filed a joint pre-hearing conference statement containing detailed factual stipulations and also submitted voluminous testimony, including the testimony of experts and present and former execution team members, by means of deposition excerpts. The evidentiary hearing recommenced on September 26 and concluded on September 29, 2006. Following the evidentiary hearing, the parties submitted closing briefs.

From the evidence in the record and the parties' extensive briefing, the Court has learned a great deal about executions by lethal injection in general and their implementation in California in particular. The opportunity to make first-hand observations at San Quentin was quite useful, and the oral testimony and written declarations of well-qualified experts on both sides have been very helpful. Yet in many respects, the Court finds itself in virtually the same position today that it was in when it considered Plaintiff's motion for a preliminary injunction in February 2006.

As they did in February, the parties agree that it would be unconstitutional to inject a conscious person with pancuronium bromide and potassium chloride in the amounts contemplated by OP 770. Defendants' principal medical expert, Dr. Robert C. Singler, testified that it would be "terrifying" to be awake and injected with the contemplated dosage of pancuronium bromide and that it would be "unconscionable" to inject a conscious person with the contemplated amount of potassium chloride. The parties also agree, as they did in February, that assuming effective anesthesia, the use in executions of pancuronium bromide or potassium chloride as such does not violate the Eighth Amendment. As it has from its inception, the resolution of this case thus turns on a single factual question: whether OP 770, as implemented, provides constitutionally adequate assurance that condemned inmates will be unconscious when they are injected with pancuronium bromide and potassium chloride.

On the surface, this would appear to be a relatively straightforward inquiry. As Defendants have pointed out repeatedly and as this Court itself has found in three separate capital cases, including this one, the amount of sodium thiopental to be given to the condemned person pursuant to OP 770 is sufficient to cause virtually all persons to become unconscious or even to cease breathing within one minute. *Morales,*

415 F.Supp.2d at 1043–44; *Beardslee v. Woodford*, No. C 04 5381 JF, 2005 WL 40073, at (N.D.Cal. Jan.7, 2005); *Cooper v. Rimmer*, No. C 04 436 JF, 2004 WL 231325, at (N.D.Cal. Feb.6, 2004). Accordingly, assuming that the sodium thiopental is delivered properly, there should be virtually no risk that an inmate will suffer an unconstitutional level of pain. However, the record in this case, particularly as it has been developed through discovery and the evidentiary hearing, is replete with evidence that in actual practice OP 770 does not function as intended. The evidence shows that the protocol and Defendants' implementation of it suffer from a number of critical deficiencies, including:

> . . . Inconsistent and unreliable screening of execution team members: For example, one former execution team leader, who was responsible for the custody of sodium thiopental (which in smaller doses is a pleasurable and addictive controlled substance), was disciplined for smuggling illegal drugs into San Quentin; another prison guard led the execution team despite the fact that he was diagnosed with and disabled by post-traumatic stress disorder as a result of his experiences in the prison system and he found working on the execution team to be the most stressful responsibility a prison employee ever could have.

A lack of meaningful training, supervision, and oversight of the execution team: Although members of the execution team testified that they perform numerous "walk-throughs" of some aspects of the execution procedure before each scheduled execution, the team members almost uniformly have no knowledge of the nature or properties of the drugs that are used or the risks or potential problems associated with the procedure. One member of the execution team, a registered nurse who was responsible for mixing and preparing the sodium thiopental at many executions, testified that "[w]e don't have training, really." While the team members who set the intravenous catheters are licensed to do so, they are not adequately prepared to deal with any complications that may arise, and in fact the team failed to set an intravenous line during the execution of Stanley "Tookie" Williams on December 13, 2005. Although Defendants' counsel assured the Court at the evidentiary hearing that "Williams was a lesson well learned, one that will never occur again," the record shows that Defendants did not take steps sufficient to ensure that a similar or worse problem would not occur during the execution of Clarence Ray Allen on January 17, 2006, or Plaintiff's scheduled execution the following month.

Inconsistent and unreliable record-keeping: For example, there are no contemporaneous records showing that all of the sodium thiopental in the syringes used for injections actually was injected, and, in fact, testimony revealed that in at least several executions it was not. A number of the execution logs are incomplete or contain illegible or overwritten entries with respect to critical data such as the inmate's heart rate and the time at which observations were made. Inexplicably, Defendants use blank paper for their electrocardiogram (EKG) tracings instead of the graph paper that typically is used, and provide neither standardization markings nor paper-speed documentation, thereby precluding accurate interpretation of the tracings, even as to heart rate.

Improper mixing, preparation, and administration of sodium thiopental by the execution team: Among other things, team members' admitted failure to follow the simple directions provided by the manufacturer of sodium thiopental further complicates the inquiry as to whether inmates being executed have been sufficiently anesthetized.

Inadequate lighting, overcrowded conditions, and poorly designed facilities in which the execution team must work: The execution chamber was not designed for lethal-injection executions; San Quentin officials simply made slight modifications to the existing gas chamber, such as drilling holes in the chamber wall for intravenous lines and installing a metal hook at the top of the chamber from which the bags containing the lethal drugs are suspended. The bags are too high to permit the execution team to verify whether the equipment is working properly. The lighting is too dim, and execution team members are too far away, to permit effective observation of any unusual or unexpected movements by the condemned inmate, much less to determine whether the inmate is conscious; this is exacerbated by the fact that the chamber door is sealed shut during executions as if lethal gas were being disseminated, rendering it virtually impossible to hear any sound from the chamber. For some executions, the small anteroom from which the execution team injects the lethal drugs has been so crowded with prison officials and other dignitaries that even simple movement has been difficult.

Defendants observe correctly that Plaintiff's burden of proof at the present stage of the instant proceeding is greater than it was at the preliminary-injunction stage and that there still is no definitive evidence that any inmate has been conscious during his execution. Nonetheless, the evidence is more than adequate to establish a constitutional violation. Given that the State is taking a human life, the pervasive lack of professionalism in the implementation of OP 770 at the very least is deeply disturbing. Coupled with the fact that the use of

*(continued)*

pancuronium bromide masks any outward signs of consciousness, the systemic flaws in the implementation of the protocol make it impossible to determine with any degree of certainty whether one or more inmates may have been conscious during previous executions or whether there is any reasonable assurance going forward that a given inmate will be adequately anesthetized. The responsibility for this uncertainty falls squarely upon Defendants, and the circumstances clearly implicate the Eighth Amendment.

As this Court noted in its order of February 14, 2006, anomalies in six execution logs raise substantial questions as to whether certain inmates may have been conscious when pancuronium bromide or potassium chloride was injected. 415 F.Supp.2d at 1044–46. These substantial questions remain unanswered despite the depth and breadth of the evidentiary record and the parties' briefing. If anything, the questions have become even more substantial. One of the executions not discussed by the Court in its order of February 14 was that of Robert Lee Massie, who was executed on March 27, 2001. Massie's execution was explored in detail at the evidentiary hearing. Testifying on behalf of Defendants, Dr. Singler opined that based upon the heart rates reflected in the execution log, Massie well may have been awake when he was injected with potassium chloride. Significantly, Dr. Singler testified that he was unable to give a definitive opinion principally because of the poor quality of the log itself, and in particular an unclear entry in the log as to Massie's heart rate.

Dr. Singler's testimony regarding Massie's execution is merely the most dramatic evidence concerning the risks posed by Defendants' acts and omissions. Dr. Singler also testified to a number of additional concerns, most notably the fact that overcrowding, obstructed sight lines, and poor lighting in the execution chamber and adjoining anteroom make accurate observations of the inmate during an execution extremely problematic. Whatever the merits of the protocol in the abstract, there can be no real doubt that Defendants' implementation of OP 770 has major flaws, many of which are apparent from the undisputed facts to which Defendants stipulated in the amended joint pre-hearing conference statement.

The Framers of our Constitution were not far removed from a society in which condemned prisoners were put to death by being beheaded, drawn, and quartered. The Eighth Amendment was adopted in part as a response to such brutality, and it since has been construed by our Supreme Court to require that punishment for crimes comport with "the evolving standards of decency that mark the progress of a maturing society." *Roper v. Simmons,* 543 U.S. 551, 561, 125 S.Ct.

1183, 161 L.Ed.2d 1 (2005). While opponents of the death penalty believe that any means of execution necessarily violates such standards, the Supreme Court repeatedly has held otherwise, see, e .g., *Gregg,* 428 U.S. 153, 96 S.Ct. 2909, 49 L.Ed.2d 859, in large part because the Constitution itself makes explicit reference to capital punishment, U.S. Const. amends. V & XIV § 1. The use of lethal injection in executions represents an evolution from earlier methods such as hanging, electrocution, and lethal gas that now are viewed by most jurisdictions as unduly harsh. Needless to say, when properly administered, lethal injection results in a death that is far kinder than that suffered by the victims of capital crimes.

At the present time, however, Defendants' implementation of California's lethal-injection protocol lacks both reliability and transparency. In light of the substantial questions raised by the records of previous executions, Defendants' actions and failures to act have resulted in an undue and unnecessary risk of an Eighth Amendment violation. This is intolerable under the Constitution. See *Beardslee,* 395 F.3d at 1070–71; *Cooper,* 379 F.3d at 1033; *Taylor v. Crawford,* No. 05-4173-CV-C-FJG, 2006 WL 1779035 (W.D.Mo. June 26, 2006) (holding that Missouri's lethal-injection protocol violates Eighth Amendment).

As this Court previously has noted, "under the doctrines of comity and separation of powers, the particulars of California's lethal-injection protocol are and should remain the province of the State's executive branch." 415 F.Supp.2d at 1046. Moreover, despite its critical assessment of Defendants' performance to date, this Court has no intention of interfering with or delaying California's implementation of a constitutional execution protocol. California's voters and legislature repeatedly have expressed their support for capital punishment. This case thus presents an important opportunity for executive leadership.

The Court is prepared to issue formal findings of fact and conclusions of law with respect to the deficiencies in the administration of California's current lethal-injection protocol that have been brought to light in this case. However, it will require additional time to do so, in part because Defendants still have not fulfilled their discovery obligations. In addition, while the Court has deferred consideration of the issues raised in the PNS matter until after it issues a formal decision in this case, it still must resolve PNS in order to facilitate speedy and complete appellate review of all of the current challenges to OP 770. Finally, while it is a virtual certainty that any judgment in this case will be appealed by one party or the other, it seems fair to suggest that a judgment adverse to Defendants grounded in the extensive factual record present here is far more likely to delay the resumption of executions in California than is one favorable to Defendants. Because the Court is prepared to find that the sequence of three drugs described in OP 770 when properly administered will provide for a constitutionally adequate level of anesthesia, and given that the deficiencies in the implementation of the protocol appear to be correctable, a thorough, effective response to the issues raised in this memorandum likely will enable the Court to enter such a favorable judgment.

Accordingly, and respectfully, the Court urges the Governor's Office to take this opportunity to address seriously now, rather than later, the significant problems with OP 770 and its implementation. In light of the well-documented management issues in California's prison system generally, see, e.g., *Plata v. Schwarzenegger,* No. C 01 1351 TEH, 2005 WL 2932253 (N.D.Cal. Oct.3, 2005), the Court believes that the Governor's Office is in the best position to insist on an appropriate degree of care and professionalism in carrying out what Defendants properly characterize as the "solemn" task of executions.

Toward that end, acknowledging its own limited role and with deference to the role of the State's executive branch, and informed by what it has learned in the course of the present litigation, the Court offers the following observations:

First, given past experience, it seems unlikely that a single, brief meeting primarily of lawyers, the result of which is to "tweak" OP 770, will be sufficient to address the problems identified in this case. Rather, as contemplated by the Court in its order of February 14, 2006, "a thorough review of the lethal-injection protocol, including, *inter alia,* the manner in which the drugs are injected, the means used to determine when the person being executed has lost consciousness, and the quality of contemporaneous records of executions, such as execution logs and electrocardiograms," 415 F.Supp.2d at 1046, likely will be necessary. To be meaningful, such a review may require consultation with independent experts and with other jurisdictions, and it must be undertaken with an openness to the idea of making significant improvements in the "infrastructure" of executions.

Second, given that because of the paralytic effect of pancuronium bromide, a determination of an inmate's anesthetic depth after being injected with that drug is extremely difficult for anyone without substantial training and experience in anesthesia, the protocol must ensure that a sufficient dose of sodium thiopental or other anesthetic actually reaches the condemned inmate and that there are reliable means of monitoring and recording the inmate's vital signs throughout the execution process. An adequate protocol also must include a means of providing additional anesthetic to the inmate should the need arise. Because an execution is not a medical procedure, and its purpose is not to keep the inmate alive but rather to end the inmate's life, the Court agrees with Defendants that the Constitution does not necessarily require the attendance and participation of a medical professional. However, the need for a person with medical training would appear to be inversely related to the reliability and transparency of the means for ensuring that the inmate is properly anesthetized: the better the delivery system, the less need there is for medical participation.

Third, because the constitutional issues presented by this case stem solely from the effects of pancuronium bromide and potassium chloride on a person who has not been properly anesthetized, removal of these drugs from the lethal-injection protocol, with the execution accomplished solely by an anesthetic, such as sodium pentobarbital, would eliminate any constitutional concerns, subject only to the implementation of adequate, verifiable procedures to ensure that the inmate actually receives a fatal dose of the anesthetic. Should Defendants wish to retain a three-drug protocol, which it most certainly is their right to do, they must address in a serious way the broader structural problems in implementation outlined in this memorandum.

Accordingly, and good cause therefore appearing, within thirty days Defendants shall advise the Court and Plaintiff of their response to this memorandum, including specifically whether Defendants and the Governor's Office intend to review and revise OP 770 further and, if so, how much additional time, if any, they believe they will need to complete that task. Plaintiff may file a response to Defendants' submission within fifteen days after the submission has been served upon his counsel of record. The Court will not construe any pleading filed in response to this memorandum as a waiver of any arguments with respect to the constitutionality of the current version of OP 770, its implementation, or any other legal issue or procedural question presented by the instant case.

IT IS SO ORDERED.

## Case Review Question

If an individual commits a capital offense and is sentenced to death, why must the death be administered in a "humane" manner when most such individuals have been convicted of committing inhumane acts?

## STAGES OF CRIMINAL PROCEDURE

An understanding of the rights of accused persons in the criminal process allows a much clearer sense of the reasons for the various stages through which an accused must pass. These stages are all designed with the intent that every citizen shall have every available opportunity to have his or her conduct judged fairly without undue influence or unfair criticism. The following discussion of the actual stages of criminal procedure uses many of the examples already used in the discussion of the rights of the accused to illustrate the role these rights play in the criminal process.

### Pre-Arrest

Generally, before an arrest is made and a defendant is charged with a crime, the law-enforcement agencies will attempt to obtain sufficient evidence to warrant the arrest and the conviction. In fact, a standard of all arrests is that the arresting officer had probable cause to believe the suspect had committed a crime.[30] Generally, probable cause is established through introduction of evidence that connects the accused to the crime.

**Right to Privacy.** Many times, after or during the commission of a crime, the police look for evidence that will lead them to the person or persons who committed the crime. However, the constitutional rights guaranteed by the Fourth Amendment prevent the police from rampantly searching among members of the public and their belongings. Such searching would violate all rights of privacy and notions of fairness. The police are entitled to obtain whatever evidence exists publicly, but before they may delve into private property and dwellings, they must establish that there is probable cause to believe evidence of a crime exists there.

As indicated earlier in the chapter, items or occurrences in public view do not require probable cause because it would be unreasonable for a person to consider such things private. Such items include things that are on private property but can be viewed from outside the property. It is also permissible to use the assistance of such items as binoculars. If the item only enhances natural ability, it is acceptable.

In addition, individuals do not have a right to privacy with regard to such matters as the phone numbers they have called. No one can reasonably expect that the phone company will not be allowed to know what numbers are called from a private telephone. Indeed, these records are necessary to the phone company's business. Therefore, because this is common knowledge to a third party such as the phone company, individuals should not expect that no other third party could obtain the information. Thus, phone registers, which record the numbers called from a private phone, require no showing of probable cause. Nor do conversations made on public telephones. There can be no reasonable expectation of privacy in the use of public facilities.

Before the police may enter the private property of an individual, they must have probable cause to suspect a connection between the property and the crime committed. As stated earlier, the police must have more than mere suspicion. They must have access to other evidence or testimony that would indicate the likelihood of criminal activity. For example, the police may have information from informants who have had contact with the person or persons suspected of criminal activity and can provide specific information regarding their conduct (such as phone conversations about the crimes) or the exact location of criminal evidence. If the police have conducted surveillance of the persons or property and have discovered highly suspicious activities taking place, then a court may find probable cause.

**Search Warrant.** If a court finds that there is probable cause to suspect that evidence of a crime exists in or on private property, then it will issue an appropriate search warrant. Search warrants must be specific concerning the objective, location, and scope of the search.[31] If, for example, the warrant is issued to determine whether the suspects are discussing crimes on the telephone, then only wiretaps on the telephones may be placed. If the warrant is issued to search the premises for evidence of a crime, then only the premises can be searched and no wiretaps would be allowed. The requirement that warrants must be specific prevents unreasonable invasions of privacy by some overzealous law-enforcement officers.

**Plain View Rule.** What happens if a search is being conducted for specific evidence and evidence of other criminal activity is discovered? This falls under the plain view rule. If police are lawfully on property (public, with consent, or with a search warrant) and discover evidence of any crime in plain view, then that evidence can be used against its owners in a criminal prosecution.

**Arrest Warrant.** If the police can demonstrate to the court that there is enough criminal evidence to support a conviction, then the court will issue an arrest warrant. When the warrant is issued, the police have the authority to take the defendant into custody and make initial criminal charges. At this point, the defendant's constitutional protection against being deprived of life or liberty without due process of law becomes a concern of law-enforcement personnel.

In certain situations, no search or arrest warrant is required. In such special circumstances, police have the authority to stop, search, and make an arrest if necessary. If there is probable cause to believe that individuals are committing— or have in the immediate past committed—a crime, then the police have the authority to stop these individuals. When the individuals are stopped, the police have the authority to pat them down and search areas within their reach to determine whether anything is available that the individuals could use to harm the officers. The police then have the option of questioning the persons and releasing them or, if probable cause exists, the persons can be placed under arrest, and the property in their immediate reach can be searched.

**Grand Jury.** Another method used in federal criminal prosecutions and some states for prosecutions of serious crimes is the **grand jury,** which consists of twenty or more citizens who, for a period of approximately six months, hear evidence of criminal activity in various cases presented by the prosecution. The duty of the grand jury is to determine whether there is enough evidence to prosecute someone for a crime. A grand jury proceeding often occurs even before an initial arrest has been made.

Much of the evidence the grand jury hears has been obtained through government investigation, the use of various search warrants, and the testimony of informants or other persons with relevant information. Suspects have no absolute right to appear at grand jury proceedings or to introduce evidence. The purpose of such proceedings is solely to determine whether enough evidence exists that a jury could find a person guilty of criminal conduct.

If the grand jury finds that sufficient evidence exists to formally charge an individual with a crime, then it will issue an *indictment* (pronounced "in-dite-ment"), which gives law-enforcement personnel the authority to arrest and charge the individual with the crime. An indictment operates in much the same fashion as an arrest warrant issued by a judge. After apprehension, the person is taken into custody and advised of his or her rights. At that point, the stages of actual prosecution begin.

**grand jury**
A group of individuals (often more than twenty) that reviews evidence to determine whether a defendant could be convicted of a crime if charged and tried.

## Arrest and Interrogation

**Arrestee's Rights.** Persons who are initially arrested must be advised of their basic rights on arrest.[32] They must be told that they have the right to remain silent, that anything they say can and will be used against them in a court of law, that they have the right to an attorney, and that if they cannot afford an attorney, then one will be appointed for them at no cost. Law-enforcement agencies are making it a common practice to require all arrestees to sign a statement that indicates they have been notified of and understand their rights. These written statements have greatly reduced the number of arrestees who claim they were never advised of their rights or that the advisement came after they had incriminated themselves.

**Interrogation.** After an arrest, the law-enforcement officers and prosecutors may question (interrogate) the accused person about the crime with which he or she is charged. Identification proceedings such as lineups, where the victims or witnesses to the crime are asked to identify the alleged criminal from a group of persons, may also take place.

The arrestee has the right to have an attorney present to ensure that identification proceedings are not conducted in a way that would unduly influence the victims or witnesses to name the accused.[33] For example, if the police have information from a witness that the suspect was of a particular race and present a lineup of persons of other races except for the actual suspect, then the witness would have no choice but to indicate the actual suspect as the criminal. Such an identification proceeding is unfair. Lineups must be conducted in such a way that they truly test the ability of the witness to identify the criminal.

Many law-enforcement agencies avoid the necessity of providing attorneys for all those who are suspected of criminal activity. Instead, the police ask the individual before arrest to answer questions voluntarily or to take part in an identification proceeding. If the individual voluntarily complies, then the police have complete consent and do not have to advise the person of his or her rights or provide counsel. The individual does, however, have the right to obtain his or her own counsel or to refuse to cooperate. An exception occurs when a grand jury issues a subpoena to the individual. In that situation, the person is required to appear to be questioned but may avoid answering on the basis of the Fifth Amendment guarantee against self-incrimination.

**Confession.** A particular concern arises when an arrestee confesses to a crime. At this point, law-enforcement personnel are under a particular duty to establish that the individual was not coerced in any way or misled into an involuntary confession. It must be established that the confession was given freely and without undue influence. Further, it must be shown that the individual understood the possible consequences of a confession.[34] Increasingly, law-enforcement agencies are establishing that a confession was made in fair circumstances by videotaping it. This is relatively inexpensive compared to the cost of trying the issue of a confession in court. Also, when a confession is videotaped and the court can actually observe the circumstances under which it was made, a defendant is much less likely to claim that it was unfairly obtained unless such circumstances truly existed.

## Bail

Shortly after arrest, the accused person is entitled to request release from custody before trial in exchange for bail. Bail—or *bond,* as it is sometimes called—is the amount paid to the court as an assurance that the suspect will not flee the jurisdiction or commit additional crimes before trial. It operates as an insurance policy against such conduct by the accused.

Many persons utilize the services of bail bondsmen. For a fee, the bondsman will issue a bond to the court stating that if the accused flees the jurisdiction or commits a crime while the prosecution is pending, then the bondsman will be responsible for the entire amount of bail. The bondsman acts as a sort of insurance company that issues the policy for the accused. If the accused violates the terms of the bail release and flees or commits a crime, then the bondsman has the right to be reimbursed by the accused.

One method utilized when larger amounts of bail are imposed is a payment of 10 percent of the amount of bail. Many jurisdictions allow the accused to make this 10 percent payment. If the accused then violates the terms of the bail release, full payment is required, and the accused will be taken back into custody.

The decision of how much bail to require—or whether to grant release on bail at all—is generally left to the discretion of the judge. The judge has the duty to determine (1) what would be a reasonable amount to assure the court of the accused's good conduct and presence at future hearings and (2) what is within the means of the defendant to pay. Although these two factors are balanced against each other, the more important factor, of course, is the first.[35]

If the judge determines that no amount would be assurance that the accused will not leave the jurisdiction or commit other crimes, then bail may be denied. To be justified, this usually requires substantial evidence that the accused has ignored court orders in the past or has engaged in other conduct that would indicate a likelihood that bail would be ignored.

Another option is to require no security at all in the form of bail for release. When this occurs, as previously mentioned, the person is released on his or her own recognizance. The judge makes a finding that the person's contacts to the community, such as family and work, are strong enough to prevent the person from fleeing the jurisdiction. Further, there must be evidence that the person is not likely to commit additional crimes. Release on one's own recognizance is issued most often when the charge is less serious or when it is the person's first criminal offense.

Once the issue of bail has been determined, the accused is either released or returned to the physical custody of law-enforcement personnel. The next stage of prosecution is the preliminary hearing.

## Preliminary Hearing and Arraignment

Shortly after the accused's arrest, a preliminary hearing is scheduled. At this time, the defendant and the prosecution appear for a decision by the judge of whether sufficient admissible evidence exists to warrant further prosecution. The prosecution introduces evidence of the defendant's guilt. The defendant has the opportunity to challenge the admissibility of this evidence under the exclusionary rule. Generally, the defendant is not allowed to introduce evidence of defense. The burden is on the prosecutor to prove that a finding of guilty is possible. The purpose of the preliminary hearing is simply to determine whether there is enough admissible evidence to meet this burden. Because no conviction can result at this stage, there is no need for a defense at this point.

If the court finds that insufficient evidence exists that would be admissible in court, then the case will be dismissed and all charges will be dropped. In the event the court finds sufficient evidence to prosecute, the court will arrange an **arraignment** and schedule the case for trial. In less serious matters, the stages of bail, preliminary hearing, and arraignment may be combined into a single proceeding. In more complex cases, each side must prepare a presentation for the various issues, and the three stages are scheduled separately.

Arraignment follows the preliminary hearing. At this stage, defendants are informed of the actual charge of which they are accused and for which they will be tried, and the charge is recorded in the court files. Often this charge is related to,

**arraignment**
Stage of a criminal proceeding in which the accused is formally charged.

but different from, the charge for which the defendant was initially arrested. This occurs because some evidence may have been excluded by the court or because additional evidence has been accumulated since the time of arrest. Either development may affect the ability of the prosecution to prove guilt on a particular charge. Thus, the charge may be modified. Another possibility is that the judge during the preliminary hearing will determine that there is insufficient evidence for one charge but adequate evidence for another. In that event, the judge will order that the latter be the basis for prosecution.

During arraignment, the defendant is formally advised of the crime charged. Bail may also be reviewed by the court at this time. It may be increased, decreased, or withdrawn, with the accused placed back into custody. Most important, the defendant pleads on the issue of guilt at the arraignment.

Typically, a defendant pleads one of three ways. If the plea is guilty, then the defendant is making an admission of responsibility for the crime committed. Thus, there is no need for a trial to prove guilt, and the procedure moves directly to sentencing. If the plea is not guilty, then the court will schedule a trial date. At trial, the prosecution will attempt to prove the guilt of the defendant beyond a reasonable doubt. The third type of plea sometimes accepted by a court is *nolo contendere,* also known as *no contest.* This plea means that the defendant will not plead guilty but will raise no defense to the claims of the prosecutor. In essence, the defendant takes the position, "I am not saying I am guilty or innocent, but I will not defend myself at trial or challenge a conviction."

As a result of a *nolo contendere* plea, the defendant has no recorded confession of guilt, but no trial is required for a finding of guilt. Sentencing occurs immediately after this plea, just as it would on a plea of guilty. Many times a defendant will plead *nolo contendere* in a situation where someone injured by the crime may bring a civil suit against the defendant in addition to the criminal charge. If a defendant pleads *nolo contendere,* the injured party in a civil trial cannot introduce an admission of guilt for the act that caused the injury. Thus, it may be in the defendant's interest to plead *nolo contendere* in the criminal suit to increase his or her chances of success as a defendant in a civil suit.

## APPLICATION 16.5

Suzette and Janet are young women at the same party. During the course of the evening, they become involved in an argument that escalates into a physical fight. Suzette strikes Janet with a lamp, breaks her jaw, and causes a laceration on her face that requires plastic surgery. Suzette is charged with assault. Janet also brings a civil suit against Suzette for her injuries and related damages such as pain and suffering and disfigurement. If Suzette pleads no contest or not guilty to the charges, then the charges cannot be admitted in the civil case even if she is convicted. However, if she pleads guilty, the criminal charge can be admitted as a legal admission of guilt for the assault.

*Point for Discussion:* Why is the plea of no contest inadmissible?

**Plea Bargaining.** Plea bargaining has become an integral part of the criminal process for several reasons. It occurs when the prosecution agrees to a lesser charge or a reduced sentence in exchange for a plea of guilty by the defendant. The benefit to the defendant is that he or she will not have to stand trial and face the possibility of a more serious conviction or penalty. The government is saved the expense of a trial and, perhaps more important, is able to impose a penalty on the defendant in some degree. When the prosecution is required to go to trial, the burden of proof is so severe that there is always the possibility of acquittal.

## APPLICATION 16.6

Rose is arrested and charged with shoplifting. Rose had been arrested previously and always managed to avoid conviction. She is well known to local shop owners, however, as someone who is in their stores before the discovery of missing inventory. In this instance, the angle of the store surveillance camera did not show Rose actually taking the merchandise but did show her handling several items and then making a purchase. She continued to wander around the store before leaving. Several stolen items were found in the shopping bag in Rose's possession. Rose claimed that she had accidentally picked up the bag of another customer who was shoplifting. Because the video evidence is questionable, the prosecution offered to lower the charges in exchange for a guilty plea. Rose does not know the details of any eyewitness testimony. She did not steal from that department. However, she did steal some expensive jewelry from another part of the store on the same day. The jewelry was not identified as stolen when Rose was arrested. She accepted the offer and entered a plea agreement whereby she will plead guilty but will only have to pay a fine.

*Point for Discussion:* Assume Rose is, in fact, innocent of stealing the items for which she is accused. Why would someone ever plead guilty in a plea bargain if they did not commit a crime?

## Trial, Appeal, and Sentencing

The crucial stage of any prosecution is the trial. At this point, the trier of fact—usually the jury—will determine the guilt or innocence of the defendant based on the evidence of the prosecution. Guilt must be established beyond a reasonable doubt. In practical terms, this means that one who considers the situation logically and rationally must have no doubt that the defendant committed the crime with which he or she is charged. Guilt cannot be based on prejudice or bias or pure circumstance. There must be no other reasonable explanation than that the accused committed the crime.

This burden of proof is quite severe to help ensure that innocent individuals will not be convicted because of questionable circumstances. In the U.S. legal system, individuals are considered innocent until proven guilty. Furthermore, they cannot be compelled to testify about information that might incriminate them. Some defendants, regardless of innocence, simply are not effective witnesses in a criminal prosecution because they do not communicate well, and they do their defense more harm than good by attempting to tell their story to the trier of fact. For this reason, a defendant is not required to testify at trial. Further, a jury may not consider such a refusal to testify as evidence of guilt. The evidence of guilt must be established by the prosecutor.

If the trier of fact determines that the prosecution has met its burden, then a conviction will result. If the burden is not met, the charges are dismissed, and the defendant is released from further proceedings. On dismissal, bail is returned to the defendant if its terms were not violated during the prosecution. With a conviction, bail may be returned or applied to a fine imposed as a penalty for a conviction.

After conviction, the court may sentence the defendant immediately, or sentencing may be scheduled for a later time. In some instances, a jury is asked to impose the sentence on the defendant. This usually occurs in extremely serious cases that require much thought and consideration of the circumstances of the crime—for example, a capital offense where the sentence could be death. The reasoning is that, in such a serious matter, several of one's peers can determine just punishment as well as or better than a single judge. The prosecution and defense are both allowed to introduce evidence that will enable a fair sentence to be imposed based on all of the circumstances. Such factors include the state of mind of the defendant, such as malice or premeditation, and the extent of the criminal conduct, such as extreme violence. Other factors such as intelligence, maturity, or likelihood of rehabilitation may also affect sentencing.

If a defendant chooses to appeal, it is up to the trial court to determine whether the defendant will be released during the appeal. In more serious cases, the defendant is usually required to begin serving the sentence, because appeals can take a long time. Further, after conviction and sentencing, a defendant may be tempted to flee the jurisdiction. If an appeal is successful and the conviction is overturned, then the defendant is not entitled to any compensation for time served or inconvenience caused by the prosecution of the crime. In most of these cases, a new trial is granted and the procedure starts over again. A defendant who is granted a new trial is treated as if the first trial never occurred. Therefore, the sentence can be greater or lesser if conviction is obtained a second time.

## ASSIGNMENT 16.4

Consider the following facts and identify any challenges that the defendant could make with regard to the charges against her and the procedure that has occurred.

Judy was a college student in her senior year. The college was a small one in a rural community. As she walked back to her dorm one night, a young man she recognized from having seen around campus asked to escort her. She thanked him and he walked her home. The next night the two went on a date. At the end of the evening, the young man sexually assaulted Judy. She reported the incident, but the police determined it was a consensual act by both parties. Enraged, Judy began to stalk the young man and record his movements. She thought if he committed a similar act against another student, then he might be charged in the assault against her. She had even told a few classmates of her plan and asked them to let her know if they heard of any suspicious activity by the young man.

One night in January, Judy was following him as he walked down an icy street. However, as the street turned into a downhill slope, her car began to slide and pick up speed. She struck and killed the young man and then careened into a tree. Judy was rendered unconscious. When she awoke, she used her cell phone to call 911 for herself. She was unaware of the young man lying dead between her car and the tree. The investigating officer recognized her and immediately gave his partner instructions to search Judy's car and dormitory room. The notes of the young man's

movements were found in her room and seized. When she realized what had happened, Judy was nearly hysterical at the scene of the accident and made no acknowledgement of having been advised of her rights. Ultimately, she was taken to a local hospital to be sedated before being taken to jail. Judy was charged with murder. She spent most of the night of the accident in an interrogation room following the administration of a sedative. During the interrogation she was lethargic but answered the following questions.

Question: "When you found out the boy wasn't going to be charged last fall, did you wish he was dead?"

Answer: "I wished he would never hurt anyone again. I wished that he would be stopped from hurting women like he had hurt me."

Question: "What do you want to do right now?"

Answer: "I just want to buy a plane ticket to get me as far away from here as I can get. I just want to go somewhere and pretend this never happened."

Based on the interrogation, Judy was denied bail because she was determined to be a flight risk. She had been in custody seventy-two hours when frantic family members reported her missing and were told she was in custody and charged with murder. Approximately two weeks after being taken into custody, a court-appointed attorney from a nearby town (there were no public defenders in the town where the accident occurred) came to visit Judy for the first time. She remembered virtually nothing

*(continued)*

## ASSIGNMENT 16.4 (Continued)

of the night of the accident or her subsequent arrest and interrogation. The attorney asked for a speedy trial. However, the week before trial, the local judge suffered a stroke and was rendered incapacitated. Judy was in custody a full fourteen months before another judge was appointed and her trial began. During that time, several of her classmates had graduated and moved to other parts of the country. Many were no longer willing to come and testify in the case on her behalf.

## ETHICAL CONSIDERATIONS

Criminal defense lawyers are commonly asked, "How can you represent someone that you know is guilty?" This seems to be a concept that the general public has great difficulty in reconciling as ethical behavior. However, representation of the accused is a cornerstone right guaranteed to all citizens under the U.S. Constitution. In the U.S. system of justice, certain principles prevail. First, everyone is innocent until proven guilty by evidence in a court of law—not by the media, or by speculation, or by circumstance, or even by the accused's own lawyer. Second, it is not the function of a criminal defense lawyer to judge the client. Rather, it is to see that the client's defense is heard in the best light possible and to take all necessary measures to achieve a fair trial for the client. The criminal defense lawyer is assisted in this endeavor by the Bill of Rights. Consequently, the answer to the preceding question is frequently not one of the ethics of the lawyer but one of the general public. It is important to view anyone accused of criminal conduct objectively until such time as the evidence is fully reviewed. This was the goal of the Constitution's framers, who sought primarily to reverse the standard of guilty until proven innocent.

## Question

Why should the standard of guilty until proven innocent be reversed?

## ETHICAL CIRCUMSTANCE

Meg is a paralegal working for attorney Russel. The two represent a man who claims his home and belongings were destroyed in a house fire; the insurance company, however, refuses to pay on the allegation the fire was deliberately set. No charges have been filed. A neighbor of the man calls the office and speaks with Meg. He informs her that two days before the fire, he was home from work sick and observed the man bring his travel trailer from a nearby storage lot where he kept it and spend the better part of the day filling it with boxes of what appeared to be personal items, photos, and documents. He then returned the trailer to the storage lot. Meg gives this information to the attorney. If, in fact, the man was removing items of value from his house two days before it was coincidentally consumed by fire, then there is an ethical obligation to confront the man with the information and request answers. Although attorney–client privilege may prevent them from disclosing the information to the authorities, they could certainly withdraw from representation if they believe the man is attempting to commit insurance fraud and they could also encourage him to go to the authorities and admit his actions.

## CHAPTER SUMMARY

The U.S. legal system is committed to fairness to persons accused of criminal conduct, and every attempt is made to ensure that innocent persons are not convicted and punished. Much of the U.S. Constitution was written with this objective in mind, and it continues to be the basis for all aspects of criminal procedure.

Criminal procedure begins at the moment law-enforcement authorities suspect criminal activity; accused individuals are often afforded constitutional protections before they are even aware that they are suspects. An example of such a protection is the requirement of probable cause before any search, seizure, or arrest can be made. When possible, this probable cause must be determined by a judicial officer who can view the situation more objectively than a law-enforcement officer.

After a person's arrest, the Constitution continues to influence the proceedings through its mandates regarding bail, specific charges, right to counsel, and a speedy trial. In spite of all these protections, innocent persons have still been convicted. In the majority of these cases, however, the mistaken conviction occurred as a result of misconduct by witnesses or, in some instances, prosecutors. When properly applied, the system provides greater protection from improper convictions than perhaps any other legal system in the world.

## CHAPTER TERMS

| | | |
|---|---|---|
| arraignment | due process | probable cause |
| critical stage | grand jury | selective incorporation |
| double jeopardy | | |

## REVIEW QUESTIONS

1. Selective incorporation is designed to do what?
2. Which guarantees of the Bill of Rights are currently adopted into the definition of due process?
3. What is probable cause?
4. When does double jeopardy not apply after trial has begun?
5. At what stages does a defendant have the right to counsel?
6. When can bail be denied?
7. When is an arrest warrant not necessary?
8. What is the function of a grand jury?
9. What happens when there is no grand jury?
10. What takes place at an arraignment?

## HELPFUL WEB SITES

| | |
|---|---|
| Criminal law | http://www.nolo.com/lawcenter |
| About the law | http://www.lawyers.com/common/content/ |
| | http://public.findlaw.com/ |

## INTERNET ASSIGNMENT 16.1

Using Internet resources, determine the penalty, if any, for refusing a breathalyzer test in an alleged driving-under-the-influence case. Trace your research steps.

## INTERNET ASSIGNMENT 16.2

Determine when your jurisdiction most recently considered whether it would apply the death penalty.

## ENDNOTES

1. United States Constitution, Amendments 4, 5, 8, 14.
2. *Palko v. Connecticut,* 302 U.S. 319, 58 S.Ct. 149, 82 L.Ed. 288 (1937).
3. *Id.*
4. *Mapp v. Ohio,* 367 U.S. 643, 81 S.Ct. 1684, 6 L.Ed.2d 1081 (1961).
5. *Id.*
6. *Weeks v. United States,* 232 U.S. 383, 34 S.Ct. 341, 58 L.Ed. 652 (1914).
7. 338 U.S. 25, 69 S.Ct. 1359, 93 L.Ed. 1782 (1949).
8. See note 4.
9. 468 U.S. 897, 104 S.Ct. 3405, 82 L.Ed.2d 677 (1984).
10. *Katz v. United States,* 389 U.S. 347, 88 S.Ct. 507, 19 L.Ed.2d 576 (1967).
11. *Brinegar v. United States,* 338 U.S. 160, 69 S.Ct. 1302, 93 L.Ed. 1879 (1949).
12. *Vale v. Louisiana,* 399 U.S. 30, 90 S.Ct. 1969, 26 L.Ed.2d 409 (1970).
13. *Hester v. United States,* 265 U.S. 57, 44 S.Ct. 445, 68 L.Ed. 898 (1924).
14. *United States v. Dunn,* 480 U.S. 294, 107 S.Ct. 1134, 94 L.Ed.2d 326 (1987).
15. See note 10.
16. *New York v. Class,* 475 U.S. 106, 106 S.Ct. 960, 89 L.Ed.2d 81 (1986).
17. *New York v. Belton,* 453 U.S. 454, 101 S.Ct. 2860, 69 L.Ed.2d 768 (1981).
18. *Id.*
19. *Terry v. Ohio,* 392 U.S. 1, 88 S.Ct. 1868, 20 L.Ed.2d 889 (1968).
20. *Crist v. Bretz,* 437 U.S. 28, 98 S.Ct. 2156, 57 L.Ed.2d 24 (1978).
21. *Id.*
22. *Arizona v. Washington,* 434 U.S. 497, 98 S.Ct. 824, 54 L.Ed.2d 717 (1978).
23. 384 U.S. 436, 86 S.Ct. 1602, 16 L.Ed.2d 694 (1966).
24. *Brewer v. Williams,* 430 U.S. 387, 97 S.Ct. 1232, 51 L.Ed.2d 424 (1977).
25. *Barker v. Wingo,* 407 U.S. 514, 92 S.Ct. 2182, 33 L.Ed.2d 101 (1972).
26. *Id.*
27. See note 24.
28. *United States v. Salerno,* 481 U.S. 739, 107 S.Ct. 2095, 95 L.Ed.2d 697 (1987).
29. *Schilb v. Kuebel,* 404 U.S. 357, 92 S.Ct. 479, 30 L.Ed.2d 502 (1971).
30. See note 20.
31. See note 28.
32. See note 19.
33. *Marron v. United States,* 275 U.S. 192, 48 S.Ct. 74, 72 L.Ed. 231 (1927).
34. See note 23.
35. See note 24.

## STUDENT CD-ROM

For additional materials, please go to the CD in this book.

## ONLINE COMPANION™

For additional resources, please go to www.paralegal.delmar.cengage.com

# The Constitution of the United States

## PREAMBLE

We the People of the United States, in Order to form a more perfect Union, establish Justice, insure domestic Tranquility, provide for the common defence, promote the general Welfare, and secure the Blessings of Liberty to ourselves and our Posterity, do ordain and establish this Constitution for the United States of America.

## Article I

**Section 1.** All legislative Powers herein granted shall be vested in a Congress of the United States, which shall consist of a Senate and House of Representatives.

**Section 2.** The House of Representatives shall be composed of Members chosen every second Year by the People of the several States, and the Electors in each State shall have the Qualifications requisite for Electors of the most numerous Branch of the State Legislature.

No Person shall be a Representative who shall not have attained to the Age of twenty five Years, and been seven Years a Citizen of the United States, and who shall not, when elected, be an Inhabitant of that State in which he shall be chosen.

Representatives and direct Taxes shall be apportioned among the several States which may be included within this Union, according to their respective Numbers, which shall be determined by adding to the whole Number of free Persons, including those bound to Service for a Term of Years, and excluding Indians not taxed, three fifths of all other Persons. The actual Enumeration shall be made within three years after the first Meeting of the Congress of the United States, and within every subsequent Term of ten Years, in such Manner as they shall by Law direct. The Number of Representatives shall not exceed one for every thirty Thousand, but each State shall have at Least one Representative; and until such enumeration shall be made, the State of New Hampshire shall be entitled to chuse three, Massachusetts eight, Rhode Island and Providence Plantations one, Connecticut five, New York six, New Jersey four, Pennsylvania eight, Delaware one, Maryland six, Virginia ten, North Carolina five, South Carolina five, and Georgia three.

When vacancies happen in the Representation from any State, the Executive Authority thereof shall issue Writs of Election to fill such Vacancies.

The House of Representatives shall chuse their Speaker and other Officers; and shall have the sole Power of Impeachment.

**Section 3.** The Senate of the United States shall be composed of two Senators from each State, chosen by the Legislature thereof, for six Years; and each Senator shall have one Vote.

Immediately after they shall be assembled in Consequence of the first Election, they shall be divided as equally as may be into three Classes. The Seats of the Senators of the first Class shall be vacated at the Expiration of the second Year, of the second Class at the Expiration of the fourth Year, and of the third Class at the Expiration of the sixth Year, so that one third may be chosen every second Year; and if Vacancies happen by Resignation, or otherwise, during the Recess of the Legislature of any State, the Executive thereof may make temporary Appointments until the next Meeting of the Legislature, which shall then fill such Vacancies.

No Person shall be a Senator who shall not have attained to the Age of thirty Years, and been nine Years a Citizen of the United States, and who shall not, when elected, be an Inhabitant of that State for which he shall be chosen.

The Vice President of the United States shall be President of the Senate, but shall have no Vote, unless they be equally divided.

The Senate shall chuse their other Officers, and also a President pro tempore, in the Absence of the Vice President, or when he shall exercise the Office of President of the United States.

The Senate shall have the sole Power to try all Impeachments. When sitting for that Purpose, they shall be on Oath or Affirmation. When the President of the United States is tried, the Chief Justice shall preside: And no Person shall be convicted without the Concurrence of two thirds of the Members present.

Judgment in Cases of Impeachment shall not extend further than to removal from Office, and disqualification to hold and enjoy any Office of honor, Trust, or Profit under the United States: but the Party convicted shall nevertheless be liable and subject to Indictment, Trial, Judgment, and Punishment, according to Law.

**Section 4.** The Times, Places and Manner of holding Elections for Senators and Representatives, shall be prescribed in each State by the Legislature thereof; but the Congress may at any time by Law make or alter such Regulations, except as to the Places of chusing Senators.

The Congress shall assemble at least once in every Year, and such Meeting shall be on the first Monday in December, unless they shall by Law appoint a different Day.

**Section 5.** Each House shall be the Judge of the Elections, Returns, and Qualifications of its own Members, and a Majority of each shall constitute a Quorum to do Business; but a smaller Number may adjourn from day to day, and may be authorized to compel the Attendance of absent Members, in such Manner, and under such Penalties as each House may provide.

Each House may determine the Rules of its Proceedings, punish its Members for disorderly Behavior, and, with the Concurrence of two thirds, expel a Member.

Each House shall keep a Journal of its Proceedings, and from time to time publish the same, excepting such Parts as may in their Judgment require Secrecy; and the Yeas and Nays of the Members of either House on any question shall, at the Desire of one fifth of those Present, be entered on the Journal.

Neither House, during the Session of Congress, shall, without the Consent of the other, adjourn for more than three days, nor to any other Place than that in which the two Houses shall be sitting.

**Section 6.** The Senators and Representatives shall receive a Compensation for their Services, to be ascertained by Law, and paid out of the Treasury of the United States. They shall in all Cases, except Treason, Felony and Breach of the Peace, be privileged from Arrest during their Attendance at the Session of their respective Houses, and in going to and returning from the same; and for any Speech or Debate in either House, they shall not be questioned in any other Place.

No Senator or Representative shall, during the Time for which he was elected, be appointed to any civil Office under the Authority of the United States, which shall have been created, or the Emoluments whereof shall have been increased during such time; and no Person holding any Office under the United States, shall be a Member of either House during his Continuance in Office.

**Section 7.** All Bills for raising Revenue shall originate in the House of Representatives; but the Senate may propose or concur with Amendments as on other Bills.

Every Bill which shall have passed the House of Representatives and the Senate, shall, before it become a Law, be presented to the President of the United States; If he approve he shall sign it, but if not he shall return it, with his Objections to the House in which it shall have originated, who shall enter the Objections at large on their Journal, and proceed to reconsider it. If after such Reconsideration two thirds of that House shall agree to pass the Bill, it shall be sent together with the Objections, to the other House, by which it shall likewise be reconsidered, and if approved by two thirds of that House, it shall become a Law. But in all such Cases the Votes of both Houses shall be determined by Yeas and Nays, and the Names of the Persons voting for and against the Bill shall be entered on the Journal of each House respectively. If any Bill shall not be returned by the President within ten Days (Sundays excepted) after it shall have been presented to him, the Same shall be a Law, in like Manner as if he had signed it, unless the Congress by their Adjournment prevent its Return in which Case it shall not be a Law.

Every Order, Resolution, or Vote, to which the Concurrence of the Senate and House of Representatives may be necessary (except on a question of Adjournment) shall be presented to the President of the United States;

and before the Same shall take Effect, shall be approved by him, or being disapproved by him, shall be repassed by two thirds of the Senate and House of Representatives, according to the Rules and Limitations prescribed in the Case of a Bill.

**Section 8.** The Congress shall have Power To lay and collect Taxes, Duties, Imposts and Excises, to pay the Debts and provide for the common Defence and general Welfare of the United States; but all Duties, Imposts and Excises shall be uniform throughout the United States;

To borrow Money on the credit of the United States;

To regulate Commerce with foreign Nations, and among the several States, and with the Indian Tribes;

To establish an uniform Rule of Naturalization, and uniform Laws on the subject of Bankruptcies throughout the United States;

To coin Money, regulate the Value thereof, and of foreign Coin, and fix the Standard of Weights and Measures;

To provide for the Punishment of counterfeiting the Securities and current Coin of the United States;

To establish Post Offices and post Roads;

To promote the Progress of Science and useful Arts, by securing for limited Times to Authors and Inventors the exclusive Right to their respective Writings and Discoveries;

To constitute Tribunals inferior to the supreme Court;

To define and punish Piracies and Felonies committed on the high Seas, and Offenses against the Law of Nations;

To declare War, grant Letters of Marque and Reprisal, and make Rules concerning Captures on Land and Water;

To raise and support Armies, but no Appropriation of Money to that Use shall be for a longer Term than two Years;

To provide and maintain a Navy;

To make Rules for the Government and Regulation of the land and naval Forces;

To provide for calling forth the Militia to execute the Laws of the Union, suppress Insurrections and repel Invasions;

To provide for organizing, arming, and disciplining, the Militia, and for governing such Part of them as may be employed in the Service of the United States, reserving to the States respectively, the Appointment of the Officers, and the Authority of training the Militia according to the discipline prescribed by Congress;

To exercise exclusive Legislation in all Cases whatsoever, over such District (not exceeding ten Miles square) as may, by Cession of particular States, and the Acceptance of Congress, become the Seat of the Government of the United States, and to exercise like Authority over all Places purchased by the Consent of the Legislature of the State in which the Same shall be, for the Erection of Forts, Magazines, Arsenals, dock-Yards, and other needful Buildings;—And

To make all Laws which shall be necessary and proper for carrying into Execution the foregoing Powers, and all other Powers vested by this Constitution in the Government of the United States, or in any Department or Officer thereof.

**Section 9.** The Migration or Importation of such Persons as any of the States now existing shall think proper to admit, shall not be prohibited by the Congress prior to the Year one thousand eight hundred and eight, but a Tax or duty may be imposed on such Importation, not exceeding ten dollars for each Person.

The privilege of the Writ of Habeas Corpus shall not be suspended, unless when in Cases of Rebellion or Invasion the public Safety may require it.

No Bill of Attainder or ex post facto Law shall be passed.

No Capitation, or other direct, Tax shall be laid, unless in Proportion to the Census or Enumeration herein before directed to be taken.

No Tax or Duty shall be laid on Articles exported from any State.

No Preference shall be given by any Regulation of Commerce or Revenue to the Ports of one State over those of another: nor shall Vessels bound to, or from, one State be obliged to enter, clear, or pay Duties in another.

No Money shall be drawn from the Treasury, but in Consequence of Appropriations made by Law; and a regular Statement and Account of the Receipts and Expenditures of all public Money shall be published from time to time.

No Title of Nobility shall be granted by the United States: And no Person holding any Office of Profit or Trust under them, shall, without the Consent of the Congress, accept of any present, Emolument, Office, or Title, of any kind whatever, from any King, Prince, or foreign State.

**Section 10.** No State shall enter into any Treaty, Alliance, or Confederation; grant Letters of Marque and Reprisal; coin Money; emit Bills of Credit; make any Thing but gold and silver Coin a Tender in Payment of Debts; pass any Bill of Attainder, ex post facto Law, or Law impairing the Obligation of Contracts, or grant any Title of Nobility.

No State shall, without the Consent of the Congress, lay any Imposts or Duties on Imports or Exports, except what may be absolutely necessary for executing it's inspection Laws: and the net Produce of all Duties and Imposts, laid by any State on Imports or Exports, shall be for the Use of the Treasury of the United States, and all such Laws shall be subject to the Revision and Controul of the Congress.

No State shall, without the Consent of Congress, lay any Duty of Tonnage, keep Troops, or Ships of War in time of Peace, enter into any Agreement or Compact with another State, or with a foreign Power, or engage in War, unless actually invaded, or in such imminent Danger as will not admit of delay.

## Article II

**Section 1.** The executive Power shall be vested in a President of the United States of America. He shall hold his Office during the Term of four Years, and, together with the Vice President, chosen for the same Term, be elected, as follows:

Each State shall appoint, in such Manner as the Legislature thereof may direct, a Number of Electors, equal to the whole Number of Senators and Representatives to which the State may be entitled in the Congress; but no Senator or Representative, or Person holding an Office of Trust or Profit under the United States, shall be appointed an Elector.

The Electors shall meet in their respective States, and vote by Ballot for two Persons, of whom one at least shall not be an Inhabitant of the same State with themselves. And they shall make a List of all the Persons voted for, and of the Number of Votes for each; which List they shall sign and certify, and transmit sealed to the Seat of the Government of the United States, directed to the President of the Senate. The President of the Senate shall, in the Presence of the Senate and House of Representatives, open all the Certificates, and the Votes shall then be counted. The Person having the greatest Number of Votes shall be the President, if such Number be a Majority of the whole Number of Electors appointed; and if there be more than one who have such Majority, and have an equal Number of Votes, then the House of Representatives shall immediately chuse by Ballot one of them for President; and if no Person have a Majority, then from the five highest on the List the said House shall in like Manner chuse the President. But in chusing the President, the Votes shall be taken by States, the Representation from each State having one Vote; A quorum for this Purpose shall consist of a Member or Members from two thirds of the States, and a Majority of all the States shall be necessary to a Choice. In every Case, after the Choice of the President, the Person having the greater Number of Votes of the Electors shall be the Vice President. But if there should remain two or more who have equal Votes, the Senate shall chuse from them by Ballot the Vice President.

The Congress may determine the Time of chusing the Electors, and the Day on which they shall give their Votes; which Day shall be the same throughout the United States.

No person except a natural born Citizen, or a Citizen of the United States, at the time of the Adoption of this Constitution, shall be eligible to the Office of President; neither shall any Person be eligible to that Office who shall not have attained to the Age of thirty five Years, and been fourteen Years a Resident within the United States.

In Case of the Removal of the President from Office, or of his Death, Resignation or Inability to discharge the Powers and Duties of the said Office, the same shall devolve on the Vice President, and the Congress may by Law provide for the Case of Removal, Death, Resignation or Inability, both of the President and Vice President, declaring what Officer shall then act as President, and such Officer shall act accordingly, until the Disability be removed, or a President shall be elected.

The President shall, at stated Times, receive for his Services, a Compensation, which shall neither be increased nor diminished during the Period for which he shall have been elected, and he shall not receive within that Period any other Emolument from the United States, or any of them.

Before he enter on the Execution of his Office, he shall take the following Oath or Affirmation: "I do solemnly swear (or affirm) that I will faithfully execute the Office of President of the United States, and will to the best of my Ability, preserve, protect and defend the Constitution of the United States."

**Section 2.** The President shall be Commander in Chief of the Army and Navy of the United States, and of the Militia of the several States, when called into the actual Service of the United States; he may require the Opinion, in writing, of the principal Officer in each of the executive Departments, upon any Subject relating to the Duties of their respective Offices, and he shall have Power to grant Reprieves and Pardons for Offenses against the United States, except in Cases of Impeachment.

He shall have Power, by and with the Advice and Consent of the Senate to make Treaties, provided two thirds of the Senators present concur; and he shall nominate, and by and with the Advice and Consent of the Senate, shall appoint Ambassadors, other public Ministers and Consuls, Judges of the supreme Court, and all other Officers of the United States, whose Appointments are not herein otherwise provided for, and which shall be established by Law; but the Congress may by Law vest the Appointment of such inferior Officers, as they think proper, in the President alone, in the Courts of Law, or in the Heads of Departments.

The President shall have Power to fill up all Vacancies that may happen during the Recess of the Senate, by granting Commissions which shall expire at the End of their next Session.

**Section 3.** He shall from time to time give to the Congress Information of the State of the Union, and recommend to their Consideration such Measures as he shall judge necessary and expedient; he may, on extraordinary Occasions, convene both Houses, or either of them, and in Case of Disagreement between them, with Respect to the Time of Adjournment, he may adjourn them to such Time as he shall think proper; he shall receive Ambassadors and other public Ministers; he shall take Care that the Laws be faithfully executed, and shall Commission all the Officers of the United States.

**Section 4.** The President, Vice President and all civil Officers of the United States, shall be removed from Office on Impeachment for, and Conviction of, Treason, Bribery, or other high Crimes and Misdemeanors.

## Article III

**Section 1.** The judicial Power of the United States, shall be vested in one supreme Court, and in such inferior Courts as the Congress may from time to time ordain and establish. The Judges, both of the supreme and inferior Courts, shall hold their Offices during good Behaviour, and shall, at stated Times, receive for their Services a Compensation, which shall not be diminished during their Continuance in Office.

**Section 2.** The judicial Power shall extend to all Cases, in Law and Equity, arising under this Constitution, the Laws of the United States, and Treaties made, or which shall be made, under their Authority;—to all Cases affecting Ambassadors, other public Ministers and Consuls;—to all Cases of admiralty and maritime Jurisdiction;—to Controversies to which the United States shall be a Party;—to Controversies between two or more States;—between a State and Citizens of another State;—between Citizens of different States;—between Citizens of the same State claiming Lands under Grants of different States, and between a State, or the Citizens thereof, and foreign States, Citizens or Subjects.

In all Cases affecting Ambassadors, other public Ministers and Consuls, and those in which a State shall be a Party, the supreme Court shall have original Jurisdiction. In all the other Cases before mentioned, the supreme Court shall have appellate Jurisdiction, both as to Law and Fact, with such Exceptions, and under such Regulations as the Congress shall make.

The Trial of all Crimes, except in Cases of Impeachment, shall be by Jury; and such Trial shall be held in the State where the said Crimes shall have been committed; but when not committed within any State, the Trial shall be at such Place or Places as the Congress may by Law have directed.

**Section 3.** Treason against the United States, shall consist only in levying War against them, or, in adhering to their Enemies, giving them Aid and Comfort. No Person shall be convicted of Treason unless on the Testimony of two Witnesses to the same overt Act, or on Confession in open Court.

The Congress shall have Power to declare the Punishment of Treason, but no Attainder of Treason shall work Corruption of Blood, or Forfeiture except during the Life of the Person attained.

## Article IV

**Section 1.** Full Faith and Credit shall be given in each State to the public Acts, Records, and judicial Proceedings of every other State. And the Congress may by general Laws prescribe the Manner in which such Acts, Records and Proceedings shall be proved, and the Effect thereof.

**Section 2.** The Citizens of each State shall be entitled to all Privileges and Immunities of Citizens in the several States.

A Person charged in any State with Treason, Felony, or other Crime, who shall flee from Justice, and be found in another State, shall on Demand of the executive Authority of the State from which he fled, be delivered up, to be removed to the State having Jurisdiction of the Crime.

No Person held to Service or Labour in one State, under the Laws thereof, escaping into another, shall, in Consequence of any Law or Regulation therein, be discharged from such Service or Labour, but shall be delivered up on Claim of the Party to whom such Service or Labour may be due.

**Section 3.** New States may be admitted by the Congress into this Union; but no new State shall be formed or erected within the Jurisdiction of any other State; nor any State be formed by the Junction of two or more States, or Parts of States, without the Consent of the Legislatures of the States concerned as well as of the Congress.

The Congress shall have Power to dispose of and make all needful Rules and Regulations respecting the Territory or other Property belonging to the United States; and nothing in this Constitution shall be so construed as to Prejudice any Claims of the United States, or of any particular State.

**Section 4.** The United States shall guarantee to every State in this Union a Republican Form of Government, and shall protect each of them against Invasion; and on Application of the Legislature, or of the Executive (when the Legislature cannot be convened) against domestic Violence.

## Article V

The Congress, whenever two thirds of both Houses shall deem it necessary, shall propose Amendments to this Constitution, or, on the Application of the Legislatures of two thirds of the several States, shall call a Convention for proposing Amendments, which, in either Case, shall be valid to all Intents and Purposes, as part of this Constitution, when ratified by the Legislatures of three fourths of the several States, or by Conventions in three fourths thereof, as the one or the other Mode of Ratification may be proposed by the Congress; Provided that no Amendment which may be made prior to the Year One thousand eight hundred and eight shall in any Manner affect the first and fourth Clauses in the Ninth Section of the first Article; and that no State, without its Consent, shall be deprived of its equal Suffrage in the Senate.

## Article VI

All Debts contracted and Engagements entered into, before the Adoption of this Constitution shall be as valid against the United States under this Constitution, as under the Confederation.

This Constitution, and the Laws of the United States which shall be made in Pursuance thereof; and all Treaties made, or which shall be made, under the Authority of the United States, shall be the supreme Law of the Land; and the Judges in every State shall be bound thereby, any Thing in the Constitution or Laws of any State to the Contrary notwithstanding.

The Senators and Representatives before mentioned, and the Members of the several State Legislatures, and all executive and judicial Officers, both of the United States and of the several States, shall be bound by Oath or Affirmation, to support this Constitution; but no religious Test shall ever be required as a Qualification to any Office or public Trust under the United States.

## Article VII

The Ratification of the Conventions of nine States shall be sufficient for the Establishment of this Constitution between the States so ratifying the Same.

## AMENDMENT I [1791]

Congress shall make no law respecting an establishment of religion, or prohibiting the free exercise thereof; or abridging the freedom of speech, or of the press; or the right of the people peaceably to assembly, and to petition the Government for a redress of grievances.

## AMENDMENT II [1791]

A well regulated Militia, being necessary to the security of a free State, the right of the people to keep and bear Arms, shall not be infringed.

## AMENDMENT III [1791]

No Soldier shall, in time of peace be quartered in any house, without the consent of the Owner, nor in time of war, but in a manner to be prescribed by law.

## AMENDMENT IV [1791]

The right of the people to be secure in their persons, houses, papers, and effects, against unreasonable searches and seizures, shall not be violated, and no Warrants shall issue, but upon probable cause, supported by Oath or affirmation, and particularly describing the place to be searched, and the persons or things to be seized.

## AMENDMENT V [1791]

No person shall be held to answer for a capital, or otherwise infamous crime, unless on a presentment or indictment of a Grand Jury, except in cases arising in the land or naval forces, or in the Militia, when in actual service in time of War or public danger; nor shall any person be subject for the same offence to be twice put in jeopardy of life or limb; nor shall be compelled in any criminal case to be a witness against himself, nor be deprived of life, liberty, or property, without due process of law; nor shall private property be taken for public use, without just compensation.

## AMENDMENT VI [1791]

In all criminal prosecutions, the accused shall enjoy the right to a speedy and public trial, by an impartial jury of the State and district wherein the crime shall have been committed, which district shall have been previously ascertained by law, and to be informed of the nature and cause of the accusation; to be confronted with the witnesses against him; to have compulsory process for obtaining witnesses in his favor, and to have the Assistance of Counsel for his defence.

## AMENDMENT VII [1791]

In Suits at common law, where the value in controversy shall exceed twenty dollars, the right of trial by jury shall be preserved, and no fact tried by jury, shall be otherwise re-examined in any Court of the United States, than according to the rules of the common law.

## AMENDMENT VIII [1791]

Excessive bail shall not be required, nor excessive fines imposed, nor cruel and unusual punishments inflicted.

## AMENDMENT IX [1791]

The enumeration in the Constitution, of certain rights, shall not be construed to deny or disparage others retained by the people.

## AMENDMENT X [1791]

The powers not delegated to the United States by the Constitution, nor prohibited by it to the States, are reserved to the States respectively, or to the people.

## AMENDMENT XI [1798]

The Judicial power of the United States shall not be construed to extend to any suit in law or equity, commenced or prosecuted against one of the United States by Citizens of another State, or by Citizens or Subjects of any Foreign State.

## AMENDMENT XII [1804]

The Electors shall meet in their respective states, and vote by ballot for President and Vice-President, one of whom, at least, shall not be an inhabitant of the same state with themselves; they shall name in their ballots the person voted for as President, and in distinct ballots the person voted for as Vice-President, and they shall make distinct lists of all persons voted for as President, and of all persons voted for as Vice-President, and of the number of votes for each, which lists they shall sign and certify, and transmit sealed to the seat of the government of the United States, directed to the President of the Senate;—The President of the Senate shall, in the presence of the Senate and House of Representatives, open all the certificates and the votes shall then be counted;—The person having the greatest number of votes for President, shall be the President, if such number be a majority of the whole number of Electors appointed; and if no person have such majority, then from the persons having the highest numbers not exceeding three on the list of those voted for as President, the House of Representatives shall choose immediately, by ballot, the President. But in choosing the President, the votes shall be taken by states, the representation from each state having one vote; a quorum for this purpose shall consist of a member or members from two-thirds of the states, and a majority of all states shall be necessary to a choice. And if the House of Representatives shall not choose a President whenever the right of choice shall devolve upon them, before the fourth day of March next following, then the Vice-President shall act as President, as in the case of the death or other constitutional disability of the President.—The person having the greatest number of votes as Vice-President, shall be the Vice-President, if such number be a majority of the whole number of Electors appointed, and if no person have a majority, then from the two highest numbers on the list, the Senate shall choose the Vice-President; a quorum for the purpose shall consist of two-thirds of the whole number of Senators, and a majority of the whole number shall be necessary to a choice. But no person constitutionally ineligible to the office of President shall be eligible to that of Vice-President of the United States.

## AMENDMENT XIII [1865]

**Section 1.** Neither slavery nor involuntary servitude, except as a punishment for crime whereof the party shall have been duly convicted, shall exist within the United States, or any place subject to their jurisdiction.

**Section 2.** Congress shall have power to enforce this article by appropriate legislation.

## AMENDMENT XIV [1868]

**Section 1.** All persons born or naturalized in the United States, and subject to the jurisdiction thereof, are citizens of the United States and of the State wherein they reside. No State shall make or enforce any law which shall abridge the privileges or immunities of citizens of the United States; nor shall any State deprive any person of life, liberty, or property, without due process of law; nor deny to any person within its jurisdiction the equal protection of the laws.

**Section 2.** Representatives shall be apportioned among the several States according to their respective numbers, counting the whole number of persons in each State, excluding Indians not taxed. But when the right to vote at any election for the choice of electors for President and Vice President of the United States, Representatives in Congress, the Executive and Judicial officers of a State, or the members of the Legislature thereof, is denied to any of the male inhabitants of such State, being twenty-one years of age, and citizens of the United States, or in any way abridged, except for participation in rebellion, or other crime, the basis of representation therein shall be reduced in the proportion which the number of such male citizens shall bear to the whole number of male citizens twenty-one years of age in such State.

**Section 3.** No person shall be a Senator or Representative in Congress, or elector of President and Vice President, or hold any office, civil or military, under the United States, or under any State, who having previously taken an oath, as a member of Congress, or as an officer of the United States, or as a member of any State legislature, or as an executive or judicial officer of any State, to support the Constitution of the United States, shall have engaged in insurrection or rebellion against the same, or given aid or comfort to the enemies thereof. But Congress may by a vote of two-thirds of each House, remove such disability.

**Section 4.** The validity of the public debt of the United States, authorized by law, including debts incurred for payment of pensions and bounties for services in suppressing insurrection or rebellion, shall not be questioned. But neither the United States nor any State shall assume or pay any debt or obligation incurred in aid of insurrection or rebellion against the United States, or any claim for the loss or emancipation of any slave; but all such debts, obligations and claims shall be held illegal and void.

**Section 5.** The Congress shall have power to enforce, by appropriate legislation, the provisions of this article.

## AMENDMENT XV [1870]

**Section 1.** The right of citizens of the United States to vote shall not be denied or abridged by the United States or by any State on account of race, color, or previous condition of servitude.

**Section 2.** The Congress shall have power to enforce this article by appropriate legislation.

## AMENDMENT XVI [1913]

The Congress shall have power to lay and collect taxes on incomes, from whatever source derived, without apportionment among the several States, and without regard to any census or enumeration.

## AMENDMENT XVII [1913]

1. The Senate of the United States shall be composed of two Senators from each State, elected by the people thereof, for six years; and each Senator shall have one vote. The electors in each State shall have the qualifications requisite for electors of the most numerous branch of the State legislatures.

2. When vacancies happen in the representation of any State in the Senate, the executive authority of such State shall issue writs of election to fill such vacancies: Provided, That the legislature of any State may empower the executive thereof to make temporary appointments until the people fill the vacancies by election as the legislature may direct.

3. This amendment shall not be so construed as to affect the election or term of any Senator chosen before it becomes valid as part of the Constitution.

## AMENDMENT XVIII [1919]

**Section 1.** After one year from the ratification of this article the manufacture, sale, or transportation of intoxicating liquors within, the importation thereof into, or the exportation thereof from the United States and all territory subject to the jurisdiction thereof for beverage purposes is hereby prohibited.

**Section 2.** The Congress and the several States shall have concurrent power to enforce this article by appropriate legislation.

**Section 3.** This article shall be inoperative unless it shall have been ratified as an amendment to the Constitution by the legislatures of the several States, as provided in the Constitution, within seven years from the date of the submission hereof to the States by the Congress.

## AMENDMENT XIX [1920]

1. The right of citizens of the United States to vote shall not be denied or abridged by the United States or by any State on account of sex.
2. Congress shall have power to enforce this article by appropriate legislation.

## AMENDMENT XX [1933]

**Section 1.** The terms of the President and Vice President shall end at noon on the 20th day of January, and the terms of Senators and Representatives at noon on the 3d day of January, of the years in which such terms would have ended if this article had not been ratified; and the terms of their successors shall then begin.

**Section 2.** The Congress shall assemble at least once in every year, and such meeting shall begin at noon on the 3d day of January, unless they shall by law appoint a different day.

**Section 3.** If, at the time fixed for the beginning of the term of the President, the President elect shall have died, the Vice President elect shall become President. If the President shall not have been chosen before the time fixed for the beginning of his term, or if the President elect shall have failed to qualify, then the Vice President elect shall act as President until a President shall have qualified; and the Congress may by law provide for the case wherein neither a President elect nor a Vice President elect shall have qualified, declaring who shall then act as President, or the manner in which one who is to act shall be selected, and such person shall act accordingly until a President or Vice President shall have qualified.

**Section 4.** The Congress may by law provide for the case of the death of any of the persons from whom the House of Representatives may choose a President whenever the right of choice shall have devolved upon them, and for the case of the death of any of the persons from whom the Senate may choose a Vice President whenever the right of choice shall have devolved upon them.

**Section 5.** Sections 1 and 2 shall take effect on the 15th day of October following the ratification of this article.

**Section 6.** This article shall be inoperative unless it shall have been ratified as an amendment to the Constitution by the legislatures of three-fourths of the several States within seven years from the date of its submission.

## AMENDMENT XXI [1933]

**Section 1.** The eighteenth article of amendment to the Constitution of the United States is hereby repealed.

**Section 2.** The transportation or importation into any State, Territory, or possession of the United States for delivery or use therein of intoxicating liquors, in violation of the laws thereof, is hereby prohibited.

**Section 3.** This article shall be inoperative unless it shall have been ratified as an amendment to the Constitution by conventions in the several States, as provided in the Constitution, within seven years from the date of the submission hereof to the States by the Congress.

## AMENDMENT XXII [1951]

**Section 1.** No person shall be elected to the office of the President more than twice, and no person who has held the office of President, or acted as President, for more than two years of a term to which some other person was elected President shall be elected to the office of President more than once. But this Article shall not apply to any person holding the office of President when this Article was proposed by the Congress, and shall not prevent any person who may be holding the office of President, or acting as President, during the term within which this Article becomes operative from holding the office of President or acting as President during the remainder of such term.

**Section 2.** This article shall be inoperative unless it shall have been ratified as an amendment to the Constitution by the legislatures of three-fourths of the several States within seven years from the date of its submission to the States by the Congress.

## AMENDMENT XXIII [1961]

**Section 1.** The District constituting the seat of Government of the United States shall appoint in such manner as the Congress may direct:

A number of electors of President and Vice President equal to the whole number of Senators and Representatives in Congress to which the District would be entitled if it were a State, but in no event more than the least populous state; they shall be in addition to those appointed by the states, but they shall be considered, for the purposes of the election of President and Vice President, to be electors appointed by a state; and they shall meet in the District and perform such duties as provided by the twelfth article of amendment.

**Section 2.** The Congress shall have power to enforce this article by appropriate legislation.

## AMENDMENT XXIV [1964]

**Section 1.** The right of citizens of the United States to vote in any primary or other election for President or Vice President, for electors for President or Vice President, or for Senator or Representative in Congress, shall not be denied or abridged by the United States, or any State by reason of failure to pay any poll tax or other tax.

**Section 2.** The Congress shall have power to enforce this article by appropriate legislation.

## AMENDMENT XXV [1967]

**Section 1.** In case of the removal of the President from office or of his death or resignation, the Vice President shall become President.

**Section 2.** Whenever there is a vacancy in the office of the Vice President, the President shall nominate a Vice President who shall take office upon confirmation by a majority vote of both Houses of Congress.

**Section 3.** Whenever the President transmits to the President pro tempore of the Senate and the Speaker of the House of Representatives his written declaration that he is unable to discharge the powers and duties of his office, and until he transmits to them a written declaration to the contrary, such powers and duties shall be discharged by the Vice President as Acting President.

**Section 4.** Whenever the Vice President and a majority of either the principal officers of the executive departments or of such other body as Congress may by law provide, transmit to the President pro tempore of the Senate and the Speaker of the House of Representatives their written declaration that the President is unable to discharge the powers and duties of his office, the Vice President shall immediately assume the powers and duties of the office as Acting President.

Thereafter, when the President transmits to the President pro tempore of the Senate and the Speaker of the House of Representatives his written declaration that no inability exists, he shall resume the powers and duties of his office unless the Vice President and a majority of either the principal officers of the executive department or of such other body as Congress may by law provide, transmit within four days to the President pro tempore of the Senate and the Speaker of the House of Representatives their written declaration and the President is unable to discharge the powers and duties of his office. Thereupon Congress shall decide the issue, assembling within forty-eight hours for that purpose if not in session. If the Congress, within twenty-one days after receipt of the latter written declaration, or, if Congress is not in session, within twenty-one days after Congress is required to assemble, determines by two-thirds vote of both Houses that the President is unable to discharge the powers and duties of his office, the Vice President shall continue to discharge the same as Acting President; otherwise, the President shall resume the powers and duties of his office.

## AMENDMENT XXVI [1971]

**Section 1.** The right of citizens of the United States, who are eighteen years of age or older, to vote shall not be denied or abridged by the United States or by any State on account of age.

**Section 2.** The Congress shall have power to enforce this article by appropriate legislation.

## AMENDMENT XXVII [1992]

No law varying the compensation for the services of the Senators and Representatives shall take effect, until an election of Representatives shall have intervened.

# NALA Code of Ethics and Professional Responsibility

A legal assistant must adhere strictly to the accepted standards of legal ethics and to the general principles of proper conduct. The performance of the duties of the legal assistant shall be governed by specific canons as defined herein so that justice will be served and goals of the profession attained. (See Model Standards and Guidelines for Utilization of Legal Assistants, Section II.)

The canons of ethics set forth hereafter are adopted by the National Association of Legal Assistants, Inc., as a general guide intended to aid legal assistants and attorneys. The enumeration of these rules does not mean there are not others of equal importance although not specifically mentioned. Court rules, agency rules and statutes must be taken into consideration when interpreting the canons.

**Definition:** Legal assistants, also known as paralegals, are a distinguishable group of persons who assist attorneys in the delivery of legal services. Through formal education, training and experience, legal assistants have knowledge and expertise regarding the legal system and substantive and procedural law which qualify them to do work of a legal nature under the supervision of an attorney.

## Canon 1

A legal assistant must not perform any of the duties that attorneys only may perform nor take any actions that attorneys may not take.

## Canon 2

A legal assistant may perform any task which is properly delegated and supervised by an attorney, as long as the attorney is ultimately responsible to the client, maintains a direct relationship with the client, and assumes professional responsibility for the work product.

## Canon 3

A legal assistant must not: (a) engage in, encourage, or contribute to any act which could constitute the unauthorized practice of law; and (b) establish attorney-client relationships, set fees, give legal opinions or advice or represent a client before a court or agency unless so authorized by that court or agency; and (c) engage in conduct or take any action which would assist or involve the attorney in a violation of professional ethics or give the appearance of professional impropriety.

## Canon 4

A legal assistant must use discretion and professional judgment commensurate with knowledge and experience but must not render independent legal judgment in place of an attorney. The services of an attorney are essential in the public interest whenever such legal judgment is required.

## Canon 5

A legal assistant must disclose his or her status as a legal assistant at the outset of any professional relationship with a client, attorney, a court or administrative agency or personnel thereof, or a member of the general public. A legal assistant must act prudently in determining the extent to which a client may be assisted without the presence of an attorney.

## Canon 6

A legal assistant must strive to maintain integrity and a high degree of competency through education and training with respect to professional responsibility, local rules and practice, and through continuing education in substantive areas of law to better assist the legal profession in fulfilling its duty to provide legal service.

## Canon 7

A legal assistant must protect the confidences of a client and must not violate any rule or statute now in effect or hereafter enacted controlling the doctrine of privileged communications between a client and an attorney.

## Canon 8

A legal assistant must do all other things incidental, necessary, or expedient for the attainment of the ethics and responsibilities as defined by statute or rule of court.

## Canon 9

A legal assistant's conduct is guided by bar associations' codes of professional responsibility and rules of professional conduct.

# NALA Model Standards and Guidelines for Utilization of Legal Assistants

NALA's study of the professional responsibility and ethical considerations of legal assistants is ongoing. This research led to the development of the NALA Model Standards and Guidelines for Utilization of Legal Assistants. This guide summarizes case law, guidelines, and ethical opinions of the various states affecting legal assistants. It provides an outline of minimum qualifications and standards necessary for legal assistant professionals to assure the public and the legal profession that they are, indeed, qualified. The following is a listing of the standards and guidelines.

The annotated version of the Model was revised extensively in 1997. It is on-line at www.nala.org and may be ordered through NALA Headquarters.

## INTRODUCTION

Proper utilization of the services of legal assistants affects the efficient delivery of legal services. Legal assistants and the legal profession should be assured that some measures exist for identifying legal assistants and their role in assisting attorneys in the delivery of legal services. Therefore, the National Association of Legal Assistants, Inc., hereby adopts these Model Standards and Guidelines as an educational document for the benefit of legal assistants and the legal profession.

Comment—NALA Definition

## STANDARDS

A legal assistant should meet certain minimum qualifications. The following standards may be used to determine an individual's qualifications as a legal assistant:

1. Successful completion of the Certified Legal Assistant certifying (CLA) examination of the National Association of Legal Assistants;
2. Graduation from an ABA approved program of study for legal assistants;
3. Graduation from a course of study for legal assistants which is institutionally accredited but not ABA approved, and which requires not less than the equivalent of 60 semester hours of classroom study;
4. Graduation from a course of study for legal assistant, other than those set forth in (2) and (3) above, plus not less than six months of in-house training as a legal assistant.
5. A baccalaureate degree in any field, plus not less than six months in-house training as a legal assistant;
6. A minimum of three years of law-related experience under the supervision of an attorney, including at least six months of in-house training as a legal assistant; or
7. Two years of in-house training as a legal assistant.

For purposes of these Standards, "in-house training as a legal assistant" means attorney education of the employee concerning legal assistant duties and these Guidelines. In addition to review and analysis of assignments the legal assistant should receive a reasonable amount of instruction directly related to the duties and obligations of the legal assistant.

## GUIDELINES

These guidelines relating to standards of performance and professional responsibility are intended to aid legal assistants and attorneys. The responsibility rests with an attorney who employs legal assistants to educate them with respect to the duties they are assigned to supervise the manner in which such duties are accomplished.

## Guideline 1

Legal assistants should:

1. Disclose their status as legal assistants at the outset of any professional relationship with a client, other attorneys, a court or administrative agency or personnel thereof, or members of the general public;
2. Preserve the confidences and secrets of all clients; and
3. Understand the attorney's Code of Professional Responsibility and these guidelines in order to avoid any action which would involve the attorney in a violation of that Code, or give the appearance of professional impropriety.

## Guideline 2

Legal assistants should not:

1. Establish attorney–client relationships; set legal fees, give legal opinions or advice; or represent a client before a court; nor
2. Engage in, encourage, or contribute to any act which could constitute the unauthorized practice of law.

## Guideline 3

Legal assistants may perform services for an attorney in the representation of a client, provided:

1. The services performed by the legal assistant do not require the exercise of independent professional legal judgment;
2. The attorney maintains a direct relationship with the client and maintains control of all client matters;
3. The attorney supervises the legal assistant;
4. The attorney remains professionally responsible for all work on behalf of the client, including any actions taken or not taken by the legal assistant in connection therewith; and
5. The services performed supplement, merge with and become the attorney's work product.

## Guideline 4

In the supervision of a legal assistant, consideration should be given to:

1. Designating work assignments that correspond to the legal assistant's abilities, knowledge, training and experience.
2. Education and training the legal assistant with respect to professional responsibility, local rules and practices, and firm policies;
3. Monitoring the work and professional conduct of the legal assistant to ensure that the work is substantively correct and timely performed;
4. Providing continuing education for the legal assistant in substantive matters through courses, institutes, workshops, seminars and in-house training, and
5. Encouraging and supporting membership and active participation in professional organizations.

## Guideline 5

Except as otherwise provided by statute, court rule or decision, administrative rule or regulation, or the attorney's Code of Professional Responsibility; and within the preceding parameters and proscriptions, a legal assistant may perform any function delegated by an attorney, including but not limited to the following:

1. Conduct client interviews and maintain general contact with the client after the establishment of the attorney–client relationship, so long as the client is aware of the status and function of the legal assistant, and the client contact is under the supervision of the attorney.

2. Locate and interview witnesses, so long as the witnesses are aware of the status and function of the legal assistant.

3. Conduct investigations and statistical and documentary research for review by the attorney.

4. Conduct legal research for review by the attorney.

5. Draft legal documents for review by the attorney.

6. Draft correspondence and pleadings for review by and signature of the attorney.

7. Summarize depositions, interrogatories, and testimony for review by the attorney.

8. Attend executions of wills, real estate closings, depositions, court or administrative hearings and trials with the attorney.

9. Author and sign letters provided the legal assistant's status is clearly indicated and the correspondence does not contain independent legal opinions or legal advice.

The notes to accompany the NALA Model Standards and Guidelines for Utilization of Legal Assistants are updated regularly by the NALA Professional Development Committee. The standards and guidelines are adopted by the NALA membership, and changes to these provisions must be brought before NALA members during their annual meeting in July.

# National Federation of Paralegal Associations, Inc. Model Code of Ethics and Professional Responsibility and Guidelines for Enforcement

## PREAMBLE

The National Federation of Paralegal Associations, Inc. ("NFPA") is a professional organization comprised of paralegal associations and individual paralegals throughout the United States and Canada. Members of NFPA have varying backgrounds, experiences, education, and job responsibilities that reflect the diversity of the paralegal profession. NFPA promotes the growth, development and recognition of the paralegal profession as an integral partner in the delivery of legal services.

In May 1993 NFPA adopted its Model Code of Ethics and Professional Responsibility ("Model Code") to delineate the principles for ethics and conduct to which every paralegal should aspire.

Many paralegal associations throughout the United States have endorsed the concept and content of NFPA's Model Code through the adoption of their own ethical codes. In doing so, paralegals have confirmed the profession's commitment to increase the quality and efficiency of legal services, as well as recognized its responsibilities to the public, the legal community, and colleagues.

Paralegals have recognized, and will continue to recognize, that the profession must continue to evolve to enhance their roles in the delivery of legal services. With increased levels of responsibility comes the need to define and enforce mandatory rules of professional conduct. Enforcement of codes of paralegal conduct is a logical and necessary step to enhance and ensure the confidence of the legal community and the public in the integrity and professional responsibility of paralegals.

In April 1997 NFPA adopted the Model Disciplinary Rules ("Model Rules") to make possible the enforcement of the Canons and Ethical Considerations contained in the NFPA Model Code. A concurrent determination was made that the Model Code of Ethics and Professional Responsibility, formerly aspirational in nature, should be recognized as setting forth the enforceable obligations of all paralegals.

The Model Code and Model Rules offer a framework for professional discipline, either voluntarily or through formal regulatory programs.

## § 1. NFPA MODEL DISCIPLINARY RULES AND ETHICAL CONSIDERATIONS

### 1.1 A Paralegal shall Achieve and Maintain a High Level of Competence

**Ethical Considerations**

EC-1.1(a) A paralegal shall achieve competency through education, training, and work experience.

EC-1.1(b) A paralegal shall aspire to participate in a minimum of twelve (12) hours of continuing legal education, to include at least one (1) hour of ethics education, every two (2) years in order to remain current on developments in the law.

EC-1.1(c) A paralegal shall perform all assignments promptly and efficiently.

## 1.2 A Paralegal shall Maintain a High Level of Personal and Professional Integrity

### Ethical Considerations

EC-1.2(a) A paralegal shall not engage in any ex parte communications involving the courts or any other adjudicatory body in an attempt to exert undue influence or to obtain advantage or the benefit of only one party.

EC-1.2(b) A paralegal shall not communicate, or cause another to communicate, with a party the paralegal knows to be represented by a lawyer in a pending matter without the prior consent of the lawyer representing such other party.

EC-1.2(c) A paralegal shall ensure that all timekeeping and billing records prepared by the paralegal are thorough, accurate, honest, and complete.

EC-1.2(d) A paralegal shall not knowingly engage in fraudulent billing practices. Such practices may include, but are not limited to: inflation of hours billed to a client or employer; misrepresentation of the nature of tasks performed; and/or submission of fraudulent expense and disbursement documentation.

EC-1.2(e) A paralegal shall be scrupulous, thorough and honest in the identification and maintenance of all funds, securities, and other assets of a client and shall provide accurate accounting as appropriate.

EC-1.2(f) A paralegal shall advise the proper authority of non-confidential knowledge of any dishonest or fraudulent acts by any person pertaining to the handling of the funds, securities or other assets of a client. The authority to whom the report is made shall depend on the nature and circumstances of the possible misconduct, (e.g., ethics committees of law firms, corporations and/or paralegal associations, local or state bar associations, local prosecutors, administrative agencies, etc.). Failure to report such knowledge is in itself misconduct and shall be treated as such under these rules.

## 1.3 A Paralegal shall Maintain a High Standard of Professional Conduct

### Ethical Considerations

EC-1.3(a) A paralegal shall refrain from engaging in any conduct that offends the dignity and decorum of proceedings before a court or other adjudicatory body and shall be respectful of all rules and procedures.

EC-1.3(b) A paralegal shall avoid impropriety and the appearance of impropriety and shall not engage in any conduct that would adversely affect his/her fitness to practice. Such conduct may include, but is not limited to: violence, dishonesty, interference with the administration of justice, and/or abuse of a professional position or public office.

EC-1.3(c) Should a paralegal's fitness to practice be compromised by physical or mental illness, causing that paralegal to commit an act that is in direct violation of the Model Code/Model Rules and/or the rules and/or laws governing the jurisdiction in which the paralegal practices, that paralegal may be protected from sanction upon review of the nature and circumstances of that illness.

EC-1.3(d) A paralegal shall advise the proper authority of non-confidential knowledge of any action of another legal professional that clearly demonstrates fraud, deceit, dishonesty, or misrepresentation. The authority to whom the report is made shall depend on the nature and circumstances of the possible misconduct, (e.g., ethics committees of law firms, corporations and/or paralegal associations, local or state bar associations, local prosecutors, administrative agencies, etc.). Failure to report such knowledge is in itself misconduct and shall be treated as such under these rules.

EC-1.3(e) A paralegal shall not knowingly assist any individual with the commission of an act that is in direct violation of the Model Code/Model Rules and/or the rules and/or laws governing the jurisdiction in which the paralegal practices.

EC-1.3(f) If a paralegal possesses knowledge of future criminal activity, that knowledge must be reported to the appropriate authority immediately.

## 1.4 A Paralegal shall Serve the Public Interest by Contributing to the Improvement of the Legal System and Delivery of Quality Legal Services, Including Pro Bono Publico Services

### Ethical Considerations

EC-1.4(a) A paralegal shall be sensitive to the legal needs of the public and shall promote the development and implementation of programs that address those needs.

EC-1.4(b) A paralegal shall support efforts to improve the legal system and access thereto and shall assist in making changes.

EC-1.4(c) A paralegal shall support and participate in the delivery of Pro Bono Publico services directed toward implementing and improving access to justice, the law, the legal system or the paralegal and legal professions.

EC-1.4(d) A paralegal should aspire annually to contribute twenty-four (24) hours of Pro Bono Publico services under the supervision of an attorney or as authorized by administrative, statutory or court authority to:

1. persons of limited means; or
2. charitable, religious, civic, community, governmental and educational organizations in matters that are designed primarily to address the legal needs of persons with limited means; or
3. individuals, groups or organizations seeking to secure or protect civil rights, civil liberties or public rights.

## 1.5 A Paralegal shall Preserve all Confidential Information Provided by the Client or Acquired from other Sources Before, During, and After the Course of the Professional Relationship

### Ethical Considerations

EC-1.5(a) A paralegal shall be aware of and abide by all legal authority governing confidential information in the jurisdiction in which the paralegal practices.

EC-1.5(b) A paralegal shall not use confidential information to the disadvantage of the client.

EC-1.5(c) A paralegal shall not use confidential information to the advantage of the paralegal or of a third person.

EC-1.5(d) A paralegal may reveal confidential information only after full disclosure and with the client's written consent; or, when required by law or court order; or, when necessary to prevent the client from committing an act that could result in death or serious bodily harm.

EC-1.5(e) A paralegal shall keep those individuals responsible for the legal representation of a client fully informed of any confidential information the paralegal may have pertaining to that client.

EC-1.5(f) A paralegal shall not engage in any indiscreet communications concerning clients.

## 1.6 A Paralegal shall Avoid Conflicts of Interest and shall Disclose any Possible Conflict to the Employer or Client, as Well as to the Prospective Employers or Clients

### Ethical Considerations

EC-1.6(a) A paralegal shall act within the bounds of the law, solely for the benefit of the client, and shall be free of compromising influences and loyalties. Neither the paralegal's personal or business interest, nor those of other clients or third persons, should compromise the paralegal's professional judgment and loyalty to the client.

EC-1.6(b) A paralegal shall avoid conflicts of interest that may arise from previous assignments, whether for a present or past employer or client.

EC-1.6(c) A paralegal shall avoid conflicts of interest that may arise from family relationships and from personal and business interests.

EC-1.6(d) In order to be able to determine whether an actual or potential conflict of interest exists a paralegal shall create and maintain an effective recordkeeping system that identifies clients, matters, and parties with which the paralegal has worked.

EC-1.6(e) A paralegal shall reveal sufficient non-confidential information about a client or former client to reasonably ascertain if an actual or potential conflict of interest exists.

EC-1.6(f) A paralegal shall not participate in or conduct work on any matter where a conflict of interest has been identified.

EC-1.6(g) In matters where a conflict of interest has been identified and the client consents to continued representation, a paralegal shall comply fully with the implementation and maintenance of an Ethical Wall.

## 1.7 A Paralegal's Title shall be Fully Disclosed

### Ethical Considerations

EC-1.7(a) A paralegal's title shall clearly indicate the individual's status and shall be disclosed in all business and professional communications to avoid misunderstandings and misconceptions about the paralegal's role and responsibilities.

EC-1.7(b) A paralegal's title shall be included if the paralegal's name appears on business cards, letterhead, brochures, directories, and advertisements.

EC-1.7(c) A paralegal shall not use letterhead, business cards or other promotional materials to create a fraudulent impression of his/her status or ability to practice in the jurisdiction in which the paralegal practices.

EC-1.7(d) A paralegal shall not practice under color of any record, diploma, or certificate that has been illegally or fraudulently obtained or issued or which is misrepresentative in any way.

EC-1.7(e) A paralegal shall not participate in the creation, issuance, or dissemination of fraudulent records, diplomas, or certificates.

## 1.8 A Paralegal shall not Engage in the Unauthorized Practice of Law

### Ethical Considerations

EC-1.8(a) A paralegal shall comply with the applicable legal authority governing the unauthorized practice of law in the jurisdiction in which the paralegal practices.

## § 2. NFPA GUIDELINES FOR THE ENFORCEMENT OF THE MODEL CODE OF ETHICS AND PROFESSIONAL RESPONSIBILITY

### 2.1 Basis for Discipline

2.1(a) Disciplinary investigations and proceedings brought under authority of the Rules shall be conducted in accord with obligations imposed on the paralegal professional by the Model Code of Ethics and Professional Responsibility.

### 2.2 Structure of Disciplinary Committee

2.2(a) The Disciplinary Committee ("Committee") shall be made up of nine (9) members including the Chair.

2.2(b) Each member of the Committee, including any temporary replacement members, shall have demonstrated working knowledge of ethics/professional responsibility-related issues and activities.

2.2(c) The Committee shall represent a cross-section of practice areas and work experience. The following recommendations are made regarding the members of the Committee.

    1. At least one paralegal with one to three years of law-related work experience.
    2. At least one paralegal with five to seven years of law related work experience.
    3. At least one paralegal with over ten years of law related work experience.

4. One paralegal educator with five to seven years of work experience; preferably in the area of ethics/professional responsibility.
5. One paralegal manager.
6. One lawyer with five to seven years of law-related work experience.
7. One lay member.

2.2(d) The Chair of the Committee shall be appointed within thirty (30) days of its members' induction. The Chair shall have no fewer than ten (10) years of law-related work experience.

2.2(e) The terms of all members of the Committee shall be staggered. Of those members initially appointed, a simple majority plus one shall be appointed to a term of one year, and the remaining members shall be appointed to a term of two years. Thereafter, all members of the Committee shall be appointed to terms of two years.

2.2(f) If for any reason the terms of a majority of the Committee will expire at the same time, members may be appointed to terms of one year to maintain continuity of the Committee.

2.2(g) The Committee shall organize from its members a three-tiered structure to investigate, prosecute and/or adjudicate charges of misconduct. The members shall be rotated among the tiers.

## 2.3 Operation of Committee

2.3(a) The Committee shall meet on as-needed basis to discuss, investigate, and/or adjudicate alleged violations of the Model Code/Model Rules.

2.3(b) A majority of the members of the Committee present at a meeting shall constitute a quorum.

2.3(c) A Recording Secretary shall be designated to maintain complete and accurate minutes of all Committee meetings. All such minutes shall be kept confidential until a decision has been made that the matter will be set for hearing as set forth in Section 6.1 below.

2.3(d) If any member of the Committee has a conflict of interest with the Charging Party, the Responding Party, or the allegations of misconduct, that member shall not take part in any hearing or deliberations concerning those allegations. If the absence of that member creates a lack of quorum for the Committee; then a temporary replacement for the member shall be appointed.

2.3(e) Either the Charging Party or the Responding Party may request that, for good cause shown, any member of the Committee not participate in a hearing or deliberation. All such requests shall be honored. If the absence of a Committee member under those circumstances creates a lack of a quorum for the Committee, then a temporary replacement for that member shall be appointed.

2.3(f) All discussions and correspondence of the Committee shall be kept confidential until a decision has been made that the matter will be set for hearing as set forth in Section 6.1 below.

2.3(g) All correspondence from the Committee to the Responding Party regarding any charge of misconduct and any decisions made regarding the charge shall be mailed certified mail, return receipt requested, to the Responding Party's last known address and shall be clearly marked with a "Confidential" designation.

## 2.4 Procedure for the Reporting of Alleged Violations of the Model Code/Disciplinary Rules

2.4(a) An individual or entity in possession of non-confidential knowledge or information concerning possible instances of misconduct shall make a confidential written report to the Committee within thirty (30) days of obtaining same. This report shall include all details of the alleged misconduct.

2.4(b) The Committee so notified shall inform the Responding Party of the allegation(s) of misconduct no later than ten (10) business days after receiving the confidential written report from the Charging Party.

2.4(c) Notification to the Responding Party shall include the identity of the Charging Party, unless, for good cause shown, the Charging Party requests anonymity.

2.4(d) The Responding Party shall reply to the allegations within ten (10) business days of notification.

## 2.5 Procedure for the Investigation of a Charge of Misconduct

2.5(a) Upon receipt of a Charge of Misconduct ("Charge"), or on its own initiative, the Committee shall initiate an investigation.

2.5(b) If, upon initial or preliminary review, the Committee makes a determination that the charges are either without basis in fact or, if proven, would not constitute professional misconduct, the Committee shall dismiss the allegations of misconduct. If such determination of dismissal cannot be made, a formal investigation shall be initiated.

2.5(c) Upon the decision to conduct a formal investigation, the Committee shall:

1. mail to the Charging and Responding Parties within three (3) business days of that decision notice of the commencement of a formal investigation. That notification shall be in writing and shall contain a complete explanation of all Charge(s), as well as the reasons for a formal investigation and shall cite the applicable codes and rules;
2. allow the Responding Party thirty (30) days to prepare and submit a confidential response to the Committee, which response shall address each charge specifically and shall be in writing; and
3. upon receipt of the response to the notification, have thirty (30) days to investigate the Charge(s). If an extension of time is deemed necessary, that extension shall not exceed ninety (90) days.

2.5(d) Upon conclusion of the investigation, the Committee may:

1. dismiss the Charge upon the finding that it has no basis in fact;
2. dismiss the Charge upon the finding that, if proven, the Charge would not constitute Misconduct;
3. refer the matter for hearing by the Tribunal; or
4. in the case of criminal activity, refer the Charge(s) and all investigation results to the appropriate authority.

## 2.6 Procedure for a Misconduct Hearing Before a Tribunal

2.6(a) Upon the decision by the Committee that a matter should be heard, all parties shall be notified and a hearing date shall be set. The hearing shall take place no more than thirty (30) days from the conclusion of the formal investigation.

2.6(b) The Responding Party shall have the right to counsel. The parties and the Tribunal shall have the right to call any witnesses and introduce any documentation that they believe will lead to the fair and reasonable resolution of the matter.

2.6(c) Upon completion of the hearing, the Tribunal shall deliberate and present a written decision to the parties in accordance with procedures as set forth by the Tribunal.

2.6(d) Notice of the decision of the Tribunal shall be appropriately published.

## 2.7 Sanctions

2.7(a) Upon a finding of the Tribunal that misconduct has occurred, any of the following sanctions, or others as may be deemed appropriate, may be imposed upon the Responding Party, either singularly or in combination:

1. letter of reprimand to the Responding Party; counseling;
2. attendance at an ethics course approved by the Tribunal; probation;
3. suspension of license/authority to practice; revocation of license/authority to practice;
4. imposition of a fine; assessment of costs; or
5. in the instance of criminal activity, referral to the appropriate authority.

2.7(b) Upon the expiration of any period of probation, suspension, or revocation, the Responding Party may make application for reinstatement. With the application for reinstatement, the Responding Party must show proof of having complied with all aspects of the sanctions imposed by the Tribunal.

## 2.8 Appellate Procedures

2.8(a) The parties shall have the right to appeal the decision of the Tribunal in accordance with the procedures as set forth by the Tribunal.

## DEFINITIONS

"Appellate Body" means a body established to adjudicate an appeal to any decision made by a Tribunal or other decision-making body with respect to formally-heard Charges of Misconduct:

"Charge of Misconduct" means a written submission by any individual or entity to an ethics committee, paralegal association, bar association, law enforcement agency, judicial body, government agency, or other appropriate body or entity, that sets forth non-confidential information regarding any instance of alleged misconduct by an individual paralegal or paralegal entity.

"Charging Party" means any individual or entity who submits a Charge of Misconduct against an individual paralegal or paralegal entity.

"Competency" means the demonstration of: diligence, education, skill, and mental, emotional, and physical fitness reasonably necessary for the performance of paralegal services.

"Confidential Information" means information relating to a client, whatever its source, that is not public knowledge nor available to the public. ("Non-Confidential Information" would generally include the name of the client and the identity of the matter for which the paralegal provided services.)

"Disciplinary Hearing" means the confidential proceeding conducted by a committee or other designated body or entity concerning any instance of alleged misconduct by an individual paralegal or paralegal entity.

"Disciplinary Committee" means any committee that has been established by an entity such as a paralegal association, bar association, judicial body, or government agency to: (a) identify, define and investigate general ethical considerations and concerns with respect to paralegal practice; (b) administer and enforce the Model Code and Model Rules and; (c) discipline any individual paralegal or paralegal entity found to be in violation of same.

"Disclose" means communication of information reasonably sufficient to permit identification of the significance of the matter in question.

"Ethical Wall" means the screening method implemented in order to protect a client from a conflict of interest. An Ethical Wall generally includes, but is not limited to, the following elements: (1) prohibit the paralegal from having any connection with the matter; (2) ban discussions with or the transfer of documents to or from the paralegal; (3) restrict access to files; and (4) educate all members of the firm, corporation, or entity as to the separation of the paralegal (both organizationally and physically) from the pending matter. For more information regarding the Ethical Wall, see the NFPA publication entitled "The Ethical Wall—Its Application to Paralegals."

"Ex parte" means actions or communications conducted at the instance and for the benefit of one party only, and without notice to, or contestation by, any person adversely interested.

"Investigation" means the investigation of any charge(s) of misconduct filed against an individual paralegal or paralegal entity by a Committee.

"Letter of Reprimand" means a written notice of formal censure or severe reproof administered to an individual paralegal or paralegal entity for unethical or improper conduct.

"Misconduct" means the knowing or unknowing commission of an act that is in direct violation of those Canons and Ethical Considerations of any and all applicable codes and/or rules of conduct.

"Paralegal" is synonymous with "Legal Assistant" and is defined as a person qualified through education, training, or work experience to perform substantive legal work that requires knowledge of legal concepts and is customarily, but not exclusively performed by a lawyer: This person may be retained or employed by a lawyer, law office, governmental agency, or other entity or may be authorized by administrative, statutory, or court authority to perform this work.

"Pro Bono Publico" means providing or assisting to provide quality legal services in order to enhance access to justice for persons of limited means; charitable, religious, civic, community, governmental and educational organizations in matters that are designed primarily to address the legal needs of persons with limited means; or individuals, groups or organizations seeking to secure or protect civil rights, civil liberties or public rights.

"Proper Authority" means the local paralegal association, the local or state bar association, Committee (s) of the local paralegal or bar association(s), local prosecutor, administrative agency, or other tribunal empowered to investigate or act upon an instance of alleged misconduct.

"Responding Party" means an individual paralegal or paralegal entity against whom a Charge of Misconduct has been submitted.

"Revocation" means the recision of the license, certificate or other authority to practice of an individual paralegal or paralegal entity found in violation of those Canons and Ethical Considerations of any and all applicable codes and/or rules of conduct.

"Suspension" means the suspension of the license, certificate or other authority to practice of an individual paralegal or paralegal entity found in violation of those Canons and Ethical Considerations of any and all applicable codes and/or rules of conduct.

"Tribunal" means the body designated to adjudicate allegations of misconduct.

**actus reus** Element of physical conduct necessary for someone to commit a criminal act.

**administrative agency** Government office created by the legislature and overseen by the executive branch. The purpose of such an agency is to apply certain specified laws created by the legislature.

**administrative law** Regulations and decisions that explain and detail statutes. Such regulations and decisions are issued by administrative agencies.

**Administrative Procedure Act (APA)** Congressional enactment that requires all federal administrative agencies to follow certain procedures in the issuance of administrative law.

**administrative regulation** Form of administrative law; a regulation that defines, clarifies, or enforces a statutory objective.

**agency** When one party known as the *agent* acts on behalf of another party known as the *principal*. In a valid agency relationship, the agent can legally bind the principal.

**agent** A person authorized, requested, permitted, by another to act on his or her behalf.

**ancillary jurisdiction** Authority of a court over issues in a case that is subject to the court's authority on other grounds.

**annulment** Court order that restores the parties to their positions before the marriage. The marriage of the parties is void and treated as if it never existed. It is permissible in situations in which a particular legal disability prevented the marriage from becoming valid.

**antenuptial agreement (prenuptial agreement)** Agreement between parties who intend to marry that typically provides for the disposition of the property rights of the parties in the event the marriage ends by death or divorce.

**appellate court** A court that reviews the actions of a trial court and determines whether an error has been committed that requires corrective action.

**arbitration** Third-party resolution of a legal issue that has arisen between two or more parties. Typically, parties are agreed (arbitration clause) or court ordered (compulsory) to submit evidence to an arbitrator for a binding decision.

**arraignment** Stage of a criminal proceeding in which the accused is formally charged.

**articles of incorporation** Document filed with the state at the time of incorporation that states the purpose of the corporation and defines the corporate structure.

**assumption of risk** Defense to negligence on the basis that the plaintiff knew of, appreciated, and voluntarily encountered the danger of defendant's conduct.

**bilateral contract** An agreement between two or more persons in which each party promises to deliver a performance in exchange for the performance of the other.

**bill** Proposed law presented to the legislature for consideration.

**bylaws** Document of a corporation that details the methods of operation such as officers and duties, chain of command, and general corporate procedures.

**civil law** Law that governs the private rights of individuals, legal entities, and government.

**client confidentiality** The obligation to retain all communications of any sort that occur within the attorney–client relationship as private and privileged.

**Code of Federal Regulations (CFR)** Publication that contains all current administrative regulations.

**codification** Process of incorporating newly passed legislation into the existing law code.

**comparative negligence** Degree of plaintiff's own negligent conduct that was responsible for plaintiff's injury.

**compensatory damages** An award of money payable to the injured party for the reasonable cost of the injuries.

**competence** Having adequate knowledge, skill, and training to undertake specific legal representation in a matter.

**complaint** Also known as a *petition*. The document that apprises the court and the defendant of the nature of the cause of action by plaintiff.

**concurrent jurisdiction** Situation in which more than one court has authority to hear a particular case.

**conflict of interest** Either the appearance of or actual divided loyalty by one who is a fiduciary.

**contract** A legally binding agreement that obligates two or more parties to do something they were not already obligated to do or refrain from doing something to which they were legally entitled.

**contractual agreement** A promise or set of promises for the breach of which the law provides a remedy and the performance of which the law recognizes a duty.

**contractual capacity** The ability to enter into and be bound by a legal contract; the ability is not diminished by age of minority or adjudicated incompetence.

**contributory negligence** The doctrine that maintains a plaintiff who contributes in any way to his or her injury cannot recover from a negligent defendant.

**corporation** Entity legally recognized as independent of its owners, who are known as *shareholders*. A corporation can sue or be sued in its own name regarding its own rights and liabilities.

**critical stage** Stage of a criminal proceeding in which the presumed innocence of the accused is in jeopardy, and therefore the accused is entitled to the representation of counsel.

**criminal law** Law created and enforced by the legislature for the health, welfare, safety, and general good of the public.

**custody (parental rights)** The rights to oversee the care, education, and rearing of a child.

**delegation doctrine** Principle that Congress may not assign its authority to create statutory law and no other government entity can assume such authority.

**discovery** Court-supervised exchange of evidence and other relevant information between parties to a lawsuit.

**dissolution of marriage** The end of the marriage relationship (also known as *divorce*).

**domestic violence** Violence perpetrated by one member of a household onto another.

**double jeopardy** Being placed on trial for the same crime twice.

**due process** That which is necessary to fundamental fairness in the U.S. system of justice.

**enabling act** Congressional enactment that creates the authority in the executive to organize and oversee an administrative agency by establishing specific legislative goals and objectives.

**exclusive jurisdiction** Authority of a court to hear a case, that authority being superior to the authority of all other courts.

**excusable conduct** Conduct by one who, under the color of authority, is considered to be innocent of otherwise criminal behavior.

**exhaustion of administrative remedies** The requirement that anyone having a dispute with an administrative agency must first follow all available procedures to resolve the dispute within the agency before taking the issue before the judiciary.

**federal court** A court that is part of the U.S. court system, has limited authority, and hears only cases involving the U.S. government, federal laws, or appropriate cases of diversity of citizenship.

**federal question** Authority of a federal court to hear a case on the basis of the Constitution and other federal law.

**fee simple** In U.S. law, this involves absolute ownership of real property.

**felony** Serious crime punishable by imprisonment in excess of one year or by death.

**fiduciary** One who is in a position of trust by another with respect to rights, person, or property.

**fixture** An item of personal property that has been affixed to real property for a specific purpose and in a semipermanent manner.

**forced (elected) share** The legal right of a surviving spouse to receive a statutorily designated percentage of the estate of a deceased spouse that is superior to the terms of a will or other rights of inheritance of heirs.

**freehold estate** An interest in real property that involves certain rights of ownership.

**grand jury** A group of individuals (often more than twenty) that reviews evidence to determine whether a defendant could be convicted of a crime if charged and tried.

**guardianship** One who has legal and fiduciary responsibility to care for the welfare of another as court ordered.

**in personam (personal) jurisdiction** Authority of a court to render and enforce rulings over a particular individual and the individual's property.

**in rem jurisdiction** Authority of a court over a specific item of property regardless of who claims the property or an interest in it.

**intentional tort** An act that the actor knows or should know with substantial certainty will cause harm to another.

**intestate** Dying without a valid will.

**joint tenancy** A form of multiple property ownership whereby the property owners have fee simple and share four unities, and each owner shares in the right of survivorship.

**judicial law** Opinions that are issued by members of the judiciary in legal disputes that have the effect of law.

**jurist (judge)** Judicial officer who presides over cases in litigation within the court system.

**justifiable conduct** Conduct by one who, under the circumstances, is considered to be innocent of otherwise criminal behavior.

**last clear chance** Defense of plaintiff responding to defenses of allegedly negligent defendant, in which plaintiff claims defendant had the last opportunity to avoid plaintiff's injury irrespective of plaintiff's own negligence.

**lawyer (attorney)** Individual who has completed the necessary requirements of education and training and who has been licensed to practice law in a jurisdiction.

**legal analysis** The process of examining precedent in detail in order to predict its effect on future similar circumstances.

**legal separation** Legal document that establishes the property rights of the parties without effecting a dissolution of the actual marriage relationship.

**legal standard** Legal principle, point of law. May appear in the form of statutory, judicial, or administrative law.

**life estate** The right to possess and use real property for the duration of one's life with limited ownership rights.

**limited partnership** Partnership of two or more persons in which the limited partners can be held liable for partnership debts only to the extent of their investment and cannot take part in the general management and operation of the partnership business.

**lobbyist** Individual hired to meet with legislators regarding proposed laws.

**long-arm statute** Authority of a court to impose *in personam* jurisdiction over persons beyond the court's geographical boundaries (allowed only in statutorily specified circumstances).

**material evidence** Evidence necessary to a fair and informed decision by the trier of fact.

**mens rea** Mental state required on the part of the accused as an element to convict him or her of criminal conduct.

**misdemeanor** Criminal offense punishable by a fine or by imprisonment of less than one year.

**modern balance** Goal of lawmaking authorities to balance the need for consistency and stability against the need for a flexible and adaptive government.

**motion** Formal request by a party to a lawsuit for court-ordered action or nonaction.

**naturalist theory** Philosophy that all persons know inherently the difference between right and wrong.

**negligence** An act or failure to act toward another when (1) a duty was owed to the other person; (2) the act or failure to act was less than a reasonable person would have done under the circumstances; (3) the act or failure to act was the direct cause of injury to the other person; and (4) the injury resulted in measurable financial, physical, or emotional damage to the other person.

**nonfreehold estate** An interest in real property that is limited in duration and involves the right of possession but not ownership.

**original jurisdiction** Authority of a court to determine the rights and obligations of the parties in a lawsuit (e.g., trial court).

**paralegal (legal assistant)** One who has training and knowledge in legal principles and practices and who supports and assists an attorney in the practice of law.

**partnership** An agreement of two or more parties to engage in business or enterprise with profits and losses shared among all parties.

**pendent jurisdiction** Authority of a federal court, presented with a federal claim, to also determine interrelated claims based on state law.

**per capita distribution** Distribution of an estate in equal shares, with each person representing one share.

**permanent injunction** An injunction that remains effective until an order of the court removes it; sometimes such orders are left in force forever.

**personal property** Movable items that are not land or items permanently affixed to land. Personal property includes tangible (physical) and intangible items such as rights of ownership in property held by others (e.g., bank accounts or ownership in legal entities such as stock). It does not include the rights to bring legal action against others, commonly known as a *chose in action*.

**per stirpes distribution** Distribution of an estate in equal shares to one level or class of persons. If a member of this level or class is deceased, then his or her heirs divide the share.

**positivist theory** Political belief that there should be a superior governmental entity that is not subject to question or challenge.

**precedent** Existing legal standards to which courts look for guidance when making a determination of a legal issue.

**preliminary injunction** Court order that orders a party to act or refrain from acting in a particular manner for a specified period of time (often during the pendency of a legal proceeding).

**probable cause** More than mere suspicion of criminal activity but less than evidence adequate to justify conviction.

**probate** Process of paying creditors and distributing the estate of one who is deceased.

**procedural law** Law used to guide parties fairly and efficiently through the legal system.

**promoter** One who is hired as a fiduciary to recruit investors in a proposed corporation.

**property settlement** Agreement as to the property rights and obligations of co-owners or co-debtors such as parties to a marriage.

**proximate cause** The direct cause that is sufficient to produce a result. There can be no other intervening force that occurs independently and before the result that is also sufficient to produce the result.

**quasi in rem jurisdiction** Authority of a court over a person's interest in certain property.

**real property** Land or anything permanently affixed to land and no longer movable.

**reasonable conduct** That action or nonaction that is appropriate under the circumstances when all risks and benefits are taken into account.

**relevant evidence** Evidence that tends to establish an essential fact in the dispute.

**representative** A person elected to the U.S. House of Representatives, which is designed to ensure equal representation of all citizens.

**right of survivorship** A characteristic associated with multiple property ownership in which the ownership interest transfers automatically to surviving co-owners on death of an owner rather than passing by will or intestate succession.

**selective incorporation** Process of expansion of the definition of due process to include certain guarantees enumerated in the Bill of Rights.

**senator** A person elected to the U.S. Senate, which is designed to ensure equal representation of all states.

**session law** Law passed during a particular session of Congress.

**sociological theory** Doctrine that follows the principle that government should adapt laws to reflect society's current needs and beliefs.

**stare decisis** "Let the decision stand." Method used by the judiciary when applying precedent to current situations.

**state court** A court that is a part of the judicial branch in the state in which it is located. Typically, state courts hear cases that involve state law.

**statute of frauds** Statutory law that specifies what contracts must be in writing before they will be enforced.

**statutory law** A statute. Law created by the legislature.

**strict liability** Liability without fault. Applied in situations where the intention or neglect of the party is immaterial. The mere performance of the act will result in liability.

**subject matter jurisdiction** Authority of a court to determine the actual issue between the parties.

**substantive law** The law that creates and resolves the issue between the parties. Legal standards that guide conduct and that are applied to determine whether conduct was legally appropriate.

**temporary restraining order** Court order that temporarily orders a party to act or refrain from acting in a particular manner until such time as the court has the opportunity to consider a more permanent ruling on an issue.

**tenancy by the entirety** A form of multiple ownership of property between spouses that includes the characteristics of joint tenancy, including the right of survivorship.

**tenancy in common** A form of multiple ownership of property whereby each tenant (owner) shares with the other(s) an undivided interest in the property.

**testate** Dying with a valid will.

**third-party beneficiary** One who, as the result of gift or collateral agreement, is entitled to the contractual performance owed another.

**traditional balance** Goal of the judiciary to allow maximum personal freedom without detracting from the welfare of the general public.

**trial court** A court that has authority to hear the evidence of the parties before it and render a verdict.

**unilateral contract** A contractual agreement in which one party makes a promise to perform on the actual performance of another.

**veto** Presidential power to invalidate a law passed by a majority of Congress; a two-thirds majority of each house is needed to override a veto.